D1233946

The New York
Botanical Garden
Illustrated Encyclopedia
of Horticulture

The New York Botanical Garden Illustrated Encyclopedia of Horticulture

Thomas H. Everett

Volume 9
Q-Sta

Garland Publishing, Inc.
New York & London

15 14 13 12 11 10 9 8 7 6 5 4 3 2

Library of Congress Cataloging in Publication Data

Everett, Thomas H
    The New York Botanical Garden illustrated encyclopedia of horticulture.

    1. Horticulture—Dictionaries. 2. Gardening—Dictionaries. 3. Plants, Ornamental—Dictionaries. 4. Plants, Cultivated—Dictionaries. I. New York (City). Botanical Garden. II. Title.
SB317.58.E94   635.9'03'21   80-65941
ISBN 0-8240-7239-1

PHOTO CREDITS

Black and White

All-American Rose Selections: Hybrid tea roses (part c), p. 2986; Floribunda roses (part a), p. 2986; Grandiflora roses (part a), p. 2986. American Association of Nurserymen: A fountain and statue backed by fencing clothed with English ivy, p. 2964. Armstrong Nurseries: Hybrid tea roses (part a), p. 2985; Grandiflora roses (part b), p. 2987. The British Travel and Holidays Association: Climbing roses at Bodnant Gardens, Wales, p. 2982. Estelle Gerard: The Cranford Rose Garden, Brooklyn Botanical Garden, p. 2983; A combination of bush roses and climbers, p. 2989. Jackson & Perkins Company: 'Blaze', a large-flowered climbing rose, p. 2988; A pillar in full bloom, p. 2988; Climbing roses trained (parts a & b), p. 2989; *Rudbeckia* 'White King', p. 3006. Joseph Harris Co., Inc.: Spinach, p. 3200. The New York Botanical Garden: *Quercus palustris* (leaves), p. 2868; *Quercus prinus* (acorns), p. 2869; *Quercus rubra* (female flowers), p. 2870; *Quercus velutina* (leaves), p. 2870; *Raphanus raphanistrum*, p. 2883; *Rehmannia elata*, p. 2892; *Reseda odorata*, a garden variety, p. 2896; *Rhizophora mangle*, p. 2909; Part of the collection of "ironclad" rhododendrons in bloom, p. 2912; *Rhododendron catawbiense* hybrid, p. 2913; *Rhus radicans* (foliage), p. 2932; *Rhus radicans* (fruits), p. 2933; *Rhus typhina* (fruits), p. 2933; *Robinia viscosa* (fruits), p. 2942; *Rosa spinosissima* (flowers), p. 2973; *Sabal causiarum*, Fairchild Tropical Garden, Miami, Florida, p. 3017; *Sabatia grandiflora*, p. 3018; *Salix lucida* (foliage), p. 3031; *Sanchezia speciosa*, p. 3044; *Sassafras albidum* (foliage), p. 3061; *Saururus cernuus*, p. 3063; *Saxifraga stolonifera*, p. 3070; *Sedum telephioides*, p. 3103; Bearded irises, normally sun-lovers, here flourish in part-day shade, p. 3142; *Shepherdia argentea* (fruits), p. 3145; *Silene hookeri*, p. 3153; *Sisyrinchium idahoense*, p. 3161; *Sium suave*, p. 3161; *Smilacina racemosa*, p. 3164; *Smilacina racemosa* (fruits), p. 3164; *Smilax glauca* (fruits), p. 3165; *Solanum dulcamara* (flowers), p. 3175; *Solanum dulcamara* (fruits), p. 3175; *Spiranthes cernua*, p. 3205; *Spiranthes lucida*, p. 3205; *Spondias mombin* (fruits), p. 3206. New York State Agricultural Experiment Station: Red raspberries, p. 2886. United States Department of Agriculture: *Rosmarinus officinalis* as a pot plant, p. 2998. United States National Arboretum: *Quercus phellos* (part b), p. 2868. University of Redlands, Redlands, California: Miniature *Rhapis* palms of Japan (parts a & b), p. 2902. Other photographs by Thomas H. Everett.

Color

The New York Botanical Garden: *Rhabdadenia biflora, Rhynchostylis* variety, *Ricinus communis* (young fruits), *Romanzoffia sitchensis, Salix arctica, Salix retusa, Saxifraga oppositifolia, Saxifraga pensylvanica, Silene acaulis.* Other photographs by Thomas H. Everett.

Published by Garland Publishing, Inc.
136 Madison Avenue, New York, New York 10016

Printed in the United States of America

This work is dedicated to the honored memory of the distinguished horticulturists and botanists who most profoundly influenced my professional career: Allan Falconer of Cheadle Royal Gardens, Cheshire, England; William Jackson Bean, William Dallimore, and John Coutts of the Royal Botanic Gardens, Kew, England; and Dr. Elmer D. Merrill and Dr. Henry A. Gleason of The New York Botanical Garden.

Foreword

According to Webster, an encyclopedia is a book or set of books giving information on all or many branches of knowledge generally in articles alphabetically arranged. To the horticulturist or grower of plants, such a work is indispensable and one to be kept close at hand for frequent reference.

The appearance of *The New York Botanical Garden Illustrated Encyclopedia of Horticulture* by Thomas H. Everett is therefore welcomed as an important addition to the library of horticultural literature. Since horticulture is a living, growing subject, these volumes contain an immense amount of information not heretofore readily available. In addition to detailed descriptions of many thousands of plants given under their generic names and brief description of the characteristics of the more important plant families, together with lists of their genera known to be in cultivation, this Encyclopedia is replete with well-founded advice on how to use plants effectively in gardens and, where appropriate, indoors. Thoroughly practical directions and suggestions for growing plants are given in considerable detail and in easily understood language. Recommendations about what to do in the garden for all months of the year and in different geographical regions will be helpful to beginners and will serve as reminders to others.

The useful category of special subject entries (as distinct from the taxonomic presentations) consists of a wide variety of topics. It is safe to predict that one of the most popular will be Rock and Alpine Gardens. In this entry the author deals helpfully and adequately with a phase of horticulture that appeals to a growing group of devotees, and in doing so presents a distinctly fresh point of view. Many other examples could be cited.

The author's many years as a horticulturist and teacher well qualify him for the task of preparing this Encyclopedia. Because he has, over a period of more than a dozen years, written the entire text (submitting certain critical sections to specialists for review and suggestions) instead of farming out sections to a score or more specialists to write, the result is remarkably homogeneous and cohesive. The Encyclopedia is fully cross referenced so that one may locate a plant by either its scientific or common name.

If, as has been said, an encyclopedia should be all things to all people, then the present volumes richly deserve that accolade. Among the many who call it "friend" will be not only horticulturists ("gardeners," as our author likes to refer to them), but growers, breeders, writers, lecturers, arborists, ecologists, and professional botanists who are frequently called upon to answer questions to which only such a work can provide answers. It seems safe to predict that it will be many years before lovers and growers of plants will have at their command another reference work as authoritative and comprehensive as T. H. Everett's Encyclopedia.

John M. Fogg, Jr.
Director Emeritus, Arboretum of the Barnes Foundation
Emeritus Professor of Botany, University of Pennsylvania

Preface

The primary objective of *The New York Botanical Garden Illustrated Encyclopedia of Horticulture* is a comprehensive description and evaluation of horticulture as it is known and practiced in the United States and Canada by amateurs and by professionals, including those responsible for botanical gardens, public parks, and industrial landscapes. Although large-scale commercial methods of cultivating plants are not stressed, much of the content of the Encyclopedia is as basic to such operations as it is to other horticultural enterprises. Similarly, although landscape design is not treated on a professional level, landscape architects will find in the Encyclopedia a great deal of importance and interest to them. Emphasis throughout is placed on the appropriate employment of plants both outdoors and indoors, and particular attention is given to explaining in considerable detail the how- and when-to-do-it aspects of plant growing.

It may be useful to assess the meanings of two words I have used. Horticulture is simply gardening. It derives from the Latin *hortus*, garden, and *cultura*, culture, and alludes to the intensive cultivation in gardens and nurseries of flowers, fruits, vegetables, shrubs, trees, and other plants. The term is not applicable to the extensive field practices that characterize agriculture and forestry. Amateur, as employed by me, retains its classic meaning of a lover from the Latin *amator*; it refers to those who garden for pleasure rather than for financial gain or professional status. It carries no implication of lack of knowledge or skills and is not to be equated with novice, tyro, or dabbler. In truth, amateurs provide the solid basis upon which American horticulture rests; without them the importance of professionals would diminish. Numbered in millions, amateur gardeners are devotees of the most widespread avocation in the United States. This avocation is serviced by a great complex of nurseries, garden centers, and other suppliers; by landscape architects and landscape contractors; and by garden writers, garden lecturers, Cooperative Extension Agents, librarians, and others who dispense horticultural information. Numerous horticultural societies, garden clubs, and botanical gardens inspire and promote interest in America's greatest hobby and stand ready to help its enthusiasts.

Horticulture as a vocation presents a wide range of opportunities which appeal equally to women and men. It is a field in which excellent prospects still exist for capable entrepreneurs. Opportunities at professional levels occur too in nurseries and greenhouses, in the management of landscaped grounds of many types, and in teaching horticulture.

Some people confuse horticulture with botany. They are not the same. The distinction becomes more apparent if the word gardening is substituted for horticulture. Botany is the science that encompasses all systematized factual knowledge about plants, both wild and cultivated. It is only one of the several disciplines upon which horticulture is based. To become a capable gardener or a knowledgeable plantsman or plantswoman (I like these designations for gardeners who have a wide, intimate, and discerning knowledge of plants in addition to skill in growing them) it is not necessary to study botany formally, although such study is likely to add greatly to one's pleasure. In the practice of gardening, many botanical truths are learned from experience. I have known highly competent gardeners without formal training in botany and able and indeed distinguished botanists possessed of minimal horticultural knowledge and skills.

Horticulture is primarily an art and a craft, based upon science, and at some levels perhaps justly regarded as a science in its own right. As an art it calls for an appreciation of beauty and form as expressed in three-dimensional spatial relationships and an ability to translate aesthetic concepts into reality. The chief materials used to create gardens are living plants, most of which change in size and form with the passing of time and often show differences in color and texture and in other ways from season to season. Thus it is important that designers of gardens have a wide familiarity with the sorts of plants that lend themselves to their purposes and with plants' adaptability to the regions and to the sites where it is proposed to plant them.

As a craft, horticulture involves special skills often derived from ancient practices passed from generation to generation by word of mouth and apprenticeship-like contacts. As a technology it relies on this backlog of empirical knowledge supplemented by that acquired by scientific experiment and investigation, the results of which often serve to explain rather than supplant old beliefs and practices, but sometimes point the way to more expeditious methods of attaining similar results. And from time to time new techniques are developed that add dimensions to horticultural practice; among such of fairly recent years that come to mind are the manipulation of blooming season by artificial daylength, the propagation of orchids and some other plants by meristem tissue culture, and the development of soilless growing mixes as substitutes for soil.

One of the most significant developments in American horticulture in recent decades is the tremendous increase in the number of different kinds of plants that are cultivated by many more people than formerly. This is particularly true of indoor plants or houseplants, the sorts grown in homes, offices, and other interiors, but is by no means confined to that group. The relative affluence of our society and the freedom and frequency of travel both at home and abroad has contributed to this expansion, a phenomenon that will surely continue as avid collectors of the unusual bring into cultivation new plants from the wild and promote wider interest in sorts presently rare. Our garden flora is also constantly and beneficially expanded as a result of the work of both amateur and professional plant breeders.

It is impracticable in even the most comprehensive encyclopedia to describe or even list all plants that somewhere within a territory as large as the United States and Canada are grown in gardens. In this Encyclopedia the majority of genera known to be in cultivation are described, and descriptions and often other pertinent information about a complete or substantial number of their species and lesser categories are given. Sorts likely to be found only in collections of botanical gardens or in those of specialists may be omitted.

The vexing matter of plant nomenclature inevitably presents itself when an encyclopedia of horticulture is contemplated. Conflicts arise chiefly between the very understandable desire of gardeners and others who deal with cultivated plants to retain long-familiar names and the need to reflect up-to-date botanical interpretations. These points of view are basically irreconcilable and so accommodations must be reached.

As has been well demonstrated in the past, it is unrealistic to attempt to standardize the horticultural usage of plant names by decree or edict. To do so would negate scientific progress. But it is just as impracticable to expect gardeners, nurserymen, arborists, seedsmen, dealers in bulbs, and other amateur and professional horticulturists to keep current with the interpretations and recommendations of plant taxonomists; particularly as these sometimes fail to gain the acceptance even of other botanists and it is not unusual for scientists of equal stature and competence to prefer different names for the same plant.

In practice time is the great leveler. Newly proposed plant names accepted in botanical literature are likely to filter gradually into horticultural usage and eventually gain currency value, but this sometimes takes several years. The complete up-to-dateness and niceties of botanical naming are less likely to bedevil horticulturists than uncertainties concerned with correct plant identification. This is of prime importance. Whether a tree is labeled *Pseudotsuga douglasii*, *P. taxifolia*, or *P. menziesii* is of less concern than that the specimen so identified is indeed a Douglas-fir and not some other conifer.

After reflection I decided that the most sensible course to follow in *The New York Botanical Garden Illustrated Encyclopedia of Horticulture* was to accept almost in its entirety the nomenclature adopted in *Hortus Third* published in 1976. By doing so, much of the confusion that would result from two major comprehensive horticultural works of the late twentieth century using different names for the same plant is avoided, and it is hoped that for a period of years a degree of stability will be attained. Always those deeply concerned with critical groups of plants can adopt the recommendations of the latest monographers. Exceptions to the parallelism in nomenclature in this Encyclopedia and *Hortus Third* are to be found in the CACTACEAE for which, with certain reservations but for practical purposes, as explained in the Encyclopedia entry Cactuses, the nomenclature of Curt Backeburg's *Die Cactaceae*, published in 1958–62, is followed; and the ferns, where I mostly accepted the guidance of Dr. John T. Mickel of The New York Botanical Garden. The common or colloquial names employed are those deemed to have general acceptance. Cross references and synonymy are freely provided.

The convention of indicating typographically whether or not plants of status lesser than species represent entities that propagate and persist in the wild or are sorts that persist only in cultivation is not followed. Instead, as explained in the Encyclopedia entry Plant Names, the word variety is employed for all entities below specific rank and if in Latin form the name is written in italic, if in English or other modern language, in Roman type, with initial capital letter, and enclosed in single quotation marks.

Thomas H. Everett
Senior Horticulture Specialist
The New York Botanical Garden

Acknowledgments

I am indebted to many people for help and support generously given over the period of more than twelve years it has taken to bring this Encyclopedia to fruition. Chief credit belongs to four ladies. They are Lillian M. Weber and Nancy Callaghan, who besides accepting responsibility for the formidable task of filing and retrieving information, typing manuscript, proofreading, and the management of a vast collection of photographs, provided much wise council; Elizabeth C. Hall, librarian extraordinary, whose superb knowledge of horticultural and botanical literature was freely at my disposal; and Ellen, my wife, who displayed a deep understanding of the demands on time called for by an undertaking of this magnitude, and with rare patience accepted inevitable inconvenience. I am also obliged to my sister, Hette Everett, for the valuable help she freely gave on many occasions.

Of the botanists I repeatedly called upon for opinions and advice and from whom I sought elucidation of many details of their science abstruse to me, the most heavily burdened have been my friends and colleagues at The New York Botanical Garden, Dr. Rupert C. Barneby, Dr. Arthur Cronquist, and Dr. John T. Mickel. Other botanists and horticulturists with whom I held discussions or corresponded about matters pertinent to my text include Dr. Theodore M. Barkley, Dr. Lyman Benson, Dr. Ben Blackburn, Professor Harold Davidson, Dr. Otto Degener, Harold Epstein, Dr. John M. Fogg, Jr., Dr. Alwyn H. Gentry, Dr. Alfred B. Graf, Brian Halliwell, Dr. David R. Hunt, Dr. John P. Jessop, Dr. Tetsuo Koyama, Dr. Bassett Maguire, Dr. Roy A. Mecklenberg, Everitt L. Miller, Dr. Harold N. Moldenke, Dr. Dan H. Nicolson, Dr. Pascal P. Pirone, Dr. Ghillean Prance, Don Richardson, Stanley J. Smith, Ralph L. Snodsmith, Marco Polo Stufano, Dr. Bernard Verdcourt, Dr. Edgar T. Wherry, Dr. Trevor Whiffin, Dr. Richard P. Wunderlin, Dr. John J. Wurdack, Yuji Yoshimura, and Rudolf Ziesenhenne.

Without either exception or stint these conferees and correspondents shared with me their knowledge, thoughts, and judgments. Much of the bounty so gleaned is reflected in the text of the Encyclopedia, but none other than I am responsible for interpretations and opinions that appear there. To all who have helped, my special thanks are due and are gratefully proferred.

I acknowledge with much pleasure the excellent cooperation I have received from the Garland Publishing Company and most particularly from its President, Gavin Borden. To Ruth Adams, Geoffrey Braine, Nancy Isaac, Carol Miller, and Melinda Wirkus, I say thank you for working so understandingly and effectively with me and for shepherding my raw typescript through the necessary stages.

How to Use This Encyclopedia

A vast amount of information about how to use, propagate, and care for plants both indoors and outdoors is contained in the thousands of entries that compose *The New York Botanical Garden Illustrated Encyclopedia of Horticulture*. Some understanding of the Encyclopedia's organization is necessary in order to find what you want to know.

Arrangement of the Entries

Genera

The entries are arranged in alphabetical order. Most numerous are those that deal with taxonomic groups of plants. Here belong approximately 3,500 items entered under the genus name, such as ABIES, DIEFFENBACHIA, and JUGLANS. If instead of referring to these names you consult their common name equivalents of FIR, DUMB CANE, and WALNUT, you will find cross references to the genus names.

Bigeneric Hybrids & Chimeras

Hybrids between genera that have names equivalent to genus names—most of these belonging in the orchid family—are accorded separate entries. The same is true for the few chimeras or graft hybrids with names of similar status. Because bigeneric hybrids frequently have characteristics similar to those of their parents and require similar care, the entries for them are often briefer than the regular genus entries.

Families

Plant families are described under their botanical names, with their common name equivalents also given. Each description is followed by a list of the genera accorded separate entries in this Encyclopedia.

Vegetables, Fruits, Herbs, & Ornamentals

Vegetables and fruits that are commonly cultivated, such as broccoli, cabbage, potato, tomato, apple, peach, and raspberry; most culinary herbs, including basil, chives, parsley, sage, and tarragon; and a few popular ornamentals, such as azaleas, carnations, pansies, and poinsettias, are treated under their familiar names, with cross references to their genera. Discussions of a few herbs and some lesser known vegetables and fruits are given under their Latin scientific names with cross references to the common names.

Other Entries

The remaining entries in the Encyclopedia are cross references, definitions, and more substantial discussions of many subjects of interest to gardeners and others concerned with plants. For example, a calendar of gardening activity, by geographical area, is given under the names of the months and a glossary of frequently applied species names (technically, specific epithets) is provided in the entry Plant Names. A list of these general topics, which may provide additional information about a particular plant, is provided at the beginning of each volume of the Encyclopedia.

Cross References & Definitions

The cross references are of two chief types: those that give specific information, which may be all you wish to know at the moment:
Boojam Tree is *Idria columnaris.*
Cobra plant is *Darlingtonia californica.*
and those that refer to entries where fuller explanations are to be found:
Adhatoda. See Justicia.
Clubmoss. See Lycopodium and Selaginella.

Additional information about entries of the former type can, of course, be found by looking up the genus to which the plant belongs—*Idria* in the case of the boojam tree and *Darlingtonia* for the cobra plant.

ORGANIZATION OF THE GENUS ENTRIES

Pronunciation

Each genus name is followed by its pronunciation in parentheses. The stressed syllable is indicated by the diacritical mark ´ if the vowel sound is short as in man, pet, pink, hot, and up; or by ˋ if the vowel sound is long as in mane, pete, pine, home, and fluke.

Genus Common Names
Family Common Names
General Characteristics

Following the pronunciation, there may be one or more common names applicable to the genus as a whole or to certain of its kinds. Other names may be introduced later with the descriptions of the species or kinds. Early in the entry you will find the common and botanical names of the plant family to which the genus belongs, the number of species the genus contains, its natural geographical distribution, and the derivation of its name. A description that stresses the general characteristics of the genus follows, and this may be supplemented by historical data, uses of some or all of its members, and other pertinent information.

Identification of Plants

Descriptions of species, hybrids, and varieties appear next. The identification of unrecognized plants is a fairly common objective of gardeners; accordingly, in this Encyclopedia various species have been grouped within entries in ways that make their identification easier. The groupings may bring into proximity sorts that can be adapted for similar landscape uses or that require the same cultural care, or they may emphasize geographical origins of species or such categories as evergreen and deciduous or tall and low members of the same genus. Where the description of a species occurs, its name is designated in **bold italic.** Under this plan, the description of a particular species can be found by referring to the group to which it belongs, scanning the entry for the species name in bold italic, or referring to the opening sentences of paragraphs which have been designed to serve as lead-ins to descriptive groupings.

Gardening & Landscape Uses
Cultivation
Pests & Diseases

At the end of genus entries, subentries giving information on garden and landscape uses, cultivation, and pests or diseases or both are included, or else reference is made to other genera or groupings for which these are similar.

General Subject Listings

The lists below organize some of the Encyclopedia entries into topics which may be of particular interest to the reader. They are also an aid in finding information other than Latin or common names of plants.

PLANT ANATOMY AND TERMS USED IN PLANT DESCRIPTIONS

All-America Selections
Alternate
Annual Rings
Anther
Apex
Ascending
Awl-Shaped
Axil, Axillary
Berry
Bloom
Bracts
Bud
Bulb
Bulbils
Bulblet
Bur
Burl
Calyx
Cambium Layer
Capsule
Carpel
Catkin
Centrals
Ciliate
Climber
Corm
Cormel
Cotyledon
Crown
Deciduous
Disk or Disc
Double Flowers
Drupe
Florets
Flower
Follicle
Frond
Fruit
Glaucous
Gymnosperms
Head
Hips
Hose-in-Hose

Inflorescence
Lanceolate
Leader
Leaf
Leggy
Linear
Lobe
Midrib
Mycelium
Node
Nut and Nutlet
Oblanceolate
Oblong
Obovate
Offset
Ovate
Palmate
Panicle
Pedate
Peltate
Perianth
Petal
Pinnate
Pip
Pistil
Pit
Pod
Pollen
Pompon
Pseudobulb
Radials
Ray Floret
Rhizome
Runners
Samara
Scion or Cion
Seeds
Sepal
Set
Shoot
Spore
Sprigs
Spur
Stamen
Stigma
Stipule

Stolon
Stool
Style
Subshrub
Taproot
Tepal
Terminal
Whorl

GARDENING TERMS AND INFORMATION

Acid and Alkaline Soils
Adobe
Aeration of the Soil
Air and Air Pollution
Air Drainage
Air Layering
Alpine Greenhouse or Alpine House
Amateur Gardener
April, Gardening Reminders For
Aquarium
Arbor
Arboretum
Arch
Asexual or Vegetative Propagation
Atmosphere
August, Gardening Reminders For
Balled and Burlapped
Banks and Steep Slopes
Bare-Root
Bark Ringing
Baskets, Hanging
Bed
Bedding and Bedding Plants
Bell Jar
Bench, Greenhouse
Blanching
Bleeding
Bog
Bolting
Border
Bottom Heat
Break, Breaking
Broadcast
Budding
Bulbs or Bulb Plants

Gardening Terms and Information (Continued)

State Agricultural Experimental Stations
Stock or Understock
Straightedge
Strawberry Jars
Strike
Stunt
Succession Cropping
Sundials
Syringing
Thinning or Thinning Out
Tillage
Tilth
Tools
Top-Dressing
Topiary Work
Training Plants
Tree Surgery
Tree Wrapping
Trenching
Trowels
Tubs
Watering
Weeds and Their Control
Window Boxes

FERTILIZERS AND OTHER SUBSTANCES RELATED TO GARDENING

Algicide
Aluminum Sulfate
Ammonium Nitrate
Ammonium Sulfate
Antibiotics
Ashes
Auxins
Basic Slag
Blood Meal
Bonemeal
Bordeaux Mixture
Calcium Carbonate
Calcium Chloride
Calcium Metaphosphate
Calcium Nitrate
Calcium Sulfate
Carbon Disulfide
Chalk
Charcoal
Coal Cinders
Cork Bark
Complete Fertilizer
Compost and Composting
Cottonseed Meal
Creosote
DDT
Dormant Sprays
Dried Blood
Fermate or Ferbam
Fertilizers
Fishmeal
Formaldehyde
Fungicides
Gibberellic Acid
Green Manuring
Growth Retardants
Guano
Herbicides or Weed-Killers
Hoof and Horn Meal

Hormones
Humus
Insecticide
John Innes Composts
Lime and Liming
Liquid Fertilizer
Liquid Manure
Manures
Mulching and Mulches
Muriate of Potash
Nitrate of Ammonia
Nitrate of Lime
Nitrate of Potash
Nitrate of Soda
Nitrogen
Orchid Peat
Organic Matter
Osmunda Fiber or Osmundine
Oyster Shells
Peat
Peat Moss
Permanganate of Potash
Potassium
Potassium Chloride
Potassium-Magnesium Sulfate
Potassium Nitrate
Potassium Permanganate
Potassium Sulfate
Pyrethrum
Rock Phosphate
Rotenone
Salt Hay or Salt Marsh Hay
Sand
Sawdust
Sodium Chloride
Sprays and Spraying
Sulfate
Superphosphate
Trace Elements
Urea
Urea-Form Fertilizers
Vermiculite
Wood Ashes

TECHNICAL TERMS

Acre
Alternate Host
Annuals
Antidessicant or Antitranspirant
Biennals
Binomial
Botany
Chromosome
Climate
Clone
Composite
Conservation
Cross or Crossbred
Cross Fertilization
Cross Pollination
Cultivar
Decumbent
Dicotyledon
Division
Dormant
Endemic
Environment
Family

Fasciation
Fertility
Fertilization
Flocculate
Floriculture
Genus
Germinate
Habitat
Half-Hardy
Half-Ripe
Hardy Annual
Hardy Perennial
Heredity
Hybrid
Indigenous
Juvenile Forms
Juvenility
Legume
Monocotyledon
Monoecious
Mutant or Sport
Mycorrhiza or Mycorhiza
Nitrification
Perennials
pH
Plant Families
Photoperiodism
Photosynthesis
Pollination
Pubescent
Saprophyte
Self-Fertile
Self-Sterile
Species
Standard
Sterile
Strain
Terrestrial
Tetraploid
Transpiration
Variety

TYPES OF GARDENS AND GARDENING

Alpine Garden
Artificial Light Gardening
Backyard Gardens
Biodynamic Gardening
Bog Gardens
Botanic Gardens and Arboretums
Bottle Garden
City Gardening
Colonial Gardens
Conservatory
Container Gardening
Cutting Garden
Desert Gardens
Dish Gardens
Flower Garden
Fluorescent Light Gardening
Formal and Semiformal Gardens
Greenhouses and Conservatories
Heath or Heather Garden
Herb Gardens
Hydroponics or Nutriculture
Indoor Lighting Gardening
Japanese Gardens
Kitchen Garden
Knot Gardens

Types of Gardens and Gardening (Continued)

Miniature Gardens
Native Plant Gardens
Naturalistic Gardens
Nutriculture
Organic Gardening
Rock and Alpine Gardens
Roof and Terrace Gardening
Salads or Salad Plants
Seaside Gardens
Shady Gardens
Sink Gardening
Terrariums
Vegetable Gardens
Water and Waterside Gardens
Wild Gardens

PESTS, DISEASES, AND OTHER TROUBLES

Ants
Aphids
Armyworms
Bagworms
Bees
Beetles
Billbugs
Biological Control of Pests
Birds
Blight
Blindness
Blotch
Borers
Budworms and Bud Moths
Bugs
Butterflies
Canker
Cankerworms or Inchworms
Casebearers
Caterpillars
Cats
Centipede, Garden
Chinch Bugs
Chipmunks
Club Root
Corn Earworm
Crickets
Cutworms
Damping Off
Deer
Die Back
Diseases of Plants
Downy Mildew
Earthworms
Earwigs
Edema
Fairy Rings
Fire Blight
Flies
Fungi or Funguses
Galls
Gas Injury

Gophers
Grasshoppers
Grubs
Gummosis
Hedgehog
Hornworms
Inchworms
Insects
Iron Chelates
Iron Deficiency
Lace Bugs
Lantana Bug
Lantern-Flies
Larva
Leaf Blight
Leaf Blister
Leaf Blotch
Leaf Curl
Leaf Cutters
Leaf Hoppers
Leaf Miners
Leaf Mold
Leaf Rollers
Leaf Scorch
Leaf Skeletonizer
Leaf Spot Disease
Leaf Tiers
Lightening Injury
Maggots
Mantis or Mantid
Mealybugs
Mice
Midges
Milky Disease
Millipedes
Mites
Mold
Moles
Mosaic Diseases
Moths
Muskrats
Needle Cast
Nematodes or Nemas
Parasite
Pests of Plants
Plant Hoppers
Plant Lice
Praying Mantis
Psyllids
Rabbits
Red Spider Mite
Rootworms
Rots
Rust
Sawflies
Scab Diseases
Scale Insects
Scorch or Sunscorch
Scurf
Slugs and Snails
Smut and White Smut Diseases
Sowbugs or Pillbugs

Spanworms
Spittlebugs
Springtails
Squirrels
Stunt
Suckers
Sun Scald
Thrips
Tree Hoppers
Virus
Walking-Stick Insects
Wasps
Webworms
Weevils
Wilts
Witches' Brooms
Woodchucks

GROUPINGS OF PLANTS

Accent Plants
Aquatics
Aromatic Plants
Bedding and Bedding Plants
Berried Trees and Shrubs
Bible Plants
Broad-Leaved and Narrow-Leaved Trees
    and Shrubs
Bulbs or Bulb Plants
Bush Fruits
Carnivorous or Insectivorous Plants
Dried Flowers, Foliage, and Fruits
Edging Plants
Epiphyte or Air Plant
Evergreens
Everlastings
Fern Allies
Filmy Ferns
Florists' Flowers
Foliage Plants
Fragrant Plants and Flowers
Gift Plants
Graft Hybrids
Grasses, Ornamental
Hard-Wooded Plants
Houseplants or Indoor Plants
Japanese Dwarfed Trees
Medicinal or Drug Plants
Night-Blooming Plants
Ornamental-Fruited Plants
Pitcher Plants
Poisonous Plants
Shrubs
State Flowers
State Trees
Stone Fruits
Stone or Pebble Plants
Stove Plants
Succulents
Tender Plants
Trees
Windowed Plants

The New York
Botanical Garden
Illustrated Encyclopedia
of Horticulture

QUAIL BRUSH is *Atriplex lentiformis*.

QUAKER BONNETS is *Lupinus perennis*.

QUAKER LADIES is *Hedyotis caerulea*.

QUAMASH is *Camassia quamash*.

QUAMOCLIT. See Ipomoea, and Mina.

QUASSIA (Quás-sia) — Bitterwood. Depending upon the botanical authority followed, the genus *Quassia*, of the quassia family SIMARUBACEAE, consists of from one to forty species. One is accepted here. The name commemorates a black man named Quasi who used the bark of the bitterwood for treating fevers. Known as Surinam quassia, the dried bark of the bitterwood is used medicinally, as an insecticide, and as a substitute for hops in beer. The species from which it is obtained is a native of tropical America and the West Indies. The product known as Jamaica quassia is derived from the related Asian and Malasian tree *Picrasma quassioides*.

Bitterwood (*Q. amara*), a shrub or tree up to 25 feet tall, is a close relative of the tree-of-heaven (*Ailanthus altissima*). It has alternate, pinnate leaves up to 10 inches long, with three, five, or seven elliptic-oblong leaflets up to 6 inches long, with their stalks and the parts of the midribs between the leaflets conspicuously winged. Showy, red-stalked racemes or panicles of bright red blooms develop from the branch ends. The slender flowers, 1 inch to 2 inches long, do not open widely. They have a five-lobed calyx, five petals, ten stamens, hairy at their bases and fully developed in male blooms, but rudimentary in female flowers, and one style. The fruits, which contain a single seed and resemble little purple-black plums, are usually in fives on red receptacles. All parts of the plant are intensely bitter. Commercial quassia is obtained from the yellowish-white wood.

Garden and Landscape Uses and Cultivation. In the humid tropics, bitterwood prospers in any fairly good soil and is attractive when planted alone, in groups, or with other shrubbery. Because of its medicinal uses it is sometimes grown in greenhouse collections of plants useful to man. There, it thrives without trouble where the atmosphere is humid in a minimum temperature of about 60°F. Repotting and pruning to shape is done in late winter. Propagation is by seed and by cuttings.

QUEEN or QUEEN'S. One or the other of these words are part of the vernacular names of these plants: Queen Anne's lace (*Daucus carota*), Queen Anne's pocket melon (*Cucumis melo dudaim*), queen cup (*Clintonia uniflora*), queen-lily (*Phaedranassa*), Queen-of-Sheba vine (*Podranea brycei*), queen-of-the-meadow (*Filipendula ulmaria*), queen-of-the-prairie (*Filipendula rubra*), queen orchid (*Grammatophyllum speciosum*), queen palm (*Arecastrum romanzoffianum*), queen's delight (*Stillingia sylvatica*), and queen's wreath (*Petrea volubilis*).

QUEENSLAND. This word is part of the common names of these plants: Queensland gold blossom tree (*Barklya syringifolia*), Queensland-hog-plum (*Pleiogynium cerasiferum*), Queensland kauri-pine (*Agathis robusta*), Queensland nut (*Macadamia integrifolia*), Queensland-poplar (*Homalanthus populifolius*), Queensland pyramid tree (*Lagunaria patersonii*), and Queensland umbrella tree (*Brassaia actinophylla*).

QUERCIFILIX (Querci-fílix). The only species of this genus of ferns belongs in the aspidium family ASPIDIACEAE and is native to China, Hong Kong, Taiwan, Borneo, Ceylon, and Mauritius. The name *Quercifilix* alludes to the shape of the leaves. It is derived from *Quercus*, the genus of the oaks, and the Latin *filix*, a fern.

Creeping by rather slender rhizomes, *Q. zeylanica* has two distinct types of fronds. The sterile ones have a stalk as long or longer than the blade and clothed with a fuzz of yellow hairs. The blades are trian-

Quercifilix zeylanica

gular and have a pair of basal leaflets in addition to the much larger center one. All are irregularly-round-lobed in the manner of the leaves of certain oaks and have, extending to each lobe, but not actually reaching the margin, a chief lateral vein. The leaf blade is 2 to 4½ inches long by 1 inch to 1½ inches wide. The fertile ones have much longer, slender stalks than the sterile ones and similarly-lobed, but very much more slender blades. The spore capsules are closely and evenly distributed along the veins and to some extent on the other parts of the blade.

Garden and Landscape Uses and Cultivation. This attractive fern is appropriate for rock gardens and other intimate plantings in the humid tropics and subtropics and for tropical greenhouses and terrariums. It needs porous soil well supplied with leaf mold or peat moss, a humid atmosphere, shade from strong sun, and for plants grown indoors, a minimum night temperature of 55°F, rising by five to fifteen degrees by day. For more information see Ferns.

QUERCUS (Quér-cus) — Oak. Confined in the wild to temperate parts of the northern hemisphere and to mountains in the tropics, *Quercus*, of the beech family FAGA-

CEAE, includes approximately 450 species of deciduous and evergreen trees or much less commonly shrubs. Some kinds, symbols of strength and majesty, are among the noblest of trees. The name *Quercus* is an ancient Latin one for oaks.

Oaks have twigs that if cut through transversely reveal a characteristic five-rayed pith. Their winter buds are in clusters at the shoot ends. The leaves, deciduous or evergreen according to sort, are pinnately-lobed or toothed or less commonly have smooth margins. Those of some deciduous kinds remain on the trees, especially young specimens, long into the winter, but drop before new growth begins. Appearing with or before the new foliage, the small, inconspicuous flowers are unisexual with both sexes on the same tree. The males, in drooping slender catkins, generally consist of a six-parted calyx and four to twelve stamens. The females have a six-lobed calyx, a three- or less commonly a four- or five-celled ovary, and as many styles as cells. They are solitary or in spikes from the axils of the young leaves. They are surrounded by an involucre (collar) of overlapping bracts that develops into the cups of the acorns (the fruits) in which the nuts sit. These cups, their scales loose and spreading or pressed closely together, may surround only the bases of the nuts or almost completely enclose them.

Acorns are much appreciated as food by deer, squirrels, pigs, and some other animals. Those of a few kinds have been used as human food. The oldest known dye Turkey red, made by a process developed in India before 2000 B.C., and in wide use until production of synthetic dyes began in the late nineteenth century, was made from scale insects that infest *Q. coccifera*, a native of Cyprus and western Asia. An extract from galls that develop on the Aleppo oak (*Q. infectoria*), of Cyprus and western Asia, was used to dye hair black at least as far back as Roman times and is still a constituent of indelible inks used by the United States Treasury, the Bank of England, and governmental institutions of some other countries. Commercial cork is a product of the cork oak. It is stripped from the trees, without injury to them, at intervals of nine to ten years. Oak leaves and acorns have been much employed as motifs in design.

Botanically, oaks are classified in two subgenera, which, in turn, are divided into lesser groups. The subgenera are *Cyclobalanopsis*, which has the scales of its acorn cups fused into rings, and *Euquercus* in which the scales are separate and arranged spirally. The species of *Cyclobalanopsis* are evergreen natives of Asia; few are cultivated. Those of *Euquercus* are grouped in six sections. Representatives of all except one of these, *Macrobalanus*, are described further on in this entry. The sorts

of *Macrobalanus*, little known in cultivation, are natives of Mexico and Central America. The other five sections of *Euquercus* are these:

Section 1 (*Cerris*) consists of natives of the Old World. The leaves of its deciduous sorts most often have bristle-tipped, triangular lobes, the usually small leaves of the evergreen kinds are variously-toothed. The female flowers have long styles. The cups holding the acorns have usually long scales.

Section 2 (*Mesobalanus*) consists of natives of the Old World. The leaves are deciduous and usually large. In botanical details, they are intermediate between the sorts of Section 1 and Section 4.

Section 3 (*Lepidobalanus*) includes deciduous, partly evergreen, and evergreen species of the Old World and the New World. Their female flowers are long-styled. The cups of the acorns are not woolly on their insides.

Section 4 (*Protobalanus*) comprises evergreen species native to western North America that differ from those of Section 3 in the cups of the acorns being woolly on their insides.

Section 5 (*Erythrobalanus*) includes deciduous and evergreen species, all natives of North America. The female flowers have long, spatula-shaped styles.

Three subsections of Section 5 are recognized:

(a) The willow oak group, which comprises deciduous or rarely semievergreen species with lobeless, smooth-edged leaves

(b) The black and red oak group, which comprises deciduous sorts, usually with leaves with triangular, bristle-pointed lobes

(c) The evergreen group, with more or less holly-like, evergreen leaves

American oaks of the sections *Lepidobalanus* and *Protobalanus* constitute what is known as the white oak group. Section *Erythrobalanus* constitutes the red oak group.

In the presentation that follows, deciduous and evergreen sorts are dealt with separately and within those categories are arranged alphabetically according to their botanical names. The botanical standing of each is indicated in parentheses after its name. If of subgenus *Cyclobalanopsis* by (cycl.); if of *Euquercus* by a number indicating the section or subsection of that subgenus to which it belongs.

Deciduous oaks in cultivation include those now to be described. Because of the variability of some species and more especially because of the readiness with which many kinds hybridize in the wild and in cultivation, identification of particular specimens is sometimes puzzling. The ap-

proximate hardiness of native American oaks may be deduced from the natural ranges given for each, that of other kinds is indicated in their descriptions. The sawtooth oak (*Q. acutissima*) (1), of Japan, China, and Korea, and hardy about as far north as New York City, attains a height of nearly 50 feet; it has a rounded head of wide-spreading branches. Its chestnut-like, pointed, obovate-oblong to oblong leaves 3½ to 6 inches long, lustrous and hairless on their upper surfaces, have tufts of hairs in the axils of the veins on their undersides. They have twelve to sixteen pairs of parallel veins ending in bristle-like teeth. The stalkless acorns have cups two-thirds as long as the nut, clothed with long, slender, spreading and recurved scales. The white oak (*Q. alba*) (3), one of

Quercus alba: (a) In winter

(b) In summer

Quercus alba (foliage and acorns)

the most impressive and massive of its genus, rarely attains 150 feet in height, but more commonly is not over two-thirds that height. Native from Maine to Minnesota, Florida, and Texas, it has a rounded head of sturdy, spreading, chiefly horizontal branches and blunt, smooth buds. Its bright green leaves, 4½ to 10 inches long and oblong to oblong-obovate, are deeply-cleft into five to nine oblongish, blunt, usually toothless lobes, some often shallowly indented at their apexes. At first downy, but soon hairless, in fall they become dark wine-red to purplish. The short- to long-stalked acorns have cup-shaped cups about one-quarter the length of the nuts and with much-thickened basal scales. Variety *Q. a. latiloba* has leaves with broader lobes that extend less than half-way to the midrib. The swamp white oak (*Q. bicolor*) (3) has much the aspect of the white oak, but is smaller and less wide-spreading, with coarser foliage. Native to damp and wet soils from Quebec to Michigan, Georgia, and Arkansas, this has a comparatively narrow, round-topped head. Its terminal clusters of buds have often fine scales. The obovate to oblong-obovate leaves, dark, 4 to 6 inches long, and velvety or white-downy on their undersides, have six to ten pairs of coarse, blunt teeth or lobes. The acorns are ovoid-oblong, ¾ to a little over 1 inch long, and have cups about one-third as long as the nuts. The chestnut-leaved oak (*Q. castaneaefolia*) (1)

Quercus castaneaefolia, the Royal Botanic Gardens, Kew, England

hardy in southern New England, which attains a height of 120 feet or sometimes more, is handsome. It holds its foliage until very late in the fall, then its leaves drop without changing color. Of thin, firm texture, they are elliptic to oblongish and coarsely-toothed or lobed from one-third to two-thirds to the midrib. Varying considerably in shape and size, they mostly are 2½ to 5 inches long by 1 inch to 3 inches wide. Both the upper dark green surface and the lower grayish-green one are clothed with fine down. Solitary or paired, the nearly cylindrical nuts of the very short-stalked, 1- to 1¼-inch-long acorns protrude from cups covered with a moss of long, slender scales. The scarlet oak (*Q. coccinea*) (5b), native from Maine

Quercus cerris (acorns)

to Minnesota, Florida, and Missouri, differs from the red oak in its oblong to elliptic leaves being much more deeply-cleft into seven or sometimes nine lobes. In

Quercus coccinea: (a) A young specimen in winter

Quercus bicolor

Quercus cerris

has a native range from Iran to the Caucasus. An impressive, round-headed, wide-topped tree, up to 100 feet tall, it has downy young shoots and chestnut-like, narrow-elliptic to oblongish leaves 4 to 7 inches long. Eight to ten pairs of veins, each ending in a marginal triangular tooth, angle outward from the midrib. The shaggy-cupped acorns, ¾ inch to 1¼ inches long, have a nut embedded for one-third to one-half of their lengths in the cup. This oak is perhaps not hardy in climates colder than that of Long Island, New York. The Turkey oak (*Q. cerris*) (1), of southern Europe and Asia Minor and

Quercus cerris (leaves)

(b) A young specimen in summer

Quercus coccinea (male flowers and young leaves)

length 3 to 6 inches, they have tufts of hair in the vein axils on their undersides, and in fall turn brilliant scarlet. The ovoid nuts of the acorns, ½ to ¾ inch long, are seated for one-half their lengths in the cups. Native to Japan, China, and Korea, **Q. dentata** (2) is a round-headed species up to 75 feet tall remarkable for its large leaves, sometimes 1 foot long by 9 inches wide. Bluntly-obovate, they have four to nine pairs of broad, round lobes, hairless above, except when young, and grayish-downy on their undersurfaces. The usually clustered, nearly stalkless, spherical-ovoid acorns, ½ to ¾ inch long, have their basal halves in cups with long, spreading scales. The jack oak (**Q. ellipsoidalis**) (3) shares with the shingle oak its vernacular name. Native from Michigan to Minnesota

Quercus falcata

Quercus coccinea (leaves and acorns)

Quercus dentata (leaves)

and Missouri, it favors dry, upland soils. Up to 75 feet tall and in habit and leaf style resembling the pin oak, this has leaves with five or six deep, conspicuously bristle-pointed lobes. They are 3½ to 4½ inches long, except when young, hairless, but for tiny tufts in the vein axils on their undersides. From ½ to ¾ inch long, the acorns, ellipsoid to subspherical, have a cup less than one-half the length of the nut. The Spanish oak (**Q. falcata**) (5b), untrue to its colloquial name, is a native of dry or moist soils from New Jersey to Ohio, Indiana, Florida, and Texas. Up to 75 or rarely nearly 100 feet tall and with an open, round-topped head of stout

branches, this has leaves of very various shapes, but most often ovate to broadly-elliptic. They have one to four pairs of conspicuously bristle-pointed, usually long, narrow-triangular side lobes in addition to a long terminal one. Their undersides and stalks are gray-downy. The ovoid acorns, their lower one-third enclosed by the cup, are up to ½ inch long. The Oregon oak (**Q. garryana**) (3), native from British Columbia to California, is round-headed and 25 to 60 feet tall; it has stout, spreading branches. Obovate to oblong and 3½ to 6 inches long, its leathery leaves have upper surfaces slightly hairy, undersides with pale or rust-colored hairs. They are coarsely-pinnately-cleft into toothless or few-toothed, oblong-ovate lobes. The acorns, ovoid and 1¼ to 2¼ inches long, have shallow cups. The Lucombe oak (**Q. hispanica lucombeana**) (1), a chance hybrid between *Q. cerris* and *Q. suber* that originated in an English nursery about 1765, is a deciduous or sometimes semi-evergreen tree up to 100 feet tall. Of handsome appearance, it has elliptic to ovate leaves 2 to 5 inches long, clothed with gray felt on their undersides. The ¾- to 1-inch-long acorns, their cups enclosing over one-half of the nuts, are fertile. Seedling trees exhibit considerable variation. The scrub oak (**Q. ilicifolia**) (5b), a native of poor, often rocky or sandy soils from Maine to Ohio, North Carolina, and West Virginia, and sometimes a tree up to 15 feet tall, is more frequently a densely-branched shrub. Oblong to obovate in outline and generally with five bristle-pointed, broad-triangular lobes, the leaves are 2 to 4 inches long by one-half to two-thirds as broad. Their undersides are minutely-gray-hairy. From ½ to ¾ inch long, the acorns have deep saucer- to top-shaped cups from one-third to one-half as long as the nut. The shingle oak or jack oak (**Q. imbricaria**) (5a) inhabits dry soils in upland regions from Pennsylvania to Iowa, Kansas, Georgia, and Arkansas. Attaining heights up to 60 feet or rarely more, this has firm-textured, lobeless, toothless, bristle-tipped, elliptic to narrowly-obovate-oblong leaves 4 to 7 inches long by up to 3 inches wide, softly-hairy beneath and with the veins of their hairless upper surfaces raised. In fall they change to russet-red. The ovoid acorns, from a little under to slightly over ½ inch long, have cups approximately one-half as long as the the nuts. The California black oak (*Q. kelloggii*) (5b) is native from Oregon to California. Handsomer than the common black oak, this sort is used as an ornamental in its native area and elsewhere where climates are reasonably similar. It develops a dense, rounded head, up to 100 feet in height, of spreading branches. Its leaves, divided into usually seven-toothed lobes, glossy above, when young pubescent on their undersides, are 3 to 6 inches long. The short-stalked acorns have ovoid to oblong nuts, their lower one-third to one-half seated in hairless cups. The laurel oak (*Q. laurifolia* syn. *Q. hemispherica*) (5a), native in moist or wet soils from Virginia to Florida and Louisiana, which retains its foliage until very late in the winter, is often semievergreen. Up to about 75 feet in height and with a dense, rounded head, it has leathery, lobeless, toothless, usually hairless, narrowly-oblong to lanceolate, elliptic, or narrowly-obovate, sometimes bristle-tipped leaves 2 to 4 inches long by up to 1½ inches wide. From those of the willow oak they differ in being not over three times as long as broad and being glossy on their undersides. The ovoid acorns, in hemispherical cups that enclose one-quarter of the nut, are about 1 inch long. This species is not hardy in the north. The valley oak (*Q. lobata*) (3), a stately, elegant native of California, attains heights of 40 to 110 feet. This has an open head and oblong to obovate leaves 2 to 4 inches long, deeply-cleft into seven to eleven blunt lobes usually coarsely-toothed at their apexes. Their upper surfaces are nearly hairless, their undersides are paler and hairy, as are the leafstalks. The conical acorns, 1¼ to 2 inches long, have nuts contained in warty cups that enclose one-quarter to one-third of them. The overcup oak (*Q. lyrata*) (3) is native from New Jersey to Illinois, Florida, and Texas. A round-headed tree up to 100 feet high and with slightly pendulous branches, this has leaves much like those of the white oak, but with fewer lobes. From 4 to 7 inches long and with wedge-shaped bases, they are hairless above and usually white-hairy on their undersides. The nearly spherical acorns, generally almost completely enclosed in their cups, are up to 1 inch long. The burr or mossy cup oak (*Q. macrocarpa*) (3), exceptionally exceeding 150 feet tall, but more often not over 80 feet, is native from Nova Scotia to Manitoba, Pennsylvania, and Texas. Broad-

Quercus macrocarpa

headed, it has obovate to oblong-obovate leaves 4 to 10 inches long, usually wedge-shaped at their bases. They are deeply-lobed with the terminal lobe much the largest, and coarsely-toothed or shallowly-lobed. The upper surfaces of the leaves are lustrous, the undersides white-hairy. The nuts of the 1- to 1½-inch-long acorns are seated for about one-third of their length in cups fringed around their rims with slender scales much longer than those below. The black jack oak (*Q. marilandica*) (5b), up to 30 or occasionally 50 feet tall, inhabits dry, poor, often sandy soils from New York to Michigan, Iowa, Florida, and Texas. It has an often irregular, narrow head of spreading branches and broad-ovate to triangular-obovate, lustrous leaves 4 to 8 inches long that turn brown or yellow in fall. They have three or five bristle-pointed apical lobes and, occasionally, side lobes. They are minutely-brownish-hairy or rarely downy on their undersides. From ½ to ¾ inch long, the acorns have top-shaped cups about one-half as long as the nuts. The yellow chestnut oak (*Q. muehlenbergii*) (3) ranges from Vermont to Nebraska, Virginia, New Mexico, and Texas. It occasionally attains 100 feet, but more often not over about 60 feet in

Quercus muehlenbergii

height. It has oblong to oblong-lanceolate leaves 4½ to 6 inches long and coarsely-toothed. Their upper surfaces are usually yellowish-green, their lower ones whitish-hairy. From ½ to ¾ inch long, the ovoid to roundish acorns are seated for about one-half their length in a thin cup with small, tightly-fitted scales. The water oak (*Q. nigra*) (5a), which chiefly favors moist and wet soils, is native from Delaware to Florida and Texas. Sometimes 75 feet tall,

Quercus nigra

usually very much smaller, this has a round-topped, conical head of rather slender branches and lobeless and toothless or sometimes irregularly, shallowly two- to five-lobed, dull, bluish-green leaves, obovate narrowing to a long, wedge-shaped base, and barely bristle-tipped. They are hairless or sometimes have a little hair in the axils of the veins. From ⅓ to ½ inch long, the ovoid acorns have a saucer-shaped cup about one-third the length of the nut. The pin oak (*Q. palustris*) (5b), native from Massachusetts to Wisconsin, Delaware, and Arkansas, is one of the

Quercus palustris, a young specimen

most beautiful oaks. It grows rapidly when young, more slowly later. Approximately 75 feet or rarely up to more than 100 feet in height, it has drooping lower branches, horizontal middle ones, and upright upper ones. Comparatively slender, they form shapely and conical crowns in young trees, in older specimens the crown is irregular and narrowly-oblongish. The

Quercus phellos: (a) A young specimen

Quercus phellos (leaves)

Quercus palustris, an older specimen

slender-stalked leaves, up to about 4½ inches long, are elliptic to elliptic-oblong and cleft into five to seven toothed lobes. Their upper surfaces are lustrous and bright green, their lower ones paler and with tufts of hair in the axils of the veins. In fall they change to scarlet. Nearly hemispherical, the stalkless or short-stalked

Quercus palustris (leaves)

acorns have thin, saucer-shaped cups one-third as long as the nuts. The willow oak (**Q. phellos**) (5a) has foliage of most unoak-like aspect that, as its vernacular name implies, is remindful of that of a willow. A splendid ornamental, this native of the eastern seaboard and Gulf States from New York to Texas is much used as a street tree. As a young tree it grows rapidly. Usually about 50 feet in height, exceptionally nearly twice as tall, the willow oak has a conical to rounded, densely-branched head and pointed, linear-oblong to narrowly-elliptic, lustrous leaves, 2 to 5 inches long, when young downy on their undersides. In fall they become pale yel-

(b) A mature specimen

low. The hemispherical nearly stalkless acorns have shallow cups that enclose about one-quarter of the nut. The chinquapin oak (**Q. prinoides**) (3) in botanical detail closely resembles *Q. muehlenbergii*, but differs in its smaller, fewer-lobed, shorter-stalked leaves and acorns with slightly deeper cups. Usually a shrub 2 to 3 feet tall, it sometimes is a tree 10 to 15 feet in height. The native range of this oak is Maine to Nebraska, North Carolina, and Texas. The basket or chestnut oak (**Q. prinus**) (3), up to 100 feet in height, is native from Delaware to Indiana, Florida, and Texas. Forming a dense, rounded head, it has pointed, hairless, yellowish buds and obovate to oblong leaves, 4 to 7 inches long, with many regularly-spaced, coarse, blunt teeth. Bright green above and gray-

Quercus prinus (acorns)

hairy on their undersides, in fall they change to crimson. From 1 inch to 1½ inches long, the oblong-ovoid acorns have nuts fitted in cups extending for from one-third to one-half their lengths with at their rims a distinct fringe of slender scales. English oak (**Q. robur**) (3) has somewhat the aspect of the American white oak to which it is closely related, but is smaller and has smaller leaves. In eastern North America, it is less satisfactory than most native species, often dying inexplicably and suddenly when quite large. A native

Quercus robur in southern California

of Europe, including the British Isles, and of North Africa and western Asia, and hardy through much of New England, this species sometimes, but uncommonly exceeds 75 feet in height. It has an irregular, open head of wide-spreading, stout branches. The buds are short, thick, and blunt, the leaves obovate to obovate-oblong, 2 to 4½ inches long, and with three to seven pairs of rounded lobes and usually earlike bases. Hairless, they have dark green upper surfaces, bluish-green lower ones. From one to five on a stalk 1¼ to 3 inches long, the ovoid acorns have cups one-third as long as the nuts. The golden English oak (*Q. r. concordia*), more upright, has bright yellow young foliage that be-

Quercus robur fastigiata

Quercus robur variegata (leaves)

comes greener as the season advances. Erect, narrow, and with upright branches so that it has much the habit of a Lombardy poplar, *Q. r. fastigiata* breeds fairly true from seed. Leaves attractively edged or variegated with creamy-white are characteristic of *Q. r. variegata*. The Durmast oak (**Q. petraea**) (3), of Europe, including the British Isles, and western Asia, scarcely differs from *Q. robur* except for its acorns having short or nonexistent stalks.

The common red oak (**Q. rubra** syn. *Q. borealis*) (5b) is a member of the black oak group. Native from Nova Scotia to Pennsylvania, Minnesota, and Iowa, this becomes 80 feet tall and has a broad, rounded head with a few large branches. Elliptic-oblong to obovate, and 4 to 9 inches long, its leaves, dull green changing in fall to dark red, are cut about half-

Quercus rubra, a group of trees

Quercus rubra (male flowers)

Quercus rubra (female flowers)

Quercus rubra (leaves)

way to their midribs into seven to eleven triangular to oblong, irregularly-toothed lobes, with hairs only in the axils of the veins of the leaf undersides. The ovoid nuts, about 1 inch long, are one-third embedded in their flat-bottomed cups. The Shumard oak (*Q. shumardii*) (5b) resembles the scarlet oak in aspect and foliage. A handsome native of damp soils from North Carolina to Michigan, Florida, and Texas, it is sometimes 120 feet in height. When mature its leaves are hairless, except for tufts in the axils of the veins on their undersides. Obovate in outline and deeply-seven-lobed or less often five-lobed, they have several conspicuously bristle-pointed teeth at the apex of each lobe. The acorns, ½ to ¾ inch long, have a shallow, saucer- to more or less top-shaped cup covering up to one-third of the nut. The post oak (*Q. stellata*) (3), native from Massachusetts to Nebraska, Florida, and Texas, is up to 60 feet or rarely 100 feet tall. Round-headed, it has blunt, hairy buds and obovate leaves with usually wedge-shaped bases, 4 to 8 inches long, and with two or three pairs of blunt, squarish side lobes in addition to the terminal one. The upper leaf surfaces are furnished with scattered hairs, whereas the undersurfaces have denser, yellow hairs. From ½ to 1 inch in length, the stalkless,

ovoid acorns possess hemispherical cups from one-third to one-half as long as the nuts. The Oriental oak (*Q. variabilis*) (1) is notable for its corklike bark, which is, however, very much thinner than that of the cork oak. Native to Japan, China, and Korea, and hardy in southern New England, and attaining a height of about 75 feet, it has a rather open head. Its pointed, chestnut-like leaves, 3 to 7 inches long and up to 2 inches wide and elliptic-oblong to elliptic, have nine to sixteen pairs of parallel side veins, which terminate at the margins in bristle-like teeth. The upper leaf surfaces are dull green and hairless, the undersides felted with minute, whitish hairs. The nearly stalkless acorns, their spherical-ovoid nuts nearly completely enclosed by the cups, are ½ to ¾ inch long. The common black oak (*Q. velutina*) (5b), one of the biggest North American species, is native from Maine to Florida, Minnesota, and Texas. Of quite rapid growth, this attains an eventual height up to 100 to

Quercus velutina

Quercus velutina (trunk)

Quercus velutina (branching habit)

Quercus velutina (leaves)

150 feet, and has a rather narrow, open head of comparatively slender branches. Its inner bark is orange. The variable, ovate to oblong leaves are, when young, brownish-pubescent on their undersides. Up to 10 inches long, they have seven or nine broad, toothed lobes. They turn dullish red to orange-brown in fall. The short-stalked acorns, ½ to 1 inch long, have ovoid nuts with their lower halves embraced by densely-hairy cups.

Evergreen oaks or live oaks include several native species as well as the cork oak, holm oak, and other exotic kinds. None is hardy in the north. Here belong these sorts: The Japanese evergreen oak (*Q. acuta*) (cycl.), in its native state attains heights of 30 to 40 feet; in cultivation it is usually much lower and often shrublike. It has leathery, elliptic to ovate leaves, 2½ to 5½ inches long, with lobeless, toothless, wavy margins and eight to ten veins on each side of the midrib. Their upper surfaces are lustrous and dark green, their undersides dull and yellowish. In crowded spikes of several, the ¾-inch-long acorns have hemispherical nuts, their lower thirds covered by the cups. The California live oak (*Q. agrifolia*) (5c), endemic to coastal regions from northern California to Baja California, dome-shaped, and up to 100 feet tall by 150 feet wide, has a short trunk and massive, crooked branches, the lowermost often resting on the ground.

Quercus agrifolia, Rancho Santa Ana Botanic Garden, Claremont, California

Somewhat resembling those of American and English hollies, the glossy leaves, usually prickly along their margins, are paler on their undersides than above, and hairy there when young. They are 1½ to 3 inches long. Individuals remain for not over a year, then shed while new foliage is developing. The usually stalkless, long-pointed acorns mature in their second year. Up to 1½ inches long, they possess cups one-quarter to one-third their lengths. The maul or canyon oak (*Q. chrysolepis*) (4) is a very beautiful California endemic. Up to 60 feet tall or rarely taller, but generally lower, it has a short trunk and a head of massive, often horizontal or pendulous branches. Its short-stalked leaves, broad-elliptic to oblong-ovate, spiny-toothed or smooth-edged, are 1 inch to 4 inches long. Their upper surfaces are yellowish- or bluish-green. Beneath they are glaucous, covered when young with reddish hairs. Ripening in their second year, the short-stalked acorns have cups commonly densely clothed with reddish hairs, one-quarter as long as the nuts. The Engelmann oak (*Q. engelmannii*) (4), a handsome native of southern California and Baja California, is 50 to 60 feet tall, with a head of branches that spread nearly hori-

Quercus engelmannii

zontally. It has oblongish to obovate, remotely-toothed or toothless evergreen leaves about 2 inches long, bluish-green

above and with pale undersides. The usually stalked but sometimes stalkless acorn, ¾ to 1 inch long and about ½ inch wide, has a cup that contains about one-third of the nut. The holm oak (*Q. ilex*) (3), a native of the Mediterranean region, develops a large, round-topped head up to 60 feet in height. Very variable, its distantly-toothed to nearly toothless, evergreen leaves are dark green above, yellowish or whitish on their undersides. They are 1 inch to 3 inches in length and have rolled-back margins. The usually stalked acorns

Quercus ilex, the Royal Botanic Gardens, Kew, England

have egg-shaped nuts, their lower halves seated in cups with thin, rarely slightly spreading scales. Variety *Q. i. rotundifolia* (syn. *Q. ballota*) has smaller, broadly-ovate to nearly round leaves. Those of *Q. i. fordii*, a small pyramidal tree, are narrower than those of the typical species. Japanese *Q. myrsinaefolia* (cycl.) is not hardy in the north. A beautiful species up to about 50 feet in height, this has pointed, hairless, lanceolate to oblanceolate, toothed, evergreen leaves 3 to 5 inches long by ¾ inch to 1¼ inches wide, with upper sides lustrous green and undersides somewhat glaucous. In short spikes, the acorns have hairless cups concealing the lower one-third of the nut and formed of about six concentric rings. The cork oak (*Q. suber*)

Quercus suber, the National Botanic Garden, Glasnevin, Dublin, Ireland

(1), of the Mediterranean region, broad, round-topped, and up to about 60 feet high, is remarkable for its very thick, deeply-furrowed, elastic bark. Its re-

Quercus suber (trunk)

Quercus suber (leaves and male flowers)

motely-toothed evergreen leaves, 1 inch to 3 inches long, are whitish on their undersides. The short-stalked acorns have the lower thirds to halves of their ovate to oblong nuts seated in cups with thick scales, often with recurved tips. The eastern North American live oak (*Q. virginiana*) (3), native from Virginia to Florida

Quercus virginiana, young trees at Williamsburg, Virginia

and Mexico, is a massive tree with a spread twice as great as its up to 75 foot height. A splendid ornamental, it has a trunk that divides within a few feet of the ground and branches that spread horizontally. Whitish and hairy on their undersides, the glossy, scarcely-toothed, dark green, usually blunt, evergreen, obovate to elliptic or oblong leaves, 1½ to 5 inches long, have rolled-under, scarcely-toothed margins. The approximately 1-inch-long, ovoid acorns have cups one-quarter as long as the nuts, with thin nonspreading scales. The interior live oak (*Q. wislizenii*) (5c), of southern California and New Mexico, is a slow grower used to some extent ornamentally in its native regions. Attaining a height of 75 feet, this has evergreen, usually oblong leaves, glossy-green above, yellowish on their undersides, smooth-edged or spiny-toothed, and about 4 inches long. The conical or tapering acorns, 1½ inches long or slightly longer, have cups one-quarter to one-half as long as the nuts.

Garden and Landscape Uses. Although mostly handsome, stately, little subject to storm damage, and possessed of many other virtues, because of their need for considerable space, oaks are generally not well suited for small home grounds. Old specimens in place when such sites are developed are, however, frequently and quite rightly preserved as noble adornments and for shade. But it is in more expansive landscapes, such as parks, areas around institutions and industrial buildings, estate-size home grounds, and as avenue and street trees, that oaks are most often planted.

In choosing sorts, consider their adaptability to local climate and other environmental circumstances. The pin oak, willow oak, and evergreen *Q. acuta*, for example, will not tolerate alkaline soils, and some kinds, such as the chestnut oak and Oregon oak, adapt better than others to somewhat dryish ones. Give thought to habits of growth. The white oak, with its eventual immense spread of branches, is clearly less promising as a street tree than are pin and willow oaks. Others, which as they approach maturity demand much space and may eventually exceed 100 feet in diameter, include the live oak of the southern United States, the maul oak, and the Oregon oak. Less demanding of space are the burr, chestnut, common black, shingle, red, scarlet, laurel, and water oaks. The shingle oak, sheared regularly, makes a very good tall hedge or windbreak, and doubtless other sorts could serve this purpose also.

Beautiful fall foliage colors are special dividends provided by many oaks. Absent, or but slightly developed in European species, such as the English, Durmast, and Turkey oaks, such hues are most strikingly evident in many natives of North America. Among the most brilliant are the scarlet and pin oaks, with leaves that turn brilliant scarlet; the basket, red, and shingle oaks, bright red to russet-red; and the overcup oak, scarlet to orange. With the coming of fall, the leaves of the chestnut oak change to orange or orange-brown, those of the water oak to duller shades of the same colors. Then too, the foliage of the Spanish and scrub oaks becomes dull orange-brown or yellow and that of the willow oak yellow or yellowish. The white oak signals fall's arrival by its leaves changing to various shades of wine-red to violet-purple.

Many species, notably the white, scarlet, and black oaks, have deep taproots and, except when very young, much resent transplanting. Others, of which the red, pin, willow, laurel, and water oaks are examples, can be moved with greater expectation of success, but with all kinds care is needed and it is important to take good-sized balls of earth and to prune the tops fairly heavily at planting time.

Cultivation. Because oaks are predominately deep-rooting and strong-branched they are little subject to storm damage and in reasonably acceptable environments prosper with little or no special care. Regular pruning is not needed. Except for horticultural varieties, which are usually multiplied by grafting onto seedling understocks in greenhouses in late winter or early spring, seeds provide the most satisfactory means of propagation.

As understocks for grafting, deciduous kinds of the same subgenera or sections of subgenera are usually preferred. Favored kinds are the English oak, common black oak, common red oak, and basket oak or chestnut oak. Evergreen oaks are sometimes increased by layering and sometimes by summer cuttings in a greenhouse propagating bench, preferably under mist.

Seeds of sorts of the white oak group, under favorable conditions, begin root developent as soon as they are mature and drop from the tree, but do not develop shoots until spring. The germination of those of many other sorts is delayed until spring. With all kinds it is fatal to allow them to dry out before sowing. Either sow in fall as soon as ripe or store in slightly damp peat moss, sand, or vermiculite in a temperature of 40°F until spring, and then sow. To avoid unnecessary root disturbance, some propagators advocate sowing seeds of sorts difficult to transplant singly in individual pots and later to repot the seedlings into larger containers and grow them there until they are in their permanent locations.

During their years in nursery rows, as they grow to sizes suitable to moving to their permanent quarters, it is important to transplant oaks every two or three years to favor the development of compact masses of roots.

Pests and Diseases. Oaks are subject to what might be considered more than their fair share of pests and diseases, some serious, others less so. Not all occur in all parts of North America, and comparatively few are likely to be prevalent in any one locality. Still, watchfulness must be maintained and if trouble appears the services of the local Cooperative Extension Agent, State Agricultural Experiment Station, or other reliable authority should be enlisted to identify the pest or malady and to prescribe control measures.

Galls caused by insects or mites that live inside them, and number hundreds of kinds, develop on oaks. Most, unless considered disfiguring, do no appreciable harm, but heavy infestations of a few kinds may kill branches. Application of a dormant-strength lime-sulfur or miscible oil spray in early spring is the recommended control. The same sprays applied at the same time are advised for dealing with infestations of the different sorts of scale insects that infest oaks.

Leaf-eating caterpillars and weevils of several sorts, including annoying canker-worms or inchworms, may be checked with stomach poison contact sprays, applied when they first become active. Contact sprays may be used also to check such sucking pests as lacebugs and mites.

Diseases that affect oaks include anthracnose, cankers, leaf blisters, leaf spots, and powdery mildew, as well as twig blights and rust. Extremely destructive in some parts of North America, oak wilt is a fungus disease that usually kills infected tress within a year or two. Shoestring root rot is also serious, more especially to specimens in weak condition from other causes. The black, rootlike strands of mycelium of this fungus surround the roots and grow under loosened bark at the base of the trunk, causing rotting and death of the living tissues. A distinct mushroom-like odor is detectable near affected parts, and toadstools eventually appear around the trees. There is no practicable control.

QUESNELIA (Ques-nèlia). Native only to eastern Brazil, the possibly thirty species of *Quesnelia* belong in the pineapple family BROMELIACEAE. Their name commemorates M. Quesnel, French Consul at Cayenne, French Guiana, who first introduced this genus into cultivation.

Botanically, *Quesnelia* stands midway between *Aechmea* and *Billbergia*. From *Aechmea* it differs in its flowers not having sharp-pointed sepals, from *Billbergia* in its blooms being neither asymmetrical nor having petals strongly coiled backward. Quesnelias are generally stemless, evergreen, herbaceous perennials. Most kinds normally grow in the ground rather than, like the majority of the pineapple family, perched on trees. Often in the wild they favor places near the ocean, some growing on sandy shores not much above high tide, others in peat bogs and swampy forests back from the shore. Some few kinds grow as tree-perchers (epiphytes) in coastal mountain ranges. The leaves of quesnelias, usually in rosettes, are generally strap-shaped. They have spiny margins. The blooms are arranged variously, loosely or crowded, on branchless or branched flowering stalks. Each has three, more or less asymmetrical sepals, the same number of separate, similar, erect or nearly erect petals longer than the six stamens and furnished at their bases with a pair of small scales, and a three-cleft style. The fruits are berries.

These species are cultivated: *Q. arvensis,* native to wet places in humid forests, has rosettes of prominently spined, green leaves obscurely cross-banded with silver on their undersides. The leaves are up to 2 feet long by 2 inches broad above, and wider at their bases. The stout, flowering stalks clothed with pointed-ovate bracts terminate in a dense, cylindrical head 3 to 4 inches long of salmon-pink bracts that practically conceal the blue-petaled flowers. *Q. blanda (syn. Q. strobilispica),* a tree-perching inhabitant of forests, has rosettes of up to six erect, sword-shaped leaves up to 2 feet long by 2 inches wide or somewhat narrower, and green with obscure silvery cross-bands on their undersides. Erect, slender, and 1 foot to 1½ feet long, the flowering stalks terminate in a crowded, cylindrical to ellipsoid head 3 to 4 inches long of greenish-blue- to violet-petaled blooms. The bracts are red. *Q. humilis* spreads by stolons to form broad patches. Its tubular rosettes, 1 inch to 1½ inches in diameter, are of blue-green, channeled to flattish leaves 9 inches to 2 feet long that spread above their middles and have minutely-toothed margins. The branchless flowering stalks, which may or may not extend beyond the foliage, carry crowded, cerise heads of blooms with bright red calyxes and rich blue petals. *Q. lateralis* is a mountain plant, in habit much resembling *Billbergia,* but distinct by reason of its flowering stalks coming from the sides of the plant (laterally) as well as from their centers. The bright green leaves, eight to ten to each rosette, are up to 2 feet long or sometimes longer. The cylindrical heads of bloom top slender stalks 1 foot to 2 feet in length. The flowers have blue petals. The bracts are red-tinged to flame-red, the lower ones up to 1 foot long. *Q. liboniana* is a forest dweller spreading by stolons. Of *Billbergia*-like aspect, it has rosettes of narrow, green leaves, 1 foot to 2 feet long by up to 1½ inches wide. The pendulous flowering stalks carry small heads of dark purple blooms and orange bracts. *Q. marmorata* (syn. *Aechmea marmorata*) has narrow fans rather than typical rosettes of five or six

two-ranked, erect leaves, 1 foot to 1½ feet long by about 2 inches wide. They are blue-green, decoratively mottled or marbled with maroon. Not much longer than the leaves, the branched, slightly drooping flower stalks have blooms with blue petals that contrast beautifully with the showy, pink bracts. Short-stalked offsets are produced from the bases of the plants. *Q. quesneliana* is vigorous, in the wild making tremendous jungles 3 to 4 feet tall along seashores and in fields. It also perches on trees. Its fine-toothed leaves are light green cross-banded with gray on their undersides. The flowering stalks, up to 3 feet tall, end in a cone-shaped head with overlapping, white-edged, rose-pink bracts and blooms with lavender-edged, white petals. *Q. siedeliana* has erect rosettes of dark-spined, green, white-scale-covered leaves up to 1¼ feet long. Slender and erect, the flowering stalks, up to about 1½ feet tall, terminate in an egg-shaped head or spike, 2 inches long, composed of pale bracts and blooms with white sepals and pale blue petals. *Q. testudo* is a tree-percher with leaves up to 2

Quesnelia testudo

Quesnelia testudo (flower head)

feet in length and breadth; they have small marginal spines and on their undersurfaces many fine whitish cross-bands. The stout, erect flowering stalks, 1 foot or so tall, end in an ovoid-cylindrical, dense

head, 4 to 8 inches long, composed of rosy-to purplish-red bracts and blooms with violet or white petals.

Garden Uses and Cultivation. These plants make their chief appeal to bromeliad fanciers. In addition, they are useful furnishings for gardens in the humid tropics and subtropics. They respond to environments and care that suit aechmeas, billbergias, and many other bromeliads. For additional information see Bromeliads or Bromels.

QUIABENTIA (Quia-béntia). Five species of leafy cactuses, with much the appearance of *Pereskia* and *Pereskiopsis,* are contained in *Quiabentia,* of the cactus family CACTACEAE. They are most closely related to *Pereskiopsis,* but differ in having smooth instead of hairy seeds. The name is from *quiabento,* a native name for *Q. zehntneri.* All are natives of South America. The blooms more closely resemble those of *Pereskia.*

Quiabentias are bushy, more or less vinelike or treelike, and have slender, cylindrical stems. Typically, their alternate leaves are fleshy and oval. From the areoles (points of origin of spines) develop many usually small spines and glochids (barbed bristles). The red blooms expand widely. The fruits contain white seeds.

Native to Brazil, *Q. zehntneri* is 6 to 10 feet tall. It has broad-ovate to roundish leaves ¾ inch to 1½ inches long and from each areole numerous small, whitish spines. Its blooms are bright red, its slender fruits up to 3 inches long. A tree up to 45 feet tall, *Q. pflanzii* is indigenous to Bolivia. It has short, thin spines and ovate leaves about 1½ inches long by one-half as broad. Its flowers are light red. Also Bolivian, *Q. verticillata* is a shrub some 6 feet in height, with pointed-lanceolate leaves 2 inches long, spines that may be nearly 3 inches long, and light red flowers.

Garden and Landscape Uses and Cultivation. These are as for *Pereskia.* For general information see Cactuses.

QUICK STICK is *Gliricidia sepium.*

QUILLAJA (Quil-làja) — Soap-Bark Tree. The name of this genus of three species of trees of temperate South America is derived from the Chilean name *quillai,* a modification of *quillean,* to wash. It alludes to the suds-making qualities of the soap-bark tree, the result of the presence in its tissues of saponin. Quillajas belong in the rose family ROSACEAE and are sparsely foliaged evergreens, with stalked, undivided, thick leathery leaves. The flowers, solitary or more usually three to five together in terminal and axillary clusters, are unisexual or sometimes bisexual. They have leathery, persistent, five-cleft calyxes, five small, spatula-shaped petals, and five stamens. The fruits consist of five leathery, many-seeded follicles (pods), joined at their bases.

The only kind likely to be cultivated is the soap-bark tree (*Quillaja saponaria*). This is hardy in southern California and in areas with climates similarly mild. Up to 60 feet tall, it has ovate, slightly toothed leaves up to 2 inches long, and white flowers, ½ inch or slightly more in diameter, that are usually terminal and may be in clusters or solitary.

Garden and Landscape Uses and Cultivation. The soap-bark tree is of interest for planting in climates where there is little or no frost. It succeeds in ordinary soil and is increased by seed and by cuttings planted in a greenhouse propagating bench or in a similar environment.

QUINCE. Here we are concerned with quinces cultivated chiefly for their edible fruits, which, although too harsh to be eaten out of hand, are esteemed for jellies, jams, and similar preserves. For the ornamental shrubs called flowering- or Japanese-quinces, see Chaenomeles.

The quince (*Cydonia oblonga*), cultivated since ancient times, is without importance as a commercial orchard fruit and is rarely planted in home gardens. Yet besides supplying useful produce, it is an attractive, rather slow-growing tree that with age becomes quite picturesque. Its flowers are white. Seedling quinces are used as dwarfing understocks upon which to graft pears. Native from Iran to Turkestan, this tree, which usually does not much exceed 15 feet in height, develops a bushy head. For more details see Cydonia.

Quinces respond to sunny locations and well-drained soils such as suit apples, pears, and most other fruit trees of temperate regions. Plant one- or two-year-old specimens where there is adequate space for them to develop spreads of 15 feet or more. In their early years, prune and train as for apples, but allow more branches to develop. Little pruning is needed later. Excessive cutting is likely to stimulate too vigorous growth, which is susceptible to

Quince (foliage and fruit)

Quince (*Cydonia oblonga*)

fire blight, the most serious disease of quinces. Ordinarily the removal of crossing branches and a little thinning is all that is needed. Do not, unless absolutely necessary, make large cuts.

Avoid excessive use of fertilizers that stimulate vigorous, succulent growth. Shoots of this character invite fire blight. Often it is best to refrain entirely from using nitrogenous fertilizers and to rely instead on mulching with hay or compost.

Harvesting must not be done until the fruits are fully mature, as indicated by their readiness to part from the branch when gently lifted to a horizontal position. When this condition is reached, they are wonderfully fragrant. Wipe the fruits when dry with a clean cloth and spread them in single layers in a cool, frostproof room or cellar. But do not keep them with other fruits, such as apples or pears, or they will impart something of their characteristic odor and flavor to them.

Propagation is by budding onto seedling quinces or 'Angus' quince understocks and by mound, stool, or trench layering.

A favorite variety and the earliest to ripen is 'Orange'. This has yellow, apple-shaped fruits and is hardy about as far north as southern New York. Slightly more cold-resistant and somewhat later

ripening are 'Van Deman', a hybrid of 'Orange', which fruits when quite young, and 'Burbank Jumbo', which also fruits when young and ripens rather later than 'Van Deman'. Quinces are subject to the pests and diseases that affect pears.

QUININE BUSH is *Garrya fremontii*. The drug quinine is a product of species of *Cinchona*.

QUINOA is *Chenopodium quinoa*.

QUINTINIA (Quin-tínia). Of the saxifrage family SAXIFRAGACEAE, this genus of twenty species ranges from New Guinea, the Philippine Islands, and New Caledonia to Australia and New Zealand. It is related to *Escallonia*. Except for one New Zealand species, it is little known in cultivation. The name commemorates the French botanist, Jean de la Quintinie, who died in 1688.

Quintinias are nonhardy trees and shrubs with undivided, alternate, usually toothed leaves, and small blooms in axillary or terminal racemes. The flowers have five each calyx lobes, petals, and stamens, and a pistil with a three- to five-lobed stigma. The fruits are capsules.

Endemic to New Zealand, *Quintinia*

Harvesting radishes

mustard family CRUCIFERAE, is one of the most ancient of cultivated plants. More than 4,500 years ago, radishes were included in the rations of workers who built the Great Pyramids of Egypt. In the Orient many more varieties are cultivated than in American or European gardens and they are used in more ways. One, the rat-tailed radish (*R. s. caudatus*) does not produce edible roots, but develops curved, twisted pods, 8 inches to 1 foot long, that are used in the same way as the roots of more familiar sorts.

Radishes are annuals eaten chiefly as salads. The common sorts have small, swollen roots, when young crisp and tender, but as they age becoming pithy and bitingly hot. Other varieties, listed in catalogs as fall and winter radishes, have larger roots that do not behave in this way and are suitable for storage.

The common, small-rooted radish is a cool weather crop that matures rapidly. Where climate permits it is usual to make several sowings at intervals of ten days to three weeks.

For best success sow rather thinly and about ½ inch deep in fertile, well-tilled soil in full sun for early sowings, where there is just a little shade during the heat of the day for later ones. Make the drills 9 inches to 1 foot apart or locate them between rows of wider-spaced vegetables for the radishes to serve as a catch crop to be harvested before they are crowded by or crowd the other kind. It is also practicable to scatter seeds at the rate of three or four to the foot, say, along with seeds of onions, parsnips, and other vegetables that develop slowly. Because radishes germinate quickly the young plants mark the rows and so facilitate cultivating between them; as they mature they provide welcome pickings.

Should the weather be dry, water copiously to keep the ground always reasonably moist. If birds prove troublesome, it may be desirable to protect the crop by covering the rows with netting or cheesecloth supported on short stakes. Harvest by pulling selected individuals from the row as soon as they are big enough.

Early crops may be had by sowing in frames or hot beds two weeks to a month before outdoor seeding is feasible. Where the climate is too hot for summer crops, it is often practicable to obtain harvests from sowings made in early fall. At that time, too, sow seeds of fall and winter radishes for storage or in mild regions for harvesting through the winter.

Popular varieties of common radish include 'Cherry Belle', with globular, red-skinned roots; 'French Breakfast', with olive-shaped to oblongish, red-skinned roots; and 'White Icicle', with long, white-skinned roots. Fall and winter radishes include 'Round Black Spanish', with black-skinned, globular roots 3 to 4 inches in diameter, and 'White Chinese', a variety with white-skinned roots 6 to 8 inches long by 2 to 3 inches wide.

RAFFENALDIA (Raffen-áldia). A genus of the mustard family CRUCIFERAE, containing two species, *Raffenaldia* is native to North Africa. Its name commemorates Alire Raffeneau Delile, an early nineteenth-century professor of botany in France.

Low plants, of the style of *Morisia*, raffenaldias are tap-rooted and have rosettes of narrow, lobed or toothed leaves. The flowers, typical of their family, have four sepals, four petals spreading to form a cross, four long and two shorter stamens, and one style. The fruits are capsules.

The oblanceolate to inversely-fiddle-shaped, pinnately-lobed leaves of *R. primuloides* (syn. *Cossonia africana*), 1 inch to 4 inches long, are thickish and glaucous. They have a terminal lobe much larger than the others. Numerous and opening in succession over a long period, the blooms, about 1¼ inches wide, are on stalks 2 inches long that thicken upward. They are primrose-yellow to lilac, with lilac veins. This native of Morocco and Algeria is a perennial.

Garden Uses and Cultivation. The only appropriate uses for this plant are in rock gardens and alpine greenhouses. It is probably not hardy where winters are severe. Very porous, well-drained soil, on the poor side rather than too fertile, and full sun are necessary to maintain a desirable, neat habit. Propagation is very easy by seed.

RAFFIA. Less used than formerly for tying plants to stakes and similar supports, raffia is a thin, strong, pliable material consisting of strands of the leaves of the palm *Raphia farinifera*, a native of Malagasy (Madagascar). They are prepared by drying young leaves, shredding them into long strips, and then plaiting and baling them for market. For tying plants, raffia is easier to handle if it is first soaked in water.

RAFT. This is the name gardeners use for platforms, usually 1 foot to 3 feet square, constructed of strips of rot-resistant wood such as cypress, redwood, or teak as supports for certain orchids, ferns, and other epiphytes such as bromeliads. The strips are spaced to form an open grid and the raft is suspended in a horizontal position in the fashion of a hanging basket by wires or chains attached to its corners and their free ends connected to a hook. Other rafts are simply slats of cork bark or tree fern trunks. Osmunda fiber or other rooting medium is piled on and sometimes is wired to the raft.

RAG GOURD. See Luffa.

RAGWORT. See Senecio.

RAILROAD CREEPER is *Ipomoea cairica*.

RAILROAD WORM. See Maggots.

RAIN-LILY. See Zephyranthes.

RAIN TREE is *Samanea saman*. The golden-rain tree is *Koelreuteria paniculata*.

RAINBOW SHOWER is *Cassia hybrida*.

RAINIERA. See Luina.

RAISIN TREE, JAPANESE is *Hovenia dulcis*.

RAJANIA (Raj-ània)—Cockscomb-Yam. This West Indian genus of twenty-five species belongs in the yam family DIOSCOREACEAE. The tubers of some kinds of *Rajania* are believed to be edible. The name commemorates an English botanical author, the Reverend John Ray, who died in 1705.

Rajanias are twining, perennial, tuberous-rooted vines with alternate, undivided, heart-shaped to linear leaves. Their unisexual flowers, the sexes often on separate plants, are small, greenish, in clusters or racemes, or solitary. Each has six perianth segments (petals). The males have six stamens. The fruits are small carpels with a large wing.

The cockscomb-yam (*R. pleioneura*) is so called because its large aerial tubers are irregularly-branched and have lobed or crested margins suggestive of a cock's comb. A subshrubby species, up to 6 feet tall, this has pointed, heart-shaped leaves, 2 to 6 inches in diameter, with nine prominent longitudinal veins, and quite long stalks at the bases of which the aerial tubers grow. Male and female flowers are on separate plants, in racemes, and often clustered.

Garden and Landscape Uses and Cultivation. In the tropics and warm subtropics, the cockscomb-yam is grown as an ornamental and something of a curiosity. It thrives in fertile soil and is propagated by aerial tubers.

RAKES and RAKING. Rakes are basic garden tools used for a variety of purposes and worthy of thought in their selection and care. As with all hand tools, competence in their use comes only with practice.

The rigid iron-toothed rake with usually twelve or fourteen teeth is employed to

A fourteen-toothed iron rake in use

even surfaces left rough after spading or forking and to gather into piles debris to facilitate picking up for removal. It also serves as the gardener's equivalent of a harrow for breaking the surface soil into a fine tilth in readiness for sowing seeds and planting. To perform this last operation effectively calls for considerable skill. If the surface is suitably graded, but rough, the objective is to break the lumps and sift the soil through the teeth of the rake without creating hills and hollows by dragging or pushing too much from place to place. To achieve this, do not bear down heavily on the handle with the lower hand (the left, if you are right-handed). Instead, hold it loosely so the handle can slide through that hand, and accept with it the

A wooden rake in use

weight of the head to prevent the teeth digging in too deeply. Break lumps of soil that do not disintegrate easily by tamping them with the flat side of the head of the rake. If large stones are encountered, re-

A bamboo lawn rake in use

move them as the work proceeds but do not bother about any less than ½ inch or perhaps even 1 inch in diameter.

The wooden rake, because its head is much wider than that of the iron rake, is often preferable for final preparation for seeding and planting large areas. Because it is lighter and has a greater span it is easier, especially for the relatively unskilled, to attain an even surface with it than with an iron rake. But these same features render it less effective when dealing with heavy, clayey soils that do not break up easily.

Lawn rakes with long flexible teeth of bamboo or steel curved at their ends are used for picking fallen leaves and other light debris from lawns, flower and shrub beds, and other areas.

RAMBUTAN is *Alectryon subcinereum*.

RAMIE is *Boehmeria nivea candicans*.

RAMONDA (Ramón-da). The gesneria family GESNERIACEAE is primarily a tropical one. Few of its members survive freezing winters. The present genus is an exception. It consists of three late-spring-blooming species that in the wild chiefly inhabit cracks and crevices in shaded places, generally in limestone, in the mountains of southern Europe. The name *Ramonda*, sometimes spelled *Ramondia*, commemorates the French botanist L. F. E. von Ramond de Carbonnieres, who died in 1827.

Ramondas are stemless, evergreen, herbaceous plants with much the general appearance of African-violets, to which they are related. Their roughish, undivided leaves, in basal rosettes, are hairy. The asymmetrical flowers, few together or occasionally solitary, on erect, leafless stalks, have four-, five-, or rarely six-parted ca-

lyxes and corollas, the latter with short tubes. There are the same number of short stamens as petals. The fruits are many-seeded capsules.

Native to the Pyrenees, *R. myconi* (syn. *R. pyrenaica*) forms rosettes that may be 6 inches or somewhat more in diameter, of deeply-toothed, wrinkled leaves with a few pale hairs on their upper surfaces and

Ramonda myconi

many reddish ones beneath. The flower stalks, 3 to 4 inches tall, have usually three to five lavender-blue to purple flowers, about 1¼ inches wide, with five sepals and five petals. The seed capsules are ½ to 1 inch long. A distinguishing feature is the sharp-pointed, yellow anthers. This species exhibits some variation in leaf form as well as in flower color. In *R. m. alba*, the blooms are white, in *R. m. rosea*, pink. The latter variety is especially beautiful.

Similar to *R. myconi* but with smaller, more cup-shaped flowers, smaller seed capsules, and blunt anthers is *R. serbica*, of the Balkans. Its leaves, obovate to spatula-shaped, are wrinkled and have irregularly-toothed, slightly upturned edges. They are furnished with brownish hairs, especially on their edges and undersides. Each 2- to 4-inch-long flower stalk normally has one to three lilac-blue blooms with yellow throats that do not expand as

Ramonda myconi alba

widely as those of the other species. Their calyxes have four or five, their corollas, four to six lobes. The anthers are blunt and lilac-blue. The seed capsules do not exceed ½ inch in length. Also from the Balkans, *R. nathaliae* differs from the last in having flatter rosettes of rounded-ovate, wrinkled leaves, not upturned at their shallowly-toothed edges, and flatter flowers. Both leaf surfaces, but more especially the lower, are covered with reddish hairs. On stems up to 4½ inches tall are carried up to six orange-eyed, lavender-violet flowers. Most commonly these have four, rarely five or six, petals. The seed capsules are about ⅓ inch in length. Variety *R. n. alba* has white flowers. This species and its variety bloom earlier than the others.

Garden Uses and Cultivation. Choice plants for rock gardens and alpine greenhouses, ramondas are primarily of interest to alpine gardening enthusiasts. Under favorable conditions they are not extraordinarily difficult to grow, but they do need careful placement and intelligent care. They cannot be expected to survive where the environment is not reasonably to their liking. The essentials are loose earth that contains a large proportion of leaf mold or other decayed organic matter, and is uniformly moist from spring to fall, and a shaded, cool-in-summer location. An ideal place for them is a deep vertical crevice in a north-facing rock garden cliff. Many growers assert that such a situation is the only one that ramondas find agreeable, and in the wet climate of England this may be true, but in the northeastern United States excellent specimens have been had planted on the flat on the tops of low-cut rotting tree stumps. They can also be grown in well-drained pans (shallow pots) kept buried to one-half their depth in a bed of sand, sand and peat moss, or cinders, in a cold frame. Under these conditions it is possible to prevent water from lying in the rosettes of foliage for long periods, a condition that may cause rotting. Ramondas can be increased by leaf cuttings planted in a greenhouse propagating bench or under approximately similar conditions, but the best results are generally had by raising them from seeds. These are extremely minute. They are sown in spring in pots or pans of sandy, peaty soil. The seeds are pressed into the surface, but are not covered with soil. Instead, a shaded piece of glass is placed over the container to conserve moisture and assure a humid atmosphere. All needed watering is done by immersing the containers partway in water and allowing the moisture to seep from below to the surface. After the seedlings have germinated, the glass cover is removed. At all times the plants are shaded from strong sun.

RAMONTCHI is *Flacourtia indica.*

RAMPION is *Campanula rapunculus.* Horned-rampion is *Phyteuma.*

RAMPS is *Allium tricoccum.*

RAMSONS is *Allium ursinum.*

RANDIA (Rán-dia). Between 200 and 300 species of tropical trees and shrubs, many spiny, constitute *Randia,* of the madder family RUBIACEAE. The name commemorates Isaac Rand, an apothecary and Director of the Chelsea Physic Garden in London, England, who died in 1743. The plant previously known as *R. dumetorum* is *Rothmannia longiflora,* the sort once known as *R. macrantha* is *Rothmannia macrantha.*

Relatives of gardenias, randias have opposite, undivided leaves and solitary or clustered, mostly white or yellowish flowers from the leaf axils, or less frequently terminal on the stems. The blooms have an often lobeless and toothless calyx, a funnel-shaped or narrowly-tubular corolla, with usually spreading lobes (petals), five stamens, and one style. The fruits are berries.

Native to Central America, tropical South America, and the West Indies, *R. formosa* is a beautiful spineless shrub 3 to 12 feet tall. It has short-stalked, pointed, elliptic to ovate or obovate leaves 1 inch to 3 inches long or less often longer, clustered near the tips of the branches. Solitary at the ends of the shoots and short branchlets, its fragrant flowers have a white corolla with a slender tube 2 to 4½ inches long and lobes (petals) that spread to form a star 2 to 3 inches across. The fruits, ellipsoid and approximately 2 inches long, have thin rinds, which, when ripe, are yellowish. They contain edible, pleasantly sweet, black pulp, and flat, brown seeds.

Garden and Landscape Uses and Cultivation. The species described succeeds under conditions that suit gardenias and is readily propagated by cuttings and seed.

RANGER'S BUTTON is *Sphenosciadium capitellatum.*

RANGOON CREEPER is *Quisqualis indica.*

RANGPUR is *Citrus limonia.*

RANUNCULACEAE — Buttercup or Crowfoot Family. Comprising some 800 species of dicotyledons distributed among fifty genera, many of which contain sorts of ornamental merit, this family, which chiefly inhabits north temperate regions, is less abundantly represented in the natural floras of the tropics and the southern hemisphere. Its members are annuals or herbaceous perennials with basal and alternate leaves, or shrubs or vines with opposite leaves often composed of several leaflets. Solitary or in branched clusters or panicles, the flowers have usually five to eight sepals, less often fewer, rarely more, sometimes petal-like. There are generally five petals, but there may be more, fewer, or none. The stamens are numerous. There are usually many carpels, less often few or only one. The fruits, usually bunches of dry achenes, sometimes with long feathery tails, less often are berry-like. Among genera included in this Encyclopedia are *Aconitum, Actaea, Adonis, Anemone, Anemonella, Anemonopsis, Aquilegia, Caltha, Cimicifuga, Clematis, Consolida, Coptis, Delphinium, Eranthis, Glaucidium, Helleborus, Hepatica, Hydrastis, Isopyrum, Leptopyrum, Nigella, Paeonia, Ranunculus, Thalictrum, Trautvetteria, Trollius,* and *Xanthorhiza.*

RANUNCULUS (Ranúnc-ulus)—Buttercup, Crowfoot, Fair-Maids-of-France, Lesser Celandine. Few of the about 400 species of *Ranunculus,* of the buttercup family RANUNCULACEAE, have garden merit, but among those that do are some of considerable charm. Others, familiar as weeds of waysides and meadows, are not generally important pests of cultivated grounds, although on occasion they invade lawns. The genus is native throughout practically the entire cold and temperate regions of the world and on mountains in the tropics. Its name, from the Latin diminutive of *rana,* a frog, alludes to the moist places many buttercups favor.

Buttercups display a wide variety of forms. Chiefly herbaceous perennials, less often annuals or biennials, the various kinds occur natively in dry, moist, or wet soils and a few in water, sometimes as floating aquatics. Most have fibrous roots. A few have tubers. There are short and tall, erect and spreading kinds, some with creeping runners. The leaves are alternate, divided or undivided, frequently lobed or toothed. Rarely the blooms are without stalks. Much more frequently they are stalked and are displayed in variously branched arrangements, including panicles. By far the most common flower color is yellow, but some buttercups have white- and some red-petaled blooms.

Each flower has generally five sepals, usually five, sometimes fewer or no petals, or in double-flowered horticultural varieties, considerably more. There is a small nectar gland at the bottom of each petal. In most kinds the stamens are numerous. The female element consists of five to many pistils, each with one persistent style. The pistils develop into the fruits, which are small seedlike achenes tightly clustered in heads.

Persian and Turban ranunculuses and the more recent sorts called French and peony-flowered ranunculuses are the showiest buttercups. They are horticultural developments of *R. asiaticus,* a na-

Persian or turban ranunculuses: (a) Semidouble-flowered

(b) Double-flowered

tive of southeast Europe and adjacent Asia. From 9 inches to 1½ feet tall or taller, these sorts have stems without branches or are branched from their bases. Their leaves are two- or three-times-divided in palmate (handlike) fashion, the segments three-cleft or toothed. The blooms, which come in white and a wide range of colors except blues and violets, are single, semidouble, or fully double, and 1½ to 3 inches in diameter. The wild, single-flowered forms of *R. asiaticus*, although showy, are rarely cultivated. They have yellow or red blooms, or in *R. a. albiflorus* white ones with a suffusion of green, 1 inch to 1½ inches in diameter.

The double-flowered creeping buttercup, or yellow bachelor's button, generally cultivated as *R. repens pleniflorus* (syns. *R. r. flore-pleno*, *R. acris flore-pleno*), is of somewhat uncertain origin, and there is some small doubt as to its precise identity. A vigorous spreader that rapidly extends itself by sending out runners that root from their joints, this has dark green, nearly round, long-stalked leaves three-times-cleft and coarsely-toothed. Rising to heights of 1 foot to 2 feet, the flowering stalks are erect and branched. The many fully double blooms, about ¾ inch wide and deep, are bright yellow. The species **R. repens,** a vigorous, creeping European, occurs freely as an introduced weed of fields, roadsides, and lawns in North America. Another common native of Europe naturalized in North America, **R. bulbosus** differs from *R. repens* in not creeping and in having bulbous-based, erect stems. The species is not of horticultural merit,

Ranunculus bulbosus pleniflorus

but its double-flowered variety *R. b. pleniflorus* is attractive enough to warrant planting it at the fronts of mixed flower borders. About 1 foot tall, it has ovate to roundish leaves of three lobed leaflets or three deep lobes, which are again lobed. The glossy, bright yellow flowers are about 1 inch in diameter.

Fair-maids-of-France or fair-maids-of-Kent (**R. aconitifolius**) is a native of Europe cultivated since the sixteenth century

Ranunculus aconitifolius

Ranunculus aconitifolius flore-pleno

in its double-flowered variety. From 1 foot to 2 feet tall, this has leaves deeply-cleft into three or five ovate to lanceolate-ovate segments, those of the upper parts of the stems very pointed. The segments are lobed or deeply-toothed. The hairless or nearly hairless stems branch above. They carry many usually white, sometimes yellow blooms, up to about 1 inch wide and with calyxes with few or no hairs, those of cultivated sorts more or less double. The cultivated kind with rosette-like double flowers is *R. a. flore-pleno.*

Greater spearwort (*R. lingua*) is a robust, wet-soil native of Europe suitable for

Ranunculus lingua

planting at watersides. It has hollow stems 2 to 4 feet tall and hairless, undivided, short-stalked, lanceolate leaves up to 1 foot long by ¾ to 1 inch broad, toothed or not, the upper ones stem-clasping. The clear yellow, more or less panicled blooms are 1 inch to 2 inches in diameter. Less meritorious than the last, the lesser spearwort (*R. flammula*) is native in wet soils in Europe, Asia, and North America. Typically, it has erect or reclining stems up to 1½ feet long and branched in their upper parts. The lower leaves are stalked and ovate; the upper, elliptic-lanceolate to lanceolate ones are stalkless. The yellow flowers are nearly or quite ¾ inch in diameter.

Ranunculus flammula

The lesser celandine (*R. ficaria*) comes in several easy-to-grow, pretty varieties. A native of Europe and temperate Asia naturalized in North America, this inhabits moist, shady places and watersides. Usually 2 to 6 inches high, but sometimes taller, it has clusters of small tubers and glossy, long-stalked, triangular-heart-shaped, shallowly-lobed, but not dissected leaves that die down in late spring or early summer. New foliage does not appear until the following spring. The highly lustrous flowers are from a little over ½ inch to somewhat over 1 inch in diameter. They have three or four green sepals and eight to twelve spreading petals. Attractive varieties are *R. f. albus,* with white flowers; *R. f. cuprea,* early-blooming and with cop-

Ranunculus ficaria cuprea

pery blooms; *R. f. flore-pleno,* its flowers fully double; and *R. f. grandiflorus,* which is larger in all its parts.

Sorts suitable for rock gardens include *R. gramineus,* a variable native of southwest Europe that has glaucous, hairless, linear-lanceolate leaves, and flowering stalks 6 inches to 1 foot tall, carrying one to three citron-yellow flowers ¾ to 1 inch across. Variety *R. g. flore-pleno* has double

Ranunculus ficaria flore-pleno

Ranunculus gramineus

flowers. Appropriate for similar use, *R. montanus,* native from the Pyrenees to the Caucasus, has short, creeping rootstocks and chiefly basal leaves, few in number and rounded in outline, with stalks mostly longer than the blades. They are cleft into three- or five-lobed segments, ½ to 1 inch in diameter, and more to less hairy. The flowering stalks, 2 to 6 inches long and erect, have one or two small narrow-lobed leaves and usually solitary, bright yellow blooms, ¾ to 1 inch across. Another adaptable for rock garden cultivation, *R. parnassifolius,* native from the Pyrenees to Austria, is hairy and up to 9 inches tall. Its round-ovate to heart-shaped, often red-margined basal leaves are woolly-hairy along the veins beneath. The white or sometimes pinkish blooms, about 1 inch in diameter, are up to six on each flowering stalk. Their overlapping petals are not notched at their apexes.

The mountain-lily (*R. lyallii*), of New Zealand, is one of the choicest, and in cultivation one of the rarest of alpines. A perennial 1 foot to 5 feet tall, it has fleshy roots and long-stalked lower leaves with nearly circular blades 4 inches to 1 foot in diameter jointed to their stalks well in from their round-toothed margins. The stem leaves are smaller and deeply-lobed. White to creamy-white, the very beautiful flowers, 1 inch to 3 inches in diameter, are in panicles. Another New Zealander, reported to be more amenable to cultivation than *R. lyallii*, is related **R. insignis.** From

Ranunculus insignis

1 foot to 3 feet tall, this has nearly circular to kidney-shaped, stout-stalked lower leaves, with round-toothed blades 4 to 6 inches across. They are dark green and, especially on their undersides, hairy. The smaller upper leaves are more deeply toothed or cleft. From 1 inch to 2 inches or sometimes more in diameter, the flowers are in erect panicles of ten to forty. Each has five to ten, or occasionally more, golden-yellow petals.

Garden and Landscape Uses. Persian and Turban ranunculuses and their variants are excellent for outdoor gardens in mild climates and for cultivation in frames protected from frost and in cool greenhouses. Their cut blooms last well in water. As a flower border plant, *R. repens pleniflorus* grows vigorously and makes a fine display. Its one fault is its tendency to overrun its neighbors, but this can be checked by chopping off with a spade from time to time its overambitious runners. Shady, moist soil places beneath trees and shrubs and at watersides afford suitable accommodations for the lesser celandine and its varieties. There they will prosper and increase without becoming aggressive. The greater spearwort is an appropriate furnishing near water. It succeeds in wet soils and in water an inch or two deep. Lovely *R. montanus* is best fitted for sunny places in rock gardens, preferably under moraine conditions. In similar places, *R. lyallii* may be tried in regions of

Persian ranunculuses: (a) Outdoors in California

(b) In a heated frame

(c) As a greenhouse pot plant

cool summers by those who welcome challenges to their skills as growers.

Cultivation. The planting and care of Persian and Turban ranunculuses and their kin are identical to those that satisfy poppy anemones (see Anemone). The other kinds discussed here are all hardy and once planted need no special attention beyond perhaps limiting their spread. Ranunculuses are increased by tubers, offsets, division, and seed.

RANZANIA (Ran-zània). One species endemic to mountain woodlands in Japan, and rare in the wild and in cultivation, constitutes *Ranzania*, of the barberry family BERBERIDACEAE. It is related to *Diphylleia*. The name honors the distinguished Japanese naturalist Ono Ranzan, who died in 1810.

A hardy, deciduous, herbaceous perennial, **R. japonica** has creeping rhizomes and erect, branchless stems 1 foot to 1½ feet tall, each with two leaves of three short-stalked, thin leaflets at its summit. The blades of the leaflets, 3½ to 4½ inches

Ranzania japonica

Ranzania japonica (foliage)

long and glaucous on their undersides, are nearly circular to broadly-ovate, three-lobed, or cleft. In terminal clusters, the 1-inch-wide, pale purple, nodding flowers make no great show. Each has three petal-like sepals, the same number of tiny petals with a pair of nectar glands at the base of each, and six stamens. The fruits are egg-shaped berries.

Garden Uses and Cultivation. A collector's item agreeable for planting in woodlands and shady rock gardens, *Ranzania* needs conditions and care that suit *Diphylleia*.

RAOULIA (Ra-oùlia). Except for a few species in Australia and New Guinea, this genus of twenty-five of the daisy family COMPOSITAE is endemic to New Zealand. Its name commemorates Edouard Raoul, a French naval surgeon who collected and wrote about New Zealand plants. He died in 1852.

Raoulias are related to *Helichrysum* from which they differ in the arrangement of the hairs of the pappus (appendages to the florets and fruits). They are low shrubs or herbaceous perennials that fall conveniently into two groups, those that are compact true shrubs, with woody, more or less erect, branching stems, and those that are mat-forming, carpeting kinds with creeping stems. Although highly interesting, so far as is known members of the first group have rarely, if ever, been successfully cultivated. To them belongs remarkable *Raoulia eximia*, which forms a dense billowy mound up to 3 feet broad and 2 feet tall, and which because of its appearance is sometimes called vegetable sheep (a name shared by related and rather similar *Haastia pulvinaris*, of New Zealand). The leaves of raoulias are tiny, alternate, and undivided, overlap to hide their stems, often and are clothed with woolly hairs. The stalkless or almost stalkless little flower heads terminate the stems and branches. They are composed of disk florets (the type of which the center eyes of daisies are formed), without any surrounding ray florets (the petal-like ones of daisies), but with an involucre (collar) of dry, papery or membraneous, white or yellow bracts. The seedlike fruits are achenes.

Silvery *R. australis* (syn. *R. lutescens*) has been so admirably described by one writer as "clinging to rock and scree like a coat of cracked and dirty aluminum paint" that further description is hardly needed. It is indeed one of the lowest of carpeters, one that exactly follows with its rooting stems the contours of the ground or rocks it clothes. The extremely abbreviated,

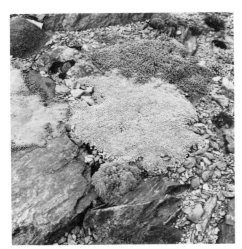

Raoulia australis in a Scottish rock garden

crowded branches have leaves with silvery hairs that lie flat on their surfaces. On wild plants the leaves are not longer than 1/12 inch, but on cultivated specimens they may be up to 1/4 inch long. The flower heads are yellow. Less compact, and green-foliaged, *R. glabra* has prostrate, rooting stems and narrowly-ovate to linear leaves, hairless except for a tiny tuft on their undersides near the apex. Its minute flower heads are white. Similar, but more compact, and with leaves conspicuously clothed on their undersides with silvery or yellow hairs, *R. subsericea* has white flower heads. From prostrate, much-branched, slender, rooting stems, *R. hookeri* produces numerous short, erect, leafy branches crowded together to form

Raoulia hookeri

flat patches up to 1¼ feet in diameter. The stems are furnished with closely overlapping, round-ended, ovate-spatula-shaped leaves, less than 1/10 inch long, that spread radially so that, viewed from above, the plant appears to be a mat of tiny rosettes. Except toward their apexes, the leaves are hairless. The flower heads are yellowish. Rather more compact, *R. h. albo-sericea* has both surfaces of its leaves clothed with silvery-white hairs.

Garden Uses and Cultivation. In regions favored with mild winters and not too sultry summers, the raoulias described above may be grown in rock gardens. They are also suitable for pans (shallow pots) in alpine greenhouses. They need perfect drainage and a porous soil on the lean side rather than rich in nitrogen. Full sun with just a little shade to temper middle-of-the-day temperatures is best for these plants. Propagation is by division and by seed.

RAPE is *Brassica napus oleifera*.

RAPHANUS (Ráph-anus)—Radish. Except for cultivated radishes, this group of the mustard family CRUCIFERAE is without interest to gardeners. It consists of annuals, biennials, and herbaceous perennials, tall, branched, and generally of weedy appearance. Indigenous to Europe and Asia, it comprises about eight species. The name is from the ancient Greek one for the radish, *raphanis*.

The leaves of *Raphanus*, at least the basal ones, are more or less pinnately-lobed, and hairy or hairless. On the stems they are alternate. The white, yellowish, pink, or purplish flowers have slender stalks and are in loosely-branched racemes. They have four sepals, four petals arranged to form a cross, and four comparatively long and two shorter stamens. The slender style ends in a slightly-lobed stigma. The fruits are long, slender, beaked pods, often somewhat constricted between the spherical, wingless seeds, which are embedded in spongy tissue.

The garden radish (*R. sativus*) is unknown as a truly wild plant, although it occurs as a weed in many temperate parts of the world, including North America. It is conjectured that it is an ancient horticultural development of *R. raphanistrum*, a variable native of Europe and adjacent Asia, but that species has yellowish flowers and its fruits, when dry, are constricted between the seeds, which is not true in *R. sativus*. The radish is a thick-

Raphanus raphanistrum

rooted biennial (cultivated as an annual). Its stems are erect and somewhat glaucous, its leaves oblanceolate, pinnately-few-lobed, and hairless to somewhat rough-hairy. The flowers, white, pinkish, or lilac, are usually dark-veined and approximately ½ inch in diameter. They are succeeded by few-seeded, non-splitting pods 1 inch to 3 inches long. There are numerous garden varieties. For their cultivation see Radish.

RAPHIA (Ráph-ia)—Raffia Palm. Except for one indigenous to South America, all thirty species of tropical and subtropical palms that constitute *Raphia*, of the palm family PALMAE, are natives of Africa and Malagasy (Madagascar). The name is derived from the Greek *rhaphis*, a needle, and alludes to the beaked fruits. These palms are remarkable because of the immense size of the leaves of some species. Those of the Madagascan raffia palm, the longest of any known plant, are up to 65 feet in length. From this species is obtained commercial raffia fiber used by gardeners for tying, in handicrafts such as bag- and mat-making, and for other purposes. The fiber consists of strips of epidermis from the undersides of the leaves. This species and others provide fibers for native arts and crafts. Palm wine is also a product of these trees.

Raphias have comparatively short trunks and pinnate leaves. The gigantic, arching and erect leaves of many species tower high into the air so that the total height of the trees is much greater than the length of their trunks, which occasionally are branched. The pendulous flower clusters, several feet in length, develop from among the upper leaves and are much-branched, with the branchlets arranged along the stalks like the teeth of a comb. Toward the ends of the branchlets, the flowers are female, those nearer their bases, male. There are six to sixteen stamens. The ellipsoid to top-shaped fruits are beaked and covered with scales. These palms die after their first flowering and fruiting.

The Madagascan raffia palm (*R. farinifera* syn. *R. ruffia*) inhabits tropical Africa and Malagasy. It has a trunk up to 30 feet tall and leaves up to 65 feet in length that stand almost erect and have numerous slender leaflets up to 5 feet long that are green above and whitish-powdery beneath. The American species *R. taedigera*, indigenous from Central America to Brazil, often occupies swamps and in places covers tremendous areas. Characteristically, it has three to five trunks from 30 to 65 feet tall and great pinnate leaves up to 56 feet in length, with almost 100 leaflets on each side of the midrib. The leafstalks are spiny. The flower clusters arch or hang from among the upper leaves and are 8 to 16 feet long. The ellipsoid fruits, 2 to 2½ inches in length, are covered with glossy, brownish-orange scales. They have sharp beaks.

Garden and Landscape Uses and Cultivation. These palms are little known in cultivation in the United States. They may be grown in Hawaii and southern Florida and are of interest for large conservatories where plants of use to man are emphasized. They succeed in fairly moist, fertile soil in sun or light shade. In greenhouses a minimum winter night temperature of 60 to 65°F, with a five to ten degree rise during the day, is appropriate. At other seasons day and night temperatures should be several degrees higher. Coarse, fertile, well-drained soil is suitable and this should be watered sufficiently often to keep it always moist, but not constantly saturated. From spring to fall biweekly applications of dilute liquid fertilizer benefit well-rooted specimens. Propagation is by seed sown in a temperature of 75 to 90°F in sandy, peaty soil. For additional information see Palms.

RAPHIDOPHORA (Raphidó-phora)—Taro Vine. The name of this genus of about sixty species of evergreen, stem-rooting vines from Indomalaysia and islands of the Pacific is sometimes misspelled *Rhaphidophora*. It comes from the Greek *rhaphis*, a needle, and *phoros*, to bear, and acknowledges the presence in the plant cells of sharp crystals of calcium oxalate called raphides. It is these that cause the intense burning pain that results from chewing raw parts of plants of the arum family ARACEAE, to which *Raphidophora* belongs. The common name taro vine is applied to both *Raphidophora* and closely allied *Epipremnum*.

Raphidophoras are high-climbing plants of tropical forests that support themselves by roots from the stems grasping and adhering to tree trunks and similar supports. As with many vining aroids (plants of the arum family), these have two kinds of foliage, a juvenile type and the usually very much larger and often quite differently shaped or lobed adult leaves. This, together with the fact that many kinds seldom bloom, at least in cultivation, tremendously complicates the problem of the identification of species and even of genera. With certain kinds there is no unassailable botanical opinion as to whether they properly belong in *Raphidophora*, *Scindapsus*, or *Epipremnum*.

Raphidophoras have alternate, two-ranked leaves, the stalks of which angle sharply upward to the blades and whose bases sheathe the stems. Generally the blades are lanceolate to broadly-ovate and spreading. As is usual in the arum family, the tiny flowers are crowded in spikes called spadixes from the bottoms of which comes a more or less petal-like bract called a spathe bract (in the calla-lily the central yellow column is the spadix, the trumpet-shaped part that surrounds it, the spathe). The tiny flowers of *Raphidophora* cover the entire spadix and, except for a few at its base, are bisexual. Without sepals or petals, they have usually four stamens. The spathe is large, boat-shaped, and early deciduous. The fruits are berries crowded along the spadix and angled by compression.

Common in cultivation, *R. decursiva*, in its juvenile stage, has leaves that are

Raphidophora decursiva (juvenile foliage)

Raphidophora decursiva (inflorescence — spadix and spathe — and adult leaf)

pressed flat against the support up which it grows and more or less overlap like shingles on a house. It is one of several plants called shingle plants. Adult leaves have stalks over 1 foot long and ovate blades up to 3 feet long by up to 2 feet wide that spread outward from the plant's support. They are broad-ovate and are slit in pinnate fashion almost or quite to their midribs into closely spaced, narrow lobes. Native from Vietnam to India and Ceylon, this noble vine is much admired for the handsome pattern of its bold, lustrous, dark green foliage.

Called shingle plant, *R. celatocaulis*, of Borneo, is often misnamed *Marcgravia paradoxa*. A high climber, on juvenile shoots it has elliptic-ovate leaves that overlap and press closely to their supports. Later, adult leaves are produced. They have blades up to 1¼ feet long and 1 foot wide, irregularly pinnately-lobed. Another species sometimes cultivated, *R. silvestris*, of Indonesia, is a tall vine with short-stalked, leathery, lobeless, lanceolate leaves up to 5 inches long by 1 inch wide.

Garden and Landscape Uses and Cultivation. The chief uses of these plants are as vigorous, root-clinging climbers in the humid tropics and in tropical greenhouses. In their juvenile, shingle plant stages, *R. celatocaulis* and *R. decursiva* are unusual and fascinating conversation pieces. Raphidophoras respond to the same cultural care as philodendrons and are propagated in the same ways.

RAPHIOLEPIS (Raphió-lepis)—India-Hawthorn, Yeddo-Hawthorn. This name has been spelled *Rhaphiolepis*, but *Raphiolepis* is correct. It is that of a genus of fifteen species of evergreen shrubs of China and Japan. They belong to the rose family RO-SACEAE. The Greek words *rhaphis* and *lepis*, the first meaning a needle, and the other a scale, are the bases of the name, which alludes to the bracts of the flower clusters.

Thornless, raphiolepises have alternate, short-stalked, leathery, undivided, toothed or toothless leaves. Their apple-blossom-like, white or pink flowers are clustered in racemes or panicles. Each has five spreading or erect sepals, five wide petals, fifteen to twenty stamens, and two or three styles with their bases united. Resembling small, hard beads, the fruits technically, like apples, are pomes. Each contains one or two seedlike stones. When ripe, purple-black to black, they remain for a long time.

India-hawthorn (**R. indica**), a native of southern China, is 4 to 5 feet tall and

Raphiolepis indica

variable. Its obviously-toothed, pointed leaves, oblong- to obovate-lanceolate and 1½ to 3 inches long, when young are sometimes somewhat hairy. The pale to light pink or pink-tinged-white blooms, about ½ inch in diameter and with usually red, lanceolate sepals, are in rather loose racemes or panicles, their stalks sometimes sparingly pubescent when young. The fruits, up to ½ inch in diameter, are blue-black. Varieties include *R. i. rosea* with deeper pink flowers than the species, a variety with variegated foliage, and many varieties selected chiefly on the basis of stature, compactness of growth, and flower colors, that carry horticultural names such as 'Apple Blossom', 'Bill Evans', 'Clara', 'Coates' Crimson', 'Cool-

idge Primrose', 'Enchantress', 'Jack Evans', 'Santa Barbara', 'Springtime', and 'W. B. Clarke'.

Yeddo-hawthorn (**R. umbellata** syn. *R. japonica*), a native of Japan and the Ryukyu Islands, is a rounded shrub more rigid than the last. It reaches a maximum height of about 12 feet, but is often much lower,

Raphiolepis umbellata (leaves and fruits)

and commonly is broader than tall. Its short-stalked leaves, thicker than those of India-hawthorn, with rolled-under margins, are usually blunt or bluntish, and round-toothed to practically toothless. From 1½ to 4 inches long, when young they are loosely felted on both sides with downy hairs that soon fall. About ¾ inch wide, the fragrant, pure white flowers are clustered in dense, rigid, downy-stalked, upright racemes or panicles, 3 or 4 inches long. The erect, blue-black, pear-shaped fruits are ½ inch long. Variety *R. u. ovata*

Raphiolepis umbellata ovata

has broader obovate, toothless or few-toothed leaves. Variety *R. u. liukiuensis* (syn. *R. liukiuensis*), of the Ryukyu Islands and perhaps Korea, has leaves narrower than those typical of the species, with undulate, obscurely-toothed or toothless margins. This variety has proved more successful than any other in southern Florida.

Hybrid **R. delacouri,** the parents of which are *R. indica* and *R. umbellata,* has characteristics intermediate between those of its parents. Its short-stalked, blunt to pointed-obovate leaves, toothed above

Raphiolepis delacouri (flowers)

their middles and 1½ to 3½ inches long, are hairless except perhaps when very young. They are proportionately broader than those of *R. indica* and not as rigid and thinner than those of *R. umbellata.* The rosy-pink flowers, ½ to ¾ inch across, are in erect, pyramidal, downy-stalked panicles 3 or 4 inches tall. The calyx lobes are downy.

Garden and Landscape Uses. Among the most satisfactory shrubs for mild-climate regions, and particularly well adapted for seaside planting, raphiolepises are charming in foliage and flower and attractive in fruit. They succeed in sun or partial shade in ordinary soils and may be employed in a wide variety of ways. They make good single specimens, look well in groups, and can be combined with other shrubs in beds, borders, and foundation plantings. They are also effective as informal and semiformal hedges. In containers raphiolepises are useful for decorating patios, terraces, steps, and suchlike places. Because they bloom when quite small, they make pleasing pot plants for cool greenhouses.

Cultivation. No special difficulties attend growing these shrubs. Because they tend to resent root disturbance it is best to set out specimens from cans or pots. Any pruning needed to keep the plants shapely or to prevent them from becoming too large for their sites should receive attention as soon as blooming is through or in early spring. In containers these plants do well in any hearty potting soil such as suits chrysanthemums and geraniums. It must be drained adequately and maintained in a moderately moist, but not constantly wet state. Well-rooted specimens benefit from regular applications of dilute liquid fertilizer. A winter night temperature of 45 to 50°F is adequate with a rise of five to fifteen degrees by day. During the summer the plants benefit from being put outdoors with their pots buried nearly to their rims in sand or similar material. Propagation is by cuttings, layering, grafting on understocks of *Crataegus*, and seed.

A hedge of *Raphiolepis delacouri* in California

RAPHIONACME (Raphion-ácme). The approximately twenty species of *Raphionacme*, of the milkweed family ASCLEPIADACEAE, are natives of tropical and South Africa.

They are nonhardy, milky-juiced herbaceous perennials with tuberous rootstocks or clusters of fleshy roots, and opposite leaves. The stems of raphionacmes, usually short and sometimes twining, may branch or not. Of small to moderate size, the flowers are in clusters of few to many from the leaf axils or from the forks or ends of the stems. They have a five-parted calyx, a bell-shaped, five-lobed corolla, and a crown or corona with five two- or three-cleft, sometimes recurved lobes. There are five stamens, the anthers of which form a cone united to the style. The fruits are podlike follicles, often solitary, sometimes in pairs.

Native to South Africa, *R. divaricata* has a large tuber, and much-branched, hairy stems up to 8 inches high. Its leaves, pubescent on their undersides and up to 1¼ inches long, are elliptic to almost round. The purple flowers, up to ½ inch long and clustered, are succeeded by minutely-hairy pods.

Garden Uses and Cultivation. This collectors' item is a rare one, suitable for including with choice succulent plants outdoors in warm, semidesert regions, or in greenhouses. It needs porous soil and exposure to sun. Water moderately when the plant is in foliage, keep it dry when resting. Propagation is by seed.

RASPBERRY. Raspberries belong to the genus *Rubus*, of the rose family ROSACEAE. Kinds commonly cultivated for their edible

Red raspberries

Blackcap raspberries

fruits are derived from three species, the European red raspberry (*R. idaeus*), the American red raspberry (*R. i. strigosus*), both sorts with red fruits and the parents of garden varieties of red and yellow raspberries, and North American *R. occidentalis*, the blackcap raspberry, which has black fruits. Purple raspberries, hybrids between blackcap and red raspberries, have, but for fruit color, the characteristics of blackcaps. For the flowering raspberry and Rocky Mountain or Boulder flowering raspberry, see Rubus.

Raspberries are hardier than blackberries and differ in that when the fruits are picked the central core remains, so that the harvested berry is a hollow cone. For satisfactory growth, these fruits need a fairly cool climate. They do not do well in the Plains and Mountain states where summers are hot and arid and winters severe. Nor are they well adapted for regions south of Virginia, Tennessee, and Missouri. Where they prosper they are rewarding crops in home gardens. Except in the method of propagation the cultural needs of all raspberries is basically similar.

Soils of widely different types, provided they are deep and well drained, suit. The planting site should be open and have good air drainage; avoid low-lying frost

pockets. A sunny location is essential. In the southern part of the range where they may be grown, north-facing slopes afford better chances for success than warmer ones. Do not plant on land that has been cropped with eggplants, peppers, potatoes, or tomatoes during the previous three years. Such ground may be infected with a verticillium wilt that also attacks these berries. Remove all wild red raspberries and abandoned and nondescript cultivated ones from the vicinity well before planting. These are likely to harbor pests and virus diseases that may be transmitted to the new planting.

Soil preparation must be thorough. It consists of spading, rototilling, or plowing deeply and incorporating liberal amounts of manure, compost, or other agreeable organic matter such as one or two green manure crops grown in succession and turned under. It is important that all perennial weeds be eliminated and it is advantageous to finish the preparation in fall in readiness for early spring planting. Immediately before setting the plants, loosen the ground by forking or harrowing.

Planting may be in rows or hills, the latter spaced 5 to 6 feet apart each way. The

Red raspberries planted in rows supported by wires stretched between upright posts

first method is generally best in home gardens. Space the rows 6 or 7 feet apart. Set red raspberries 2 feet apart, black and purple raspberries 3 feet apart in the rows. Red and purple varieties will remain as individual plants, but by the production of suckers red kinds, which include variants with yellow fruits, will form uninterrupted hedgerows of fairly closely spaced canes (stems). Before planting prune the canes to a length of about 6 inches. Set red raspberries an inch or two deeper than they were previously, black and purple varieties at their previous depth or not over 1 inch deeper. Immediately after planting, as a helpful disease control measure, cut the shortened canes of red and purple varieties back to ground level.

Supports are needed in some regions and for some varieties of red raspberries.

If they are planted in individual hills stakes may be used, if in rows, two or three wires stretched taut between posts about 5 feet high set 15 to 30 feet apart are satisfactory. Supports are not needed for black and purple raspberries.

In fall, shorten the ends of red raspberry canes newly tied to wire supports

Routine care following planting involves keeping down weeds. To do this, cultivate shallowly and frequently in the early part of the season. If practicable, mulch with straw, hay, or similar material before the onset of hot weather. In any case cease cultivating soon after harvest. If continued too late it stimulates new growth, which is susceptible to winter injury. For their best success, raspberries need ample moisture. Water or irrigate deeply at regular intervals in dry weather. This is particularly important from blossoming time until the fruits are harvested. Raspberries respond to generous fertilizing, nitrogen being the element they most need, but too much nitrogen may result in too vigorous, soft growth likely to suffer from winter injury. For this reason, stable and poultry manures, which are excellent when used with caution, should not be applied in excess. Nitrate of soda used at the rate of about one pound to ten or twelve square yards, or its equivalent in some other fertilizer, is satisfactory.

Prune annually immediately after the summer harvest, but not after the fall crop of autumn-fruiting varieties. Raspberry canes are biennial. They grow one year, fruit the next, and then die. Two or three new canes develop each summer from the base of each old cane. Red raspberries develop, in addition, sucker shoots from the roots. Pruning consists of cutting out at their bases all two-year-old canes and of thinning out new ones. Thinning black and purple raspberries consists of cutting out all canes under ½ inch in diameter. If none is so thick, leave the two strongest. With red raspberries grown in hills, leave

seven or eight strong canes to each plant. Thin rows so that the new canes stand about 6 inches apart in rows not over 1 foot wide.

Harvest not less often than two or three times a week. To avoid bruising, pluck the berries carefully with the thumb and next two fingers. Deposit them gently in a basket or basin and avoid rehandling. After the receptacles are filled keep them out of the sun. Discard all overripe and decayed fruit.

In the western-northcentral states, winter protection is generally needed. It is usually sufficient to bend the canes over all in the same direction and hold them close to the ground by weighting them with clods of soil. The clods are removed in spring.

Propagation of red raspberries is usually by transplanting suckers, their tops cut back to within 1 foot of the ground, in early spring. It can also be done by root cuttings. Cut stout roots into pieces 2 to 3 inches long, scatter them over the surface of a bed made ready as for seeds, and cover them with 2 inches of soil. Tip cuttings afford the readiest means of propagating black and purple raspberries. Pinch out the tips of new canes 1 foot to 1½ feet tall. This will cause branching. In late summer take a fork, loosen the soil, bend the branches so that their ends point straight down, and bury their tips to a depth of 2 to 4 inches in a circle around the plants.

Recommended varieties (consult Cooperative Extension Agents for those best suited for particular localities) include, among the reds, 'Canby', 'Chief', 'Hilton', 'Latham', 'Milton', 'Taylor', 'Washington', and 'Willamette'. Everbearing or fall- as well as summer-bearing varieties, are 'Falbred' and 'September'. Purple raspberry varieties are 'Clyde', 'Marion', and 'Sodus'. Black varieties include 'Allen', 'Black Hawk', 'Black Pearl', 'Cumberland', 'Huron', 'New Logan', 'Morrison', and 'Munger'. Raspberries are susceptible to a number of serious diseases including mosaics and other diseases caused by viruses as well as anthracnose, crown gall, and wilt. Although usually less serious, insects of several kinds infest raspberries. They include aphids, beetles, borers, caterpillars, scale insects, spittle-bugs, weevils, and whiteflies.

RAT TAIL CACTUS is *Aporocactus flagelliformis.*

RATA. See Metrosideros.

RATAMA is *Parkinsonia aculeata.*

RATHBUNIA (Rath-bùnia). This genus of the cactus family CACTACEAE is dedicated to Dr. Richard Rathbun, zoologist and Secretary of the Smithsonian Institution, who

died in 1918. There are four species of *Rathbunia*, all natives of Mexico.

Rathbunias have slender, rather weak, few-ribbed stems, erect, arching, or bent, and with clusters of awl-shaped spines. Open during the day, the solitary, asymmetrical, scarlet flowers commonly develop from near the tops of the stems. Narrowly-tubular with the upper parts of the petals spreading, they have long scales hugging the perianth tube. The stamens and slender style protrude. Spherical, spiny or sometimes smooth, the fruits are capped by the withered remains of the blooms.

Forming broad clusters or thickets up to 25 feet across, **R. alamosensis** (syns. *R. so-*

Rathbunia alamosensis

norensis, Cereus pseudosonorensis) has blunt-ribbed stems 6 to 10 feet long by a little over 3 inches thick that at first are erect, but later bend over and often root into the ground from near or at their tips. Each stem has five to eight ribs with clusters of one to four stout central spines up to 2 inches long and eleven to eighteen much weaker, whitish radial spines. The blooms are scarlet and 1½ to 4 inches in length. The spiny or spineless, spherical fruits are approximately 1½ inches in diameter.

Garden and Landscape Uses and Cultivation. These rather rapid-growing cactuses succeed under conditions that suit most desert types. They are suitable for outdoors in warm, dry climates, and for greenhouses. For additional information see Cactuses.

RATIBIDA (Ratíb-ida)—Coneflower. This is a North American genus of six species of the daisy family COMPOSITAE that by some botanists has been called *Lepachys*. The group is closely related to *Rudbeckia* and the kinds here discussed were originally described as such. The name *Ratibida* is of uncertain origin and the common one of the genus, coneflower, is used also for *Dracopis, Echinacea,* and *Rudbeckia,* all of which have elevated central disks that give reason for the designation, and all of which were once included in *Rudbeckia*.

Consisting of perennial and biennial herbaceous plants, *Ratibida* has all or some of its leaves pinnate or pinnately-lobed and flower heads with yellow, orange, or purple-brown ray florets. The fruits are achenes.

Remarkable because of the height, sometimes 2 inches, of the central column-like disks of its flower heads, **R. columnifera** (syns. *R. columnaris, Lepachys columnifera, L. columnaris, Rudbeckia columnifera, R. columnaris*) is native from southwestern Canada to Minnesota, Texas, and northern Mexico. A biennial or short-lived perennial 1 foot to 3 feet tall, this kind has flower heads with bright yellow, slightly drooping or spreading ray florets shorter than or equal in length to the comparatively slender, erect central column. In variety *R. c. pulcherrima* they are purplish-brown, at least at their ends. A double-flowered variety is sometimes cultivated.

A coarser perennial plant, **R. pinnata** (syns. *Lepachys pinnata, Rudbeckia pinnata*), 2 to 4 feet tall, has woody, rhizome-like roots and the central disks of the flower heads much shorter than the drooping ray florets, which are 2 inches long or longer and bright yellow. This kind is native from Ontario to Georgia, Minnesota, and Oklahoma. Another perennial, one with less showy flower heads, **R. tagetes** is native from Kansas to Colorado and northern Mexico. Sometimes this may slightly exceed 1½ feet in height but is often somewhat lower. It has very tiny, yellow to purplish-brown ray florets and oblong or ellipsoid disks about ½ inch high.

Garden Uses and Cultivation. These are decidedly decorative plants for sunny flower beds and borders, informal garden areas, and native plant gardens, and their blooms are useful for cutting. They grow without difficulty in any ordinary, well-drained garden soil, stand heat and humidity well, and are easily raised from seeds sown in a cold frame or outdoors in May or June. The seedlings are transplanted when big enough to handle to nursery beds in rows about 1 foot apart, with 6 inches between the plants in the rows. In fall or the following spring they are ready for shifting to their flowering locations where they may be spaced 1 foot to 2 feet apart. No special routine care is needed and usually no staking is required. Alternatively, *R. columnifera* can be treated as an annual. To do this, sow the seeds in a temperature of about 60°F in a greenhouse in March and transplant the seedlings 2 inches apart in flats. Grow them in these in a sunny greenhouse or similar place where the night temperature is 50 to 55°F until danger of frost has passed, then plant them where they are to bloom, which they will do freely throughout late summer and fall.

RATSTRIPPER is *Paxistima canbyi*.

RATTLE BOX. These plants are known by the vernacular name of rattle box: *Crotalaria, Ludwigia alternifolia,* and *Rhinanthus crista-galli*.

RATTLESNAKE. This word forms parts of the common names of these plants: rattlesnake fern (*Botrychium virginianum*), rattlesnake master (*Eryngium yuccifolium* and *Manfreda virginica*), rattlesnake orchid (*Pholidota*), rattlesnake-plantain (*Goodyera*), and rattlesnake root (*Prenanthes*).

RAUVOLFIA (Rauvòlf-ia). A complicated genus of tropical woody plants that range in height from 6 inches to 100 feet, *Rauvolfia* is imperfectly understood botanically. Sometimes spelled *Rauwolfia*, it consists of perhaps a hundred or more species, natives of warm parts of South America, Central America, the West Indies, Africa, Asia, Indonesia, and Hawaii. A member of the dogbane family APOCYNACEAE, this genus is named in honor of Leonhart Rauwolf, a German physician and traveler, who died in 1596.

For those interested only in ornamental plants, *Rauvolfia* holds little interest, but because of the medicinal virtues of some species it is of importance for display in collections of plants that are sources of useful products. West Indian *R. nitida* has been recommended in Florida as a good windbreak tree for seashores, and two fragrant-flowered Cuban species, *R. salicifolia* and *R. cubana*, have been suggested as ornamental shrubs for tropical and subtropical gardens.

As a source of reserpine and other drugs, *Rauvolfia* was unknown to Western medicine until the middle of the twentieth century, although *R. serpentina* had for long been used in India by practitioners of Ayurvedic medicine as an antidote against the bites of reptiles and insect stings and as a specific for diarrhea and other afflictions, including nervous ailments; in the Americas *R. tetraphylla* and *R. nitida* were widely used in indigenous medicine. The drug rauwolfia consists of dried roots from which are prepared reserpine and other alkaloids used to treat hypertension, nervous disorders, and insanity. The source species include *R. serpentina* and *R. tetraphylla*, the former native of tropical Asia, the latter of tropical America, and *R. vomitoria*, of Africa. Several other species are exploited as drug sources.

Rauvolfias are milky-juiced plants with lobeless leaves in whorls (circles) of three to five, small flowers in terminal or axillary clusters, and berry-like fruits, technically drupes (a plum is a typical drupe). There are glands in the leaf axils and in some kinds on the leafstalk.

A variable shrub up to 5 feet in height, **R. tetraphylla** has ovate to ovate-elliptic,

Rauvolfia hirsuta (fruits)

hairy or smooth leaves with glands on their stalks and axils. At each node there are four leaves, two very much bigger than the others. The flower clusters, usually branchless, consist of a few blooms. When ripe the fruits, the size of small peas, are black. This is native from Mexico to South America and the West Indies. Having approximately the same natural distribution as the last, **R. hirsuta** (syn. *R. canescens*) is a freely-branched shrub 3 to 7 feet tall. Mostly in whorls (circles) of four, but sometimes of three or five, those of each whorl varying in size, the hairy to nearly hairless leaves are narrow-elliptic-oblong to obovate-elliptic and from ¾ inch to 4½ inches long. The tiny flowers, in clusters of few to several in the leaf axils, are succeeded by spherical black fruits ¼ to ⅓ inch in diameter. Asian **R. serpentina** is a low subshrub with elliptic-ovate leaves in threes and flower clusters of many blooms. Its egg-shaped fruits, which have pointed ends, are about ¼ inch long. A native of Africa, **R. vomitoria** is a tree with broad-elliptic leaves, the four from each node of approximately equal size. West Indian **R. nitida,** from 6 to 50 feet tall, has glistening, elliptic leaves usually in whorls

Rauvolfia verticillata

Quercus alba in fall

Ranunculus asiaticus

Rhabdadenia biflora

Raoulias in a rock garden

Ranunculus ficaria

Rhododendron augustinii

Rhododendron carolinianum

Rhododendron catawbiense

A *Rhododendron cinnabarinum* hybrid

A *Rhododendron catawbiense* hybrid

Rhododododendron 'Conewago', a *R. carolinianum* × *R. mucronulatum* hybrid

of four, more rarely in twos, threes, or fives. Its terminal and lateral flower clusters have few to many blooms. The small, two-seeded fruits are notched at their ends. Native to China, Indochina, and Taiwan, **R. verticillata** is a slender-branched shrub 3 to 5 feet tall with elliptic to oblanceolate leaves 3 to 5 inches long in whorls (circles) of three or occasionally four. Its ¼-inch-wide, white flowers, in longish-stalked clusters, are succeeded by about ½-inch-long, ellipsoid, red fruits.

Cultivation. In tropical regions and in warm, humid greenhouses rauvolfias present no particular difficulties to the cultivator. They thrive in a variety of soils, but especially in fertile ones, and in sun or part-shade. They may be increased by cuttings and by seed sown in sandy, peaty soil in a temperature of about 75°F. In many cases the percentage of seeds that germinate is low and investigation has revealed that some fruits of some kinds, although of quite normal appearance, contain seeds without embryos.

RAVENALA (Raven-àla)—Travelers' Tree or Travelers'-Palm. The very distinctive travelers' tree is commonly cultivated for ornament in the tropics and sometimes in large conservatories. The genus to which it belongs, *Ravenala*, of the banana family MUSACEAE, has an unusual natural distribution, the travelers' tree being endemic to Malagasy (Madagascar) and the only other species, a smaller plant not known to be in cultivation, a native of tropical South America. The generic name is Madagascan.

Ravenalas have stout, palmlike trunks and huge, long-stalked leaves that resemble those of bananas (*Musa*) and spread in one plane in two rows like an immense fan from the top of the trunk. The blooms, borne in the leaf axils, do not extend far from the trunk. They are whitish, bisexual, and arise several together from boat-shaped bracts. Each flower has three sepals, two of the side ones resembling petals, and the other smaller, and three petals. Those of the travelers' tree have six stamens, those of the South American species, five stamens. The fruits are many-seeded, dry, woody capsules. From the nearly related bird-of-paradise plant (*Strelitzia*), ravenalas differ in the bases of their petals not being united.

The travelers' tree or travelers'-palm (**R. madagascariensis**) was given its common names because the bases of its leafstalks form cups that hold considerable amounts of water. According to popular stories, this was used by travelers to slake their thirst. Realistic appraisals point out that such water is scarcely potable and would appeal only if none other were available. The travelers' tree has an erect trunk 30 feet or more tall. Its paddle-shaped leaves have stalks, longer than the blades, that

Ravenala madagascariensis, young specimens in South Africa

broaden to conspicuous sheaths in their lower parts and overlap toward their bases. The total length of stalk and blade may be 20 feet. Although naturally undivided, like those of bananas, the leaves are ordinarily much shredded by wind. The white flowers are succeeded by blue seeds, which are used as food in Malagasy. The travelers' tree is put to other uses. From its sap, sugar is obtained. Its wood is used in construction and its leaves for thatching.

Garden and Landscape Uses and Cultivation. This, one of the most striking of all trees, has considerable ornamental merit

as a lawn specimen, for planting in association with buildings and other architectural features, and for use along boundaries. It is seen to best advantage when its silhouette is presented against a clear sky without a background clutter of other trees or hillside. Then its effect is dramatic, especially by moonlight. Not difficult to cultivate, it thrives best in deep, fertile soil, not excessively dry, and in full sun. Suckers arise rather infrequently from the base of the trunk and can be used to start new plants. They should be carefully removed with as many roots, with soil adhering to them, as possible when they are 1½ to 2 feet tall. Seed sown in sandy, peaty soil may also be used for propagation. This remarkable plant grows well in large greenhouses where a minimum night temperature of 50 to 60°F is maintained. In greenhouses it prospers in full sun or with slight shade in summer. Good soil drainage, fairly generous supplies of water, and occasional fertilizing encourage the production of large leaves.

RAVENIA (Rav-ènia). The rue family RUTACEAE includes *Ravenia*, a genus of the West Indies, Central America, and tropical South America that comprises eighteen species. The significance of its name is not known.

These are shrubs with opposite leaves of one to three leaflets. The flowers, solitary or in racemes from the leaf axils, have five

Ravenala madagascariensis planted in South America as an ornamental

unequal sepals, a tubular, asymmetrical corolla with five spreading lobes (petals), and five stamens. The fruits are berry-like.

Native to Cuba, **R. spectabilis** is an attractive tall shrub with rather thick,

Ravenia spectabilis

smooth leaves with pubescent stalks and three oblong leaflets each with a conspicuous mid-vein. Bright pink to red with cream-colored stamens, the flowers, in clusters of few from the leaf axils and ¾ to 1 inch in diameter, have rather fleshy, blunt petals.

Garden and Landscape Uses and Cultivation. Suitable for general landscape planting in the tropics and warm subtropics and for cultivation in tropical greenhouses, the sort described above succeeds in well-drained fertile soil in sun or part-day shade. Propagation is by seed and by cuttings, the latter preferably planted in a propagating bench with slight bottom heat.

RAVNIA (Ráv-nia). Four species of tree-perching (epiphytic) shrubs constitute *Ravnia*, of the madder family RUBIACEAE. The name honors Peter Ravn, a Norwegian ship's surgeon, who collected plants in the West Indies. He died in 1839.

Natives of Central America, these plants have opposite, rather fleshy leaves and flowers in terminal clusters of three, each with a five- or six-parted calyx, a slender-tubed, five- or six-parted corolla, and five or six stamens. The fruits are slender, cylindrical capsules.

From 1 foot to 3 feet tall, **R. triflora** has very short-stalked, long-pointed, elliptic to lanceolate-oblong leaves up to 4 inches long, and bears, rather sparsely, 2-inch-long, rose-red flowers.

Garden Uses and Cultivation. But little information is recorded about the needs of this plant. It should interest collectors of the rare and unusual and may be expected to respond to conditions that suit *Aeschynanthus*, *Nematanthus*, and other epiphytic gesneriads.

RAY FLORET. The flower heads of plants of the daisy family COMPOSITAE consist of usually few to many florets. They may be all similar, but often, as in daisies, they are of two distinct types, disk florets that form a central eye and, surrounding the disk, petal-like ray florets.

REBUTIA (Re-bùtia). Among the more popular genera of the cactus family CACTACEAE is *Rebutia*, variously accepted as comprising four to fourteen species depending upon the interpretations of different botanists. They are natives of South America. The name commemorates a French dealer in cactuses of the late nineteenth and early twentieth centuries.

Rebutias are small and have much the aspect of mammillarias. They have spherical to flattish-spherical, solitary or clustered plant bodies without clearly defined ribs but with many tubercles (fleshy protrusions) and clusters of almost hairlike to needle-like spines. The funnel-shaped flowers, from the sides or near the bottoms of older tubercles, are of various shades of red, orange-red, and yellow. Certain cactuses admitted to this genus by some authorities are treated in this Encyclopedia in *Aylostera* and *Mediolobivia*.

Except Bolivian *R. krainziana*, the species described here are natives of Argentina. **R. calliantha** closely resembles *R. hyalacantha*, but has much shorter spines. Its nearly spherical plant bodies, up to 3½ inches tall by 2½ inches wide, have clusters of fifteen to eighteen white spines under ½ inch long. The flowers, about 1¾ inches wide, are cinnabar-red with orange throats and petals with a center stripe of violet. **R. chrysacantha** has generally solitary plant bodies, about 2 inches in diameter, and slightly taller. Lustrous green, they have tubercles in spirals. At first white, changing to yellow, the spines are in clusters of twenty-five to thirty, the largest ½ inch long. Yellowish-orange, the blooms are 2 inches long. **R. grandiflora** has spherical to flattened-spherical plant bodies about 3 inches wide by two-thirds as high encircled by spirals of tubercles, with spines in clusters of about thirty. The brick- to carmine-red blooms are 2½ inches long. **R. hyalacantha** (syn. *R. wess-*

Rebutia hyalacantha

neriana) has flattened-spherical plant bodies 2 to 3 inches wide with clusters of about twenty-five brown-tipped, white spines about ¾ inch long, and 2-inch-wide vermilion to crimson flowers, their stamens tipped with yellow anthers. **R. krainziana** has clustered plant bodies, when young flattish-spherical, 1 inch to 1½ inches in diameter, with age becoming taller than wide. The tubercles make slight spirals around them. Large and white-woolly, the areoles sprout clusters of eight to twelve bristly, white spines. Bright red with a purplish overcast, the flowers, from near the bases of the plants are 1½ inches wide. **R. marsoneri**, small and approxi-

Rebutia marsoneri spathulata

mately spherical, has yellowish-brown spines, green flower buds, and light to golden-yellow, 1-inch-wide blooms. Variety **R. m. spathulata** has spatula-shaped petals and, on the perianth tube, violet-red scales. **R. minuscula** has plant bodies about 2½ inches wide by 1½ inches tall, with tubercles spiraled around them. The abundant, whitish spines are in clusters of twenty-five to thirty. Bright crimson and 1 inch to 1½ inches long, the flowers, open by day, originate from the sides of the plant. **R. senilis** has clustered, usually flattened-spherical plant bodies 2½ to 3½ inches in diameter, which sometimes are columnar and two to four times as tall as wide. They have spiraled tubercles and are thickly clothed with clusters of thirty-five to forty translucent, bristly spines a little over 1 inch long. Arising from the bases of the plants, the carmine blooms are 1½ to 2 inches long. This is a variable species of which several varieties have been named. One of these, **R. s. steumeri**, has somewhat laxer plant bodies than the typical species and flowers with a brick-red throat and often yellowish margins to the petals. **R. violaciflora**, which rather resembles *R. marsoneri*, has solitary, depressed-spherical plant bodies about ¾ inch wide with clusters of about twenty brownish-yellow spines and 1¼-inch-wide violet-purple blooms with white stamens and stigmas. The flowers of **R. v. knuthiana** are crimson.

Rebutia senilis steumeri

R. xanthocarpa has plant bodies approximately 2 inches across with clusters of fifteen to twenty bristly, white to yellowish, ¼-inch-long spines. The flowers are red and ½ inch wide or a little wider. This is variable, especially as to the shade of red of the blooms.

Garden Uses and Cultivation. These attractive plants are delightful for rock gardens in mild desert climates and are greatly esteemed for inclusion in indoor collections of cactuses. They thrive and usually bloom well in greenhouses and sunny windows, responding to environments and care appropriate for mammillarias and similar small desert cactuses. For more information see Cactuses.

RECHSTEINERIA. See Sinningia.

RED. The word red forms parts of the colloquial names of these plants: Australian-red-cedar (*Cedrela australis*), little red elephants (*Pedicularis groenlandica*), red Africaner (*Homoglossum priori*), red-alder (*Cunonia capensis*), red-almond or Bushman's red-ash (*Alphitonia excelsa*), red-barked-apple (*Angophora lanceolata*), red-bay (*Persea borbonia*), red-bean (*Kennedia rubicunda*), red berry (*Rhamnus crocea*), red bloodwood (*Eucalyptus gummifera*), red-box (*Eucalyptus polyanthemos*), red campion (*Silene dioica*), red-cedar (*Juniperus occidentalis*, *J. silicicola*, *J. virginiana*, and *Thuja plicata*), red-ginger (*Alpinia purpurata*), red-hot-cat-tail (*Acalypha hispida*), red hot poker (*Kniphofia*), red ironbark (*Eucalyptus sideroxylon*), red maids (*Calandrinia*), red mombin (*Spondias purpurea*), red puccoon (*Sanguinaria canadensis*), red ribbons (*Clarkia concinna*), red root (*Amaranthus retroflexus*), red-sandalwood tree (*Adenanthera pavonina*), red sapote (*Pouteria mammosa*), red shank (*Adenostoma sparsifolium*), and red-valerian (*Centranthus ruber*).

RED SPIDER. Because the common plant pest often called red spider is not a spider, but a kind of mite, it is more correctly identified as red spider mite. See Mites.

REDBUD. See Cercis.

REDROOT is *Lachnanthes caroliana*.

REDWOOD is *Sequoia sempervirens*. Dawn-redwood is *Metasequoia glyptostroboides*.

REDWOOD-IVY is *Vancouveria planipetala*.

REED. This is a name used for various tall grasses, including certain bamboos, that grow in damp or wet soils. Examples are to be found in the genera *Arundinaria*, *Arundo*, *Calamagrostis*, *Glyceria*, *Phalaris*, and *Phragmites*.

REGELIA. See Neoregelia.

REGISTRATION OF PLANT NAMES. As part of an attempt to bring some degree of order to the application to cultivated plants of varietal and other names not covered by the International Code of Botanical Nomenclature, efforts have and are being made in America, Europe, and elsewhere to register new names with designated authorities. A common requirement for registration is that the name be published in accordance with the International Code of Nomenclature for Cultivated Plants approved by the International Society for Horticultural Science, and usually additional information and perhaps photographs or specimens are requested. There is no legal requirement that plant names be registered or that the name of a variety follow the rules of the International Code, but if all or most do, a desirable degree of uniformity may result.

REGNELLIDIUM (Regnel-lídium). The one species of this genus, a relative of the water-clover (*Marsilea*) and generally resembling it, is a native of southern Brazil where it grows in wet soils and shallow water. It belongs in the marsilea or water-clover family MARSILEACEAE and thus is a fern rather than a seed plant. It has no flowers and is sexually reproduced by spores. From *Marsilea* and other fern allies

Regnellidium diphyllum

and ferns it differs in containing latex. Its name honors the Swedish doctor and naturalist Anders Fredrik Regnell, who died in 1884.

From creeping, much-branched, rooting rhizomes **Regnellidium diphyllum** sends up fronds (leaves) with long, slender stalks topped by two stalkless, spreading, oval leaflets that are broader than long and have many fine, forking veins fanning outward from their bases. The nearly round, spore-bearing organs develop from near the bases of the fronds.

Garden Uses and Cultivation. Of considerable botanical interest, this unique species may be grown in fertile mud or in shallow water over a mud bottom. It is suitable for gardens in the tropics and for tropical greenhouses, and in the north can be used in outdoor pools in summer. It thrives in pans (shallow pots) kept standing in saucers of water or sunk to their rims in a pool. Rich soil, shade from strong sun, and a minimum winter greenhouse temperature of 60°F are conditions for good growth. Propagation is very easy by division. New plants can also be raised from spores in the same way as ferns.

REHDERODENDRON (Rehdero-déndron). Its name commemorating Alfred Rehder, distinguished botanist of the Arnold Arboretum, Jamaica Plain, Massachusetts, who died in 1949, *Rehderodendron* comprises nine species of Chinese and Indochinese deciduous trees. The name combines that of Rehder with the Greek *dendron*, a tree. Rehderodendrons belong to the storax family STYRACACEAE. From *Styrax* they differ in the ovaries of their flowers being below or behind the petals and sepals and from *Halesia* in having more than four corolla lobes (petals). Leafless flowering shoots distinguish *Rehderodendron* from *Pterostyrax* and *Sinojackia*. Only one species, *R. macrocarpum*, is known to be cultivated. It is not hardy in the north, nor, probably, would the others be.

Introduced to cultivation in America

Rehderodendron macrocarpum (foliage and fruits)

and Europe in 1934, *R. macrocarpum,* about 30 feet in height, has alternate, undivided, pointed, elliptic to elliptic-ovate or oblongish leaves 3½ to 4½ inches long, minutely-toothed, and with short, reddish stalks. The veins on the undersides of the leaves are furnished with star-shaped hairs. Coming in spring before the foliage, the racemes of six to ten flowers have finely-hairy stalks and are up to 2 inches long. The blooms have calyxes with five short, triangular lobes, five elliptic-oblong, white petals, pubescent on both surfaces, about ½ inch long, and joined only at their bases, ten unequal stamens with conspicuous yellow anthers, and a slender style a little longer than the stamens. The thick-shelled fruits, containing one to three seeds, are oblong-egg-shaped, eight- to ten-ribbed, woody, and about 3 inches in length. This is native to western China.

Garden and Landscape Uses and Cultivation. Chiefly a tree for arboretums and collectors of the rare and unusual, *R. macrocarpum* succeeds in ordinary soils and locations in fairly mild climates and may be expected to be hardy about as far north as Virginia. It can be raised from seed and probably from summer cuttings under mist.

REHMANNIA (Reh-mánnia). The somewhat foxglove-like plants that comprise *Rehmannia* are natives of eastern Asia. There are ten species, generally regarded as members of the figwort family SCROPHULARIACEAE, although they exhibit similarities to the gesneria family GESNERIACEAE. None is hardy in the north. The name commemorates a physician, Joseph Rehmann, of St. Petersburg (Leningrad), who died in 1831.

Rehmannias are clammy herbaceous perennials that branch from near their bases and have leafy or nearly leafless stems. Their alternate, pinnately-lobed or toothed leaves, the basal ones in rosettes, are obovate to oblong. Their attractive, medium-sized to large flowers are in leafy, terminal, spikelike racemes. They have ovoid to bell-shaped, five-cleft calyxes and tubular, pubescent, obliquely-two-lipped corollas with brightly colored throats and five spreading brownish or purplish lobes (petals). There are four stamens and one pistil. The fruits are many-seeded capsules.

One of the best, *R. elata,* in gardens often misidentified as *R. angulata,* attains heights of 3 or 4 feet and has leaves with two to six pointed, toothless lobes along each side. Its flowers have red-spotted, yellow throats and bright rosy-purple petals.

With rather smaller blooms than the last, *R. angulata* is 1 foot to 3 feet tall. Its leaves have a few toothed lobes along each margin, or are toothed and without lobes. The bracts in the axils from which the

Rehmannia elata

flowers arise narrow abruptly at their bases instead of tapering gradually. The flowers are purplish-red with a scarlet margin to the upper petals, and the lower petals marked with orange spots.

From 1 foot to 2 feet tall, *R. glutinosa* has usually purplish stems and obovate, coarsely-toothed leaves 3 to 5 inches in length. Its blooms, 1 inch long or a little longer, are 1 inch to 1½ inches across their faces. Buff-yellow to purplish and veined with purple, they have purple throats and often purplish calyxes. Not over 1½ feet tall, *R. henryi* has elliptic-oblong leaves with tapered bases, the largest 3 to 7 inches long. Its flowers, white to yellowish, dotted with red in their throats, are 1¾ to 2 inches long.

Hybrid rehmannias are generally intermediate between their parents. The hybrid of *R. elata* and *R. henryi, R. briscoei,* has dark-veined leaves and pale pink flowers. The one between *R. glutinosa* and *R. henryi, R. kewensis,* has creamy-yellow blooms marked on the upper petals with a dark red blotch.

Garden and Landscape Uses. Rehmannias stand considerable cold, but not hard freezing. They may be grown outdoors in California, the Pacific Northwest, and other mild areas, and are adapted for pots in cool greenhouses. They thrive in fertile, well-drained, but not dry soil. Where hardy the taller kinds are good flower border plants. The shorter ones are suitable for the fronts of flower beds and rock gardens. All do well in partial shade.

Cultivation. Propagated from seed sown about midsummer, or from cuttings or root cuttings, rehmannias bloom freely the following year and, in greenhouses, at least, it is often preferable to treat them as biennials by raising new plants each year and discarding the old ones when blooming is through. Cuttings are made from basal shoots that develop after the old flower stalks are cut down. The young plants are potted individually and, in re-

gions where hardy, are later planted in nursery beds to be transplanted in fall or the following spring to their flowering quarters. For greenhouses the young plants are potted successively into bigger pots as growth makes necessary. This usually means that before fall they will occupy 5-inch-wide containers, and the following spring will be potted into 7- or 8-inch pots. During winter they should be kept as cool as possible without freezing. Night temperatures of 40 to 45°F are adequate. Then, the soil should be kept dryish, but not dry. At all other times moderate to generous watering is in order. After the final pots are well filled with roots, weekly applications of dilute liquid fertilizer stimulate vigorous growth. Always, the greenhouse must be ventilated as freely as weather conditions permit. Rehmannias are nearly hardy and any suspicion of "coddling" brings inferior results. Shade from strong summer sun is needed by plants in greenhouses.

REICHARDIA (Reich-árdia). It is important not to confuse *Reichardia* with *Richardia.* The latter name, that of a genus in the family RUBIACEAE, has also been used for the calla-lily (*Zantedeschia*). The genus *Reichardia,* with which we are concerned, belongs in the daisy family COMPOSITAE and consists of eight to ten species, natives from the Canary Islands and the Mediterranean region to India. Its name honors Johann Jacob Reichard, a German botanist, who died in 1782.

Reichardias are annuals and herbaceous perennials with basal or alternate leaves and flower heads topping long stalks. The heads are composed of all ligulate florets (similar to the petal-like ones of daisies rather than the disk florets of a daisy's eye). The fruits are achenes.

An often glaucous perennial, *R. picroides* (syn. *Picridium vulgare*), of southern Europe, has erect, branched, few-leaved stems 1 foot to 2 feet tall. Its leaves are lanceolate to spatula-shaped, the lower ones commonly pinnately-lobed. The

Reichardia tingitana

heart-shaped bases of the upper ones clasp the stems. The solitary pale yellow flower heads are about ¾ inch across and have involucres (leafy collars at the backs of the flower heads), more than one-half as long as the florets, of white-margined, green bracts. An annual or less often a perennial, *R. tingitana* (syn. *Picridium tingitanum*), native from the Canary Islands to India, 6 inches to 1½ feet tall, has pinnately-lobed or toothed to nearly toothless, oblanceolate basal leaves up to 5 inches long and smaller oblanceolate to linear stem-clasping leaves. The flower heads, yellow with purple centers, are about 1½ inches across.

Garden Uses and Cultivation. For providing variety in flower borders, the plants described have modest merit. They prosper in well-drained soil in full sun and are easily raised from seed sown in spring where the plants are to bloom. Thin the seedlings out sufficiently to avoid overcrowding. No special care is needed.

REINECKEA (Rein-éckea). To the lily family LILIACEAE belongs *Reineckea carnea*, the only species, a native of Japan and China. Its name commemorates a German gardener, J. Reinecke.

An evergreen, herbaceous perennial, *R. carnea* has greenish, prostrate, or when

Reineckea carnea

grown in pots, sometimes partially erect stems, and tufts of broad-linear to narrowly-lanceolate, dark green, hairless leaves that narrow gradually to stalklike bases. They are up to 1 foot long or longer. Shorter than the foliage, the leafless flower stalks are 1½ to 4 inches long. Their upper parts are densely crowded spikes of fragrant, pale pink, stalkless blooms ⅓ to nearly ½ inch long. Each has six slightly fleshy petals (more correctly tepals) joined below into a tube and reflexed above, six stamens, and a style as long or a little longer than the stamens and tipped with a three-lobed stigma. The fruits are small, spherical, few-seeded berries. In Japan *Reineckea* favors woodlands at low alti-

tudes. Variety *R. c. variegata* has its leaves conspicuously longitudinally banded with white.

Garden Uses and Cultivation. Not hardy in the north, this species withstands light frosts and, where winters are not too severe, may be grown outdoors in partial shade in woodland-type soil. It is also suitable for greenhouses and as a window plant. For these purposes it may be accommodated in well-drained pots 4 or 5 inches in diameter, in porous, fertile potting soil watered to keep it always moderately moist. Good light, with some shade from summer sun, and a moderately humid atmosphere are needed. In greenhouses a minimum winter night temperature of 40 to 50°F suits, with a daytime rise of five to fifteen degrees, but the plant is fairly tolerant and will stand higher temperatures. Propagation is by division, cuttings, and seed.

REINHARDTIA (Reinhár-dtia). There are eight or fewer species of *Reinhardtia*, of the palm family PALMAE. Unfortunately they are little known in horticulture. They are natives of southern Mexico, Central America, and northern South America. Their name honors Johannes Theodor Reinhardt, a Danish botanist, who died in 1882.

Reinhardtias are small to medium-sized palms with nonprickly, solitary or clustered stems from subterranean rhizomes. Their leaves are pinnate or pinnately-lobed, without the segments being divided so deeply that they form separate leaflets. The lobes or segments have numerous, fine parallel veins and a main central one that forms a point at the leaf end. Their margins are jagged-toothed. In some species there are comparatively large spaces or openings called "windows" between the divisions of the leaf blades. The flower clusters, branched and arising from the axils of the lower leaves, at first are enclosed in two papery bracts. Their branches are creamy-white later changing to orange-red. The individual small blooms, also creamy-white, are chiefly in threes, each group consisting of a female flanked by two males. The more or less egg-shaped fruits are small and, at maturity, red, dark purple, or purple-black.

Two or three sorts are cultivated to a limited extent in the warmest parts of the United States. These include *R. simplex*, native from Honduras and Nicaragua to Panama, which has one to several canelike stems up to 4 feet in height and about ¼ inch in diameter furnished at their tops with dark green leaves without openings or windows and cleft very shallowly at their ends, but often with a pair of narrow leaflets beneath the larger, ovate main leaf blade, which is 6 to 8 inches long by slightly over one-half as wide. From the last, *R. gracilis* differs in having leaves

deeply-cleft at their ends, with spaces or windows between most of their few segments, and in the leaves being deeply-cleft at their tops. The leafstalks are pale beneath. This species, which attains a height of 10 feet, is represented by four varieties. The typical kind, native to Guatemala and Honduras, does not appear to have been cultivated. It has leaves up to 2 feet long with fourteen to twenty-two veins on each side of the rachis (central axis). Its stems are usually clustered. Its male flowers have sixteen to twenty-two stamens. Variety *R. g. tenuissima*, a native of Oaxaca, Mexico, has much smaller leaves with only eight or nine veins on either side of the rachis. Variety *R. g. gracilior*, from southern Mexico to Honduras, differs in having male flowers with eight to ten stamens. Its leaves have eight to eleven veins on each side of the rachis, and its fruits have pointed-tipped crowns. Variety *R. g. rostrata* has staminate flowers with eight to ten stamens, leaves with eleven to fifteen veins on either side of the rachis, and fruits with blunt crowns.

Garden and Landscape Uses. Reinhardtias are attractive for tropical gardens and make effective pot plants. Because they are low and slender they do not take up much room.

Cultivation. Information about the outdoor cultivation of these palms is limited and there is need for trials. It seems probable that they would be most likely to succeed in fertile, well-drained, fairly moist soil in part-shade in warm regions where they would not be subjected to frost. In greenhouses they prosper in rich, porous soil kept always moist where the atmosphere is highly humid and there is shade from strong sun. Propagation is by fresh seed sown in sandy, peaty soil in a temperature of 80 to 85°F. For further information see Palms.

REINIKKAARA. This is the name of orchid hybrids the parents of which include *Aerides*, *Ascocentrum*, *Euanthe*, and *Vanda*.

REINWARDTIA (Rein-wárdtia) — Yellow-Flax. One or two species of evergreen shrubs or subshrubs are the only members of the northern Indian genus *Reinwardtia*. They belong to the flax family LINACEAE. Although one is known by the colloquial name yellow-flax, they are distinct from true flaxes (*Linum*), differing markedly in their habits of growth and in having larger and broader leaves, and blooms with usually fewer than five styles. Their name commemorates a Dutch scientist, Kaspar Georg Karl Reinwardt, who died in 1822.

Reinwardtias have alternate, undivided leaves and numerous individually short-lived blooms that provide a gay succession over long periods. Their symmetrical flowers, solitary or more usually in terminal clusters, have five persistent sepals and

Reinwardtia indica

the same number of spreading petals and stamens, the latter with the bases of their stalks united. The fruits are spherical capsules.

The yellow-flax (**R. indica** syns. *R. trigyna*, *Linum trigynum*) must not be confused with yellow-flowered *Linum flavum*. The most commonly cultivated reinwardtia, it is 2 to 4 feet tall and has thin, elliptic-obovate, toothless leaves 1 inch to 3 inches long. Bright golden-yellow, the nearly circular blooms, solitary or in few-flowered clusters, are up to 2 inches in diameter. They have three styles and the bases of the petals are united to form a slender tube.

Garden and Landscape Uses. In warm, frostless or practically frostless regions, and especially humid ones, reinwardtias are splendid outdoor shrubs for sunny locations in fertile, reasonably moist soils. They also make attractive pot plants for warm greenhouses.

Cultivation. Well-drained, fairly fertile soil that never becomes excessively dry produces the best results. In spring old plants should be pruned to shape. Then, cuttings to give new plants may be planted in a propagating bed where the atmosphere is humid, or under mist. New plants can also be had from seed. To encourage branching and prevent straggly growth the young plants should have the tips of their shoots pinched out occasionally. Although reinwardtias will not tolerate excessive dryness, care must be taken not to maintain the soil in an over-wet condition, for if this is done leaf drop is sure to occur. Full exposure to sun, or in greenhouses light shade only in high summer, is needed. Reinwardtias do best in pots rather small for size of the plants. When the containers are fairly filled with roots it is necessary to fertilize regularly, preferably with liquid fertilizer. A winter night temperature of 55 to 60°F, with a daytime rise of five to fifteen degrees, is satisfactory. From spring to fall higher temperatures are favorable. Attention must be given to controlling red spider mites, which are especially partial to these plants.

REMUSATIA (Re-musátia). Four species of the arum family ARACEAE constitute *Remusatia*. They are natives of tropical Africa and Asia and Taiwan and are related to the jack-in-the-pulpit (*Arisaema*). Their name commemorates the French scholar and professor of Chinese, Abel Remusat, who died in 1832.

Rare in cultivation, remusatias are tuberous herbaceous perennials that send from the sides of their tubers leafless shoots bearing tiny scaly tubers. Each tuber has one or two undivided, shield-to heart-shaped leaves. Flowers are very rarely borne, at least by the kind discussed here. As is usual in the arum family, they are minute and crowded and in spikes (spadixes), with a spathe or bract at its base. In *Remusatia* the spadixes are very short, and male and females are separated by neuter flowers. None has decorative significance, but the spathes may be somewhat showy. The fruits are berries.

Native to India, **R. vivipara** (syn. *Arum viviparum*) occurs as an epiphyte in clefts and crotches of tree trunks and in pockets or soil on practically bare cliffs. Its tubers are up to 1½ inches across. The long-stalked leaves have heart-shaped blades up to 1½ feet long by 1 foot wide. The slender, erect shoots bearing the bristly tiny tubers are up to 1½ feet long. The yellow spathes that accompany the flowers are 4 to 5 inches long.

Garden Uses and Cultivation. This is an interesting and rare plant for lovers of the curious. It requires the same conditions and care as *Alocasia* and *Anthurium*.

RENAGLOTTIS. This is the name of orchid hybrids the parents of which are *Renanthera* and *Trichoglottis*.

RENANCENTRUM. This is the name of orchid hybrids the parents of which are *Ascocentrum* and *Renanthera*.

RENANTHERA (Ren-anthéra). About thirteen species, natives of tropical Asia, Indonesia, the Philippine Islands, and New Guinea, comprise decidedly ornamental *Renanthera*, of the orchid family ORCHIDACEAE. The name, derived from the Latin *renis*, a kidney, and *anthera*, an anther, refers to the kidney-shaped pollen masses of the first known species of these usually epiphytic (tree-perching) orchids.

Renantheras, without pseudobulbs, have branching stems and alternate, two-ranked leaves. There are two distinct types, those with comparatively short, erect, self-supporting stems, and vinelike kinds that may have stems 10 to 20 feet long or longer. The flowers, predominantly brilliant orange, scarlet, or crimson, are in horizon-

Remusatia vivipara

Renanthera hybrid 'Brookie Chandler'

tally spreading racemes or panicles of many individual blooms. The sepals and petals spread and are similar, or the lateral sepals may be bigger and of a different color. The small, movable lip, attached to the column and spurred or not, often has two small, erect side lobes. Attractive hybrids exist between species of *Renanthera* and also between that genus and *Arachnis, Phalaenopsis, Vanda,* and *Vandopsis,* the latter named, respectively, *Aranthera, Renanthopsis, Renantanda,* and *Renanopsis.*

Vining renantheras include brilliant-bloomed *R. coccinea* and *R. storiei,* the first native from southern China to Thailand, the other of the Philippine Islands. Its stems up to 15 feet long or sometimes longer, sparingly-branched, and well furnished with oblong, leathery leaves 4 to 6 inches long that spread at right angles, *R. coccinea* has usually branched panicles of up to 150 blooms. These come from the upper parts of the stems. The long-lasting flowers are 3 to 3½ inches long. The upper (dorsal) sepal and the petals are brilliant red spotted with yellow, the glossy side sepals are a darker, richer red. The lip is red and yellow. Very robust, usually branchless stems are characteristic of *R. storiei.* They sometimes exceed 20 feet in length. Up to about 1 foot long by 1½ inches wide, the leaves are unequally two-lobed at their tips. There is a brief projection between the lobes. Much branched, and up to 4 feet long or longer, the horizontal flower panicles may have 150 or more blooms 2½ inches across. The upper sepal and the petals are orange with crimson blotches and spots. The considerably larger side sepals are bright scarlet with darker blotches. The lip, predominantly scarlet, is marked with yellow.

Shorter, erect-stemmed renantheras are

R. imschootiana, up to about 3 feet, and *R. monachica,* which usually is less than 2 feet, in height. Native to Indochina and Assam, **R. imschootiana** has solitary, densely-foliaged stems that become woody as they age. The fleshy leaves, mostly under 4 inches long by ¾ inch broad, are oblong, with notched apexes. The horizontally spreading panicles, 1½ to 2 feet long, are of many bright blooms 2 to 2½ inches across. Their narrow-strap-shaped upper sepal and usually red-spotted petals are yellow. The lateral sepals are larger, elliptic, and light scarlet. The 2-inch-long, scarlet lip has yellow keels. The Philippine Islands is the home territory of **R. monach-**

Renanthera monachica

ica. Its very thick, rigid leaves, about 5 inches long, are often mottled with dull purple or brown. The flowers, 1 inch to 1½ inches across, are in panicles up to 1½ feet long. They have fiery-red-spotted, orange sepals and petals, the upper sepal and petals narrower than the down-pointing lateral sepals, and a small blood-red lip.

Garden and Landscape Uses and Cultivation. In Hawaii and other humid, tropical places, renantheras are splendid for outdoors. They provide showy displays of long-lasting blooms. They are also satisfactory in warm greenhouses. For the best results these orchids must be given a brightly lighted site, with only just sufficient shade to prevent the foliage from scorching. The vining kinds respond to conditions and care that suit *Aerides,* the shorter ones to those appropriate for *Vanda.* For more information see Aerides, Vanda, and Orchids.

RENANTHOCERAS. This is the name of orchid hybrids the parents of which are *Pteroceras* and *Renanthera.*

RENEALMIA (Ren-eálmia). Related to *Alpinia,* but differing in having flowers with an erect lip and in other botanical details, *Renealmia,* of the ginger family ZINGIBERACEAE, consists of seventy-five species of aromatic herbaceous perennials of the American tropics. Its name commemorates Paul Reneaulme, a French botanist, who died in 1624.

Renealmias have fleshy rootstocks and erect, somewhat canelike stems with many leaves arranged in two ranks. Stalkless or stalked, the leaves are lanceolate or oblong. In panicles or racemes terminating the leafy stems or on separate leafless ones, the blooms have a short, three-lobed calyx, a short-tubed corolla with three erect or spreading, unequal to nearly equal lobes (petals), and one fertile stamen. The fruits are spherical capsules.

For long grown in conservatories as *Alpinia vittata,* a name that correctly belongs

Renealmia ventricosa

to a similar variegated-leaved member of the ginger family, *R. ventricosa,* of the West Indies, is vigorous, clump-forming, and up to 6 feet tall or taller. Its short-stalked leaves have pointed blades up to 10 inches long by 2½ inches broad. Borne from the ends of leafy stems, the 1-inch-long white flowers, in half-nodding panicles, are solitary or paired in the axils of the bracts. The hairless fruits are about ½ inch in diameter.

Other species cultivated in Hawaii and elsewhere in the tropics are *R. exaltata* and *R. strobilifera.* About 12 feet tall, *R. exaltata* has leaves 1 foot to 3 feet long by 2 to 5 inches wide. On stalks separate from its leafy ones and up to 3 feet tall are carried 1-foot-long clusters of red flowers, from two to four in each bract axil. About 6 feet tall, *R. strobilifera* has leaves about 1 foot long and 2 inches wide or slightly wider. Its yellow flowers, solitary in the axils of the bracts, are in orange clusters up to 4 inches in length.

Garden and Landscape Uses and Cultivation. These are as for *Alpinia* and *Hedychium.*

RESEDA (Res-èda) — Mignonette. An old-fashioned garden annual enjoyed chiefly for the delightful, distinctive fragrance of its flowers, common mignonette is the most important sort of *Reseda.* The name is from the Latin *resedare,* to assuage, in allusion to the ancient use of the plants for treating bruises. There are about sixty species. The group is native from Europe to North Africa, and central Asia. A few kinds are naturalized in North America. It belongs in the mignonette family Resedaceae.

Resedas are erect or more or less prostrate, hairless or hairy annuals, biennials, and perennials, with stems sometimes rather woody at their bases. They have undivided leaves that may be lobed, or pinnately-divided ones, and rather insignificant flowers in terminal spikes or racemes. The sepals and the cleft or toothed petals are four to eight. There are eight to forty stamens, joined to one side of the flower, and three or four stigmas. The fruits are bottle-shaped, angled, or horned capsules containing small seeds that are released through an opening at the top.

Reseda odorata, a garden variety

Common mignonette (*R. odorata*), a native of North Africa, in its wild form is a branching annual or biennial up to 2 feet tall, with stems more or less horizontal below, and then erect, and oblanceolate to obovate leaves 2 to 4 inches long and generally with one or two pairs of shallow lobes. The yellowish-white flowers, in loose spikes, have finely-cleft petals about ⅙ inch long and yellow anthers. They are very fragrant and are succeeded by three-angled, nodding capsules. There are many excellent garden varieties of mignonette, mostly with bigger flower spikes and larger and richer-colored blooms.

A nonfragrant kind, *R. alba,* of southern Europe, is occasionally grown in flower beds. In the wild it is annual, biennial, or perennial. It is generally cultivated as an annual. From 6 inches to 2½ feet tall and upright, its stems branch in their upper parts. The long-stalked leaves are irregularly-deeply-pinnately-cleft into five to fifteen pairs of narrow, wavy-margined, sometimes toothed lobes. Greenish-white, the small flowers, with usually five, rarely six petals, are in very long, slender spikes,

Reseda alba

sufficiently numerous to make a very creditable display of bloom. The seed capsules have four horns.

Dyer's-rocket (*R. luteola*) was once esteemed as a dye plant. From its seeds an

Reseda luteola

illuminating oil was obtained. A biennial, with a basal rosette of leaves that overwinters and the following year develops flower stems 1½ to 4 feet tall, it is a hardy native of Europe, naturalized in North America. It has slender leaves without lobes and yellow blooms with four each sepals and petals; the upper petal is cleft into four to eight lobes, and the lateral ones sometimes into four. The three-lobed seed capsules are roughly spherical.

Garden Uses. Garden varieties of common mignonette are delightful in flower gardens and herb gardens and supply excellent material for bouquets. The penetrating, slightly spicy, characteristic fragrance of their blooms is liked by all. As well as being appreciated as outdoor annuals, they are very useful for growing in greenhouses as sources of out-of-season cut flowers and as pot plants. The other resedas described may be grown in naturalistic, semiwild landscapes and in flower borders, and the dyer's-rocket as a species of interest in collections of plants once useful to man.

Cultivation. Resedas succeed in porous, moderately fertile soil. Those slightly alkaline are especially to their liking. Good outdoor results are had by sowing seed in early spring where the plants are to bloom and thinning the seedlings to 4 to 5 inches apart. Common mignonette does best where it receives a little shade during the hottest part of the day, but too much is detrimental. To secure early flowers in the garden it is practicable, where mild winters prevail, to sow in fall where the plants are to remain. Alternatively, and this is the best plan where winters are severe, seeding may be done, as described below for plants to bloom in greenhouses, indoors in a temperature of 55 to 60°F eight weeks before the last spring frost is expected. In the greenhouse the young plants are grown in full sun and under airy conditions in a night temperature of 50°F, and day temperatures five to ten degrees higher. A week or ten days before they are to be planted in the garden, which should be as soon as all danger from frost has passed, they are stood in cold frames or in a sheltered, sunny place outdoors to harden. In the garden they are planted about 6 inches apart.

To bloom mignonette in greenhouses in winter and spring as decorative pot plants and to provide cut flowers it is necessary to maintain cool temperatures. Under too warm conditions the shoots become "blind," that is, they fail to produce flower spikes. On all favorable occasions the structure must be ventilated freely. After the seedlings are well up, whenever outdoor temperatures make it possible, the greenhouse should be held at 45 to 48°F at night and not more than five to ten degrees warmer by day. A rather heavy, but porous, fertile soil gives the best results. The plants may be grown in benches, ground beds, or pots. To have flowers in December seeds are sown in August. September and October sowings provide a succession of blooms, a January sowing a spring crop. Seeds are sown five or six in a 2½-inch pot and kept at a temperature of 55°F. As soon as the seedlings are big enough to handle, pull all except the two strongest out of each pot. Before the roots crowd excessively, set young plants for cut flowers, spaced 1 foot apart in each direction, in benches or beds. At this time cut off at ground level (pulling at this stage is too disturbing to the roots) the weaker of the two plants. Take care not to break the root balls. When the plants are 4 inches tall, pinch out their tips to encourage branching. Three to eight shoots may be allowed to each plant. All side shoots that develop on those are removed as soon as they are big enough to be seized between finger and thumb. Supports, preferably in the form of wires such as are favored for carnations, are positioned when the shoots that develop after the first pinching are 4 inches tall; at that time the soil surface is lightly cultivated.

To have pot plants for greenhouse display, essentially the same procedure as for cut flowers is followed except that instead of being planted in benches or beds the young plants are potted into successively larger pots until they occupy containers of 5- to 7-inch size. Also, if more, but somewhat smaller flower spikes are preferred, the young plants may be pinched a second time when the shoots from the first pinch are 4 inches long.

Mignonette "trees" developed from *Reseda odorata* were pleasing conceits of old-time gardeners. They must not be confused with the mignonette tree (*Lawsonia inermis*). A mignonette "tree" is an ordinary mignonette plant trained in tree form. The word "tree" is a little ambitious, for the finished result is not over 3 to 4 feet tall. Nevertheless, it has a single stem or "trunk," and a well-rounded top of branches, foliage, and flowers. It is what sophisticated gardeners call a "standard" specimen. Other plants such as fuchsias, geraniums, lantanas, and heliotropes are often grown in this way.

To develop a mignonette "tree" it is best to begin in July or August, preferably with cuttings made from sturdy shoots of strong-growing plants, otherwise by sowing seeds. Cuttings root quickly in a humid, shaded cold frame or a greenhouse propagating bench. The rooted cuttings are potted singly in sandy soil in 3-inch pots and are kept growing in a cool greenhouse or cold frame. As soon as roots have well penetrated the available soil, and before the plants become starved and stunted because of insufficient root room, they are repotted into larger pots and this is repeated until they occupy containers 6 or 7 inches in diameter. The soil should be coarse, rich, and porous. Some crushed limestone mixed with it is advantageous. At all stages care must be exercised not to allow the plants to suffer from dryness, but at the same time, not to permit long periods of soil saturation. A nice balance is needed. Training begins early. It consists of pinching out all side shoots that appear as soon as they are big enough to be taken between thumb and finger. To neglect this and allow them to drain strength from the main stem, which is to become the trunk, is fatal. Equally important is to provide a stout bamboo cane as a stake and to keep the future trunk tied neatly, but not excessively tightly, to it. Through the winter the future "trees" are grown under conditions recommended above for mignonette in greenhouses. They need plenty of room and full sun. Crowding soon spoils them. When the main stem has attained a height of 2 to 3 feet its tip is pinched out and several side shoots are permitted to develop from below the top. When these are 4 inches long their ends are pinched out with the result that they branch and produce a fine head of flowering shoots.

RESEDACEAE — Mignonette Family. This family of dicotyledons consists of six genera embracing seventy species, mostly natives of the Mediterranean region, but including some indigenous from Europe to India and others from South Africa and California. Members of the family are annuals and perennial, herbaceous or rarely woody-stemmed plants with alternate, undivided or pinnately-divided leaves. Their usually asymmetrical flowers are in terminal racemes or spikes. They have a persistent calyx of two to eight lobes or sepals, a corolla of eight or fewer petals, or wanting, from three to forty-five stamens protruding even when the flowers are in bud, and six or fewer pistils with stalkless stigmas. The fruits are capsules, with often gaping apexes, or less often are berries or consist of separate follicles. Only *Reseda* is of horticultural importance.

RESERVE BORDER. This is a name sometimes given to a border or bed set aside as a small home nursery in which to raise plants to sizes suitable for planting elsewhere. Besides such biennials as Canterbury bells, English daisies, forget-me-nots, pansies, and sweet williams, many young perennials and propagations of trees and shrubs can be conveniently accommodated in an area of this kind where they can be cared for with a minimum expenditure of labor. A reserve border may often be appropriately associated with a vegetable or a cut flower garden.

REST HARROW. See Ononis.

RESTESIA. This is the name of orchid hybrids the parents of which are *Orleanesia* and *Restrepia*.

RESTING. Most plants that live for more than one season experience periods of active growth and periods of rest during which growth is apparently suspended. During the latter periods, which usually correspond with the cool or dry seasons of the plant's native habitats, deciduous sorts lose their leaves.

The successful cultivation and particularly the successful flowering of many kinds of plants depend upon observing their resting periods. Indoors this is commonly done by withholding water completely or supplying it less frequently than during growing periods, by ceasing to fertilize, and by keeping the plants at lower temperatures. The end of a resting period or beginning of the growing period that follows is appropriate for repotting many plants and for pruning some kinds.

RESTREPIA (Res-trèpia). Some authorities include this genus of the orchid family OR-CHIDACEAE in *Pleurothallis,* to which it is closely related. As a separate entity, *Restrepia* consists of sixty species, natives from Mexico to Brazil. The name compliments Joseph Emanuel Restrep, a naturalist, who traveled in South America and died in 1864.

Restrepias are epiphytes (tree-perchers that do not take nourishment from their hosts). They include tufted and creeping kinds, mostly with solitary flowers, very rarely with more than one bloom on a stalk. The stems are sheathed with bracts. They terminate with a solitary leaf. The upper (dorsal) sepal and petals are slender and threadlike, with broadened bases and clublike apexes. Very much larger and showy, the two lateral sepals are joined except at their tips. The scarcely evident lip rests on the bases of those sepals.

These sorts are cultivated: *R. antennifera* (syn. *Pleurothallis ospinae*), of Venezuela and Colombia, has clustered, slender stems up to about 1 foot long, sheathed with black-spotted bracts and terminated with an elliptic to ovate leaf 3 to 5 inches long. The slender-stalked, showy flowers, ¾ inch to 1¼ inches long, have a white upper sepal and petals. The boat-shaped, purple-striped, yellow-brown lateral sepals are joined almost to their tips. Shorter than the petals, the fleshy, warty lip is pink spotted with dark brown. *R. guttulata* (syn. *R. maculata*), from Ecuador to Venezuela, resembles the last, but has stems not over 3 inches long and flowers with linear-lanceolate upper sepals and petals that are white with a red center line. The lateral sepals are greenish-yellow spotted with purple. *R. xanthophthalma* (syn. *Pleurothallis xanthophthalma*), from Mexico to Panama, is from 3 to 8 inches high. It has tightly-clustered stems. Its leaves, three-toothed at their apexes, are at most 3 inches long by 1 inch wide, and frequently smaller. The red-brown-blotched, greenish-yellow or white flowers, about 1 inch long, are solitary on slender stalks.

Garden Uses and Cultivation. These are as for *Pleurothallis.* For additional information see Pleurothallis, and Orchids.

RESTREPIELLA (Restrep-iélla). The genus *Restrepiella,* of the orchid family ORCHIDA-CEAE, consists of eight species and is native from Mexico to South America. Its name is a diminutive of that of the allied genus *Restrepia.*

Tree-perchers (epiphytes), restrepiellas form tufts of one-leaved stems and have solitary, stalked, sometimes ill-scented flowers at the ends of the stems, mostly in clusters. They have separate sepals and petals and a lip jointed to the base of the arching column.

Native to Mexico and Guatemala, *R.*

ophiocephala (syn. *Pleurothallis ophiocephala*) is 6 inches to 1¼ feet high. It has stems up to about one-half that maximum and short-stalked, fleshy oblong-strap-shaped to lanceolate leaves 3 to 8 inches long by ½ inch to 1½ inches wide. Yellowish-brown spotted with dull purple, the ¾-inch-long flowers have oblong-strap-shaped petals much shorter than the elliptic-oblong sepals. The lip is fleshy and tongue-shaped.

Garden Uses and Cultivation. This is of interest chiefly to collectors of orchids. It requires cultural care appropriate for *Pleurothallis.*

RESURRECTION PLANT. This is the common name of *Anastatica hierochuntica* and *Selaginella lepidophylla.* The resurrection fern is *Polypodium polypodioides.*

RETAMA. See Genista.

RETARDING. Retarding is delaying the starting of plants into growth by prolonging their dormant season. Accomplished by keeping the plants at carefully regulated temperatures in cold or cool storage, it is most commonly employed to make available for out-of-season flowering pips of lily-of-the-valley and bulbs of certain sorts of lilies. It is also used by nurseries to "hold back" trees and shrubs that have been dug for landscape planting so that they can be planted later in spring than would otherwise be feasible.

RETINOSPORA. See Chamaecyparis.

REUSSIA (Re-ússia). At one time included in *Pontederia,* the genus *Reussia,* of the pontederia family PONTEDERIACEAE, consists of three species. From *Pontederia* they differ in having flowers with the upper lip five-lobed and the lower lip one-lobed. The name presumably honors Gustav Reuss, a Hungarian botanist, who died in 1861. This genus is endemic to South America.

Reussias are freshwater aquatic plants with long floating stems that root freely from the nodes. They have ovate to heart-shaped leaves with long stalks that broaden toward their bases to sheathe the stem. The flowers are in stalked spikes. Each has a corolla-like, six-lobed perianth, six stamens, and one style. After the flowers are fertilized, the spikes, previously held erect above the water, bend downward and dip beneath the surface where the fruits, which are capsules, mature.

Widely distributed in tropical South America, *R. rotundifolia* (syn. *Pontederia rotundifolia*) has stems up to several feet long and long-stalked orbicular-heart-shaped leaves with blades 2 to 4 inches across. Crowded in more or less cylindrical spikes about 2 inches long, with on the stalk just beneath the spike a conspicuous

Reussia rotundifolia

bract, the flowers are lilac-blue with an orange spot.

Garden and Landscape Uses and Cultivation. Reussias are attractive ornamentals for water gardens and pools, for year-round display in the tropics and subtropics where little or no frost occurs and in tropical greenhouses. In regions of severer winters, they may be summered in outdoor pools and overwintered in a greenhouse. They prosper under conditions that suit tropical water-lilies, reveling in rich soil, which may be contained in tubs or large pots, and a sunny location. Water temperatures of 70°F or higher are appreciated. Propagation is easy by division and by seed.

REVERSION. True genetic reversion to ancestral species is rare, but the term is applied horticulturally to changes in form, color, or other characteristics of plants that suggest a "throw back" to an earlier, usually less desirable stock. Plants that exhibit such reversion include varieties that originated as mutants (sports) but which develop branches similar to or identical with those of the plants that gave rise to them. Many dwarf varieties of conifers at times exhibit this type of reversion. A circumstance sometimes mistaken for reversion is when one characteristic in a population of mixed varieties, for example, one flower color of gladioluses of different colors, over a period of years becomes predominant. This usually results from one of the sorts being more vigorous and prolific than the others, and so it becomes more numerous, but it may be caused by infection with a virus as is true of the "breaking" of colors in tulips. Another circumstance that may be mistaken for reversion is when shoots develop from the understock of a grafted or budded tree or shrub.

REWAREWA. See Knightia.

REYNOUTRIA. See Polygonum.

RHABDADENIA (Rhabdad-ènia) — Rubber Vine. Four species constitute *Rhabdadenia,* of the dogbane family APOCYNACEAE. The genus inhabits tropical America, the West Indies, and southern Florida. The name, from the Greek *rhabdos*, a rod, and *aden*, a gland, alludes to a technical botanical feature of the genus.

Rhabdadenias are perennial woody vines, or more rarely are suberect or erect plants. They have opposite leaves and clusters of trumpet-shaped blooms. The flowers have deeply-five-cleft calyxes and corollas with straight tubes and five flaring, overlapping lobes (petals). There are five stamens and one style. The fruits are paired, but not joined, podlike, many-seeded follicles.

Native to southern Florida, the West Indies, Mexico, and Central America, and often favoring the margins of mangrove swamps and thickets near the sea, *R. biflora*, which like its relative *Echites umbellata* and unrelated *Cryptostegia* is called rubber vine, has narrow- to broad-ovate-oblong to lanceolate, short-stalked leaves 2 to 4½ inches long. Usually lateral, the flower clusters have stalks one-half as long as the leaves or longer. The white blooms are sometimes flushed with delicate pink. They have calyxes with five short, spreading lobes. Their corolla tubes, much narrowed in their lower one-third, broaden above and are 1½ to 2 inches long. The faces of the blooms are 1½ to 2 inches across. Smaller than the last and shrubby rather than high-climbing, *R. corallicola* has elliptic leaves up to 1¼ inches long and yellow flowers 1 inch or a little more in length and width. It is wild in southern Florida, including the Keys.

Garden and Landscape Uses and Cultivation. Attractive for tropical and subtropical gardens and for greenhouses, *R. biflora* responds to conditions and care appropriate for *Trachelospermum* and *Mandevilla*. Less showy *R. corallicola* responds to the same conditions.

RHABDOTHAMNUS (Rhabdo-thámnus). The one species of this genus occurs wild only in the North Island of New Zealand. It is the only member of the gesneria family GESNERIACEAE native to that country. Its name, from the Greek *rhabdos*, a rod, and *thamnos*, a bush, alludes to its many branches.

A shrub 2 to 6 feet tall, with numerous grayish-hairy branches, *Rhabdothamnus solandri* has opposite, slender-stalked, coarsely-toothed, broad-ovate to nearly round, grayish-green leaves, rough with conical hairs and ½ inch to 2 inches long. Its nodding, slender-stalked blooms, ¾ to 1 inch long, are solitary from the leaf axils. They have hairy, five-lobed, persistent calyxes and somewhat bell-shaped corollas with five flaring lobes (petals) up to about ¾ inch long and spaced to form a slightly two-lipped face to the bloom. Most commonly, the corollas are orange with red veins, but they vary from bright brick-red

to pale yellow and are variously striped. The slender style is tipped with a two-lobed stigma. The fruits are small egg-shaped capsules containing minute seeds. Dry woodlands, often beside streams, are the preferred natural habitats of this species.

Garden Uses and Cultivation. An attractive, rather slow-growing plant, *Rhabdothamnus* is best adapted for humid greenhouses where a minimum temperature of 55°F is maintained. Shade from strong sun is needed. Well-drained, fertile soil, coarse and containing an abundance of organic matter suits it, and should be kept always moderately moist. Excessive wetness is to be avoided. Seed form a satisfactory means of securing new plants, as do cuttings and leaf cuttings.

RHAGODIA (Rhag-òdia)—Australian-Saltbush. The sorts of *Rhagodia*, of the goosefoot family CHENOPODIACEAE, are shrubs and herbaceous plants, natives of Australia. There are about fifteen species. The name, derived from the Greek *rhagodes*, bearing berries, alludes to the fruits.

These plants have alternate or opposite, undivided, toothless leaves, and small flowers, both unisexual and bisexual, in terminal panicles or spikes up to about 1 inch long. The fruits are berries. Several sorts are grown for fodder.

Probably the only species cultivated in North America, the Australian-saltbush (**R. nutans**), is an evergreen herbaceous perennial with prostrate or climbing, weak stems about 2 feet tall. Its limp, slender-stalked, green, lanceolate leaves, usually somewhat arrow-shaped at their bases, are mostly opposite and up to 1¼ inches long. The flowers, mealy and in short, terminal spikes or panicles, are succeeded by tiny red fruits, to which remain attached the red, or sometimes yellow, perianths.

Garden and Landscape Uses and Cultivation. Not hardy in the north, the kind described is sometimes cultivated for ornament in mild, dryish climates. It does well near the sea and prospers in well-drained soil, in sun. It is increased by seed.

RHAMNACEAE — Buckthorn Family. Comprising 900 species of dicotyledons accommodated in fifty-eight genera, the buckthorn family is widely distributed in tropical, subtropical, and temperate regions. Chiefly trees, shrubs, and woody vines, rarely herbaceous plants, its members are often spiny. They most commonly have alternate, rarely nearly opposite, undivided leaves and small, symmetrical, generally bisexual flowers that have a four- or five-lobed calyx, four, five, or no petals, four or five stamens, and a short, lobed style. The fruits are fleshy drupes or capsules. Genera cultivated include *Alphitonia, Berchemia, Ceanothus, Colletia, Con-*

dalia, Discaria, Hovenia, Krugiodendron, Noltea, Paliurus, Phylica, Pomaderris, Rhamnella, Rhamnus, Sageretia, Spyridium, Trevoa, and *Ziziphus*.

RHAMNELLA (Rham-nélla). This horticulturally little known genus, of the buckthorn family RHAMNACEAE, consists of six species, natives of eastern Asia. Its name is a diminutive of that of closely related *Rhamnus*, from which it differs in its fruits having only one stone.

Rhamnellas are deciduous trees or shrubs with alternate, undivided, toothed leaves veined in pinnate fashion. Their tiny green bisexual flowers are in clusters from the leaf axils. They have five each sepals, petals, and stamens, and one two-lobed style. The fruits are black, berry-like drupes.

Occasionally cultivated **R. franguloides**, of eastern China, Japan, and Korea, is hardy in Philadelphia, Pennsylvania, and perhaps somewhat further north. It is a tree up to 30 feet tall with short-stalked, long-pointed, ovate-oblong, finely-toothed leaves 2 to 4½ inches long and hairless except on the veins on their undersides. In short-stalked clusters of five to fifteen, the tiny flowers are succeeded by cylindrical-oblong fruits ⅓ inch long.

Garden Uses and Cultivation. The species described is chiefly of interest because of its rarity. It succeeds in sun or partial shade in reasonably moist and fertile soil. Propagation is by seed and by cuttings.

RHAMNUS (Rhám-nus) — Buckthorn. Deciduous and evergreen trees and shrubs numbering 160 species (including kinds separated by some botanists as *Frangula*) constitute *Rhamnus*, of the buckthorn family RHAMNACEAE. As wildlings, they are widely distributed through the northern hemisphere with a few extensions into the tropics and south of the equator. Their name is an ancient Greek one for certain of the species.

Usually the leaves of rhamnuses are alternate, rarely are they opposite. They are stalked, pinnately-veined, and toothed or toothless. Greenish-white or yellowish, the small unisexual or bisexual flowers are in clusters, umbels, or racemes from the axils of the lower leaves of the current season's growth. Sometimes they are without petals or they may have four or five, often minute ones. There are four or five each sepals and stamens and a style ending in a lobed stigma. The fruits are pea-sized, berry-like drupes with two to four seedlike stones.

Several buckthorns have economic uses. Cascara sagrada, the name means sacred bark, is used medicinally, and the common buckthorn and some others have similar medicinal properties. The wood of the alder buckthorn is a source of the finest charcoal for gunpowder. Several kinds have been used as sources of green and yellow dyes.

Common buckthorn (**R. cathartica**), of Europe and temperate Asia, is deciduous and extremely hardy. In eastern North America it is widely naturalized, mostly in dryish soils, in some places to the extent that it has become something of a pest. A tall shrub or more rarely a small tree up to 20 feet in height, it generally has few to many of its branches terminated with a short, stiff spine. It has opposite, broad-elliptic to broad-ovate, toothed leaves, 1½ to 2½ inches long, with usually three veins on each side of the midrib. The flowers, the sexes commonly on separate plants, have four each sepals and petals. There are four stamens. The style has four branches. Generally containing four stones, the berries are ¼ inch in diameter and black. Similar to the common buckthorn, **R. davurica**, of Japan and Korea, differs in its somewhat larger and proportionately narrow leaves being grayish on their undersides and commonly having four or more veins on each side of the midrib. This is a large, wide shrub or small tree up to 30 feet in height. In **R. d. nipponica** the leaves are narrowly-oblong, 2 to 6 inches long by 1 inch to 2 inches wide.

One of the best deciduous species is the alder buckthorn (**R. frangula** syn. *Frangula alnus*). This native of Europe, North Africa, and western Asia is naturalized, especially in wet soils, from Nova Scotia to Quebec, New Jersey, and Indiana. It is a dense shrub or small tree up to 20 feet high, valued for its extreme hardiness, rapid growth, and handsome appearance. Its lustrous, dark green leaves are broad-elliptic to obovate and 1½ to 3 inches long. They have eight or nine pairs of veins and are usually toothless. Sometimes their undersides are slightly hairy. In clusters of eight to ten, the bisexual flowers, each with four sepals, four petals, and four stamens, are succeeded by ¼-inch-wide, two- or three-stoned berries that change from green to red to purple-black as they ripen. A very distinct and useful variety named 'Tallhedge' (**R. f. columnaris**) is dis-

tinct because of its erect, very narrow habit. Variety **R. f. aspleniifolia** has wavy-margined, linear to linear-lanceolate leaves up to 2½ inches long and under ¼ inch wide. The lanceolate leaves of **R. f. heterophylla** have wavy, often lobed margins. The leaves of **R. f. angustifolia** are lanceolate to oblong-lanceolate and ⅜ to ¾ inch wide.

Native to moist soils from Virginia to Missouri, Kansas, Florida, and Texas, the Indian-cherry (**R. caroliniana**) is a tall shrub or sometimes a tree up to 30 feet high. It has obscurely-toothed, elliptic to oblong leaves 2 to 6 inches long and one-third as wide. They have eight to ten pairs of veins and are more or less hairy on their undersides, especially when young. The flowers, with stalks usually shorter than the leafstalks, and solitary or in umbels, are bisexual. They have five each sepals, petals, and stamens and an undivided style. The fruits are three-stoned, sweet berries, ⅓ inch in diameter, that change from green to red to black as they ripen.

Among other eastern North American natives are **R. alnifolia** and **R. lanceolata**, inhabitants of wet or moist soils, the last favoring those of limestone derivation. Mostly about 3 feet high but sometimes taller, **R. alnifolia** is a fairly compact, deciduous, wide shrub. Its alternate, oblong-lanceolate to ovate-lanceolate, toothed, bright green leaves, up to 4 inches long, have six to eight pairs of veins. The unisexual flowers, in clusters of two or three, are without petals, but have five sepals. There are five stamens. The black fruits contain three stones. This, the most widely ranging North American buckthorn, occurs wild from Newfoundland to British Columbia, New Jersey, and California, and in Tennessee. An erect, slender-branched, deciduous shrub 3 to 6 feet tall, **R. lanceolata** is wild from Pennsylvania to Nebraska, Alabama, and Texas. From **R. alnifolia** it differs in its unisexual flowers having four each sepals and petals, in the stamens numbering four, in the style being forked, and in the ¼-inch-wide, black berries having two stones. Its alternate, bright green, finely-toothed, lanceolate to elliptic leaves, 1½ to 3½ inches long, have seven to nine pairs of veins.

Cascara sagrada (**R. purshiana**), a deciduous tree up to 25 feet or more in height, is native from Montana to British Columbia, and California. Its elliptic to ovate-oblong leaves, crowded at the branch ends, are toothed or nearly toothless, and 2 to 6 inches long. They have ten to fifteen pairs of veins. Many together in pubescent-stalked umbels, the flowers are bisexual. Their parts are in fives. About ¼ inch in diameter, the berries as they ripen change from green to red to black.

An excellent rock garden plant, **R. pumila**, a native of European mountains, is a

Rhamnus pumila: (a) With elliptic leaves

(b) With roundish leaves

beautiful ground-hugging, deciduous shrub only a few inches high. Its branches are prostrate. Its finely-toothed, elliptic to roundish leaves, ¾ inch to 2¼ inches long and finely-toothed, have four to nine pairs of veins. The fruits, about ¼ inch in diameter, are black.

The coffee berry or pigeon berry (**R. californica**) earned its second-mentioned vernacular name because wild pigeons are so fond of its fruits that they often strip all ripe ones from the bushes. An evergreen, this is so variable that botanists recognize at least half a dozen varieties. Its natural range is from Nevada to Oregon, New Mexico, California, and Mexico. Typically, it is a rounded shrub 6 to 8 feet tall. Its dark green leaves with paler green, usually hairless undersides, elliptic and 1 inch to 4½ inches long, have about nine pairs of veins. The bisexual flowers have their parts in fives. The nearly spherical, mostly two-stoned berries, ⅓ to ½ inch in diameter and edible, but not particularly palatable, change as they ripen from green to red to black. Variety **R. c. tomentella** attains heights up to 15 feet and has narrow-elliptic leaves densely-clothed on their undersides with short, white, velvety hairs. This tolerates higher temperatures and more intense sun than the typical species. Vari-

Rhamnus frangula columnaris (foliage, flowers, and fruits)

ety *R. c. occidentalis* (syn. *R. occidentalis*) differs from the typical species in its leaves having yellow undersides, and its fruits usually three stones. A nearly prostrate variety that attains a height of 2 to 3 feet and a spread of 4 to 6 feet is known horticulturally as *R. c. compacta.*

The red berry (*R. crocea*) is an evergreen shrub distinctive because its ripe fruits are bright red. Native to California, its offshore islands, Arizona, and Mexico, this species is very variable. Botanists recognize at least five varieties. Typically, it is 1 foot to 2 or less commonly up to 6 feet tall, usually much broader than high, and much branched, with the branches often rooting where they contact the ground. The branches, especially on plants in dry locations, are usually spine-tipped. The obovate to elliptic leaves, hairless or somewhat hairy, are ⅓ to ⅔ inch long. The fragrant flowers, without petals, are unisexual with the sexes on different plants. The globular fruits are about ¼ inch in diameter. Less compact and sometimes treelike, *R. c. ilicifolia* is 3 to 15 feet in height. Its leaves, slightly bigger than those of the typical species, and broadly-elliptic to nearly round, usually have spiny margins. The fruits are up to ⅓ inch long. A tree up to 30 feet high or a single-trunked, treelike shrub, *R. c. pyrifolia* is native to Santa Barbara Islands. It has larger berries than *R. c. ilicifolia*, and less prominently toothed leaves.

An evergreen or sometimes partially deciduous shrub 15 to 20 feet tall, *R. alaternus,* of southern Europe, has ovate to lanceolate leaves, remotely-toothed or nearly toothless, 1 inch to 2 inches long, and with three to five pairs of veins. Its flowers, with five each sepals and petals, are mostly unisexual. They are in short racemes. The ¼-inch-wide berries are black. Variety *R. a. argenteo-variegata* has leaves attractively edged with creamy-white.

Other deciduous kinds, black-fruited shrubs hardy in southern New England, include these: *R. alpina,* of southwest Europe, is up to 10 feet tall. It has broad-elliptic, finely-toothed leaves with nine to twelve pairs of veins. *R. a. fallax* (syn. *R. fallax*), the Carniolian buckthorn, is a beautiful-foliaged shrub 5 to 10 feet tall. Native to southeast Europe, it has broadly-elliptic to obovate leaves, finely-toothed, 2 to 5 inches long, and with twelve to twenty pairs of veins. *R. crenata,* up to 10 feet tall and a native of Japan and China, has oblongish, finely-toothed leaves up to 4 inches long and berries that change from red to black as they ripen. *R. dumetorum,* of China, has spine-tipped branchlets and distantly-toothed, obovate leaves ¾ inch to 1½ inches long. *R. imeretina,* the largest-leaved buckthorn, is up to 10 feet tall. From 4 to 10 inches long and finely-toothed, its leaves are oblong to broadly-elliptic. They have fifteen to twenty-eight pairs of veins, and in fall become bronzy-purple. It is native to the Caucasus. *R. infectoria,* the Avignon berry, a native of southwest Europe and up to 10 feet high, has broad-elliptic to obovate leaves up to 1½ inches long, finely-toothed, and with three or four pairs of veins. *R. utilis,* native to China and about 10 feet tall, has finely-toothed, oblongish, yellowish-green leaves up to 5 inches long.

Garden and Landscape Uses. The extreme hardiness of several deciduous buckthorns renders them distinct assets in cold climates. They, and other deciduous kinds, can be employed with good effects as general-purpose shrubs, screens, and hedges. For these last uses the alder buckthorn and especially its variety 'Tallhedge' are outstanding. The variety can be maintained as a high hedge 3 to 4 feet wide simply by shearing its top every year or two. Its sides need little or no such attention. Used as a hedge, typical *R. frangula* needs shearing at sides and top as do *R. cathartica* and *R. davurica.* Especially well suited for rock gardens, where it will closely follow the contours of the ground and rocks, is *R. pumila.* Partially evergreen or evergreen *R. alaternus* may be employed south of Washington, D.C. for the purposes, except as a rock garden plant, suggested above for deciduous kinds.

The landscape use of the evergreen western North American species described above is practically restricted to their home regions and places with approximately similar climates. The red berry prospers in California in stony, very well-drained soils. It endures a little shade, but prefers warm, sunny locations. Even more demanding of sun and warmth is variety *R. crocea ilicifolia.* Less finicky and more tolerant of cooler, moister, shadier environments, the coffee berry thrives in California with little care and survives under adverse conditions.

Cultivation. Except for the western North American evergreens, the needs of which are given above under Garden and Landscape Uses, and the common buckthorn, which grows well in dryish earth, buckthorns do best in fairly moist, reasonably fertile soils in sun or part-shade. Once planted they make few demands on the time or skill of the gardener. The only pruning needed is any to keep the plants in bounds and shapely. This is best done in late winter or spring. Propagation is easy by seed, layering, and cuttings. Rare kinds may be grafted onto seedlings of other buckthorns.

RHAPHIODORA. See Raphiodophora.

RHAPHIOLEPIS. See Raphiolepis.

RHAPHITHAMNUS (Rhaphi-thámnus). To the vervain family VERBENACEAE belong the two species of shrubs or trees that constitute *Rhaphithamnus.* The name is from the Greek, *rhaphis,* a needle, and *thamnos,* a shrub, and alludes to the spines. In the wild the genus is restricted to Chile and the islands of Juan Fernandez.

Rhaphithamnuses have small, opposite, undivided, smooth-margined leaves and, in their axils, solitary or in pairs, tubular flowers with five-toothed, bell-shaped calyxes, corollas with four or five unequal lobes (petals), and four stamens. The fruits are berry-like.

Suitable only for mild climates (even in the south of England it needs a very sheltered location), *R. cyanocarpus* is a pretty, dense evergreen 15 to 25 feet tall. Its branches have slender spines ½ to 1 inch long. Opposite or in threes, and crowded along the shoots, the very short-stalked, pointed, broad-ovate leaves are ¼ to ¾ inch long. Their upper sides are dark green, beneath they are paler. The pale blue flowers show in early spring along shoots of the previous year. They have bristly stalks and are about ½ inch long. More decorative than the blooms are the beautiful bright blue berries that succeed them. Spherical, they are ⅓ to ½ inch in diameter.

Garden and Landscape Uses and Cultivation. Decidedly ornamental, this shrub or small tree deserves to be planted more freely. It is not hardy in the north, but is adapted to California and other places where Chilean plants thrive. It succeeds in well-drained, fertile soil and needs little routine attention. The only pruning needed is any essential to keep the specimens shapely and within bounds. Any cutting is best done immediately after flowering even though this inevitably results in a reduced display of fruit. Propagation is by seed, by summer cuttings under mist, in a cold frame, or greenhouse propagating bed, and by layering.

RHAPIDOPHYLLUM (Rhapidophýl-lum)— Needle Palm. The only species of *Rhapidophyllum* is a low fan palm of the palm family PALMAE, a native of the coastal plain of the southeastern United States from South Carolina to Florida and Mississippi. Its name is derived from the Greek *rhaphis,* a needle, and *phyllon,* a leaf, and refers to the needle-like appendages of the leaf sheaths.

The needle palm (*R. hystrix*) has no aboveground stem or trunk over a few inches high. It appears as a neat cluster of foliage 3 to 5 feet in height and in width. The leaves, bright green above, are grayish-glaucous and finely-pubescent beneath. They have fan-shaped blades 1½ to 3 feet in diameter and long, slender, smooth stalks with the sheaths at their bases intermixed with 6- to 12-inch-long spines and fibers among which the purple flowers are borne, the males and females usually on separate plants. The leaf blades

Rhapidophyllum hystrix

are divided nearly to their bases into five to twelve, strongly ribbed divisions, up to 1½ inches broad and notched or toothed at their tips. The red, pubescent, egg-shaped fruits are up to 1 inch long.

Garden and Landscape Uses. The needle palm is decidedly ornamental and well worth planting as a lawn specimen or in association with other plants in beds and groups. It is one of the hardiest palms and may be cultivated outdoors as far north as North Carolina. It may also be grown indoors in pots and tubs.

Cultivation. This palm succeeds in a wide range of soils and is not particular as to moisture. It grows well in sun or shade, but for the best results some shade is desirable. When grown in greenhouses a minimum winter night temperature of 55 to 60°F, with a few degrees rise in the day permitted, is appropriate. Propagation is by fresh seed sown in sandy, peaty soil in a temperature of 75 to 80°F. The chief pests are scale insects, mealybugs, and red spider mites. For further information see Palms.

RHAPIS (Rhà-pis) — Lady Palm. Fifteen species of Asian cluster-stemmed palms are accommodated in *Rhapis,* but only two are in general cultivation. Long popular for planting outdoors in mild climates and as pot and tub plants, they are easy to grow and highly decorative. Lady palms belong in the palm family PALMAE. The name of their genus is from the Greek *rhapis,* a needle, and perhaps refers to the shape of the leaf segments.

Lady palms are low-growing and form dense clusters of erect, reed- or bamboo-like, leafy stems with peculiar long leaf sheaths that form an open network of fibers encasing them. The plants are unisexual, male and female flowers developing on separate individuals in short branching clusters among the foliage. Seeds are rarely produced in cultivation, chiefly perhaps, because plants of one sex only are likely to be grown, and these often are of one clone reproduced vegetatively by di-

vision. The slender-stalked leaves are divided almost to their bases into several segments that spread like the fingers of a hand, and are either alternate along the stems or mostly at the ends of the shoots. The ends of the leaf segments are toothed or cleft.

Up to 15 feet tall, **R. excelsa** (syn. *R. flabelliformis*) is usually considerably lower

Rhapis excelsa in Brazil

when grown in containers, but is quite variable and some forms seem to remain quite low. Its stems, up to 2 inches in diameter, have spreading, puckered-looking leaves with stalks at least as long as the blades. The main segments of fully developed leaves are 1¼ inches broad or broader at their centers and are mostly blunt and toothed at their ends. From the last, **R. humilis** differs in being normally much lower and more compact and in

Rhapis humilis, Garfield Park Conservatory, Chicago, Illinois

having canes not over ¾ inch in diameter. Its leaves are smaller, with stalks considerably shorter than the blades and segments up to 1 inch broad at their centers and toothed and pointed at their tips; they are not puckered.

Dwarf varieties of both *R. humilis* and *R. excelsa* are cultivated by enthusiastic hobbyists in Japan in great numbers, and in the 1970s some were introduced to the United States and made commercially available. In Japan the sorts of *R. humilis* are called shurochiku and those of *R. excelsa* kannonchiku. A society, the Kansokai, dedicated to promoting interest in collecting and cultivating these small palms was organized shortly after World War II. Of the more than 100 varieties currently grown in Japan, approximately half have leaves beautifully variegated, usually longitudinally-striped, with yellow or white.

Shurochiku and kannonchiku have been grown in Japan for nearly 400 years. At first ownership was restricted to nobility, but after the feudal system of government was replaced the hobby was open to everyone. Good specimens of shurochiku and kannonchiku command very high prices. As early as 1938 approximately $3,000 was paid for one specimen of a variegated variety and in the late 1970s a specimen of variety "Eizannishiki" was reported to have sold for about $10,000. Many varieties are available at more modest prices.

Miniature *Rhapis* palms of Japan: (a) A plain green-leaved variety

(b) A variety with leaves longitudinally striped with yellow

Garden and Landscape Uses. Because of their handsome appearance, durability, and ability to accommodate to difficult environments, these are among the most useful of low palms. They are excellent evergreen shrubs for use in warm climates in outdoor borders, foundation plantings, and as lawn clumps and underplantings beneath trees. They are also splendid ornamentals for growing in pots and tubs as decorations for halls, lobbies, rooms, and conservatories.

Cultivation. Lady palms represent no unusual difficulties to the gardener. They succeed in any ordinary, well-drained soil kept reasonably moist and are easily increased by division of the clumps in spring. Newly potted divisions should be kept in a warm, humid atmosphere and shaded until their roots have reestablished themselves, say, for a period of six to eight weeks. Outdoor clumps benefit from having the ground around them mulched. Container-accommodated specimens should be watered freely from spring through fall and moderately in winter; well-rooted specimens benefit from being given dilute liquid fertilizer at two-week intervals from spring through fall. A minimum winter night temperature of 55 to 60°F is satisfactory; at other times it may with advantage be a few degrees higher and at all seasons the day temperature should exceed the night temperature by five to ten degrees. A humid atmosphere and shade from strong sun are needed. Dwarf varieties, as grown in Japan and by some enthusiasts elsewhere, are accommodated in comparatively small pots, usually not exceeding 6 inches in diameter and often smaller, but with a large drain hole. For more information see the Encyclopedia entry Palms.

RHAZYA (Rhà-zya). Subshrubs related to, and in appearance much like, *Amsonia* constitute *Rhazya*, of the dogbane family APOCYNACEAE, a genus native from the Mediterranean region to India. There are

Rhazya orientalis (flowers)

two species. The name honors Abu Bekr-er-Rasi, an Arabian physician and author, who lived in the ninth and tenth centuries.

Rhazyas have erect, clustered stems and alternate, rather thick leaves. The blue, purple, or white flowers are in loose, terminal panicles. They have a five-parted calyx, a corolla with a slender tube and five wide-spreading lobes (petals), and five stamens. The fruits, slender paired pods, are in clusters.

A pretty ornamental, *R. orientalis* has ovate, dark green leaves with paler midveins about 2½ inches long. The clusters of lavender to violet flowers, sometimes suffused with pink toward the ends of the petals, are 3 to 4 inches across. Individual blooms are about ¾ inch in diameter.

Garden and Landscape Uses and Cultivation. Not hardy in the north, *R. orientalis* is a satisfactory flower garden decorative for beds and informal plantings in regions of mild winters. It succeeds in sunny locations in fertile, well-drained earth, and blooms in summer. It is also a worthwhile greenhouse pot plant, prospering where the winter night temperature is 45 to 50°F, and daytime levels are five to ten degrees higher. Airy conditions and a moderately humid atmosphere are appreciated. The pots must be well drained, the soil a fertile, porous, loamy mix, watered to keep it always moderately moist, but not for long periods wet. Propagation is easy by seed and by cuttings. Old plants are refurbished and repotted in late winter. In greenhouses flowers are displayed in June.

RHEEDIA (Rheèd-ia). Rheedias, trees of tropical America, the West Indies, and Malagasy, belong to the garcinia family GUTTIFERAE. There are forty-five species, many with edible fruits. The name commemorates the botanical author Hendrik Adrian van Rheede tot Drakestein, who died in 1691.

Rheedias have yellow sap and opposite, rigid, leathery, undivided, toothless leaves, with at the bases of their short stalks a large pit. The flowers, clustered in the leaf axils or along the branches, and usually small, are bisexual and unisexual. They have two sepals and four petals. In bisexual blooms the stamens are in a single circle, in male flowers they are numerous. The stigma may be stalkless or atop a short style. The fruits are leathery berries, with the pulp enclosing one to five seeds, crowned with the persistent stigma.

Native to the West Indies, *Rheedia aristata* is a shrub or small tree with branches spreading nearly at right angles. Its glossy, prickle-pointed, elliptic to broad-elliptic leaves are 1 inch to 3 inches long. Many together in clusters below the ends of short side shoots, the white flowers are ⅓ to ½ inch across. The globular

fruits are about ¾ inch in diameter. Very different *R. lateriflora* is a West Indian tree 50 feet tall or perhaps taller, with glossy, oblong-elliptic, short-stalked leaves up to 1 foot long and 5 inches wide. The longish-stalked, translucent white flowers, about ¾ inch in diameter, are in bunches from small knobs on the branches. The fruits are yellow.

Garden and Landscape Uses and Cultivation. The species described above are sometimes planted for ornament in the tropics and near-tropics. Raised from seed, they may be grown in ordinary soils in sun or part-day shade.

RHEKTOPHYLLUM (Rhekto-phýllum). The only species of this genus of the arum family ARACEAE is a tall, thick-stemmed, milky-juiced vine of tropical West Africa. Its name, from the Greek *rechtos*, torn, and *phyllon*, a leaf, alludes to the ovate or oblong-ovate leaves of mature plants being lobed and perforated.

The leaves of young specimens are heart-shaped and somewhat wavy, but are not lobed and are without holes. The areas between the veins are variegated with pale green. The flowers, as is characteristic of the arum family, are small and arranged along a spikelike axis called a spadix (in the calla-lily represented by the central yellow column) from the base of which a spathe (in the calla-lily the white, trumpet-shaped part) grows. The spathe in *Rhektophyllum* is about 4 inches long, red-purple on the inside and green outside.

A handsome tropical foliage plant that in the wild ascends trees by fastening itself by roots from the nodes (joints) of its stems, *R. mirabile* (syn. *Nephthytis pictur-*

Rhektophyllum mirabile, a young specimen

ata) has leaves on mature specimens with stalks 1 foot to 3 feet long and blades up to 3 feet long by 2 feet broad that are deeply-two- or three-times-pinnately-lobed or have a few holes in them.

Garden and Landscape Uses and Cultivation. Only in the humid tropics is this bold aroid of value for outdoor landscaping. It can be used effectively to clothe the trunks of palms and other trees to produce luxuriant effects, and in its younger stages for underplanting. In greenhouses and conservatories where night temperatures in winter are 60°F or higher, the atmosphere is humid, and shade from strong sun is available, it grows without difficulty. Like many of its family, *Rhektophyllum* prefers coarse, fertile soil with a generous organic content, kept always moist, but not saturated. Pot specimens that have filled their containers with roots benefit from regular applications of dilute liquid fertilizer. Propagation is very easy by cuttings of short pieces of stem with one or two nodes (joints) and by air layering. Seeds germinate readily if sown when fresh in peaty soil in a temperature of 70 to 75°F.

RHEUM (Rhèum) — Rhubarb. Except for common rhubarb or pie plant, for the cultivation of which see Rhubarb or Pie Plant, the genus *Rheum* is little known to gardeners, yet it includes handsome kinds splendid for bold landscape effects. The group belongs in the buckwheat family POLYGONACEAE and consists of fifty species, all natives of temperate and subtropical Asia. The name comes from *rha*, the ancient Greek name for the common rhubarb.

Rheums are stout, deciduous, perennial herbaceous plants that form clumps with thick roots and large, broad, thick-stalked leaves with sheathing stalks. In some sorts the leaves are deeply-lobed or divided and often toothed, in others they are not. The small, bisexual, greenish or whitish flowers, quickly succeeded by triangular and usually showy fruits, are developed in great numbers and displayed in erect, more or less pyramidal clusters of impressive size. They have six-parted spreading perianths, usually nine, sometimes fewer stamens, and three styles. The fruits are winged achenes.

Besides the common rhubarb or pie plant (*R. rhabarbarum*), the leafstalks of which are cooked as substitutes for fruit

Rheum alexandrae

and from which wine is made, some other species have other than decorative uses. The most important is the medicinal rhubarb (*R. officinale*). This, one of the ingredients of Gregory's powder, is a laxative, stomachic, and tonic. Chinese rhubarb (*R. palmatum*), Himalayan rhubarb (*R. australe* syn. *R. emodii*), and other species are also used medicinally.

Of the rhubarbs grown for ornament, *R. alexandrae*, a native of Tibet and western China, has long-stalked, lobeless, ovate-oblong leaves, with heart-shaped bases, that toward the tops of its stout, erect stems, gradually give way to pale green or greenish-yellow, leafy bracts beyond which the flowering branches protrude but a short way. This kind is 4 to 5 feet tall. Chinese *R. collinianum* attains a

Rheum collinianum

height of 4 to 7 feet and has deeply-lobed, heart-shaped leaves, reddish at first, with their margins unevenly cut. Its dull red flowers are in loose, branching clusters. Hailing from Tibet and one of the most luxuriant, *R. officinale* has roundish kid-

Rheum officinale

ney-shaped leaves with five unequally-toothed short lobes. Its flowering stems attain heights up to 10 feet. The flowers are greenish and in short-branched clusters. One of the most satisfactory and hardiest ornamental species is *R. palmatum*,

Rheum palmatum, the Royal Botanic Gardens, Kew, England

Rheum palmatum tanguticum (flowers)

a native of the Chinese-Tibetan border region, that, in bloom, is 7 to 10 feet tall and has boldly-lobed and toothed leaves 2 to 3 feet long. The depth of the lobing varies considerably with individual specimens. *R. p. tanguticum* is even more robust and has more coarsely-cut foliage. The flowers of these kinds are in upright, branched, more or less pyramidal clusters that much overtop the foliage. They are white, pink, or reddish. The flowers of *R. p.* 'Bowle's Crimson' are red.

Garden and Landscape Uses. The ornamental rhubarbs are picturesque plants of bold appearance that can be elements of strength in landscape pictures. Their massive leaves and stout flower clusters are effective in naturalistic and informal settings where they have plenty of space to develop and display themselves. They are very effective by watersides if they are planted sufficiently high above the water so that the soil is not saturated.

Cultivation. Deep, rich, moderately moist soil and locations in full sun suit these plants best. They benefit from being kept mulched and from a dressing of complete fertilizer applied each spring. In dry weather, watering is likely to be needed. The plants may be set 5 to 7 feet apart in early spring or early fall. They should be lifted, divided, and replanted at long intervals only, when, by producing smaller leaves, they evidence signs of deterioration. Seeds, sown in sandy, peaty soil kept moderately moist, germinate well; they may be sown in pots indoors or in cold frames or outdoor beds protected from interference by animals, and other disturbances.

RHEUMATISM ROOT is *Jeffersonia diphylla.*

RHEXIA (Rhéx-ia) — Meadow Beauty. The North American genus *Rhexia,* of the melastoma family MELASTOMATACEAE, is an outlying representative of the about 4,500 species of melastomes, as members of the family are called. It occurs further north than any other genus of this predominently tropical and subtropical family. The name is an ancient Latin one for some unknown plant, possibly an *Echium.*

There are eleven species of *Rhexia,* rather easy to recognize as to genus, but a little harder to determine as to species. Their pink, crimson, yellow, or white flowers have somewhat the form of those of evening primroses (*Oenothera*). They have four each sepals and petals and eight stamens. But in leafage and fruit, rhexias are very different from evening primroses. Their leaves are distinctly those of melastomes. Characteristically they have three or five distinct longitudinal veins that belly outward from the base of the leaf and in-

Unidentified species of the melastoma family MELASTOMATACEAE

ward toward its tip. The fruits are capsules that develop within the ends of the stems at the bases of the flowers and at maturity are flask- or urn-shaped.

The hardiest kind, **R. virginica,** also enjoys the widest natural distribution. It is found in wet, sandy soils from Nova Scotia to Ontario, Florida, and Louisiana. A distinguishing feature is its square stems with prominent wings or flanges at each corner. The plant, up to 2 feet in height, is often lower. Its usually tuberous roots are without horizontal rhizomes. Ovate-lanceolate to ovate, the leaves are 1 inch to 3 inches long and nearly or quite one-half as broad. They are stalkless and hairless or nearly so. This kind has bright rose- to purple-pink flowers, each about 1½ inches wide, in much-branched clusters. Unlike the last-named, the roots of **R. mariana** are never tuberous and send out horizontal rhizomes. It has nearly round to quadrangular stems without wings and is 8 inches to 1½ feet tall. The stalkless or shortly-stalked, lanceolate or lanceolate-oblong leaves are 1 inch to 2 inches long or sometimes longer. The flowers, in loose clusters, vary from pure white to rose-purple and are about 1 inch in diameter. The fruits are hairy. This kind inhabits moist sandy soils from Massachusetts to Kentucky, Oklahoma, Florida, and Texas. Closely resembling the last-named, but with usually more lanceolate leaves and nonhairy fruits, **R. nashii** is native from Maryland to Florida and Louisiana.

Other species include these: **R. alifanus,** about 3 feet tall, has roundish stems and pink flowers in clusters. It is native from North Carolina to Florida and Texas. **R. aristosa,** 1 foot to 2 feet tall, has square stems, bristly where the leaves join them, and dark pink to rose-purple blooms. It inhabits pine barrens from New Jersey to Georgia and Alabama. **R. cubensis,** 1 foot tall, indigenous from North Carolina to Florida and Louisiana, and in the West Indies, has rose-purple blooms. **R. lutea,** the only yellow-flowered kind, has small blooms and is much branched. It ranges from North Carolina to Florida and Texas. **R. petiolata,** 1 foot to 1½ feet tall, has square stems, and few-flowered clusters of pink blooms. It is native from Virginia to Florida and Texas.

Garden Uses. Meadow beauty is an appropriate name for these charming natives. Both in the wild and in cultivation they exhibit an endearing elegance and grace. This belies the great English authority on rock garden plants, Reginald Farrer, who peevishly wrote "R. virginica has been unwisely praised. It is at once a worthless and impossible species—it is an erect and gawky grower, suggesting a stiff and inferior Loosestrife. In the same condemnation, and no less impracticable as well as ugly, are R. mariana, R. ciliosa and R. aristosa." But then Farrer had a noto-

rious blind spot when it came to evaluating American plants; he rarely found anything good to say about them, and he never saw them in their native land. True, the pink of their blooms is sometimes a little harsh; it may exhibit that cursed suggestion of magenta prevalent in certain phloxes, and then again it may not. But even that difficult hue can be lived with and actually turned to advantage by locating it appropriately in reference to nearby colors. Other pinks and, above all, reds must not be close, and it is wise to avoid purples and lavenders unless of just the right shades. Whites are safe, and pale yellows complement these phlox-pinks to the extent that each does something for the other, as the ladies say. Logical places to grow meadow beauties are in rock gardens, bog gardens, and wild gardens.

Cultivation. Acid, moist or wet, sandy soil provides the right conditions for these plants. The liberal admixture of peat moss and coarse, gritty sand with any soil other than one excessively alkaline is likely to produce a good growing medium. Sunny locations are appropriate. Planting may be done in spring or early fall. Once established, practically no care is required by rhexias beyond keeping weeds down. In climates markedly colder than those of their natural ranges, the protection of a light winter covering of branches of evergreens, salt-hay, or other suitable loose material is helpful. Meadow beauties are very easily raised from seed sown in sandy, peaty soil kept always evenly moist. They can also be increased by division in spring or early fall.

RHIGOZUM (Rhigò-zum). About nine African species of the bignonia family BIGNONIACEAE constitute *Rhigozum.* The name, of uncertain application, comes from the Greek *rhigos,* frost, cold, or the sensation of cold.

Rhigozums are erect, freely-branching, spiny shrubs. They have undivided, three-parted or pinnate leaves and white, yellow, or salmon flowers with a five-toothed calyx, a funnel- to bell-shaped, slightly-two-lipped corolla with five spreading lobes (petals), five fertile stamens, and a slender style. The fruits are flattened, oblong to elliptic-oblong capsules.

Native to South Africa, **R. obovatum** is 5 to 8 feet tall. Its leaves or leaflets are up to ½ inch long and obovate to obovate-oblong. The 1-inch-long flowers are yellow, the fruits elliptic-oblong and 1½ to 2 inches in length.

Garden and Landscape Uses and Cultivation. The species described is suitable for outdoor cultivation in dryish tropical and subtropical climates. It can be propagated by seed and by cuttings.

RHINANTHUS (Rhin-ánthus) —Yellow Rattle. The genus *Rhinanthus,* of the figwort family SCROPHULARIACEAE, consists of about fifty species of semiparasitic plants, natives of cool parts of North America, Europe, and Asia. The generic name, from the Greek *rhis*, a snout, and *anthos*, a flower, refers to the shape of the upper lip of the corolla. The common name yellow rattle alludes to the flower color of some kinds and the sound made by the seeds when the ripe husklike capsules are shaken.

Yellow rattles are close relatives of two other groups that parasitize the roots of other plants, *Euphrasia* and *Pedicularis*. They are annuals with opposite, stalkless or short-stalked, pinnately-veined leaves and much smaller and proportionately broader bracts with veins that spread like the fingers of an open hand. In the axils of the bracts are the markedly asymmetrical flowers. They have a membranous, net-veined, persistent, four-toothed calyx that enlarges as the seed pod develops and encloses it. The corolla has a strongly-hooded upper lip, with two small lateral lobes near its apex, and a three-lobed lower lip. There are four stamens in two pairs of different lengths, positioned under the upper lip. The fruits are nearly round, flat capsules containing large, flat, winged seeds. From the species described below a yellow dye for home use was obtained and the plant was thought to be effective in treating diseases of the eye. Yellow rattles are reported to be poisonous to livestock, but are not usually eaten by them.

The common yellow rattle or rattle box (**R. crista-galli**) is variable, especially with regard to the color patterns of its blooms, which are in loose spikes and are basically yellow, but may have dark markings on the lower lips and pale or colored teeth on the upper. They are ⅓ to ⅔ inch long. This species is 8 inches to 2 feet tall and may be branched. Its narrowly-oblong to triangular-lanceolate, deeply-toothed, stalkless leaves are ¾ inch to 2 inches long. The seed pods are approximately ½ inch in diameter. This kind is native from New York to Labrador, British Columbia, and Alaska, as well as in Europe and Asia. By some botanists it is regarded as comprising several species.

Garden Uses and Cultivation. Yellow rattles are of little significance as garden plants, but occasionally they may be grown because of their former home uses. Their cultivation is complicated by the fact that host plants with roots to which yellow rattles are partial must be available. These are chiefly grasses, including cultivated grains. The procedure is to sow the yellow rattle seeds in early spring among or close to grass plants.

RHINEPHYLLUM (Rhin-ephýllum). Small, nonhardy succulents of the *Mesembryanthemum* relationship belonging in the carpet-weed family AIZOACEAE constitute *Rhinephyllum*. Natives of South Africa, they number about fourteen species that, except for technical distinctions in the flowers and fruits, closely resemble *Stomatium*. The name, from the Greek *rhine*, a file, and *phyllon*, a leaf, alludes to the rough surfaces of the foliage.

The genus includes short-stemmed plants with leaves so close together that no stem shows between, and others that branch freely and have leaves more distantly spaced. Two or four pairs of opposite, toothed or toothless leaves are borne on each shoot. Club-shaped, with flat tops and rounded or slightly keeled undersides, the leaves are freely sprinkled with tiny, hard, white warts. Golden-yellow to yellowish-white, the solitary, terminal flowers, like other members of the *Mesembryanthemum* group, are daisy-like in appearance, although very different in structure. Each is a single bloom not, as is true of daisies, a head of many small florets. Usually the blooms open in afternoons and evenings. The stamens are grouped in a dense cone. There are five stigmas. The fruits are capsules.

Compact and little over 1 inch in height, **R. broomii** has shoots with four or six notched leaves so close together that no stem shows between them. The lower leaves are spatula-shaped, those above nearly spherical. The yellow blooms are from a little under to slightly over ½ inch in diameter. The leaves of **R. comptonii** are up to almost 1 inch long and ⅜ inch wide and thick and have short, soft teeth along their edges. Of medium size, the yellow flowers open at night. With prostrate stems and short, erect, four- or six-leaved branches, cushion-forming **R. macradenium** has banana-shaped, greenish, toothless leaves, three-angled toward their apexes and 1 inch to 2¼ inches in length. On stalks shorter than the leaves the yellowish blooms are about 1 inch wide.

Garden Uses and Cultivation. Rhinephyllums are appropriate for collectors of choice, dwarf succulents. They are not difficult to grow. They respond to the care that suits *Stomatium*. Propagation is by seed and by cuttings. For additional information see Succulents.

RHIPOGONUM. See Ripogonum.

RHIPSALIDOPSIS (Rhipsal-idópsis)—Easter Cactus. This genus of two species of the cactus family CACTACEAE is separated from *Rhipsalis* because of its large, terminal blooms as well as other more recondite characteristics. Native to Brazil, *Rhipsalidopsis* has a name contrived from that of the genus *Rhipsalis*, and the Greek *opsis*, resembling.

In habit of growth these plants, called Easter cactuses, have much the aspect of the Christmas cactus (*Schlumbergera*), but their flowers are very different. These are bushy plants. Their stems are jointed and flat or sometimes angled. Their flowers differ from those of *Schlumbergera* in having shorter perianth tubes, stamens that are separate from each other, and a stigma with spreading lobes.

Its beautiful rose-pink flowers about 1¼ inches in diameter, **R. rosea** blooms freely

Rhipsalidopsis rosea

in spring on specimens up to 6 inches in height and over six inches in diameter. Its rose-red blooms, about 1¼ inches in diameter, are produced with great freedom. Quite distinct is **R. gaertneri** (syns. *Schlum-*

Rhipsalidopsis gaertneri in a hanging basket

bergera gaertneri, Epiphyllopsis gaertneri). This robust plant has bright scarlet blooms composed of numerous long, narrow sharply-pointed petals. The flowers, about 1½ inches long, most commonly develop in spring, but sometimes in fall. Whether this variation in flowering time is an inherent feature of some stocks of this species or whether it is a response to environmental conditions has not been determined.

Hybrids between *R. rosea* and *R. gaertneri* are named **R. graeseri** (syn. *Rhipsaphyllopsis graeseri*). They are intermediate

Rhipsalidopsis 'Peter Pan'

between the parents and have blooms about as big as those of *R. rosea*. They are available in various shades of red.

Garden Uses and Cultivation. These are the same as for *Schlumbergera*. More care must be exercised in watering *R. rosea* than the others, since it is especially sensitive to over-wetness. For more information see Cactuses.

RHIPSALIS (Rhíp-salis)—Mistletoe Cactus. This genus is intensely interesting to the student of the natural distribution of plants because it is the only representative of the vast cactus family CACTACEAE that is possibly native outside the western hemisphere. Possibly, because although a few species of *Rhipsalis* are apparently indigenous in Africa, Malagasy (Madagascar), and Sri Lanka, most botanists believe that they are derived from plants introduced there by man since the discovery of the New World. Still, no one can be sure. It is not impossible that they are true natives of the Old World. Be that as it may, *Rhipsalis* consists of about sixty species the great majority of which inhabit the Americas, where they are wild, from Florida to Argentina. The name, from the Greek *rhips*, wickerwork, refers to the slender, cylindrical, interlaced stems of some sorts.

As with many groups of the cactus family, *Rhipsalis*, as conceived broadly, has suffered from botanical monkeyshines that have resulted in splitting it into several lesser genera. Not without reluctance, but with some attempt at uniformity of treatment, these are recognized in this Encyclopedia. Treatments of certain species included by conservative botanists in *Rhipsalis* will be found under the names of the satellite genera *Acanthorhipsalis*, *Erythrorhipsalis*, *Hatiora*, *Lepismium*, *Pfeiffera*, and *Rhipsalidopsis*.

Rhipsalises are mainly epiphytic, that is, they perch on trees, but take no nourishment from them. They are not parasites. Their life-style is that of many orchids and bromeliads. Sometimes they grow on rock ledges, dead tree stumps, or other places where a little organic debris or moss and moisture are available. These are forest cactuses, not inhabitants of deserts or semideserts as are so many of their kin. In appearance the species exhibit considerable variation. Some have long, slender, whiplike, cylindrical stems. In others the stems are slender and angled. Yet a third group has broad, thin, leaflike stems resembling those of *Epiphyllum*. Often the stems are drooping or lax and clambering,

Rhipsalis, undetermined species

but in some kinds are erect. Mostly they produce aerial roots. Like all cactuses they have on their stems specialized areas called areoles, which morphologically are vestigial branches. These frequently have wool, hairs, or bristles and from them the flowers develop. The blooms, usually solitary, but sometimes clustered, are small and have few to several perianth segments (sepals and petals). They remain open at night. The juicy fruits are globular or nearly globular, white, pinkish, or red berries resembling those of mistletoe.

Common mistletoe cactus (**R. baccifera** syn. *R. cassutha*) ranges in the wild from Florida to Peru and southern Brazil, and in Africa and Ceylon. It is the only rhipsalis native in the United States. Forming considerable bushes, its much-branched, light green, pendulous stems up to 3 feet long are all alike. Circular, their segments are 4 to 8 inches or sometimes more in length and up to ⅙ inch in diameter. On very young stems the areoles have one or two brief bristles. The solitary yellowish or greenish-white blooms, scarcely ¼ inch long, are studded along the stems. They have spreading petals and nine to twelve stamens. The style is longer than the petals. There are three to five reflexed lobes

Rhipsalis baccifera

to the stigma. Under ¼ inch in diameter, the fruits are white. Much like the last, but less markedly pendulous, **R. virgata** is Brazilian. It has freely-branched, ascending, arching, or drooping stems, up to about 3 feet long, with branches toward their ends not over 2½ inches long by ¼ inch thick and more or less in spirals. Sparsely furnished with woolly hairs, their areoles bear occasional pinkish bristles. The cream-colored flowers, ½ to ¾ inch wide, are succeeded by pinkish berries about ¼ inch in diameter.

Others with circular stems include these: **R. burchellii**, of Brazil, has pendulous, usually forked stems with ultimate branches mostly up to 4 inches long. Coming from near their ends, the bell-shaped, white flowers, under ½ inch long, are followed by top-shaped, rose-pink fruits. **R. cereuscula** is a slender, erect to drooping

Rhipsalis cereuscula

Brazilian with mostly long stems that toward their ends bear a cluster of short branches with minutely-bristly areoles. Coming from near the ends of the branches, the flowers, ½ inch or a little more in diameter, have petals pinkish to white with yellowish midribs. The fruits are white. **R. grandiflora**, of Brazil, has long, branching stems up to ⅓ inch thick

Rhipsalis grandiflora

and areoles, often red-ringed, without bristles. The about 1-inch-wide, white or pink flowers, borne laterally along the branches, are succeeded by purplish or white fruits about ¼ inch in diameter. **R. lumbricoides**, of Uruguay and Paraguay, has cylindrical to slightly-angled, creeping

Rhipsalis lumbricoides

or hanging, ¼-inch-thick stems up to 3 feet long or sometimes considerably longer. They branch freely with the ultimate branches not markedly shorter than the others. From the areoles of the younger shoots sprout a few white bristles. The orange-blossom-scented, pale straw-yellow, wheel-shaped flowers, approximately 1½ inches wide, have about a dozen petals. The pea-sized fruits are greenish becoming brown and finally purplish-brown. **R. mesembryanthoides** is a distinctive, very attractive ornamental. Native to Brazil, bushy, and 1 foot tall or somewhat taller, it has comparatively long, slender, cylindrical stems with much shorter branches. The final club-shaped

branchlets, which suggest the leaves of certain *Mesembryanthemum*-type plants, are exceedingly numerous, stubby, and scarcely ½ inch long. The areoles are woolly, and those at the branch tips have a few bristles. The approximately ½-inch-wide flowers, with about ten white petals with yellowish midribs, are borne at the branch ends. The spherical to oblongish fruits, produced in great quantities, are white sometimes tinged with red. **R. puniceodiscus**, Brazilian, has slender, pendent,

Rhipsalis puniceodiscus

freely-rooting stems, with red-tinged areoles without bristles, and 3- to 4-inch-long branches in terminal whorls (circles) of up to six. About ¾ inch in diameter, the white flowers have orange stamens. At first dark red, the fruits become orange with age.

Stems with five or sometimes six prominent angles or wings are characteristic of **R. pentaptera** (syn. *R. pentagona*), of Brazil. Their shallowly-notched segments are 3 to 4½ inches long. The areoles, in the notches of the wings, sometimes bear a few bristles. White and about ten-petaled, the blooms, about ⅓ inch long, are succeeded by small, spherical, white or pale pink fruits. This is an erect, bushy plant up to 1¼ feet tall by 3 feet wide. Its ¼- to ⅓-inch-wide stems erect or drooping, the young ones with six to nine low ribs, the more mature ones weakly to more evidently three- to five-angled, **R. dissimilis**,

Rhipsalis mesembryanthoides

Rhipsalis dissimilis

of Brazil, has areoles with or without bristles and solitary, ¾-inch-wide, pink flowers succeeded by red fruits ½ inch in diameter.

The chain cactus (*R. paradoxa*), of Brazil, has drooping stems of sharply three- to four-angled, 1- to 2-inch-long segments,

Rhipsalis paradoxa

the angles of each alternating with those of the adjacent segments. The white, ¾-inch-wide flowers originate from woolly areoles and are succeeded by red fruits.

Broad, two-edged leaflike stems are typical of Brazilian *R. pachyptera,* but an occasional one may have three broad wings. They are 3½ to 8 inches long by 2 to 4½ inches wide and more or less arched, with a heavy mid-vein and coarsely-notched margins. Solitary or in small clusters from areoles along the stem edges, the yellowish flowers are about ½ inch long. This is bushy, erect, and up to 3 feet tall. The attractive Brazilian *R. warmingiana* has stems at first erect, later arching or hanging, with segments 4 inches to 1 foot long by about ¾ inch wide. Usually flat, they occasionally have three or four wings and often are purplish. The more or less fragrant, white flowers, displayed along the edges of the stems, are under ½ inch long. The fruits are deep violet to nearly black. Having both slender cylindrical or three-angled and broad, flat, thin, leaflike stems, Brazilian *R. houlletiana* is 3 to 6 feet tall. The flat stems, 4 to 8 inches long by up to 2 inches wide, have jagged-

toothed margins along which are borne ¾-inch-long, creamy-white flowers that yellow as they age; they are followed by red fruits.

Garden and Landscape Uses. These are delightful plants for growing outdoors on trees in the humid tropics, for cultivating in lath houses in drier warm climates, and for greenhouses. The sorts with pendulous stems are most conveniently grown and displayed in lath houses and greenhouses in hanging baskets.

Cultivation. Being epiphytes, rhipsalises need like others of that group a very loose planting medium that assures the roots an ample air supply. One that more or less simulates the organic debris likely to collect in crotches of trees in the humid tropics is ideal. Accordingly, the mix should be of a type that suits epiphyllums and tree-perching orchids. It may consist of osmunda or tree fern fiber with coarse leaf mold, a little topsoil, sand or perlite, and perhaps a sprinkling of crushed charcoal or of any similar chiefly organic material that ensures free passage of air and water. Keep it moderately moist at all times, never soaking wet for long periods. Well-established specimens benefit from biweekly applications of dilute liquid fertilizer from spring to fall.

Shade from strong sun and a decidedly humid atmosphere are needed. But shade must not be over-dense, otherwise flowering and fruiting are inhibited. As for temperatures, in winter 55 to 60°F at night, with a daytime increase of five to fifteen degrees, is satisfactory. At other seasons more warmth is appreciated. Repotting is best done in late winter or early spring. Increase is very easy by cuttings and by seed. For further information see Cactuses.

RHIZOME. A prostrate aboveground stem or a usually horizontal underground one that generally roots from the nodes, a rhizome has rudimentary, scalelike leaves along its length and eventually develops from its tip more ordinary leaves. The term is practically synonymous with stolon.

RHIZOPHORA (Rhiz-óphora)—Mangrove. There are about seven species of *Rhizophora*, of the mangrove family RHIZOPHORACEAE. The name, derived from the Greek *rhiza*, a root, and *phoreo*, to bear, alludes to their habit of growth. Like other genera of their family, rhizophoras are mangroves, a designation not restricted to one genus or even to one family, but used rather to describe a mode of growth and a way of life. Rhizophoras are native to many parts of the tropics.

Mangroves are among the most useful elements of the world's vegetation. Because of their peculiar growth they not only protect shorelines from erosion by

waves and other forces but are helpful in building new land. These trees and shrubs inhabit tropical and subtropical seashores from low-water mark to the limits of high tides or a little further, and along the banks of rivers as far as the water is brackish. They show peculiar adaptations to their specialized habitats. Notably, they develop an abundance of aboveground, interlacing, horizontal roots from which descend into the mud anchor roots; the ascending trunks branch and, in *Rhizophora*, produce roots from the branches. These reach down into the water and mud and support the superstructure. If mangroves shed their seeds in the manner of most plants they would simply be washed away by the tides and mostly lost. This danger is overcome by another peculiar adaptation. The fruits remain on the trees long after they are ripe and until the seeds germinate and make substantial rootlike growth from their lower ends. Only then does the young plant, now well started in life, separate from its parent and plummet like a streamlined bomb. If this happens at low tide it buries itself in the mud, soon becomes established, and develops into a new tree. At other times the newly dropped germinating seeds float to sea, generally to be washed in by the next tide and planted, possibly on some other part of the strand or even on some new shore. Mangrove roots, aerial roots, and "breathing roots" form tangles that entrap various kinds of debris and sediments and provide habitats for barnacles and oysters, as well as hideouts and feeding grounds for crabs and other sea creatures. Gradually, as mud banks and finally land are built from the materials captured by their roots, the mangroves march outward from the shore and slowly add to the land.

Rhizophoras have thick, leathery, opposite, undivided, stalked, ovate to elliptic, hairless leaves and bisexual blooms in clusters of few. The leathery flowers are rather large and have four-lobed calyxes, four petals, and eight to twelve stamens. The fruits are leathery.

The American or red mangrove (*R. mangle*), native from Florida to the West

Rhizophora mangle

Indies and the warmer parts of South America, is naturalized in Hawaii. Commonly a dense, bushy-topped shrub or tree up to 30 feet tall, it sometimes attains 75 feet or more. Its many arching branches, aerial roots that eventually become new trunks, and masses of basal roots form impenetrable tangles. The bluntish leaves, 2 to 6 inches long and 1½ to 4 inches wide, have prominent midribs. The yellow blooms, two or three together in forked clusters, have lanceolate sepals and much narrower, linear, hairy petals that alternate with them, and eight stamens. They are about ¾ inch in diameter. The greenish-brown fruit, ¾ inch to 1¼ long, develops, before it parts from its parent, a root growth 4 to 10 inches long. Edible, but not palatable, the fruits were famine foods of the Indians. The wood of this species is red and so heavy that it sinks in water. Cutch is obtained from it. It can be also used for tanning and dyeing, and for fences, building, and fuel. It makes excellent charcoal.

Garden and Landscape Uses and Cultivation. Where mangroves grow naturally, clumps are often very acceptable features in the landscape and form good backgrounds for more sophisticated plantings, for which they supply shelter. In addition, they protect the shoreline. New plantings can be established by setting seedlings where the soil is inundated with salt water or brackish water. Germinating seeds are sometimes planted in pots and grown as novelties in greenhouses and windows. They are more interesting than beautiful. They succeed in ordinary soil, but the pots in which they grow should be kept standing in saucers of water so that the soil is always wet.

RHIZOPHORACEAE — Mangrove Family. Sixteen genera of trees and shrubs of the tropics and subtropics comprise this chiefly Old World family of dicotyledons. Generally opposite, their undivided leaves are without lobes or teeth. Symmetrical and prevailingly bisexual, the flowers have three to sixteen each sepals and petals, two to four times as many stamens as petals, and one style. The fruits are technically berries, drupes, or capsules. The only genus cultivated is *Rhizophora*.

RHODANTHE. See Helipterum.

RHODESIAN-WISTERIA is *Bolusanthus speciosus*.

RHODOCHITON (Rhodó-chiton) — Purple Bell Vine. One attractive Mexican species closely related to *Maurandia* is the only representative of this genus of the figwort family SCROPHULARIACEAE. It is a tender perennial vine that blooms profusely the first year from seed and is commonly grown as an annual. Its name is from the

Rhodochiton atrosanguineum as a greenhouse vine

Greek, *rhodon*, red, and *chiton*, a cloak, in allusion to the calyx.

The purple bell vine (*Rhodochiton atrosanguineum* syn. *R. volubile*) has slender stems 6 to 8 feet long and heart-shaped leaves, toothed at their margins, with stalks that twist around available supports in the manner of tendrils. This is how the plant supports itself and climbs. Beautiful and distinctive flowers hang on slender stalks. At first their only showy part is the large, reddish-pink, shallow-bell-shaped calyx, with the clapper of the bell represented by a small, incipient corolla. This gradually elongates to about 2½ inches in length and becomes tubular and rich reddish-purple. It has five slightly spreading lobes. Finally it opens at its apex to show four white stamens. After pollination the corolla falls away leaving the long-persistent calyx. The fruits are capsules.

Garden Uses. This very graceful vine is attractive for screening porches, fences, and other supports, and for grouping in flower borders. It is also attractive for the summer decoration of greenhouses.

Cultivation. Seeds germinate irregularly, taking from twelve to forty days. Fresh ones respond fastest. They are usually sown indoors in porous soil in a temperature of 60 to 65°F in February. The seedlings are potted individually in 2½- or 3-inch pots and later into those 4 or 5 inches in size. The young plants are grown in a sunny greenhouse in a minimum night temperature of 55 to 60°F. Their stems are trained to strings stretched below the greenhouse roof, and the strings are cut and moved with the plants when the latter are transplanted to the

outdoors, which may be done when it is safe to set out such tender subjects as begonias, coleus, and peppers. Prior to planting in the garden, they should be hardened for a week or ten days in a cold frame or sheltered place outdoors. They are spaced 9 inches to 1 foot apart. For supports, strings or wires stretched tautly will do, or pyramids of leafless brushwood with the base of each branch sharpened and pushed deeply into the ground, as is done with pea stakes, may be used. In the south, where the growing season is long, seeds of the purple bell vine may be sown outdoors as soon as warm settled weather arrives. Specimens to be bloomed in greenhouses may be trained to wires stretched just below the roof bars.

RHODOCODON (Rhodo-còdon). This not-very-well-known genus of the lily family LILIACEAE is endemic to Malagasy (Madagascar). It comprises eight species. The name, derived from the Greek *rhodon*, red, and *kodon*, a bell, is not of obvious application.

Botanically intermediate between *Muscari* and *Urginea*, the sorts of *Rhodocodon* are herbaceous perennials with bulbs and basal linear leaves. The leafless flowering stalks terminate in a raceme of small, nodding, bell-shaped flowers with a perianth with six short lobes. Each has six stamens and one style. The fruits are capsules.

A native of mountains in central Malagasy, *R. urgineoides* has a small spherical

Rhodocodon urgineoides

bulb and two or three lax, lanceolate-strap-shaped leaves ½ to ¾ inch wide. In lily-of-the-valley-like racemes, the white flowers, about ¼ inch long, are without fragrance.

Garden Uses and Cultivation. An interesting plant for growing in pots and pans (shallow pots) in greenhouses and, in mild climates, for planting outdoors, the species described above responds to well-drained, moderately fertile soil and a location that afforts light shade from strong sun. In greenhouses, a winter night temperature of 50 to 55°F with a daytime rise of five or ten degrees is agreeable. Water freely through the season of active growth; withhold water during the season of rest.

RHODODENDRON (Rhodo-déndron). This well-known genus, of the heath family ER-ICACEAE, contains a very large number of attractive, horticulturally important ornamentals, but is nearly without other practical values. It consists of between 500 and 600 species and several thousand varieties and hybrids. In excess of 4,000 kinds are reported to be cultivated in North America; more are grown in Europe. The genus *Rhododendron* chiefly inhabits cool regions including many mountainous parts of the northern hemisphere, but it is also represented at high altitudes in tropical and subtropical regions both north and south of the equator. The name *Rhododendron* derives from the Greek *rhodon*, a rose, and *dendron*, a tree.

Rhododendrons are shrubs or much less frequently trees of great diversity. In size they range from only a few inches high to giants that in their Asian homelands attain nearly 100 feet. As garden plants the tallest rarely exceed 10 to 20 feet in height. A few tropical kinds are epiphytes, which grow perched on trees after the fashion of many orchids and bromeliads. Not only do rhododendrons vary tremendously in size, they also vary in other ways. For example, the leaves of some are no bigger than the nail of a little finger whereas those of others exceed 1 foot in length. Great differences in flower size and color also occur between different kinds.

As now understood, *Rhododendron* includes the plants that previously constituted the genus *Azalea*. Botanically azaleas are accepted as a subgenus of *Rhododendron*, but in gardens it is usual to consider them separately, and as a matter of convenience this is done in this Encyclopedia, but without implication that they are not indeed rhododendrons. The following species of rhododendrons are described in the Encyclopedia entry Azaleas: *R. alabamense, R. albrechtii, R. arborescens, R. atlanticum, R. austrinum, R. bakeri, R. calendulaceum, R. canadense, R. canescens, R. dauricum, R. flammeum, R. indicum, R. japonicum, R. kaempferi, R. luteum, R. mucronatum, R. mucronulatum, R. nakaharai, R. oblongifolium, R. obtusum, R. occidentale, R. pentaphyllum, R. periclymenoides, R. poukhanense, R. prunifolium, R. quinquefolium, R. reticulatum. R. roseum, R. schlippenbachii, R. serrulatum, R. simsii, R. tsusiophyllum, R. vaseyi, R. viscosum, R. yedoense.* Hybrid rhododendrons treated in the Encyclopedia entry Azaleas that have Latin-form names are *R. gandavense, R. kosteranum,*

and *R. mixtum.* The plant once named *R. chamaecistus* is *Rhodothamnus chamaecistus.*

Rhododendrons are evergreen or deciduous. They have alternate, short-stalked leaves and flowers most often in terminal, umbel-like racemes usually called trusses, much less commonly in clusters from the leaf axils or solitary. The blooms have an often minute calyx usually with five lobes or five separate sepals, a generally five-lobed but sometimes six- to ten-lobed, often two-lipped, funnel-, bell-, or wheel-shaped corolla, most frequently five or ten stamens, but sometimes an intermediate number or more than ten, enclosed by or protruding from the corolla, and a slender style terminated by a knoblike stigma. The fruits are capsules containing many tiny seeds.

The cultivation of rhododendrons began with the British and their interest in the group is still extraordinarily high. In North America the climate of the Pacific Northwest is well suited for success with them and gardeners there devote much attention to their cultivation. Selected kinds also find favor in other regions, notably in the northeast.

So far as is known, the first rhododendron to be introduced to England was the European *R. hirsutum.* This was planted in the garden of that most remarkable collector of plants and other items known to the English of the day as oddities, John Tradescant. Before the middle of the eighteenth century the first native American species to reach Europe *R. maximum* had been sent to England by John Bartram of Philadelphia, but not until 1809 did *R. catawbiense*, that other great American contribution to the parentage of modern hybrids, reach Britain's shores. Meanwhile, *R. ponticum* from Spain, Portugal, and Asia Minor, *R. minus* from eastern North America, and *R. caucasicum* from the Caucasus had arrived, the first in 1763, the second in 1786, the third in 1803.

Not over fifteen species of rhododendrons including azaleas were being grown in gardens at the end of the first decade of the nineteenth century. Then in 1811 *R. arboreum*, of the Himalayas, was introduced. This later became the parent of many of the best red-flowered hybrids.

The list of sorts of *Rhododendron* in cultivation remained pretty much unchanged until the middle 1800s when Joseph Dalton Hooker's exploration of the Himalayas enriched English gardens by nearly fifty new species including *R. barbatum, R. fulgens, R. hookeri,* and *R. thomsonii,* all with red flowers. About the same time Robert Fortune discovered *R. fortunei* in eastern China and sent seeds of this species to England in 1856.

Although botanical exploration by the French missionaries David, Dalavay, Farges, and others earlier revealed the existence of rhododendrons in central and

western China, it was not until the last decade of the nineteenth century that seeds of any of these reached Europe, and although by 1900 most of the rhododendrons of Europe, the Caucasus, and eastern Asia, as well as of India and North America, were well known, no one had any true idea of the vast number of species that existed in central and western China and adjacent Tibet and Burma.

Then the very active nursery firm of Messrs. Veitch, of Chelsea, London, England, decided to send someone to China to collect seeds of the dove tree (*Davidia involucrata*), which had become known from explorations of the French missionary the Abbé Armand David, and, as a side issue, to gather and send home any other promising horticultural items. On the advice of the Director of the Royal Botanic Gardens, Kew, a young student of horticulture there was chosen. In 1899 Ernest H. Wilson, later to be become known worldwide as "Chinese" Wilson, left England on the first of four of what were to prove tremendously successful collecting trips to China, the first sponsored by Veitch, the others by the Arnold Arboretum, Jamaica Plain, Massachusetts. During the first two years of his exploration Wilson sent home seeds of about forty new species of *Rhododendron* in addition to seeds of numerous other sorts of plants.

The first of a small group of twentieth-century plant hunters in China, Wilson was soon followed by George Forrest, Reginald Farrer, Frank Kingdon-Ward, Joseph Rock, Frank Ludlow, and George Sherriff, all of whom added greatly to the sorts of rhododendrons in cultivation and to the store of knowledge about the genus.

Hybridizing rhododendrons began early and in England. The first successful cross recorded was made about 1820 between *R. catawbiense* and *R. ponticum.* Shortly afterward a hybrid between *R. maximum* and *R. ponticum* was produced. Following the first blooming in England, in 1825, of gorgeously red-flowered, but decidedly tender *R. arboreum*, that species became available as a parent and hybrids between it and *R. catawbiense* and hardy hybrids of *R. catawbiense* were obtained. First results were disappointing because the hybrids, although of improved flower color, lacked the ability to survive the winters in most parts of the British Isles. But breeders persisted in their efforts, and back-crossing some of the first hybrids of *R. arboreum* with their hardier parents produced reliably hardy hybrids in a considerable range of flower colors, including some good reds. These were the beginnings of the catawbiense hybrids, including the famous "ironclads," that were to become the mainstay of rhododendron plantings until well into the twentieth century. Doubtless some other species were crossed with these to produce some of the later devel-

A Dexter hybrid rhododendron

Part of the collection of "ironclad" rhododendrons in bloom at The New York Botanical Garden in 1970

oped catawbiense hybrids. In any case, by the middle of the century, a large number of hybrids were available.

In America first acquaintance with the new hybrids came in 1876 when the English hybridist and nurseryman Anthony Waterer exhibited 1,500 of his plants at the Century Exposition at Chicago. These created a sensation among horticulturists, and a demand for the plants. At the conclusion of the Exposition the plants were sold and they and other shipments from England were planted mostly in gardens of estate owners in New England, New York, Pennsylvania, and Maryland and one very complete collection at the Arnold Arboretum near Boston, Massachusetts. Not all proved hardy in the vicinity of Boston but some did and were later called the "ironclads." A notable collection was maintained at The New York Botanical Garden until the late 1970s.

The ironclads a full century after their debut in America are still the most cold-resistant hybrid rhododendrons suitable for growing in the northeastern United States. They are R. album elegans, lavender fading to white; R. album grandiflorum, white; R. atrosanguineum, bright red; R. 'Boule de Neige', white; R. 'Charles Dickens', medium red; R. everestianum, rosy-lilac and frilled; R. 'Henrietta Sargent', crimson; R. 'Lady Armstrong', rose-pink, paler in the throat; R. purpureum elegans, purple; R. purpureum grandiflorum, purple; and R. roseum elegans, rosy-pink.

Dexter hybrid rhododendrons are an outstanding group of varieties, the outcome of breeding carried out by Charles O. Dexter on Cape Cod, Massachusetts, during the third and fourth decades of the twentieth century. For many years Dexter

Dexter hybrid rhododendrons in bloom at The New York Botanical Garden

raised from 5,000 to 10,000 seedlings annually from which he rigorously selected for retention individuals that met his exacting standards. Unfortunately he distributed some inferior individuals before they bloomed and equally regretably no adequate record was kept of the parentage of the many splendid superior sorts he re-

tained. It is known, however, that the parents included some of the ironclads, as well as R. fortunei, and other Chinese species.

After Dexter's death in 1943, an unofficial committee of members of the American Rhododendron Society engaged in locating, collecting, testing, and evaluating the best of the Dexter hybrids. A survey in 1972 revealed 141 named selections in cultivation, too many for convenience and including too many similar or in some cases inferior sorts. In 1975 Herman A. Howard, an authority on this group of rhododendrons, published a list of thirty he considered superior. Here it is. Red-flowered: 'Acclaim', 'Accomac', 'Dexter's Brick Red', 'Dexter's Giant Red', 'Gigi', 'Glenda Farrell', 'Red Velvet', 'Todmorden'. Pink-flowered: 'Ben Moseley', 'Josephine Everitt', 'Madison Hill', 'Mrs. W. R. Coe', 'Newport Belle', 'Parker's Pink', 'Sagamore Bayside', 'Sagamore Bridge', 'Scintillation', 'Skerryvore Monarch', 'Skyglow', 'Westbury', 'Willard'. Purple-flowered: 'Amethyst', 'Dexter's Orchid', 'Lavender Princess'. Apricot-flowered: 'Champagne', 'Honeydew'. Cream-flowered: 'Dexter's Brandy', 'Dexter's Vanilla'. White-flowered: 'Dexter's Spice', 'Helen Everitt'.

The Dexter hybrids are mostly tall, some exceeding 15 feet in height and having as wide a spread. They have large trusses of often fragrant blooms, many with the seven corolla lobes (petals) characteristic of R. fortunei. The color range includes admirable pastels as well as much more brilliant hues, and individual flowers of some varieties are as much as 5 inches in diameter. Although probably a little less hardy than the ironclads, the Dexter hybrids survive much lower temperatures than many other large-leaved hybrids, particularly those of European origin.

Although the ironclads, Dexter hybrids, and a few other sorts are the best hybrid rhododendrons for the northeast, a magnificent array of other kinds, some imported from Europe and others raised in America, are grown successfully in the Pacific Northwest and parts of California, and breeders will undoubtedly continue to add new ones.

Species rhododendrons in cultivation as distinct from hybrids and excluding azaleas and *R. albiflorum, R. dauricum,* and *R. mucronulatum,* which look like azaleas, but do not belong in the subgenus *Azalea,* are very numerous, but many are known only in botanical collections or other special plantings. In the treatment that follows, native American and exotic (foreign to North America) sorts are presented separately. First, all the former are discussed, then a considerable selection of the exotics.

Native American rhododendrons are few in number, but include the hardiest of the taller growers *R. maximum* and nearly as hardy *R. catawbiense,* which has been of such inestimable value to breeders of hybrids. Four other species of the eastern part of the continent, one of the west, and one of boreal and subarctic regions complete the roll of Americans. Here they are in alphabetical sequence of their botanical names.

The Catawba rhododendron (**R. catawbiense**), named after the Catawba river that was itself named after the Catawba tribe of Indians that inhabited the region through which it flows, occurs at high elevations in the southern Alleghany mountains from Virginia to Georgia. This handsome sort, under favorable circumstances, forms a shapely, wide to rounded bush mostly 5 to 6 feet tall, but exceptionally approaching 20 feet. Its blunt, broad-elliptic to oblong, leathery leaves, dark green above and with paler undersurfaces, are

Rhododendron catawbiense hybrid

2½ to 5 inches long. In showy, subspherical trusses the about 2½-inch-wide, broadly-bell-shaped flowers are displayed many together in May or June. Usually they are lilac-purple spotted with olive-green, but occasional variants have blooms of more pleasing pinks and those of rare *R. c. album* are pure white. They have ten stamens, downy at their bases, and a hairless style. The flowers of *R. c. tomopetalum* are deeply-cleft into lobes

Rhododendron catawbiense fastuosum-plenum

(petals) with two to four coarse teeth. Beautiful semidouble or double blooms, unusual among rhododendrons other than those of the azalea group, are borne by *R. c. fastuosum-plenum.* They are rosy-lavender with the base of the upper petal spotted with brown. The Catawba rhododendron is hardy in sheltered locations throughout much of New England.

The West Coast equivalent of the Catawba rhododendron, *R. macrophyllum* (syn. *R. californicum*), is much less hardy. Native from California to British Columbia, this differs from its eastern counterpart in having leaves with blades narrowed to points at both ends, in the stalks of its flowers being hairless or practically so, and in the ovaries of the blooms being clothed with silky hairs instead of glandular ones. There are ten stamens, downy at their bases. This may survive in climates not more severe than that of Philadelphia, Pennsylvania, but except on the West Coast it is rarely employed for landscaping.

The rose-bay rhododendron or great-laurel (*R. maximum*), indigenous from Nova Scotia and Ontario to Georgia, Alabama, and Ohio and most cold tolerant of evergreen rhododendrons, is less showy in bloom than other American sorts, but has the most handsome, dark green foliage. This is commonly a large, sometimes rather loose bush 10 to 12 feet high, but on occasion considerably taller; it may even become treelike and up to 35 feet tall. About three times as long as wide, the ob-

Rhododendron maximum

Rhododendron maximum (flowers)

long, oblong-ovate, or lanceolate-oblong leaves are 4½ to 10 inches long. Their undersurfaces, paler than the upper ones, nearly always are thinly-hairy. The bell-shaped blooms, up to 1½ inches in diameter, are in smallish trusses of many, partly hidden by new leafy shoots that develop in June or July when the flowers are displayed. Normal flower color is rose-pink to purple-pink, mottled with olive-green to orange spots. The individual stalks and the ovaries of the flowers are glandular-hairy. There are usually ten stamens, sometimes as few as eight or up to twelve.

The Carolina rhododendron (**R. carolinianum**), a native of North Carolina, is hardy as far north as southern New England. Very beautiful, this sort blooms in May or June well before the Catawba rhododendron and its hybrids. A neat-foliaged shrub of compact habit generally 3 to 4 feet tall, but sometimes attaining 6 feet, the Carolina rhododendron has elliptic to narrow-elliptic leaves 2 to 3 inches long or slightly longer, hairless above, with rusty-brown scales on their undersides or sometimes slightly glaucous there. The flowers, in freely-produced and well-displayed trusses of usually ten or fewer, are

Rhododendron carolinianum

broadly-funnel-shaped and 1¼ to 1½ inches wide. Varying in color from light rose-purple to clear pink, they have few or no spots, and the outsides of their corolla tubes are without scales or have few. There are ten downy stamens and a hairless style. The blooms of *R. c. album* are white or nearly white, those of rare *R. c. luteum,* reported to be less hardy than the typical species, are described as being mimosa-yellow, certainly a unique and unexpected hue among North American evergreen rhododendrons.

Close relatives of the Carolina rhododendron are *R. minus* and *R. chapmanii.* Native from South Carolina to Georgia and Alabama and hardy in southern New England, *R. minus* is less compact than *R. carolinianum* and from 6 to 10 feet tall. Its narrowly-elliptic to lanceolate leaves, 1½ to 4 inches long, are hairless on their upper surfaces, scaly and frequently glaucous beneath. The greenish-spotted, rosy-pink flowers in clusters of up to ten and 1 inch to 1¼ inches in diameter differ from those of *R. carolinianum* in having corolla lobes (petals) shorter than the corolla tube and in the lobes being distinctly scaly on their outsides. Scarcely known in cultivation and extremely rare in the wild, *R. chapmanii* occurs natively in sandy areas in northwestern Florida, a most unlikely habitat for a rhododendron species. Almost certainly not hardy in the north, its greatest worth would seem to be as a possible parent from which to derive varieties adaptable to warmer climates. Up to approximately 6 feet in height, this species is rigidly upright.

Hardiest of evergreen rhododendrons, *R. lapponicum* is a prostrate, mat-forming shrub 6 inches to 1½ feet tall that inhabits mountain tops in the northeastern United States, as well as in eastern Canada, Newfoundland, northern Europe, and northern Asia. This kind has thick, scaly, elliptic to broad-lanceolate or narrowly-obovate leaves ¼ to ¾ inch long. The bright purple blooms, ½ to ¾ inch wide, are in clusters

of up to six. Their five to eight stamens, as long as the corolla, are hairless, as is the style, which equals or exceeds the stamens in length.

Exotic rhododendrons, sorts native elsewhere than in North America, are very numerous. Here is a selection of those most frequently cultivated: *R. ambiguum,* of China, is a somewhat variable, rather compact shrub mostly not over 5 to 6 feet tall and with ovate-lanceolate to elliptic leaves 1½ to 3 inches long, densely-scaly on their undersides and less densely so above. The green-spotted, lemon-yellow to greenish, funnel-shaped, 2-inch-wide, five-lobed flowers are less attractive than those of related *R. keiskei.* They have ten downy stamens. *R. arboreum,* native to the Himalayas and not hardy in the northeast, is a magnificent tree, reported to attain in the wild heights up to 100 feet and in cultivation in Cornwall, England, to have reached 70 feet. A chief interest in it is the important part it played as the source of good red flower color in hybrid rhododendrons, including the ironclads and other *R. catawbiense* hybrids. A variable sort, *R. arboreum* usually is moundlike in outline and broader than tall. Its lustrous, more or less hanging, bronzy-green, oblong-lanceolate leaves 4 to 8 inches long have depressed veins and are clothed on their undersides with silvery, white, tan, or brown hairs. Globular trusses 5 inches or more in diameter of twelve to twenty bell-shaped, five-lobed, blood-red blooms each with ten stamens appear in early spring. This describes the typical species, which, unfortunately, is not hardy in climates harsher than that of San Francisco. Much more cold tolerant is white-flowered *R. a. cinnamomeum,* which has smaller leaves, but it is not sufficiently hardy to survive in northeastern North America. *R. augustinii* is Chinese and not reliably hardy in climates colder than that of Philadelphia, Pennsylvania. From 6 to 10 feet in height or sometimes taller and tending to become rather loose and straggly, this is variable in flower color and only its better forms are worth growing. Its leaves, oblanceolate-lanceolate to elliptic-obovate, are 1½ to 3¼ inches long. Their upper surfaces are dark green, finely-wrinkled, and furnished with short hairs. On their undersides they are minutely-scaly and along the midrib bristly-hairy. In clusters of three or four, the deeply-five-lobed, broadly-bell-shaped flowers, 1½ to 2 inches in diameter, are pale pink to purple-pink, grayish-blue and lavender-blue, or rarely white. The ten stamens, nearly or quite as long as the corolla, are exceeded in length by the style. *R. auriculatum* is a late-blooming native of Chinese woodlands. Up to 20 feet tall, it has oblong leaves 4½ inches to 1 foot long or longer, rusty-hairy on their undersides, with a pair of earlike lobes at the bottom

of the blade on each side of the midrib, and glandular-pubescent stalks. The bell- to funnel-shaped, fragrant flowers, up to more than 4 inches across and in clusters of seven to fifteen, are white to pinkish spotted with pink or green. They have seven or eight corolla lobes (petals), fourteen to rarely sixteen hairless stamens, and a glandular style longer than the stamens. This sort, hardy almost as far north as New York City, needs a decidedly humid atmosphere for its best development. *R. baileyi,* of Tibet, 3 to 5 feet tall, has oblong to obovate leaves 1 inch to 2½ inches long, scaly on both surfaces. Appearing in early spring in clusters of five to eighteen, the flattish, approximately 1-inch-wide, dark red-purple flowers, deeply-five-lobed, have ten hairy stamens and a conspicuously bent style. *R. barbatum,* of the Himalayas, is not hardy in the northeast. From 15 to 40 feet tall, it has dull, oblong, 4- to 9-inch-long leaves with heart-shaped bases clustered at the twig ends. The blood-red flowers in closely packed clusters, and 1½ inches across, are bell-shaped, five-lobed, and have ten stamens with purple-black anthers and a hairless style. In cultivation this sort is regarded as being rather difficult to satisfy. *R. bullatum* is a Chinese species much like *R. edge-*

Rhododendron bullatum

worthii, but it differs in its flowers having scaly instead of shaggy-hairy calyxes and in being a little hardier, although not sufficiently so to survive in the northeast. *R. bureavii,* of western China, outstanding for the Pacific Northwest, is not hardy in the northeast. Up to about 6 feet high and usually broader than tall, it has tan to rusty-red young growth and glossy, leathery, broadly-elliptic leaves rusty-woolly on their undersides. In compact trusses of ten to fifteen, the 1½-inch-wide, bell-shaped flowers are rose-pink with crimson markings. *R. burmanicum,* native to Burma, is hardy only in very mild climates. A distinguished species usually not more than 6 feet tall, it has leaves densely-hairy on both surfaces up to about 2¾ inches long. The fragrant, greenish-yellow to yellow, often fading to ivory-yellow, 2½-inch-wide blooms are in clusters of three to six. **R. caeruleum,** of western China, up to 6 feet tall, has leathery, elliptic leaves about 1¼ inches long with a few scales on their undersides. The ¾-inch-long, deep-rose-lavender or less often white, five-lobed flowers, in clusters of three or four, have ten stamens and a hairless style. **R. callimorphum,** of western China and Burma, is not hardy in northeastern North America. Attaining a height of about 9 feet in the wild, in cultivation it is usually lower. It has thinnish-roundish-elliptic to nearly circular leaves 1 inch to 2 inches long, glaucous on their undersides and with scattered hairs above. Deep rose-pink in the bud stage, the bell-shaped flowers have five lobes notched at their apexes and usually a crimson blotch at the base of the corolla. There are ten stamens, sometimes with a few hairs near their bases, and a style that is hairy toward its base. **R. calophytum,** of western China, is hardy perhaps in climates not harsher than that of Philadelphia, Pennsylvania. One of the finest species, this in the wild attains heights of 40 feet or more, in cultivation it is rarely one-half as tall. For its best success it needs a shaded, fairly moist location. It has oblong-obovate to oblanceolate leaves 9 inches to 1 foot long, and in early spring white to rose-pink flowers 2½ to 3 inches wide, with a red blotch at the base of the upper of the usually seven or eight corolla lobes (petals). They have sixteen to twenty stamens and a stout, hairless style. **R. calostrotum,** of Burma, about 1 foot tall, has broad-elliptic to obovate leaves from a little under ½ inch to slightly over 1 inch long, fringed with hairs and scaly on their undersides. Chiefly paired, the shallow, pale pink to purplish-crimson flowers have five overlapping lobes, ten stamens hairy at their bases, and a hairless or nearly hairless style. This is hardy in climates not more severe than that of Philadelphia, Pennsylvania. **R. campanulatum,** of Himalayan provenance, is attractive, adaptable, and although best suited for the Pacific Northwest has one pink-flowered form hardy in sheltered locations at Philadelphia, Pennsylvania. Usually 8 to 10 feet in height, but on occasion attaining 20 feet, this has lustrous, elliptic to elliptic-oblong leaves 2½ to 6½ inches long, felted, in some forms attractively with tawny hairs, on their undersides. Opening early in the year and in clusters of about eight, the five-lobed, bell-shaped, 2-inch-wide flowers, white, white-edged with violet, rosy-purple, or in some seedlings unattractive pale magenta flowers are spotted on their upper petals. They have ten stamens hairy at their bases and a hairless style. **R. campylocarpum,** the honeybell rhododendron, is a truly lovely native of

the Himalayas that has been much used by hybridists. Remarkable for its clear canary-yellow to paler yellow flowers, it unfortunately is not adaptable to northeastern North America, but thrives in the Pacific Northwest. From 4 to 10 feet in height and the dwarfer forms said to be somewhat hardier than the taller, it becomes a rounded bush with ovate to elliptic leaves 1½ to 4 inches long. The flowers, mostly in clusters of six or seven, bell-shaped and five-lobed and 2¼ to 3 inches in diameter, have ten stamens. The ovary and lower part of the style are glandular. **R. caucasicum,** of the Caucasus, was employed early as a parent in hybridizing. Hardy in southern New England, compact, and 1½ to 3 feet tall, this has pointed, narrow-elliptic to obovate-oblong leaves 2 to 4 inches long, rusty-hairy on their undersides. The bell- to funnel-shaped, 2-inch-wide flowers, in clusters of seven to ten, have notched corolla lobes (petals). They are pink to creamy-white with greenish spots. Their ten stamens are hairy near their bases. **R. chartophyllum,** of western China, scarcely fully evergreen,

Rhododendron chartophyllum

is more correctly described as semideciduous. Shapely and free-flowering and up to 8 feet tall or taller, it has elliptic to oblanceolate leaves, slightly scaly on their undersides, up to 2½ inches long. The broad-funnel-shaped flowers, in compact clusters at the branchlet ends, are up to 2 inches in diameter, light purple or white with lavender-pink and brown spots on the upper petal. They have long-protruding stamens. **R. chryseum,** of western China, is hardy in southern New England. From 1½ to 2½ feet tall, it has broad-elliptic to obovate leaves from ½ inch to nearly 1 inch long. Its ¾- to 1-inch-wide, sulfur-yellow to bright yellow, five-lobed flowers, in clusters of four to six, have five stamens and a hairless style. **R. ciliatum,** of Sikkim, called the fringed rhododendron, suitable for gardens in the Pacific Northwest, is not hardy in the northeast. Varying in height from 3 to 6 feet and as wide

or wider than tall, this has hairy, elliptic leaves 1½ to 4 inches long, and in spring broadly-bell-shaped, five-lobed, pale pink blooms that fade to white and are 2 to 2½ inches across and in loose clusters of three to five. They have ten stamens. Variety *R. c. bergii* is especially fine. The species has been used in hybridizing. **R. ciliicalyx,** of western China, is appropriate for planting outdoors only where little or no frost is experienced, as in the region of San Francisco. Up to 10 feet in height, it has narrow-elliptic leaves, 2½ to 4½ inches long, with scaly, glaucous undersurfaces and bristly stalks. Mostly in threes, the fragrant, 4-inch-wide, white or pink-tinged flowers have corollas with funnel-shaped tubes and five spreading lobes. The ten stamens are conspicuously hairy at their bases. **R. cinnabarinum,** of the Himalayas, from 6 to 10 feet tall, has elliptic, grayish-green leaves 2 to 4 inches long with rather glaucous, scaly undersides. In clusters of five to eight, the pendulous, short-stalked, thick-textured, tubular, five-lobed blooms come in a considerable color range, from buff to orange, yellow, purple, cinnabar-red and a combination of orange and scarlet. They are 1½ to 2¾ inches long, up to 1¾ inches wide. They have ten stamens a little shorter than the corolla and a hairy style. The blooms of *R. c. blandfordiaeflorum* have yellow outsides, are red within. Those of *R. c. roylei* are bright rosy-red. **R. crassum,** of western China, Burma, and Tibet, is not hardy in the northeast. Up to 20 feet tall, it blooms late and has narrowly-obovate to oblanceolate leaves, 2 to 4½ inches long, with wrinkled upper surfaces, densely covered with rust-colored scales on their undersides. Sweetly-scented and funnel-shaped, the creamy-white to pink, five-lobed flowers, in clusters of three to six, are sometimes blotched with yellow. From 2 to 2½ inches long, they have fifteen to twenty stamens. **R. davidsonianum,** of China, is a variable sort about 10 feet tall. Not hardy in the northeast, it has pointed, elliptic to oblong or less commonly lanceolate leaves 1½ to 2½ inches long. Their two halves angle upward from the midrib in V-shape fashion. Their uppersides have scattered scales, beneath they are glaucous and densely-scaly. In loose terminal and axillary clusters of usually three to seven, the pink, five-lobed, funnel- to bell-shaped flowers 1 inch wide or a little wider, have ten slightly protruding stamens, hairy at their bases, and a hairless style longer than the stamens. **R. decorum,** of China, is hardy in southern New England. A close ally of *R. fortunei* and *R. discolor,* and, like those sorts, an attractive ornamental, it differs from them in the stamens of its flowers being clothed with short hairs toward their bases. From 6 to 20 feet in height, *R. decorum* has round-ended, oblong to oblong-obovate leaves 2 to 6 inches long, their

Rhododendron decorum

undersides glaucous and with scattered minute hairs. In clusters of eight to ten and with glandular individual stalks, the broad-funnel-shaped, fragrant, waxy, white to pink, usually greenish-spotted flowers, with six to eight lobes (petals), are about 2 inches in diameter. They have twelve to sixteen hairy stamens. The ovary and the style, throughout its length, are densely-glandular. **R. diaprepes**, of western China and Tibet, is 10 to 25 feet tall. Unfortunately not hardy in the northeast, this fine ornamental has oblong-elliptic leaves 6 inches to 1 foot in length. In loose trusses of seven to ten, its slightly fragrant, bell-shaped flowers have seven-lobed, white or pink-tinged, fleshy corollas 4 to 5 inches across and with a funnel-shaped tube. They have eighteen to twenty stamens, downy toward their bases. **R. discolor**, of China, is close kin to R. fortunei and R. decorum. From 10 to 15 feet tall, this late-blooming sort has pointed, narrow-elliptic to oblanceolate leaves 4 to 9 inches long with wedge-shaped bases. With dark green upper surfaces, they are whitish beneath. In clusters of about ten, the wax-like, bell- to funnel-shaped, fragrant, white to pale pink flowers are 2½ to 4 inches in diameter. They have six or seven

lobes (petals) and twelve to fourteen hairless stamens. The ovary and the style throughout its length are glandular. **R. drumonium** is Chinese. From 1 foot to 2 feet in height, it has elliptic to narrow-elliptic leaves under ½ inch long, densely-scaly on both surfaces, rust-colored beneath. The broadly-funnel-shaped, bluish-purple flowers are solitary. From a little under to somewhat over ½ inch wide and scaly on their undersides, they have stamens slightly longer than the hairless style. This is hardy about as far north as New York City. **R. edgeworthii**, of the Himalayas, is hardy only in regions of very mild winters. More attractive when fairly young than when older, when it tends to become straggling, 6 to 8 feet tall, it has broad-elliptic to ovate leaves 2 to 4½ inches long and with the veins on their wrinkled upper surfaces depressed. Their undersides are felted with tawny hairs. The strongly fragrant, funnel-shaped, five-lobed, pink-tinged, waxy-white blooms are in clusters of two to four. They have shaggy-hairy calyxes and ten stamens. This is a parent of many splendid hybrids. **R. fargesii**, an excellent Chinese species, is hardy in sheltered sites as far north as New York City or perhaps somewhat fur-

ther north. From 10 to 15 feet in height, this has elliptic to elliptic-oblong or ovate-oblong, blunt leaves 2 to 3½ inches long, with glaucous undersides. The flowers, in clusters of five to ten, have corollas about 2 inches wide with seven lobes (petals). They are white to rose-pink spotted with red. There are fourteen hairless stamens. The ovary is glandular, the style not at all or only at its base. **R. ferrugineum**, the alpine-rose of the mountains of central Europe, is very like R. hirsutum, which is also called alpine-rose. From that it differs most obviously in its leaves not being fringed with hairs and the calyxes of its flowers being extremely short. The blooms, in clusters of six to twelve, are funnel-shaped, pink to carmine-red, and scaly on their outsides. A little over ½ inch in diameter, they have ten hairy stamens. The flowers of R. f. album are white, those of R. f. atrococcineum almost scarlet. This sort, not adaptable to northeastern North America, thrives in the Pacific Northwest. **R. fictolacteum**, of western China, up to 20 feet tall or sometimes taller, is hardy in climates not harsher than that of Philadelphia, Pennsylvania. It has narrow-elliptic leaves clustered at the ends of the twigs and 5 to 8 inches in length. Their undersides are clothed with a felt of reddish-brown hairs. The bell-shaped flowers appear early. About 2 inches wide, and white with a crimson blotch at their centers, they have seven or eight corolla lobes and fourteen to sixteen stamens of markedly uneven lengths. **R. flavidum** (syn. R. primulinum), of western China and Tibet, upright and 1 foot to 3 feet tall, has lustrous, ovate-oblong leaves up to 1 inch long, which are aromatic when crushed. The funnel-shaped flowers are 1¼ inches wide and pale primrose-yellow, with corollas with five crinkled lobes. There are ten stamens and a style hairy toward its base. The blooms of R. f. album are white. This species and its varieties are hardy where winter cold is not more severe than in Philadelphia, Pennsylvania. **R. forrestii** (syn. R. repens) is a prostrate alpine species with rooting stems, native of Burma, Tibet, and western China, and in North America adaptable only to the Pacific Northwest. Over a period of years it forms a mat up to 4 feet wide or wider and not over 1 foot tall. The leaves, purplish on their undersides, broadly-obovate to orbicular, are ¼ inch to 1¼ inches long. Displayed in spring, the sparingly-produced, solitary or paired, bell-shaped, bright scarlet flowers, about 2¼ inches in diameter, have five lobes (petals) notched at their apexes. Variety R. f. repens, some horticultural forms of which bloom with great freedom, is distinguished by the undersides of its leaves being green. This has been of value as a parent of dwarf hybrids. It is closely similar to somewhat taller R. f. chamaethomsonii. **R. fortunei** is one of the

Rhododendron fortunei

the entire length of the style are sparingly glandular. This is a parent of numerous hybrids, including many of the Dexter group. **R. fulvum** (syn. *R. fulvoides*), of western China, Assam, Burma, and Tibet, is not hardy in the northeast. From 9 to 20 feet tall, it has glossy-oblong to broad-elliptic leaves 3 to 10 inches long with undersides clothed with a felt of cinnamon-brown or orange hairs. Blush-pink to rose-pink and with or without a crimson blotch, the five- or six-lobed, bell-shaped flowers, about 1½ inches wide, are white suffused with rose-pink and blotched with crimson. They have ten stamens. **R. grande,** of the Himalayas, is hardy only in very mild climates. Handsome and up to

4 to 9 inches long and with buff-colored, woolly-hairy undersides. In loose clusters of five to twelve, the geranium-scarlet, trumpet-shaped, 2½-inch-wide flowers have corollas very downy on their outsides, ten stamens, and a hairy ovary and style. **R. griffithianum,** one of the largest flowered and one of the most magnificent species native in the Himalayas, and hardy only in very mild climates, has played a part as parent of many splendid hybrids, among them the old favorite 'Pink Pearl', collectively known as 'Loderi' varieties. Up to 20 feet tall and with oblong leaves 8 inches to 1 foot long and slightly glaucous on their undersides, this species has, in clusters of about six, white to light pink, five-lobed, slightly fragrant blooms suffused with yellow in their throats, 5 to 6 inches or sometimes more in diameter, with large, smooth, saucer-shaped calyxes and twelve to sixteen hairless stamens. **R. haematodes** is Chinese, the parent of several hybrids. A beautiful sort, up to 10 feet high in the wild, but in cultivation decidedly dwarf and compact, this has glossy, oblong-obovate leaves 1½ to 3½ inches long, thickly felted on their undersides with rust-red woolly hairs. The brilliant red, bell-shaped flowers, in clusters of six to ten, and about 1½ inches wide, have five lobes, ten stamens, and a hairless style. This is not hardy in the northeast. **R. hanceanum,** of western China, is related to *R. keiskei.* From 3 to 4 feet tall, it has slightly-scaly shoots. Its pointed, lanceolate to narrowly-obovate leaves, which range from ½ inch to 4 inches long, are furnished with small scales especially on their undersides. White, creamy-white, or yellow, with ten protruding, often pinkish stamens conspicuously downy in their lower halves and a hairless style, the 1-inch-long, deeply-lobed, funnel-shaped flowers are in solitary or paired clusters at the branch ends. Variety *R. h. nanum* is smaller. **R. hippophaeoides,** of China, is hardy about as far north as Philadelphia, Pennsylvania. From 2 to 3 feet tall and compact, it has

Rhododendron fortunei (flowers)

most satisfactory Chinese evergreen species for gardens in northeastern North America and one of the most beautiful of all rhododendrons. Hardy in sheltered locations in southern New England and 10 to 12 feet tall, this has abruptly-pointed, oblongish, rather pale green leaves 4 to 8 inches long and with rounded or somewhat heart-shaped bases. Their slightly glaucous undersides are furnished with minute, scattered hairs. Blush-pink to rosy-lilac, the fragrant, waxy-looking flowers, on slender, glandular stalks, have seven corolla lobes (petals) and fourteen to sixteen hairless stamens. The ovary and

30 feet tall, it has oblong to oblanceolate, leathery leaves 6 inches to over 1 foot long, lustrous above and with a cover of silvery-white or buff-colored hairs on their undersides. From 2 to 3½ inches across and in dense clusters of up to thirty, the bell-shaped, eight-lobed flowers are ivory-white blotched with purple within. From 2 to 3 inches across, they have sixteen stamens downy at their bases and a style tipped with a large disk-shaped stigma. **R. griersonianum,** of western China and not hardy in the northeast, has been much employed by hybridists as a parent. Up to 7 feet tall or taller, it has lanceolate leaves

Rhododendron hanceanum nanum

elliptic-oblong to oblong, blunt leaves thickly-scaly on both surfaces. In clusters of eight or fewer, the purplish-blue to bluish-pink, broadly-bell-shaped flowers are ¾ to 1 inch wide or sometimes wider. A little shorter than the corolla, the ten stamens are hairy at their bases. The style equals the stamens in length. *R. hirsutum*, the alpine-rose of the mountains of southern Europe, is hardy about as far north as Philadelphia, Pennsylvania. Up to 3 feet tall, in its native state it grows only on soils of limestone origin, which is extremely unusual for a rhododendron. Resembling *R. ferrugineum*, which is also called alpine-rose, this has elliptic-oblong to obovate, round-toothed, hair-fringed leaves up to a little over 1 inch long, with bright green upper surfaces and lower ones with scattered scales. The flowers resemble those of *R. ferrugineum*, but have longer calyxes. Those of *R. h. albiflorum* are white. Although hardy in northeastern North America, this has not proved easy to grow there. *R. impeditum*, of Western China, is hardy in many parts of the northeast, but usually does poorly there because of the hot, dry summers. From 6 inches to 1½ feet tall, it has broad-elliptic to ovate leaves, up to slightly over ½ inch long, of which both surfaces are densely-scaly. The slightly fragrant, 1-inch-wide, five- or six-lobed, mauve to purplish-blue flowers, in twos or threes, have ten stamens. *R. intricatum* is a western Chinese species hardy in the region of New York City, but not easy to grow. Rarely exceeding 1½ feet in height, it has broad-ovate to elliptic leaves, dark green above, paler on their undersides, and densely-scaly on both surfaces. The broadly-funnel-shaped, five-lobed flowers, a little over ½ inch in diameter, are in clusters of five or six. Violet-purple, the ten stamens, which do not protrude, are hairy toward their bases. They exceed the very short, hairless style in length. This is hardy about as far north as Philadelphia, Pennsylvania. *R. keiskei*, of Japan, rarely exceeds 4 to 5 feet in height, and with age tends to become a

little straggly. Its leaves, 1½ to 2¼ inches long and scaly, especially on their undersides, are pointed-ovate-lanceolate. The flowers, which expand earlier than those of most evergreen rhododendrons, have five lobes and are a light yellow without spots. From 1¼ to 2 inches wide and in clusters of three to five, they have ten stamens and a hairless style. This, quite the hardiest of yellow-flowered evergreen species, does well outdoors in southern New York. *R. keleticum*, of Tibet, is semiprostrate and up to 1 foot tall. It has elliptic to

Rhododendron keleticum

obovate leaves about ½ inch long by ¼ inch wide, each tipped with a short point. Hairless on their upper sides, they have densely-scaly undersurfaces. Solitary or in twos at the branchlet ends, the short-stalked, up-to-1-inch-wide flowers are purplish-crimson with darker markings. They have ten stamens. *R. keysii*, of Bhutan, hardy in mild climates only, is 6 feet

tall or taller. Its young shoots, leafstalks, undersides of the leaves, and flower stalks are thickly clothed with brownish-red scales. Short-stalked and elliptic, the leaves are 2 to 4 inches long by ⅔ inch to 1¼ inches wide. Crowded in short clusters, the flowers are ¾ to 1 inch long by about ¼ inch wide. They have a cylindrical, brick-red to deep peach-pink corolla with five small teeth at its mouth. *R. leucaspis*, of the Burma-Tibet region, 1 foot to 3 feet tall, has elliptic to obovate, hairy leaves up to 2¼ inches long, with a tiny usually reflexed point at the apex. Saucer-shaped, about 2 inches wide, and with a deeply-five-lobed calyx, the flowers, in clusters of two or three or occasionally solitary, appear early; they are milky-white. They have five overlapping petals, ten stamens with chocolate-brown anthers, and a bent style. This, the parent of several good hybrids, succeeds only where winters are very mild. *R. macabeanum*, of the Himalayas, one of the handsomest species, is only for decidedly mild climates. In the wild up to 45 feet tall, but lower in cultivation, this has oblong-elliptic, leathery leaves up to 1 foot long, felted with grayish hairs on their undersides. The bell-shaped flowers, pouched at their bases, are in clusters of many. They are eight-lobed, about 2½ inches across, and pale to rich yellow, spotted purple toward their middles. There are fourteen to twenty stamens. *R. maddenii*, of Sikkim, is especially well suited for coastal northern California and other places with similarly mild climates, but not for harsher regions. Of dense habit and 6 to 9 feet tall, it accommodates well to cultivation. Its dull lanceolate to oblong-lanceolate leaves, 3 to 6 inches long, are densely-clothed on their undersides with reddish-brown

Rhododendron keiskei

Rhododendron keysii

Rhododendron maddenii

scales. White or white suffused with yellow and flushed with pink on their outsides, the strongly fragrant, five-lobed flowers, three or four in a cluster and about 4 inches wide, have twenty stamens. Several hybrids are derived from this species. **R. metternichii,** of mountain woodlands in Japan, is hardy in northeastern North America, at least as far north as New York City. Up to 12 feet tall, it has oblanceolate leaves 3½ to 8 inches long, felted beneath with rust-colored hairs. In clusters of many, the widely bell-shaped, rose-pink flowers, 2 inches or more in diameter and with seven corolla lobes (petals), have fourteen stamens and

Rhododendron micranthum (flowers)

a hairless style. **R. micranthum,** of China, Korea, and Manchuria, in foliage and in bloom has much the aspect of *Ledum.* Compact, rounded, and 4 to 7 feet tall, it has pointed, elliptic-oblong to oblanceolate leaves ¾ inch to 1½ inches long, thickly clothed on their undersides with rust-colored scales. Many together in crowded clusters up to 1½ inches wide, the five-lobed, bell-shaped, white flowers, ⅓ inch wide or a little wider, have ten hairless stamens and a somewhat shorter style. These protrude from the clusters like pins from a pin cushion. This is hardy in southern New England. **R. moupinense** is a Chinese species not hardy in climates

Rhododendron micranthum

appreciably harsher than that of the Pacific Northwest, but it is one of the finest early bloomers for that region. About 4 feet tall, this has lustrous, ovate-elliptic to oblong-elliptic leaves ¾ inch to 1¾ inches long. They have hairy stalks and are densely-scaly on their undersides. Broadly-funnel-shaped, five-lobed, and fragrant, the flowers are in twos or threes or occasionally are solitary. About 2 inches across, they have scaly stalks and are white, pink, or rosy-red, red-spotted on the upper lobes of the corollas and with ten hairless stamens. Some hybrids of this are hardier than the parent. **R. neriiflorum,** of western China, Burma, and Tibet, is not hardy in the northeast. From 4 to 9 feet tall, it has oblong to narrow-obovate leaves 2 to 4 inches long and glaucous on their undersides. The flowers, bell-shaped and rose-pink to scarlet or crimson, are in clusters of six to twelve. They are up to 1½ inches wide and longer than wide. They have calyxes colored like the crimson corollas, with five lobes notched at their apexes, and ten hairless stamens. Taller, variety *R. n. euchaites* has bigger crimson-scarlet blooms. **R. nuttallii,** of Bhutan, is one of the most impressive and largest-flowered rhododendrons. Hardy in the Pacific Northwest, but not in northeastern North America, and 12 to 15 feet tall, this often tends to become somewhat lanky. It has elliptic leaves 5 inches to 1 foot long with depressed veins. When they first expand they are bronzy-maroon. In clusters of three to six, the white or pale yellow blooms, sometimes flushed with pink, are lily-like, up to 5 inches long by 6 inches wide, and have ten stamens. **R. orbiculare,** of western China, 5 to 10 feet tall or on occasion taller, forms a symmetrical bush. It has rounded-heart-shaped leaves 1½ to 4 inches long, glaucous on their undersides. Bell-shaped and seven-lobed, the pink flowers, red in the bud stage and in loose clusters of seven to twelve, are 2 to 2½ inches in diameter and have fourteen stamens and a hairless style. They expand in early spring. This sort is not hardy in climates appreciably colder than that of Philadelphia, Pennsylvania. **R. oreotrephes,** a native of western China, Burma, and Tibet, is hardy in climates not colder than that of Philadelphia, Pennsylvania. In the wild it attains heights of 15 to 25 feet; in cultivation it rarely exceeds 8 feet. It has dullish gray-green, broad-elliptic leaves 1½ to 3 inches long. Generally funnel-shaped and mauve, pinkish-lavender, or rose-colored and usually spotted with crimson, the five-lobed flowers, 2 to 2½ inches in diameter, have funnel-shaped corolla tubes. They have ten stamens and are in clusters of four to twelve. **R. pemakoense,** of Tibet, one of the earliest to bloom and most charming of dwarf rhododendrons, is unusual in that it spreads by suckers. Up to 2 feet tall, but often lower, it has oblong-obovate to obovate leaves ½ to ¾ inch long with slightly scaly, glaucous undersides. Solitary or paired, the broadly-funnel-shaped, deeply-five-lobed flowers, 1½ inches wide, come in shades of lilac, mauve, and pink. They have ten stamens and a short style. Although hardy in climates as severe as that of Philadelphia, Pennsylvania, this has not proved generally amenable to cultivation in the eastern United States. *R. praevernum*, of western China, and hardy in southern New England, is more cold-tolerant than its close ally *R. sutchuenense*. Some 3 feet tall, compact, and generally broader than high, *R. praevernum* has oblanceolate leaves 4 to 7 inches long, completely hairless at maturity. In clusters of about ten, the flowers open in early spring. Bell-shaped and about 2 inches wide, they are white or pink blotched at the downy base of the corolla with wine-red. There are fifteen stamens, downy at their bases. *R. racemosum*, sometimes called mayflower

Rhododendron racemosum

rhododendron and a variable native of China, is hardy in southern New England. From under 1 foot to well over 6 feet tall, it has elliptic leaves ¾ inch to 2 inches long, glaucous and scaly on their undersides. The flowers are in clusters of three to six from the axils of the upper leaves. Funnel-shaped, five-lobed, and about 1 inch across, they come in various shades of pink or less commonly white. They have ten stamens. This sort in the wild inhabits limestone as well as more acid soils. *R. rubiginosum*, of southwest China, is hardy in eastern North America about as far north as Washington, D.C. In the wild it may be 25 feet tall, but in cultivation it is usually less than one-half that height. Much resembling American *R. carolinianum*, this has elliptic leaves, aromatic when crushed and 1½ to 3½ inches long, their lower surfaces clothed with reddish-brown scales. In clusters of four to eight, the funnel-shaped flowers, nearly 2 inches wide, are pink, mauve, or bright rose-pink spotted with maroon-red on the upper co-

rolla lobe. They have ten stamens, downy at their bases. Unlike most rhododendrons, this is said to tolerate limestone soils. *R. russatum*, of western China, is an excellent sort hardy in southern New England, but is highly intolerant of high summer temperatures and dry atmospheric conditions. Usually about 2 feet tall, much less commonly up to 4 feet or even higher, it has ¾- to 2-inch-long leaves that are elliptic to oblong-elliptic and rusty-green and thickly-scaly on both surfaces. The funnel-shaped flowers, about 1 inch in diameter and with five overlapping lobes, are in compact clusters of four to ten. Varying from deep reddish-purple to blue-purple, they sometimes have white throats. There are ten prominent stamens and a longer style hairy in its lower part. *R. smirnowii*, of the Caucasus, is of much merit. Hardy through much of New England, this has been used to a considerable extent in hybridization. From 10 to nearly 20 feet tall and of rather loose habit, its dark green, oblong leaves, 3½ to 6 inches long, are felted on their undersides with whitish to light brown hairs. The bell- to funnel-shaped blooms in clusters of many have rosy-red corollas with five frilled lobes (petals). There are ten hairy stamens. The ovary is downy, the style hairless. *R. souliei*, of western China, is highly decorative. Possibly hardy in sheltered locations in climates as severe as that of Philadelphia, Pennsylvania, this sometimes but not commonly exceeds 7 feet in height. Its broad-ovate to nearly heart-shaped, bluish-green leaves are 2 to 3½ inches long. The cup-shaped, pale pink to white flowers, 2 to 3 inches across and with five or sometimes six lobes, are in clusters of six to eight. They have eight to ten stamens and a glandular ovary and style. *R. sutchuenense* is Chinese. An admirable early-flowering shrub or tree 10 to 25 feet in height, it is hardy in climates not more severe than that of Philadelphia, Pennsylvania, or, in sheltered locations, as far north as Boston, Massachusetts. Its oblong-elliptic, conspicuously-veined leaves are 5 inches to almost 1 foot long. Up to 3 inches wide and in clusters of eight to fourteen, the bell-shaped, light lavender-pink flowers, densely-short-hairy on their outsides, are spotted with purple on the upper of their five lobes. They have twelve to fifteen stamens tipped with dark purple anthers and a longer style with a large reddish stigma. A natural hybrid between this and closely allied *R. praevernum* is known as *R. s. geraldii*. *R. tephropeplum*, of western China, Burma, and Tibet, unfortunately is not hardy in the northeast. Attaining a height of 3 to 6 feet, it has oblong-obovate leaves tipped with a tiny sharp point. From 1¼ to 5 inches long, they have glaucous and very scaly undersides. Narrowly-bell-shaped, five-lobed, and approximately 1 inch wide, the flow-

ers are brilliant pink, purplish-pink, rosy-crimson, or sometimes white. Borne in clusters of three to nine, and without scales on their undersides, they have ten stamens and a slender style capped with a large crimson stigma. This species is reported to adapt to limestone soils. *R. thomsonii*, a Himalayan species not hardy in the northeast, in favorable climates attains heights of 12 to 20 feet. Often wider than tall, it has roundish-elliptic to nearly round, bluish-green leaves 1½ to 4 inches long, often with slightly-heart-shaped bases and with glaucous-bluish-white undersides. The bell-shaped, blood-red or much less commonly magenta-blotched, light red or rose-pink, five-lobed flowers are 2 to over 3 inches across, in clusters of six to ten. They have large cup-shaped calyxes and ten hairless stamens. Often individuals of this species tend to become lanky as they age. Differences in the quality of bloom of individual seedlings is quite marked; select only the better ones for retention and propagation. *R. ungernii*, of the Caucasus and hardy in southern New England, differs from allied *R. smirnowii* in being of somewhat coarser growth, in having usually larger leaves ending in a short point, and in its flowers not having frilled corollas. From 10 to 20 feet tall, this sort has oblongish leaves up to 8 inches long furnished at their apexes with a short point and with a felt of pale hairs on their undersurfaces. The nearly 2-inch-wide, five-lobed, pale rose-pink to white flowers, in candelabra-like clusters of up to twenty, are displayed well after midsummer. They have ten stamens. *R. wardii*, in its best forms outstanding among yellow-flowered species, is a variable native of western China and Tibet. Hardy in mild climates only, this is mostly 4 to 10 feet tall in cultivation, but considerably taller in the wild. It has lustrous, roundish to oblong leaves 1½ to 5 inches long, with glaucous or light green undersides. The bowl-shaped, five-lobed blooms, in clusters of seven to fourteen and 2½ inches wide, are deep to very pale yellow sometimes with a basal blotch of red. They have ten hairless stamens and a style glandular throughout its length. *R. williamsianum*, a beautiful native of western China and a parent of several hybrids, is not hardy in the northeast, but is well adapted to the Pacific Northwest. From low and prostrate to nearly 5 feet tall and neatly dome-shaped, it has slightly bluish, broad-elliptic to nearly round leaves, ½ inch to 1½ inches long, with heart-shaped bases and when very young bronze to chocolate-brown. The nodding, bell-shaped, pale-pink to rose-pink flowers, in clusters of two to four, are 2¼ inches wide. They have five, six, or sometimes seven corolla lobes, ten stamens, and a style glandular throughout its length. *R. yakusimanum*, of Japan, is closely allied to

Rhododendron fortunei

Rhododendron keiskei

Hybrid *Rhododendron* 'P.J.M.'

Hybrid *Rhododendron* 'Strawberry Ice'

A groundcover of *Rhoeo spathacea* beneath palms in Florida

Rhus toxicodendron

Rhus typhina (fall foliage)

Rhynchostylis variety

Ribes sanguineum

Robinia ambigua

Ricinus communis (young fruits)

Rhododendron yakusimanum

the total number of species of *Rhododendron*, and a few of its sorts have been sparingly cultivated by enthusiasts since the middle of the nineteenth century and hybrids between them have been raised, not until after World War II did botanists have opportunity to study and classify its sorts in some detail. In the wild, many species of this group perch as epiphytes on trees, but some are terrestrial and some adapt to either life-style. None is hardy, and practically no experience is recorded about growing them, other than in greenhouses, anywhere. Peculiarities of the native environments of these Malaysian rhododendrons include but little change in temperature or in day length throughout the year.

Among the species of Malaysian rhododendrons cultivated are these: **R. jasminiflorum,** of Malacca, up to 10 feet tall, has very short-stalked, elliptic to ovate or obovate, hairless leaves 1 inch to 2½ inches long. In trusses of up to twenty, its white flowers have corollas with slender

Rhododendron jasminiflorum

and by some authorities considered a variety of *R. metternichii*. Compact, and of fairly recent introduction, this probably will not exceed 4 to 5 feet in height at full maturity; as presently known in cultivation, it is not more than 4 feet tall. It has linear-oblong, lanceolate, or oblanceolate leaves up to 3 inches long, when young hairy on their undersides. The broadly-bell-shaped, white or pink flowers are five-lobed and 2½ inches across. **R. yunnanense,** of western China, is hardy in well-sheltered locations in the vicinity of New York City. An early-bloomer, it attains a height of 9 to 12 feet and has elliptic-lanceolate to oblanceolate leaves 1½ to 3 inches long, fringed with hairs and slightly hairy on their upper surfaces. Pinkish to almost white and spotted with red or sometimes pale mauve, the flowers, in twos or threes, have five corolla lobes and ten stamens.

Malaysian rhododendrons constitute a group of species that are native to high altitudes in Malaya, Java, Borneo, the Philippine Islands, New Guinea, and northern Australia. Although this remarkable assemblage accounts for nearly one-third of

tubes up to 1½ inches long and five spreading lobes (petals). The ten downy stamens have pink anthers. **R. javanicum,** of Java, 4 to 6 feet tall, has pointed, elliptic-lanceolate, lustrous leaves 4 to 7 inches long. Its orange-yellow flowers, in trusses up to 6 inches wide, have corollas with a narrow tube and five wide-spreading lobes (petals) that form a face to the bloom 1½ to 2½ inches across. **R. lochae,** endemic to Australia and the only *Rhododendron* native to that continent, occurs natively at about a 5,000-foot altitude in Mount Bellenden Ker, in Queensland. A rather straggly shrub up to 20 feet tall, this has, in whorl-like arrangements near the branch ends, ovate leaves 2 to 3 inches long. Its pendulous, bell-shaped, red, waxy flowers, in few-flowered terminal trusses, have a small calyx, a corolla with

Rhododendron yunnanense

Rhododendron yunnanense (flowers)

Rhododendron lochae

five spreading lobes (petals), and ten stamens. **R. macgregoriae,** of New Guinea, is
a rather straggling shrub with, often in
whorls (circles of three or more), short-
stalked, hairless, elliptic-ovate leaves up to
about 3 inches long. The flowers, in
trusses about 6 inches wide consisting of
eight to fifteen yellowish to reddish-or-
ange blooms, have a rudimentary calyx
and a scarcely 1-inch-long corolla, which
has five wide-spreading lobes (petals).
There are ten stamens.

Hybrid rhododendrons are very numerous, and thousands of varieties are cultivated. A survey by the Brooklyn Botanic
Garden, and published in 1971, gave the
favorites of specialists in representative
geographical regions. The letters in parentheses following each sort, and defined as
follows, indicate the region or regions for
which they were chosen: (A) the Upper
Northwest, (B) the Northwest, (C) the Pacific Coast south, (D) the Rocky Mountain
area, (E) the Great Lakes region, (F) New
England, (G) the Greater New York–Long
Island area, (H) the Greater Philadelphia
region, (I) the Middle Atlantic region, and
(J) the Southeast. These favorite sorts are
album elegans, a *R. catawbiense* hybrid and
one of the "ironclads," tall, late-flowering,
flowers pale mauve fading to white (J);
'Alice', a *R. griffithianum* hybrid, tall, flowers deep pink fading to pale rose-pink (A,
J); 'America', a hybrid of 'Parson's Grandiflorum', bushy and broad, flowers dark
red, in ball-like clusters (D, F, J); 'Amy', a
R. griffithianum hybrid, flowers bright
rose-pink (J); 'Anah Kruschke', of compact
growth, flowers lavender, expanding late
(C, I); 'Anne Rose Whitney', a *R. griersonianum* hybrid, tall, flowers pink (J); 'An-
toon van Welie', a hybrid of 'Pink Pearl',
large trusses of deep pink flowers (C);
'Azor', a hybrid of *R. griersonianum* and *R.
discolor*, flowers deep salmon-pink with

paler streaks and some yellow (A); 'Beau-
fort', a *R. fortunei* hybrid, flowers white,
fragrant (I); 'Blue Diamond', a *R. augustinii*
hybrid, leaves small and small clusters of
lavender flowers (A, B, D); 'Blue Peter',

Rhododendron macgregoriae

Rhododendron 'Boule de Neige'

fringed lavender-blue flowers with a dark
blotch (F, near the coast, G, J); 'Bonito', a
R. discolor hybrid, large clusters of white
flowers with a chocolate blotch (B); 'Boule
de Neige', one of the "ironclads," a hybrid
between *R. catawbiense* and *R. caucasicum*,
compact, flowers white (E, F, G, H); 'Bow
Bells', a *R. williamsianum* hybrid, flowers
clear pink (A); 'Caractacus', a *R. catawbiense* hybrid, flowers purple-red (F); 'Car-
men', a *R. forrestii repens* hybrid, up to 2
feet tall, considerably wider than tall, 1-
inch-long leaves, flowers dark red (A); *catawbiense album*, tall, buds pale lilac, flowers white (D, F, G, H, I); *chionoides*, a *R.
ponticum* hybrid, low and compact, flowers
white (I); 'Crest', a *R. wardii* hybrid, flowers large, yellow (B); 'Cynthia', a *R. catawbiense* hybrid, flowers large, rose-crimson
(D, J); 'Dame Nellie Melba', a *R. arboreum*
hybrid, flowers bright pink with crimson
dots (C); 'Dora Amateis', a hybrid between
R. carolinianum and *R. ciliatum*, compact,
flowers white lightly spotted with green
(H); *everestianum*, a *R. catawbiense* hybrid,

Rhododendron 'Blue Peter'

one of the "ironclads," rosy-lilac flowers with frilled petals (G); *forsteranum*, a hybrid between *R. veitchianum* and *R. edgeworthii*, flowers white and fragrant (C); 'Goldsworth Yellow', a *R. campylocarpum* hybrid, yellow flowers dotted on their upper petals with bronze open from apricot-colored buds (I); 'Graf Zeppelin', a hybrid between 'Pink Pearl' and 'Mrs. C. S. Sargent', vigorous, flowers bright pink (I); 'Jan Dekens', tall, compact clusters of ruffled, pink, fragrant flowers (J); 'Jean Marie de Montague', a *R. griffithianum* hybrid, flowers bright scarlet, crinkle-edged, in compact clusters (A, B, I, J); 'Lady Roseberry', a hybrid of *R. cinnabarinum royleyi*, flowers pendulous, rosy-red, crimson on their outsides (A); 'Leo', a hybrid of the "ironclad" variety 'Britannia' and *R. elliottii*, flowers dark red (B, C); *Loderi* 'King George', a hybrid between *R. griffithianum* and *R. fortunei*, large, pure white, fragrant blooms with green spot at base (A, B, C); 'Loder's White', a hybrid of *R. griffithianum* and perhaps *R. arboreum album*, white flowers, frilled and edged with pink (B); 'Mars', a *R. griffithianum* hybrid, dark red flowers with pale stamens (G); 'Mary Fleming', a hybrid between *R. racemosum* and *R. keiskii*, flowers salmon-colored tinged with yellow (H); 'Mrs. Betty Robertson', a *R. campylocarpum* hybrid, broad, cream-colored, funnel-shaped flowers in trusses of ten or more (A); 'Mrs. Charles S. Sargent', a *R. catawbiense* hybrid, one of the "ironclads," flowers carmine-rose spotted with yellow (E, F); 'Mrs. Furnival', a hybrid between a *R. griffithianum* hybrid and a hybrid of *R. caucasicum*, funnel-shaped, crimson-blotched, pink flowers (B); 'Mrs. P. den Ouden', a *R. catawbiense* hybrid, compact, flowers deep crimson (F); 'Montchanin', a hybrid of *R. keiskii* and *R. pubescens*, flowers small, white, and abundant (H); 'Naomi', a *R. fortunei* hybrid, large, slightly fragrant, yellow-tinged pink flowers (A, B); 'Nova Zembla', a hybrid of 'Parson's Gloriosum', flowers dark red (D, E, F, G, H); 'Noya Chief', handsome, glossy foliage, long-lasting red blooms (C); 'Parson's Gloriosum', a *R. catawbiense* hybrid, abundant trusses of large, light, rosy-lavender flowers (D, E); 'Pinnacle', a *R. catawbiense* selection, very hardy, pure pink blooms (E); 'P.J.M.', a *R. carolinianum* hybrid, lavender-pink flowers in early spring, foliage in winter bronze to purple (E); 'P.J.M. Victor', a superior selection of the 'P.J.M.' group (F); 'Purple Gem', a hybrid of *R. carolinianum* and *R. fastigiatum*, dwarf, leaves small, flowers violet-purple (F); 'Purple Splendour', a *R. ponticum* hybrid, flowers ruffled, deep purple with a darker blotch (B, D); *purpureum grandiflorum*, a *R. catawbiense* hybrid, one of the "ironclads," flowers lilac-purple (H); 'Ramapo', a hybrid between *R. carolinianum* and *R. fastigiatum*, low and spreading, leaves tiny and blue-green, little vi-

olet-blue flowers (D, E); 'Rocket', a *R. catawbiense* hybrid, flowers coral-pink (I); *roseum elegans*, a *R. catawbiense* hybrid, one of the "ironclads," rosy-lilac flowers in dome-shaped trusses (D, E, F, H, J); 'Saphire', a hybrid between the *R. impeditum*

Rhododendron 'Scintillation'

hybrid 'Blue Tit' and *R. augustinii*, low, flowers lavender-blue (C); 'Scintillation', a Dexter hybrid, flowers pink (F, G, H, I, J); 'Tally Ho', late-blooming, flowers glowing orange-scarlet with black anthers (C); 'The General', a *R. catawbiense* selection, rich crimson blooms with dark blotches in their throats (E); 'Trilby', a *R. griffithianum* hybrid, gray-green foliage, ball-like trusses of deep crimson flowers with darker markings at their centers (D); 'Vulcan', a *R. griersonianum* hybrid, compact, flowers brick-red (I, J); 'Weston', a *R. fortunei* hybrid, flowers pink (F); 'Wheatley', a Dexter hybrid, flowers delicate pink (G); and 'Windbeam', a *R. carolinianum* hybrid, low, flowers apricot-pink fading paler and to white (E, H, J).

Among the many other noteworthy hybrid rhododendrons are the following, probably none of which are hardy in the north: **R. cilpinense**, its parents *R. ciliatum*

Rhododendron cilpinense

Rhododendron 'Lady Chamberlain'

and *R. moupinense*, rarely exceeds 3 feet in height and commonly is wider than high. A choice sort, this has glossy, elliptic to slightly obovate leaves and, in clusters of two or three, broad-funnel-shaped flowers 2¾ to 3 inches wide that are pale pink shading to deeper pink at their edges and often with two lines of tiny crimson spots. *R.* 'Lady Chamberlain' is a name applied to a group of variants that resulted from crossing *R. cinnabarinum* with *R. maddenii* and back-crossing the first generation with

Rhododendron 'Cunningham's White' blooming outdoors in October, Long Island, New York

R. cinnabarinum. The hybrid much resembles *R. cinnabarinum*, but has larger flowers and is rather less hardy. Up to 8 feet tall and erect, it has pendent blooms, somewhat *Lapageria*-like in aspect, in trusses of four or five. They range in color from orange-red with paler corolla lobes to shades of orange suffused with pink. *R.* 'Cunningham's White', a hardy old hybrid between *R. caucasicum* and *R. ponticum album*, is noteworthy for its propensity in some regions, including the vicinity of New York City, for blooming quite freely in late fall. In times past this variety was much favored in Europe for forcing into winter bloom in greenhouses. A compact shrub up to 10 feet tall, it has oblanceolate leaves

Rhododendron loderi

up to 4 inches long. About 2 inches wide, its funnel-shaped flowers are in trusses of six to eight. Opening pale mauve, they change to pure white with some yellow, brown, or purple spots on the upper corolla lobe. **R. loderi,** its parents *R. fortunei* and *R. griffithianum,* is represented by several variants. Typically tall and vigorous, they have elliptic leaves 8 inches to 1 foot long. The fragrant, six- or seven-lobed flowers, in trusses of up to twelve, are funnel-shaped and up to 6 inches wide or even wider. They vary in color from white to pink.

Garden and Landscape Uses. Wherever they can be grown successfully, and for selected sorts that includes all except the coldest, hottest, and driest parts of North America, rhododendrons are accounted among the most useful shrubs for landscaping. Their frequently very handsome evergreen foliage gives life to winter landscapes. The freedom with which most sorts bloom; according to kind, the wide diversity in color, size, and to a lesser extent form of bloom; and, given a suitable selection of kinds, the long season during which flowers can be had places them in the forefront among flowering shrubs.

An important consideration is the pH of the soil, that is its degree of acidity or alkalinity. With extremely few exceptions rhododendrons will not tolerate other than acid soils. A pH reading between 4.5 and 5 is ideal, but if the ground contains an abundance of organic matter, such as leaf mold or peat moss, good results can be had up to pH 5.6 or perhaps somewhat higher. At the other end of the scale success may be achieved in ground with a reading as low as 4. In limestone regions, it is possible to attain a measure of success by planting in raised beds of specially prepared, acid soil, but only for very special purposes is this worthwhile, and considerable attention is needed afterward to prevent the medium from becoming alkaline as a result of water from the understratum of limestone rising by capillarity.

Rhododendrons are seen at their best perhaps in naturalistic and other informal settings, yet they may be used with excellent effects in more structured beds and borders and as screens and foundation plantings. They look well in groups, as free-standing specimens to give emphasis and serve as focal points, and as flanking supports of other plantings. The dwarf sorts are admirable furnishings for rock gardens.

Select sites for rhododendrons with considerable care. Success is likely to depend upon wise choices. Shelter from sweeping winds is of prime importance, consequently hilltops, exposed locations near the sea, and drafty corners of buildings are unsuitable unless they can be sheltered by windbreak plantings of more tolerant evergreens or in other ways.

A certain amount of shade is highly desirable, although if other conditions, such as adequate moisture, approach the ideal it is not absolutely necessary. Certainly too dense shade can lead to the development of loose and rangy rather than compact specimens, and it seriously inhibits blooming. Ideal shade is the dappled kind provided by a woodland of deep-rooted trees, such as oaks, that is sufficiently open or has been thinned out and "limbed up" so that the lowest tree branches are 20 feet or more from the ground, thus permitting side light, as well as rays that break through the foliage from above, to reach the plants. Filtered, as contrasted with full sunlight, not only makes for better growth, but prolongs the life of the blooms and prevents the bleaching of delicate pink and lavender flowers that occurs when they are fully exposed.

Favorable locations include dells and valleys where air drainage is adequate to prevent them from becoming frost pockets on cold winter and early spring nights, and places partway down from crests of north- and west-facing slopes. Land sloping to the south and east is in regions of cold winters less favorable, because plants so placed are exposed to strong sun while still frozen, which may result in the foliage suffering from winter burn (scorching). This last, a desiccation and killing of the leaf tissues caused by excessive loss of moisture when the ground is frozen so solidly that the roots cannot replace the moisture transpired, is less likely to occur if the plants are sheltered from wind and shaded early in the day. A deep mulch, by preventing the ground from freezing deeply, does much to prevent winter burn.

When planting on sites other than north- and west-facing slopes, the same consideration for avoiding exposure to morning sun in winter applies. When set near buildings or walls that face east or south, reflected heat can work havoc; therefore confine plantings to those with other aspects. Tall evergreens, such as pines or arborvitaes, located on the sunny side of the rhododendrons can also give sufficient shade to prevent harm.

Cultivation. The care of rhododendrons, appropriately placed as to soil, shelter, and shade, is not demanding, and even where environmental factors are not ideal much can be done both before and after planting to render them acceptable.

A first consideration is the soil. If unsuitable, spare no effort to improve it. Equally distressing are hard-packed clayey ground and sandy earth lacking abundant humus. Most impossible is wet, waterlogged soil. The last must be corrected by draining before planting. In some situations, breaking through a shallow layer of clay or hardpan that lies up to a couple of feet or so beneath the surface, or even raising the bed a few inches above its present level, may correct the drainage, but more often an adequate system of land drains will prove the best and perhaps only means of relief. It is quite useless to dig deep holes in impermeable clay and fill their bottoms with stones in the expectation that by so doing you are improving drainage. This will only work if the holes break through the barrier layer that impedes the flow of water to a substratum that is pervious.

Nor need a site be constantly waterlogged to render it unsuitable. Stagnant water around the roots for even comparatively short periods each year, say in spring, can wreck havoc. As a result death may come rapidly or after months or even years of unsatisfactory growth. Often chlorosis (yellowing of the foliage with the veins remaining green), which may be mistaken as a signal that the soil is too alkaline, results from poor subsurface drainage.

Excessively compact earth is inimical to the growth of rhododendrons. Their numerous fine roots, many close to the surface, need air, and penetrate most readily into fairly loose soil with a high organic content. This last, of prime importance, can be implemented by mixing in before planting very generous proportions of compost, leaf mold, peat moss, well-decayed sawdust, or old rotted manure, not merely into the bottoms of the planting holes and with the soil back-filled immediately around the root balls, but also into the adjacent ground which the roots will, if conditions are favorable, ramify as the bushes grow. It is a grave mistake to set the root balls, underlaid and surrounded with a little agreeable earth, in basins cut in inhospitable ground.

Sandy soils that drain quickly and so dry out in summer are most easily conditioned. Mix with them thoroughly and to a depth of at least 1 foot, and deeper is better, generous amounts of compost, leaf mold, peat moss, or other humus-producing organic matter. It is all to the good if as much as one-third of the soil consists of such additives. And afterward keep the surface of the ground constantly mulched with the same sorts of material.

Planting is best done in fall or spring, with fall preferred in all but the coldest climates in which rhododendrons will grow. Dig the hole at least twice the diameter of and 6 to 8 inches deeper than the root ball. Fill into its bottom a fifty-fifty mixture of sandy soil and peat moss or leaf mold and pack this firmly. Then position the plant so that the top of the ball, as indicated by the soil mark on its stem or trunk, is flush with the ground surface. Fill around it with, and press moderately firmly, the same mix used in the bottom of the hole. Then erect a ridge of soil about 4 inches high around the circumference of the filled hole so that a "saucer" to hold water is formed. Fill this two or three times with water and then complete the job by mulching with peat moss, partly decomposed leaves, pine needles, wood chips, or other suitable organic material. If you use wood chips it is well to anticipate possible temporary reduction of available nitrogen in the soil by spreading, before applying the mulch, a 10-6-4 fertilizer at the rate of 3 ounces to 10 square feet, or other fertilizer in amounts that will supply similar amounts of nitrogen.

Routine care of established rhododendrons may involve deep watering at intervals of ten days to two weeks during spells of dry weather or drought, but the need for this is greatly reduced if, as it should be for good results, the ground is kept constantly covered with an organic mulch. Mulching not only conserves moisture, but keeps the soil temperature relatively even and promotes conditions favorable to root growth. It also reduces the necessity for weeding and eliminates need for cultivating or hoeing, both very harmful because they disturb or destroy surface roots.

In exposed locations and in climates in which winter cold is something of a problem, temporary shelter is sometimes very advantageous. It can be given by erecting screens of burlap on the exposed sides or by covering or by sticking into the ground around small specimens, such as are accommodated in rock gardens, branches of pine or other evergreens to temper wind and sun.

Fertilizing is not needed as long as the plants are making thrifty growth, and if kept mulched with nourishing organics this growth may continue indefinitely. But old specimens that have partially exhausted the soil of nutrients, and others that because of insufficient nourishment are growing poorly, are improved by judicious fertilizing. Assistance of this sort may be given by mulching with half-rotted manure, by using cottonseed meal as a fertilizer, or by employing, according to the

When planting rhododendrons: (a) Choose plants with large balls of healthy roots

(b) Dig holes of ample size

(c) After the plant is positioned, fill around the root ball with agreeable soil

(d) Tamp the soil moderately firm with a wooden stick and finish the surface to form a shallow saucer

(e) Fill the saucer two or three times with water

(f) Spread an organic mulch around the plant

manufacturer's directions, one of the fertilizers especially compounded for rhododendrons and other acid-soil plants.

Pruning rhododendrons is not needed on a routine basis and should be done only to repair damage by storms or other cause, to correct obvious growth imbalances, and to rejuvenate neglected, straggly specimens. When a branch is to be shortened, cut it back to a strong side branch. If this is not done the stub will almost surely die back.

Rejuvenation of old, overgrown, unshapely specimens of many species and varieties can be achieved by the drastic procedure of cutting them down in early spring to within a foot of the ground, then fertilizing and mulching and making sure the ground is kept well watered through any dry spells that occur in the summer. This procedure gives the best results in humid regions where summers are not excessively hot; it is not practical in many parts of North America.

A few sorts, some varieties of Dexter hybrids, for instance, fail to respond to this severe cutting and are likely to die if it is employed. Should an examination of old specimens being considered for drastic pruning reveal young shoots appearing spontaneously from low down on old stems, have no hesitation about following the procedure outlined, but if there are no young growths test the plant's capabilities of producing such by cutting one or two main stems or trunks to within a foot of the ground and observing the result. If new growth develops the remaining main stems may be cut back severely the following early spring.

The special needs of Malaysian rhododendrons, which are intolerant of both winter cold and extreme heat, are best met by growing them in a greenhouse with a minimum winter night temperature of 55 to 60°F and a daytime temperature not more than five to ten degrees higher. Summer temperatures should not exceed 60 to 70°F at night or up to ten degrees higher by day. These sorts seem to thrive best when accommodated in pots in freely-drained, coarse, peaty soil kept uniformly moist, but not saturated. Shade is needed from spring through fall.

Propagation of rhododendrons, including the sorts commonly called azaleas, may be by seed, layering, grafting, and cuttings. The first is appropriate only for multiplying species and for breeding new varieties. Plants raised from seed from hybrids usually exhibit much variation.

Seeds of rhododendrons are very small. They may be sown as soon as they are ripe or they may be stored in a cool place in paper bags for up to a year. Sow in well-drained, sandy, peaty soil in a cold frame or in pots or pans in a greenhouse where the winter night temperature is about 50°F. If containers are used, milled sphagnum moss may, if desired, be substituted for soil. Water the soil or moss thoroughly before scattering the seeds. Sprinkle them thinly and sift a little soil over the surface afterward but do not cover the seeds entirely. Place polyethylene plastic film over the container or if a frame is used cover it with the sash. Shade from direct sun.

Under favorable conditions the seeds will germinate in a month or less. Water with great care so as not to disturb the surface soil and to keep the rooting medium moist, but not constantly saturated. Gradually accustom the seedlings to more air and light, but not strong sun. As soon as the tiny plants are big enough to handle with fair ease, transplant them to pots,

Rhododendron seedlings: (a) Ready for transplanting

(b) Transplanted to a flat and growing vigorously

pans, flats, or into a cold frame, spacing them about 2 inches apart and using sandy, peaty soil. The next transplanting will usually be to a cold frame with about 4 inches between individual plants. From there, when they begin to crowd, transfer the young plants to outdoor nursery beds to grow on to planting size.

Layering, the bending down of a suitably placed branch to the ground, notching it where it makes contact and then pegging it securely in soil mixed with generous amounts of peat moss and sand, and heaping soil over the place of operation, is a reliable, but exceedingly slow method of increase. It may take two years before the layer is sufficiently rooted to warrant removing it from its mother plant, and during this time the soil into which it is rooting must be kept moderately moist, if necessary by watering during dry spells.

Grafting, until the middle of the twentieth century the most popular commercial method of raising rhododendrons, has, except for some sorts of azaleas (see Azaleas), been almost completely superseded by the cutting method of propagation. This last technique, developed chiefly in the United States, makes possible the rapid and sure production of plants.

Take cuttings of evergreen rhododendrons in late summer and fall and insert them under mist in a greenhouse propagating bench in peat moss mixed with perlite or coarse sand. Growers vary somewhat in the proportions they use, but many favor about fifty percent peat moss. The propagating bed should be supplied with bottom heat sufficient to maintain the rooting mixture at 70°F. The best cuttings are made from thin side growths; stout, heavy, terminal shoots will not do. Cuttings taken from the undersides of large old plants root more readily than those made from young specimens.

Good shoots from which to make cuttings are produced by pinching out the terminal buds of plants growing in nurseries as soon as the first of the normally two summer flushes of growth are completed (about the first of June in the vicinity of New York City). With old plants likely to make only one flush of growth, the ends of the shoots are nipped out before this begins. As a result of pinching, several thinnish, relatively short side shoots develop; these are ideal for use as cuttings.

It is advisable to cut the shoots early in the morning when they are well charged with water, and turgid. Moisten them and put them in a cool, shady place until they are prepared for planting, which should be as soon as possible. Preparation consists of removing all leaves except the upper four or five, or if they are very small possibly six, and cutting the base of the stem cleanly across just beneath a node. The length of the cuttings should be 3 to 4 inches. There is no advantage in retaining a heel of older wood at the base.

It is helpful to wound the cutting by removing a narrow, longitudinal slice of bark or bark and underlying wood from down the side of the stem for a length of about 1½ inches, beginning the cut at that distance from the base and slicing down to it. Many propagators take such a slice from opposite sides of the stem. Roots develop from the wounds as well as from the bottom of the cutting. Before the cuttings are inserted, treat them with a hormone rooting preparation.

Light is an important factor to success. Some shade may be needed from strong sun, but too much can be fatal. One experienced propagator recommends a minimum of 450 foot-candles of light during the brighter part of the day if the rooting medium is maintained at 70°F. If the light is weaker it is better that the temperature at the roots be reduced to 60 or 65°F. Rooting usually takes place within two months. It has been found that cuttings that have not rooted in three months do so more quickly if the bottom temperature is then reduced to 60°F.

Remove the cuttings from the bench and pot them individually or plant them in flats as soon as they have made a root mass about as big as a golf ball. A mixture of peat moss, sedge peat, and perlite or coarse sand is satisfactory at this first planting, but fine leaf mold or other nourishing humus material may be substituted for the sedge peat.

At the time of transplanting pinch out the tip of each young plant to encourage branching. Place the pots or flats in a greenhouse or cold frame where a temperature of 45 to 50°F can be maintained, and grow the plants there until all danger of spring frost is past; then transplant them to outdoor nursery beds.

Pests and Diseases. Black vine weevil is a serious pest of rhododendrons. In the larval stage it feeds on the roots and when mature chews pieces out of the edges of the leaves. Control is best had by spraying the foliage with a contact insecticide. Japanese beetles, also sometimes troublesome, may be dealt with in the same way. Lace bugs, transparent-winged insects that congregate on the undersides of the leaves, which as a result of their activities become sickly, grayish or silvery, and speckled on their undersides with black spots of excreta, are especially troublesome in sunny locations. This too can be controlled by spraying, taking care to thoroughly wet the undersides of the leaves. Other pests include borers, leafhoppers, mealybugs, mites, whiteflies, and thrips. Fungus diseases include bud and twig blight, canker, crown rot, die-back, various leaf spots, powdery mildew, shoestring root rot, and wilt.

RHODOHYPOXIS (Rhodo-hypóxis). South Africa is the homeland of the one or, according to some authorities, two species of this genus of the amaryllis family AMARYLLIDACEAE. It differs from *Hypoxis* in the bases of its perianth segments (petals or, more truly, tepals) being joined to form a short tube. The close relationship between the two genera is recognized in the name, which is derived from the Greek *rhodon*, rose-colored, and *Hypoxis*.

A low, deciduous, herbaceous perennial, **Rhodohypoxis bauri** has small, cylindrical to ovoid tubers covered with the persistent bristly bases of old leaves. Its erect, all-basal leaves have two chief veins and are sparingly furnished on both sides with white, stellate (star-shaped) hairs. They are about 4 inches long and strap-shaped. The solitary blooms, from the leaf axils, are on long, stellate-hairy stalks that lift them about as high as the foliage. The flowers are rich carmine-red to white with all manner of intermediates, and a little over 1 inch in diameter. They have six spreading petals, six stalkless or stalked stamens, and a very short style ending in a minute stigma. The fruits are capsules. Pure white-flowered *R. b. platypetala* is

Rhodohypoxis baurii platypetala

sometimes accorded specific status as *R. platypetala*, but except in flower color does not differ significantly from the typical kind. Rock garden enthusiasts have selected variations having larger blooms, wider petals, and especially worthy, distinctive flower colors, and apply to them such identifying names as 'Margaret Rose' for a bright, pink-flowered one and 'The Major' for another with glowing pink blooms.

Garden Uses and Cultivation. Rhodohypoxises are unfortunately not hardy in the north. Little known in America, they can be expected to succeed outdoors only where winters are mild and summers moderate. Adversely sensitive to extremes of cold and heat, they are also intolerant of winter wetness.

Worth trying in rock gardens in the few places where climate is close to ideal, rhodohypoxises are generally more likely to succeed in alpine greenhouses and cold frames. Usually they are accommodated in very well-drained pans (shallow pots). A porous, peaty, lime-free soil suits them. This must be kept nearly dry in winter, but quite moist during the growing season. Repotting or replanting is done after growth begins, not when the plants are dormant. Essential for the multiplication of superior varieties, and generally the best method of increase, is division at repotting time. Seed can be used, but the resulting plants are likely to exhibit considerable variation.

RHODOLEIA (Rhodo-lèia). Asian evergreen trees numbering seven species constitute *Rhodoleia*, of the witch-hazel family HAMAMELIDACEAE. The name comes from the Greek *rhodon*, a rose, and *leios*, smooth, in allusion to the appearance of the flowers and their smooth stamens.

Rhodoleias have alternate, undivided, leathery leaves with glaucous undersides. Their small flowers are five to ten together in pendulous heads surrounded by colored bracts. They have two to four rose-pink petals, seven to ten stamens. The fruits are clusters of radiating capsules.

Native to China, **R. championii** is a small tree with elliptic-ovate, hairless leaves up to 3½ inches long and heads of flowers about 2½ inches wide.

Garden and Landscape Uses and Cultivation. Rare in cultivation and adaptable only to mild, essentially frost-free climates, the species described is worth growing as an ornamental and responds to conditions that suit gardenias.

RHODOMYRTUS (Rhodo-mýrtus) — Downy-Myrtle or Hill-Gooseberry. This genus of twenty species of trees and shrubs native from tropical Asia to Australia contains only one of horticultural significance. It is the downy-myrtle or hill-gooseberry. The genus *Rhodomyrtus* belongs in the myrtle family MYRTACEAE. Its name comes from the Greek *rhodon*, rose, and *myrtos*, myrtle, and alludes to the pink, myrtle-like blooms. It is most easily distinguished from the true myrtle (*Myrtus*) by its leaves being prominently three-veined. Its flowers are pink or white. They have a usually five-lobed persistent calyx, generally five petals, and many stamens. The fruits are berries.

The downy-myrtle (**R. tomentosa**) is indigenous from Japan and China to the Philippine Islands. A shrub 4 to 10 feet tall, like other members of the genus, it has opposite, lobeless leaves and fruits that are berries. The leaves of the downy-myrtle are pubescent, elliptic-ovate, 1½ to 3 inches long, and approximately 1 inch wide. They are hairless above and white-woolly on their undersides. The rose-pink to purplish flowers, solitary or in twos or threes, 1 inch to 2 inches across, and borne profusely in spring and early summer, are followed by downy, greenish-purple, edible, spherical fruits about ½ inch in diameter. Each bloom has five sepals, five petals, and many pink stamens with yellow anthers. As they age the petals fade to white or nearly white. The fruits are sweet and pleasantly flavored and contain several seeds in their soft, purplish flesh.

Garden and Landscape Uses and Cultivation. This warm-climate shrub is quite ornamental, especially early in the season when it is covered with blooms that look like single roses. It is suitable for planting in parts of Florida and California and in other places in the subtropics and tropics. Although not among the most important of fruits, those of the downy-myrtle provide variety both for eating fresh when they are mature, and for harvesting before they are ripe for use in pies. The fruits are produced in abundance. Cultivation presents no special problems. Sandy, loamy, or clayey soils of an acid character suit this species well, preferably they should be deep. The plant is not adaptable to limestone soils. Seeds, removed from the pulp of the fruits as soon as they are ripe and sown at once, form an easy means of increase. In dry climates abundant water should be supplied.

RHODOPHIALA. See Hippeastrum.

RHODORA. See *Rhododendron canadense* (Encyclopedia entry Azaleas).

RHODOSPATHA (Rhodo-spàtha). Fifteen tropical American evergreen vines of the arum family ARACEAE comprise *Rhodospatha*, a genus closely related to *Stenospermation* and by some authorities included there. The name, referring to the color of the designated floral part comes from the Greek *rhodo*, red, and *spathe*, a spathe.

Rhodospathas have large oblong-elliptic leaves with stalks the bases of which sheathe the stems. The inflorescences, commonly called "flowers," but each actually an assemblage of flowers and related parts, have a slender, spikelike spadix crowded with little bisexual, four-stamened flowers without perianths, and, rolled around the spadix, a spathe that soon falls away. The fruits are berries.

Native to Brazil and Peru, *R. latifolia* has leaves with stalks as long as the broad-elliptic blades, which are up to 1½ feet long by nearly two-thirds as wide and have angled from each side of the midrib thirty or more lateral veins. The inflorescences have a rose-pink spathe up to 7 inches long and a violet spadix almost as long. Of unknown provenance, *R. picta* has leaves with blades up to 2 feet long by two-thirds as wide and stem-sheathing stalks a little over one-half as long. The inflorescences have a nearly 1-foot-long yellow spathe and a slightly shorter, rose-pink spadix.

Garden and Landscape Uses and Cultivation. These are as for philodendrons. See Philodendron.

RHODOSPHAERA (Rhodo-sphaèra)—Australian-Yellow-wood. Differing from *Rhus* in that its flowers have ten instead of five stamens, the Australian genus *Rhodosphaera* consists of one species. It belongs to the cashew family ANACARDIACEAE. In allusion to its spherical, reddish fruits its name derives from the Greek *rhodon*, rose, and *sphaeron*, a sphere.

Australian-yellow-wood (*R. rhodanthema*) is a good-looking evergreen tree up to 60 or 70 feet tall, with lustrous, pinnate leaves of seven or nine oblong-ovate leaflets, 2 to 3 inches long, and hairless except for tufts in the axils of the veins on the undersides. The numerous minute flowers, in terminal and axillary panicles about 4 inches long, are red or pink and include unisexual and bisexual individuals. The fruits, structured like plums and hence technically drupes, are reddish-brown, globose, and about ½ inch in diameter. Australian-yellow-wood is a source of lumber esteemed for cabinet work, and of a yellow dye.

Garden and Landscape Uses and Cultivation. In California and other warm-climate regions, this handsome tree is planted for ornament. It succeeds in ordinary soils and is propagated by seed.

RHODOSTACHYS. See Fascicularia, and Ochagavia.

RHODOTHAMNUS (Rhodo-thámnus). One species of evergreen shrub, of the heath family ERICACEAE, constitutes *Rhodothamnus*. Native to the European Alps and eastern Siberia, in sheltered locations it is probably hardy as far north as southern New England. The name, alluding to the blooms, comes from the Greek *rhodon*, rose, and *thamnos*, a shrub.

Rarely over 1 foot tall, freely-branched, and semiprostrate, *R. chamaecistus* (syn. *Rhododendron chamaecistus*) has downy young shoots and alternate, nearly stalkless, bristle-margined, narrow-elliptic, lustrous leaves ¼ to ½ inch long. They are without lobes or teeth. Borne in late spring at the branch ends, the *Cistus*-like flowers, 1 inch to 1½ inches in diameter, are in clusters of two to four. They have five-lobed calyxes, a pale rose-pink corolla with five spreading lobes (petals), ten stamens with dark purple anthers, and a style about as long as the stamens. The fruits are globular, hairy capsules, with the persistent sepals attached. A hybrid between this species and *Phyllodoce empetriformis* is *Phyllothamnus erectus*.

Garden Uses and Cultivation. The most suitable accommodation for this choice plant is an unshaded rock garden, or perhaps better a rock garden with just a little shade from the most intense sun. It grows well in well-drained, moderately moist soil that contains much leaf mold or peat. In the wild *Rhodothamnus* commonly grows on limestone, but the presence of lime in the soil does not seem to be essential. No pruning is required, except, if the branches become crowded, a few of the oldest may be cut out as soon as blooming is over. Propagation is by seed and by careful removal and transplanting of rooted pieces from specimens already established.

RHODOTYPOS (Rhodotȳp-os) — Jetbead. One deciduous shrub of Japan and China is the only species of *Rhodotypos*, of the rose family ROSACEAE. It is remarkable as being the only member of the family with opposite leaves except that young seedlings of *Prunus* exhibit this phenomenon. The name derives from the Greek *rhodon*, a rose, and *typos*, form or shape, and refers to the general resemblance of the flowers to those of single roses.

The jetbead (*R. scandens* syns. *R. tetrapetala*, *R. kerrioides*) forms a bushy speci-

Rhodotypos scandens (flowers)

Rhodotypos scandens (fruits)

men 6 feet high or higher with many erect stems and short-stalked, long-pointed, ovate, double-toothed leaves 2½ to 4 inches long and about one-half as broad. Bright green and soon hairless above and paler and hairy below, they have prominent parallel veins angled from the midrib. The pure white flowers, which appear with the leaves, are solitary and about 2 inches across. They have four rounded petals that spread widely and numerous stamens about one-half as long as the petals. Each flower usually generates four very distinctive, slightly-ellipsoid, shining jet-black, hard, berry-like fruits about the size of small peas. They are surrounded by a ruff of large, persistent leafy bracts and remain attractive throughout the winter. The jetbead is hardy in southern New York and southern New England.

Garden and Landscape Uses. This good general purpose shrub tolerates a wide variety of locations and conditions that would be unfavorable to many more finicky kinds. Although less showy than many popular shrubs, it makes a pleasing display of bloom in spring and of fruits in fall and winter. Its form and foliage associate well with other garden plantings. This is a useful "workhorse" type of plant that can be used in many places with confidence of its survival and certainty of its looking well. It stands sun and considerable shade.

Cultivation. No problems attend the cultivation of the jetbead. When the bushes become too crowded with stems they may be thinned out after flowering, and old, much overgrown bushes may be thinned out and pruned back as severely as desired in late winter. This procedure, of course, results in loss of all or part of the current spring's bloom. Propagation is easy by seed, leafy cuttings in summer, and hardwood cuttings in fall.

RHOEO (Rhoè-o)—Oyster Plant or Moses-in-a-Boat or Moses-in-a-Cradle. The genus *Rhoeo*, of the spiderwort family COMMELI-NACEAE, consists of one species native to Mexico, Central America, and the West Indies. The meaning of the genus name is unknown.

Semisucculent *R. spathacea* (syn. *R. discolor*) has a short, erect stem closely furnished with spreading, sword-shaped leaves with overlapping bases that partly envelop the stem. Their upper sides are metallic-green, their undersides purplish and shining. They are 6 inches to 1 foot long and 1 inch to 3 inches broad. From

Rhoeo spathacea

Rhoeo spathacea (flowers)

the leaf axils are produced the flower clusters, usually solitary, but sometimes paired, and each is enclosed by two boat-shaped bracts, which give reason for the common names applied to *Rhoeo*. Each small white flower has three sepals, three petals, and six stamens. The individual blooms soon wither. Variety *R. s. vittata* (syn. *R. s. variegata*) is distinguished by

Rhoeo spathacea vittata

having the upper sides of its leaves longitudinally streaked with pale yellow. Their undersides are glossy-purple. Another variety, with leaves green on both sides, is *R. s. concolor*.

Garden and Landscape Uses. The oyster plant is commonly used in warm climates in beds at airports, shopping centers, and other public places, as well as in private gardens. This speaks well for its toughness and ease of cultivation. It is also popular as a greenhouse and a window garden plant. In New York and other northern cities, one not infrequently comes upon it in varying degrees of health

A groundcover planting of *Rhoeo spathacea* at the Fairchild Tropical Garden, Miami, Florida

in the windows of barbers and other fanciers of potted vegetation. It is an appealing plant that submits to domestication as willingly as a puppy dog and as readily shows tolerance of partial neglect. In foliage it is attractive and its small flowers, crowded in boat-shaped spathes and opening one after the other over a long period, never fail to interest the curious. Rhoeos succeed in sun or part-shade. They resist drought and grow in any soil not too infertile, provided it is well drained.

Cultivation. This is of the simplest. Minimum care is needed. Container-grown specimens are watered to keep their soil moderately moist and are repotted annually in spring. When their pots are well filled with roots, occasional applications of dilute liquid fertilizer are beneficial. Winter night temperatures of 55 to 70°F are satisfactory. By day, and at other seasons, they may be higher. Propagation is by division and by cuttings, which root with great ease.

RHOICISSUS (Rhoicís-sus). Formerly included in *Cissus*, this South African genus of a dozen species is now regarded as a separate entity. It is different from *Cissus* in that its flowers have five to seven instead of four petals. Like those of *Cissus*, but unlike those of the nearly related *Vitis*, the petals fall separately. From *Ampelopsis* it may be distinguished by the disk surrounding the bottom of the ovary being flattened or ringlike (not bowl-shaped) and the style being conical rather than awl-shaped. The genus *Parthenocissus* differs from *Rhoicissus* in its flowers lacking disks around their ovaries and the tendrils of most kinds ending in hold-fast disks. All of these genera belong in the grape family VITACEAE. The generic name is derived from the Greek *rhoia*, a pomegranate, and the name of the genus *Cissus*.

Only one species, *R. capensis*, is presently cultivated in North America, a tender, vigorous, evergreen vine with un-

Rhoicissus capensis

Rhoicissus capensis (leaves)

derground tubers up to 6 inches in diameter, brownish-hairy shoots, and long-stalked, triangular-ovate, coarsely-toothed, grapelike leaves. Its glossy dark red berries are in short clusters.

Garden Uses and Cultivation. As a vine for frost-free and nearly frost-free climates for covering fences and other supports to which it can attach itself by tendrils, *R. capensis* is esteemed. Its merits are its vigorous growth and attractive foliage. It is well suited for patios, terraces, conservatories, large greenhouses, and other indoor locations where good light is assured. It ordinarily performs better when planted in a ground bed than in containers. Any fer-

tile, well-drained garden soil suits. Watering should be adequate to keep the earth evenly moist, but not constantly saturated, from spring through fall and somewhat drier in winter. Indoors a winter night temperature of about 50°F, with a daytime rise of five to ten degrees, is adequate; at other seasons, temperatures may be higher. Ventilation sufficient to maintain an airy, buoyant atmosphere is necessary whenever weather permits. Pruning, consisting of shaping the plant and restraining unruly shoots, is best done in late winter or early spring. This vine is readily increased by cuttings taken in late winter, spring, or early summer and inserted in a propagating bench in a greenhouse or under approximately similar conditions, in coarse sand, vermiculite, or perlite. It can also be propagated by layering.

RHOMBOPHYLLUM (Rhombo-phýllum). Among the most attractive of the many dwarf succulents that hail from South Africa and belong in the *Mesembryanthemum* section of the carpetweed family AIZO-ACEAE are the three species of *Rhombophyllum*. The name, from the Greek *rhombos*, a lozenge, and *phyllon*, a leaf, alludes to the leaf shapes of some kinds.

Rhombophyllums are shrublets or clump-forming plants with crowded foliage and mostly swollen, fleshy, sometimes turnip-like roots. Their smooth, opposite leaves, the successive pairs commonly set at right angles to each other, are more or less joined at their bases and keeled toward their tips. Borne in summer or fall, three to seven on a stalk, the golden-yellow flowers superficially resemble daisies, but are very different in structure from those familiar blooms, which are really flower heads composed of a large number of florets. The flowers of *Rhombophyllum* are single blooms. The fruits are capsules.

When old, branching freely and up to 1 foot in height, but when young forming lower tufts, *R. dolabriforme* has spreading, laterally-compressed, hatchet-shaped leaves 1 inch long or somewhat longer. They have flat, tapering, upper surfaces, subcylindrical undersides with extended keels, and a tooth at their tips. The flowers, from three to five on a stalk, are about 1½ inches in diameter. Differing in its light bluish-gray leaves being distinctly two-lobed and clawlike and about ¾ inch long, *R. nelii* has short, branching stems. Its flowers, about 1½ inches across, are one to several on each stalk.

Very different, *R. rhomboideum* is tufted and stemless. Its lozenge-shaped, thick leaves, of unequal size and up to 2 inches long, are in rosettes. Grayish-green with white dots, they are flatter than those of the other kinds and are slightly hollowed above and rounded on their undersides with the keel usually extending to form a

chinlike extremity. The whitish margins occasionally have one or two teeth. About 1¼ inches in diameter, the flowers are reddish on their undersides.

Garden Uses and Cultivation. Rhombophyllums are among the easiest dwarf succulents of the *Mesembryanthemum* relationship to grow. They are not hardy, but may be accommodated in sunny greenhouses or windows. As with all their kin they need thoroughly drained, porous soil and a dry atmosphere. Their soil must be kept dry in winter and watered moderately from late spring or early summer to late fall. In general their treatment is that of *Stomatium*. They come readily from seed and cuttings. For more information see Succulents.

RHOPALOBLASTE (Rhopalo-blást-e). Six or seven species, rare in cultivation, belong in *Rhopaloblaste*, of the palm family PALMAE. The genus is native from Malaya and the Nicobar Islands to New Guinea and the Solomon Islands. The name derives from the Greek *rhopalon*, a club, and *blastos*, a bud or shoot. It alludes to a feature of the flower buds. It is pronounced as five syllables.

These are slender palms with ringed trunks and pinnate leaves with pointed leaflets. Their flower clusters, borne below the foliage, are composed of groups of one female and two males.

Native to the Nicobar Islands, *R. augusta* (syn. *Ptychoraphis augusta*) has a solitary trunk up to 100 feet tall or taller. It has short-stalked leaves up to 10 feet long with on each side of the midrib ninety to one hundred drooping leaflets up to 2½ feet long by 1½ inches wide. Its ellipsoid fruits are red. Indonesian *R. ceramica* has a single trunk, 40 to 60 feet tall, and short-stalked leaves up to 10 feet long with eighty to ninety drooping leaflets up to 3 feet long and 1¼ inches wide on each side of the midrib. The scarlet fruits are about 1½ inches long. A native of Singapore and the nearby mainland, *R. singaporensis* (syn. *Ptychoraphis singaporensis*) has usually clusters of trunks 6 to 9 feet tall. Its 3- to

Rhopaloblaste singaporensis, a young specimen

6-foot-long leaves have forty to fifty up-to-1-foot-long leaflets with threadlike apexes on either side of the midrib. Its orange-yellow fruits are about ½ inch long.

Garden and Landscape Uses and Cultivation. These are essentially plants for palm specialists and collectors. Little information is available regarding their landscape uses and cultivation. They need humid tropical conditions and may be expected to grow under the treatment suggested for *Verschaffeltia*. For more information see Palms.

RHOPALOSTYLIS (Rhopalósty-lis)—Nikau Palm. The name of this genus is derived from the Greek *rhopalon*, a club, and *stylis*, a pillar. It alludes to the club-shaped stalks of the flower clusters. The genus *Rhopalostylis*, consisting of three graceful pinnate-leaved palms of New Zealand, Norfolk Island, and Kermadec Islands, belongs to the palm family PALMAE. The Nikau palm is native farther south than any other member of the family.

Of small to moderate size, these palms have trunks ringed with leaf scars, and compact terminal crowns of foliage, which because of the upswept angle at which the leaves are held, remind one of giant shaving brushes or feather dusters. The branches of the flower clusters are short, spreading, and densely-flowered. Each has two papery spathes that soon fall. The blooms are in groups of three. The fruits are ellipsoid, smooth, brownish or red, and nearly ¾ inch long. They contain one seed.

The Nikau palm (*R. sapida*), of New

Rhopalostylis sapida, the Palmengarten, Frankfurt-am-Main

Zealand, most common in cultivation, but rarer than its merits deserve, thrives in southern California and is suitable for other warm subtropical climates. At one time it was fairly plentiful in Santa Barbara. It attains a maximum height of about 30 feet and has leaves 4 to 6 feet in length with very narrow leaflets. The basal parts of its leafstalks form a bulbous, short crownshaft that looks like a continuation

of the trunk. The much-branched flower clusters are up to 2 feet long and have pale pink flowers succeeded by brownish fruits. Taller and more slender than the last, *R. baueri*, of Norfolk Island, has leaves up to 9 feet long. Its flowers are white, in clusters longer than those of the New Zealand species, and are followed by red fruits. The Kermadec Island species, *R. cheesemanii*, very like *R. baueri*, is rare in cultivation.

Garden and Landscape Uses. These are attractive for outdoor cultivation in frost-free and essentially frost-free climates. They lend themselves for use as accents and as single specimens, and for spotting among lower plants to relieve monotony in the landscape. They are also appropriate for greenhouses.

Cultivation. Ordinary garden soil and full sun or part-shade suit these palms. They are easily raised from seed sown in sandy, peaty soil in a temperature of 70 to 80°F. When grown indoors in containers they need sharp drainage, porous, fertile soil, shade from strong summer sun, a humid atmosphere, and a minimum winter night temperature of 55°F, with an increase of five to fifteen degrees by day. At other seasons higher temperatures are needed. Specimens that have filled their containers with roots may be kept thrifty by biweekly applications of dilute liquid fertilizer from spring through fall. For further information see Palms.

RHUBARB. The plant known as bog-rhubarb is *Petasites hybridus*. Spinach-rhubarb is *Rumex abyssinicus*. For common rhubarb or pie plant see the next entry.

RHUBARB or PIE PLANT. The usable parts of this agreeable vegetable are its thick, succulent, acid leafstalks. These are cut into pieces, cooked with sugar, and eaten like stewed fruit, or in pies and jams. The leaf blades must not be eaten. They contain calcium oxalate, which in sufficient amounts is harmful and sometimes causes death. Botanically *Rheum rhabarbarum*, a native of Siberia, rhubarb is one of the few

Rhubarb or pie plant

Rhubarb flowers

vegetables cultivated as a perennial. A robust, thick-rooted, deciduous herbaceous plant, belonging to the buckwheat family POLYGONACEAE, it thrives in cool climates, in North America best in the northern states and Canada. It is poorly adapted to the southern half of the United States.

Rhubarb succeeds in a wide variety of drained, fertile soils, preferring those slightly to moderately acid. Fertility is important because quality is measured by the size, thickness, and succulence of the leafstalks, and the excellence of these depends to a large degree on the ready availability of nutrients. Poor soils produce small, inferior leaves with thin, stringy stalks. For best results, a sunny location is needed. One at the margin of the vegetable garden or bordering a path, where this perennial crop will not be in the way of the annual soil preparation necessary for most vegetables, is likely to be convenient.

Soil preparation should be thorough. Under favorable conditions plants may remain without replanting for twenty years or more, although it is often better to divide and reset them after about ten years or less. But even ten years is a long period for such a hungry crop to go without deep soil refurbishment, depending upon surface applications only of fertilizer. Before planting rhubarb, spade or otherwise loosen the earth to a depth of at least 10 inches (more is better) and mix with it very generous amounts of half-decayed manure or compost and a complete garden fertilizer, such as a 5-10-5 or 10-10-10, with a comparatively high phosphorus and potash content.

Plant in early fall or spring, in regions of very severe winters in spring only. Among the most popular varieties are 'Crimson Wine', 'German Wine', 'McDonald', 'Ruby', 'Valentine', and 'Victoria', the last one of the best for early forcing. Set out divisions of strong clumps each consisting of one to three dormant buds or eyes and a substantial section of root. Space the sets at least 4 by 3 feet apart, at such a depth that they are covered with 2 to 3 inches of soil. If space is available an extra foot each way may be afforded with advantage. During the first summer water thoroughly at intervals in dry spells. Mulching to conserve moisture and reduce weeds is advantageous. Do not harvest any stalks the first year. Rather, leave all leaves to nourish the roots and encourage their establishment.

Routine care of established clumps includes applying a complete garden fertilizer each spring before new growth begins and, in fall, a heavy mulch of manure, compost, or other suitable material to limit the depth to which the soil freezes. Deep freezing does not harm the roots, but delays the development of the spring crop. The mulch is pulled away from the crowns and removed or forked into the soil as soon as the ground is workable in spring. The surface soil is then cultivated. Summer care consists of keeping weeds down, removing flower stalks as soon as they show, and in dry weather watering periodically. The quality and quantity of the following season's crop depends to a very large extent upon the vigor of the summer growth. After killing frost, remove the tops prior to applying the winter mulch.

Harvesting should not begin until the second season after planting and then should be very light. In the third and subsequent years, normal numbers of leaves may be taken over a period of six to eight weeks from the time the first are ready. All subsequent foliage is left to mature and to strengthen the roots for the following season's effort. Harvest only large leaves.

Harvesting rhubarb

To do this grasp the stalks firmly and pull steadily. Do not twist, jerk, or cut them. To keep the stalks crisp, trim the leaf blades to within 2 or 3 inches of the top of the stalk as soon as they are pulled.

Forcing early crops of rhubarb is easily done indoors and in the garden. Garden-forced produce cannot be had as early as that from greenhouses, cellars, and other heated accommodations, but may be avail-

able two or three weeks before the normal outside crop. To force rhubarb outdoors it is not necessary to dig up the roots. Simply cover them in fall with barrels or large boxes, fitted with removable tops. Fill the insides of the receptacles with straw or dry leaves and heap around their outsides sufficient strawy manure, loose compost, leaves held in place with chicken wire, or other insulating material to prevent the ground from freezing deeply. In late winter remove the insulating materials from inside and outside the coverings and if available pile around their outsides hot, fermenting horse manure. If this is not practicable, the production of harvestable stalks will be slower, but still in advance of those from uncovered crowns. Individual roots should not be forced in this way more often than in alternate years.

To force rhubarb indoors, dig roots in fall. The best are strong, well-grown ones, two to three years old. Before forcing they must be held for at least seven weeks at temperatures below 50 and above 28°F. Forcing may be done under greenhouse benches or in a cellar or similar place where temperatures between 50 and 60°F are maintained and the air is humid. If the humidity is deficient, place a framework covered with polyethylene plastic film over the roots. Set the roots closely together and pack soil between them. Keep this moist. Exclude light during the forcing process. Harvesting begins, depending upon temperatures, in one month to six weeks and may continue for four to eight weeks. To maintain a continuous supply, two or more batches of roots may be started from mid-December at about monthly intervals. Roots forced indoors are discarded after harvesting is through. Propagation is usually be division at planting time. Seeds may be used, but seedlings are less uniform than plants raised from division. Seeds are sown in spring in drills about 1 inch deep. The seedlings are thinned or transplanted to 1 foot apart and the following spring are transplanted to their permanent locations.

Diseases and Pests. The chief disease of rhubarb is foot rot (phytophthora crown rot). This causes lesions at the bases of the stalks and eventual collapse of the stalks. No practical control is known. Destroy affected plants. Rhubarb curculio, a snout beetle, bores into the stalks, crown, and roots. Control consists of digging and burning infested plants and destroying all dock weeds in the vicinity, in July. Docks (*Rumex*) harbor this pest.

RHUS (Rhús) — Sumac, Poison-Ivy, Poison-Oak. Several genera of the cashew family ANACARDIACEAE include members that contain resins or nonvolatile oils that upon contact with the skins of sensitive individuals cause severe dermatitis. Certain kinds of *Rhus* are examples. The names

poison-ivy, poison-oak, and poison sumac designate noxious natives of North America. Others occur elsewhere. Not all rhuses are poisonous. Many are quite harmless, and some are attractive ornamentals. The name *Rhus* is the Greek one of *R. coriaria*.

The genus consists of 250 species of trees, shrubs, and vines, the latter clinging by aerial roots, of temperate, warm-temperate, and subtropical regions. Some are thorny. They have alternate, deciduous or evergreen leaves, pinnate with usually an odd number of generally opposite leaflets, of three leaflets, or more rarely of five arranged in palmate (handlike) fashion. The leaflets may be lobed, toothed, or smooth-edged; they may be stalkless or have tiny stalks. The small to minute flowers are in panicles or racemes, unisexual with the sexes on separate plants, or unisexual and bisexual with the sexes on the same plant. The blooms have five-lobed, usually persistent calyxes, five greenish-white to yellowish or rarely pink petals, five stamens, or in female flowers, small staminodes (nonfunctional stamens), and a pistil, vestigial in male flowers, with three styles and three stigmas. The fruits are berry-like, more or less globular, white, brownish, red, or black, and hairy or hairless.

Useful products are obtained from some sumacs. The syrupy juice of the varnish tree (*R. verniciflua*) is the source of a natural varnish called Japanese or Chinese lacquer. In its Asian homelands, this species occasionally is 100 feet high. Oil expressed from the seeds is used as an illuminant and sometimes as an adulterant of tung oil. A commercial wax is obtained from the fruits of *R. succedanea*, of eastern Asia. Some species, including the shining and staghorn sumacs of North America, *R. coriaria*, of the Mediterranean region, and Asian *R. chinensis*, are exploited as sources of tanning materials.

Sumacs to avoid are those with skin-irritating sap, even although some, including poison-ivy, are decidedly ornamental. Among such poisonous kinds are the vining poison-ivy (*R. radicans*) and its nonvin-

Rhus radicans (foliage)

Rhus radicans (fruits)

Rhus diversiloba

ing relative *R. toxicodendron*, of eastern North America; poison-oak (*R. diversiloba*), a shrub of western North America; poison sumac (*R. vernix*), a North American shrub or small tree; and the varnish tree (*R. verniciflua*), a tree of Japan, China, and the Himalayas.

Shining sumac (**R. copallina**) is one of the most attractive ornamentals of the ge-

Rhus copallina (flowers)

nus. Native from Maine to Minnesota, Florida, and Texas, it is a shrub or tree up to 30 feet tall with rich green, lustrous foliage, in fall changing to reddish-purple and then associating well with the decorative, crimson fruits. The leaves are of nine to fifteen oblong-ovate to lanceolate-ovate leaflets 1½ to 4 inches long, toothless or with a few teeth near their tips. Unusual for the genus, although it occurs also in *R. chinensis*, this has the midribs of the leaves along which the leaflets are arranged winged. The greenish flowers are in crowded panicles. The fruits are hairy. From the smooth sumac, Chinese **R. chinensis** is readily distinguished by the seven to thirteen, 2- to 4½-inches-long, pointed, ovate to oblong leaflets of its leaves having coarsely-round-toothed margins and its flowers being creamy-white, in broad pyramidal panicles 6 inches to 1 foot long. They are displayed in late summer. The orange-red fruits are subspherical and densely-hairy. The leaves have winged midribs and often winged stalks. Their undersides are brownish-hairy.

Staghorn sumac (**R. typhina**), the largest native American species, sometimes 30

Rhus typhina (fruits)

feet high or taller, is often lower. It has densely-velvety-hairy shoots, deciduous, pinnate leaves up to 1¼ feet long or longer of eleven to thirteen pointed, lanceolate-oblong, toothed leaflets with glaucous undersides. The leaflets are 2 to 4½ inches long. Handsome, tall cones or spindles of crowded, crimson fruits decorate the branches of female trees in fall. Then, the foliage assumes striking hues of orange and scarlet. This is a native of Quebec to Ontario, Georgia, Indiana, and Iowa. Variety *R. t. laciniata* has leaflets deeply-cleft

Rhus typhina laciniata

into lacy fringes. Those of *R. t. dissecta* are even more finely pinnately-dissected.

Smooth sumac (**R. glabra**), native from Maine to British Columbia, Florida, and Arizona, is 10 to occasionally 15 feet tall. From the staghorn sumac it is readily dis-

Rhus glabra

tinguished by its shoots being hairless and glaucous. Its deciduous leaves have eleven to thirteen pointed, lanceolate-oblong, toothed leaflets 2 to 4½ inches long, glaucous on their undersides. Greenish, the flowers are crowded in panicles up to 1 foot long. The females are succeeded by decorative, sticky-hairy, scarlet fruits. In fall the foliage becomes bright red. Variety *R. g. laciniata* with pinnately-cut leaflets is less hardy than the species. It survives in southern New England. An intermediate natural hybrid between the smooth sumac and the staghorn sumac is *R. hybrida*.

Fragrant sumac (**R. aromatica** syn. **R. canadensis**) and rather similar **R. trilobata** are very different from any of the foregoing.

Rhus trilobata (young fruits)

going. They have leaves of three leaflets. The yellowish flowers come in spring before the new foliage. They are in short, dense, solitary or clustered spikes up to ¾ inch long at the branchlet ends, catkin-like before they open. Fragrant sumac rarely exceeds 3 feet in height. When bruised pleasantly aromatic, it has hairy shoots and leaves, the latter with pointed leaflets, the side ones ovate, the center one often wedge-shaped or obovate. They are 1 inch to 3 inches long. In fall they assume brilliant shades of orange and scarlet. The subspherical, hairy fruits are red. This species is native from Ontario to Minnesota, Florida, and Louisiana. Variety *R. a. illinoensis*, erect and up to 6 feet tall, has leaves with blunt, few-toothed leaflets. Up to 6 feet tall, the skunk bush (*R. trilobata*) is ill-scented when bruised. Its leaves, ¾ to 1 inch long, with a few teeth or lobes, are less hairy than those of *R. aromatica*, its flowers are slightly smaller. Otherwise flowers and foliage resemble those of fragrant sumac.

Native to the Mediterranean region, **R. coriaria** is a shrub or tree up to 20 feet in height. Its short-stalked, pinnate leaves have nine to fifteen broad-elliptic to oblong, coarsely-toothed leaflets, hairy on their undersides, 1 inch to 1½ inches long, and with their midribs winged at least toward their apexes. The flowers are in loose terminal panicles up to 2 inches long. The crimson fruits are hairy.

Evergreens with generally undivided leaves, the sourberry or lemonade berry (*R. integrifolia*), the laurel sumac (*R. laurina*), and the sugar bush (*R. ovata*), all natives of southern California, are not hardy in the north. Up to 12 feet tall or sometimes taller, **R. integrifolia** has hairless, short-stalked, blunt, broad-elliptic leaves with smooth or spine-toothed edges. They are 1 inch to 2 inches long. The hoary-hairy panicles of white or pinkish flowers are 1 inch to 3

inches long. The ½-inch-long fruits are dark red. Similar to the above, *R. ovata* differs chiefly in its leaves being pointed-ovate. A hairless, aromatic shrub ordinarily up to 7 feet high, **R. laurina** is sometimes twice as tall. Its glossy, ovate to lanceolate, toothless leaves, short-pointed at their apexes, are 1½ to 5 inches in length. The greenish-white flowers are in dense panicles up to 4 inches in length. The fruits are white and very small. This is esteemed as a good bee plant.

Garden and Landscape Uses. Despite their undeniably attractive foliage, fruits, and sometimes flowers, as a group sumacs are not esteemed very highly by gardeners and landscapers. Their most serious shortcomings are their propensity for spreading by suckers and the weak wood of the tall shrub and tree types being subject to storm damage. Most are more adaptable for naturalizing in extensive areas than for use in gardens. In such places they can be very effective. They are especially adapted for poor, sandy, and dry soils. For the best results they need full sun. The kinds of most refined appearance are the cut-leaved varieties of the staghorn and smooth sumacs, both of which color handsomely in fall. These, like the species they represent, should be in groups. Solitary specimens are rarely shapely. This, however, is not true of *R. copallina*, which makes a good single specimen, or of *R. chinensis*, which is worth considering for its summer display of bloom. Excellent uses for *R. aromatica* and *R. trilobata* are as coverings for sunny slopes and shallow-angled banks. Once established the only attention they need is trimming back every two or three years or at longer intervals with a sickle or brush scythe to maintain an even appearance. A possible disadvantage in some places is that its foliage, being hairy, tends to accumulate dust.

Cultivation. Routine care of established sumacs consists of nothing more than any cutting back needed to keep them within bounds. Propagation is simple by division and by root cuttings. Plants are also easily had from seed. However, most individual sumac plants are unisexual and since males do not fruit and females fruit only if a male is nearby, seedlings are less satisfactory than plants raised in other ways from stocks of known performance. A small proportion of sumacs are bisexual and fruit independently. Obviously, nurseries and other propagators should concentrate their efforts on such bisexual individuals.

RHYNCHELYTRUM (Rhyn-chélytrum) — Natal Grass or Ruby Grass. To the grass family GRAMINEAE belongs this genus of about thirty-five species. Its name, from the Greek *rhynchos*, a beak, and *elytron*, a scale, has reference to parts of the flower spikelets that end in beaks.

Rhynchelytrums are indigenous to India, Arabia, tropical Africa, South Africa, and Malagasy (Madagascar). One species is grown for ornament and, in the southern United States, for forage. There are annuals and perennials. They are tufted plants with linear to very slender, almost threadlike leaf blades and tight or loose panicles of bloom. The slender-stalked spikelets of flowers are compressed, keeled, and often open-mouthed. Each usually has one male and one bisexual flower.

Natal grass or ruby grass (**Rhynchelytrum repens** syns. *Tricholaena rosea, T. vio-*

Rhynchelytrum repens

lacea), native to tropical South Africa, is an annual or short-lived perennial naturalized in parts of the United States. From 2 to 4 feet tall, it has slender, erect, hairless or slightly hairy stems and slender-pointed leaves with blades up to ¼ inch wide by up to 1 foot long. Loose or compact, its graceful flower panicles, 3 to 9 inches long and up to 4 inches broad, have lustrous spikelets clothed with purplish, reddish, pinkish, or white, silky hairs.

Garden Uses and Cultivation. This plant is ordinarily cultivated as an annual. It is admirable as an ornamental for beds and borders and for cut flowers for mixing in bouquets. Seeds are sown outdoors in spring in sunny locations in ordinary garden soil. The seedlings are thinned so as not to crowd unduly. Alternatively, sowing is done in 4-inch pots in a cool greenhouse and the young plants transplanted outdoors after danger of frost is gone. Indoor sowing is done about six weeks before the expected time of transfer to the garden. The outdoor site should be one sheltered from strong winds.

RHYNCHOGLOSSUM (Rhyncho-glóssum). In pronouncing *Rhynchoglossum* the "ch" takes the sound of "k." Consisting of about six species, this genus belongs in the gesneria family GESNERIACEAE. It is unique in being the only genus of the group native both to the Americas and to the Old World.

The name, from the Greek *rhynchos,* a beak, and *glossa,* a tongue, presumably refers to the form of the flowers.

As now interpreted, *Rhynchoglossum* includes the plants formerly segregated as *Klugia.* It is indigenous from Mexico to Central America and South America, and from tropical Asia to Indonesia, the Philippine Islands, and Taiwan.

Rhynchoglossums are herbaceous perennials with upright stems and opposite leaves. One of each pair is markedly smaller than the other and often is early deciduous so that to a casual observer the leaves may appear alternate. They are asymmetrical, with one side at the base obviously bigger than the other. There may or may not be branched hairs on their undersurfaces. The flowers are in one-sided, often curved racemes. They have a five-angled, five-lobed calyx and a tubular corolla with two lips, one much bigger than the other. There are two or four stamens, their anthers united, and a style tipped with a slightly lobed or lobeless stigma. The fruits are capsules.

The only species known to be cultivated, *R. notonianum* (syn. *Klugia zeylan-*

Rhynchoglossum notonianum

ica) inhabits wet and moist woodland soils in India and Sri Lanka. From 1 foot to 1½ feet high, it has somewhat fleshy stems, like those of *Chirita lavandulacea* rather translucent. The light green, pointed-ovate leaves, shaped like those of angel-wing begonias, are 2 to 8 inches in length and somewhat under one-half as broad. They are paler on their undersides than above. The lax, terminal racemes of flowers droop. The blooms have sepals with pointed lobes, and 1-inch-long corollas with a broad, rich dark blue lower lip, a white upper lip, and a pair of yellow spots in the throat. Occasionally the tip flower of the raceme is symmetrical and trumpet-shaped with the lower part white and the upper blue.

Garden Uses and Cultivation. The species described, scarcely spectacular enough

to be grown by other than fanciers of the gesneria family, who are numerous, is easy to manage in greenhouses and terrariums, and perhaps under favorable conditions as a houseplant. It does well in porous, fertile soil that contains a moderate to generous proportion of organic matter and is kept moderately moist. This species will not tolerate dryness at the roots. Some shade from strong sun is needed. A winter night temperature of 55 to 60°F, from five to fifteen degrees higher by day, is satisfactory. A fairly humid atmosphere is needed. Specimens that have filled their containers with roots are greatly benefited by regular applications of dilute liquid fertilizer. Seed afford a ready means of raising new plants, which if kept growing without interruption make quite nice specimens and bloom within four to six months. Cuttings root readily and also provide a convenient means of increase. For additional information see the Encyclopedia entry Gesneriads.

RHYNCHOSIA (Rhyn-chòsia). Natives of the tropics and subtropics, the 300 mostly prostrate or twining species that constitute *Rhynchosia* are most numerous in the Americas and Africa. They belong to the pea family LEGUMINOSAE and have a name alluding to the beaked seed pods of some kinds, derived from the Greek *rhynchos,* a beak.

Perennial herbaceous plants, subshrubs, or low shrubs, rhynchosias have alternate leaves of three or more leaflets, resinous-dotted on their undersides. The pea-like flowers, yellow, with the standard petal sometimes striped or purple, are in racemes or rarely are solitary. They have two-lipped calyxes, the upper lip with two partly united teeth, the lower usually the longer. The spreading or reflexed standard or banner petal is spurred at the base. There are ten stamens, of which nine are joined and one is free, and an incurved style sometimes swollen toward its apex. The flattened pods are two- or more rarely one-seeded.

Native to South Africa, *R. capensis* (syn. *Desmodium ciliatum*) has trailing or twining, slender stems up to 3 feet long, and leaves with three ovate-oblong to oblong-lanceolate leaflets ¾ inch to 1¼ inches long terminating a stalk shorter or as long. The clusters of up to six or sometimes solitary flowers are on slender stalks from the axils of the upper leaves. Their calyxes are sticky and slightly hairy. Of approximately equal lengths, the petals are about ⅓ inch long. Slightly hairy, the reflexed short-stalked, narrow-elliptic seed pods are ¾ inch long.

Species of the American tropics sometimes cultivated include *R. pyramidalis* and *R. minima.* A vine, *R. pyramidalis* has leaves of three triangular leaflets 1 inch to 5 inches long, and reddish-yellow, 1-inch-

long blooms followed by pods as long containing red and black seeds much like, and used similarly to, those of the rosary-pea (*Abrus precatorius*), but usually with a small pit in the red instead of in the black portion. Also a trailer or vine, *R. minima* has rhomboid-ovate leaves with three leaflets up to ½ inch long, flowers ¼ inch long, and pods ½ to ¾ inch long, which contain brown or black seeds.

Garden and Landscape Uses and Cultivation. Of minor importance as ornamentals, these plants are occasionally grown in warm climates. They succeed in ordinary soils and are increased by seed.

RHYNCHOSPERMUM JASMINOIDES is *Trachelospermum jasminoides.*

RHYNCHOSTYLIS (Rhynchó-stylis) — Foxtail Orchid. Members of this genus of possibly fifteen species are often grown under the misleading name *Saccolabium,* a designation that correctly belongs to a related group of orchids not known to be in cultivation. An inhabitant of the Indo-Malaysian region, *Rhynchostylis* consists of tree-perching (epiphytic) or occasionally rock-perching plants of the orchid family ORCHIDACEAE. Its name, derived from the Greek *rhynchos,* a beak, and *stylos,* a pillar, was applied because of the shape of the column of the flower.

Rhynchostylises are sometimes called, in allusion to the appearance of their thick, cylindrical racemes of blooms, foxtail orchids. They have erect leafy stems. Their leaves are flat or channeled, leathery or fleshy, and in two ranks. Displayed in showy, many-flowered racemes, the long-lasting blooms have similar, spreading sepals and petals, the upper sepal usually somewhat smaller than the side ones. The lip, which is joined to the short, thick, blunt column, has a backward-pointing spur. The plant sometimes grown as *R. densiflora* and *R. grandiflora* is *Anota densiflora.*

Fairly frequently cultivated, *R. retusa* (syn. *Saccolabium blumei*) is widely distributed in tropical Asia. It has stems 1 foot to 2 feet tall and arching, channeled, strap-shaped leaves approximately as long, with overlapping bases. The pendulous, densely-flowered, tail-like racemes of fragrant blooms come in summer or early fall. About ¾ inch in diameter, the flowers have lanceolate, usually entirely violet lips and white sepals and petals distinctly spotted with discrete markings of the same color. Several varieties are recognized by orchid specialists; they differ slightly in the lengths of their racemes, flower color, and other details. One such, *R. r. russellianum,* has racemes, up to 2 feet in length, of flowers larger than those of the typical species. The blooms of *R. r. alba* and *R. r. holfordiana* are white, those of the latter are also spotted with crimson and have a crimson lip. Variety *R. r. gigantea* is more robust than the typical species.

Late-summer- and fall-blooming *R. coelestis* (syn. *Saccolabium coeleste*) is very beautiful. It has a stem rarely more than 9 inches, but sometimes up to 1 foot tall and closely spaced leaves 4 to 8 inches long. The erect, many-flowered racemes are of fragrant, waxy blooms up to ¾ inch wide. They are white, with the apexes of the sepals and petals, and most of the lip, sky-blue to indigo-blue. This is a native of Thailand.

Garden Uses and Cultivation. Rhynchostylises find favor with orchid fanciers who can provide conditions that suit vandas. They grow readily in intermediate- and warm-temperature greenhouses in osmunda, tree fern fiber, and other rooting mediums suitable for epiphytic orchids. They are impatient of root disturbance, and great care must be taken when transplanting to keep this to a minimum. They should not be transplanted more often than necessary. Usually rhynchostylises succeed best in suspended baskets or pans that permit free circulation of air about them. As much light as possible, short of scorching the foliage, is appreciated. Water to keep the roots moderately moist at all times. For more information see Orchids.

RHYNDOROPSIS. This is the name of orchid hybrids the parents of which include *Doritis, Phalaenopsis,* and *Rhynchostylis.*

RHYTICOCOS (Rhyticò-cos) — Overtop Palm. Columbus was undoubtedly the first European to see this native of Dominica, Guadeloupe, Martinique, and a few other West Indian islands, for it was on the first of these islands that the Italian mariner landed on his second voyage in 1493. The only palm common on the coast he touched is the overtop palm, which towers conspicuously above the surrounding vegetation. It is unlikely that Columbus missed observing it. In all probability he assumed it to be the coconut, which the overtop palm closely resembles, for in that day botanical niceties were less well defined than now. Belonging in the palm family PALMAE, the genus *Rhyticocos* consists of one species. Its name is derived from the Greek *rhytis,* wrinkled, and *Cocos,* the coconut palm, in allusion to the mottled seeds. It also has something of the aspect of the queen palm (*Arecastrum romanzoffianum*).

The overtop palm (**R. amara**) has an erect, ringed trunk up to 50 or 60 feet tall and a great crown of large, dark green, glossy, pinnate leaves that spread in many directions and have numerous long, slender leaflets. The fruits, covered with a thick, fibrous coat and resembling miniature coconuts, are in clusters. They are orange, 2 to 3 inches long, and when young contain "milk," which, as the botanical *amara* indicates, is bitter. Associated with each cluster of flowers and fruits are large, conspicuous, pendulous, woody spathes. The Carib Indians made a fermented beverage from the sap of this palm and extracted an oil from its seeds, which they mixed with coloring obtained from annatto (*Bixa orellana*) to paint their bodies. Carib children ate the bitter kernels of the nuts.

Garden and Landscape Uses. This species is elegant for planting singly or in groups and is particularly adapted for locations near the sea. Like the coconut palm, it is tolerant of high winds, salt spray, and strong sun. It is more resistant to cold than one might expect. At Daytona Beach, Florida, it has survived 25°F, but with severe damage to its foliage.

Cultivation. Any reasonably good soil suits the overtop palm. In greenhouses it is best with a minimum winter night temperature of 55 to 60°F, high humidity, and shade from strong summer sun. Pot or plant in coarse, porous, fertile soil and keep this reasonably moist. Well-established specimens benefit from biweekly applications of dilute liquid fertilizer from spring through fall. Common pests are scale insects, mealybugs, and red spider mites. For additional information see Palms.

RHYTIDOPHYLLUM (Rhytid-óphyllum). Most cultivated members of the gesneria family GESNERIACEAE, to which belong African-violets, gloxinias, and episcias, are nonwoody. An exception is *Rhytidophyllum,* a West Indian genus of about twenty species of shrubs or small trees. Its name, an apt one derived from the Greek *rhytidos,* a wrinkle, and *phyllon,* a leaf, refers to the crinkled foliage.

Rhytidophyllums are generally hairy. They have alternate, round-toothed or toothless, often long leaves, sometimes white-woolly on their undersides. The flowers, clothed with soft hairs, are in clusters at the ends of long stalks that come from the leaf axils. The five-lobed calyxes have top-shaped to nearly globular tubes. The corollas, usually greenish on their outsides, have tubes that broaden above and end in five short, erect or spreading lobes (petals). There are four fertile stamens, one rudimentary stamen, and one style. The fruits are capsules.

Up to 5 feet in height, **R. tomentosum** has woody stems and drooping, lanceolate to oblong-lanceolate, slightly clammy, toothed leaves 8 to 10 inches long by up to 2 inches wide. They are aromatic, and on their lower sides white-woolly. The flower clusters are of twenty to thirty musky-scented, yellowish-green blooms, about ¾ inch long by about ½ inch wide. The flowers have green-tipped petals and throats spotted purplish-red.

Garden Uses and Cultivation. This rare plant is only likely to be cultivated by fanciers and collectors of gesneriads (plants belonging to the gesneria family), in greenhouses and similar indoor environments, and outdoors in the tropics. It requires the same soil and environment as African-violets and most other tropical gesneriads. Being evergreen, it has no season of rest and so must be watered throughout the year. Propagation is by seed, cuttings, and leaf cuttings.

RIBBON BEDS. Narrow flower beds very much longer than wide and often bordering paths are sometimes called ribbon beds.

RIBBON BUSH. This is the common name of *Adenostoma sparsifolium* and *Homalocladium platycladum.*

RIBBONWOOD. See Hoheria.

RIBES (Rí-bes)—Currant, Gooseberry. The name *Ribes* is derived from the Arabic name *ribas,* that of a kind of rhubarb. The genus, a member of the saxifrage family SAXIFRAGACEAE, inhabits many temperate and cold regions of the world, extending into the southern hemisphere in South America. It consists of about 150 species of deciduous, much less frequently evergreen, shrubs, some prickly, some not.

The leaves of *Ribes,* according to species, are alternate or clustered. They are undivided, but usually palmately-lobed (in hand-fashion), and toothed. The flowers are bisexual or unisexual with the sexes on different plants. Small, but sometimes brightly colored, the blooms are solitary or in racemes. They have tubular to wheel-shaped calyxes with usually five, rarely four lobes (sepals). There are as many petals as sepals, or sometimes none. When present the petals are usually smaller than the sepals. There are commonly five, less often four stamens, and two, more rarely one, styles. The fruits are many-seeded berries, with the remains of the calyx attached at their tips.

Serious limiting factors to growing *Ribes* in North America are the parts many kinds play as alternate hosts to white pine blister rust and wheat black stem rust diseases. In regions where white pines are native or where wheat is grown commercially, it is generally illegal to plant some or all kinds, or they may be planted only under approved regulations. Before planting, consult local authorities, such as Cooperative Extension Agents. White pine blister rust affects not only native white pines, but other kinds that have needles (leaves) in bundles of five.

Kinds grown for their fruits include the common garden currant (*R. sativum*), a deciduous European cultivated only in its improved pomological varieties that include white-fruited as well as red-fruited

Currants (*Ribes sativum* variety)

Ribes speciosum

English gooseberries (*Ribes uva-crispa*)

sorts, the black currant (*R. nigrum*), of Europe and Asia, much grown in northern Europe for its edible fruits, but little known in North America, the English gooseberry (*R. uva-crispa*), a native of Europe, North Africa, and western Asia, and somewhat naturalized in North America, and the American gooseberry (*R. hirtellum*), native from Newfoundland to Manitoba, West Virginia, and South Dakota. None of these pomological kinds is cultivated in its wild type, nor are their natural species employed for ornament. For information about the cultivation of the improved varieties and hybrids grown for their fruits see the Encyclopedia entries Currants and Gooseberry.

The fuchsia-flowered gooseberry (*R. speciosum*) is the only evergreen sort considered here. Endemic to California and Baja California, where it inhabits shaded canyons, this is 3 to 12 feet tall. It has spreading, bristly and spiny stems and roundish, somewhat three-lobed, glossy leaves up to 1½ inches long. The bright red, drooping, bell-shaped flowers, in clusters of two to four, have stamens ¾ to 1 inch long, much exceeding the sepals and petals. The bristly-hairy fruits are red.

Highly ornamental *R. sanguineum*, often simply called flowering currant, although

the alpine currant and buffalo currant would seem as worthy of that designation, is native from northern California to British Columbia. A bushy, branched shrub 4 to 10 feet tall or sometimes taller, this has hairy young shoots and bluntly three- or five-lobed, triangular-ovate to kidney-shaped or roundish, usually toothed leaves, up to 4 inches in diameter, softly-hairy on their undersides, nearly hairless above. The showy, prevailingly pink to rich crimson flowers are in ascending to erect racemes. The individual flower stalks are glandular, as to some extent are the petals. The latter, white to reddish, are approximately one-half as long as the sepals. The usually somewhat glandular fruits are glaucous-blue-black. Restricted in the wild to the southern reaches of the range of the species, *R. s. glutinosum* and horticultural varieties of it are most common in cultiva-

Ribes sanguineum glutinosum, Rancho Santa Ana Botanic Garden, Claremont, California

tion. From the typical species, *R. s. glutinosum* differs in its leaves being somewhat less hairy and having shorter, wider terminal lobes and in the usually deep pink to pale pink flowers being in pendulous racemes of fifteen to forty. Very popular in the British Isles and other parts

of Europe, *R. sanguineum* or *R. s. glutinosum* is cultivated in a number of horticultural varieties, among them white-flowered *R. s. album*, blush-pink-flowered *R. s. albescens*, pink-flowered *R. s. carneum*, and with deep red blooms, *R. s. atrorubens* and *R. s.* 'King Edward VII', the last comparatively low. Double flowers are borne by *R. s. plenum*, especially long racemes of rosy-crimson ones by *R. s. splendens*. Deep-red-flowered *R. s.* 'Elk River Red' is grown in the Pacific Northwest.

The alpine or mountain currant (*R. alpinum*), broad, dense, and 6 to 8 feet tall, has erect stems, whitish shoots, and hairless foliage. Its mostly three-lobed leaves have broad-ovate to triangular-ovate, irregularly-toothed blades 1 inch to 2 inches across. The little greenish-yellow flowers, the sexes on separate bushes, are in erect racemes, those of male flowers 1 inch to 2½ inches long, those of females shorter. Bright scarlet and long-persisting, the fruits are attractive. Male plants of this European native seemingly do not serve as alternate hosts to white pine blister rust.

The buffalo currant, Missouri currant, or clove currant (*R. odoratum*) is charm-

Ribes odoratum (foliage and flowers)

ing in bloom. Native from South Dakota to Texas and the Rocky Mountains, this has plentiful, aromatically-scented, bright yellow, bisexual flowers in usually nodding, hairy racemes of up to ten that make a bright display in spring. The sepals of the blooms are not over one-half as long as the calyx tube. The black fruits are about ⅓ inch in diameter. This 5- to 7-foot-tall shrub has ovate to ovate-kidney-shaped, deeply-three- or five-lobed, coarsely-toothed leaves, wedge-shaped at their bases. At first somewhat hairy, later hairless, they are 1 inch to 3 inches in length and width. In fall they turn bright scarlet. Variety 'Crandall' is cultivated for its edible fruits. Variety *R. o. xanthocarpum* has orange-yellow fruits. Similar to the buffalo currant, but smaller, more slender, and less ornamental, the golden currant (*R. aureum*) has hairless or scarcely-hairy young shoots. Its leaves, less coarsely-toothed than those of the buffalo currant, are mostly somewhat heart-shaped at their bases. The flowers, otherwise like those of the buffalo currant, have calyxes with sepals over one-half as long as the calyx tube. Variety *R. a. chrysococcum* has orange-yellow fruits. The golden currant is native from the Rocky Mountains to Washington and California.

Garden and Landscape Uses. Where government regulations permit their planting, ornamental currants are delightful shrubs for mixed beds and borders and as single specimens. Evergreen *R. speciosum* is hardy only where there is little or no frost and where summers are dry. Much hardier, it may live outdoors in sheltered places in southern New England, *R. sanguineum* is nevertheless most commonly planted in gardens in the Pacific Coast region. The buffalo currant and golden currant are extremely hardy, surviving well north in Canada. The alpine currant is a good cold region hedge plant that does well in partial shade. All kinds give good results in ordinary garden soils of fair quality, not excessively dry, and thrive in sun or part-day shade.

Cultivation. Little or no routine attention is needed. Any pruning to prevent the plants becoming too big is acceptable, and a little thinning out of branches tending to become crowded may be done as soon as blooming is through. If needed, severe cutting back to restore old overgrown specimens may be done. Increase is easily had by summer leafy cuttings planted under mist or set in a greenhouse or cold frame propagating bed, and by hardwood cuttings taken in fall. Some kinds can be divided. Seeds sown in a cold frame in fall, or mixed with slightly damp sand or vermiculite, stored for three months at 40°F, and then sown, are also satisfactory.

RICCIA (Rícc-ia)—Crystalwort. The genus *Riccia* includes many species of hardy plants belonging to the liverwort family RICCIACEAE. They are cryptogams (nonflowering plants related to mosses and ferns). Most inhabit damp soil, but a few are aquatics, and one is cultivated in aquariums. They have no true stems, leaves, or flowers; the plant body consists of a thallus of flat green ribbons of tissue. The name commemorates P. F. Ricci, an Italian nobleman.

The crystalwort (*R. fluitans*) is cosmopolitan in its natural distribution. It floats at or near the water surface, forming freely-branching, light- or blue-green spongy masses of slender, flat strands, at their ends divided into two strongly diverging lobes, or it grows on mud bottoms or on wet land. Only on land are spores formed.

Garden Uses and Cultivation. This is a favored plant for aquariums because it forms a good spawning and hiding place for fish and provides some shade. It grows readily in cool or warm, slightly acid water and multiplies very rapidly if the light is good. It requires at least six hours of sunlight each day. Propagation is by division.

RICCIACEAE — Riccia Family. Here belong about 200 species of lowly, nonflowering plants called liverworts. The family is of nearly worldwide natural distribution. Its members have a flat plant body called a thallus that has divergent forked branches. The only genus is *Riccia*.

RICE is *Oryza sativa*. Wild-rice is *Zizania aquatica*. The rice paper plant is *Tetrapanax papyriferum*. For rice flower see Pimelea.

RICHARDIA (Richárd-ia)—Mexican-Clover. The name of this genus, once applied to the calla-lily (*Zantedeschia*), properly belongs to a group of South American plants of the madder family RUBIACEAE, one of which is cultivated. The name *Richardia* commemorates Richard Richardson, an English student of botany, who died in 1741.

Mexican-clover (*R. scabra*) is an annual, naturalized from Virginia to Arkansas, Florida, and Texas. It has erect or lax, much-branched stems about 2 feet long, and rough, ovate to lanceolate leaves up to 3 inches long. Its white, funnel-shaped flowers, with four to eight, but most commonly six, spreading corolla lobes (petals), ¼ inch long, are in close clusters backed by an involucre (collar) of leafy bracts.

Garden Uses and Cultivation. Of no ornamental value, Mexican-clover is grown in warm regions as a cover crop, for green manure, and for forage. It grows readily from seed sown in spring and thrives in sandy soil.

RICHEA (Rích-ea). Little known horticulturally, *Richea*, of the epacris family EPACRIDACEAE, consists of ten species of Australian and Tasmanian evergreen trees and shrubs adaptable for outdoor cultivation only where no more than mild frosts are experienced and where summers are relatively cool. The genus was named in honor of the French naturalist Colonel A. Riche, who died in 1791.

Richeas have narrow, sheathing leaves and flowers in closely packed, branched or branchless terminal heads or in axillary panicles. The flowers are peculiar in that the petals do not separate, but are closed or nearly closed at their tips. When mature they split transversely near their bases and the upper parts, joined to form a cap like that of a clown, fall away leaving a cuplike lower portion and exposing the stamens. In this regard they resemble the flowers of *Eucalyptus*. The fruits are tiny capsules.

One of the hardiest sorts, *R. scoparia* is a bushy native of Tasmania 2 to 9 feet tall

Richea scoparia

and much-branched. Its overlapping, stiff, pointed-lanceolate, dark green leaves, up to 3 inches long, clothe the stems. The latter end in erect, cylindrical, spikelike panicles of pink, orange, red, or creamy-white flowers up to 5 inches long. Also Tasmanian, *R. sprengelioides* is a spreading shrub 1 foot to 4 feet tall with broadly-ovate, sharply-pointed leaves up to ½ inch long. Its solitary, cream-colored flowers are in small, terminal, spherical, leafy heads. From 6 to 30 feet high, *R. pandanifolia* is a Tasmanian with arching, narrow leaves 3 to 5 feet in length that resemble those of a *Cordyline*. Its inconspicuous white or reddish blooms are in axillary panicles 4 to 6 inches long.

Garden and Landscape Uses and Cultivation. Richeas are choice subjects for collectors of the unusual; where cool summers prevail they are well adapted for shrub beds and similar landscape uses. For best success they should be planted in well-drained, sandy, peaty soil that is never dry, but is not saturated, and in sunny locations.

They can also be grown in large pots or tubs in well-ventilated greenhouses where the winter night temperature is 40 to 50°F,

Riccia fluitans

with day temperatures slightly higher. A moderately humid atmosphere is desirable. Plants grown in this fashion benefit from being placed outdoors during summer. Repotting or top dressing should be done when needed in late winter or spring. Increase is by cuttings planted in late summer in a greenhouse propagating bench in a mixture of peat moss and sand or by seed sown in porous, sandy, peaty soil in a cool greenhouse in late winter or spring.

RICINUS (Rícin-us)—Castor-Bean or Castor Oil Plant or Palma Christi. A single notable species is the only member of *Ricinus*, of the spurge family EUPHORBIACEAE. The castor-bean, or castor oil plant or palma christi, is of great commercial importance as well as being an ornamental of dramatic aspect for gardens and other landscapes. Originally a native of Africa, but now widely naturalized throughout warm parts of the world, it has a name that was the Latin one for this plant, presumably applied because of a fancied resemblance of its seeds to a kind of European tick.

The seeds of the castor-bean are extremely rich in oil, which is used medicinally as well as for many other purposes, such as lubricating fine machinery, and in the manufacture of linoleum, plastics, paints, soaps, and inks. The coats of the seeds contain ricin, one of the deadliest poisons known. Because of this, it is extremely important not to plant castor-beans where there is any chance that children or others will eat the attractive looking seeds, or alternatively, as a precautionary measure, to break the flower panicles off the plants before seeds develop.

Many varieties of **R. communis** are cultivated. In warm regions it becomes a

Ricinus communis

shrub or small tree, but it is often grown satisfactorily as a fast-growing annual. Its leaves, alternate and long-stalked, are peltate (the stalk is attached to the blade

Ricinus communis (flowers and fruits)

some little distance in from the margin). Their blades, 1 foot to 3 feet wide, are lobed palmately (in hand-fashion) to below their middles, and the five to eleven lobes are toothed. The flowers are not showy or colorful. They are unisexual, with males and females mixed in terminal panicles on the same plant. The tiny blooms, without petals, have three- to five-parted calyxes, the males many much-branched stamens, the females a feathery style. The fruits are capsules covered with long, soft spines, containing large, smooth, beautifully colored and variegated seeds, the castor-beans.

Varieties of castor-beans commonly cultivated are *R. c. africanus,* with extraordinarily big green leaves; *R. c. borboniensis arboreus,* red-stemmed and with glaucous foliage; *R. c. cambodgensis,* with dark foliage; *R. c. coccineus,* with red leaves; *R. c. gibsonii,* a compact, fairly small variety with leaves metallic red; *R. c. hybridus panormitans,* a big variety with very glaucous, dark foliage; *R. c. laciniatus,* with leaves with deeply-cleft lobes; *R. c. macrocarpus, R. c. macrophyllus,* and *R. c. purpureus,* all with purplish-red foliage; *R. c. sanguineus,* with red leaves; and *R. c. zanzibarensis,* with white-veined, bright green leaves.

Garden and Landscape Uses. Where shrub-size or larger plants are needed for bold foliage effects, castor-beans serve usefully, in the tropics and near tropics as perennials, there and elsewhere as quick-

growing annuals. They are effective in mixed plantings and in groups and in beds alone. They associate pleasingly with architecture and so can be set with good effects near buildings. They make striking contrast with finer-foliaged plants. Castor-beans can also be grown in large pots, tubs, and planters to decorate patios, terraces, and similar places. They are sun-lovers, but stand part-day shade. They grow in a variety of soils, but those well drained and fertile are best to their liking.

Cultivation. Few plants are easier to grow than castor-beans. All that is necessary is to plant seeds in spring, after the ground has warmed and the weather is settled, where the plants are to remain, and to thin out the seedlings so that they do not unduly crowd each other. The seeds are set about 1 inch deep. Alternatively, in the preferred procedure where the growing season is short, the seeds are started indoors in a temperature of about 70°F eight to ten weeks before the resulting plants are to be planted outdoors. This is done about the time it is safe to set out tomatoes, peppers, and other warm-weather crops. When sowing indoors plant two or three seeds in a 4-inch pot and if more than one germinate pull out, while quite small, all except the strongest. Keep the young plants growing in a sunny greenhouse, window, or similar location, and pot them into 5- or 6-inch pots as growth makes necessary. From ten days to two weeks before planting out time, harden them by standing them in a cold frame or sheltered, sunny place outdoors. Spacing in the garden may be 2 to 3 feet between individuals. As the plants grow, staking to prevent storm damage becomes necessary.

RICOTIA (Ricòt-ia). Belonging in the mustard family CRUCIFERAE, the genus *Ricotia* includes nine species, natives of the eastern Mediterranean region. The name commemorates an obscure French botanist, Ricot.

Ricotias are hairless, branched annuals with mostly pinnately-lobed leaves and four-petaled flowers, with the petals narrowed to claws at their bases. The fruits are broad, flat pods.

One species, **R. lunaria,** is sometimes cultivated. A native of Egypt and Syria, and 6 inches to 1½ feet tall, it is somewhat spreading. Its pale lavender flowers have petals notched at their ends. These are followed by attractive, oblong-oval seed pods that look somewhat like those of honesty (*Lunaria*), but are smaller. They are suitable for using in arrangements of dried flowers.

Garden Uses and Cultivation. Appropriate employments for this annual are as edgings to paths or borders, in patches at the fronts of flower beds, and in drifts in rock gardens. It grows and blooms quickly. Sow seeds in early spring where the plants are to bloom or, where mild winters prevail, in fall. Beyond thinning the seedlings to about 4 inches apart and keeping down weeds, no further attention is needed. This plant needs full sun and responds best to a well-drained neutral or slightly alkaline soil.

RIGIDELLA (Rigid-élla). Consisting of four species, *Rigidella,* of the iris family IRIDA-CEAE, is native from Mexico to Peru. The name, referring to the erect stalks of the fruits, is a diminutive of the Latin *rigidus,* stiff.

Rigidellas have bulblike organs called corms that differ from true bulbs in being solid instead of being formed of concentric or overlapping scales. From tigridias they differ in having flowers with three erect, very small inner petals, of little display value, and three much larger outer ones with reflexed or spreading blades. They have three stamens, the stalks of which are joined to form a tube, and one style. The fruits are capsules.

Up to 5 feet tall, **R. flammea** has broadly-linear-lanceolate, longitudinally-pleated

Rigidella flammea

leaves, the bases of which sheathe the stem, and terminal clusters of fleeting, flame-scarlet, nodding blooms, with purple-black-striped throats or with a purple-black spot at the bottom of each petal, that come from between spathelike bracts.

Garden Uses and Cultivation. Rigidellas are of interest to collectors of unusual bulbs. They are grown under conditions that suit tigridias.

RIMARIA. See Dinteranthus, and Gibbaeum.

RIMU is *Dacrydium cupressinum.*

RIPOGONUM (Ripo-gònum). Native to New Guinea, Australia, and New Zealand, *Ripogonum,* of the lily family LILI-ACEAE, contains seven species. Its members are climbing shrubs with generally opposite, sometimes alternate, net-veined leaves. The jointed stems give reason for the name, from the Greek *rhips,* a rod, and *gony,* a joint or knee.

The leaves of ripogonums have three or five chief veins. The rather small blooms are in terminal panicles or axillary spikes or racemes. They have six petals (more correctly, tepals) and six stamens. The fruits are berries.

Native to New Zealand, *R. scandens* has leathery, ovate-oblong to oblong-lanceolate leaves, up to 5 inches long, and axillary panicles, up to 6 inches long, of ⅓-inch-wide, greenish flowers. The bright red berries, ⅓ inch in diameter, are very decorative.

Garden and Landscape Uses and Cultivation. Suitable for mild climates only, this vine needs partial shade and fertile soil. It is not common in cultivation and gardeners report difficulty in getting it established. It is increased by seed.

RITTEROCEREUS (Rittero-cèreus). Conservative botanists include *Ritterocereus,* of the cactus family CACTACEAE, in *Lemaireocereus.* When considered separately it includes a dozen species, natives from Mexico to northern South America and the West Indies. The name honors Friedrich Ritter, a twentieth-century student of the CACTACEAE of Chile.

Treelike, ritterocereuses have thick, markedly-ribbed stems with clusters of usually strong spines, and when young often with a thin waxy coating. The flowers open in the evening or at night. Funnel-shaped, they have scaly perianth tubes and ovaries. The fruits are large, spherical to egg-shaped, and spiny.

Commonly cultivated **R. pruinosus** (syn. *Lemaireocereus pruinosus*), of Mexico, up to

Ritterocereus hystrix

25 feet tall, has bluish-green stems, waxy when young and with five or six ribs. In clusters of five to eight, the brown-tipped, gray spines are 1 inch to 2 inches long. The off-white flowers are about 3½ inches long. West Indian **R. hystrix** (syn. *Lemaireocereus hystrix*), up to 20 to 40 feet in height, has a short trunk and several to many erect branches 3 to 4 inches thick. They have nine, ten, or occasionally up to twelve ribs with clusters of about ten radial and usually three central, brown-tipped, gray spines, one generally longer than the others and up to 1½ inches in length. The white flowers are 3½ inches long.

Other kinds include these: **R. deficiens** (syn. *Lemaireocereus deficiens*), of Venezuela, up to 40 feet high, has a distinct trunk and shiny green, erect branches with seven or eight sharp ribs. Its black-tipped, gray spines, ½ inch to 1½ inches long, are in clusters of about eight. The white flowers are 2½ inches long. **R. eichlamii,** of Guatemala, has dark green stems with eight to ten rounded ribs and clusters of four to six ½- to 1-inch-long, grayish spines. The pink flowers are 2½ to 3 inches long. **R. queretaroensis** (syn. *Lemaireocereus queretaroensis*), of Mexico, about 20 feet tall, has a short trunk and dark green branches with six to eight ribs and clusters of eight to twelve whitish spines 1½ to 2 inches long. The flowers are light red and 3½ inches long.

Garden and Landscape Uses and Cultivation. These are excellent for outdoor landscaping in areas with warm, dry, frost-free climates and for inclusion in greenhouse collections of cactuses. For further information see Cactuses.

RIVER-ROSE is *Bauera rubioides.*

RIVINA (Riv-ìna)—Rouge Plant or Bloodberry. There are three species of *Rivina,* one and a variety of it known to gardeners. The genus belongs in the pokeweed family PHYTOLACCACEAE and is native from the southern United States to South America. Its name commemorates Augustus Q. Rivinus, professor of botany at Leipzig, who died in 1723.

These are bushy, evergreen herbaceous plants with forking stems and alternate, ovate, heart-shaped, or lanceolate, toothless or more or less round-toothed leaves. Their many small, bisexual blooms are in racemes. Without petals, they have four-parted, persistent calyxes that look like four-petaled corollas. There are four stamens. The blooms are succeeded by small, red or yellow berries.

Rouge plant or bloodberry (**R. humilis**) is a native of the southern United States, the West Indies, and South America. Bushy, slender-stemmed, and somewhat woody toward its base, it is 1 foot to 3 feet tall and slightly hairy. Its pointed, scarcely

Rivina humilis

toothed leaves are 1 inch to 4 inches long. The numerous pink-tinged, white flowers, about ¹⁄₁₂ inch across, are in slender, more or less erect racemes, longer than the leaves, that become pendulous in fruit. Currant-like, the one-seeded berries of the typical species are bright red, those of *R. h. aurantiaca* yellow to orange.

Garden and Landscape Uses. Rivinas are pleasing, easy-to-grow decoratives. Their shiny berries last well and are in evidence almost continuously. Outdoors these plants succeed only in the tropics and warm subtropics. They are delightful greenhouse ornamentals and can be raised as window plants in rooms where the atmosphere is not excessively dry.

Cultivation. Rivinas respond to not-too-dry, moderately fertile soil. They prosper in part-shade or sun, with little or no care beyond the suppression of weeds. Seeds supply means of increase, and young plants from self-sown ones spring up in great numbers around fruiting specimens.

For pot plants, seeds are sown in sandy soil in well-drained containers in a temperature of 60 to 70°F. When the seedlings are just big enough to handle conveniently, they are transplanted individually to small pots and later to larger ones. As finals, containers 4 or 5 inches in diameter are satisfactory. The plants are grown throughout in a humid atmosphere where the night temperature is 60 to 65°F and by day five to fifteen degrees higher. At all times the soil is kept moderately moist, and after the pots are filled with roots regular applications of dilute liquid fertilizer are given. Good light and shade from strong sun are necessary.

ROBINIA (Robín-ia) — Locust or False-Acacia, Rose-Acacia. This strictly North American genus contains a number of useful and attractive sorts. It consists of twenty species of deciduous trees and shrubs, natives of the United States and Mexico. It belongs in the pea family LEG-UMINOSAE. The name honors Jean and Vespasien Robin, father and son, six-

teenth- and seventeenth-century herbalists to the king of France. The father was the first to introduce *Robinia* to Europe. He obtained seeds of the black locust from America in 1601 and raised plants in a botanic garden he had established in Paris a little more than a decade previously. In 1624 his son planted one of the resulting trees in the Jardin des Plantes in Paris and that specimen, ancient, revered, and skillfully propped and cared for, survives. The common name locust reflects the confusion of early settlers in America who identified the tree with the carob (*Ceratonia*), the fruits of which were thought to be the locusts that John the Baptist ate in the wilderness.

The wood of the black locust, heavy, strong, and hard, is extremely durable in contact with wet ground or other moisture and is greatly esteemed for fence posts and rails, the construction of pergolas and similar garden uses. It has the virtue, too, of neither shrinking nor swelling much and was used for tree nails in the building of wooden ships and for other construction. A principal modern use is for pins to secure glass insulators for telephone and telegraph wires. The wood, reported to be one and one-half times as hard, tough, and strong as that of the white oak (*Quercus alba*), is an excellent fuel. The heartwood of the variety of black locust called shipmast locust is twice as durable when used for fences as that of the typical kind. Authentic records exist of posts being in good condition after being in the ground for 125 years.

Robinias have alternate, pinnate leaves with stalked leaflets, with all but the terminal one in opposite pairs. The base of the leafstalk fits over and conceals the axillary winter buds that lie, protected by scales, in small clusters in depressions not visible until they start to grow in spring. Most robinias are spiny, the spines being modified stipules. The slender-stalked, often showy, pea-shaped flowers are in pendulous racemes borne in summer when the plants are in leaf. The fruits, flattened pea-like pods, contain several seeds.

Black locust, yellow locust, or false-acacia (*R. pseudoacacia*), noblest of the genus and probably originally native of the Allegheny Mountains, is now spontaneous over a much wider range in North America, extending even into southern Canada and westward to Missouri and Oklahoma. Nor has this ambitious colonizer confined its territorial gains to its native continent. Through much of Europe and many parts of Asia and some places in South America it holds its own against native vegetation. Indeed it is probably the only native American tree that has established itself as more than an adventive element in the flora of Europe. Black locust prospers in the Old World without the aid of man and is there to stay.

Robinia pseudoacacia, an aged specimen

Robinia pseudoacacia (flowers)

This species, often 70 or 80 feet, rarely 100 feet high, has a trunk diameter of up to 4 feet. Its bark is dark brown and furrowed. The narrow-oblong crown consists of comparatively few, upright, sinuous, more or less contorted branches. Characteristically, its shoots are armed with paired spines, but a spineless variety exists. Not until late spring do the beautiful lacy green leaves appear. In fall, before they drop, they change to yellow. In bloom the black locust is one of the prettiest trees of temperate regions. Its white flowers hang in a profusion of miniature wisteria-like clusters and in early summer scent the air with their delicious fragrance. They are succeeded by clusters of hairless, brown pods that remain through the winter. Black locust produces an abundance of suckers from its roots, and colonies spread by this means. After specimens are felled sucker development is likely to be especially vigorous. This characteristic, together with the ability of the species to adapt itself to poor, infertile soils, has led foresters to employ it for erosion control.

Shipmast locust (*R. p. rectissima*) is one of the most noteworthy of the many varieties of black locust. This was not formally described until 1936, although foresters and other practical tree men recognized it long before. Botanists have difficulty finding characters to distinguish this variety from the typical species. It has a solitary, more erect and straighter trunk, less flared at its base, and a narrower crown as well as thicker, more deeply furrowed bark and greener sepals to its fewer flowers than the typical species. The shipmast locust rarely produces seeds. Its heartwood is canary-yellow rather than brownish or olive-brown, and its sapwood is comparatively thin.

Other varieties of black locust are these: *R. p. bessoniana* has an ovoid head of spineless branches; *R. p.* 'Burgundy' has deep pink flowers; *R. p.* 'Frisia' has orange branchlets with red spines and bright yellow foliage; *R. p. inermis* (syn. *R. p. spectabilis*) has spineless branchlets; *R. p. monophylla fastigiata* (syn. *R. p. erecta*) is a narrow, columnar tree with leaves of one to few leaflets; *R. p. pendula* has somewhat drooping branches; *R. p. pyramidalis* (syn. *R. p. fastigiata*), columnar, has spineless branches; *R. p. rehderi* is low and nearly spherical; *R. p. semperflorens* blooms intermittently through most of the summer; *R. p. tortuosa*, with short, contorted

Robinia pseudoacacia tortuosa

branches, grows slowly; and *R. p. umbraculifera* has a somewhat spherical head, denser than that of rather similar *R. p. bessoniana*, of stouter, spineless branches. It seldom blooms.

Hybrid **R. ambigua,** its parents *R. pseudoacacia* and *R. viscosa*, is a tree with slightly sticky shoots and small spines. Its leaves have six to ten pairs of leaflets. The flowers are pale pink. Variety *R. a. bellarosea* has larger, deeper pink flowers and much stickier branchlets. Variety *R. a. decaisneana* (syns. *R. pseudoacacia decaisneana, R. decaisneana*) has pale rose-pink blooms. The flowers of *P. a. idahoensis* (syn. *P. pseudoacacia idahoensis*) are pink to lavender.

Clammy locust (**R. viscosa**), a native of the southeastern United States, is sometimes 40 feet in height. It has dark red-brown branches and a dense sticky cover-

Robinia ambigua decaisneana

Robinia viscosa (flowers)

Robinia viscosa (fruits)

ing of glandular hairs on its young shoots and usually on its leafstalks, flower stalks, and seed pods. It is often spineless or it may have small spines. The leaves, usually pubescent beneath, have thirteen to twenty-five ovate leaflets each. The attractive flowers have red calyxes and pink corollas with a yellow blotch on the upper petal. Despite its southern origin, the clammy locust is hardy into southern Canada.

Rose-acacia (**R. hispida**) is one of the most beautiful species in flower. A shrub up to 7 feet tall with bristly-hairy, but not sticky shoots, this has leafstalks and flower stalks clothed with bristly hairs. The leaves are of seven to thirteen hairless or nearly hairless leaflets. The flowers vary from

Robinia hispida (flowers)

rose-pink to pale purplish-pink. Only rarely do glandular-hairy pods develop. The rose-acacia produces a great abundance of root suckers. Variety *R. h. macrophylla* has slightly bigger leaflets and flowers and is almost without bristly hairs. These are hardy through most of New England. About as hardy is **R. kelseyi,** a highly decorative shrub, a native of North Carolina, which has rose-pink flowers and pods densely covered with purple hairs. About 10 feet in height, this differs from rose-acacia in its shoots not being glandular, bristly, or sticky. Hairless, they are furnished with some slender prickles.

Additional sorts are these: **R. boyntonii** is a shrub 10 feet tall with hairless or minutely-pubescent shoots, leaves with seven to thirteen leaflets, glandular-hairy pods, and pink or rose-purple and white flowers. It is native from North Carolina to Georgia and Alabama. **R. elliottii,** about 4½ feet tall, has hairless or pubescent, but not bristly, wandlike branches, leaves with eleven to fifteen leaflets, rose-purple or white flowers, and bristly pods. It is native from North Carolina to Georgia. **R. hartwegii,** native from North Carolina to Alabama, is a shrub up to 12 feet tall with

Robinia hartwegii (flowers)

the mid-veins of its leaves, stalks of its rosy-purple flowers, and seed pods thickly covered with stalked glands. *R. holdtii,* a hybrid between *R. luxurians* and *R. pseudoacacia,* originated before 1890. It is a tree with pink flowers. *R. luxurians,* native from Colorado to Utah and New Mexico, is a shrub or tree up to 30 feet in height with glandular-pubescent or viscid shoots, leaves of fifteen to twenty-one leaflets, and pale pink to almost white flowers. *R. neomexicana,* a shrub about 6 feet tall, is closely related to *R. luxurians.* A native of New Mexico, it has grayish-pubescent branches, leaves of nine to fifteen leaflets, pink flowers, and smooth or sparsely-hairy pods.

Garden and Landscape Uses. Despite its obvious merits, very careful consideration should be given before planting black locust. It is extremely susceptible to two serious pests difficult to control, the locust borer and the locust leaf miner. The former causes tremendous damage by tunneling into trunk and branches and seriously weakens and eventually kills infested trees; the leaf miner mars the beauty of the foliage in late summer. Where these pests are prevalent, maintenance care of black locusts is likely to be high. Black locust is attractive as a single specimen, and in groups or groves, it casts light shade. It seems that its roots have a harmful effect on conifers, in any case these and black locusts do not grow well in close association.

Other robinias are useful for screening and for the graceful appearance of their lacy foliage and summer flowers. Some, especially rose-acacia, may be troublesome in some areas because of the invasive character of the suckers that spring from the roots. In other places, for example where it is desired to stabilize a bank or provide a screen, this very quality may be advantageous.

Cultivation. Robinias thrive best in deep, fertile, well-drained soil, but they tolerate much poorer land and indeed must be accounted among the most-likely-to-be-successful trees and shrubs for dry and comparatively barren sites. Like most members of the pea family, they have on their roots nodules in which live nitrogen-fixing bacteria, an arrangement that enables the tree or shrub to secure part of its nitrogen needs from the air instead of being, as most plants are, wholly dependent upon the soil. Locusts are sun-lovers; they do not prosper in shade. They transplant easily and in their early years grow rapidly. At transplanting time it is well to prune them severely. No regular systematic pruning is necessary later, but if any becomes desirable it may be done with the sure knowledge that the cut trunks and branches will respond with an abundance of new growth. Locusts are easy to raise from seeds sown in spring in sandy soil. They can also be increased by

transplanting suckers that arise from the roots. Root cuttings are successful with many kinds, and horticultural varieties can be grafted onto seedlings or onto pieces of root in the greenhouse in winter or early spring.

Diseases and Pests. Diseases that attack locusts include cankers, leaf spots, powdery mildews, wood decay, and a virus-caused witches broom condition. In addition to locust borer and locust leaf miner, discussed under Garden and Landscape Uses, they may be infested with insects that cause galls and with scale insects.

ROBINSONELLA (Robinson-élla). To the mallow family MALVACEAE belongs *Robinsonella,* a genus of seven species of much-branched shrubs and small trees, native from Mexico to Costa Rica. The name honors Dr. Benjamin Lincoln Robinson, American botanist, who died in 1935.

Robinsonellas have alternate, undivided, generally ovate to rounded, sometimes lobed leaves with five or seven main veins radiating from their bases. The white to rosy-purple flowers are in panicles or small clusters. Each has five deep calyx lobes, five petals, and a column of many united stamens surrounding the pistil. The fruits consist of nine to thirteen thin carpels much inflated at maturity.

A variable tree 15 to 40 feet tall and about as wide, *R. cordata,* of Mexico, is cultivated in southern California and perhaps elsewhere. It has pointed-ovate, softly-hairy leaves slightly lobed near their ends, with stalks about 2 inches long. The flowers, in twos or threes on short branchlets, are 1½ to 2 inches across and pale lilac, rosy-purple, or rarely white. Differing in its numerous 1-inch-wide, white, or lilac-veined, white flowers being in leafy panicles up to 1 foot long from the leaf axils, *R. lindeniana,* of Central America, a slender tree 18 to 30 feet tall, has rather rough-hairy, broad-ovate to nearly round, deeply- to shallowly-lobed leaves, the largest up to about 9 inches long. Their undersides are densely-hairy, the upper sides sparsely so. Variety *R. l. divergens* (syn. *R. edentula*) is a tree with slightly three-lobed or lobeless leaves and more crowded panicles of bloom.

Garden and Landscape Uses and Cultivation. Although not frequent in cultivation, robinsonellas are worth planting wherever the climate is suitable for their beautiful displays of bloom. They succeed in ordinary well-drained soils in sunny locations and are increased by seed and by cuttings.

ROBLE is *Platymiscium pinnatum.* Roble amarillo is *Tecoma stans.*

ROCAMBOLE. Sometimes called giant-garlic, rocambole (*Allium scorodoprasum*), a native of Europe, Asia Minor, and the

Caucasus, is little known in North America. An onion relative, it is cultivated for its strongly-flavored bulbs used for the same purposes as those of garlic.

The underground bulbs, like bulbs of garlic, form cloves (clusters of bulblets contained within a common skin). The stems, up to about 3 feet tall, are furnished below their middles with flat or keeled leaves ⅓ inch wide or wider and with their upper parts spirally twisted. They terminate in an umbel of small bulblets, of bulblets interspersed with a few purple, six-petaled, bell-shaped flowers, or more rarely of all flowers. Seeds are seldom produced.

Cultivation is very easy. In earliest spring or in mild climates in fall, separate the cloves into segments and plant in a sunny place in moderately fertile soil in rows 1 foot to 1½ feet apart with 6 to 8 inches between individuals in the rows. Alternatively, plant bulblets from the tops of the stems, but these take longer to develop into sizable cloves.

Summer care consists of keeping down weeds. When in late summer or fall the leaves die naturally, lift the bulbs, dry them in the sun, and store in trays or suspended in net bags or old stockings in a cool, dry cellar or similar place.

ROCHEA (Ròch-ea). All natives of South Africa, and so admired there that the law forbids collecting them, the four species of *Rochea* belong in the orpine family CRASSULACEAE. The name honors François de la Roche, a French botanical author, who died in 1813. For this reason it is preferable that it be pronounced with a soft "ch" rather than with the hard "k" sound so often used.

From closely related *Crassula,* rocheas differ in having petals united at least to

Rochea coccinea

their middles into a tube, but they are tenuously joined; they separate as the flowers age. The upper parts of the petals spread widely in the manner of those of phlox flowers.

The genus *Rochea* consists of somewhat succulent subshrubs with opposite, undivided leaves, and upturned flowers in dense, terminal heads. Each bloom has a five-parted calyx, a corolla with five petals very much longer than the calyx, five stamens, and five pistils. The fruits are pod-like structures called follicles. The plant sometimes called *R. falcata* is *Crassula falcata*.

Excellent for pots in greenhouses and cool window gardens, **R. coccinea** (syns. *Kalosanthes coccinea, Crassula coccinea*) is a native of Table Mountain. Taken in the early part of the eighteenth century to Europe, it has been popular there since, but it is less well known in North America. Showy and attractive, this species, 1 foot to 2 feet tall, has red stems thickly clothed for much or all of their lengths with overlapping, ovate leaves 1 inch to 1½ inches long, spreading or up-pointing, and in four distinct rows. The bright scarlet flowers are almost 2 inches long and one-half as wide. They are in small clusters in heads, 3 inches or more across, at the branch ends.

Other kinds, rarer in cultivation, are **R. versicolor**, a hybrid with longer leaves than *R. coccinea* and usually white, fragrant flowers that are red, pink, or yellowish on the undersides of the petals, or sometimes are red throughout; **R. jasminea**, with spatula-shaped leaves ¾ inch long with hairy margins, and fragrant, white blooms that fade to pink; and less beautiful **R. odoratissima**, which has ascending, pointed-linear leaves up to 1½ inches long by under ¼ inch broad, and yellowish to pinkish blooms. Hybrids between *R. coccinea* and *R. jasminea* have been cultivated.

Garden Uses. Rocheas are highly satisfactory for greenhouse and window garden embellishment. They are suitable for outdoor flower beds, rock gardens, and similar plantings in areas with warm, dry, frost-free climates. They flower freely in spring or summer and are attractive in bloom for three or four weeks.

Cultivation. These plants can be raised from seed, but cuttings root so readily at any time that they are used more commonly. To have good plants in bloom the following spring or summer, cuttings taken from April to June are planted in sand, sand and peat moss, or other rooting medium. They are shaded from strong sun and kept moist, but not wet, in a temperature of 55 to 60°F where the air is moderately, but not oppressively humid. There is no need to keep them in a propagating case or under an inverted glass jar as is done with cuttings of many plants. The cuttings soon root and then are potted in porous, sandy, peaty soil in 2½- or 3-inch pots. As soon as new growth begins, the tips of the young plants are pinched out to force branching. Exposure to full sun in

a well-ventilated greenhouse or sunny window, or outdoors during the summer, provides a suitable environment for the young plants. They are transferred to successively bigger pots as the ones they occupy become well filled with roots. The soil used should be coarse, porous, fertile, and of a loamy, peaty character. By early September the plants should be ready for 5- or 6-inch containers. Throughout the growing season water moderately, the objective being to avoid long periods of saturation without permitting the earth to become really dry. Plants grown outdoors in summer are brought inside before frost. From late fall to late winter they are kept where the night temperature is 40 to 45°F and by day not over five to ten degrees higher. During that period water sparingly. Beginning in March or April, a temperature of 50 to 55°F at night and a few degrees higher by day, together with more generous watering and biweekly or weekly applications of dilute liquid fertilizer, are in order. Large specimen plants in 9- or 10-inch pots can be grown by preventing the plants from blooming the second spring by pinching out the tips of the shoots, potting them on, and keeping them growing until their third year before they are allowed to develop flowers.

An alternative method of cultivation involves rooting cuttings in late spring, potting about five in a 5-inch pot, and growing them without pinching under the conditions described above.

ROCK. The word rock forms parts of the common names of these plants: rock beauty (*Petrocallis*), rock-brake (*Cryptogramma*), rock-cress (*Arabis*), rock-jasmine (*Androsace*), rock-lily (*Arthropodium cirrhatum*), rock-pink (*Phlox subulata*), rock-rose (*Cistus*), rock-spirea (*Holodiscus discolor*), and rock spray (*Cotoneaster horizontalis*).

ROCK AND ALPINE GARDENS. Gardens in which rocks and plants appropriate to them are the chief landscape elements are called rock gardens or sometimes, if the plants are entirely or mainly sorts that grow natively at high altitudes or under subarctic or arctic conditions, alpine gardens. Well planned and well executed rock gardens are aesthetically agreeable as well as horticulturally stimulating, but when ill-considered and poorly developed, they are likely to represent the nadir of landscape gardening.

The satisfactions of rock gardening lie not alone in creating and maintaining pleasing landscapes, but also in developing intimate acquaintance with and caring for the plants accommodated. At its best, rock gardening is a splendid hobby, not excessively demanding, yet sufficiently challenging to reward reasonable dedication and attention.

Because the plants used are chiefly small,

many sorts can be accommodated in quite limited areas. This appeals to gardeners with a well-developed instinct for collecting, a commendable expression of horticultural interest displayed by many amateurs.

Another attraction of rock gardening is that, apart from initial construction perhaps, the tasks connected with it are generally light and agreeable. Most can be accomplished while puttering around the garden at odd hours rather than by working for longer periods on more fixed time schedules as some other types of gardening demand.

Historically, rock gardening began in the British Isles, its development an outcome of the greatly increased numbers of travelers from there who from early in the nineteenth century on visited Switzerland and other mountainous parts in Europe. Enamored by the great wealth of beautiful alpine plants they saw, unknown in their own countries, they were inspired to bring some back and attempt to grow them at home.

Because of a nearly complete lack of understanding of the needs of alpine and other mountain plants most early attempts at domesticating them were dismal failures. A few of the toughest and more adaptable sorts survived in the generally atrocious "rockeries" built by Victorians, but in the main those horticultural conceits, which sometimes included grottos, arches, bridges, and other elaborate architectural features, became graveyards for the choicer alpines enthusiasts had plucked from their mountain homes.

But gradually improvement came. As early as 1870, William Robinson, in his book *Alpine Flowers for English Gardens*, attempted to give some guidance, and by the early years of the twentieth century, an altogether better appreciation of the needs of mountain plants had developed and skills in cultivating them improved. Nevertheless, for a long time, rock gardens continued to be poorly made and many esthetically unsatisfactory ones were established, as, sadly, are some modern ones. The least attractive belong in the groups the inspired English authority Reginald Farrer characterized as the almond pudding, dog's grave, and devil's lapful styles and that later in America became known as peanut-brittle rock gardens.

Before the end of the first decade of the twentieth century, capable Europeans were advocating sound principles for constructing and planting rock gardens and for caring for plants appropriate to them. Among the books in that decade are *My Rock Garden*, by Reginald Farrer, whose famous garden was in Yorkshire, England, and *Rock Gardens* by Lewis Meredith, who gardened in County Wicklow, Ireland.

Completed in 1913, but not published until six years later, Farrer's book *The En-*

In the Thompson Memorial Rock Garden, The New York Botanical Garden

glish Rock Garden became the bible of rock gardeners everywhere. A master of English prose, the author stimulated thousands to attempt the cultivation of the plants he so beautifully, entrancingly, and sometimes extravagantly described.

Another benchmark was the publication, in English, in 1930, of *Rock Garden and Alpine Plants* by Henri Correvon, the distinguished Swiss pioneer in the cultivation of alpine plants. As early as 1877, Correvon exhibited at a horticultural flower show in Geneva a small collection of alpines he had grown from seeds, for which pains he was accounted "a young enthusiast who does not realize the needs of the gardening world." Nevertheless, at the urging of one of the judges who thought the Société d'Horticulture de Genève should "give him something as evidence that the Société is interested in encouraging young beginners," Correvon was awarded a prize, four little silver teaspoons.

In North America, interest in rock gardens began later than in Europe, yet in 1890 an example patterned after that at the Royal Botanic Gardens, Kew, England, but much smaller, was constructed at Smith College Botanic Garden, Northampton, Massachusetts. In the 1920s, another was installed at the Brooklyn Botanic Garden

in New York City, and in 1932, construction began on the Thompson Memorial Rock Garden at The New York Botanical Garden in New York City. It is interesting to note that the men who designed these gardens and supervised their construction and planting, Robert Cameron, Montague Free, and Thomas H. Everett, respectively, were all graduates of the school of horticulture at the Royal Botanic Gardens, Kew, England.

Part of the rock garden at the Brooklyn Botanic Garden

Meanwhile keen amateurs were furthering the cause of rock gardening in America; among pioneers in the East were Clarence Lown, of Poughkeepsie, New York, F. Cleveland Morgan, of Montreal, Canada, Louise Beebe Wilder, of Bronxville, New York, and Mrs. Clement Houghton, of Boston, Massachusetts. On the West Coast others were experimenting with rock gardens. The publication in 1923 of Mrs. Wilder's delightful book *The Rock Garden* and the many other writings of this competent cultivator and talented author stimulated many Americans to engage in the new hobby.

Other circumstances that in the period between the two world wars encouraged the rapid expansion of enthusiasm for rock gardening were the organization, in 1934, of the American Rock Garden Society and the truly marvelous examples of planted rock gardens staged as exhibits at the great spring flower shows at Boston, New York, and Philadelphia, by the superb artists of rock garden design and construction, Marcel Le Piniac, Ralph Hancock, and Zenon Schrieber. The American Rock Garden Society continues to flourish and to attract to its membership people interested in its special field.

Partly because of climate, which in many parts of North America precludes or makes extremely difficult the cultivation of many true alpines that are the glories of European rock gardens, and partly because of the availability of numerous charming small plants native to the continent that are not alpines, most American rock gardeners wisely do not limit their plantings to inhabitants of high mountains, but include other neat and choice kinds that look as if they properly belong. And this is as it should be.

Traditionally, and as generally interpreted, rock gardening involves the cultivation of mountain plants and other low sorts that withstand severe winter cold with impunity. It is thought of as belonging only in temperate climates, and this of course is true if alpines are to be accommodated.

But viewed as an art form based on the agreeable use of rocks in the landscape, the development of rock gardens is as appropriate in warm-temperate, subtropical, and tropical climates as in temperate ones. Certainly there are many places in such regions where cliffs, outcropping rocks, and similar formations are as inspiring as those of colder regions, and the principles of adapting or constructing such features as garden landscapes are not different.

The kinds of plants to employ in warm climates quite obviously differ from those useful in colder ones, but plenty are available. Fit choices to local conditions. In desert and semidesert areas, cactuses and other succulents in nearly endless array are obvious possibilities. They look especially well in association with rocks. For humid warm climate regions, there are available just as many sorts of plants appropriate for displaying in rocky environments. They include ferns, as well as many kinds of begonias, gesneriads, peperomias, and other plants, many of which as wildlings inhabit cliffs and other rock features.

There are two chief types of rock gardens, natural and artificial. The first represents the development of sites on which native rocks are prominent as outcrops, cliffs, or perhaps strewn boulders. The others are made in areas in which all or most of the rocks used must be imported.

Existence of a site of the first description is reason enough for adapting it as a rock garden, but constructed gardens are generally only justified by a genuine desire to grow and display small plants the majority of which are not well suited for flower beds and borders. There are sometimes rockless sites, such as banks and steep slopes, where the development of a rock garden presents less problems than other treatments.

To begin a natural rock garden, first make a careful survey of the site and identify the plants growing there. Some, especially well-located, deep-rooted trees such as oaks and hickories that can be relied upon to provide light shade for part or all of each day in summer, besides adding to the charm and perhaps majesty of the area, should be preserved, but remove overcrowded, spindly specimens and weedy sorts of little garden merit along with tangles of brushwood and similar undesirable growth. There may be too, evergreen or deciduous shrubs or herbaceous perennials, such as ferns, bulbs, and other wildlings, that should be retained where they are or transplanted elsewhere.

Clearing the area of unwanted vegetation may then be done by digging out completely all roots as well as tops. Then give attention to any pruning retained trees and shrubs need. Cut out all dead and seriously diseased wood and, if desirable, thin out branches from dense specimens. It is often advantageous to provide for more side light by removing some lower branches to "raise the heads" of trees that cast too dense shade.

Rearrangement of a few rocks, or even supplementing those on the site with others brought in, is permissible, but it must be done so skillfully that even persons knowledgeable about natural formations cannot easily detect the artifice. Transported rocks must match precisely those of the site and be positioned as though placed by nature.

Improving the soil is the next order of business. Unless you are dedicated to growing plants that need quite different types of soil than what you have, do not attempt drastic changes in its basic character. For example, if it is naturally acid or alkaline accept the condition and select plants adapted to it. Concentrate on bettering soil texture where needed by mixing in such additives as chips of crushed rock, coarse sand, perlite, or, for alkaline soil plants, crushed limestone or crushed clam or oyster shells. For woodland or moorland plants, add generous amounts of leaf mold, peat moss, compost, or similar organic material.

Make certain there is adequate depth of soil, especially in the crevices and crannies you intend to plant. It is usually desirable to rake out existing soil and, if necessary after deepening or enlarging the clefts or crevices, to replace it with a better mix packed firmly so no voids are left.

Planting is best done in early fall or early spring, but not until disturbed ground has had time to settle or before it is reasonably certain that it is essentially free of pestiferous perennial weeds. Whenever practicable, it is advantageous to allow an entire growing season to elapse between the preparation of the site and actual planting. This permits clearing the soil of weeds and ensuring clean planting areas by pulling up or hoeing off every one as soon as it shows aboveground.

The sorts of plants appropriate for natural rock gardens are likely to include many native to the region as well as others that thrive under similar conditions. In selected spots and corners, avid rock gardeners are likely to try a few more challenging sorts.

To be convincing, placement of the plants calls for an appreciation of how vegetation is disposed on natural rocky sites. Seek inspiration from such places, noting the unstrained informality that prevails. Here, irregular drifts of low plants may carpet the soil surface or occupy ledges, shelves, or miniature plateaus, with very likely outlying smaller groups or individuals, often at lower levels or to the lee of the main groups, the outcome of seeds that have fallen and been washed away or have drifted down from the main colonies. Note how plants run along narrow crevices or congregate at the bases of miniature cliffs. Without slavishly copying such native features, let your natural rock garden epitomize them and represent a distillation of what is good about what you find in the wild, miniaturized and tailored to accommodate the plants you want to grow.

Rock gardens constructed on sites devoid of native rock or where little is present clearly offer opportunities for imaginative development, yet in such places the most inappropriate examples are often perpetrated. Farrer's almond pudding, dog's grave, and devil's lapful styles unfortunately are usual in rockless country and often even where native rocks that should supply inspiration are more plentiful.

Following Farrer's castigation, the better examples of British rock gardens were made in what their builders fondly imagined was a natural fashion, but because many of those who made such gardens failed to study rock formations as they occur in the wild, they were usually unconvincing.

At first, great emphasis was placed on creating "pockets" to be planted with individual kinds of plants and the structure was likely to consist of a series of such little flat or nearly flat terraces backed by and supported by more or less vertical walls of stone. Such was the rock garden at the Royal Botanic Garden, Kew, England, until the 1930s, and many others constructed in Great Britain and elsewhere followed the same general plan. The pockets, frequently referred to in garden writings of the time, were well drained and bottomless so the soil with which they were filled connected directly with the main body of earth beneath and made it entirely practicable for plants to grow and flourish, but the overall esthetic effect was rarely satisfactory. But gradually improvement came, and between the two world wars, gardens more suggestive of native rock formations were developed both in Europe and America.

The choice of a site for a rock garden may be wide or limited depending upon the extent and character of the property. The advice so often given in older writings to locate the garden well out of sight of buildings and other formal features, is, on small grounds, often not tenable, and certainly is not essential to success in cultivating alpines and other rock garden plants.

It is by no means necessary to duplicate or even approximate an alpine scene to achieve a satisfying and beautiful rock garden. Such styles may be admirable in suitable surroundings, but so are rock gardens of other types. It is even possible to install a garden adjacent to a building or cropping out of a lawn without being incongruous, possibilities earlier advocates of rock gardens and some contemporaries completely reject. Furthermore, garden features suitable for embellishment with rock plants that make no pretense of naturalness, and yet are congruous and beautiful, can be developed. To this category belong what are known as dry walls, of which more will be discussed later. See also the Encyclopedia entry Wall Gardens.

A secret of success of rock gardens that aspire to naturalness, be they near or remote from man-made structures, be they large or small, is the placement of the rocks. To be convincing the effect *must* be that they were positioned by nature without aid from man. Here, if ever, true art is to conceal art.

The surest ways of obtaining such effects are (1) to use the same type of rock throughout the garden or at least throughout major parts of it, (2) to position each piece so that it appears stable and, except for minor crevices, connected with neighboring pieces aboveground such that the whole apparently represents the exposed part of a massive underground formation, and (3) if the rock be stratified, to lay the pieces with the strata lines all in one direction. Granted, because of geological or other disturbances the disposition of rocks in the wild does not always conform to these principles, the departure from them, unless carried out very skillfully by one who has carefully studied natural deviations from them, is very likely to produce uneasy, unconvincing effects.

Especially appropriate sites for rock gardens are slopes, banks, and small valleys or dells, natural or created, but flat areas can also be utilized. A first necessity is to evaluate the area, particularly with reference to any contouring that may be desirable. If a pool, stream, or waterfall is contemplated, and these can add greatly to the charms of rock gardens, their locations and courses must be planned, and so, especially if the garden is sizable, must be paths needed to enjoy and service the area.

Contouring is usually best achieved by stripping and stockpiling the topsoil,

Construction of the Thompson Memorial Rock Garden at The New York Botanical Garden: (a) In a broad, shallow valley, ground was broken in late summer 1932; the only native rock outcrop can be seen in the background

(b) Throughout the winter, rocks were collected and brought to the site on a horse-drawn, low-slung, flat-bed cart

(c) A block and tackle suspended from a wooden tripod was used to position the rocks

(d) A rock being positioned

(e) Meanwhile, soil made agreeable by the addition of sifted coal cinders (to improve porosity) and organic material was screened and made ready

fashioning the undersoil to the convolutions and grades deemed appropriate (this may involve bringing in additional material), then after modifying it in any way that seems desirable, and if necessary supplying additional soil to achieve a depth of at least 1 foot, replacing the topsoil. Modification, if the soil is not sufficiently porous, will involve mixing in generous amounts of coarse sand, grit, or small chips of stone, and if woodland plants are to be grown probably the admixture of leaf mold, peat moss, or other suitable partially decayed organic material. If a section of the garden is to be devoted to plants that need alkaline soil, crushed limestone or limestone chips may be included in the topsoil mix.

The kind of rock used is usually determined by availability. Where choice may be had, one that is porous, rather than such hard, impervious types as granite and schist, is to be preferred. Hard sandstones, millstone grits, and not excessively soluble limestones are very satisfactory. But remember, limestones, and waterworn limestone is one of the most beautiful rocks, are distasteful or unacceptable to such acid-soil plants as heaths, heathers, and rhododendrons. Tufa, a soft, light-weight, porous limestone-type rock formed by calcium carbonate deposited in springs and streams, is easy to handle and congenial to plants, but of undistinguished appearance. Harder rocks can be used, but take longer to weather because they are less encouraging to the growth of mosses, lichens, and other primitive vegetation that soon conceals freshly exposed portions of softer rocks.

Unless no other is available do not use newly quarried rock. Its raw surfaces are likely to take a long time to weather and, even worse, may display marks of drilling. Weathered pieces collected from the surface of the ground and of a character and color that suggest age are likely to be ideal. In some parts of the country suitable material can be obtained from old stone walls. The pieces must be of manageable

(f) As the work proceeded, but prior to planting, the rockwork seemed to some to be too massive; note the original rock outcrop at the top, right of center, and the beginning of the construction of a waterfall, just left of center

(g) Part of the waterfall with new planting established

Types of rock that may be used include: (a) Hard sandstone

(c) Even less porous rocks such as schist

sizes and of acceptable relation to the size of the garden, although here some "cheating" can be done for, by careful placement, it is possible to arrange several comparatively small rocks so skillfully that they appear to be a creviced bigger one. When the chinks between them are filled with plants that effect is greatly enhanced.

Boulders are generally considered unsatisfactory for rock gardens, and certainly they should not be mixed with angular rocks, but if boulders are all that is available it is not impossible to fashion a con-

(b) Water-worn limestone

In the Thompson Memorial Rock Garden: (a) Installing rocks, about two dozen in all

(b) Produces the effect of a massive outcrop

(c) Abundant plant growth masks minor faults and "ties" the rocks together

vincing garden from them as was done at the Brooklyn Botanic Garden.

The secret is to use boulders of different sizes and to position them, some partly buried, some exposed, as they would be in the bed of a dry stream or wash. Let the areas between the stones slope gently except for some accumulations of what represent washed-down, stony, gravelly, or sandy soil piled on the "upstream" sides of boulders. These accumulations may be level-topped or even tilted slightly against the prevailing slope.

Take care not to scar rocks when collecting and handling them. To minimize this danger it may be worthwhile wrapping choice pieces in burlap. Use crowbars, often necessary for levering large pieces, although sometimes staves of wood or pieces of two-by-four can be used for this purpose, with care to avoid bruising the rocks. If possible have rocks delivered to the tops of slopes. It is easier to move them downhill than up.

When constructing the garden, do not distribute the rock evenly throughout; instead, make massive use of it in some parts, employ it sparingly or not at all in others. Take a cue from natural rocky places where accumulations of detritus and washed or blown soil form slopes and terraces about and between bold protrusions of rock. In gardens, rockless areas afford relief to the eye, splendid opportunities for planting attractively, and by contrast give seemingly greater massiveness and importance to the rocky portions.

Areas that lend themselves to rocklessness or to not more than suspicions of rock poking through the surface are gentle slopes downward and backward from the tops of cliffs, moraine-type slopes forward and downward from the fronts of cliffs, valley-like depressions between outcrops, and little flats bordering streams and pools.

Install the most massive features of the garden first. These may include bold outcrops, cliffs, and perhaps a waterfall. Give

An alpine meadow-like area provides visual relief from rock outcrops in the Thompson Memorial Rock Garden

Pools and watercourses call for special thought. The supply may be natural, piped in, or recycled by a pump. If artificial, be sure its source is concealed. With careful planning, a comparatively small flow can be managed so that it is seen more than once to give the impression that the garden is much better supplied with water than it really is.

When placing the rocks begin at the low parts of slopes and work upward, carefully setting each piece with its most attractive weathered side exposed and, so far as consistent with naturalness, with its top sloped slightly backward to direct rain or water from sprinklers to the roots. With this same thought in mind avoid overhangs that keep water from reaching rock faces below them.

Strive to achieve a feeling of stability. Leave no impression that the rocks are separate pieces susceptible to being easily loosened and removed. This is most surely done, so far as practicable, by setting each with its broadest side as its base, a positioning that suggests the most common aspect of exposed portions of outcropping rocks and the usual attitude of surface rocks in the wild. To achieve stability, with the rocks in their best possible positions, it is sometimes desirable to prop a large rock on several smaller ones and then to fill the voids with firmly-packed soil.

A variation of this procedure that, if skillfully done, carries conviction and is highly satisfactory, is to stand flat rocks, much thinner than long or wide, on edge

Here the effect of a rocky alpine field with an inconspicuous path and an abundance of low flowering plants is achieved

special attention to the location of the last as well as to other water features. Water spouting from the top of a hill or cliff is all wrong; it lacks the appearance of naturalness. To seem plausible, there must be, or by skillful construction or planting the viewer must be led to believe there is, a catchment area of considerable size above the point of emergence to account for the volume of water.

A small waterfall adds life to this rock garden

A small flow of water tumbling into small pools at different levels gives the impression of a much larger volume of water

with their most attractive broad sides facing outward to form miniature cliffs. In this way height is achieved with much less bulk of stone than is required if one or two or more superimposed pieces are set widest side down to produce similar effects. When using flakes take special care to set them in positions of repose that allow of no easy disturbance. This is particularly important in regions where strong outward thrusting comes from the soil freezing deeply.

No matter how individual pieces are positioned, they must relate to each other as though representing bedrock exposed by natural weathering or as a result of gulleying by water or wind. This means the major rock faces will have the same general direction throughout the garden, and if the stone shows lines of stratification they will be at the same angle throughout. Minor exceptions are when rocks represent pieces broken away from the main body and that angle downward from the clifflike margins of a gullied stream or have tumbled from a cliff to repose on a slope or plateau below.

Fairly small rocks may be effectively employed to give the impression of being a bold outcrop, as here in the Royal Botanic Garden, Edinburgh, Scotland

Although it is true that natural outcrops occur in which, as a result of geological upheavals, their lines of stratification run vertically or nearly so, and there are others in which they are approximately horizontal, it is much easier and generally makes for the most satisfactory accommodation of a considerable variety of plants if in constructed rock gardens they are established at an angle of from ten to forty

Rocks, all at a similar angle, produce the effect of a massive outcrop

degrees from the horizontal. This means of course that the joints between the long sides of adjacent stones will run similarly, which emphasizes the stratification.

In natural formations of stratified rock, fractures, called primary joints, spaced from 1 foot or so to up to about 5 feet apart, commonly occur along the sides of uptilted masses, but not along their faces. These are at right angles to the lines of stratification and cleft the rock into approximately rectangular blocks. They may be simulated in constructed rock gardens by positioning the ends of individual stones

to produce chinks and crevices that cross the lines of stratification at right angles and where exposed surfaces, which consist of superimposed pieces of rock, extend through more than one layer. To accomplish this, take care not to place the rocks like bricks in a wall with their vertical separations staggered, but have them above one another, with the chinks thus formed angling downward from the tilted top of the exposed rock.

The ends of uplifted masses of stratified rock show no regular system of primary joints, such as just described, but they may be creviced vertically by frost action or as a result of water running down them.

Whether the garden be big or whether it occupies no more space than an average living room, the principles discussed are applicable. Only scale differs. In large gardens, bolder features necessitating the use of larger rocks are needed, and by the same token, rockless or sparingly rocked portions can be more expansive.

The final effect must be one of rightness, of belonging. If the development adjoins a house or other building, make sure it seems that the rock is native and the structure was built upon it, rather than rocks have been brought in and piled or positioned against or in front of the building. And if your rock garden is to outcrop from a lawn or meadow, perhaps rising no more than a couple of feet or so above ground level, perhaps higher, let it, by the way it slopes into the ground, suggest firm ties with imaginary underlying bedrock.

A scree or moraine is often included as part of a rock garden. Such developments are patterned after natural features of the same names that occur in mountain regions. Their special characteristic depends upon the material of which they are formed and into which the plants root. This mostly consists of fragmented rock, in natural screes detritus collected in rock slides and at the bases of cliffs, and in moraines along the fronts and sides of glaciers. Natural moraines are further commonly characterized by having flowing through them some distance below the surface cold melt water from the ice. It is less natural for screes to have any constant flow beneath the surface.

Rock garden screes and moraines simulate to a degree natural ones. Their purpose is to provide plants with extremely well aerated rooting mixes of low fertility. Surface water should drain through them rapidly, leaving a film around each particle to meet the needs of the plants.

To make a scree, which may well slope away from the base of a clifflike rock or occupy a sloping gulley, install over a base of crushed stone or other very adequate drainage a foot or more of a mix consisting very largely of crushed stone or gravel, grit,

Rocks angled downward from each side give a realistic appearance to this reproduction of a mountain stream

and coarse sand with a small admixture of topsoil. Approximate proportions may well be one-half by bulk crushed stone or gravel, and one-quarter part each grit or sand and soil, but these proportions may be varied somewhat depending upon the character of ingredients.

A moraine, in the horticultural sense, differs from a scree, although the words

Shallow concrete basins at different levels, with water to eventually flow slowly from the highest to the lowest, are the basis of the moraine installed in this rock garden

A portion of a planted moraine

Two large rocks propped into place with smaller rocks, before soil is packed into the voids

are often used interchangeably, in that a foot or two below its surface there is a constant slow flow of water. This may be arranged by a shallow basin of concrete or one formed of clay or of earth covered with heavy polyethylene film as a base, with faucet or other source of a trickle of water supplying one end and an outlet at the other. To be most harmonious, arrange for the surface of the scree or moraine to slope gently away from the base of a cliff or down a gulley and have a few pieces of rock a little bigger than the average, of which the rooting mix largely consists, showing at the surface.

Planting a newly built rock garden is best, but not necessarily, delayed for a few weeks to allow for any settling of the soil or rocks that may occur. But if each rock is set on a firm base and the soil is packed well around it and between neighbor rocks there will be little, if any, movement and planting may begin as soon as convenient. Early spring and early fall are the most propitious seasons for this work.

When placing the plants keep two objectives in mind, any special needs of individual kinds and the overall effect you are creating. If the first is not respected, as for instance the need of dianthuses for exposure to sun, of primulas for some shade, of ramondas for a vertical crevice, of sorts finicky about the pH of the soil for acid or alkaline areas, and of other kinds for drier or moister soils, the growth, the flowering, and even the permanence of the plants may be adversely affected.

Endeavor to achieve a relaxed landscape, a feeling of naturalness. If too many single plants of different kinds are spotted around, or if there are not some areas, fair-sized in relation to the extent of the garden, clothed with low creepers such as thymes, creeping phloxes, or *Mazus* to afford rest for the eye, the effect will be too busy. If groups of the same kind are too equal in size, are of too formal an outline, or are of individuals too evenly spaced, the effect will be unnatural.

Some single specimens advantageously located may serve as special points of interest. Especially appropriate for such use

A selection of rock garden plants displayed as single specimens:
(a) A dwarf spruce (*Picea*)

(b) A dwarf boxwood (*Buxus*)

(c) *Campanula elatines fenestrellata*

(d) Edelweiss (*Leontopodium alpinum*)

(e) *Erinacea pungens*

(f) *Eriogonum umbellatum*

(g) *Primula auricula*

(h) *Umbilicus repestris*

are selected varieties of dwarf conifers, among them arborvitaes, cedars, false-cypresses, firs, hemlocks, junipers, pines, and spruces. Occasional individuals of other kinds of plants may be used similarly.

But for the most part, plant in informal groups and drifts that suggest a natural ecological association of kinds. This requires knowledge about how different sorts will grow after planting. You may have this information. If not, acquire as much as you can by observing other gardens and by reading.

Groups of iris and other flowering plants well placed near a rock garden cascade

Groups may drift down gentle slopes, with the plants closer together in the upper than the lower end of the group and with perhaps a few specimens irregularly placed some little distance from the low side of the main planting. Such outliers

Informal groups displayed to good advantage: (a) *Iberis sempervirens* on a rocky slope

(b) *Anemone pulsatilla*, the plants in the front suggesting chance seedlings

suggest the results of seeds dropped or washed from a higher place.

Other groups may occupy little plateaus, hang from the tops of cliffs, or follow crevices. They need not be clearly de-

Armeria maritima laucheana blooms freely on a small plateau

Alyssum serpyllifolium decorates the face of a cliff

fined. If adjacent groups mingle somewhat at their margins, and if an occasional plant of one crops up as it were as a seedling inside a group of another kind, the effect of naturalness is enhanced.

Crevice plantings: (a) *Phlox subulata* variety

(b) *Sempervivum*, unidentified species

No matter how knowledgeable and careful you are, it is not improbable that some errors of judgment will creep into your selection of spots for some plants, but if these be comparatively few they can be corrected later by transplanting to sites that afford better growing conditions or more appropriate display.

Choose times for planting when the soil is pleasantly damp, neither wet nor dust dry. Make sure the roots of plants dug in readiness for planting are protected from exposure to sun and wind. Space individuals with some regard for the amount of top growth they are expected to make. Do not break the balls of soil in which roots are growing, but spread roots not encased in soil in their natural positions and work soil between them. Set the plants at the same depths or very slightly deeper than they were previously, firm the soil around them, and soak with a fine spray of water.

Depending upon the kind of plant and the part of the rock garden it is to occupy, the surface between individual plants may be mulched lightly with chips or fragments of stone or, about woodland plants in shaded areas, with screened leaf mold or peat moss mixed with grit or coarse sand. For the best effect see that the stone chips consist of a mixture of sizes

and are of the same or closely matching kind of rock to that of which the garden is constructed.

Routine care of rock gardens demands regular attention, but not arduous toil. Beginning in late winter or early spring, the first task in regions of cold winters without an adequate blanket of snow is the removal of the winter covering. Do this before growth is well advanced and in two or three stages rather than all at one time, so that new shoots and foliage become gradually accustomed to full exposure.

Choose dull, humid, quiet days rather than sunny, windy ones for taking off the cover. Push back into place any plants that have been heaved up by frost action and replace any labels that have been disturbed.

Do not be in too great haste to cut back what appears to be the lifeless tops of woody-stemmed plants. Some may surprise you by leafing later. But if you are certain they are dead, do not hesitate, and at the same time clear away dead foliage and any weeds overlooked from the previous year.

Top-dressing is next. Prepare a porous mix of topsoil, peat moss, and grit or coarse sand as a base and modify it as needed for particular areas of the garden devoted to plants with special needs by adding additional peat moss for acid-soil plants, crushed limestone or agricultural lime for lovers of alkaline soils, bonemeal for plants likely to benefit from some extra nutrients, and for kinds known to appreciate richer diets, such as primulas, some old rotted or dried commercial cow manure. But beware of using too much fertilizer. The vast majority of rock garden plants thrive in rather lean soils and become too lush and gross in those too fertile. Before spreading the top-dressing, stir the soil shallowly with a hand cultivator so that the new layer will integrate with the old.

Summer care consists chiefly of weeding, watering (do this only when clearly needed and then soak the ground to a

Weeding in a rock garden with the aid of a small hand cultivator

depth of several inches), and taking off faded flowers, plus a certain amount of propagation. Weeding calls for special knowledge. In a garden containing many species and varieties it is not a job for a tyro or an odd-job man. Not infrequently, choice plants that perhaps have defied the gardener's best efforts to propagate reproduce voluntarily and one or more precious seedlings will appear in some unlikely spot, in a crevice, on a little plateau, or perhaps among some spreading plant of another kind. Only the keen eye of an experienced rock gardener is likely to detect such dividends, with the result that instead of being ruthlessly rooted out they are nurtured to add yet further glory to the garden. Besides, weeding in a rock garden can be a delightful task, one that gives opportunity to know one's plants more intimately, to observe their manners of growth, and to note their individual idiosyncrasies—that is, if weeding is done when it should be, at the very earliest

Plant spring-flowering bulbs of *Muscari* among carpeting *Mazus reptans* in fall

evidence of the weed growth and before it has begun to take over from the rightful occupants.

In the fall a general cleanup is needed. Cut back the dead tops of plants that are

Spreading salt hay for winter protection

not evergreen and make comfortable for the winter all that are perennial. This is the time, too, to plant hardy spring-flowering bulbs.

Winter protection in regions where hard freezing is experienced, but a continuous snow cover cannot be relied upon, is necessary, but it is easy to overdo this. Do not install the cover until the ground is frozen to a depth of 2 or 3 inches, otherwise mice or other rodents may establish winter quarters and harm plants. A covering of branches of evergreens (discarded Christmas trees are fine for this purpose), such as pines, spruces, or hemlocks, is ideal. Or salt hay can be used. It is important that air circulates freely through the covering. Common errors are to put it in place too early and too thickly.

Propagation is an important phase of rock gardening. Many of the very finest rock plants are comparatively short-lived or are fickle in cultivation. This makes it necessary always to have at hand a stock of young plants to replace those that may succumb to the heat and humidity of the summer, to the extreme conditions of winter, or to other causes. Raising young plants is fascinating work and makes a particular appeal to the real plant lover.

Rock garden plants are increased in several ways, and the method followed in any particular case will depend upon the character of the plant, the availability of propagating material, and the percentage of increase desired.

Plants of a mat-forming type, such as creeping thymes, *Mazus*, and *Draba repens*, are easily increased by a simple division of old sods. This method also serves splendidly for many kinds that form clumps, as do most veronicas, primulas, and asters. If more rapid increase is desired, or if divisions are not obtainable, cuttings afford an alternative method of securing additional stock. Seed provides an excellent means of obtaining stock of many wild species of plants, but it is not reliable for garden varieties or for improved kinds that you may want to grow. Then again, the species of certain genera hybridize very freely if they are grown near to one another, thus seed collected from any such species growing in a garden where others of the same genus are grown will very likely result in hybrid progeny of unpredictable characteristics and desirability. Dianthuses, aquilegias, saxifrages, and sempervivums are typical of this group.

Many rock garden plants can be propagated in the spring. September is also an excellent time to attend to this work, for at this season the trying conditions that have prevailed during July and August no longer have to be faced, and the young plants still have an opportunity to become established before the onset of winter. Stock of kinds known or suspected not to be reliably hardy must be established in pots

and plunged to the rims of the pots in a bed of ashes in a cold frame for the duration of the winter.

Division is, of course, the simplest means of propagation. All that is necessary is to lift the parent plant and carefully divide it into suitably sized portions, each with some roots attached. If the plant has a great deal of top growth, this is usually cut back somewhat to compensate for the unavoidable root disturbance caused by the operation. The divisions are then planted directly back into the rock garden or potted into the smallest size pot into which their roots can be comfortably fitted in a soil mixture similar to, but lighter than that in which established plants of the same kind are known to thrive. The addition to the soil mixture of a liberal proportion of grit or coarse sand ensures lightness. Shade from strong sunlight must be provided, at least until new roots have thoroughly taken possession of the medium in which divisions are growing.

A cutting is essentially a division without roots that, if placed in an appropriate environment, may be expected to develop a new root system. Until new roots are sent out, cuttings require special care, and every effort must be made to provide conditions favorable to root development. The medium in which cuttings are planted is usually clean, coarse sand or perlite kept constantly and evenly moist, but some kinds, for instance heaths and heathers, root more readily in a mixture of sand or perlite and peat moss. Protection from currents of moving air, shade from direct sunshine, and the maintenance of a humid atmosphere check excessive transpiration and evaporation. This is important because if the cutting continues to lose from its tissues more moisture than it is able to replace, it quickly withers and dies. A well-managed cold frame provides suitable conditions for rooting cuttings of a great many rock garden plants. If a considerable number are to be inserted, install a 3- to 4-inch-deep bed of the rooting medium in the frame. For lesser quantities, a flat will suffice. Be sure that the medium is moist and packed down firmly by pounding it with a brick or an equivalent tool.

The cuttings will vary in length according to kind, the smallest perhaps not exceeding ½ inch, the largest up to 3 inches. Cut them cleanly across with a keen knife or razor blade at the base just below a joint or node, and trim off the lower leaves. Plant them so the base of each sits squarely on the bottom of the hole it occupies, and pack the sand firmly against it. After the cuttings are planted, water them thoroughly with a fine spray and then cover the frame with the sash. In the beginning, ventilate not at all or at most sparingly and provide shade from direct sunshine. But when the cuttings com-

mence to form roots, more ventilation and less shade are in order and finally the young plants should be exposed to the ordinary outdoor conditions that suit their kind.

As soon as good root systems have developed, transplant the new plants into small pots. Use a gritty or sandy soil mix and make sure of good drainage by putting into the bottom of each pot a few crocks. After potting, sink the plants to the rims of their pots in ashes, sand, or peat moss in a cold frame.

Raising alpine and other rock garden plants from seed sometimes brings interesting problems, but it is impossible to generalize as to procedures except in the broadest way. Experience and observation suggest that the importance of compounding exact soil mixes to meet the requirements of individual species is frequently overstressed. In their early stages at least, the vast majority of plants can be successfully raised in one of three distinct types of soil. The first contains lime, preferably in the form of ground limestone, but ordinary builders lime will do. The second is free of lime, but contains an abundance of leaf mold or peat moss. The latter is particularly desirable for plants known to need an acid soil. The third is an ordinary, porous seed soil, such as you would use for the majority of garden annuals, but considerably more gritty. This type will be used most often, since the majority of plants thrive in it during their early stages. Lime-loving plants, such as encrusted saxifragas, need the first mixture. Woodland plants in general prefer the second mix. Of far more importance for most sorts than the exact chemical reaction of the soil is its physical condition. It must be porous and drain freely.

Pots, pans, or flats, according to the amount of seed to be sown, may be used. Most gardeners agree that it is desirable, after sowing, to expose seeds of alpines to freezing or near freezing temperatures for a few weeks before putting them into a cool greenhouse or similar environment to germinate. But often the most practical plan is to sow seeds of all rock garden plants as soon as they are obtainable. Many will germinate in a few days to a few weeks, others may take several months, even a year or longer. Keep those that do not germinate quickly moist, and in fall sink their containers to their rims in a bed of sand or peat moss in a cold frame or outdoors. They may be left there until they germinate, or to hasten germination, they may be brought into a cool greenhouse in February. Alternatively, mix the seeds with slightly damp sand or peat moss and store them in a plastic bag in a refrigerator at 35 to 40°F for three or four months before sowing.

Detailed care following germination plays an important part in the degree of success attained. It is particularly important that the soil be kept uniformly moist. When the seedlings are of such size that they can be transplanted, a little more thought than when seed sowing should be given to the exact soil mix most suitable for each particular kind. Only by experience and experiment, and often a certain amount of error, can these facts be determined, for above all, it is unwise to be too dogmatic about a subject having such wide ramifications as this. Frequently, gardeners following widely different practices get equally good results provided fundamental principles are not violated.

Rock garden plants for temperate and cold-temperate climates include a vast array of alpines as well as natives of lower elevations that, by custom and for convenience, are accepted as appropriate. Most are species and varieties that somewhere occur as wildlings, but practically all rock gardeners admit a selection of garden varieties and man-made hybrids. These are usually limited to sorts that look as if they could be natural species and varieties, although this is scarcely true of a few that have double flowers. Nevertheless, it is generally considered inappropriate to admit plants of distinctly gardenesque appearance, those that strongly suggest the hand of the plant breeder.

Because of this, common garden annuals such as begonias, petunias, verbenas, and zinnias are taboo. Some rock gardeners bar all annuals, but that is scarcely defensible, for plants of annual and biennial duration occur in mountain regions, although perennials are more plentiful there. The only valid measure of a plant's suitability for inclusion is the distinctly subjective one of, does it look as though it belonged? As you gain experience, your taste in this matter is likely to become refined and your judgments more critical. Base the selection of plants for rock gardens in the subtropics, tropics, and desert regions on the same principle of excluding those that strongly suggest horticultural origin, and depend upon sorts that believably could belong in such environments in the wild.

Among plants suitable for rock gardens in temperate regions are a wide variety of dwarf conifers, notably arborvitaes (*Thuja*), cedars (*Cedrus*), cryptomerias, false-cypresses (*Chamaecyparis*), firs (*Abies*), hemlocks (*Tsuga*), junipers (*Juniperus*), pines (*Pinus*), and spruces (*Picea*). There are other dwarf evergreens and some dwarf deciduous shrubs that are suitable.

Other categories from which selections may be made are deciduous and evergreen herbaceous perennials in great variety and some subshrubs. Included with the perennials are a considerable selection of bulbous plants, as well as plants suitable for carpeting places where bulbs are planted. There are groundcovers and little

plants well suited for filling chinks and crannies between rocks.

The individual requirements of this immense selection of plants as to types of soil, amount of sun or shade needed, preference for moist or dry locations, and so on, are discussed in the Encyclopedia entries under the genera to which each belongs. In the lists now to be presented a separation has been made of sorts that generally do best in sunny places and those that need or tolerate shade. But these are only loose guidelines, for other factors may determine reactions, and sometimes particular species within a genus have different needs. In using the lists, it must not be assumed that all sorts of any one genus are appropriate for rock gardens. Often that is not so. Nor are these the only genera that contain desirable rock garden plants. The lists are intended only to afford some guidance to beginners.

Plants for sunny locations include these: acaenas, achilleas, aethionemas, alliums, alyssums, arabis, arenarias, armerias, belliums, brodiaeas, *Bulbocodium vernum*, callunas, calochortuses, chionodoxas, colchicums, cooperias, corydalises, crocuses,

Rock garden plants for sunny locations:
(a) *Allium karataviense*

(b) *Dianthus monspessulanus sternbergii*

(c) *Geranium cinereum subcaulescens*

(d) *Iberis saxatilis*

cytisuses, daboecias, some daphnes, dianthuses, *Doronicum cordifolium*, douglasias, drabas, dryases, empetrums, eranthises, ericas, erigerons, eriogonums, erodiums, erysimums, euphorbias, genistas, gentianas, geraniums, geums, globularias, gypsophilas, helianthemums, hutchinsias, hypericums, iberises, some irises, jasiones, leiophyllum, *Leontopodium alpinum*, leucojums, lewisias, linarias, lychnises, *Muehlenbeckia axillaris*, muscaris, narcissuses, oenotheras, papavers, parnassias, penstemons, *Petrophytum caespitosum*, some phloxes, phyteumas, polemoniums, potentillas, *Pterocephalus parnassi*, puschkinias, ranunculuses, raoulias, santolinas, saponarias, satureias, some saxifragas, scabiosas, *Schivereckia doerfleri*, scutellarias, sedums, sempervivums, most silenes, sisyrinchiums, talinums, teucriums, thymuses, tulipas, tunicas, verbenas, and veronicas.

Plants for shade or partial shade include these: ajugas, androsaces, anemonellas, anemones, aquilegias, arisaemas, asarums, asperulas, *Bletilla striata*, campanulas, *Chrysogonum virginianum*, *Claytonia virginianum*, colchicums, *Cornus canadensis*, corydalises, *Cotula squalida*, cyclamens, cymbalarias, cypripediums, *Dalibarda repens*, certain daphnes, dicentras, dodecatheons, edraianthuses, *Epi-*

Rock garden plants for shady locations:
(a) *Aquilegia flabellata*

(b) *Chrysogonum virginianum*

(c) *Cornus canadensis*

(d) *Erythronium americanum*

(e) *Primula denticulata*

(f) *Ramonda myconi*

(g) *Sanguinaria canadensis*

gaea repens, epimediums, *Erinus alpinus*, erythroniums, fritillarias, galanthuses, *Galax aphylla*, *Gaultheria procumbens*, gentianas, hedyotises, some heucheras, some irises, jeffersonias, *Linnaea borealis*, *Mazus reptans*, mertensias, *Mitchella repens*, mitellas, myosotises, *Nierembergia repens*, some phloxes, polemoniums, primulas, pulmonarias, pyrolas, *Pyxidanthera barbulata*, ramondas, *Sanguinaria canadensis*, some saxifragas, shortias, a few silenes, symphyandras, synthyrises, thalictrums, trilliums, uvularias, vancouverias, and *Waldsteinia trifoliata*.

ROCK PHOSPHATE. This natural rock contains 20 to 30 percent phosphoric acid, but unless treated by heating or in other helpful ways, the nutrient content is unavailable or available only very slowly. To be useful, raw rock phosphate must be ground exceedingly fine. It produces better results on acid than on alkaline or neutral soils. There is little advantage in applying it to land with a pH of 6.2 or higher. Plants of the pea family LEGUMINOSAE seem able to benefit from its use better than grasses. It may be added to compost piles. Apply in fall or spring at 4 to 8 ounces to 10 square feet.

ROCKBERRY is *Empetrum eamesii*.

ROCKET. The word rocket forms parts of the common names of these plants: double yellow-rocket (*Barbarea vulgaris florepleno*), dyer's-rocket (*Reseda luteola*), rocket salad (*Eruca sativa*), sweet rocket (*Hesperis matronalis*), and wall-rocket (*Diplotaxis*).

ROCKFOIL. See Saxifraga.

RODGERSIA (Rodgérs-ia). Commemorating John Rodgers, a nineteenth-century commodore of the United States Navy and commander of an expedition the results of which included the discovery of *Rodgersia*, the genus here treated comprises six species. It belongs in the saxifrage family SAXIFRAGACEAE and inhabits Japan and China.

Rodgersias are deciduous, bold-foliaged, herbaceous perennials. They have short, thick rhizomes and alternate, long-stalked, large leaves variously divided or lobed or peltate (with the leafstalk joined to the blade some distance from the margin). Many together in panicles terminating long stalks, the flowers are tiny. They have petal-like calyxes with five lobes, but usually are without true petals. There are ten stamens and two or three carpels, which, unlike those of nearly related *Astilbe*, are united.

Beautiful foliage, green at first and bronzy later, is reason enough for growing the most popular species **R. podophylla.** This has lower leaves with five-angled, toothed leaflets up to 10 inches long

Rodgersia podophylla

by two-thirds as broad. The upper stem leaves are smaller and of three leaflets, or are three-lobed. Its 1-foot-long sprays of yellowish-white flowers, carried to heights

Rodgersia aesculifolia

Rodgersia pinnata

of 3 to 4 feet, are added attractions. From 2½ to 5 feet in height, *R. aesculifolia* has leaves, the lowermost up to about 1½ feet across, with usually seven coarsely-toothed leaflets 4 to 10 inches long. The leaflets spread from the tops of the leafstalks. The white flowers are in ample panicles 1 foot to 2½ feet long.

Leaves with pinnately-arranged leaflets are typical of *R. pinnata.* From 3 to 4 feet tall, this has hollow, somewhat branched stems and leaves with five, seven, or nine obovate to oblanceolate, toothed leaflets 6 to 8 inches long. In much-branched, red-stalked panicles, the flowers are commonly reddish, but in varieties *R. p. elegans, R. p. rosea,* and *R. p. rubra* they are pink, as they are in taller *R. p. superba.* White blooms in bigger, looser panicles characterize *R. p. alba.* Also pinnate-leaved, *R. sambucifolia* is 2 to 3 feet tall. This has rather small, crowded panicles of white flowers. Its leaves have seven, nine, or eleven leaflets that, except the terminal one, are in widely separated pairs.

Leaves with stalks that join the 1- to 3-foot-wide blades some way in from their edges distinguish *R. tabularis.* The leaf margins have many short lobes. In aspect resembling those of astilbes, the panicles are of numerous white flowers.

Rodgersia tabularis

Garden and Landscape Uses. Rodgersias are much less well known to American than to European gardeners, perhaps because they are a little too tender to winter cold, and impatient of summer heat, to be entirely satisfactory in many parts of the continent, including much of the northeast. Where less extreme conditions prevail they are outstanding ornamentals, especially well adapted for watersides, but succeeding wherever there is deep, fertile, moist soil and full sun. They may be colonized in massive clumps in informal places and used effectively in perennial beds. Because of the wide spread of their foliage they need ample space.

Cultivation. Propagation of rodgersias is easy by seed and by division. Routine care calls for little attention. An annual spring application of a complete fertilizer encour-

ages vigor. Because the soil must always be moist, in some locations periodic deep watering may be needed. Where winters are cold, heavy protective winter covering is advisable. Replanting is necessary only at long intervals. Gradual loss of vigor indicates the need for this.

RODRIGUEZIA (Rodri-guèzia). Mostly showy-flowered, the about thirty species of *Rodriguezia,* of the orchid family ORCHIDACEAE, are natives of tropical South America. They are epiphytes, perching on trees without taking nourishment from their hosts. The name commemorates Manuel Rodriguez, eighteenth-century Spanish physician and botanist.

Rodriguezias are small orchids. Their pseudobulbs, their bases sheathed with leafy bracts, are clustered or spaced more distantly along slender rhizomes. Each has usually one, sometimes two leaves at its apex. The flowers, often borne in great profusion, are in racemes from the bases of the pseudobulbs. They have three sepals, the upper (dorsal) one resembling the two petals, the lateral ones different and united, and an obovate to reverse-heart-shaped lip with a usually crested disk and a short basal spur. The erect, slender column of the flower has two projections from its base.

Peruvian *R. batemanii* has clusters of flattened, ovoid pseudobulbs each with a

Rodriguezia batemanii

solitary, leathery, strap-shaped leaf up to 4 inches long. The abundant flowers, in arching to pendulous racemes of three to eight, are 1½ to 2½ inches long. They have a prominent spur and are white, spotted or flushed with rose or rosy-lavender and with a center band of the same color on the lip. Native from Panama to northern South America and Trinidad, *R. secunda* has light pink to bright rose-red blooms up to about 1 inch long in densely-flowered, arching, one-sided racemes that may exceed 1 foot in length. The clustered, compressed pseudobulbs are 1 inch to 2 inches

Rodriguezia secunda (flowers)

tall. The leaves, narrow-strap-shaped to elliptic-oblong, are up to about 9 inches long by somewhat over 1 inch wide. Smaller pseudobulbs less densely clustered are typical of **R. venusta,** of Peru and

Rodriguezia venusta

Brazil. Borne in pendulous racemes, and fewer-flowered and looser than those of *R. secunda*, its fragrant, 1½-inch-long blooms, white or pink-tinged, have a yellow patch on the wavy-edged, triangular lip. The stiffish leaves, linear-oblong, are 5 to 9 inches long by up to 1 inch wide. The 1-inch-tall pseudobulbs of **R. decora,** of Brazil, are spaced at wide intervals along creeping, wiry rhizomes often several feet long. The solitary leaf of each pseudobulb is 3 to 4 inches long by approximately 1 inch wide. The sometimes branched, arching racemes, up to 2 feet in length, have a dozen or fewer blooms about 1½ inches long. The white to yellowish flowers, sometimes flushed with pink, are dotted on their faces with deep red-purple. The lip is kidney-shaped.

Garden Uses and Cultivation. Among the easiest tropical orchids to grow, and needing little space, rodriguezias are ad-

mirable for collectors with limited greenhouse accommodations, as well as for others. In the humid tropics and subtropics they succeed outdoors. They may be grown in pans (shallow pots), hanging baskets, or attached to pieces of tree fern trunk or other agreeable support. This last method is particularly recommended for kinds with long rhizomes and distantly spaced pseudobulbs. Osmunda fiber, tree fern fiber, and fir bark are suitable rooting media. Perfect drainage is necessary, and the containers should be smallish in comparison to the size of the plants. Stagnancy about the roots soon brings trouble, and too frequent repotting is to be avoided. A minimum winter night temperature of 60°F is satisfactory, rising on sunny days to up to fifteen degrees higher. A humid atmosphere and sufficient shade, but no more than is necessary to prevent the foliage scorching, are needed. Watering is done throughout the year, less often in winter than when the plants are in active growth. For more information see Orchids.

RODRIOPSIS. This is the name of orchid hybrids the parents of which are *Ionopsis* and *Rodriguezia.*

ROEMERIA (Roemèr-ia). The slender annuals that constitute *Roemeria*, of the poppy family PAPAVERACEAE, are natives from the Mediterranean region to central Asia. There are seven species. The name commemorates Johann Jakob Roemer, Professor of Botany at Zurich, Switzerland, who died in 1819.

Roemerias have deeply-pinnately-lobed, ferny leaves and solitary, long-stalked violet, blue, or lavender, poppy-like flowers succeeded by long, slender seed pods. The blooms have two sepals, four petals, and many stamens. The fruits are slender pod-like capsules. All their parts contain yellow juice.

Native to Asia Minor and the Caucasus, **R. refracta,** up to 1 foot high, has showy, blue flowers 2 to 3 inches wide marked with black at the bottom of each petal. Variety *R. r. albomarginata* has the black blotch bordered with a white band; variety *R. r. setosa* has black-blotched red flowers and bristly seed pods. The leaves of **R. hybrida** are two- or three-times-divided and have bristle points to the divisions. The comparatively short-stalked flowers are pale lilac. This native of the Mediterranean region, up to 1½ feet tall, was previously known as *R. violacea.*

Garden Uses and Cultivation. Roemerias are pleasing flower garden ornamentals well suited for beds and borders, but, as with so many of the poppy family, their blooms do not last when cut. These plants need full sun and porous, well-drained soil. Seeds, sown in early spring where the plants are to bloom, are covered very shal-

lowly with soil. The young plants are thinned to about 6 inches apart. No regular attention other than the elimination of weeds is required.

ROHDEA (Ròh-dea). Long considered to consist of only one species, *Rohdea,* of the lily family LILIACEAE, is now regarded as composed of two or three natives of China and Japan. The generic name honors a physician and botanist of Bremen, Germany, Michael Rohde, who died in 1812.

Rohdeas are herbaceous plants with tufts of crowded evergreen leaves terminating short, stout, upright rhizomes, and dense, short-stalked spikes of insignificant deep-bowl-shaped, whitish, fleshy flowers that have six perianth lobes, six stamens, and a short style. They are succeeded by showy, spherical, usually one-seeded berries that change from green to bright red when they ripen. The flower spikes are 1 inch to 2 inches long.

Probably the only species cultivated, **R. japonica,** of China and Japan, has stout

Rohdea japonica

rhizomes and, more or less in two ranks, arching to erect, lanceolate to oblanceolate, thick-leathery leaves 9 inches to 2 feet long by 2 to 3 inches wide. Hidden among the foliage, the pale yellow flowers, in short spikes that suggest the spadix of an aroid, are succeeded by red or sometimes yellow fruits. Nearly black-green leaves edged with white are characteristic of *R. j. marginata.* In Japan, the cultivation of *R. japonica* is a popular and highly developed hobby. Hundreds of horticultural varieties are recognized by fanciers and an extensive literature about them exists. The varieties vary in height, shape of leaves, coloring, habit of growth, and other details. Very high prices are paid for choice and scarce kinds. Societies dedicated to furthering interest in rohdeas, cultivating them, and breeding new varieties are extant. No comparable interest in these plants exists in North America or Europe.

Garden and Landscape Uses. Rohdeas are excellent houseplants and greenhouse plants and may be grown outdoors in climates not more severe than that of Washington, D.C. They suggest themselves as being suitable for rock gardens and for planting beneath shrubs and trees. They are not particular as to soil and stand considerable neglect. However, they are at their best in fertile, porous soil, neither excessively dry nor wet. They need shade from strong sun.

Cultivation. Rhodeas grow slowly. Planted permanently outdoors, they need practically no attention. Pot-grown specimens are repotted at infrequent intervals, certainly not every year. Early spring is the most favorable season for the operation. Water to keep the soil moderately moist. When thoroughly well rooted, rohdeas benefit from occasional applications of dilute liquid fertilizer. They are temperate rather than tropical plants and are best in coolish rooms in houses or greenhouses where night temperatures range from 45 to 55°F and day temperatures are not more than five to ten degrees higher. At other seasons approximately normal outdoor temperatures are appropriate. Propagation is by division and by seed.

ROLLINIA (Rol-línia). To the annona family ANNONACEAE belong the about sixty-five species of *Rollinia*. This genus is endemic to Central America, South America, Mexico, and the West Indies. Its name honors the French historian, Charles Rollin, who died in 1741.

Rollinias are trees and shrubs with alternate, undivided leaves, and flowers that are solitary or more often in clusters of few. The blooms have three sepals much smaller than the six petals. The three outer petals are lanceolate, and on their backs winged or spurred. The inner three are shorter and ovate. The stamens are tightly grouped into an ovoid mass. The compound fruits are formed, like those of the cherimoya and other annonas, by the uniting of many fleshy capsules. Those of some species are greatly esteemed in their homelands for eating.

Native to Mexico and the West Indies, *R. mucosa* is a small tree with elliptic leaves, pubescent on their undersides and up to 8 inches long. The 1-inch-long flowers are rusty-hairy. About 3 inches in diameter and nearly spherical, the fruits are edible. A slender-branched shrub or small tree of Brazil that favors moist soils, *R. emarginata* has ovate to elliptic leaves. Its egg-shaped to roundish fruits are 1 inch or a little more in diameter and much like but smaller than those of the sweetsop or sugar-apple (*Annona squamosa*). Hailing from Brazil, where it is known as biriba, *R. orthopetala* is a small tree that closely resembles *R. mucosa*. Native to Brazil and Guiana, *R. pulchrinervis* is a tree with rusty-silky-hairy young shoots and oblong to oblong-elliptic leaves up to 1 foot long, pubescent on their undersides. The silky-hairy flowers are 1 inch or more across. Of indifferent eating quality, the subspherical fruits are 3 to 4½ inches in diameter.

Garden and Landscape Uses and Cultivation. These are as for *Annona*.

ROMAN CANDLE is *Yucca gloriosa*.

ROMAN NETTLE is *Urtica pilulifera*.

ROMANZOFFIA (Roman-zóffia). Four species of low deciduous herbaceous perennials and one, as yet undescribed, apparently an annual, of the water leaf family HYDROPHYLLACEAE, constitute *Romanzoffia*, of western North America. The name honors Count Nikolai von Romanzoff, who promoted a Russian expedition to California in 1816.

The kinds of this genus are generally very similar to and in aspect resemble delicate saxifragas. They have mostly basal, long-stalked, round to kidney-shaped, crenately-toothed or lobed leaves, and stalks with a few smaller leaves and creamy-white or pink blooms in loose, curled, raceme-like clusters. Their broadly-funnel-shaped corollas have five spreading lobes (petals) and enclose the five stamens and slender style. The stigma is scarcely or not lobed. The fruits are ovoid capsules containing many seeds.

Inhabiting moist cliffs and rocks in alpine, subalpine, and arctic regions from California to Montana and Alaska, *R. sitchensis* is without tubers, but has swollen bulblike bases to its leafstalks. From 1½ to 8 inches or rarely up to 1 foot tall, it has leaves with blades mostly up to 1 inch across and few-toothed or lobed. The corolla, about ⅓ inch in length, has shallow, oval lobes. This sort blooms in summer. Differing in having clustered, woolly, ovoid tubers, *R. suksdorfii* (syn. *R. californica*) occurs as a native of California and Oregon, favoring moist, rocky woodland locations at lower elevations that *R. sitchensis*. Blooming in spring, it is 4 to 10 inches tall and has leaves ½ inch to 1½ inches in diameter. In the axils of the loose flower clusters tiny tubers often develop. The blooms, in elongated clusters, are ¼ to ½ inch long and banded with yellow below the throat. Another tuberous species, *R. tracyi* grows on ocean cliffs from California to Vancouver Island. Differing from the last named in being conspicuously hairy and in its flower stems being scarcely taller than the foliage and from 2 to 5 inches in height, it often forms mats of succulent foliage up to 1 inch tall. Native to Alaska and the Aleutian Islands, *R. unalaschensis* has succulent, generally hairy leaves about 1 inch in diameter and comparatively large blooms or stalks 2 to 8 inches tall.

Garden Uses and Cultivation. Romanzoffias are rock garden plants adapted best for lightly shaded locations and dampish, gritty soil that contains an abundance of organic matter. They can be raised from seed without difficulty and may be increased by dividing the roots during their summer period of dormancy.

ROMNEYA (Romnèy-a) — Matilija-Poppy. The only species of *Romneya*, of the poppy family PAPAVERACEAE, is a somewhat shrubby herbaceous perennial endemic to southern California and Baja California. The name honors the Irish astronomer, Thomas Romney Robinson (a friend of the botanist Thomas Coulter), who discovered it about 1845.

Romneyas, bushy plants 3 to 8 feet tall, have essentially glabrous, glaucous-blue-gray stems and foliage and gorgeous large white flowers borne over a long summer period. The blooms have three sepals, six white petals, and many stamens and stigmas. The fruits are capsules clothed with yellowish bristles. The stems are much branched above, and the leaves are alternate, deeply-lobed, and sparingly-toothed. All parts of the plants contain a bitter colorless sap.

The matilija-poppy (*R. coulteri*) has leaves 2 to 4 inches long, their margins sparsely fringed with hairs. The quite

Romneya coulteri (flower)

hairless flower buds expand into fragrant blooms about 6 inches in diameter with beautifully crinkled, crepy petals. Distinguishing features are that the upper parts of the flower stalks are not very leafy, and their tops and the sepals are without hairs. Variety *R. c. trichocalyx* differs in having ill-scented blooms atop stalks that are leafy above and, near the flowers, clothed with bristly hairs. Its leaves are dissected into narrower lobes than those of *R. coulteri*, and their margins are without hairs.

Garden Uses. These are not plants for cold climates, although even in New York City they survive outdoors if planted in sheltered locations at the bases of south-facing walls and are well protected over winter by a thick layer of coal ashes, sand, or some other mulch that prevents the ground from freezing too deeply. But basically they belong in regions of warmer winters. They are drought resistant and thrive in the hot, dry summers of the Pacific Southwest even without irrigation. That they tolerate wetter conditions, if soil drainage is sharp, is apparent from the fact that they are cultivated with success in England. These handsome plants are splendid as lawn bed specimens, for fronts of shrub plantings, and for inclusion in foundation plantings.

Cultivation. Romneyas have deep, wide-spreading roots and because it is impossible to dig them up without destroying or seriously damaging these they are difficult to transplant successfully. Best results are had by setting out young plants from pots or by transplanting young suckers with as many roots as can be taken, with a good ball of soil adhering to them. Cut the suckers back to a few inches in length at transplanting time.

These plants thrive in various soils, but not if they are wet or waterlogged. They need full sun. If, as may happen, the tops are killed to the ground, but the roots survive the winter, cut the plants completely back in spring. New shoots will develop and bloom the same year. Even where they are not killed back, this same practice may be followed if it is desired to limit the size of the plants, otherwise the recommended procedure is to prune out in spring all weak and crowded shoots and shorten any that have had their tops damaged by winter cold.

Pieces of thickish roots 3 to 4 inches long taken in spring and planted about ½ inch deep in sandy soil in a cold frame or cool greenhouse afford a simple means of propagation. Pot the young plants individually into 5-inch pots and when well established in these set them in their permanent locations in the garden. Fresh seeds sown in sandy soil in a greenhouse in spring offer an alternative mode of securing increase. Shade the seed pots until germination takes place and keep the soil evenly moist. When large enough to han-dle, pot the seedlings into 3-inch pots, later into 5-inch pots.

ROMULEA (Romu-lèa). The possibly ninety species of *Romulea*, of the iris family IRI-DACEAE, are natives of western Europe, the Mediterranean region, and South Africa. None is hardy in the north. The name honors Romulus, the founder of Rome.

Romuleas are crocus-like plants with corms, underground food storage organs that look like bulbs, but instead of being composed of concentric layers as are onions, or of overlapping scales as are lily bulbs, are solid throughout. They are without true stems, but unlike crocuses they have aboveground, sometimes branched, stemlike flower stalks with a solitary bloom terminating each stem or branch. The leaves are linear and few in number. Each bloom has at its base a bractlike spathe longer than the short perianth tube. There are six nearly equal yellow, white, lilac, or purple perianth lobes (petals, or more correctly, tepals), three stamens, and a three-branched style. The fruits are cylindrical capsules.

Although there are several attractive species, romuleas are not well known in cultivation. They are mostly 4 to 6 inches tall with blooms 1 inch wide or wider. Among kinds worth trying in regions of mild winters are these: *R. bulbocodioides,* of South Africa, has usually two leaves, 6 inches to 1 foot long, and starry, yellow, or yellow-centered white to cream blooms with petals up to ½ inch long. *R. bulbocodium,* a variable Mediterranean species, has three or four slender, nearly cylindrical, 3- to 5-inch-long leaves. Its flowers, on stalks shorter than the leaves that sometimes scarcely, if at all, lift the cup-shaped flowers above ground level, are ¾ to 1 inch long. They are lilac, veined with purple, and with yellow throats, or yellow may predominate with only the apexes of the petals lilac. *R. chloroleuca,* of South Africa, has three to five slender leaves from 6 inches to 1¼ feet long and much exceeding the flower stalks. About ½ inch long, the flowers are white with yellow or green throats. *R. hirsuta,* of South Africa, has two to four leaves and flowers with ¾- to 1-inch-long petals, the lower halves of which are bright yellow to orange-yellow, the upper magenta- to brick-red. *R. rosea,* also South African, generally has four leaves, 6 inches to 1 foot long, and pale pink, mauve, magenta, or rarely white flowers with yellow centers and up to 1½ inches long. The flower stalks of robust specimens are up to 1 foot long. *R. sabulosa,* of South Africa, has two to four slender, cylindrical leaves and on stalks longer than the leaves, almost tubeless, bell-shaped, deep rose-pink to reddish-lilac blooms veined with yellow on their outsides and with a brownish-purple blotch in their throats. They are up to 2½ inches in diameter. *R. sublutea,* a native of South Africa and one of the handsomest species, unfortunately may not be in cultivation. It usually has two slender leaves and showy, short-stemmed, golden-yellow flowers, about 1¼ inches long, with distinctly hairy stamens and sulfur-yellow anthers.

Garden and Landscape Uses and Cultivation. The most appropriate outdoor use for these plants in regions such as California, which have mild, Mediterranean-type climates, is for embellishing rock gardens, naturalistic areas, and similar developments. Some, notably *R. rosea,* may generate new plants from self-sown seeds to the extent that they may become something of a nuisance. Romuleas are also of interest for growing in pans (shallow pots) and pots in cool, sunny greenhouses. They need well-drained, moderately nourishing soil, full sun, and growing conditions that suit freesias, sparaxises, and ixias. Propagation is by seed and offsets.

RONDELETIA (Ron-delètia). Tropical American evergreen trees and shrubs numbering more than 100 species constitute *Ron-*

Romulea chloroleuca

deletia. A few are cultivated as ornamentals. The group belongs to the madder family RUBIACEAE. Its name is a memorial to the French naturalist and physician Guillaume Rondelet, who died in 1566.

The leaves of rondeletias, opposite or rarely in threes, have usually persistent stipules (appendages) at the bottoms of their stalks. The red, orange-red, yellow, or white, often fragrant flowers are in clusters or panicles from the leaf axils or rarely terminal. Each small bloom has a persistent four- or five-lobed calyx, a usually slender-tubed corolla with four or five spreading lobes (petals), four or five stamens, and one style. The fruits are capsules.

Most frequent in cultivation, **R. odorata**

Rondeletia odorata

(syn. *R. speciosa*) is poorly named. Neither its foliage nor its flowers are fragrant. A native of Panama and Cuba, this shrub, 3 to 6 feet tall, has downy branches and short-stalked, ovate to elliptic or oblongish leaves, some 2 inches long, commonly wrinkled and with rolled-back margins. In terminal groups of three, the flower clusters, suggesting those of lantanas, are of slender-tubed, yellow-throated, bright orange- to brick-red or yellow blooms about ½ inch long and as much across. They are without beards in their throats.

Pink to dullish red blooms are borne by *R. cordata* and *R. amoena*, the first native of Guatemala, the other from Mexico to Panama. A shrub 4 to 7 feet tall, **R. cordata** has stalkless or nearly stalkless, pointed, ovate to ovate-oblong, nearly hairless leaves 2½ to 7 inches long, about one-half as broad, and somewhat heart-shaped at their bases. Not over ¼ inch across, and less long, its pink to red, short-stalked flowers, with densely yellow-bearded throats, are in crowded, branched, terminal clus-

Rondeletia cordata

ters up to 4½ inches wide. From the last, pink-flowered **R. amoena,** a shrub or small tree, differs in its young shoots being densely-hairy and its leaves having rounded bases and densely-brownish-hairy undersides. They are short-stalked, 3 to 6 inches long, and ovate with short-pointed apexes. The flowers, about ½ inch long and hairy, have thick yellow beards in their throats. Another native of Mexico, **R. leucophylla** is a shrub up to 4 feet tall with young shoots densely clothed with white-woolly hairs. The opposite, elliptic to oblong or obovate leaves, 2 to 4 inches long, have sparsely-hairy upper surfaces and undersides densely felted with white hairs. The rose-crimson flowers, in headlike clusters terminating the branches and branchlets, are about ¾ inch long by ½ inch wide. Each has a four-lobed calyx, a four-lobed corolla, white-hairy on its underside, and four stamens.

Quite distinct **R. thyrsoides,** of Jamaica, is a shrub or small tree up to 20 feet tall with ovate to pointed-elliptic leaves 4 to 6 inches long and hairy on their undersides. The tiny, tawny-yellow blooms are in loose, pyramidal panicles 1 inch to 2½ inches long.

Garden and Landscape Uses and Cultivation. As garden decoratives for the tropics and warm subtropics rondeletias have much merit. With little care they succeed in ordinary soil in sun or part-day shade. They are also satisfactory in pots and tubs in greenhouses. When so grown they need a winter night temperature of 55 to 60°F, with five to ten degrees higher by day. At other seasons higher night and day temperatures are in order. A humid atmosphere and good light with just a little filtered shade from the strongest sun give the best results. Too heavy shade inhibits blooming. Fertile, porous soil kept evenly moist, but rather drier in winter than at other times, is requisite. Specimens that have filled their containers with roots are encouraged to remain in good condition by fairly frequent applications of

dilute liquid fertilizer from spring to fall. In late winter or early spring, old plants should be pruned to shape and repotted or top-dressed according to their needs. Following this, somewhat higher temperatures and on sunny days light overhead spraying with water, done early enough in the day that the foliage dries before night, promotes the production of healthy new growth. As young plants, rondeletias grow rather slowly. During their early stages occasional pinching out of the tips of the shoots may be done to promote shapeliness and encourage branching. Propagation is easily accomplished by cuttings, usually taken in spring. Seeds afford an alternative means of increase.

RONNBERGIA (Ronn-bèrgia). Eight species of the pineapple family BROMELIACEAE constitute *Ronnbergia,* a genus named in honor of Monsieur Ronnberg, Director of Agriculture and Horticulture, Belgium.

Natives of Brazil and Colombia, ronnbergias have rosettes of stalked and spineless leaves or stalkless, spiny leaves. The flowers, without individual stalks, are in compact and crowded to longer and looser spikes, the stalks of which are furnished with leafy bracts. The blooms have three each sepals and petals, six stamens, and a three-parted style. The fruits are berries.

A native of Colombia, **R. columbiana** has leaves up to about 1¼ feet long by 2 inches wide. Its erect, branchless flowering stalks, shorter than the leaves, carry two rows of fairly widely spaced, 1¼- to 1¾-inch-long violet flowers.

Garden and Landscape Uses and Cultivation. These are as for *Aechmea* and *Billbergia.*

ROOF AND TERRACE GARDENING. In its broadest sense, roof gardening includes what is sometimes called terrace gardening and sometimes balcony gardening, that is, growing plants on flat, balcony-like areas at the sides of apartment houses or other buildings. Such terraces or balconies, although usually smaller, much resemble roofs in the opportunities they afford and the problems they present. The last are chiefly occasioned by the lack of connection between the soil in the containers or beds and the ground, and from greater exposure to wind and reflected heat from walls and other surfaces than is common in more conventional gardens.

Before engaging in roof or terrace gardening on any substantial scale, give careful consideration to the load-bearing capacity of the structure and have it determined that there is no danger that water draining from the garden will cause damage. Certainly with rented properties the landlord's permission should be obtained.

Careful planning of roof gardens is just as important as it is with ground-level gar-

A fountain and statue backed by fencing clothed with English ivy is an attractive feature of this roof garden

New York City roof gardens, strolling and sitting areas

dens, more so in fact because weight and its distribution are factors to consider seriously. Locate heavy beds, planters, and tubs around the perimeter of roof areas, not toward their centers. Unless the roof has been specially constructed to accept greater weights, use long planter boxes up to 1 foot wide and deep, and round or square tubs to 2 feet wide and deep. Another point to bear in mind is not to locate beds or planters over drain holes or in low areas. Ideally, the floor should slope gently away from them.

Containers of masonry, brick, or, for preference, light cinder blocks are perma-

nent and generally more attractive than wooden ones, although the latter can be satisfactory and fairly long-lasting if well made of such rot-resistant lumber as redwood or cedar. Even so, before planting treat the wood with a wood preservative other than creosote (which is deadly to plants). Commercially available plastic or metal window boxes can also sometimes conveniently be used as roof and terrace garden containers. In any case, planters must have drainage holes in their bottoms, and beds similar provision, called weep holes, at the bottoms of their sides.

A sense of enclosure, as well as an opportunity for training vines, is often desirable and can be achieved by the thoughtful placement of fencing or trellis. Open-work fences that permit some air to flow through them are better than solid types, which are much more liable to blow over in heavy winds. Trellis can be used to mask and to decorate blank walls and to support vines and espaliered trees and shrubs.

An awning or other cover to allow protection from too-strong sun and rain makes a roof garden more enjoyable by extending its leisure time usefulness to include inclement periods. If a waterproof cover is not desired or is impracticable, a vine-covered arbor will at least afford shade. You may want also to consider installing lights so that the garden may be enjoyed after dark. And do not forget the need for one or more faucets as a source of water.

The soil for "gardens in the sky," as roof gardens are sometimes called, and for terrace gardens needs special consideration. Clearly, the lighter it can be without detracting from its capability to serve its primary functions of providing anchorage, nutrients, and moisture, the better. Another usually important consider-

ation is that it be long lasting, that it will serve its purposes for several years at least. Apart from the high cost, in labor if not in money and frequently in both, of installing soil on a roof or terrace, it is usually a disruptive and sometimes rather messy procedure, a procedure that one does not want to undertake more often than is necessary.

Minimum weight can be achieved by maximizing the employment of light-weight ingredients, such as peat moss and perlite, in the mix and reducing its soil content proportionately. There are those who carry this to the extreme of using completely soil-less mixes, but these give less secure anchorage for tall plants and make fertilizing a matter of more detailed concern. Best results are commonly had if at least one-third, by bulk, of the mix consists of fertile topsoil, and it is generally unwise to reduce the proportion of topsoil to under 10 percent. The remaining bulk can be equal parts of peat moss and perlite laced with bonemeal at the rate of a pint to each bushel of the mix and with a generous sprinkling of dehydrated cow manure added. Good compost may be substituted for one-half the peat moss, but it is heavier and breaks down (decays) more rapidly.

Put in the bottom of each bed or container a layer at least 2 to 3 inches deep of drainage material. Coke, coal cinders (not fine ash), and perlite are light weight and highly effective, or oyster or clam shells may be used. If weight is not an important consideration, crushed bricks, gravel, or similar material may be substituted. Before putting in the soil cover the drainage with a layer of straw, hay, or fallen leaves or with fine mesh aluminum or plastic screening, this to prevent the soil mix clogging the drainage.

Deciduous shrubs for roof gardens:
(a) Butterfly bush

Deciduous vines for roof gardens:
(a) Akebia

ing quinces (*Chaenomeles*), ginkgos, hawthorns (*Crataegus*), honey-locusts (*Gleditsia*), Japanese maples (*Acer*), mountain ash (*Sorbus*), purple leaf plum (*Prunus cerasifera* varieties), Russian-olive (*Elaeagnus angustifolia*), Siberian pea tree (*Caragana arborescens*), and willows (*Salix*).

Deciduous shrubs that have responded well to roof conditions in New York City include azaleas (hardy sorts), Japanese barberry (*Berberis thunbergii*) and its pur-

(b) Deutzia

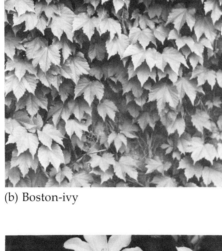

(b) Boston-ivy

Evergreens for sheltered roof gardens:
(a) Pachysandra

(c) Firethorn

(c) Clematis

(b) Pieris

In selecting plants for roof and terrace gardens, choose sorts that can withstand the desiccating effects of strong winds and, except for shaded locations, brilliant sun. Trees, shrubs, and other permanent plants must be hardy. Not all that prosper at ground level are sufficiently cold resistant and tough to survive in elevated gardens. Roof garden environments possess many of the characteristics of seaside ones, and many plants that do well near the shore succeed on roofs and terraces.

Trees, shrubs, and perennial vines that lose their leaves in winter are generally more adaptable than evergreens. Not only are they more resistant to the drying effects of cold winter winds combined with bright sun, but they have the great advantage of ridding themselves once a year of accumulations of oily deposits from chimneys and other grime that accumulates on foliage, and of making a fresh start each spring.

Deciduous trees that have proved successful in New York City are birches (*Betula*), Callery pear (*Pyrus calleryana*), crab apples (*Malus*), flowering almond (*Prunus*), flowering cherries (*Prunus*), flower-

(c) Skimmia

(d) English ivy

(c) Squash

(e) Onions and herbs

ple-leaved variety, blueberries (*Vaccinium*), butterfly bush (*Buddleia*), chokeberries (*Aronia*), *Cotoneaster horizontalis*, deutzias, *Euonymus alata*, firethorn (*Pyracantha*), forsythias, hydrangeas, *Magnolia stellata*, mock-oranges (*Philadelphus*), privets (*Ligustrum*), *Rosa rugosa* and other hardy shrub roses as well as roses of the hybrid tea, floribunda, and grandiflora classes, rose-of-Sharon (*Hibiscus syriacus*), spireas (*Spi-*

(d) Tomatoes

Vegetables are featured in this New York City roof garden: (a) Cabbage

(b) Corn

raea), sweet shrub (*Calycanthus floridus*), tamarisks (*Tamarix*), viburnums, weigelas, and witch-hazels (*Hamamelis*).

Deciduous vines successful in New York City include *Akebia quinata*, bittersweet (*Celastrus*), Boston-ivy (*Parthenocissus tricuspidata*), clematises, climbing hydrangea (*Hydrangea anomala* and similar *Schizophragma hydrangeoides*), climbing roses, Dutchman's pipe (*Aristolochia durior*), grapes (*Vitis*), honeysuckles (*Lonicera*), silver lace vine (*Polygonum aubertii*), Virginia creeper (*Parthenocissus quinquefolia*), and wisterias.

Evergreens successfully used in roof gardens in New York City include, among trees, arbor-vitaes (*Thuja*), hollies (*Ilex*), junipers (*Juniperus*), Austrian and Japanese black pines (*Pinus*), and yews (*Taxus*). Evergreens of shrub dimensions that have proved adaptable, at least in sheltered places and where they receive part-day shade, are *Aucuba japonica*, arbor-vitaes (*Thuja*), *Euonymus fortunei* and *E. kiautschovica*, *Ilex crenata*, junipers (*Juniperus*), *Leucothoe fontanesiana*, mugo pine (*Pinus mugo mugo*), pachysandra (a ground cover), *Pieris floribunda* and *P. japonica*, skimmias, and yews (*Taxus*). Evergreen vines that can

be recommended for roof gardens at New York City, and then only for sheltered places shaded from strong sun, are English ivy (*Hedera*) and varieties of *Euonymus fortunei*.

Other plants to use may include a considerable variety of annuals, biennials, bulb plants, and herbaceous perennials. Even some vegetables, certainly tomatoes, may be grown as well as a selection of such herbs as basil, mint, and thyme. For floral display dependence should largely rest with the first three categories mentioned.

Among annuals are a few reliable vines that supply quick coverage if strings or wires are supplied for supports. Annual hops (*Humulus*), black-eyed-Susan-vine (*Thunbergia*), cardinal climber (*Ipomoea*), hyacinth-bean (*Dolichos*), moonflowers (*Ipomoea*), and morning glories (*Ipomoea*) belong in this group. Best choices among other annuals are those that bloom continuously over a long season, such as celosias, dwarf dahlias, gloriosa-daisies (*Rudbeckia*), ice plant (*Mesembryanthemum crystallinum*), impatiens, marigolds, petunias, portulacas, salvias, sweet alyssum (*Lobularia*), torenias, wax begonias, and zinnias.

Annuals for roof gardens:
(a) Black-eyed-Susan-vine

Biennials for roof gardens: (a) English daisy

(b) Daffodil

(b) Dwarf dahlia

(b) Primrose

Bulb plants of all hardy spring-blooming kinds bloom well the first season, but rarely do well subsequently, and it is well to plan on replacing such sorts as crocuses, daffodils (*Narcissus*), glory-of-the-snows (*Chionodoxa*), grape-hyacinths

(*Muscari*), hyacinths (*Hyacinthus*), squills (*Scilla*), and tulips (*Tulipa*) each year. The same is true of such summer bulb plants as caladiums, cannas, gladioluses, and tuberous begonias.

(c) Marigold

Biennials and plants grown as biennials are discarded at the end of their first season of bloom. Those practical for roof gardens are English daisies (*Bellis*), forget-me-nots (*Myosotis*), pansies, and polyanthus primroses (*Primula*). These may be purchased in bud or bloom in spring and after they are through blooming may be replaced with annuals.

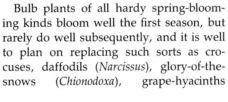

Bulbs for roof gardens: (a) Hyacinth

(c) Tulips

Herbaceous perennials upon which reliance may be placed if their individual needs for shade or sun are observed, include chrysanthemums, creeping charlie (*Lysimachia*), day-lilies (*Hemerocallis*), evergreen candytuft (*Iberis*), plantain-lilies (*Hosta*), and sedums. Many others are possibilities.

Planting, except for spring-flowering bulbs, which must be set out in fall, should always be done in spring. If the site has been planted previously, that is if the soil is not new, revitalize it by forking it over and mixing in a generous scattering of bonemeal and dehydrated cow manure. If it is in really poor condition and if it is practicable, remove the top 3 inches or so and replace it with new. Except where rhododendrons or other plants of known preference for acid soils are growing, every second or third year work into the top 2 or 3 inches of soil ground agricultural limestone at the rate of ½ to 1 pound per 10 square feet.

Routine care, except that it is somewhat more intensive, is not vastly different from that of looking after a garden at ground level. More frequent watering is likely to be needed to maintain the soil desirably damp. Be sure when you water to give enough to drench the whole body of soil. Dribbles that wet only the top 3 or 4 inches will not do. Because the volume of soil is strictly limited and as a result of frequent watering nutrients are soon leached out of it, more frequent fertilization is required. From spring to fall, a once-a-month application of a dry fertilizer or weekly or biweekly application of a liquid fertilizer will probably be about right, but be guided by the appearance and response of the plants.

Give frequent attention to such matters as picking dead leaves, snipping faded blooms, pinching out tips of shoots to encourage branching as needed, and tying in unruly shoots of vines. Pests and diseases are usually rather easily controlled by spot-spraying with aerosols or other simple means, but it is important to be alert for such troubles and to take prompt action. Good housekeeping or rather good gardenkeeping does much to keep a roof garden attractive and enjoyable.

Winter is especially trying for plants in roof gardens in regions where there is severe freezing. This is because their roots are confined to limited volumes of soil isolated from the natural ground. If the entire mass of soil remains frozen for an extended period, the roots are unable to obtain or transmit the moisture needed to replace that lost by transpiration from the aboveground parts of trees, shrubs, and woody vines, and these parts are injured or die of dehydration.

Damage can be forestalled, at least to some extent, by surrounding and covering the planters, tubs, and beds with a thick layer of branches of evergreens (old Christmas trees are splendid for this purpose) or with salt hay or straw held in place with wire netting. As an additional help, in late December and again a month later spray deciduous trees and shrubs as well as evergreens with an antitranspirant (antidesiccant).

ROOKSBYA (Roòks-bya). The plant previously known as *Cephalocereus euphorbioides* and *Neobuxbaumia euphorbioides* is by botanists, who split cactus genera finely, classified as the only species of *Rooksbya*, of the cactus family CACTACEAE. The name presumably honors Ellen Rooksby, who in the twentieth century wrote about desert plants.

Well known in cultivation, but its provenance not surely known, handsome *R. euphorbioides* is possibly a native of Mexico. Up to 20 feet tall, it has erect, columnar stems branched from and above the ground and up to 4 inches in diameter. They have eight prominent pointed ribs and clusters of two to six stiff, white spines ½ to 1 inch long. The flowers are pink to red. Variety *R. e. olfersii* has softer, brown spines 1 inch to 2 inches long in clusters of five to ten.

Garden and Landscape Uses and Cultivation. An easy-to-grow cactus, this responds to conditions that suit *Cephalocereus*. It perhaps does better in partial shade than full sun. For more information see Cactuses.

ROOSTER FLOWER is *Aristolochia brasiliensis*.

ROOTSTOCK. A rhizome or underground stem or a compact collection of these at the base of a plant is called a rootstock.

ROOTWORMS. Not true worms, these are the larvae of beetles that feed on roots, sometimes confining their activities to quite different plants than those upon which the adult insects feed. The Southern corn rootworm, for example, is the larvae of the spotted cucumber beetle. Among plants harmed by rootworms are corn, grapes, and strawberries. Consult Cooperative Extension Agents, Agricultural Experiment Stations, or other authorities about best controls.

ROQUETTE. See Eruca.

RORIPPA (Rorìp-pa). One species of the approximately seventy of *Rorippa*, of the mustard family CRUCIFERAE, is cultivated. The generic name, in allusion to the plants' habitats, comes from the Latin *roris*, dew or moisture, and *ripa*, a bank or shore. Horseradish, previously named *R. armoracia*, is *Armoracia rusticana*.

Rorippas are annual and perennial herbaceous plants, some aquatic, of the northern hemisphere. They have undivided to pinnate leaves and racemes of small yellow flowers. The fruits are capsules.

Apparently the only sort cultivated, *R. amphibia*, of North Africa, Europe, and eastward to Siberia, is a perennial with hollow, branched stems up to 5 feet tall and elliptic to oblanceolate lobeless or pinnately-lobed, bright green leaves. The ¼-inch-wide flowers are of little ornamental appeal.

Garden Uses and Cultivation. This is sometimes cultivated in aquariums.

ROSA (Rò-sa). Less appreciated as garden plants in America than in Europe, the wild species and natural varieties of *Rosa*, of the rose family ROSACEAE, as well as some of their simple hybrids include a fair number of worthwhile ornamentals. From some of these the garden roses, dealt with in the Encyclopedia entry Roses, have been derived. The genus *Rosa*, of some 250 species, is widely distributed throughout the northern hemisphere and on some mountains in the tropics. The name is the ancient Latin one of the rose.

The sorts of *Rosa* are deciduous or less often evergreen shrubs, usually prickly and with erect, trailing, or clambering stems. Their alternate leaves, generally pinnate with a terminal leaflet, less often are undivided. At the bases of the leafstalks are a pair of usually conspicuous appendages called stipules. Solitary or in branched clusters at the ends of short branchlets, the flowers characteristically have five, less commonly four, each sepals and petals. There are semidouble and double varieties of some kinds that have more petals. The stamens and pistils are numerous. Called hips, the more or less berry-like, most frequently urn-shaped fruits contain several to many seeds (technically achenes). Because of the variability within species and the freedom with which they hybridize, precise identification is not always easy. In the presentation that follows, species and some hybrids that have been accorded botanical names and that are the bases of well-defined groups are treated first in alphabetical sequence of their botanical names, followed by other sorts similarly arranged.

The white rose of York, Jacobite rose, or cottage rose (**R. alba**), hardy about as

Rosa alba

far north as New York City, was cultivated by the Greeks and Romans; much later it was adopted as a symbol by the Yorkists in the English War of the Roses. One or more of its varieties are cultivated in southern Europe for making attar of roses. Of hybrid origin, its parents probably the dog rose and Damask rose, *R. alba* has stout, prickly stems up to about 6 feet tall and leaves with five or seven broad, grayish-green leaflets. Its more or less double white to blush-colored, fragrant blooms are 2¼ to 3¼ inches wide. The fruits are oblong-ovoid, red, and about ¾ inch long. Variety *R. a. incarnata* has double pink flowers. Garden varieties and hybrids include 'Celestial', with 4-inch-wide white flowers, pink in the bud stage; 'Maiden's Blush', which has clusters of nearly spherical 3-inch-wide, very double flowers; 'Mme. Plantier', with long-stalked clusters of creamy-white flowers that become pure white; and 'Koenigin von Daenemarck', which has 4-inch-wide double pink flowers with darker centers. Lady Bank's rose (*R. banksiae*), not hardy in the north, and a beautiful climber up to 20 feet tall, is lightly furnished with, or is without, prickles. Its leaves have usually three or five, less often seven, elliptic-ovate to oblong-lanceolate, toothed leaflets from less than 1 inch to a little over 2 inches long, and hairless except near the bottom of the midrib on the under surface. Slightly fragrant, 1 inch in diameter, and in many-flowered clusters, the smooth-stalked, white or yellow flowers are succeeded by small red fruits. Known as *R. b. normalis*, the typical form has single, creamy-white flowers. Those of *R. b. alba-plena* are double and white. Scentless, double yellow blooms are borne by *R. b. lutea*, single yellow flowers by *R. b. lutescens*. The Bourbon rose (*R. borboniana*), is believed to be a hybrid of *R. chinensis* and probably *R. damascena* or possibly *R. gallica*. Discovered in 1877 on Réunion Island (Isle de Bourbon) in the Indian Ocean, and parent of hybrid perpetual garden roses, its sorts are rare in cultivation. They have stout, erect stems up to 6 feet or more in height, with strongly-hooked prickles and leaves of five to seven lustrous leaflets. The usually semidouble flowers, solitary or in clusters of few, in the typical sort are rose-pink. Varieties include 'Boule de Neige', with creamy-white blooms; 'Bourbon Queen', the flowers of which are magenta and pink; 'La Reine Victoria', its rosy-pink blooms with outer petals shading to deeper rose-pink; 'Madame Ernest Calvat', with rich pink flowers. 'Madame Isaac Pereire' has big rose-madder flowers shaded with magenta; 'Madame Pierre Oger', flowers with blooms creamy-pink becoming deep rose-pink; 'Souvenir de la Malmaison', flesh-pink blooms; 'Variegata di Bologna', white flowers striped with deep magenta to purple; and 'Zepherine

Drouhin', bright clear pink blooms. The cabbage rose (*R. centifolia*) is of complex hybrid origin. Although the cabbage rose is extremely ancient and was described by

Rosa centifolia

Herodotus more than 2,000 years ago, it seemingly did not emerge in its present form until the eighteenth century. It is hardy in southern New England. It was much portrayed by Dutch painters and is especially esteemed for the rich fragrance of its always double flowers. Its foliage is also scented. From 4 to 6 feet tall, it has prickly stems. Its leaves, hairy on their undersides and sometimes above, have usually five toothed leaflets. Typically pink, the nodding flowers have long, slender glandular stalks and many incurved petals. The fruits are ellipsoid to nearly spherical. From its close ally, the French rose, this differs in having larger, less leathery leaves. The moss rose (*R. c.*

Rosa centifolia muscosa

muscosa) is distinguished by having a "moss" of green hairs on its flower stalks and calyxes, as also does white-flowered *R. c. muscosa alba*. The "moss" of *R. c.*

Rosa centifolia cristata

cristata is only along the edges of the sepals. Called the pompon rose, *R. c. pomponia* is a dwarf with small leaves and bright red flowers up to 1½ inches across with densely-bristly stalks. Similar to the last, *R. c. parvifolia*, the Burgundian rose, has leaves with leaflets up to ¾ inch long and flower stalks only slightly bristly. Garden varieties and hybrids of the cabbage rose include 'Petite de Hollande', with long-stalked clusters of miniature pink, green-eyed flowers; 'Red Provence', with dark-centered, rose-pink flowers; 'Rose des Peintres', with large, purplish-rose-pink flowers; and 'Vierge de Clery', with big white blooms. Garden varieties and hybrids of the moss rose include 'Blanche Moreau', with clusters of white flowers; 'Comtesse de Murinais', with pink-tinted buds that open as pure white flowers; 'Deuil de Paul Fontaine', with big blooms of deepest crimson, orange-brown, and purple; 'Duchesse de Verneuil', with flesh- to salmon-pink, camellia-shaped flowers; 'Mme Louis Leveque', with

Rosa 'Duchesse de Verneuil'

double, light pink flowers; 'Robert Leopold', with flowers of pink, yellow, and orange; 'Salet', with flat, double, rose-pink blooms; and 'Striped Moss', with flowers sometimes striped with white and crimson, but sometimes plain pink. The China rose (**R. chinensis**) was introduced to Europe from China in several varieties long cultivated in the Orient in the latter part of the eighteenth century and the early part of the nineteenth century, but it was 1900 before the wild species, sometimes identified as *R. c. spontanea*, was discovered in China. The last, not hardy in the north, is not much cultivated, but horticultural varieties are more popular and some are represented in the parentage of hybrid perpetual, hybrid tea, and many other sorts of garden roses. From 2½ to 3 feet tall and with stout, prickly or sometimes nearly unarmed stems, the China rose characteristically has leaves of three or five ovate-oblong leaflets 1 inch to 2¼ inches long. Usually in clusters of few, less often solitary, the generally long-stalked, 2-inch-wide flowers are crimson to pink or almost white. The ovoid fruits are ½ to ¾ inch long. Varieties of *R. chinensis* include

Rosa chinensis minima

R. c. minima (syn. R. roulettii), the fairy rose, from which has been bred a whole race of varieties of miniature roses. A variable sort up to 1½ feet high, this has much smaller leaves than other kinds and single or double pink or red flowers ¾ inch to 1½ inches wide. The flowers, 1½ to 2 inches wide, of *R. c. mutabilis* in the bud are bright orange, open buff-yellow, and change successively to orange, red, and crimson. Called the Chinese monthly rose, crimson China rose, or Bengal rose, *R. c. semperflorens* has slender stems with or almost without prickles, thinnish leaves usually suffused with purple, and long-stalked, generally solitary, crimson or deep pink flowers a little over 1 inch across and produced over a long season. This is a parent of certain varieties of floribunda roses of gardens. The fine old variety 'Old Blush', with pink flowers with darker veins

that deepen in color as they age, belongs here. The so-called green rose, *R. c. viridiflora* is curious rather than beautiful. Said to have been cultivated as early as 1753,

Rosa chinensis viridiflora

it is a low bush that has flowers with small green leaves in place of petals. Garden varieties of *R. chinensis* include 'Archduke Charles', with double flowers marbled with light and deeper pink, changing to red. The Damask rose (**R. damascena**), an ancient garden hybrid, was brought to Europe from Asia Minor by sixteenth-cen-

tury Crusaders. Recent authorities recognize two types, the summer Damask, thought to be a hybrid of *R. gallica* and *R. phoenicea*, and the autumn Damask, thought to be a hybrid of *R. gallica* and *R. moschata*. Previously identified as *R. d. semperflorens*, the autumn Damask is now named **R. bifera**. Damask roses, up to 8 feet tall, have arching stems with many hooked prickles and prickly-stalked leaves, softly-hairy on their undersides, of five or less frequently seven leaflets about 2½ inches long. In clusters, the semidouble, rose-red to pink, fragrant flowers range from white through pink to red. They have prickly stalks and are succeeded by large, obovoid, red fruits. Much grown in Europe for use in the production of attar of roses, *R. d. trigentipetala* has smallish, loosely-double, very fragrant, soft pink blooms. Those of *R. d. versicolor*, the York and Lancaster rose, a variety in cultivation before 1629 and sometimes confused with *R. gallica versicolor*, has white flowers irregularly patched and flaked with pink. Garden varieties and hybrids include 'King George IV', which has double crimson flowers; 'Madame Hardy', with big, very double, white flowers; 'Marie Louise', with double, deep pink blooms; 'Oratam', the flowers of which are rosy-orange-pink; 'Rose du Roi', its bright red flowers with lighter undersides to the

Rosa damascena

petals and the outer petals with almost black shading; and 'York and Lancaster', which has semidouble blooms variously marked pink, or white flowers with a few red petals. The eglantine or sweetbrier (**R. eglanteria** syn. *R. rubiginosa*), a native of Europe naturalized in parts of North America, and hardy through most of New England, is parent of numerous hybrids. Vigorous and about 6 feet tall, this has arching, prickly stems and delightfully apple-fragrant foliage. The leaves have five or seven roundish leaflets up to 1½ inches long, and hairy on their undersides. Solitary or in twos or threes, the flowers are bright pink and 1¼ to almost 2 inches wide. The orange to scarlet fruits are subspherical to egg-shaped. A double-flowered variety is known. This species, kept sheared, forms a good hedge. The Austrian brier (**R. foetida**), a native of southwest Asia naturalized in southern and central Europe, has been cultivated since the sixteenth century and in America since colonial times. Up to 10 feet tall, this has arching, slender, prickly, chestnut-brown stems, and leaves up to 1½ inches long of mostly seven or nine leaflets. The somewhat ill-scented, solitary, rich yellow flowers are 2 to 2½ inches across. The fruits are spherical and red. Outstanding varieties are *R. f. bicolor* or 'Austrian Copper', which has flowers or-

Rosa 'Star of Persia'

rootstock and stems usually densely-prickly and bristly. Its dark green, wrinkled leaves are of three, five, or sometimes seven broad leaflets up to 2¼ inches long. Their stalks and midribs are bristly. Pink or crimson and solitary, the 2- to 3-inch-wide, rather long-stalked flowers are succeeded by subspherical to top-shaped, brick-red fruits. Called the red rose of Lancaster or apothecaries' rose, *R. g. officinalis*, known to have been cultivated as early as 1310, has deliciously fragrant, double, rose-crimson blooms with prominent yellow stamens. From the last, *R. g. versicolor* or 'Rosamundi' originated as a sport (mutant). It has semidouble flowers generally

rose-red and striped or parti-colored with white, with usually some all-red blooms, or, in some seasons, all of that sort. This is sometimes confused with *R. damascena versicolor*. Other varieties or hybrids include 'Belle de Crecy', which has green-centered blooms with cerise-pink petals shaded with violet, the outer ones becoming blue-violet; 'Belle of Portugal', with large, flesh-pink flowers; 'Boule de Nanteuil', with rose-pink blooms; 'Cardinal de Richelieu', which has rich velvety purple flowers; 'Camaieux', with semidouble, white to blush-pink blooms striped with rose-pink; 'Charles de Mills' which has flowers of deep rose-pink, lavender, and purple, with silvery undersides to the petals; and 'Tuscany Suberb', which has blackish-crimson flowers with yellow stamens. The musk rose (**R. moschata**), of uncertain provenance, but presumably native of southern Europe, North Africa, and western Asia, has arching or sprawling stems with straight or slightly curved prickles and leaves of five or seven elliptic-ovate leaflets. The musky-scented flowers, 1½ to 2 inches wide, are white and usually in clusters of seven. They are succeeded by small, egg-shaped fruits. Variety *R. m. nastarana*, more vigorous, has more numerous, pink-tinged flowers over 2 inches in diameter. Double flowers are borne by *R. m. plena*. Garden varieties and hybrids of *R. moschata* are notable for their general high resistance to disease. They

Rosa foetida bicolor

ange-scarlet or coppery-red on their undersides, and *R. f. persiana* or 'Persian Yellow', with double yellow blooms, called the Persian yellow rose. Other varieties or hybrids include 'Lawrence Johnston', which has semidouble, bright yellow flowers, and 'Star of Persia', with medium-sized yellow flowers with golden stamens. The French rose (**R. gallica**), a remote ancestor of many modern garden varieties and cultivated since ancient times, is native to central and southern Europe and adjacent Asia. Hardy in southern New England and occasionally naturalized, and from 2½ to 4 feet tall, this has a creeping

Rosa 'Belinda'

Rosa 'Clytemnestra'

Rosa multiflora platyphylla

include 'Belinda', which has huge clusters of semidouble, bright pink, 1-inch-wide blooms; 'Buff Beauty', with old-gold- to cream-colored blooms, apricot-yellow in the bud stage; 'Bishop Darlington', with semidouble flowers of a peaches-and-cream hue that develop from coral-colored buds; 'Clytemnestra', bearing over a long season coppery buds and salmon-pink flowers; 'Cornelia', with coral-pink flowers that become paler as they age; 'Kathleen', which has pink buds that open to white flowers; 'Lavender Lassie', with long-stemmed clusters of double lavender-pink flowers; 'Pax', with very large, almost single, creamy-white flowers; 'Penelope', which has salmon-pink buds that expand into creamy-white or delicate pink blooms; 'Vanity', with bright pink single flowers; 'Will Scarlet', its semidouble, light scarlet flowers in sprays; and 'Wild Chimes', which has small pink flowers with white centers. The Japanese rose (**R. multiflora** syn. *R. polyantha*), ancestor of the hybrid polyantha group of garden roses and sometimes called the living fence rose, is an extraordinarily vigorous native of Japan and Korea. It forms a bush up to 8 feet tall and wider than tall of very prickly stems. The pubescent leaves have seven to eleven leaflets ½ inch to 1½ inches long. In many-flowered, conical clusters, the white or rarely pink-tinged, fragrant blooms are ½ to ¾ inch wide. The spher-

Rosa multiflora

ical, pea-sized, long-lasting fruits are bright red. Pink flowers few to many together in flattish clusters are borne by *R. m. cathayensis*. A variant of the last, *R. m. carnea* has light pink, double flowers. Similar to *R. m. carnea*, but with bigger leaves, and flowers that open cerise-purple and then change to lavender-pink and finally white, *R. m. platyphylla* is the 'Seven Sisters' rose. To this the old garden variety 'Crimson Rambler' is closely related. The very hardy Japanese rose is the most popular understock for use in budding (grafting) garden roses. For this purpose variety *R. m. inermis*, which is without

prickles, is preferred. The noisette rose (**R. noisettiana**) is a hybrid between *R. chinensis* and *R. moschata* that originated about 1816 at Charleston, South Carolina. The original, called 'Champney's Pink Cluster', up to 10 feet tall, has upright or spreading stems with reddish prickles, and leaves with five or seven leaflets. In many-flowered, large clusters, the semidouble, 2-inch-wide blooms are delicate pink. Varieties and hybrids of *R. noisettiana* include 'Chromatella', a climber with dark-centered, creamy-yellow flowers; 'Maréchal Niel', a climber with pale yellow blooms; 'Reve d'Or', a climber with coppery-yellow flowers; and 'William Allen Richardson', which has small buff-colored to bronzy-orange flowers. The tea rose (**R. odorata**) unfortunately is hardy in mild climates only. Developed in China as a result of hybridizing *R. chinensis* and *R. gigantea*, it was introduced to Europe in 1810. An evergreen or semievergreen tall climber or trailer with stems and scattered prickles, this has leaves of five or seven ovate-lanceolate, lustrous, hairless leaflets ¾ inch to 2 inches long. The shortish-stalked, loosely-double, pink flowers, solitary or in twos or threes, are 2 to 3½ inches across. When supported up to 30 feet tall, *R. o. gigantea* has smooth-stalked, single, creamy-white flowers 4 to 6 inches in diameter. A variant of the last, *R. o. erubescens* has usually smaller blush to pale pink flowers. Pale yellow double flowers are borne by *R. o. ochroleuca*. Called 'Fortune's Double Yellow' and 'Gold of Ophir', *R. o. pseudindica* has double salmon-yellow blooms tinted red on their outsides and 3 to 4 inches across. Horticultural varieties include 'Catherine Mermet', with long-stalked, double flowers opening from flesh-pink buds; 'Duchesse de Brabant', with pearly-pink, double flowers; 'Safrano', which has apricot-yellow blooms; 'Gloire de Dijon' a climber with blush-pink blooms shaded with buff, salmon-pink, and orange; and 'Sombreuil', a climber with rich cream-colored flowers. The rugosa rosa (**R. rugosa**), of Japan, Korea, and China, is a source of many varieties and hybrids, notable for their hardiness and ability to prosper in exposed places and notably near the sea. This forms sturdy bushes 4 to 6 feet tall that spread by suckers and have very

red flowers with toothed petals; 'Roseraie de l'Hay', which has large deep crimson blooms suffused with purple; and 'Ruskin', with flowers of brilliant red. 'Therese Bugnet' has fragrant, double, 4-inch-wide, red blooms that fade to a pinkish color. The Scotch or burnett rose (**R. spinosissima** syn. *R. pimpinellifolia*), a suckering shrub up to 3 or 4 feet tall, is remarkably disease-resistant and the source of numerous varieties. Extremely hardy, and in the wild more widely dispersed than any

Rosa 'F. J. Grootendorst'

Rosa rugosa

other species, this occurs through much of Europe and temperate Asia, not uncommonly as an inhabitant of coastal sand dunes. In cultivation it does best in rather sandy soils. Its erect or arching stems are thickly clothed with straight or nearly straight spines and bristles. Its leaves are fernlike and of five to eleven, but most often nine, almost round to obovate leaflets ¼ to ½ inch long. The solitary white, pale pink, or sometimes yellowish, very fragrant flowers, 1½ to 2 inches wide, festoon the branches. Becoming nearly black at maturity, the spherical fruits are up to ¾ inch wide. Larger in all its parts and with fewer bristles, variety *R. s. altaica* has white flowers. Garden varieties and hybrids include 'Fruhlingsgold', with golden-yellow flowers; 'Stanwell Perpetual', which has double flesh-pink blooms; and 'Susanne', with flowers of coral-pink.

Rosa spinosissima (flowers)

prickly stems. The leaves, which in fall become bright orange and red, of five to nine wrinkled leaflets, are downy on their undersides. Produced throughout summer and fall, the purplish-rose-pink, fragrant flowers, 3½ to 4 inches across, are succeeded by 1-inch-wide, bright red, tomato-shaped fruits. Varieties include *R. r. alba*, with single white flowers; *R. r. alboplena*, with double white blooms; and *R. r. plena*, with double, dark purple-red flowers. Among other varieties and hybrids of *R. rugosa* are 'Agnes', with very double, 3-inch-wide pale yellow flowers; 'Blanc Double de Coubert', with white, moderately-double flowers; 'Delicata', which has semidouble, lilac-pink flowers; 'F. J. Grootendorst', with double, bright

Rosa rugosa (fruits)

Additional species and hybrids with botanical (Latin-form) names in cultivation include these: **R. acicularis**, native from New York to Michigan, Wyoming, and Alaska and also of northern Europe and Asia, which rarely exceeds 3 feet in height, has densely-bristly stems, and leaves with three to nine leaflets up to 2 inches long. The solitary, fragrant, rose-pink flowers are 1½ to 2 inches across. The usually pear-

Rosa amblyotis

shaped fruits are ½ to ¾ inch long. **R. amblyotis,** of Kamchatka, is extremely hardy. From 3 to 5 feet tall, and with stems with slender, straight, upward-pointing prickles, it has leaves of seven to nine leaflets 1¼ to 2 inches long. The 2-inch-wide flowers are red. **R. arkansana,** of from Wisconsin to Colorado and Kansas, about 1½ feet tall, has very prickly and bristly stems. Its lustrous, essentially hairless leaves are of seven to nine pointed leaflets ¾ inch to 2¼ inches long. The flowers are clustered, pink, and almost 1½ inches wide. The subspherical fruits are not over ½ inch across. **R. arnoldiana,** an intermediate hybrid between *R. rugosa* and *R. borboniana,* 5 feet tall, has 2-inch-wide, semidouble, bright pink flowers. **R. blanda,** the meadow rose, and native from Newfoundland to Manitoba, Pennsylvania, and Missouri, is up to 6 feet tall. Its slender stems are without prickles, but sometimes when young have a few bristles. The leaves are of five, seven, or rarely nine dull leaflets. Solitary or in clusters of few, the flowers are pink and 2 inches or a little more in diameter. The usually subspherical fruits are ½ inch across. **R. bracteata,** the Macartney rose, not hardy in the north, is a Chinese species naturalized from Virginia to Florida and Texas. It has procumbent or trailing stems with strong, hooked prickles and lustrous leaves of five, seven, or nine leaflets ½ inch to 2 inches long. The usually solitary flowers are white and 2 to 2¾ inches wide. The woolly, spherical, orange-red fruits are about 1¼ inches across. **R. brunonii,** the Himalayan musk rose, is closely related to and often confused with

the musk rose (*R. moschata*), from which it is distinguishable by the undersides of its leaves being decidedly hairy instead of hairless or nearly so and its flowers being in larger clusters. **R. californica,** indigenous from Oregon to Baja California and hardy in southern New England, up to 9 feet tall, has stems with flattened, hooked prickles. Its leaves are of five or seven leaflets up to 1¼ inches long and hairy on both surfaces. The pink flowers, approximately 1½ inches wide, are in clusters of a dozen or more. The fruits are spherical, but have a distinct neck, and are from somewhat under to somewhat over ½ inch across. The flowers of *R. c. plena* are semidouble to double. **R. canina,** the dog rose, a widespread native of Europe, is sparingly nat-

Rosa canina

uralized in North America. Hardy throughout New England and up to 9 feet tall, it has usually arching branches with stout, hooked prickles. Its leaves have five or seven leaflets ¾ to 1 inch long. Solitary or in twos or threes, the light pink to white flowers, 1½ to 2 inches across, are succeeded by ellipsoid, scarlet fruits ½ to ¾ inch long. **R. cantabrigiensis,** a hybrid of *R. hugonis* and *R. sericea,* and handsome, has densely-bristly stems and ferny leaves

with seven to eleven leaflets. The about 2-inch-wide flowers are pale yellow passing to cream. They are succeeded by rather small, globular, orange-red fruits. **R. carolina,** the pasture rose, native from Maine to Wisconsin, Florida, Kansas, and Texas, is a handsome species up to 1 foot tall that spreads by suckers. Its stems have straight, slender prickles; its leaves have usually five, sometimes seven leaflets up to 1¼ inches long. Usually solitary, the rose-pink, approximately 2-inch-wide flowers are succeeded by pea-sized fruits. The blooms of *R. c. grandiflora* are larger, those of *R. c. alba* are white. **R. dumalis** (syn. *R. coriifolia*), of Europe and western Asia, up to 5 feet high, has rather sparingly-prickly stems. The leaves are of five to seven leaflets. The pink, solitary or clustered flowers are followed by spherical fruits ¾ inch in diameter. The creamy-white blooms of *R. d. froebelii,* a taller, more robust variety, are about 2½ inches in diameter. **R. ecae,** of Afghanistan, is less common in cultivation than closely related *R. primula,* which often passes for it. From the last, *R. ecae,* which is probably hardy about as far north as New York City, differs in being more compact and in having leaves ¾ to 1 inch long with five to nine leaflets. Also, the buttercup-yellow flowers are not over 1 inch wide. The fruits are small, spherical, and red. **R. harisonii,** called Harison's yellow rose, a hybrid of *R. foetida* and *R. spinosissima,* is hardy through most of New England. From 5 to 6 feet tall, this beautiful rose has foliage intermediate between that of its parents and semidouble, yellow flowers 2 inches in diameter. The fruits are small and almost black. **R. helenae,** a Chinese species hardy in southern New England, has sprawling to erect stems up to 18 feet tall, with stout, hooked prickles. Its leaves have seven or nine or, less frequently, five leaflets 1 inch to 2 inches long. The fragrant, white, 1- to 2-inch-wide flowers, in clusters of many, are succeeded by scarlet, ovoid to ovoid-oblong fruits approximately ½ inch in length. **R. hugonis,** of China, is without doubt one of the finest and most serviceable of the

Rosa cantabrigiensis

Rosa hugonis

Rosa hugonis (fruits)

Rosa micrantha

yellow-flowered species. Hardy in southern New England, it is 6 to 7 feet high and with arching stems furnished with bristles and straight prickles. Father Hugo's rose has leaves of five to thirteen leaflets up to ¾ inch long. The light yellow, solitary flowers, 2 inches in diameter, and borne profusely, are followed by dark red to

blackish-red, flattened-spherical fruits ½ inch or slightly more across. *R. laevigata,* the Cherokee rose, despite its vernacular name a native of China, is naturalized from Georgia to Florida, and Texas. Not hardy in the north and up to 15 feet high, it has stems with scattered, hooked prickles and lustrous leaves of usually three, less frequently five, pointed leaflets 1¼ to 2½ inches long. The fragrant, white or rarely pink flowers give way to bristly, pear-shaped fruits nearly or quite 1½ inches long. *R. l'heritierana,* the Boursault rose, is a hybrid between *R. pendulina* and *R. chinensis.* Hardy through much of New England, this robust, sparingly-prickly climber, up to 20 feet high, has leaves of three to seven leaflets, and light to dark purple, double to semidouble flowers in clusters. *R. longicuspis,* a clambering or climbing native of China, is not hardy in the north. Semievergreen or evergreen, it has leaves 5 inches to 1 foot long or longer of five to nine slender-pointed, lustrous leaflets 2 to 4 inches long. Borne in large terminal panicles, the banana-scented, white flowers, 2 inches across, are followed by scarlet to orange-red, ovoid fruits. *R. micrantha,* of Europe and the Mediterranean region and naturalized in North America, is a shrub up to 6 feet tall. It has curved prickles, and leaves with five or seven broad-ovate leaflets. The pink to white blooms, in clusters of up to four or solitary, are nearly 1½ inches wide. The fruits are ovoid or subspherical. *R. moyesii,* a Chinese species especially admired for its fruits, is hardy in southern New England. From 7 to 9 feet tall, it has stems with short, straight prickles and leaves with seven to thirteen pointed leaflets up to 1½ inches long. Solitary or paired, the dark blood-red flowers are 1½ to 2 inches wide or slightly wider. The long-necked, fla-

Rosa moyesii (fruits)

Rosa 'Nevada'

gon-shaped, orange-red fruits are 2 inches long or somewhat longer. The blooms of *R. m. fargesii* are glowing carmine. Variety 'Geranium' has bright geranium-red blooms, and is slightly more compact and has larger, smoother fruits than the species. A popular hybrid of *R. moyesii* or *R. m. fargesii* and, it is thought, the hybrid tea rose 'La Giralda', profusely flowering 'Nevada' is a vigorous grower up to 7 feet tall. From pink or apricot-pink buds open short-stalked, single, white flowers sometimes splashed with carmine on the backs of the petals. *R. multibracteata,* of China, is hardy about as far north as New York City. Graceful and up to about 6 feet tall, it has slender stems with prickles in pairs. The leaves are of seven to nine leaflets scarcely exceeding ½ inch in length, or smaller. Pink and about 1½ inches wide, the flowers are in branched clusters or panicles. The fruits are ovoid, orange-red, and up to slightly over ½ inch long. *R. nitida,* native from Newfoundland to Connecticut, is a pretty sort. From 1 foot to 2 feet tall and spreading by suckers, it has stems densely-clothed with bristles and short slender prickles. The glossy leaves have seven to nine leaflets, up to 1¼ inches long, which in fall turn bright red. Solitary or in clusters of five or fewer, the rose-pink flowers are 1½ to 2 inches wide. The slightly-bristly, scarlet fruits are under ½ inch in diameter. *R. omeiensis* is a beautiful Chinese species hardy about as far north as New York City. From 8 to 12 feet tall, it has bristly stems with flattened, red prickles conspicuously widened at their

Rosa omeiensis (fruits)

bases. The fernlike leaves are of nine to seventeen leaflets ⅓ to 1 inch long. The white flowers, 1 inch to 1½ inches in diameter and unusual among roses in having only four petals, festoon the branches. Pear-shaped and edible, the crimson and yellow fruits have stout yellow stalks. Those of *R. o. atrosanguinea* are deep crimson, those of *R. o. chrysocarpa,* yellow. Yellow flowers are borne by *R. o. lutea.* One of the most attractive roses, *R. o. pteracantha* is furnished with large, translucent, red prickles that form wings along

the stems and are especially lovely when seen with the sun shining through them. ***R. palustris,*** the swamp rose, is native from Nova Scotia to Minnesota, Florida, and Mississippi. Up to 6 feet tall, it has slender stems with few stout thorns. Its leaves are of seven or rarely nine leaflets ¾ inch to 2 inches long, usually more or less hairy on their undersides. Generally clustered, the rose-pink flowers are approximately 2 inches wide. The fruits are globular, bristly,

and fragrant leaves of seven leaflets. The flowers are single or semidouble and buff or yellow with shadings of copper. Favorite varieties are 'Lady Penzance' and 'Lord Penzance'. ***R. pisocarpa,*** the cluster rose native from California to British Columbia, has slender stems 3 to 6 feet tall with few straight prickles or sometimes none. The leaves have five or seven leaflets ½ inch to 1½ inches long. The flowers, pink and about 1¼ inches

Rosa palustris

Rosa omeiensis pteracantha

and somewhat under ½ inch wide. ***R. paulii,*** its parents *R. rugosa* and *R. arvensis,* is a low and sprawling shrub with clusters of 2½-inch-wide white flowers. ***R. pendulina,*** a handsome native of mountains in central and southern Europe, is hardy in southern New England. From 2 to 3 feet in height, it has slender stems, usually without bristles or prickles, and leaves of five to thirteen generally hairy leaflets ¾ inch to a little over 2 inches long. Solitary or in clusters of up to five, the rose-red to red-purple flowers are 1½ inches wide. The usually nodding, long-necked, oblongish, bright red fruits are ¾ to 1 inch long. ***R. penzanceana*** is the name of hybrids between *R. foetida* and *R. eglanteria.* These, called Lord Penzance briers, are moderately low and have arching stems

Rosa piscocarpa

wide, are succeeded by spherical fruits about ⅓ inch in diameter. *R. primula,* which has been confused in gardens with *R. ecae,* is more commonly cultivated than the latter. Native from Turkestan to China, hardy in southern New England, and about 6 feet tall, it is the earliest of roses to bloom. It has slender stems with many broad-based prickles and leaves of nine to fifteen or occasionally seven leaflets ½ to ¾ inch long. The solitary flowers, 1¼ to 1½ inches wide, which are light yellow when they open, fade to paler yellow. The spherical to obovoid, red fruits are under ½ inch long. *R. pruhoniciana,* a dense shrub, is an intermediate hybrid between *R. moyesii* and, probably, *R. multibracteata.* It has 2-inch-wide pink flowers, and ellipsoid, bright red fruits that are ¾ inch long. *R. pterogonis* is an intermediate hybrid between *R. omeiensis pteracantha* and *R. hugonis.* Variety

Rosa pruhoniciana (foliage and fruit)

'Redwing' has stems with very big brilliant red prickles and rich yellow, 1½-inch-wide flowers. *R. roxburghii,* of Japan and China, is hardy in southern New England. Up to 8 feet tall, it has wide-spreading, vi-

Rosa roxburghii (foliage and fruit)

ciously-prickly stems, and leaves of nine to fifteen leaflets up to ¾ inch long. The wild form, *R. r. normalis,* has single, fragrant, pale pink, prickly-stalked flowers 2 to 3 inches in diameter. The very prickly, flattened-spherical fruits are 1¼ to 1½ inches across. Variety *R. r. plena* has double flowers. *R. richardii,* its parents *R. gallica* and *R. phoenicia,* is a spreading bush

Rosa richardii

approximately 3 feet tall with rose-pink flowers that are 2 to 2½ inches in diameter. *R. rubrifolia,* of central Europe, and extremely hardy, is admired chiefly for its handsome foliage. It has reddish-violet stems almost devoid of prickles and attains a height of about 6 feet. Its leaves, glaucous-purple or bluish-green tinged with purplish-red have seven or nine leaflets. Rather sparsely borne, the clear pink 1- to 1½-inch-wide flowers are followed by subspherical, bright red fruits a little over ½ inch in diameter. *R. sericea,* of the Himalayan region, a close ally of *R. omeiensis,* is much like that species, but of more upright habit. Its leaves have seven to eleven small, roundish leaflets silky-hairy on their undersides. The white to lemon-yellow, cupped flowers, 1 inch to 2 inches wide, have four or five petals. The small red fruits have slender, not thickened stalks. This is probably not hardy in the north. *R. setigera,* the prairie rose, is native from Ontario to Nebraska, Florida, and Texas. A

Rosa setigera

Rosa ultramontana (foliage and fruits)

late-bloomer, it makes thickets of arching or climbing stems up to 15 feet long with stout, hooked prickles or in some forms with few or none. The leaves occasionally have five, more commonly three, leaflets 1¼ to 3½ inches long. About 2 inches in diameter, the rose-pink, nearly scentless flowers are in clusters of rather few. As they age they fade to blush-white. The fruits are spherical, about ⅓ inch in diameter. The rose named 'Baltimore Belle' is a variety or hybrid of this species. *R. ultramontana,* native to western North America, is 3 to 8 feet tall and has slender, straight prickles. Its leaves are of five to seven oval to oval-oblong, toothed leaflets, with short pubescence on their undersides. The pink flowers are single and 1½ to 2 inches in width. The bright red, elliptic to spherical fruits are up to ⅞ inch in length. *R. villosa* (syn. *R. pomifera*), the apple rose, earns its vernacular name by reason of its very large fruits. Native to Europe and western Asia and hardy in southern New England, this attains a height of 6 feet. It has stems with nearly straight spines and leaves with five, seven, or less often nine hairy leaflets ¾ inch to 2 inches long. Solitary, or in clusters of two or three, the flowers are pink and 1½ to 2 inches across. The fruits are crimson, generally subspherical, bristly, and up to 1 inch in diameter. Variety *R. v. duplex,* probably of hybrid origin, has semidouble flowers. *R. virginiana,* native from Newfoundland

Rosa villosa

Rosa villosa (fruits)

Rosa wichuraiana as a bank planting

Rosa villosa duplex

bler roses. Hardy in southern New England, and in mild climates partially evergreen, this is one of the latest rose species to bloom. It has long, trailing or prostrate stems, with strong, curved prickles, and lustrous leaves of seven or nine ½- to 1-inch-long leaflets. The fragrant, white flowers, in small to large pyramidal clusters, are 1½ to 2 inches wide. They are followed by ovoid, red fruits ⅓ inch long or a little longer. **R. willmottiae,** of western China, hardy about as far north as New York City, is very lovely. Densely-branched and 6 to 9 feet tall, it has stems with pairs of straight prickles. Its ferny leaves, fragrant when crushed, are of seven or nine leaflets up to slightly over ½ inch in length. Generally solitary, the rose-purple flowers are about 1¼ inches wide and are followed by orange-red, pear-shaped fruits approximately ⅓ inch long. Variety *R. w.* 'Wisley' has blooms of deeper pink. **R. xanthina,** of China and Korea, is a close ally of *R. hugonis,* differing chiefly in its shoots being without bristles even at their bases and the more bluntly-toothed leaves being usually hairy when young. Hardy in southern New England, *R. xanthina,* up to 9 feet tall, has stems with stout, straight prickles. Its leaves are of seven to thirteen leaflets up to ¾ inch long. The solitary,

to Virginia, Alabama, and Missouri, up to 6 feet in height, makes few or no suckers and has stems with often hooked prickles. The leaves are of seven to nine lustrous leaflets ¾ inch to 2¼ inches long. Solitary or in clusters of few, the pink flowers are 2 to 3 inches wide. They are followed by spherical, bright red, ½-inch-wide fruits. The blooms of *R. v. plena* are double. Variety *R. v. lamprophylla,* very compact, rarely exceeds 3 feet in height. **R. wichuraiana,** the memorial rose, a native of Japan, Taiwan, China, and Korea, and naturalized in parts of North America, has played an important part as a parent of hybrid ram-

Rosa wichuraiana

Rosa wichuraiana (flowers)

Rosa xanthina spontanea

golden-yellow flowers, about 1½ inches across, are semidouble or double. Those of the wild form *R. x. spontanea* are single.

Garden and Landscape Uses. The species, varieties, and simple hybrids of roses dealt with here are mainly less formal than such more familiar garden groups as hybrid perpetuals, hybrid teas, floribundas, grandifloras, ramblers, and large-flowered climbers, which represent the outcome of involved hybridization and selection. These last are treated, together with a selection of fairly complex hybrids grouped as shrub roses, in the Encyclopedia entry Roses.

The sorts with which we are immediately concerned are also shrubs, mostly bushy, but some climbing and some trailing. The majority of the roses we are considering have prickly stems, those of *R. omeiensis pteracantha* and some others brightly colored. The foliage is generally attractive, and most sorts bloom freely, the great majority for a comparatively short period in early summer, but a few others, notably *R. rugosa* and its hybrids, more protractedly, flowers being produced intermittently long after the main display. The fruits of many are highly ornamental and long lasting. As landscape furnishings, these roses are admirable when employed like the majority of garden shrubs. In congenial environments they flourish for many years, indeed more or less indefinitely. They may be used alone or mixed with other shrubs in beds and borders. Such plantings are often appropriate on the outskirts of rose gardens. Selected sorts of these roses make excellent informal hedges, screens, and barriers. Trailing kinds, notably *R. wichuraiana*, are splendid for clothing banks. In exposed locations near the sea and elsewhere, few deciduous shrubs equal *R. rugosa* and its hybrids.

Cultivation. None of the roses treated here poses serious problems in regions climatically adapted to them. Soil and fertilizer requirements are as for more sophisticated sorts (see the Encyclopedia entry Roses) and so are methods for controlling diseases and pests.

Propagation is often most conveniently accomplished by cuttings of firm, leafy shoots in summer or of leafless hardwood stems in fall, but layering affords an alternate and sure method with kinds with trailing or procumbent stems or with stems that can conveniently be bent to the ground. Species, as distinct from hybrids and varieties, are easily raised from seed sown as soon as ripe in a cold frame or a location outdoors protected from disturbance, or they may be stratified by mixing with slightly damp peat moss, storing in a plastic bag or other container at about 40°F until late winter or spring, and then be sown indoors in well-drained pots or flats in sandy, peaty soil in a temperature of 60 to 70°F.

Pruning these kinds of roses is based upon their being shrubs. No more is necessary than needed to keep them shapely, uncrowded with superfluous stems, and of sizes appropriate to their sorts and sites. Try to preserve their natural growth habit, erect, arching, spreading, or prostrate as may be, so grace and elegance are displayed to best advantage.

Late winter or earliest spring is the time to attend to the chief pruning, which usually involves taking out badly placed branches completely and possibly one or more older ones, and shortening others lightly to moderately. Sometimes it is desirable to cut back neglected, overgrown specimens severely, possibly to within 1 foot of the ground, and to make a new start at creating a framework of permanent or semipermanent branches, but this is exceptional rather than routine. For additional information see Roses.

ROSA DE MONTANA is *Antigonon leptopus.*

ROSACEAE — Rose Family. Horticulturally outstandingly important, the ROSACEAE, in the wild of cosmopolitan distribution, is especially numerous as to species in temperate regions. It comprises 100 genera totaling 2,000 species of dicotyledons. To it belong such familiar fruits as apples, apricots, blackberries, cherries, loquats, peaches, pears, plums, raspberries, strawberries, and, in addition, numerous evergreen and deciduous trees, shrubs, herbaceous perennials, and annuals highly esteemed as ornamentals. Members of the family have usually alternate, rarely opposite, undivided or divided leaves and generally symmetrical flowers with four or five sepals or calyx lobes, the same number of petals or sometimes none or in horticultural varieties that have double or semidouble blooms often many more than five. There are generally many stamens, rarely a definite number of just one or two, and as many styles as there are carpels. The fruits, very various, are achenes, follicles, drupes, pomes (as in apples), or hips (as in roses). Genera of the rose family treated in this Encyclopedia include *Acaena, Adenostoma, Agrimonia, Alchemilla, Amelanchier, Amelasorbus, Aronia, Aruncus, Cercocarpus, Chaenomeles, Chamaebatia, Chamaebatiaria, Chrysobalanus, Cotoneaster, Cowania, Crataegomespilus, Crataegus, Crataemespilus, Cydonia, Dalibarda, Docynia, Dryas, Duchesnea, Eriobotrya, Exochorda, Fallugia, Filipendula, Fragaria, Geum, Gillenia, Heteromeles, Holodiscus, Horkelia, Ivesia, Kageneckia, Kelseya, Kerria, Leucosidea, Luetkea, Lyonothamnus, Maddenia, Malus, Margyricarpus, Mespilus, Neillia, Neviusia, Oemleria, Osteomeles, Peraphyllum, Petrophytum, Photinia, Physocarpus, Potentilla, Poterium, Prinsepia, Prunus, Purshia, Pyra-*

cantha, *Pyracomeles, Pyrus, Quillaja, Raphiolepis, Rhodotypos, Rosa, Rubus, Sanguisorba, Sibbaldia, Sibiraea, Sorbaria, Sorbaronia, Sorbopyrus, Sorbus, Spenceria, Spiraea, Stephanandra, Stranvaesia,* and *Waldsteinia.*

ROSARY-PEA is *Abrus precatorius.*

ROSARY VINE is *Ceropegia woodii.*

ROSCHERIA (Roschèr-ia). One species, endemic to the Seychelles Islands, is the only representative of this genus of the palm family PALMAE. Its name commemorates Albrecht Roscher, a traveler in Africa killed in 1860.

Rare in cultivation, small to medium-sized **Roscheria melenochaetes** has a solitary trunk that, when young, is encircled with rings of black spines. These are mostly absent from older specimens. From *Verschaffeltia,* this differs in that, except on very young specimens, its leaves are divided to their midribs into ten to twelve pairs of distinctly separate, irregularly-sized leaflets, the broader ones toothed at their ends. The flower clusters arise from among the foliage. The fruits are shotlike, up to ¼ inch in diameter, and red at maturity.

Garden Uses and Cultivation. This is a plant for collectors. It has the same uses and requires the same conditions as *Verschaffeltia.* For additional information see Palms.

ROSCOEA (Ros-còea). William Roscoe, founder of the first botanical garden at Liverpool, England, who died in 1831, is commemorated by *Roscoea,* a genus of low, deciduous, herbaceous plants of the ginger family ZINGIBERACEAE. The group is endemic from the Himalayas to China, mostly at high altitudes. None of its about seventeen species is reliably hardy in the north. It differs from *Cautleya* in its flowers having an upper petal much wider than the two lateral ones.

Roscoeas have fleshy roots and short rhizomes from which develop erect, vase-like clusters of sheathing, lanceolate to oblong, parallel-veined leaves. From the centers of the vases, the orchid-like, blue, purple, yellow, or white flowers, solitary or in spikes or heads, are displayed. They have long, tubular calyxes split down one side and with two or three teeth. Their generally long corolla tubes are dilated in their upper parts and end in three perianth lobes (petals), an upper erect one, the others spreading or deflexed. Another showy feature of the flower, a large, petal-like lip, is morphologically a nonfunctional stamen or staminode. In addition, there are two smaller, erect staminodes. There is one fertile stamen and one style. The fruits are capsules.

Beautiful primrose-yellow-flowered **R. cautleoides** is especially pleasing. Its lustrous, green or grayish leaves, up to six in

Roscoea cautleoides

a cluster, are lanceolate and about 5 inches long. There are seven or fewer blooms in each rather crowded spike. The upper petals are hooded. The two-lobed, obovate lip of the flower is 1¼ inches long. A variety with broader leaves and nearly stalkless flower spikes is *R. c. grandiflora.* Another, *R. c.* 'August Beauty', blooms later than the typical species.

Purplish-blue flowers of rather thin texture are borne by **R. purpurea,** a robust

Roscoea purpurea

kind up to about 1 foot tall. In the wild this ranges from the Himalayas to Burma and Assam. Its broadly-linear to linear-lanceolate leaves nearly hide the short-stalked spikes of two to four flowers. The large, deeply-two-lobed, obovate lip is longer than wide. Variety *R. p. procera* is

taller and has considerably larger blooms with lips 2 inches long. Wider leaves, and flowers with lips broader than long, distinguish **R. humeana** from *R. purpurea.* Also, it is usually somewhat lower. The flowers, two to four together, are violet-purple. They have hooded upper petals 1½ inches long and lips 1 inch long by 1¼ inches wide. Its flowers usually solitary and scarcely topping the lanceolate or linear-lanceolate leaves, **R. alpina** is a native of the Himalayas. It has usually three

Roscoea alpina

slender-pointed lanceolate to linear leaves in each cluster. Its purple flowers have a rounded upper petal and an obovate, two-lobed lip. This species is ordinarily up to 6 inches tall.

Garden Uses and Cultivation. Roscoeas are not plants for regions of climatic extremes. Mild winters and coolish, humid summers best suit them. Under such conditions, they thrive in lightly shaded places in sandy woodland soil that contains abundant leaf mold or other decayed organic material and that is reasonably moist, but not wet. Some gardeners recommend the addition of lime to the soil for *R. cautleoides,* but this does not appear to be necessary. Roscoeas are increased by division and by seed. Agreeable locations in rock gardens, at the fringes of woodlands, and similar places afford opportunities to nurture these choice plants. It is beneficial to maintain an organic mulch about them. In addition to their suitability for outdoor cultivation in favorable climates, they are admirable for growing in pots in cold frames and greenhouses devoted to alpine plants.

ROSE. Besides true roses (members of the genus *Rosa*), which are treated in this Encyclopedia in the entries Rosa and Roses, many other plants have the word rose as a part of their common names. Among such are these: African-dog-rose (*Xylotheca kraussiana*), alpine-rose (*Rhododendron ferrugineum* and *R. hirsutum*), California-rose (*Calystegia hederacea flore-pleno*), Christmas-rose (*Helleborus niger*), Confederate- or cotton-rose (*Hibiscus mutabilis*), desert-rose (*Adenium obesum, Alyogyne huegelii, Hibiscus farragei,* and *H. huegelii*), dog- or river-rose (*Bauera rubioides*), green water- or underwater-rose (*Samolus parviflorus*), guelder-rose (*Viburnum opulus roseum*), Lenten-rose (*Helleborus orientalis*), mountain-rose (*Orothamnus zeyheri*), rock-rose (*Cistus*), rose-acacia (*Robinia hispida*), rose-apple (*Syzygium jambos*), rose-bay (*Rhododendron maximum*), rose-campion (*Lychnis coronaria*), rose geranium (*Pelargonium graveolens*), rose-mallow (*Hibiscus* and *Lavatera trimestris*), rose-moss (*Portulaca grandiflora*), rose-of-China (*Hibiscus schizopetalus* and *H. rosa-sinensis*), rose-of-heaven (*Lychnis coeli-rosa*), rose-of-Jericho (*Anastatica hierochuntica* and *Selaginella lepidophylla*), rose-of-Sharon (*Hibiscus syriacus* and *Hypericum calycinum*), rose-of-Venezuela (*Brownea grandiceps*), rose plantain (*Plantago major rosularis*), sage-rose (*Turnera ulmifolia*), small-wood-rose (*Argyreia nervosa*), sun-rose (*Helianthemum*), underwater-rose (*Samolus parviflorus*), and wood-rose (*Merremia tuberosa*).

ROSELINGS. See Cuthbertia.

ROSELLE or JAMAICA-SORREL. This, cultivated in the tropics and subtropics and sometimes in warm parts of the United States for its thickened calyxes and floral bracts, which are esteemed for the acid flavor they impart to jams, jellies, sauces, and beverages, is *Hibiscus sabdariffa*, a native annual of the tropics of the Old World.

Roselle, which attains a height of 4 to 6 feet, is usually grown in rows about 3 feet apart with 1½ to 2 feet between the plants in the rows. It is easily raised from seed sown where the plants are to remain or, where the growing season is not long enough, started early indoors to give plants to set out after the weather is warm and settled. This crop responds to conditions that suit eggplants and tomatoes. The red or yellow heads or bolls are harvested in an immature stage and used fresh or after drying.

ROSEMARY is *Rosmarinus officinalis*. Australian- or coast-rosemary is *Westringia fruticosa*, bog-rosemary *Andromeda polifolia*, and wild-rosemary *Ledum palustre*.

ROSEOCACTUS (Roseo-cáctus) — Living Rock or Star Cactus. The genus *Roseocactus*, of the cactus family CACTACEAE, is, by those who prefer lumping genera separated by minute technical differences into fewer, more embracing genera, included in *Ariocarpus*. Treated separately, it contains about four species. Native chiefly of Mexico with a minor extension into Texas, this genus has a name that honors the American botanist Dr. Joseph Nelson Rose, who died in 1928.

Roseocactuses have more or less turnip-like roots and flattened to hemispherical, fleshy plant bodies of rugged appearance, with spirals of thick tubercles. The flowers, which remain open for a short time only, come from the centers of the plants, arising from woolly grooves or fissures on the upper sides of the tubercles. This distinguishes *Roseocactus* from *Ariocarpus*. The blooms of the latter originate in the axils of the tubercles.

Living rock or star cactus (**R. fissuratus** syn. *Ariocarpus fissuratus*) has gray-green to

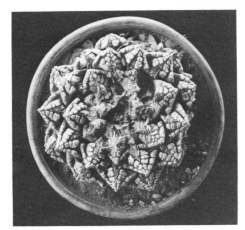
Roseocactus fissuratus

yellowish, flattish-topped plant bodies 2 to 4 or rarely up to 6 inches in diameter and broader than high. Their much roughened, triangular tubercles, not spreading or leaflike, resemble rather craggy pieces of rock. A little broader than long, along the entire upper surface they have a woolly groove flanked on each side by one naked of wool. The magenta-pink to nearly white blooms are 1 inch to almost 2 inches wide. From this, **R. intermedius** differs in the woolly grooves of its tubercles, which extend for their entire lengths, not being accompanied by side grooves. The plant bodies of **R. lloydii** (syn. *Ariocarpus lloydii*) are more hemispherical than those of the preceding sorts, and as they grow in the wild stand higher out of the ground. Their tubercles are rhomboidal. Each has a woolly groove extending for only one-half its length. The flowers resemble those of *R. fissuratus*.

Considerably smaller than other species, **R. kotschoubeyanus** has cylindrical to somewhat turnip-shaped roots and flattish plant bodies, 1½ to 3 inches wide, with triangular tubercles each with a woolly groove along their entire length. The 1½-inch-wide flowers are purple. Variety *R. k. albiflorus* has white blooms. Tiny *R. k. macdowellii* has plant bodies 1 inch in diameter and 1-inch-wide, purple-crimson flowers.

Garden Uses and Cultivation. These slow-growing cactuses are choice for collections, outdoors in warm, desert climates, and in greenhouses. They respond to environments and care that suit *Ariocar-*

pus. They need very porous sandy earth, preferably containing some limestone, but with little or no organic content. Some cultivators believe that the addition of gypsum to the soil promotes flowering. Great care must at all times be exercised with watering, especially in winter. Excessive moisture is disastrous. Roseocactuses need full sun. Propagation is by seed and by offsets and sometimes by grafting onto other genera of cactuses. They grow very slowly. For further suggestions on cultivation see Cactuses.

ROSEOCEREUS (Roseo-cèreus). Included in *Trichocereus* by conservative botanists, one handsome species of cactus is segregated as *Roseocereus* by those who split genera finely. It belongs in the cactus family CACTACEAE. Its name commemorates the American botanist Dr. Joseph Nelson Rose, who died in 1928.

Native to Bolivia, **R. tephracanthus** (syns. *Cereus tephracanthus, Eriocereus teph-*

Roseocereus tephracanthus

racanthus), bushy to treelike, usually has several to many erect, 4- to 8-foot-tall stems, 1½ to 2¼ inches thick, glossy gray-green, and with eight blunt, wide, notched ribs. The clusters of rigid, awl-shaped, brown-tipped, whitish spines consist of four to seven ½-inch-long radials and one ¾- to 1-inch-long central. The flowers are white, 7 to 8 inches long by up to 6 inches wide, with the innermost segments bright rose-pink and the outermost segments greenish with brown margins. Their perianth tubes and ovaries, like the fruits, are covered with reddish scales and plentiful white hairs.

Garden and Landscape Uses and Cultivation. This adapts well to a variety of environments and grows with vigor. In warm, desert and semidesert climates, it is a useful landscape subject for sunny locations where the soil is nourishing and slightly acid. It also does well in greenhouses. Propagation is easy by cuttings and by seed. For more information see Cactuses.

ROSEROOT is *Sedum rosea*.

ROSES. Probably the most widely grown of flowers and certainly among the most beautiful, roses are cultivated practically everywhere that gardening is done. Only in parts of the tropics where continuous warmth and availability of moisture denies them a season of dormancy are they likely to be omitted from garden plantings.

Here our concern is limited to horticultural varieties of more or less complex hybrid origin, but these encompass the vast majority of sorts that come to mind when the word roses is mentioned. Species roses, kinds that occur as natives in some part of the world, and their varieties and simple hybrids are dealt with in this Encyclopedia under Rosa.

The literature of roses is vast and ever increasing. Throughout the world from 1920 to 1970 approximately 400 books on the subject were published in addition to numerous bulletins, magazine articles, and the like. Plato's pupil Theophrastus wrote of roses and how to grow them as early as the fourth century B.C., but ap-

proximately nine centuries were to pass before a book devoted exclusively to roses was to appear. It was *Rosa et Partibus* by Nicolas Monardes, better known as the author of a treatise on the Americas titled *Joyful Newes Out of the Newe Founde Worlde*, published at Antwerp in 1551. From the early years of the sixteenth century to the early ones of the seventeenth, herbals devoted to the virtues or supposed virtues of plants as cures or alleviants of bodily ills were produced. Invariably roses were included and sometimes the sorts cultivated were described. The last of the great English herbalists, John Parkinson discusses in *Paradisi in Sole Paradisus Terrestris*, published in 1629, twenty-four varieties and supplies hints on how to grow them.

The history of roses in cultivation stems from antiquity. Some 4,750 years ago they were brought by King Sargon of Ur and Akkad from across the Taurus Mountains and planted in the fertile land between the Euphrates and Tigris rivers. Seneca describes how in ancient Rome they were forced into bloom in December in struc-

tures heated with piped hot water, and the Emperor Charlemagne, who died in 814, or perhaps his son, sponsored the planting of rose gardens, chiefly because of the medicinal value roses were, in those days, believed to possess.

Yet by modern standards progress in developing new sorts was slow. In the middle of the fourteenth century only fourteen kinds were grown in England, scarcely more 200 years later. As such, those that existed had arisen as chance hybrids or as mutants (sports) of older kinds.

By the end of the eighteenth century, a great many of what are now called old-fashioned shrub roses had come into being. Chiefly variants of *Rosa gallica*, *R. damascena*, and *R. centifolia*, these are discussed under these names in the Encyclopedia entry Rosa. But the possibilities of obtaining new varieties by sowing seeds of the old-timers had by then been pretty well explored, and the art of artificial hybridization had not yet arrived.

Then came a great breakthrough for which two events were largely responsible. One was the development of the technique of hybridizing, the other, the introduction from southern China to Europe between 1792 and 1824 of varieties of *R. chinensis*, the China rose, and of closely related *R. odorata*, the tea rose. The new-

Climbing roses at Bodnant Gardens, Wales

Hybrid China rose 'Hermosa'

comers were hybridized among themselves and with European varieties to produce completely new classes of garden roses, among the first, teas, hybrid chinas, and bourbons.

Great impetus was given to the developing interest in roses by Napoleon's Empress Josephine, who, in 1799, while Napoleon was away on his Egyptian campaign, purchased a chateau at Malmaison near Paris. Extravagant alterations and additions to both house and grounds included expanding the latter to several hundred acres. Josephine's passion for

The Cranford Rose Garden, Brooklyn Botanic Garden

gardening was expressed in many ways, but in none more completely than in the establishment of the roseraie at Malmaison. She maintained such close contact with John Kennedy of the nursery firm of Kennedy and Lee, of Hammersmith, London, that he was issued a special passport that allowed him, even during the continental blockade and throughout the Napoleonic wars, to pass freely through the English and French lines to advise Josephine about her garden.

It was Josephine's ambition to assemble at Malmaison all known species and varieties of roses and to add to her collection new sorts as they became available. This, to a very large extent, she succeeded in doing. Estimates have been made that at her death in 1814 some 250 varieties of rose were being grown at Malmaison, but this may be somewhat of an exaggeration. Sad to say, within a few years of Josephine's death the roseraie at Malmaison had mostly disappeared. Many of the roses that prospered at Malmaison are illustrated in the magnificent folio edition of *Les Roses* by Pierre Joseph Redouté and Claude Antoine Thory. Redouté was originally commissioned by the Empress to produce these stippled engravings in color, but they were not published until 1817–1820, after her death.

Crossing and recrossing was continued with such enthusiasm by breeders that well before the first third of the century had passed a spate of varieties of mixed ancestry, the parentage of which often could only be conjectured, had come into being. Out of this complex, by about 1837, had evolved a totally new class, the hybrid perpetual, of which some 3,000 varieties were eventually introduced, the last in 1926.

Tea roses, chiefly derived from *R. odorata* and decidedly tenderer than hybrid teas, acquired their name because the delightful spicy scent of their blooms reminded some of crushed tea. Introduced from China, the first of its class, 'Pink Tea', was brought to England in 1810, to be followed fourteen years later by double-flowered, pale yellow *R. o. ochroleuca* and others. Subsequently, many varieties were developed by intercrossing these and by hybridizing them with *R. chinensis*.

Until the coming of the sturdier hybrid teas, tea roses were very popular outdoors, in regions where winters were not too severe, and in greenhouses. To them the hybrid teas owe their propensity for continuous blooming. The flowers of tea roses are quite large and well formed, but often have somewhat weak stems and petals of rather poor substance. Among varieties extant are 'Catherine Mermet', 'Duchesse de Brabant', 'Maman Cochet', 'Rosette Delizy', and 'Safrano'. Climbing varieties include 'Gloire de Dijon' and 'Sombreuil'.

Hybrid perpetuals, among the most cold resistant of garden roses, may be grown where winters are too severe for most hybrid teas, floribundas, and grandifloras. The immediate predecessors of hybrid teas, these were the most important garden roses of the last half of the nineteenth century. Vigorous, often tall bushes, some 4 to 6 feet in height, they are not as reliable continuous bloomers as hybrid teas and most

Hybrid perpetual roses: (a) 'Baroness Rothschild'

(b) 'Earl of Dufferin'

(c) 'Mrs. John Laing'

Polyantha roses originated in France sometime after 1862 as chance hybrids between *Rosa multiflora* and *R. chinensis*. The earliest included 'Mignonette', which was crossed with a tea rose by the French breeder Joseph Pernet-Ducher to produce 'Mlle Cecile Brunner', introduced in 1881. One of the great roses of all time, this became widely known as the sweetheart rose. Roses of this class still grown, some of which in favorable climates attain a 3-foot height, although many are shorter, include these: 'Mlle Cecile Brunner', which unlike most polyanthas has high-centered blooms resembling those of perfect tea or hybrid tea form, but tiny and clustered. Delightfully fragrant, they are soft pink with a yellow background. 'Charlie McCarthy', free-flowering and very dwarf, has white blooms. 'Margo Koster' has pink-flushed, orange-colored blooms. 'Perle d'Or', similar to 'Mlle Cecile Brunner', but dwarfer, has flowers scarcely as exquisitely formed of a slightly more golden hue. 'Red Sweetheart' is a red-flowered variant of 'Mlle Cecile Brunner'.

Nineteenth-century climbing roses include several extant that, besides being beautiful and worthy, excite pleasurable nostalgia. Possibly the oldest, the *Rosa setigera* hybrid 'Baltimore Belle', introduced in 1843 and vigorous and hardy, has fully double, fragrant blooms of blush-pink. Unfortunately so tender that in the United States it succeeds outdoors only in the south and the far west, glorious 'Maréchal Niel', of the noisette class, is well worthy of cool greenhouse accommodation. Over a long season this introduction of 1864 produces very large, superbly fragrant, golden-yellow flowers, in the bud stage beautifully pointed. Hardier than 'Maréchal Niel', but not sufficiently so to survive outdoors in the north, except perhaps in a few very sheltered sites, the noisette climber 'William Allen Richardson', introduced in 1878, has pointed buds that open into delightfully fragrant, buff-yellow to apricot blooms. Introduced in 1879, 'Mme Alfred Carriere', hardier than most

other noisettes, bears very fragrant, blush-white flowers over a long season.

Early twentieth-century climbers other than ramblers, sorts introduced to cultivation before 1925, include some still cultivated. Among the best known are these: 'Belle of Portugal', a hybrid of *Rosa gigantea* introduced in 1903, has very large, semidouble, flesh-pink flowers, but is not hardy in the north. 'Dr. Van Fleet', a hybrid of *R. wichuraiana*, was introduced in 1910. This, which has soft-pink buds and a profusion of fragrant double flowers, later gave rise to an ever-blooming variant named 'New Dawn'. Another debutant of 1910, the very vigorous *R. wichuraiana* hybrid 'Silver Moon' has big semidouble creamy-white, faintly-fragrant flowers that open from pointed, yellow buds.

Rambler roses, the first of which, 'Crimson Rambler', was introduced from the Orient about 1893, are less commonly grown than formerly, but a few older kinds are extant and, hardier than many modern climbers, are well suited for planting in exposed places and especially near the sea. Ramblers, some like 'Crimson Rambler', derivatives of *Rosa multiflora*, but most of *R. wichuraiana* ancestry, differ from other climbers in producing in one great flush in early summer, large clusters of small single, semidouble, or double flowers. Their canes are comparatively slender and weak and an abundance of new ones develops from the base of the plant each year at about the time flowering is through, making pruning necessary before entanglement results.

Older ramblers still cultivated include these: 'American Pillar', with single, white-centered, crimson blooms; 'Dorothy Perkins', which has double, rose-pink blooms, but unfortunately is very susceptible to mildew; 'Excelsa', its flowers crimson, also has the fault of being very mildew prone; and mildew-resistant 'Minnehaha', with bright pink flowers.

Modern roses are classified into several more or less distinct groups based upon

other modern roses, although most make some display after the first early summer flush of bloom and many produce a second, lesser display in fall. The blooms, generally lacking the high, pointed centers of most hybrid teas, and often very fragrant, range in color from white through various shades of pink to deep rich red. There are no yellows. Most of the many varieties once grown are no longer extant. The few available are treasured by collectors of old roses. Representative varieties are 'Arrillaga', 'Baronne Prevost', 'Baroness Rothschild', 'Candeur Lyonnaise', 'Captain Hayward', 'Earl of Dufferin', 'Ferdinand Pichard', 'Frau Karl Druschi', 'General Jacqueminot', 'Georg Arends', 'Mrs. John Laing', 'Paul Neyron', and 'Reine des Violettes'.

Noisette rose 'Maréchal Niel' in a greenhouse

Rambler roses: (a) 'Dorothy Perkins' on an arbor

Romanzoffia sitchensis

A rose garden in bloom

A hybrid pòlyantha rose

Rosa centifolia variety

Climbing rose 'Blaze'

Rothmannia capensis

Rudbeckia, gloriosa-daisy variety

Rubus cockburnianus

A hybrid tea rose

(b) 'Minnehaha' trained to a tall post

Hybrid tea roses: (a) 'Charlotte Armstong'

habit of growth, manner of flowering, and type of bloom. According to habit they are listed as bush, shrub, climbing, pillar, and trailing or creeping varieties. The first two groups include all of shrublike form that stand upright without support. Climbing, pillar, and trailing roses have comparatively slender stems that, unless supported, sprawl or spread over the ground. None climbs by twining or attaching itself to a support like a vine. To achieve height the stems must intertwine with the support or be tied into place. Pillar roses are sorts that ordinarily do not exceed 8 feet in height and have stems sturdier than those of more typical climbers. Trailing or creeping varieties have long, slender stems well adapted for covering slopes and banks.

The most popular bush roses are the hybrid teas, floribundas, grandifloras, and miniatures. Introduced in 1867, the first hybrid tea, 'La France', was a cross between a hardy hybrid perpetual variety and a nonhardy tea rose. Since then, thousands of varieties of similar parentage and some resulting from crossing with other kinds have been raised to constitute the hybrid tea class, varieties of which in large measure provide the standard of excellence against which other roses are judged. About 1900, a decided step forward was taken when the French rosarian Pernet-Ducher crossed *Rosa foetida* with a hybrid tea variety to produce the first hybrid teas with yellow and coppery-yellow flowers.

Hybrid teas, if in cold regions afforded appropriate winter protection, can be grown practically throughout the United States. Most have beautifully formed, often fragrant, comparatively long-stemmed, usually fully double flowers with high, pointed centers, but there are sorts with semidouble and single blooms. They come

(b) 'Miss Rowena Thom'

(c) 'Yankee Doodle'

Floribunda roses: (a) 'Cathedral'

(b) 'Fanfare'

in a wide range of colors and are produced over a long summer and fall season. Hybrid tea rose bushes, mostly 2 to 4 feet high, are sometimes as tall as 6 feet. A group of varieties called subzero hybrid teas, raised in the 1930s by Dr. Walter Brownell of Little Compton, Rhode Island, by crossing hybrid teas with hybrids of *Rosa wichuraiana*, proved much hardier than other sorts, but their blooms were often less refined in form.

Floribunda or hybrid polyantha roses came into being in 1924 as a result of the

Grandiflora roses: (a) 'Arizona'

American rosarian Dr. J. H. Nicolas crossing a hybrid tea with a polyantha variety to produce the floribunda 'Rochester'. The long succession of floribundas that followed have added immensely to the wealth of garden roses. Considerable variation occurs among varieties, but all have much bigger blooms than those of polyantha roses, although like the flowers of those, they are in clusters. The blooms of floribundas, single, semidouble, or fully double, come in a wide spectrum of colors and are often as beautifully formed as the best hybrid teas. Generally vigorous, these roses have the great advantage of tolerating much lower temperatures than hybrid tea roses.

Grandiflora roses are really a subgroup of floribundas segregated on the basis of having blooms resembling and approaching in size those of hybrid teas, but in long-stalked clusters of fewer individuals than is usual with floribundas. The first of this class, 'Queen Elizabeth' was raised about 1950, the result of crossing hybrid tea 'Charlotte Armstrong' with floribunda 'Floradora'.

Hybrid polyanthas or baby ramblers, less popular than formerly, but still useful, are bush varieties of hybrid origin with large clusters of many small, flattish, red, pink, or white flowers that are without the high, pointed centers typical of many hybrid teas.

Miniature roses are bush sorts, ordinarily not over 1½ feet tall and often smaller, that have diminutive leaves and blooms. The earliest varieties and many later ones resulted from crossing *Rosa chinensis minima* with varieties of hybrid teas, but other sorts have played a part in the parentage of some varieties. Kinds with long slender stems and diminutive foliage and flowers are called climbing miniatures.

Climbing roses, sorts that ordinarily need support and are best suited for training against walls and fences, over arches and pergolas, and up poles and posts, are of varied origin, and their classification, like the ancestries of some sorts, is blurred. Those with thin, pliable canes and great crowded clusters of flattish flowers not over 2 inches in diameter are called ramblers. These bloom profusely on short side

Rose, hybrid polyantha variety

(b) 'Montezuma'

A miniature rose in a 5-inch pot

A rambler rose clothing an archway

growths from one-year-old canes and most typically are not remontant. That is, they bloom but once in early summer and devote the rest of the season to developing an abundance of new canes that will flower the following year. However, some of the newer rambler-type roses flower more or less recurrently so that their season of bloom is more extended.

Large-flowered climbers characteristically have more rigid, stouter canes than ramblers, and flowers over 2 inches in diameter, often, but not always, with higher pointed centers so that they more nearly resemble those of hybrid teas, in clusters of fewer than is typical of ramblers. Many, but not all, large-flowered climbers have a second flowering after the first one in early summer, or they bloom fairly continuously throughout the summer.

Climbing hybrid teas, climbing floribundas, and climbing hybrid polyanthas are sorts that are known to have originated as mutants (sports) from bush varieties. For example, 'Climbing Peace' is a climbing mutant from 'Peace'. Except in their very much more robust growth, climbers of this origin do not differ materially from their bush counterparts.

Pillar roses belong with climbers. They are simply sorts that have a less rambunctious habit of growth than many climbers and so are likely to require, for the purposes of their adequate containment, less effort in pruning and in tying in their shoots.

Trailing roses are sorts that can be trained to supports, but that have shoots sufficiently prostrate that if denied support, can trail or flop along the ground surface and so serve well as covers for slopes and banks.

The landscape use of roses should obviously take aesthetics into account, but even more important is the practicability of the proposed locations. These are sun-loving plants. There is little purpose in attempting to grow them where less than six hours exposure daily is assured, and longer is better. Good air circulation, but without exposure to strong winds, is important. Black spot, mildew diseases, and red spider mites are much more prevalent in small enclosed areas, bays and interior corners of walls and hedges, corners, and in hollows where air tends to be stagnant than where moderate breezes have access and good air drainage is assured. For this same reason avoid crowding roses among other plants or planting them too closely together. Also, and this is important, keep roses far enough from trees and shrubs, especially those, such as beeches, elms, willows, and privets, with invasive near-the-surface roots, so that they do not have to compete for moisture and nutrients.

Gardens devoted entirely or chiefly to roses are traditional features of many large public and private gardens as well as some

'Blaze', a large-flowered climbing rose

A pillar rose in full bloom

Rose gardens: (a) Gravel paths give access to the beds here

(b) A pool and statue provide a focal point in this formal garden

(c) A combination of bush roses and climbers are featured in the Cranford Rose Garden of the Brooklyn Botanic Garden

sundial, or piece of statuary as a focal feature. But semiformal and informal layouts can be just as charming, and sometimes more appropriate. The lay of the land—its natural contours as well as the locations of existing trees and other major features—should be considered when determining the character a rose garden is to assume.

Many other possibilities for employing roses in gardens can be explored. It is by no means necessary to set aside a special garden to display them effectively, to en-joy their lovely blooms. This is especially true of modern hybrid teas, floribundas, and grandifloras, many of which are really quite robust shrubs, the old-fashioned shrub roses, and of course, the climbers and trailers. Climbers lend themselves to espaliering against walls and fences, to training up pillars and posts and over arches and pergolas, and for planting where they cascade over low walls, large rocks, or old tree stumps. Trailers are ex-cellent for covering banks and steep

Climbing roses trained: (a) Against a wall

(b) Along a fence

smaller ones. Such developments, well planned and maintained, are splendid and enjoyable examples of the art of gardening at its best. Most often rose gardens are of formal design with the beds arranged geo-metrically. Such gardens often lend them-selves well to the inclusion of a bird bath,

(c) To metal arches

slopes. Bush roses of upright habit are suited for planting by themselves in lawn beds, and this is a most effective way of displaying low-growing hybrid teas and floribundas. Beds paralleling a straight or curving path with a strip of grass 1½ to 3 feet wide between the bed and the path can be quite stunning. Tall, vigorous hybrid teas, floribundas, and grandifloras are excellent in beds and make good informal hedges; they can also be used as single specimens along with herbaceous perennials and other plants in mixed flower borders.

Tree or "standard" roses, not a class by themselves, but products of the grafter's art, can be employed to give emphasis and interest. Such specimens have a single, trunklike, leafless stem, generally 3 to 4 feet high, crowned with a sizable head of branches, and in season, foliage and flowers. Such specimens are had by budding onto a tall stem of a suitable understock, such as *Rosa rugosa,* at an appropriate height from the ground, a hybrid tea, floribunda, or other rose selected to form the head.

Flowers for cutting may, without much adverse effect on the display, be taken in reasonable numbers from plantings intended chiefly for garden embellishment,

Standard roses, in a trial garden, showing the trunklike stem and rounded head

but where a large demand for cut blooms exists it is better to establish a row or two or more of plants in a special cut flower garden or in a vegetable garden, from which harvests may be gathered without affecting display areas. Roses are also grown in greenhouses, both for cut flowers and to a lesser extent as flowering pot plants.

Selecting and buying rose plants needs thought. Although most varieties are remarkably adaptable, some are less so than others, and in all regions there are sorts most likely to give satisfaction. Consultation with local growers, advice offered by reliable nurseries, and observation of how different varieties respond to local conditions are the best guides.

The number of plants required for a particular planting depends upon the space each individual is allowed, and this in turn should relate to the variety and the region in which the planting is to be made. As a rough guide, in the northeastern and northcentral United States, 2 feet may be accepted as reasonable spacing for hybrid teas, floribundas, grandifloras, and polyanthas; 3 feet for hybrid perpetuals and many other old-fashioned roses; and 5 to 6 feet for climbers, pillars, and shrub roses. Miniatures may be planted from 6 inches to 1 foot apart. In the middle Atlantic and midcentral states, these distances may be increased by up to 20 percent and in the mild climates of Florida, the Gulf States, and California by up to 50 percent. In all cases some adjustment may be desirable for the known vigor or lack of vigor of individual varieties and for local conditions, including soil fertility.

Rose plants are a long-term investment. It is folly to plant less than first-class stock. Deal only with reliable suppliers. These include most nurseries specializing in roses and the majority of well-established neighborhood nurseries held in high local esteem. With dormant stock accept nothing less than meets the American Association of Nurserymen's standard for two-year-old, No. 1 grade, field-grown plants. Grades with higher numbers may prove less satisfactory.

The surest and best results are usually had from dormant plants, but more and more amateurs rely upon those started in cans or other containers that are in leaf and often flower at the time of purchase. Frequently these are No. 1½ grade plants. If managed properly they can give satisfaction, but the vast majority of experienced growers opt for dormant stock. It is important that bare-root plants be handled and packed so the roots do not dry. Fall planting is advisable in regions of reasonably mild winters, but in harsher climates it is usual to delay planting until early spring even though, if plants are obtainable, and with appropriate winter covering, early fall planting is likely to be suc-

cessful and may be preferable to planting in spring, bushes that have been overwintered in storage.

When dormant plants arrive open the package immediately to determine whether the roots are damp. If they are not, moisten them and the packing material that surrounds them thoroughly and, if planting cannot be done the same day, stand them in a cool, shaded place. Should it not be possible to plant within a week to ten days, remove the plants from the package and plant them temporarily closely together (heel them in) at an angle of forty-five degrees in a shaded place outdoors. Firm the soil about the roots and cover the tops with loose soil or peat moss. Plants received in fall may, if necessary, be left heeled in over winter, but those that come in spring only until their buds begin obvious growth, usually not longer than one to three weeks. Plants in containers can be accepted and planted at any convenient time. If planting must be delayed, keep them in a sunny, sheltered place outdoors and water them regularly.

Soils in which roses can be successfully grown are of many types and even those not especially favorable can usually be made satisfactory by conditioning them properly before planting. And it is worth going to some trouble with this because once the bushes are installed they are likely to remain undisturbed for several years during which time it is impossible to do much about bettering conditions beneath the surface.

Ideal conditions are provided by a foot or more of fertile, reasonably porous topsoil of a medium loam or slightly more clayey type, containing seven to ten percent organic matter and overlying a porous substratum. In practice, any ground capable of producing satisfactory crops of cabbage, corn, potatoes, and most other vegetables suits roses.

If your soil approaches this quality, readying it for planting is simple. Spade or plow it to a minimum depth of 9 inches, or very much better, disturb it to at least twice that depth by double digging or by removing the upper 9 inches, forking over, loosening, and incorporating with the subsoil a generous amount of manure, compost, or other organic matter and a liberal dressing of superphosphate or bonemeal, and then replacing the topsoil and mixing with it the same amendments as well as a dressing of an all-purpose garden fertilizer. A pH of 6.5 is ideal, but good results can be achieved anywhere between pH 5.5 and 7.5.

But roses can be grown successfully in soils that differ widely from the ideal, in clayey ground, in sandy and even gravelly earths, and on land naturally too acid or too alkaline for their satisfactory performance. Such results are achieved by sound initial preparation of the soil, including measures to modify its less desirable characteristics.

Special treatments of soils that differ quite markedly from the ideal are necessary or at least desirable. Ground with inadequate subsurface drainage, where the water table stands within 2 feet of the soil surface, must be drained artificially, most usually by the installation of agricultural land drains. The often made suggestion that deep holes be dug for the roses and be partly filled with stones has merit only if the holes reach a porous substratum that allows surplus water to escape. Otherwise the holes act as sumps to collect and hold water. As an alternative to lowering the water table by draining, good results can sometimes be had by raising the beds 4 to 9 inches above the natural surface of the ground.

Complete soil preparation, if possible, at least a few weeks before planting, to permit the ground to settle and the leavening effects of its microorganisms and chemical reactions to affect it favorably. Except where high water tables make raised beds advantageous, and in some regions of high rainfall, it is desirable, in order to hold irrigation water, that the finished surface of rose beds in lawns be 1 inch to 3 inches below the level of the turf.

Sandy and gravelly soils can be made more favorable by mixing with them really large amounts, up to one-fourth or even one-third of their total bulk, of organic matter, such as compost, peat moss, or well-rotted manure. If some heavier (more clayey) soil can be had to mix with sandy or gravelly ground that is all to the good. In addition to these amendments add generous dressings of superphosphate or bonemeal and of a slow-release complete garden fertilizer.

Planting is a simple, but important operation. Choose a time when the soil is easily workable and not so wet that it sticks to shoes and tools. For each plant dig a hole of ample width and depth to accommodate the roots easily without bending or crowding. Take care not to expose the roots to the drying effects of sun or wind, examine them, cut off any broken parts, and shorten back to living tissue any dead extremities. Also, prune the tops, if this has not been properly done before you receive the plants, by removing thin, twiggy stems as well as any seriously injured or badly placed, and shortening others to 8 inches to 1 foot long.

With the holes dug and pruning and root trimming completed, you are ready to plant. Take the bush in one hand and lower it into the hole with its roots well spread and angled generally downward and with the bud-union (the swollen, knuckle-like part where top and understock are united) at the correct depth.

Now with the other hand or with a fork wielded by a companion, trickle loose, not lumpy soil among the roots. Firm it with your fingers or a stick as the filling proceeds until the plant will stand upright in the right position and at the proper depth without support. Next, with a fork or trowel, add soil until the hole is two-thirds to three-fourths full. Then tread it by exerting all your weight on the sole of your shoe until it is held so firmly that it would be difficult to pull out with even a powerful tug. But do not "stomp" the soil.

Follow this by filling space left at the top of the hole two or three times with water. Allow this to completely drain away before filling to ground level and packing the added soil, not hard, but moderately firm.

This procedure is illustrated in the Encyclopedia entry Planting.

The next step, an important one, completes the job. Mound soil against the plant and between its canes to a height of several inches. If it is practical to cover them almost entirely, all to the good. This gives protection from desiccation by sun and wind until new feeding roots, sufficient to adequately replace moisture lost from the tops, develop, and with fall-planted roses, affords considerable winter protection.

Watch carefully for new growth (it may be necessary to pull a little soil from one side of the mound to check this), and before incipient shoots are ½ inch long break the mounds down and spread the soil, or if additional soil was brought in remove it.

Planting container-grown roses calls for a different technique to that appropriate for bare-root, dormant plants. Because they were pruned when planted in the containers there is no need for any cutting back, and because they are in active growth and possibly full foliage, it is important not to disturb their roots.

Water them very thoroughly a few hours before planting. Dig holes of ample size to accommodate the root balls and leave a few inches all around to pack with fertile soil. Fork into the bottom of each hole one or two spadefuls of rotted manure or rich compost and a handful or two of bonemeal or superphosphate and then pack the bottom soil firmly and level it so that when the rose bush is positioned the top of its root ball will be at the correct level for planting.

Remove the container from the plant (not the reverse) by splitting down the side of the container and unwrapping it without breaking the soil ball. Position it in the hole and fill around it with good topsoil mixed

Unpack dormant rose bushes promptly and keep their roots moist until they are planted; prior to planting or immediately afterward, prune dormant roses by:
(a) Cutting out thin, weak, and badly placed canes

(b) Shortening the other canes to lengths appropriate for the variety

(c) A newly-purchased hybrid tea rose pruned for planting

with peat moss or compost with which some bonemeal or other fertilizer has been incorporated and then pack it firmly with a stick of about the diameter of a broom handle. When the hole is filled to within about 4 inches of its top, fill it three or four times with water and allow this to drain. Finish the surface as a very shallow saucer (to hold future applications of water). Then install a mulch of leaves, hay, straw, or other suitable material that will check loss of evaporation around the newly set plants. This procedure is illustrated in the Encyclopedia entry Planting.

Transplanting established roses, if this becomes necessary, is best done in fall or early spring. Begin by pruning them quite severely, bush sorts to a height of about 1 foot, climbers less severely, but enough to make them manageable, shrub roses to one-half or less of their heights. Prepare the planting holes in advance and if the soil is dry, soak the ground around the plants to be moved, very thoroughly a few hours before digging them. Retain, if possible, good balls of soil about their roots and replant immediately. Soak the ground around the newly set specimens as soon as planting is completed.

Routine care of roses calls for fairly constant attention from spring through fall. Although not arduous, and often pleasant, needful tasks must be done on time if good results are to be had. Roses are extremely tolerant and tend to cling to life even if neglected, but the quantity and quality of the blooms they produce deteriorates rapidly if care is stinted.

Pruning probably looms most forbidingly in the minds of most beginner rose growers. It is important, of course, but fortunately a more simple task than inexperienced gardeners often suppose. The extent, method, and timing is governed chiefly by the type of rose, to a lesser extent by the purpose for which it is being grown and its actual geographical location. There are ground rules of universal application. Use sharp pruning shears and make slanting cuts about ¼ inch above live buds, preferably ones that point outward.

Begin by cutting out or shortening to beyond the region of damage all dead, injured, broken canes and any that are cankered or otherwise seriously diseased. Finally, cut out promptly any shoots that sprout from the understock (the root portion upon which the superior variety has been grafted). As a precaution against entry of borers and possibly disease organisms, some growers advocate painting the cuts with tree wound paint or other deterrent, but there is little evidence to suggest that much advantage comes from this.

Bush roses should be pruned in late winter or in early spring just as their buds swell, but before they expand. The severe cutting back once favored, which with hybrid teas and some other types promotes longer-stemmed blooms of exhibition quality, is now rarely advocated, first because the number of flowers produced is greatly reduced and second because, practiced over a few years, this sort of butchery has a debilitating effect on the plants.

After clearing away dead and damaged wood, snip out weak, twiggy growth and remove any ill-placed canes, especially one of any pair that may rub together and cause injury. If the remaining canes are too

To prune a bush rose: (a) For example, this hybrid tea

(c) Shorten canes to be retained to lengths appropriate for the variety

(d) Vigorous new growth starting from the pruned plant

crowded, thin them by removing some of the older and weaker ones. Where winters are severe, little more may be needed, but in milder climes well-placed canes that remain will need shortening to from one-third to two-thirds of their total lengths, depending upon their thickness. The objective is to finish with a reasonably symmetrical bush with well-disposed, not overcrowded branches.

Climbing roses need different attentions, which vary somewhat with the classes to which they belong. Do the main pruning of all as soon as flowering is

(b) First remove all thin, weak, and ill-placed canes

On canes to be retained, make pruning cuts with sharp shears just above a growth bud

Rambler roses: (a) In early summer they produce numerous new canes from their bases

(b) At that time prune out old canes that are through blooming

(c) Tie new canes fairly loosely into place so that the ties will not cut into the canes

A climbing rose: (a) After pruning, the retained canes tied into place

(b) New shoots sprouting directly from a retained new cane of a climbing rose

(c) New shoots sprouting from pruned-back side branches of a two-year-old cane

through. The rambler class of roses at that time produces an abundance of new canes from near their bases. This makes it practicable, and indeed if the plant is not to become a tangled mass of briers, necessary, to cut out completely all the old flowering canes; to prevent undue crowding, it is often necessary to remove some of the weaker (thinner) new ones also. The others are then tied into place on their supports.

Large-flowered climbers are mostly much less productive of new growth than ramblers. Attend to those that bloom but once during the season by cutting out, as soon as flowering is through, branches for which there are strong replacements, and taking care to retain a framework of well-placed stems both old and new. At the same time shorten side branches that have flowered on old canes to within two or three eyes (buds) of their bases. They will then develop shoots to bloom the next year.

Repeat-blooming climbers, including climbing hybrid teas, climbing floribundas, climbing grandifloras, and climbing polyanthas, normally are not given to producing much new growth, but when such appears in advantageous places, some older

wood may be removed to make place for the new. The chief summer pruning of these sorts is limited to the prompt removal of faded flowers by cutting just above the first leaf, but below the blooms. In early spring shorten these side growths still further, and at that time cut out any wood that has been killed or injured during the winter and any that is obviously ill-placed or crowded.

Trailers need little systematic pruning. On banks and in similar locations they may be allowed to run pretty much as they please, subject to being restrained from outgrowing allotted space. Every two or three years it may be desirable to thin them out or shear them back as soon as they have finished blooming, and after severe winters there may be a little dead wood to remove in spring.

Standard or tree roses are pruned in the way applicable to the kind of roses of which the head is formed, teas, hybrid teas, floribundas, and the like in early spring, ramblers (used to form the heads of weeping standards) in summer as soon as their display of bloom is over.

Shrub roses are pruned in the same manner as many other flowering shrubs, with the purpose of keeping the bushes to a reasonable size, shapely, and not so crowded with branches that the quantity or quality of flowers suffers. Look them over in early spring, and cut out or shorten shoots as may be desirable to achieve your objective, but retain their typical shrublike appearance. Only if they have been neglected to the extent that they become straggly and clearly overgrown is it desirable to prune more severely. Then, they may be cut down nearly to the ground in late winter, and fertilized to encourage new shoots. These should then be thinned to leave only enough to form a shapely new aboveground part to the plant. Too many shoots results in inferior flowers.

Fertilizing is another matter of concern. Frequently too much attention is bestowed on it by inexperienced growers, who tend to believe that therein lies the answer to inadequacies and failures. Roses need nourishment, of course, but they are less hearty feeders than many garden plants. Only if the soil is decidedly poor in nutrients or is of a sandy character that favors rapid leaching are more than two modest applications a year needed. If the ground has been properly conditioned before planting, no further fertilization will be required during the first growing season. Timing applications is important. Make the first in early spring, shortly after pruning, the second from soon after midsummer to early August.

Which fertilizer to use, so long as it supplies the basic elements, nitrogen, phosphorus, and potassium, needed in reasonably balanced proportions, is less important than sometimes thought. For the spring dressing a 3-inch layer of half-rotted cow manure supplemented by a light application of superphosphate is adequate except on soils known to be deficient in potash. They need, in addition, a dressing of unleached wood ashes or sulfate of potash. But most gardeners will find it more practicable and convenient to substitute a complete fertilizer for the spring dressing suggested above; in any case such a fertilizer should be used for the summer application.

Fertilizers formulated especially for roses are available and generally satisfactory, but ordinarily they are more expensive than complete fertilizers recommended for growing vegetables and flowers and not formulated for a particular crop. And these last are likely to bring as good results with roses as special formulations. Depending somewhat on local soils, complete garden fertilizers are likely to be rated as 5-10-5 or 4-12-4. Other formulations may be found locally. The numbers relate to the proportions of nitrogen, phosphorus, and potassium, in that order, they contain. Distribute the fertilizer evenly over the entire area occupied by the roots, which are likely to range more widely than you may think. Lime will be needed if a test shows the soil rates pH 5 or lower. Used indiscriminately, lime may raise the pH to above an acceptable level with the result that the plants become chlorotic, a condition related to nitrogen deficiency evidenced by a yellowing of the leaves with the veins remaining green.

Summer care calls for a number of attentions, weed control and watering among them. The need for both can be minimized by surfacing the ground with a mulch that reduces evaporation and checks weed growth or at least makes easy pulling of any weeds that appear. Some mulches also add to the appearance of a garden, others have less aesthetic appeal. Among those used, and choice may very well depend upon availability and cost, are bagasse (sugar cane refuse), buckwheat hulls, cotton seed hulls, peanut hulls, ground corncobs, peat moss, pine needles, and wood chips. Even lawn mowings can be used and so can sawdust, but with this last it is necessary to apply some additional nitrogen fertilizer to compensate for the nitrogen that the organisms that cause the decay of the sawdust will otherwise abstract from the soil.

If you do not mulch, weeds must be controlled by surface cultivation supplemented with a little hand pulling close to the plants, and it must be repeated faithfully as often as is needed to eliminate weeds before they have made any substantial growth. When cultivating, do not stir the soil more than about 1 inch deep. If you do, substantial harm will result from cutting feeder roots. A scuffle or Dutch hoe is by far the best tool with which to cultivate.

Watering is important. Less than adequate supplies of water reduce vigor and limit the production of foliage and blooms. True in all but desert and semidesert regions, unsupplemented rainfall allows roses to survive, but not give of their best. Just a few rules should govern watering. The first is that when you water give enough to soak the soil to a minimum depth of 8 inches, then give no more until the ground once more approaches a state where it will be too dry for the best well-being of the plants. Shallower and more frequent watering does more harm than good. If you can, water at such times or in a way, as with a porous soil-soaker hose, so that the foliage is dry by nightfall. Foliage that remains wet for long periods encourages black spot disease. If overhead sprinklers are used, turn them off early enough for the plants to dry before darkness comes. One last thought about watering, keep it up regularly, as needed, throughout the season. It is folly to make a good start and then taper off or quit, perhaps because of a long vacation, when really hot, dry summer weather comes. It may be even better to water seldom or never from the beginning than this.

Spraying or dusting, the former usually to be preferred, at weekly intervals when growth is rapid, and preferably when it is slower too, although the lapse between applications may be stretched a few days more then, is necessary in most parts of North America to give reasonable control of a variety of pests and diseases. Excellent commercially prepared, all-purpose (combinations of insecticides, miticides, and fungicides) sprays and dusts are available, or one may elect to employ kinds more specific for particular pests and diseases.

Disbudding to achieve stems with single blooms as perfect as possible is chiefly confined to hybrid teas, and among older roses, teas and hybrid perpetuals. A "must" if exhibition-quality blooms are desired, it consists of removing all except the center flower bud that terminates each stem. Do this just as soon as the buds are big enough to take between finger and thumb and break off cleanly with a sideways and downward motion. To delay may result in an ugly scar and in any case defeats to some extent the purpose of pre-

(b) The result, a long-stemmed, solitary flower of superior quality

(c) Without disbudding, each stem produces several blooms, often of lesser quality

Disbudding: (a) Pinching out incipient side shoots that develop below the terminal flower

venting the side buds competing with the terminal one for nourishment and water.

Training climbing and pillar roses and, in the technique called pegging, other sorts, calls for timely attention. It consists of positioning and tying into place canes to clothe attractively a wall, fence, trellis, pole, arch, or pergola, or in pegging a ground bed, to encourage the best display of flowers. It is done when the plants are pruned, with possible minor adjustments made at other times.

Arrange the stems without having them cross awkwardly to assure a fair share of sun. If the support is a wall, fence, or other surface that reflects much heat, keep them 4 to 6 inches away from it by attaching them to trellis or to wires stretched tautly through eye bolts. Canes trained more or less horizontally are likely to bloom more freely than canes allowed to grow vertically. When arranging them against a flat surface, have the outer ones of the plant occupy the lowest positions. Let the others rise vertically for some distance before bending them to the left or right.

Pegging has been used chiefly for strong-growing hybrid perpetuals, but would undoubtedly be successful with more modern strong-growing types. It is done by bending until they form low arches almost parallel with the ground and radiating from the plant's center, four or fewer 3- to 4-foot-long canes and securing them a little distance from their ends to pegs driven into the soil. A notch cut into each peg will prevent the ties from slipping in response to the upward pull of the cane. The canes are positioned so they extend between pairs of those of neighbor bushes to form an interlocking pattern of horizontally held stems over the whole bed.

Preparations for winter vary according to climate. Everywhere an end-of-season cleanup is in order, including, as a measure of tidiness as well as to prevent them being whipped by wind, the shortening of tall, unruly canes that overtop or extend much beyond the general limits of the plant. In regions of cold winters, more

Shorten excessively tall canes of roses in late fall to prevent them from being damaged by winter storms

preparation may be needed. But low temperatures are not the only determiners of winter damage. Were that so, it would be easy to establish where and where not particular roses could be relied upon to survive without special protection.

Factors that affect winter killing include cold, but anything that causes drying of the stems, such as too-strong winds and reflected heat from nearby walls, markedly accentuates the danger. The condition of the plant also is important. One kept

healthy throughout the summer is much more likely to survive than one debilitated by damage to foliage by disease or insects or by serious leaf loss caused by overenthusiastic harvesting of blooms or by lack of adequate nutrition or moisture.

Overvigorous, soft, succulent growth is much more subject to winter-kill than firm, "well-ripened" shoots. Such growth can result from shade and other causes. To promote production of resistant growth do not overfertilize. And without allowing the plants to actually suffer, be wary of watering at the end of summer or in early fall. This does not exclude, if the ground is dry, giving a thorough soaking shortly before hard freezing is expected, when it is too late to stimulate new growth.

Winter protection is desirable for many varieties where temperatures may be expected to go below 10°F. But this is only an approximation because the degree of damage likely to be sustained is related not only to temperature, but, to an extent, to when in winter the lows occur. Alternate freezing and thawing does more harm than steady cold, whereas deep snow affords natural protection against much lower temperatures than would be endured without it.

Where extremely cold winters prevail, winter protection is necessary or highly desirable. In mild climates it is totally unnecessary and can be harmful. It is areas where winters are intermediate between these extremes that give cause for questioning and often spark heated controversy among rose growers. Southern New York is a case in point. There temperatures down to 10°F, with an occasional dip to 0 or −1 or −2°F, are normal. But in exceptional winters, ten or even twenty below zero may be experienced for brief periods and snow cover is decidedly uncertain. Under such circumstances one must balance the possibility or probability of losses against the certainty of the considerable work of covering and uncovering.

Hilling with soil affords by far the most satisfactory protection down to temperatures of −20°F. Properly done, it prevents desiccation by sun and wind, and by conducting heat present in even frozen ground to the mound of soil, improves its temperature to the extent that it never drops below the critical level at which canes are killed. It is important to remember that the principle involved is not that of supplying insulation to keep heat in the ground, but rather to provide a heap of conductive material that itself will be warmed by heat absorbed from the ground. Retention of heat within the hill of soil is desirable and can be promoted by covering it with an insulating mulch. Mulching without first mounding with soil is likely to do more harm than good.

If you hill your roses, do so just before the first hard freeze, and do not use any-

Roses hilled with soil as winter protection from excessive cold and dehydration

thing but soil. Materials such as manure or compost that remain or become wet and soggy promote disease. Loose, dry stuffs including leaves, salt-hay, and peat moss are insulators that retain heat in the ground instead of conducting it to the canes.

Bring soil in from outside. Perhaps you can borrow it from a vegetable garden or flower bed and return it in spring. It is not good practice, as some amateurs do, to scrape it from between the plants to hill around them. To do this exposes roots to more cold than desirable and even mulching between the hills does not compensate fully for this.

Use loose, not lumpy soil and about bush roses make hills 9 or 10 inches tall or in very cold climates a few inches higher. If you plan to add an insulating mulch of littery manure, dry leaves, straw, or other material, delay this until the top inch or two of the hills of soil are frozen, to discourage mice taking up residence in the mulch.

Climbing and standard roses need somewhat different handling. To protect them by hills of soil, it is necessary to bring them to ground level. This involves the considerable task of loosening climbers from their supports (unless they are on a trellis hinged at its bottom so that it can be laid over), and of digging around the roots of standards to the extent that they can be laid horizontally. Then both climbers and standards are pegged into place, covered with soil and later with a mulch of loose, insulating material. As an alternative, standards can be grown in large wire baskets dug up in fall, stored in a cool cellar or shed, and replanted in spring.

In extreme climates where temperatures may go seriously below −20°F, hilling may not be enough. Some authorities recommend digging the plants up, tying their tops together, and burying them 3 to 4 feet deep in the ground, but that involves a tremendous amount of labor. An alternative reported to have given good results is to surround the plants with a wooden box or frame 1½ feet wide and high and long enough to accommodate four plants. Then fill this with crushed corn cobs and cover it with waterproof building paper or polyethylene plastic.

Greenhouse rose growing, for cut flowers, once engaged in to a very considerable extent by owners of private estates, is now almost exclusively a commercial procedure. For the best results entire greenhouses must be devoted to them, with temperature, humidity, ventilation, and light intensity carefully adjusted to seasonal requirements.

Plants, usually raised by grafting (not budding) on *Rosa manettii* or other stock especially favorable for greenhouse cultivation, are planted from pots into the ground beds, or more often in raised deep benches, in fertile, well-drained soil at almost any season, with May or early June generally preferred. A usual spacing is about 1¼ feet apart.

Support for the growing stems is provided by stout wire stakes 4 to 5 feet long, one to each plant, pushed into the soil and secured near their tops to a horizontal wire stretched between sturdy frames, which may be of galvanized iron pipe, positioned at the ends of the beds or benches, with, if necessary, some at intermediate points.

Routine care, besides maintaining favorable temperatures and adequate air circulation, consists chiefly of watering, fertilizing, controlling diseases and pests, and harvesting the blooms.

Watering newly planted stock must be done with some reserve until the roots have taken possession of the new soil, but once the plants are well established and in active growth, supplies should be generous. Because repeated heavy watering leaches nutrients, fertilizing must also be rather lavish. A once-a-week application of a completely soluble sort is not too much when the plants are in active growth and are flowering well. When growth slows a little and there are fewer blooms, reduce slightly the frequency of watering and fertilizing.

A period of dormancy or near dormancy is required by roses. Indoors, a summer rest period, induced by keeping the plants dry, substitutes satisfactorily for the natural one outdoors triggered by winter cold. It furthermore makes practicable harvesting cut flowers when they are most in demand. To bring about this artificial dormancy, for about a month withhold water except any minimum that may be needed to prevent the bark from shriveling, and keep the greenhouse ventilated much more freely than at other times.

When the soil has dried sufficiently, the upper about 1½ inches is removed and replaced with fresh soil. Also, the bushes are pruned by cutting out weak and unwanted canes and by shortening others to one-half or less of their lengths.

Forcing roses as pot plants to bloom in late winter or early spring is a rewarding procedure practicable for operators of amateur as well as commercial greenhouses. Best suited for this purpose, be-

Dwarf polyantha roses are attractive for growing in pots

cause they produce such abundances of bloom at one time, are dwarf polyantha varieties, but hybrid teas, floribundas, and other sorts also respond. Obtain top quality bushes for delivery in November. Prune them upon arrival about as severely as you would outdoor roses of the same sorts, and pot them at once in containers just big enough to hold their roots without excessive crowding. Then stand them in a cold frame or sink them to the rims of their pots in a bed of peat moss, sand, sawdust, or similar material in a sheltered place outdoors.

In January bring them into a sunny greenhouse where, if possible, the temperatures are held for a couple of weeks a few degrees below those maintained later, which should be 55 to 60°F at night and, depending upon the brightness of the weather, five to ten degrees higher by day. Water moderately at first, more freely as roots and foliage develop. Spray the tops lightly with water on sunny days sufficiently early that the foliage dries within about an hour and is never wet at nightfall. If a nutritious potting mix was used fertilizing is not needed.

After flowering is through, the plants may be planted permanently in the garden or they may be kept in their pots for forcing the following year.

Propagation of most roses for commercial purposes is accomplished effectively by T- or patch-budding or, for those to be grown in greenhouses, by grafting. Shrub

roses and some climbers are often increased by cuttings, species from cuttings and seed. These techniques and in some cases others can be practiced successfully by amateurs, although few will have occasion to graft.

Budding and grafting require the availability of suitable understocks. For outdoor roses, *Rosa multiflora* or climbing rose 'Dr. Huey' are usually preferred. For greenhouse roses, *R. manettii* raised from cuttings made about a year earlier is usually used. Budding is done outdoors from late May to early August. For a description of the T- or patch-budding method used consult the Encyclopedia article Budding. Except for standards, the buds are inserted very low on the understocks.

Grafting is done in a propagating case or under mist in a greenhouse where a temperature of 75°F is maintained from January to April, two months before the resulting plants are to be planted in beds or benches. When grafting roses for greenhouse cultivation, understocks two to three months old raised from cuttings rooted in a greenhouse are employed. Prune these back to within 1½ to 2 inches of the soil, then cut them appropriately for splice grafting. The scions should have not more than three eyes (buds). The manner of making a splice graft is described in the Encyclopedia article Grafting. The graft must be kept moist until union is effected.

Cuttings of most roses give satisfaction, but are especially reliable with strong, vigorous growers. With outdoor plants make them from firm, but not hard, leafy shoots in June or July or in fall from fully mature leafless canes. Because a cutting must establish a new root system as well as grow a new top, it usually takes a year longer to achieve the same size plant than is achieved by budding, disregarding of course the time taken to raise the understock of the budded specimen.

To make summer cuttings, select strong stems, originating low on the plant of flowers that have just dropped their petals. Remove the portion of stem with the upper two or three leaves and the flower and cut the remainder into sections 5 to 8 inches long. Make the basal cuts squarely across just beneath a node (joint), the upper ones slantwise ¼ inch above a bud. Snip or cut off (do not pull off) all leaves except the top two or three. Keep the prepared cuttings wrapped in wet burlap or other material or in water until they are planted, which should be as soon as possible.

For successful rooting, the cuttings must have a humid atmosphere and good light without exposure to direct sun. A cold frame located on the north side of a wall, fence, or hedge provides ideal conditions. If the cuttings are few, Mason jars or similar glass containers inverted over them can serve as miniature cold frames.

The rooting medium must be porous and well-drained. Coarse sand or perlite mixed with one-third its bulk of topsoil gives good results. Plant the cuttings to one-half to two-thirds of their lengths and pack the medium firmly against them. Then water thoroughly and close the frame, or cover the cuttings with jars.

Subsequent care calls for checking the frames or jars to make sure the atmosphere inside does not become saturated. This is evidenced by droplets of water gathering on the inside of the glass. If this occurs, ventilate by opening the frame sash a little, but only a little, or by propping the jars on stones or pegs so that air enters from below.

Roots should develop in five or six weeks. A general perkiness in the appearance of the cuttings and the beginning of new shoot growth signal this. Now, a little at a time over a period of three weeks or a month, increase the ventilation of the cold frame or jars until the cuttings stand full exposure without the slightest wilting. Then uncover the cuttings completely. Depending upon the climate, some winter protection may be needed. The following spring transplant the young plants to a nursery bed, to remain for a year, or plant them in their permanent locations.

Hardwood cuttings are prepared similarly from fully mature, approximately pencil-thick canes; the uppermost, unripened portions are discarded. Make the cuttings 8 to 10 inches long in autumn before the first killing frost.

In regions where the ground freezes no deeper than 2 or 3 inches, plant the cuttings directly in sandy soil outdoors. With a spade nick out a trench of such depth that after planting, 1 inch of each cutting will protrude above the surface. Have one side of the trench form a wall very slightly angled from the vertical, the other sloped away from it at a considerably greater angle. To achieve this, if the soil is dry, it is helpful to soak it deeply a few hours before cutting the trench. Sprinkle 2 or 3 inches of sand or perlite along the bottom of the trench and position the cuttings 4 to 6 inches apart against the wall, with their bases in the sand or perlite. Taking care not to disturb the cuttings, shovel soil into the trench and tread it firmly against them. Winter protection, afforded by a covering of peat moss, loose, strawy material, or branches of evergreen may be desirable later.

Callusing and very often some rooting will take place before new top growth starts in spring. But do not move the plants then. Leave them undisturbed until the fall or following spring. Then lift and prune them and transplant them to nursery beds for another season's growing or to their permanent locations.

Where the ground freezes to depths greater than 2 or 3 inches, a somewhat different procedure is preferable. After the cuttings are made, tie them in bundles of up to twenty or so, with their upper ends facing one way, and store them until spring where they will be kept damp, but not wet, at as near as possible a temperature of 35 to 40°F, where they are not denied air. Such an environment is provided by burying them under 6 to 8 inches or more of sandy soil, sand, or peat moss, outdoors, in a cold frame, or in an unheated building. After the top couple of inches of the cover freezes spread over it sufficient leaves, straw, or branches of evergreens to prevent further penetration. In early spring take up the bundles, separate the cuttings, and plant them as advised for fall planting in milder climates.

Division is sometimes done to multiply own-root (not budded or grafted) rambler-type climbers and shrub roses that produce clusters of stems from the base. To accomplish this, prune the plant back severely. Dig it up and with a spade or machete chop it into two or more parts. Sometimes it is possible to remove a division without digging the whole plant up.

Layering is a simple and sure method of securing increase of roses that have canes that can be brought into contact with the ground. Take a young, but firm one and bend it to touch the soil about 1 foot to 1½ feet from its tip. At that point, and preferably through a joint, make on its lower side a slit 1½ to 2 inches long in the direction of the tip and extending nearly to the center of the cane. Prop the slit open with a sliver of wood or small stone. Then, having previously forked over a patch of soil and mixed in a generous amount of coarse sand or perlite, bury the wounded part of the stem to a depth of about 3 inches, allowing the end to protrude. Peg it into position so securely that there is no danger of it moving, tie its free end to a stake, and mound soil over the buried part. In dry weather water regularly. About a year later, the layer will have made sufficient roots to warrant severing it from its parent and transplanting it to a new location.

Pests and diseases of roses include several that are serious and widespread, others are of lesser or more local importance. In addition, malfunctions caused by malnutrition or other faulty environmental circumstance can cause trouble.

Chief among animal pests are aphids; beetles of various sorts including those called Asiatic, blister, dialrotica, Fuller rose, Japanese, June, and spotted cucumber beetles; rose chafer or rose bug; rose curculio; strawberry rootworm; various kinds of borers; caterpillars of several sorts, among them budworms, webworms, leaf tiers, leaf rollers, and tent caterpillars; earwigs; galls; leaf hoppers; rose midge; nematodes; red spider mites; scale insects; and thrips.

Diseases causes by funguses include black spot and other leaf spots; a number of blights, chief among them botrytis and cane blight; cankers, the most prevalent of which are brown canker, cane canker, and stem canker; galls; powdery mildew; root rots; rusts; sooty mold; and wilt. Crown gall is a serious bacterial affliction.

Keeping roses healthy in the face of all these threats may well strike the beginner as an impossible or at least a too-demanding task, but in practice this need not be so. In the first place not all of the afflictions listed are prevalent in any one area,

Black spot disease of roses

A rose infected with mildew

Mossy galls on a rose

and of those that are possible, it is improbable that more than few will prove troublesome in any one garden. Spraying or dusting, the first preferable, at weekly intervals or, in periods of slow growth and no rain, at ten-day intervals from the time when growth begins in spring until fall with an all-purpose rose spray or dust will keep most pests and diseases in check. Supplement this with strict sanitation. This involves taking care that only healthy bushes are planted, picking up fallen leaves, and pruning out all cankered shoots.

ROSEWOOD. See Dalbergia.

ROSINWEED. See Silphium.

ROSMARINUS (Rosmar-ìnus)—Rosemary. "There's rosemary, that's for remembrance, pray, you love, remember" admonishes Shakespeare's Ophelia. Probably the most familiar, this is only one of perhaps hundreds of references in classical literature to *Rosmarinus officinalis*, a charming and delightfully aromatic, evergreen shrub of the Mediterranean region. A member of the mint family LABIATAE and the only species of its genus, it is surely the subject of more studies and legends than any other legitimate occupant of herb gardens. According to one belief, it was originally named Rose Mary in honor of the Virgin and its flowers reflect the blue of her raiment, however, the fact is that Pliny applied to this plant the apt designation *rosmarinus*, which translates as sea dew.

Rosemary is a native of sea cliffs and adjacent grounds in southern Europe and Asia Minor. An old English belief holds that "rosemary grows best where the mistress is master," and has resulted, it is said, in insecure husbands employing pruning shears or more drastic measures to curb its vigor. Rosemary is quite distinct from and not related botanically to the plant called wild-rosemary (*Ledum palustre*). In the south another entirely different plant, *Ceratiola ericoides*, is called rosemary.

A well-branched, leafy, broad, upright shrub, **R. officinalis** is 6 feet or so high

Rosmarinus officinalis as a pot plant

and ashy gray-green in general appearance. Its young shoots are whitish-pubescent, and its narrow-linear leaves, ⅓ inch to 1½ inches long and with rolled-under margins, are lustrous dark green above and white-hairy on their undersides. The almost stalkless, asymmetrical, tubular blooms are in clusters of two or three in the leaf axils of the previous year's shoots; they appear in spring. Their corollas, up to ½ inch long, have a notched or two-lobed upper lip and a lower one with a central concave large lobe and two smaller lateral ones. There are two functional stamens and two tiny staminodes (sterile stamens). The fruits, often called seeds, are small, smooth, nearly spherical nutlets. Commonly the flowers are light blue, but a white-flowered variety (*R. o. albiflorus*) is

Rosmarinus officinalis prostratus draped down the face of a wall in California

in cultivation as also is a low, prostrate one, *R. o. prostratus*. The latter is somewhat more tender to cold than the typical kind. Other varieties are *R. o. angustifolius*, with very narrow leaves; *R. o. aureus*, with leaves marked with yellow; and *R. o. erectus*, of very upright growth.

Rosemary has but limited uses as a culinary herb and modern medicine places no reliance on virtues once attributed to it. It is esteemed for the very pleasing fragrance of the oil it contains in some abundance. This is extracted commercially and used in perfumery; it is an ingredient of eau de cologne. Rosemary is an excellent bee plant and the honey derived from it is of high quality.

Garden and Landscape Uses. This native of the sunny Mediterranean does not adapt to cold, wet winters in the north, and except in possibly a few very favored and well-protected sites, will not survive outdoors there. It is grateful for a climate not colder than that, say, of Washington, D.C., and earth that is porous and on the dryish side. It thrives in limestone soils and appreciates warmth. Reflected heat, of which it frequently endures much from cliffs that back it in its native haunts, does not affect it adversely. Because of this, rosemary is satisfactory for planting at the bases of sunny walls and for use in patios and other paved areas. Well suited for growing in containers, it makes a fine subject for furnishing pots, tubs, and urns used to decorate terraces, steps, and other parts of the garden. It suggests itself as being worth the attention of devotees of the art of bonsai (the Japanese method of growing dwarfed trees and shrubs in containers). Rosemary can be used effectively to form hedges, and it is an excellent shrub for seaside gardening. Most characteristically, it belongs in herb gardens. Where it will not winter outdoors it is quite usual to grow specimens in pots to add to the herb garden in summer and to winter indoors in a cool, light place where little or no frost is experienced.

Rosmarinus officinalis

Rosmarinus officinalis albiflorus

Cultivation. The environmental needs of rosemary are explained above. Provided these are reasonably satisfied, no difficulty attends its cultivation. It is durable and increases in size at a moderate rate or slowly. No pruning is ordinarily needed other than any deemed necessary to restrict the size of the plant or to correct any tendency to straggliness. Such as is needed is best done as soon as the flowers fade. In acid soils the application of lime at intervals of two or three years is beneficial and in poorish soil gentle fertilization may occasionally receive attention, but this must not be overdone lest the plant grows so vigorously that it loses its character and charm. Propagation is easily accomplished by cuttings taken in late summer or early fall and by seed sown in sweet (non-acid), porous soil. Layering may also be successfully practiced.

ROSULARIA (Rosu-lària). The approximately twenty-five species of *Rosularia*, of the orpine family CRASSULACEAE, are natives of Asia and Asia Minor. The name is derived from the Latin *rosula*, a rose. It alludes to the appearance of the rosettes of foliage.

Succulent, mostly tuberous perennials, rosularias have rosettes of flat, broad-based leaves and, usually from the leaf axils, panicles of small flowers with five or six sepals, a corolla with a tubular base and five or six lobes, ten or twelve stamens, and erect pistils. The fruits are of several follicles.

Native to Asia Minor, *R. pallida* (syns. *Cotyledon chrysantha*, *Umbilicus chrysanthus*) has rosettes 1 inch to 1½ inches across of glandular-pubescent, oblong-spoon-shaped, blunt leaves. Up to 8 inches high, the flowering stalks carry erect, white to yellowish blooms sometimes striped with red. Ranging in the wild from Asia Minor to the Caucasus, *R. sempervivum* (syn. *Umbilicus sempervivum*) has rosettes of minutely-glandular-hairy, spatula-shaped, toothed, hair-fringed leaves, up to ¾ inch long, and flowering stalks, 2 to 4 inches long, bearing up-facing, reddish blooms about ⅜ inch long.

Garden and Landscape Uses and Cultivation. These are as for cotyledons.

ROTALA (Ro-tàla) — Tooth-Cup. Belonging to the loosestrife family LYTHRACEAE and comprising about forty species of annuals and a few herbaceous perennials, *Rotala* occurs in wet places in temperate, subtropical, and tropical regions. Its name, presumably alluding to the whorls of leaves of some sorts, derives from the Latin *rotalis*, of wheels.

The plants of this genus have stalkless or very short-stalked leaves, usually opposite or in whorls (circles of more than two). Their inconspicuous flowers are from the leaf axils, sometimes in umbels, or are

in terminal spikes. They have a three- or six-lobed calyx, three, six, or sometimes no petals, and one to six stamens. The fruits are capsules.

A native of Japan to Malaya and India, *R. indica* has stems up to somewhat over 1 foot long and opposite, elliptic to elliptic-lanceolate leaves up to 4 inches long. The purplish-violet flowers are solitary in the axils of upper, small, bractlike leaves.

Garden Uses and Cultivation. The species described is sometimes grown in aquariums.

ROTARY TILLERS. These are power-driven implements designed to loosen ground to a depth of several inches and mix in manure, compost, and other amendments. They do work traditionally done by plows and harrows or manually with spades or spading forks and rakes.

Rotary tillers churn the soil with blades or pronglike tines fixed to a power-driven shaft set at right angles to the direction of travel. These are covered with a hood that prevents earth or stones being flung to endanger the operator.

The rotary tiller was invented in Switzerland in the 1920s and manufactured there under the trade name Rototiller. It soon achieved a well-deserved popularity there and in other parts of Europe, but several years elapsed before it was introduced to and found acceptance in the United States.

The word rototiller, in common usage, is often applied generally to all makes of rotary tillers. Not all, however, are heavy enough or have sufficient power to turn the ground as deeply as desirable for optimum results. Some light models designed for sale to amateur gardeners, and decidedly ineffective for heavy work, are little more than rotary hoes.

ROTATION OF CROPS. It is usually considered advantageous to rotate crops, that is, not to succeed a harvested crop with another of the same or botanically nearly related kind. The rationale is that various sorts of plants need nutrients in somewhat different proportions and that by rotating them the resources of the soil are used most effectively and also that there is less danger of soil pests and diseases partial to specific plants building up to extraordinary degrees.

Crop rotation is chiefly practiced with vegetables; less often considered important in flower gardens, if conditions permit, it is wise to adopt there, too. Obviously, large gardens afford better opportunity to rotate crops than small ones.

In vegetable gardens, a favored method is to plant the few perennials, such as asparagus and rhubarb, in one area, and divide the remainder into three parts. One of these is planted to members of the cab-

bage tribe, such as broccoli, brussels sprouts, cabbage, cauliflower, and kale, another with root crops, such as carrots, onions, parsnips, potatoes, rutabagas, turnips, and the third with such crops as beans, corn, eggplants, peas, and tomatoes. In this rotation, the plot planted with the cabbage group one year is the next given over to root crops and in the third season is planted to the beans, corn, etc., selection. Short-term items, such as lettuce and radishes, are treated as catch crops to be sown wherever it is most convenient on any plot.

ROTENONE. Because it is harmless to man and other warm-blooded creatures, but deadly to many kinds of insects, rotenone is especially suitable for use as an insecticide on fruits and vegetables. It kills both as a contact and a stomach poison and may be applied as a dust or spray. Derived from several tropical trees, shrubs, and vines, notably *Derris* and *Lonchocarpus*, rotenone is poisonous to fish. Because of this, great care must be exercised that none of it contaminates water in which fish live. Most of the plants from which rotenone comes are or have been in their native lands employed as fish poisons.

ROTHMANNIA (Roth-mánnia). Horticulturally little known, *Rothmannia* comprises twenty or more species of tropical and subtropical evergreen shrubs and trees of Africa, Malagasy, and Asia. Related to *Gardenia*, from which it is distinguished by technical details of the ovary, and belonging in the madder family RUBIACEAE, it has a name that commemorates the Swedish botanist, a pupil of Linnaeus, Goran Rothman, who died in 1778.

Rothmannias are shrubs and trees, with opposite, usually leathery, lanceolate to obovate leaves. The short-stalked or stalkless, white, yellowish, greenish, or less commonly reddish-brown blooms are solitary or in axillary or terminal clusters of few. They have usually tubular, rarely toothed or lobed calyxes, and tubular corollas, funnel- or bell-shaped or cylindrical. There are usually five, occasionally more, spreading, twisted lobes (petals) and five stamens. The fruits are technically berries.

Sometimes 30 feet tall, but often much lower, *R. macrantha* (syn. *Randia macrantha*) inhabits equatorial Africa. A straggly, more or less climbing shrub, it has short-stalked, slender-pointed, obovate-oblong, lustrous leaves 2½ to 8 inches long by 1 inch to 3½ inches wide, hairless except on the midrib beneath, clustered mostly at the ends of its shoots. The solitary, red-spotted, white to pale yellowish, fragrant blooms, often suffused with reddish-brown on their outsides, are at the ends of the shoots or in the leaf axils. They have slender corolla tubes, 6 to 10 inches in length,

Rothmannia macrantha

and spreading or recurved, blunt, ovate petals; they are borne in winter.

Introduced from the Cape of Good Hope to Kew Gardens in England by the first professional plant collector, Francis Masson, in 1774, **R. capensis** (syn. *Gardenia capensis*), in its native South Africa called wild-gardenia, is a small evergreen tree. It has short-stalked to nearly stalkless, glossy, elliptic leaves 3 to 4 inches long by 1 inch wide. The solitary, nearly stalkless, sweetly-scented, white, creamy-white, or delicate yellow flowers are sprinkled in their throats and at the bases of their pointed, spreading petals with purple dots. The blooms are 2 to 3 inches long and wide. They have spreading or reflexed petals with stamens conspicuously alternating with them. The

Rothmannia capensis

nearly spherical, ribbed, leathery fruits, about 2 inches long, contain many flattened seeds surrounded by pith. They are a favorite food of baboons and monkeys. A smaller tree, evergreen or deciduous **R. globosa** (syn. *Gardenia globosa*) has lanceolate to ovate leaves up to 4 inches long by 1 inch wide. The nearly stalkless, bell-shaped flowers, about 1½ inches wide, are clustered on short side branches. Sweetly-scented, they are white and often marked inside with pink or red. The corolla lobes (petals), which are triangular, curve gracefully outward and backward. The nearly globular fruits are ¾ to 1 inch in diameter. This species in its native South Africa is called September bells.

Other sorts cultivated are *R. longiflora* (syn. *Randia maculata*) and *R. urcelliformis* (syn. *Gardenia urcelliformis*), both natives of tropical Africa. A shrub or tree, **R. longiflora** is up to 15 feet high with pointed-elliptic leaves 2½ to 5 inches long. Its flowers have a corolla tube up to 6½ inches long, slender for most of its length and becoming funnel-shaped in its upper third. They are greenish to reddish on their outsides and on their insides are white spotted with red or purple at the bases of the petals. Up to 25 feet tall, **R. urcelliformis** has elliptic to broad-elliptic leaves, 3 to 5 inches long, and from the leaf axils solitary, bell-shaped, white flowers marked with purple and 2 to 3 inches long.

Garden and Landscape Uses and Cultivation. These are good ornamentals for gardens in the humid tropics and subtropics and for greenhouses and conservatories. Their cultivation presents no special difficulties. They prefer fertile, well-drained, acid to neutral soil that contains a fair amount of organic matter and is kept moderately moist. They grow well in light shade or sun. Any pruning needed to keep them shapely or limit their size should be done at the beginning of a new period of growth. In greenhouses a minimum winter night temperature of 55 to 60°F is satisfactory, with a rise of a few degrees by day permitted. At other seasons both day and night temperatures may with advantage be considerably higher. Propagation is by cuttings in spring or summer and by seed. From cuttings rooted in early spring, good plants in flower in 5-inch pots can be had by the following January. In summer well-rooted specimens benefit from regular applications of dilute liquid fertilizer. In general, environments satisfactory for gardenias suit *Rothmannia*.

ROTOTILLER. See Rotary Tillers.

ROTS. These diseases are characterized by decomposition and putrefaction of plant parts caused by invasion of the cells by pathological organisms. The most common causal agents are bacteria and funguses. Affected parts, which may be dry

Fungus rot: (a) Of a caladium tuber

(b) Of a cactus

and firm or soft and mushy, are often foul-smelling. Among more common kinds are bud rot of cannas, blossom end rot of tomatoes, crown rot of delphiniums and other plants, rhizome soft rot of iris, and stem rots of begonias, cactuses, geraniums, and other plants. There are many more. Control measures vary widely with the kind of plant and particular disease. Consult Cooperative Extension Agents or up-to-date books on plant diseases for treatment.

ROUGE PLANT is *Rivina humilis*.

ROUPALA (Roú-pala). Differing chiefly in seed characteristics from *Grevillea* and *Hakea*, the Mexican, Central American, and South American genus *Roupala*, like them, belongs to the protea family PROTEACEAE. It consists of fifty species of mostly small trees and shrubs, and has a name stemming from a native one of Guiana.

Roupalas have alternate, rigid, leathery, toothed or toothless leaves, usually undivided, but those of young specimens and younger parts of older trees pinnate, and all those of older trees of some species pinnate. The bisexual flowers are in pairs along axillary and terminal racemes. They have cylindrical perianths of four segments (petals), recurved at their tips and with a stamen inserted at the middle of each. The fruits are short-stalked, hard capsules.

A handsome tree 20 to 30 feet tall, *R. macrophylla* (syns. *R. pohlii, R. corcovadensis*), because of the distinctive odor of its foliage when brushed against or bruised, is called skunkwood. It has shoots, young leaves, and flower buds clothed with short, rust-colored hairs. Its leaves, generally

Roupala macrophylla

pinnate, are up to 1 foot long or longer and have four to eight pairs and a terminal one of stalked, ovate or oblique, coarsely-toothed leaflets 3 to 5 inches long. Less often the leaves are undivided. The whitish flowers, ⅓ inch long, are crowded in slender, cylindrical racemes 3 to 5 inches long.

Garden and Landscape Uses and Cultivation. Roupalas may be used as specimens to add distinction and interest to landscape plantings. Southern California and other areas with similar or warmer climates provide environments suitable for their outdoor cultivation. They are also sometimes grown in greenhouses. They make no particular demands, but succeed under conditions appropriate for grevilleas and hakeas. They may be increased by seed, and by cuttings under mist or in a greenhouse propagating bed with a little bottom heat.

ROWAN TREE is *Sorbus aucuparia*.

ROYAL. This word occurs as parts of the common names of these plants: royal climber (*Oxera pulchella*), royal fern (*Osmunda regalis*), royal palm (*Roystonea*), royal poinciana (*Delonix regia*), and royal waterlily (*Victoria amazonica*).

ROYENA (Roy-èna). Consisting of evergreen or rarely deciduous shrubs and small trees of the ebony family EBENACEAE, the genus *Royena* is endemic to Africa. It contains about twenty species, and by some authorities is included in *Diospyros*. Its name commemorates Adrian van Royen, a Dutch professor of botany, who died in 1779.

Royenas commonly have alternate, undivided, toothless leaves. Coming from the leaf axils and solitary or sometimes in twos or threes, the small blooms have five- or rarely four-parted, persistent calyxes that enlarge and surround the bases of the fruits, a bell- to urn-shaped corolla with five spreading lobes (petals), and usually ten stamens. The fruits are spherical, ovoid, or oblong, and leathery. They do not split to release the seeds. This genus is unusual in its family in having bisexual blooms.

Called wild-coffee in South Africa, *R. lucida* is a shrub or tree up to 25 feet in height, but often lower. It has hairy shoots, and two-ranked, nearly stalkless, broadelliptic to ovate leaves 1¼ to 2 inches long by up to ¾ inch broad, and heart-shaped at their bases. Their upper surfaces are polished green, beneath they are paler and hairy. In racemes of two or three, with two small bracts on their short stalks, the white or cream-colored flowers are urn-shaped and about ⅓ inch long. They have reflexed petals, and hairy anthers. The spherical red or purple fruits, up to ¾ inch across, are enclosed by the enlarged calyxes. The fruits are red or purple and fleshy.

About 3 feet tall or sometimes taller, *R. glabra,* of South Africa, is an erect, branching shrub. Its leaves, up to ¾ inch long by ⅕ inch wide, are lanceolate to elliptic. When young, hairy, they soon become hairless. The cream-colored flowers are in drooping, hairy-stalked racemes about 1½ inches long. The hairy, spherical, green or yellow fruits are slightly over ¼ inch in diameter.

Garden and Landscape Uses and Cultivation. The species discussed above are suitable for planting to add distinction and interest to landscapes in California and elsewhere where little or no frost is experienced. They succeed under ordinary garden conditions and are easily raised from seed, and by summer cuttings planted under mist or in a greenhouse or cold frame propagating bed. No special care is needed.

ROYOC is *Morinda royoc*.

ROYSTONEA (Roystò-nea) — Royal Palm, Cabbage Palm. Confined in its natural distribution to the warmer parts of the Americas, including southern Florida, *Roystonea* includes some of the most beautiful and impressive members of the palm family

PALMAE. Its name honors the United States Army engineer, General Roy Stone, who served with distinction in Puerto Rico during the Spanish-American war. He died in 1905. There are seventeen species of which two or three are widely cultivated. By some authorities these palms have been named *Oreodoxa*.

Roystoneas have solitary, strictly vertical, columnar, smooth trunks topped by prominent, green crownshafts (columns formed of the sheathing basal parts of the leafstalk) and graceful heads of many large, pinnate leaves. The flowers, in heavy, branched clusters that come from the base of the crownshaft, are in groups of three, one female flanked by two males. The fruits are up to ½ inch long and bluish.

The Cuban royal palm (*R. regia*) is a native of the island from which it takes its name and perhaps other West Indian is-

Roystonea regia in Florida

Roystonea oleracea, the botanic garden, Rio de Janeiro, Brazil

lands. It attains a height of about 70 feet and has a trunk thickest near its middle, which distinguishes it from the Caribbee royal palm, which has a trunk that tapers upward from a broad base. The Caribbee royal or cabbage palm (*R. oleracea*) at times exceeds 100 feet in height. Its leaves, unlike those of other species, have leaflets in two instead of three rows. The Puerto Rico royal palm (**R. borinquena**), normally up to 60 feet in height, has a trunk that narrows upward from a swollen base, then thickens, and finally narrows again toward the crownshaft and foliage. Its leaves are up to 10 feet long. This, one of the most common and most characteristic palms of Puerto Rico, is also indigenous to St. Croix and Vieques. The Florida royal palm (**R. elata**) is a rare native of the state after which it is named. Somewhat taller than the Cuban royal palm, its trunk thickens at its base

Roystonea elata in Florida

and usually narrows and then widens again to form a broad shoulder at the top. This sort is very closely related to the Cuban royal palm.

Garden and Landscape Uses. These stately trees are of great worth as ornamentals. They may be used with grand effects as single specimens and in groups. They lend themselves especially well to use as avenue trees, and for this purpose they are much used in the Americas and other parts of the humid tropics. Kinds most favored for avenue planting are the Cuban and the Caribbee royal palms. The famous Alamedas de Palmeiras in the botanical garden at Rio de Janeiro and the great avenue of royal palms in the botanical garden at Peradeniya in Ceylon are of the Caribbee royal palm. In Florida the Cuban royal palm is most commonly planted. Roystoneas are sometimes grown in large conservatories.

Cultivation. Royal palms thrive in any reasonably moist, fertile soil, in full sun. In tropical greenhouses they can be grown while young in pots and tubs, but they soon outgrow these and the most satisfactory results are obtained in a deep bed of rich, well-drained soil in a conservatory tall enough to allow for considerable height. The soil should be evenly moist at all times. Container-grown specimens benefit from regular applications of dilute

liquid fertilizer from spring through fall. Seeds afford the only means of propagation. They must be fresh and should be sown in a sandy, peaty soil in a temperature of 80 to 85°F.

Pests and Disease. In addition to scale insects, mealybugs, and red spider mites, royal palms are subject to attacks of an insect called the royal palm bug and by thrips. A wilt and trunk rot disease sometimes infects them. For additional information see Palms.

RUBBER. The chief natural source of rubber is the rubber tree (*Hevea brasiliensis*). Other plants called rubber tree include *Euphorbia tetragona, E. triangularis,* and *Ficus elastica,* the last also known as rubber plant. The Ceara rubber is *Manihot glaziovii;* Mexican or Panama rubber, *Castilla elastica.* Rubber vine is a common name for *Cryptostegia, Echites umbellata,* and *Rhabdadenia.*

RUBIA (Rù-bia) — Madder. None of the sixty species of *Rubia* is of horticultural importance except that madder, because of its former importance, is occasionally included in collections of dye plants. The genus, which belongs to the madder family RUBIACEAE, is a widely dispersed native of both the Old World and the New World. Its name derives from the Latin *ruber,* red, and alludes to the color of the roots. For centuries the dye obtained from madder, called turkey red, was of great importance. Burial wrappings of Egyptian mummies were colored with it. The development of synthetic dyes practically eliminated the commercial importance of natural madder.

Rubias are often somewhat prickly, trailing, lax, or erect herbaceous perennials and subshrubs with leaves generally in circles of four to eight, or very rarely paired. The tiny wheel- or slightly bell-shaped flowers, with small tubular calyxes, and five-parted corollas, are in axillary or terminal clusters. The fruits are berry-like.

Madder (**R. tinctoria**) has long fleshy roots, vining stems up to about 4 feet long, and mostly lanceolate, stalkless or very short-stalked leaves 2 to 4 inches long, finely-prickly along their margins and midribs, and in circles of four to six. The flower clusters form terminal panicles of greenish-yellow blooms under $\frac{1}{10}$ inch in diameter. The fruits resemble tiny burrs and ripen from red to black. They are $\frac{1}{8}$ to $\frac{1}{4}$ inch in diameter.

Cultivation. Well-drained soil and a sunny location suit madder. It is propagated by seed.

RUBIACEAE — Madder Family. Chiefly tropical and subtropical in its natural distribution, but including some genera and species of cooler regions, this family of dicotyledons comprises about 6,000 species distributed among 500 genera. Its mem-

bers, some sources of dyes, medicines, edibles, and beverages, include trees, shrubs, and herbaceous plants. They have undivided, usually lobeless and toothless leaves, opposite or in whorls (circles) of four, six, eight, or ten. The flowers, rarely solitary, more commonly in branched clusters, have two- to six-cleft calyxes or are without calyxes, a four- to six-lobed corolla, four to six stamens, and one style. The fruits are berries or drupes. Among genera cultivated are *Adina, Asperula, Bouvardia, Burchellia, Calycophyllum, Catesbaea, Cephaelis, Cephalanthus, Chiococca, Cinchona, Coccocypselum, Coffea, Coprosma, Coutarea, Crucianella, Damnacanthus, Duggena, Emmenopterys, Galium, Gardenia, Genipa, Hamelia, Hedyotis, Hoffmannia, Hydnophytum, Isertia, Ixora, Kraussia, Leptodermis, Luculia, Manettia, Mitchella, Morinda, Mussaenda, Myrmecodia, Nertera, Oxyanthus, Paederia, Palicourea, Pavetta, Pentas, Portlandia, Posoqueria, Psychotria, Putoria, Randia, Ravnia, Richardia, Rondeletia, Rothmannia, Rubia, Serissa, Vangueria, Warszewiczia,* and *Xeromphis.*

RUBUS (Rù-bus) — Bramble, Blackberry, Raspberry, Baked Apple Berry. The genus *Rubus,* belonging to the rose family ROSACEAE, its members collectively called brambles, is of very wide natural distribution, the preponderance of its kinds natives of the northern hemisphere. Botanically, it is one of the most confused genera. Hundreds of species names have been applied, many apparently with little justification, to American and European kinds. Fairly conservative authorities recognize the probability of there being about 250 species. They include hardy and nonhardy ones. The name, a classical Latin one, stems from *ruber,* red. It refers to the fruits of some species.

The most familiar representatives of *Rubus* are the blackberries, raspberries, dewberries, and loganberries cultivated for their fruits, so delicious raw, so excellent for pies, preserves, jellies, and wines. These pomological brambles are mostly improved selections and hybrids of natural species. They and other kinds cultivated for their fruits are dealt with under Blackberry, and Raspberry. In addition *Rubus* contains kinds of ornamental merit. These are our concern here.

Rubuses, or rubi if one prefers the Latinized version, are mostly shrubs, deciduous or evergreen, with canelike stems. A few are herbaceous perennials. They are erect, spreading, sprawling, or creeping, according to kind. Often the prickly or sometimes nonprickly stems root where they come into contact with the ground. The leaves are alternate, usually divided into leaflets arranged pinnately, pedately, or less commonly palmately, or are sometimes undivided. Their flowers, generally coming from canes (stems) of the previous year's growth, are in clusters, racemes, or panicles, or sometimes are solitary. Having much the aspect of small single roses, they are generally white, less commonly pink to rosy-purple. They have a calyx of five lobes or sepals, frequently accompanied by the same number of bracts, five petals, numerous stamens, and few to many pistils clustered on a cone-shaped core (the receptacle). The fruits, usually called berries, are not berries in the botanical sense. They are coherent aggregations of many tiny drupes, each berry-like and containing one small seedlike stone. The fruits of rubuses belonging to the raspberry section, when picked, separate from the receptacles and so are hollow cones. The receptacles of blackberries and dewberries remain with the picked fruits, which thus are solid cones. Unless otherwise stated the kinds discussed below are deciduous shrubs.

The flowering raspberry (**R. odoratus**) is wild from Nova Scotia to Michigan, Georgia, and Tennessee. From 5 to 9 feet tall, it has arching stems without prickles. The quite handsome leaves, palmately-three- or five-lobed, are maple-like and 4 to 10 inches wide. Rosy-purple or rarely white, the 2-inch-wide, fragrant blooms are displayed for a long period. The crumbly, red fruits

Rubus odoratus

Rubus parviflorus

Rubus 'Tridel'

are without merit for eating. Similar to the last, but with white flowers and longer-pointed leaf lobes, the thimbleberry (**R. parviflorus**) is widely distributed in northern North America. Another American worth planting for its flower display, and in bloom perhaps the most beautiful of all brambles, the Boulder raspberry or Rocky Mountain flowering raspberry (**R. deliciosus**) is wild in Colorado and Wyoming. Graceful, this is 3 to 9 feet tall and has arching stems without prickles. Its undivided currant-like leaves are heart-shaped-ovate, toothed, and 1½ to 3 inches long. Mostly solitary, the white flowers, 2 inches across, strongly resemble single roses. The purple fruits belie the implication of the botanical name. They are insipid rather than delicious. An especially lovely, double-flowered variety is R. d. plena. A hybrid between the Boulder raspberry and Mexican R. trilobus named R. 'Tridel', raised in England in 1950, promises well as a flowering ornamental shrub. Probably hardy in southern New England, it is about 10 feet tall and has white flowers up to 3½ inches in diameter. The salmonberry (**R. spectabilis**), native from Idaho to Alaska and California, has erect or sprawling stems up to several feet long. They are without prickles and sometimes persist for over two years. The thinnish, nearly hairless, toothed leaves have three or five pointed, ovate to heart-shaped leaflets 4 to 6 inches long. About 1 inch wide, the long-stalked, reddish-purple flowers, few together or solitary, are succeeded by large, edible, red or yellow fruits.

The wineberry (**R. phoenicolasius**), a native of eastern Asia and naturalized in North America, is 4 to 6 feet tall and has arching stems thickly clothed with red, gland-tipped, bristly hairs. The stems root freely where their ends touch the ground. White-hairy on their undersides and less hairy above, the leaves are of three or rarely five toothed, triangular-ovate leaflets, the middle one, much the biggest, 2 to 4 inches long. The small, white flowers, in long terminal panicles, are succeeded by red

fruits, at first enclosed by the calyxes. The cut-leaved blackberry (**R. laciniatus**), presumably of European origin, but unknown in a truly native state, has escaped from cultivation and occurs spontaneously in North America. Its sprawling or erect stems, 10 to 12 feet in length, are abundantly furnished with hooked prickles. The leaves, in mild climates somewhat evergreen and almost fernlike in aspect, are softly-hairy beneath, hairless on their upper surfaces. Including their stalks 6 inches to 1 foot long, they are mostly of five leaflets arranged palmately (in hand-fashion). The leaflets are pinnately-lobed or jaggedly-cleft, and toothed. About 1 inch in diameter, the rose-pink flowers are in long panicles. The large, spherical, black fruits are edible. Selected varieties are grown for their fruits. A variety with nonprickly stems is known.

The dewberry (**R. macropetalus**), native from California to British Columbia, is a more or less procumbent, weak-prickly, vining shrub, with stems at first erect. Green on both sides, its leaves have three sharp-toothed leaflets. Of varying size, the white, often functionally unisexual flowers are in short clusters. The fruits are black. This species is very similar to the Pacific dewberry (**R. ursinus**) from which cultivated sorts known as boysenberries, loganberries, and youngberries have been derived.

White-stemmed blackberries, little grown in America, are excellent winter ornaments. Most noteworthy are R. cockburnianus (syn. R. giraldianus) and R. lasiostylus, of China, and R. biflorus, of the Himalayas. The beauty of these lies in the brilliant white waxy coatings of their first-year stems, fully apparent only after the foliage drops in fall. This gives the canes the appearance of having been whitewashed. The first two are hardy in southern New England, the other perhaps as far north as Philadelphia. Up to about 10 feet tall, **R. cockburnianus** has arching, sparingly-prickly stems, branched in their upper parts, and leaves 5 to 8 inches long of

Rubus cockburnianus

Rubus ulmifolius bellidiflorus

seven to nine oblong-lanceolate, prickly-stalked, coarsely-toothed leaflets, white-hairy on their undersides, the terminal one often lobed. The small, rosy-purple blooms, in terminal panicles, are succeeded by black fruits. The usually erect stems of **R. lasiostylus,** clad with bristle-like prickles, are 3 to 6 feet tall. The leaves, 5 to 8 inches long or longer, have three or five double-toothed leaflets, white-hairy on their undersurfaces, and the terminal one conspicuously the biggest. The nodding, reddish flowers, five or fewer together, with hairy styles, are succeeded by agreeably flavored reddish fruits. From the last, **R. biflorus** differs in having stems armed with straight, broad-based prickles, white flowers ¾ inch wide, two or three together or sometimes solitary, terminal or from the leaf axils, and with hairless styles. Also, the edible fruits are yellow and some ¾ inch in diameter. This robust kind is up to 10 feet tall. Even more vigorous and somewhat hardier is R. b. quinqueflorus, which has flowers prevailingly in clusters of five, and up to as many as eight.

Double-flowered **R. linkianus** (syn. R. thyrsoideus plenus) is an attractive, robust ornamental with long, lax, green stems armed with scattered, hooked prickles. It has coarsely-double-toothed, prickly-stalked leaves of five leaflets, hairless above, white-hairy on their undersides. Its 1-inch-wide, white or pinkish blooms are in erect, conical panicles up to 1½ feet long. The origin of R. linkianus, which has been cultivated since the eighteenth century, is not known. Another beautiful double-flowered black-berry is R. ulmifolius bellidiflorus. This vigorous kind has plum-colored stems with nearly straight prickles, and leaves, white-felted on their undersides, of three or five toothed leaflets. Its double, pink, narrow-petaled flowers are in large panicles. The species of which this is a variety is native to Europe. Another variety, R. u. variegatus, has leaves with bright yellow veins. The double-flowered kinds just described and the one with variegated foliage are

hardy in southern New England. The double-flowered variety of R. deliciosus, the Boulder raspberry, is described above under that name.

Evergreen rubuses are mostly less hardy than the deciduous ones considered here. One of the most noteworthy, a kind hardy only in warm, frost-free or nearly frost-free climates, is **R. reflexus.** This native of Hong Kong has long, lax stems, which, like the leafstalks and undersides of its undivided leaves, are clothed with rust-colored hairs. The leaves are three- to five-lobed, with the center lobe long-triangular. The tiny white flowers, in close clusters, are succeeded by dark purple fruits. Prostrate, prickly or nonprickly stems, and undivided, round-heart-shaped leaves 4 to 6 inches across and white- or rusty-hairy on their undersides, are characteristic of evergreen **R. irenaeus,** of China. Its few nearly ½-inch-wide white flowers are succeeded by large red fruits. This is hardy perhaps as far north as Philadelphia. Na-

Rubus irenaeus

Rubus calycinoides

tive to Taiwan, normally evergreen **R. calycinoides** in gardens has been misidentified as allied R. fockeanus, of China. It is very attractive, and although the harsh winters experienced in the vicinity of New

York City cause it to lose its foliage, it thrives there and leafs out each spring. A dense, matting creeper, this has little mallow-like, three- to five-lobed leaves with granular, green upper surfaces and white-felted lower ones. Its white flowers, mostly concealed by the foliage, are without ornamental significance. The fruits are scarlet and ½ inch long or slightly longer. Chinese **R. tricolor** has prostrate, prickle-less, yellowish-hairy stems and undivided, sharply-toothed, evergreen, or in cold localities, deciduous leaves 3 or 4 inches long, dark green and hairy above, and white-hairy on their undersides. On erect stalks, the white flowers are 1 inch across. The fruits are bright red. This does well in damp soils in part-shade. A vigorous kind, its stems make an annual growth of several feet. This is hardy about as far north as New York City, but near this limit of its cold tolerance it loses its leaves in winter. Native to moist and wet soils from Nova Scotia to Georgia and Kansas, R.

Rubus tricolor with spikes of immature fruits

hispidus has slender, bristly stems and thick, usually persistent, lustrous, hairless leaves, generally of three broadly-ovate, double-toothed leaflets 1 inch to 1¾ inches long, that in sunny locations assume attractive bronzy hues in winter. The small white flowers, in clusters of few, are succeeded by sour, red to blackish berries.

Sometimes called the strawberry-raspberry, **R. illecebrosus** is a Japanese subshrub or herbaceous perennial with a creeping rootstock. From 6 inches to 1¼ feet tall, its stems are angular and prickly. They bear pinnate leaves 5 to 9 inches long, each with a terminal leaflet and two to seven side leaflets. The nearly hairless leaflets are ovate-lanceolate, sharply-toothed, and 1½ to 3 inches long. Solitary or in threes at the shoot ends, the white flowers, with numerous stamens with yellow anthers, are 1 inch to 1½ inches wide. The more or less cylindrical, somewhat insipid, sweet fruits are red and about 1¼ inches long.

Rubus illecebrosus (fruits)

Herbaceous perennials without woody stems include the baked apple berry or cloudberry (**R. chamaemorus**). This native of far northern reaches of Europe, Asia, and North America is found from the Atlantic to the Pacific and as far south as northern New England. It has creeping stems and long-stalked, shallowly-three- or five-lobed, finely-toothed, round-heart- to kidney-shaped leaves 1½ to 3½ inches across. The white flowers, solitary and terminal, are succeeded by red to orange fruits of excellent eating quality. The cloudberry favors cool, moist, peaty soils and bogs. Growing in similar situations, from Newfoundland to Alaska, New Jersey, and Nebraska, **R. pubescens** has slender, trailing, almost or quite hairless, sometimes somewhat woody stems, without prickles, 1 foot to 2 feet in length. Its soft, thin, coarsely-toothed leaves are of three or five ovate leaflets. The small, white flowers, one to three on a stalk, are succeeded by small, red berries. This grows in cool woodlands and is native from Idaho to Alaska and California. It has thin leaves of three or five irregularly lobed and toothed, hairless or sparsely-hairy leaflets, and at the ends of short shoots, solitary, 1-inch-wide, white flowers.

Garden and Landscape Uses. Although comparatively few brambles have garden merit, and may if not properly cared for become impenetrable, annoying tangles of viciously thorny stems, the tribe must not be denigrated to the extent that the virtues of its more admirable members are neglected. For clothing arbors, trellises, pillars, and other supports, double-flowered *R. linkianus* and *R. ulmifolius bellidiflorus* and the cut-leaved blackberry have virtue. In mild climates and greenhouses, *R. reflexus* can be used similarly. As flowering shrubs, the Boulder raspberry and its double-flowered variety rank highly, as does *R.* 'Tridel', and surely the whitestemmed blackberries should not be overlooked. Like colored-stemmed dogwoods

and willows these brighten winter landscapes. They are especially effective in front of evergreens. As groundcovers and in rock gardens, trailing and creeping kinds, evergreen and deciduous, and woody and herbaceous, are useful when appropriately located. Species indigenous to North America are suitable for native plant gardens.

Cultivation. Brambles adapt readily to a variety of soils, preferring those reasonably fertile and not excessively dry. Most do well in sun, but a few, notably *R. reflexus*, prefer light shade. The chief attention needed is pruning to keep them tidy and orderly. Some kinds have stems that die or are considerably weakened after their first flowering, which takes place in their second year. With such, pruning consists of cutting the old canes out completely as soon as blooming or fruiting is over. This encourages the production of strong new canes from the bases of the plants that will flower and fruit the following year. Whitestemmed blackberries are good examples of kinds that must be treated in this way if best results are to be had. Most other kinds respond to the same management or to simple modifications of it. Propagation of superior and distinct varieties is, according to kind, by suckers, division, layering, and cuttings taken in early fall. This last method is appropriate for the doubleflowered kinds. The young plants of these, which resent root disturbance, do not transplant well. They should be grown in pots until they are set in their permanent locations. Species, in contrast to varieties, are easily raised from seed, which germinate readily in well-drained, sandy soil.

RUDBECKIA (Rud-béckia) — Coneflower, Black-Eyed Susan, Gloriosa-Daisy, Golden Glow. Some plants previously included in *Rudbeckia*, of the daisy family COMPOSITAE, now belong in *Dracopis, Echinacea,* and *Ratibida*. The about twenty-five species that remain are annuals, biennials, and hardy herbaceous perennials, all natives of North America. Their name commemorates a father and son, both named Olaf Rudbeck and both professors of botany before Linnaeus at the University of Upsala, Sweden. Rudbeckias are called coneflowers because of the high disks or central portions of their flower heads. They share that vernacular name with *Dracopis, Echinacea,* and *Ratibida.*

Members of this genus are somewhat coarse. Cultivated kinds have showy, terminal, daisy-like flower heads, with yellow ray florets and with rounded to tall-columnar, yellowish, greenish, or purplish-black disks at their centers. Some cultivated sorts have double flowers consisting of all ray florets. The fruits are seedlike achenes.

Among the perennials, *R. fulgida* is popular. Quite variable, it includes several varieties some of which in the past were accepted as species. Thus we have *R. f. deamii* (syn. *R. deamii*), *R. f. speciosa* (syn. *R. speciosa*), and *R. f. sullivantii* (syn. *R. sullivantii*). The plant grown in gardens as *R. newmanii* (syn. *R. speciosa newmanii*) is correctly *R. fulgida speciosa*. All of these spread by underground stolons and have tufts of long-stalked, lanceolate to broad-lanceolate, more or less hairy basal leaves as well as stem leaves that become gradually shorter-stalked above, until the up-

Rudbeckia fulgida

Rudbeckia 'White King'

of its disk florets are reflexed. The yellow ray florets, 1¼ to 2¼ inches long, are distinctly drooping. The disks are conical and brownish-purple. Ranging as a wild plant from Wisconsin to Texas and Louisiana, the sweet coneflower (**R. subtomentosa**) is attractive. From 3 to 4½ feet in height, it has a woody rhizome, rather stiff stems, and ascending branches ending in flower heads with conical, purple-brown disks and bright yellow ray florets ¾ inch to 1½ inches long. The stems bear lanceolate to ovate, toothed leaves softly-pubescent on their lower sides and harsh above. The bottom leaves commonly are markedly three-lobed. The flower heads of the sweet coneflower are pleasingly anise-scented, which accounts for the vernacular name.

Old-fashioned golden glow (**R. laciniata hortensia**) is one of the most familiar coneflowers, but because its flower heads are "double" (composed of all or nearly all ray florets without a distinct conelike center) it is not always recognized as such. Because of its somewhat aggressive character and the fact that its stems do not support its heavy flower heads well, it is planted less than formerly. The newer variety, 'Goldquelle' is much superior to golden glow and like it, has double flower heads. It is reputed to be a hybrid between *R. nitida* 'Herbstsonne' and golden glow and is more compact, less invasive, and has more consistently double flower heads on stronger stems. It attains a height of about 3 feet. The species **R. laciniata** is coarse and vigorous. A perennial, it is 6 to 9 feet tall and hairless. Its pinnate leaves have deeply-lobed or divided leaflets. The

permost are stalkless. Usually the stems branch in their upper parts with the branches terminating in flower heads with orange-yellow ray florets and short-conical or hemispherical, dark brownish-purple disks. The disk flowers have erect corolla lobes. In *R. f. deamii*, the basal leaves are coarsely-toothed, those on the stems have distantly spaced, small, sharp teeth. The variety *R. f. speciosa* has coarsely-toothed or dissected stem leaves and basal ones toothless or with only obscure rounded teeth. The stem leaves of *R. f. sullivantii* are gradually reduced in size from the base to the top of the stem until the upper ones are merely bracts. The ray florets, 1 inch to 2 inches long, are larger than those of any other natural variety of this species. In addition to these natural variants of *R. fulgida*, a number of improved horticultural varieties are cultivated. These include 'Goldsturm' (syn. 'Gold Storm'), 'Oriole', and 'White King'.

Perennial **R. grandiflora**, native from Missouri and Oklahoma to Louisiana and Texas, grows from 1½ to 3 feet tall and has long-stalked, ovate basal leaves and stalkless upper ones. The corolla lobes

Rudbeckia subtomentosa

flower heads have low, greenish-yellow disks that become conical as they mature and reflexed yellow ray florets 1¼ to 2¼ inches long. This species occurs as a native from southern Canada to Florida and westward beyond the Rocky Mountains. Variety *R. l.* 'Soleil d'Or' has showier flower heads with broader ray florets than those of the typical species.

Less resistant to cold than the kinds discussed above and not reliably hardy in the north, **R. nitida** is a perennial native from Georgia and Florida to Texas. This hairless species is about 3 feet in height and has lobeless, but toothed, ovate to lanceolate, leathery, lustrous green leaves and flower heads with greenish-yellow conical to cylindrical disks and yellow ray florets 1 inch to 2 inches long. A variety, *R. n.* 'Herbstsonne', is taller and has bigger flower heads. Another southern species, **R. maxima** ranges as a native from Missouri to Louisiana and Mississippi. From 3 to 9 feet in height, this perennial has glaucous, lobeless, toothed leaves progressively smaller from the base to the tops of the stems, and flower heads with drooping, yellow ray florets 1 inch to 2 inches long and conical disks at maturity 1½ inches high. As its name implies, a native of California, **R. californica** is a coarse, leafy, branchless perennial about 5 feet tall with broad-lanceolate to oblanceolate, lobeless, sometimes toothed, more or less hairy leaves and solitary flower heads with greenish disks and medium-yellow ray florets 1 inch to 2¼ inches long. Variety *R. c. glauca*, with glaucous, hairless foliage, is a native of coastal California and Oregon.

The black-eyed Susan (**R. hirta**) is an outstanding biennial or short-lived perennial. Believed to have been confined originally to the prairie states, it or its western variety *R. h. pulcherrima* are now spontaneous throughout most of the United States. As may be expected with a species so widely dispersed, it is variable and most of its many horticultural varieties behave as annuals. These have been given fancy horticultural names, such as 'Goldflamme'

Rudbeckia 'Goldflamme'

(syn. 'Gold Flame'), 'Herbstwald' (syn. 'Autumn Forest'), 'Kelvedon Star', and 'Monsplasir' (syn. 'My Joy'), and are described under such in seed catalogs. The gloriosa-daisy is the most remarkable hor-

Gloriosa-daisies bloom profusely

Gloriosa-daisy: (a) Single-flowered

(b) Semidouble-flowered

ticultural development of *R. hirta*. This magnificent and variable strain consists of perennial plants that can, however, be cultivated as annual or biennials. They bloom freely the first year from seed. Attaining heights of 2½ to 3 feet, they are

robust and freely-branched and carry a plentitude of magnificent, single, semidouble or double flower heads 3 to 5 inches or even more in diameter. Their central "eyes" or disks are brown, and their striking ray florets golden-yellow or chestnut-red or parti-colored with those hues. The brown-eyed Susan (**R. triloba**) is another worthwhile biennial. A little weedier in appearance than the better forms of the black-eyed Susan, it occurs spontaneously from southern New England to Minne-

Rudbeckia triloba

sota, Oklahoma, and Georgia and differs from the black-eyed Susan in having some of its stem leaves deeply-three-lobed. Its basal leaves are ovate to ovate-heart-shaped and long-stalked. Like the narrower and shorter-stalked stem leaves, they are toothed. From 1½ to 4½ feet high, the brown-eyed Susan has stiff, much-branched stems and numerous, short-stalked flower heads 1½ to 3 inches in diameter with brown-purple centers and ray florets yellow or yellow with orange bases.

Garden Uses. Rudbeckias are generally rewarding plants in American gardens because with little or no trouble they provide showy displays of bloom during hot summer and fall weather that is not kindly to some other desirable flowers. It may be argued, with slight justice, that they are a little lacking in refinement, that their great dark-eyed, sometimes slightly ragged, predominantly yellow daisies are just a trifle too brassy and blatant. Yet theirs is an honest assertiveness that fits well in the American landscape. In bright sunshine they are brilliant. Never do they seem to be struggling in an alien clime. And of course they are not, for they are representatives of a great group of showy, daisy-like composites that bespangle America's fields, hills, roadsides, and open woodlands with bright yellow daisies in summer. Their kin include sunflowers, blanket flowers, sneezeweeds, tickseeds, and *Heliopsis*.

Rudbeckias are grand plants for beds and borders, for informal areas, for naturalizing, for inclusion in native plant gardens, and for supplying cut flowers that last remarkably well in water. They flourish in ordinary garden soil and are content in full sun or even where they receive a little part-day shade, but cannot be expected to thrive under shadier conditions.

Cultivation. No great skill is needed to succeed with rudbeckias. Once planted, the perennials pretty much take care of themselves. The more vigorous, such as the popular golden glow, may even invade neighboring plants' territories, unless curbed occasionally, which can be done appropriately by reducing with a spade in spring the sizes of clumps that threaten to grow out of bounds. Perennial rudbeckias are planted in early spring or early fall about 1½ to 2 feet apart, depending upon the vigor of the species or variety. When they become too large or show evidence of deterioration, usually every four or five years, they are dug up, divided, and replanted in newly spaded earth improved by mixing in compost, peat moss, or other organic matter, and fertilizer. In intervening years, a spring application of a complete fertilizer encourages satisfactory growth. Summer care may involve staking and certainly will include suppressing weeds by frequent shallow surface cultivation or by mulching, watering during dry weather, and removing faded blooms. After killing frost the tops are cut off at ground level and later, in harsh climates, a light winter covering of salt-hay or branches of evergreens may be placed over the ground to minimize the ill effects of alternate freezing and thawing. Choice perennial varieties are increased by division in early spring or early fall. Unimproved species can be reproduced in the same way or by seeds sown in May in a cold frame or outdoor seedbed.

Annual rudbeckias and biennial or short-lived perennial kinds cultivated as annuals, including the magnificent gloriosa-daisies, are among the easiest of plants to raise from seeds. These may be sown outdoors in early spring where the plants are to bloom and the seedlings thinned to 6 inches to 1½ feet apart if in informal groups that result from broadcast sowing, or slightly closer together in rows spaced 1½ to 2 feet apart if they are being grown for cut flowers. The exact thinning distance should depend upon the vigor of the variety. To secure early flowers or to have young plants to set out after spring-blooming plants, such as pansies, English daisies, Siberian wallflowers, tulips, and hyacinths, have been removed from the beds, seeds may be started about eight weeks before planting out time, in a greenhouse in a temperature of about 60°F. The seedlings are transplanted about 2 inches apart in flats and are grown in a sunny greenhouse where the night temperature is 50°F, and the day temperature

is five to ten degrees higher, until it is safe to put them outside, which can be done as soon as all danger of frost is passed. Final spacing of plants started indoors may be 8 inches to 1½ feet. Annual rudbeckias respond to fertile, well-drained garden soil. They need full sun. Routine care is not exacting; it consists of keeping down weeds, watering in dry weather, removing faded blooms, and staking the taller growing varieties.

To grow brown-eyed Susan and black-eyed Susan and its varieties, including the gloriosa-daisies, as biennials, seed may be sown outdoors or in a cold frame in May or June and the seedlings transplanted, spaced 6 inches apart in rows 1 foot apart, in nursery beds where they remain until early fall or early spring, when they are transferred to their flowering locations.

RUDOLFIELLA. See Bifrenaria.

RUE. See Ruta. Bush-rue is *Cneoridium dumosum;* Goat's-rue, *Galega officinalis* and *Tephrosia virginiana;* meadow-rue, *Thalictrum.*

RUE-ANEMONE is *Anemonella thalictroides.*

RUELLIA (Ru-éllia). The genus *Ruellia,* of the acanthus family ACANTHACEAE, is composed of herbaceous plants, subshrubs, and shrubs. Considered broadly, it numbers in excess of 200 species and is widely distributed, chiefly in tropical, subtropical, and warm-temperate regions, especially in the Americas. Its name commemorates Jean de la Ruelle, a French physician and botanist, who died in 1537.

Ruellias have opposite, undivided, toothed or toothless leaves. Solitary or in clusters in the leaf axils or in terminal branched clusters or panicles, the flowers have calyxes deeply-cleft or parted into slender lobes or sepals, and tubular corollas enlarged in their upper parts and with five equal or nearly similar spreading lobes (petals). There are four fertile stamens with dilated stalks more or less united at their bases. Usually with a recurved apex, the style is slender and sometimes two-lobed. The fruits are cylindrical or club-shaped capsules.

Attractive purple leaves boldly midveined with white characterize *R. devosiana* and *R. makoyana,* both subshrubs 9 inches to 1½ feet tall, native to Brazil. Their stems are somewhat procumbent at their bases, their branches erect. They have elliptic, short-pointed, velvety leaves 1½ to 2 inches long. The stalkless blooms, solitary from the upper leaf axils, are about 1¾ inches long. Those of *R. devosiana* are white with lilac-colored throats and streakings, those of *R. makoyana* bright carmine-red.

A shrub up to 6 feet high, *R. macrantha,* of Brazil, has sparsely-hairy shoots and foliage. Its stems, conspicuously thick-

Ruellia makoyana

Ruellia macrantha

ened at the nodes and branched, bear essentially toothless, ovate-lanceolate leaves 2 to 5 inches in length. The showy, distinctly veined, bright rosy-purple, round-petaled blooms are 3 inches long and broad. Their corolla tubes are much expanded in their upper parts. Also Brazilian, *R. graecizans* (syn. *R. amoena*) is a subshrub 1 foot to 2 feet in height. Its short-stalked, short-

Ruellia graecizans

hairy, more or less toothed, ovate- to oblong-lanceolate leaves are 2 to 5 inches long. The bright red blooms are on branched, several-flowered, slender stalks that come from the leaf axils. They have evidently-pouched, 1-inch-long corolla tubes and short spreading petals. A pretty mound-forming plant 9 inches or so tall, *R. elegans* (syn. *R. formosa*), of Brazil, has four-angled stems that, like the 3- to 4-inch-long, light green, ovate leaves, are pubescent. The long-stalked, light scarlet and cream-colored flowers, in twos or threes from the upper leaf axils, are 1½ to 1¾ inches long. The two uppermost petals are united below their middles. The stamens and style protrude.

Mexican *R. malacosperma*, up to 3 feet tall, has four-angled, hairless or sparingly-hairy stems and short-stalked, narrow-lanceolate leaves up to 6 inches in length. The forking, flowering stalks carry few to several lavender-blue blooms approximately 2 inches long that remain open for a few hours only, falling in the afternoon of the day they open. Sometimes confused with this, *R. brittoniana*, native to Mexico and naturalized in Florida and the Gulf States, is about as tall, but has linear leaves up to twice as long as those of *R. malacosperma*. Its lavender-blue to blue-violet blooms, 1 inch to 1½ inches long, are in leafy clusters. Pale yellow blooms are borne by *R. speciosa* (syn. *R. pulcherrima*), a

Mexican shrub 3 to 6 feet tall. The flowers, solitary or in twos or threes on stalks from the leaf axils, are up to 2 inches long or a little longer and nearly as wide. The young shoots are glandular-hairy. The ovate to oblong-ovate leaves are clammy and, especially on their undersides, downy. They are 1½ to 3 inches long.

Other tropical and subtropical sorts sometimes cultivated include *R. affinis*, of Brazil, a hairless shrub up to 3 feet tall with short-stalked, elliptic leaves 3 to 5 inches long. Its broad-funnel-shaped flowers, red and about 3½ inches long, have spreading corolla lobes and are solitary in the leaf axils. West Indian *R. coccinea* is herbaceous or subshrubby, and 3 to 6 feet tall; it has round-toothed, downy or hairless, ovate leaves up to 4 inches long and 1-inch-long, stalked or stalkless, red flowers, solitary or more than one from the leaf axils. *R. squarrosa* is a name used without botanical approval for an otherwise unidentified low sort with elliptic to ovate leaves and attractive bright blue flowers.

Hardier sorts, natives of the United States, are scarcely prepossessing out of flower and less than splendid in bloom. Nevertheless, they have an attraction for plant enthusiasts, in part perhaps because they represent a chiefly tropical genus. Here belong *R. caroliniensis, R. ciliosa, R. humilis, R. nudiflora, R. pedunculata, R. purshiana*, and *R. strepens*. With the pos-

sible exceptions of *R. ciliosa* of the southeastern states and *R. nudiflora* of southern Texas and adjacent Mexico, all are reliably hardy in the vicinity of New York City and quite probably in harsher climates. Typical of this group, the others differ in detail only, *R. caroliniensis* is a variable, deciduous herbaceous perennial 1 foot to 2½ feet tall, with pubescent, lanceolate to ovate leaves 1½ to 4 inches long or sometimes longer. Its stalked or nearly stalkless flowers, from the axils of the upper leaves, are produced over a long summer and early fall season. They have a slender-tubed, funnel-shaped, lilac to lavender-blue corolla, about 2 inches long and wide, and are suggestive of primitive, small petunias. Usually few are open at one time and each lasts for only a few hours. The stems of this are usually solitary and without branches. Those of *R. ciliosa*, which is usually not over 1 foot tall, and *R. humilis* are mostly few to several together or are branched from near their bases. The flowers of *R. nudiflora* are in terminal panicles rather than solitary or in clusters from the leaf axils. Branched stems are characteristic of *R. pedunculata*, a feature that distinguishes it from *R. purshiana*, the stems of which are usually branchless. Vigorous *R. strepens*, up to 3 feet tall, has leaves up to 6 inches long. Its flowers are solitary or clustered.

Garden and Landscape Uses and Cultivation. Except for hardy and near-hardy sorts native to the United States, ruellias are suitable only for the tropics and subtropics and for greenhouses. The lower ones are also appropriate in terrariums. They prosper in well-drained, reasonably moist soil that contains an abundance of peat moss, leaf mold, or similar decayed organic matter, and need shade from strong sun. Fairly high humidity, and indoors on winter nights a minimum temperature of 60°F, suits. By day and at other seasons higher temperatures are appreciated. The sorts native to the United States may be planted in rock gardens, native plant gardens, and naturalistic areas. They succeed in moderately moist to somewhat dryish soils and appreciate slight shade from strong sun. Without that their foliage often assumes a rather unpleasant rusty appearance. These sorts are most conveniently increased by seed.

RUKAM is *Flacourtia rukam*.

RUMBERRY is *Myrciaria floribunda*.

RUMEX (Rù-mex) — Dock, Sorrel, Canaigre. The often coarse and troublesome weeds of meadows, waste places, and lawns that belong in this genus of 200 species are generally more familiar to gardeners than the few kinds that possess decorative or other useful qualities. The genus belongs in the buckwheat family POLY-

Ruellia squarrosa

GONACEAE and is widely spread throughout much of the world, mostly in temperate regions. The name is its ancient Latin one.

Docks are mostly annuals and herbaceous perennials. A few kinds develop woody stems and become subshrubs or shrubs. All are remarkable for the considerable variation of foliage they exhibit, often on the same plant. Characteristically the lower leaves are large and those above progressively smaller. At the bottoms of the leafstalks are stem-sheathing appendages (stipules). Individually small, and unisexual or bisexual, the greenish to reddish flowers are clustered, often in large, conspicuous panicles. They have six persistent sepals, the inner three of which usually enlarge considerably as the fruits form, no petals, six short-stalked stamens, and three styles each ending in a star-shaped stigma. The fruits are achenes. A few species, including garden sorrel (*Rumex acetosa*), French sorrel (*R. scutatus*), herb patience or spinach-dock (*R. patientia*), and spinach-rhubarb (*R. abyssinicus*), are sometimes cultivated as edible greens. The tubers of *R. hymenosepalus* contain tannin, for which this species is sometimes cultivated.

The canaigre or wild-rhubarb (**R. hymenosepalus**) is a bold-appearing perennial,

Rumex hymenosepalus

native from Oklahoma to California. From a cluster of spindle-shaped tubers it develops a little-branched stem up to 3 feet tall. The short-stalked, crinkled, oblong-lanceolate leaves are up to 1 foot long. The panicle of fairly large, bisexual flowers is brownish-rose-pink and 6 inches to 1 foot in length. The great water dock (**R. hydro-lapathum**), a perennial native of Europe, from 3 to 6 feet high, has broad oblong-lanceolate, wavy-edged, pointed, toothed leaves up to 2 feet long. Its bisexual flowers are in very large panicles.

Garden and Landscape Uses and Cultivation. The generally hardy species described above have ornamental merit and are occasionally cultivated in sunny, naturalistic areas. The great water dock looks well at watersides, the other succeeds under drier conditions. Neither is difficult to grow. Both appreciate deep, fertile soil. Propagation is by seed and by division.

RUMOHRA (Ru-mòhra) — Leather-Leaf Fern. This genus of one species of the aspidium family ASPIDIACEAE is, by some authorities, included in the polypody family POLYPODIACEAE. It is a widely dispersed native of warm parts of the southern hemisphere. The name honors Dr. Carolus de Rumohr Holstein. Formerly other species, now referred to *Arachniodes*, were included in *Rumohra*.

The leather-leaf fern (**R. adiantiformis** syns. *Polystichum adiantiforme, Polypodium*

Rumohra adiantiformis

adiantiforme) is vigorous, has somewhat the aspect of *Davallia bullata*. It has long, creeping, brown rhizomes and dense clusters of leathery, triangular-bladed leaves 1 foot to 3 feet in length, pinnate in their upper parts, twice- or thrice-pinnate below. Their rather coarsely-toothed ultimate segments are oblongish and up to 1 inch in length. The clusters of spore capsules are between the mid-veins of the segments and the leaf margins.

Garden Uses and Cultivation. These are as for *Davallia*. For more information see Ferns.

RUMRILLARA. This is the name of orchid hybrids the parents of which include *Ascocentrum, Neofinetia,* and *Rhynchostylis*.

RUNNERS. These are slender shoots that trail (run) over the ground for some considerable distance outward from certain kinds of perennial plants and develop at their extremities or at intervals along their lengths young plants (plantlets). At first the connecting stem serves as a sort of umbilical cord between the mother plant and the plantlets, but after the latter take root, the stem dies and decays leaving the young plants established as separate individuals.

The strawberry is one of the best-known producers of runners. Others include the strawberry-begonia (*Saxifraga stolonifera*) and the spider plant (*Chlorophytum comosum*), both popular indoor plants. These and all other runner-producing plants are easily increased by removing the plantlets as soon as they have developed sufficient roots and planting or potting them separately. To facilitate this it is often advantageous to pin young plantlets on runners to the surface of soil contained in small pots. Use pieces of wire bent like hairpins to do this, and keep the soil in the pots moist. When the plantlets are well rooted, cut the stem that leads from the mother plant and treat the propagations as separate individuals.

RUNNING. This word forms parts of the names of these plants: running-myrtle (*Vinca minor*), running-pine (*Lycopodium clavatum*), and running postman (*Kennedia prostrata*).

RUPICAPNOS (Rupi-cápnos). More than thirty species, of Spain and North Africa, constitute *Rupicapnos,* of the fumitory family FUMARIACEAE. The name, from the Greek *rupi*, rock, and *knapnos*, smoke, alludes to the habitat and appearance of the plants.

These are low, nearly stemless, evergreen natives of cliffs and rocky places. They have pinnate leaves with pinnately-lobed leaflets. The long-stalked flowers, in racemes, have a pair of tiny sepals, four petals, the uppermost with a spur, the lowest standing apart from the others. The fruits are capsules.

Variable **R. africana,** of North Africa, much resembles a *Corydalis* and inhabits limestone areas. It has more or less glaucous leaves with ovate, oblong, or linear leaflets. The ½-inch-long flowers, smokey-

Rupicapnos africana

pink with darker extremities, rarely are white.

Garden Uses and Cultivation. A choice item for alpine greenhouses or where winters are fairly mild for rock gardens, this responds to well-drained, limy soil and partial shade. Propagation is by seed or by very carefully dividing the plants in early spring.

RUPRECHTIA (Ru-préchtia). Related to buckwheat and rhubarb and belonging to the buckwheat family POLYGONACEAE, the genus *Ruprechtia* comprises about thirty species of trees and shrubs. It ranges in the wild from Mexico to Argentina. The name honors Franz Josef Ruprecht, of the botanic garden at St. Petersburg, Russia. He died in 1870.

Ruprechtias are trees and shrubs with alternate, undivided leaves and clusters or short spikes of little unisexual flowers, the sexes on separate plants. The flowers have winged, petal-like sepals and no petals, and the males nine stamens. The fruits are three-angled achenes.

The only species known to be cultivated in the continental United States, *R. coriacea* is an evergreen, 20-foot-tall tree, a

Ruprechtia coriacea

native of Venezuela and Curacao. Its ovate to elliptic, short-stalked, leathery leaves, with shallowly-wavy margins, are 2 to 4 inches long by up to 2 inches wide. Male flowers are red, tiny, and inconspicuous. The female blooms, red, abundantly produced and showy, are succeeded by fruits that are enclosed and exceeded by the winglike, persistent calyxes, which have bright red, narrow lobes ¾ inch long. Normally trees of this species bear all male or all female flowers, but at least one instance is recorded of a specimen in Florida that produced only female flowers for several years, then after transplanting, only male blooms. Three or four years later it again produced only female flowers.

Garden and Landscape Uses and Cultivation. The species described has merit as an ornamental for general-purpose planting in warm climates where little or no frost occurs. Female trees are especially worth while because of their showy displays of flowers and fruits. However, the sex of specimens raised from seed is not determinable until they first bloom, and this may require seven to fifteen years. Little information is available about other methods of propagation, but it seems likely that cuttings, layering, or grafting would afford means of multiplying known females.

RUPTUREWORT. See Herniaria.

RUSCHIA (Rùs-chia). The genus *Ruschia*, restricted in the wild to South Africa, chiefly to the southern, western, and central parts, is one of the largest of the many segregates formerly included in *Mesembryanthemum*. It comprises 350 species and belongs to the carpetweed family AIZOACEAE. Its name commemorates Ernst Rusch, of southwest Africa.

Ruschias are small to moderate-sized evergreen, succulent subshrubs or small shrubs with woody, rarely tuberous roots and erect, sprawling or prostrate stems or sometimes shorter, tufted ones. The lower parts of the branches are often clothed with persistent remains of dead leaves. The firm, fleshy, bluish-green, usually dark-dotted leaves are in pairs, their bases united and continued down the stems. The free portions are usually three-angled and long in relation to their width. Less often they are nearly hemispherical. Generally they terminate in a brief point and not uncommonly have blunt teeth along their keels. They are fringed with hairs or are hairless. Solitary or clustered, terminal or from the leaf axils, the white, pink, red, purple, or violet, stalked or stalkless flowers may suggest to the casual observer the flower heads of daisies. Actually they are very different. Each is a single bloom, not a head of florets. They have four or five sepals, and numerous petals and stamens. A few sorts expand their blooms only at night, but most are day-bloomers. The fruits are capsules.

More sorts than listed here are perhaps cultivated by fanciers of succulent plants, but none seems to be commonly grown. Sorts most likely to be cultivated include these: *R. acuminata* (syn. *Mesembryanthemum exacutum*), 4 to 8 inches tall, has erect to reclining wandlike stems and pointed leaves ½ inch to 1¼ inches long by not over ¼ inch wide and thick. Its white or pinkish flowers, ½ inch to 1¼ inches in diameter, have stalks up to 1¼ inches long. *R. crassa* (syn. *Mesembryanthemum crassum*) is a vigorous small shrub with fleshy leaves up to ¾ inch long and almost as wide as broad, with soft, white

hairs. Their upper surfaces are flat, their under ones keeled. The flowers, shortstalked and white, are 1 inch across. *R. derenbergiana* (syn. *Mesembryanthemum derenbergianum*) forms compact cushions up to 8 inches in diameter of crowded shoots, each with two or three pairs of wedge-shaped, blunt, three-angled leaves 1 inch long or a little longer and with scarcely visible dots. The short-stalked flowers are pale pink, ¾ to 1 inch in diameter. *R. dualis* forms clumps of shoots up to 2 inches high. Their pairs of ¾-inchlong, ¼-inch-wide leaves, united for one-third of their lengths from their bases, have flat tops and rounded and partly keeled undersides. The stalkless, magenta-pink flowers are a little over ½ inch wide. *R. granitica* (syn. *Mesembryanthe-*

Ruschia granitica

mum graniticum) has prostrate stems and crowded, erect, short flowering branches each with a few pairs of short, thick, oblong to ovate, flat-topped, glaucous leaves that are keeled on their undersides. Rather under ½ inch in diameter, the flowers are pink. *R. impressa,* compact and 1 inch to 3 inches high, has spreading stems with erect branchlets, and blunt-keeled leaves ½ inch long or slightly longer, at their apexes about ¼ inch thick. The flowers, under ½ inch across, are pink. *R. karrooica* (syn. *Mesembryanthemum karrooicum*), an erect, hairless subshrub up to about 1 foot tall, has green-dotted, bluish leaves ⅓ to ¾ inch long by under ¼ inch wide and thick. They have a spinypointed, recurved apex, a slightly channeled upper surface, and a rounded underside. The solitary flowers, 2 inches in diameter and on stalks 1¾ inches long, have purplish petals with a darker stripe down the center of each. *R. rostella* (syn. *Mesembryanthemum rostellum*) has prostrate stems with many branchlets. The conspicuously-dotted, subcylindrical leaves, three-angled below the leaf tip, are up to ¾ inch long by about ⅛ inch wide. The solitary, stalkless, 1-inch-wide blooms are white.

Garden Uses and Cultivation. These are admirable in collections of choice succulents, outdoors in warm desert regions and in greenhouses. Most are not difficult to grow in full sun in thoroughly well-drained soil. Indoors, a winter night temperature of 45 to 50°F suits, with a daytime increase, adjusted to the brightness of the weather, of up to fifteen degrees. Water with moderate caution spring to fall, sparingly in winter. Propagation is easy by seed and by cuttings. For more information see Succulents.

RUSCUS (Rús-cus) — Butcher's-Broom. The lily family LILIACEAE, which consists largely of plants with bulbs and bulblike organs, contains a few nonbulbous shrubs and subshrubs, among them this genus of about half a dozen species of the Mediterranean region and vicinity of the Black Sea. The name *Ruscus* is an ancient Latin one.

Ruscuses have tough, usually green, semiwoody stems from underground rootstocks. The apparent leaves are alternate, persistent, evergreen cladodes (branches modified to function as leaves) that grow from the axils of the small, membranous bractlike organs that are the true leaves. Close to the center of each cladode is a bract from the axil of which develops a brief stalk bearing one to several tiny, generally unisexual, green or purple-tinged blooms. The flowers have six perianth segments (properly tepals, but often called petals), three united stamens or staminodes (infertile stamens), and a pistil, vestigial in male blooms, in females topped by a sticky stigma. The fruits are one- to few-seeded berries. Branches of *R. aculeatus* are often dried and dyed for use as florists' ornamentals. For *R. racemosus* see *Danae racemosa*.

Butcher's-broom (**R. aculeatus**), a native of Europe, the Black Sea region, and

Ruscus aculeatus

the Azores, differs from other kinds in having stems that branch freely from more than one level. From 1½ to 4 feet tall, they bear numerous, rigid, ovate, sharp-pointed cladodes ¾ inch to 1½ inches long, with the flower clusters from their upper surfaces. Typically, they are unisexual with the sexes on separate individuals, but a variant that has male and female flowers on the same plant, and another that bears bisexual flowers, are known and esteemed because they can fruit in the absence of plants of separate sexes. The berries are bright red or, in *R. a. fructuluteo*, yellow. Variety *R. a. angustifolius* is low growing, less stiff, and has narrower cladodes. In *R. a. platyphyllus* (syn. *R. a. latifolius*) the cladodes are 2 inches long or longer and up to 1½ inches broad. Differing from *R. aculeatus* in branching only from the tops of its stems, **R. hyrcanus** is native to western Asia.

Branchless, arching stems, up to 1¼ feet tall, and spineless cladodes are typical of *R. hypoglossum*, indigenous from south-

Ruscus hypoglossum

ern Europe to Turkey and the Crimea. Obovate to broadly-ovate or ovate-lanceolate, its cladodes, which bear the flowers on their top surfaces in the axils of green, leaflike bracts are 1½ to 4 inches long by from ½ inch to 1½ inches wide. The plants are unisexual, the berries red. Closely related *R. hypophyllum*, of the western Mediterranean region, has erect, branchless stems, up to 3 feet in height, and thinner cladodes than *R. aculeatus*. The bracts in the axils of which the flowers develop are narrower and have five or fewer, rather than five to fifteen veins.

A possible hybrid between *R. hypoglossum* and *R. hypophyllum* is **R. microglossus**. This has been much confused with its supposed parents. Only female plants of *R. microglossus* are known, and these differ from *R. hypoglossum* in being up to 2 feet in height, having somewhat larger cladodes more uniformly obovate-lanceolate to oblanceolate, and in the bract from which the flowers arise having only three or four veins. Its stems arch. The flowers

appear from either the upper or lower sides of the cladodes and generally from both locations on the same plant.

Two other species that have been confused with *R. hypophyllum* are *R. colchicus* and *R. streptophyllus*, the former of western Asia, the other of Madeira. Both differ from *R. hypophyllum* in their stems usually being arched. Generally the flowers of **R. colchicus** are on the undersides of the cladodes, rarely on the upper. The flowers of **R. streptophyllus** are technically on the upper sides of the cladodes, but, because the latter are twisted, face downward.

Garden and Landscape Uses. Not hardy in the north, but suitable for milder climates such as those of the south and California, ruscuses are highly tolerant of environments unacceptable to many plants. They grow in quite heavy shade, but do best in light shade, and stand dryness well. They are useful for planting under trees, for fronting shrub plantings and for other places where tough, low evergreens can serve usefully. The spiny character of *R. aculeatus* discourages walking upon or among; it may be employed to discourage minor trespasses.

Cultivation. Division, best done in spring, is the usual means of propagation. Plants can also be raised from seed sown as soon as ripe in a cold frame or outdoor bed. When the growths of established plants become too crowded, the oldest may be pruned out at ground level.

RUSH. See Juncus.

RUSH FEATHERLING is *Pleea tenuifolia*.

RUSH, FLOWERING- is *Butomus umbellatus*.

RUSH, SCOURING-. See Equisetum.

RUSH, WOOD-. See Luzula.

RUSH, ZEBRA- is *Scirpus tabernaemontani*.

RUSPOLIA (Rus-pòlia). Native to Africa, this genus of the acanthus family ACANTHACEAE consists of four species. Its name honors the Italian explorer of Africa, Prince Eugenio Ruspoli, who died in 1893. From related *Pseuderanthemum*, the genus *Ruspolia* is most readily distinguished by its flowers being red or red and yellow. In addition there are technical differences between the two genera.

Ruspolias are shrubs with short-stalked, opposite, ovate leaves and flowers in spikes or panicles. The flowers have a deeply-five-cleft calyx, a corolla with a long, cylindrical tube and much shorter lobes (petals), two slightly protruding stamens, and a slender style tipped with a somewhat two-lobed stigma. The fruits are capsules.

Small, somewhat straggling, and hairless, **R. hypocrateriformis**, of tropical Africa, has four-angled stems and 2- to 3-inch-long leaves. The flowers have corollas with yellow tubes and are yellow inside, but the outsides of the petals are crimson. From

Ruspolia hypocrateriformis

the last, **R. seticalyx** (syn. *Pseuderanthemum seticalyx*), of tropical Africa, differs in its stems being cylindrical, its leaves somewhat hairy, and in its flowers being less brilliantly colored.

Garden and Landscape Uses and Cultivation. These are as for *Eranthemum*.

RUSSELIA (Rus-sèlia) — Coral Plant or Coral Blow or Fountain Plant. The twenty or so species of shrubs that comprise *Russelia*, of the figwort family SCROPHULARI-ACEAE, are of distinct appearance. Although often leafless, or rather having only tiny scales in place of leaves, they are evergreen in the sense that their slender stems, which actually perform the life functions the leaves of most plants do, are green, so that the bushes present a lively appearance at all seasons. The genus was named in honor of Alexander Russell, an English physician and traveler, who died in 1768.

Russelias are natives of warm parts of the Americas. Their leaves, or scales representing leaves, are opposite or in whorls (circles of three or more). The slender, tubular, red flowers with five sepals, five corolla lobes, four stamens included in the corolla tube, and one style are usually in many-flowered clusters; rarely they are solitary. The fruits are subglobose capsules.

The coral plant, coral blow, or fountain plant (**R. equisetiformis** syn. *R. juncea*) is best known in cultivation. A native of Mexico, naturalized in Florida and the West Indies and 1 foot to 4 feet in height, it has numerous arching or drooping, four-angled, rushlike stems, and leaves mostly reduced to minute scales. Those that are not are about ¼ inch long and ovate to linear-lanceolate. The 1-inch-long, fire-cracker-like flowers are in loose clusters and on long, slender stalks; their corolla tubes end in five short, rounded lobes. Differing from *R. equisetiformis* in having ovate, toothed leaves up to 2 inches long, and being without leafless stems, **R. sarmentosa** is also a native of Mexico. Presumed hybrids between these two species, of intermediate characteristics, are **R. elegantissima** and **R. lemoinei.**

A newer introduction, **R. lilacina** (syn. *R. campechiana lilacina*) is a sprawly subshrub, a native of Honduras, with broad, more or less heart-shaped, toothed or toothless leaves up to 4 inches long. Its blooms, in clusters near the branch ends, are purple and about ¾ inch long.

Garden and Landscape Uses. These warm-climate plants revel in sun, but stand a fair amount of shade, although they bloom less freely then than when fully exposed. They withstand drought and wind well. Exceedingly graceful, they are extremely useful for fronting borders of shrubs and trees, for foundation plantings, and for lawn beds. They are effective when located just behind the top of a retaining wall so that their branches cascade down its face, and are first-rate plants for hanging baskets. They have the great virtue of blooming more or less continuously. Russelias are easily grown in greenhouses and are charming for conservatory decoration.

Cultivation. Provided the soil is well drained, no difficulty attends the cultivation of russelias. They grow in any ordinary soil and even in those somewhat below par in fertility. They are readily increased by division, by cuttings, and by bending the stems to the ground, pegging them in place, and covering their ends with a little soil that is kept moist until they root and develop new plants from the buried portions. In greenhouses a minimum winter night temperature of 50 to 55°F is satisfactory. Day temperatures in winter, and night and day temperatures at other seasons, may be higher.

RUSSIAN ALMOND. See *Prunus tenella.*

RUSSIAN COMFREY is *Symphytum uplandicum.*

RUSSIAN-OLIVE is *Elaeagnus angustifolia.*

RUSSIAN-SAGE is *Perovskia atriplicifolia.*

RUSSIAN WORMWOOD is *Artemisia gmelinii.*

RUST. Gardeners not uncommonly call any reddish discoloration of foliage rust, but the term is most properly restricted to diseases that exhibit such symptoms caused by pathogenic funguses that live only in the tissues of live plants and not, as do some funguses that cause plant diseases, for parts of these lives on other media or in the soil. Some sorts, such as cedar-apple rust, white pine blister rust, and wheat rust, live for part of each year on one kind of plant, and the remainder upon an entirely different sort or sorts. Others, including carnation rust, chrysanthemum rust, hollyhock rust, mint rust, and rose rust, spend their entire lives on one type of plant.

Control of rust diseases dependent upon alternate hosts is often best achieved by eliminating one of the hosts or series of hosts. This is the reason for laws forbidding the cultivation of certain barberries in wheat-growing regions. Similarly, in areas where cedar-apple rust is troublesome, red-cedars and other junipers known to be host to the disease should, if practicable, be eliminated within about a mile radius of crab-apples and hawthorns, for example.

Other control techniques, applicable to both two-host and one-host rust diseases include, as with asparagus and snapdragon rusts, reliance upon resistant varieties; as with hollyhock rust, growing the plants as biennials instead of perennials; and as with susceptible greenhouse crops, avoiding splashing the foliage with water.

RUTA (Rù-ta) — Rue or Herb of Grace. Common rue or herb of grace is by far the best known of this genus of sixty species that inhabits the Mediterranean region and western Asia, and typifies the rue family RUTACEAE. The name *Ruta* is the classical Latin one of the common rue.

Consisting of subshrubs and herbaceous perennials notable for their bitterness or pungency, rutas have alternate, divided or undivided leaves and terminal clusters of small, yellowish or greenish blooms. The flowers have mostly four each sepals and petals, although the central blooms may have five of each, and eight or ten stamens. The fruits are lobed capsules.

Common rue, well known and highly regarded since ancient times, is frequently mentioned in literature, including the writings of Milton and Shakespeare. It was considered to be a specific against all manner of poisons, such as those of toadstools, serpents, scorpions, and insects, and to be a powerful antidote against spells of magic and the machinations of witches. Particularly, it was believed to benefit the sight, prevent blindness, and ward off contagious diseases. This last virtue was recognized in the custom of placing rue before judges, hopefully to protect them from pestilences that might be brought into their courts by prisoners from the jails. The name herb of grace refers to a former use of brushes made of rue to sprinkle holy water before the celebration of the Roman Catholic High Mass. This is reason for

Shakespeare's "There's rue for you; and here's some for me; we may call it herb of grace o' Sundays." Contact with the foliage of common rue, especially in hot weather, may cause a mild dermatitis.

Common rue (*R. graveolens*), native from the Balkan Peninsula to the Crimea, is widely naturalized through southern Eu-

Ruta graveolens

Ruta graveolens (flowers)

rope, more sparingly in North America. It is a strongly acrid-aromatic, glaucous, hairless, evergreen subshrub, 1 foot to 2½ feet tall, with many erect stems and bluish, two-or-three-times pinnate leaves 3 to 5 inches long, with oblanceolate to obovate leaflets. The lower leaves have much longer stalks than the upper ones, which are very short-stalked. The dull greenish-yellow flowers, about ½ inch wide, are in loose clusters. They have pointed-lanceolate se-

pals and concave, toothed petals, not fringed with long hairs. The foliage of *R. g. variegata* is white-edged. Dwarf, compact *R. g.* 'Jackman's Blue' has rich blue foliage.

Native to southern Europe, **R. chalepensis** differs from common rue in having in dense clusters flowers with broader,

Ruta graveolens variegata

blunt sepals, and petals fringed with long hairs that do not equal the width of the petals. Its leaves are once- or twice-pinnate. Closely allied **R. angustifolia,** also of southern Europe, differs from *R. chalepensis* in having short-glandular hairs on the branches of its flower clusters, bracts, and sepals, and in the hairs that fringe the petals often being as long as the petals are wide. The plant formerly named *R. patavina* is *Haplophyllum patavinum.*

Garden Uses and Cultivation. These plants are chiefly of service in herb gardens, where they are included for their historic interest as well as for their attractive foliage and quite pretty, although certainly not spectacular, muted blooms. Hardy in southern New England, they are best accommodated in very well-drained soil where they are exposed to full sun. As young specimens rues are attractive pot plants for greenhouses and windows. They grow readily in any ordinary potting soil kept moderately moist, and in good light. Winter night temperatures of 45 to 50°F are adequate with rise of ten degrees or so by day permitted. Propagation is easy by cuttings and by seed.

RUTABAGA or SWEDE TURNIP. This, a cultivated development of *Brassica napobrassica,* an Old World native belonging in the mustard family CRUCIFERAE, is adapted for temperate and cool climates, in eastern North America thriving best north of Washington, D.C. It differs from the common turnip in having larger, more or less pointed-ovoid to nearly globular, never flattened or oblate, tuberous roots that have longer necks and finer-textured flesh than ordinary turnips. Their flesh is yellowish or whitish. The foliage is hairless and bluish-green. Rutabagas, usually grown for fall and winter use, need a longer season of growth than ordinary turnips. They are eaten boiled.

Soil requirements for this crop are as for ordinary turnips. Sow from mid-June to early July in rows 1¼ to 2 feet apart, ½ to ¾ inch deep, scattering the seeds at a rate of about six to the foot. Good varieties are 'Laurentian' and 'Purple Top Yellow'. Before they crowd, thin the seedlings to 6 to 9 inches apart. Care until harvest consists of frequent shallow cultivations between the rows and hand pulling along them to eliminate weeds and watering deeply every five to seven days during dry weather.

Harvest after light frost, but before hard freezing. After removing the tops and side roots, store in a root cellar or other cool place where the air is humid (if it is dryish, bed the roots in slightly damp soil, sand, or peat moss) or in outdoor covered pits. The commercial practice of coating the roots with paraffin to prevent moisture loss is not generally recommended for home gardeners.

RUTACEAE—Rue Family. Consisting chiefly of trees and shrubs, often evergreen, but including a few herbaceous perennials, this family of dicotyledons totals 150 genera and possibly 1,600 species. Predominantly natives of tropical, subtropical, and temperate regions, especially those with dry climates, these plants are especially numerous in South Africa and Australia. Oranges, lemons, and other citrus fruits are among the most familiar representatives of the family.

Frequently aromatic because of the essential oils they contain, members of the rue family have alternate or opposite, undivided or pinnate leaves, commonly with tiny translucent dots most easily seen by viewing them against the light. Generally bisexual, rarely unisexual, the flowers are arranged variously in different genera and species. They have three to five calyx lobes or sepals, three to five or rarely no petals, two to ten or less commonly numerous stamens, sometimes united in bundles, and one to five styles, if more than one often united. The fruits are berries, capsules, drupes, follicles, or samaras, sometimes separating into sections. Genera most commonly cultivated include *Acronychia, Adenandra, Aegle, Aeglopsis, Agathosma, Atalantia, Balsamocitrus, Boenninghausenia, Boronia, Calamondin, Calodendrum, Casimiroa, Choisya, Citrofortunella, Citroncirus, Citropsis, Citrus, Clausena, Cneoridium, Coleonema, Correa, Crowea, Dictamnus, Diosma, Eremocitrus, Eriostemon, Esenbeckia, Evodia, Feronia, Feroniella, Fortunella, Geijera, Glycosmis, Haplophyllum, Hesperethusa, Luvunga, Melicope, Microcitrus, Murraya, Orixa, Paramignya, Peltostigma, Phebalium, Phellodendron, Pilocarpus, Poncirus, Ptelea, Ravenia, Ruta, Severinia, Skimmia, Swinglea, Thamnosma, Triphasia, Vepris,* and *Zanthoxylum.*

RUTTYA (Rút-tya). Half a dozen African and Madagascan species constitute *Ruttya,* of the acanthus family ACANTHACEAE. The name commemorates an Irish naturalist, Dr. John Rutty, who died in 1775.

Ruttyas are shrubs with opposite leaves and with blooms that have associated with them small linear bracts. They have asymmetrical, tubular flowers with deeply-five-parted calyxes, the lobes of which are of approximately equal size, and a five-lobed, two-lipped corolla. There are two stamens. The style has two short branches. The fruits are capsules, normally four-seeded.

Evergreen, and up to 12 feet in height, *R. fruticosa* has slender, somewhat four-angled branches at first minutely-hairy. Its leaves, ovate to elliptic and not toothed, are somewhat hairy at first, but later smooth. They are 1¼ to 2¼ inches long by ½ inch to 1¼ inches wide. From the leaf axils are produced the short-stalked blooms

Ruttya fruticosa

in panicles or clusters of one to three. The flowers are 1 inch to 2¼ inches long. They have very asymmetrical corollas, typically orange-red, brick-red, or scarlet, but in one form bright yellow, with a conspicuous, irregular, purple-black, tarry-looking blotch at the base of the center lobe. The lateral lobes (petals) bend strongly backward. This quite showy species is native to tropical East Africa. A yellow-flowered plant cultivated under the botanically invalid name *R. scholesei* is perhaps a color variant of *R. fruticosa.*

Garden Uses and Cultivation. For gardens in the humid tropics and for cultivation in pots in tropical greenhouses *R. fruticosa* is a very worthwhile ornamental. Easily raised from cuttings, it blooms when a year or two old, while yet quite small. It succeeds in any ordinary soil, well drained and moderately moist, and thrives in sun or part-shade.

In greenhouses it needs some shade from strong summer sun. A minimum winter

Seed of winter rye

night temperature of 55 to 60°F is suitable. By day and at other seasons somewhat higher temperatures are favorable, as is a humid atmosphere at all times. Pruning to shape and repotting established specimens is done in spring. Well-rooted plants benefit from regular applications of dilute liquid fertilizer.

RYDBERGIA. See Hymenoxys.

RYE GRASS. Not to be confused with winter rye (see next entry), rye grass is the name of species of *Lolium,* of the grass family GRAMINEAE. Horticulturally, Italian rye grass (*L. multiflorum*) and English rye grass (*L. perenne*) are employed as nurse grasses in lawn-seed mixtures and for making temporary lawns.

RYE, WINTER. Winter rye is a form of the cereal rye (*Secale cereale*) employed horticulturally as a temporary cover crop to check erosion and to serve as green manure. Most commonly, it is sown in late summer or fall on land cleared of vegetables or other crops that will not be planted again until spring.

Winter rye germinates rapidly, makes sturdy growth until the ground freezes, and stores in its parts nutrients that would otherwise be leached from the soil. The crop is plowed, spaded, or rototilled under as soon as the ground is workable in spring. It tops and roots soon rot with the result that the organic content and texture of the soil are markedly improved.

A stand of young winter rye

S

SABAL (Sà-bal) — Palmetto, Puerto Rican Hat Palm. The genus *Sabal*, which consists of nearly twenty species of fan-leaved palms, is endemic to warm parts of North America including the southeastern United States, as well as Bermuda, the West Indies, and Central and South America. The genus belongs in the palm family PALMAE. The derivation of its name is unexplained.

A young *Sabal*, species undetermined

Some species of *Sabal* are imposingly tall, others are dwarfs with short trunks, yet others have subterranean trunks. The leaves, approximately orbicular and divided from the margin part way to the center into many hanging segments, are notched at their ends and frayed into filaments along their margins. In most kinds a continuation of the leafstalk extends well into the leaf blade, sometimes almost the entire length of it, and is conspicuously curved downward, the curve being most apparent when the leaf is viewed from the side, but this is not true of the dwarf palmetto. The small white or green, bisexual flowers have six stamens. The fruits are globular to pear-shaped and small. After the leaves fall the basal parts of their stalks often remain attached to the trunk for many years and sometimes entire dead leaves remain for many months or longer.

The Seminole Indians use the trunks of the cabbage palmetto for constructing their huts. They are also employed as wharf piles because of their resistence to decay when immersed. Cross sections of the trunks are polished and used as small table tops. The leaves are employed for thatching huts and for handicrafting into baskets and mats, and from the stiff leafstalks rough brushes are made. The aboriginal indians ate the fruits, and bees made honey from the nectar of the flowers. The leaf buds of the crowns are eaten as hearts of palm and the unfolded leaves are used in Palm Sunday religious ceremonies. The leaves of the Texas palmetto are used for thatching and for chair seats. The leaves of the Puerto Rican hat palm are made into hats and the leaf fibers are used for baskets, mats, and hammocks. The older leaves are used for thatching. In the past the Bermuda palmetto (*S. bermudiana*) supplied material for thatching roofs and for plaiting baskets and other handmade items, as well as hearts for eating, but limited supplies have greatly reduced its exploitation for these purposes. With the passing from the picture of the Bermuda-cedar (*Juniperus bermudiana*), the Bermuda palmetto is the most

Sabal mexicana, a young specimen

important arboreal element of the island's indigenous flora.

The cabbage palmetto (*S. palmetto*), a native of the southeastern United States, varies tremendously in stature, at its maximum 90 feet tall, but more often lower. It often begins flowering and fruiting when scarcely 3 feet high. The leaf blades, 5 to 8 feet long and usually somewhat broader, are green with, on large leaves, up to sixty or more, long, slender, drooping, deeply-two-lobed segments with many filaments hanging from the clefts between them. A stout down-curved midrib extends from the leafstalk well into the blade. The crown of foliage, especially on older plants, is compact and spherical. The flower clusters are much branched and on old trees are as long as or longer than the leaves. The fruits are black and nearly or quite ½ inch in diameter.

The Texas palmetto (*S. mexicana* syns. *S. texana, S. guatemalensis*), of Texas, Mexico, and Guatemala, is up to 60 feet tall or sometimes taller. As it ages it sheds its old leaf bases leaving a comparatively smooth trunk. Its yellowish-green leaves, with blades, are up to about 3 feet long and about as broad. They are cleft halfway or more from their margins to their midribs into long-pointed segments with filaments in the clefts. A down-curved midrib extends from the leafstalk into the leaf blade. The flower clusters are as long or longer than the leaves. The dull black, globular or kidney-shaped fruits are ¾ to 1 inch in diameter. The plant called the Victoria palmetto, and previously named *S. exul,* belongs here.

The dwarf palmetto (*S. minor*) is native from North Carolina to Missouri, Florida, and Texas. The hardiest of its genus and one of the most cold-tolerant palms, it often favors wet ground, where it grows with special luxurance. It is quite variable and is distinct from other sabals in its leaf blades being flat or nearly flat and in the leafstalk not being continued as a strong, curved midrib of the blade for any very considerable proportion of the length

Ruellia macrantha

Ruta graveolens

Ruta graveolens 'Jackman's Blue'

Ruttya scholesei

Sabatia dodecandra

Salix arctica

Saintpaulia ionantha variety

Salix retusa

Salpiglossis, garden variety

Salix gracilistyla melanostachya

of the blade. This species usually has no emergent trunk, but only a stout, curved, subterranean rootstock with a short erect part, which may reach the surface and from which develops the crown of leaves. However, an aboveground, upright trunk may develop, sometimes to a height of 18 feet. This form with aerial trunks is by some botanists segregated as **S. louisiana** (syn. *S. deeringiana*). The leaves of the dwarf palmetto are green or bluish and firm, 2 to 4 feet across, and divided for two-thirds or more of their depth into sixteen to forty segments forked at their tips. The margins of the leaf segments have few filaments. Because of the absence of long strengthening midribs, the blades of mature leaves often flop and hang vertically like partly folded umbrellas. The flower clusters at first are erect and overtop the foliage, but they arch downward under the weight of the developing fruits, which at maturity are glossy or dull black and about ⅓ inch in diameter.

Another low sort, **S. etonia** normally has a subterranean crooked or S-shaped rootstock, but on occasion develops an emergent erect trunk up to 6 feet tall or taller. This kind, a native of dry ground in Florida, has green, arched leaves about 3 feet in diameter, with the leafstalks extending as strong midribs for a long distance into the blades, with the margins of the forty to sixty leaf segments extending more than halfway into the blade, and with abundant filaments in the clefts between them. The globose black or nearly black fruits are about ½ inch in diameter.

The Bermuda palmetto (**S. bermudana**), endemic to Bermuda, one of the handsomest of its genus, is 30 to 40 feet tall and characteristically has a trunk that is commonly crooked or leaning. Dead leaves often hang for a while, but it soon divests itself of old leafstalks. An open crown of bright green foliage tops the trunk. The deeply-cleft leaves, slightly paler beneath than above, are 6 to 9 feet in diameter and have few or no filaments along their margins. The flower clusters are shorter than the leaves. The pear-shaped, black fruits are about ¾ inch wide. This is sometimes confused with *S. blackburniana* and *S. domingensis*.

The Puerto Rican hat palm (**S. causiarum**), endemic to Puerto Rico and up to 50 feet tall, has a stout trunk from the lower parts of which the old leaf bases soon drop. The large, loose crown consists of dull bluish-green or sometimes glaucous-blue leaves with blades 3 to 6 feet across and stalks 3 to 8 feet long. The blades have long, definite, down-curved midribs and are cleft halfway from margin to midrib. There are loose fibers in the notches. The many-branched clusters of white, slightly fragrant flowers extend beyond the foliage and are up to 10 feet

long. The globose to pear-shaped fruits are dark brown or black. This is the only native palm of Puerto Rico with fan leaves and a stout trunk.

Sabal causiarum, Fairchild Tropical Garden, Miami, Florida

Other sorts cultivated include these: **S. blackburniana** (syn. *S. umbraculifera*), of unknown origin, is not adequately known botanically. It has leaves up to a little over 6 feet in diameter, cleft into segments from their margins halfway to their centers and with filaments in the clefts. The white flowers have orange anthers. The spherical fruits are ¾ inch in diameter. **S. do-**

Sabal blackburniana

mingensis, of Hispaniola, attains a height of 60 feet or more and is likely the largest and most stately of the palmettos. Its trunk is bare and smooth below like that of a royal palm (*Roystonea*). The crown consists of grayish-green leaves with blades to 6 feet in length. The handsome trunks often carry skirts of old leaves similar to those of *Washingtonia*. The fruits, spheri-

cal to pear-shaped, are brown-black and ½ to ¾ inch in diameter. This species is commonly misnamed *S. blackburniana* and *S. umbraculifera*. **S. jamaicensis**, of Jamaica, is occasionally 40 feet tall, but often lower, and forms a rather loose crown of long-stalked, green leaves with few or no marginal filaments. The flattened, brown-black or black fruits are a little over ⅓ inch in diameter. **S. mauritiiformis** (syn. *S. glaucescens*), of Mexico to Venezuela and Trinidad, a slender, graceful palm up to 75 feet tall, has very deeply-divided leaves, light green above and slightly glaucous to silvery beneath. They have long, slender stalks and blades 3 to 6 feet across. The basal parts of the leafstalk soon fall from the trunks. The black fruits are about ⅓ inch in diameter. **S. parviflora**, of Cuba, has a thick trunk up to 50 feet tall that does not retain its old leaves. Its crown is of leaves 3 feet or more long; the leaves are cleft for up to three-fourths of their lengths into deeply-two-lobed segments with prominent filaments between them. The flower clusters are not longer than the leaves. The spherical, brownish-black fruits are ½ inch or a little more in diameter. **S. princeps** (syn. *S. beccariana*), of unknown origin, is a tall tree that retains the basal parts of its leafstalks on its trunk for long periods. The leaves, green on both sides, have long stalks. The pear-shaped, dark gray or black fruits are about ¾ inch in diameter. **S. uresana**, the Sonoran palmetto, of Mexico, is up to 30 feet tall. It has a slightly-ringed trunk and glaucous-blue leaves, up to 6 feet long, with the leaf stalks continued as pronounced extensions well into the blades, which are cleft for one-half their lengths into deeply-two-lobed segments with filaments between. The flower clusters are about as long as the leaves. The fruits are ¾ inch across. **S. yapa** (syns. *S. japa, S. mayarum, S. peregrina*), of Yucatan, Cuba, and Belize, has a trunk up to 20 feet tall or sometimes higher, topped with a very open, loose crown of long-stalked, deeply-incised, light green leaves with few filaments. The trunks soon shed the bases of the old leaves. The spherical or somewhat pear-shaped fruits are about ⅓ inch in diameter.

Garden and Landscape Uses. The native sabals of the United States are fairly hardy. The cabbage palmetto can be grown outdoors as far north as coastal North Carolina. Kinds from more tropical regions are generally less cold resistant, but *S. causiarum* and *S. yapa* have withstood a temperature of 25°F at Daytona Beach, Florida, without injury. Where they are native these palms are attractive for landscaping. The low ones make good groundcovers under taller palms or other trees. The tree types are effective planted singly or in groups. All adapt well to cultivation in tubs and other large containers.

Cultivation. Although at their best in rich earth, these palms will grow in any moderately fertile soil and even in those that offer little nourishment. The cabbage palmetto, particularly, succeeds even in poor, sandy soils. Sabals transplant without difficulty even when large. For the best results they should be fertilized generously and in dry periods kept well watered. They are propagated from fresh seed sown in sandy, peaty soil in a temperature of 70 to 80°F. When accommodated in containers, good drainage and porous, fertile soil must be provided. An indoor winter minimum night temperature of 50°F is satisfactory for species native to the United States. Tropical kinds are better with a winter minimum of 55 to 60°F. At other seasons night temperatures should be higher and day temperatures at all times should be five to ten degrees above those maintained at night. Light shade from strong summer sun is advisable. Water freely from spring through fall, more cautiously in winter. Biweekly applications of dilute liquid fertilizer from spring through fall are helpful to well-rooted specimens. For more information see Palms.

SABATIA (Sabàt-ia) — Marsh-Pink. These very lovely annuals, biennials, and perennials, belonging to the gentian family GENTIANACEAE, are natives of the eastern and southern United States, Mexico, and the West Indies. There are about seventeen species. Few are cultivated, but many are well worth growing and should receive more attention from gardeners. The name commemorates the eighteenth-century Italian botanist Liberato Sabbati.

Sabatias are erect, often slender, branching plants with undivided, linear to ovate, stalkless or nearly stalkless leaves that in some species are stem-clasping. The flowers, few to many in terminal clusters or loosely arranged, are from deep magenta-pink to white, and have five to thirteen calyx lobes and usually as many spreading corolla lobes (petals) and stamens. The corollas have short tubes. The style is split into two lobes or branches. The fruits are many-seeded capsules.

Annual kinds with five petals (or rarely four or six) and normally pink flowers include Sabatia campestris, S. grandiflora, and S. stellaris. Growing chiefly in sandy, moist soils in prairies and light woodlands from Illinois to Kansas, Mississippi, and Texas, **S. campestris** is up to 1 foot tall or somewhat taller, and has alternate upper branches and thin, somewhat stem-clasping, ovate-lanceolate to lanceolate leaves up to 1¾ inches long. The long-stalked blooms, loosely arranged in many-flowered clusters, are 1¼ to 1¾ inches across. They have conspicuously ribbed calyxes, and bright pink petals with, at the base of each, a white-margined, greenish-yellow blotch.

Sabatia grandiflora

Confined as a wildling to Florida and Cuba, and growing in pine lands and grasslands, **S. grandiflora** blooms more or less throughout the year. From 9 inches to 3 feet tall, it has alternate upper stem branches, and succulent, slender leaves, the upper ones usually narrower than the stems and up to 2 inches long. Bright pink, the flowers, 1¼ to 2 inches across, have petals blotched at their bases with yellow, and often edged with red. Very dainty and variable, **S. stellaris** inhabits brackish and salt marshes from Massachusetts to Florida, Louisiana, Mexico, and the West Indies. It blooms throughout the year in the southern part of its range. This species merges into or hybridizes with the closely allied perennial **S. campanulata.** In the latter the main foliage leaves have blunt or rounded bases; those of S. stellaris narrow at their bases. The leaves of S. stellaris are thin and elliptic to very narrow and up to 2 inches long. The bottoms of the petals are marked with a three-lobed blotch of yellow usually edged with red and sometimes white.

A fine annual with flowers having more than five petals is **S. gentianoides**. This native of North Carolina to Florida and Texas, 1½ to 2 feet or sometimes more tall, has thickish leaves, the basal ones in rosettes, the upper markedly tapering to their lower ends. The blooms, 1½ to 2 inches across, are almost stalkless and in tight heads. They are pink with greenish-yellow bases to the petals.

Normally having white flowers with five petals, **S. difformis** and **S. macrophylla** are native perennials of pine lands and wet, acid bogs. Indigenous from New Jersey to Florida, **S. difformis** attains a height of 1½ to 3 feet and has lanceolate to linear-lanceolate, succulent leaves up to 1½ inches long. Its usually many, well-branched stems have generally opposite upper branches. The many blooms, ¾ inch to 1½ inches wide, are in compact, roundish or flattish clusters. Native from Georgia to Florida and Louisiana, **S. macrophylla** is 2 to 4 feet tall. In summer it has many ½-inch-wide blooms in compact, flattish or rounded clusters. Its succulent stems, coated with whitish, waxy bloom, on their upper parts are opposite-branched. Its leaves, ¾ inch to 2 inches long or slightly longer, are elliptic- to ovate-lanceolate.

Handsome perennial sabatias with usually pink flowers are **S. bartramii, S. dodecandra,** and **S. kennedyana.** These have rhizomes, and large blooms with seven to thirteen petals ranging in color from deep purplish-pink to rarely white. One of the most striking of the genus, **S. bartramii**, native to grasslands and pine barrens from Georgia to Alabama, Mississippi, and Florida, is 1½ to 2½ feet tall. It has usually solitary stems that branch, mostly alternately, in their upper parts. Each branch bears one or rarely two usually pink blooms, 2 to 2½ inches in diameter, with a toothed yellow blotch at the base of each petal. Its broad, succulent basal leaves form rosettes; those of the upper part of the stem are very narrow. From the last, *S. dodecandra* and *S. kennedyana* differ in having upper leaves much wider than the diameters of the stems, linear to lanceolate or no basal leaves, and flowers 1½ to 2 inches, sometimes slightly less or more, wide. In *S. dodecandra* the main branches are usually alternate and the terminal bloom is long-stalked. The main branches of *S. kennedyana* are commonly opposite and the terminal bloom is short-stalked. In the wild, *S. dodecandra* is found from Connecticut to Louisiana, and *S. kennedyana* from Nova Scotia to South Carolina. Blooming in summer and fall, and native to brackish marshes from New York to Florida and Louisiana, *S. dodecandra* is 1 foot to 2 feet in height. It has narrowly-lanceolate to narrowly-elliptic leaves from ¾ inch to 2 inches long. The lobes of the calyx and corolla number eight to twelve, the latter may be pink or white with yellow bases. The diameter of the blooms is 1½ to 2 inches. Freshwater marshes are the favored habitat of *S. kennedyana*, which attains heights of 1 foot to 2½ feet and blooms in summer and fall. It has lanceolate to linear-lanceolate leaves ¾ inch to 2 inches in length, and pink flowers 1½ to 2½ inches across, with yellow bases to the petals.

Garden Uses and Cultivation. These charming and graceful American plants appeal particularly to lovers of wild gardens. Many are well adapted to waterside locations and even bog conditions. Their soil requirements vary considerably and must be determined by studying the habitats in which they naturally occur or by trial and error. Certain it is that some kinds, particularly those that inhabit bogs, must have acid soil, whereas others seem to prefer neutral or even alkaline ones. Even for those that are not bog plants fairly moist conditions are required. They grow best in sun. They are propagated by seed.

In especially favorable places it is possible to scatter seeds of sabatias where the plants are to remain and thin the seedlings if they come up too thickly. A surer procedure is to sow about midsummer or a little earlier in pots in a shaded cold frame (to ensure the soil being evenly moist it is a good plan to keep the pots covered with a sheet of glass and standing in saucers or other receptacles containing an inch or two of water). The seedlings are transplanted individually to small pots, or to flats, and are grown in cold frames until fall or the following spring when they are transferred to their blooming stations.

SABIACEAE — Sabia Family. Dicotyledonous trees, shrubs, and vines totaling about 160 species and distributed in four genera native to tropical, subtropical, and warm-temperate parts of the Americas and Asia consitute this family. Their undivided or pinnate leaves are alternate. Usually bisexual and often in panicles, the asymmetrical flowers are generally small, less often rather large. They have four or five sepals; five, or less often four or six, petals, the inner ones commonly smaller than the others; four, five, or six stamens of which sometimes only two bear pollen; and two more or less united styles. The fruits are berry-like or are dry and do not split open. The only genus ordinarily cultivated is *Meliosma*.

SABICÙ is *Lysiloma latisiliqua*.

SABINEA (Sab-ínea). This West Indian genus of three species of shrubs and small trees is of the pea family LEGUMINOSAE. Its name honors Joseph Sabine, a founder and secretary of the Horticultural Society of London, who died in 1837.

Sabineas have deciduous, pinnate leaves with even numbers of small, toothless leaflets. Their pea-like blooms are few together in clusters from the leaf axils. They have short-toothed calyxes, red or purple corollas with a spreading or reflexed, roundish standard or banner petal, and ten stamens, nine of which are joined and one free. The fruits are long-stalked, flattish, linear pods.

Native to dryish soils in Puerto Rico, the Virgin Islands, and Dominica, **Sabinea florida** is a shrub or tree attaining a maximum height of about 20 feet, but commonly lower. Its leaves, with eight to fifteen pairs of oblong or elliptic-oblong leaflets from a little under to a little over ½ inch long, are up to 4 inches long. The pretty, lilac to light purple flowers, ½ to ¾ inch long, are displayed along the branches for lengths of 2 to 3 feet. Each bloom has five stamens about twice as long as the other five. From the last, **S. carinalis**, of Dominica, differs in its leaves having six to eight pairs of leaflets up to ¾ inch in length, and in its few-flowered clusters of 1 inch to 1½ inches long, scarlet to crimson blooms.

Endemic to Puerto Rico, **S. punicea** is a shrub up to 6 feet tall. It has hairy shoots and leaves. The latter, 2 to 4 inches long, have five to ten pairs of oblong to obovate leaflets about ½ inch long. The flowers, in small clusters, are up to almost 1 inch in length and are pink to purplish carmine. From *S. florida* this species differs in its stamens being of nearly equal lengths.

Garden and Landscape Uses and Cultivation. These are attractive ornamentals for the tropics and warm subtropics. They succeed in sunny locations and prefer fertile, reasonably moist soils. They are propagated by seed.

SACALINE is *Polygonum sachalinense*.

SACASIL is *Wilcoxia poselgeri*.

SACCHARUM (Sácchar-um) — Sugar Cane. Only one of the eight to ten species that comprise *Saccharum*, of the grass family GRAMINEAE, is at all well known. It is the sugar cane, one of the most important crop plants of the world. Besides sugar, this species is a source of molasses, rum, and alcohol, and its stems are used for fiber board and as bagasse for fertilizer and mulch and for other purposes. The foliage provides fodder for cattle. Indigenous to the tropics of Asia and Africa, *Saccharum* has a name derived from *saccharon*, the ancient Greek name for sugar.

All species of *Saccharum* are robust perennials with tall, stout stems and long, usually flat leaf blades. The silky-hairy flower panicles are composed of many racemes of paired, two-flowered spikelets. One spikelet of each pair is stalked, the other stalkless. By some botanists the genus *Erianthus* is included in *Saccharum*.

Sugar cane (**S. officinarum**) is a clump-forming grass with solid, short-jointed

Saccharum officinarum in a tropical greenhouse

stems up to 15 to 20 feet in height and up to 2 inches or more in diameter. The hairless leaf blades, 1½ to 2 inches wide or wider, are 1 foot to 6 feet long and rough-edged. The fragile, loose or fairly dense panicles of bloom are pyramidal and 1 foot to 3 feet long with spikelets, furnished with tufts of white hairs, about ⅙ inch long. Now widely grown in many varieties, this species has been cultivated since prehistoric times and may be of hybrid ancestry. It originated in tropical Asia or Polynesia. Variety *S. o. violaceum* has handsome violet-purple stems and foliage. Sugar is prepared from the juice of the stems (canes).

Occasionally grown for ornament, *S. bengalense* has tall stems and glaucous, very rough-to-the-touch leaves. Its ¼-inch-long flower spikelets are crowded in slender, silvery panicles up to 2½ feet long. This is native from Iran to India.

Garden Uses and Cultivation. In the tropics sugar cane is grown as a crop plant and at times for ornament. Its handsome panicles of bloom are sometimes cut and used as decorations. In temperate regions it is occasionally grown in greenhouses devoted to plants useful to man. It thrives in rich, moist soil in full sun. In greenhouses it needs a minimum temperature of 55 to 60°F and a humid atmosphere. It is planted or potted in spring in well-drained containers and watered freely at all times. Sugar cane is propagated by sectional stem cuttings and division. The other species described here requires the same conditions and management as does sugar cane.

SACCOLABIUM (Sacco-làbium). Many species previously included in this genus, of the orchid family ORCHIDACEAE, have been transferred to other genera including *Anota, Ascocentrum,* and *Rhynchostylis.* As now understood, *Saccolabium* consists of six species, natives of tropical Asia and the Malay Archipeligo. The name, alluding to the pouchlike lip of the flowers, comes from the Greek *saccus,* a bag, and *labium,* a lip.

Saccolabiums are tree-perchers (epiphytes). They have stems furnished with leaves that are flat or folded lengthwise, and in erect racemes, panicles, or clusters from the leaf axils, usually small flowers. These have spreading or backward-pointing similar sepals and petals and a lip with a strap-shaped center lobe and two triangular side lobes.

Its stems drooping and up to 3 feet long, *S. trichromum,* of Assam, has strap-shaped leaves notched at their apexes and 4 to 6 inches long. Pale yellow striped with pink, the about 1-inch-long flowers are in racemes of few. Native to Thailand and Java, *S. rhopalorrhachis* has a stout stem 2 to 4 inches long and, in two ranks, strap-shaped leaves 2½ to 4 inches long and about 1 inch wide. The flowers, on short stalks from the axils of the lower leaves, are about ⅝ inch across. Their sepals and petals are cream-colored with a band of brownish-red near the base. The lip is cream-colored, touched with orange.

Saccolabium rhopalorrhachis

Garden Uses and Cultivation. Rare in contemporary collections, saccolabiums are unlikely to appeal to other than avid orchid enthusiasts. They respond to environments and care agreeable to *Aerides.* For more information see Orchids.

SADLERIA (Sad-lèria). Known in the wild only in Hawaii, *Sadleria* comprises six or seven species of tree ferns closely related to *Blechnum* and belonging in the blechnum family BLECHNACEAE. The name commemorates Joseph Sadler, Professor of Botany at Budapest, who died in 1841.

From *Blechnum* this genus differs in its trunks being typically stout and woody and its leaves (fronds) twice-pinnate or pinnately-lobed, as well as in technical details. The linear clusters of spore capsules form rows on each side of the midribs. One species, *S. polystichoides,* has trunkless variants as well as forms with trunks.

Common throughout the Hawaiian Islands and sometimes planted outdoors in warm, humid climates, and grown in greenhouses, *S. cyatheoides* has a trunk that attains a maximum height of about 5 feet, but is often considerably shorter. It is crowned with many stout-stalked, leathery, fleshy, smooth fronds, reddish when young, 2 to 3 feet long by 1 foot to 1½ feet wide or a little wider, and at maturity dark green. Their bases are covered with masses of soft brownish scales called pulu, which have been used as pillow and mattress stuffings. In times of famine the Hawaiians ate the pith of this fern. They used its fronds to mulch their crops.

Garden and Landscape Uses and Cultivation. No particular difficulties attend the cultivation of these vigorous ferns where the temperature is above 60°F, where there is shade from strong sun, and where the soil contains abundant humus and is moist yet sufficiently porous and well drained, never to be waterlogged. Regular applications of dilute liquid fertilizer from spring through fall help container specimens that are well rooted. Propagation is by spores. For further information see Ferns.

SAFFLOWER is *Carthamus tinctorius.*

SAFFRON. The saffron crocus (*Crocus sativus*) is the source of saffron. The false-saffron is *Carthamus tinctorius;* the meadow saffron, *Colchicum autumnale* and *C. speciosum.*

SAGE. Besides its employment as a common name for sorts of *Salvia* and *Artemisia* (see the following entry) the word sage forms part of the common names of these plants. Bethlehem-sage (*Pulmonaria saccharata*), Jerusalem-sage (*Phlomis fruticosa* and *Pulmonaria officinalis*), pitcher-sage (*Lepechinia calycina*), Russian-sage (*Perovskia atriplicifolia*), sage-rose (*Turnera ulmifolia*), and sweet- or white-sage (*Eurotia lanata*).

SAGE. As a common name sage is sometimes used to encompass all members of the genus *Salvia,* and in western North America is occasionally employed as a shortened form of sagebrush for *Artemisia tridentata* and *A. arbuscula.* More specifically sage is the culinary or sweet herb *Salvia officinalis.* That is what we are concerned with here. It and its varieties are botanically described under Salvia.

Sage (*Salvia officinalis*)

Sage is one of the most popular and commonly cultivated herbs. A bushy shrub, rarely more than 1½ feet high, its leaves are used in dressings to stuff pork, veal, goose, duck, and other meats and to flavor soups, stews, sausages, and cheeses. Preferably used fresh, it can also be dried and stored in tightly stoppered jars or other containers. Sage was once popular as an ingredient of home medicines.

For the best results choose for this herb a sunny place where the soil is well drained, fertile, and well supplied with organic matter. Planting stock may be had by dividing old plants about every second year in spring, but it is usually better to raise new plants from seed or cuttings or by layering. The last operation may be done in spring or late summer. To propagate by cuttings, take young, firm shoots 3 to 4 inches long in early summer before flower buds develop. Remove their lower leaves and slice the stems cleanly across just beneath a node. Before they wilt, plant them in sand or other suitable rooting material in a greenhouse propagating bench, or in sand or very sandy soil in a cold frame or under similar conditions, such as beneath an inverted glass jar, in a shaded place outdoors. Keep the rooting medium moist, and until roots have formed, give only sufficient ventilation to prevent water accumulating on the inside of the glass covering. Later, ventilate more freely, and when well rooted transplant to small pots, flats, or a nursery bed outdoors. Alternatively, cuttings of mature wood may be taken in early spring and rooted in a cold frame.

To raise sage from seed, sow in a nursery bed outdoors in early spring or in a greenhouse or other suitable place indoors some two months earlier. Transplant seedlings from indoor sowings to small pots or flats and grow them indoors until danger from frost has gone. Then transplant them to the open ground. Seedlings from outdoor sowings may be transplanted to their permanent locations when 2 or 3 inches tall.

In herb gardens sage may be planted 1 foot to 1½ feet apart in casual groups, or it may be set at about the same spacing or a little closer as edgings to paths. Elsewhere, plant in rows 1½ feet apart with 9 inches between the plants in the rows. Subsequent care consists chiefly of regular shallow surface cultivation to keep down weeds and watering at intervals in dry weather. It may be desirable at the end of the first year to remove alternate plants in the rows to prevent overcrowding. Generally sage plants are not productive after three or four years. Replace them then with young, vigorous stock.

Harvest by cutting the leafy stems before flower buds appear. For drying, tie them in bundles and hang them upside down, or spread them thinly on racks, in a shaded, airy place. When thoroughly dry, rub between the palms of the hand and store the crumbled leaves in air-tight containers. Under favorable conditions two and sometimes three harvestings can be made each year. Sage can also be preserved by freezing.

SAGERETIA (Sager-ètia). Chiefly tropical, this genus of about thirty species is represented in the wild in North America by three. It also occurs in Central America, South America, Asia, Australia, and Africa. It belongs in the buckthorn family RHAMNACEAE and is much like Rhamnus and Berchemia, but Rhamnus differs from Sageretia in its flowers being distinctly stalked and its leaves usually being alternate, and Berchemia differs in having alternate leaves,

and fruits with only one stone. The name commemorates the French horticulturist and botanist Augustin Sageret, who died in 1851.

Sageretias are evergreen or deciduous, often spiny, sometimes straggly shrubs, or low trees, with opposite or nearly opposite, toothed leaves, and minute bisexual, usually stalkless, whitish flowers in terminal and axillary, spikelike or rarely raceme-like clusters. There are five calyx lobes, five petals, five stamens, and a short style. The fruits are berry-like and contain three or rarely two seedlike stones. Those of the pauper's-tea, S. thea, are edible. The leaves of that species are used by the poor in China as a substitute for tea.

Occasionally cultivated in the south, S. minutiflora is a straggling or trailing, spiny shrub, commonly 6 to 10 feet tall, but under favorable conditions sometimes ascending tall trees. Its finely-toothed, lustrous, ovate leaves are mostly up to 1½ inches long and leathery. The very fragrant flowers, in slender spikes up to 1½ inches long, come in fall and are succeeded in spring by purple fruits ⅓ inch in diameter. This species inhabits the coastal plain, often favoring limestone and sandy soils, from South Carolina to southern Florida and Mississippi. It is not hardy in the north.

Hardy as far north as southern New England, S. pycnophylla is a spiny, clambering shrub about 6 feet tall. It has short-stalked, elliptic to obovate, toothed, yellowish-green leaves, up to ¾ inch in length and lustrous on their undersides. The flowers are in spikes, ½ inch to 1½ inches long, in groups of up to four. This is a native of western China. Hailing also from western China, S. thea is similar to the last, but has larger leaves and has terminal panicles of flower spikes. It is not hardy in the north.

Garden and Landscape Uses and Cultivation. Not commonly cultivated, sageretias have been recommended for hedges and screens. They are not fussy as to soil and are propagated by seed, cuttings, and layering.

SAGINA (Sa-gìna)—Pearlwort. Humble relatives of carnations, pinks, and bouncing bet (Saponaria officinalis), pearlworts reveal little to the untrained eye of this botanical affinity. The tyro might well be excused for mistaking certain of their number, when out of bloom, for mosses. Unlike mosses they bear flowers, studies of which resulted in the group being assigned to the pink family CARYOPHYLLACEAE. There are about twenty-five species of Sagina, natives of temperate and arctic North America, Asia, and Europe; the Andes; and the mountains of East Africa. Many are too weedy in appearance to be admitted to cultivation, and a few are weeds of cultivated and neglected places. The name, from the

Latin, sagina, fattening, refers to the supposed nutritive qualities of some kinds eaten by sheep.

Pearlworts are mat-forming or tufted herbaceous perennials and annuals. They have small, linear, linear-lanceolate, or awl-shaped, opposite leaves, often in rosettes, and tiny flowers, solitary or in clusters of few. The flower stalks are erect or else are more or less prostrate toward their bases and upturned at their ends. There are four or five sepals and usually the same number of petals, but some species are without petals. The stamens are as many or twice as many as the sepals. There are four or five styles. The fruits are small, many-seeded capsules that split to the base in four or five sections.

Pearlworts sometimes cultivated include S. glabra, a rather loose, creeping or prostrate perennial up to 4 inches tall, with hairless, almost threadlike leaves, the upper ones nearly as long as the lower and spaced apart by about the lengths of the leaves on the stems. The solitary, white, five-petaled flowers, on stems up to 1 inch long, have petals up to twice as long as the sepals and are ⅕ to ⅖ inch in diameter. This is a native of the European Alps and Pyrenees. From the mountains of Corsica and Sardinia comes S. pilifera, similar to the last, but dwarfer, more compact, and with petals more than twice as long as the sepals. Also, its leaves are tipped with much longer bristles.

A tight mat-forming, mosslike perennial, S. subulata, a native of dryish soils in western, central, and southern Europe, has bristle-tipped, linear-awl-shaped leaves up to about ½ inch long. Usually solitary and mostly with glandular-hairy stalks up to ¾ inch long, its tiny blooms have four or five petals about as long as the sepals. This species, often confused with Arenaria verna caespitosa, is, like it, sometimes called Irish-moss. Its yellowish-foliaged variety S. s. aurea shares with Arenaria verna aurea the common name Scotch-moss. These arenarias differ from Sagina in their flowers having only three styles.

Sagina subulata

Its generally solitary tiny flowers with four petals or sometimes none, *S. procumbens* is indigenous to northern North America, Europe, and Asia. Usually a mat-forming perennial, it sometimes is an annual. Not uncommonly it occurs as a weed in garden paths and similar places. It has prostrate or ascending stems, linear leaves up to ½ inch long, and slender flower stalks with usually solitary blooms about ⅕ inch across. The narrowly-linear leaves, ¼ to ½ inch long, are tipped with bristles. Similar to the last, but less spreading, with solitary or occasionally paired flowers, generally with five petals about as long as the sepals, perennial *S. saginoides* occurs in northern North America, Europe, and Asia. A natural hybrid between these last two species, *S. normaniana* has rosettes of leaves up to 1 inch long and solitary or paired flowers. This rarely produces viable seeds.

A diminutive curiosity treasured by collectors of choice alpines, *S. boydii* has not been found in the wild since it was collected in Scotland in 1878. It forms a tight, bright green humplet of almost unreal appearance, that scarcely grows and rarely blooms and never sets seeds. Its stems are erect and crowded with little, stiff recurved leaves. Its tiny flowers have four or five petals.

Garden Uses. The fantastic and rare *S. boydii* is cared for by dedicated rock gardeners in alpine greenhouses, cold frames, and choice spots in favored rock gardens. It is a cool-climate plant unlikely to succeed where summers are torrid. The other kinds are more robust and less fastidious. They are suitable for establishing in crevices between flagstones and for providing carpets of greenery and very modest summer displays of bloom in rock gardens. They are appropriate elements in alpine lawns and are useful for surfacing the ground above small bulbs. They should not be placed where their stems are likely to thread their way among and perhaps choke out less vigorous small plants treasured by rock gardeners.

Cultivation. No difficulty attends the cultivation of most pearlworts (*S. boydii* is something of an exception). All prosper in gritty, not too dry soils rather poor in nutrients, in sun or part-shade. They are increased by seed and by division, which is best done in spring or early fall.

SAGITTARIA (Sagit-tària) — Arrowhead. The species of this cosmopolitan genus are mostly American. About twenty, they belong to the water-plantain family ALISMATACEAE. From nearly related *Echinodorus* they differ in their seedlike fruits (achenes), in burrlike heads, being winged. The name *Sagittaria*, from the Latin *sagitta*, an arrow, alludes to the shape of the leaf blades of some kinds.

Arrowheads are aquatics, in deep or fast-moving water often floating or completely submersed, but more commonly with only their bases under water. Their roots anchor them to soil bottoms. They have milky sap, and rhizomes at the ends of which tubers, those of some kinds edible, often form. The leaves of submersed forms are usually ribbon-like without definite blades. Above-water leaves are mostly arrow-shaped, halberd-shaped, ovate, or lanceolate. The blooms are unisexual on separate plants or on the same plant, or sometimes are bisexual. Often the upper flowers are bisexual or male and those below female. In panicles or racemes the blooms are in whorls (circles). Each has three sepals, and the same number of white petals sometimes purple at their bases. The stamens number half a dozen or more, the pistils few to several.

Giant arrowhead (*S. montevidensis*), a native of South America, is naturalized from Delaware to South Dakota, Texas, and California. In northern parts of this range it is usually markedly smaller than in warmer climates, where it is not uncommonly 6 feet tall. Characteristically its long-stalked, hairless leaves have arrow-shaped blades with sharp-pointed, widely-spreading basal lobes, but they vary to halberd-shaped and sometimes are lobeless. The blades are up to 2 feet long and 1 foot wide. The flowers are ¾ to over 1 inch across, often with a purple spot at the bottom of each petal. The sepals enlarge and become erect after the flowers fade.

Old World arrowhead (*S. sagittifolia*) is a variable native of Europe and Asia. In the Orient its tubers are used for food. From 3 to 4 feet tall, it has leaves with linear or arrow-shaped blades with basal lobes longer or shorter than the center one.

About 1 inch in diameter, the flowers have petals blotched at their bases with purple. The sepals fall when the flowers fade. Variety *S. s. flore-pleno*, sometimes cultivated as *S. japonica*, has handsome double blooms. From the Old World arrowhead, American *S. latifolia*, native from Nova Scotia to British Columbia, Florida, California, and Mexico, differs in its seedlike fruits having beaks nearly four times as long as the bodies of the fruits instead of only short ones. Its blooms have twenty-five to forty stamens. A double-flowered variety is *S. l. flore-pleno*.

Sagittaria latifolia

Linear-lanceolate to broadly-elliptic leaves, with blades up to 1 foot long and 4 inches wide and without basal lobes, are

Sagittaria montevidensis

characteristic of *S. graminea*, but sometimes its leaves are without blades. Rarely they have lobed blades. Native from Newfoundland to Saskatchewan, Florida, and Texas, this is up to 2 feet tall and has blooms ¾ inch to 1½ inches wide, each with twelve to twenty stamens.

Often not over 6 inches high, but taller in the southern part of its range, *S. subulata* is a native of New York to Alabama and Florida. Occasionally it produces leaves with elliptic to ovate-oblong blades up to 2 inches long, more commonly the leaves are bladeless, strap-shaped, and 1 inch to, the submersed ones, 2 feet long. The few flowers, up to ¾ inch wide, have ten or fewer stamens.

Native from southeastern United States to the American tropics, *S. lancifolia* is about 5 feet in height and has usually lobeless, lanceolate to narrowly-oblong leaves. Its large white flowers are attractive. Closely similar *S. falcata* (syn. *S. lancifolia media*) ranges from Delaware to Florida, Texas, and Mexico.

Garden and Landscape Uses. Hardy arrowheads, which include all discussed above except *S. montevidensis* and *S. lancifolia*, are useful for permanent colonization at the margins of ponds, streams, and other waters. The exceptions can be used similarly in the south and other mild-climate regions. Grown in tubs or other containers, they can be employed with waterlilies and other low aquatics to provide welcome height and variation in foliage and flower patterns. They succeed in sun or partial shade in water from an inch or two to about 1½ feet deep.

Cultivation. Planting in fertile, loamy soil is done in early spring or early fall. In soil-bottomed pools this may be accomplished by wrapping each tuber and a stone to weight it in a piece of burlap and dropping it into the water. Planting in containers is done in more normal fashion after raising the receptacles or lowering the water so that the soil surface is well above its level. Following planting, an inch or two of sand is spread over the soil to prevent organic debris or other matter from floating upward or muddying the water. Established arrowheads need little or no care beyond pulling out any shoots necessary to keep the plants within their allotted space. Container specimens need dividing and replanting in fresh soil every two or three years. Where their roots are likely to freeze, tender kinds should be wintered indoors in water in a temperature of about 50°F. Propagation is usually by division, which is the only way with double-flowered varieties, and by seed sown in containers of soil immersed beneath 1 inch to 3 inches of water. A layer of sand is spread over the soil surface before immersion. The seeds must be kept in water or constantly moist from the time of gathering to sowing.

SAGO FERN is *Cyathea medullaris*.

SAGO PALM. This is a common name of *Cycas revoluta* and *Metroxylon sagu*.

SAHUARO is *Carnegiea gigantea*.

SAINFOIN or SAINTFOIN is *Onobrychis viciaefolia*.

SAINT. For plants with common names beginning with the word saint, see the entry St.

SAINT, PATRON OF GARDENERS. Saint Fiacre, patron saint of gardeners and of the taxi drivers of Paris, France, lived in the seventh century. Born in Ireland of noble parentage, as a young man he went to France to seek solitude as an anchorite. There, he cleared a tract of forest near the town of Brie made available to him by Saint Faro, Bishop of Meaux, and built a cell for himself, an oratory dedicated to the Virgin Mary, and a hospice. He also established an extensive garden in which he grew vegetables, fruits, and flowers.

As word of the holiness and good deeds of Saint Fiacre (Celtic, Fiachra) become widely known, pilgrims in search of spiritual guidance, comfort, and healing came in large numbers. Many of these he accommodated overnight or for longer periods, feeding them on the produce of his garden, which he also shared with those who in times of need sought his charity.

St. Fiacre would not permit women to enter his hermitage or chapel. According to legend, this was because of a happening during his early days at Meaux. When awarding him a tract of ground, the Bishop told Fiacre he could have as much as he could turn over in a single day. Without plow or tools to undertake the task, Fiacre prayed, then attempted the work with his staff. As he did so a great furrow miraculously appeared in the earth. An evil peasant woman, observing this, reported it to the Bishop as the work of the Devil. Hastening to the scene, the Bishop found the young foreigner kneeling in devotion and, in his native Gaelic, thanking God for the miracle. Without further inquiry the Bishop blessed the project Saint Fiacre had so well begun.

For sixty years St. Fiacre lived at Brie; he died at age eighty. For centuries after his death crowds of pilgrims came to his chapel, where he was buried and which contains his relics. Many miraculous cures attributed to him include the recovery of Louis XIII from a dangerous illness he contracted in 1641.

When, in the middle of the seventeenth century, carriages as public conveyances first became available in Paris they were hired from an establishment on the rue Saint Martin near the hotel Saint Fiacre. As a result they became known as fiacres,

the word used to this day in France for taxicabs. Symbolic of his tilling of the soil, statues of Saint Fiacre invariably show him holding a spade. The feast of Saint Fiacre is celebrated September 1st.

SAINTPAULIA (Saint-paùlia) — African-Violet, Usambara-Violet. The genus *Saintpaulia* is one of the most popular in the gesneria family GESNERIACEAE. As a native it is confined to a limited region of East Africa. Its closest relatives, *Platystemma*, *Linnaeopsis*, and *Boea*, are Asian. From *Saintpaulia* the first two differ markedly in the forms of their flowers, from *Boea* in its fruits not being twisted spirally. The genus was discovered in 1892 by Baron Adalbert Emil Walter Redcliffe le Tanneux von Saint Paul-Illaire, District Governor of Usambara, in what was then the German colony of Tanganyika. The Baron sent seeds and probably plants to his father in Germany, the Baron Ulrich von Saint Paul, who shared his gift with Herman Wedland, Director of the Royal Botanic Garden at Herrenhausen, Hamburg. Wedland described the new plant and named it, after its discoverer and his father, *Saintpaulia*, adding *ionantha*, meaning violet flower, as its specific epithet. Much later it was discovered that this original introduction also included *S. confusa*. Not until 1910 were other species found. By 1921 four were known and by 1964, twenty-four. Others may await discovery.

African-violets or saintpaulias are known to everyone familiar with indoor plants. They are cultivated by amateurs and professionals in countless variety and are sold in enormous numbers from ultra-fashionable florist shops to dime stores. They come with typically violet-colored blooms as well as in blues, pinks, near reds, whites, and bicolors. There are no yellows or oranges. There are single- and double-flowered kinds, as well as those with foliage variously frilled or variegated or just plain green. The horticultural development of African-violets and the tremendous interest in them was at first almost exclusively American and is of the twentieth century, but the discovery and introduction of wild species has been largely the work of Europeans.

Saintpaulias are nonhardy, evergreen herbaceous plants with leaves in rosettes or nearly opposite to each other. Some kinds are stemless or nearly so, others have fleshy, more or less prostrate stems up to a few inches long. The leaves are fairly long-stalked and have heart-shaped, heart-shaped-elliptic, or nearly round blades with often scalloped-toothed margins. Generally they are hairy, and the character of the hairiness, whether it consists of a mixture of long and short hairs or of hairs of essentially the same length, and whether the hairs are erect or lie more along the plane of the leaf surface, is often important in identifying species. The hairs can be examined most easily by slicing a leaf through and observing the cut edge. From the centers of the rosettes, or from the leaf axils of kinds without rosettes, the flower stalks arise, each terminating in a cluster of usually up to a dozen violet-like blooms. Each bloom has a calyx of five lanceolate or linear sepals and a very short-tubed, two-lipped corolla with, except in double-flowered, many-petaled horticultural varieties, five spreading, rounded lobes (petals), two of which form the upper lip, and three the lower. The normal number of fertile stamens is two, but sometimes there are four; they protrude slightly from the corolla tube, as does the style, which is tipped with a slightly lobed stigma. The fruits are capsules.

Species with rosettes of foliage and usually very short, branchless stems or no stems include that most important progenitor of modern African-violets, *S. ionantha.* From it, the first kind known, have been derived as mutants ("sports"), se-

Saintpaulia ionantha variety

lections, and hybrids the vast majority of African-violet varieties now cultivated. As it grows in the wild *S. ionantha* has thickish, densely-hairy, shallowly-toothed, nearly round to oblong-ovate leaves, dark green on their upper sides and often purplish beneath. Their stalks are up to 2½ inches long. The violet flowers, in clusters of two to eight, are 1 inch to 1¼ inches in diameter. This species was once mistakenly named *S. kewensis.* Rather similar, but having thinner leaves with blades green above and paler beneath covered with hairs of two distinct lengths (those of *S. ionantha* are all about the same length), is **S. confusa.** Its leaves have round-toothed margins, stalks up to 3 inches long, and elliptic to ovate blades up to 1½ inches long by slightly less broad. The violet to violet-blue blooms, 1 inch to 1¼ inches wide, are in clusters of about four. For long this species was misidentified as *S. diplotricha.* True **S. diplotricha** differs from *S. confusa* in that its thicker,

Saintpaulia confusa

purplish leaves have a covering of intermixed long-spreading and short-erect hairs, instead of all spreading hairs approximately parallel with the leaf surface. An identifying characteristic of *S. diplotricha* is that the lower lip of the flower juts forward at an angle from the upper lip, so that if the latter is held vertically the lower lip is about midway between being vertical and horizontal.

Like *S. ionantha* in its leaves being in rosettes, **S. tongwensis,** with age, develops a short, very thick stem. The leaves, with

Saintpaulia tongwensis

stems up to 3½ inches long and thickish, toothed, elliptic or ovate-elliptic blades up to 3¼ inches long by 2 inches wide, are dark green with pale midribs and lighter green or purplish-red undersides. Four to six blooms slightly over 1 inch wide are on stalks longer than the leaves. They are pale blue and more opaque than similarly colored varieties of *S. ionantha.* A distinguishing characteristic is the length of the seed pods, ½ to ¾ inch as compared with slightly over ¼ inch for *S. ionantha.* Also with very short branchless stems, sometimes scarcely apparent, is **S. orbicularis.** Its leaves have nearly circular to broad-ovate, light green, coarsely-toothed blades

1¼ to 2¼ inches long on stalks up to 3 inches long. The hairs that cover them lie approximately parallel with the surface. The long-stalked flower clusters have eight to ten pale blue to white blooms a little under 1 inch in diameter, with violet eyes. Variety *S. o. purpurea* differs most markedly in having rich purple blooms.

Saintpaulia orbicularis

Two especially vigorous close allies of *S. ionantha* are *S. grandifolia* and *S. difficilis.* With rosettes of thin, clear green leaves, **S. grandifolia** has stalks 3 to 4 inches long, and broad, ovate-elliptic, toothed blades up to 4 or 5 inches long and nearly as broad. The blue-violet flowers, darker at their centers, 1 inch or a little more in diameter, have petals fringed with glandular hairs. They are in clusters of up to a dozen. The saw-toothed, light yellowish green leaves of **S. difficilis** are usually markedly longer than broad. They have stalks up to 4½ inches long and quilted-surfaced, elliptic blades 2½ to 3½ inches long. The 1-inch-wide blooms, light violet with darker centers, are borne in great abundance.

Saintpaulia difficilis

Also robust, **S. rupicola** has thick, rhizome-like stems that may be eventually up to 8 inches long and rosettes of lustrous, heart-shaped, light green leaves, paler on their undersides, with blades up to 2½ inches long. The leaves are clothed with a mixture of long and short hairs; their margins are faintly toothed. The 1-inch-wide or slightly wider flowers are blue-purple. Closely related **S. brevipilosa** is much less robust. Its nearly round leaves, in rosettes, have stalks and blades each 1½ inches long or slightly longer. The most obvious characteristic is that, except at the edges, the leaves appear to be hairless; actually they are thickly clothed with very short hairs visible under a good lens or microscope. The flowers are purple and about 1 inch across. Another close relative of *S. ionantha* is **S. teitensis.** It is the most northerly of the known species of *Saintpaulia.* Short-stalked, and the older ones slightly peltate (with the stalks joining the blades in from their margins), the leaves have blades 2½ to 3 inches long, broad-elliptic to nearly round, dark, lustrous green above, and purplish below. On young leaves the hairs are erect, on older ones more nearly horizontal. The flower stalks are shorter than the leaves. The flowers are about 1¼ inches across. Rosettes of rather glossy leaves with stalks 2 to 3½ inches long and shallowly-toothed, broad-ovate to nearly circular, inconspicuously-hairy blades with slightly convex upper surfaces are characteristic of **S. nitida.** The ¾-inch-wide, violet blooms are several together on stalks not longer than the leaves.

Saintpaulia nitida

Three small species with short stems or none and leaves in rosettes are *S. shumensis, S. velutina,* and *S. pusilla.* Compact, with ovate to nearly round, toothed leaves with thick, olive-green blades up to 1½ inches in length by scarcely as broad and sparingly clothed with long, erect, white hairs, **S. shumensis** is an attractive miniature. Its very delicate gray-blue to almost white blooms, ¾ to 1 inch in diameter, and with violet centers, are not very freely produced. They are in clusters of about five. Dull velvety, dark green upper surfaces and reddish-purple undersides

characterize the thinnish leaves of *S. velutina.* They are toothed and covered with a mixture of short and long hairs. Their stalks are up to 3½ inches long, the roundish blades under 2 inches long. Abundantly produced, the dark violet blooms, up to ¾ inch in diameter, have petals sometimes tipped with white. Quite commonly there are four fertile stamens, and the upper lip of the corolla is often doubled. Smallest of saintpaulias, **S. pusilla** is not known to be in cultivation. Its toothless leaves, green with paler veins and often with purplish undersides, have ovate blades up to 1⅜ inches long and 1 inch wide. The flowers, ⅜ inch in diameter, have blue upper petals and white lower ones. They are in clusters of few on stalks under 1½ inches long.

Species with obvious prostrate stems, and leaves not in rosettes, are less well known. One of the best is **S. grotei.** It has branching stems several inches in length and rounded, coarsely-toothed leaves with stalks up to 10 inches long and blades 1 inch to 3½ inches long and nearly as wide. Paler beneath than on their upper surfaces, they are sparsely covered with a mixture of long and short hairs. On stalks usually shorter than the leaves, the two to four 1-inch-wide to a little larger flowers are blue-violet with violet centers. The edges of their petals are fringed with glandular hairs. The hairs that margin the petals of **S. magungensis** (syn. *S. amaniensis*) are a mixture of gland-tipped and nonglandular ones, in proportions that differ considerably in individuals. This species has procumbent branching stems a few inches long. Its leafstalks are 2 to 4 inches long, and the ovate to rounded, toothed leaf blades 1½ to 2½ inches long. They are covered with a mixture of long and short hairs that lie along the leaf surfaces. The dark-centered, blue-violet flowers, a little over ½ inch to somewhat under 1 inch in diameter, are in twos or threes. Variety *S. m. minima* has smaller leaves and flowers than the typical species. Variety *S. m. occidentalis,* more attractive than the typical species, has stout, thick, rhizome-like stems, and thick, brittle leaves.

Toothless or scarcely toothed leaves distinguish **S. goetzeana** from most other *Saintpaulia* species. Its trailing, branching stems, up to 6 inches long, are thickly clothed with white hairs. The nearly round blades are on stalks about 1½ inches in length. Above, they are green with paler veins; their undersides are purplish. Usually two flowers are on each stalk. Each is a little over ½ inch in diameter. They are blue-and-white. Nearly related **S. intermedia** differs in having leaves with stalks about 3½ inches long and ovate to nearly orbicular blades, round-toothed at their edges at least when young, purplish or reddish on their undersides, and 1½ to 2 inches long. The blooms, about 1 inch

wide, are deep violet and in clusters of several. Their edges are fringed with glandular hairs. This species develops its stems very slowly. From it, **S. pendula** differs in having laxer stems that develop more rapidly and exuberantly, light green leaves with nearly erect hairs, and usually one, but sometimes two, flowers on each stalk. The blooms, about 1 inch across, are fringed with glandular hairs. They are deep violet. The leaves, toothed at least when young, have stalks 1½ inches long and ovate to nearly round blades up to nearly 2 inches long by 1½ inches wide. Variety *S. p. kizarae,* more compact, with darker foliage, has leafstalks noticeably tinged brownish-red.

Of strange appearance, **S. inconspicua** looks less like an African-violet than other kinds. It has weak stems, more or less elliptic leaves with stalks ¾ inch to 1½ inches long and blades up to 2 inches long and two-thirds as broad. On their upper surfaces the leaves are hairy only at their margins; the undersides have hairy veins. Blue with white centers, the flowers, up to six on each stalk, are about ½ inch in diameter.

The most popular African-violets are horticultural varieties and hybrids. They comprise by far the greater number of those cultivated. In the main only collectors and hybridizers interest themselves with the natural species described above, although the trailers among them are sometimes favored for furnishing hanging baskets. Horticultural varieties and hybrids are so numerous and various that to describe all even briefly would require a sizable book, and would serve little purpose because of the great number of new kinds introduced each year. These, as well as older ones available, are described and often illustrated in publications devoted to this popular group of plants and in the catalogs of specialist dealers. The African-violet enthusiast is indeed fortunate in having abundant literature, books and periodicals, dedicated to his or her hobby, as well as special societies. Most prominent of the latter is the African-Violet Society of America.

Garden Uses. Unquestionably the most popular flowering houseplants in America, African-violets are grown in countless thousands, indeed millions, by amateurs, including those who care for one to a few on a window sill and others who collect and cultivate them as a major hobby. They are produced in enormous quantities by commercial growers and are often displayed in amateurs' greenhouses, along with other plants, by gardeners who do not make a specialty of African-violets. Usually they are accommodated in pots, but the trailing kinds are pleasing in hanging baskets. In the humid tropics, African-violets can be used effectively in rock gardens. The great appeals these plants have, in addition to their ob-

Horticultural varieties of African-violets:
(a) Single-flowered

(b) Double-flowered

An African-violet as a window plant

vious beauty, are their adaptability and ease of propagation and cultivation in homes as well as greenhouses, in natural light and under artificial illumination, the moderate amount of space they occupy, their extended seasons of bloom, and their almost endless variety.

Cultivation. The needs of African-violets are simple. They succeed in winter temperatures of 60 to 75°F. Night temperatures may be a little lower than those maintained by day, but except possibly for occasional very short periods, should not

drop below 60°F. In summer the plants accommodate to natural temperatures above 75°F, but growth practically ceases and the plants are not benefited when the thermometer reads significantly above 90°F. If kept too cool too long growth is checked and blooming is inhibited, and such flowers that do develop have shorter stalks and are inferior in size. Also, the leaves may harden and tend to curl downward. Excessively high temperatures for long periods, especially if accompanied by insufficient light, are likely to result in soft, weak, pale foliage that may tend to wilt, excessively long leafstalks, and few flowers on weak stalks. Adequate moisture in the atmosphere is a necessity. A relative humidity of 60 to 75 percent is favorable, but the plants will get along with less, down to between 40 and 50 percent, as well as with more humid conditions.

Light is very important. It controls not only growth, but also blooming. Unlike some plants, African-violets are not significantly influenced by day length, but the intensity of the illumination determines to a very great extent their behavior. Shade from strong sun is a necessity. Only in winter and in northern latitudes is full exposure tolerated. Experience shows that when grown in natural light its intensity should not be under 600 or over 1,500 foot-candles. Under artificial light, which normally is kept on for longer periods than natural day length, they succeed with down to about 300 foot-candles, but may bloom better with more. Foot-candles is a scientific unit of measurement for light intensity (on a sunny day in summer in the north natural light intensity may be in the neighborhood of 10,000 foot-candles). As houseplants, African-violets commonly succeed best in east- or north-facing windows, but in winter the latter may not admit enough light and supplemental illumination may be desirable. In all locations some shade in summer is needed. Exposure to too strong light causes the foliage to bleach and become yellowish and the stalks of the leaves to be shorter than normal and to turn downward so that the leaf blades are against the containers. In extreme cases, flower production is reduced. Too little light, especially if temperatures are high, induces long leafstalks, soft foliage often of rather light color, and either a paucity of bloom or none.

Artificial light is a satisfactory substitute for sunlight for African-violets. It may be used to supplement natural light, or alone. Because they do not generate excessive heat, and thus may be placed closer to the plants, fluorescent tubes are generally more satisfactory than incandescent bulbs. Various arrangements are possible (see Indoor Light Gardening), but as an approximate guide, 40-watt tubes located about 6 inches above the rims of the pots of small specimens in the growing stage, or 9 to 11

inches above those of mature plants, will give good results. To encourage more rapid flower development, 75-watt tubes 9 inches to 1 foot above mature plants may be used. Although the exact day length is unimportant to African-violets, it is necessary for them to experience at least six hours of darkness in each twenty-four. Fourteen to sixteen hours of illumination, followed by eight to ten hours of darkness, works out best.

Artificial light as a supplement to daylight often benefits African-violets: (a) A plant blooming well where it receives daylight and artificial light

(b) Leaf cuttings rooting in vermiculite receive artificial light here

Soils and soil substitutes for African-violets must be porous enough to admit air, allow water to drain through freely, and be sufficiently loose to admit easy root penetration. A high organic content is desirable. To achieve this, leaf mold, woods soil, peat moss, or other suitable decayed vegetable matter is used for one-third to one-half, by bulk, of the soil mixture, with the remainder consisting of good topsoil, coarse grit, sand, vermiculite, or perlite, and perhaps a little crushed charcoal, and a sprinkling of bonemeal. Some very rotted, dried manure can with advantage be included. In place of soil, various mixes of an organic nature, such as peat moss and vermiculite, peat moss and perlite, or just sphagnum moss, may be used. The potting material, soil or otherwise, should be slightly acid. The rooting mediums for African-violets must be kept always moist, but not soggy and stagnant. To preclude danger of this, care is taken that the containers are very well drained. Porous clay, glazed porcelain, or plastic pots are satisfactory. Because the last two are not porous, plants in them require less frequent watering than those in ordinary clay pots.

Watering African-violets calls for some care. It is advisable to use water at room temperature and to avoid wetting the foliage, at least if conditions are such that it is unlikely to dry within an hour. Provided this receives attention and the soil is wetted through, it matters not whether the water is applied from above or seeps from below. Before water is supplied the soil should be dryish, but not dry.

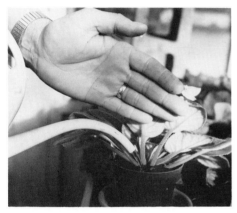

When watering African-violets avoid wetting the foliage by: (a) Lifting the leaves out of the way of the stream

(b) Or pouring water into saucers or other containers from which it will rise by capillarity and moisten all of the soil

Fertilizing specimens that are in containers filled with healthy roots is necessary for their well-being. Complete soluble fertilizers (such as those prepared for houseplants) applied in liquid form are satisfactory, and weekly or biweekly applications from spring to fall normally are adequate. In winter less frequent fertilizing is recommended.

Repotting and dividing old plants needs attention from time to time. These operations may be done at any season, but spring and early summer are most favorable because then the plants are likely to reestablish themselves most quickly. When repotting it is important not to set the plants too deeply, so that soil does not wash into their centers later, and not to pack the earth too firmly. Another point to remember is not to use too large pots. Beginners often do this to the detriment of the plants; African-violets thrive best when their roots are a little crowded. Division is done either by carefully pulling, or by cutting with a sharp knife, the plants apart. Each division should retain a generous portion of roots. African-violets are best when grown as single-crowned specimens. Those that develop multicentered crowns (centers of more than one rosette) should be divided, or the offset crowns removed early.

Potting African-violets: (a) An established plant into a larger pot

(b) Divisions of an old plant into small pots

Propagation is extraordinarily simple. Seeds germinate readily, but are rarely used except when the objective is to raise new varieties. Sown on fine sandy, peaty soil, they are scarcely covered with soil or sand and are kept uniformly moist in a temperature of 70 to 80°F. Alternatively,

they may be sown on milled sphagnum moss or other favored medium. The containers in which they are sown are covered with a piece of glass, to conserve humidity, until germination takes place, and are shaded. The most common means of increase is by leaf cuttings. Single leaves root and soon develop new plants. Firm, healthy leaves of medium size are best. The stalks are shortened to approximately 1½ inches, or less in the case of short-stalked kinds. The leaves may be rooted in any of various materials that will hold the leaves upright, supply moisture, and admit air; coarse sand, vermiculite, perlite, and mixtures of these and peat moss are satisfactory. The leaves are planted leaning slightly from the vertical, with up to ½ inch of their stalks in the rooting

Propagating African-violets by leaf cuttings: (a) Select mature, healthy leaves and shorten their stalks to 1 inch to 1½ inches in length

(b) Plant them, slanted upward with only their stalks in the rooting medium, in pots or pans, or in a greenhouse propagating bench

medium. The blades may be supported by a plant label or by a thread stretched taut or in other suitable manner. Amateurs frequently root leaves in water, but young plants so raised, when potted find it a little more difficult to accustom themselves to soil than do those propagated in non-liquid mediums.

(c) Or in a glass or plastic container; water them lightly with a fine spray

(d) Cover with glass or transparent plastic, leaving an opening for ventilation

(e) After a few weeks the cuttings will have produced a mass of roots and tiny shoots and are ready for potting individually in small pots in loose, humusy soil

Leaf cuttings of African-violets rooting in water

Pests and Diseases. The major insect and insect-like pests of African-violets are mealybugs, mites, nematodes, and springtails. Diseases caused by funguses are blight, crown rot, and petiole (leafstalk) rot. The last occurs, perhaps, as a result of fertilizer elements absorbed by porous clay pots, on leafstalks in contact with the rims. The best preventatives are to mold a strip of aluminum foil around the rims of the

An African-violet severely injured by mites

pots, or to use plastic or other nonabsorbant containers. Two troubles not known to be associated with organisms are rather common afflictions of African-violets. One is that the flower buds may fail to open, turn brown, and fall off. This results from such unfavorable environmental conditions as too low temperatures, poor soil aeration, too wet soil, and excessively dry atmosphere. The second, the distressing appearance resulting from rings and lines of yellow on the foliage, is apparently caused by unfavorable environment and faulty culture. Wetting the foliage with water appreciably below air temperature, especially in sunlight, is thought to be a prime reason for this unsightly condition. Inadequate aeration of the soil, with resulting stagnation, and too low temperatures, especially likely to be experienced by plants in windows on cold nights, are also probable causes.

SALAD BURNET. Salad burnet (*Poterium sanguisorba*) is a lacy-leaved herb sometimes cultivated for flavoring soups, vinegars, claret cup and other cold drinks, and salads. It has a cucumber-like flavor. Although perennial, salad burnet is sometimes short-lived. Because of this, it is well to raise young plants fairly frequently. This herb thrives in sunny locations and dry soils. It is easily raised from seed, and by division in spring or early fall. Space the plants about 1 foot apart, and prevent blooming by picking off all flower buds. The young, tender leaves are the parts to use.

SALAL is *Gaultheria shallon*.

SALICACEAE — Willow Family. Three genera, *Populus*, *Salix*, and *Chosenia*, the first two widely distributed chiefly in temperate regions of the northern hemisphere, the last consisting of one Asian species probably not in cultivation, constitute this family of dicotyledons of about 500 species. Its sorts are mostly deciduous trees, shrubs, and subshrubs. They have alternate, undivided leaves and, densely crowded in erect or pendulous catkins often displayed before the foliage, tiny to minute flowers, each in the axil of a deciduous or persistent scale or bract. Unisexual with the sexes on separate plants, they are without a perianth or have one represented by a pair of glandular scales or a cuplike disk. The two to thirty stamens of male flowers may be separate or united. The style of the female flowers has two or four branches. The fruits are many-seeded, small capsules.

SALIX (Sà-lix) — Willow, Weeping Willow, Pussy Willow, Osier, Permanent Wave Tree. About 500 species, chiefly natives of north temperate regions but indigenous to all continents except Australia, constitute *Salix*. In addition there are many natural and some man-made hybrids. Because of this, and because male and female flowers are borne on separate plants, willows are often difficult to identify as to kind. They and poplars (*Populus*) are the only cultivated members of the willow family SALICACEAE. The name *Salix* is the ancient Latin one for these plants.

Willows vary from tall, stately trees to alpine and arctic prostrate shrubs not over an inch or two high. With few exceptions they are deciduous. All have alternate or rarely nearly opposite, undivided, lobeless leaves, often with conspicuous stipules (appendages at the bases of the leafstalks) and tiny, petal-less flowers in erect, cylindrical to egg-shaped, usually densely-silky-hairy catkins. Male flowers have usually two, sometimes fewer or more stamens; females two, often cleft stigmas on a short style. Usually the leaves are narrow in comparison to their length, but this is not true of all kinds. The flowers of many willows are displayed in later winter or spring before the leaves appear, those of others expand after the leaves. They are wind-pollinated.

Most willows inhabit moist soils, naturally favoring stream sides, lake sides, and wet ground. A few occur in drier locations. They grow rapidly and have extensive root systems that often serve to prevent erosion of river banks. Although not of primary importance as lumber, the light, soft wood of willows has many uses. That of *S. alba calva* is quite fine for the bats used in the British game of cricket. The wood of the white willow (*S. alba*) is made into wooden shoes, toothpicks, sieves, boxes, tool handles, and paper pulp and is used for boat-building and carpentry. In Japan the Yeddo willow (*S. jessoensis*) supplies wood for geta (clogs), toothpicks, matches, and boxes. The wood of the black willow (*S. nigra*) is used for pulp and excelsior.

Osiers and withes used for basketwork are a very important product of willows. They are pliable young stems. In Europe, selected willows are cultivated in wet areas unsuitable for other agriculture as sources of osiers. For this purpose the plants are pruned close to the ground every year or two. A familiar sight in Europe are pollarded willows, trees with a definite trunk with branches only from the top. These are pruned by cutting their branches back close to the trunk every few years. The prunings are used for stakes, fuel, and other purposes. Old, pollarded willows, along the banks of rivers, canals, and ponds, are very picturesque. Among sorts grown for osiers are the almond-leaved willow (*S. triandra*), white willow (*S. alba*), crack willow (*S. fragilis*), purple osier (*S. purpurea*), and common osier (*S. viminalis*). In Central America and South America Humboldt's willow (*S. chilensis*) is similarly used.

High grade charcoal for gunpowder is made from the wood of the goat willow (*S. caprea*), the crack willow (*S. fragilis*), and the black willow (*S. nigra*). Alaskan Eskimos eat the catkins and young shoots of *S. daphnoides*. In South Africa, native species are considered good fodder for domestic animals.

That certain willows have pain-relieving properties was known to the Greek physician Dioscorides who, in the first century A.D., recommended the use of decoctions of the white willow (*S. alba*) as fomentations to relieve the agonies of gout. From then on infusions of willows were used in Europe as external applications to treat gout, toothache, neuralgia, and other ills, but were not taken internally because of their extreme bitterness. Early in the nineteenth century, a French chemist sought to isolate the pain-relieving principle believed to be present in willows as well as in certain other plants. His first success was in 1827 when, from *Spiraea*, he obtained a glucoside he

named salicin, the word salicin derived from the botanical name of the willow, *Salix*. Some ten years later salicylic acid was refined from salicin. The German name for salicylic acid is spirsaure, a word derived from *Spiraea*, the original source of salicin and salicylic acid. When, in 1899, a German chemist isolated from the bark of willows the related product acetylsalicylic acid, he gave it a name based on spirsaure and called it aspirin. And so both the popular and technical names of one of the most commonly used pain-killing drugs are derived from the botanical names of two plants, *Spiraea* and *Salix*. Salicin, salicylic acid, and acetylsalicylic acid are used medicinally and it is of interest that the Hottentots use the young shoots of the Cape willow (*S. capensis*), the commonest South African species, in the treatment of rheumatic fever.

That the Israelites, captive in Babylon, wept and hung their harps on willow trees is commonly believed because of an error in the translation of the Bible into English. It seems certain that the trees in question were not willows but poplars (*Populas euphratica*). The pretty legend that the weeping willow originally had erect branches and was weighed down with sorrow at the plight of the Israelites can thus have no foundation in fact. The great Swedish botanist Linnaeus, unaware that the weeping willow was not indigenous to Babylon, assumed that it was the tree of the Bible story and because of this named it *S. babylonica*.

In the British Isles and some other parts of northern Europe where palms were unknown or were unavailable, willow branches bedecked with catkins have for a long time been used with religious significance on Palm Sunday. In the British Isles they are called palm.

In the treatment that follows, the sorts are grouped in this order. First, weeping willows (those with strongly pendulous secondary branches), then upright tree and shrub willows that bloom as the leaves develop or later. Next, the most popular sorts of pussy willows followed by other kinds that bloom on naked shoots before the coming of the leaves, and last the low ground-hugging or carpeting kinds favored for growing in rock gardens.

Weeping willow is a name applied to several different willows, all of which bloom as their leaves expand, or after. The best known by name is the Babylon weeping willow (**S. babylonica**). This willow, unknown in the wild, was introduced to European gardens from the Middle East before 1730. It is thought to be a man-selected variant of a northern Chinese species, possibly *S. matsudana*, that was brought originally and very early from China to the Middle East along one of the ancient trade routes. One of the most graceful weeping willows, this 30- to 60-foot-tall tree has a rugged trunk that

Salix babylonica

branches low and a wide crown with long, slender, drooping secondary branches that reach to the ground. Its yellowish-green twigs are reddish on their upper sides. The slender-pointed, lanceolate, finely-toothed leaves, 3 to 4 inches long by ½ to ¾ inch wide, are hairless except when very young. Their uppersides are green, their lower surfaces bluish-gray. Although male trees are known in parts of Asia, specimens cultivated elsewhere are invariably female. Their catkins are slender and about 1 inch long. A specimen of the Babylon weeping willow that grew on St. Helena was a favorite of Napoleon during his sojourn there. He spent much time sitting beneath it and was buried under it. The Babylon weeping willow, which is less tolerant of cold than many other sorts, cannot be relied upon for hardiness appreciably north of New York City. The leaves of *S. b. crispa* are curiously curled into circles.

Salix babylonica crispa (foliage)

Hybrids between the Babylon weeping willow and the white willow (*S. alba*) are correctly identified as *S. sepulcralis*. Most frequent in cultivation, *S. s. salamonii* is a handsome, broad-headed tree up to 60 feet in height, rather less "weeping" in habit than *S. babylonica*. From 2½ to 5 inches long and up to ⅞ inch wide, its finely-toothed leaves have green upper surfaces and bluish-white undersides. The female, or sometimes bisexual, stalked catkins are about 1¾ inches long.

The hardiest weeping willow, possibly, but not certainly, a variety of *S. sepulcralis*, is the lovely golden weeping willow (*S. chrysocoma* syn. *S. alba tristis*). Hardy throughout New England, southern Quebec, and southern Ontario, this resembles the Babylon weeping willow in being a large tree with secondary branches that hang perpendicularly and reach to the ground. From 30 to 40 feet tall, this has bright yellow current season's shoots. Its narrow-lanceolate to narrow-elliptic, tapered leaves, glaucous on their undersides, are 3 to 4½ inches long by up to slightly over ½ inch wide. Appearing with the new foliage, the slender catkins, on leafy twigs, are 1½ to 2 inches long. Male, female, and sometimes bisexual catkins are borne by the same tree.

The Thurlow weeping willow (*S. elegantissima*), its botanical name the subject of some confusion, is believed to be a hybrid between *S. babylonica* and *S. fragilis* or perhaps *S. babylonica* and the hybrid *S. rubens*, which itself is a hybrid between *S. alba* and *S. fragilis*. Up to about 40 feet tall and considerably hardier than the Babylon weeping willow, it is satisfactory well into central New England and is the preferred substitute for the Babylon weeping willow in climates too cold for the latter. The Thurlow weeping willow has pendulous secondary branches that reach almost or quite to the ground. Presumably of the same parentage as the Thurlow weeping willow, the Wisconsin weeping willow or Niobe weeping willow (*S. blanda*) is about as hardy. A wide-spreading tree up to about 40 feet tall, it has pendulous secondary branches about one-half as long as those of the Thurlow weeping willow. Its shoots are green. Its lustrous leaves tend to be wider than those of the Babylon weeping willow and are thicker and blunt-toothed.

Yet another weeping willow is *S. matsudana pendula*. The species *S. matsudana* is described in the next paragraph under tree and shrub willows of erect growth. The weeping variety is a graceful tree known in China as the upside-down-willow and there popularly but, erroneously, believed to be produced by planting cuttings upside down.

Tree and shrub willows of erect growth that bloom as or after the foliage expands include those now to be described in the

Salix alba

alphabetical sequence of their botanical names. The white willow (*S. alba*), of Europe, Asia, and North Africa, and escaped in North America, is up to 90 feet tall. It has finely-toothed, silky-hairy, narrow-lanceolate leaves 1½ to 3½ inches long and catkins 1½ to 2 inches long. *S. a. calva* (syn. *S. coerulea*), the blue or cricket bat willow, is a variety or possibly hybrid of *S. alba*. Most common in eastern England and known only as a female tree, this last is more upright-branched and pyramidal than *S. alba* and has leaves with bluish-gray undersides. *S. a. britzensis* (syn. *S. a. chermesina*) is distinguishable by its bright orange-scarlet branchlets. *S. a. argentea* (syn. *S. a. sericea*) is especially noteworthy because of its intensely silvery-white foliage. *S. a. vitellina* has yellow branchlets. The peach-leaved willow (*S. amygdaloides*), of North America, differs chiefly from *S. alba* in having glandless leafstalks. It attains a height of 60 feet or more. One of the most ornamental of willows is *S. bockii*, a native of western China introduced to America by the Arnold Arboretum in 1908 or 1909. Eventually 3 to 10 feet tall or sometimes taller, it has oblong to obovate, short-stalked leaves, up to ⅝ inch long and ¼ inch wide. Their blue-white undersides are covered with silky hairs, the upper sides are dark green. The catkins, the females 1½ inches long by ½ inch wide, the males, shorter, are produced in late summer in the leaf axils of shoots of the current season's growth. Native to Central America and South America, *S. chilensis* (syn. *S. humboldtiana*) is evergreen or nearly so and up to 60 feet tall. It is slender-topped and has narrow-linear, saw-toothed leaves up to 6 inches long. The furry willow (*S. cordata* syn. *S. adenophylla*) is a handsome North American species up to 12 feet tall with gray-downy branchlets and broad-elliptic to ovate-lanceolate, fine-toothed, densely-silky-hairy leaves up to 5½ inches long. Its catkins are showy, the males 1 inch to 2¼ inches long, the females smaller. Interesting because of its feathery, grayish foli-

Salix elaeagnos

age, slender-branched *S. elaeagnos*, a shrub or more rarely a tree up to 45 feet tall, is a native of the mountains of southern and central Europe and Asia Minor. It has linear to narrow-lanceolate leaves 2 to 5 inches long by up to ¾ inch wide, glistening white on their undersides, and catkins ¾ inch to 1½ inches long. The leaves of *S. e. augustifolia* are not over ³⁄₁₆ inch wide. The crack willow or brittle willow (*S. fragilis*), so called because its branchlets break away readily

Salix fragilis

from where they join their parent branch, attains a height of 60 feet and has lanceolate, hairless, toothed leaves up to 7 inches long. The slender catkins are 2 to 2½ inches long. This, a native of Europe and Asia, is naturalized in the United States. The halberd-leaved willow of Europe and Asia, *S. hastata*, is a much-branched shrub up to 5 feet tall with ovate to obovate leaves 1 inch to 4 inches long and glaucous beneath. The catkins are silky-hairy, the males short-stalked and up to 2 inches long, the females longer-stalked. Variety *S. h. wehrhanii* is a slow-growing, decidedly ornamental sort decorated in early spring with silvery male catkins, which later are yellow. In its native Japan, *S. jessoensis* grows up to 90 feet tall. It has narrow-

Salix lanata

Salix lucida (foliage)

from 20 to 60 feet tall and one of the handsomest species, is a hardy, round-topped native of Europe and Asia that is naturalized in parts of North America. It has shiny, brownish twigs and glossy, dark green, elliptic-lanceolate to ovate, pointed, aromatic leaves, 1½ to 4½ inches long, that somewhat resemble those of laurel (*Laurus nobilis*). The catkins are cylindrical, the males bright yellow and up to 1½ inches long, the females mostly slightly longer. Native to eastern and northcentral North America, *S. petiolaris* is a shrub 4 to 6 feet tall or taller. It has purple twigs and finely-toothed lanceolate leaves 1½ to 4 inches long, silky-hairy when young but not later, and with bluish undersides. The catkins, except that the females lengthen in fruit, are under 1 inch long. The almond-leaved willow of Europe and temperate Asia, *S. triandra* (syn. *S. amygdalina*) is a shrub or tree up to 30 feet tall with flaking bark. It has hairless, lanceolate leaves, 2 to 4 inches long, glossy dark green above, paler and sometimes glaucous beneath. The male catkins are up to 2½ inches long and fragrant, the female catkins are shorter.

Pussy willow is the vernacular name of *S. discolor* and *S. caprea*, both of which display their catkins on leafless shoots in late winter or early spring. The latter is also called goat willow and sallow. Native in wet soils throughout much of eastern North America, extremely hardy *S. discolor* is a tall shrub or tree up to 20 feet in height. It has wavy-toothed to nearly toothless, oblong leaves, glaucous on their undersides, which distinguishes it from *S. caprea*, and up to 4 inches long. The gray-silky-hairy male catkins are up to 1½ inches long. In fruit the females are longer. A native of Europe and adjacent Asia, much cultivated in North America, *S. caprea* is less hardy than *S. discolor*, but survives through much of New England. A shrub or tree up to 25 feet tall, it has broad-ovate to oblong or obovate, slightly-toothed or toothless leaves, 2½ to 4 inches long, with gray-hairy undersides. The catkins are stalkless. The softly-silky-hairy males, about 1 inch long, when ripe are bedecked with golden anthers. The female catkins in fruit attain a length of 2 inches. *S. c. pendula*, the Kilmarnock willow, comprises two varieties, one male, the other female. Both have stiff, crooked, drooping branches and are usually propagated by grafting onto erect-growing understocks to form weeping, tree-type specimens.

Other willows that, like pussy willows, display their catkins in late winter or spring on leafless shoots include those now to be described alphabetically according to their botanical names. Handsome *S. aegyptiaca* (syn. *S. medemii*), native to Armenia and Iran, is erect and up to 12 feet in height or rarely is a tree up to 30 feet tall. Stout-branched, it has ob-

lanceolate, finely-toothed leaves 2 to 4 inches long that when young are very silky-hairy. The male catkins are ¾ inch to 1¼ inches long, the females up to 1¾ inches long. The red willow or polished willow, *S. laevigata*, of western North America, is 20 to 50 feet tall. It has reddish-brown to yellow branchlets and nearly toothless, broadly-oblong to lanceolate leaves 2½ to 7½ inches long with glaucous undersides. The male catkins are slender and 1½ to 4½ inches long, the females are ¾ inch to 2 inches long. The

Salix lanata (foliage)

woolly willow (*S. lanata*) is one of the handsomest low willows. Usually not over 3 feet high, but sometimes attaining 4 feet, it is a sturdy, slow-growing bush with oval to obovate leaves 1 inch to 2½ inches long and ¾ inch to 1½ inches wide that are densely covered with silvery-woolly hairs on both surfaces, and have stipules as long as the leafstalks. Its male catkins are 1 inch to 2 inches long, the females, in fruit, up to 4 inches long. They are often solitary at the termination of the previous year's shoots. The woolly willow is native at high altitudes in northern Europe and temperate Asia. The shining willow of from Newfoundland to Nebraska, *S. lucida*, is about 18 feet high. It has lanceolate to ovate-lanceolate leaves 2 to 6 inches long and glossy on both surfaces. The oblong to ovoid catkins are up to 3 inches long.

Chinese *S. magnifica* is about 18 feet tall. It has magnolia-like, elliptic leaves up to 8 inches long. Its male catkins are up to 7 inches long, the females up to 1 foot. The Peking willow (*S. matsudana*), botanically closely related to *S. babylonica* and native to semiarid regions in northern China and Korea, is much planted in China. A tree 40 to 50 feet tall with erect to spreading branches, the Peking willow has short-stalked, slender-pointed, mostly finely-toothed, linear-lanceolate leaves, 2 to 4 inches long, with bright green upper surfaces and whitish-glaucous undersides. Its cylindrical male catkins are slightly more than ½ inch long, the females about 1 inch long. A variety represented by both male and female trees, *S. m. pendula* has pendulous branches. Variety *S. m. umbraculifera* is rounded, compact, and without a dominant central leader. The most popular variety, *S. m. tortuosa*, called permanent wave tree and dragon's claw willow,

Salix matsudana tortuosa (young branches)

has markedly spirally-contorted branches and branchlets. The black willow of North America (*S. nigra*) is up to 60 feet tall. It has blackish bark and finely-toothed, linear-lanceolate to lanceolate, often slightly sickle-shaped leaves, 3 to 4½ inches long and pale green on their undersides. The slender catkins are 1 inch to 3½ inches long. The laurel willow (*S. pentandra*), long leaves 2½ to 6 inches long, toothed, and on their undersides gray-hairy, and very attractive catkins about 1½ inches long. Sometimes male and female catkins occur on the same bush and sometimes male and female flowers in the same catkin. **S. boydii,** a hybrid between *S. lapponum* and *S. reticulata,* looks like a gnarled, miniature tree 1 foot to about 3 feet tall. It has broad-ovate to short-stalked, nearly round, leathery leaves up to about 1 inch long, at first silvery-gray but becoming dark green as they age. Their undersides are clothed with whitish wool. The veins are conspicuously indented. This willow bears catkins sparingly. A chance hybrid discovered in Scotland toward the end of the nineteenth century, *S. boydii* has been found only once in the wild; all cultivated specimens are derivatives of the original find. The gray willow of Europe, North Africa, and temperate Asia (**S. cinerea**) is up to 15

Salix cinerea (male catkins)

feet in height and has elliptic to obovate-lanceolate, wavy leaves that are gray-hairy beneath and 2 to 4 inches long. The silky-hairy catkins resemble those of *S. caprea,* but are rather smaller and are displayed somewhat later. From *S. caprea* the gray willow is distinguishable by its persistently hairy twigs and its narrower leaves. The common sallow (*S. c. oleifolia*) is a taller shrub than the typical species or may become a tree up to 40 feet tall. It has hairless or nearly hairless twigs and leaves rarely exceeding 2½ inches in length, with on their undersides a mixture of gray and brown hairs. Unusual rather than attractive, *S. c. tricolor* has leaves variegated with yellow and white and sometimes red. Possibly of hybrid origin, and as known in cultivation undoubtedly including hybrids, **S. dasyclados** is by some authorities accepted as a good species, a native of eastern Europe to eastern Siberia. It is closely related to *S. viminalis,* which is one of the parents of the hybrids grown as *S. dasyclados.* Most common in cultivation is

Salix dasyclados (male catkins)

the male variety *S. d. grandis.* A shrub up to about 18 feet tall, this has pointed-oblong-elliptic leaves up to 7 inches long by 1 inch wide or a little wider that are gray-hairy on their undersides. Its handsome, slightly-curved catkins, from 1½ to 2 inches long, look like great hairy, yellow caterpillars. Their long cream-colored stamens are tipped with bright yellow. Native to China, Japan, and Korea, **S. gracilistyla,** a spreading shrub of erect habit, is up to 9 feet tall. It has gray-downy young shoots and more or less oval leaves 2 to 4 inches long by up to 1¼ inches wide, gray-green above and glaucous and silky-hairy beneath. Its pretty 1- to 1½-inch-long catkins are gray toned with red. *S. g. melanostachya* (syn. *S. melano-*

Salix gracilistyla (male catkins)

stachya), introduced from Japan to Europe in 1950, is a distinctive variety that differs most obviously from *S. gracilistyla* in having very dark brownish-black catkins that at maturity are peppered with anthers that at first are brick-red then change to yellow. The prairie willow (**S. humilis**), native from Newfoundland to Minnesota and North Carolina, is up to 8 feet tall. It has oblong-lanceolate leaves, 2 to 4 inches long and glaucous and hairy beneath, and brick-red, ellipsoid catkins,

Salix gracilistyla melanostachya (male catkins)

Salix humilis (male catkins)

½ inch to 1½ inches long. An erect shrub up to 15 feet tall or less often a small tree, **S. irrorata** is attractive because of the white, waxy bloom that covers its branchlets. Its linear-lanceolate leaves, 2½ to 4 inches long, have lustrous upper surfaces and are glaucous beneath. Its catkins are ¾ to 1 inch long. The males have reddish anthers. From *S. daphnoides* this species is distinguishable by its buds being pressed against the stems, by its very short-stalked, scarcely toothed leaves, and by its smaller catkins. The beauty of the stems in winter of this native from Colorado to New Mexico and Arizona is best displayed when the shrub is planted in front of evergreens. A dense, much-branched shrub, 2 to 5 feet tall, **S. lapponum** has more or less downy young shoots and elliptic to obovate, hoary leaves narrower than those of *S. lanata*, 1 inch to 2½ inches long, and woolly-hairy beneath. It is a native of alpine and arctic regions of Europe and temperate Asia. Its male catkins are about 1 inch long, the female catkins 1 inch to 2 inches long. The arroyo willow (*S. lasiolepis*), native from Washington to Mexico, is a shrub or tree 10 to 18 or rarely 35 feet tall. It has yellowish to brown, usually pubescent branchlets, and oblanceolate to linear, nearly toothless leaves, up to 4 inches long, with glaucous or white-pubescent undersides. The catkins are stalkless, the males ¾ inch to 1½ inches long, the females, in fruit, up to 2½ inches long. The purple osier (*S. purpurea*), a shrub from 9 to 18 feet tall or less frequently a small tree, is native to Europe, North Africa, and temperate Asia. Its glossy, tough young stems, at first purplish, are later olive-gray. Its linear to oblanceolate, often nearly opposite, linear to oblong leaves are 1½ to 3 inches long, lustrous green above and paler and more or less glabrous beneath. The attractive, slender, usually curved catkins are beautiful because of their red anthers. They are ½ to 1 inch long. Variety *S. p. nana* grows to about 3 feet in height or somewhat higher and has

A hedge of *Salix purpurea nana*

smaller leaves than the typical species. It may be sheared to form low hedges. The branches of *S. p. pendula* droop. This sort is often grafted onto tall erect understocks to produce weeping standard specimens. Native to Japan and the Sakhalin Islands, *S. sachalinensis* is a tree up to 30 feet tall. It has dark green, lanceolate leaves up to 6 inches long by about 1 inch wide, glaucous, and slightly hairy on their undersides. The male catkins are about 1½ inches long. The female catkins are more slender. *S. s.* 'Sekka', the fan-tail willow, is a male variety, from 9 to 15 feet tall, with flattened, curiously contorted, twisted branchlets and 2-inch-long leaves silvery on their undersides. The branchlets find much favor with flower arrangers. A na-

Salix sachalinensis 'Sekka' (male catkins)

tive of eastern and central North America, *S. tristis* is a shrub 1 foot to 3 feet tall. Its toothless leaves, crowded toward the ends of the branchlets and on their undersides clothed with white hairs, are up to 2 inches long. The catkins are ⅓ to ⅔ inch long. The common osier or basket willow of Europe, *S. viminalis* is naturalized to some extent in eastern North America. A shrub or tree up to 20 feet tall, it has linear to linear-lanceolate, toothless leaves up to 4 to 10 inches long and up to ½ inch wide. Their upper surfaces are dull green, their undersides clothed with shining, silvery-gray hairs. The catkins are up to 1 inch long and ¾ inch wide.

Prostrate and creeping willows include these now to be described: *S. arctica* (syn. *S. petrophila*), the Arctic willow, native from North America to the mouth of the St. Lawrence River, the Gaspé Peninsula, Colorado, and New Mexico, is a very variable, loose-mat-forming species up to 4 inches tall or sometimes a little taller. It has creeping, sometimes buried stems with more or less erect branches. Its elliptic to broad-oblanceolate leaves, hairy when young, later hairless, are ¾ inch to nearly 2 inches long by up to ⅝ inch wide. Borne on leafy side shoots, the catkins, of twenty-five to fifty flowers, are hairy and 1 inch to 1¾ inches long. *S. cascadensis*, of western North America, much resembles *S. arctica*, from which it differs most obviously in having leaves rarely attaining a length of 1 inch and smaller catkins having not more than twenty-five flowers. *S. glacialis*, of the Arctic coast of western North America, is a prostrate shrub with blunt, ovate to obovate leaves up to ½ inch long, sometimes with a few teeth at their bases and, except when young, hairless. The ovoid to nearly spherical catkins are

S. herbacea, native to Arctic North America and southward to New Hampshire, indigenous also to Iceland and to mountains in Europe, including those in the British Isles. A shrub up to 1 foot tall, but more often 2 to 4 inches tall, this species has stems that creep along or just beneath the ground surface. Its suborbicular to broad-obovate, finely-toothed leaves are lustrous green on both surfaces. Usually not more than three near the end of each shoot, and ¼ to ¾ inch long, they are often notched at their apexes. From ¼ to ¾ inch long, the few-flowered catkins are borne on short stalks in early spring. *S. repens*, native to wet soils in Europe, including those in the British Isles, and northern Asia, in its

Salix repens (male catkins)

typical wild form is 1 foot to 1½ feet tall, but planted in fertile soil may attain a height of 6 feet or more. From stems that creep along or just beneath the surface of the ground, it produces erect branches. The ovate-elliptic to lanceolate leaves, silky-hairy on their undersides and in gardens up to 1½ inches long, on wild specimens rarely exceed one-half that length. The stalkless catkins, displayed on leafless shoots in late winter or spring, are ovoid to cylindrical and up to ¾ inch long. The leaves of *S. r. argentea*, a bigger, more erect shrub than the typical species, are usually silky-hairy on their upper surfaces as well as on their undersides. *S. reticulata*, native to arctic and subarctic regions throughout the northern hemisphere and southward to the Rocky Mountains and the European Alps, is rarely over 6 inches tall, but sometimes twice as tall. *S. retusa*, native to the mountains of central Europe, has procumbent stems and branches and obovate, hairless, seemingly parallel-veined leaves, green on both surfaces and up to ¾ inch long. Its cylindrical catkins, erect and about ⅔ inch long, are borne at the ends of short, leafy shoots. *S. serpyllifolia* (syn. *S. retusa serpyllifolia*) differs most obviously from *S. retusa*, which it otherwise much resembles, in having smaller leaves, those of specimens in the wild typically not

Salix reticulata

more than ⅓ inch long, those of cultivated specimens up to a little over ½ inch long. A native at usually higher altitudes than *S. retusa* in the European Alps, *S. serpyllifolia* favors limestone soils. **S. uva-ursi,** the bearberry willow, forms mats up to several feet in diameter. Native to Greenland and in eastern North America from the Arctic to some mountain peaks in New England, it differs from *S. retusa,* to which it is closely allied, in technical details of its flowers. Its narrow-elliptic to broad-elliptic or obovate leaves are up to 1 inch long. On leafy shoots, the catkins are up to ¾ inch long.

Garden and Landscape Uses. In gardens and landscapes, willows have rather limited uses. They have weak wood and are somewhat subject to storm damage, their roots ramify widely and may enter and clog nearby drains, and in many regions they are subject to various serious diseases and insect pests. Despite this there are some places where some willows can be used to distinct advantage and the catkins of some kinds that bloom before they leaf out are useful as cut flowers. The really low growing kinds, such as *S. repens, S. reticulata,* and *S. herbacea,* are appropriate for rock gardens, and *S. purpurea nana* is useful for low hedges. Tall willows grow rapidly and prosper in wetter soils than most trees. Surely there are few more lovely landscape scenes than that of a shapely weeping willow by the waterside. Given a suitable location one should not hesitate to plant to achieve such effects, but beware of setting a willow tree on a small lawn near a house where it will soon be overpoweringly big and a threat to drains, cesspools, and possibly foundations.

Cultivation. Willows thrive best in damp, heavy soils, but will grow in most soils that are not excessively dry. When setting out tree kinds it is important to allow ample space for growth because they are not seen to advantage when crowded, but shrubby kinds may be set fairly close together to form bold groups. If we con-

sider the ease with which they root from cuttings, it is rather surprising that they do not withstand transplanting well and often recover slowly following this operation. It is best to plant only young trees and to prune them back rather severely at planting time. Pruning of established specimens should be done as necessary to keep them shapely. Shrubby kinds cut hard back soon renew themselves by the production of new branches. The commonest method of increase is by hardwood cuttings. These root so readily that leafless pieces several feet long of one-year or older wood placed in moist soil will usually take root and develop into new individuals; however, hardwood cuttings 9 to 12 inches long are more commonly used. Shoots stood in containers of water in late winter or spring usually root quickly and leafy summer cuttings also root without difficulty. The dwarf creeping willows, such as *S. repens,* may be increased by dividing them and setting rooted pieces in new locations. Pendulous varieties are grafted onto erect growers to produce weeping trees. Willows can be raised from seeds, but these do not retain their vitality for long and often many are sterile. If sown in moist soil as soon as they are ripe, the fertile seeds will germinate in a few days time.

Diseases and Pests. Willows are subject to bacterial twig blight, leaf blight, various cankers, scab, leaf spot diseases, powdery mildew, and rust. Insects that attack them are aphids, European willow beetle, galls, lace bug, flea weevil, borers, willow sawfly, and scales.

SALLOW is *Salix caprea.*

SALMONBERRY is *Rubus spectabilis.*

SALPICHROA (Salpi-chroà) — Lily-of-the-Valley Vine or Cock's Eggs. South American *Salpichroa,* of the nightshade family SOLANACEAE, consists of twenty-five species. Few have been cultivated. The name, alluding to the shape and texture of the blooms, is from the Greek *salpinx,* a tube, and *chroa,* skin.

Salpichroas include herbaceous perennials, subshrubs, and shrubs, some vining. They have undivided, often hairy leaves. Their flowers have five-lobed or five-parted calyxes and tubular or urn-shaped corollas with five, often short lobes (petals), five stamens, and one style. The fruits are berries containing flattened seeds.

Lily-of-the-valley vine or cock's eggs (*S. origanifolia* syn. *S. rhomboidea*), a perennial not hardy in the north, is sometimes grown as an annual. It climbs or forms tangled masses of square, slender stems and has foliage with a strong odor. It is attractive to bees. A native of Argentina and Paraguay, this has fleshy roots and

slender-stalked, rhomboid-ovate leaves, with blades up to 1½ inches long. Its solitary or paired, white flowers, about ⅜ inch long, are succeeded by many-seeded, bright red, yellowish, or white, ellipsoid fruits, about ½ inch long, that are edible, but not very flavorful. These are the "cock's eggs" sold for eating in parts of South America.

Garden and Landscape Uses and Cultivation. The vine described grows rapidly, and although a trifle weedy in appearance, it is useful for clothing walls, trellises, and other supports. Tender to frost, it is perennial outdoors in mild climates only. It makes no special demands regarding soil, growing satisfactorily in any of ordinary garden quality and succeeding even in alkaline ones. Good drainage is needed, and sun. This plant stands high summer temperatures.

SALPIGLOSSIS (Salpiglós-sis) — Painted Tongue. This Chilean group of annuals, of the nightshade family SOLANACEAE, consists of eighteen species, but only one appears to be cultivated. The name *Salpiglossis* derives from the Greek *salpinx,* a tube, and *glossa,* a tongue. It alludes to the form of the corolla and the shape of the style.

Erect and usually covered with slightly sticky hairs, these plants have alternate, broadly-lanceolate, long-stalked leaves with wavy or sometimes shallowly-indented margins. The flowers are in loose clusters, terminating the main stem and branches. They have five-lobed calyxes and broadly-funnel-shaped, five-lobed corollas in a variety of gay patterns and colors. There are four fertile stamens, two short and two long, and sometimes a staminode (sterile stamen). The fruits are capsules.

Cultivated sorts, varieties of **S. sinuata,** outdoors attain heights of 2 to 3 feet, but in greenhouses are often taller. They branch freely and have bluntly-toothed, wavy-margined leaves. Because of their covering of glandular hairs, stems and foliage are

Salpiglossis sinuata variety, flowers cream with purple streakings

Salpiglossis sinuata variety, flowers clear yellow

decidedly clammy to the touch. The very beautiful blooms are up to 2½ inches long and wide. Their colors include cream, straw-yellow, primrose-yellow, golden-yellow, orange, brown, red, scarlet, violet, and nearly blue, usually overlaid with brightly colored veinings in contrasting hues.

Garden Uses. These plants are elegant for outdoor garden decoration and for cutting and are exquisite when grown in greenhouses to bloom in late winter and spring.

Cultivation. As outdoor plants, salpiglossises succeed best where summers are not excessively hot. They need a sunny location and fertile soil that does not become exceedingly dry, but nevertheless is porous and well drained. Sow outdoors where the plants are to bloom in spring as soon as the ground can be brought into condition and there is no longer danger of severe frost. If the plants are to be in patches in flower beds and borders, the seeds may be broadcast, but if they are being raised for cut flowers, sow in rows 1½ to 2 feet apart. Thin seedlings in patches to about 9 inches apart, those in rows to about 6 inches between plants in the rows.

Alternatively, sow in a greenhouse in a temperature of 55 to 60°F eight to ten weeks before the plants are to be set in the outdoor garden, which may be done when the weather is right for planting tomatoes. Transplant the seedlings individually to 2½- or 3-inch pots or 2½ inches apart in flats and grow them in a sunny greenhouse with a night temperature of 55°F and daytime temperatures five to ten degrees higher. Before transferring outdoors harden them in a cold frame or sheltered outdoor location for a week or two. Plant 10 inches to 1 foot apart in a sunny, sheltered location. Care during the growing season includes keeping down weeds and staking or providing other suitable support. In dry weather thorough watering at intervals of a few days is necessary. When hot weather

arrives mulching is helpful. Pick faded blooms promptly.

For winter and spring bloom in sunny greenhouses, sow in September or October in sandy soil in a temperature of 60°F. Transplant the seedlings to small pots and later to benches filled with soil or ground beds or pot them successively to bigger pots until they occupy 6- to 8-inch pots. In beds and benches space them 8 inches apart each way. Use porous, decidedly sandy, but fertile soil and keep a night temperature of 45 to 50°F, with a daytime increase of five to fifteen degrees. Maintain a dryish atmosphere. Whenever weather is favorable promote airy conditions by opening the greenhouse ventilators. Never water excessively. The soil must not be constantly wet, but allowed to dry appreciably between soakings. When the final pots are filled with roots give dilute liquid fertilizer at seven- to ten-day intervals.

SALPINGA (Salpín-ga). Belonging to the melastoma family MELASTOMATACEAE, the genus *Salpinga* consists of ten species of low herbaceous perennials of the rain forests of tropical South America that resemble and are closely related to *Bertolonia*. The name comes from the Greek *salpinx*, a trumpet, and alludes to the shape of the calyx.

Salpingas have opposite, ovate leaves with five to seven prominent veins running from base to apex and white or pink flowers with five petals, ten stamens, and one style, in one-sided, curved spikes or branched clusters. The fruits are capsules.

One of the handsomest of the group, *S. margaritacea,* of Brazil, has dull green leaves with blades up to 6 inches long by one-half as wide, on their upper sides marked with a single row of conspicuous white spots between each pair of veins, a very distinctive form of variegation and similar to that exhibited by *Sonerila margaritacea.* The leaves of *Salpinga margaritacea* are green or reddish beneath. Those of *S. longifolia,* bright green above, are downy on their undersides.

Garden Uses and Cultivation. These plants have the same uses and need the same care as bertolonias.

SALPINGOSTYLIS (Salpingó-stylis). William Bartram, pioneer American botanist, first described and illustrated the only species of this genus in 1791. "Behold," he wrote, alluding to the landscape of northern Florida, "the azure fields of cerulean Ixea." Following its discovery, Bartram's *Ixea* (the modern spelling is *Ixia*) was lost to science and not seen again for more than a century. Some botanists thought it extinct, others that it had never existed. In 1931 it was rediscovered and, as it clearly was not an *Ixia* as that genus is presently understood, was given the name *Salpin-*

gostylis coelestina. The name, constructed from the Greek *salpinx*, a trumpet, and *stylos*, a little column, alludes to the shape of the style.

This plant belongs to the iris family IRIDACEAE and differs from related *Nemastylis* in having a curious, long, trumpet-shaped, pendulous style. The rediscovery revealed an important reason why this quite showy species had remained hidden from searching botanists for so long. Its blooms open a little before dawn and close by eight to ten o'clock in the morning. As can be readily imagined, wide comment about the "rising hours" of botanical collectors were occasioned by this discovery.

Lovely in bloom, *S. coelestina* is 1 foot to 1½ feet tall. It has a corm (bulblike organ that is solid rather than composed of concentric layers or overlapping scales as are onion and lily bulbs). The corm, ½ to ¾ inch in diameter, produces narrow-linear, pleated leaves 5 to 6 inches in diameter. The flowers are nodding and 2 to 3 inches wide. They are violet, lavender-violet, or purple, sometimes with a white eye, or rarely are white. They have six perianth parts (commonly called petals, but more correctly tepals) and three stamens. The fruits are capsules containing small, brick-red seeds.

Garden and Landscape Uses. Because of its limited natural distribution the possibility exists that this rare endemic of the United States will become extinct in the wild in the face of advancing agriculture and other operations of man. Fortunately it is easily raised from seed and cultivated. A delightful plant for those to whom the rare and botanically interesting is alluring, it is adaptable to flower beds and rock gardens and for greenhouse cultivation.

Cultivation. Fertile, sandy, somewhat acid soil that contains an abundance of decayed organic matter and is well drained, but uniformly moist during the spring to fall season of growth, suits *Salpingostylis*. New growth begins in spring and ripens and dies after the seeds mature. Propagation by seed is the most practical means of increase. Under good cultivation plants can be had in bloom in their second year from seed sowing. In greenhouses the soil should be kept dry during the bulbs' dormant season. In late winter or spring repotting is done and watering resumed. A night temperature of 50°F, with a daytime rise of five to fifteen degrees, depending on the brightness of the day, is appropriate. On all favorable occasions the greenhouse is ventilated freely. Very light shade in summer, just sufficient to break the full intensity of the strongest sunlight, is beneficial. It seems probable that in the north, where it is not hardy, this interesting species could be managed like gladioluses, by storing the bulbs over winter and planting them outdoors in spring.

SALSIFY, OYSTER PLANT, or VEGETABLE OYSTER. The last two names allude to the flavor of the roots of this comparatively little known vegetable. They are boiled, or cooked in other ways, before eating. Botanically *Tragopogon porrifolius*, of the daisy family COMPOSITAE, salsify in its cultivated forms scarcely differs from the wild plant, a native of Europe naturalized in North America.

Prepare the ground deeply as for parsnips. Let it be in a sunny spot, well drained, and fertile without containing fresh manure or excessive nitrogen. Sow the long, sticklike seeds in early spring in rows 1 foot apart. Cover them to a depth of 1 inch. When large enough to handle, thin the seedlings to 3 to 5 inches apart. Keep the soil free of weeds and in dry spells watered regularly.

Ready for harvest in fall, the crop may be dug then and stored like parsnips in a root cellar, or similar place, or in outdoor pits or left in the ground until spring to be taken up as needed. It is perfectly hardy. The only flaw in the last procedure is that when the ground is frozen hard, digging becomes impossible.

SALT HAY or SALT MARSH HAY. Hay made from grasses that inhabit salt marshes is especially useful as winter covering for hardy herbaceous perennials and low evergreens, as well as for mulching strawberries to prevent the fruits being splashed with mud. Its special virtues are that its wiry stems neither mat down nor rot as quickly as ordinary hay and straw and that, because any seeds it sheds will not germinate except in wet saline soil, it is not a source of weeds.

SALT TREE. See Halimodendron.

SALTBUSH. See Atriplex. For Australian-saltbush see Rhagodia.

SALVIA (Sál-via) — Sage, Clary. Widely distributed as natives throughout temperate and tropical regions of the Old World and the New World, *Salvia* is a genus of about 700 species. Most gardeners are familiar with at least a few, and even people not horticulturally inclined are likely to recognize common sage, a popular flavoring herb. The name of this genus, of the mint family LABIATAE, comes from the Latin *salveo*, to save or heal. Used by Pliny, it alludes to the supposedly curative properties of some species. In the American west, sage is also used as a common name for certain artemisias.

Salvias include annuals, biennials, herbaceous perennials, subshrubs, and shrubs. Some are hardy in the north, others are much too tender to cold to live as perennials away from the subtropics and tropics. They have square stems and opposite leaves. The latter, according to kind, may be toothless or variously toothed, pinnately-cleft or -divided. Occasionally the leaves of the flowering parts are similar to those lower on the stems or basal, more often they are bractlike, and in some species highly colored. The flowers are in whorls of few or many arranged loosely or crowded in interrupted or continuous terminal spikes, racemes, or panicles. More rarely they are from the leaf axils. Their calyxes commonly have two lips, the upper often three-toothed, the lower deeply-two-lobed. There are two fertile stamens that may or may not protrude, sometimes a pair of staminodes (rudimentary stamens), a style, two-branched at its summit, and two stigmas. The tubes of the asymmetrical corollas extend beyond or are included in the calyx. They are strongly-two-lipped, with the upper lip straight or arched and sometimes notched, the lower three-lobed with the center lobe the biggest, and often notched or forming a pouch. The fruits generally consist of four more-or-less seedlike nutlets.

Common sage (*S. officinalis*) is a hardy, aromatic, freely-branched shrub up to about

Salvia officinalis

Salvia officinalis (foliage)

2 feet tall. It has white-hairy shoots, and stalked, wrinkled, oblong, gray-green leaves, 1 inch to 2 inches long, with finely-round-toothed margins. The many-flowered whorls of bloom are in interrupted, branchless or little-branched racemes. The blooms have purplish, bell-shaped, pointed-toothed calyxes, and purple, blue, or white corollas, ½ to ¾ inch long, with a ring of hairs on their insides. The best known varieties are *S. o. albiflora*, white-flowered; *S. o. rubriflora*, with red flowers and leaves three times or more as long as wide; *S. o. aurea*, yellow-foliaged and compact; *S. o. purpurascens*, with reddish-purple leaves; *S. o. tricolor*, with leaves veined with yellowish-white and pink, becoming

Salvia officinalis aurea

Salvia officinalis tricolor

deep rose-pink; *S. o. latifolia*, with leaves one-half as long as broad; *S. o. salicifolia*, its leaves four times or more as long as wide; and *S. o. crispa*, with crinkled, variegated foliage.

Pineapple sage (*S. elegans* syn. *S. rutilans*), of Mexico, is a nonhardy subshrub up to 3 feet in height; this, when brushed against or bruised, has a strong odor of pineapple. It has pointed, softly-hairy, toothed, ovate leaves. The red flowers, about 1¼ inches long, are in leafy panicles. Their stamens protrude.

Clary (*S. sclarea*), a hardy biennial or sometimes perennial native to Europe and western Asia, is used as a flavoring herb. This is 2 to 4 feet tall. Its stems are hairy-glandular above. The leaves are stalked, broadly-ovate, round-toothed, and hairy.

Salvia elegans

Salvia sclarea

They are up to 9 inches long. The large, blunt, broad bracts of the flowering parts are white toward their bases, pink or lilac at their tips. The pinkish to purplish blooms, in distantly-spaced whorls of about six, are approximately 1 inch long. The corollas do not protrude beyond the calyxes. Their upper lips are three-toothed. Variety *S. s. turkestaniana*, of Turkestan, has larger, showier floral bracts and whitish flowers.

Scarlet sage (*S. splendens*), a nonhardy perennial usually grown as an annual, is

Salvia splendens

popular. Most often its blooms, brilliant scarlet or crimson, are accompanied by showy bracts of the same hue, but varieties with white, pink, and purple flowers and bracts are available. Except for colored hairs in the floral parts, this species and its varieties are hairless. Their heart-shaped leaves are stalked and 2 to 3½ inches long. The blooms, in terminal spikelike racemes, branched or not, are 1½ to 2 inches in length. The scarlet sage is native to Brazil. It is reported to attain heights of 8 feet in the wild, but as known in gardens is generally 2 to 3 feet tall. There are compact varieties not over 1 foot in height.

Several nonhardy, red-flowered salvias besides the scarlet sage and the pineapple sage are cultivated. Sometimes called Texas sage, *S. coccinea* is native from South Carolina to Florida, Texas, and tropical America. A more or less hairy annual or perennial, this is 1 foot to 2 feet high. It has slender-stalked, toothed, ovate leaves 1 inch to 2 inches long. Scarlet, often with a purplish upper lip, the flowers, ¾ to 1 inch long, are in rather widely spaced tiers forming erect, slender racemes. Variety *S. c. pseudococcinea*, of Mexico, up to 4 feet tall, has leafstalks and the margins of its

Salvia coccinea pseudococcinea

bracts furnished with long hairs. Horticultural varieties are *S. c. alba*, with white flowers; *S. c. bicolor*, with flowers that have red lower lips and white upper ones; and

S. c. major, up to 4½ feet high and with larger blooms. Rose-red to magenta-red blooms about 2½ inches long are borne in loose spikes by *S. dorisiana*, of Honduras. This is a hairy, shrubby perennial 2

Salvia dorisiana

to 3 feet tall and freely-branched. Its thinnish leaves are long-stalked and have ovate blades 3 to 7 inches long. The showy flowers, in tiers of up to ten, are in loose terminal spikes about 6 inches long. Called cardinal sage or Mexican red sage, *S. fulgens* is a 3-foot-tall, woody-based, freely-branched subshrub. It has slightly round-toothed, triangular-ovate leaves, green and hairy above, white-hairy on their undersides. The showy, hairy, scarlet flowers, 1½ to 2 inches long, are in racemes up to 1 foot long. This is a native of Mexico. Another Mexican, *S. grahamii* is a shrub up to 4 feet tall with hairless or nearly hairless stems and foliage. It has round-toothed, blunt-ovate leaves and, in racemes 1 foot long or longer, deep crimson to purplish flowers with hairy calyxes and corollas with a lower lip twice as long as the upper. Also Mexican, but extending as a wildling into Texas, *S. greggii* is a subshrub 2 to 3 feet tall. It has short-stalked or nearly stalkless, dull green, linear-oblong to spatula-shaped, toothless, glandular leaves, ¾ inch to 1½ inches long, and clustered. The red or purplish-red blooms, with much swollen corolla tubes and 1 inch to 1½ inches long, are in few-flowered racemes. A garden variety of pink-flowered, shrubby *S. involucrata*, of Mexico, *S. i. bethellii* is a shrub 3 to 4 feet tall or taller with large, pointed-ovate-

Salvia involucrata bethellii

heart-shaped leaves and, at the shoot ends, ample spikes of bright rosy-crimson flowers accompanied in the bud stage by colored bracts. Mexican *S. neurepia*, a strongly aromatic subshrub up to 7 feet tall

Salvia neurepia

and akin to *S. grahamii*, has stalked leaves with ovate blades about 3 inches long that are softly-hairy on their undersides and have scattered hairs above. They are toothed except at their bases. In erect spikes the carmine flowers are in whorls of up to six. About 1 inch long, they have a large, flat lower lip, notched at its apex and about ⅝ inch wide, and a narrow, arched upper lip. The stamens do not protrude. The pitcher sage of California (*S. spathacea*) is a nonhardy herbaceous perennial with creeping rhizomes and mostly basal, oblongish to triangular, rough-surfaced leaves, 4 to 8 inches long and with a pair of well-developed basal lobes. The 1- to 2½-foot-tall, erect, flowering stalk terminates in a dense, narrow-pyramidal spike with purplish bracts and purplish-red flowers 1¼ to 1½ inches long.

Salvia spathacea

Nonhardy blue-flowered salvias are splendid for mild climates and greenhouses. Here belong the gentian sage (*S. patens*), the mealycup sage (*S. farinacea*), *S. guaranitica*, and *S. clevelandii*. Native to mountains in Mexico, *S. patens* is a tuberous-rooted, deciduous herbaceous pe-

Salvia patens

rennial. A summer bloomer, it is less happy in hot, humid climates than in less tropical conditions. It will not survive much frost. From 1½ to 2½ feet tall, glandular and clammy, the gentian sage has ovate to triangular or arrow-shaped, toothed leaves, downy on their undersides, less hairy above. Its blooms, in pairs in loose spikes, are deep blue and 2 inches long or longer. Variety *S. p. alba* has white flowers. The blooms of *S. p.* 'Cambridge Blue' are light blue. Mealycup sage (*S. farinacea*), of Texas, a herbaceous perennial in mild climates, is commonly grown as a summer annual. About 2 to 4 feet tall and pubescent, it has ovate to linear-lanceolate, blunt-toothed leaves, up to about 4 inches long, and slender racemes of flowers, up to 9

Salvia farinacea

inches long, with violet-blue, ½-inch-long corollas that contrast pleasingly with their white-woolly calyxes. Garden varieties, notably 'Blue Bedder', more compact than the typical species, are available. The corollas of *S. f. alba* are white. Native to southern Brazil, Paraguay, and Argentina, *S. guaranitica* (syn. *S. ambigens*) is a herbaceous perennial or subshrub often cul-

Salvia guaranitica

tivated as an annual. From 2 to 3½ feet tall and bushy, it has round-toothed, wrinkled, ovate leaves 2 to 5 inches long. Its rich blue flowers, in erect, loose spike-like racemes, spread at right angles to the stem and are 1½ to 2 inches long. Native to southern California and Baja California, *S. clevelandii* is a much-branched shrub, 1 foot to 2 feet in height, with oblong, short-stalked leaves ½ inch to 1½ inches long, round-toothed, and more or less white-hairy especially on their undersides. The flowers are in solitary or few, rather distant headlike whorls at or near the tops of erect, slender stems furnished with distant pairs of small leaves. They have sticky-hairy calyxes and blue corollas about ¾ inch long.

Because the stems and the calyxes of its flowers are thickly clothed with violet hairs, even though the corollas of its blooms are white, violet is the predominant hue of the flowering racemes of Mexican S. leucantha. A nonhardy, woolly-stemmed shrub or subshrub 2 to 3 feet tall, this species thrives in hot weather and is mostly cultivated for blooming in greenhouses in early winter. It has wrinkled, pointed, narrow-oblong-lanceolate, toothed leaves 2½ to 5 inches long, white-woolly-hairy on their undersides and nearly hairless above. From 6 inches to 1 foot long, the slender flower spikes have stems and calyx thickly clothed with violet, woolly hairs. The white corollas are about ¾ inch long.

Salvia leucantha

Popular hardy herbaceous perennials include **S. azurea** and its variety **S. a. grandiflora** (syn. *S. a. pitcheri*), both blue flowered. The first is native from South Carolina to Florida and Texas, the other in the more western part of that range. The variety, a finer garden plant than the species, differs in having more and bigger blooms, and in the hairs of its 4- to 6- or sometimes 8-foot-tall stems pointing downward. Both kinds have toothed, lanceolate to elliptic, or toothless, linear leaves 1½ to 4 inches long, and long, slender, interrupted spikes of blooms. The stems of the floral parts are glandular. The flowers of *S. azurea* are about ½ inch, those of *S. a. grandiflora* approximately ¾ inch, long. Its flowers violet-purple, **S. superba** (syn. *S. virgata nemorosa*) a sterile (non-seed-producing) hybrid of complex parentage that in gardens is often mis-identified as *S. nemorosa*. True **S. nemorosa** appears not to be in cultivation. The bushy hybrid is 2½ to 4 feet tall and has erect, branched stems, somewhat woody at their bases, and ovate-oblong to ob-

Salvia superba

Salvia superba (flowers)

long, round-toothed, grayish-green leaves 1 inch to 3 inches long, the lower ones mostly stalkless. The flowers, in crowded spikes 4 to 9 inches long, are associated with red-purple bracts. From 1 foot to 3½ feet tall, hardy herbaceous perennial **S. pratensis** (syn. *S. haematodes*) is a highly variable native of Europe occasionally naturalized in the United States. It has wrinkled, toothed, often red-spotted leaves, the basal ones long-stalked, with oblong to ovate blades, 2 to 6 inches long, with heart-shaped bases. The few stem leaves are smaller and stalkless. The bright blue flowers have a markedly sickle-shaped, hooded upper lip longer than the lower one. There are a number of varieties including *S. p. alba*, with white flowers; *S. p. atroviolacea*, the blooms of which are dark violet; *S. p. baumgartenii*, with violet blooms; *S. p. lupinoides*, which has bluish-purple and white flowers; *S. p. rosea*, with rosy-purple blooms; *S. p. rubi-*

cunda, the flowers of which are rose-red; *S. p. tenori*, its blooms deep blue; and *S. p. variegata*, which has a white center lobe to the lower lip of its light blue blooms.

Salvia pratensis

Other hardy herbaceous perennials are cultivated, among them *S. lyrata*, *S. nutans*, and *S. verticillata*. A native of woods and thickets from Connecticut to Illinois, Missouri, Florida, and Texas, **S. lyrata** has stems 1 foot to 3 feet tall. Its thinly-hairy principal leaves are in a basal rosette. From 4 to 9 inches long, stalked, generally obovate-oblong, they are deeply-pinnately-cleft into broad, rounded lobes. There is usually only a single pair of shorter-stalked, much smaller stem leaves of similar shape. The flowers, in rather distantly spaced tiers, are blue or violet and ¾ to 1 inch long. Southern Europe is home to **S. nutans**, a 3- to 4-foot-tall kind with mostly basal foliage. Its leaves are long-stalked. They have wrinkled, ovate-oblong blades, 4 to 7 inches long, with heart-shaped bases and double-toothed margins. Their undersides are white-woolly. Nodding in bud, so that they are upside down, the deep violet-purple blooms, about ⅓ inch long, are crowded in slender racemes. The floral bracts are very small. From 2 to 3 feet high, **S. verticillata** is indigenous from Europe to the Caucasus and Asia Minor and naturalized in North America. Erect and more or less bristly-hairy, it has stalked, broadly-ovate to fiddle-shaped, wavy-edged lower leaves, up to 6 inches long, and stalkless, smaller, toothless upper ones. The lilac-blue flowers, about ⅜ inch long, are crowded in distantly spaced whorls (tiers).

A good rock garden plant, **S. jurisicii** is very distinct by reason of its finely once- or twice-pinnately-divided upper leaves. Its

Salvia jurisicii

lower leaves are not cleft. They are ovate-oblong and toothed. Native to the Balkans, this hardy kind, 9 inches to 1½ feet tall, is hairless except along the margins of its leaves. The deep purple-blue or less commonly pink or white flowers, carried upside down, are hairy and about ¼ inch long and have widely divergent lips.

Annual salvias, as distinct from such nonhardy perennials as *S. farinacea*, *S. splendens*, and *S. guaranitica*, commonly cultivated as annuals, are *S. viridis*, *S. carduacea*, and *S. columbariae*. Most popular is southern European *S. viridis* (syn. *S. horminum*). Erect, branched, 1 foot to 2

Salvia viridis

feet tall, and with white-hairy stems and foliage, this has stalked, elliptic-oblong leaves. Its flowers, in distantly spaced whorls (tiers) of about six and from pale lilac to purple, are not showy. The chief display is made by the highly colored, or in one variety white, upper floral bracts.

These are longer than the blooms, broad, and purple, pink, or white. Referring to the colors of the bracts, garden varieties are named *S. v. alba*, *S. v.* 'Bluebeard' (syn. *S. v. violacea*), *S. v.* 'Oxford Blue', *S. v. purpurea*, and *S. v.* 'Rose Bouquet'. The thistle-sage, **S. carduacea** does indeed to the casual observer have much the aspect of a thistle. Native to California, 1 foot to 2 feet tall, and conspicuously white-hairy, it has elliptic to oblong basal leaves, that are pinnately-lobed, spiny-toothed and commonly 3 to 6 inches long. Erect and leafless, the flower stalks are 9 inches to 1½ feet in length. Their upper parts are occupied by close or well-separated whorls of lavender-blue to bluish-purple blooms from the axils of large, woolly-hairy spiny bracts. They have woolly-hairy calyxes, and corollas ¾ to 1 inch long. A quite different Californian annual, **S. columbariae** is 1 foot to 2 feet tall and softly-hairy. Its leaves are wrinkled and mostly basal. Those at the base of the plant are stalked and once- or twice-pinnately-cleft into blunt, not spine-tipped lobes. They are 2 to 5 inches long. The few stem leaves are smaller, once-pinnately-divided, and without stalks. The flowers, up to ½ inch long and bright blue, are many together interspersed with stiff, spine-tipped rosy-purple bracts in one or two nearly globular, headlike whorls 1 inch to 1½ inches in diameter at and near the ends of the stems and branches.

Biennial **S. argentea**, a native of the Mediterranean region, is 2 to 4 feet in height and softly-hairy. Its broad-ovate, stalked leaves, with blades 6 to 8 inches long by two-thirds as broad, are irregularly-toothed and sometimes shallowly-lobed. Their branches wide-spreading, the impressively large panicles are of whitish, yellowish, or reddish blooms, nearly 1 inch long, and in tiers (whorls) of six to eight. Also indigenous to the Mediterranean region, **S. barrelieri** (syn. *S. bicolor*) usually biennial, is sometimes perennial. From 2 to 3 feet in height and sparsely, if at all branched, this has stalked, toothed or lobed basal leaves up to 10 inches long, passing gradually to stalkless, ovate-lanceolate, toothless upper stem leaves. The slender, erect flower spikes are little or not branched. They have whorls of four to six blooms with white lower lips and upper ones bluish-violet spotted with yellow.

Garden and Landscape Uses. The garden and landscape employments of salvias are, according to kind, many and varied. Common sage, clary, and some others obviously belong in herb gardens. Probably the most widely cultivated ornamental salvias are the the annuals and nonhardy perennials grown as annuals for temporary summer flower displays. Chief among these are the scarlet and mealycup sages. The first in its several varieties and color forms is admirable for formal and

informal beds, edgings, porch and window boxes, and similar locations. The other, especially in its dwarfer varieties, is suitable for formal beds and excellent for grouping in mixed borders. Its blooms are useful for cutting. In mild climates scarlet and mealycup sages are permanent perennials. Where summers are not excessively hot the gentian-sage is also a good candidate for summer bedding. Other nonhardy perennial kinds are grown outdoors in regions of little frost, and especially those such as *S. leucantha*, and *S. dorisiana* that bloom in winter, in greenhouses. For warm, dry climates shrubby *S. clevelandii* is suitable. The not inconsiderable number of hardy herbaceous perennial salvias are admirable for grouping in mixed flower beds, and some, such as *S. superba*, are effective in large landscapes in beds by themselves. Except that they must be raised annually from seed, biennial salvias serve the same purposes as the hardy perennials.

Cultivation. As a group salvias are easy to manage. The hardy herbaceous perennials respond to deep, fertile soil, well-drained and moderately moist. They are easy to propagate by division and, except improved horticultural varieties, by seed. Early fall or spring are the best times to divide, and it is generally advisable to do this about every third year, planting the divisions in soil that has been improved by deep spading and adding organic material and fertilizer. In intervening years a spring application of a complete fertilizer is appropriate. Tall kinds need staking. After fall frost kills the foliage, remove the tops, and in harsh climates, after the ground is frozen to a depth of an inch or two, give a protective covering of salt or marsh hay, branches of evergreens, or other such material.

Nonhardy perennial salvias are grown permanently outdoors in warm, frostless or nearly frostless regions, and in greenhouses. They give of their best in fertile, well-drained, moderately moist soil in sun, and are easily increased by seed and by cuttings. Sunny, arid and semiarid climates are to the liking of *S. clevelandii*. In greenhouses, the nonhardy perennials are satisfied with winter night temperatures of 50°F with a daytime increase of five to fifteen degrees permitted. Full sun, or at most very light shade in summer, and airy conditions are needed. Environments satisfactory for geraniums and chrysanthemums suit these salvias. Plants started in late winter, spring, or early summer from seed or cuttings are first potted individually in small pots and successively into larger ones until they occupy the ones in which they are to bloom. Depending upon the species and the time of propagation these may be from 5 to 8 inches in diameter. When the final pots are filled with roots, weekly applications of dilute liquid fertilizer are in order. To ensure shapely, bushy specimens of such kinds as *S. leucantha* and *S. dorisiana* it is necessary during their early stages to pinch out the tips of their shoots occasionally to encourage bushiness. The gentian-sage has tuberous roots. It is possible to winter this by storing the clumps of roots like those of dahlias, but in general it is better to raise new plants each year from seed sown early indoors.

For summer bedding, the scarlet, mealy-cup, and gentian-sages and *S. guaranitica* are most commonly raised from seed sown in a greenhouse or other place indoors. They are successful, but come into bloom later, when seeded directly outdoors. Ten to twelve weeks before it is safe to set the plants in the garden, which in the case of the mealycup sage is as soon as all danger of frost is passed, and with the other sorts about the time it is safe to plant tomatoes or a little later, is the time to sow indoors. Grow the resulting plants of the scarlet sage in a night temperature of 60°F and daytime temperatures up to fifteen degrees higher. For mealycup sage and gentian-sage, temperatures ten degrees lower are appropriate. The young plants, preferably grown singly in pots rather than in flats, when 3 or 4 inches high should have the tips of their shoots pinched out to promote branching. Before planting outside, harden the plants by standing them in their containers in a cold frame or sheltered, sunny place outdoors for a couple of weeks.

Annual and biennial salvias are raised by sowing seed outdoors, those of the annuals in spring where the plants are to remain, those of the biennials in May or June in a cold frame or an outdoor nursery bed. All that is needed with the annuals is to thin out the seedlings so that they are not unhappily crowded. As soon as the biennials are big enough to handle, transplant them about 6 inches apart in nursery beds or cold frames to make their first season's growth. In fall or early spring carefully transplant to their flowering sites. For cultivation of common sage as a culinary herb see Sage.

SALVINIA (Sal-vínia) — Floating-Moss. This genus and *Azolla* constitute the salvinia family SALVINIACEAE, a group of ferns of wide distribution in the tropics and warm parts of the world. The name *Salvinia* honors Antonio Maria Salvini, a professor of Florence, Italy. He died in 1729.

Salvinias are floating plants, with larger leaves than *Azolla*, borne in threes, two of which are floating and two-ranked, but not dissected, and the other submersed and divided into slender lobes that look like roots. The upper sides of the floating leaves are covered with tiny pustules, the lower sides with densely matted hairs. There are about ten species.

Salvinia auriculata

Frequently cultivated *S. auriculata* is often misidentified by having attached to it the name of another species, *S. natans*. It is a native of tropical South America and the West Indies. This has broadly-elliptic leaves with heart-shaped bases, the upper sides of which are clothed with erect, stiff hairs arising from minute protuberances. Its appearance varies considerably according to the conditions under which it is grown. In strong daylight the leaves are over 1 inch in length and crowd so that their edges are lifted above the water level. Under less favorable circumstances they are smaller and lie flat on the water and some little distance apart. The plants are up to 10 inches long.

Floating-moss (*S. rotundifolia*), of tropical America, has nearly circular floating leaves up to ¾ inch long, with erect, stiff hairs sprouting from minute protuberances, on plants up to 2¾ inches long. In this species the hairs of each cluster of four are quite separate and not, like those of *S. auriculata*, united.

Garden Uses and Cultivation. Salvinias afford shelter, shade, and spawning places for fish. Because of this, they are useful in

aquariums as well as for decorating surfaces of pools in greenhouses and similar environments. They thrive, with little care, in water 65 to 75°F. Good light with shade from strong sun is needed and for their best development the air above the water should be constantly humid. This can be assured by covering aquariums with a sheet of glass or transparent plastic. Water that contains some nutritious detritus of soil or mud is most favorable to growth. Because of this, they usually do best in shallow water. Propagation is rapid by natural division and spores.

SALVINIACEAE — Salvinia Family. About sixteen species of little, free-floating, aquatic ferns distributed in two genera constitute this family. Widely distributed as natives in the tropics, they have undivided, lobeless or two-lobed leaves. The spore cases are in soft, spore-bearing organs called sporocarps on the undersides of the leaves. The genera are *Azolla* and *Salvinia*.

SAMANEA (Sam-anèa)—Rain Tree or Monkey Pod or Samen. By some authorities included in *Pithecellobium*, the genus *Samanea*, of the pea family LEGUMINOSAE, considered separately consists of approximately twenty species indigenous to tropical America and Africa. Its name is derived from a native South American one.

Samaneas are thornless shrubs and trees with alternate, twice-pinnate leaves. Their small flowers, in spherical or pompon-like heads, have five-parted calyxes, five petals, and many stamens united at their bases. The fruits are pods.

The rain tree or monkey pod (*S. saman* syn. *Pithecellobium saman*) is unlikely to be overlooked by visitors to the tropics and warm subtropics who are interested in plants. One of the most impressive and distinctive of large trees, it is commonly planted for shade and for ornament. In

Samanea saman

Spanish-speaking lands it is called samen or zamen. The common name rain tree refers to the leaflets of its leaves folding together in dull, cloudy weather and at night. Not infrequently this magnificent species attains heights of 60 to 70 feet and spreads its branches over a circle up to 100 feet in diameter. Its umbrella-shaped crown is very characteristic. Nor are the dimensions given maximums. From Trinidad is recorded a specimen 147 feet in height with a branch spread of 187 feet.

The rain tree has leaves 9 inches to 1¼ feet long, with two to six pairs of primary divisions each with three to eight pairs of asymmetrical, obscurely-diamond-shaped leaflets that have undersides, like the midrib and lateral ribs that bear them, velvety-hairy. The leaflets are up to about 1½ inches in length. About 2½ inches in diameter, the long-stalked *Albizzia*-like, powder-puff heads of flowers, with long-protruding stamens, are grouped near the ends of the branchlets. They are attractive to bees. Each head consists of many flowers with slender, pinkish-green, five-lobed corolla tubes, up to ½ inch long, and clusters of stamens about 1½ inches long. The stamens, white toward their bases and pink in their upper parts, are the showy parts of the flowers. Straight or slightly curved, the flat seed pods, blackish or brown, have much thickened margins and are 4 to 8 inches long by up to ¾ inch wide. Their several seeds are embedded in sweetish pulp. They have a licorice flavor and are relished by cattle, hogs, and goats and are sometimes eaten by humans.

Garden and Landscape Uses and Cultivation. As an ornamental, and for providing shade, the rain tree or monkey pod is highly desirable in humid tropical and subtropical regions. A noble species, it is only seen to best advantage where there is ample room for it to spread its mighty branches and to display its beauty. In dryish soils it grows more slowly and never becomes as big as where adequate continuous moisture is available; nevertheless it can be very satisfactory under dryish conditions and is less likely to suffer storm damage than in places where it develops a huge crown. It provides abundant shade and because of this is appreciated in pastures, parks, and public and home grounds and at roadsides. It has certain disadvantages. One is that its many surface and shallow roots, avid searchers for moisture and nutrients, so deplete the soil that it is often difficult or impossible to persuade other plants to grow under or near rain trees. Another point to remember is that large specimens are apt to be uprooted by gales. Because of this it is not wise to plant this tree close to buildings or other places where serious harm could result from such a happening. Established specimens need little attention. Propagation is by seed.

SAMARA. A dry, winged fruit that does not split to release the seed is a samara. The fruits of ashes and maples are examples of these.

SAMBUCUS (Sam-bùcus) — Elder or Elderberry, Danewort. Probably few nonbotanists connect elders (*Sambucus*) with honeysuckles (*Lonicera*), yet they belong in the honeysuckle family CAPRIFOLIACEAE. The name *Sambucus* is the Roman one of *S. nigra*. Most of the forty species of the genus are deciduous shrubs, a few are herbaceous perennials. They are natives of many temperate parts of the northern and southern hemispheres and of mountains in the tropics. Several are indigenous to North America.

From viburnums, abelias, weigelas, kolkwitzias, and other shrubs with which they share kinship, elders or elderberries differ in having pinnate leaves, always with an odd number of leaflets. The leaves are opposite, the leaflets toothed. The white or whitish, wheel-shaped flowers, up to ¼ inch in diameter, are in terminal panicles or flattish, often large clusters. They have a calyx with five or rarely fewer teeth, a wheel-shaped corolla with usually five, sometimes fewer lobes (petals), five or less often fewer stamens, and one three- to five-lobed style or sometimes none. The fruits are small, juicy, and berry-like drupes. Those of some species are pleasant to eat, certain others are reported to be poisonous. The cultivated elders are all deciduous.

The sweet elder or American elder (*S. canadensis*) is indigenous from Nova Scotia to Florida and Texas. It closely resem-

Sambucus canadensis

bles the European elder (*S. nigra*), a native of Europe, western Asia, and North Africa, and like it has large flat clusters of white flowers in summer, and edible fruits. There are a few garden varieties that have been selected because of the good quality of their fruits; these have horticultural names. From its European counterpart, the American elder differs in having less warty

Sambucus nigra

shoots and leaves of usually seven instead of mostly five leaflets. Also, it does not grow as tall as *S. nigra*, which at its best may reach 30 feet; maximum height for *S. canadensis* is about 12 feet. Both species have shoots with large cores of white pith. Their flowers, and their foliage and stems if bruised, emit a characteristic, not particularly pleasant odor. The fruits are glossy-black, but not glaucous.

Varieties of the American elder are *S. canadensis acutiloba*, with much-dissected foliage; *S. c. aurea*, with yellow foliage; *S. c. chlorocarpa*, with light green leaves and greenish fruits; *S. c. maxima*, with flower clusters up to 1 foot or more across; *S. c. rubra*, with bright red fruits; and *S. c. submollis*, which has the undersides of its leaves softly-grayish-hairy. Varieties of the European elder are *S. nigra albo-variegata*, with white-variegated leaves; *S. n. aurea*, with yellow foliage; *S. n. aureo-variegata*, with leaves variegated with yellow; *S. n. flore-pleno*, with double flowers; *S. n. heterophylla*, with leaves irregularly-toothed and cut into threads or sometimes reduced to little more than midribs; *S. n. laciniata*, with deeply and evenly dissected leaves; *S. n. pendula*, with drooping or prostrate branches; *S. n. pyramidalis*, an upright, columnar kind; *S. n. rosea flore-*

Sambucus nigra laciniata

pleno, with double pinkish flowers; and *S. n. rotundifolia*, which has nearly round leaves of usually three leaflets.

Sambucus nigra tricolor

The blue elder (**S. caerulea** syn. *S. glauca*), native from California to Utah and British Columbia, is a slender-branched shrub or tree up to 30 or sometimes 50 feet in height. When young, its shoots are glaucous. The leaves have five to seven bright green, coarsely-toothed, oblong to oblong-lanceolate leaflets. The yellowish flowers, in clusters 4 to 6 inches or sometimes more in diameter, appear in late spring or summer. Especially striking are the blue-black fruits, so thickly glaucous (covered with a waxy deposit) that they appear bluish or almost white. They are edible. This species is hardy in southern New England.

Two red-fruited elders are *S. pubens* and *S. racemosa*. Both are hardy in New England. They bloom in spring. The American red elder **S. pubens** is native from New Brunswick to Georgia and Colorado. Up to 15 feet tall, it has stems with brownish-red pith. Its shoots, and its leaves on their undersides, are hairy, at least when young. Each leaf has five to seven oblong, toothed leaflets 2 to 4 inches long. The yellowish flowers are in terminal, loose, pyramidal panicles, up to 4 inches in length, with their lower branches spreading nearly horizontally. The fruits, ¼ inch in diameter, are bright red. From *S. pubens* the European red elder **(S. racemosa)** differs in having stems with light brown pith, the young shoots and undersides of its leaves hairless, and the lower branches of the dense flower clusters, up to 3 inches long, reflexed. The European red elder attains a height of about 12 feet.

Varieties of the American red elder are *S. pubens dissecta*, with deeply dissected leaflets; *S. p. leucocarpa*, with white fruits; and *S. p. xanthocarpa*, with fruits amber-yellow. Varieties of the European red elder are *S. racemosa flavescens*, with fruits yellow or yellow flushed with red on one side; *S. r. laciniata*, with deeply-dissected leaf-

Sambucus racemosa

lets; *S. r. ornata*, with the leaflets of its lower leaves very deeply-toothed (to about their middles) and those nearer the ends of the shoots deeply-dissected into slender segments; *S. r. plumosa*, with very deeply-toothed leaflets (the teeth extending almost to the centers of the leaflets); *S. r. plumosa-aurea*, similar to the last, but with golden-yellow foliage; *S. r. purpurea*, with flowers purple in the bud and later purplish or pinkish on their outsides; and *S. r. tenuifolia*, with very finely-dissected foliage purplish when young.

A non-shrubby herbaceous kind that dies to the ground each winter is the dwarf elder or danewort **(S. ebulus)**. This native of Europe, western Asia, and North Africa oc-

Sambucus ebulus

curs spontaneously as a rare escape from cultivation from Quebec to New Jersey. About 3 feet in height, it has spreading underground stems, and leaves with five to nine leaflets, the lateral ones very un-

equal at their bases. Its pleasantly fragrant flowers are creamy to pinkish, with purple anthers. The berries are black.

Garden and Landscape Uses. Elders are seen to best advantage in extensive landscapes where they can be massed and viewed from some distance. They are generally too vigorous and coarse for small properties; they do not lend themselves to the ornamentation of intimate gardens. Their fruits are appreciated by birds, and for this reason are worth planting in some areas. The American species are appropriate in native plant gardens. All grow with great vigor in moistish soils and adapt well to drier ones. They grow in sun or part-day shade and withstand windy and seaside environments well. For floral effect, the large-trussed *S. canadensis maxima* is the best of the black-fruited kinds. If fruits for pies, jellies, or wines are the chief interest, one of the improved horticultural varieties of *S. canadensis*, selected especially for superior size and quality of its berries, such as 'Adams', should be chosen. The typical species *S. nigra* is so similar to, and no better than, *S. canadensis* that, except as a collection item, there is no advantage in planting it. As foliage shrubs, where golden leafage is appropriate *S. canadensis aurea* and *S. nigra aurea*, are worthwhile; because of their vigor they do not have the sickly appearance characteristic of golden-leaved varieties of many shrubs. Kinds with finely-cut leaves, *S. canadensis acutiloba*, *S. nigra laciniata*, and *S. pubens dissecta* also offer a change of pace, their foliage differing in texture and effect from that of the species from which they derive. The usually red-cheeked, yellow fruits of *S. racemosa flavescens* offer variety from the scarlet ones typical of the species. Change from the scarlet fruits of *S. pubens* is provided by *S. p. leucocarpa* and *S. p. xanthocarpa*, with white and yellow fruits, respectively. The gray-blue fruits of *S. caerulea* are unique among elders.

Cultivation. Elders are tough plants that persist even under ill-treatment, but are likely to become straggly and unkempt under such circumstances. They have the ability to renew themselves from their bases after being cut back, even severely. This treatment is used to rehabilitate ill-shaped and overgrown specimens. Late winter or early spring is the best time to prune. Beyond occasional attention to this detail no particular care is needed. Propagation is by seed, by hardwood and leafy cuttings, and in some cases by removal of rooted portions of established plants.

SAMOLUS (Sámol-us)—Water-Pimpernel, Green Water-Rose, Underwater-Rose. The genus *Samolus*, of the primrose family PRIMULACEAE, consists of some ten species of perennial herbaceous plants, sometimes woody at their bases, natives of temperate North America, South America, Europe,

Asia, South Africa, and Australia. The name was employed by the Romans for a plant used by the Druids and is probably Celtic in origin.

Samoluses have undivided, lobeless leaves, sometimes in basal rosettes, and small white flowers in terminal racemes. The blooms have deeply-five-lobed corollas with a tiny scalelike appendage between each pair of lobes. There are five stamens and a very short style. The fruits are capsules.

An amphibious plant (one that lives on water and land), *S. parviflorus* (syn. *S. floribundus*) inhabits muddy stream banks, sandbars, and brackish shores through much of the United States and parts of Canada, as well as Central America, South America, and the West Indies. From 4 inches to 1 foot tall and branching, it has a rosette of leaves at the base and alternate ones on the stems. Usually 1 inch to 2 inches long, but sometimes longer, the leaves are spoon-shaped to obovate. The flowers, up to ⅛ inch across, are in loose racemes. When growing as an underwater plant this species does not bloom, but multiplies by offset shoots. A similar species, European *S. valerandi*, has narrower leaves.

Garden Uses and Cultivation. Although not showy in bloom, the kinds cultivated are attractive because of their basal rosettes of foliage, fancifully likened to green roses. They are grown submersed in aquariums, in shallow water in pools, and in wet soils by watersides. In aquariums they require strong illumination and water not above 68°F. Under such conditions they are evergreen. They thrive in sandy earth and in neutral or slightly acid water.

SAMPHIRE. See Crithmum.

SAMUELA (Samu-éla) — Date-Yucca. This genus of two species is endemic to Texas and Mexico. Closely related to *Yucca*, it belongs in the lily family LILIACEAE. Its name commemorates Dr. Sam Farlow Trelease, American botanist, who died in 1958.

Samuelas are trees with erect trunks and, crowded in tufts at their tops, many sharp-pointed, grooved, slender leaves with filamentous frayings at their margins. The white flowers, with six united perianth segments (petals, or more correctly, tepals) and six stamens, are in dense panicles. The fruits are capsules 2 to 3 inches long. In Mexico the flowers and fruits are eaten. The pulp of the trunks is used for stock feed.

Native to Texas and adjacent Mexico, *Samuela faxoniana*, up to 15 feet in height, is often branched at the top and has leaves up to 4 feet long by 3 inches wide. The broadly-pyramidal flower clusters have blooms up to 4 inches in diameter, with perianth tubes up to ½ inch long. Mexican

S. carnerosana, up to 18 feet tall, rarely branches. Its leaves are about 1½ feet long by 3 inches broad. The blooms, as large as those of *S. faxoniana*, have 1-inch-long perianth tubes.

Garden and Landscape Uses. These are attractive small trees of distinctive form and appearance, suitable for garden and landscape use in warm, dry climates such as that of the southwestern United States. Their trunks provide strong vertical lines topped by feather-duster heads of foliage and, in season, decorative clusters of flowers. Samuelas associate well with succulents and other dry-region plants and are effective near buildings and other architectural features.

Cultivation. Well-drained soil and a sunny location are needed. Established specimens need no special care. Seed affords an easy means of propagation. Transplanting is best done just before new growth begins. In greenhouses and conservatories, samuelas may be accommodated among collections of succulent plants. They respond to the care that suits yuccas, dasylirions, and other thin-leaved desert plants. For general information see Succulents.

SANCHEZIA (San-chèzia). The genus *Sanchezia*, of the acanthus family ACANTHACEAE, includes about sixty species of vigorous, erect or climbing herbaceous plants and shrubs of Central and South America. One is cultivated. The name commemorates Josef Sanchez, an eighteenth-century professor of botany at Cadiz, Spain.

Sanchezias, mostly hairless, have large, opposite, conspicuously-veined, somewhat toothed or smooth-margined leaves and generally both terminal and axillary spikes of showy orange, red, or purple, tubular flowers interspersed with calyx-like bracts that hide the five-lobed calyx. The usually curved corolla tube enlarges in its

upper part and expands into five short, broad lobes of equal size. There are two fertile stamens and two staminodes (nonfunctional stamens). The slender style is slightly two-lobed at its apex. The fruits are capsules containing six to eight seeds.

Known only as a cultivated plant, but perhaps a native of Ecuador or Peru, *S. speciosa*, in gardens often misidentified as *S. nobilis*, is sometimes named *S. glaucophylla*. A rounded, dense, hairless shrub 3 to 5 feet in height, it has four-angled shoots and short-pointed, oblong-ovate leaves that taper to short stalks and are widest near their middles. Up to 1 foot long or longer, and sparsely-toothed or toothless, they usually have well-defined yellow or whitish veins. The rich yellow flowers, in erect spikes, are about 2 inches long and interspersed with red bracts about 1½ inches long. The species *S. nobilis*, a native of Ecuador probably not in cultivation, differs from *S. speciosa* in its leaves being widest well above their middles and in the staminodes of the flowers being ¹⁄₁₆ instead of ¾ to 1 inch long.

Garden and Landscape Uses. In the far south and in the tropics, *S. speciosa* is a

Sanchezia speciosa (flowers)

Sanchezia speciosa

handsome ornamental for fertile, not-too-dry soil and sunny locations. It is also grown in tropical greenhouses and conservatories and may be used in the north for outdoor summer bedding.

Cultivation. Among the easiest of tropical shrubs to grow, the sort commonly cultivated responds to adequately drained, rich soil and an abundance of water. If it outgrows the space allotted or becomes straggly it may be pruned with impunity, after which it soon renews itself by new shoots from the base. Pruning is best done at the beginning of a new growing season, or in the tropics, as soon as flowering is through. Young plants are improved by pinching out the tips of their shoots once or twice to encourage branching. In greenhouses a minimum night temperature of 60°F is best, but five degrees or so lower is acceptable. By day the temperature may rise five to ten degrees above that maintained at night and in summer both day and night temperatures will of course exceed those maintained in winter. A humid atmosphere and good light are needed. Give only enough shade to prevent scorching of the foliage. Keep the soil at all times fairly moist and from spring through fall provide weekly or biweekly applications of dilute liquid fertilizer. Propagation is simply accomplished by cuttings set in a greenhouse propagating bed and by seed.

SAND. The best sand for horticultural employments, which include its use as an ingredient of potting soils and as a medium in which to root cuttings, consists of angular particles of silica or quartz of pinhead size or slightly bigger, free of clay and other fine particles.

Called coarse or sharp sand, such material may be obtained from banks or pits. Because of the salts it contains, seashore sand is not suitable for use unless it has been leached by leaving it exposed to rains over a period of several weeks or months or by washing it thoroughly several times with water, pouring the water off between successive washings. See also the Encyclopedia discussion in the entry Soils and Their Management.

SAND. The word sand occurs as parts of the vernacular names of these plants: sand cherry (*Prunus besseyi* and *P. pumila*), sand-lily (*Leucocrinum montanum*), sand- myrtle (*Leiophyllum buxifolium*), sand pear (*Pyrus pyrifolia* and *P. p. culta*), and sand-verbena (*Abronia*).

SAND-CORN is *Zigadenus paniculatus*.

SANDALWOOD is *Santalum album*. Bastard sandalwood is *Myoporum sandwicense*.

SANDALWOOD TREE or RED SANDAL-WOOD TREE is *Adenanthera pavonina*.

SANDBOX TREE is *Hura crepitans*.

SANDERSONIA (Sander-sònia). To the lily family LILIACEAE belongs the only species of this South African genus. It is named after John Sanderson, a nineteenth-century secretary of the Horticultural Society of Natal.

An elegant, tuberous-rooted, herbaceous plant 1 foot to 2 feet tall, *Sandersonia aurantiaca* has slender, upright stems foliaged throughout their lengths.

Sandersonia aurantiaca

The leaves are alternate or occasionally opposite, and stalkless. The lower ones are oblong-lanceolate; those on the upper parts of the stems are narrowly-lanceolate and more or less erect and often end in curving slender points that look like the beginnings of tendrils. They are 2 to 4 inches long. The charming flowers, suggesting gay, Chinese lanterns, nod from each of three to eight upper leaf axils. On longish stalks, and bright orange-yellow, they have six perianth segments, free at their tips as short, spreading petals, but joined for most of their lengths into a nearly globose bell ¾ to 1 inch in diameter. This contains six short stamens much overtopped by a three-branched style. The fruits are capsules.

Garden and Landscape Uses and Cultivation. This gracious species is an asset to collectors of summer-flowering bulbs. It is not hardy in the north, but is reliably so in warm-temperate and subtropical regions where the ground does not freeze in winter. It is attractive for flower borders and rock gardens. Where content, it self-sows with agreeable freedom. Seedlings first bloom when about three years old. In addition to its usefulness outdoors, this species grows well in pots or ground beds in cool, sunny greenhouses, responding to the environment and care appropriate for gloriosas.

SANDPAPER TREE is *Ficus exasperata*.

SANDPAPER VINE. See Petrea.

SANDWORT. See Arenaria.

SANGUINARIA (Sanguin-ària) — Bloodroot, Red Puccoon. One rather variable North American species constitutes this genus. It inhabits rich woods from Nova Scotia to Ontario, Manitoba, Florida, Alabama, and Oklahoma. It belongs in the poppy family PAPAVERACEAE and earns its colloquial name by reason of its red or reddish-yellow sap. Its generic name also alludes to that characteristic. It is derived from the Latin *sanguis*, blood.

The bloodroot (*Sanguinaria canadensis*) is a spring-blooming, deciduous herba-

Sanguinaria canadensis

ceous perennial with a fleshy underground rhizome several inches long. Each bud on the rhizome usually develops only one leaf, rounded in outline and with three to nine toothed or wavy-edged lobes arranged palmately (in handlike fashion). The leaves have stalks about 8 inches long and their blades are about as wide. They are only partly developed at blooming time. The pure white or pinkish flowers, 1 inch to 1½ inches in diameter, are on stalks up to 8 inches tall. Each usually has eight or sometimes up to sixteen petals, in two to four rows, and numerous stamens. They are succeeded by seed capsules about 1 inch long. A very lovely variety is *S. c. multiplex* (syn. *S. c. plena*), the blooms of which have additional petals in place of stamens

Sanguinaria canadensis multiplex

and are fully double. This garden treasure flowers a few days later than the single-flowered kind and has blooms that last considerably longer.

Garden Uses. Bloodroots, both single- and double-flowered, are splendid additions to wild gardens, rock gardens, and native plant gardens and can be used to good purpose among open shrubbery and beneath trees that do not cast too dense shade if the ground is not too impregnated with hungry roots and is moderately moist. They succeed in full sun in adequately humid soil and are also most effective when set out in natural-looking drifts or colonies.

Cultivation. Bloodroots, without pronounced soil preferences, grow as well in alkaline earth (above pH 7) as in a somewhat acid medium. Whether clayey or sandy, enriched with some nourishing leaf mold or other decayed organic matter, any ordinary garden soil is likely to prove agreeable. In poorish soil a spring application of a complete fertilizer promotes growth, and under any circumstances the plants benefit from a mulch of compost, leaf mold, peat moss, or sawdust. If sawdust is used, it is advisable to make a second application of fertilizer some few weeks after the first to supply additional nitrogen. Propagation of the double-flowered kind is by division of the rhizomes only. These may be broken or cut into pieces so small that each contains only one eye or bud, or larger pieces may be used. Division is done in late summer or early fall after the foliage has ripened and may be repeated every two or three years until an adequate stock of plants is attained. Unless increase is desired, established plants may be left undisturbed for many years. The single-flowered kind can be multiplied in the same way or raised from seeds sown in a shaded cold frame or outdoor bed where they will not be subject to disturbance. A sandy, peaty soil is suitable for seed sowing. When transplanting bloodroots it is important not to allow their roots to dry. A planting distance of 6 to 8 inches between individuals is adequate. Late August and September is the best time for transplanting.

SANGUISORBA (Sangui-sòrba) — Burnet. Consisting of perhaps as many as five species of hardy herbaceous perennials, *Sanguisorba*, of the rose family ROSACEAE, inhabits temperate parts of the northern hemisphere. Its name, from the Latin *sanguis*, blood, and *sorebere*, to absorb, alludes to supposed styptic properties of some kinds. The genus *Poterium*, in this Encyclopedia treated separately, is by some authorities included in *Sanguisorba*.

Sanguisorbas have short, thick rhizomes and pinnate leaves with few to many toothed or lobed, opposite leaflets and a terminal one. In dense spikes or heads, the small blooms are without petals. They have four petal-like sepals united at their bases, four to numerous or rarely only two stamens, and one or two pistils and styles. The fruits are achenes.

American burnet (**S. canadensis** syn. *Poterium canadense*) inhabits damp and wet

Sanguisorba canadensis

soils from Labrador to Manitoba, New Jersey, and Indiana, in the mountains to North Carolina, and perhaps in Asia. It has stems, usually branched only above, up to 6 feet in height. The leaves, of seven to seventeen ovate to oblong or elliptic, toothed leaflets 1½ to 3½ inches long, are up to 1½ feet long, the lower ones the largest, those above progressively smaller. The long-stalked, cylindrical spikes of bisexual, white flowers are 1½ to 5 inches long. The stamens protrude conspicuously to produce a feathery effect. Each bloom has one pistil. From all other sanguisorbas this differs in its flowers opening in succession from the tops of the spikes downward.

Great burnet (**S. officinalis**) is much like the last, but usually not over 3 feet in height. It has leaves with three to seven pairs of stalked leaflets, and purple-brown flowers in thick spikes up to 1¼ inches long. Their stamens do not protrude. The flowers have one branchless style. Native to Europe and Asia, this is sparingly naturalized in North America. Japanese *S. o. carnea* has flesh-red flowers.

Endemic to moist subalpine meadows in northern Italy, **S. dodecandra** is 1½ to 3 feet tall. Its leaves have up to ten pairs of elliptic, stalked leaflets about 3 inches long. Its greenish to whitish flowers, in cylindrical spikes up to 3 inches long, have four to fifteen protruding stamens.

Variable northern Asian **S. tenuifolia** (syn. *Poterium tenuifolium*) has mostly basal foliage and attains heights up to 4 feet. Its leaves have thirteen to twenty-one deeply-toothed, long, linear-oblong leaflets. The flowers, in spikes up to 2 inches long, are white to purple-red. Variety *S. t. alba* is a Japanese variant with greenish-white or white blooms; *S. t. purpurea*, also Japanese, has blood-red flowers; and *S. t. grandiflora*, of northern Japan, is an alpine with comparatively shorter stems and thicker flower spikes.

Japanese **S. obtusa** (syn. *Poterium obtusum*) is a rare native of alpine meadows.

Sanguisorba obtusa

From 1 foot to 2 feet in height, or sometimes taller in cultivation, it has leaves of thirteen to seventeen densely-arranged, toothed, oblong, almost stalkless leaflets, usually with brown hairs on the veins on their undersides. The pale rose-pink flowers are in nodding spikes 1½ to 3½ inches in length.

Garden and Landscape Uses and Cultivation. Sanguisorbas are suitable for grouping in beds and borders and for planting in naturalistic surroundings. The American kinds are appropriate for native plant gardens. They are easy to manage, and thrive in ordinary, reasonably fertile garden soil in full sun or where shaded for only a small part of each day. Propagation is very easy by division, in spring or early fall, and by seed.

SANSEVIERIA (Sansev-ièria)—Snake Plant, Bowstring-Hemp. The genus *Sansevieria* belongs in the lily family LILIACEAE. It comprises about seventy species of the tropics and subtropics of Africa, Malagasy (Madagascar), and Asia. It was named in honor of an eighteenth-century Prince of Sansevicro.

Sansevierias have stout, horizontal rhizomes or erect stems and stiff, upright or more or less spreading, flat, concave or cylindrical leaves containing many strong fibers. At the bases of the leaves are prominent bracts. The white, greenish, or creamy flowers are in long spikes, racemes, or clusters. They are tubular, with usually swollen bases, six narrow spreading perianth lobes (petals), six stamens, and a slender style tipped with a knoblike stigma. The fruits are berries containing one to three seeds.

Few indoor plants are more familiar or are as tolerant of abuse as the common snake plant and its varieties. In their ability to survive under difficult conditions and to withstand ill-treatment, these are the donkeys of the houseplant world, and like those patient beasts, they are often mildly despised by those they serve; contempt born of familiarity and perhaps because they ask for so little seems often to be their lot. Yet the common snake plant and its kin, and there are a good many more kinds than we shall discuss here, are quite handsome and useful decoratives. Some, called bowstring-hemps, are sources of useful fibers. In Africa, parts of Asia, and other warm regions, their products are used for bowstrings, fishing lines, cordage, mats, sails, and hammocks. Among the several species so employed are *S. hyacinthoides* and *S. zeylanica*.

The common snake plant (**S. trifasciata**) has horizontal rhizomes from which

Sansevieria trifasciata (flowers)

Sansevieria trifasciata (fruits)

arise erect, rigid, linear-lanceolate to sword-shaped, pointed leaves, channeled toward their bases, and up to 4½ feet tall and 1½ inches broad, but often smaller. Each cluster consists of eight to fifteen

leaves, dark green marked with broad, light gray, horizontal bands. The many-bracted flower stalks have very fragrant, greenish-white blooms that open at night. Variety *S. t. laurentii* is distinguished by its leaves having longitudinal marginal

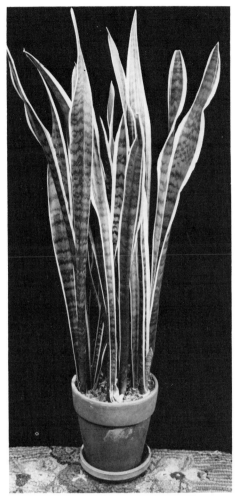

Sansevieria trifasciata laurentii

bands of golden-yellow. A variant, known as *S. t. l. compacta,* with richer colored leaves, is less than 1½ feet in height. Somewhat slower growing *S. t. craigii* is similar to *S. t. laurentii,* but has broader, paler yellow marginal stripes. Creamy-white marginal bands with occasional additional longitudinal bands distinguish *S. t. goldiana.* Quite distinct is *S. t.* 'Bantel's Sensation'. Its slender leaves are very variable. Commonly, one-half is plain green with whitish crossbars and the other golden-yellow with adjoining bands of white margined with green. Some leaves may display only one of these patterns exclusively.

Very dwarf, broadly-vase-shaped variants of *S. trifasciata* are *S. t. hahnii, S. t.* 'Golden Hahnii', and *S. t.* 'Silver Hahnii'. Except for their colors, these are similar. They have rhizomes and increase by offsets. Not over a few inches tall, and rather resembling small agaves, they have broad, short, pointed leaves more or less spirally arranged and bending outward to form

Sansevieria trifasciata hahnii

vase- or bird-nest-shaped plants. In *S. t. hahnii* the color is dark green with cross-bands of light gray. The leaves of *S. t.* 'Golden Hahnii' have, in addition, broad, golden-yellow to cream-colored bands. Those of *S. t.* 'Silver Hahnii' are narrower than those of the other two and evenly pale metallic-silvery-green with a few darker spots.

African **S. hyacinthoides** (syns. *S. guineensis, S. thyrsiflora*) has rhizomes from

Sansevieria hyacinthoides

which arise clusters of two to four flat or nearly flat, lanceolate leaves up to 1½ feet long by 3½ inches wide, tapering toward their bases into channeled leafstalks. The dark green leaves, narrowly-edged with brownish-red, are cross-banded with lighter green, which tends to fade or disappear with age. The flowers, in spikelike racemes, are greenish-white and fragrant. In cultivation this species is often misidentified as *S. zeylanica*.

Cylindrical leaves, pointed, rigid, arching, and usually furrowed, are borne by **S. cylindrica.** They are up to 5 feet long by 1¼ inches in diameter, and are in clusters

Sansevieria cylindrica

Sansevieria ehrenbergii

Sansevieria patens

Sansevieria nelsonii

Sansevieria powellii

of three or four from horizontal rhizomes. Dark green, when young they are cross-banded with gray-green. The flowers of this African species are pinkish. Its leaves also cylindrical, grooved, and from horizontal rhizomes, but very much more flexible than those of the last, *S. canaliculata* is a slow-growing, tropical African kind that does not ordinarily exceed 3 feet in height.

Other sansevierias sometimes culti-vated include the following kinds: *S. arborescens,* of East Africa, has stems up to 4 feet tall, and slender, channeled, horny-white-edged, spreading leaves. *S. aubry-tiana,* of East Africa, has erect, sword-shaped, dark green leaves up to 4 feet long by 4 to 7 inches broad, marked with hori-zontal silvery-gray bands. *S. ehrenbergii,* of Ethiopia and southward, has erect stems concealed by the clasping bases of its up-right, two-ranked, bluish-green leaves. *S. grandicuspis,* a native of tropical Africa, has leaves approximately 1½ feet long and up to 1¼ inches wide. They are dull green,

cross-banded with pale grayish-green. *S. grandis,* of East Africa, perches on trees as an epiphyte (not taking nourishment from its hosts). It has few, short, dull green, silver-banded, red-edged leaves up to 6 inches broad and dense panicles of white flowers. *S. intermedia,* of East Africa, has many gray-green, deeply-chan-neled, thick, spreading, recurving leaves marked with paler horizontal bands. *S. kirkii,* of East Africa, has flat or concave leaves up to 6 feet tall and 3½ inches broad. They are grayish-green mottled or barred with pale green. *S. grandicuspis* is often grown under the name of this last. *S. liberica,* of West Africa, is 2 to 3 feet tall and has erect, thick leaves with verti-cal bands of white or greenish-white. *S. metallica,* of tropical Africa, resembles *S. hyacinthoides,* but has strap-shaped leaves up to 5 feet long by 2 to 5 inches wide. *S. nelsonii,* of apparently unrecorded prove-nance, is an attractive sort with oblanceo-

late, dark green, erect leaves up to 1 foot long or a little longer and, although usu-ally somewhat narrower, up to 1¾ inches wide. Their upper surfaces are longitudi-

nally channeled. Their apexes are finely-pointed. *S. parva,* of East Africa, has a short stem and forms a dense rosette of narrow-lanceolate, concave leaves 1 inch to 1½ inches long, with long, pointed-cylin-drical apexes. They are green with darker bandings. *S. patens* is stemless and has two-ranked, more or less recurved, pointed leaves 1½ to 3 feet long, with narrow,

white margins. It is indigenous to East Africa. *S. pearsonii,* of tropical Africa, is stemless. It has stout, two-ranked, rigid, dull dark green leaves 2 to 3 feet long, obscurely horizontally banded with lighter green and tapering to a sharp point. *S. powellii,* from East Africa, has stems 3 to 4 feet tall, and channeled, bluish-green,

spirally arranged, slender leaves 1 foot to 2 feet in length. *S. senegambica,* of West Africa, has pointed, oblanceolate, some-what spreading leaves, channeled toward their bases, and dull green with faint markings on their lower sides. *S. singu-laris,* of East Africa, is essentially stem-less. Its channeled, cylindrical, erect, rigid leaves are 1½ to 8 feet long by up to nearly 2 inches in diameter. *S. subspicata* is South African. It has broad-lanceolate, some-times stalked, flat leaves, about 1½ feet

Sansevieria senegambica

long, in loose rosettes. They are dark green with narrow red margins. *S. suffruticosa,* from East Africa, has branching stems, and thick, rich green leaves up to 2 feet long, with paler bands. The leaves, cylindrical toward their apexes, are channeled below. *S. zanzibarica,* native to Zanzibar, has a short stem and two-ranked, nearly cylindrical, somewhat channeled rigid leaves 5 to 6 feet in length and dark green with paler cross-bands. *S. zeylanica,* of Sri Lanka (Ceylon), forms a more shapely rosette than *S. hyacinthoides* (often misnamed *S. zeylanica*). Its grayish-green, channeled leaves, cylindrical at their tips, are recurved and have cross-bands of darker green.

Garden and Landscape Uses. In the tropics and subtropics, sansevierias play useful roles in landscaping. Other than "wet feet" resulting from water-saturated soil, there are few conditions they will not tolerate. In hot, humid climates where the soil contains moderate moisture, they luxuriate almost beyond belief. Under less encouraging conditions they develop more slowly and may not be as tall, but flourish. Even where long periods of drought are a constant threat to their existence, they struggle and are likely to live unless conditions preclude the growth of almost any vegetation. Sansevierias stand occasional light frosts, but basically are warm weather plants. One of their greatest virtues is their ability to grow with minimal light. Because of this they are extremely useful for planting in quite dense shade. Interestingly enough, they also thrive in full sun, although their color then is likely to be paler and less attractive than when they have at least some shade. Where they may be grown permanently outdoors they are useful as underplantings beneath palms and other trees, for grouping in beds and borders, and particularly for planting near stonework and masonry, with which they associate well. Locations on terraces and near steps or the bases of buildings are often ideal. The taller kinds can be used as fences and to mark boundaries.

In greenhouses and conservatories, humid or dry, sansevierias may be grown in containers or ground beds, preferably where the minimum winter temperature is not below 50°F, but surviving, although not liking, drops to almost freezing. Their ability to get along with low light intensities and arid atmospheres ensures their survival as indoor plants where most other kinds would perish. Their merits are many, but their popularity as ornamentals is, alas, limited. On the rare occasions when an old specimen grown in a home blooms, some excitement is generated, only, most often to pass with the fading of the flowers.

Cultivation. Coarse, porous, loamy, rather heavy soil of moderate fertility suits these plants best. Beds or containers for them must be thoroughly drained. Watering should be moderate to sparing, never excessive. When done, soak the earth thoroughly and give no more until it becomes nearly completely dry. Very well-rooted specimens in pots or other containers benefit from once-in-a-while applications of dilute liquid fertilizer, given a few hours after a regular watering. Repotting is ordinarily necessary at intervals of three to many years. Propagation is commonly by division and by cutting the leaves into pieces 3 to 4 inches long and using these as cuttings. They are planted with their bases in sand, sand and peat moss, or other propagating medium, with most of their lengths standing erectly in the air. A temperature of 70°F or higher promotes root formation, and if the medium, kept slightly moist, but not wet, is warmed to a few degrees higher than the atmosphere, so much the better. An interesting phenomenon is that leaf cuttings of most,

To divide a *Sansevieria:* (a) Slice the root ball with a sharp knife

(b) Then pull it apart into suitably sized pieces

(c) Place one large crock hollow side down in the bottom of a pot

(d) Cover with smaller crocks

(e) Then some coarse leaves followed by a little soil

(f) Center the division in the pot and pack soil firmly around it

Leaf cuttings of *Sansevieria* sprouting new roots and shoots

and possibly all, variegated-leaved kinds produce plain green plants. Variegated sansevierias can be propagated true to type only by divisions consisting of leaves and a part of the rhizomes. Seeds also provide a satisfactory way of obtaining new green-leaved plants, but because of the ease with which vegetative propagation is done, they are rarely used.

SANTA MARIA is *Calophyllum brasiliense*.

SANTALACEAE — Sandalwood Family. Comprising about 400 species of semiparasitic and parasitic trees, shrubs, and herbaceous plants distributed among some thirty genera, of which *Buckleya* and *Santalum* are cultivated, the dicotyledonous family SANTALACEAE is of small horticultural importance. It is represented in the native floras of many tropical, subtropical, and temperate regions. Its sorts have alternate or opposite, undivided leaves or these may be represented only by scales. The symmetrical, bisexual or unisexual, greenish, yellowish-green, or rarely orange flowers are in spikes, racemes, or heads. Without petals, they have an often somewhat fleshy, sometimes corolla-like, four- or five-lobed, rarely three- or six-lobed calyx, usually the same number of stamens as calyx lobes, and one style. The fruits are drupes or nuts.

SANTALUM (Sán-talum)—Sandalwood. The name of the genus *Santalum* is a modification of its Persian name *chandal*. Belonging in the sandalwood family SANTALACEAE, it comprises twenty-five species of evergreen trees and shrubs, and ranges in the wild from southeastern Asia to Australia and islands of the Pacific, including Hawaii.

Santalums are semiparasitic. Their roots attach themselves to those of other plants and extract some of the water and nutrients they need from their hosts. The most important species, the sandalwood (*S. album*) has since ancient times been esteemed for its fragrant wood which, in addition to being used for making boxes and chests, and for carpentry, is the source of sandalwood oil used in perfumes and pharmaceuticals. In the Orient it is employed as incense, by Buddhists for funeral pyres. It is also ground, colored, and used by Brahmans to decorate their faces with caste insignia.

Santalums have opposite, thickish or leathery leaves and terminal or axillary panicles of flowers, with usually four-, but sometimes five-lobed perianths, and five or four stamens. The fruits are drupes (fruits constructed like plums). Species native to Hawaii were nearly exterminated in the late eighteenth and early nineteenth centuries as a result of an active export trade of the very valuable wood to China. This trade was the first serious exploitation, for export, of the resources of the Hawaiian Islands.

Sandalwood (*S. album*) is a small tree with hairless shoots and foliage. Its opposite, elliptic-ovate to ovate-lanceolate, more or less pointed leaves, 1½ to 2 inches long, have slender stalks. The bell-shaped to obovate flowers, in panicles usually shorter than the leaves, at first pale yellow, change to red. The black fruits are about the size of cherries.

Garden and Landscape Uses and Cultivation. Adaptable for outdoor cultivation only in the tropics and warm subtropics, sandalwood is sometimes planted for interest and ornament. It succeeds in ordinary soils in sun or part-day shade and is raised from seed. Occasionally sandalwood is cultivated in greenhouses where plants useful to man are displayed. A winter night temperature of 60°F, raised five to fifteen degrees by day, and higher from spring to fall, is suitable. A humid atmosphere and shade from summer sun are needed. Fertile, porous earth kept moderately moist gives good results. Pruning to shape and repotting receives attention in late winter or early spring.

SANTOLINA (Santo-lìna) — Lavender-Cotton. A few popular garden plants belong to this group of ten aromatic species of the daisy family COMPOSITAE. The genus, native chiefly to the Mediterranean region, consists of low shrubs and shrublets and fewer herbaceous plants. The name is probably derived from *sanctum linum* (holy flax), an ancient name of *Santolina virens*. One species, *S. chamaecyparissus*, has medicinal uses.

Santolinas have alternate, pinnate or pinnately-lobed, or toothed leaves, green or felted with gray or white hairs. Their long-stalked, button-like, rayless flower heads consist of all disk florets (the kind that form the central eyes of daisies). They are bisexual, and yellow, cream, or white. The seedlike fruits are achenes.

Lavender-cotton (*S. chamaecyparissus* syn. *S. incana*) is a compact, bushy, evergreen shrub about 2 feet tall with, except for the earliest leaves which are green,

Santolina chamaecyparissus

Santolina chamaecyparissus (flowers)

gray- to whitish-hairy shoots and foliage. Crowded, its leaves are 1 inch to 1½ inches long and about ⅛ inch wide. They are pinnately-cut into short thick segments arranged in two to four rows. Borne freely in summer, the bright yellow, solitary flower heads, ½ to ¾ inch in diameter, are carried well above the foliage on stalks up to 6 inches long. An attractive, dwarf, compact variety is *S. c. nana*. Native to the Mediterranean region, lavender-cotton is naturalized somewhat in North America. It is the hardiest species. From lavender-cotton and its variety, *S. neapolitana*, which is at times cultivated as *S. rosmarinifolia*, differs in having leaves, 1½ to 3 inches long, dissected into threadlike segments disposed in two to four rows, and always densely-white-felted. On slender, erect stalks up to 6 inches long, the yellow flower heads are displayed in summer. This native of southern Italy is an evergreen shrub up to 2½ feet tall.

Two species with green foliage, both evergreen shrubs, are cultivated. Native to Italy and almost or quite hairless, *S. pinnata* (syn. *S. leucantha*) is 1 foot to 2 feet tall. From 1 inch to 1½ inches long by ¼ to ⅜ inch wide, its leaves are pinnately-divided into segments that form two to four rows. The creamy-white, solitary flower

Santolina neapolitana

Santolina virens (flowers)

Santolina pinnata

heads come in summer on rigid stalks up to 6 inches long. From it, **S. virens** (syn. *S. viridis*) differs in its solitary flower heads being yellow, ¾ inch in diameter, and on stalks 6 to 10 inches long. They are displayed in summer. This forms a wide bush 1 foot to 2 feet tall. It has hairless stems and foliage. From 1 inch to 2 inches long and about ⅛ inch broad, the leaves are pinnately-cut into numerous small sharp teeth.

Santolina virens

Garden and Landscape Uses. Santolinas are appropriate furnishings for herb gardens, rock gardens, terraces, and similar locations and can be kept trimmed to form neat, attractive low hedges. When so grown they are effective components of knot gardens. With the exception of *S. neapolitana*, the kinds discussed above are fairly hardy in sheltered locations as far north as New York City, and lavender-cotton even into southern New England. But so far north their foliage may not, as it does in milder climes, remain evergreen, and their tops may be more or less winter-killed. For safety it is advisable to carry a few stock plants over in a cold frame or cool greenhouse.

Cultivation. Santolinas need full sun, and, for their best comfort, thoroughly well-drained, poorish earth. They are intolerant of "wet feet" and need no rich diet. Soils of a limy nature are to their liking, but they also succeed in slightly acid ones. Planting may be done in spring or early fall. As soon as flowering is through the faded flower heads should be cut off. A spring shearing to promote neatness is helpful, as are one or two additional clippings through the summer to maintain them as low hedges. In cold climates it is inadvisable to do this much later than midsummer. Propagation is very easily accomplished by cuttings taken in spring and planted in a greenhouse propagating bed, or in early fall and set similarly or in a propagating bed in a cold frame. Plants may also be raised from seeds.

SANTONICA is *Artemisia cina*.

SANVITALIA (Sanvità-lia) — Creeping-Zinnia. Seven species of the southwestern United States and Mexico belong in *Sanvitalia*, of the daisy family COMPOSITAE, but only one is commonly cultivated. The name probably commemorates Federico Sanvitali, a professor at Brescia, Italy. He died in 1761.

Sanvitalias are chiefly low branching annuals with stalked, opposite, usually undivided leaves and small, solitary, daisylike flower heads at the branch ends. The disk florets are brown to purple, the rays yellow or white. The fruits are seedlike achenes.

The cultivated species, **S. procumbens**, a native of Mexico, is a pretty annual 6 to 8 inches tall that blooms throughout the summer. Hairy, it has trailing stems. Its ovate leaves are stalked and up to 1 inch long. The flower heads, ¾ to 1 inch wide, are borne in profusion. They have yellow rays and dark purple centers. Beneath each is a pair of leafy bracts. Garden varieties with double flowers are cultivated.

Sanvitalia procumbens

Garden Uses and Cultivation. Sometimes called creeping-zinnia, *S. procumbens* is among the simplest of annuals to grow. Well adapted for the fronts of flower beds, low edgings, and rock gardens, it thrives in full sun in any ordinary garden soil. All that is necessary is to sow seeds in early spring where the plants are to bloom, or in fall in regions of mild winters, and cover them to a depth of about ¹⁄₁₀ inch with soil. The young plants are thinned to leave those that remain about 3 inches apart.

SAPINDACEAE — Soapberry Family. Approximately 2,000 species of trees, shrubs, and woody vines that climb by tendrils, apportioned among about 150 genera and mostly natives of the tropics and subtropics, constitute this family of dicotyledons. Many are sources of valuable lumber, some, including *Euphoria* and *Litchi*, have edible fruits. The kinds of SAPINDACEAE have alternate or very rarely opposite, undivided or pinnate leaves. Functionally unisexual (even though the females have apparently well-developed stamens, they do not produce fertile pollen) and generally with both sexes on the same plant, the flowers are symmetrical or asymmetrical. They have five or four sepals; usually five but sometimes more, fewer, or no petals; generally eight or ten stamens, less often more or as few as five or four; and the females, one or rarely two or four styles. The fruits are of many kinds including capsules, berries, drupes, and nuts.

Cultivated genera include *Alectryon*, *Blighia*, *Cardiospermum*, *Cupaniopsis*, *Dip-*

loglottis, Dodonaea, Euphoria, Harpullia, Koelreuteria, Litchi, Melicoccus, Paullinia, Sapindus, Serjania, Talisia, Ungnadia, and *Xanthoceras.*

SAPINDUS (Sapín-dus) — Soapberry, Soap Nut, Aulu, Wild China Tree. Trees and shrubs, chiefly tropical, but with one species extending north to Missouri, compose *Sapindus.* Natives of the Old World and the Americas, the thirteen species belong to the soapberry family SAPINDACEAE. The name comes from the Latin *sapo,* soap, and *indicus,* Indian. Both botanical and vernacular names refer to the use, still practiced in many regions where the plants grow natively, of the fruits as soaps. Because of their high saponin content, they lather freely in water. However, some people are allergic to saponin and develop severe skin irritations after contact with it. In Hawaii the seeds of the soapberry and soap nut are strung in leis. Elsewhere they are made into necklaces, bracelets, and rosaries. They are poisonous if eaten. In parts of the Orient the fruits of the soap nut are employed as a lice-killing shampoo.

Sapinduses usually have alternate, abruptly-pinnate leaves with toothless or toothed leaflets. One species has undivided leaves. The tiny flowers are in ample, terminal or axillary panicles or racemes. Each has, in two rows, four or five sepals. There are four or five petals, eight or ten separate stamens, and a style with a two- to four-lobed stigma. Individual plants chiefly bear flowers of one sex, along with a few of the opposite sex or bisexual ones. The fruits are berries containing bony, black seeds.

The common soapberry, a native of southern Florida, the West Indies, Mexico, Central America, South America, and Hawaii, is *S. saponaria,* a broad, densely-foliaged tree ordinarily up to 35 feet high, but in Hawaii sometimes 80 feet tall. Usually evergreen, in some areas, including Hawaii, it is deciduous. It has lustrous, bright green, pinnate leaves with generally seven to nine, sometimes less or more, often somewhat sickle-shaped, elliptic to oblong-lanceolate leaflets up to 6 inches long. The midribs of the leaves may or may not be winged. The leaflets are 2 to 6 inches in length and hairless above and sometimes have somewhat wavy edges. Their undersides are finely-hairy. In terminal panicles up to 10 inches long, the flowers have white petals with hair-fringed margins. The stalks of the stamens are hairy. The lustrous, brown, translucent-fleshed, spherical or lobed fruits are nearly or quite ¾ inch in diameter.

The soap nut (*S. mukorossii*), native to Japan, Taiwan, and from China to India, and up to 50 feet tall, is a deciduous or evergreen tree of good form. It has leaves with narrowly-winged stalks and eight to

sixteen, more or less alternate, oblong-ovate or oblong-lanceolate, wavy leaflets 3 to 6 inches long. The white or lilac flowers have petals fringed with hairs. The stalks of the stamens are hairy. The smooth, spherical, yellow to orange-brown, thick-skinned fruits, solitary or in pairs, are ¾ to 1 inch in diameter.

The aulu (*S. oahuensis*), endemic to Hawaii, is the only kind with undivided leaves. They are hairless, ovate, and 4 to 8 inches long by 2 to 5 inches broad. The yellowish-white flowers are in panicles with rusty-hairy stalks that come from the axils of smaller leaves toward the branch ends. This species, which attains a height of about 30 feet, inhabits drier parts of the Hawaiian Islands.

The hardiest species, the wild China tree (*S. drummondii*) is indigenous from Missouri to Kansas, Louisiana, Texas, and Mexico. Deciduous and up to 50 feet tall, this tree has less coarse leaves with much smaller leaflets than the soapberry and soap nut. They have eight to eighteen lanceolate leaflets 2 to 3 inches long, short-hairy on their undersides, hairless above. Its yellowish-white flowers, in panicles 6 inches to 1 foot long, are succeeded by spherical fruits, ½ inch in diameter, that are yellow, but become black as they age. They have semitranslucent flesh.

Garden and Landscape Uses and Cultivation. Sapinduses are attractive general-purpose ornamental trees well suited for dryish, sandy and rocky soils. The only kind hardy in the north, *S. drummondii* survives in southern New England. Propagation is easy by seed and can also be accomplished by cuttings.

SAPIUM (Sà-pium) — Chinese Tallow Tree. The genus *Sapium,* of the spurge family EUPHORBIACEAE, inhabits the tropics and subtropics of the eastern and western hemispheres. Its name is one used by Pliny for a species of pine. Some sorts are minor sources of rubber, and from the fruits of the Chinese tallow tree, wax used for candles, soaps, and dressing cloth is obtained. In China a black dye is prepared from the leaves of this species and its wood is used in the manufacture of furniture and printing blocks. There are about 120 species of *Sapium.*

Sapiums are trees, some very large, and shrubs. They contain a poisonous, milky sap. They have alternate, lobeless, hairless leaves with two glands at the top of the leafstalk. The flowers are unisexual and in terminal or lateral spikes with the female blooms solitary at the bases of spikes and the males above them usually three together beneath each bract. The bracts have two glands. The calyx is two- or three-lobed, petals are lacking, and there are two or three stamens. The fruits are more or less fleshy capsules.

The only kind of horticultural signifi-

cance is the Chinese tallow tree (*S. sebiferum*), a native of China, Japan, and Taiwan and naturalized in the southern United

Sapium sebiferum

States. An evergreen tree up to 45 feet in height, it has somewhat the appearance of a poplar. Its abruptly-pointed leaves, up to 3 inches in length, are rhombic-ovate or top-shaped and have long slender stalks. They become brilliant red with age. The flowers are in terminal spikes up to 4 inches in length. The females are succeeded by three-lobed capsules, about ½ inch in diameter, that have three large black seeds covered with a thick layer of white wax. The seeds adhere to a central column.

Garden and Landscape Uses and Cultivation. In the southern United States the Chinese tallow tree is used for shade and ornament. Of attractive appearance, it succeeds without difficulty in regions where little frost is experienced. It is propagated by seed and by cuttings. Selected forms or varieties may be grafted onto seedling understocks.

SAPODILLA is *Manilkara zapota.*

SAPONARIA (Saponàr-ia) — Soapwort, Bouncing Bet. Annuals and herbaceous perennials, nearly all of easy culture, constitute this genus of thirty species of the pink family CARYOPHYLLACEAE. Erect and spreading plants, they are natives of Europe, Asia, and North Africa. The name *Saponaria* refers to the bruised leaves of some kinds producing a lather when rubbed in water. It is derived from the Latin *sapo*, soap.

Saponarias have opposite, undivided, more or less lanceolate, hairy or hairless leaves. The usually showy pink or white flowers, in loose or fairly compact clusters, have a five-toothed calyx, five petals, in double-flowered varieties more, ten stamens, and two or less often three styles. The fruits are capsules. The plant previously known as *S. vaccaria* is *Vaccaria pyramidata*.

Bouncing Bet (*S. officinalis*) is one of the most familiar perennials. In most parts of temperate North America it colonizes rail-

Saponaria officinalis

road embankments, roadsides, and waste places and blooms abundantly in summer. This species, a native of western Asia, spreads vigorously and has erect stems 1½ to 3 feet tall clothed with broadly-lanceolate, nonhairy leaves up to 3 inches long. The stems are but sparsely branched, and the pink or whitish flowers, about 1 inch in diameter and in close clusters, are not unlike those of phlox. Variety *S. o. florepleno* has double flowers.

Saponaria officinalis flore-pleno

Quite different in appearance and excellent and useful, perennial *S. ocymoides* in its native Alps and elsewhere in Europe clothes mountainsides, banks, and rocky places with sheets of bright color in summer. This is a loose, much-branched, trailer about 9 inches tall and softly-hairy. It has broadly-ovate or broadly-lanceolate leaves and small starry pink flowers abundantly produced in loose clusters in late spring and summer. The flowers of *S. o. alba* are white; those of *S. o. rosea*, rose-pink; those of *S. o. splendens*, larger than those of the typical species and of a deeper rose-pink; and those of *S. o. rubra*, red.

Saponaria ocymoides

Other perennial kinds grown in gardens include these: *S. bellidifolia*, of Greece and other parts of eastern Europe, is akin to *S. lutea*. It is a nonhairy, tufted perennial with mostly basal leaves that are spoon-shaped and flower stems up to 1¼ feet in height that bear one or two pairs of leaves. The small clustered heads are of straw-yellow flowers with yellow stamens. *S. caespitosa*, a tufted native of high elevations in the Pyrenees, has reddish

Saponaria caespitosa

stems, up to 6 inches in height, that bear one or two pairs of leaves and are topped with two or three large oval-petaled, bright pink blooms. *S. lutea*, of the European

Alps, forms mats of bright green foliage and has pale yellow, purple-stamened blooms of not great attraction on 2- to 3-inch-long stems. *S. pumila*, of the European Alps and Carpathian Mountains, which forms cushions about 3 inches tall, has linear leaves up to 1 inch long, and solitary, 1-inch-wide, rose-pink or white flowers with three styles. *S. pumilio*, of Turkey, forms dense cushions or mats up to 1 foot or more across. Its linear leaves, all or mostly basal, are not over ¼ inch long. The glandular-hairy flowering stems carry three to ten crimson to purple flowers on each branch. *S. sicula* (syn. *S. depressa*) is a tufted or mat-forming native of Greece and Sicily with bluish-green, spoon-shaped to obovate-elliptic, basal leaves 3 to 4 inches long. Its flowers are in clusters atop stems 3 inches to 1 foot tall that bear two pairs of leaves. They are pink and about ¾ inch across.

Hybrid perennial saponarias include sorts of interest. An altogether admirable one between *S. ocymoides* and *S. caespitosa* is *S. boissieri*, which has excellent pink flowers twice as large as those of its first-named parent on much dwarfer mats of stems and foliage. A hybrid of *S. ocymoides* and *S. bellidifolia* is *S. peregrina*. This has larger leaves, heavier growth, and denser flower clusters than *S. boissieri*. Its blooms are pale yellow flushed with pink. Hybrid *S. wiemannii*, which forms mats of stems and foliage 2 to 3 inches high, has heads of bright rose-pink flowers.

Annual species sometimes cultivated include *S. calabrica* (syn. *S. multiflora*). A native of Greece, this has branching stems about 6 inches in height, oblong or lanceolate leaves, and clusters of pale rose-pink flowers each ½ inch in diameter. Variety 'Scarlet Queen' has deeper pink blooms; *S. c. alba* has white flowers; and *S. c. compacta* is dwarfer than the typical species. *S. cerastioides*, native to the Caucasus, sometimes exceeds 2 feet in height. It is glaucous and has obovate to nearly round leaves and branched panicles of small flowers with notched petals. Its flower stalks are glandular-hairy.

Garden Uses. Because of its invasiveness, bouncing Bet is too much of a problem child to establish near choice, weaker-growing garden plants, yet it can be used, especially in its better color forms, in semiwild and natural areas. Even there, unless self-sown seedlings can cause no trouble, it is usually advisable to rely upon the double-flowered variety. In any case this makes a rather better display, and the plants do not look quite as messy as the flowers fade. Provided it is prevented from spreading by reducing the sizes of the clumps when necessary with a spade or by lifting, splitting, and replanting them, the double-flowered bouncing Bet is also quite an attractive addition to the fronts of flower borders.

Really excellent garden plants, *S. ocymoides* and its varieties can be used at the fronts of flower beds and borders, as broad edgings to paths, in rock gardens, and to cascade over the tops of soil-retaining walls. They are attractive planted in the crevices of dry walls and at the sides of garden steps. The other perennial kinds described above are all primarily plants for rock gardens. The annual soapworts are suitable for flower beds and borders.

Cultivation. The soapworts are sun-loving plants, but bouncing Bet tolerates a little shade. It and *S. ocymoides* grow without difficulty in almost any well-drained soil; they are not fussy. For that matter, none is at all finicky as to soil, but to be sure it is best to plant the rock garden kinds in a porous, gritty medium that contains some organic matter in the form of leaf mold or humus, but that is rather lean in available nitrogen; in any case this encourages desirable compact growth. The annual kinds grow best in regular fertile garden soil such as suits most annuals and vegetables. Perennial soapworts are raised from seed, division, and cuttings. Double-flowered and other horticultural varieties cannot, of course, be increased by seed. For the double-flower bouncing Bet, division in spring or fall is a simple and sure method, but cuttings taken in summer and planted in a propagating bed under mist or in a humid, shaded cold frame is usually a better way with *S. ocymoides* varieties. Typical *S. ocymoides*, as well as other natural species, is very easily reproduced from seed sown in porous soil in containers, a cold frame, or a seed bed outdoors. The seeds may be sown indoors in late winter or in a frame or outdoors in spring. Routine care of perennial soapworts is minimal. Cutting back somewhat after flowering is over is in order, and it is well to lift, divide, and replant flower border patches of bouncing Bet occasionally, but *S. ocymoides* seems to have no need of such periodic transplanting. It does benefit from an annual top dressing or fertilizing in spring. So long as the rock garden species flourish, they, too, can be left in place, unless they are lifted to be divided to increase their number. An annual spring top dressing of gritty soil with some leaf mold or peat moss and bonemeal mixed in benefits them.

The annual kinds are grown from seed sown in early spring as soon as the ground is ready to work or, where winters are moderate, in fall, where the plants are to bloom. The seedlings are thinned to about 6 inches apart.

SAPOTA ACHRAS is *Manilkara zapota*.

SAPOTACEAE — Sapodilla Family. This family of dicotyledons is variously defined as comprising thirty-five to seventy-five genera, approximating 800 species. Its sorts, chiefly natives of the tropics and subtrop-

ics, contain milky sap and have alternate, undivided, more or less leathery leaves. Several are esteemed for their edible fruits. Generally rather small and symmetrical, the flowers, bisexual and solitary or in clusters, come from the leaf axils or not infrequently are produced directly from old branches or trunks. Both calyx and corolla are four-, six-, or eight-lobed. The stamens ordinarily equal the corolla lobes or petals in number. In addition there are sometimes staminodes (nonfertile stamens). There is one style. The fruits are one- or few-seeded berries, sometimes large, or rarely capsules.

Genera cultivated include *Argania, Bumelia, Chrysophyllum, Manilkara, Mastichodendron, Mimusops, Palaquium, Planchonella,* and *Pouteria*.

SAPOTE. This is a common name of *Pouteria sapota*. The black sapote is *Diospyros digyna*, the white sapote, *Casimiroa edulis*.

SAPPHIRE BERRY is *Symplocos paniculata*.

SAPROPHYTE. Plants without chlorophyll are unable to photosynthesize foods from simple elements contained in soil, water, and air, as do the vast majority of plants with which gardeners are familiar. They must obtain their nutrients from the bodies or remains of other organisms. Those that obtain their foods from living plants or animals are called parasites, those that use dead organic materials or organic wastes as sources of nutrients are called saprophytes.

SAPUCAIA NUT is *Lecythis zabucajo*.

SARACA (Sar-àca) — Asoka or Sorrowless Tree. The genus *Saraca* consists of about twenty tropical Asian species of the pea family LEGUMINOSAE. Its name is a modification of a vernacular one of India.

In open locations, saracas are rarely over 30 feet tall, but in forests they may be twice that height. Their leaves, large, dark green, and pinnate, have an even number of short-stalked leaflets. When young, like those of *Amherstia, Brownea,* the mango (*Mangifera*), and cacao (*Theobroma,*) they are grayish-pink to purplish and dangle limply like wet rags. Soon they stiffen, straighten, and become green. From the trunk, branches, or twigs the flowers develop in small dense clusters. Red, orange, or yellow, mostly with dark centers, they are without petals. Their showy parts are the brightly colored tubular calyxes with four spreading lobes that look like petals. There are three to nine stamens. The fruits are large, flat, leathery, purple-black pods.

The asoka or sorrowless tree (*S. indica*) is a native of India and Malaya. An evergreen about 30 feet in height, with a dense crown of spreading branches, it has alternate leaves with three to seven pairs of el-

liptic, hairless, leathery, leaflets, 3 to 6 inches long. Shorter than the leaves and arising from the trunk and older branches the numerous flower clusters are strongly reminiscent of those of *Ixora*, although the plants that bear them are not related. The showy calyxes, first yellow to orange, change to brilliant vermilion as they age. The six or seven slender stamens protrude far from the calyxes. The seed pods, 4 to 10 inches long, contain four to eight seeds.

By Buddhists and Hindus the asoka is considered sacred. Its blooms, fragrant after nightfall, are much used to decorate temples and the tree is commonly planted near sacred buildings. Buddhists believe that the Buddha was born under this tree. By Hindus the asoka is dedicated to Kama, the god of erotic desire, who carries a quiver of five arrows that are flowers used to arouse passion in celestials and humans. One of these five potent blooms is that of the asoka tree. Many charming stories are told of this revered species. According to Sanskrit poetry, it blushes into crimson bloom if touched by a beautiful woman. The name asoka means without sorrow. It is a reported practice of Hindu women to drink water in which six asoka blooms have been immersed to protect their children from grief and pain.

The red saraca (*S. declinata*) is much like the asoka, but has larger leaves with longer stalks to the leaflets and its blooms are more richly colored. It is a native of Malaya, Thailand, Sumatra, and Java. Similar, but smaller and with redder blooms, *S. thaipingensis*, of Malaya, is sometimes cultivated. Also smaller and of shrubby habit, *S. cauliflora* is a native of India. Its leaves have ten or twelve leaflets 1 foot long or longer. Its clusters of scarlet flowers, in Florida borne in March and April, are 4 to 6 inches in diameter. There are seven stamens.

Garden and Landscape Uses and Cultivation. Species of this genus are suitable for warm, humid climates only; to some extent they are planted in Florida and Hawaii. Those cultivated flourish in ordinary soils, preferably where there is a little shade. They are propagated by seed.

SARCANTHUS (Sar-cánthus). Consisting of perhaps 100 species, *Sarcanthus*, of the orchid family ORCHIDACEAE, is native from southeastern Asia to Australia. Its name, alluding to the fleshy flowers, derives from the Greek *sarkos*, flesh, and *anthos*, a flower.

Epiphytes (tree-perchers), these orchids have pendent or erect, long and slender or short, stouter stems, arranged in two ranks. The fleshy leaves range, according to species, from slender and cylindrical to flat. In racemes or panicles that originate opposite a leaf, the flowers have spreading sepals and petals, the upper sepal concave and arched over the column, the petals a little smaller. The lip is three-lobed, rather fleshy, short-spurred, and joined to the base of the column. There is a callus at the mouth of the spur.

These sorts are cultivated: *S. filiformis,* of northern India, Thailand, and Indo-

Sarcanthus filiformis

china, has pendent stems and 2- to 4-foot-long, slender, cylindrical leaves. Its small, violet-scented flowers, in drooping racemes 6 to 8 inches in length, have chocolate-brown sepals and petals, and a white, yellow, or orange lip. *S. pallidus,* of Indochina, has a thick stem 4 to 6 inches long with, near its base, flat, leathery leaves up to 1 foot long. Freely-branched and 1 foot to 1½ feet long, the flowering stalk carries many ½-inch-wide, greenish-white blooms with the lip longer than the petals. *S. teretifolius,* a native of China and Hong Kong, has jointed stems sometimes over 1 foot long that produce adventitious roots freely. Its cylindrical leaves are 3 to 4 inches in length. Spreading more or less horizontally, the flowering stalks have six to eight blooms up to ¾ inch wide, with elliptic, dull green sepals and petals, lined with brownish-red, and a longer, drooping, yellowish-white, slipper-shaped lip margined with red.

Garden Uses and Cultivation. Of interest to orchid fanciers, sarcanthuses succeed in environments and with care appropriate for *Aerides* and *Vanda.* Those with pendulous stems are best displayed in baskets, on rafts, or growing on slabs of tree fern trunk. Because these plants are intolerant of root disturbance do not pot or replant them more often than necessary. For more information see Orchids.

SARCOBATUS (Sarco-bàtus) — Greasewood. To the goosefoot family CHENOPODIACEAE belongs the only species of *Sarcobatus,* a native of alkaline soils in desert and semidesert habitats from North Dakota to Alberta, Washington, Texas, and California. Its name derives from the Greek *sarx,* fleshy, and *batos,* a bramble, blackberry, or raspberry, and probably relates to the spiny stems and fleshy foliage.

The greasewood (*S. vermiculatus*) is an erect or spreading, freely-branching, spiny shrub up to 6 feet tall, with alternate or opposite, stalkless, fleshy leaves and unisexual flowers on the same or separate plants. It has thick, gray older branches and yellowish to whitish younger ones, sometimes with white hairs. The leaves, from ⅒ inch to over 1 inch long, may have a few hairs. The blooms are small, the males in terminal, catkin-like spikes ½ to slightly over 1 inch in length. Their perianths have a membranous, shield-shaped scale concealing the two or three stamens. The females, stalkless and solitary or in pairs in the leaf axils, have a calyx joined to the ovary and two stigmas. The winged fruits are disklike, erect, and ⅓ inch across. Variety *S. v. baileyi,* more densely-hairy than the species and differing somewhat in other aspects, is found in California and Nevada. Greasewood is hardy in climates as cold as that of southern New England.

Garden Uses and Cultivation. Rarely planted except occasionally in regions where it is native, greasewood needs conditions approximating those of its natural habitats. It is propagated by seed.

SARCOCAULON (Sarco-caùlon) — Bushman's Candle. The sorts of *Sarcocaulon* are *Pelargonium* relatives that inhabit stony, sometimes saline soils in coastal deserts in southern Africa. Belonging to the geranium family GERANIACEAE, they number twelve species. The name comes from the Greek *sarkos,* fleshy, and *caulon,* a stem.

These plants have adapted to the harsh conditions of their natural environments, which include exposure to blazing sun, high temperatures, low humidity, and wind, by adopting several devices common to other completely unrelated desert plants. The stems of most are thickened to store water and those of all kinds are protected from excessive transpiration by corky layers that contain so much wax and resin that if ignited they burn like torches. Because of this, one kind is called bushman's candle. The leaves are comparatively small, offering limited surfaces for dehydration, and are in evidence for only brief periods following rains. Sarcocaulons are capable of surviving droughts lasting several years; then, when moisture becomes available, they break out displays of foliage and blooms.

Sarcocaulons are subshrubs, mostly with stems abundantly armed with spines that

An undetermined species of *Sarcocaulon* with finely-divided gray foliage and pink flowers

are leafstalks that remain and harden after the blade of the leaf falls, but some kinds are spineless or nearly so. Their leaves, small and often in tufts, have blades that persist for a short time only. The flowers, solitary, symmetrical, and usually with longish stalks, are white, yellow, orange, pink, or red. They have five each sepals and petals, and distinguishing them from all other members of the geranium family, fifteen united stamens. The fruits are long, slender capsules.

Bushman's candle (*S. spinosum* syn. *S. burmannii*) has the widest natural range. Up to 1 foot in height, with branches about 6 inches long, this has round-toothed, hairless or downy leaves, ½ to ¾ inch long, with short fleshy stalks. From 1½ to 2 inches across, its white to pale pink flowers have petals twice as long as the sepals. The longest spines, up to 4 inches, are those of sparingly-branched, thin-stemmed *S. l'heritieri.* They are in four rows. About 1 foot in height, this species has hairless, toothless leaves. The flowers, with petals approximately as long as the sepals, are yellow and nearly 1 inch in diameter.

A variable kind, *S. patersonii* is typically a low shrub with branches up to 8 inches long, and straight spines. Fringed with short hairs, its leaves are about ⅓ inch long. The flowers are red and 1 inch wide or slightly wider. Varieties of this have pink blooms. Very beautiful *S. multifidum* has thick, horizontal branches and tufts of leaves ⅓ inch long, from two rows of wartlike tubercles. Its large pink blooms have a conspicuous dark red blotch at the bottom of each petal. Up to approximately 1 foot tall, *S. crassicaule* has stout, fleshy stems with recurved spines. The leaves have thickish, glaucous, ovate to wedge-shaped blades, ½ to ¾ inch long and with a few coarse teeth. Yellowish or white, the flowers have petals about 1 inch long. The fruit capsules stick out from the mass of stems and foliage like pins from a pin cushion.

Sarcocaulon crassicaule

Garden Uses and Cultivation. Out of doors sarcocaulons can be expected to succeed only in frost-free desert regions where rain does not fall for most of the year. More usually, they are accommodated in greenhouses devoted to succulents. Full sun, dry atmospheric conditions, and a winter night temperature of about 50°F, with a few degrees higher by day allowed, are to their liking. They succeed in slightly acid soil with a moderate organic content. This is kept quite dry during the resting season and watered moderately during the period of active growth and when leaves are in evidence. It is especially important not to keep the thick-stemmed kinds too wet. Propagation is very easy by seeds, which germinate very quickly. However, young seedlings are much given to damping off, and extreme care with watering must be taken at this stage. Cuttings, taken from plants in active growth and treated with a root-inducing hormone, root with fair success; those of thin-stemmed kinds more readily than those with thick stems.

SARCOCHILUS (Sarco-chìlus). Not often cultivated, *Sarcochilus*, of the orchid family ORCHIDACEAE, broadly interpreted includes more than fifty species, natives of tropical Asia, Indonesia, Polynesia, Australia, and New Zealand. It is closely allied to *Thrixspermum*. Some authorities assign many of the species accepted under this liberal interpretation to other genera. The name comes from the Greek *sarkos*, flesh, and *cheilos*, a lip, in allusion to the thick lips of the flowers.

Sarcochiluses are mostly epiphytes (plants that perch on trees without taking nourishment from them). They are without pseudobulbs. Their stems are short and leafy. The racemes or panicles of often handsome, generally short-lived flowers come from the leaf axils. The blooms have the upper (dorsal) sepal and the petals similar. The lateral sepals are broader and are continued down the foot of the col-

umn. The three-lobed lip has a spur or shoe-shaped pouch.

Native to Malaya, Indonesia, and the Philippine Islands, *S. pallidus* (syn. *S. unguiculatus*) has much the appearance of a vigorous *Phalaenopsis*. Its brief stems have few two-ranked, fleshy, oblong leaves up to somewhat over 1 foot long by 2 inches wide or wider. The few- to several-flowered, pendulous racemes, shorter than the leaves, are of fragrant blooms from a little under to a little over 2 inches wide. Their narrow-elliptic sepals and petals are white to creamy-yellow. The considerably shorter, spurred lip, of similar base color, or pinkish in hue, is barred with red-brown or purple.

Native to Sikkim, *S. mannii* (syn. *Camarotis mannii*) has drooping, leafy, sometimes branched stems up to 1 foot long. Its leaves are leathery, linear, 3 to 4 inches long, and notched at their apexes. In racemes shorter than the leaves, the ¼-inch-wide flowers are pale pink spotted toward their centers with crimson.

Usually without leaves, but sometimes with tiny ones, *S. luniferus*, of Burma, has slender, gray, rootlike stems radiating from a central crown. In pendulous racemes, its ½-inch-wide flowers have yellow-margined, light brown sepals and petals.

Sarcochilus luniferus

Australian *S. ceciliae* has stems 3 to 5 inches tall with linear leaves up to 3½ inches long. Its fragrant, bell-shaped flowers, in erect, very slender racemes of eight or fewer, have about ¼-inch-long, similar, bright pink sepals and petals and a lip with three lobes, the center one fleshy and above densely-hairy. Also Australian, *S. hartmannii* has vigorous, erect stems furnished with deeply-channeled, fleshy leaves. The long-stalked, many-flowered racemes are of 1- to 1½-inch-wide blooms with converging sepals and petals and a tiny lip often streaked with red inside.

Garden Uses and Cultivation. These are as for *Vanda*. For more information see Vanda, and Orchids.

SARCOCOCCA (Sarcocóc-ca). About fourteen species of evergreen shrubs of Asia, Taiwan, the Philippine Islands, Sumatra, and Java belong in *Sarcococca*, of the boxwood family BUXACEAE. The name, from the Greek *sarkos*, fleshy, and *kokkos*, a berry, alludes to the fruits.

These attractive plants have alternate, stalked, toothless, usually pinnately-veined, leathery leaves, and unisexual, whitish or greenish flowers in axillary racemes, the lowermost blooms females, those above males. The flowers, with four to six sepals, are without petals. Males have four to six stamens, females two or three styles. The fruits, berry-like and containing one or two seeds, remain on the plants for a long time. Although they look quite different, sarcococcas are botanically closely related to *Pachysandra*.

Himalayan *S. hookerana*, up to 6 feet tall, spreads slowly by underground rhizomes. Its glossy, pointed leaves are lanceolate to elliptic and 1½ to 4 inches long. The fragrant flowers are in short racemes. The males have cream-colored or pink anthers, the females two or three stigmas. Purplish-black to black, the fruits are about ⅜ inch long. This sort is unlikely to succeed where winters are colder than those of Philadelphia, Pennsylvania. Somewhat hardier, *S. h. digyna*, of western China, is also more slender and has narrower leaves.

Sarcococca hookerana digyna

Its female flowers have two stigmas. The fruits are black with a purplish bloom. This variety exists in two forms. The better, sometimes identified as 'Purple Stem', has reddish-purple young stems, leafstalks, and leaf midribs. Its lanceolate leaves are 3 to 4 inches long by slightly over ½ inch wide. The male flowers are very fragrant and have cream-colored anthers. The other variant is lower and has green stems, paler green leaves, and male flowers with pink anthers. Also western Chinese, *S. h. humilis* overwinters satisfactorily outdoors in sheltered locations at Boston, Massachusetts. From 1 foot to 1½ feet tall or a little taller, this spreads slowly by underground

Sarcococca hookerana humilis

rhizomes from which rise numerous erect stems. The leaves are lanceolate, up to 3 inches long by about one-fourth as wide, and glossy. The flowers are fragrant; the males have bright pink anthers, the females two stigmas. The fruits are black, egg-shaped, and covered with a purplish bloom.

Native to limestone regions in central China, **S. ruscifolia** is a sturdy, single-stemmed shrub up to 6 feet or perhaps

Sarcococca ruscifolia with flower buds

sometimes more in height, with dark green, ovate to elliptic-ovate leaves 1½ to 2½ inches long. Its very fragrant flowers, males with cream-colored anthers, females with three stigmas, are borne profusely. The rich scarlet fruits are attractive, but tend to be hidden among the foliage. This is rather more tender than *S. hookerana*. Western Chinese *S. r. chinensis* is lower than *S. ruscifolia* and has paler foliage and lighter colored fruits. Its leaves have longer points and it blooms later. A native of the Himalayas, **S. saligna,** about 5 feet high, has slender, pendulous branches and oblong-lanceolate to oblong-ovate leaves up to 6 inches long by 1

inch broad. Its greenish flowers are not fragrant. The fruits, up to ½ inch long, are purple. This suffers winter damage even in San Francisco.

The uncertainty surrounding the origin of *S. confusa* is reflected in its name. The plants in cultivation came from seeds sent from China by plant explorer Ernest H. Wilson about the beginning of the twentieth century, but no herbarium record of wild-collected plants has been found. Because this sort is intermediate in appearance between *S. hookerana, S. humilis,* and *S. ruscifolia* it is possibly a hybrid between them. However, insofar as it breeds true from seed, it behaves like a good species. A vigorous, single-stemmed bush up to about 6 feet in height, **S. confusa** has elliptic leaves about 2¼ inches long by somewhat under 1 inch wide. Its many fragrant male flowers have cream-colored anthers. Females have two or three stigmas and are succeeded by glossy-black berries not hidden by the foliage. This sarcococca is suitable only for regions of comparatively mild winters.

Sarcococca confusa with fruits

Garden and Landscape Uses. Of the sorts discussed, *S. hookerana humilis* is a choice groundcover and the others attractive ornamental evergreens for shrub borders, foundation plantings, and other purposes. In mild climates *S. confusa* can be used as a hedge. With the exception of *S. saligna,* cultivated kinds have fragrant flowers pleasant for cutting for use in indoor decorations.

Cultivation. Sarcoccas need no special care. They grow in any ordinary garden soil and are best in part-shade. It is helpful to keep the soil around them mulched and to water periodically in very dry weather. Propagation is simply accomplished by division in the case of suckering kinds, and with all sorts by cuttings taken in late summer or early fall and set in an indoor propagating bed or under mist outdoors. Seeds also give satisfactory results.

SARCOPOTERIUM. See Poterium.

SARCORHIZA. This is the name of orchid hybrids the parents of which are *Rhinerrhiza* and *Sarcochilus.*

SARCOSTEMMA (Sarco-stémma). Succulent-stemmed plants of the milkweed family ASCLEPIADACEAE compose *Sarcostemma,* a genus of fifty species, natives of tropical and subtropical America, Africa, Asia, and Australia. By some authorities the New World species are segregated as the genus *Philibertia.* The name, in allusion to the fleshy corona of the blooms, is from the Greek *sarkos,* fleshy, and *stemma,* a crown.

Straggling shrubs, subshrubs, and vines, sarcostemmas contain milky sap. Their stems are slender, often twining, and bear evident leaves or are apparently leafless, the leaves then being represented by tiny bracts. White, yellowish, or greenish, the small flowers are in umbels or racemes. In form, but not size, they resemble those of stapelias. They have deeply-five-lobed calyxes, wheel-, bell-, or salver-shaped corollas, five stamens, their stalks (sometimes absent) united to form a tube, and two carpels. The fruits are paired podlike follicles.

Favoring less arid habitats than most species, *S. clausum* (syn. *Philibertia clausa*) ranges in the wild from Florida to the West Indies, Mexico, and Argentina. A few-branched vine with twining or trailing stems densely-white-hairy at the nodes, this has leaves, sometimes soon falling, and sometimes much reduced in size, but commonly elliptic to broadly-elliptic and ¾ inch to 2 inches long by ½ to 1 inch wide. Its sweetly fragrant, wheel- to shallowly-bell-shaped, white flowers, ½ inch wide, are in umbels of up to fifteen.

Sometimes cultivated under the obviously misapplied name *Euphorbia pendula,* African *S. viminale* is essentially leafless. It has lax stems, up to ¼ inch in diameter, with distantly spaced nodes (joints). From the upper ones, the white, greenish-white, or yellowish, lemon-scented, ½-inch-wide flowers are produced. This rampant climber in the wild clambers over and drapes over shrubs.

Garden Uses and Cultivation. Primarily for the collector of succulents, *S. viminale* can be grown outdoors in warm, dry climates, and in greenhouses. It needs very porous, well-drained soil, never overwet. Indoors, the soil is kept nearly dry in winter, somewhat moister at other times. A sunny location is needed. Winter temperatures indoors should be 55°F at night and five to fifteen degrees higher by day. An unusual vine for outdoors in mild climates, *S. clausum* requires a sunny location and a trellis or other support around which its stems can twine. Although this sort stands more humid environments than *S. viminale,* and indoors should not be kept as dry in winter, too much moisture soon brings disaster. In greenhouses the general conditions suggested for *S. viminale* suit *S. clausum*. Propagation of both kinds is by cuttings, layers, and seed.

SARCOTHERA. This is the name of orchid hybrids the parents of which are *Renanthera* and *Sarcochilus*.

SARGENTODOXA (Sargent-odóxa). A native of central China, the only species of *Sargentodoxa* constitutes the sargentodoxa family SARGENTODOXACEAE, which is allied to the barberry family BERBERIDACEAE. Its name commemorates Charles S. Sargent, founder and first director of the Arnold Arboretum, Jamaica Plain, Massachusetts. He died in 1927.

Rare in cultivation, *S. cuneata* is a twining, deciduous vine up to about 25 feet tall. It has alternate, hairless, long-stalked, glossy leaves suggestive of those of scarlet runner beans (*Phaseolus*), each with a 2- to 4-inch-long stalk and three leaflets. The center leaflet is obovate to lozenge-shaped and smaller than the side ones, which are up to 4½ inches long and obliquely-ovate to extremely lopsided-ovate. The unisexual, yellowish-green flowers are in pendulous, loose racemes, those of males 4 to 6 inches long, those of females up to 4 inches long. They have six slender, yellowish-green, petal-like sepals about ½ inch long and the same number of minute petals. Males have six stamens and are fragrant. Females have at their centers a little cone of carpels, each of which later develops into a short-stalked, dark purplish-blue, berry-like, single-seeded fruit about ¼ inch across, and six staminodes (non-functional stamens). The fruits are hairy pods.

Garden and Landscape Uses and Cultivation. Interesting for clothing trellises and other supports about which its stems can twine, this vine, hardy only in regions free of severe frost, succeeds in ordinary soils. It may be propagated by seed and by cuttings.

SARGENTODOXACEAE. The characteristics of this family of dicotyledons are those of its only genus, *Sargentodoxa*.

SARITAEA (Sarit-aèa). The only species of *Saritaea*, formerly included in *Arrabidaea*, sometimes cultivated in warm parts of the United States, in the tropics and subtropics, and in greenhouses, belongs in the bignonia family BIGNONIACEAE. The name honors the wife of the twentieth century botanist Armando Dugan, of Colombia, who first described the genus. Her name is Saritaea.

Native to Colombia, *S. magnifica* (syns. *Arrabidaea magnifica*, *Bignonia magnifica*) is a robust woody vine with opposite, leathery leaves each with two leaflets and a terminal, branchless tendril, or with three leaflets. In this they resemble the leaves of *Clytostoma*, but the leaflets are obovate. The

leaflets, short-stalked and usually bluntish, are up to 4 inches long. The narrowly-bell-shaped, pale purple to rose-pink flowers, up to 3 inches long, are in clusters. They have more or less round, spreading corolla lobes (petals). The fruits are flattened, slender capsules.

Garden and Landscape Uses and Cultivation. These are as for *Clytostoma*.

SARMIENTA (Sarm-iénta). The only species of *Sarmienta*, of the gesneria family GESNERIACEAE, inhabits cool, humid mountain forests in Chile. Its name honors the Spanish botanist Mart. Sarmiento.

A very beautiful evergreen trailer, *S. scandens* (syn. *S. repens*) has slender, woody stems and opposite, short-stalked, elliptic to obovate leaves up to about 1 inch long by one-half as wide. They are minutely-glandular on both surfaces and at their apexes are shallowly- to deeply-three- to five-lobed. Solitary from the leaf axils, the flowers are on stalks with two bracts near their apexes. They have five sepals and a corolla with a ¾-inch-long, coral-pink tube that from a narrowed base broadens to become urn-shaped and then narrows to the throat. The five short corolla lobes (petals) are rose-pink. There are two stamens and one style. The fruits are berries.

Garden Uses and Cultivation. Of special appeal to collectors of gesneriads (members of the gesneria family), this very lovely plant is delightful for use in hanging baskets. It thrives with minimum care in humid, warm conditions that suit African-violets, gloxinias, and many other gesneriads, but to bloom satisfactorily it must spend three months or so in winter in temperatures lower than those in order at other times. Then, the greenhouse at night should be 40 to 45°F and not more than five or ten degrees warmer by day. Without this, the plant grows well, but does not flower. During this period of partial rest the foliage is retained and so the soil must be kept reasonably moist. From spring through fall, night temperatures of 60°F or higher are satisfactory with increases of five to fifteen degrees by day. Loose, humus-rich soil that permits the free passage of water and air agrees with *Sarmienta*. Propagation is very easy by cuttings, division, and seed. For additional information see Gesneriads.

SAROTHAMNUS. See *Cytisus scoparius*.

SARRACENIA (Sarra-cènia)—Pitcher Plant or Side Saddle Flower, Trumpets, Huntsman's Cup. This remarkable North American genus of up to ten species and several natural and horticultural hybrids occurs wild chiefly on the coastal plain from New Jersey to Texas, with one species extending as far north as Labrador and Saskatchewan. Belonging, along with the California pitcher plant (*Darlingtonia*) and South

American *Heliamphora*, to the sarracenia family SARRACENIACEAE, the genus we are considering is named after Dr. Michel Sarrasin de l'Etang, of Canada, who sent the first pitcher plants to Europe. He died in 1734. In addition to American *Sarracenia* and *Darlingtonia*, the tropical Asian genus *Nepenthes* and the Australian genus *Cephalotus*, of quite different families, are called pitcher plants.

Carnivorous bog and wet-lands plants, sarracenias entrap insects and other small prey that drown in water held in the pitchers. Their bodies decay and supply part of the sustenance needed by the plants. But sarracenias are not dependent upon this source of nutrients. They contain chlorophyll and like other green-leaved plants are able to synthesize the food they need from simple elements absorbed from the soil and air. The animal bodies they secure serve only as supplements.

Sarracenias are stemless herbaceous perennials with horizontal rootstocks and hollow, trumpet- or urn-shaped leaves called pitchers, winged down one side, and topped with a lid or hood. The large, nodding, solitary blooms have five sepals, the same number of petals or none, a dozen or more stamens, and a style expanded at its apex to form a five-notched, umbrella-like disk over the five stigmas. The fruits are capsules.

The common pitcher plant or side saddle flower (*S. purpurea*) is the hardiest and natively the most widely distributed kind.

Sarracenia purpurea

It occurs in acid sphagnum bogs and suchlike habitats from Labrador to Saskatchewan, Florida, and Louisiana. Variable, in the southern part of its range its pitchers are squatter than those of more northerly plants. This southern manifestation is sometimes distinguished as *S. p. venosa*. The common pitcher plant has approximately obovate pitchers 4 inches to 1 foot long. They are green, often variegated with reddish-purple. Markedly lopsided, they radiate in loose clusters, with their rounded bases resting on the ground, and have half-obovate or half-oblanceolate wings broadest near their tops, a wide open mouth, and a nearly erect, broader-than-long hood. The flowers, on stalks 8 inches to 1¼ feet tall, are 2 inches or a little more in diameter. They have purple, fiddle-shaped petals and a style disk 1¼ to 1¾ inches in diameter. Intermediate hybrids between this and *S. flava* are named *S. catesbaei.* From the common pitcher plant, *S. psittacina* differs in its up-to-6-inch-long decumbent pitchers being tubular-club-shaped and having the opening at one side rather than terminal. Green, with purple veins and white blotches, they have kidney-shaped hoods. The flowers, on stalks up to 8 inches long, are up to 2 inches wide and have purple petals. This is native to Georgia, Florida, and Louisiana. Native from North Carolina to Florida and Mississippi, *S. rubra* (syn. *S. jonesii*) has fragrant, red blooms 1¼ to 2 inches across with a style disk about 1¼ inches in diameter. They have stalks that usually lift them above the pitchers. The narrow-winged, nearly cylindrical pitchers, up to 1½ feet tall and at least ten times as long as their diameters, are faintly veined with purple and downy inside.

Sarracenia rubra

Trumpets (*S. flava*) is wild from Virginia to Florida and Alabama. It has erect, slender, fluted pitchers, 1 foot to 3 feet tall or taller and not more than one-tenth as wide. These widen gradually from base to summit, have narrow wings, and have an erect hood, 2 to 5 inches wide, with reflexed margins, that narrows significantly where it joins the top of the trumpet. Yellow to yellowish-green, the pitchers are faintly

Sarracenia flava

veined with red. The flower stalks, up to 3 feet tall, bear blooms 3½ to 4 inches wide, commonly with bright yellow petals, but in one variant with red petals. The style disk is 3 inches or more in diameter. A hybrid between *S. flava* and *S. leucophylla* named *S. mooreana* has erect, trumpet-shaped, green pitchers up to about 2 feet tall. The hood or lid, green with crimson veins, is about 3 inches across and subcircular with wavy margins. About 4 inches in diameter, the fragrant flowers have greenish sepals flushed with pink on their outsides, and petals that are pale pink on their insides and rose-pink on their outsides. Its slender, erect pitchers veined with purple, up to 2½ feet long, and with ovate hoods, *S. alata* (syn. *S. sledgei*), native from Alabama to Texas, has flowers up to 2½ inches wide with fiddle-shaped, cream to greenish-yellow petals. This species is called yellow trumpets.

Pitchers 1½ to 4 feet tall, slender-trumpet-shaped, narrowly-winged, the lower portions green, the upper, like the erect, wavy-edged hood, white netted with purple, are characteristic of *S. leucophylla* (syn. *S. drummondii*). This native from Georgia to Florida and Alabama has flowers 3 to 4 inches wide, with fiddle-shaped, dark red petals atop stalks scarcely longer than the pitchers. Pale yellow flowers, 1½ to a little over 2 inches wide, with style disks 1 inch or a little more across, are borne by clump-forming *S. minor,* native from North Carolina to Florida. Its pitchers, erect and 8 inches to 3 feet long, are trumpet-shaped and variegated near their tops with purple veins and white or yellowish scarlike patches. The wing nar-

rows from its middle to both ends. The hood arches to nearly close the mouth of the pitcher. Native from Alabama to Georgia, *S. oreophila* has erect, trumpet-shaped, green pitchers 1 foot to 2½ feet long. The flowers, on stalks about as long as the trumpets, are green and nearly or quite 2 inches long, with slightly longer yellowish-green petals. The hood is approximately erect.

Garden and Landscape Uses. These American pitcher plants, in addition to being intensely interesting because of their peculiar adaptations to their mode of life, are attractive ornamentals for bog gardens and other wet places. The common pitcher plant is hardy far north. The cold tolerances of others can be judged approximately from the climates of their natural ranges, although most can be grown somewhat north of regions where they are native. All kinds withstand winter temperatures down to freezing. Trumpets (*S. flava*) stands drier summer conditions than most kinds; *S. psittacina* thrives with most of its roots submerged.

Cultivation. Sarracenias, once their simple needs are understood, are not difficult to grow. They must have a soil at least somewhat acid that contains a very large proportion of humus (decayed organic matter) and is always wet, one similar to the mucks in which they commonly grow in the wild. Full sun is to their liking. Without it, the full beauty of their coloring is not developed.

In greenhouses, the pots or pans (shallow pots) in which the plants are accommodated should be kept standing in saucers or other receptacles containing an inch or two of water. A humid atmosphere is needed for the best development of pitcher plants. Indoor winter night temperatures in the 40 to 50°F range are adequate. Repotting or replanting when needed is done in late winter or spring.

It is most important not to feed the plants insects, scraps of meat, or other such tidbits. Despite the fact that they entrap small creatures, the presence of too much animal material in the pitchers is likely to cause them to become brown and to decay. Some gardeners recommend plugging the pitchers with cotton to prevent this, but this is usually unnecessary.

Propagation is by division and by seed. Seeds do not develop unless the plants are cross-pollinated. This is easily done by wetting ripe pollen of one flower with nectar from the surface of the ovary, which is at the base of the style, and placing it on the dry, receptive stigmas of the blooms of another plant. Hybrids are easily obtained in this way. Sown in pots or pans containing chopped sphagnum moss or sandy muck soil, kept uniformly moist, in a temperature of about 60°F, the seeds germinate in a month or less and produce plants that may attain full size in two or three years.

SARRACENIACEAE — Sarracenia Family. Three genera totaling seventeen species constitute this family of dicotyledons. All are carnivorous herbaceous perennials, inhabitants of bogs and swamps. The genera *Sarracenia* and *Darlingtonia* are restricted in the wild, respectively, to eastern and western North America; *Heliamphora* is endemic to a restricted region in northeastern South America. The sorts of the SARRACENIACEAE have basal rosettes of leaves developed as pitchers that entrap insects and other small creatures and by their form prevent their escape. The pitchers contain watery fluid in which the prey drowns. Solitary or in racemes of few on leafless stalks, the nodding, bisexual flowers have four or five often attractively colored, persistent sepals, five or no petals, many stamens, and one style, often expanded at its apex. The fruits are many-seeded capsules.

SARSAPARILLA. This is the name of various species of *Smilax*, some of which are used in the preparation of the beverage of the same name. Australian-sarsaparilla is *Hardenbergia*; bristly-sarsaparilla, *Aralia hispida*; wild-sarsaparilla, *Aralia nudicaulis* and *Schisandra coccinea*.

SASA (Sá-sa). About 200 species of eastern Asian bamboos, of the grass family GRAMINEAE, belong in *Sasa*. Closely related *Pseudosasa*, which differs in having fewer stamens than the six that each flower of *Sasa* has and in other botanical details, is sometimes included, but not here. The name is a Japanese one for certain small bamboos.

Sasas have slender, running rhizomes, round stems rarely over 6 feet in height, and persistent leafsheaths. There is usually one, occasionally two, branches at each node with the tessellated leaves crowded toward their tips. Several kinds are sufficiently hardy to survive outdoors in sheltered locations in southern New York, but in cold winters the margins and tips of their leaves may wither, die, and turn yellow or whitish.

Among the tallest sorts in cultivation are *S. chrysantha*, *S. palmata*, and *S. tessellata*. Native of Japan, **S. chrysantha** is a hardy, rampant grower with dark olive-green canes up to about 6 feet tall and ¼ inch wide. The branches are divided into numerous branchlets. The leaves, up to 7 inches long by 1 inch wide, taper to long points; they are smooth on both sides and conspicuously tessellated. Their upper surfaces are bright green often with yellow variegation, their undersides duller. As a garden ornamental this is less desirable than *Arundinaria viridistriata*. In gardens often misnamed *S. senanensis*, a name that by right belongs to a quite different plant, **S. palmata** is vigorous, invasive, and suitable only for planting where there is

Sasa palmata

ample room for it to spread. Also native to Japan, this is hardy in sheltered places in southern New York and attains a height of up to 7½ feet. About ½ inch in diameter, its canes are waxy below the nodes, bright green when young, and dull at maturity. The branches are mostly solitary, less often there are two or three from a node. The thick leaves, up to 1¼ feet long by 7½ inches wide, are bigger than those of any cultivated sasa except *S. tessellata*. They have smooth margins and prominent yellow midribs, bright green upper surfaces and silvery-grayish-green lower ones. In places where the spreading rhizomes can be allowed to run or can be kept under control, this bamboo forms an effective screen. A sort grown as *S. p. nebulosa* has green canes blotched with purple. It is perhaps the kind called *S. nebulosa* by some authorities. Easily identified by the size of its leaves, which are up to 2 feet long by 4 inches wide, **S. tessellata** has canes about 6 feet tall by ½ inch wide, bright green, and waxy. The branches, usually solitary, are sometimes paired. The leaves, glossy-green above, are markedly tessellated and have the bases of the midribs yellow. Their undersides are dull grayish-green. Under favorable conditions this is a rampant spreader. A native of Japan, it is hardy in sheltered places in southern New York.

Dwarfer kinds include **S. veitchii**, which rarely attains 3 feet in height but occasionally is up to 1 foot taller. Native to Japan, its canes about ¼ inch wide, it is dull purple at maturity. The branches, usually solitary, are occasionally two from a node. They bear leaves up to 10 inches long by 2½ inches wide with both edges fringed with fine, bristly hairs. Their upper surfaces are deep green and their undersides dull gray-green. This spreads rapidly and makes a dense cover. In southern New York, it is hardy in sheltered places. A lower variety, *S. v. nana* has somewhat smaller, more pointed leaves. Another low grower, Japanese **S. borealis** has dull, purplish-green canes 2½ to 3½ feet tall by ¼

inch thick and long-tapered leaves up to 1 foot long by 2 inches wide. The upper sides of the leaves are medium green, beneath they are duller. Another native of Japan, **S. nipponica**, 4 feet or less in height, has green, ½-inch-thick canes, usually solitary branches, and medium-green leaves up to 10 inches long by 1¼ inches wide. The plant often grown in gardens as *S. pygmaea* is *Arundinaria pygmaea*.

Garden and Landscape Uses and Cultivation. For information on these subjects see Bamboos.

SASH. The window-like sections that form the top of garden frames and hotbeds are called sashes. Usually removable, they consist of wood or metal frames fitted with panes of glass or covered with fiberglass or other transparent or translucent plastic.

SASKATOON is *Amelanchier alnifolia*.

SASSAFRAS (Sássa-fras). The familiar sassafras of eastern North America is one of a genus of three species of aromatic deciduous trees of the laurel family LAURACEAE. The others are natives of eastern Asia. The name, from the Spanish *salsafras*, refers to reputed medicinal virtues.

These trees have alternate, three-lobed or lobeless leaves. Their greenish-yellow flowers, unisexual with the sexes on separate trees or sometimes bisexual, come before or with the leaves and are in racemes. They have six-parted calyxes, but no petals. Male blooms have three circles of three stamens each, the inner three with a pair of glands at their bases. Female flowers have a slender style. The fruits are small drupes (fruits structured like plums).

The sassafras of North America (***Sassafras albidum*** syns. *S. officinale*, *S. variifolium*) occurs in the wild from Maine to Michigan, Florida, and Texas. Rarely it at-

Sassafras albidum

Sassafras albidum (male flowers)

Sassafras albidum (foliage)

tains a height of 125 feet, more commonly about one-half that. It has deeply-furrowed bark and a flat-topped, irregularly-pyramidal head. Bright green above and glaucous on their undersides, the hairless leaves, even on the same tree, vary considerably in shape, being roughly ovate to elliptic and very frequently with one or two side lobes, those with one lobe being somewhat mitten-like in outline. The leaves are 3 to 6 inches long. In fall they assume rich tones of orange and red. The flowers are in racemes about 2 inches long. Egg-shaped and about ⅓ inch long, the slightly wax-coated fruits, on fleshy, red stalks, are dark blue. Sassafras wood is very durable. It is used for fence posts, and for cooperage. An essential oil from this species is used for flavoring root beer and other beverages, chewing gum, candies, and pharmaceuticals.

Garden and Landscape Uses and Cultivation. The planting of sassafras as an ornamental is undoubtedly hindered by its intolerance of root disturbance. Specimens to be moved should be small and preferably root pruned a year previously. Alternatively, young trees can be grown in containers until they are set in their permanent locations. As an ornamental, sassafras is effective at all seasons, but most strikingly so when its foliage colors in fall. It is seen to particularly good advantage in

groups of three or more. It has the ability to grow in poor, gravelly soils as well as in those of better quality. No special care is needed by established trees. Propagation is by seeds sown in a cold frame or protected bed outdoors as soon as they are ripe, or stratified for a period of three months at 40°F and then sown in a greenhouse. Root cuttings also afford simple means of increase.

SATIN FLOWER. See Lunaria, and Sisyrinchium.

SATIN LEAF is *Chrysophyllum oliviforme.*

SATUREJA (Satur-èja) — Savory, Yerba Buena. Many plants once included in this genus, the name of which is sometimes spelled *Satureia*, are now placed in other genera, notably *Acinos*, *Calamintha*, *Clinopodium*, and *Micromeria*. The genus *Satureja*, as now understood, comprises thirty species, natives chiefly of the Mediterranean region, but some indigenous elsewhere, including North America. It belongs in the mint family LABIATAE. The name is derived from the Latin one of the summer savory.

Saturejas are aromatic herbaceous plants and subshrubs. From nearly related genera they are distinguished by their flowers having bell-shaped, ten- to thirteen-veined calyxes with five nearly equal, pointed lobes. The leaves are opposite. The blooms have straight, tubular, two-lipped corollas, with the upper lip erect and in some species notched, and the lower one three-lobed. There are four stamens and a two-lobed style. The fruits consist of four seedlike nutlets.

Summer savory (*S. hortensis*) is an annual 6 inches to 1 foot tall or taller. It has slender, finely-hairy stems and soft, usually hairless, grayish foliage. The spaces between the pairs of leaves are longer than the leaves. The latter are ½ to 1 inch in length, oblong-linear, and nearly stalkless. The white or pale lilac-pink flowers, up to ¼ inch long and nearly stalkless, have calyxes with tubes shorter than their lobes and corollas scarcely longer than the calyxes. The blooms, in short-stalked clusters of three to six from the axils of the upper leaves, form loose, one-sided spikes. This is a native of the Mediterranean region.

Winter savory (*S. montana*), up to about 1¼ feet tall, is generally similar to the last, but is a semievergreen perennial with the spaces between its pairs of up to 1-inch-long, oblong-linear, stalkless leaves shorter than the leaves. The white or lilac flowers, their lower lips spotted with purple, are ⅓ inch long or longer. Their calyxes are usually hairy and have tubes exceeding the lobes in length. The blooms are in slender panicles. This variable species is native to the Mediterranean region.

Satureja montana

Attractive yerba buena (*S. douglasii* syns. *Micromeria douglasii*, *M. chamissonis*), native from California to British Columbia, has slender, trailing, rooting stems up to about 2 feet long and evergreen, ovate, toothed, hairless to somewhat hairy leaves up to 1¼ inches long by 1 inch wide. The flowers, solitary and long-stalked from the leaf axils, and white to purplish, are approximately ⅜ inch long.

Satureja douglasii

Other natives of North America include *S. georgiana* (syns. *Clinopodium georgianum*, *C. carolinianum*) and *S. glabella* (syn. *Calamintha glabella*). A shrub up to 2 feet tall, **S. georgiana** has slightly-round-toothed, blunt-elliptic leaves up to 1 inch long and ½ inch wide, hairless on their upper surfaces. The pink to lavender flowers, about ½ inch long, are in whorls (tiers) of nine or fewer. Native from Kentucky to Arkansas, **S. glabella** is a 1-foot-high herbaceous perennial with stems hairy only at the nodes. The few-toothed leaves are oblanceolate, ordinarily from ¾ inch to 1¼ inches long by ½ to ¾ inch wide. The flowers, light purple and two to eight from a node, are 1 inch or a little more in length.

Garden Uses and Cultivation. The chief employments of winter and summer savories are as culinary sweet herbs and garnishes. The latter has also been employed as a vermifuge. Winter savory may not be reliably hardy in climates harsher than that of New York City. Yerba buena, not hardy in the north, where it survives winters is an attractive herb in herb gardens and for use as a groundcover, thriving in light shade in ordinary soil and especially suitable for herb gardens and, in appropriate regions, native plant gardens. It is also interesting for growing in pots or hanging baskets indoors. The other native American sorts discussed are adapted for native plant gardens and herb gardens. All thrive in ordinary soil and are easily increased by seed and cuttings. For further information see Savory.

SATYRIUM (Satýr-ium). More than 100 species, natives of South Africa, the Mascarene Islands, India, and China, constitute *Satyrium*, of the orchid family ORCHIDACEAE. The name is an adaptation of Satyrion, used by Dioscorides as the name for an unidentified orchid.

Satyriums are ground orchids. They have tuberous roots and usually few, sometimes only two, basal or near-basal leaves. More rarely, they have stems with many leaves. The flowers, in dense spikes, have separate, spreading or reflexed sepals and petals and a hooded or broad-concave, erect lip.

South African *S. erectum*, 1 foot to 2 feet tall, has spreading, broad-oblong basal

Satyrium erectum in South Africa

leaves and, completely hiding the stem, down-pointing, concave bracts. The handsome, rather crowded spike of flowers has bracts about as long as its numerous yellowish-orange to light purple blooms, which have sepals and petals scarcely longer than the hooded lip. Also South African, *S. coriifolium* is up to 1 foot tall. It has spreading, pointed-oblanceolate leaves with slightly-roughened margins. In spikes on stalks with ovate bracts, its yellow flowers have linear sepals and petals, a longer, nearly circular lip, and a cylindrical spur hairy on its inside. Variety *S. c. aureum* has golden-yellow flowers suffused with crimson.

Satyrium coriifolium in South Africa

Cultivation. Rare in cultivation, the sorts of this genus mostly do best in cool, humid greenhouses. A winter night temperature of 50°F with an increase of five degrees by day is appropriate. It is probable that the species described above would accommodate to outdoor cultivation in essentially frost-free climates, such as that of California. Pot or plant in a well-drained mixture of peat moss, topsoil, and coarse sand. Water freely when in growth, seldom or not at all when dormant. For more information see Orchids.

SAURAUIA (Saurau-ia). The name of this genus of about 300 species of trees and shrubs of the tropics and warm subtropics of the Americas and Asia has also been spelled *Saurauja*. It commemorates Fr. J. von Saurau, Austrian statesman, who died in 1832. The group belongs to the dillenia family DILLENIACEAE, or according to those who favor splitting that family, to the actinidia family ACTINIDIACEAE.

Saurauias are small trees and shrubs with undivided, usually toothed leaves. The flowers, generally bisexual, are in axillary, mostly many-flowered, panicles. They have five overlapping sepals, five overlapping petals united at their bases or nearly separate, and many stamens. The fruits are berries.

A bold-foliaged shrub 6 to 8 feet tall, *Saurauia subspinosa* is native to Burma. It has oblanceolate, toothed leaves with blades 5 to 9 inches long by 2 inches broad. Their upper sides are lustrous and have prominent parallel veins curving upward and outward from the midribs, and short stalks, densely-hairy, as are the veins on the lower sides of the leaves. The flowers have broadly-bell-shaped corollas ⅓ inch wide or a little wider. Pale pink to nearly white, with deep red interiors, they have bristly stalks.

Saurauia subspinosa

Garden and Landscape Uses and Cultivation. Little experience has been had with this impressive, shapely shrub in America. It would seem to be well suited for warm climates where little or no frost is experienced. At Longwood Gardens, Kennett Square, Pennsylvania, it is a handsome embellishment in a large conservatory. Ordinary, moderately moist, fertile soil supports satisfactory growth. No systematic periodic pruning is required. Propagation is by cuttings, air layering, and seed. Indoors, a winter night temperature of 50 to 55°F suits. Day temperatures in winter are five to fifteen degrees higher. Warmer conditions both night and day are in order at other seasons.

SAUROMATUM (Sauró-matum) — Voodoo-Lily or Monarch-of-the-East. The half dozen species of *Sauromatum*, of the arum family ARACEAE, in the wild inhabit the tropics and subtropics of Africa and Asia. Relatives of the jack-in-the-pulpit and the calla-lily, they have a name, referring to the spotted surface of the inside of the spathe, that comes from the Greek *sauros*, a lizard.

Sauromatums are jack-in-the-pulpit-like, tuberous, herbaceous perennials. Each tuber produces a solitary, long-stalked leaf, the blade palmately-three-lobed, with the side lobes again deeply-cleft. As is common in the arum family, what are seemingly and are usually called flowers are inflorescences consisting of many small, inconspicuous, unisexual blooms grouped along a central, spikelike organ called a spadix, from the base of which comes a bract (modified leaf) called a spathe. In *Sauromatum* the female flowers on the lower portion of the spadix are separated from the males above by a section of spadix bearing club-shaped, rudimentary blooms. The fruits are berries.

Voodoo-lily or monarch-of-the-East (*S. guttatum* syn. *S. venosum*), a native of northwest India, has tubers up to 6 inches

Sauromatum guttatum

in diameter and a leaf usually developed after, but sometimes at, flowering time. The leafstalk is 1 foot to 2 feet long, and spotted or not. The roundish-ovate blade is deeply-divided into up to eleven oblong-lanceolate to oblong segments up to 1 foot in length. The inflorescence has a stalk 2 to 4 inches long, a slender, tapering spadix, and a spathe with its base wrapped around to form a cylindrical lower part 2 to 4 inches long, and with a 1-inch-wide, drooping, somewhat twisted blade 1 foot to 2 feet in length, green or purplish, and on the inside green, beautifully marked with irregular black-purple spots. For two or three days when the flowers are fully mature they emit a powerful, foul odor of putrid flesh. At this time specimens grown as houseplants must be banished temporarily to a porch, garage, or other place where their evil

smell cannot offend, or at least not much. The voodoo-lily is sometimes wrongly identified as *Arum cornutum*.

Garden Uses and Cultivation. The voodoo-lily, the only kind commonly cultivated, is grown as a curiosity outdoors in warm regions and in greenhouses, and sometimes as a houseplant. Advertisers are likely to offer it as a remarkable plant that blooms without soil or water, if flowering-size tubers are set in a fairly warm place. In so doing, however, the tubers exhaust themselves and will not bloom again. As permanent plants, sauromatums thrive in fertile, humus-rich soil kept moist from the time the new leaf begins to grow until it dies, and dry during the season of dormancy. When resting, the tubers may be stored in or out of soil. In mild climates where little or no frost is experienced, the voodoo plant can remain permanently in the ground outdoors, and even in the vicinity of New York City this can be done if it is planted in a sheltered location and if the ground is covered over winter with 1 foot of leaves or other loose mulch. The tubers should be planted about 6 inches deep where there is light shade. In pots, this species thrives with minimum attention. In summer the pots may be put outdoors, sunk nearly to their rims in sand, peat moss, or earth. Propagation is by offsets and by seed.

SAURURACEAE—Lizard's Tail Family. The seven species of this North American and eastern Asian family of dicotyledons are accommodated in four genera. They are herbaceous perennials with alternate, undivided leaves, the upper ones often colored, petal-like, and forming an involucre or collar beneath the flowers. The latter are small, symmetrical, and in dense spikes or racemes. They are without calyxes, have a corolla of three, six, or eight petals or, by abortion, rarely fewer. The pistil is composed of three or four separate or joined carpels each with its own style. The fruits are dry.

Cultivated genera are *Anemopsis*, *Houttuynia*, and *Saururus*.

Saururus cernuus

SAURURUS (Saur-ùrus) — Lizard's Tail. One species of this genus is a native American, the other three are indigenous to eastern Asia. They belong in the lizard's tail family SAURURACEAE, a group related to the pepper family PIPERACEAE. The name is from the Greek *sauros*, a lizard, and *oura*, a tail. It refers to the slender flower spikes. The sorts of this genus are herbaceous perennials.

The only kind likely to be cultivated is the American *Saururus cernuus*, which inhabits swamps and marshlands from southern Quebec and southern New England to Michigan, Minnesota, Florida, and Texas. It has extensively creeping, slender, aromatic rhizomes from which spring erect, branching stems 1½ to 4 feet tall. The long-stalked leaves are pointed-heart-shaped with several veins that spread from the base and converge at the tip. The spikes of bloom are terminal and overtop the foliage. They are 4 inches to 1 foot long with their tips recurved or nodding. Each spike consists of a large number of small white flowers crowded along its length. They are without sepals or petals, being reduced to the functional parts necessary for sexual propagation, the male organs or stamens, and the female parts or pistils. Nevertheless, there are enough of these to form decorative flower spikes, and being fragrant, they are the more pleasing.

Garden Uses and Cultivation. The lizard's tail is suitable for bog gardens, watersides, and for planting in tubs or beds in ornamental pools. It grows without difficulty in swampy land or shallow water and is quite pretty both in foliage and bloom. It may be planted in spring or early fall, the former being preferable. Rich soil that contains a goodly supply of organic matter is most to its liking, but it is not fussy. It needs a sunny location. Once established it may be left undisturbed for several years. Only if it begins to deteriorate or to exceed its allotted space is it necessary to take it up, divide it, and replant. Propagation is by division or by seeds sown in soil maintained in a muddy condition. Sowing should be done as soon as the seeds are ripe.

SAUSAGE TREE is *Kigelia pinnata*.

SAUSSUREA (Saus-sùrea). Of its estimated more than 400 species, one of *Saussurea* inhabits western North America, one Europe, one Australia, and the remainder temperate Asia, mostly in the mountains. This is indeed a curious natural distribution. The genus, of the daisy family COMPOSITAE, has a name commemorating Horace Benedict de Saussure, a Swiss philosopher, who died in 1799.

Saussureas are somewhat thistle-like herbaceous plants. They have alternate, generally lobed or toothed, but spineless leaves and solitary or loosely clustered, purplish or bluish flower heads consisting of all disk florets. The involucre (collar of bracts at the back of the flower head) is spherical to egg-shaped and of many overlapping bracts. The seedlike fruits are achenes.

Native to the Himalayas, *S. albescens* is 2 feet tall or taller. It has branchless stems and stalkless, scarcely-lobed or lobeless, broad-elliptic leaves, white-hairy on their undersides. The flower heads, with slightly hoary involucres and reddish-purple florets, are about ¾ inch in diameter. Its stems 4 to 8 inches tall, *S. densa* (syn. *S. alpina densa*) has lanceolate, elliptic-lanceolate, toothed leaves 2 to 3 inches long and webbed with fine hairs. The purple flower heads are 1½ to 2 inches across. An inhabitant of the mountains of central Europe, *S. pygmaea* has solitary stems 3 to 8 inches tall and, chiefly in a basal rosette, stalkless, hairy, linear to linear-lanceolate leaves 1½ to 3 inches long. The blue-violet flower heads are solitary and about 1¼ inches across.

Garden Uses and Cultivation. Low saussureas are suitable for rock gardens, taller ones for naturalistic plantings. They respond to ordinary well-drained soil and need sunny locations. Most are easy to grow, but those from alpine regions may not thrive where summers are hot and humid. Propagation is by seed.

SAVORY. Two species of sweet herbs of the genus *Satureja* are called by this name. They are grown in herb and vegetable gardens and are used fresh and dried for flavoring and seasoning, and fresh for garnishing. They were among the first plants introduced from Europe to America by the early colonists. Summer savory (*S. hortensis*) is considered superior to winter savory (*S. montana*). It has been employed as a vermifuge. Both are good bee plants.

Summer savory is raised from seeds sown in well-drained, moderately fertile soil in spring, in rows 1 foot to 1½ feet apart, or in ornamental herb gardens, scattered in patches. In either case, before they crowd, the seedlings are thinned out from 5 to 6 inches apart.

Winter savory can be propagated in the same way as summer savory or by summer cuttings each consisting of a short side shoot with a heel (small piece of older stem) attached to its base. The cuttings root easily in a shaded cold frame, under mist, or even in a shaded, sheltered place outdoors in sandy soil kept moist. Division in early spring is yet another way of increasing stocks of winter savory. This kind seems to do best in soils rather low in nutrients. Too lush a diet does not produce the best results.

Harvesting for drying is done as soon as the flower buds begin to open. Then the stems are cut, tied together in small bundles, and hung in a cool, airy place in shade until quite dry.

SAWDUST. In moderate quantities sawdust can be employed in much the same ways as peat moss to add organic matter to the soil, and as a mulch. If it has been used for bedding animals, or composted with vegetable refuse, or if, as a result of being piled in the open for a considerable period, it is half decayed, its suitability for these purposes is enhanced. Unless a readily available source of nitrogen is used with it, fresh sawdust added to soil temporarily reduces the amount available to plants of this essential element, even to the extent that growth may be seriously checked. This is because the bacteria of decay that work upon the sawdust and multiply, rapidly abstract nitrogen from the soil to build their own bodies (later, when they die, this is returned).

Sawdust employed as a mulch should generally not exceed 1 inch in depth and it is advisable to spread with it 1 pound of sulfate of ammonia (or other fertilizer that will supply an equivalent amount of quickly available nitrogen) to each 100 square feet.

SAWFLIES. Stingless relatives of bees and wasps, these insects differ in having no waist (constriction between the thorax and abdomen) and in the females possessing a pair of "saws," pointed, flattened plates at the tip of the abdomen that slide between two guide plates. With this equipment she cuts into plant tissues and then deposits her eggs in the cuts.

The larvae of sawflies, many of which resemble caterpillars of butterflies and moths, differ in having a solitary simple eye (ocellus) instead of several on each side of the head and also in being usually without legs on the abdomen or, if these are present, in not having the circles of hooks common on the legs of caterpillars.

The larvae of practically all sawflies feed on plants, upon which they live in colonies or singly. A few sorts spin webs, a few are leaf miners. There are many sorts, often named after the kinds of plants upon which they chiefly or exclusively feed. Examples are the arbor-vitae sawfly, cherry fruit sawfly, coiled rose sawfly, dogwood sawflies, elm sawfly, European apple sawfly, European pine sawfly, introduced pine sawfly, and mountain-ash sawfly. In addition there are pestiferous sawflies usually identified by other names. Here belong the rose-slug, bristly rose-slug, pear slug and California pear-slug, and imported currant-worm. Controls consist chiefly of spraying with stomach poison insecticides.

SAXEGOTHAEA (Saxegothaè-a) — Prince-Albert-Yew. One species is the only member of the genus *Saxegothaea*, of the podocarpus family PODOCARPACEAE. Native to the Andes of Argentina and Chile, it was named in honor of Prince Albert of Saxe-Coburg-Gotha, consort of Queen Victoria.

He died in 1861. Although called Prince-Albert-yew, this unusual evergreen tree is more closely related to *Podocarpus* and *Araucaria* than to the yew (*Taxus*); indeed, it is considered a connecting link between the families PODOCARPACEAE and ARAUCARIACEAE. However, trees of *Saxegothaea* resemble yews in gross appearance, which is the reason for their common name.

Prince-Albert-yew (*S. conspicua*) may become 40 to 60 feet tall, but often is

Saxegothaea conspicua

lower. Its branches spread widely and are pendulous at their ends. They bear branchlets in opposite pairs or in whorls of three or four. Male and female flowers are on the same plant, the former in cylindrical spikes, clustered near the tips of the branchlets, the latter solitary at the branchlet ends. The fruits are fleshy cones resembling those of junipers. They are formed of grooved scales and are up to ½ inch long. Each contains six to twelve small flattened seeds.

Garden and Landscape Uses and Cultivation. This rare conifer is a collector's item scarcely known in cultivation in North America. It is hardy only in regions of mild winters and is probably best adapted for the Pacific Northwest. It succeeds in good garden soil, well drained, but not excessively dry, and may be propagated by seeds sown in sandy, peaty soil or by cuttings inserted under mist or in a propagating bench in a humid, cool greenhouse or cold frame in summer. Increase may also be had by veneer grafting onto yew (*Taxus*) or *Podocarpus*.

SAXIFRAGA (Saxí-fraga)—Saxifrage, Rockfoil, Strawberry-Geranium, London Pride, Prince's Feather. This, the name genus of the saxifrage family SAXIFRAGACEAE, consists of about 370 species, mostly of temperate, alpine, and subarctic regions, and in addition, a number of natural hybrids as well as many of garden origin. The name, derived from the Latin *saxum*, a rock, and *frango*, to break, alludes to these plants frequently inhabiting rock crevices and by doing so giving the impression that they are responsible for the cleavages. By extension of this reasoning, under the doctrine of signatures, they were thought to have medicinal value in treating stones of the bladder. Some large-leaved plants of easy cultivation previously included in *Saxifraga* and still sometimes grown as such, belong in *Bergenia* and *Peltiphyllum*.

The horticultural popularity of saxifrages in North America is much less than in northern Europe, where it is not unusual for rock garden enthusiasts and operators of alpine greenhouses to care for extensive collections and where some easy-to-manage saxifrages are common garden plants. With few exceptions, the sorts of *Saxifraga* abhor high temperatures and arid atmospheres and, except in specially favored areas, such as parts of the Pacific Northwest and northern New England and adjacent Canada, most do poorly in North America.

Saxifrages vary much in habit and aspect. The vast majority are low, some are mosslike. Others are notable for white encrustations that decorate their foliage. These consist of lime absorbed in solution by the roots and deposited on the leaf surfaces as transpired water evaporates. Mostly herbaceous perennials, but including a few annuals and biennials, saxifragas are usually tufted and have stems that are subterranean or emerge for only a little distance, but there are some of more wandering, even trailing growth. Generally the foliage is all or mostly basal. Stem leaves are usually alternate. White, pink, yellow, or purple, the symmetrical or less frequently asymmetrical flowers are in panicles, racemes, or other grouped arrangements or are in some sorts solitary. Of small to medium size in relation to the sizes of the plants, they are generally produced in such abundance that the total effect is showy. Each has a five-parted calyx, usually five petals, ten stamens, and generally two styles. The fruits are capsules.

The saxifragas native in North America, except for a very few circumboreal sorts that also inhabit Europe and Asia, a selection of which is described later under their respective sections, practically all belong to the not very exciting section *Boraphila*. This group is distinguished by possessing comparatively few soft, hairy, usually toothed leaves in basal rosettes and in spring or early summer little white or whitish, sometimes pink-spotted flowers in loose or less often crowded panicles or spikes. These sorts mostly inhabit woodlands where the soil is dampish and they receive light shade. The most garden worthy of the boraphilas, none of which approaches in beauty the better sorts of other sections of the genus, are nevertheless worth considering for use in wild gardens and native plant gardens. Among such are *S. ferruginea*, native from Montana to British Columbia and Alaska; *S. mertensiana*, native from California to Alaska; *S. occidentalis*, native from Montana to Alberta; *S. pensylvanica*, native from Maine and Ontario to Minnesota, Virginia, and Missouri; *S. rhomboidea*, native from Idaho to British Columbia, and Colorado; *S. tennesseensis*, of Tennessee; and *S. virginiensis*, native from New Brunswick to Arkansas, Georgia, and Tennessee.

Saxifraga tennesseensis

Saxifraga virginiensis

The yellow mountain saxifrage (*S. aizoides*), of the section *Xanthizoon*, is a variable native of Europe, Asia, and arctic North America. Typically it forms loose mats with linear-oblong, toothed or bristle-margined, thick leaves up to 1 inch in length. Its flowers, in loose clusters or less often solitary on leafy stems up to 6 inches or so tall, are yellow to orange, often spotted with red, or less often are red or purple.

The purple mountain saxifrage (*S. oppositifolia*), of the *Porphyrion* section of the genus, which occurs in northern latitudes around the world, inhabits usually north-facing mountain slopes in Oregon and Washington and in the northern Rocky Mountains. This produces dense, tangled mats of prostrate stems and opposite, blunt, obovate, keeled leaves up to ⅜ inch long, with hairy margins. Its rose-pink to purple, ½-inch-wide flowers have the briefest of stalks.

Mossy saxifragas (section *Dactyloides*) comprise a delightful lot that contains numerous hybrids and varieties as well as a considerable quota of species. Those that do well (there are a few high alpine ones of tight cushion-like habit that, even where others succeed, do not adapt easily to cultivation) form thick to somewhat looser mats of little rosettes of foliage and in early summer carry an abundance of white, pale to deep pink, or red flowers. Hairless to moderately hairy, mossy saxifrages have green leaves variously cleft or lobed. They favor dampish, gritty soils and need slight shade from strong sun. Very variable *S. caespitosa*, a widely distributed native of cool regions throughout the northern hemisphere, is a mossy that forms mostly loosely-leafy mats or patches with broad, glandular-hairy leaves cleft into wide and blunt, or narrow and pointed lobes. Its flowers, on stalks about 4 inches long, when fully open are flat. They have white petals two or three times as long as the sepals and not narrowed at their bases into claws. Variety *S. c. compacta*, which forms tight tufts or cushions, is dwarfer than the species. Variety *S. c. hirta* is distinct because of its white-woolly foliage. Many hybrids are cultivated as *S. caespitosa*, some with red or pink blooms, which usually indicates *S. muscoides atropurpurea* has played a part in their parentage. Spanish *S. camposii* (syn. *S. wallacei*) is one of the most attractive mossies. Robust, it forms cushions, 4 to 6 inches high, of clammy, hairy stems and leaves, the latter sharply-three-lobed. Freely produced and long-lasting, the white flowers are ¾ inch in diameter. Especially richly-silvered foliage is characteristic of densely-tufted *S. crustata* (syn. *S. incrustata*), of the eastern European Alps and Yugoslavia. This has linear leaves up to 1½ inches long and, in season, stalks up to 6 inches tall or taller displaying ⅜-inch-wide white flowers sometimes marked with purple at the bases of their petals. Fragrant-foliaged *S.*

geranioides, of the Pyrenees, is particularly lovely. Densely-tufted, it has thickish, long-stalked, hairy leaves, often slightly clammy and with blades variously cleft and abruptly narrowed to their

Saxifraga geranioides

Saxifraga moschata

Saxifraga rosacea (flowers)

stalks. Not widely expanded, the snow-white flowers are in open panicles reaching heights of 6 to 8 inches. Cushion-forming, variable **S. hypnoides,** of North America as well as western Europe, is often very compact. Bulbils form in the axils of its long-stalked, emerald-green leaves, which are very-finely-three- to five-cleft with each segment tipped with a bristle. The up-to-1-inch-wide, creamy-white flowers, nodding in bud and in clusters of mostly four to six, are on stems 6 to 9 inches tall. Bright green, sometimes glandular but not clammy, **S. moschata** forms loose to crowded tufts with blunt-lobed leaves. In the typical species the flowers are yellowish-white to whitish, less commonly purplish or deep purple. Their petals are 1¼ to 1½ times as long as the sepals. Garden plants frequently of questionable parentage and grown as *S. moschata* often have pink flowers. There are also light yellow-flowered varieties, one with double blooms. A native of high altitudes in the Pyrenees, **S. muscoides** is very dwarf and much more densely tufted than allied *S. moschata,* with which it is often confused. Its blunt, linear to lanceolate, lobeless leaves are without narrow, transparent margins. The ¼-inch-wide, white to yellow flowers on stalks 2 to 3 inches tall have petals twice as long as the sepals. The blooms of *S. m. atropurpurea* are red. Another charming, variable mossy, **S. pedemontana,** native to the central European Alps and with varieties inhabiting the Maritime Alps and the Carpathians, is densely-foliaged and has rather fleshy, short-stalked, obovate to fan-shaped, glandular-hairy, lobed leaves. Its white flowers, in clusters of three to seven on stalks 1 inch to 2½ inches long, have petals two or three times as long as their narrow sepals. Akin to *S. geranioides,* from

which it differs in the bases of its leaf blades tapering gradually rather than abruptly to their stalks, **S. prostii** forms semishrubby tufts of firm stems and long-

Saxifraga prostii

stalked, hair-fringed, five- to eleven-cleft leaves. Its goblet-shaped, pure white blooms are in clusters of five to ten on stalks 4 to 6 inches tall. The name of **S. rosacea** (syn. *S. decipiens*) is an embracing one for a vast and intergrading array of

Saxifraga rosacea

forms or varieties, many of the more distinct of which have been given identifying names. This species is akin to *S. caespitosa* and intermediate forms connect these species. A distinctive, woody-stemmed native of Spain, hairless **S. trifurcata** (syn. *S. ceratophylla*) has clammy, long-stalked, thick, leathery, aromatic leaves cleft in staghorn fashion into up to thirteen recurved segments. The numerous large white flowers in reddish-branched, loose sprays somewhat resemble those of *S. geranioides,* but are more goblet-shaped. This stands exposure to sun better than most mossy saxifrages.

The *Trachyphyllum* section of *Saxifraga* consists of mat-forming sorts with most of the attributes of the mossies, but having lanceolate to wedge-shaped, bristle-tipped or three-toothed, bristly-margined leaves. The flowers are commonly white, very much less frequently purple. Belonging to this group, Siberian **S. bronchialis** is represented in the flora of alpine and arctic North America by its varieties *S. b. austromontana* and *S. b. funstonii.* Of mosslike aspect, these have crowded, rigid, more or less glandular-hairy leaves, ¼ to ½ inch long, and in loose raceme- or panicle-like arrangements 2 to 8 inches tall, whitish flowers, those of the first spotted with red, those of the other with yellow.

Encrusted or silvery saxifragas (section *Euaizoonia*) include some of the loveliest of the genus, splendid in foliage, marvelous in bloom. The common designations of the group allude to very obvious crustations of lime that decorate their leaves. The species that belong here are nearly all variable, often to the extent that precise identification is difficult. Referring to cultivated specimens of particular species is further complicated because encrusted saxifrages hybridize with such abandon that seeds collected in gardens, unless special precautions have been taken to prevent cross-pollination, almost always produce mongrel swarms of individuals that may be charming, but are not repli-

A pot-grown encrusted saxifrage

cas of the mother plant. Characteristically, encrusted saxifrages have rosettes that die after they bloom. With a few sorts the life of the plant then ends, but well in advance of blooming the rosettes of most kinds develop offsets that persist and bloom in future years. These in time build into sizable clumps or cushions. The flowers, in moderately to decidedly long, loosely- to densely-flowered panicles, come in summer.

Mats of large rosettes are formed by *S. callosa* (syn. *S. lingulata*), of the European Alps. Their long, narrow, pointed, more

Saxifraga callosa

or less erect, gray leaves, thickened and recurved at their apexes, are decorated along their margins with limy beads. The white flowers are in gracefully arching panicles 1 foot to 1½ feet long. Variety *S. c. australis* has leaves greener than those of the typical species, hairy toward their bases, broadest above their middles. Its flowers are sometimes spotted with pink. More spreading to prostrate, shorter, blunt, spatula-shaped leaves with hollowed upper surfaces and continuous

rather than beaded limy crustations along their margins characterize *S. c. lantoscana.* The flowers of this, in panicles up to 1 foot high, tend to be more crowded than those of the species. The foliage rosettes of *S. cochlearis,* of the European Alps, are of obscurely to more obviously toothed,

Saxifraga cochlearis

spatula-shaped leaves up to 1 inch long, narrowed at their bases, abruptly expanded and then subcircular toward their apexes, with the widened portion hairfringed at its base. The stems of the graceful panicles of bloom branch below their middles. Up to over ½ inch long, the white flowers are often spotted toward their centers with purple. From the species, *S. c. minor* differs in its much smaller rosettes and shorter sprays of bloom. One of the noblest encrusted saxifrages, *S. cotyledon* has rosettes 6 inches to exceptionally 1 foot across of broad, strapshaped leaves. Its bold pyramidal panicles, under favorable conditions 2 to 3 feet long, are of sometimes pink-spotted, snowwhite flowers. Most impressive of the many variants is *S. c. icelandica,* the rosettes of which may exceed 1 foot in diameter, the panicles 4 feet in length. Also

Saxifraga cotyledon icelandica

of special merit is *S. c. pyramidalis,* its panicles of white or pink-spotted white blooms branching from close to their bases. Clustered rosettes that produce offsets freely and develop into wide patches are typical of *S. hostii,* of limestone habitats in the European Alps. The strap-shaped leaves, down-turned at their tapered apexes, are beaded with deposits of lime along their margins. The pinkish-spotted, yellowish-white flowers are in flattishtopped panicles up to 1 foot or sometimes more in height. Rivaling *S. cotyledon* in impressiveness, *S. longifolia,* of the

Saxifraga longifolia

Pyrenees, has rosettes 4 to 7 inches in diameter of many linear-lanceolate leaves with lime-encrusted margins. From the centers of the rosettes rise conical panicles 1 foot to 2 feet in length branched from their bases and with glandular-pubescent stalks. The numerous ½-inch-wide blooms are white, sometimes spotted with pinkish-purple. Specimens of this species take a few years to gain strength enough to flower. Extremely rarely, they develop offsets that live after the chief rosette has flowered and set seeds, but there is little doubt that most specimens reported to have done this were hybrids. This is not surprising because, to quote the renowned English alpine gardener Clarence Elliott, "In the garden *longifolia* contracts alliances with every other silver saxifrage within working radius of a bee, and garden-saved seed of *longifolia* will give a most astonishing range of beautiful mongrels, whose distinguishing feature is that no two are alike, and scarcely one will be true *longifolia*." A notable hybrid of *S. longifolia,* which probably has as its other parent *S. callosa* and has not undeservedly been called the queen of saxifragas, is *S.* 'Tumbling Waters'. This develops giant rosettes of beautifully silvered foliage and in due time curved plumes 2 to 3 feet long, larger and of more virginal white blooms than those of the finest *S. longifolia.* But best of all, 'Tumbling Waters' develops offsets and these provide a ready means

Saxifraga 'Tumbling Waters'

of assuring its continuance after rosettes that have flowered die. The mountains of central Europe are the home of **S. mutata**, which has stout rhizomes and rosettes of thick, blunt, spatula-shaped, horny-margined leaves up to 3 inches long and green with little or no silvering. This sort appreciates some shade. The tawny-yellow to orange, narrow-petaled, starry flowers, about ½ inch across, are in sprays up to 1 foot long. Variable **S. paniculata** (syns. *S. aizoon*, *S. cartilaginea*), of Europe and

Saxifraga paniculata

northern North America, is densely encrusted. It has rosettes of incurved, blunt, obovate-oblong to narrowly-spatula-shaped, toothed leaves 1 inch to 1½ inches long, margined with white-encrusted teeth. Erect and nearly always glandular-hairy, its panicles of bloom begin branching at one-

third of their heights from their bases. White or white spotted with pink, the flowers are up to ½ inch wide. Notable varieties are *S. p. balcana*, with red-spotted white flowers; *S. p. baldensis*, which forms very compact cushions of short, thick, ashy-gray leaves and has red young shoots and whitish flowers; *S. p. flavescens*, its blooms lemon-yellow; and *S. p. rosea*, with pink flowers. Also of the European Alps, **S. valdensis**, which has much the aspect of a miniature *S. paniculata*, is densely-tufted and has narrow-spatula-shaped leaves and, on 2-inch-tall stalks, compact heads of creamy-white flowers.

Kabschia or cushion saxifragas (section *Kabschia*) afford a bewildering array of species and hybrids that include some of the most fascinating and beautiful members of the genus, mostly not very easy to grow. From encrusted saxifragas, kabschias differ chiefly in their offsets not separating from the rhizomes, but instead building into tight cushions or mounds. Their flowers, fairly large for the sizes of the plants, are white, yellow, pink, or purple, without spotting, and solitary or few to several on each stalk. Here belong as a subsection of the group sorts often distinguished in gardens as *Engleri* saxifragas.

Among the best-known kabschias, **S. aretioides**, of limestone regions in the Pyrenees, holds an honored place because of its importance as parent of numerous superior garden hybrids generally easier to grow than the typical species. This forms exceedingly compact, irregular cushions of woody stems up to 2 inches long and firm, linear, glaucous-gray-green, horny-margined leaves up to ¼ inch long. Its golden-yellow flowers are three to five or more on stalks that come from the tops of the stems. The plant frequently cultivated as *S. a. primulina* is *S. diapensioides lutea*. Variable **S. burserana** is an especially lovely native of limestone screes in the European Alps. Characteristically it forms dome-shaped cushions of rosettes of pointed, narrow, horny-edged leaves up to ½ inch long, the younger ones with limy incrustations. Usually solitary on red stalks 1 inch to 2 inches long, and opening from red buds, its brilliant white flowers are about 1 inch across. Varieties include *S. b. crenata*, the flowers of which have petals with frilled margins; *S. b.* 'Gloria', with red stems and large white blooms; *S. b. major*, with larger blooms; and *S. b. minor*, neat and dwarf and with flowers on ½-inch-long stalks. Native in limestone soils from the Pyrenees to the Alps of Europe, **S. caesia** forms wide, dense mats of stems and gray-green foliage. The former are slender, branched, and about 2 inches long. In small rosettes, the leaves are small, flattish, and when young crusted with lime. The white flowers are in panicles 2 to 3 inches high of three to four. Variety *S. c. major* has larger leaves and

flowers. This species, which has given rise to many varieties recognized horticulturally, is parent of numerous attractive hybrids. Tiny, slow-growing **S. diapensioides**, of the European Alps, forms very firm, compact hummucks 1 inch to 2 inches tall of stems and silvery-gray to blue-gray, blunt leaves, hairy at their bases and up to ¼ inch long. The milky-white flowers, in twos to fives or sometimes solitary, are on hairy stems 1 inch to 3 inches high. Possibly a hybrid, *S. d. lutea* (syn. *S. aretioides primulina*) is similar, but has pale yellow flowers. Perhaps the finest species of the group, Balkan **S. ferdinandi-coburgii**, parent of many hybrids, has compact cushions of spiny, silver-gray leaves and displays, on 2-inch-tall stems, of ½-inch-wide bright yellow flowers. **S. grisebachii**, of the *Engleri* subsection, is native to the Balkan Peninsula and Greece. This has clusters of a few symmetrical rosettes of spatula-shaped leaves up to 1½ inches long, heavily incrusted with lime and with horny margins. At flowering time the center of the rosette turns crimson and develops an arching stem that, like the narrow, scalelike leaves it bears and the baggy calyxes of the rose-pink, ³⁄₁₆-inch-long flowers that form the spike of bloom, is clothed with crimson, glandular hairs. Superior *S. g.* 'Wisley Variety' is larger, more intensely colored, and displays its flowers more advantageously. Named be-

Saxifraga grisebachii 'Wisley Variety'

cause of the juniper-like fragrance its foliage emits when bruised, variable Bulgarian **S. juniperifolia** (syn. *S. juniperina*) forms rosettes of up to ¾-inch-long, dark green (hair-fringed) leaves and bears ovoid to rounded heads of yellow flowers a little over ¼ inch across. Southern European *S. marginata* (syn. *S. coriophylla*) is a variable, tufted sort with silvery rosettes of up to ½-inch-long, translucent-edged, linear-oblong to ovate-spatula-shaped leaves. About ½ inch across, the pure white to delicate pink flowers are up to four on stalks about 2 inches tall. Belonging to *Engleri*, a subsection of the section *Kabschia*, *S. media*, of the Pyrenees, has symmetrical rosettes of silvery, about 1-inch-long leaves with lime-incrusted margins. Its small, purple-pink flowers, in racemes 3 to 4 inches long, have red-hairy calyxes. Also of the *Engleri* subsection, variable *S. porophylla*, of southern Europe, in effect is a smaller edition of *S. grisebachii*. It has horny-margined, oblong-spatula-shaped to linear leaves up to ½ inch long and pink to purple flowers slightly under ¼ inch wide. The Balkan Peninsula is home to *S. scardica*, which forms domed mounds of columnar rosettes of rigid, blue-gray, oblong to lanceolate, up to ½-inch-long leaves, keeled on their undersides and with horny, more or less hair-fringed margins. The pure white or pink-tinted flowers, a little over ¼ inch long, are clustered on 2- to 3-inch-long stalks. The smallest and one of the slowest-growing *Kabschia* saxifragas, densely-tufted *S. squarrosa*, of limestone regions in the Tyrolean mountains of Europe, has rosettes of linear to linear-lanceolate leaves ⅛ inch long. Its heads of white flowers are on 2-inch-tall, glandular stems. Excellent *S. stribrnyi*, of the *Engleri* subsection of the genus, is parent of several good hybrids. Native of Bulgaria and Greece, it has handsome rosettes of silvery-gray, oblong-spatula-shaped leaves up to 1 inch long. Its 3- to 5-inch-long stems branched, with the branches terminating in flat rosettes of silvery-gray, oblong-spatula-shaped leaves up to 1 inch long, *S. s. stribrnyi* has, in panicles of ten to thirty, purplish-pink blooms ⁵⁄₁₆ inch wide with baggy calyxes clothed with rich red glandular hairs.

Hybrid *Kabschia* saxifragas are numerous. Among those best known are these: *S. apiculata*, its parents *S. juniperifolia sancta* and *S. marginata rocheliana*, forms loose tufts of sharp-pointed basal leaves up to 6 inches long and smaller, spatula-shaped stem leaves. The flowers, five to nine to each stem, are yellow. *S. boeckeleri*, the result of mating *S. ferdinandi-coburgii* and *S. stribrnyi*, has rosettes of leaves under ½ inch long in clusters and flowering stems up to 3 inches tall carrying red-flushed, yellow blooms. *S. elizabethae*, its parents *S. burserana* and *S. juniperifolia sancta*, forms mats of rosettes of blue-green foliage and has heads of small yellow flowers on 3-inch-tall stems. *S. sundermannii*, the parents of which are *S. burserana* and *S. marginata*, has rosettes scarcely more than ½ inch across of ¼-inch-long, triangular leaves with lime-white

margins. Its ¾-inch-wide flowers are solitary or in twos. *S. tirolensis*, its parents *S. caesia* and *S. squarrosa*, has small rosettes of gray leaves and, on stems usually not over 2 inches tall, well-rounded, pure white flowers.

London pride, prince's feather, St.-Patrick's-cabbage, and mother-of-thousands are names by which *S. umbrosa*, of the section *Robertsonia*, and its hybrid *S. urbium* are affectionately known in the British Isles. There it grows lustily with little or no attention in city as well as country gardens and is frequently employed as edgings to flower beds and borders and vegetable plots, as well as for other purposes. It is coyer about making itself at home in most parts of North America. This sort typifies the section of *Saxifraga* named *Robertsonia*, of which only two other species are cultivated. Plants of this group have aboveground rhizomes, basal rosettes of leathery, toothed, spatula-shaped leaves, and, in graceful, loose panicles, little starry, white, pink-spotted or pink flowers that appear in early summer. A native of Europe, including the British Isles, variable *S. umbrosa* has ovate to oblong-ovate or spatula-shaped, obscurely-round-toothed

Saxifraga umbrosa

leaves, up to 2½ inches long, narrowly-margined with white and tapered to short, usually hairy stalks. The panicles, up to 1½ feet tall, have glandular-pubescent stalks and red-dotted, white to pink flowers, with on each petal a yellow spot. Smaller and neater *S. u. primuloides* has foliage suggesting that of a primrose and pale pink flowers in panicles 3 to 6 inches high. The form called 'Elliott's Variety', decidedly superior, has deeper pink blooms. About as tall, *S. u. covillei* has pink and white blooms. Hybrid *S. urbium*, its parents *S. umbrosa* and *S. spathularis*, much resembles *S. umbrosa*, but differs in its larger, more pointed leaves with many rounded teeth and less hairy stalks, and its bigger flowers.

The meadow saxifrage (*S. granulata*), of Europe, also called fair-maids-of-France, belongs in the section *Nephrophyllum*. It is a pretty sort with a bulbous base and erect stems 6 inches to 1½ feet tall with little bulbils in the axils of its lobed, kidney-shaped leaves. The latter have blades 1 inch to 1½ inches wide. The white flowers are about 1 inch across. Variety *S. g. flore-pleno* has double flowers. Shortly after blooming, this species and its variety die to the ground and fail to show any further signs of life until the next spring.

Saxifraga granulata

The strawberry-geranium (*S. stolonifera* syn. *S. sarmentosa*), of the section of the genus called *Diptera*, is native to eastern Asia. Its common name alludes to the somewhat geranium-like appearance of its leaves and its strawberry-like habit of producing slender runners bearing plantlets. Loosely-hairy throughout, it has rosettes of long-stalked leaves with slightly round-toothed, round-heart-shaped blades, 2 to 4 inches in diameter, their upper surfaces olive-green with whitish veins, their undersides purplish or reddish. The markedly asymmetrical flowers are in erect, slender-stalked, airy panicles 6 inches to 2 feet tall. Two lower white petals, about ½ inch long, much exceed in length the others, which are white usually spotted with yellow or purple. Very beautiful *S. s. tricolor*, its leaves splendidly variegated with green, cream, and rose-pink, is very much more challenging to grow then the species.

Others of the *Diptera* group well worth growing are *S. cortusaefolia*, *S. c. fortunei*, and *S. veitchiana*, all admirable outdoor plants particularly for lightly shaded locations where the soil is not excessively dry. Not the least of the virtues of the first two is their very late season of bloom, which comes in northern gardens about the time of the flowering of outdoor chrysanthemums. The other blooms in summer. The species *S. cortusaefolia* flourishes at Poughkeepsie, New York, and probably in colder climates, but *S. c. fortunei* is not reliably hardy even in the environs of New York

gradually narrow to their bases rather than being broadly-ovate or oblong and abruptly narrowed to a claw. The variety *S. c. compacta* is dwarfer. Native to western China, **S. veitchiana** has thick, roundish-heart-shaped, shallowly-lobed, sometimes

Saxifraga stolonifera

Saxifraga cortusaefolia compacta

Saxifraga stolonifera, a young plant

Saxifraga stolonifera tricolor

Saxifraga veitchiana

City. In this last region, however, *S. veitchiana* seems to be reliable.

Inhabiting shaded, wet rocky places and the banks of streams in Japan and mainland eastern Asia, **S. cortusaefolia** has short rhizomes and deciduous, leathery, very long-stalked, lobed and toothed, hairy leaves roundish or kidney-shaped in outline and mostly 2 to 6 inches wide. Their undersides are reddish. In erect, loose panicles 9 inches to 1½ feet tall, the white flowers, like those of all *Diptera* saxifrages, have the two lower petals much longer than the three upper. In this the broadly-ovate upper petals narrow to claws at their bases and are marked with a yellow spot. Japanese *S. c. fortunei* differs in minor details only. In the main it has shorter and fewer hairs and the upper petals of its white, spotless flowers are lanceolate and

Saxifraga cortusaefolia

marbled leaves. In loose panicles 6 to 9 inches tall, the flowers are white generally with a few yellow spots at the bottoms of the petals. This species sometimes develops plantlet-bearing runners.

Annual and biennial saxifrages are less important horticulturally than perennial kinds. Among those with charm, **S. cymbalaria,** of the Mediterranean region, and superior **S. sibthorpii,** of Greece, which differs in its flowers having pointing instead of spreading sepals, are quite similar. They have weakly erect to prostrate, slender stems, long-stalked, kidney-shaped, bright green, fleshy leaves, and golden-yellow, starry flowers ⅜ to ½ inch in diameter. Both belong in the *Cymbalaria* section of the genus.

Garden and Landscape Uses. In favorable climates, which in the main means regions of cool summers, saxifrages are among the most satisfactory and useful plants for furnishing rock gardens, dry walls, sink gardens, and other accommodations favorable to the cultivation of alpine plants. A few, including sorts of the mossy section and London pride, in agreeable climates make attractive edgings to paths and flower beds, and a few native Americans are satisfactory for wild gardens and naturalistic plantings. The sorts of the *Diptera* group are appropriate for naturalizing informally and one, the strawberry-geranium, although hardy outdoors at New York City and perhaps in harsher climates, is frequently grown in pots and hanging baskets in greenhouses, and as a houseplant. Unfortunately its colorful variety *S. stolonifera tricolor* is not hardy.

Cultivation. As to be expected in a genus as diverse as this, cultural requirements vary considerably. Sorts of the *Boraphila, Diptera, Dactyloides,* and *Robertsonia* sections do best in porous, neutral to slightly acid soil well supplied with leaf mold or other decayed organic matter, which does not dry markedly from spring through fall. Encrusted, kabschia, and other alpine saxifrages thrive only under scree, or under moraine conditions or in chinks or cliffs where drainage is very sharp, but where adequate supplies of moisture are assured throughout the growing season. All those encrusted with lime and many others require gritty limestone soil testing from pH 7 to 8. In their native homes and in gardens in the far north, the alpines flourish when exposed to full sun, but elsewhere, especially at low altitudes, some shade from strong summer sun is needed; even then difficulties attending their cultivation become progressively more pronounced as one goes southward, until in climates with notably hot, dry summers, they become virtually impossible to maintain. In southern New York a few can be coaxed to grow if sites and soils for them are selected with care, but none prospers as it does where the heat of summer is less intense. The discouragement imposed by low altitudes and hot summers can, to some extent, be alleviated by selecting for their accommodation a north-facing slope or cliff where light shade filters all but early morning and late afternoon sun. But even so, the plants may suffer to such an extent in July and August that they show stress by their generally unhappy mein and their browning leaves. However, with the coming of cooler weather they perk up and regain some semblance of what they are at their best. Propagation of saxifrages is easily accomplished by seeds sown in soil of a type favored by mature plants of the same kind. Division and removal and planting of offsets are also easy means of multiplying many sorts.

SAXIFRAGACEAE—Saxifrage Family. Some authorities divide this family of dicotyledons into several smaller ones with such names as Escalloniaceae, Grossulariaceae, Hydrangeaceae, and Philadelphaceae. Considered broadly, the Saxifragaceae consists of approximately 1,200 species and eighty genera, chiefly of temperate and cold regions. It includes many ornamentals. Some sorts of *Ribes* (currants and gooseberries) are much esteemed for their fruits. Included are herbaceous plants, shrubs, a few woody vines, and a few small trees. The leaves of the members of this family are alternate, less often opposite, or are all basal. They are undivided or variously divided, lobed or lobeless, with or without teeth. Solitary or in racemes, panicles, or clusters, the usually bisexual, symmetrical flowers generally have a calyx with four or five lobes or sepals, four or five petals or rarely none, as many or twice as many stamens as sepals or petals, and a pistil of two to five united carpels each with one style. The fruits are capsules or berries.

Among genera cultivated are *Abrophyllum, Anopterus, Astilbe, Bauera, Bensoniella, Bergenia, Bolandra, Boykinia, Brexia, Cardiandra, Carpenteria, Carpodetus, Chrysosplenium, Decumaria, Deinanthe, Deutzia, Dichroa, Elmera, Escallonia, Fendlera, Francoa, Heuchera, Heucherella, Hydrangea, Itea, Jamesia, Kirengeshoma, Leptarrhena, Lithophragma, Mitella, Mukdenia, Parnassia, Peltiphyllum, Peltoboykinia, Philadelphus, Pileostegia, Platycrater, Quintinia, Ribes, Rodgersia, Saxifraga, Schizophragma, Suksdorfia, Tanakaea, Telesonix, Tellima, Tiarella, Tolmiea,* and *Whipplea.*

SAXIFRAGE. See Saxifraga.

SCAB DISEASES. The symptoms of scab diseases, which vary with the kind of plant, usually consist of often raised or depressed, crustlike, rough surfaces on corms, tubers, roots, stems, leaves, or fruits. Twigs may die back and leaves may wither and drop. Most scab diseases are caused by funguses, a few by bacteria. Among the many plants susceptible are apples, avocados, beets, cabbage, cotoneasters, dahlias, English ivy, gladioluses, hickories, oleanders, pansies, parsnips, radishes, spinach, Swiss chard, turnips, and willows.

Control measures, depending upon the sort of plant, may involve crop rotation, the employment of resistant varieties, prompt removal and destruction of affected parts, spraying with fungicides, and, especially with potatoes, avoiding the use of lime or other alkalizing materials and where possible maintaining the soil acidity at about pH 4.5. For more specific suggestions consult local Cooperative Extension Agents or State Agricultural Experiment Stations.

SCABIOSA (Scabi-òsa) — Scabious or Mourning Bride or Pincushion Flower, Carmel-Daisy. The approximately 100 species of *Scabiosa*, of the teasel family Dipsacaceae, inhabit Europe, Asia, and Africa with the greatest concentration of kinds endemic to the Mediterranean region. Few are cultivated. The name, derived from the Latin *scabies*, the itch, was given because some species were believed to cure this once-prevalent affliction.

Scabiouses are hardy annuals, biennials, and herbaceous perennials, the latter sometimes more or less woody at their bases. The leaves are opposite and undivided and without lobes or teeth or are variously toothed, cleft, or dissected. The flat, hemispherical, or more or less egg-shaped to conical flower heads generally terminate long stalks or rarely are almost stalkless. Like those of the daisy family Compositae, some of which they casually resemble, the flower heads are composed of tiny individual flowers or florets with at the base of each head an involucre (collar) of leafy bracts. In *Scabiosa* these are in one or two rows. Again, as in many Compositae, the florets are usually of two types, the marginal ones larger than those that form the center of the flower head and spreading outward like the ray florets of daisies. Each floret has a persistent calyx of five bristle-like sepals, a white, yellowish, pink, lavender, blue, purple, or maroon, markedly two-lipped to nearly symmetrical corolla cleft into four or five lobes (petals), four or rarely two stamens, and one style. The fruits are seedlike achenes.

Sweet scabious, mourning bride, or pincushion flower (**S. atropurpurea**) is a popular, variable, free-branching annual 1½ to 2½ feet tall and native to southern Europe. It has nearly hairless stems, coarsely-toothed, lobeless to fiddle-shaped basal leaves, those higher on the stems deeply-pinnately-cleft or pinnate. The about 2-inch-wide flower heads, white, pink, lavender-blue, to dark purple-maroon, flattish at first, become ovoid to oblong as they pass into the seed stage. This sort is available in a choice of garden varieties, some double-flowered.

Carmel-daisy (**S. prolifera**) is an annual less common than sweet scabious. A na-

Scabiosa prolifera

tive from Turkey to Israel and in Libya and Cyprus, this is clothed with hairs that lie flat on the surfaces of its stems and foliage. From 1 foot to 2 feet tall, it has oblong-lanceolate to linear leaves and short-stalked or nearly stalkless, cream-colored flower heads 1 inch to 2 inches wide.

Yellowish, long-stalked flower heads, ¾ to 1 inch wide or a little wider, are borne by European and western Asian *S. ochroleuca.* Perennial or biennial, 1 foot to 2½ feet tall, this has grayish-pubescent stems and foliage. The basal leaves are lobeless to fiddle-shaped, the upper ones once- or twice-pinnate with narrow leaflets. From 6 to 9 inches tall, *S. o. webbiana* has wrinkled foliage, creamy-white flowers.

Lilac flower heads are characteristic of European *S. columbaria,* the only scabious indiginous in the British Isles. From 1 foot to 2 feet tall, this hairless or hairy perennial has broadly-ovate, usually lobeless basal leaves with round-toothed edges, and once- or twice-pinnately-cleft stem leaves. Its long-stalked flower heads of florets with five-lobed corollas and yellow anthers are about 1 inch in diameter.

Scabiosa columbaria

Beautiful hardy perennial *S. caucasica,* as its name indicates, is a native of the Caucasus. From 1½ to 2½ feet in height, this has hairless or slightly hairy stems. Its lobeless or pinnately-lobed basal leaves have oblongish blades tapering to long stalks. The upper stem leaves are pinnately-divided into narrow lobes. From 2 to 3 inches across, or in garden varieties larger, the flattish flower heads are of various shades of blue and lavender or are white. Good varieties are *S. c.* 'Clive Greaves', with large mauve flower heads, and *S. c.* 'Miss Willmott', the flower heads of which are pure white.

Other species cultivated include these: *S. graminifolia,* which has a somewhat woody base, is about 1 foot tall. A native of Europe, this has silvery, linear leaves and light blue to lavender flower heads 1 inch to 1¼ inches in diameter. *S. japonica*

is a biennial native of Japan closely allied to *S. atropurpurea.* From 1 foot to 2½ feet tall, it has branched stems with pinnately-cleft leaves 2 to 4 inches long. The blue flower heads, 1 inch to 2 inches in diameter, have large ray florets. Dwarfer *S. j. alpina* grows at high altitudes. *S. lucida,* a native of the mountains of Europe, is a perennial up to about 1 foot tall with practically hairless, somewhat glossy foliage. Its rosy-lilac, deep mauve, or violet flower heads are up to ¾ inch wide. *S. stellata,* native from Portugal to Italy, is a rough-hairy annual 1 foot to 1½ feet tall. It has pinnately-cleft stem leaves and globular, yellowish-white to bluish-lilac flower heads ¾ inch to 1½ inches wide.

Garden Uses. Scabiouses are useful for sunny flower beds and borders and for supplying cut blooms. Some lend themselves to planting in informal, naturalistic areas, and sweet scabious, besides being an excellent summer annual, is very satisfactory for growing in cool greenhouses for late winter and spring bloom. All are easy to grow. Some of the perennials are short-lived and in cultivation tend to behave like biennials.

Cultivation. Scabiouses adapt to any moderately fertile, well-drained soil. Most do well in those of a limestone nature. Propagation is chiefly by seed, but garden varieties of *S. caucasica* are multiplied by division and some other perennial sorts can be.

Sow seeds of sweet scabious and other annual kinds outdoors in friable, moderately fertile soil in early spring, broadcast in patches in flower borders or for cut flowers in rows 1 foot to 1½ feet apart. Cover to a depth of about ⅛ inch. They take two to four weeks to germinate. Thin the seedlings to 8 inches to 1 foot apart. Light staking to prevent storm damage is likely to be needed. In regions of mild winters, fall sowing gives earlier flowers the following year. The same result may be had by sowing indoors in a temperature of 55 to 60°F, transplanting the seedlings to flats or individual small pots, and growing them under cool, sunny conditions in a greenhouse or equivalent place until all danger of frost has past and it is safe to set them in the garden. For this use, sow eight weeks before the anticipated date of planting outdoors.

For winter and spring bloom in greenhouses, sow in September, transplant the seedlings to small pots, and later as growth makes necessary, successively transplant to bigger ones until they occupy containers 5 to 7 inches in diameter, or from the small pots plant 8 inches apart in beds or benches of soil. Maintain a night temperature of 50 to 55°F, with a five to ten degree increase by day. Keep a somewhat dryish, airy atmosphere rather than an excessively humid one, water moderately and after the pots in which the plants are to

bloom are well filled with roots give regular applications of dilute liquid fertilizer. Early flowering is induced by using, after the plants have become well established, artificial light to extend the day length to sixteen hours.

Provide *S. caucasica* and other perennial sorts with well-drained, fertile, mellow soil. Plant in spring in a sunny location. In cold climates protect in winter by covering with salt hay or similar loose material or with branches of evergreens. Perennial scabiouses may be increased by seed and by division in spring or early fall.

SCABIOUS. See Scabiosa. Devil's-bit-scabious is *Succisa pratensis;* field-scabious, *Knautia arvensis.* Sheep's-bit-scabious is a common name of *Jasione montana* and *J. perennis.*

SCAEVOLA (Scae-vòla) — Naupaka. Belonging to the goodenia family GOODENI-ACEAE, the genus *Scaevola* comprises from eighty to 100 species widely distributed as natives in the tropics and subtropics, especially Australia and islands of the Pacific. Sorts that grow in Hawaii are there called naupakas. The botanical name, a diminutive of the Latin *scaeva,* left-handed, probably alludes to the peculiar handlike aspect of the blooms.

Scaevolas are herbaceous plants, shrubs, and trees with alternate leaves and solitary or clustered flowers. The blooms have a five-lobed calyx or none, a five-petaled, asymmetrical corolla with its tube slit down one side to its base, five stamens, and one bent style. The drupelike or berry-like fruits are or more less succulent.

Beach naupaka (**S. frutescens sericea** syn. *S. sericea*) is a spreading, somewhat succulent shrub 3 to 10 feet tall that inhabits beaches and coasts of tropical Asia and islands of the Pacific. The typical sort is smooth, but a more or less downy variety is best known. Branching freely from their bases, the plants have obovate, bright green leaves, notched at their apexes, 3 to 5 inches long, with convex upper surfaces. The fragrant flowers are in clusters of five to nine in the leaf axils. About ¾ inch long and white streaked with purple, they are succeeded by succulent, white berries about ½ inch long.

Native to coastal sand dunes in Florida and the West Indies, **S. plumieri** spreads by underground stems to form large clumps. A shrub 2 to 6 feet in height, this has short-stalked, fleshy, obovate to spatula-shaped leaves 1½ to 4½ inches in length. Its 1-inch-long white to pinkish flowers, woolly within, are in stalked, loose clusters. The juicy, black berries are spherical, almost or quite ½ inch in diameter.

Garden and Landscape Uses and Cultivation. These plants are employed to some extent in Hawaii and other warm regions as soil binders and windbreaks, and around beach homes for hedges and other ornamental purposes. They thrive in sandy soils in full sun, and can be propagated by seed, division, layering, and cuttings.

SCALE INSECTS. The numerous and very various sorts of insects that belong here constitute a complex and, so far as their entomological identification and classification goes, difficult group. Although they technically include mealybugs, these are usually considered separately by gardeners and are so treated in this Encyclopedia.

Convenient groupings of scale insects are armored or hard-shelled scales and soft scales. The former are covered with a protective layer of usually hard wax and cast the skins of early moltings separate from the body. Soft scales, or tortoise scales as they are sometimes called, may have bodies equally as hard, but are without a separate layer of armor.

Not all scale insects are useless, although admittedly the great majority are. Shellac, for which various substitutes have been developed, but none with all the fine qualities of the natural material, is a commercial product obtained from the Indian lac insect, a species of scale. Once of considerable commercial importance, but now practically supplemented by analine dye substitutes, cochineal is a preparation of the bodies of the females of a scale insect that infests certain species of cactuses. Other usable products of this group of insects is a white wax secreted by males of the Chinese wax scale and a sweet substitute for sugar called manna and thought by some to be the "manna of the wilderness" of the Bible. This, the dried secretions of honeydew from female insects, may still be used locally by inhabitants of the Sinai mountains.

Damage by scale insects is chiefly debilitation caused by the females sucking sap. Unsightliness results from the presence of the insects and in some cases from deposits of the sticky honeydew they secrete, which attracts ants and on which grows a disfiguring black fungus mold. The males, which at maturity look like gnats and are then without mouth parts, do little harm other than the part they play in assuring new generations. Females begin life as scarcely visible six-legged crawlers. Soon they puncture the skin of a plant with their slender mouth parts, and become immobile. They molt twice, lose their legs and antennae, and devote the rest of their lives to feeding, breeding, and either laying eggs or bearing live young.

Harmful scales infest a very wide range of plants, especially those abundant in warm regions, but are by no means limited to such. Some sorts feed only on one or a few related kinds of plants, others are less selective. A brief listing of the more common kinds includes the acuminate scale, azalea bark scale, barnacle scale, black scale, brown soft scale, cactus scale, California red scale, camellia parlatoria, citricola scale, cottony cushion scale, cottony maple scale, cottony Taxus scale, cyanophyllum scale, euonymus scale, fern scale, Florida red scale, Florida wax scale, hemispherical scale, juniper scale, oleander scale, oystershell scale, pine scales, rose scale, San Jose scale, scurfy scale, tea scale, tulip tree scale, and white peach scale.

Brown scale insects on a greenhouse plant

Scale insects on *Euonymus*

SCALLIONS. Young onions and shallots that have fresh and tasty green foliage and have not yet developed bulbs of appreciable size, although their bases may be somewhat swollen, are called scallions; in the British Isles they are known as spring onions. They are much appreciated in salads. Young leeks are also occasionally known as scallions.

Scallions are obtained by planting sets or seeds especially for the purpose or they are the early thinnings from crops planted to produce mature crops. For further information see Onions, and Shallots.

SCANDIX (Scán-dix) — Venus' Comb or Shepherd's Needle. One of the fifteen or more species of this group, of the carrot family UMBELLIFERAE, is occasionally grown in gardens. In many parts of North America it naturalizes in waste places, having been brought from Europe or temperate Asia, which are the homes of the genus. This kind has the rather unusual name of *Scandix pecten-veneris*, the last part of which is a translation into scientific Latin of its vernacular name Venus' comb. The peculiar fruits give reason for this fanciful designation. They are in clusters, and each has a flattened beak, much longer than the part that contains the seeds, that suggests the tooth of a comb. The name is the ancient Greek one for chervil (*Anthriscus*), a related plant.

The genus *Scandix* consists of annuals or biennials with pinnately-dissected leaves and small white flowers in simple or compound (umbels of smaller umbels) umbels without leafy bracts. The sepals are tiny or wanting. There are five petals; those toward the margins of the umbels are bigger than the others, so that the outer flowers are asymmetrical. Individual blooms are nearly stalkless and about 1/20 inch in diameter. They are pure white and in the aggregate make a good show. Their sepals are absent or very small.

Venus' comb (*S. pecten-veneris*) is nearly hairless and branches freely from its base. It has feathery three-times-pinnate foliage, with the ultimate divisions very slender. Its umbels are solitary or in twos or sometimes threes. The cylindrical fruits have flattened beaks three to four times as long as the seed-containing part. Overall they are 3/4 inch to 3 inches long. When ripe they split with a violent jerk into two parts.

Scandix pecten-veneris

Garden Uses and Cultivation. Because its young shoots may be used in salads there is reason for including Venus' comb in herb gardens. Consideration should be given also to displaying it in wild gardens, rock gardens, and even more formal places.

Managed as a biennial, it comes into full bloom in spring at about tulip time. Then it is seen to best advantage and, if given a sunny location and poorish soil, will remain compact and not become taller than about 6 inches. The seeds are sown in late summer where the plants are to remain, and the seedlings thinned to 3 to 4 inches apart.

SCAPHYGLOTTIS (Scaphy-glóttis). Native from Mexico to tropical South America and the West Indies, *Scaphyglottis*, of the orchid family ORCHIDACEAE, comprises thirty-five or perhaps more species. Its name, derived from the Greek *skaphe*, a bowl, and *glotta*, a tongue, alludes to the concave lip of the flower.

Chiefly epiphytes (tree-perchers), the sorts of this genus vary greatly in habit of growth. Often new pseudobulbs develop from the apexes of the most recent ones, so that they pile up on top of one another, but some sorts do not do this but instead have pseudobulbs, often stalked, without others surmounting them. The flowers are small and in terminal clusters from the upper parts of the pseudobulbs.

Native from Mexico to Panama and perhaps northern South America, *S. lindeniana* has clusters of spindle-shaped, stalked pseudobulbs 2 inches to 1 foot tall

Scaphyglottis lindeniana

by up to 1 inch wide. Each has usually two leathery leaves from 2 to 10 inches long. From ¼ to ¾ inch across, the drooping, yellow-green to reddish-green flowers, commonly suffused or veined with purple and not opening wide, are in clusters of few to several.

Garden Uses and Cultivation. Chiefly of interest to collectors of "botanical" orchids, the sorts of *Scaphyglottis* are generally not difficult to grow. They accommodate, according to kind, to environments appropriate for tropical and subtropical epidendrums. Except for a few weeks after completion of the new season's growth, generous watering is needed, but little or none should be done during their season of partial rest.

SCARLET. The word scarlet is included in the vernacular names of these plants: scarlet bugler (*Cleistocactus baumannii* and *Penstemon centranthifolius*), scarlet bush (*Hamelia patens*), scarlet coral-pea (*Kennedia prostrata*), scarlet-gilia (*Ipomopsis aggregata*), scarlet lightning (*Lychnis chalcedonica*), scarlet pimpernel (*Anagallis arvensis*), scarlet plume (*Euphorbia fulgens*), and scarlet runner bean (*Phaseolus coccineus*).

SCELETIUM (Scel-ètium). These *Mesembryanthemum* relatives contain a narcotic alkaloid called mesembrine. One or more kinds were, and to some extent still are, used by natives of South Africa to chew, to inhale as snuff, and to drink as tea. There are twenty species of *Sceletium*, of the carpetweed family AIZOACEAE, natives of deserts in southern Africa. The name comes from the Latin *sceletium*, a skeleton, and alludes to the persisting withered leaves.

Sceletiums have short stems and spreading branches. The bases of each pair of opposite, ovate-lanceolate leaves are joined. The flowers come in spring and summer, one to several on thick stalks. Comparatively large, they are white or light yellow. In appearance daisy-like, in structure they differ greatly from daisies, each bloom being a solitary flower and not a head composed of numerous florets. The fruits are capsules.

Various species may be brought into cultivation from time to time by keen collectors of succulents. One sometimes grown, **S. tortuosum** (syn. *Mesembryanthemum tortuosum*) has long, procumbent branches, and fleshy, bright green leaves with rounded, keeled undersurfaces. The leaves are about 1 inch long by one-third as wide. The flowers, white to yellowish, are 2 inches in diameter.

Garden Uses and Cultivation. Sceletiums are for collectors of choice succulents. They are easily increased by cuttings and seed and grow without undue difficulty in loamy, porous soil kept moderately moist from spring to fall, and drier in winter. Only in semidesert, frost-free, or nearly frost-free climates will they survive outdoors. Generally they are grown in greenhouses along with other desert plants. A minimum winter night temperature of 45 to 50°F is satisfactory. For further information see Succulents.

SCHAUERIA (Schau-èria). This genus of the acanthus family ACANTHACEAE contains eight rather rarely cultivated species indigenous to the humid tropics and subtropics of the Americas. The name honors Johann Conrad Schauer, a nineteenth-century German professor.

Schauerias are perennial herbaceous plants, subshrubs, or shrubs, similar to *Jacobinia*, but differing in technical details of their anthers. Their leaves are undivided and toothless. In terminal panicles or panicle-like clusters, the yellow or red flowers have conspicuously bristly or hairy, five-lobed calyxes and tubular, two-lipped corollas. They have two stamens. The fruits are capsules.

Native to Brazil, **Schaueria flavicoma** is 2 to 4 feet tall. It has cylindrical stems, and lustrous, stalked, very minutely-hairy, ovate to lanceolate-ovate leaves up to 6 inches long. The pale yellow blooms, in panicles that, because of their bracts and calyx lobes, have a distinctly shaggy appearance, have whitish-glandular-hairy calyxes, and hairless corollas 1 inch to 1½ inches long, with a notched upper lip and a three-lobed lower lip. Similar, but with downy corollas without notched upper lips, is **S. calycotricha**, also of Brazil.

Schaueria calycotricha

Garden and Landscape Uses and Cultivation. Where they can be grown outdoors, these are attractive ornamentals for the fronts of shrub borders, flower beds, and similar locations in sun or part-day shade. They thrive in fertile soil, always moderately moist, and may be pruned to shape at the conclusion of the flowering season. In greenhouses they can be grown in pots or ground beds. Nice specimens that will bloom in winter in 5-inch pots are had from cuttings rooted in spring. The tips of the young plants are pinched out to induce branching and a second pinch may be given later. Throughout they are grown in good light, but shaded from strong sun. They need a humid atmosphere. The minimum night temperature in winter should be 60°F, that by day five to fifteen degrees higher according to the brightness of the weather. Coarse, fertile soil that contains a liberal amount of peat moss or leaf mold best suits schauerias, and it should be kept moderately moist without being constantly wet. When the plants have filled the pots, in which they are to bloom, with roots, regular applications of dilute liquid fertilizer are of benefit. After blooming, the plants are rested for about a month by being kept a little drier and in a temperature a few degrees cooler than usual, and then they are cut back, repotted, and started into growth by increasing the temperature and resuming normal watering. Propagation is by cuttings and by seed.

SCHEELEA (Scheè-lea). Forty species are included in *Scheelea*, which is native from Mexico to Paraguay and the West Indies, but is chiefly Andean. Not well understood botanically and rarely cultivated, this genus belongs in the palm family PALMAE. Its names honors Karl Wilhelm Scheele, a German chemist, who worked in Sweden and died in 1786.

These massive palms usually have stout trunks, but a few, such as *S. lauromullerana*, of Brazil, have only subterranean stems. All have very large pinnate leaves. They are closely related to *Attalea* and *Orbignya* and, like those, usually have male and female blooms segregated in separate flower clusters. Individual trees may be unisexual or bisexual.

The largest native palm of the Panama Canal Zone is *S. zonensis*, which has a trunk up to 30 feet tall and leaves two-thirds as long that ascend and arch outward to form an impressive vaselike crown. The male flowers have six stamens. The trash palm (*S. curvifrons*), of Trinidad, a fine ornamental 50 feet in height, has a heavy trunk and gracefully arching leaves up to 15 feet in length with drooping leaflets. The flowers have the odor of turpentine. Known only in cultivation, *S. leandroana* attains a height of 12 feet or sometimes more and has eight rows of stubs of old leafstalks on its trunk. Its 20-foot long leaves have groups of leaflets extending in more than one plane.

Garden and Landscape Uses and Cultivation. In humid, warm climates, scheeleas should prove excellent for lush landscape effects and, at least those from the cooler parts of the range of the genus, probably will withstand occasional freezes. They are well worth trying in southern Florida and Hawaii and may be expected to grow under condtions recommended for *Areca*. For additional information see Palms.

SCHEFFLERA (Schef-flèra) — Umbrella Tree, Patete. The genus *Schefflera*, of the aralia family ARALIACEAE, is variously interpreted by botanists. Some include the popular Queensland umbrella tree or octopus tree, treated in this Encyclopedia as *Brassaia*. It contains about 150 species, trees and shrubs of the tropics and subtropics, and has a name given in honor of the nineteenth-century German botanist J. C. Scheffler.

The genus extends from Japan and China to Australia, New Zealand, South America, and the Hawaiian Islands. Its members have long-stalked leaves, usually of several leaflets arranged like fingers of a wide-spreading hand, that are toothed or smooth-edged. The small flowers are usually clustered in umbels displayed in panicles or racemes. They have five-toothed calyxes, five or more sepals, as many petals, and as many stamens as petals. The fruits are berry-like drupes.

Schefflera arboricola of gardens

Tropical Asian *S. arboricola* (syn. *Heptapleurum arboricola*) is a much-branched, evergreen shrub or tree 10 to 25 feet tall, sometimes more or less climbing and in the wild at times growing as an epiphyte (tree-percher) on other trees. Its hairless leathery leaves have slender stalks 4 to 8 inches long, with blades of seven or nine obovate-oblong to elliptic leaflets 3½ to 7 inches in length. The tiny flowers are in globose heads of five to ten, arranged in panicles about 1½ feet long with raceme-like branches. Plants grown under this name, and sometimes as miniature schefflera, may not be correctly identified.

The patete (*S. digitata*), of New Zealand, is a common endemic there. It is an evergreen shrub or tree 10 to 20 feet tall. Its stalked leaves have five- to ten-toothed or sometimes quite deeply-lobed leaflets 3 to 7 inches long. They are satiny-green above, glossier beneath, and thinner than those of the Queensland umbrella tree. The greenish-yellow flowers are displayed below the leaves in 1-foot-long panicles. Its berry-like, juicy fruits are purplish-black. The soft wood of this kind was used by the Maoris for making fire.

Beautiful *S. littorea* (syn. *S. farinosa*), of Java, Sumatra, and Malaya, is a tree with long-stalked leaves with blades 1 foot to 1¼ feet across composed of a complete circle of twelve to fifteen leathery, oblanceolate leaflets, those of the younger leaves heavily coated with white, waxy meal. The small, whitish flowers are in impressively large clusters of many incurved spikes.

Schefflera littorea

Schefflera littorea (flowers in bud stage)

Other sorts in cultivation are *S. delavayi*, of China, and *S. octophylla*, of Japan, the Ryukyu Islands, China, and Indochina. An evergreen tree up to 20 feet tall, **S. delavayi** has leaves of four to seven leaflets up to 9 inches long by approximately one-half as wide. They have dark green upper surfaces and densely-white-hairy lower ones. An evergreen shrub or tree, **S. octophylla** has thick branchlets, brown-hairy when young, and leaves with stalks up to 1 foot long and seven to ten unequal, narrow-oblong to narrow-obovate leaflets, the largest up to 8 or 9 inches by one-third to one-half as broad, and in young plants, often pinnately-cleft. The white to greenish flowers are in panicles 8 to 10 inches in length.

Garden and Landscape Uses and Cultivation. These are as for *Brassaia*.

SCHIMA (Schì-ma). The name of this genus of the tea family THEACEAE is thought to be of Arabic derivation. The group numbers fifteen species of Asian and Indonesian evergreen trees and shrubs related to *Camellia*.

The leathery leaves of *Schima* are alternate and undivided. The showy flowers, solitary or the upper ones clustered, have five nearly equal sepals, five overlapping petals much bigger than the sepals and joined at their bases, and numerous stamens. The fruits are woody capsules.

Native from India to Sumatra, **S. wallichii**, 80 to 100 feet high, has short-stalked, elliptic-oblong, slightly toothed or toothless, strongly veined leaves up to 7 inches long by 2 to 3 inches broad. They are hairless and reddish-veined above, finely-hairy and often reddish beneath. Fragrant, white, and about 1½ inches in diameter, the flowers are in short, terminal racemes. The outsides of their petals are hairy. The nearly spherical capsules are black and about ¾ inch in diameter.

Garden and Landscape Uses and Cultivation. Only in climates essentially free of frost is this handsome tree hardy. It succeeds in well-drained soil, preferably one with a fairly high organic content, that does not become excessively dry, in sun or part-day shade. It is handsome as a single specimen or in groups. No pruning or special care is needed, but an organic mulch maintained on the soil around it is helpful. Propagation is by cuttings made from firm shoots planted under mist or in a greenhouse propagating bench supplied with a little bottom heat, and by seed.

SCHINUS (Schìn-us) — California Pepper Tree, Brazilian Pepper Tree or Christmas Berry Tree. As a native confined to South America, *Schinus*, of the cashew family ANACARDIACEAE, is familiar in warm, nearly frost-free climates because two of its kinds are widely planted for shade and ornament. The name, one used by the ancient Greeks for the mastic tree, *Pistacia*, is applied to this genus because of the mastic-like sap of some species. In Mexico and probably elsewhere an intoxicating beverage is prepared from the fruits of *S. molle*. Its fruits and other parts are used medicinally and its seeds are ground as a substitute for pepper. The bark is employed to some extent for tanning.

Twenty-seven species of shrubs and trees comprise this genus. Their leaves are undivided or are pinnate with usually stalkless or nearly stalkless leaflets. The small flowers, functionally male or female and in terminal or axillary panicles, have five or sometimes four sepals, as many petals, and twice as many stamens, the latter of two lengths. There are three styles, occasionally joined to appear as one. The fruits are small, berry-like drupes.

The kinds most frequently cultivated are readily distinguished from each other. The leaves of the California pepper tree or Peruvian mastic tree (**S. molle**) have seven to twenty pairs of mostly alternate leaflets,

Schinus molle

and a terminal one, while those of the Brazilian pepper tree or Christmas berry tree (**S. terebinthifolius**) have one to six pairs of opposite leaflets, and a terminal one. If tiny, freshly broken pieces of the leaf of the California pepper tree are dropped lightly onto still water they soon move about erratically because the oil they exude lowers the surface tension of the water.

The California pepper tree is a broad-headed evergreen that attains a height of about 25 feet, and is as elegant as a weeping willow. Fernlike leaves, up to 1 foot long, clothe its slender, gracefully pendulous branches. The yellow flowers are in much-branched panicles. The fruits are rose-pink.

The Brazilian pepper tree is of much more rigid aspect and less graceful than the last. It is a round-headed shrub or tree up to 20 or 25 feet in height. The midribs of its leaves are often winged. The obovate to elliptic or oblong-lanceolate leaflets, ¾ inch to 3 inches long and 1½ inches

Schinus terebinthifolius with fruits

wide, are dark green above and paler on their undersides. They have strong midveins and are toothed or toothless, and hairy or not. The flower panicles, often raceme-like, are axillary and up to 5 inches long, but often considerably shorter. The blooms are white. The red fruits are up to ¼ inch long. This species, believed to be a native of Brazil, and perhaps of Paraguay, is naturalized in some other parts of the tropics and subtropics.

Other species cultivated include these: **S. latifolius**, of Chile, is a small tree with undivided, irregularly-toothed, oblong-ovate leaves 1½ to 3 inches long. Its white flowers, in short racemes, are succeeded by lavender fruits. **S. lentiscifolius** is Brazilian. A tall shrub, it has graceful leaves of four to seven pairs of toothed or practically toothless, elliptic to lanceolate leaves ¾ to 1 inch long, and white to straw-colored flowers succeeded by white to pink fruits in panicles about 3 inches long. **S. longifolius**, of Argentina, is a small tree with undivided, narrow-oblanceolate to spatula-shaped leaves, 1 inch to 2 inches long, and in racemes from the leaf axils, white flowers succeeded by lavender fruits.

Garden and Landscape Uses and Cultivation. The kinds described are highly ornamental, but the California pepper tree is in some places looked upon with disfavor because it is very subject to infestations of scale insects that also infest citrus fruits. It has the disadvantage, too, of being a shedder of litter that looks out of place in well-groomed surroundings. These trees are well suited to dryish soils and generally rather arid environments. They revel in full sun. The Brazilian pepper tree is much used for street planting and as a lawn specimen, and its great clusters of beautiful fruits are esteemed for indoor decorations and, in Hawaii, for leis. No special care is required. Propagation is very easy by seed.

SCHIPPIA (Schípp-ia) — Silver Pimento. One species constitutes *Schippia*, of the palm family PALMAE. Its name honors William A. Schipp, a twentieth-century Australian botanical collector.

Native to British Honduras, attractive *S. concolor* in appearance is intermediate between *Coccothrinax* and *Thrinax*. From both it differs in having bigger white fruits. At maturity ranging in height from 8 to 30 feet, this fan-leaved palm has a whitish, decidedly corky trunk about 4 inches in diameter. The leaves have stalks up to 7 feet in length. Its blades, about 2 feet across and green on both surfaces, are deeply-cleft into thirty-two to thirty-eight pointed lobes or segments, the basal ones considerably shorter than those above. The white or yellow, spherical, 1-inch-wide, berry-like fruits are in clusters 2 feet long.

Garden and Landscape Uses and Cultivation. In southern Florida this attractive palm, which has adapted well in cultivation, gives good results in ordinary soils and locations. For additional information see Palms.

SCHISANDRA (Schis-ándra). The name of this genus of vining magnolia relatives is sometimes incorrectly spelled *Schizandra*. One species is native in North America, the other twenty-four in warm-temperate and tropical Asia. Traditionally considered to be a primitive member of the magnolia family MAGNOLIACEAE, by some authorities *Schisandra* is separated, with *Kadsura*, as the family SCHISANDRACEAE. Its name, from the Greek *schizein*, to split, and *andros*, male, refers to the cleft anther cells of *S. coccinea*.

Schisandras include deciduous and evergreen, more or less aromatic, twining, perennial, woody vines. They have alternate or sometimes somewhat clustered, long-stalked, toothed or toothless leaves. Their smallish, mostly cup-shaped, white, pink, magenta-pink, or red blooms are few together in slender-stalked clusters from the leaf axils. They are unisexual, the sexes usually on separate plants. The sepals and petals, both from now on for convenience referred to here as petals, are indistinguishable and together number five to twenty. There are four to sixty more or less united stamens. The axis that carries the many female flower elements (carpels) after pollination lengthens into a drooping spike to which are attached the quite showy, orange-red, red, or rarely black, berry-like fruits. In the Orient those of some kinds are eaten.

The hardiest schisandra, deciduous *S. chinensis*, of eastern Asia, is hardy in southern New England. It attains heights of up to 25 feet and has reddish, hairless shoots and lustrous, broad, elliptic to obovate, toothed leaves 2 to 4 inches long, often slightly glaucous on their undersides. The flowers, over ½ inch wide and

fragrant, creamy-white to pinkish, have six to nine petals notched at their apexes and five stamens. The fruits are small and scarlet. Probably slightly less hardy, *S. sphenanthera*, of China, differs chiefly in its orange-yellow flowers having ten to fifteen stamens.

Not hardy in the north, *S. propinqua* is worth growing in milder climates for its attractive orange blooms. The leaves, elliptic to oblong-lanceolate and 3 to 4½ inches long, are nearly always toothed. They are leathery and have undersides paler than the upper sides. Almost or quite ¾ inch in diameter, the male blooms have nine or ten, the females eleven to sixteen petals. The ten to sixteen stamens are united in a globose mass. The fruits are red. This species is Chinese.

Other Chinese schisandras sometimes cultivated, none of which is hardy in the north, are *S. henryi*, *S. rubriflora* (syn. *S. grandiflora rubriflora*), and *S. sphaerandra* (syn. *S. grandiflora cathayensis*). With ovate to ovate-elliptic, remotely toothed leaves 2½ to 5 inches long and glaucous on their undersides, *S. henryi* has flowers with six to ten broad, white petals up to ½ inch long and, united only at their bases, fourteen to forty stamens. The red fruits ¼ to ⅓ inch long. The leathery leaves of *S. rubriflora* are oblanceolate to obovate-elliptic, 2 to 6 inches long by ¾ inch to 2½ inches wide.

Schisandra rubriflora

Paler on their undersides than above, they are quite prominently toothed. Its flowers are bright red and exceed 1 inch in diameter. Quite distinct *S. sphaerandra* is a hairless shrub with lanceolate to oblong-elliptic or oblanceolate leaves, paler on their undersides than above, and usually 1½ to 4 inches long by ¾ inch to 1½ inches wide. The flowers, red, crimson, or magenta, are ¾ to 1 inch or slightly more across. They have five to eight petals and twenty to fifty nearly stalkless stamens. The fruits are red. Variants with flowers ranging from pink to white are segregated as *S. s. pallida*.

The only American schisandra, the wild-sarsaparilla (*S. coccinea*) grows in rich woodlands from South Carolina to Flor-

Schisandra sphaerandra

ida, and in Texas. A deciduous high climber, it has thickish, ovate to elliptic or broad-elliptic, toothed or toothless leaves 2 to 6 inches in length. The red flowers have five stamens. The berries are crimson. This is not hardy in the north.

Garden and Landscape Uses and Cultivation. Although rarely planted, schisandras are rather good-looking vines, worth growing particularly for their foliage and fruits. Their flowers are neither showy nor long-lasting. They prefer fertile, well-drained, reasonably moist soil and appreciate a little shade from intense sun. Because they twine, schisandras must either have supports their stems can embrace or be allowed to scramble over rocks, walls, or tree stumps. Pruning, consisting of cutting out whatever stems are necessary to contain the plants to size and to prevent them from developing into overgrown tangles, is done in late winter or spring. Propagation is by seed, layering, and summer cuttings 3 or 4 inches long planted in a greenhouse propagating bench, preferably with a little bottom heat, or under mist. Schisandras do not transplant readily, so it is advisable to keep young plants in pots or cans until they are set in their permanent locations. Only female plants fruit, and then only if a male to supply pollen is growing nearby.

SCHISANDRACEAE — Schisandra Family. Two genera totaling fewer than fifty species of dicotyledons constitute this family, which in the wild is confined to the southeastern United States, eastern Asia, and western Malaysia. Of very ancient origin and related to the magnolia family MAGNOLIACEAE in which it was formerly included, the SCHISANDRACEAE consists of climbing and trailing shrubs with alternate, undivided leaves, often with tiny translucent dots visible when the leaf is viewed against the light. The small, unisexual flowers, the sexes on the same or separate plants, are solitary from the leaf axils. They have a perianth of nine to fifteen overlapped, spirally-arranged sepals and petals scarcely distinguishable from each other, four to numerous short stamens more or less united into a rounded, fleshy mass, and many carpels crowded into a head. The fruits are berry-like. The genera are *Katsura* and *Schisandra,* the first perhaps not cultivated.

SCHISMATOGLOTTIS (Schismato-glóttis). Related to the American genus *Dieffenbachia,* and chiefly native to Indonesia, the Philippine Islands, and tropical Asia, but with at least two species in tropical America, *Schismatoglottis* belongs in the arum family ARACEAE. There are 100 species. Its name, from the Greek *schismas,* division, and *glotta,* a tongue, makes reference to the division between the blade of the spathe, which is early deciduous, and its basal part. From *Dieffenbachia* this genus differs in its stamens not being united, and from *Aglaeonema* in its female flowers possessing staminodes. (imperfectly developed stamens). Plants sometimes named *S. marantifolium maculatum, S. roebelinii,* and *S. siamensis* are presumably, respectively, *Aglaeonema commutatum maculatum, A. crispum,* and *A. siamense.*

Schismatoglottises are evergreen perennials with horizontal surface or subterranean rhizomes and sometimes erect stems. Their oblong to ovate-heart-shaped or sometimes somewhat arrow-shaped leaves are undivided, lobeless, and toothless. As is typical of the arum family, the true flowers, scarcely recognizable as such, are assembled in structures called inflorescences, which are often referred to as "flowers." Each inflorescence consists of a spikelike spadix, with from its base a petal-like or leaflike bract called a spathe. The tiny flowers are crowded on the spadix, the females on the lower part, the males above, and above them sterile flowers. The structure is that of the calla-lily, in which the central yellow organ is the spadix and the enveloping white trumpet the spathe. In *Schismatoglottis* the lower part of the spathe envelops the female flowers, and later the berry-like fruits.

Best known in cultivation, *S. picta* of Java, has aboveground stems. Its leaves have long stalks, and thinnish, lanceolate to ovate blades, heart-shaped at their bases, pointed at their apexes. They have on each side of center, and midway between the leaf margins and midrib, an irregular band of light gray. From its underground stems *S. calyptrata* sends leaves with 1-foot-long stalks and somewhat shorter, thick, pointed, ovate-oblong to heart-shaped blades, in forms cultivated for ornament usually spotted or striped with white. Green-leaved forms of this species are cooked for food in the Asian tropics, where they are native.

Native to Borneo, tufted *S. concinna* has long-stalked, lanceolate, lanceolate-oblong, or narrow-ovate leaves, not heart-

Schismatoglottis calyptrata

Schismatoglottis tecturata

shaped at their bases, and with blades about 6 inches long. Above, they are blotched with white. Variety *S. c. immaculata* is without white variegation and has purple-red undersides to its leaves. Another Bornean, *S. emarginata* has a very short stem and stalked leaves with heart- to arrow-shaped blades up to 6 inches long, dark grayish-green with a clear broad, feather-edged band of pale silvery-gray straddling the midrib. Without aboveground stems, *S. neoguineensis* has long-stalked leaves with thin ovate-heart-shaped blades irregularly spotted or blotched with pale yellow-green. It is from New Guinea. Native to the Molucca Islands, *S. rutteri* is a low kind with underground rhizomes, and bright green, slightly corrugated, ovate leaves. Crowded, short-stalked leaves are characteristic of low, tufted *S. tecturata,* of Borneo. They have asymmetrical, oblong-oblanceolate blades, 5 to 7 inches in length, pointed at their apexes, and lustrous-green relieved only by a faint band of paler green down their centers. Their undersides are glaucous.

Natives of Venezuela, but perhaps not in cultivation, are *S. bolivarana* and *S. spruceana.* These are attractive, low kinds. The first has pointed-heart-shaped leaves with long stalks, and blades up to 7 inches long and as broad. The leaves of the other have narrow- to broad-oblong blades, pointed at their apexes, 6 inches long, with stalks about as long as the blades. The blades are striped with dark and light green and have red edges.

Garden and Landscape Uses and Cultivation. For the humid tropics and greenhouses where similar environments are maintained, these are excellent foliage ornamentals. They also are useful as houseplants. Their cultural needs are those of dieffenbachias and most other evergreen aroids of tropical origin. They revel in fertile soil that contains abundant organic matter and is always moderately moist, and do well in quite deep shade. Strong sun is not to their liking. Increase is easy by division, cuttings, and when available, seed. In greenhouses the minimum winter night temperature should be 60 to 65°F. Higher day temperatures are needed.

Schismatoglottis neoguineensis

SCHIVERECKIA (Schiver-éckia). Five species of low, hardy herbaceous perennials closely related to *Alyssum* and *Draba* compose *Schivereckia*, of the mustard family CRUCIFERAE. Inhabitants of Europe, temperate Asia, and Asia Minor, they differ from *Alyssum* in technical details, and from *Draba* in having the stalks of their four longest stamens winged. The name commemorates S. B. Schivereck, a Swiss professor, who died in 1805.

Schivereckias are branching plants with rosettes of leaves more or less silvery with minute, stellate (star-shaped) hairs. Their flowers are in terminal racemes. They have four sepals, four petals that spread to form a cross, two short and four long stamens, and a style ending in a knoblike or slightly two-lobed stigma. The filaments (stalks) of the inner stamens are winged and have a short tooth at their tops. The seed pods contain four to seven seeds in each of two compartments.

A crowded, tufted, cushiony plant about 4 inches tall, but with flower stems of up to 10 inches high, **S. podolica** (syn. *Alyssum podolicum*) has oblanceolate to oblong-spatula-shaped basal leaves under ½ inch long, with two to five teeth along each side. The leaves of the branched or branchless flowering stems partly embrace them and have one to four teeth along each side. Each stem may carry as many as thirty pure white flowers up to ½ inch across. The stigmas are not lobed. The seed pods are 1 inch to 2 inches long. This is a native of eastern Europe and adjacent Asia. The only other European, **S. doerfleri** (syn. *S. bornmuelleri*) differs from the last in having leaves that are toothless or at most have

Schivereckia doerfleri

one tooth on each margin. The stem leaves scarcely or do not embrace the stems. This kind is less compact than *S. podolica*. Its flower stems, about 6 inches tall, may be branched. They have up to fifteen blooms up to ½ inch in diameter. The stigma is two-lobed.

Garden Uses and Cultivation. Schivereckias have about the same uses in gardens and need about the same treatment as perennial alyssums. They are useful in rock gardens, wall gardens, and as edging plants. They need full sun and grow in any ordinary well-drained soil. In hot, muggy weather older plants tend to die and because of this where torrid summers prevail fairly frequent propagation should be done. After flowering it is well to shear the spent flower heads. Propagation is by seed, summer cutting, and division.

SCHIZAEA (Schi-zaèa) — Curly-Grass Fern. The diminutive curly-grass fern, a wet-acid-soil native from Newfoundland to the pine barrens of New Jersey, is the only one of the thirty species of this group likely to receive attention from American gardeners. The genus, mostly tropical, belongs in the schizaea fern family SCHIZAEACEAE. It consists of small ferns with threadlike fronds (leaves) that in many species are divided, a circumstance that explains the name, from the Greek *schizein*, to split. Schizaeas have erect rhizomes and spirally arranged leaves. There are both sterile and spore-bearing fronds, the latter divided and forming terminal spikes with the sori (clusters of spore-bearing organs) in rows.

Curly-grass fern (*S. pusilla*) is so called because its very narrow-linear, stalkless leaves, scarcely ever over 2 inches long and often less, are spiraled or curled and grasslike. They are hairless. The fertile fronds are erect and 3 to 4½ inches tall. They do not curl. Each ends in a pinnate arrangement of four to seven pairs of segments ¾ inch to 1½ inches long with eight to fourteen spore-producing organs on each division.

Garden Uses and Cultivation. It is something of a horticultural triumph to persuade this dainty unfernlike-looking fern to make itself at home in gardens. It does not take kindly to cultivation and is a challenge to connoisseurs of choice native wildlings. The best chance of success lies in duplicating as nearly as possible the conditions under which this rare plant grows in it native bogs, where it favors above-water-level hummocks, and in wet grassy places. Propagation is by spores.

SCHIZAECEAE — Schizaea Fern Family. Four genera, totaling about 150 species, most native to the tropics, few to subtropical and temperate regions, constitute this family of ferns. Many sorts have climbing stems. The leaves (fronds) are undivided or pinnate. The spore capsules, borne on specialized, often spikelike segments of the fronds, are in rows. Genera cultivated are *Lygodium* and *Schizaea*.

SCHIZANDRA is Schisandra.

SCHIZANTHUS (Schizán-thus) — Butterfly Flower or Poor-Man's-Orchid. That these popular, flowering annuals belong in the same family as potatoes, tomatoes, eggplants, and tobacco may surprise non-botanists, yet all are members of the nightshade family SOLANACEAE. The fifteen species of *Schizanthus* are natives of Chile. They are called butterfly flower and poor-man's-orchid because their irregularly-shaped, variously-colored blooms with spreading winglike petals are suggestive of certain butterflies and orchid flowers. These plants are not, of course, related to orchids, nor does their habit of growth or foliage suggest that. The name *Schizanthus*, from the Greek *schizo*, to cut, and *anthos*, a flower, alludes to the corolla of the flower being deeply cleft.

Schizanthuses are erect, and branched. Their alternate leaves, broadly-lanceolate in outline, are usually much divided and of distinctly ferny aspect. The numerous very asymmetrical and usually showy flowers are in large, branched clusters. They have a tubular, five-cleft calyx, a short- or long-tubed corolla with two wide-spreading lips, the upper two-lobed, the lower three-lobed. There are two protruding stamens and three staminodes (abortive stamens), one minute. There is one style. The fruits are capsules.

An attractive species about 4 feet tall, *S. pinnatus,* often cultivated as *S. grandiflorus,* has blooms about 1¼ inches across, of various colors and markings, but most commonly with the lower lip violet-purple, the upper one paler with a purple-spotted, yellow blotch. The corolla tube is shorter than the calyx. The stamens protrude considerably. Prevailingly white-, pink-, and lilac-flowered varieties have been named *S. p. candidissimus, S. p. carmineus,* and *S. p. lilacinus,* respectively. Similar to *S. pinnatus* but differing in its flowers having a corolla as long or longer than the calyx and with a shorter lower lip, *S. retusus* has usually rose-pink flowers, approximately ¾ inch across, with the

Schizanthus retusus

upper lip marked at its center with orange. The flowers of *S. r. grahamii* are lavender with the middle lobe of the upper lip yellow.

Hybrid *S. wisetonensis*, intermediate between its parents *S. pinnatus* and *S. retusus grahamii,* and up to 4 feet tall, has a profusion of beautiful white, pink, lavender, blue, or reddish-brown flowers, variously blotched or marked and with the upper lip streaked with yellow. The stamens are slightly exserted. Variety *S. w. compactus* is shorter and of denser growth.

Schizanthus wisetonensis

Garden Uses and Cultivation. The chief use of schizanthuses is as pot specimens for blooming in greenhouses in late winter and spring. Where summer temperatures are not excessively high, they can be used as garden annuals, but rarely as successfully as many other plants. For outdoor display sow seeds in early spring where the plants are to remain and thin the seedlings to about 1 foot apart or sow indoors seven to eight weeks before the plants are to be set out in the garden. As soon as they are big enough to handle readily, transplant the seedlings from indoor sowings individually to 2½- to 3-inch pots or 2½ inches apart in flats in porous soil. Grow them on in a sunny greenhouse in a 50°F night temperature until a week or two before planting-out time, which is when it is safe to set out tomatoes, then harden by standing them in a cold frame or sheltered place outdoors. Except *S. retusus,* which is better left without pinching, the plants should have their tips pinched out when they are a few inches high to encourage branching. Sunny, sheltered locations where the soil is encouraging to root growth are congenial for schizanthuses. Staking is needed.

For flowering in greenhouses, sow seeds in porous soil from early September to January. The earlier sowings give the largest plants. Under good cultivation and if kept potted into successively larger containers before their roots really become pot bound, they may be finished in 9-, 10-, or

even 12-inch pots or tubs and will measure 3 feet or more in diameter and bear thousands of flowers. Smaller plants in pots 6 to 8 inches in diameter are very serviceable. The seeds germinate well in a temperature of 55 to 60°F. Transplant the seedlings individually to small pots and shift them successively to larger ones as root growth indicates need. Crowding of their roots tends to induce schizanthuses to bloom; therefore, when large specimens are grown for late flowering, the plants must never become really pot bound until after the final potting in February. On the other hand, plants intended to bloom as fairly small specimens in late December, January, and early February should be established in their final pots not later than the beginning of November.

The soil for indoor-grown schizanthuses must be fertile and porous. One of rather coarse, loose texture that contains a fair proportion of peat moss or other organic matter, as well as sufficient fertilizer to make it moderately nourishing, is ideal.

As cut flowers, schizanthuses are elegant and last well in water. They can be grown indoors in greenhouse ground beds or benches from seed sown in September or October. The young plants are transferred to 2½-inch pots and from these are planted 1 foot apart in beds or benches in January. Whether grown as pot plants or for cutting, the young plants, with the exception of those of *S. retusus,* should be pinched once, and plants to be grown into large pot or tub specimens from early-sown seeds must be pinched several times during the winter to promote branching. Because schizanthuses are brittle rather special care must be taken to avoid breakage. This is especially true when potting and planting. Give careful attention to staking and tying well before the stems become twisted.

Grow these plants in full sun and under cool, airy conditions. A night temperature of 45 to 50°F is ample. When day temperatures reach 55 to 60°F, ventilate the greenhouse freely.

Take care not to overwater schizanthuses, especially when the plants are small and in the depth of winter. With the coming in of longer days and more intense light and after the plants have filled their available soil with roots, more frequent applications are necessary. Excessive dryness at that stage can lead to yellowing and loss of leaves. After the final pots are well filled with roots, weekly applications of dilute liquid fertilizer greatly help to maintain green and healthy foliage.

SCHIZOBASOPSIS. See Bowiea.

SCHIZOCAPSA. See Tacca.

SCHIZOCASIA. See Xenophya.

SCHIZOCENTRON. See Heterocentron.

SCHIZOLOBIUM (Schizo-lòbium) — Bacurubu. Native from Central America to Brazil, *Schizolobium* consists of five species of tall trees of the pea family LEGUMINOSAE. One is cultivated in the tropics and warm subtropics. The name is from the Greek *schizo,* split, and *lobos,* a lobe, and refers to the manner of opening of the seed pods.

The large leaves of *Schizolobium* are twice-pinnately-divided into numerous small leaflets. The flowers have asymmetrical calyxes with five sepals overlapping in bud and bent backward when the blooms open. There are five petals of unequal size and shape, and ten stamens. The flat or flattish seed pods contain a solitary seed.

Deciduous, the bacurubu (*S. parahybum* syn. *S. excelsum*) is a handsome, slender, fast-growing tree with foliage somewhat resembling that of the royal poinciana (*Delonix regia*) and Colville's glory (*Colvillea racemosa*), but with a not wide-spreading crown and with bigger leaves than those trees. The leaves are 3 feet long or longer. Each has fifteen or more primary divisions, with ten to thirty pairs each of oblong, short-stalked leaflets, ½ to 1 inch long, and whitish or grayish on their undersides. The bright yellow blooms are in large, erect, terminal, 1-foot-long panicles. Each flower is about 1 inch in diameter. The seed pods are flattish, obovate, and about 4 inches long. The solitary seed has a long wing.

Garden and Landscape Uses and Cultivation. This is a beautiful ornamental for the tropics and warm subtropics. Its branches are brittle and because of this it is not recommended as a street tree nor for planting where harm is likely to result from a falling branch. This species grows in ordinary soil in full sun and is propagated by seed.

SCHIZOPETALON (Schizo-pétalon). One species of *Schizopetalon,* of the mustard family CRUCIFERAE, is the only cultivated member of this South American genus of eight species. The generic name, derived from the Greek *schizo,* cut, and *petalon,* a petal, alludes to the dissected petals.

Schizopetalons are annuals with alternate, wavy-edged, toothed, or pinnately-lobed leaves and terminal, bracted racemes of smallish flowers with four sepals, four petals narrowed conspicuously to basal claws and with blades irregularly pinnately-cleft. There are four long and two short stamens and one style. The fruits are pods.

Dainty *S. walkeri* has slender, branched stems up to 1 foot in height and deeply-divided, rough, wavy leaves. In racemes and almond-scented, its white flowers have feathery, deeply-pinnately dissected and fringed petals.

Garden Uses and Cultivation. This plant is useful for edgings, rock gardens, flower

Salvia officinalis purpurascens

Salvia officinalis tricolor

Salvia patens

Sandersonia aurantiaca

Saxifraga oppositifolia

Sassafras albidum (fall foliage)

Saxifraga pensylvanica

Schizanthus wisetonensis variety

Schaueria flavicoma

beds, and window and porch boxes, and also for cultivation in pots in greenhouses for spring flowering. For blooming outdoors, sow in early spring directly where the plants are to bloom or alternatively sow indoors eight weeks before it is safe to transplant the resulting young plants to the garden, which may be done as soon as there is no longer danger of frost. Transplant seedlings from early indoor sowings individually to small pots as soon as they have their second pair of leaves. Because schizopetalons are sensitive to root disturbance it is much better to do this than to transplant to flats and from them to the outdoors. Grow the young plants in a sunny greenhouse with a night temperature of 50°F, and a day temperature five to ten degrees higher.

Thin seedlings from seed sown outdoors to leave them 4 or 5 inches apart, space plants from pots 6 inches apart. No special summer care is required. Schizopetalons prefer a porous, moderately rich soil and a sunny location.

To raise plants for spring blooming in greenhouses sow seeds in September in a temperature of about 60°F and transplant the seedlings individually to 2½-inch pots. Later pot three together in a 5- or 6-inch pot, in which they will bloom. Use porous, nourishing soil. A suitable environment is that of a sunny greenhouse where the temperature is 50°F by night, five to ten degrees higher by day. Water rather sparingly in the early stages of growth, more generously as spring approaches. Weekly applications of dilute liquid fertilizer are helpful after the final pots are well filled with roots.

SCHIZOPHRAGMA (Schizo-phrágma). The genus *Schizophragma*, of which there are eight species in eastern Asia and the Himalayas, belongs in the saxifrage family SAXIFRAGACEAE. The formidably long name *Schizophragma hydrangeoides* probably limits the popularity of a very good hardy vine. This is regrettable, for it is a handsome one. Yet the name has meaning. The first part of the generic title comes from the same Greek source as the initial syllables of schizophrenia; it derives from *schizo*, to split. The phragma part is the Greek *phragma,* a screen or fence. Combined, they allude to the skeletonized, fencelike appearance of the seed capsules after parts have split away. Then, the seed pods resemble tiny Japanese lanterns. Greek also gives meaning to the specific epithet of *S. hydrangeoides,* which consists of a slightly abbreviated "hydrangea" married to *oides,* resembling, and resemble hydrangeas schizophragmas certainly do, to the extent that they are sometimes known as climbing-hydrangeas. But that is confusing because there are also true hydrangeas that climb.

Members of this genus ascend trees in the manner of trumpet vine, poison-ivy,

and English ivy, by attaching themselves by aerial roots that develop from their stems. They also grow on cliffs and sprawl over rocks. All are deciduous.

From *Hydrangea* this genus differs in its flowers having their styles united, so that there is apparently one instead of two to five separate ones, and in its showy sterile blooms having a solitary petal-like part instead of four or five such. These petal-like organs are really sepals. In *Schizophragma,* but not *Hydrangea,* they are long-stalked.

The leaves of *Schizophragma* are opposite. The flowers are white or creamy-white and in large, flat, much-branched clusters. The fertile blooms are tiny and have four or five each sepals and petals, eight or ten stamens, and one short style. The fruits are capsules.

Native only in Japan and Korea, *S. hydrangeoides* is hardy at least as far north as Boston, Massachusetts, and probably in

Schizophragma hydrangeoides

colder climates. At the Arnold Arboretum, Jamaica Plain, Massachusetts, it is at its best on a northeast-facing wall. Its fresh green leaves appear in early spring. Ovate to heart-shaped and coarsely-toothed, they are up to 6 inches long and wide. They do not change color in fall. The flower clusters are at the ends of branches, rarely more than 3 feet long, that develop at right angles from the main stems. The blooms are showy for a long period in July and August. Each cluster, 5 or 6 inches in diameter, consists of very many fertile flowers and, around the edges of the cluster, possibly a dozen sterile ones, their showy petal-like sepals ovate to lanceolate and ½ inch to 4 inches long by ½ inch to 3 inches wide.

Much rarer in cultivation and less hardy is *S. integrifolium*, a native of China and Taiwan. This is much more variable than the last and usually is showier in bloom. Its leaves, darker on their undersides than above and hairless to densely-felted with hairs beneath, range in size from 2½ to 8 inches in length and 1¾ to 5 inches in

Schizophragma hydrangeoides (flowers)

width. They are broadly-elliptic to ovate and toothless, minutely-toothed, or coarsely wavy-dentate. The flower clusters are 6 inches to 1 foot wide. In general, except for size, they resemble those of *S. hydrangeoides.* The enlarged sepals of the sterile blooms are white to creamy-yellow and ¾ inch to 3½ inches long by ⅜ inch to 2 inches broad. Several variants have been described and named, but as these graduate almost imperceptibly into each other, with many intermediates, as varieties they are of horticultural rather than botanical significance.

Garden and Landscape Uses. As self-clinging vines for covering masonry and tall tree trunks and for scrambling over large rocks and stumps, schizophragmas are very useful. Because of their method of supporting themselves they are not suitable for planting against wooden structures. Their foliage patterns are distinctive and they bloom at a season when flowering vines are not too plentiful. In temperate regions where fairly mild winters prevail every effort to obtain the finest blooming types of *S. integrifolium* should be made. The other species is also a very worthwhile planting. These plants grow best in partial shade in moistish soil, but will succeed in sunny locations if they do not lack for moisture.

Cultivation. Schizophragmas are often a little more difficult to get started than true hydrangeas that are climbers, but they are worth the slight effort needed. Young pot-grown plants should be chosen for setting out in spring, close to the bases of their supports. They should be cut back to a height of about 6 inches, the objective being to encourage the development of new shoots because only these cling. No special attention, except whatever pruning is necessary to control their spread, is needed. Pruning is done in late winter or spring.

SCHIZOSTYLIS (Schizó-stylis) — Crimson Flag or Kafir-Lily. This genus, of the iris family IRIDACEAE, is endemic to South Africa. Unlike the great majority of its relatives there, such as *Gladiolus*, *Watsonia*, and *Ixia*, it has rhizomes instead of bulblike corms. There are two species of *Schizostylis*, and an exceedingly beautiful variety of one. The name, from the Greek *schizo*, to split, and *stylos*, a pillar, alludes to the style being split for almost half its length into three spreading branches.

Schizostylises have few, linear, slightly sickle-shaped leaves in fans, and branchless, one-sided spikes of up to eight loosely arranged blooms carried in two ranks on erect stalks well above the foliage. The bracts of the flower spikes are lanceolate and green. The blooms have perianths with straight, cylindrical tubes 1 inch to 1½ inches long, and six pointed lobes (petals, or more properly, tepals) cupped to produce shallowly-bell-shaped blooms. There are three slender stamens. The fruits are capsules.

The best-known species, **S. coccinea**, has hairless basal leaves up to 1 foot long, and with distinct midribs. The stems have three sheathing leaves smaller than those below. The brilliant scarlet flowers are 2 to 2½ inches wide. They have yellow anthers. Very beautiful **S. c. 'Mrs. Hegarty'** has clear pink flowers. From **S. coccinea** and its variety, **S. pauciflora** differs in having more slender rhizomes, and stouter stems up to 2½ feet tall. In few-flowered spikes, its blooms are purple-pink.

Garden and Landscape Uses. These lovely South Africans have much the appearance of gladioluses and the same uses. Because they need a much longer season of growth, and because they are without corms that can be stored dry through the winter, their cultivation is somewhat different. They are splendid for flower beds where fall frosts do not come early and for supplying late fall and early winter color in greenhouses. They are excellent cut flowers.

Cultivation. In climates where frost does not enter the ground deeply enough to injure the rhizomes, schizostylises can be grown permanently outdoors. Rather sandy, loamy soil fairly well supplied with organic matter in the form of peat moss, compost, or similar material gives the best results. It should be moderately moist, but never remain for long wet. Locations in full sun, with shelter from strong wind, are ideal.

Spring is the time to plant. Space divisions of the rhizomes, each of about three shoots, 6 inches apart to form clumps in flower beds, or for cut flowers in rows about 1½ feet apart. Where hardy allow the plants to remain undisturbed until they become overcrowded or begin to deteriorate. This will usually happen after three or four years. Then, dig them up in spring, divide the rhizomes, and replant the strongest divisions in newly spaded ground improved by adding peat moss or compost and a complete garden fertilizer. Each spring give a dressing of such fertilizer to established plants, and lighter applications once or twice during the summer. Where winters are reasonably mild yet are such that frost may reach the rhizomes unless protection is given, mulch the ground heavily in late fall with salt hay, dry leaves, or other suitable insulation.

Schizostylises can be grown in cold frames as far north as southern New York. These afford the protection needed to prevent the flowers being harmed by fall frosts and so make possible the raising of flowers for cutting. The trick is to construct the frames with sides that can be built higher in fall so that glass or plastic sash can be placed over them without damaging the blooms. Alternatively, frameworks of wood or metal covered with polyethylene plastic can be erected over the plants before frost. Adequate provision for ventilation must be made. Schizostylises grown in this way should be divided each spring and replanted 6 inches apart in newly prepared earth. They are kept over winter by cutting them down after flowering and covering them with a heavy mulch of salt hay or dry leaves over which is placed the glass or plastic sash. On warm winter days the sash must be lifted or removed to permit free ventilation. An alternative plan is to dig the rhizomes after blooming and store them until spring, packed closely together in slightly damp peat moss or sand in a cellar or similar place in a temperature of 35 to 40°F.

As pot plants for greenhouse adornment schizostylises are lovely. To have them, plant five strong, single-shoot divisions together in well-drained, 6-inch pots, or more in larger containers, in early spring. Use porous, fertile soil, and after potting stand them in a cold frame or outdoors where there is no danger from frost. Water sparingly at first, more generously as rooting takes place. Later, when the weather is warm and settled bury the pots to their rims in a bed of peat moss, sand, or soil in a sunny location. Before frost remove them to a greenhouse where the night temperature is 45 to 50°F and by day five to ten or fifteen degrees higher. During their growing season water freely, but not so that the soil is for long periods saturated. Give dilute liquid fertilizer regularly. Through the winter, pot specimens may be kept in a cold frame, very cool greenhouse, or cellar. Divide and repot them in early spring.

SCHLUMBERGERA (Schlum-bèrgera) — Crab Cactus, Thanksgiving Cactus, Christmas Cactus. Belonging to the cactus family CACTACEAE, the genus *Schlumbergera* consists of three or according to some authorities five species, endemic to Brazil. Its name commemorates Friedrich Schlumberger, a Belgian cactus fancier of the late nineteenth century.

Schlumbergeras are epiphytes (tree-perchers) with arching or drooping, much-branched, conspicuously-jointed (segmented), thin, flat, green stems, or the older ones becoming rounded, woody, and brown. The joints of the stems are truncated-ovate and have toothed margins with areoles from which sprout short bristles. The showy symmetrical or asymmetrical flowers are solitary or in pairs at the ends of the stems. Their inner perianth parts (petals) are united to form a tube. There are numerous protruding stamens, the inner ones united as a tube surrounding the long, slender style. The fruits are berries.

The application of correct names to Thanksgiving, Christmas, and Easter cactuses has long bedeviled gardeners and botanists. Recent investigations and reappraisals have resulted in discarding the old familiar name *Zygocactus* and transferring the plant formerly called *Z. truncatus* to the genus *Schlumbergera* as *S. truncata*. The Easter cactus, formerly named *S. gaertneri*, is transferred from *Schlumbergera* to *Rhipsalidopsis* as *R. gaertneri*. An added complication is that this plant has also been known as *Epiphyllopsis gaertneri* and, according to some botanists, should be *Rhipsalis gaertneri*. At least the specific epithet *gaertneri* endures no matter the genus.

The crab cactus (**S. truncata**), one variety of which is a parent of the Christmas

Schlumbergera truncata (flower)

cactus, has closely overlapping stems with segments 1½ to 2½ inches long and up to 1½ inches broad. Each segment has two to four sharp teeth along each margin as well as one at each corner at the apex. The teeth are progressively larger from the bases to the apexes of the segments. The tubular, gaping-mouthed, cerise flowers are highly asymmetrical. The corolla tube just above the ovary bends sharply at almost right angles. The petals spread and lay backward, the upper ones usually hooded over the stamens. The stamens have white filaments (stalks). The style is markedly curved. The fruits are round, not angled. Several varieties, characterized by different flower colors and some differences in their times of blooming, are grown.

Schlumbergera truncata variety 'White Christmas'

The Thanksgiving cactus is *S. t. bicolor*, an early blooming plant, the flowers of which have white tubes and deep rose-pink margins to the petals. In *S. t. delicata* the flowers, at first white, develop a blush of pink at their edges when two days old, the style is magenta. Late-flowering, *S. t. salmonea* has salmon-pink blooms with some white in the corolla tubes. There are other varieties with horticultural names, such as 'Gertrude W. Beahm', red, 'Llewellyn', orange; and 'Parna', light crimson with an orange throat. Others are described in catalogs of specialists.

The other parent of the Christmas cactus, the seed bearer, is **S. russelliana.** This differs markedly from the crab cactus. Its stem segments, rarely exceeding 1½ inches long by ½ inch wide, are without sharp teeth, but do have one or two notches on each edge. The magenta-pink flowers, 2 to 2½ inches long, have straight corolla tubes that do not bend sharply above the ovaries. The blooms are almost symmetrical and their petals spread, but scarcely bend backward. The stalks of the stamens are pink. At night the flowers partially close. The fruits have four, or rarely five, angles. This species is notoriously a shy bloomer and more difficult to grow than the crab cactus, Christmas cactus, or Thanksgiving cactus.

The Christmas cactus (**S. bridgesii** syn. *S. buckleyi*) originated in a London, England, nursery shortly before the middle of the nineteenth century and was first named *Epiphyllum buckleyi*. Its parents are

S. russelliana and *S. truncata ruckeri.* This fine kind seems to display hybrid vigor and is probably the easiest of the schlumbergeras to grow and flower well. In growth and flower characteristics, it is midway between its parents. The apexes of the leaf segments are blunt, sometimes with hairs. There are no obvious claws on the leaf margins. The blooms are bright purplish-pink and have pink-stalked stamens. Despite its appellation Christmas cactus, this kind is highly variable in its blooming, the flowers appearing from November to March. A sister hybrid raised at the same time by the same breeder, and sometimes confused with the Christmas cactus, was originally named *Epiphyllum rollissonii.* Its correct name now is *Schlumbergera bridgesii rollissonii.* This has wide-spaced, less closely overlapping stems than the Christmas cactus and pinker, less magenta blooms with the stalks of the stamens white instead of pink. Otherwise it is similar.

Garden and Other Uses. Schlumbergeras are, of course, of special interest to cactus fanciers. They are also first-rate greenhouse plants and houseplants. They bloom at times of the year when their brightly colored blooms are especially welcome and, with the exception of the somewhat cantankerous *S. russelliana*, are easy to grow. In addition to being attractive as pot plants they are splendid in hanging baskets.

Cultivation. Conflicting reports regarding the behavior of these plants, of success and nonsuccess in persuading them to flourish and bloom, is surely, in part at least, associated with the shocking confusion of identities that has and still does prevail. The names Thanksgiving cactus and Christmas cactus have been applied indiscriminatingly to *S. truncata, S. russelliana,* and *S. bridgesii.* The first and last of these are easy to grow and ordinarily bloom freely, but even when tiny, *S. russelliana* is much less obliging. Gardeners

Schlumbergera bridgesii (flowers)

who acquire that kind are likely to experience difficulty in bringing it to bloom. It probably grows better and flowers more surely and freely when grafted onto *Pereskia* than on its own roots. There are other reasons, however, for low success with these cactuses, even with *S. truncata* and *S. bridgesii.* Chief among these is a not sufficiently porous soil kept in a constantly too wet condition. This often causes yellowing of the stems, bud dropping, and poor growth. Extremely dry, hot rooms are inhibiting and may cause shriveling of the stems. Another possible cause of failure to bloom may be exposure to artificial light. Schlumbergeras normally bloom during short days. Denying them the long night of about sixteen hours that they may need to bloom, is a likely reason for nonflowering. Yet another cause of this trouble is insufficient intensity of light. Except in summer, when a little shade from the strongest sun is in order, exposure to full sunlight should be the rule with schlumbergeras.

Provided the soil is well drained and porous enough to pass water through it readily, its exact composition is not of great importance. A somewhat loamy earth containing a generous amount of organic matter, such as peat moss or leaf mold, satisfies. Older plants accommodated in largish containers need repotting at intervals of several years only. In intervening years it suffices to scrape away a little of the topsoil and replace it with nourishing earth to which has been added some bonemeal. Repotting and top dressing are done in spring. Small plants, those in pots up to 4 inches in diameter, may be transferred to slightly larger receptacles every year or two if growth warrants. From repotting or top dressing until well into August, when the end segments of the shoots are maturing and flower bud formation is to be stimulated, watering is done fairly freely so that the soil is always moderately moist, but never sodden. Beginning in August or September less water is given. The soil is allowed to become decidedly dryish between waterings, but not to an extent that there is danger of the stems shriveling. Then, too, all shade is removed and the plants are exposed to full sun. Once flower buds are well formed, more generous watering may be initiated and continued until after flowering is through, then once again, lesser amounts are given until after spring potting or top dressing, and the start of a new cycle of growth. Well-rooted specimens benefit from occasional applications in summer of dilute liquid fertilizer.

In greenhouses these plants grow well in a 50 to 55°F night temperature from fall through spring with a five to ten, and in sunny weather fifteen degree daytime increase permitted. At other times natural outdoor temperatures suffice. Plants cultivated in homes should be given conditions as close to these as possible. A fairly humid atmosphere is desirable; since these are not desert cactuses, too arid conditions harm them. In bright weather from spring until August daily spraying with a fine mist of water favors good growth. Propagation is easy by cuttings of two or three stem segments inserted in sand, vermiculite, or perlite early in the year. Plants started then bloom, tiny though they are, before they are one year old. Grafting onto understock of *Pereskia* is resorted to when tree-form (or standard) specimens are desired and

Schlumbergera grafted on *Pereskia*

may be the best method of inducing *S. russelliana* to bloom. It is easily done. A single-stemmed *Pereskia* plant has its top cut off at the height that the trunk of the future standard plant is to have. The cut end of the stem is cleft and into the incision is inserted a two- or three-segment section of *Schlumbergera*, with the part that will be inside the cleft shaved to a broad wedge. After insertion the scion of *Schlumbergera* is fastened into place with spines removed from the *Pereskia* and used as pins to stick through the two halves of the stem of the understock that result from the cleft and the scion grasped between them. In a few weeks a good union will have taken place. Other erect-stemmed cactuses, such as *Selenicereus*, *Hylocereus*, and similar ones, can be used as understocks, but *Pereskia* is generally preferred. Scale insects and mealybugs are likely insect pests.

SCHOLAR TREE is *Alstonia scholaris*. The Chinese scholar tree is *Sophora japonica*.

SCHOMBONITIS. This is the name of orchid hybrids the parents of which are *Schomburgkia* and *Sophronitis*.

SCHOMBURGKIA (Schom-búrgkia). Its name commemorating its discoverer, the great botanical explorer of South America, Robert Hermann Schomburgk, of Germany, who died in 1865, *Schomburgkia* consists of seventeen species of the orchid family ORCHIDACEAE. Natives of Mexico, Central America, tropical South America, and the West Indies, these orchids are by some authorities included as a distinct section of closely related *Laelia*. From *Laelia*, interpreted narrowly, they differ in their flowers having lips united for a short distance to the column, which is not, as is usual with *Laelia*, ordinarily markedly enfolded by the side lobes of the lip, and in the petals and sometimes the sepals being wavy, which is unusual in *Laelia*.

Schomburgkias are evergreen epiphytes (plants that perch on trees without absorbing nourishment from them) or sometimes cliff- or rock-perchers. They have clustered pseudobulbs, most often with two or three leaves, and flowers in racemes or panicles from the tops of the pseudobulbs.

Native to tropical South America, fall-blooming *S. crispa* (syns. *S. gloriosa*, *Laelia gloriosa*) has spindle-shaped pseudobulbs about 8 inches tall, usually with a pair of pointed-lanceolate leaves up to 1 foot long. Sometimes 4 feet in length, the flowering stalks have crowded racemes of many 2- to 2½-inch-wide, waxy blooms with very wavy, dark-veined, brownish-yellow sepals and petals. Their slightly three-lobed lips are oblongish, pale pink deepening in hue toward their tips. Its club-shaped pseudobulbs up to 10 inches long and slenderer than those of allied *S. crispa*, Venezualan *S. lueddemannii* has flowers in clusters of up to twenty atop tall, slender

Schomburgkia lueddemannii

stalks. From 3 to 3½ inches wide, they have similar, tongue-shaped sepals and petals, wavy-margined and light brown to clear chestnut-brown with darker margins. The rosy-violet lip, tipped with brown, has three short, yellow keels. The pollinia (pollen masses) are yellow. This species blooms in winter and spring.

Hollow, spindle-shaped, densely-clustered pseudobulbs up to more than 2 feet long by 3 inches in diameter, and in the wild usually inhabited by fierce ants, are typical of *S. tibicinis* (syn. *Laelia tibicinis*). From two to four oblong-elliptic, bluntish

Schomburgkia tibicinis

leaves, up to 1½ feet long by 3 inches broad, sprout from each pseudobulb. Native from Mexico to Costa Rica, this has branched or branchless flowering stalks up to 10 feet long or longer. The many 2- to 3½-inch-wide, very fragrant blooms vary in color. Most often their very wavy-margined sepals and petals are chiefly bright purplish-magenta, sometimes brownish-orange. The lip may be whitish-yellow to glowing purple with a yellow patch at its base. This is a spring to early summer bloomer. In aspect much like the last, but smaller, *S. thomsoniana* (syn. *Laelia thomsoniana*) has pseudobulbs 6 to 8 inches in length with two or three leaves about as long. Its 2½-inch-wide flowers, in panicles 2 to 4 feet long, are creamy-white to yellow with the lip tipped with deep maroon-purple to almost black. Native to Cuba and the Cayman Islands, this blooms in spring.

Robust *S. humboldtii* (syn. *Laelia humboldtii*), of Venezuela, is allied to *S. thomsoniana*. Flowering in winter and spring, it has from stout rhizomes rather loosely-clustered pseudobulbs 6 to 8 inches long, each with two or three oblongish leaves about 6 inches in length. The 3- to 4-foot-long, usually branched, flowering stalks carry many 2½- to 3-inch-wide fragrant blooms with pale lilac to nearly white sepals and petals, the latter usually stained amethyst-purple toward their tips, the three-lobed lip, with its center lobe cleft and fringed, rich purple streaked with paler purple and with a yellow patch at its base.

Pseudobulbs, 1½ to 2 feet tall, spindle-shaped and most commonly with two pointed-oblong leaves not over 1 foot long are characteristic of *S. undulata* (syn. *Lae-*

lia undulata), of Venezuela and Colombia. Produced in winter and spring, its almost 2-inch-wide, fragrant or scentless flowers have mostly dark brown-purple to maroon-purple, very wavy sepals and petals and a three-lobed pink to rose-purple lip with a white basal patch. They are in loose terminal racemes, with stalks 2 to 6 feet long. Rather similar to *S. undulata* but with somewhat smaller flowers produced in winter and spring, *S. rosea,* of Colombia, has pseudobulbs with usually two leaves. Its flowers are similar, wavy-margined, reddish-purple sepals and petals, a rose-purple lip with three white keels, and a purple-spotted white column. They are clustered at the tops of slender, erect stalks.

Schomburgkia rosea

Schomburgkia rosea (flowers)

Vigorous and handsome winter-blooming *S. superbiens* (syn. *Laelia superbiens*), of Mexico and Central America, has club-shaped pseudobulbs, about 1½ feet tall by 1½ inches wide, each with 1- or 2-foot-long, 2½-inch-wide, stiff, leathery leaves. The stout flowering stalks are up to 4 feet tall or taller. They have racemes of fragrant, long-lasting, about 5-inch-wide blooms. The linear-strap-shaped to lanceolate sepals and oblong to oblanceolate-oblong petals are wavy, rose-purple paling somewhat toward their bases. Bright magenta-crimson and folded around the column, the three-lobed lip has a notched center lobe much longer than the lateral ones and a yellow disk.

Schomburgkia superbiens

Garden Uses and Cultivation. These are as for *Laelia* and *Cattleya*. For more information see Orchids.

SCHOTIA (Schòt-ia). Handsome shrubs or small trees of the pea family LEGUMINOSAE compose *Schotia*, a genus confined in the wild to South Africa and adjacent territory. There are possibly eighteen species. The name commemorates Richard van der Schot, a Dutch head gardener at Schoenbrunn botanic garden, Austria, who accompanied Jacquin on his botanical exploration of North America. He died in 1819.

Schotias have pinnate leaves with an uneven number of leaflets, and showy red flowers in crowded racemes or panicles. The blooms are not pea-like, but are structured like those of *Cassia*. They have four-parted calyxes and five nearly equal petals. The ten stamens are not united except briefly at their bases. They protrude and add notably to the showiness of the blooms. The fruits are flattened, often curved, leathery pods.

From 6 to 15 feet tall, rigid-branched *S. afra* (syn. *S. speciosa*) is a shrub or small tree with leaves, 1½ to 2½ inches long, crowded from the base to the tip of the midrib with up to twenty pairs of mostly oblong leaflets ⅓ to ¾ inch long. The terminal flower clusters, 3 to 4 inches across, are composed of crowded panicles and originate from the upper leaf axils. The blooms have calyxes of the same color, but shorter than the ½-inch-long broad-elliptic petals. The pods are 3 inches long by about 1 inch wide. A variety with leaflets broader than those of the typical species is *S. a. tamarindifolia*.

Very different and very beautiful, *S. brachypetala* is a nearly evergreen tree 20 to 40 feet in height. In South Africa called boerboon, it has lustrous, hairless leaves up to about 8 inches long. They have three or four pairs of blunt, broad-elliptic leaflets 1 inch to 2½ inches long and approximately one-half as wide. The pyramidal panicles of brilliant red flowers are 3 to 5 inches long and terminal. They have calyxes ⅓ inch long, and minute, bristle-like petals. The pods are 2 to 4 inches in length. They contain three or fewer seeds.

Schotia brachypetala

From the last, *S. capitata,* a slender shrub up to 20 feet tall, differs in having flowers with normally developed, narrowly-obovate petals, ½ inch long or longer, and in the rachises (mid-veins to which the leaflets are attached) of its leaves being narrowly-winged.

A tree 15 to 45 feet in height, with leaves with two to four pairs of broad-elliptic to obovate leaflets, *S. latifolia* has lustrous, hairless foliage. The freely-branched, dense, terminal flower panicles are pyramidal and 3 to 5 inches long. The blooms have green calyxes, pink petals ¼ inch long, and pink stamens. The pods are straight and about 4 inches long by 1 inch wide.

Garden and Landscape Uses and Cultivation. Only in climates essentially free of frost are schotias hardy. They are suitable for parts of California and similar regions and need sunny locations and well-drained, ordinary soil. They are propagated by seed and from cuttings of firm shoots under mist or in a greenhouse propagating bench.

SCHRANKIA (Schránk-ia) — Sensitive-Brier, Cat's Claw. Although of minor horticultural importance, *Schrankia* is of interest because its twice-pinnate leaves, like those of its close relative the sensitive plant (*Mimosa*), are often highly responsive to touch, their leaflets folding quickly upon slight contact. There are about thirty species, natives of chiefly warmer parts of the Americas. Belonging in the pea family LEGUMINOSAE, this genus consists of perennial herbaceous plants and subshrubs with tiny pink or purplish flowers in spherical or cylindrical stalked heads. It differs from *Mimosa* in technical characteristics of the fruits. The name commemorates the German botanist Franz von Paula von Schrank, who died in 1835.

The cat's claw (*S. nuttallii* syn. *S. uncinata*), a herbaceous perennial, has prostrate or arching, branched stems up to 3 feet in length and prominently ribbed and furnished with stout, hooked thorns. Its highly sensitive leaves are 2½ to 6 inches long, with thorny midribs and about six main divisions each of sixteen to thirty small, prominently veined leaflets. The globose heads of pink flowers are almost or quite 1 inch in diameter. The blooms are succeeded by slender, thorny-ribbed seed pods. This species inhabits dry, poor soils from Illinois to South Dakota, Arkansas, and Texas. Differing in having less conspicuously veined leaves, flower heads up to ¾ inch in diameter, and stems and seed pods finely-pubescent as well as thorny, *S. microphylla* grows in similar terrain from Virginia to Kentucky, Florida, and Texas.

Garden Uses and Cultivation. The sensitive-briers are sometimes cultivated as curiosities in rock gardens and similar places. They are best accommodated in well-drained, not excessively fertile soil in full sun and are easily raised from seed. They can also be grown from cuttings. They are probably not hardy in climates much harsher than those of their natural ranges.

SCHWALBEA (Schwál-bea) — Chaffseed. A lone species, native to the United States from New England and New York to Florida and Texas, comprises this genus of the figwort family SCROPHULARIACEAE. Its name honors an eighteenth-century German traveler and botanical author, Christian Georg Schwalbe.

A hardy perennial of minor horticultural importance, the chaffseed (*Schwalbea americana*) inhabits moist, sandy soils. It is finely-hairy, with branchless stems 1 foot to 2 feet tall. Its alternate, stalkless, three-veined, lanceolate leaves, without lobes or teeth, are 1 inch to 2 inches long. They diminish in size progressively from the base of the stem upward, until finally they are represented by bracts. The very asymmetrical flowers, solitary in the axils of the upper leaves or bracts, are in terminal spikelike racemes. They are 1¼ to 1½ inches long or slightly longer and have yellowish corollas stained with purple. The five-lobed calyxes have two very unequal lips, the lower much longer. The upper lip of the corolla is concave and sometimes notched at its apex. The lower one is approximately as long as the upper and shallowly-three-lobed. There are four stamens, not protruding. The fruits are capsules containing slender, winged seeds.

Garden Uses and Cultivation. Other than for native plant gardens or as a perennial occasionally to be set in semiwild places, *Schwalbea* is not of great value for garden planting. It grows without difficulty in moist soils and is easily propagated by seed and by division.

SCHWANTESIA (Schwant-èsia). All ten species of *Schwantesia* are natives of South African deserts where they inhabit granite and quartzite rocky outcrops. They belong in the *Mesembryanthemum* section of the carpetweed family AIZOACEAE. Their name honors the distinguished twentieth-century student of this family, Dr. G. Schwantes, of Kiel, Germany.

Schwantesias are low, short-stemmed, tufted or clustered succulents with the older parts of the stems thickly clothed with the remains of old leaves. The keeled, toothed or toothless, very succulent, bluish-white to greenish-white, opposite leaves are in alternate pairs at right angles to each other. The flowers, solitary and yellow or rarely orange, superficially resemble daisies, although structurally they are entirely different; each is a single bloom, not, as in daisies, a head of many florets. The blooms open in the afternoons. The fruits are capsules.

One of the easiest species to grow, *S. triebneri* has stems each with three pairs of elongated, triangular, gray-green,

Schwantesia triebneri

toothless leaves up to 2¼ inches long, broadening toward their apexes. They are clothed with minute hairs. The undersides of the leaves toward their bases are rounded, near their apexes they are keeled. The leaf edges are often red near their tips and in summer the leaves may be dotted with red. The stalked blooms are up to 2 inches in diameter. Forming compact clumps 3 to 4 inches tall, *S. ruedebuschii* has beautiful blue-gray, boat-shaped leaves mottled with white, ending in coarse, short teeth that spread like abbreviated fingers each with a tiny brown tip. Cushion-forming *S. herrei* has smooth, bluish-gray, keeled leaves about 1¼ inches long, often with a few teeth. Its flowers are 1¼ to 1¾ inches in diameter.

Garden Uses and Cultivation. These are among the many small succulents that attract collectors of such intriguing and delightful plants. They can be grown in outdoor rock gardens in mild desert regions, but much more commonly are accommodated in pots, or more appropriately in pans (shallow pots), in cool greenhouses or sunny windows. They are less difficult to satisfy than is sometimes thought. Conditions and care appropriate to *Lithops* and similar plants are likely to produce satisfactory results. The greatest dangers are from too fertile earth and excessive watering. Schwantesias succeed best in soil consisting largely of decomposed granite or sandstone with a little good topsoil mixed in. Limestone is not to their liking, and it is better not to include organic matter. Schwantesias grow slowly, summer being their active season. Then, they should be watered moderately to rather sparingly; in winter they are kept nearly dry. Seeds germinate readily, but unless carefully managed the seedlings are likely to damp off. Cuttings root easily. For additional information see Succulents.

SCIADOPITYS (Sciadóp-itys) — Umbrella-Pine. One endemic Japanese species of unusual aspect constitutes *Sciadopitys*, of the taxodium family TAXODIACEAE. Its name derives from the Greek *skias*, a parasol, and *pitys*, a pine or fir tree. It alludes to the arrangement of leaves.

The umbrella-pine (*S. verticillata*) in its native country is sometimes 120 feet high

Sciadopitys verticillata

Sciadopitys verticillata (foliage)

and may develop a trunk 4 feet in diameter, but is less than one-half as tall in cultivation in North America. It is easily distinguished from all other evergreens by the arrangement of its leaves or leaflike organs. These are in whorls of ten to thirty and spread like the ribs of an umbrella. Difference of opinion exists among botanists as to what these apparent leaves are. One school holds that they represent true leaves joined in pairs along their edges with only a central channel on top and bottom and a notch in the top to indicate the line of fusion. Others are of the opinion that, morphologically, they are short shoots or cladodes that function as leaves and that the true leaves of the plant are represented by the small scales that surround their bases. Because they look like leaves and are commonly so regarded, we shall refer to them as such. Male and female flowers are borne on the same tree, the males in tight terminal clusters about 1 inch long. The females are also terminal and develop into oblong-ovoid cones, 2½ to 4 inches long by almost or quite one-half as wide. The cones take two years to mature. Some of the leaves of *S. v. pendula* are yellow.

In youth and middle age the umbrella-pine is handsome and narrowly-pyramidal with ascending branches and lustrous, needle-like leaves 3 to 4½ inches long, notched at their tips and grooved above and below. In old age the branches tend to be pendulous and the crown is looser than in younger trees.

Garden and Landscape Uses. The umbrella-pine is so distinct in habit and appearance that it is seen to best advantage when used as a specimen, standing by itself and not crowded by other trees or shrubbery. It needs a sunny location not exposed to sweeping winds. It grows rather slowly.

Cultivation. This species needs deep, fertile, somewhat acid or neutral soil never excessively dry, but not poorly drained. It does not prosper in alkaline soils. No regular pruning is needed, but if a branch

shows a tendency to rival the central leader it should be removed. Propagation is by seeds sown in a greenhouse in winter or in a cold frame or outdoors in spring. Seedling plants often exhibit considerable differences in their rates of growth even when planted under identical conditions.

SCILLA (Scíl-la) — Squill. The genus *Scilla*, of the lily family LILIACEAE, is a mightier one than *Chionodoxa*, the other predominantly blue-flowered genus sometimes confused with it. It includes eighty to ninety species, not all of which flower in spring, and some of its lesser known ones are considerably more massive than chionodoxas. It is more widely distributed in the wild than *Chionodoxa*, ranging through temperate Europe, Asia, and South Africa, and represented by a few species in tropical Africa. The name *Scilla* is an old Greek and Latin one. The sorts of this genus are distinguished from chionodoxas and hyacinths (*Hyacinthus*) by their petals not being joined at their bases to form a distinct corolla tube. From chionodoxas they also differ in having stamens that do not hug each other in a central cone, but flare outward from their bases. Plants previously included in *Scilla* now assigned to other genera are the English bluebell (*Endymion nonscriptus* syns. *Scilla nonscripta* and *S. nutans*), the Spanish bluebell (*Endymion hispanicus* syns. *Scilla hispanica*, *S. campanulata*), *Endymion italicus* (syn. *Scilla italica*), and *Ledebouria socialis* (syn. *Scilla violacea*). Plants listed by bulb dealers as *S. amethystina* may be *Brimeura amethystina* or a robust form of *Scilla litardierei*.

Scillas are bulbous with few to several, mostly narrow, linear basal leaves that usually appear with the flowers, and erect, leafless flower stalks of few to many blue, purple, white, or pink blooms that may be bell-shaped or have spreading petals. There are six petals (properly tepals), six stamens with slender stalks sometimes widened at their bases, and one pistil. The fruits are three-lobed or three-angled capsules.

The small squills of spring are typified by the Siberian squill (*S. siberica*) and rather less well-known *S. bifolia*. Both may be had in various color forms and both bloom early, the latter ten days to two weeks ahead of the former. But even the Siberian squill is in bloom before the last snowdrops have faded. From the Siberian squill the other can be distinguished by the stalks of its individual blooms being two to five times as long as the flowers and there being none or only very minute bracts at their bases. In *S. siberica*, quite evident bracts are found at the bases of the stalks of the individual flowers, and the flower is at least one-half as long as its stalk. The Siberian squill is a native of Russia, including Siberia, and Asia Mi-

nor. Each purplish-skinned bulb produces one to six flower stalks, 4 to 6 inches long, with one to three flowers that are open bells, nodding or held more or less horizontally. They are about ½ inch across and long, and characteristically are brilliant Prussian blue. The leaves, of which there are two to four, are strap-shaped, with convex upper surfaces and apexes that bend outward. The blooms of *S. s. alba* are pure white. In *S. s. atrocaerulea* the flowers are deeper colored and the racemes of flowers taller than those of the typical species. This is similar to or identical with *S. s.* 'Spring Beauty'. With paler blue flowers with a darker stripe down the center of each petal, *S. s. taurica* is very early flowering.

Scilla siberica 'Spring Beauty'

In keeping with its name, **S. bifolia** usually has two leaves, but sometimes there is a third smaller one. They are linear, convex on their upper sides, and 3 to 6 inches long. The starry flowers with spreading petals face upward like glories-of-the-snow. There may be six to twelve, each up to ½ inch across, in each 3- to 6-inch-long raceme. Typically the blooms of *S. bifolia* are a more muted, slaty-blue than those of the Siberian squill. Varieties with flowers of white and shades of pink are cultivated.

A comparative newcomer, **S. tubergeniana** is native to northern Iran. In appearance it resembles *Puschkinia scilloides*. Each bulb has up to four flower stalks 3 to 4 inches tall, usually with three or more blooms. The latter are delicate milky-blue with a darker blue stripe down each petal. A variety with deeper blue flowers is *S. t.* 'Zwanenburg'.

The only other hardy spring-blooming squills much cultivated are the star-hyacinth (*S. amoena*), the "starry Jathinth of Constantinople" as Parkinson called it, and the meadow squill (*S. litardierei* syn. *S. pratensis*). Probably native of southern Europe or Asia Minor, **S. amoena** has purplish bulbs from which develop early in

Scilla tubergeniana

Scilla scilloides

the year to seven narrow, channeled leaves, up to 1 inch broad and 4 to 8 inches long. There are several slender, purplish flower stalks scarcely as long as the leaves, each with five to six violet-blue, star-shaped blooms that have blue anthers. The flowers, about ¾ inch in diameter and splashed with white at their centers, are usually carried horizontally or face upward. They rarely nod. The meadow squill (**S. litardierei**) has white bulbs and three to six broadly-linear leaves 8 inches to 1 foot long. Its flower stalks are about the same length. Borne in a dense raceme, the soft purple, fragrant flowers are less brilliant than those of many species. This is the latest of spring-blooming kinds. In the neighborhood of New York City it is at its best in mid-May. It is a native of Dalmatia. The vernal squill

Scilla verna

(**S. verna**) blooms only just ahead of the tardy meadow squill. Not as precocious as its name might suggest, it is a native of western Europe, including parts of Great Britain and Ireland. This is a dainty plant with sweetly-scented, erect, starlike flowers of quite clear blue arranged six to ten together in half-round rather than elongated clusters. The flower stalks are shorter than the slender, linear leaves of which there are four to six from each bulb. The blooms, about ½ inch in diameter, less brilliant than those of some squills, have violet-blue anthers.

Two species that bloom later are fairly common in gardens, one appropriately named **S. autumnalis.** A native of Great Britain and southern Europe to the Caucasus, this has bulbs covered with thin, gray tunics. There are four or five slender, rigid leaves 3 to 4 inches in length. The one to three stiff flower stems, about as long as the leaves, carry eight to sixteen small, erect, bell-shaped, bluish-lilac to pinkish-lilac blooms, their petals about ¼ inch long. It is a plant of no great ornamental import, but may have appeal for the collector of the unusual. It blooms in August and September and retains its foliage through the winter. The other available fall bloomer finds much of North America agreeable, and self-sows and reproduces with considerable abandon. This widespread native of eastern Asia, **S. scilloides** (syn. *S. chinensis, S. japonica*) blooms in August. It is quite pretty, but because of the abundance of plants in colorful bloom then, unless planted among greenery away from more brilliantly-hued competition, its racemes of pale pink blooms may not be displayed to best advantage. This squill has slender, bright green, grassy leaves and racemes 6 inches to 1 foot tall, each with many starry blooms approximately ¼ inch wide.

Scilla litardierei

Less often grown hardy squills include *S. hyacinthoides,* of the Mediterranean region, which is up to 3 feet tall and has six to twelve leaves up to 1½ feet long by 1¼ inches broad, hair-fringed along their margins. The bell-shaped, violet-blue flowers, many in each loose raceme, about ¾ inch wide, have greenish anthers. As its name implies, *S. monophyllos,* of Spain and Portugal, usually produces only one leaf, which is strap-shaped and up to 1 foot long by ½ inch wide. Bell-shaped and lilac-blue, the flowers, little over ¼ inch long, are in racemes of up to a dozen. Their stamens have blue stalks and violet anthers.

Tender squills, those that fail in the cold of northern winters, are fairly numerous, but few are cultivated. Most are natives of South Africa. An exception to both statements is the Cuban-lily. Lest names common and botanical betray the unsuspecting into false assumptions, let it be said that this species is without ancestral connection with Cuba or Peru. Rather it is a native of the Mediterranean region and Madeira. The why of the name Cuban-lily is unexplained. The botanical misnomer is attributed to faulty understanding by the botanist Clusius of information given to him by a gardener. On a visit to England, Clusius for the first time saw the squill in bloom, inquired whence it came, and was told, so he thought, from Peru. Actually he was given the name of the ship that transported the bulbs to England. The Peru traded between England and the Levant. A tiny error, reflected in the name of a plant, for all time may lead the unwary to suppose that *Scilla* is represented in the native flora of the New World. It is not.

The Cuban-lily (*S. peruviana*) is a handsome species with ovoid bulbs over 2 inches in diameter, six to nine broad-strap-shaped leaves, and stout flower stalks, one to three from each bulb and mostly shorter than the leaves. They bear fifty to 100 blooms in a broad pyramidal cluster. The lower flowers have very long individual stalks, those above shorter ones. The starry flowers are over 1 inch in diameter, their petals blue, blue-purple, pale lilac, or white. Each spreading stamen ends in a yellow anther.

Another squill not hardy in the north, South African *S. natalensis* attains a height of 3 feet and has nine or fewer lanceolate-strap-shaped leaves up to 1 foot long by 4 inches wide and stout-stalked, crowded racemes of fifty to 100 starry, ¾-inch-wide, blue flowers with white anthers and yellow stamens.

Garden and Landscape Uses. The spring-blooming hardy squills are among the most charming of bulb plants. Along with grape-hyacinths, glories-of-the-snow, puschkinias, and crocuses, their flowering overlaps and trails that of snowdrops, and pays colorful tribute to the waning winter. It brings promise of gardens dressed in new leafage, gay with spring and summer bloom. Squills should be planted generously. They are at their best when strewn quite thickly over large or at least largish areas. They do not lend themselves to pinch-penny planting, nor is this necessary, for the bulbs are inexpensive and under reasonable conditions multiply with some degree of abandon. These squills must be planted in hundreds or thousands for really stunning effects, although it must be conceded that in intimate spots in rock gardens, groups of two or three dozen provide worthwhile spots of interest. Wherever planted they do not give of their best the first spring. It is only after they have settled down and begin to multiply that their full charm is apparent. They prosper in sun or light shade and in any ordinary well-drained garden soil. Sandy loams are especially agreeable to them. They are at their best when used to carpet places beneath deep-rooting trees and shrubs where sufficient sun filters down to satisfy the needs of their foliage even after their blooms have faded. Such places are to be found at the fringes of tree and shrub plantings, in open places in woodlands, around the bases of lawn trees, and at the edges of foundation plantings. They may also be planted in groups at the fronts of flower borders and in drifts in rock gardens. The ingenious gardener will have no trouble finding congenial spots where squills can be displayed to good advantage.

Autumn-blooming hardy squills are of lesser importance. Although pleasing and of interest to lovers of uncommon plants, they are unlikely to appeal to the extent that they will be planted with the prodigality that befits the squills of spring. They are primarily items for the rock gardener, although *S. scilloides* multiplies so rapidly and grows so easily that there is no reason why it should not be used in more extensive colonies than in the often limited space that rock gardens usually permit. The spring-blooming squills are delightful for forcing early into bloom indoors.

The Cuban-lily and *S. natalensis* are admirable outdoors in frost-free, dryish climates and for use as spring-blooming greenhouse plants. The Cuban-lily is also adaptable as a cool-room window garden plant, but *S. natalensis* is a little too tall to be widely used as a houseplant.

Cultivation. If soil and location are reasonably to their liking, outdoor squills grow vigorously, bloom generously, and usually multiply. They are planted in fall with the bulbs spaced 2 to 3 inches apart, but for best effect, not with studied, geometrical precision. The most satisfactory results are had from scattering the bulbs rather haphazardly and planting them approximately where they fall. If this is done the groups are not sharply defined, but will feather out at their edges as would drifts from self-sown seeds. And this is as it should be. The bulbs should be set with their tips about 2 inches beneath the soil surface. An annual early spring application of a complete fertilizer is beneficial. Every few years it may be desirable to lift and replant the bulbs to compensate for overcrowding. Under no circumstances should the foliage be cut until it has died naturally, and seed pods should not be removed if increase is desired.

To force into early bloom indoors, the bulbs of spring-blooming squills are planted, as soon as they can be obtained in fall, in well-drained pans (shallow pots) in porous soil. They are set closely together, but not quite touching, with their tips at about the soil surface. After planting they are buried outdoors or in a cold frame under 6 to 8 inches of sand or sandy soil, which, after its surface is frozen to the depth of an inch or two, in cold climates is covered with leaves, salt hay, straw, or other insulator to prevent the frost from reaching the bulbs (this only because it delays rooting). Alternatively, they may be placed in a very cool, but frost-free cellar or similar dark place. In either case they remain until after the New Year. Then, they may be brought indoors in successive batches and forced into bloom. At first they should be shaded from sun, but after about a week exposed to all available. A temperature of 45 to 50°F at night, and a few degrees warmer by day, is adequate. Ample water is needed. Bulbs forced in this way may be planted outdoors later if through blooming and until their foliage dies naturally they are kept watered and in a cool, sunny, growth-encouraging place. Occasional applications of dilute liquid fertilizer during this period are helpful.

Scilla peruviana

The Cuban-lily grows best in fertile, well-drained soil, in the open with the neck of the bulb 2 or 3 inches beneath the surface, in pots or other containers, with it barely covered. Single bulbs may be accommodated in pots about 5 inches diameter. A winter night temperature of 50°F is satisfactory, with a five or ten degree daytime rise permitted. At other seasons the temperature should be that of the outdoors. Full sun and good air circulation are requisite. During the fall to late spring growing season, ample supplies of water are needed and regular applications of dilute fertilizer are beneficial. In summer the soil is kept quite dry. Repotting is likely to be needed about every third year. Overcrowding of the bulbs due to their multiplication signals the need for this.

SCINDAPSUS (Scin-dápsus). A variety of one species of *Scindapsus*, of the arum family, ARACEAE, is frequently cultivated and is familiar in florists' shops, greenhouses, and as an outdoor ornamental in the tropics. The genus to which it belongs comprises about twenty species of evergreen vines, natives of Indo-Malaysia. The name is an adaptation of an ancient Greek one for some kind of vine.

Mostly large at maturity, scindapsuses climb by means of aerial roots that develop from their stems. They have leaves with pointed, oblong-lanceolate to oblong-ovate or heart-shaped blades, and abruptly bent, wide, stem-sheathing stalks. The inflorescences (assemblages of flowers and associated parts) are by all but the botanically informed called the flowers. Constructed on the pattern of calla-lily and jack-in-the-pulpit inflorescences, each consists of a spikelike spadix on which the true tiny flowers are clustered, from the base of which originates a bract called a spathe. In the calla-lily the spadix is yellow, and the white, petal-like organ surrounding it is the spathe. In *Scindapsus*, the inflorescences are short-stalked, with the spadix and spathe about equal in length. The latter is densely beset with tiny, bisexual flowers, each with four more or less cohering stamens and a pistil without a style. The spathe is boat-shaped and early deciduous. The fruits are berries clustered on the spadix. The plant previously known as *S. aureus* (syn. *Pothos aureus*) is *Epipremnum aureum*.

Tall and angular-stemmed, *S. pictus* has two ranks of alternate, thickish, hairless, asymmetrical, waxy leaves, rounded to heart-shaped at their bases, and at their apexes narrowed and ending in a short point. They lie flat against the support up which the plant climbs and are ovate to broad-ovate to lanceolate, green with greenish or greenish-silver spots or blotchings. The inflorescences have pointed, ovate-oblong, white spathes. Much more frequent in cultivation than the species,

S. p. argyraeus differs in its smaller foliage being conspicuously and attractively decorated with silvery spots.

Garden and Landscape Uses and Cultivation. These are as for vining philodendrons. See Philodendron.

SCION or CION. A shoot with two or more buds that is to be or has been grafted or inarched upon another plant is called a scion or cion. If only one bud is involved it is called a bud and the operation of implanting it on an understock is known as budding.

SCIRPUS (Scírp-us) — Bulrush. This genus of about 300 species of perennials and a few annuals is represented in the native floras of almost all parts of the world. It belongs in the sedge family CYPERACEAE and typically inhabits watersides, marshes, bogs, and wet moorlands. It does not include the bulrush of the Bible, in which the infant Moses was hidden; that was probably *Cyperus papyrus*. The tubers of some species of *Scirpus* provided food for American Indians. The stems of *S. lacustris* are used in Europe for making mats and baskets. The name *Scirpus* was used by Pliny for plants of this genus.

Scirpuses have erect, angular stems and three rows of grasslike leaves, often reduced to mere sheaths, clasping the stems at least at their bases. The stems, rather than the leaves, perform the chief work of photosynthesis (food manufacturing).

Scirpus lacustris

Scirpuses sometimes have creeping rhizomes, and in some species, shoots from these produce tubers at their ends. The sepals and petals of the minute flowers are represented by one to eight bristles. The individual blooms have no decorative merit, but the clusters of blooms of some sorts are showy. The fruits are seedlike achenes.

Great bulrush is a name applied to the American *S. acutus*, *S. heterocaetus*, and *S. validus*, and to the European *S. lacustris* and *S. tabernaemontani*. These are similar perennials, up to 9 feet tall, with flexible triangular stems, leaves reduced to sheaths, and usually loosely-branching compound clusters of flowers. One or more of the American kinds occurs in swamps and at watersides throughout most of the United States and southern Canada; the European sorts are found in similar habitats through most of Europe. These bulrushes differ in technical details only. The zebra-rush (*S. tabernaemontani zebrinus*) is a handsome and popular variety that rarely attains 3 feet in height and has its stems attractively banded horizontally, alternately with green and creamy-white. In another pleasing variety, *S. t. albescens*, the stout, erect, cream-colored stems are marked longitudinally with narrow stripes of green.

Scirpus tabernaemontani albescens

The wool-grass (*S. cyperinus*) is a highly variable perennial from 8 inches to 6 feet in height with loose flower clusters and leaflike bracts. It occurs in wet places from Newfoundland to Saskatchewan, Florida, and Louisiana. *S. robustus*, a native of brackish and saline wet soils chiefly in coastal areas from Nova Scotia to Texas, forms dense clumps of slender stems up to 3 feet tall.

As a pot plant for growing in greenhouses, *S. cernuus* (syn. *Isolepis gracilis*) is

Scirpus robustus

Scirpus cernuus

popular. Entirely different from the other species discussed, it is a perennial with tufts of very many, rich green, slender, hairlike stems, each tipped with a usually solitary, ovoid-lanceolate, whitish or pale brown flower spikelet. The stems are 6 inches to 1 foot in length, at first erect, but later gracefully drooping. This species is a widely distributed native of Europe and perhaps elsewhere.

Garden and Landscape Uses. The tall-growing species discussed above are suitable for locating beside water to give height and to provide contrast in foliage sizes, shapes, and textures with other wet-soil and aquatic plants. For small ornamental pools, the variegated-stemmed varieties are most adaptable. Low-growing *S. cernuus* is also a good plant for small pools and is highly desirable as a decorative edging to benches in humid greenhouses in which

orchids and other tropical and subtropical plants are grown. This is not hardy in the north.

Cultivation. Wet soil and a sunny location are about the only requirements of the tall growing species; *S. cernuus* also needs wet soil, but when grown in greenhouses some shade from strong sun is advisable. This species may be conveniently accommodated in 4- to 6-inch pots and prefers soil that contains an abundance of organic matter. When its pots are well filled with roots, regular applications of dilute liquid fertilizer do much to keep the plants vigorous and of a healthy green color. Propagation of bulrushes is easily accomplished by division and, except in the case of varieties with variegated stems, by seed. Variegated varieties sometimes develop tufts of plain green stems of the kind normal to the typical species; these must be removed promptly at their source, otherwise they are likely to grow so vigorously that they will crowd and replace the desirable variety.

SCLERANTHUS (Scler-ánthus) — Knawel. There are about ten species of *Scleranthus*. They belong in the pink family CARYOPHYLLACEAE. The name, from the Greek *skleros*, hard, and *anthos*, a flower, alludes to the rigid calyxes. Native to all continents of the Old World, and Australia and New Zealand, and naturalized in North America, the genus offers little to gardeners. It is best known to them as the somewhat pesky, low weed of roadsides, fields, and waste places, *S. annuus*. One or more New Zealand species are sometimes cultivated.

The group consists of prostrate or low, tufted annuals and perennial, herbaceous plants with forking stems, small, awl-shaped, opposite leaves, and tiny greenish, axillary or terminal flowers, solitary or clustered. The blooms have calyxes with four or five teeth or lobes. There are no petals. The stamens number one to ten, the styles two. The fruits are one- or rarely two-seeded nutlets enclosed within the hardened calyx.

The New Zealand perennial *S. biflorus* forms a yellowish-green, not very compact mat. From its crown it spreads to a diameter of several inches, and is 3 or 4 inches tall. Its awl-shaped leaves are up to ⅓ inch long. The four-sepaled flowers are in pairs. They have one stamen. Another perennial New Zealander, *S. uniflorus* is much more compact. It has mosslike cushions of yellowish-green stems and foliage. The solitary flowers have four sepals and one stamen. From the above two kinds, *S. brockiei* differs in its flowers, which are in pairs, having five sepals and one stamen. A perennial, this makes tight green mats. The stems that spread from the central rootstock of this New Zealander root freely into the ground.

Garden Uses and Cultivation. The species described above are not hardy where severe cold is experienced, but may be grown in rock gardens in the Pacific Northwest and other places where winters are mild and summers neither extremely hot nor arid. They succeed in gritty, well-drained soil and are easily increased by seed and, *S. brockiei,* by division. They form neat mats or cushions of greenery, but because they make no floral display can only be rated as plants of secondary or minor horticultural importance.

SCLEROCACTUS (Sclero-cáctus). The six species of *Sclerocactus*, of the cactus family CACTACEAE, by some botanists included in *Echinocactus*, are natives of the southwestern United States and northern Mexico. The name comes from the Greek *skleros*, harsh or cruel, and *Cactus*, the name of a related genus.

Sclerocactuses have usually solitary, globose, flattened-globose, egg-shaped or obovoid stems or plant bodies 2 to 8 inches tall and 1½ to 6 inches wide. Occasionally they exceed 1 foot in height. They have rows of tubercles (bumps), those of their lower halves more or less joined into continuous ribs. From each areole (spine-bearing area) sprout spine clusters with one to eleven or sometimes no centrals ½ inch to 3½ inches long, and six to fifteen shorter, radial spines. Usually some of the spines are strongly hooked. Appearing from felted areas near the apex of the stem, the short-tubed, funnel- to somewhat bell-shaped blooms are ¾ inch to 2 inches in diameter. They are white, yellow, pink or reddish-purple. The fruits become dry and reddish as they age. From *Echinocactus* and *Ferocactus*, these plants differ in their fruits being devoid of wool and having few or no scales.

A variable native of the southwestern United States, **S. whipplei** (syn. *Echinocactus whipplei*) has one or sometimes two or three stems usually not over 6 inches tall by 4 inches in diameter, but on occasion up to 1 foot high and 6 inches wide. They have thirteen to fifteen ribs, and spine clusters of up to twelve radial spines ½ to 1 inch long and often hooked at their ends and, on mature specimens, up to five straight centrals 1 inch to 2 inches long. Some of the spines of each cluster are white, others tan, pink, or reddish. The pink, purple-pink, yellow, or rarely white blooms are 1 inch to 2½ inches long and almost as wide. The fruits have a few fringed scales.

Garden Uses and Cultivation. Except in regions very similar climatically to their native haunts, sclerocactuses usually prove challenging to grow. They are plants for the keen collector of succulents. For cultural suggestions see Cactuses.

SCOKE is *Phytolacca americana*.

SCOLYMUS (Scóly-mus)—Spanish Oyster Plant. Thistle-like annual, biennial, and perennial herbaceous plants constitute *Scolymus*, of the daisy family COMPOSITAE. There are three species, inhabitants of the Mediterranean region. The name is an ancient Greek one for these plants.

Scolymuses have erect stems and alternate, spiny-toothed, pinnately-lobed, or wavy-edged leaves. Their yellow, stalkless flower heads are terminal or lateral. The bracts, the outer ones leafy, of their long involucres (collars of bracts at the rears of the heads) are spine-tipped. All the florets are of the ray type (similar to the petal-like ones of daisies) rather than of the disk type that compose the eyes of daisies. The seedlike fruits are achenes.

Spanish oyster plant (*S. hispanicus*) is a very spiny biennial 1 foot to 3 feet tall and branching above. It has slightly hairy, deeply-pinnately-cleft leaves and clusters of golden-yellow flower heads, about 1¼ inches long, closely surrounded by spiny-toothed bracts. The anthers are yellow.

An annual, *S. maculatus* is similar in size and appearance to the Spanish oyster plant. Its foliage is often more or less spotted with white. The golden-yellow flower heads are solitary or in clusters of up to four. Their florets have dark brown anthers.

Garden and Landscape Uses. The Spanish oyster plant is sometimes grown as a vegetable for its edible roots, which are cooked and eaten like those of the common oyster plant or salsify (*Tragopogon porrifolius*). The annual species is occasionally cultivated as an ornamental in flower beds and naturalistic plantings.

Cultivation. The cultivation of the Spanish oyster plant is the same as for salsify. The other species is managed by sowing seeds in spring in ordinary soil, in a sunny location, and thinning out the seedlings to 9 inches to 1 foot apart.

SCOPOLIA (Scop-òlia). The European and Asian genus *Scopolia*, of the nightshade family SOLANACEAE, comprises four species of perennial herbaceous plants. Its name commemorates Giovanni Antonio Scopoli, Italian professor of natural history and botanical author, who died in 1788.

Scopolias have alternate, undivided leaves. Their solitary, tubular, bell-shaped to cylindrical, distinctly-veined, lurid purple to greenish or yellow flowers, nodding from the leaf axils, have corollas with five angles or short lobes (petals), five stamens, and one style. The fruits are capsules. This last characteristic distinguishes *Scopolia* from similar *Atropa*, the fruits of which are berries.

Native to western Asia and naturalized in Europe, *S. carniolica* is a much-branched, leafy, hardy species 1 foot to 2 feet tall. Its short-stalked, long-pointed, elliptic to obovate, toothless leaves are 3½ to 4 inches long. About ¾ inch in length, the blooms are brownish-purple to lurid red, with yellowish olive-green interiors. Hardy Japanese *S. japonica*, 1 foot to 2 feet tall, has narrowly-oblong, stalked leaves pointed at both ends, 4 to 8 inches in length by up to 3 inches wide. From 1¼ to 2 inches long, the flowers have five-lobed, purplish-yellow, bell-shaped corollas.

Garden and Landscape Uses and Cultivation. Scopolias are suitable for half-shaded locations in well-drained, dryish soils. They are readily increased by division and by seed.

SCORCH or SUNSCORCH. These are terms for injuries caused to foliage and sometimes bark as a result of exposure to strong sun, especially during exceedingly hot weather and under some circumstances in winter when the ground is so frozen that the roots cannot replace quickly enough moisture transpired from aboveground parts. Similar damage occurs to plants in greenhouses and windows denied the degree of shade they need.

Foliage of *Clivia* scorched by strong sun

Apparently both heat and light rays can cause scorch. The harm is manifested by yellowing, browning, blistering, shriveling, or drying and dying of leaves, parts of leaves, and sometimes other tissues most exposed to intense light, while at the same time shaded parts of the plant, the north side and lower foliage, for example, are unaffected. Sun-scorched bark of exposed trunks and branches of trees, especially thin-barked ones, become pale, a condition that may indicate serious damage to underlying water-conducting tissues.

Newly transplanted trees, especially if moved from partial shade or shade to full sun, and specimens with trunks previously shaded by their tops, but exposed as a result of severe pruning, can be protected by wrapping their trunks in strips of burlap or of paper made especially for the purpose. When severe thinning of a heavy crown of a tree has to be done, it is often advisable to spread the work over two or three years rather than to open the head too drastically in one operation.

In greenhouses, timely application of shade and the avoidance of transferring plants from shade to very bright sunny areas without allowing them a couple of weeks or more of intermediate illumination to give them time to adjust eliminates danger of sunscorch. It is helpful too, to make certain the greenhouse is adequately ventilated so that temperatures do not reach excessive highs. It is worth noting that many desert cactuses and succulents can suffer from sunscorch in cultivation. This because some kinds in the wild are partly shaded by other plants, cliffs, or boulders and also because, in a greenhouse or similar environment, their tissues are likely to be softer and more susceptible to damage than in the dry, arid atmosphere in which they grow natively.

SCORPION-SENNA is *Coronilla emerus*.

SCORPIURUS (Scorpi-ùrus) — Worm Plant or Caterpillar Plant. This genus of the pea family LEGUMINOSAE ranges in the wild from the Mediterranean region to the Caucasus. It comprises eight species. The name, from the Greek *skorpios*, a scorpion, and *oura*, a tail, alludes to the fruits.

The sorts of *Scorpiurus* are prostrate or spreading herbaceous plants with undivided leaves, and nodding, mostly yellow, pea-like blooms, solitary or in clusters of few in the leaf axils. Each flower has ten stamens, of which nine are joined and one is separate. The fruits are pods, curiously and variously coiled and contorted and longitudinally ridged, with the ridges often warty or spiny.

Chiefly restricted in the wild to southern Europe, *S. muricatus* is a variable annual now interpreted as including kinds previously regarded as separate species and named *S. subvillosus* and *S. sulcatus*. It has hairy or hairless stems, up to 2½ feet in length, and flowers mostly two to five together, but occasionally solitary, and ¼ to nearly ½ inch long. The fruits have spines or tubercles on their outer ridges. The chief differences between this and *S. vermiculatus,* of southwestern Europe, are that the blooms of the latter are usually solitary, rarely in pairs, and that their seed pods have knob-tipped tubercles along their outer ridges.

Garden Uses and Cultivation. Because of their wormlike seed pods these annuals are sometimes grown, but have little to offer in the way of beauty. The seeds are sown in spring where the plants are to remain in sunny, well-drained locations, and the young plants are thinned out to avoid excessive overcrowding. No special care is needed.

SCORZONERA (Scorzon-èra) — Black Salsify or Viper's-Grass. Most familiar of the about 150 species of *Scorzonera*, a milky-juiced genus of the daisy family COMPOSITAE, is the vegetable black salsify. Related to *Tragopogon*, scorzoneras differ in that the involucre (collar) at the base of the flower head is composed of several overlapping rows of bracts instead of one row. The origin of the name is in doubt. Some believe it to derive from the French *scorzon*, a serpent, in allusion to its supposed virtues as an antidote for snake bite, others that it is from the Italian *scorza*, bark, and *nera*, black, and refers to the roots. The genus is native to Europe and Asia.

Scorzoneras are mostly hardy herbaceous perennials, rarely annuals or biennials. They have usually narrow, grasslike foliage, but sometimes the leaves are dissected or lobed. The pink, purple, or yellow flower heads, like those of dandelions, are of all strap-shaped florets; there is no central eye of disk florets as in daisies.

Black salsify or viper's-grass (*S. hispanica*) is so called because its roots are black. A native of central and southeast Europe, and sparingly naturalized in California, it is a usually hairy, fleshy, tap-rooted biennial or perennial, generally with branched stems 1 foot to 4 feet tall, and variable, sometimes toothed, linear to ovate-lanceolate, stem-clasping leaves. The one to five flower heads are yellow and about 2 inches long. Sometimes called purple viper's-grass, *S. purpurea* is a hairless, tuberous-rooted perennial of central Europe. Branching sparsely and 1 foot to 2½ feet tall, it has narrowly-linear leaves under 1 foot long, and two to five violet-purple flower heads 1½ inches across. More vigorous *S. p. grandiflora* has larger flower heads.

Garden Uses and Cultivation. As ornamentals the kinds mentioned are rarely cultivated, in informal landscapes, as they do not have a great deal of beauty to recommend them. They prosper in ordinary, deep, well-drained soil in sun and are easily grown from seed. For use as a vegetable, cultivate black salsify in the manner recommended for salsify (*Tragopogon porrifolius*) in the entry Salsify, Oyster Plant, or Vegetable Oyster.

SCOTCH. This word forms parts of the vernacular names of these plants: Scotch attorney (*Clusia rosea*), Scotch broom (*Cytisus scoparius*), Scotch-lovage (*Ligusticum scoticum*), Scotch-moss (*Arenaria verna aurea* and *Sagina subulata aurea*), and Scotch thistle (*Onopordum acanthium*). The Scottish bluebell is *Campanula rotundifolia*.

SCOURING-RUSH is *Equisetum hyemale*.

SCREE. See Rock and Alpine Gardens.

SCREW-BEAN is *Prosopis pubescens*.

SCREW-PINE is *Pandanus*.

SCROPHULARIA (Scrophul-ària) — Figwort. Of small interest to gardeners, *Scrophularia*, of the figwort family SCROPHULARIACEAE, consists of some 300 species of herbaceous plants, mostly perennial, and except for a dozen North Americans, natives of Europe and Asia. The name, from the Latin *scrofula*, was given in recognition of some kinds being used to treat disease.

Figworts have opposite, undivided, stalked, lobed or toothed leaves and large panicled clusters of little brownish, greenish, or yellow flowers of little or no decorative merit. Each bloom has a deeply-saucer-shaped, five-lobed calyx and a broad-tubed corolla, with a forward-pointing upper lip and a lower lip of three lobes, the center one deflexed, the side ones directed forward. There are two long and two short stamens and one staminode (nonfunctional stamen). The fruits are small capsules.

The only *Scrophularia* usually thought worth growing is perennial *S. nodosa variegata*, a variety of an Old World species (*S. nodosa*) very similar to American *S. marilandica*. About 2 feet tall, it has square

Scrophularia nodosa variegata

Scrophularia nodosa variegata (foliage)

stems, and foliage beautifully and generously variegated along the leaf margins with creamy-white. The leaves, ovate or ovate-lanceolate and coarsely-toothed, are 3 to 6 inches long.

Garden and Landscape Uses and Cultivation. The variegated figwort is hardy and succeeds in damp, rich soil, preferably where it receives a little shade from the strongest sun. It is useful for watersides, and for flower beds where it is not subjected to excessive competition from the roots of neighbor plants. It is very easily increased by division and by seed.

SCROPHULARIACEAE — Figwort Family. This horticulturally extremely important family of dicotyledons comprises many splendid ornamentals including one, *Digitalis*, that is the source of the drug digitalin. Consisting of about 3,000 species accommodated in more than 200 genera, the SCROPHULARIACEAE is widely distributed throughout the world, most abundantly in temperate regions. It consists of mostly herbaceous plants and subshrubs as well as a few shrubs and trees. Some sorts are vines. Its leaves are alternate, opposite, or whorled (in circles of three or more). The flowers, characteristically markedly asymmetrical, less often nearly symmetrical, are in terminal or axillary spikes or racemes, or clusters, or are solitary. They have a persistent calyx of four or five sepals or lobes, a five- or less commonly four-lobed or rarely six- or eight-lobed, two-lipped corolla, four or less often two stamens, and sometimes one staminode (nonfunctional stamen). The style is simple or two-lobed. The fruits are capsules or rarely berries containing many seeds.

Among genera cultivated are *Agalinis, Alonsoa, Anarrhinum, Angelonia, Antirrhinum, Asarina, Aureolaria, Bacopa, Bowkeria, Calceolaria, Campylanthus, Castilleja, Celsia, Chaenorrhinum, Chelone, Chionophila, Collinsia, Craterostigma, Cymbalaria, Dermatobotrys, Diascia, Digitalis, Erinus, Galvezia, Gratiola, Hebe, Hebenstretia, Isoplexis, Jovellana, Kickxia, Lagotis, Leucophyllum, Linaria, Lindernia, Manulea, Mazus, Mimulus, Mohavea, Nemesia, Orthocarpus, Ourisia, Parahebe, Pedicularis, Penstemon, Phygelius, Phyllopodium, Rehmannia, Rhinanthus, Rhodochiton, Russelia, Schwalbea, Scrophularia, Sibthorpia, Sutera, Synthyris, Tetranema, Tonella, Torenia, Verbascum, Veronica, Veronicastrum, Wulfenia*, and *Zaluzianskya*.

SCRUB-ASH is *Acronychia baueri*.

SCRUB PALMETTO is *Serenoa repens*.

SCRUB-YELLOWWOOD is *Acronychia baueri*.

SCURFY-PEA. See Psoralea.

SCURVY-GRASS is *Cochlearia officinalis*.

SCUTELLARIA (Scutel-lària)—Skullcap. The skullcaps are hardy and nonhardy annuals, herbaceous perennials, and subshrubs of the genus *Scutellaria*, of the mint family LABIATAE. In the wild they are widely distributed through much of the world, especially in temperate regions and in mountains in the warmer parts. There are approximately 300 species. The name, from the Latin *scutella*, a small dish or saucer, alludes to the calyx in the fruiting stage.

Scutellarias have four-angled stems and opposite leaves, often toothed, more rarely deeply-pinnately-lobed or without lobes or teeth. The flowers, from the leaf axils or in spikes or racemes with leafy bracts and decidedly asymmetrical, have a bell-shaped, persistent calyx with two lobeless lips, or the upper lobe notched and with a fold or crest on its back. When the flowers fade the lips of the calyx close. The tubular, blue, purple, white, yellow, or red corolla, which projects well out from the calyx, has an upper lip of two lobes, a lower one of three. There are four fertile stamens and one style with two stigmas. The fruits are of four seedlike nutlets.

Hardy perennial sorts include *S. alpina*, of Europe and temperate Asia. From 6

Other hardy perennials are *S. indica* and *S. baicalensis*. Asian *S. indica* differs from *S. alpina* in its leaves being rounder and having heart-shaped bases and its blooms being ½ to ¾ inch long. This has slender, densely-hairy, procumbent stems up to 1 foot long or longer and upturned at their ends. The leaves have round teeth and are ½ inch to 1¼ inches in length. The bluish flowers are crowded in terminal racemes 3 to 4 inches long. Variety *S. i. parvifolia* (syn. *S. japonica*), 4 to 6 inches tall, has bluish-purple to lilac blooms. Bushy, 9 inches to 1 foot tall, nearly hairless, and with stems procumbent at their bases, then erect, *S. baicalensis* is eastern Asian. It has blunt, lanceolate, lobeless, toothless, almost stalkless leaves four times or more as long as wide and with hair-fringed margins. Its about 1-inch-long blue to blue-purple flowers are in branchless, one-sided racemes. Native to China, *S. b. coelestina* has big, bright blue blooms.

Brilliant orange-scarlet blooms with orange-yellow mouths are displayed by nonhardy, subshrubby *S. costaricana*, a native of Costa Rica. They are 1¾ to 2¼

Scutellaria javanica

inches long, and one-sided terminal racemes of small tubular flowers that are dark purple with paler blue-purple lips.

Garden Uses and Cultivation. The hardy skullcaps described here are useful in rock gardens and similar places, and *S. baicalensis* for the fronts of flower borders. They are easily satisfied, responding to well-drained soil of poorish to moderate rather than high fertility and sunny locations. They are easily increased by seed, cuttings, and division.

The nonhardy sorts, appropriate for cultivation outdoors only in humid tropical regions and in greenhouses, thrive best in fertile soil that contains abundant organic matter and is moderately moist. Light shade from strong sun is desirable. In greenhouses, winter night temperatures of 60 to 65°F are suitable, with an increase of five to fifteen degrees by day. The atmosphere should be humid. Specimens that have filled their pots with roots benefit from weekly or biweekly applications of dilute liquid fertilizer. Propagation is usually by cuttings, which root readily in a temperature of about 70°F if planted in sand, perlite, or vermiculite. If seeds are available these may be used. It is advisable to pinch the tips out of young plants to encourage branching. Shade from strong sun is needed.

SCUTICARIA (Scutic-ària). The three species of this genus of the orchid family OR-

Scutellaria alpina

inches to 1 foot tall and tending to be sub-shrubby, this hairy species has many semiprostrate, branched, leafy stems. Its mostly stalkless, lanceolate-ovate to ovate leaves, ½ to ¾ inch long and not heart-shaped at their bases, have coarse, rounded teeth. In crowded, terminal, quadrangular racemes 2 to 3 inches long and with conspicuous pale or purple-flushed bracts, the ¾- to 1-inch-long flowers are blue-violet with white lower lips, less commonly all purple or yellowish to white. Similar to the last, hardy perennial *S. orientalis*, of Spain and southeastern Europe, differs in having stalked leaves with silvery hairs on their undersides and yellow flowers with pinkish lower lips.

Scutellaria costaricana

inches long, very erect, and in short, terminal racemes. From 1½ to 3 feet tall, this sort has dark purple stems and dark green, blistery-surfaced, elliptic to obovate leaves 3½ to 6 inches long by up to 3 inches wide. Subshrubby, nonhardy, and much less showy than the last, *S. javanica*, of Java, is a subshrub up to 3 feet in height. This has coarsely-toothed, hairless or nearly hairless, ovate leaves, approximately 1½

CHIDACEAE are endemic to tropical South America. Although of interesting and unusual appearance, and having quite beautiful blooms, they are rarely cultivated. The name, from the Latin *scutica*, a whip, alludes to the form of the leaves.

Scuticarias are tree-perchers (epiphytes) with woody, ringed rhizomes from which spring fleshy, stemlike pseudobulbs having as continuations solitary, erect or pendulous, slender, whiplike leaves that are grooved along one side. The handsome blooms, in twos, threes, or solitary, on short stems, have spreading sepals and petals, the latter somewhat shorter, and a three-lobed, concave lip colored differently from the sepals and petals. The two lower sepals are joined at their bases to form a small chin.

The furrowed pseudobulbs of *Scuticaria hadwenii* are clustered, pendulous, clearly jointed, and about 2½ inches long. The generally pendulous leaves are 1½ to 2 feet in length. Either from the bottoms of the pseudobulbs or on separate leafless shoots having the appearance of pseudobulbs, the solitary, waxy blooms are borne. Fragrant and long-lasting, they are up to 3 inches or sometimes more in diameter and have greenish-yellow to yellow sepals and petals boldly blotched with reddish-brown. The lip is cream-colored, spotted with red or rose-pink. It is somewhat tubular, wavy-margined, and about 1½ inches wide. The column is suffused with red. This is native to Brazil.

Having much the aspect of the last except for its longer, more flexible leaves, which may be 4½ feet long, *S. steelei* has drooping flower stems that carry three or fewer

Scuticaria steelei

blooms similar to those of *S. hadwenii*, and 3 to 4 inches in diameter. The chocolate-brown markings of the sepals and petals form more or less distinct cross-bands. The creamy-white lip is beautifully striped with brownish-purple. This is native to Brazil, the Guianas, and Venezuela.

Garden Uses and Cultivation. Admirable components of orchid collections, scuticarias are not difficult to grow in intermediate- and warm-temperature greenhouses, and bloom regularly. They are accommodated on rafts, slabs of tree fern trunk, or in baskets suspended sideways so that their leaves can droop without interference. Osmunda and tree fern fibers are satisfactory rooting mediums. Except for a rest period of two or three weeks following the fading of the blooms, they should be kept uniformly moist. Occasional applications of dilute liquid fertilizer during the season of active growth are of benefit. Scuticarias need a humid atmosphere and bright light tempered with just enough shade to preclude scorching of the foliage. For more information see Orchids.

SCYTHIAN LAMB is *Cibotium barometz.*

SEA. The word sea forms parts of the common names of these plants: sea-buckthorn (*Hippophae rhamnoides*), sea campion (*Silene vulgaris maritima*), sea-dahlia (*Coreopsis maritima*), sea-fig (*Carpobrotus chilensis*), sea-grape (*Coccoloba uvifera*), sea-heath (*Frankenia laevis*), sea-holly (*Eryngium maritimum*), sea-hollyhock (*Hibiscus moscheutos palustris*), sea-lavender (*Limonium*), sea-mulberry (*Conocarpus erectus*), sea-oats (*Uniola paniculata*), sea-onion (*Urginea maritima*), sea-pink (*Armeria*), sea-poppy (*Glaucium*), and sea urchin cactus (*Astrophytum asterias* and *Echinopsis*).

SEAKALE. The vegetable seakale, scarcely known in North America, is cultivated in Europe for its young shoots, which are blanched and then cooked and eaten like asparagus. It makes a welcome addition to the list of winter and spring vegetables and is easy to grow. Botanically, seakale is *Crambe maritima.* If you would like to try growing it, this is what to do. Because you probably will have difficulty locating in North America plants from which root cuttings (called thongs) can be taken, begin with seeds. You may have to send abroad for these. Sow in a sunny location in deep, fertile soil in spring. Let the rows be 1 foot to 1½ feet apart, and sprinkle the seeds thinly along 1-inch-deep furrows. Cover with soil. Before the seedlings crowd, thin them out to about 6 inches apart, leaving, so far as possible, the strongest. Keep the ground between the rows shallowly cultivated and about midsummer apply a light dressing of a complete fertilizer between the rows. The following spring dig the plants up, cut their tops off just below their crowns, and plant them in the manner about to be described for thongs.

Thongs are pieces of root cut off plants dug up in fall for forcing. Choose straight, pencil-thick side roots. Cut them into pieces

5 or 6 inches long, making the cut at the upper end straight across, that at the lower end slanting. Tie the thongs into bundles and stand them vertically packed in sand or soil in a root cellar or other cool place, with their tops covered to a depth of about 3 inches. In spring untie the bundles, rub off all except the strongest bud that has developed at the top of each thong, and plant vertically in deep, fertile soil with the top of the thong about 1 inch beneath the surface. Planting distances will depend upon whether you intend to force them indoors or to harvest the crop for eating directly from the garden. For plants that are to be forced indoors, set the thongs in rows 2 feet apart with 1½ feet between individuals in the rows. If the plants are to be blanched outdoors, plant in hills (individual stations) of three or four thongs set 4 to 6 inches apart, and space the hills in rows 3 feet apart and 2 feet between the hills in the rows.

Dig up plants to be forced indoors as soon in fall as the foliage has died. Trim the main root to a length of 5 or 6 inches and make throngs for spring planting out of the side roots. Store the trimmed roots, packed in soil or sand, in a root cellar or similar cool place. At intervals through the winter bring quantities of them into a basement or elsewhere where the temperature is 50 to 55°F and where they can be covered or in other ways be kept quite dark, and plant them closely together in a box or bed of fertile soil 8 or 9 inches deep. Water well and cover with hay, straw, excelsior, or similar material. Growth soon begins and the seakale will be ready for harvesting in four to five weeks. Blanching plants outdoors is done in spring by inverting over each hill, before growth begins, a tall, sturdy, completely lightproof box. Plants forced indoors are of no further use. Those blanched outdoors will produce for several seasons.

SEASIDE GARDENS. Gardening near the sea calls for special consideration because environments there are special. They differ from those of most inland regions in providing more intense light, exposure to more or less continuous wind, often chiefly from one direction and not infrequently containing traces of salt, and in some locations exposure to blown sand and salt spray. Soils near the sea vary widely. When shallow, sandy, dry, or poor in nutrients, they present special challenges.

Characteristically, winters are milder and summers cooler near the sea than inland, which makes possible, if less favorable factors are moderated, the cultivation of a considerable selection of plants. In coastal regions growth begins later in spring and continues longer in fall than inland.

The styles of gardens practicable near the sea vary from formal and informal ones that do not differ materially from landscapes appropriate inland to others peculiarly adapted to their locations and impossible to achieve except in proximity to salt-water. These last, on sites that include shorelines, dunes, beach, or ocean, if well planned, are the finest expressions of seaside gardening. In developing them it is important to exploit to the fullest the natural advantages of the site, to work with the environment rather than impose too obviously upon it man-made developments.

A seaside garden near New York City

Except in the vicinity of dwellings, where semiformal or perhaps formal treatment may be in order, keep seaside plantings as natural as practicable. Retain well-located native vegetation except, of course, undesirable sorts such as poison-ivy, and supplement it with other suitable kinds. Let paths follow natural contours and the easiest way of getting from here to there, and surface them with gravel, sand, crushed shells, or, in appropriate places, perhaps boards.

Shelter from wind is an imperative first need in developing a seaside garden that is to contain plants other than those grown natively in such places. One of the best ways of achieving this is to establish a shelter belt of trees or tall shrubs. If space permits it is advantageous to have this composed of more than one species, with a particularly tough, resistant sort windward and possibly a slightly less tolerant sort on the lee. Selection will largely depend upon climate, but nowhere is there great choice. Perhaps guidance can be had from observation of local plantings.

Hardy kinds likely to perform well in the northeast include Austrian pine (*Pinus nigra*), Japanese black pine (*P. thunber-*

giana), black locust (*Robinia pseudoacacia*), dragon spruce (*Picea asperata*), Siberian pea tree (*Caragana arborescens*), Russian-olive (*Elaeagnus angustifolia*), sea-buckthorn (*Hippophae rhamnoides*), tamarisk (*Tamarix parviflora*), and tree-of-heaven (*Ailanthus altissima*).

Kinds adaptable in milder regions include some of those already mentioned and, in addition, the Aleppo pine (*Pinus halepensis*), Australian-pine or beefwood (sorts of *Casuarina*), bishop pine (*Pinus muricata*), cajeput tree (*Melaleuca leucadendron*), California-laurel (*Umbellularia californica*), cluster pine (*Pinus pinaster*), species of *Eucalyptus*, mayten (*Maytenus boaria*), mock-orange (*Pittosporum tobira*), and Victorian-box (*Pittosporum undulatum*).

Fences as primary windbreaks in very exposed locations are less successful than belts of trees and shrubs; this is especially true of solid fences. A chief objection to them is that in storms they are very liable

A solid board fence shelters this seaside garden

to be disturbed or blown down. An open snow fence is useful for marking boundaries and encouraging dune formation, but alone affords little protection from wind. But in areas somewhat inshore or otherwise sheltered from the most savage gales, fences can play an important part not only in moderating wind, but as integral features in the design of the garden. Usually they should not be more than 3 or 4 feet high and, needless to say, must be securely anchored. It is generally advisable to have their supporting posts embedded more deeply in concrete and set more closely together than would be needed on less exposed sites. Low walls serve similarly.

Areas near buildings and adjacent to walls are often subject to sweeping or eddying winds that add to the difficulties of growing plants. An effective means of stopping or at least reducing their effect is to install at right angles to the wall baffle-

A fence of pickets spaced slightly apart and woven together with wire affords shelter here

A seaside garden compartmented with fences of glass panels fitted into wooden frameworks

Glazed cold frame sash stood vertically on edge can provide effective shelter from wind

Glass panels set in wooden frames provide sheltered bays around the foundation of this seaside home

like sections of fence or wall 3 to 4 feet tall, spaced 10 to 15 feet apart. In the bays so created you are likely to succeed with many plants that would not prosper without this aid.

Soils near the sea differ widely, and like those elsewhere, usually need some special preparation if they are to support a variety of vegetation. Frequently, but by no means always, they are sandy. Commonly they are deficient in organic matter and nutrients. Except where the substratum impedes the passage of water, they are likely to be well drained.

Methods needed to improve seaside soils are not different from those successful with inland soils with similar characteristics. Chief among them are the incorporation with the soil of large amounts of organic matter, such as compost, peat moss, or manure, and the generous use of slow-release fertilizers. Seaweed is an excellent, and often conveniently available, organic material to bury in the soil; even partly decayed sawdust may be used. Green manuring by growing buckwheat, rye

grass, winter rye, and other suitable crops to be turned under is yet another good practice. Because in many seaside environments organic matter in the soil breaks down quickly and disappears, replenishment is likely to be needed yearly.

Maintenance of seaside gardens does not differ materially from that needed by inland ones. Chief differences are that watering is likely to be needed more often, and if the soil is sandy, more frequent applications of rather light dressings of a fertilizer are desirable. Of prime importance is mulching. By covering the ground with a protective layer, loss of moisture is inhibited, erosion of surface soil by wind is prevented, and in hot weather, the roots are kept desirably cooler. In windswept places, such light mulch materials as buckwheat hulls, peat moss, and sawdust are likely to prove unsatisfactory. More stable materials, including compost, wood chips, and chips of bark are better.

Adaptability to coastal environments is often indicated by a plant's appearance and form. As with desert vegetation, that native to seashores everywhere is structured to resist desiccation by brilliant sun, strong winds, and, some of the toughest kinds, to withstand the mechanical rasping of blowing sand. Additionally, plants native near the ocean are tolerant of salt-laden air and some even of salt spray. This last attribute is not especially manifested by the plant's appearance, but clues to sun and wind tolerance are.

Succulent stems or foliage such as are possessed by opuntias and the Hottentot-fig (*Carpobrotus edulis*) signal resistance to drought and desiccation, as does a thick covering of white or silvery hairs of the kind seen in such familiar plants as beach wormwood or dusty miller (*Artemisia stellerana*) or lamb's ears (*Stachys byzantina*). Long, slender leaves, such as those of pines, tamarisks (*Tamarix*), sea-buckthorn (*Hippophae*), and most willows (*Salix*), as well as the leaflike organs of acacias and branchlets of Australian-pine (*Casuarina*) are not likely to be torn by gales as broader leaves would be. Some plants adapted to life near the sea have tough, glossy, somewhat glaucous leaves with hard, smooth surfaces resistant to mechanical damage. Here belong certain hollies (*Ilex*) and pines (*Pinus*), yews (*Taxus*), and yuccas. Others, including junipers (*Juniperus*), heaths (*Erica*), and heathers (*Calluna*), have scalelike leaves that present only small areas to the sun and wind.

Trees especially adaptable for seaside gardens, additional to those suggested earlier as being most suitable for windbreaks, include American arborvitae (*Thuja occidentalis*), catalpas, coconut palm (*Cocos nucifera*), cryptomerias, desert-willow (*Chilopsis linearis*), hawthorns (*Crataegus*), hollies (*Ilex*), honey-locust (*Gleditsia triacanthos*), horse-chestnut (*Aesculus hip-*

pocastanum), mountain-ashes (*Sorbus*), Monterey cypress (*Cupressus macrocarpa*), Norway maple (*Acer platanoides*), oaks (*Quercus alba, Q. ilex,* and *Q. virginiana*), olive (*Olea europaea*), palmetto (*Sabal palmetto*), pines (*Pinus contorta, P. mugo, P. muricata, P. radiata, P. rigida,* and *P. sylvestris*), Queensland pyramid tree (*Lagunaria patersonii*), royal palms (*Roystonea*), Sawara false-cypress (*Chamaecyparis pisifera*), sour gum (*Nyssa sylvatica*), spruces (*Picea glauca* and *P. rubens*), strawberry tree (*Arbutus unedo*), sycamore maple (*Acer pseudoplatanus*), *Washingtonia robusta*, white poplar (*Populus alba*), tall willows (*Salix*), and yews (*Taxus*).

Shrubs, including some groundcovers, of special merit for seaside gardens are bayberries (*Myrica*), bearberry (*Arctostaphylos*), beach plum (*Prunus maritima*), brooms (*Cytisus*), buddleias, cotoneasters, flowering quinces (*Chaenomeles*), groundsel bush (*Baccharis halimifolia*), heathers (*Calluna*), heaths (*Erica*), hydrangeas (especially *H. macrophylla* varieties and *H. paniculata*), inkberry (*Ilex glabra*), junipers (*Juniperus*), lavender (*Lavandula*), lavender-cotton (*Santolina*), the low form of mugo pine (*Pinus mugo mugo*), Natal-plum (*Carissa*), oleanders (*Nerium*), potentillas, rosemary (*Rosmarinus*), rose-of-Sharon (*Hibiscus syriacus*), roses (*Rosa,* many kinds but especially *Rosa rugosa* and *R. wichuraiana*), shadbush (*Amelanchier*), sumac (*Rhus*), summer sweet (*Clethra alnifolia*), sweet-fern (*Comptonia peregrina*), tamarisks (*Tamarix*), viburnums, low willows (*Salix*), and Yeddo-hawthorn (*Raphiolepis umbellata*).

Vines of special advantage for gardens near the sea include akebias, *Ampelopsis brevipedunculata*, bittersweet (*Celastrus*), clematises, climbing hydrangea (*Hydrangea anomala petiolaris*), honeysuckles (*Lonicera*), kudzu vine (*Pueraria*), silver lace vine (*Polygonum*), Virginia creeper (*Parthenocissus*), and wisterias.

Herbaceous perennials in much the same selection appropriate for inland plantings may be grown in coastal gardens. Because those with tall, brittle stems, such as delphiniums, are easily damaged by wind, they are less practicable than chrysanthemums, peonies, and other sturdy, lower sorts. Kinds with silvery-hairy or glaucous foliage are especially adaptable. Examples of these include artemisias with those characteristics, globe-thistles (*Echinops*), false-indigo (*Baptisia*), lamb's ears (*Stachys byzantina*), sea-lavender (*Limonium*), and snow-in-summer (*Cerastium*).

Also well suited for seaside gardens are achilleas, baby's breath (*Gypsophila*), butterfly weed (*Asclepias tuberosa*), day-lily (*Hemerocallis*), dianthuses, doronicums, evergreen candytuft (*Iberis*), gaillardias, gas plant (*Dictamnus*), irises, mullein-pink (*Lychnis coronaria*), oriental poppies (*Papaver*) peonies, phloxes, plantain-lilies

(*Hosta*), sea-holly (*Eryngium*), sedums, sempervivums, thrifts (*Armeria*), thymes (*Thymus*), and veronicas. There are many others.

Bulb plants of nearly all kinds, both hardy and nonhardy, if planted in acceptable soil and protected from strong winds may be depended upon for satisfactory results in seaside gardens. For sorts in this category see the Encyclopedia entry Bulbs or Bulb Plants.

Annuals and plants grown as such afford a wealth of colorful furnishings for gardens near the sea. Scarcely any are impossible in reasonably sheltered locations where the soil is at least moderately fertile and adequate water is available or provided. Among the best for garden display are those that naturally bloom for long periods and that revel in bright sun. A brief selection, there are many others, includes ageratums, black-eyed-Susan (*Thunbergia*), California-poppies (*Eschscholzia*), candytuft (*Iberis*), coreopsises, cornflowers (*Centaurea*), gaillardias, hyacinth-bean (*Dolichos*), larkspurs (*Consolida*), marigolds (*Tagetes*), mignonette (*Reseda*), nicotianas, petunias, poppies (*Papaver*), portulacas, salvias, scabiouses (*Scabiosa*), snow-in-summer (*Euphorbia marginata*), sweet-alyssum (*Lobularia*), sweet peas (*Lathyrus*), verbenas, and zinnias.

Groundcover plants that prosper in seaside gardens, besides some sorts listed under shrubs, include basket-of-gold (*Aurinia saxatilis*), beach wormwood (*Artemisia stelleriana*), bearberry (*Arctostaphylos uva-ursi*) and other low sorts of *Arctostaphylos*, evergreen candytuft (*Iberis sempervirens*), Hottentot-fig (*Carpobrotus edulis*), low junipers in considerable variety, lamb's ear (*Stachys lanata*), lampranthuses, moneywort (*Lysimachia nummularia*), creeping phloxes, sedums, sun-roses (*Helianthemum*), and thymes (*Thymus*).

SEAWEED. In a few areas of the world, including certain coastal parts of the British Isles, Brittany, and the Channel Islands, seaweed is used to a considerable extent as a fertilizer to add organic matter to the soil. It serves these purposes well. A ton of undried fresh seaweed supplies as much or slightly more organic matter than the same amount of animal manure, as much nitrogen, nearly twice as much potash, but only one-third as much phosphate. The seaweed is plowed under fresh or after being partly composted. The first method is believed to be the better. Those who have ready access to washed-up seaweed should give serious attention to collecting and using it to improve their garden soils. Commercial fertilizers in dry and liquid form made from seaweeds are available. They do not, of course, add to the soil the considerable bulk of organic matter that raw seaweed does.

SEBAEA (Seb-aèa). Comprising about 100 species, the genus *Sebaea*, of the gentian family GENTIANACEAE, is native to Africa, Malagasy (Madagascar), India, Australia, and New Zealand. The name commemorates the eighteenth-century Dutch apothecary Albert Seba, who published four large volumes of descriptions and splendid illustrations of plants.

Annual, biennial, and perennial herbaceous plants, the sorts of this genus are erect or procumbent. They have often four-angled or four-winged stems, and opposite leaves. The orange-yellow, yellow, cream, or white flowers, usually in clusters, have a four- to six-parted calyx, a tubular, cylindrical to funnel-shaped corolla with four to six spreading lobes (petals), as many stamens as corolla lobes, and one slender style. The fruits are capsules.

South African *S. thodiana* is a pretty perennial or perhaps sometimes a biennial. It has creeping rhizomes and roundish-spatula-shaped leaves ½ inch to 1½ inches long. The flowers, in compact clusters, are bright yellow and ½ to ¾ inch wide.

Sebaea thodiana

Garden Uses and Cultivation. Perhaps not in cultivation in North America, the species described above would certainly make a charming addition to gardens. Presumably adaptable to a warm climate, such as that of California, which is agreeable to so many natives of South Africa, *S. thodiana* may be expected to serve well in rock gardens and similar intimate plantings. It also suggests itself as being suitable for growing in pans (shallow pots) in cool greenhouses. Propagation is easy by division and probably by seed.

SECHIUM (Sèch-ium)—Chayote or Christophine. This very distinct genus of the gourd family CUCURBITACEAE comprises one species, a native of tropical America. Its name is believed to derive from one used for it in the West Indies. In tropical and subtropical places in the Americas and elsewhere it is greatly esteemed as a food plant and is cultivated to some extent for that purpose in the warmest parts of the United States. The tuberous roots, fruits, and seeds are eaten.

The chayote or christophine (*Sechium edule*) is a frost-tender, extremely vigorous, nonwoody, perennial, tendril-bearing vine that under favorable circumstances extends its stem to 50 feet or more in a single season. It has large tubers and rough, alternate leaves, up to 10 inches in diameter, that are broad-ovate to triangular-ovate and shallowly-lobed. Its small cream or greenish flowers arise in the leaf axils, the females solitary or in pairs, the males in racemes. The fruits are very different from those of its relatives, cucumbers and melons. They are 3 to 8 inches in length, usually pear-shaped, but varying in contour according to variety. They are fleshy and at the apex are somewhat indented or puckered inward over the end of the solitary, flattish, large seed.

Cultivation. Decidedly a warm weather crop, for its successful cultivation the chayote needs a long season of growth under tropical or subtropical conditions. It succeeds from South Carolina southward and in southern California as a perennial, and can be grown farther north as an annual by starting it from seed each year. To ensure cross pollination, more than one plant should be grown. The chayote grows well in a variety of soils, but best in loose, sandy ones of moderate fertility. Ample moisture throughout its growing season is needed. Trellis should be provided to support the vines. Propagation is usually by seed. To effect this, the entire fruit is planted where the vine is to grow, its outer fleshy portion serves as a source of food for the seedling plant. A planting distance of 8 to 10 feet between individuals is satisfactory, and the fruits are set in the earth sloped with their broad ends downward and the tops of their stem ends just showing at the surface. An alternative method of increase used for selected varieties is by cuttings made from shoots that arise from the crown of the plant, rooted in a greenhouse or cold frame. In addition to its value as a source of human food, the herbage of the chayote provides good animal forage.

SECURIDACA (Securíd-aca). There are somewhat more than seventy species of *Securidaca*, of the milkwort family POLYGALACEAE. They are trees, shrubs, and vines, natives of the warmer parts of the

Americas, Asia, and Africa. The name derives from the Greek *securis*, a hatchet, and alludes to the shape of the wings of the fruits.

Securidacas have alternate, undivided, lobeless and toothless leaves and asymmetrical, rather pea-like, usually pink or purplish flowers in racemes or panicles. The petal-like wings of the flower are formed of two of the five sepals. There are three petals, the lowest usually narrowed to a claw at its base, keeled, and fringed, and eight stamens. The fruits are dry, winged one-seeded samaras.

The violet-tree (*S. longipedunculata*), a handsome native of Africa, varies from a slender shrub to a tree 30 feet or more tall, more or less spiny, and with leaves and flowers variable as to size. The leaves are short-stalked and elliptic. The violet-scented, rosy-purple blooms are succeeded by quite decorative, maple-like, hairless fruits. A vining shrub 10 to 15 feet tall, *S. diversifolia* (syn. *S. erecta*) has thick, ovate or oblong leaves 1½ to 5 inches long. Its red or deep pink flowers in racemes almost 6 inches in length are succeeded by fruits 2½ inches long. This is a native of northern South America, Central America, and the West Indies. A native of Trinidad, *S. tenuifolia* has oblong leaves, light in color and pubescent on their undersides, and loose racemes of long-stalked, ½-inch-wide, pink blooms.

Garden and Landscape Uses and Cultivation. These are general purpose shrubs or small trees adapted for cultivation in well-drained soils in warm, frost-free climates. Usually propagated by seed, they may also be increased by cuttings.

SECURIGERA (Securíg-era)—Axe Weed or Hatchet-Vetch. This genus consists of one annual species, a native of the Mediterranean region, belonging in the pea family LEGUMINOSAE and closely related to, and often included in, *Coronilla*. Its name, from the Latin *securis*, a hatchet, alludes to the shape of the seed pods.

About 1 foot tall, *Securigera securidaca* (syns. *S. coronilla*, *Coronilla securidaca*) is a bushy plant with light green pinnate leaves and clusters of golden-yellow, nodding, pea-like flowers arising from the axils of the leaves. The broad seed pods are curved, flattened, and up to 3½ inches in length.

Garden Uses and Cultivation. Places for this plant may be found in rock gardens, semiformal gardens, and where an unusual edging to a path or border is needed. It prospers in full sun in well-drained, even dry soils and blooms freely throughout the summer, but is less likely to succeed where summer temperatures and humidity are high than where somewhat cooler, drier conditions prevail. Its cultural needs are simple. Seeds are sown in early spring

where the plants are to bloom and are covered to a depth of about ¼ inch. The seedlings are thinned to stand about 4 inches apart. Except for keeping down weeds, no particular summer care is required.

SECURINEGA (Securín-ega). The extremely hard wood of some species of *Securinega* gives reason for its name, derived from the Latin *securis*, a hatchet, and *negare*, to refuse. A member of the spurge family EUPHORBIACEAE, it comprises perhaps twenty-five species of shrubs that inhabit temperate and subtropical parts of Europe, Asia, Africa, Central America, and South America.

Securinegas have alternate, short-stalked, undivided, toothless, often small leaves. The bisexual or unisexual flowers (both sexes on the same plant) are without petals and are greenish-white. They are mostly clustered in the leaf axils. Sometimes the females are solitary. The males, which are more numerous than the females, usually have five stamens, shorter than the five sepals. The fruits are capsules.

Native to northeastern Asia, *S. suffruticosa* (syn. *S. ramiflora*) is a deciduous shrub up to about 6 feet high with many slender,

Securinega suffruticosa

yellowish-green branchlets and elliptic to lanceolate-ovate, hairless leaves, 1 inch to 2½ inches long, bright green above and paler beneath. The male blooms are in clusters of up to ten, the females are solitary. The stalked, inverse egg-shaped fruits are about ¼ inch long.

Garden and Landscape Uses and Cultivation. This species has scarcely sufficient display value to attract other than keen gardeners interested in botanical diversity. It has nothing to recommend it other than a graceful habit and pleasing bright green foliage. It is hardy in southern New England and is satisfied with ordinary garden soil and an open location. No particular care is required other than whatever pruning may be needed to keep the plants shapely. This may be done in late winter or spring. Propagation is by seed and by summer cuttings.

SEDADIA (Se-dàdia). Hybrids between *Sedum* and *Villadia*, of the orpine family CRASSULACEAE, are correctly identified as *Sedadia*, a name formed by combining parts of those of the parent genera.

Occurring spontaneously in Mexico, *S. amecamecana* (syn. *Sedum amecamecanum*) is a cross between *Sedum dendroideum* and *Villadia batesii*. An evergreen subshrub 6 to 9 inches in height, this has crowded, alternate, oblanceolate leaves about ¾ inch long, and ½-inch-wide, light yellow flowers in clusters 1 inch or so across.

Garden Uses and Cultivation. These are as for nonhardy sedums.

SEDEVERIA (Sed-evèria). The name of this bigeneric hybrid genus is derived from those of its parent genera, *Sedum* and *Echeveria*. A few such hybrids have been described. In aspect they are more or less intermediate between their parent species.

The first *Sedeveria* to be described, in 1953, *S. hummellii* is a hybrid between *Sedum pachyphyllum* and *Echeveria derenbergii*. In aspect it most strongly resembles its sedum parent. Up to 4 inches tall, it has branched stems well furnished with thick, obovate, pale green leaves tipped with red or reddish-purple. The flowers are yellow. *S. derenbergii*, its parents *Sedum allantoides* and *Echeveria derenbergii*, most closely resembles the former. It has erect to prostrate stems furnished with very fleshy, ellipsoid to ovoid, bluish-gray leaves ½ to ¾ inch long.

Garden and Landscape Uses. These are as for nonhardy sedums and echeverias.

SEDGE. See Carex.

SEDUM (Sè-dum) — Stonecrop, Orpine. The largest genus of the orpine family CRASSULACEAE is *Sedum*, which consists, depending upon the authority consulted, of from 300 to 600 species. The lower figure reflects the thinking of conservative modern botanists. Except for one sort native in Peru, all inhabit the northern hemisphere where the group has a very wide natural distribution. The name, derived from the Latin *sedo*, to sit, alludes to the manner in which some species grow on rocks, cliffs, and walls.

Sedums are mostly low, succulent, herbaceous or subshrubby, evergreen or deciduous perennials, less often biennials or annuals. Most commonly alternate, sometimes opposite, their leaves are generally in spirals and often overlap in shingle-like fashion. The rather small flowers in branched terminal clusters are often displayed along the upper sides only of coiled branches. They most often have a four- or five-parted calyx, four or five petals sometimes joined at their bases, and generally twice as many stamens as petals. Less commonly the number of stamens equals the number of petals. There are generally four or five separate pistils that later develop as small, podlike fruits.

As a matter of convenience, the sorts of *Sedum* are separated into several groups based on their botanical affinities. Some of these are recognized as subgenera by some authorities, some at times have been considered separate genera. Besides the sorts discussed here, others are likely to be cultivated by specialists.

Largest of the groups, the subgenus *Sedum* (also called *Eusedum*) contains about two-thirds of the total number of species. Widely dispersed in North America, Europe, and northern Asia, this complex consists of hardy and nonhardy herbaceous perennials, subshrubs, biennials, and annuals, mostly without rootstocks. Usually their stems are prostrate, their leaves evergreen. The flowers, generally in ample clusters, and yellow, pink, white, or greenish, have completely separate or slightly-joined petals.

Hardy perennial species of subgenus *Sedum* include many commonly cultivated. Among the best known, *S. acre* and *S. sexangulare* are of much the same aspect. They form broad, almost mosslike, sheets of bright evergreen foliage. Native to Europe and adjacent Asia and North Africa, hairless *S. acre* has erect, nonflowering shoots 1 inch to 2 inches tall

A bank planted with *Sedum acre*

thickly clothed with blunt, conical leaves not over ¼ inch long. Very plentiful, the starry, yellow, ½-inch-wide flowers are in two- or three-armed clusters atop stems 2 to 3 inches tall. Variety *S. a. aureum* has yellow foliage. The leaves and flowers of *S. a. major* are bigger than those of the typical species, those of *S. A. minor* are smaller. From *S. acre* southern European and western Asian *S. sexangulare* differs in having in six or seven rows more slender, up to ¼ inch long, linear leaves. Its yellow flowers, ⅜ inch wide, are in three-branched, flat-topped clusters. Of rampant, rather weedy growth, *S. sarmentosum*, of Japan and northern China, is a

Sedum sarmentosum

hardy evergreen species of the subgenus *Sedum*, which, although it seems not to set seeds, is widely naturalized in eastern North America. This forms mats of slender, branching, completely prostrate, pale stems that root into the ground and bear in whorls (circles) of three, broadly-lanceolate, pointed, flat, toothless leaves ½ to 1 inch long and spurred at their bases. From a little under to slightly over ½ inch in diameter, the yellow flowers are in loose clusters with usually three branches that terminate short erect stems that grow from prostrate, nonflowering ones. This sedum is invasive and can become something of a nuisance if planted among small plants. An ally of *S. sarmentosum* that differs in having pointed-linear leaves ¾ inch to 1¼ inches long, scarcely flattened at their apexes, *S. lineare*, not reliably hardy in regions of severe winters, is described later under nonhardy perennials.

Other hardy, very low carpeters of the subgenus *Sedum* include *S. brevifolium, S. anglicum,* and *S. dasyphyllum.* Native to southwest Europe and North Africa, *S. brevifolium* has erect shoots 1 inch to 2 inches long with, in four or five densely-crowded rows, ovoid leaves up to ⅛ inch in length and densely-powdered with whitish or pinkish meal. Its white flowers, approximately ⅓ inch across and with a reddish mid-vein to each petal, are in clusters of few. From the last, *S. anglicum,* of western Europe, is distinguishable by its nonmealy, nearly cylindrical leaves ¼ inch long or a little longer and its ½-inch-wide, white to pink flowers disposed along two or three branches that spread from the tops of 1- to 6-inch-tall flowering stems. Variety *S. a. minor* is smaller in all its parts. Distinct from *S. brevifolium* and *S. anglicum* in being glandular-pubescent and in tending to a more tufted habit of growth, *S. dasyphyllum* is a native of southern Europe and North Africa. From 1 inch to 3 inches tall, its nonflowering stems are freely-branched and densely-furnished with opposite, thick, spreading, ovoid to obovoid leaves up to 3⁄16 inch long. About ¼

inch across, the flowers, in clusters terminating stems taller than the nonflowering ones, have five or six white petals with pinkish undersides. Variety *S. d. glanduliferum* is more densely-glandular-hairy; *S. d. macrophyllum* is larger in all its parts.

Another trio of hardy, evergreen, mat-forming perennials of the subgenus *Sedum* comprises related *S. gracile, S. lydium,* and *S. album.* Native of the Caucasus, hairless *S. gracile* has red stems and bright green foliage. Its nonflowering shoots, up to 1 inch long or a little longer, are crowded with ¼-inch-long, blunt, linear-oblong, minutely-red-dotted leaves, flattish on their upper sides and rounded beneath. Up to 2½ inches high, the usually two-branched flowering stems bear white, ¼-inch-wide blooms. Hairless western Asian *S. lydium* has nonflowering shoots up to about 1 inch high crowded with alternate, blunt, cylindrical-linear, green leaves approximately ¼ inch long. Its ¼-inch-wide, white flowers are in flat-topped clusters that terminate stems 2 to 5 inches high. Coarser-foliaged than *S. gracile* and *S. lydium,* variable, mat-forming *S. album* is a vigorous, hairless sort with creeping stems

Sedum album

and branches 3 to 8 inches tall. Native to Europe, North Africa, and Asia, it has alternate, stalkless leaves that are more or less cylindrical, or have flattish upper surfaces, and are linear-oblong to obovate or sometimes nearly spherical. About ⅜ inch across, the slender-stalked, white flowers are in flattish to somewhat rounded, branched clusters.

Allied to *S. hispanicum,* but reliably perennial, *S. bithynicum* (syn. *S. hispanicum minus*), of the Balkans and Asia Minor, has creeping, rooting stems and nonflowering shoots crowded with alternate, linear to oblong, nearly cylindrical, glaucous leaves up to ¼ inch long. Mostly five- or sometimes six-petaled, the pink to purplish flowers are in branched clusters atop stems 1 inch to 2 inches tall.

Taller, hardy, evergreen carpeters of the subgenus *Sedum* are *S. reflexum* and *S. ru-*

pestre. Of close botanical affinity, these natives of Europe have flowers that in the bud stage are in nearly spherical clusters or heads that nod or droop from the tops of stems 6 inches to a foot tall. As the blooms open, the stems straighten and cause the ½-inch-wide yellow blooms, each usually with five and occasionally up to eight petals, to face upward. Its stems prostrate and its glaucous foliage becoming reddish with age on plants in dry locations, **S. reflexum** has alternate leaves up to ½ inch long or a little longer. Pointed-linear to linear-oblanceolate, their flat upper surfaces and rounded under ones are slightly incurved. On the nonflowering shoots they are crowded in many rows. Variety *S. r. cristatum* has crested shoots; *S. r. minus* is dwarfer. Incurved leaves crowded into subspherical to ovoid-cylindrical rosettes at the ends of nonflowering shoots most obviously distinguish **S. rupestre** from otherwise quite similar *S. reflexum*.

Often confused in cultivation, *S. spurium* and *S. stoloniferum* are hardy representatives of the subgenus *Sedum* that are of rather similar aspect. Native to the Caucasus, **S. spurium** forms wide mats of freely-branching, creeping stems and more or less evergreen, opposite, ovate-wedge-shaped, hair-fringed leaves up to 1 inch long by two-thirds as wide and toothed at their apexes. Its reddish flowering stems, 6 to 9 inches tall, terminate in flattish, about four-armed clusters of ½-inch-long flowers, typically pink, but ranging from white to deep crimson. Some of the color variants are identified by varietal names as *S. s. album*, with white flowers; *S. s. roseum*, with clear pink flowers; and *S. s. rubrum* and *S. s. splendens*, with red blooms. Western Asian **S. stoloniferum** differs from *S. spurium* in its stems being more slender and bright red, in having smaller rhomboidal leaves not fringed with hairs, and in its pink flowers being smaller and more loosely disposed.

Eastern North American natives of the subgenus *Sedum* include *S. glaucophyllum, S. nevii, S. pulchellum,* and *S. ternatum.* Native to Virginia and West Virginia, **S. glaucophyllum** has on its nonflowering shoots dense rosettes of glaucous, blunt to pointed, obovate to spatula-shaped leaves about ⅔ inch long and one-half as wide. From 4 to 8 inches tall, the flowering stalks are clothed with oblanceolate leaves up to 1 inch long by ¼ inch wide. White and mostly with four petals, the flowers are ½ inch wide. Very like the last, **S. nevii** (syn. *S. beyrichianum*) has basal rosettes of spi-rally-arranged, elliptic to oblanceolate or spatula-shaped, green or grayish-green leaves and ½-inch-wide, usually four-petaled, white flowers in two- or three-branched clusters topping stems 3 to 6 inches tall. Unusual among American species in that its leaves are nearly all linear

Sedum nevii

and cylindrical, **S. pulchellum** ranges as a wildling from Georgia to Illinois, Oklahoma, and Texas. Frequently biennial, sometimes longer-lived, in bloom this is 4 inches to 1 foot tall. Its leaves are ⅓ to 1 inch long and glaucous. The three to five spreading, recurved branches of the flower clusters carry four-petaled, rosy-purple blooms nearly ½ inch wide. The only temperate North American sedum with its leaves in whorls (circles) of three or in opposite pairs, **S. ternatum** is fairly widely distributed in the northeastern United

Sedum ternatum

States. This sort has stems prostrate in their lower parts, then upturned. The broad, obovate to spatula-shaped leaves are ½ to 1 inch long. Mostly three-branched, the clusters of white, usually four-petaled, ½-inch-wide flowers surmount stems 3 to 6 inches tall.

Nonhardy perennials of the subgenus *Sedum*, sorts that survive outdoors in mild, dry climates only, include these: **S. bellum,** of Mexico, has stems 3 to 6 inches

Sedum bellum

long with spreading, spatula-shaped or oblanceolate leaves ¾- to 1-inch-long by one-third to one-half as wide and more or less dusted with white meal. The white, ½-inch-wide flowers are many together in clusters at the ends of stems of the previous year's growth. **S. dendroideum,** of Mexico, where it often inhabits limestone cliffs, is a stout shrub 1 foot to 7 feet tall, sometimes with considerably longer trailing stems. In rosettes close to the ends of the branches, the round-ended, spatula-shaped leaves are up to 2 inches long by up to ¾ inch wide. Shining green, they have dark green or red dots along their margins. The yellow, ½- to ¾-inch-wide flowers are in up-to-1-foot-long, branched sprays from the leaf axils. The leaves of *S. d. cristatum* are crested. Lacking marginal dots, the oblong-elliptic leaves of *S. d. praealtum* are up to 3 inches long by 1 inch wide. **S. humifusum,** of Mexico, forms broad mats scarcely ½ inch high of slender stems and hair-fringed, obovate leaves about ⅛ inch long in spherical rosettes. The yellow solitary flowers, terminal on

Sedum humifusum

the shoots, are ⅓ inch in diameter. *S. lineare* is not reliably hardy in some parts of the north, but succeeds outdoors in mild areas. Closely related to *S. sarmentosum*, this native of Japan, the Ryukyu Islands, and eastern Asia, has thin, prostrate, branched stems and in whorls (circles) of three, linear-lanceolate leaves up to 1¼ inches long by ¼ inch wide. Nearly ½ inch wide, the yellow flowers are few together in terminal clusters. Pretty *S. l. variegatum* has leaves markedly variegated with silvery-white and is a good hanging basket

Sedum lineare variegatum

plant. *S. mexicanum* is a Mexican with more or less sprawling stems and, generally in whorls of four, but sometimes three or five, blunt, linear, subcylindrical leaves ¼ to ¾ inch long. Individually the practically stalkless, yellow flowers, ⅓ to ½ inch

¼ to ⅓ inch long densely clustered near the branch ends. Approximately ½ inch in diameter and in three-branched clusters terminating stems 1 inch to 3 inches long, the individually stalkless flowers are yellow. This is sometimes called miniature Joshua tree. *S. oaxacanum*, Mexican, has prostrate, rooting stems up to about 6 inches long and short nonflowering branches with alternate, spreading, thick, blunt-ovate, gray-green leaves up to ¼ inch long. Its ⅔-inch-wide, yellow flowers are in clusters of four or fewer or sometimes occur singly at the branch ends. *S. sediforme* (syns. *S. altissimum*, *S. nicaeense*), of the Mediterranean region, is a hairless perennial that forms tufts or mats of prostrate stems and alternate, spreading, narrowly-elliptic-lanceolate, green or glaucous, softly-spine-tipped leaves, ¼ to ¾ inch long, with flat upper surfaces. The flower stalks are 6 inches to 1½ feet tall. White or rarely yellow, the flowers have mostly five or six each sepals and petals. *S. stahlii* is a finely-downy, low subshrub with many usually more or less spreading branches and opposite, blunt-ovate, to nearly spherical, reddish-brown to dark green, easily detachable leaves about ½ inch long by one-half as wide and thick. The ½-inch-wide, yellow flowers are in fat, branched, terminal clusters, some 2 inches wide.

Short-lived species of subgenus *Sedum* are *S. caeruleum*, *S. hispanicum*, and *S. pilosum*. A native of the Mediterranean region, *S. caeruleum* is an annual 3 to 6 inches high with branching stems and al-

the Himalayas, is 2 to 7 inches high. It has erect stems hairless in their lower parts, glandular-pubescent above, and alternate, pale glaucous-green, oblong-linear leaves, cylindrical in section and ⅕ to ½ inch long. About ¼ inch wide, the flowers are white with green or pink keels to the backs of the petals. *S. pilosum*, of Asia Minor and the Caucasus, is a biennial of very dis-

Sedum pilosum

tinctive appearance that develops during its first season a sempervivum-like rosette of hairy leaves, and flowers and dies the following year. The leaves are linear-spatula-shaped, incurved, blunt, and about ½ inch long. The pink to rose-red flowers, about ⅓ inch wide, are in leafy-stalked, crowded clusters 2 to 4 inches tall. Biennial *S. sempervivoides* is appropriately named; the casual observer could easily

Sedum mexicanum

Sedum caeruleum

Sedum sempervivoides

wide, are in three- or four-branched clusters at the branch ends. *S. moranense*, of Mexico, forms a cushion or carpet 4 to 6 inches tall of spreading stems closely set with five or six rows of alternate, ovate to ovate-lanceolate leaves under ¼ inch long. The stalkless, white flowers, ⅕ inch wide, are in clusters of few. *S. multiceps*, of Algeria, is a 3- to 4-inch-tall subshrub with alternate, nearly cylindrical, linear leaves

ternate, ovoid leaves slightly flattened on their upper sides and ½ to ¾ inch long. Its ¼-inch-wide, pale blue to white flowers have five to nine petals and are many together in loose clusters about 1 inch across with recurved branches. A biennial or rarely a short-lived perennial, *S. hispanicum* (syn. *S. glaucum*), which as a wildling ranges from southern Europe through Asia Minor and the Caucasus to

mistake it for a *Sempervivum*. Native to Asia Minor and the Caucasus, this distinctive species forms during its first year a loose rosette of pointed-oblong-spatula-shaped, purplish leaves up to 1½ inches long. In its second year it presents its ½-inch-wide, crimson flowers in stalked panicles 6 to 10 inches tall. After flowering and producing seeds the plant dies.

The *Aizoon* group consists of hardy herbaceous perennials with tough, compact, woody rootstocks from which sprout often branchless, erect, spreading, or more or less prostrate stems bearing mostly alternate, thinnish, flat, toothed leaves. Their yellow to orange-yellow flowers have very brief individual stalks and five quite separate petals.

The type of this group, **S. aizoon,** is a variable native from the Ural Mountains through Siberia to China. It has tuberous roots and erect, generally branchless stems 8 inches to 2 feet tall. The leaves, up to 2½ inches long, are oblanceolate to broadly-oblanceolate, less often narrowly-oblong. Stalkless, they have toothed margins. The yellow flowers, many together in flat-topped or slightly concave clusters, are a little under ½ inch in diameter. Shorter than the petals, the stamens have yellow anthers. In contrast to the last, **S. hybridum,** of eastern Europe to Siberia and Mongolia, is an evergreen with prostrate, branched stems and spatula-shaped to oblong-lanceolate, 1-inch-long leaves with near their apexes usually red-tipped, coarse teeth. The yellow, ½- to ¾-inch-wide flowers are in much-branched, 2- to 3-inch-wide, flattish clusters.

Native to eastern Asia including Japan, **S. kamtschaticum** (syn. *S. aizoon kamtschaticum*) has stout rhizomes and stems up

Sedum kamtschaticum

to 1 foot long, sometimes branched near their bases. Generally alternate, occasionally opposite, the spatula-shaped to obovate, dark green leaves, always broadest above their middles and with a few shallow teeth, are ¾ inch to 1½ inches long. The yellow flowers, in flattish clusters of mostly twenty-five or fewer, and slightly over ½ inch wide, have yellow anthers. From the typical species *S. k. ellacombianum* differs in having round-toothed, spatula-shaped, light green leaves and flowers somewhat under ½ inch across. The leaves of *S. k. middendorfianum* are narrow-linear to linear-oblanceolate with round-

Sedum kamtschaticum ellacombianum

toothed apexes. Its flowers are somewhat over ½ inch wide.

Sedums of subgenus *Telephium,* all those considered here hardy, have compact rootstocks and thick, sometimes tuberous roots. Their stems die down in winter. They have flat, rather thin, toothed leaves. The flowers, always white, greenish, or pink to rosy-purple, are in usually dense terminal clusters.

The type of this subgenus, variable **S. telephium** (syn. *S. purpureum*) is native from western Europe to Japan. Called orpine and live-for-ever, it has clustered stems, 1 foot to 2 feet tall, furnished with alternate, oblong to obovate leaves 1 inch to 3 inches long and one-half as wide that become progressively smaller upward from the lower parts of the stems. Most often rosy-purple and ⅓ inch wide, the flowers, in large clusters, have stamens barely as long as the petals. Those of *S. t. pallescens* are pink. Intergrading with *S. telephium,* and native to the Caucasus, **S. maximum** differs from typical *S. telephium* in having mostly opposite leaves, broadly-ovate and 2 to 5 inches long by 1 inch to 2 inches broad. Its greenish flowers have stamens as long or longer than the petals. Variety *S. m. atropurpureum* has dark purple stems

Sedum maximum atropurpureum

and foliage, and flowers slightly tinged with pink. The leaves of *S. m. variegatum* exhibit a yellow variegation.

Similar to *S. telephium* and native from Maryland to Indiana, Illinois, and North Carolina, **S. telephioides** has elliptic-spatula-shaped leaves that scarcely diminish in size from the lower parts of the stems upward. Generally alternate, they are few-toothed or toothless and 1 inch to 2½ inches long.

Sedum telephioides

One of the handsomest tall sedums and the most commonly cultivated of the *Telephium* group, **S. spectabile** is a native of China and Korea. A robust, deciduous,

Sedum spectabile

herbaceous perennial, it has erect stems 1 foot to 2 feet tall. Its flat, fleshy, glaucous, stalkless, elliptic leaves, from 1½ to 4 inches long and approximately one-half as wide, with sparingly-toothed margins, are opposite, in whorls of three, or alternate. The flowers, ⅓ inch or slightly more across and many together in flat-topped, crowded heads, have stamens much longer than the petals. Varieties *S. s.* 'Brilliant' and *S. s. atropurpureum* have especially rich pink blooms, those of *S. s. album* are nearly white. The foliage of *S. s. variegatum* is variegated with yellow. Variable *S. maxi-*

mum, of Europe and southwest Asia, 2 to 3 feet tall, differs from *S. spectabile* in the stamens of its greenish-white flowers being at most only very slightly longer than the petals. Variety *S. m. atropurpureum* is distinguished from the species by its dark purple stems and leaves.

Hybrid *S. erythrostichum* (syn. *S. alboroseum*), its parents probably *S. spectabile* and *S. viridescens,* 1 foot to 2 feet tall, has mostly opposite, short-stalked or stalkless, obovate-wedge-shaped, blunt-toothed, pale green, often glaucous leaves 2 to 4 inches long and one-half as wide. The white or pale pink flowers, greenish down the centers of the petals, are in fairly dense to loose, terminal clusters. They rarely produce fertile seeds.

Lower sorts of the *Telephium* group include *S. anacampseros, S. sieboldii, S. cauticola,* and *S. ewersii.* An evergreen native of southern Europe, **S. anacampseros** has procumbent nonflowering shoots, ending in rosettes of foliage, and erect flowering shoots 6 inches to 1 foot tall furnished with alternate leaves. From ½ to 1 inch long, the leaves are blunt, elliptic-ovate, and glaucous. In crowded, convex clusters, the flowers, glaucous-lilac on their outsides, dark purple-red within, are about ¼ inch wide. Japanese **S. sieboldii** is a popular fall-blooming, deciduous perennial with

Sedum sieboldii

prostrate or spreading, branchless stems, 6 inches to 1 foot long, with along their lengths whorls of three broadly-obovate to nearly circular, flat leaves with wedge-shaped bases. Glaucous-blue or sometimes purplish or reddish, they are ¾ to 1 inch long and more or less toothed toward their apexes. About ¼ inch in diameter, the pink flowers are in dense, head-like clusters at the ends of the stems. They have stamens almost as long as the spreading petals. A close relative of the last, charming Japanese **S. cauticola** is a herbaceous perennial with tufts of erect or suberect stems 3 to 6 inches long from branched rhizomes. Usually opposite, sometimes alternate, the very short-

Sedum cauticola

stalked, flat leaves are glaucous, ovate-orbicular to elliptic with wedge-shaped bases, ½ to 1 inch long. They usually have a few teeth. Nearly ½ inch wide, the rosy-purple flowers are in crowded heads. The stamens, with red-purple anthers, are almost as long as the petals. Native from central China to the Himalayas, **S. ewersii,** 6 inches to 1 foot tall, has more or less prostrate, branched stems and opposite, ovate-heart-shaped, glaucous-bluish-green leaves ¼ to 1 inch long and usually toothless. The flowers, about ⅓ inch in diameter and pink, are in crowded clusters. Variety *S. e. homophyllum* is dwarfer and more glaucous.

The *Rhodiola* group inhabits temperate and cold parts of the northern hemisphere. Its sorts are hardy, hairless, herbaceous perennials with compact rootstocks from which sprout generally branchless annual stems with usually scalelike lower leaves and those above mostly alternate, thinnish, flat, and often toothed. The flowers have four or five petals separated nearly to their bases. Roseroot (**S. rosea**), its common name alluding to the fragrance of its dried roots, is native of north temperate regions throughout the world, in North America south to South Carolina and New Mexico. A variable kind, it has stems about 1 foot tall with sometimes overlapping, glaucous, stalkless, strap-shaped to obovate leaves, toothed near their apexes and ½ inch to 1½ inches long, by one-half as wide. The ¼-inch-wide, four-petaled, yellow, greenish-yellow, or purplish flowers have stamens slightly longer than the petals. The flowers of *S. r. atropurpureum* are dark purple. Usually not over 6 inches high, *S. r. integrifolium,* of the western United States, western Canada, and Alaska, has leaves ½ to 1 inch long and purple flowers.

One of the few native American sedums with pink blooms, **S. rhodanthum,** from Montana to Arizona, differs from other pink-flowered natives in having a stout rootstock and fibrous roots. Its branchless stems, up to 1¼ feet tall, have alternate,

1-inch-long, elliptic-oblanceolate to oblong, sometimes sparingly-toothed, green leaves with conspicuously depressed midveins. In densely-crowded, roundish heads, the all bisexual flowers are pink or white suffused with pink. This species has not proved tractable to cultivation in the northeast.

Subgenus *Gormania* comprises eight hardy species limited in their natural distribution to northwestern North America. Its sorts are evergreen perennials with thick rootstocks or prostrate stems, and rosettes of alternate or opposite, spatula-shaped leaves. The flowers, except those of *S. spathulifolium,* have the lower parts of their petals erect and united into a tube, the upper parts spreading.

Most commonly cultivated of the *Gormania* group are *S. oregonense* and *S. spathulifolium.* Endemic to Oregon, **S. oregonense** forms wide carpets of rather coarse rosettes of opposite or alternate, hairless, gray-green to yellowish-green, wedge-shaped leaves about 1 inch long and notched at their apexes. The erect, white to creamy-white or greenish-white flowers are in panicled clusters atop stems 4 to 10 inches tall. Closely related **S. obtusatum,** of California, is smaller and has yellow flowers. Similar, but with white to deep pink flowers, **S. laxum** hails from California and Oregon. One of the most beautiful sedums, variable **S. spathulifolium** is a slow-grower with compact, flat rosettes

Sedum spathulifolium

of more or less glaucous, blunt, spatula-shaped leaves ½ inch to 1¼ inches long. Its yellow flowers, ½ inch or a little wider and usually with five, but sometimes four, six, or seven petals, are in flat-topped clusters with three, often forked branches. The foliage of *S. s. pruinosum* is more conspicuously glaucous. That of *S. s. purpureum* is blue-purple. Especially lovely, *S. s.* Cape Blanco' is low and compact, with rosy-purple lower leaves and upper ones with a silvery-white, glaucous coating. The whole plant has a faint and elusive, but definite fragrance. Similar to *S. spathuli-*

Sedum spathulifolium 'Cape Blanco'

Sedum allantoides

Sedum cuspidatum

Sedum morganianum

Sedum adolphi

Sedum craigii

folium, but with more compact rosettes of nonglaucous leaves, **S. purdyi** is treated by some botanists as *S. spathulifolium purdyi.*

Sedums of the *Pachysedum* group are nonhardy, low shrubs or subshrubs with alternate, markedly fleshy leaves. Botanically this group shades into the subgenus *Sedum.* Its yellow or white flowers, with five separate or nearly separate petals, are often borne on stalks that originate in the leaf axils. Among cultivated sorts of this group are these: **S. adolphi,** of Mexico, is easily and frequently confused with similar *S. nussbaumeranum,* from which it differs in having larger, proportionately narrower, thick, yellow-green, pointed leaves 1½ to 2 inches long by nearly one-third as wide. The white flowers, on ½-inch-long stalks, are in panicles. **S. allantoides,** of Mexico, an erect-branched subshrub 1 foot to 1½ feet tall, has alternate, spreading, subcylindrical, slightly club-shaped, somewhat up-curved, glaucous leaves ¾ inch to 1¼ inches long. Its greenish-white flowers, ⅔ inch across, are in loose panicles up to 5 inches long. **S. craigii,** a Mexican up to 2 feet tall, has erect or prostrate stems and alternate, fleshy, flattish-club-shaped, glaucous leaves ¾ inch to 2 inches long. Its few white to yellowish-white, ¼-inch-long flowers have erect rather than wide-spreading petals, recurved at their tips. **S. cuspidatum,** of Mexico, shows an obvious relationship in its habit of growth to *S. adolphi,* but is of more refined appearance, having smaller, thinner, more abruptly-pointed leaves and more compact clusters of fewer flowers. A hairless species, it has fleshy stems with erect branches that with age become decumbent. The yellowish-green leaves are narrowly-obovate and about ¾ inch long. About ½ inch across, the white flowers are in tight clusters. **S. morganianum,** the burro's tail, has prostrate or pendulous stems, 1 foot to 3 feet long, clothed throughout their lengths with bluish-glaucous, very easily detached, slightly-curved, almost cylindrical leaves ½ to 1 inch long by up to ⅓ inch wide. In terminal clusters of a dozen or fewer, the purplish-rose-pink flowers do not spread their ½-inch-long petals. **S. nussbaumeranum,** of Mexico, much resembles *S. adolphi,* but has smaller, proportionately broader leaves that average 1¼ inches long by about one-half as wide and are yellowish-green. **S. pachyphyllum** is a Mexican subshrub up to about 1 foot tall, with branched stems. It has very fleshy ½- to 1½-inch-long leaves, for the most part crowded toward the ends of the stems, and branches about ¼ inch in diameter, club-shaped and slightly up-curved. They are glaucous-blue-green, frequently with a red tip. The individual, ⅔-inch-wide, yellow flowers, with very short individual stalks, are in a flattish cluster atop a common lateral stalk 4 to 5 inches long. **S. palmeri** (syn. *S. compressum*), of Mexico, is subshrubby, branched from the base, and has usually more or less

Sedum nussbaumeranum

Sedum hintonii

Sedum palmeri

trailing stems up to 1 foot long. Its obovate-spatula-shaped, glaucous-blue-green leaves, 1 inch to 2 inches in length and approximately one-half as wide, are in loose, flattish rosettes at the ends of the branches. The yellow to orange-yellow flowers, ½ to ⅔ inch wide, are disposed along three or four branches at the ends of stalks that apparently arise laterally from the stems. *S. rubrotinctum,* sometimes

Sedum rubrotinctum

misidentified as *S. guatemalense,* is believed to be a horticultural hybrid. A subshrub 6 inches to 1 foot tall, branched from near its base, this when grown in a sunny location is warm reddish-brown to maroon. It has slender stems, at first prostrate, later erect, furnished chiefly toward their ends with alternate, crowded, stalkless, narrow, cylindrical to club-shaped, lustrous leaves, ½ to ¾ inch long by ¼ inch wide, with slightly-flattened upper surfaces and red-brown tips. The flowers, yellow and ½ inch in diameter, are in terminal clusters. *S. trealeasii* is a Mexican subshrub with upright to procumbent stems 1 foot to 1½ feet long, branched from near their bases. Spreading at right angles from most of their lengths are very fleshy, glaucous, club-shaped leaves 1 inch to 1½ inches long and with slightly-flattened upper sides. Coming from the leaf axils, the up-to-1-foot-long flowering stalks, furnished with smaller leaves than the stems, carry ½-inch-wide, short-stalked, yellow flowers in nearly spherical clusters.

The *Sedastrum* group is endemic to Mexico. Its sorts have thick rootstocks and dense basal rosettes of usually pubescent leaves. From these are produced erect or lax stems that bear the flowers; they die to their bases after the flowers fade and seeds are developed. Displayed in panicles, the blooms have five thin, usually wavy petals. None of this group is hardy.

Species of the *Sedastrum* group in cultivation include these: *S. ebracteatum* is more or less pubescent. It has obovate to obovate-lanceolate basal leaves up to 1½ inches long. Its erect flowering stems, 6 inches to 2 feet tall, bear many white flowers about ½ inch wide. *S. glabrum* differs from *S. ebracteatum* chiefly in being smaller, from 6 inches to 1 foot tall, and except for glandular hairs on the carpels, being usually hairless. *S. hintonii* is densely pubescent with white hairs. Its crowded leaves, ½ inch to 2 inches long, are narrowly-oblong to

elliptic. The white flowers, about ½ inch wide, are borne on the wide-spreading branches of panicles terminating stems up to 10 inches tall.

Garden and Landscape Uses. The majority of low sedums are admirable for rock gardens and similar places and some of the more vigorous ones as edgings to beds and borders and as groundcovers. Taller sorts are suitable for grouping in flower beds. Nonhardy kinds, in addition to being adapted for these purposes in warm, dry climates, are favorites for inclusion in greenhouse collections of succulents and for use as window plants. They can also be employed to good advantage to furnish strawberry jars, urns, and other decorative containers.

Cultivation. Among the most accommodating of garden plants, sedums have simple needs. Perfectly drained soil, rather lean in nutrients, particularly nitrogen, and coarse enough not to compact to such an extent that water will not percolate readily through it and thus deny the roots adequate supplies of air, is needed. With extremely few exceptions, sedums crave full exposure to sun, but a very few sorts, notably *S. nevii* and other low eastern North American close relatives of it, are grateful for a little shade at least during the hottest and brightest parts of summer days. These sorts too, appreciate soil more generously supplied with leaf mold or similar organic matter than is best for most. Because sedums are well constituted to withstand drought, those planted outdoors rarely or never need watering. Too much moisture causes the plants to grow out of character and perhaps rot. This is also true of fertilizing. When grown in pots, baskets, and other containers, sedums of course need watering. But do not overdo it. Allow the soil to become decidedly dry, then soak it thoroughly and allow it to dry again before the next application. Propagation of all sorts of this genus is effected with the greatest ease by division, cuttings, leaf cuttings, and seed. Pests and diseases, other than rotting caused by compact, nonporous, poorly drained, or constantly wet soil, are rarely troublesome.

SEEDS. A seed is a ripened ovule containing an embryonic plant and frequently a store of food (endosperm) to support the seedling for a short time after germination. Most seeds result from the fusion of a male reproductive cell (gamete) with a female gamete in a sexual process called fertilization. More rarely, ovules develop without fertilization into viable seeds. This phenomenon, called apomixis, occurs in blackberries, dandelions, hawthorns, and some other plants.

Not all structures commonly called seeds are seeds in the botanical sense. Many are small dry fruits that contain a seed. This is true of the achenes of sunflowers and other members of the daisy family and the nutlets of salvias and other sorts of the mint family. The so-called seeds of beets are aggregates of tiny nutlets, each aggregate capable of giving rise to several seedlings.

Seeds vary in size from the dust-fine ones of orchids to those of the double-coconut (*Lodoicea maldivica*), which weigh up to forty pounds or more. Besides providing a chief source of food for many birds, some animals, and such creatures as beetles and ants, seeds and the fruits containing them are among the most important human foods. Here belong the cereal grains, beans, peas and other legumes, and many sorts of nuts as well as other fruits. Cocoa, coffee, and cola are products of seeds and so are many plant parts used as condiments, herbs, and spices, among them allspice, anise, caraway, dill, mustard, nutmeg, pepper, and vanilla. Other seed products of economic importance are the oils of castor bean, coconut and other palms, linseed, peanut, rape, safflower, sesame, and soybean. Cotton is another important product associated with seeds.

The longevity of seeds varies tremendously according to species, from possibly not more than a day or two for *Shortia galacifolia* and a week or less for willows, to perhaps the debatable 10,000 years suggested as the age of seeds of *Lupinus arcticus,* which in 1967, germinated within forty-eight hours of being sown after being taken from a frozen lemming burrow that contained animal remains believed to be that old. An earlier, more reliable record is of seeds of *Nelumbo nucifera* from a peat bog in Manchuria and determined by radioactive-carbon dating to be between 1,000 and 1,800 years old. These germinated quickly after their coats were filed to admit water. Seeds stored by experimental investigators have germinated after eighty years and some taken from a dried herbarium specimen after at least 150 years. The vast majority of seeds have life spans, under favorable storage conditions, of from one to a few years, but the percentage viable becomes progressively less with the passing of time.

Germination of seeds of many common domesticated crops, and in the wild of most annuals native in humid climates, occurs whenever they are afforded air, moisture, and a suitable temperature. But this is not true of all seeds. Those of desert annuals often germinate irregularly over several seasons, and complex factors govern the germination of some others. Those of dog's-tooth-violets, ginkgos, and others, for example, have embryos insufficiently developed at the time the seeds ripen to permit germination and even in favorable environments it is a few weeks or months before this occurs. Seeds of many plants have coats that, until weakened by alternate freezing and thawing, the action of microorganisms, passing through the gut of an animal or bird, or mechanical scarification, will not admit the moisture necessary to trigger germination.

Other requirements or strong stimulants for the germination of seeds of some plants in their native habitats include exposure to heat such as may result from brush or forest fires and protection from exposure to light.

After-ripening is needed to break the dormancy of many seeds that at maturity have fully developed embryos. This is especially true of those of many temperate region trees and shrubs as well as those of certain herbaceous plants including irises and lily-of-the-valley. For satisfactory after-ripening, a period of low temperature or of alternate low and higher temperatures, such as seasonal changes provide, may be needed. Much still remains to be learned about the complex factors that stimulate or inhibit seed germination.

SEEDS, PROPAGATION BY. Production of new plants from seeds is common in the wild and is freely practiced by gardeners, farmers, foresters, plant breeders, and others to raise crops, increase stocks, and develop hybrids and new varieties. With true annuals and biennials, it is usually the only available method; with many other plants, it is the most convenient. Yet it is impracticable to multiply in this way all plants that bear seeds. Hybrids and most horticultural varieties do not breed true, their offspring differ from and mostly are inferior to the plant from which the seeds are taken. In such instances, division, cuttings, separation of offsets, or other techniques afford surer or quicker ways of obtaining sizable new plants. Another common deterrent to seed propagation is the lack of readily available seeds of many sorts of plants that could otherwise be multiplied in this way.

Gardeners commonly raise from seeds most annuals and biennials and plants grown as such, nearly all vegetables (potatoes are a notable exception), certain lawn grasses, and some herbaceous perennials (delphiniums and many rock garden plants, for example). Less frequently they grow from seeds trees, shrubs, bulb plants, and others that take more than a year or two to attain appreciable size or maturity. Specialists in various plant groups are likely to adventure further into raising plants from seeds, and so of course are breeders of new plants.

Crop plants domesticated for long periods, and here belong all common vegetables and many familiar flowers, have been consciously or subconsciously selected for characteristics favorable to cultivators. One of these is the ability of their seeds to germinate whenever afforded the temperature, moisture, and presence of air that is favorable to their kind. This is true also of most natives of the humid tropics and subtropics, some of drier warm regions, and some of temperate climates. But the seeds of a great many plants, most notably those of certain trees and shrubs, will not germinate for a considerable time after they ripen or until they have undergone particular treatments. For suggestions regarding these, see the discussion of special treatments near the end of this entry.

Sowing directly outdoors is a procedure commonly used for seeds, those of lawn grasses and many vegetables, for example, and is practical with many other sorts that are often started indoors. For the most satisfactory results careful preparation of the seed bed and selection of appropriate sowing dates are necessary.

Seed bed preparation consists of spading, forking, or rotary tilling a fertile or reasonably fertile piece of ground and then raking its surface into an agreeably fine condition. To assure a friable (crumbly) state, it is often advantageous to mix additional organic material, such as compost or peat moss, into the upper two or three inches of soil.

If the seeds to be sown are of plants that are to remain without transplanting, as is true of lawn grasses, such vegetables as beets, carrots, and peas, some herbs, and many flower garden annuals, soil preparation properly includes fertilization, but this is generally not required if the seedlings are to be transplanted while quite young, as is generally done with such vegetables as broccoli, cabbage, and cauliflower; nearly all biennials including Canterbury bells, English daisies, foxgloves, and pansies; a wide variety of herbaceous perennials; and some other plants.

Fit the land for seed sowing when it is easily workable, certainly not when it is wet or sticky. This is particularly important with soils inclined to be clayey. Be especially alert to take advantage of opportunities afforded early in the season. Well before most inexperienced gardeners expect, a few sunny, windy days are likely to dry the ground sufficiently to condition seed beds for the earliest sowings of vegetables and annuals. If you miss these often all-too-brief periods, rains may deny opportunity again for a couple of weeks or more, and such delays result in later harvests and may also affect adversely the quality of such cool-weather crops as peas, radishes, spinach, and sweet peas.

Soil newly spaded, plowed, or rotary tilled is too loose for seed sowing. Reasonable consolidation is needed to ensure an even rise of moisture from below by capillarity, to guard against too rapid drying from excessive aeration, and to provide adequate anchorage for roots. On large areas rollers are used to firm the soil, but a better result is achieved by treading, a method best suited to most home gardens.

To tread the bed, walk sideways back and forth across it, placing each foot down flatly and alternately in such a way that every part of the bed is stepped on once only. Let the full weight of the body bear on each footfall. A springy, almost dance-like step may be needed to achieve the desired firmness, but do not stomp.

Raking to level the surface and bringing it to an agreeably fine condition is the next step. For large plots a wooden hay rake is often handiest and may be sufficient if the seeds to be sown are not too fine. Or a first raking may be refined by a second going over with a smaller iron rake. This last tool will generally suffice for seed plots of small to medium size. The degree of fineness to be achieved should relate to the sizes of the seeds to be sown. For beans, peas, and other large sorts it may be fairly coarse. For smaller kinds, such as beets, cabbages, and radishes, more careful raking to establish a finer surface is likely to be needed and this is even truer for smaller seeds, such as those of carrots.

Three chief methods of distributing seeds are employed: broadcasting, sowing in rows, and sowing in hills. The first, used for lawn grasses, green manure crops, small patches of seeds to give young plants for early transplanting, and sometimes for patches of annuals in flower

Preparing a seed bed with: (a) A wooden rake

(b) An iron rake

beds, is done by scattering the seeds evenly over the entire area and raking them in shallowly. Most fall into the little furrows made by the teeth of the rake and are covered by subsequent passes of the tool. If the sowing area is small, the seeds may be covered by sifting fine soil over them. To complete the operation, firm the surface by tamping it with a rake held with its prongs parallel with the ground, or, on large areas such as lawns, by rolling.

Sowing in rows has the great advantage of making it easier to control weeds that sprout as soon or perhaps sooner than those of the crop. With broadcast sowing, hand pulling is usually the only remedy. By restricting the seeds to definite rows, weeds that come up between them can be destroyed by hoeing or cultivating, or discouraged by using black plastic or other mulches.

To make drills, stretch a line (thin cord or twine attached to two stakes or spikes that can be pushed into the ground) tautly across the soil surface and with a series of short strokes pull the point of the blade of a Warren or draw hoe along it to create a shallow trench or drill, or achieve the same result by saddling over the line a deep V-shaped notch cut in the end of a wooden

To sow seeds in rows: (a) Stretch a garden line tautly across the surface of the ground

(b) Then pull either a hoe

(c) Or a rake handle or similar stake along the line to create a drill (shallow furrow)

(d) Alternatively, cut a deep V notch in the end of a 1½-inch-square stake

(e) Saddle the notch over the line, then with a to-and-fro motion push the stake forward to create a drill

stake about 1½ inches square and pushing the stake back and forth to form the drill. Alternatively, for short drills, simply draw the end of an unnotched stake, held at an angle of about forty-five degrees, through the surface soil of the seed bed.

Relate the depth of the drill to the size of the seeds, type of soil, and time of sowing. From ½ inch to 3 inches is the usual range, small seeds being sown shallowly, larger seeds more deeply. In light, sandy soils it is permissible to sow a little deeper than in clayey ones, and early spring sowings, when the ground is cooler than it will be later, may be made more shallowly. For small quantities of little seeds drills can be made by pressing the handle of a hoe or rake into the soil surface or by sliding the edge of a short piece of board to-and-fro along a line stretched tautly across the soil surface.

If the soil is at all dry, soak the bottoms of the drills *before* sowing with a gentle stream from the spout of a watering can from which the spray nozzle has been removed. This is much better than watering

If the soil is dry, soak the bottom of the drill with water

after the seeds are sown. Ample moisture rising by capillarity from below stimulates germination, drier soil used to cover the seeds checks excessive evaporation. Caking of the surface does not occur nor is the growth of weeds between the rows encouraged.

When annuals are to be sown in patches

Sow the seeds by: (a) Shaking them gently from the packet

(c) If the seeds are large, such as beans, sow them by strewing them rather thinly along the drills

(e) Or with one's feet

in flower beds, rather than broadcasting the seeds it is often preferable to sow in criss-cross patterns of shallow drills made with the end of the handle of a hoe or rake or with a thick wooden stake. This simplifies weeding and ensures that the seeds will be at the same depth and evenly covered with soil.

(b) Or sprinkling them from between the thumb and forefingers

(d) Cover the seeds by pushing or pulling soil over them with a rake

(f) Finish by raking very shallowly in the direction of the drills

To sow patches of annuals: (a) With the end of a stake, draw a crisscross of drills in finely raked soil

(b) If the soil is dry, water the drills

and 3 feet wide in the soil, heaping into it two or three good-sized pailfuls of rich compost or rotted manure and covering this with the excavated soil. For pole beans drive a stout pole firmly into the ground, then with a hoe heap soil, drawn from the surrounding area, around its base to a height of 6 to 8 inches. Hills for corn are made by chopping a shallow depression in the soil with a hoe, sowing the seeds, and covering them without raising a mound.

(c) Then sow the seeds

(d) Cover them by using the head of a rake held teeth up

To sow a hill of pole beans: (a) Heap soil around a previously implanted pole (stake)

(b) With the fingers, make a shallow furrow on the top of the hill, around the pole; position a few seeds in the furrow and cover them with soil

A common error is sowing too thickly. This is not only wasteful, but unless the seedlings are thinned out adequately at an early stage they become spindly and weak and more likely victims of pests, diseases, and drought. Too sparse sowing, especially with small seeds, is a less prevalent mistake. Seedlings seem to benefit, perhaps by sheltering each other, from reasonable proximity to others of their kind. Because of many variables, it is impracticable to suggest sowing densities with any degree of precision. Perhaps a broad general rule would be to distribute the seeds of plants that are to grow to maturity without transplanting three to four times as thickly as the mature plants are to stand. This allows for failure of some to germinate and necessitates only moderate thinning out. For sorts to be transplanted as young seedlings the chief care is to make sure they are allowed enough space to reach the transplanting stage before they become crowded too seriously.

Cover seeds in drills by pushing soil over them with a rake held with its teeth pointing upward or by shuffling along the drill and, alternately with the side of each shoe,

spreading soil over them. In either case, tamp the soil moderately firm with the head of the rake held parallel with the ground and finish the job by barely scratching the surface with the teeth of the rake to remove any footmarks and produce an even, but slightly roughened effect. When doing this, whenever practicable, rake in the direction of the drills, not across them.

Hills, in gardeners' terminology, are more or less widely separated stations, usually arranged in rows, at each of which is sown a few (generally five or six) seeds. Although for some crops, such as cucumbers and melons, they may be mounded higher than the general surface of the ground, it is not necessary for this to be done for such stations to be termed hills. Sowing in hills has the advantages of facilitating weed control by hoeing, cultivating, and sometimes by using black plastic or other types of mulches, and of not being unduly wasteful of seeds of plants that need considerable space.

For cucumbers, melons, squashes, and plants of similar growth, hills are made by forming a depression about 6 inches deep

Sow a few more seeds in each hill than the number of plants you desire and when the young plants begin to crowd pull out the surplus, leaving usually three or four of the strongest and most promising.

Cold frames are convenient protectors of newly-sown seeds and seedlings of biennials, perennials, and other kinds. They afford shelter from drying winds and other inclement weather, make it easier to shade the beds, and reduce the likelihood of disturbance by birds, animals, and careless humans. In beds of soil in cold frames, it is usual to sow broadcast or in shallow drills spaced 4 to 6 inches apart. If the amounts of seeds are small they may be accommodated in pots or pans (shallow pots), which after sowing are buried almost to their rims in a bed of sand or peat moss installed in the frame.

In cold frames: (a) Sow seeds in prewatered drills

(b) Cover the frame with a lath shade

Labeling newly sown seeds is highly important. Use labels that will remain readable for as long as necessary and inscribe on them the name of the seeds sown, the sowing date, the source from which the seeds were obtained, and any other pertinent data.

Sowing in pots, pans, and flats is the most practical way of raising many kinds of plants and is usual with sorts to be given an early start indoors, for kinds of which small amounts only are to be sown, and with seeds sown in mediums other than ordinary soil or that in other ways are to be given special attention.

It is important that containers be clean. If they have been used previously it is advantageous to sterilize them by baking, steaming, boiling, or soaking them in a suitable diluted fungicide. Minimal treatment of reused containers consists of scrubbing them thoroughly and allowing them to dry before use.

Seed soils for container use vary considerably according to the needs of the plants and the experience and sometimes idiosyncrasies of individual gardeners. The chief ingredients are topsoil (loam), peat moss, leaf mold or good compost, and coarse, gritty sand or perlite. For particular sorts of seeds other amendments, such as ground limestone, may be added in small quantities, but fertilizers are generally omitted. Sterilizing (see the Encyclopedia entry Soil Sterilization) the soil, leaf mold, and compost is a wise precaution, although unless these are contaminated with disease organisms or pests it is not essential.

Typical examples of seed soils that have proved highly successful are these: A general mix suitable for seeds of most plants consists of one part good topsoil, one part peat moss or leaf mold, and one to one-and-a-half parts coarse sand or perlite. For plants, such as African-violets, begonias, and gloxinias, that appreciate a more humus-rich mix, one part good topsoil, two parts peat moss or leaf mold, one to one-and-a-half parts coarse sand or perlite, and one-quarter part crushed charcoal passed through a ¼-inch mesh is satisfactory. For succulents, including most cactuses, a good mix consists of one part good topsoil, one part leaf mold or peat moss, and four parts coarse sand or perlite. Many variations of these and other soil mixes may be employed successfully. The essentials are that they drain freely and admit air sufficient to support root growth, that they are reasonably retentive of moisture, and that they are free of harmful organisms.

Soil-less sowing mediums are popular and generally give excellent results. Among the best known are vermiculite, perlite, and sand, and any of these mixed with peat moss. Milled (pulverized and sifted) sphagnum moss is also excellent. This can be purchased or can be prepared by rub-

bing fresh or dried sphagnum moss, picked free of twigs and any other extraneous materials it may contain, through a sieve with three or four meshes to each inch. Sphagnum has the great advantage of inhibiting the growth of fungi that cause seedlings to damp off. Because soil-less mediums contain little or no nutrients, unless seedlings raised in them are transplanted fairly promptly after their first true leaves develop, which in most cases is desirable anyway, it is important to afford nutrition by watering them every week to ten days with a very dilute solution of a complete fertilizer.

Prepare pots, pans, and flats by covering their drainage holes and bottoms with a layer at least 1 inch thick of crocks (pieces of broken flower pots), coarse cinders, nuggets of charcoal, broken oyster or clam shells, or equally effective material. This promotes free drainage. Over each drainage hole place a large crock or piece of shell, hollow side down, or a large cinder or piece of charcoal, and fill smaller pieces over them. To prevent soil washing down and clogging the drainage, cover it with some coarse dead leaves, straw, hay, or pieces of an old nylon stocking.

Next, fill the container to its top with the medium and, unless it is vermiculite, which needs no consolidating, press it moderately firm with the finger tips. Have the finished surface quite level and a little below the container rim to allow for covering the seeds and subsequent waterings.

For most seeds, soil that has passed through a ½-inch sieve will be sufficiently fine and for large sorts, such as those of cannas, sweet peas, and palms, sifting through a ¾-inch mesh is satisfactory. For very fine seeds, such as those of African-violets, other gesneriads, and begonias, use ½-inch-sifted soil in the greater part of the container and top that by sifting over its leveled surface ¼ to ½ inch of the same mix passed through a sieve having a ¼-inch mesh or one made of regular window screening. This is better than having the entire body of the soil so fine that air can not easily permeate it.

Before sowing, soak the soil thoroughly with a fine spray or immerse the filled pots or pans nearly to their rims so that water seeps to the surface from below. Allow time to drain, then scatter the seeds evenly. A usually satisfactory density is when the seeds are spaced apart about four times their average diameter.

Press the seeds lightly into the surface with a piece of board or with the bottom of a flower pot or glass and, except for extremely tiny seeds, such as those of begonias, which need no soil covering, sift fine soil over them to a depth about equal to the diameter or smallest dimension of the seeds. Press this very lightly and insert a label giving the name of the seeds and the sowing dates and any other per-

To sow seeds in a pot or pan: (a) Fill a well-drained container with suitable soil; press it moderately firmly, level its surface, and water thoroughly with a fine spray

(b) Sow the seeds evenly

(c) Cover the seeds with soil sifted through a fine sieve

(d) Press the surface lightly to firm it

(e) Cover the container with a sheet of glass and shade it with newspaper

tinent information. Then cover the containers with a sheet of glass or polyethylene plastic, shade them with paper, and put them to germinate in a location of favorable temperature that is not subject to drafts or other drying conditions.

Frequent inspection of pots, pans, and flats in which seeds have been sown is highly important. It makes possible early detection of anything that may have gone wrong, such as disturbance by worms, slugs, or other creatures or the develop-

ment of funguses, and provides an opportunity to check whether the soil or other sowing medium is drying. This is only likely to occur with seeds that take a long time to germinate. If you feel additional moisture is needed, apply water to the

To sow seeds in a flat: (a) Cover its bottom with coarse leaves

(b) Fill with suitable soil, leveled and pressed moderately firm

(c) Water with a fine spray

Sedum pachyphyllum

Sedum acre flowering on a steep slope

Seemannia latifolia

Sedum spectabile variety

Sempervivum arachnoideum

Senecio confusus

Senecio cineraria underplanted with wax begonias

Senecio hybridus

(d) Sow the seeds, if more than one variety use a flat separated by canes or thin sticks; cover with finely sifted soil, press the surface lightly, and place a sheet of glass and a sheet or two of newspaper over the flat

(e) Alternatively, if several flats are sown, stand them one on top of the other, with a small space between each for ventilation, and cover the uppermost with glass and newspaper

surface in a very fine spray or lower the container slowly into water to within about an inch of its rim and allow water to seep from below to the surface.

Most important of all, regular inspection, for most annuals and other fast growers daily after the first three or four days, promptly reveals the first evidence of germination. And this is important. Inexperienced gardeners frequently fail or suffer substantial losses because they do not notice early enough that seeds have germinated or if they do, delay taking the steps necessary to prevent the seedlings becoming "drawn" (elongated to the extent that they are weak and very subject to damping-off disease).

Inspect newly sown seed at frequent intervals for signs of germination; with small seed this is most easily detected by peering along the soil surface rather than down on it

Look closely when inspecting. With very tiny seeds it is often helpful to tilt the container a little so that the line of sight is more nearly parallel with the soil surface than at approximately right angles to it. At

the very first sign of sprouting, well before the seedlings stand any appreciable height above the surface, remove the shade and prop up the glass or polyethylene cover to admit air.

From now until the first true leaves appear is a critical period. The initial growth consists of cotyledon leaves, two if the plant is a dicotyledon, one if a monocotyledon. The cotyledon leaves, which, especially in dicotyledons, are usually very different in form and shape from true leaves, are present in embryo form in the seeds, and their later development is at the expense of stored foodstuffs they contain. The true leaves represent completely new growth.

Care at this early stage calls for exposure to light, but at first with just enough shade to slightly reduce the intensity that more mature specimens of this particular kind of plant are known to favor. For sun-loving plants a layer of cheesecloth will serve admirably. Shade-lovers need somewhat more heavy shade.

Cheesecloth may be used to provide light shade for germinating seedlings

Because at this time the entire tiny plantlet occupies only a very shallow upper layer of the sowing medium it is very important that this not be permitted to dry out. Yet saturating the entire depth of soil each time the surface dries somewhat is not good practice. If only the surface is dryish, moisten it with a fine spray that does not penetrate more deeply than nec-

Spraying with a fine mist of water may be sufficient to keep the surface soil moist

essary. Only if dryness extends to a greater depth is it desirable to soak the full depth of the rooting medium. Attend to spraying and watering early enough for the foliage to dry before nightfall.

Soon, aboveground parts increase in size and number and roots penetrate more deeply. As this occurs more normal watering practices should be initiated.

Transplanting or, as it is sometimes called, pricking off is the next step. In most cases this involves separating individuals of the several to many that have sprouted in each pot or flat and transferring them at wider spacings to other pots,

Seedlings in pots and pans can be watered effectively by standing them in water until moisture seeps to the surface

A pot of healthy seedlings

pans, or flats. Or large seedlings of vigorous plants, such as tomatoes, may at this stage be planted individually in small pots. Sometimes seeds of such plants as lupines, Mexican tulip-poppies (*Hunnemannia*), poppies (*Papaver*), and other sorts known to greatly resent root disturbance are sown three or four together in 2½- or 3-inch pots and instead of being pricked off are thinned out by pulling out the surplus and leaving only the strongest to grow without disturbance until it is big enough to be potted into a larger container or planted in a greenhouse bed or bench or outdoors.

Pricking off is best delayed until the first true leaves are fairly developed. Only if damping-off disease or some other trouble threatens loss among the seedlings is earlier transplanting advisable, and if that is done every care in handling the tiny plants is necessary. Make sure seedlings to be pricked off or potted off are watered well a few hours in advance so that their roots are moist at the time of the operation.

Special treatments to "break the dormancy" and promote the germination of

certain seeds are desirable. This is especially true of those of many temperate-region trees and shrubs and of a few herbaceous perennials that under natural conditions do not germinate until weeks or months after they ripen and fall from the parent plant. This delayed germination promotes survival of the species by keeping the seeds dormant but alive until conditions are favorable for the growth of the seedlings. It may result from the seed's coat being impermeable to moisture until, following a prolonged contact with damp soil, this is eventually remedied by bacterial or chemical action. Some sorts of seeds ripen on the parent plant before their embryos are mature. These need a period, usually a few weeks, of after-ripening to complete their development and make germination possible. In other cases a growth inhibitor within the seeds prevents germination and necessitates time-consuming changes wrought by enzymes or other agents before the seeds will sprout.

Exposure to low temperatures for a period of a few weeks is a frequent requirement to break dormancy (this is true of many cold-climate plants that mature in fall seeds that do not germinate until the next spring). Some sorts must be exposed to warm conditions for a period before they are subjected to cold, and yet others have a double dormancy. These under natural conditions take two years to germinate.

Stratifying seeds that exhibit delayed germination is an old and generally successful method of dealing with them that closely imitates natural procedures. In the past it was the practice to spread such seeds in flats or other shallow containers in layers alternated with layers of slightly damp sand, and to store them over winter or longer, where they would remain moist in a cool cellar, cold frame, or similar accommodation, until they were judged ready to germinate. Then they were sown in the ordinary way in pots, pans, flats, or cold frames. The availability of refrigerators and polyethylene plastic bags made possible a simplification of this treatment, which still however is generally referred to as stratification.

Modern practice consists of mixing seeds that exhibit simple dormancy with two to three times their bulk of damp but not wet sand, peat moss, or vermiculite, enclosing them in a tightly closed polyethylene bag, and storing them in a refrigerator at a temperature of 40°F for from one to four months (depending upon the kind of seeds) before sowing. To promote germination of seeds that exhibit double dormancy, such as those of dove trees (*Davidia*), hawthorns (*Crataegus*), hollies (*Ilex*), junipers (*Juniperus*), viburnums, and yews (*Taxus*), put them in polyethylene bags along with damp vermiculite or other material and

store in a temperature 65 to 85°F for four to six months, then at 40°F for three months before they are sown.

Several variables, including species and sometimes the part of the natural range of the species from which the seed parent came, age of the seed, and conditions of storage may influence the length of time for stratification that is most favorable for germination. Because of this, it is often worthwhile to experiment a little. The most practical procedure is to collect the seeds as soon as they are ripe, clean them of surrounding pulp, capsule parts, or other debris, and store them in a dry, cool place until such time as they can be stratified, so that the period of stratification ends at the most favorable time for sowing the seeds.

Delayed germination caused by seed coats strongly resistant to penetration by moisture can be overcome in various ways. Mechanical rupturing or scarification is practicable with many large and medium-sized seeds. Those of sweet peas (dark-seeded sorts are often slow to germinate)

To hasten germination of sweet pea seeds, chip away a small piece of their outer coat with a knife

can be chipped with a knife. Others, canna seeds, for example, respond to filing. This is easily done by placing a sharp triangular file on a firm surface and, holding the seed between finger and thumb, stroking it along the upper edge of the file until the seed coat is cut through. Smaller seeds can be scarified mechanically by placing them on a flat surface and rubbing them with emery paper attached to a piece of wood.

Hot water treatment promotes the germination of some seeds reluctant to germinate. Place the seeds in a container, pour over them water at a temperature of 190 to 200°F, allow them to stand overnight, and then sow immediately without allowing them to dry. To forestall too rapid cooling of the water, use at least a pint and the equivalent of not less than five or six times the bulk of the seeds.

Filing a nick through the hard coat of canna seeds hastens germination

Concentrated sulfuric acid (a highly corrosive substance that must be handled with the greatest respect) can be used effectively to weaken the coats of seeds not readily responsive to other methods. With small quantities of seeds the procedure is to put them dry into a glass and, pouring with great care, just cover them with the acid. After erosion of the seed coats is sufficiently accomplished, spread the seeds in a sieve and wash them with running water for several minutes to remove all traces of the acid. Then, depending upon kind, sow immediately or stratify them.

The length of time the seeds should remain in the acid varies considerably with the kind of seed, the temperature, and other factors. It is well to check from time to time the progress of the erosion of their coats by taking a few seeds from the acid, rinsing them off, and examining them under a hand lens. The procedure should stop before the coats are worn completely through. Destruction of the seed coats proceeds faster at higher than lower temperatures.

Seeds of many commonly cultivated plants stored in stoppered bottles in a cool, dry, dark place retain their ability to germinate for a few to several years. For instance, trials indicate that those of antirrhinums, aubrietas, begonias, China-asters, coleuses, cyclamens, gaillardias, lilies, nicotianas, scabiouses, violas, and wallflowers are likely to remain viable for two years, those of aquilegias, clarkias, and poppies for three years. Seeds of beans, beets, cabbage, carrots, delphiniums, and lupines stored in this way may be expected to give satisfactory results after three to four years, and those of celery, cucumbers, radishes, and turnips after as long as eight to ten years.

The percentage of germination that may be expected, as determined by recent tests, is often indicated on the packets of many sorts of seeds sold by reliable seedsmen. If such information is not available from that source or if one contemplates sowing seeds held over for a year or longer it is advisable to make a simple germination test.

To do this, take 100 seeds, representing a fair sample (if they differ in size or color, for example, include a proportionate number of each variant). Place these on a piece of wet blotting paper or flannel spread on a plate and then cover with a basin or dish slightly propped up at its base to permit a little air circulation. Keep in a temperature of about 60°F and check frequently to ascertain the percentage of the 100 seeds that germinate.

SEEMANNIA (See-mánnia). Ten species constitute *Seemannia*, a genus of the gesneria family GESNERIACEAE, native to Bolivia and Peru. The name commemorates Berthold Seemann, botanist and traveler, who died in 1871.

These nonhardy herbaceous perennials have scaly rhizomes, thickish stems, and undivided, whorled (in circles of three or more) or opposite leaves. Solitary or clustered in the leaf axils, the flowers, each with its own stalk, have a five-lobed calyx, a tubular corolla expanded at the base, or more or less bell-shaped, with five very short lobes, four stamens, their anthers joined at their tips in pairs, and one style. The fruits are capsules.

From 1½ to 3 feet tall and slight-bristly-pubescent, **S. sylvatica** (syn. *S. ternifolia*) has pointed-ovate-elliptic to narrow-elliptic leaves up to about 5 inches long by 1¼ inches wide, opposite or in whorls of three to five. Usually few together on slender stalks 1 inch to 2 inches long from the axils of the rather distantly spaced upper leaves, the flowers have narrow-ovate calyx lobes not over ⅛ inch long, and a ½-inch-long, orange-red, red, or rarely yellow corolla with maroon-edged, yellow lobes. From 9 inches to 1¼ feet in height, **S. latifolia** is slightly-bristly-hairy, with finely-hairy stems and opposite, short-stalked, conspicuously-veined, pointed, elliptic to lanceolate-elliptic leaves from 3 to 6 inches long. Its flowers, on stalks 2½

Seemannia latifolia

to 4½ inches long, have linear-lanceolate sepals and a corolla ½ to ¾ inch long.

Garden and Landscape Uses and Cultivation. These are as for *Kohleria*.

SEERSUCKER PLANT is *Geogenanthus undatus*.

SEGO-LILY is *Calochortus nuttallii*.

SELAGINELLA (Selagin-élla)—Resurrection Plant or Rose-of-Jericho, Clubmoss. The name clubmoss is applied to *Lycopodium* as well as *Selaginella*. The latter (the "g" in the name is soft) consists of 500 or more species of more or less mosslike plants that gardeners not infrequently lump along with certain other nonflowering plants and call fern allies. Some sorts do resemble ferns, but there are good botanical reasons for keeping them separate. Constituting the only genus of the selaginella family SELAGINELLACEAE, selaginellas are cosmopolitan in the wild, inhabiting all continents except Anarctica. They are most numerous in the tropics and subtropics. The name is a diminutive of *Selago*, a name formerly used for *Lycopodium*.

Selaginellas, mostly herbaceous perennials, rarely annuals, have much the aspect of lycopodiums. Of small to moderate size, they have usually forking, often rooting stems that may trail or creep or may be erect, tufted, or rarely climbing. Some sorts have underground rhizomes. The leaves, alternate and in spirals or much more commonly opposite and in four rows, differ from those of *Lycopodium* in having on their upper sides near their bases a minute outgrowth called a ligule. When in four rows, those of the marginal rows, called leaves of the lower plane, are distinctly bigger than the leaves of the upper plane. Two types of spores are borne, small ones (microspores) and bigger ones (macrospores), in terminal, generally sharply-angled, four-sided, spikelike, loose or compact cones. Some sorts produce bulbils. The term fronds as used in this treatment must not be understood to mean, as it does when applied to ferns, single leaves, but frondlike arrangements of branched stems furnished with numerous small leaves.

In Japan there is considerable interest in collecting and growing selaginellas. Numerous horticultural varieties, presumably developed from native species, are prized by enthusiasts. Many are extremely small, many are pleasingly variegated with silver, yellow, brown, or other hues, and many exhibit very distinctive habits of growth. In recent years several varieties have been introduced to the United States by Harold Epstein who believes that some, at least, are likely to prove hardy in his garden in Larchmont, New York.

The resurrection plant or rose-of-Jericho (**S. lepidophylla**) earns the first-mentioned

Dwarf varieties of *Selaginella* brought to the United States from Japan

Selaginella lepidophylla: (a) With fronds expanded

(b) With fronds curled inward

ing spikes have scales, keeled on their backs, in four rows. Dwarfer and more compact, scarcely trailing *S. k. brownii*, a native of the Azores, is the most mosslike

Selaginella kraussiana brownii

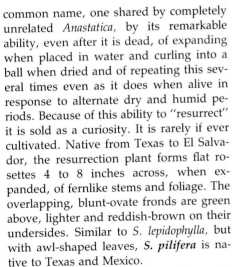

Selaginella kraussiana

common name, one shared by completely unrelated *Anastatica*, by its remarkable ability, even after it is dead, of expanding when placed in water and curling into a ball when dried and of repeating this several times even as it does when alive in response to alternate dry and humid periods. Because of this ability to "resurrect" it is sold as a curiosity. It is rarely if ever cultivated. Native from Texas to El Salvador, the resurrection plant forms flat rosettes 4 to 8 inches across, when expanded, of fernlike stems and foliage. The overlapping, blunt-ovate fronds are green above, lighter and reddish-brown on their undersides. Similar to *S. lepidophylla*, but with awl-shaped leaves, *S. pilifera* is native to Texas and Mexico.

The basket selaginella (*S. apoda* syn. *S. apus*) inhabits moist meadows and stream banks, often in limy soil, from Quebec to Maine, Wisconsin, Florida, and Texas. It has slender, prostrate stems with four rows of leaves, those of the lower plane spreading, ovate, up to ¹⁄₁₂ inch long, those of the upper erect and very tiny. The four-sided spikes containing the spores are ½ to ¾ inch long.

Most common in cultivation, *S. kraussiana* is a creeping or trailing, bright green, mosslike native of Africa and the Azores.

It grows rapidly, makes a good ground-cover, and is frequent in humid greenhouses under benches and other out-of-the-way places; it is attractive for outdoors in warm, moist climates. The slender, jointed, branched stems root freely into the ground. The leaves of the lower plane, about ⅛ inch long and close together but not touching, are lanceolate-oblong to ovate, and pointed. The leaves of the upper plane are markedly shorter and long-pointed. The short spore-bear-

of the selaginellas described here. Variety *S. k. aurea* is distinguished by its bright yellow young growth and yellow-green older parts.

Popular *S. pallescens* (syns. *S. emmeliana*, *S. cuspidata*) is a native of tropical America. It has bright green, lacy rosettes of flat, twice-pinnately-branched, broad-triangular, fernlike fronds of stems and foliage 6 inches to almost 1 foot long. The stems root only from their bases. The rather closely set leaves are in four rows. Those of the lower plane are under ¹⁄₁₆ inch long and sickle-shaped, those of the upper plane are ovate and one-half as long. Not over ½ inch long, and often shorter, the spore-bearing spikes are four-sided.

A beautiful metallic-blue luster is characteristic of *S. willdenovii* and *S. uncinata*. A robust vine 10 to 20 feet tall, *S. willdenovii* is a native of the Asian tropics, with light straw-colored to brown stems from which descend long supporting stilt roots. Its fernlike lateral fronds, fairly widely spaced and held more or less horizontally, have leaves of the lower plane crowded and overlapping. Blunt-oblong and up to ⅛ inch long, they have prominent midribs. The much shorter leaves of the upper plane are pointed-oblong-ovate. Four-sided, the spore-bearing spikes are about 1 inch long. Native to southern China, **S. uncinata** (syn. *S. caesia*) is a charming trailer. It has slender rooting stems, with widely spaced little leaves and at fairly distantly spaced intervals, forked branches with the much closer-set, heart-shaped-ovate leaves of the lower plane ⅛ inch long, spreading and with prominent midribs, and the much smaller leaves of the upper plane overlapping. When grown in shade the foliage has an iridescent metallic-blue-green sheen, in sun it assumes coppery tones.

Bright red stems naked of foliage in their lower parts are typical of **S. erythropus,** of the West Indies, Central America, and South America. This has triangular fronds

Selaginella erythropus

6 inches to 1 foot in height with leaves of the lower plane up to ⅛ inch long, oblongish to ovate, slightly sickle-shaped, and somewhat overlapping. Those of the upper plane are considerably smaller, ovate, and overlapping. The four-sided spore-bearing spikes are up to ½ inch long.

Other species in cultivation are **S. biformis,** of the Philippine Islands, which forms crowded tufts or clumps of soft, arching,

Selaginella biformis

fernlike fronds 6 to 8 inches tall and finely-divided. It is often cultivated as *S. plumosa,* a name that correctly belongs to another species. **S. braunii,** erect and of open, slender habit, sometimes 1½ feet tall, is often lower. Native to China, this has light-colored stems with a few scattered leaves, their lower halves devoid of branches. The leaves of the lower plane, not overlapping, are oval and about ¹⁄₁₆ inch long. About one-half as long, those of the upper plane are pointed-oblong-ovate. The short spore-bearing spikes are four-sided. **S. cantabricum,** a native of limestone rocks in Spain, forms mounds of dull olive-green or grayish rosettes of linear leaves, and bears on 5- to 6-inch-tall stems deep carmine flowers ¾ to 1 inch wide. **S. commutata,** of Malaya, is an attractive, compact, bushy plant 5 to 6 inches tall. It has

Selaginella commutata

many erect fronds, freely-branched, divided into a lacelike pattern of broad, rich green segments with pale midribs. **S. delicatula,** of the eastern Himalayan region, has been misidentified as *S. canaliculata* and

Selaginella delicatula

is grown under that name. It has semi-erect, forking stems 3 to 4 feet long and much-divided fronds 4 to 6 inches long and triangular in outline. The leaves are bright green, those of the lower plane oblongish, close together, and up to ⅛ inch long, those

of the upper plane about one-half as long and ovate-lanceolate. The four-sided spore-bearing spikes are ¼ to 1 inch long. **S. involvens** (sometimes misidentified as *S. caulescens*), of tropical Asia, is erect and 1 foot to 2 feet tall. The lower, branchless halves of the stems have small, narrow, separated, sharp-pointed leaves with heart-shaped bases. The leaves of the lower plane, pointed-sickle-shaped, are about ¹⁄₁₂ inch long, those of the upper plane are much smaller and overlapping. The very many four-angled, spore-bearing spikes have the appearance of firm, ½-inch-long branchlets. **S. martensii** is a variable, tufted native of Mexico, with flat, broad-triangu-

Selaginella martensii

lar fronds of decidedly fernlike aspect. From 6 inches to 1 foot tall, the stems produce aerial roots freely from their lower halves. The leaves of the lower plane, about ⅜ inch long, have prominent midribs. The much smaller, ovate to broad-elliptic ones of the upper plane overlap. The four-sided, spore-producing spikes are ¼ to ½ inch in length. In *S. m. albovariegata* (syn. *S. m. variegata*) some of the fronds are beautifully patched or tipped with white. More slender than the typical species, *S. m. divaricata* has fewer branches. The variety often identified as *S. m. watsoniana* is *S. m. albolineata.* This has firm-textured, erect growths with drooping ends and light-colored or white tips. **S. plana** (syn. *S. inaequalifolia perelegans*), of tropical Asia, has erect, wiry stems up to 1 foot tall and distinctly separated, much-divided, bright green, triangular fronds. The about 1-inch-long, spore-bearing spikes are very conspicuous. **S. pulcherrima,** of Mexico, up to 1 foot tall, has erect, yellowish stems branched in their upper parts and four-ranked, light green leaves. **S. serpens** is West Indian. It forms dense mats of trailing to pendulous stems, up to about 9 inches long, with numerous erect to spreading slender branches. The bright green leaves have distinct midribs, those of the lower plane are crowded, ovate-oblong, and spreading. The leaves of the upper plane are one-third as long and

Selaginella plana

Selaginella versicolor

Selaginella pulcherrima

Selaginella vogelii

Selaginella serpens

pointed. The spore-producing spikes are quadrangular and ¼ to ½ inch long. *S. versicolor*, of tropical West Africa, creeps by slender rhizomes. It has crowded, much-divided, erect fronds, 4 to 6 inches tall, with leaves varying from yellow-green to light green and dark green. The spore-bearing spikes are quadrangular. *S. vogelii* is native to Africa and Malagasy (Madagascar). This has fronds of stems and foliage 1 foot to 2 feet tall, without branches in their lower halves, pinnately-branched above. The leaves of the lower plane, close together but not overlapping, are about ⅛ inch long and short-pointed. The much

smaller ones of the upper plane are long-pointed. The spore-bearing spikes are not over ½ inch in length. *S. wallichii*, of tropical Asia, has creeping rhizomes and suberect stems 2 to 3 feet in length. The

Selaginella wallichii

fronds are much less finely-divided than those of other sorts considered here. The leaves of the lower plane, oblong-lanceolate and slightly sickle-shaped, are up to ⅛ inch long. Much smaller, those of the upper plane are conspicuously overlapping. From ½ to 1 inch long, the spore-producing spikes are quadrangular.

Garden Uses. Of the sorts discussed here, only the basket selaginella (*S. apoda*) is surely hardy in the north. This is appro-

priate for native plant and rock gardens. The nonhardy kinds are useful for outdoor cultivation in the humid tropics and for greenhouses and terrariums. They make few demands and are easy to grow and propagate. Trailing sorts are suitably grown in hanging baskets, or they, like nontrailers, may be grown in pans (shallow pots). These last are to be preferred to deeper containers because selaginellas do not root deeply. The creepers are also fine groundcovers, for outdoors in suitable climates, and in greenhouses and conservatories as well.

Cultivation. Well-drained soil containing an abundance of decayed organic matter, such as rich compost, leaf mold, or peat moss, some coarse sand, perlite, or grit, a sprinkling of crushed charcoal, and about one-quarter part by bulk of good topsoil suits these plants. Keep it evenly moist, but not constantly saturated. For practically all nonhardy sorts temperatures 70°F or higher give the best results, but success can be had if night temperatures are five or even ten degrees lower. A decidedly humid atmosphere and shade from all except weak sun are necessary. Avoid wetting the foliage when it is unlikely to dry within an hour. It is particularly harmful to have the foliage wet at nightfall. Well-rooted specimens benefit from biweekly applications of dilute liquid fertilizer. Propagation can be by sowing spores, as is done with ferns, but is more often accomplished by division, cuttings, or layering. Late winter and early spring are the best times to propagate, and to repot specimens in need of that attention.

SELAGINELLACEAE. The characteristics of this family are those of *Selaginella*, its only genus.

SELAGO (Sel-àgo). About 150 species constitute this infrequently cultivated genus of the figwort family SCROPHULARIACEAE. Its members are chiefly South African; a few inhabit tropical Africa. The name is one used by Pliny for an unidentified plant, gathered with mysterious ceremony by the ancient Druids.

Selagos are mostly dwarf, evergreen shrubs and subshrubs of somewhat heathlike aspect; very few are annuals. They have clustered to more distantly spaced leaves, and small, stalkless or nearly stalkless flowers in spikes, heads, or panicles. Each flower has a five-lobed calyx, a tubular corolla with five or more rarely four equal or unequal lobes (petals), and four stamens in pairs of different lengths. The fruits, included within the calyx, contain seeds flat on one side, concave on the other.

Native to South Africa, *S. hyssopifolia* has erect, branchless, thinly-downy stems furnished with many spreading, linear, few-toothed or toothless leaves up to 1¼ inches long. The tiny white flowers are in roundish-topped panicles about 1 inch across.

Selago hyssopifolia

Garden Uses and Cultivation. The species described above is suitable for planting outdoors in regions with climates similar to that of California, and for growing in sunny greenhouses. It is appropriate for the fronts of shrub beds and borders and as a pot plant. It responds to any ordinary well-drained soil that is not excessively wet or excessively dry for extended periods, and is readily propagated by cuttings and by seed. In greenhouses a winter night temperature of 50°F is adequate with an increase of five to ten degrees by day permitted. On all favorable occasions the greenhouse should be ventilated freely.

SELENICEREUS (Seleni-cèreus) — Night-Blooming-Cereus or Moon-Cereus. Among genera of the cactus family CACTACEAE, to which the name night-blooming cereus is applied, *Selenicereus* ranks highly. It inhabits subtropical and tropical America and the West Indies and includes about twenty-five species. The name comes from the Greek *selene*, the moon, and the name of the related genus *Cereus*. It alludes to the blooms of most sorts opening only at night. Plants treated in this Encyclopedia under *Deamia* are by conservative botanists included in *Selenicereus*.

Selenicereuses are climbing, clambering, or trailing cactuses with long, usually slender, more or less angled or even flattened, ribbed stems, often having aerial roots, and with the areoles (spine-bearing areas) sometimes elevated on small knobs. In the wild they grow as epiphytes (plants that perch on trees without rooting into the ground or taking nourishment from their hosts), scramble among and over rocks, or hang from cliffs. Usually the stems bear clusters of spines, bristles, or hairs. Sometimes they are naked of such. The solitary, ordinarily very large, often sweetly scented blooms are usually white. They have long slender or funnel-shaped perianth tubes

and wide-spreading petals. From the blooms of *Hylocereus*, which they much resemble, they differ in having small scales, with long hairs, bristles, or spines in their axils instead of large, leafy ones without long hairs. The fruits are large, nearly spherical, fleshy, and red and have small tufts of hairs, bristles, or spines.

The earliest known species, the West Indian endemic *S. grandiflorus* (syn. *Cereus grandiflorus*) was described in 1753 as *Cactus grandiflorus*. It has stems 1 inch in diameter, with eight or fewer ribs that have clusters of needle-like spines intermixed with white hairs. The 7-inch-long white flowers are salmon-pink on their outsides. Variety *S. g. armatus* is described as having longer spines and *S. g. tellii* as with four- or five-ribbed, ½-inch-thick stems and smaller blooms.

Popular *S. macdonaldiae* has stems about ½ inch thick, the older ones rounded, the younger five-angled and with the tiny-spined areoles on prominent knobs. The white flowers, 1 foot long or longer, are reddish or yellowish on their outsides. This is a native of Argentina and Uruguay.

Mexican *S. donkelaari* (syn. *Cereus donkelaari*) has stems up to 25 feet in length, but less than ½ inch thick. They have nine or ten, sometimes indistinct ribs and spines in clusters of ten to fifteen, of which one is central and the others radial. The 7-inch-long flowers are white, becoming reddish toward their outsides.

The snaky, bluish-green, sometimes purple-tinged stems of *S. pteranthus* (syn. *Cereus nycticallus*), 1½ inches in diameter, have four to six conspicuous angles and tiny, conical, black spines solitary or in clusters of up to four. The very fragrant white blooms, sometimes 1 foot in length, have reddish to bronzy-yellow, or purplish outer perianth segments. This, one of the most commonly cultivated species, is a native of Mexico.

Other kinds cultivated include these: *S. boeckmannii* (syn. *Cereus boeckmannii*), of Mexico and the West Indies, has ¾-inch-wide, strongly-angled stems with eight or fewer ribs and clusters of three to six spines. About 1¼ feet long, the flowers are brownish on their outsides. *S. coniflorus* (syn. *Cereus coniflorus*) has stems with five or six knobby ribs, and clusters of one central, ½-inch-long spine and four to six yellow radial ones. The blooms of this Mexican species, yellow on their outsides, are 10 inches long. *S. hondurensis*, from Central America, has stems ½ inch thick. They have seven to ten ribs and ¼-inch-long spines interspersed with many white hairs or bristles. The outer segments of the 8-inch-long flowers are yellow or brownish. *S. spinulosus*, a native of Mexico, has usually angled stems 1 inch to 2 inches in diameter with four to six or more ribs. They usually have many aerial roots. The very short spines are in clusters of two centrals

and five or six radials. The flowers, white or pinkish, are about 5 inches long. *S. vagans* has about ten-ribbed, ½-inch-thick stems, with many short spines. About 6 inches in length, the white blooms are brownish at their outsides. This sort is Mexican.

Selenicereus spinulosus

Garden and Landscape Uses and Cultivation. Most selenicereuses are among the easiest and most satisfactory cactuses to grow where there is reasonable space to train their vining stems on trellises, stakes, wires, or other supports or to grow where they can ascend trees or sprawl over rocks. They may be grown permanently outdoors in frost-free climates, and in greenhouses and sometimes as window and porch plants. Their cultural needs are those of most slender-stemmed cactuses. For most information see Cactuses.

SELENIPANTHES. This is the name of orchid hybrids the parents of which are *Lepanthes* and *Selenipedium*.

SELENIPEDIUM. See Phragmipedium.

SELENIPHYLLUM (Seleni-phýllum). This is the name, derived from those of the parent genera, of bigeneric hybrids between *Epiphyllum* and *Selenicereus*, of the cactus family CACTACEAE.

Intermediate between its parents *Epiphyllum crenatum* and *Selenicereus grandiflorus*, and existing in more than one variety, **Seleniphyllum cooperi** has fragrant, white or yellow flowers about 9 inches in diameter. The blooms of popular *S. c. pfersdorffii* are white.

Garden and Landscape Uses and Cultivation. These are as for *Epiphyllum*.

SELF-FERTILE. A plant capable of producing viable seeds as a result of its ovules being fertilized by pollen from its own flowers is said to be self-fertile.

SELF-HEAL is *Prunella vulgaris*.

SELF-STERILE. A plant incapable of producing seeds in response to pollination with pollen from its own flowers is said to be self-sterile. Self-sterility is common in almonds, apples, avocados, muscadine grapes, pears, plums, sweet cherries, Japanese quinces, carnations, gladioluses, hyppeastrums, poppies, and some other commonly grown plants.

SEMELE (Sém-e-le) — Climbing-Butcher's-Broom. Native only to the Canary Islands and Madeira, *Semele*, of the lily family LIL-IACEAE, consists of five species of evergreen vines related to *Ruscus* and *Danae*. The name honors the mother of Bacchus (Dionysus), of classical mythology.

These plants have climbing, branching stems with conspicuous alternate leaflike organs called cladodes that function as leaves, but morphologically are flattened stems. The true leaves are represented by tiny scales in the axils of which the cladodes develop. The clusters (umbels) of flowers usually develop from the edges, more rarely from the flat surfaces of the cladodes. They have six persistent, spreading perianth segments (petals) and an urn-shaped body representing the stamens, with six anthers. The fruits are berries.

Climbing-butcher's broom (*S. androgyna*) may ascend to heights of 50 feet or more. Its leathery, pointed leaves are ovate to ovate-lanceolate and up to 4 inches long by about one-half as wide. The flowers are small and greenish-white or yellowish.

Garden and Landscape Uses and Cultivation. Hardy only in warm, essentially frost-free climates, climbing-butcher's-broom is an interesting and attractive, vigorous vine for outdoors and greenhouses. It thrives in deep, rich, well-drained soil in lightly shaded locations and is easily increased by division and by seed.

SEMIARUNDINARIA (Semiarundinàr-ia). Twenty species of eastern Asian bamboos of the grass family GRAMINEAE are accommodated in *Semiarundinaria*. The name is from the Latin *semi*, half, and *Arundinaria*, another genus of bamboos, and refers to the close relationship between the genera. From *Arundinaria* the present genus differs technically in the arrangement of its flower clusters. Also, its leaf sheaths are early deciduous whereas those of *Arundinaria* are persistent.

Indigenous to Japan, *S. fastuosa* (syn. *Arundinaria fastuosa*) is hardy enough to succeed outdoors in sheltered places in southern New York. Under favorable conditions its canes are 25 to 40 feet tall. For the greater part of their lengths, they are round, but toward their tops are flattened on one side (the flattening changing to opposite sides at each node) in the fashion of those of *Phyllostachys*. Very straight and erect, they are dark glossy-green, marked with purplish-brown when young and be-

coming yellowish-brown with age. The leaves, up to 10 inches long by 1 inch wide, are prominently tessellated, bright green above and dull grayish-green on their undersides. Both margins are lined with fine bristles. A distinguishing feature is the claret color of the insides of the leaf sheaths that surround the young canes. This handsome bamboo has slender rhizomes, but is of compact habit rather than invasive.

Garden and Landscape Uses and Cultivation. For information on these subjects see Bamboos.

SEMINOLE BREAD. See Zamia.

SEMNANTHE (Semnán-the). One of the many splits from the once huge genus *Mesembryanthemum*, of the carpetweed family AIZOACEAE, this genus consists of a single species, a native of South Africa. Its name comes from the Greek *semnos*, distinguished, and *anthe*, a flower.

Closely related to *Erepsia*, and about 2 to 3 feet in height, **Semnanthe lacera** is a shrub with thick, spreading, two-angled branches and opposite, pointed, slightly sickle-shaped, fleshy, three-angled leaves, the alternate pairs at right angles to each other. The leaves, 1¼ to 2 inches long and ⅓ inch wide or a little wider, are gray marked with semitransparent dots. Their upper sides are flattish or slightly hollowed. They have deep, toothed keels that like the other edges are horny and toothed. The blooms, solitary or in pairs, come in summer and are bright rose-red. They are short-stalked, nearly or quite 2 inches in diameter, and have short inner petals. Variety *S. l. densipetala* has dark rose-purple blooms with more densely-arranged petals than the species.

Garden Uses and Cultivation. For rock gardens and other plantings of succulents in warm desert and semidesert climates, *Semnanthe* is well suited, as it is for inclusion in greenhouse collections of desert plants. Full sun, a dry atmosphere, and thoroughly well-drained soil not over-rich in nitrogen meet the needs of this plant. Indoors, a winter night temperature of 45 to 50°F, with only a few degrees more by day, satisfies. Watering must never be excessive. In summer the soil should be nearly dry between applications. In winter even more caution must be taken not to overwater. Propagation is easy by seed and by cuttings. For additional information see Succulents.

SEMPERVIVELLA (Semper-vivélla). Containing four species, *Sempervivella*, of the orpine family CRASSULACEAE, is endemic to the Himalayas. Its name, a diminutive of *Sempervivum*, alludes to a family relationship and to the aspect of its rosettes of foliage.

The first species described botanically, and perhaps the only one cultivated,

Sempervivella alba

S. alba is a low, carpeting, *Sedum*-like, herbaceous perennial clothed with small glandular hairs. It has rosettes 1 inch or a little more across of flat, fleshy, broad-oblong to slightly obovate, evergreen leaves, and similar but more distantly-spaced leaves on the stems. In strong sunlight those most exposed become bright red. Trailing to upright, the 1- to 2-inch-long flowering stems terminate in loose clusters of ½-inch-wide, starry, greenish-centered, white blooms that have six to eight each sepals, petals, and red-anthered stamens. The bases of the petals are united to form a distinct corolla tube.

Garden Uses and Cultivation. These are as for low sedums, such as are commonly accommodated in rock gardens. It is improbable, however, that this species is hardy in regions of severe winters.

SEMPERVIVUM (Semper-vìvum) — Houseleek or Hen-and-Chickens. As it is now understood, *Sempervivum*, including a few sorts some authorities set apart as *Jovibarba*, embraces about forty species of Europe, North Africa, and western Asia. It belongs in the orpine family CRASSULACEAE. Related plants formerly included in this genus, but now segregated as *Aeonium*, *Aichryson*, *Greenovia*, and *Monathes*, are still often identified by their outdated names in gardens. These, most of which are subshrubs with considerable above-ground stems, are natives of the Canary Islands, Madeira, Cape Verde Islands, and parts of North Africa; they are not hardy in the north. The name comes from the Latin *semper*, always, and *vivum*, that which is alive, and alludes to the durable qualities of the plants.

The correct identification and naming of cultivated sempervivums is beset with such extraordinary difficulties that practically hopeless confusion reigns. As long ago as 1932, Dr. R. Lloyd Praeger, the great student and monographer of the group, wrote "a large proportion of sempervivums found in gardens are unnamed and unnamable." The situation has not im-

A fine clump of *Sempervivum* undetermined as to species or variety

proved. The reasons are the considerable variability of some species and the great freedom with which many hybridize and rehybridize both in the wild and in gardens. The only sensible course for gardeners to pursue is to seek the best of the comparatively few species that are available, and their numerous and equally excellent or often superior bastard progeny, and plant and enjoy them without too much attention to the niceties of taxonomic exactitude. Here are described the commonest species to which cultivated sempervivums belong.

Sempervivums are stemless or very short-stemmed, evergreen, succulent perennials with alternate, undivided, stalkless leaves in dense, clustered rosettes. Usually the leaves are pointed-ovate with rounded undersides and have margins fringed with hairs. The flowers, in panicle-like clusters, have fleshy, green, six- to twenty-cleft, cuplike calyxes and as many separate, spreading petals as calyx lobes, or in those that some botanists segregate as the genus *Jovibarba*, with six or seven erect, fringed petals. There are twice as many stamens and as many carpels as there are petals. The fruits are capsule-like.

The common houseleek (**S. tectorum**) received its vernacular name because in

Sempervivum tectorum growing on a roof in England

parts of Europe it often grows on old walls and the roofs of houses. Originally it was planted in the latter location as a supposed protection against lightning, and to have conveniently available the leaves, which were used to poultice burns. Widespread as a wildling from the Pyrenees to the eastern Alps, it is highly variable and has given rise in innumerable hybrids. Typically it forms open, flattish rosettes, 2 to 3½ inches across, of hairless, oblanceolate, green leaves with darker apexes. Up to 1 foot or more in height, and very downy, its flower stems carry many 1-inch-wide or larger dull pink blooms with thirteen to sixteen petals marked with a few red lines. The stalks of the stamens are pinkish-purple, the anthers orange. In *S. t. calcareum* the leaves, in rosettes about 2½ inches across, are glaucous and have dark purple tips. Variety *S. t. alpinum* is smaller. The majority of commonly cultivated sempervivums are forms or hybrids of this species. Most probably, well-known **S. calcaratum** (not to be confused with *S. t. calcareum*) is one of these. It has rosettes

Sempervivum tectorum calcareum

up to 6 inches across that are glaucous or rich purple and dullish pink flowers with fine darker lines, on 8-inch-tall stalks. The flowers, 1 inch across, have twelve to sixteen petals.

The cobweb houseleek (**S. arachnoideum**), in its pure form or as varieties and hybrids of it, is almost as frequent in gardens as the common houseleek. Native from the Pyrenees to the Carpathians, this usually has 1- to 2-inch-wide or smaller, dense rosettes of more or less incurved, green or reddish leaves with their tips connected with a cobweb of fine hairs. The degree of cobwebbiness varies. It is a highly attractive feature of the best varieties and hybrids. The bright rose-red blooms, in smallish clusters and slightly over ½ inch wide, have eight to ten petals. Variety *S. a. glabrescens* (syn. *S. moggridgei*) has rosettes of hair-fringed leaves, their tips not united with a cobweb. Other variants have

Sempervivum arachnoideum

Sempervivum arachnoideum glabrescens

been named *S. a. fimbriatum*, *S. a. major*, *S. a. minor*, and *S. a. rubrum*.

Another variable, highly promiscuous species, commonly represented in gardens, is **S. montanum**. Ranging from the Pyrenees to the Carpathians and Corsica, this earliest-to-flower kind typically has dullish green, finely-hairy, glandular-sticky rosettes often 1 inch or less in diameter. From 1 inch to 1½ inches wide and in clusters of few, its bluish-purple or in the wild rarely white or yellowish blooms have slender, tapering, incurved petals. Many offsets on short to longish stolons are produced. Variety *S. m. burnatii* has white or yellowish-white blooms. The leaves of *S. m. stiriacum* are tipped with red. A commonly grown probably triple hybrid between *S. montanum*, *S. arachnoideum*, and

Sempervivum montanum stiriacum

S. tectorum is **S. funckii.** This has flattish, open rosettes of bright green, finely-hairy leaves, rounded on both sides, and with whitish bases and purple tips. Its nearly 1-inch-wide, rosy-purple flowers, with eleven or twelve petals, are in compact, flattish clusters atop about 8-inch-long, finely-hairy stalks. The numerous offsets are at the ends of 1½-inch-long stolons.

Native to southeastern Europe and Asia Minor, **S. ruthenicum** has rosettes 1½ to 3 inches wide of incurved, dull green, pubescent, pointed-oblong, lanceolate leaves with or without dark tips. From 6 inches to 1 foot long, its erect, few-leaved flower stalks end in three or four spreading branches carrying ¾- to 1-inch-wide flowers that have eleven or twelve narrow, pale green to light yellow petals and stamens with green stalks and yellow anthers. Because offsets are produced in such abundance they are the most frequently used means of increase. They may be rooted at any time, but spring is often preferred because then the young plants become well established before winter. Common in cultivation, **S. soboliferum** (syn. *Jovibarba sobolifera*), a native of Europe and Asia, has crowded clusters of flattened-spherical rosettes about ¾ inch across with sixty to eighty strongly incurving, light green, hairless leaves usually reddish on their backs toward the apex. The flower stalks, 6 to 8 inches tall and clothed with red-tipped leaves, end in flattish clusters 2 to 3 inches across of blooms with six erect, greenish-yellow petals ½ inch long. Characteristically, this develops numerous globose offsets, some often toward the centers of the rosettes and not in contact with the ground. They are on short stems that soon wither. More variable than the last, and a native of southeast Europe, **S. heuffelii** (syns. *Jovibarba heuffelii, S. patens*) has a thick rootstock and flattish, open rosettes of generally thirty to forty green or glaucous, sometimes brown-tipped, finely-hairy leaves. The rosettes may be 2 to 3 inches wide or sometimes wider. They have the rather curious habit of spontaneously

dividing into two or more rosettes approximately equal in size. Up to 8 inches in height, the flower stalks, clothed with clasping, broad-based, purple-tipped leaves, end in flattish clusters of ½-inch-long flowers with six or seven pale yellow, erect petals.

Other sorts cultivated include these: **S. allionii** (syns. *S. austriacum, Jovibarba allionii*), of the southern European Alps, has pale green, glandular-hairy rosettes that mostly do not open widely. They are about 1 inch wide. The ½-inch-long, greenish-white flowers are borne on stalks up to about 7 inches tall. **S. arenarium** (syn. *Jovibarba arenaria*), of eastern Europe, has

Sempervivum arenarium

rosettes up to ¾ inch across of fifty to sixty pale green, often brown-tipped leaves. Its offset rosettes are usually very small. The light green flowers, approximately ¾ inch in diameter, have six pale yellow petals about three times as long as the calyx lobes. **S. atlanticum,** of North Africa, has clusters of rather globular rosettes, 2 to 3 inches wide, of pale green, finely-hairy leaves, and stalks up to 1 foot tall with bronzy-red leaves. Its twelve-petaled white flowers, about 1¼ inches across, have pink petals with a dark stripe down their center. **S. barbulatum** is a variable intermediate hybrid with *S. arachnoideum* and *S. montanum* as parents. **S. ciliosum,** of the Balkan Peninsula, has flattened rosettes of gray-green, incurved, oblanceolate, 1-inch-long, conspicuously hair-fringed leaves. Its blooms have ten to twelve pale greenish-yellow petals, about 1 inch wide. **S. dolmiticum,** of the European Alps, forms numerous offsets. It has rosettes, 1½ inches wide, of glandular-pubescent, bright green, red-tipped leaves with a tuft of hair at the apex. Its ¾-inch-wide flowers have ten to fourteen pink petals with a darker band down the center. **S. erythraeum** is a native of the Balkan Peninsula. Its grayish to purplish, velvety-hairy, pointed leaves are up to eighty in each flattish rosette, 1 inch to 3 inches wide. The deep rose-pink flowers have ten to twelve petals, with a darker center band. **S. faucon-**

nettii is a hybrid between *S. arachnoideum* and *S. tectorum,* intermediate between its parents in aspect. **S. grandiflorum,** of the European Alps, has flat, loose, densely-pubescent rosettes, about 2 inches in diameter, of red-tipped leaves and purple-based yellow flowers that have purple-stalked stamens. **S. hirtum** (syn. *Jovibarba hirta*), of southeastern Europe, is rather variable. It has loose rosettes, up to 2 inches in diameter, of hairless leaves widest below their middles and numerous, easily-removed offsets. Usually glandular-hairy and 4 to 8 inches tall, the flowery stalks bear six-petaled, light yellow to greenish-white flowers ½ inch long or a little longer. The leaves of *S. h. purpureum* are purplish. **S. kindingeri,** of Macedonia, has few-leaved, loose rosettes of hair-fringed, conspicuously glandular-hairy, light green leaves. The petals of the yellow flowers are stained pink at their bases. The stalks of the stamens are striped with red. **S. leucanthum,** of the Balkan Peninsula, is much like the last. It has pubescent leaves with darker tips, and greenish-white flowers with white-stalked stamens. **S. marmoreum,** of central and southern Europe, has flattish, loose ro-

Sempervivum marmoreum

settes, 2 to 4 inches wide, of sixty to eighty leaves widest below their middles and, when young, hairy. Usually glandular-hairy, the flower stalks, 4 to 8 inches tall, display 1-inch-wide blooms with twelve or thirteen white-edged crimson petals. Variety *S. m. brunneifolium* has hairless, brown leaves that become red in winter. **S. pittonii** resembles *S. leucanthum,* but has shorter-stalked offsets and so forms denser clumps of somewhat smaller rosettes. It inhabits the European Alps. **S. pumilum,** native to the Caucasus, has loose rosettes, under 1 inch in diameter, of narrow, glandular-pubescent leaves. The ¾-inch-wide, ten- to twelve-petaled, rosy-purple flowers are on stalks 2 to 4 inches tall. **S. roseum** is a hybrid, its parents *S. arachnoideum* and *S. wulfenii.* Its rosettes, smaller than those of *S. wulfenii,* are of leaves with a tuft of hair at the apex. The flowers, intermediate between those of the parents, are of various mixes of red and yellow. *S. schottii* is a hybrid between *S. montanum* and *S. tectorum.* *S. wulfenii,* of the European Alps, has rosettes up to 2 inches across of oblong-spatula-shaped, glaucous leaves, hairless except at their margins, and lemon-yellow flowers with the bases of the petals blotched with purple, and with purple-stalked stamens.

Garden and Landscape Uses. Few hardy perennials are as easy grown or as trouble-free as houseleeks or hen-and-chickens, as they are affectionately called. They are ideally adapted for rock gardens, stony places, crevices, shallow basins or depressions in rocks, dry walls, and as edgings.

A *Sempervivum* happily located in a rock crevice

They are equally suitable for planting in such containers as strawberry barrels, shallow pots, and vases, for planting outdoors, and for display in sunny window gardens in cool rooms. They are attractive in pans (shallow pots) with a few pieces of rock partly buried to give appropriate "landscape" effects. Given two or three or more inches of soil that never remains wet for long periods and exposure to full sun, sempervivums prosper or at least survive. In too rich soil they are likely to become over-large and cabbage-like. In very poor and dry rootholds they become pinched and puny-looking even if they hang on to life. Somewhere between lie the conditions under which they thrive best. It is important that the soil be very well drained. Sempervivums revel in earth containing crushed limestone, and are likely to prosper if a goodly amount of broken brick or smashed plaster, or even finely-broken concrete, is included.

Cultivation. Seeds germinate readily in sandy, well-drained soil, but are likely to give progeny different from the parents. Because offsets are produced in such abundance, they are the most often used means of increase. They may be rooted at any time, but spring is often preferred because then the young plants are well established before winter.

SENECA SNAKEROOT is *Polygala senega.*

SENECIO (Sen-ècio). Groundsel, Cineraria, Dusty Miller, Mexican Flame Vine, Leopard's Bane, Ragwort, German-Ivy, California-Geranium, Candle Plant, String-of-Beads, Vertical Leaf. Considered in a broad sense, as it now is by most botanists and as it is presented here, *Senecio,* of the daisy family COMPOSITAE, is one of the largest genera of flowering plants, encompassing between 2,000 and 3,000 species. At various times attempts have been made to reduce this unwieldiness by splitting it into smaller genera more easy to comprehend. The names of some of the resulting segregates, including *Cineraria, Jacobaea, Kleinia,* and *Notonia,* have been and are familiar to gardeners and are still sometimes used. Nevertheless, although to nonbotanists such groups may appear distinct enough to justify recognition as separate genera, botanical differences between most of them and *Senecio* are not important enough to warrant such separation. One group previously included in *Senecio,* and still often grown under that name in gardens, but now considered to be a separate genus, is *Ligularia.* The name *Senecio* stems from the Latin *senex,* an old man, and is thought to allude to the white or grayish hairs of the flower heads.

Cosmopolitan in its natural distribution, *Senecio* includes annuals, biennials, herbaceous perennials, shrubs, vines, and even a few trees. Many of its members are succulents. There is great variation in the leaves of different kinds. They come in many forms and sizes and may be alternate, or less commonly all basal. The flower heads (usually called flowers), as is usual with nearly all members of the daisy family, are composed of numerous florets, each of which is actually a tiny flower. The florets of each head may be and most commonly are, like those of the flower heads of daisies, of two very different types, disk florets, forming a central eye, and ray florets, petal-like and encircling the disk, or all the florets may be of the disk type. The fruits are usually cylindrical, seedlike achenes, ribbed lengthwise and with a tuft of whitish hairs or bristles.

In the treatment that follows the sorts discussed are presented in groups of horticultural significance and in this order: The florests' cineraria, annuals, dusty millers, herbaceous perennials, shrubs other than dusty millers, vines, and succulents. Following this, appropriate uses for the sorts of each group are indicated under Garden and Landscape Uses and information about the cultural needs of the various kinds is given under Cultivation, which concludes this Encyclopedia entry.

The florists' cineraria, or cineraria as it is popularly called, is most familiar as a pot plant or in some mild climates as an outdoor bedding plant that makes an al-

most unbelievably prolific late winter and spring display of daisy-type flower heads in an amazing range of colors and combinations. For long thought to be horticultural selections of *S. cruentus,* these cinerarias are now accepted as being of hybrid origin with *S. cruentus, S. heritieri, S. multiflorus,* and perhaps other Canary Island species involved in their parentage. The correct group name for the florists' cineraria is now *S. hybridus.* The species *S. cruentus* is an herbaceous or slightly subshrubby perennial, native to the Canary Islands. It has large, longish-stalked, ovate-heart-shaped to triangular-ovate, shallowly-lobed, round-toothed leaves, white-hairy beneath and green above, and branched, loose clusters of flower heads, ½ to 1 inch across, with purple ray florets.

Although almost invariably grown as annuals, florists' cinerarias are in fact perennials, and in the past European gardeners sometimes perpetuated unusual types by cuttings. They have softly-hairy stems and leaves, the latter quite large, approximately circular to broadly-heart-shaped, angled and toothed, and spreading more or less horizontally. There are two chief types, the most popular, identified as the "grandiflora group," has large, very full, circular flower heads arranged in large, compact, rounded trusses that sit

Cineraria, grandiflora type

close upon the foliage and almost hide it from view. Flower colors include white, creamy-white, pink, red, lavender, blue, and purple, as well as bicolors and tricolors with the hues in concentric zones. Depending upon the strain selected and the culture given, "grandiflora" cinerarias range in height from 1 foot to 2 feet. The other main type, the "stellata group," are 2 to 3 feet tall or taller and have starry flowers in very much looser, more graceful trusses held higher above the foliage. Their flowers are most often white, pink, lilac, blue, or purple without marked zoning. A class known as the "intermediate group" has flowers of the "stellata"

Cineraria, stellata type

Senecio vira-vira

Senecio vira-vira (foliage and flowers)

Senecio cineraria variety

Senecio elegans

Senecio cineraria 'Diamond'

Senecio abrotanifolius

Lychnis) is commonly applied to **S. cineraria** (syns. *Cineraria maritima, Centaurea maritima*), of the Mediterranean region, and **S. vira-vira** (syns. *S. leucostachys, Cineraria candidissima, C. maritima candidis-*

type on plants nearly as compact as the "grandifloras."

Annual senecios are numerous in the wild, but few are sufficiently attractive to be accepted as garden plants. The best known, natives of South Africa, are the purple ragwort (*S. elegans* syn. *Jacobaea elegans*) and *S. arenarius*. Naturalized to some extent in California, *S. elegans* is from 1½ to 2 feet tall and pubescent. It has 2- to 3-inch-long, oblongish, pinnately-lobed or coarsely-toothed, more or less stem-clasping leaves and, in loose, flattish clusters, about 1-inch-wide flower heads with yellow centers and purple, reddish-purple, or rarely white ray florets. From 1 foot to 2 feet tall or sometimes higher, **S. arenarius** has pinnately-lobed, toothed leaves that, like the stems, are clothed with sticky hairs. In rather loose, flattish-topped clusters, the showy, daisy-like flower heads, ½ inch or a little more in diameter, have yellow centers and many spreading, purple, or less commonly white, ray florets. There are horticultural varieties in which the flower heads are pink, crimson, or white, some of which are double-flowered.

Dusty miller (a popular name also used for sorts of *Artemisia, Centaurea*, and

sima), of Argentina. These are confused as to names in gardens. Both are bushy subshrubs or shrubs, 2 to 2½ feet tall and not hardy in the north. The stems and foliage of both are densely-clothed with a felt of whitish hairs, but the upper surfaces of the leaves of *S. cineraria*, which are 2 to 5½ inches long, ovate, and deeply-pinnately-cleft into oblong lobes, each with a few coarse teeth, tend to become greenish as they age. The much finer-divided ovate leaves of *S. vira-vira* are 2 to 3 inches long and deeply-pinnately-cleft into two to four pairs of narrow-linear, toothless, pointed lobes. Other differences are that *S. cineraria* is more compact and rigid-stemmed than *S. vira-vira*, and its yellow flower heads possess ray florets. Those of *S. vira-vira*, nearly ½ inch in diameter, whitish to cream-colored, have only disk florets.

Herbaceous perennials are numerous in *Senecio*, but very few sorts are ordinarily cultivated. A group of very showy, hardy herbaceous perennials often called senecios more properly belong in the genus *Ligularia* and are described under that name in this Encyclopedia. Except for *S. pulcher*, the senecios now to be described are hardy in the north: **S. abrotanifolius**, of Europe, has creeping rhizomes and erect, hairless

or slightly hairy stems 1 foot to 1½ feet tall. Its leaves are 1 inch to 3 inches long, the lower ones twice- or thrice-pinnate, the upper ones pinnately-cleft. About ¾ inch across and each with ten to thirteen ray florets, the flower heads, solitary or in clusters of few, are orange-yellow to orange-red. **S. adonifolius,** native of the mountains of southern Europe, has much the aspect of *S. abrotanifolius,* but is often taller and has clusters of many smaller, bright yellow flower heads. **S. aureus,** the golden ragwort, occurs in damp soils from Newfoundland to Florida and Texas and has stems 1 foot to 2 feet tall, somewhat hairy when young. Its lower leaves are long-stalked, with undivided roundish-ovate to oblong-ovate or triangular-ovate, toothed blades 1 inch to 6 inches long. The stem leaves, smaller and mostly pinnately-lobed, become progressively shorter-stalked upward. Several to many up to ½-inch-wide flower heads, with usually six to thirteen ray florets, are carried on loosely-branched stalks 1 foot to 2½ feet tall. **S. doria,** of Europe and North Africa, robust and 3 to 4 feet tall, has glaucous, hairless, toothed or toothless leaves, 3 to 5 inches long, the basal ones short-stalked and lanceolate to oblanceolate, those above smaller and stalkless. The numerous yellow flower heads, each with five to nine ray florets and ¾ inch wide, are in clusters of many. **S. doronicum,** of Europe and North Africa, is called leopard's bane. From 1 foot to 3 feet high and cottony-hairy to almost hairless, this has irregularly-toothed, ovate to nearly lanceolate leaves up to 6 inches long. The lower ones are stalked, those above nearly stalkless. About 2 inches in diameter and solitary or in clusters of up to four, the yellow flower heads have ten to twenty ray florets. **S. incanus,** of the Alps of Europe, is densely-white-hairy. It has stalked, obovate leaves 1 inch to 4 inches long, deeply-cleft into narrow, toothed lobes. The upper leaves are oblong. In crowded terminal clusters atop 3- to 6-inch-long stalks, the golden-yellow flower heads, from a little under to a little over 3 inches wide, have three to ten ray florets. Variety *S. i. carniolicus* (syn. *S. carniolicus*), cobwebby-hairy or hairless, has bigger flower heads. **S. pulcher,** of Argentina, Uruguay, and Brazil, as its provenance suggests, is hardy only where winters are kind to somewhat tender plants. One of the latest bloomers, in fall this produces singly, or in loose, terminal clusters of few, on plants 2 to 3 feet tall, 2- to 3-inch-wide flower heads with yellow centers and many carmine-purple rays. Its younger parts clothed with cobwebs of hairs, this has leathery, elliptic to lanceolate, irregularly-toothed leaves. **S. smithii,** native to the region of the Straits of Magellan and to the Falkland Islands and naturalized in the British Isles, is best adapted for places with mild winters and cool summers. From 3 to 4 feet tall, and with a loose wool of hairs, this species has an ample mass of basal leaves with oblongish to ovate blades 8 to 10 inches long. Raised on erect stalks to just above the foliage, the rather crowded, terminal panicles, 4 to 6 inches wide, are of 1½-inch-

wide flowers with a yellow disk and twenty to thirty white florets.

Shrubs other than those called dusty millers can be conveniently separated into two groups, natives of New Zealand and natives of Mexico or South Africa. None is hardy.

New Zealand shrubby species include these: **S. compactus,** in cultivation often misidentified as *S. greyii,* is handsome and 2 to 4 feet tall. Freely-branched and compact, it has stalked, obovate to broad-elliptic leaves ½ inch to 2 inches long by ¼ to 1 inch wide and rounded at their apexes. The lower, larger ones have wavy margins, the smaller ones above, crinkled edges. Their undersides and stalks, like the young shoots, are densely-felted with soft, white hairs; their upper surfaces are dark green. In terminal racemes of three to ten, the ¾- to 1¼-inch-wide flower heads have ten to twelve bright yellow ray florets. **S. greyii,** perhaps the loveliest of the New Zealanders, and up to 8 feet tall, has young shoots, undersides of its leaves, and leaf-

Senecio greyii

stalks densely-clothed with a felt of white hairs. Its stalked leaves have oblong to oblong-ovate blades up to 4 inches long by 1 inch to 2 inches wide or slightly wider. In glandular-hairy-stalked panicles of many, up to 6 inches long and almost as broad, the 1-inch-wide flower heads have glandular-hairy involucral bracts and twelve to fifteen bright yellow ray florets. **S. kirkii,** upright, 6 to 15 feet tall, and less tolerant of cold than the others described here, is very beautiful. Its stalked, toothed or toothless, gray-green leaves, which vary in shape from linear to obovate, have blades 2 to 6 inches long by ⅓ inch to 1¾ inches wide. The yellow-centered flower heads, 1¼ to 2 inches wide, have up to ten white ray florets. They are in flattish, terminal clusters 4 inches to 1 foot wide. **S. laxifolius** resembles *S. greyii,* but has broader leaves, and flower stalks not glandular-hairy. From 2 to 4 feet tall and with its young shoots and undersides of its leaves felted with gray-white hairs, this has ellip-

Senecio laxifolius

tic to lanceolate, stalked leaves up to 3 inches long by ¾ inch wide. The ¾- to 1-inch-wide, yellow flower heads, with ten to fifteen ray florets, are in loose panicles up to 8 inches long. **S. monroi,** akin to *S. compactus,* differs from that species in having more conspicuously wrinkled leaf margins and glandular-hairy flower stalks. Much-branched, up to 6 feet tall and broader than tall, this has the undersides of its leaves and its flower stalks densely-white-felted. From ½ inch to 1½ inches long, the short-stalked leaves have oblong-elliptic to somewhat obovate blades with rounded apexes. The numerous flower heads, ½ to ¾ inch across and on longish, slender stalks, have ten to fifteen bright yellow ray florets. They are in clusters up to 6 inches wide. **S. reinoldii** (syn. *S. rotundifolia*), native to coastal New Zealand,

Senecio reinoldii (foliage)

is a stout-branched, evergreen shrub or tree up to 20 feet tall. Very leathery, its leaves are broad-ovate to subcircular. They are smooth-margined and have stalks 1 inch to 2 inches long and blades 1½ to 4 inches long. The upper surfaces of the leaves are hairless, their lower surfaces, like the branchlets, are densely-clothed with white- to buff-woolly hairs. The flower heads, of little decorative merit and about ⅓ inch wide, are assembled in panicles up to 8 inches long. They are without ray florets. This is an excellent seaside shrub for mild climates, such as found in the Pacific Northwest.

Mexican *S. petasitis*, called velvet-geranium and California-geranium, 4 to 8 feet

Senecio grandifolius

Senecio confusus

Senecio petasitis

or more high, branches freely from its base. Its ovate to almost circular leaves, up to 8 inches across, have the main veins spreading palmately (fanwise) from the base of the blade, and shallowly-wavy lobed margins. Like the shoots they are velvety-hairy, especially on their undersides. Many together in large, showy clusters, the yellow flower heads have five or six ray florets. From the last, *S. grandifolius*, which attains heights of 10 to 15 feet and is also Mexican, is distinguishable by its leaves being pinnately-veined, that is, with side veins coming from a mid-vein, which is the only one originating from the base of the leaf blade. Up to 1½ feet long and ovate to ovate-oblong, the leaves have 3- to 5-inch-long stalks and blades with shallowly-toothed or scalloped margins. Their upper surfaces are practically hair-

less, beneath they are clothed with rust-colored down. The yellow flower heads, with mostly five ray florets, are in large, showy clusters. South African *S. glastifolius* is a shrub or subshrub up to 5 feet tall with hairless stems and leaves, the latter linear to lanceolate, 2 to 3 inches long, and irregularly-toothed. In loose panicles the handsome, freely-produced, 2½-inch-wide flower heads have yellow centers and about thirteen rosy-purple ray florets.

Senecio glastifolius

Vining senecios, none hardy in the north, include these: *S. angulatus*, of South Africa, has much the aspect of *S. mikanioides*, but its flower heads have about twenty disk florets and four to six ray florets. This has stems up to several feet long and rather fleshy leaves with ovate, angularly-lobed or toothed blades 1½ to 2½ inches long. The yellow flower heads are in clusters of many. *S. confusus*, called Mexican flame vine and orange-glow vine, a sort popular for planting outdoors in California and Florida, grows rampantly, and may exceed 15 feet in height. A hairless native of Mexico, this has thickish, ovate to ovate-lanceolate, coarsely-toothed leaves 1½ to 4 inches long and approximately one-half as broad. Its showy, brilliant orange or red-orange flower heads,

¾ inch to 1½ inches in diameter and in terminal clusters, have sixty or more disk florets and about fifteen ray florets. *S. macroglossus*, the Cape-ivy, Natal-ivy, or wax vine, of South Africa, is a slender-stemmed climber or more often a trailer with stalked triangular, fleshy leaves about 2½ inches long, mostly with three or five pointed, shallow lobes. The yellow, 2-inch-wide flower heads, solitary and on about 6-inch-long stalks from the leaf axils and ends of the stems, have eight to ten 1-inch-long ray florets. The foliage of *S. m. variegatum* is variegated with yellow. *S. mikanioides*, known as German- and parlor-ivy and popular as a

Senecio macroglossus variegatum

Senecio mikanioides

houseplant, is a native of South Africa naturalized in California. Hairless and with long, twining stems, this has somewhat fleshy, ovate to triangular-ovate leaves with blades 1½ to 4 inches wide with usually deeply-indented bases. Although much softer, they are reminiscent of the leaves of English ivy (*Hedera helix*). In crowded clusters, the yellow flower heads, ⅓ inch in diameter, are without ray florets. They have eight to ten disk florets. *S. tropaeolifolius*, of South Africa, is more succulent than the others described here.

Senecio tropaeolifolius

It has a bulblike, tuberous root and trailing smooth stems. As its name suggests, its leaves have much the aspect of those of the garden nasturtium (*Tropaeolum*). Nearly circular with slightly-angled margins, the blade is about 1 inch across with the stalk attached to it some distance in from its margin. In long-stalked clusters of few, the rayless flower heads are whitish-yellow.

Succulent senecios are thick-stemmed, fleshy-leaved shrubs and subshrubs, natives of desert and semidesert regions where there is brilliant light, low humidity, and limited supplies of water. They are commonly sparsely-foliaged and protected against excessive loss of moisture by a waxy coating or by coverings of hairs. Here is a selection of the most commonly cultivated kinds: *S. acaulis* (syn. *Kleinia acaulis*), of South Africa, has tuberous rhizomes and densely-leafy, erect stems 2 to 3½ inches long. Grooved along their upper sides, the somewhat incurved, subcylindrical leaves, tipped with a small point and up to 6 inches long, broaden at their bases to partly clasp the stem. Characteristically their bases and apexes are reddish. The solitary flower heads terminate stalks 6 to 8 inches long. *S. articulatus* (syn. *Kleinia articulata*) is called candle plant. Native to South Africa and from 1 foot to 2 feet tall, it has erect, branched, thick, fleshy, cylindrical stems marked with pale gray and sharply constricted at intervals to form distinct joints (seg-

Senecio articulatus

ments). The leaves are grayish, 1 inch to 2 inches long, with stalks as long or longer than the blades. The latter are mostly deeply three- or five-lobed. The slender-stalked heads of somewhat ill-scented, off-white flowers are in clusters of few. The stem joints of *S. a. globosus* are short and nearly spherical. *S. barbertonensis* is a South African subshrub with cylindrical,

Senecio barbertonensis

fleshy stems about ¼ inch thick that become woody with age. Crowded toward the ends of the stems, the slender, slightly curved, pointed leaves, 1 inch to 3½ inches long, are flattened and grooved longitudi-

nally along their upper sides. Terminal at the ends of the branches, the erect, cylindrical heads of flowers are ½ inch long or slightly longer. Golden-yellow, they are without ray florets. *S. crassissimus*, of Malagasy (Madagascar), is called vertical leaf. A hairless subshrub up to 2½ feet tall, it has cylindrical stems and erect or spreading, broad-obovate, flat leaves up to 2¼ inches long and glaucous-green, with usually narrow, reddish margins and, at the apex, a short point. The yellow flower heads, each with several ray florets, are clustered at the ends of long stalks. *S. descoingsii* (syn. *Notonia descoingsii*), of Malagasy (Madagascar), has upright, cylindrical, sometimes sparsely-branched, grooved stems up to 1½ feet tall, with a few small, linear leaves that soon drop. The pale yellow to white, rayless flower heads are in ones, twos, or threes from the stem ends or sometimes from the leaf axils. *S. ficoides* (syn. *Kleinia ficoides*) is a South African subshrub 1 foot to 3 feet tall, with up to finger-thick, more or less sprawling, white-dotted, green stems that turn upward at their ends. Their younger parts especially, like the foliage, are coated with whitish meal. The linear leaves, tapered at both ends and compressed laterally, are 4 to 6 inches long, about ¼ inch wide, and more than twice as deep. Branched toward its top, the flowering stalk carries several stalked, white flower heads. *S. fulgens* (syn. *Kleinia fulgens*), of South Africa, a subshrub up to 3 feet tall,

Senecio fulgens

has branched, fleshy, erect to sprawling stems that, like the leaves and flower stalks, are coated with a white, waxy farina. The fleshy leaves are spatula-shaped to obovate, remotely toothed along their margins, and 3 to 4 inches long. Solitary or in twos on stalks 3 to 4 inches long, the 1-inch-wide, red or orange-red flower heads are without ray florets. *S. galpinii* (syn. *Kleinia galpinii*) is a South African subshrub 1 foot to 2 feet tall and with up to finger-thick branches that, like the foliage, have a light gray, waxy bloom. The

Senecio haworthii

Senecio jacobsenii

bluntly-tapered, oblanceolate leaves, 4 to 6 inches long by 1¼ to 1½ inches wide, with a conspicuous midrib, are partially stem-clasping. The orange-red flower heads, without ray florets, are in loose clusters of three or four. **S. hallianus,** of South Africa, forms mats of short, sticky stems from which sprout roots that, at the point they reach soil, develop sausage- or spindle-shaped tubers 3 to 4 inches long. The short-stalked, cylindrical-spindle-shaped, glaucous leaves, up to 1 inch long by 1 inch to 1¾ inches wide, have a broad, translucent stripe along the upper surface and ten less conspicuous, slimmer stripes. The flowering stalk bears one or two whitish flower heads with purple styles. **S. haworthii** (syns. *Kleinia haworthii, K. tomentosa*), of South Africa, is a very handsome subshrub of up to 1 foot tall or a little taller. It has rather few branches, chiefly erect, but sometimes becoming decumbent as they age, and, like the leaves, densely-clothed with a felt of pure white hairs. Spindle-shaped to pointed-cylindrical, the fleshy leaves are 1 inch to 2 inches long. The flower heads, without

ray florets, terminate stems 1½ to 3 inches long; they are orange-yellow. **S. herreianus** (syn. *Kleinia gomphophylla*), of South Africa, because of the appearance of its leaves is sometimes known as the gooseberry kleinia. It has slender, trailing, freely-branched, rooting stems 1 foot to 2 feet long and rather distantly-spaced, egg-shaped, berry-like fleshy leaves ½ to ¾ inch long, tipped with a tiny point, and green with translucent lengthwise lines. The small flower heads are on 2- to 3-inch-long stalks. **S. jacobsenii** (syns. *S. petraeus, Notonia petraeus*), of East Africa, has creeping, rooting, sparingly-branched, pencil-thick stems up to 1½ feet long and well furnished with more or less overlapping, thick, obovate, stalkless leaves 2 to 3 inches long by up to 1 inch wide. Furnished with small, crowded leaves the up-to-10-inch-long flowering stalks carry one to three orange flower heads. **S. kleinia** (syns. *S. neriifolius, Kleinia neriifolia*), of the Canary Islands, is a shrub up to about 3 feet tall with thick, cylindrical stems that fork or divide to produce more than two stems from the same point. The slender,

linear-lanceolate leaves, produced near the ends of the branches and slightly drooping, are 3 to 6 inches long. The yellowish-white flower heads are in loose clusters. **S. kleiniiformis** (syns. *Kleinia kleiniiformis, K. cuneatus*) is a South African subshrub 1

Senecio kleiniiformis

foot to 2 feet high with prostrate but not creeping stems and upright branches that, when broken, are pungent-scented. All its parts are coated with a white, waxy bloom. The more or less spoonlike leaves have roundish to elliptic blades with convex upper surfaces and often one to few coarse marginal teeth. From ten to thirty white or yellow flower heads are borne on branched stalks up to 2½ feet long. **S. longiflorus** (syn. *Kleinia longiflora*) is a South African shrub or subshrub 1½ to 2 feet tall and freely-branched. From ¼ to ⅔ inch thick, the dark-striped stems have rather distantly scattered, awl-shaped leaves, not over ⅓ inch long, that soon fall. The flower heads are three to five to-

Senecio herreianus

Senecio herreianus (flower)

gether on short stalks from the ends of the stems. *S. mandraliscae* (syn. *Kleinia mandraliscae*), of South Africa, is a subshrub up to 1 foot high, with more or less procumbent stems of up to finger-thickness that become woody with age. Semicylindrical and 3 to 4 inches long by ¼ inch wide or slightly wider, the sharp-pointed leaves, with flattish, often grooved upper surfaces, are incurved toward their tips. They are coated with a waxy, gray bloom. The flowering stalks, longer than the leaves and forked, carry up to thirteen flower heads. *S. medley-woodii*, of South Africa, is an attractive gray-foliaged bushy shrub 1 foot or so tall. It has woolly-hairy

Senecio medley-woodii

Senecio medley-woodii with flower head

shoots and flat, fleshy, pointed-obovate leaves, 1½ to 2 inches long and up to 1¼ inches wide, that spread widely and are bluntly-toothed. When young densely-clothed with woolly hairs, they later lose most of these and often become purplish. The about 2-inch-wide, yellow flower heads in terminal stalked clusters of few have ten to thirteen ray florets. *S. pendulus* (syn. *Kleinia pendula*), called inchworm and tapeworm plant, is native to northeast Africa and Arabia. Its curious stems sometimes grow underground, but more often arch or loop their way across its surface. Up to 1 foot long and ½ to ¾ inch

wide, they retain the dry, spinelike remains of old leaves. The latter, when fresh, are awl-shaped and about ¼ inch long. The solitary flower heads, 1 inch to 1¼ inches across and orange-red to blood-red, are borne singly or sometimes in twos on stalks 8 to 10 inches long. *S. radicans,* of South Africa, has slender, prostrate, rooting stems and plump, cylindrical, straight or somewhat curved, glaucous-green leaves, up to 1 inch long by about ¼ inch wide, pointed at the apex, and each with a short stalk and a longitudinal stripe. The flower heads, solitary or in twos on long stalks, are white and fragrant. This is an excellent hanging basket plant. *S. rowleyanus,* a South African colloquially known as string-of-beads, forms mats of prostrate, rooting stems and nearly spherical, ¼-inch-wide leaves with a "window," a band of translucent tissue ¹⁄₁₆ inch wide, which is most easily seen when a leaf is viewed against the light. The rayless, white flower heads are solitary, on stalks 1½ inches long. *S. scaposus,* of South Africa, is stemless or nearly so. Its slender, nearly cylindrical, somewhat up-curved, blunt leaves are in open rosettes. From 2 to 3½ inches long, when young they are attractively clothed with a cobweb-like white felt, which with age, disappears, leaving them green and hairless. The yellow flower heads, solitary or few on stalks longer than the leaves, have about a dozen ray florets. *S. serpens* (syns. *S. repens, Kleinia repens*), of South Africa, is a shrub up to about 1 foot tall and wide. Branched from its base, it has glaucous-blue stems. Crowded chiefly toward the tops of the stems and thinly coated with bluish-white wax easily removed by light rubbing, the nearly cylindrical, linear-lanceolate leaves are grooved along their upper sides and are 1¼ to 1¾ inches long. About twice as long as the leaves, the sparingly-branched flower stalks have at the end of each branch a head of white flowers without ray florets. *S. stapeliiformis* (syn. *Kleinia stapeliiformis*) is a South African subshrub, branched from its base and up to about 1 foot tall. Its erect, four-to seven-angled stems are dark green with paler areas between the angles. Arising from cushion-like protrusions along the angles, the awl-shaped to spinelike leaves are up to ¼ inch long. About 1½ inches wide, the red flower heads, on stalks up to 6 inches long, are without ray florets.

Garden and Landscape Uses. Because of the great variation within the genus *Senecio*, a well-chosen selection of sorts can serve many useful employments. The florists' cineraria is most familiar as a greenhouse pot plant, to be discarded at the completion of its first season of bloom, and as a colorful late winter and outdoor spring bedding plant in Mediterranean-type climates of mild, cool, but frost-free winters.

Senecio stapeliiformis

The annuals are well suited for summer display in outdoor flower beds and for use as cut blooms, but because they abhor torrid weather, especially if accompanied by high humidity, they are not satisfactory summer plants in many regions of North America. They are admirable for growing in pots and in benches in greenhouses for blooming in late winter and spring.

Dusty miller senecios are effective permanent outdoor plants for sunny locations in warm, dry climates and are much used as temporary summer furnishings for flower beds, window boxes, urns, and other decorative containers elsewhere. Their chief attraction is their handsome white-felted foliage, which provides a pleasing foil for a wide range of popular summer bedding plants, including begonias, geraniums, heliotropes, petunias, and salvias. These dusty millers are also effective cool greenhouse pot plants, their foliage contrasting pleasingly with that of other plants and with flowers.

Herbaceous perennial senecios are suitable for flower beds and borders and for naturalistic plantings. The lower ones are appropriate in rock gardens.

Shrub senecios of New Zealand nativity adapt best to relatively cool and humid climates, such as those of the Pacific Northwest and the British Isles. Excellent general-purpose plants for massing alone and for planting with other sorts, they need sunny locations and are especially well suited to coastal regions. The shrub sorts of Mexico and South Africa respond to a warmer, drier climate, such as that of California, and are also well adapted for employment as greenhouse ornamentals. The bold foliage and massive flower clusters of the Mexicans give distinction to landscape plantings. Of daintier growth, South African *S. glastifolius*, very showy in bloom, is suitable for flower beds and borders in frost-free, dryish climates and for growing in pots in greenhouses.

Vining sorts are satisfactory outdoors in fairly dry climates where little or no frost is experienced and may be used effectively in sunny places as screens and ground-covers. They are also popular as greenhouse plants and houseplants, prospering in pots, planters, and hanging baskets.

Succulent senecios are popular with fanciers of desert plants. Available in considerable assortment, they are popular for planting permanently outdoors in California, and elsewhere where mild, dry climates make that practicable, and for growing in sunny greenhouses and as window plants. These sorts vary much in size and aspect. They accommodate well to pots and hanging baskets.

Cultivation. For directions for growing the florists' cineraria, see the Encyclopedia entry Cineraria, Florists'. The annuals *S. elegans* and *S. arenarius* thrive in sunny locations in well-drained soils of moderate fertility. Because they are intolerant of high temperatures they do not remain in bloom throughout the summer in most parts of the United States, but may be grown outdoors for early summer bloom and in greenhouses for flowering in late winter and spring. They prosper under conditions that favor garden peas and sweet peas. Sow seeds of these outdoors in patches in mixed flower beds, or for cut flowers, in rows 1½ to 2 feet apart, as early in spring as the ground can be had in a crumbly, welcoming condition. Thin the seedlings to from 6 inches to 1 foot apart, and keep weeds down by frequent shallow surface cultivation. Light staking with brushwood or by other means may be needed.

To have greenhouse pot plants of annual senecios, sow seeds in September or October. Transplant the seedlings individually to 2½-inch pots, and each time they fill their containers with roots, transplant them to successively bigger ones. As finals, pots 5, 6, or 7 inches in diameter are appropriate. Use fertile, porous soil and grow throughout in a night temperature of 45 to 50°F, with a daytime increase of five to ten degrees. Ventilate the greenhouse freely on all favorable occasions and avoid excessive humidity. When the plants have filled their final pots with roots, give them biweekly applications of dilute liquid fertilizer.

Dusty miller senecios are easily raised from seed and cuttings. The first are most usually employed for *S. cineraria* and its varieties, but because seeds are less commonly available, cuttings are more often used for *S. vira-vira*. To have plants for summer beds, sow seeds in February or take cuttings in August or September.

Sow in sandy soil in well-drained pots or flats in a temperature of 65 to 70°F. Transplant the seedlings about 3 inches apart into flats of fertile, porous soil and grow them in a sunny greenhouse or similar environment where the night temperature is 55 to 60°F, that by day five to ten degrees higher. Water moderately. Constantly saturated soil causes rotting. Some two or three weeks before transplanting to the garden, harden the young plants by standing them in a sunny, sheltered place outdoors.

Make cuttings about 3 inches long of terminal pieces of leafy stems and plant them in coarse sand or perlite in a greenhouse or cold frame. Because they are so densely-hairy considerable care must be taken not to keep them too wet or to have the atmosphere excessively humid. Soak cuttings with a fine spray of water immediately after they are planted. Do not water again until the sand or perlite is nearly dry. Excessive wetness causes them to rot. In bright weather a daily fine misting with water is helpful so long as it dries within an hour. Harm may be done if the foliage remains wet for long periods. Ventilate carefully to prevent a buildup of high humidity. When rooted, pot the cuttings individually in 3-inch pots and winter the young plants in a cool, frost-free greenhouse.

Herbaceous perennial senecios give little trouble. All need sunny locations, and most do best in moderately moist, fertile soil. They are readily increased by division in spring or early fall and by seed, preferably sown in spring.

Shrub senecios prosper in ordinary, well-drained, reasonably fertile soils and are easily propagated by cuttings and by seed. Those native to New Zealand call for little maintenance other than a little occasional pruning to keep them shapely. The shrubs of Mexican and South African origin should be pruned fairly severely after flowering is through or at the beginning of each new growing season.

In greenhouses, *S. grandifolius* and *S. petasitis* may be accommodated in pots or tubs (for good results the ones in which first-year plants are to bloom should be at least 8 inches in diameter). Give specimens whose roots have filled the containers in which they are to bloom regular applications of dilute liquid fertilizer. After flowering is through, rest the plants for a month or so by withholding water. Then prune them severely, take them out of their containers, shake as much old soil from

them as practicable, repot, and resume watering. Indoors a winter night temperature of 45 to 50°F and daytime levels five to ten degrees higher suit. At other seasons normal outdoor temperatures above 50°F, with a free circulation of air, are satisfactory. Much finer-foliaged and of more airy appearance than the two species just considered, *S. glastifolius* has the same environmental needs and requires much the same care. Nice specimens of this can be bloomed in 5- or 6-inch pots, bigger ones in larger containers.

Vining senecios, except *S. tropaeolifolius*, which requires conditions and care that suit succulent kinds, flourish with minimum attention in ordinary, well-drained soil kept moderately moist. Most respond best to full exposure to sun, but will stand part-day shade, and some, including *S. mikanioides*, may benefit from this. All propagate readily from cuttings and seeds and may also be increased by layering.

Succulent senecios are among the easiest desert plants to grow, outdoors in frost-free dry climates or in greenhouses and sunny windows. Those with trailing stems may be displayed to advantage in hanging baskets. All rejoice in gritty, porous, well-drained soil, and most, particularly *S. scaposus*, benefit if some chips of limestone, crushed oyster or clam shells, or other source of lime is included in the mix. Indoor winter night temperatures of 45 to 50°F are appropriate, with a daytime increase of five to ten degrees permitted. Exposure to full sun and free circulation of air are musts. Soil that remains wet for long periods and excessively humid atmospheres are highly detrimental and result in rotting. From spring through fall, water these plants moderately, allowing the soil to become appreciably but not completely dry between soakings. In winter be rather more cautious, water only when the soil is approaching a really arid condition. Propagation of these succulents can be achieved by sowing seed, but because nearly all produce branches, offsets, or other vegetative parts that can be used as starts for new individuals, division and cuttings are the more usual methods employed.

SENNA. See Cassia. For bladder-senna see Colutea. Scorpion-senna is *Coronilla emerus*.

SENSITIVE-BRIER is *Schrankia nuttallii*.

SENSITIVE FERN is *Onoclea sensibilis*.

SENSITIVE PLANT is *Mimosa pudica*.

SEPAL. A division of the calyx or outer set of the parts of a flower, usually green or greenish and more or less leafy, but sometimes colored and petal-like, is called a sepal.

SEPTEMBER, GARDENING REMINDERS FOR. In most parts of North America, September ushers in a period of great activity in gardens. As less time is needed to keep abreast of such predominently summer chores as weed and pest control, staking, watering, lawn mowing, and the like, other pressures increase, notably those to do with harvesting, planting, transplanting, and preparing for winter. From now until the ground freezes deeply enough to end most outdoor gardening activities, and this, except in the more salubrious parts of the continent, eventually happens, gardeners can be busy indeed, especially if they have planned new construction or landscape plantings.

Fall, because it lingers longer than spring and because the ground then is drier, more easily worked, and more conducive to root growth, is the ideal time to install new gardens, renovate old ones, and make new plantings of many sorts. The beginning of September is not too early to start. In the weeks that follow, tremendous accomplishment can be achieved at a more leisurely pace than is possible in spring, and in the main, in more pleasant weather. Many tasks discussed in the Encyclopedia entries August, Gardening Reminders For, and October, Gardening Reminders For can be done as effectively now as a little earlier or somewhat later; therefore, as an extra reminder, read those entries in conjunction with this.

In the north, do not delay planting hardy evergreen trees and shrubs. Take care not to break their root balls and to water them

September is appropriate for planting evergreen trees and shrubs

very thoroughly as soon as they are installed. Mulch the soil about them with compost, peat moss, rotted manure, or other material that will conserve ground moisture and delay deep freezing. In general, it is better to postpone transplanting deciduous trees and shrubs until their natural leaf fall is fairly well advanced, which in many parts of the north will not be until October.

Making new lawns by sowing seed or laying sod can be done with greatest advantage in the first half of September, and then old lawns that lack vigor can often be greatly improved by top dressing them

Make new lawns in September by:
(a) Sowing seeds

(b) Or laying sod

Old lawns can be greatly improved by top dressing them in September

with about 1 inch of sandy soil made nutritious by the addition of screened compost or humus and a slow-acting lawn fertilizer. Mow the lawn closely before spreading and raking in the top dressing, then over-sow lightly with a suitable grass

seed mixture and rake that into the surface.

If you plan a new bed for perennials begin preparing the soil as early as convenient. For the best results choose a sunny, well-drained site and spade or rotary till the soil to a depth of at least 8 inches. Incorporate a liberal amount of compost, rotted manure, or peat moss, and a dressing of bonemeal or other slow-acting fertilizer. If the soil is too acid, add ground limestone or lime. If you intend to purchase perennials for planting this fall, place orders now for delivery late this month or early next. Also, if you have not already done so, place orders for bulbs to be set out this fall. Should they arrive before planting time, open the packages and store them in a cool, dry, airy place.

If rainfall is deficient, be sure to water evergreens, especially rhododendrons and others known to abhor dryness, at intervals of ten days to two weeks. Soak the ground to a depth of at least 1½ feet. Such attention is especially important for newly transplanted specimens. Watering, probably at more frequent intervals, will also be needed by chrysanthemums, dahlias, Michaelmas-daisies (perennial asters), and Japanese anemones in dry autumns, but unless the soil becomes extraordinarily dry refrain from watering roses and other deciduous shrubs. As preparation for winter it is better that their wood ripens under rather dry conditions.

Before they are exposed to too hard freezing, dig and prepare for winter storage such bulb and tuber plants as caladiums, cannas, dahlias, elephant's ears, gladioluses, tuberoses, and tuberous begonias. Also before frost, bring indoors abutilons, fuchsias, geraniums, heliotropes, lantanas, and other nonhardy ornamental shrubs that have been used for outdoor summer display and are to be kept for propagating next year's display.

Dahlias are among the several nonhardy bulb plants to dig up now for winter storage before severe freezing

In greenhouses, September is, in measure, a second spring. At least this is true of cool greenhouses devoted to the cultivation of many sorts of flowering plants. Now is the time to sow a wide range of annuals to flower in late winter and spring and to pot or repot many sorts of bulb plants and some others that grow throughout the winter. In contrast to spring, and sadly, the shortening days of less brilliant sun of fall are less favorable to sturdy growth; therefore make sure plants in these categories enjoy maximum exposure. See, too, that adequate air circulation is maintained by ventilating the greenhouse freely on all favorable occasions, and that temperatures, especially at night, are maintained at levels most favorable to the plants being grown. Too high levels can do much harm to cool-greenhouse plants. Avoid excessive humidity. To this end, so far as practicable, attend to watering early in the day. Avoid wetting foliage when it is likely to remain wet for more than an hour, and leave the ventilators of cool greenhouses open at least a little at night whenever outside conditions permit.

If these strictures are not followed, seedlings will be weak, lanky, and much subject to damping-off diseases, bulb plants such as freesias will make spindly growth unlikely to be productive of good flowers later, and chrysanthemums and some other greenhouse occupants are likely to become mildewed.

Tropical greenhouses sheltering foliage and flowering plants that require winter night temperatures of 60 to 70°F are now less demanding of exactitude in their management than cool greenhouses containing such one-season crop plants as cinerarias, cyclamens, primulas, and the annuals and bulb plants referred to in the last paragraphs. Maintenance of adequate temperatures is important, and excessive watering is especially to be avoided, as is wetting foliage unless it will surely dry well before nightfall.

Pot freesias and such delightful relatives of theirs as babianas, ixias, sparaxises, and tritonias, as well as calla-lilies, ferrarias, lachenalias, nerines, and some sorts of ornithogalums and oxalises. Because this month they must be grown as cool as possible short of being exposed to frost, a cold frame affords adequate protection during their early stages.

Encourage summer-growing bulb plants, such as achimenes, caladiums, gloriosas, gloxinias, hippeastrums (amaryllises), and tuberous begonias, that show little signs of beginning to die back in preparation for their season of winter rest to do so by increasing intervals between waterings and finally withholding water entirely.

Repot plants that, because they are expected to continue growing through the winter, are deemed in need of this atten-

Bulb plants to pot now for winter and spring bloom in greenhouses include:
(a) Freesias

(b) Babianas

(c) Lachenalias

tion, but exercise good judgment about this and be cautious not to use containers bigger than the roots can reasonably be expected to fill within two or three months.

Annuals to sow in September include sorts delightful as pot plants and many admirable as cut flowers. Among the wide range of kinds are annual chrysanthemums, calendulas, clarkias, gaillardias, hunnemannias, larkspurs, linarias, lupines, nasturtiums, nemesias, nicotianas,

Phlox drummondii, snapdragons, stocks, sweet peas, tithonias, ursineas, venidiums, and zinnias.

Cold frames afford the opportunity to overwinter plants that are on the borderline of hardiness and provide temporary protection to hardy and nearly hardy sorts later to be taken into a greenhouse. Among the latter are such biennials as Canterbury bells, foxgloves, polyanthus primroses, and wallflowers and such perennials as astilbes, bleeding hearts, variegated-leaved hostas, and lily-of-the-valleys. These, carefully dug to preserve as many roots as possible, potted in containers just big enough to hold them comfortably, sunk to the rims of their containers in peat moss, sawdust, sand, or similar loose material in a cold frame, watered, and shaded from strong sun for two or three weeks, soon establish themselves and become fine specimens for bringing into a cool greenhouse from January on for forcing.

The essential care of cold frames at this time involves ventilating them as freely as possible both day and night so that such occupants as Canterbury bells, English daisies, forget-me-nots, foxgloves, sweet williams, and wallflowers that will remain in them through much or all of the winter, and late crops of lamb's lettuce, lettuce, and spinach, depended upon to give harvests even after killing frost, become hardened to the more testing weather to come, and others, babianas, freesias, and ixias, perhaps, that before really severe weather comes will be transferred to a cool greenhouse, will be encouraged to make sturdy growth.

Ventilate cold frames on all favorable occasions

Houseplant care calls for a complete review of those you have and very possibly discarding or otherwise parting with specimens that have become somewhat unsightly or are too big to accommodate without serious overcrowding. Cuttings of many kinds root readily now, and it may be better to propagate oversized or straggly specimens of begonias, geraniums, and many others and winter young plants rather than to maintain the old.

Inspect your holdings carefully. If a little judicious trimming or staking is needed, attend to it. Take off any dead, dying, or seriously diseased leaves and should aphids, mealybugs, red spider mites, or whiteflies be present, take active measures to eliminate them by spraying or sponging them with an insecticide.

Bring in fairly early plants that have summered outdoors. They accommodate to the change of environment better if the transfer is made before much artificial heat is employed to warm the rooms they occupy. Possibly some specimens will benefit from repotting, but do not do this unless you are reasonably sure that they will, and at most give them a small move, into a pot, say, not bigger by 1 inch all around than the one they now occupy.

If you have available a cool (45 to 50°F at night, five to ten degrees higher by day) sunroom or similar well-lighted accommodation, dig from the garden and pot smallish plants of ageratums, calendulas, dwarf marigolds, nasturtiums, and petunias. Keep them shaded and lightly sprayed with water two or three times a day until they have recovered from the shock to their roots, then expose to full sun. They will bloom in winter and early spring. Abutilons, begonias, fuchsias, geraniums, heliotropes, and lantanas if cut back about halfway and treated similarly are also responsive.

In the south, fertilize chrysanthemums and dahlias, and if the weather is dry, water them. Disbud varieties that need this attention. Encourage roses by pruning out weak shoots, cutting very vigorous ones back by about one-quarter of their lengths, picking off any diseased leaves, and fertilizing.

Much planting can be done this month. Set out such biennials as English daisies, forget-me-nots, pansies, and wallflowers. Day-lilies and some other perennials may be divided and planted now, and evergreens, including camellias, hollies, and magnolias, may be planted.

Annuals and plants grown as annuals afford a considerable choice of kinds that will bloom in spring or early summer from seeds sown in September. Those of some sorts, including calendulas, larkspurs, pansies, snapdragons, stocks, and sweet peas, germinate more surely if their seeds are kept in a refrigerator at about 40°F for two or three weeks before sowing.

West Coast gardeners should now busy themselves making ready for seed sowing and planting. In many areas, attention to watering is still of prime importance and will continue to be until the coming of adequate rains. Take care that azaleas and rhododendrons do not suffer from lack of moisture. Clearing beds of summer an-

nuals and replacing them with winter and spring bloomers is proper in many sections now. Consider for this purpose English daisies, forget-me-nots, Iceland poppies, nemesias, pansies, polyanthus primroses, *Primula malacoides*, snapdragons, stocks, and violas. In southern parts it is well to shade these lightly until they recover from the unavoidable root disturbance.

With the coming of rains, or before if these are delayed and adequate watering can be done, planting perennials and evergreens is in order. Also, lawns sown now will have adequate time to become well established before winter.

SEQUINS. See Geissorhiza.

SEQUOIA (Sequò-ia) — Redwood. One magnificent, gigantic species of evergreen tree native to the Pacific Coast of North America is the only sort of *Sequoia*, of the taxodium family TAXODIACEAE. Previously included, the California big-tree or giant-sequoia now constitutes the genus *Sequoiadendron*. The name *Sequoia* commemorates the Indian half-breed Sequoyah, who invented the Cherokee alphabet and who died in 1843.

Fossils from widely separated regions clearly indicate that this species, or an ancestral type not materially different from it, occupied great areas of the earth's surface in the Tertiary period. All that remains is but a remnant of the vast forests of redwoods that luxuriated long before man appeared. Yet that remnant is a vigorous one that regenerates itself and if not destroyed by man is likely to persist for millennia. The closest surviving relative of the redwood is the dawn-redwood (*Metasequoia*), of China, but its foliage is deciduous.

The redwood (**S. sempervirens**), tallest of trees, exceeds its closest rival, giant *Eucalyptus regnans*, of Australia, by only a few feet. The tallest redwood, discovered in 1966 in Redwood Creek Valley, California, is 385 feet from base to summit, the max-

Sequoia sempervirens (foliage)

imum reliably reported height of the eucalyptus is 374 feet.

As a native, the redwood is restricted to a coastal strip never more than 35 miles wide and nearly 500 miles long from California to southern Oregon. Its distribution is not continuous, but occurs in groves, and it never grows away from the influence of fogs that roll in from the sea. The maximum age redwoods attain is estimated to be 2,000 years, but, from a seed one-sixteenth of an inch long that can barely cover the head of a pin, these tallest of living things attain full size much sooner.

As a forest resource, redwood is important. On a per acre basis, dense, mature groves contain more cubic feet of lumber than any other kind of forest. The wood lasts well when exposed to weather and moisture and is greatly esteemed for construction, building, shingles, greenhouse framing and benches, furniture, poles, fence posts, and railroad ties. The bark is used commercially for making roofing paper and other purposes. Burls, large wart-like structures that develop on the trunks of redwoods, if sawn off and placed cut side down in shallow containers of water, develop new shoots and live for many months or even years. They are used for indoor decoration. The redwood is one of the few conifers that sprout readily from the stumps of felled trees. So profusely does this occur that after felling, the forest soon regenerates and the sprouts, in time, attain sizes suitable for lumbering.

In youth, the redwood is a lovely and graceful, rather narrowly-pyramidal tree, that has horizontal or down-sweeping branches and attractive foliage. When it is of great age, its trunk is often bare of branches for a considerable distance and its base is conspicuously buttressed. The bark is reddish-brown, fibrous, spongy, and very thick. Undoubtedly its insulating quality has often been important in preserving old specimens through the many centuries they have lived against the heat of forest fires.

Sequoia sempervirens

The leaves of redwood and their arrangement on the shoots are totally different from those of the giant-sequoia (*Sequoiadendron*). They are of two very distinct types, those of the leading and cone-bearing shoots, about ¼ inch long, are pressed against the shoots or spread slightly, and have a horny, pointed tip that curves inward. The other leaves are narrowly-linear, ¼ to 1 inch long by about ¹⁄₁₀ inch wide, and form two rows on short shoots that look somewhat like those of yew or hemlock. The undersides of the leaves are marked with two whitish bands. Male and female cones are on the same tree, the former in the leaf axils and at the termina-

Cones, the small ones, of *Sequoia sempervirens;* the large cones are those of *Sequoiadendron giganteum*

tions of the shoots, the latter terminal. The fruiting cones have fourteen to twenty scales and are ¾ inch to slightly over 1 inch in length and rather less in width; they mature the first year. Horticultural variety *S. s. adpressa* (syn. *S. s. albospica*) has creamy-white tips to its young shoots, and leaves, up to ³⁄₈ inch long, that resemble those of the cone-producing shoots of the typical species. Although sometimes described as a dwarf, this variety, unless the tall, erect reversionary shoots it develops from time to time are cut out, eventually becomes a tree up to at least 70 feet tall. *S. s. glauca* is distinguished by its bluish leaves. *S. s.* 'Cantab' (syn. *S. s. prostrata*) is sometimes misidentified as *S. s. nana-*

Sequoia sempervirens 'Cantab'

pendula, which name correctly belongs to another variety, perhaps no longer in cultivation. *S. s.* 'Cantab' originated as a "sport" (bud mutation) on a tree in Cambridge Botanical Garden, England. Characteristically prostrate or semiprostrate, on occasion it develops tall, erect shoots that suggest that, with age, it may attain the dimensions of a tree; this variety has, in two distinct ranks, comparatively wide, glaucous leaves up to a little over ½ inch long and ¼ inch wide.

Garden and Landscape Uses. The redwood, much tenderer than the giant-sequoia or California big-tree, is suitable for planting only in regions of mild winters. As a cultivated specimen it rarely exceeds 60 to 100 feet in height, at least not within two or three generations of man, and because it responds well to pruning, it can be kept much lower, and can, in fact, be grown as a tall shrub. When left unpruned it is slender and pyramidal and excellent for establishing in groups and groves as well as for use as a single specimen. Its foliage is a good foil for other plants. Because it stands considerable shade the redwood is excellent for interspersing in open woodlands, especially those of a deciduous character that need the enlivenment of evergreens for winter effect. It is also satisfactory in full sun. For the best results this species needs deep, fertile soil, with the water table within reach of its deepest roots, and a humid atmosphere. It requires shelter from strong winds especially those from the ocean.

One other use of the redwood deserves mention. It is very attractive for growing in large tubs or other containers as a decorative foliage plant for use on terraces and suchlike places and for the ornament of large greenhouses and conservatories.

Cultivation. In suitably mild climates, there is no special difficulty in growing the redwood. If care is taken, it transplants fairly easily, although the best results are usually had by setting out comparatively young specimens than those approaching the maximum sizes that can be handled. Small ones set out in well-prepared soil and kept well-watered in dry weather make quite rapid growth. No pruning is ordinarily needed, but any necessary to restrain growth may be done at any season, but preferably just before new growth begins in spring. If the main trunk is cut back the tree soon develops new growths from near the base, and if branches are shortened or removed, the spaces opened are soon filled with new shoots and foliage. Benefit is had from the soil around the trees being kept under a permanent mulch of compost, peat moss, or some similar material.

When grown in containers, the redwood needs a porous, fertile soil kept always evenly moist and, indoors, a minimum winter temperature of 40 to 50°F, with a few degrees rise during the day. Water

well-rooted specimens with dilute liquid fertilizer about once a week from spring to fall.

Propagation of the typical species is best accomplished by seeds sown in sandy peaty soil in a protected bed outdoors or in a cold frame, or in well-drained containers in a cool greenhouse. The percentage that germinate is often rather low. During their early life the seedlings benefit from light shade from strong sun. Horticultural varieties may be multiplied by veneer grafting onto seedling understocks in winter in a greenhouse. It is possible, however, to increase all kinds by cuttings taken in summer and planted under mist or in a propagating bed in a very humid greenhouse or cold frame.

Diseases and Pests. Redwoods are sometimes affected with canker, for which there is no satisfactory control, and leaf blight, for which spraying with a copper fungicide is recommended. For additional information see the entry Conifers in this Encyclopedia.

SEQUOIADENDRON (Sequoia-déndron)—Giant-Sequoia, California Big-tree. From the redwood (*Sequoia*) the only species of *Sequoiadendron*, of the taxodium family TAXODIACEAE, differs most obviously in the arrangement of its leaves, which are all of one type and radiate all around the shoots, never in two distinct rows. Its name is that of the redwood, *Sequoia*, with as a suffix the Greek *dendron*, a tree. It refers to the close relationship between these two genera of conifers. Although now restricted as a native to an area about 280 miles long and less than twenty miles wide in California on the western slopes of the Sierra Nevada, at elevations of 5,000 to 8,400 feet, the giant-sequoia or closely similar prototypes ranged far more widely in ancient geological times. Specimens from cretaceous deposits in the Isle of Wight, off the southern coast of England, from Greenland, and elsewhere are proof of this.

The giant-sequoia or California big-tree (*S. giganteum* syn. *Sequoia gigantea*), although the most massive of trees, is not the tallest nor does it attain the greatest girth of trunk. The first distinction belongs to the redwood (*Sequoia sempervirens*), and both the Montezuma-cypress (*Taxodium mucronatum*) and the baobab (*Adansonia digitata*) are more obese. At its tallest, the giant-sequoia is about 325 feet in height and has a trunk diameter, measured above its flaring base, of about 25 feet. Measurements made closer to the ground, which are sometimes given, are considerably greater, but are really misleading as comparisons with other trees.

The maximum age attained by this species is in some doubt, but it seems probable that the sometimes quoted estimate of 4,000 years is too high. Most likely 2,500 or possibly 3,000 years is more realistic. Even this represents a very respectable age

Native stand of *Sequoiadendron giganteum* in Sequoia National Park

Trunk of a huge *Sequoiadendron giganteum* in Sequoia National Park

A multitrunked specimen of *Sequoiadendron giganteum*, the National Botanic Gardens, Glasnevin, Ireland

Sequoiadendron giganteum (foliage)

Sequoiadendron giganteum, the Royal Gardens, Brussels, Belgium

for an organism to live and function and partly because of this the giant-sequoias of California are rightly regarded as marvels of the natural world. The responsibility for preserving these unique trees for the delight and education of future generations has been met in part by incorporating some of the few dozen scattered groves that still exist in national parks. Some of the most outstanding specimens have been given individual names, such as the General Sherman and the General Grant.

The history of the naming of this famous conifer is of interest. Its discovery in 1841 aroused considerable excitement among botanists and horticulturists throughout the world. In 1853, seeds were sent to England and there the botanist Lindley described and named the new tree *Wellingtonia* (a name still often used for it, although quite wrongly, in Great Britain) in honor of the Duke of Wellington, commander of the British forces at Waterloo. Appalled that such a noble and exclusively American tree should be named after a foreigner, the American botanist Winslow the following year renamed it *Washingtonia* as a tribute to the first president of the United States.

When, with the passing years, more orderly procedures for naming plants were devised and the botanists' rule of priority became effective, it was discovered that an even earlier name than *Washingtonia* or *Wellingtonia* had been applied and the correct name of the tree became *Sequoia gigantea* for it was then regarded as belonging in the same genus as the redwood (*Sequoia sempervirens*). After further study, it was decided that the giant-sequoia was sufficiently distinct from the redwood to warrant segregating it as a separate genus and in 1939 it was given its present name of *Sequoiadendron giganteum*. The name of George Washington is honored by another genus named *Washingtonia*, a group of palms of the palm family PALMAE, but no valid genus of higher plants has been named to commemorate the Duke of Wellington.

The giant-sequoia as a young tree and through its long youth is uniformly pyramidal and clothed with branches and foliage to the ground, but as it ages it develops a more rounded, irregular crown, and old specimens may have clear trunks up to a height of 150 feet or more. The horizontal or somewhat pendulous branches do not spread widely, so the tree is comparatively narrow. On old specimens the deeply-furrowed, spongy bark is 1 foot to 2 feet thick and provides good protection from damage by fire. This, doubtless, is in part responsible for the preservation of individual trees over the many centuries. The sharp-pointed leaves, ovate to awl-shaped, and up to ½ inch or slightly more long, adhere to the shoots for more than one-half their length, so that only their ends are free and spreading. The fruiting cones, 2 to 3½ inches long by 1½ to 2 inches wide, mature in their second year. They have twenty-five to forty scales. Varieties are *S. g. argenteum*, with silver-variegated shoots and leaves; *S. g. aureum*, with yellow shoots and leaves; *S. g. glaucum*, with bluish-glaucous shoots and leaves; *S. g. pendulum*, with markedly drooping branches; and *S. g. pygmaeum*, a dwarf, bushy sort.

Garden and Landscape Uses. Young examples of this tree are of stately aspect and add quality to the landscape they adorn. Because of its comparatively narrow top, the giant-sequoia does not take up a great deal of room and so can serve well to line avenues and to provide accents. It is sufficiently formal in outline to associate well with buildings and other architectural features, and is admirable as a park tree and for use in larger landscape developments where it can be displayed singly or in groups. In favorable locations it grows throughout its early years more quickly than might be expected. Although much hardier than the redwood, the giant-sequoia cannot generally be relied upon to survive in the east much north of Washington, D.C., even though a few specimens grow on Long Island and elsewhere near New York City. A fine, 70-foot tree

exists at Bristol, Connecticut, and until the exceptional winter of 1933–34 killed it, a 60-foot tree prospered at Ithaca, New York. It seems probable that the occasional trees that have survived so far north are exceptionally resistant to cold, possibly because they are seedlings of trees growing naturally under the harshest conditions under which native specimens are found. To secure trees for the northeast, it would seem sensible to do everything possible to acquire seeds from the northernmost limit and from the highest elevations of the natural occurrence of the species.

Deep, well-drained, fertile soil best suits this conifer. Full sun is needed, and in places where the hardiness of the tree is at all suspect, shelter from strong wind, especially in the winter, is highly desirable. This can be afforded by a protective belt or border of other evergreens such as pines or arbor-vitaes.

Cultivation. Giant-sequoias can be transplanted with relative ease and certainty of success even when comparatively big. They need no regular pruning or special care. Mulching the soil about them with an organic mulch, such as compost or peat moss, is good practice, and in dry weather, periodic soakings of the soil with water are very helpful. Unlike the redwood, the giant-sequoia does not regenerate itself from stumps of cut trees. Propagation of the species is best accomplished by seeds sown in sandy, peaty soil. Varieties are veneer-grafted onto seedling understocks. The giant-redwood is remarkably free of diseases and pests. For further information see Conifers.

SERAPIRHIZA. This is the name of orchid hybrids the parents of which are *Dactylorhiza* and *Serapias*.

SERENOA (Serenò-a) — Saw Palmetto or Scrub Palmetto. The only species of *Serenoa* is native to the southeastern United States. There it is common throughout great areas of pine lands and scrub lands in the coastal plain from South Carolina to the Florida Keys, Mississippi, and Louisiana. A fan-leaved palm of the palm family PALMAE, its name honors Sereno Watson, American botanist, who died in 1892.

The saw palmetto (*S. repens*) is variable. It has a creeping, often branched, erect or leaning trunk or stem up to a few feet tall, and deeply-pleated, approximately circular, grayish-green to silvery-gray leaves 2 to 2½ feet across. They are without midribs, and are cleft to beyond their middles into twenty or more rigid segments. Their stalks are slender and sharply-toothed. The fragrant flowers, in axillary, much-branched clusters borne in summer, are succeeded by purple-black fruits ½ to 1 inch long.

Gardens and Landscape Uses. Although rarely planted, groups of saw pal-

metto that occur natively are sometimes left about homes and other buildings as landscape ornamentals, in which role they are often very attractive. Comparatively hardy, this palm withstands temperatures as low as 10°F. Specimens are sometimes grown in pots, especially by northerners, who take plants home from the south. Under such conditions the saw palmetto thrives, but grows slowly. It is considered to be difficult to transplant from the wild.

Cultivation. The saw palmetto prospers in any ordinary well-drained soil in sun or part-shade. When grown indoors in containers, it needs a moderately humid atmosphere and a minimum temperature of 55 to 65°F. It should be watered sufficiently often to keep the soil moderately moist, but not constantly saturated. Specimens that have filled their pots with healthy roots benefit from dilute liquid fertilizer once or twice a month from spring through fall. Propagation is easy by fresh seeds sown in sandy, peaty soil in a temperature of 75 to 80°F. For additional information see Palms.

SERIANIA. See Serjania.

SERISSA (Serís-sa). The eastern Asian genus *Serissa*, of the madder family RUBIACEAE, consists of three or fewer species of nonhardy, evergreen shrubs. Its name is derived from a native one of India.

Serissas have small, opposite, short-stalked or nearly stalkless leaves and little, solitary or clustered flowers in the leaf axils or at the ends of the branches. The blooms have tubular calyxes with four to six lobes, and funnel-shaped corollas, hairy on their insides, with four to six three-lobed lobes (petals). There are four to six stamens and a shorter style ending in a two-lobed stigma. The fruits are small roundish drupes (fruits similar in structure to plums).

Commonly cultivated in greenhouses, as a window plant, and in warm, essentially frost-free regions outdoors, *S. foetida* (syn. *S. japonica*), a native of southeast Asia, is a neat, stiff-branched shrub about 2 feet in height and commonly broader than tall. Its leathery, pointed-ovate leaves are ¼ to ½ inch long. Pink in bud, the pretty little blooms, up to nearly ½ inch in length and solitary or clustered, open pure white. They make a nice display. In *S. f. variegata* the leaves have narrow creamy-yellow margins. A green-leaved variety with double flowers is cultivated.

Garden and Landscape Uses and Cultivation. Outdoors serissas are useful for beds, rock gardens, and edgings and for facing down foundation plantings and other shrubbery. They are satisfied with ordinary, moderately fertile, well-drained soil that never becomes excessively dry, and succeed in sun or part-day shade. As pot plants in greenhouses and window

Serissa foetida variegata

gardens they give satisfaction with minimum care. Winter temperatures of about 50°F at night, with a daytime increase of five to fifteen degrees, are satisfactory. The atmosphere should be moderately humid, and light shade from summer sun provided. Watering is done to keep the soil always moderately moist. Potbound specimens benefit from judicious applications of dilute liquid fertilizer. Cuttings, which root readily, are the most convenient means of propagation.

SERJANIA (Ser-jània). Confined in the wild to warm parts of the Americas, *Serjania* is a genus of more than 200 species of woody vines that climb by twining or by tendrils that coil like watch springs. It belongs in the soapberry family SAPINDACEAE. Its name, honoring the French friar and botanist Philippe Serjeant, who died in the seventeenth century, has also been spelled *Seriania*.

Serjanias have alternate, usually twice- or thrice-, but sometimes only once-pinnate leaves, often with translucent dots. The tiny, asymmetrical flowers are in terminal and axillary racemes or panicles, each often with two tendrils. Unisexual and bisexual blooms are on the same plant. They have two to five, usually five, sepals, four petals, and eight stamens. The three-winged fruits are technically samaras.

Because of their high saponin content, many species of *Serjania* are poisonous and are used to poison fish and as arrow poisons. The stems of some kinds are made into string, rope, and baskets in lands where they are native.

With leaves twice- or thrice-divided into ovate to ovate-lanceolate, coarsely-toothed leaflets that have reddish hairs on their undersides, *S. fuscifolia* is a native of Brazil. Up to 30 feet tall, it has ribbed and downy branches. Its white flowers are in panicles up to 1 foot long. The wings of the fruits are ½ to ¾ inch in length and broader than long. From 10 to 30 feet tall, *S. glabrata*, widely dispersed in South

America, has, except for its youngest branches, hairless stems. Also hairless, its twice-pinnate leaves have broad, coarsely-toothed to nearly toothless leaflets up to 5 inches long by 3 inches wide. The white or pale yellow flowers are in slender-branched panicles. The fruits, ¾ to 1 inch long, have yellowish-green wings. This is native to Cuba.

Serjania glabrata

Mountain supple jack (*S. exarta*), a shrubby vine of northern South America, has leaves with hairy, ovate leaflets, up to 3 inches in length, and panicles of fragrant, white flowers. Its seeds are red. Another kind worth cultivating is dainty-foliaged *S. filicifolia*, of Hispaniola. A slender vine 6 to 12 feet tall, this has minutely-divided, fernlike foliage and white flowers. It attains a height of 6 to 12 feet.

Garden and Landscape Uses and Cultivation. These vigorous vines are cultivated outdoors, in the tropics and subtropics, and in conservatories and greenhouses. They grow with little difficulty and are useful for embellishing fences, arbors, pergolas, pillars, and other supports. In greenhouses they need a humid atmosphere, a minimum winter night temperature of 55 to 60°F, with daytime temperatures five to fifteen degrees higher. Fertile, well-drained soil kept moderately moist is to their liking. Propagation is by cuttings and by seed.

SERPENT GOURD is *Trichosanthes anguina*.

SERPENT MELON is *Cucumis melo flexuosus*.

SERRATULA (Ser-rátula). In allusion to the toothed leaves, the name of this genus, of the daisy family COMPOSITAE, is derived from the Latin *serrula*, a little saw. Related to *Centaurea*, from which it differs in the long hairs (pappus) that accompany the flowers and fruits, *Serratula* inhabits Europe, North Africa, and temperate Asia. Its members are herbaceous perennials. There are seventy species.

Serratulas have usually undivided, lobeless basal leaves and alternate, pinnately-lobed stem leaves. Their white, pink, or purple, thistle-lilac flower heads are solitary or in clusters. The bracts that form the collars (involucres) at the bases of the heads are numerous and overlapping. Each head consists of many little tubular florets with five narrow lobes. There are no petal-like ray florets. The seedlike fruits have a pappus of several rows of hairs.

Native to Europe, and 9 inches to about 1½ feet tall, *S. nudicaulis* is branched or not and has hairless, grayish-green stems and foliage. The lower leaves are ovate-lanceolate and not lobed, those above are toothed. The flower heads are purple. A quite pretty dwarf species, long grown in gardens under the untenable name *S. shawii*, is *S. seoanei*, a native of northern Spain and southwest France. A close relative of

Serratula seoanei

very variable *S. tinctoria*, it differs chiefly in its low stature and hairy leaves with narrower segments. It forms tufts of dull green, pinnate or pinnately-lobed basal leaves, about 3½ inches long by ¾ inch broad, with coarsely-bristle-toothed margins. The flower stems, loosely much-branched above, rise to a height of 6 inches to 1 foot and each branch ends in a head of lavender-pink flowers about ½ inch wide.

Garden and Landscape Uses and Cultivation. The last kind described above is a worthy, easy-to-grow sort for rock gardens and similar places. The other may, for the sake of variety, be given a minor place in informal areas. Both are hardy and succeed in well-drained, ordinary soil in full sun. They are increased by division and by seed.

SERRURIA (Ser-rúria) — Blushing Bride. The genus *Serruria*, an endemic of South Africa, belongs to the protea family PROTEACEAE. It consists of about fifty species of erect, or rarely prostrate, evergreen shrubs, and has a name honoring the French botanist Dr. Joseph Serrurier.

Serrurias have alternate leaves, usually finely-dissected into slender, cylindrical segments. Displayed in terminal clusters or panicles, or solitary on stalks from the leaf axils, the flower heads of most kinds have relatively inconspicuous bracts, but those of one of the most popular, the blushing bride, are conspicuous and showy. The individual blooms are hairy and symmetrical and have four perianth segments (petals) separated to or almost to their bases. Each bears a stalkless anther. The style is undivided. The seedlike fruits are achenes.

The blushing bride (**S. florida**), in its native land much admired and 3 to 8 feet

Serruria florida

tall, has hairless stems and foliage. Its leaves, up to 3 inches long, are once- or twice-pinnately-divided into sharp-pointed, slender segments. The flower heads, 2 to 2½ inches wide, are three to six together near the ends of the slender, arching branches. Their conspicuous elements are bracts. Those having flowers in their axils are blush-pink. The outer, sterile bracts are white. This is the loveliest of serrurias. From 4 to 6 feet tall, **S. artemisifolia** has downy shoots. Its leaves, 1 inch to 2 inches long, are twice-pinnately-divided into ultimate segments that are very slender and ¼ to ½ inch long. The pale purple flowers, about ⅓ inch long, are crowded many together in grayish, spherical heads that are 1 inch to 1¼ inches in diameter and terminate downy stalks 1½ to 3 inches long.

Garden and Landscape Uses and Cultivation. Rated difficult to grow, serrurias are perhaps not in cultivation in North America. Their cultural requirements and garden uses are similar to those of *Protea*. South African gardeners report that they respond to a slightly richer soil than most members of the protea family. They rec-

Serruria artemisifolia

ommend that seedlings not be transplanted until they are 4 to 6 inches tall, and advocate pinching out the tip of the stem when it attains a height of 6 or 8 inches and of the side branches when they are as long. Unless seeds are needed for propagation, faded flower heads should be removed promptly. The blushing bride does not normally live for more than eight years.

SERVICE BERRY. See Amelanchier.

SERVICE TREE is *Sorbus domestica*. The wild service tree is *S. torminalis*.

SESAME is *Sesasum indicum.*

SESAMOTHAMNUS (Sesamo-thámnus). This genus, of the pedalium family PEDALIACEAE, consists of half a dozen species, natives of tropical Africa. The name is derived from that of related *Sesamum* and the Greek *thamnos,* a shrub or bush.

The sorts of *Sesamothamnus* are deciduous, spiny shrubs or small trees with trunks generally swollen at their bases. Their usually obovate leaves are mostly clustered in the axils of spines. In racemes of few, the quite large, white, pink, or yellow flowers, often fragrant in the evening, have a usually glandular, five-lobed calyx, a cylindrical, five-lobed, tubular corolla, four stamens in two pairs, one staminode (nonfunctional stamen), and one style with two stigmas. The fruits are capsules.

Rare in cultivation, **S. rivae** (syn. *S. smithii*), of dry regions in tropical Africa, is a shrub or tree up to 20 feet tall, more or less swollen at the base of its trunk and with wandlike branches. The obovate, glandular leaves are ¾ inch to 3 inches long. The white to brownish flowers are 1 inch to 2¾ inches long.

Garden Uses and Cultivation. The species described, attractive for including in collections of succulents, responds to the conditions and care that satisfy a wide selection of such plants. Propagation is by seed.

SESAMUM (Sésam-um) — Sesame. The magic phrase "open sesame" from the Arabian Nights tale of Ali Baba is known to most people long before, if ever, they connect it with a plant. Yet sesame is a plant, and in the Orient and Africa a commercially important one. It is the source of benne oil used for cooking, and medicinally. Seeds of sesame are used, like those of poppy and carraway, to sprinkle on rolls, buns, and cookies; they have a pleasant aromatic flavor. Because of this, the plant that produces them is of interest to herb gardeners. It belongs to a botanical group poorly represented in gardens, the pedalium family PEDALIACEAE, the only other cultivated genus of which appears to be *Cereatotheca*. The PEDALIACEAE has affinity to the SCROPHULARIACEAE and MARTYNIACEAE. The name *sesamum* is one used by Hippocrates.

The genus *Sesamum* contains about twenty species indigenous to tropical and subtropical Africa and eastern Asia. It consists of erect and prostrate, mostly rough-hairy, tender herbaceous plants, with opposite lower leaves and upper ones approximately opposite or alternate. They are lobed, toothed, or smooth-edged, and stalked. Asymmetrical and bisexual, the flowers have bell-shaped, five-lobed, two-lipped corollas and four stamens that do not protrude. The fruits are ovoid or oblong capsules.

Sesame (**S. indicum** syn. *S. orientale*) is a rough-hairy annual, 1 foot to 3 feet tall, with ovate to lanceolate leaves 3 to 5 inches long. Those on the lower parts of the plant are often divided into three leaflets or are three-lobed. The attractive

Sesamothamnus rivae

blooms are pale pink to white and 1 inch long. The upper lip of the corolla is two-lobed and shorter than the three-lobed lower one. The four-angled, shortly beaked fruits are about 1 inch long and one-third as wide; they contain numerous small seeds. Sesame is a native of the Old World tropics.

Sesamum indicum

Other species sometimes cultivated are *S. alatum* and *S. capense*. These differ from sesame in having winged seeds. From tropical Africa, *S. alatum* is erect, about 3 feet in height, and branched. Its short-stalked leaves are divided in handlike fashion into three to five linear-lanceolate, toothless leaflets or lobes up to 3 inches long. On their undersides they are glandular-mealy. The 1-inch-long blooms are pink to carmine with dark-spotted throats. The finely-pubescent fruits are 1 inch to 1½ inches long. Native to South Africa and tropical Africa, *S. capense,* up to 6 feet tall, has leaves of three to five linear leaflets, 2 to 2½ inches long, that spread like the fingers of a hand. They are without teeth and are glandular on both surfaces. About 1½ inches long, the flowers are violet on their outsides and darker inside. The fruits are 1¾ inches in length.

Garden and Landscape Uses. Sesame is a natural for herb gardens. It and the other species described here are also acceptable decoratives for flower gardens. They are grown as annuals in sunny locations in moderately fertile, well-drained soil. They bloom freely from midsummer on. Their flowers have no value for cutting.

Cultivation. In the south, seeds may be sown directly outdoors, but because the plants need a rather long growing season, in the north, it is better to start them early indoors and set out young plants at about the same time as tomatoes, when the weather is warm and settled. This is espe-cially necessary when sesame is cultivated for its seeds. Indoors, seeds may be sown about ten weeks before the plants are to be transferred outside. A temperature of 70 to 75°F is suitable for germination. The seedlings are transplanted individually to small pots and grown until almost plant-ing out time in a sunny greenhouse at the same temperature. When the small pots become filled with roots, the plants may be repotted into others 4 or 5 inches in di-ameter. For a week or two before they are set in the garden, they are hardened by gradually accustoming them to outdoor conditions. Outdoor sowings are made in spring, as soon as the ground has warmed and the weather is settled to a promise of summer. Sesame plants may be spaced 1 foot apart and that distance, too, is satis-factory for *S. alatum*. For *S. capense* a plant-ing distance of 1½ feet is preferable. Rou-tine care is minimal. Staking may be needed for *S. capense*, but the others usually stand without support. The harvesting of se-same seeds is done after the pods ripen, but before they scatter their contents. They are thoroughly dried, freed of all particles of pod and other extraneous materials, and stored in jars, canisters, or other suitable containers. For culinary purposes they keep indefinitely.

SESBANIA (Ses-bània). Here are included seventy species of the pea family LEGUMI-NOSAE. They are small trees, shrubs, her-baceous perennials, and annuals of the tropics and subtropics of the eastern and western hemispheres. Their name is a modification of the Arabian one, *sesban*, of one species. Plants previously segregated as the genera *Agati* and *Daubentonia* be-long here.

Sesbanias have alternate leaves with many pinnately-arranged pairs of tooth-less, often glaucous leaflets, but no termi-nal one. The pea-like flowers, in loose ra-cemes from the leaf axils, are yellow, purple, white, or variegated. They have calyxes with broad, lobed or toothed tubes, a broad-ovate to nearly round, spreading or reflexed banner or standard petal, somewhat sickle-shaped wings, and an in-curved keel. There are ten stamens, of which nine are united and one is free. The fruits are usually linear and subcylindrical, less commonly flattened, four-angled or four-winged pods.

An evergreen tree, 30 to 40 feet tall, with slender, ascending branches, **Sesbania grandiflora** (syn. *Agati grandiflora*), a na-tive of tropical Asia, is naturalized in southern Florida and the West Indies. Its feathery leaves, up to 1 foot long, have ten to thirty pairs of toothless, linear-oblong leaflets 1 inch to 2 inches in length. In short racemes of two to four are borne the flat-tened, pea-shaped, red, rusty-red, or white blooms. They are 2½ to 4 inches in length and have wing petals longer than the standard or banner one. Their calyxes are ¾ inch long. The fruits are nearly straight, slender, pendulous pods, 1 foot or more long, thickened at their edges, and parti-tioned between their many seeds. There are double- as well as single-flowered forms of this species. In Asia, the flowers are eaten as a vegetable.

Naturalized from Florida to Mississippi, and native to South America, *S. punicea* (syn. *Daubentonia punicea*) is a shrub up to about 6 feet tall, or sometimes a small tree. Its leaves have six to twenty pairs of ob-long leaflets ½ to 1 inch long. The blooms are red-purple, ¾ inch long, and in ra-cemes about 4 inches long. They are suc-ceeded by 3- to 4-inch-long, four-winged, reddish-brown pods.

A shrub 6 feet tall or sometimes a small tree, *S. tripetii* (syn. *Daubentonia tripetii*), of Argentina, has dull green leaves, some-what glaucous beneath, and pendulous racemes of orange-red blooms each with a scarlet standard or banner petal, paler on its inner surface and with a yellow spot at the bottom.

Annual *S. exaltata,* in warm regions used to some extent as a green manure crop, is a native of the southern United States and Mexico. From 3 to 12 feet tall, it has hairless stems and foliage. The leaves have from twenty to seventy nar-row, 1-inch-long leaflets. The yellow blooms, in racemes up to 3 inches in length, are succeeded by seed pods up to 8 inches long.

Garden and Landscape Uses and Culti-vation. In well-drained soil of ordinary quality *S. grandiflora* thrives and grows rapidly. It blooms as early as two years from seeds, which afford the most practi-cal means of propagation. Sunny locations and warm climates that are frost-free or essentially so are to its liking. This is very well worth growing as a garden and land-scape ornamental, but is notoriously short-lived. Because of this, young specimens for replacement should be raised from time to time. The shrub species described above are also reported to be rather short-lived. They are useful for general purpose plant-ing in the deep south and other warm-cli-mate regions, and grow satisfactorily in well-drained soil in full sun without spe-cial care. They are propagated by seed and by cuttings. Any pruning needed to re-strict or shape them may be done when blooming is through.

SET. As a verb, set means to plant. As a noun it refers to small bulbs, tubers, and sometimes other plant parts used for propagation. For instance, onion sets are little onion bulbs raised from seeds to be stored over winter and planted the follow-ing spring. Another employment of the word refers to the production of young seeds or other fruits, as in a "poor set of plums" or a "good set of seeds."

SETARIA (Set-ària) — Foxtail-Millet, Palm Grass. Of the approximately 100 species of *Setaria*, a few are cultivated as ornamentals and the foxtail- or Italian-millet for grain and forage. The name, from the Latin *seta*, a bristle, directs attention to the prominent bristles of the flower panicles. The group belongs in the grass family GRAMINEAE and inhabits warm regions.

Setarias include annuals and perennials of diverse appearance. Their linear to elliptic or ovate leaf blades are in some species pleated longitudinally. Their flower panicles are fairly open, or spikelike and crowded, and have accompanying the small spikelets prominent bristles that remain on the stalks after the spikelets fall. The spikelets are not awned (bristle-tipped). Each contains one male or one sterile flower, and one bisexual one. Some species are lawn weeds in the tropics.

Palm grass (*S. palmifolia* syn. *Panicum palmifolium*), a native of tropical Asia and

Setaria palmifolia

naturalized in Hawaii, is a perennial with stout stems up to 5 or sometimes 10 feet tall. Its leaf blades, 1 foot to 3 feet long by 3 to 5 inches wide, are strongly accordion-pleated lengthways and taper to both ends. They are hairy to nearly hairless. The loose panicles of bloom, up to 3 feet long by 1 foot broad, have spreading or drooping branches, and small spikelets, some of the upper ones attended by solitary bristles.

Very like the last, *S. plicatilis* has slenderer stems and smaller leaves and is 3 to 5 feet tall. This is sometimes misnamed *Panicum plicatum*, which is a synonym of *S. plicata*, a species probably not in cultivation. Other similar tall setarias with broad, pleated, leaf blades of palmlike appearance that may be cultivated are *S. poiretiana* and *S. paniculifera* (syn. *Panicum sulcatum*), of tropical America.

Garden and Landscape Uses and Cultivation. Palm grass and its ornamental relatives are noble adornments for gardens in the tropics and subtropics, and for greenhouses and conservatories. They are

displayed to fine advantage in bold clumps in the open, and in beds, pots, or tubs indoors. They are especially effective in association with bamboos and palms. They thrive in full sun or with a little part-day shade, and need fertile, reasonably moist soil. In greenhouses they succeed where the winter night temperature is 55°F or higher, with a rise of a few degrees during the day. Foxtail-millet, an annual about 5 feet tall, is sometimes included in educational displays of plants useful to man. It is raised from seeds sown outdoors in spring where the plants are to remain.

SETCREASEA (Set-crèasea). Horticultural interest in *Setcreasea*, a genus of nine species of the spiderwort family COMMELINACEAE, was initiated or at least revived by the finding, in the early 1950s, of a specimen in a window box at the Tampico, Mexico, airport. The discoverer, a Puerto Rican nurseryman, propagated and distributed the plant, which later was named *S*. 'Purple Heart' and also became known as *S. tampicana*. In 1955 the newcomer was described and named *S. purpurea*, but later it was redefined as a variety of *S. pallida*. Native to the southern United States and Mexico, *Setcreasea* is by some authorities included in *Tradescantia*, by some it is named *Neotreleasia*. The derivation of its name is unknown.

Setcreaseas are more or less succulent, trailing, clambering, or erect, *Tradescantia*-like plants with thickish roots and fleshy stems. They have alternate, linear to ovate or oblongish, parallel-veined leaves that sheathe the stems with their bases. The white to purple flowers are in terminal or terminal and axillary clusters, each partly enveloped by a pair of leafy bracts. They have three each sepals and petals, six stamens with often hairy stalks, and one style. The fruits are capsules.

Native to dry and semidesert parts of Mexico, *S. pallida* is a trailer or creeper with the young parts of its shoots erect. Its lanceolate to oblongish, fleshy, stalkless leaves, waxy-green to purple, have glaucous undersides. They are 1½ to 2 inches long by up to 1 inch wide. The flowers, in tight clusters at the stem ends, are lavender. Variety *S. p.* 'Purple Heart' has violet-purple leaves and blooms.

Perhaps the most succulent member of the spiderwort family, *S. hirsuta* (syns. *S. hirta, Tradescantia hirta*), a Mexican species, is a low, clump-forming, evergreen perennial with dense- to sparingly-hairy, linear leaves channeled along their upper sides, rounded beneath, and up to 8 inches long by somewhat under ½ inch wide. The bright purplish-pink flowers are 1 inch to 1¼ inches across.

Garden and Landscape Uses and Cultivation. In warm, dryish, frost-free regions, these are admirable plants for permanent display outdoors in rock gardens,

Setcreasea pallida 'Purple Heart'

flower beds, window boxes, and other locations. They are attractive greenhouse plants and are well suited for sunny windows. Essentially trouble-proof, they thrive in coarse, even poorish, soil that is well drained and allows free passage of water. It should be permitted to nearly dry between applications. Indoors, a night temperature in winter of about 55°F, with a daytime rise of five to fifteen degrees, is proper. Full exposure to sun is needed by *S. hirsuta* and *S. pallida* 'Purple Heart', but *S. pallida* will stand light shade in summer. Cuttings root with such facility that they are employed almost exclusively as means of propagation. Seed may be used, but it is reported that those of *S. pallida* 'Purple Heart' produce green-leaved plants.

SETICEREUS (Seti-cèreus). The four species, of the cactus family CACTACEAE, that compose *Seticereus* are by some botanists included in nearly related *Borzicactus*. Native to Ecuador and Peru, this genus has a name derived from the Latin *seta*, a bristle, and *Cereus*, the name of a related genus. It alludes to the bristly hairs.

From upright and bushy to prostrate, seticereuses have stout, cylindrical stems with lumpy ribs decorated with clusters of spines. The flowers, from areoles near the tops of the stems furnished with long, soft bristles, are funnel-shaped. They open by day and have a cylindrical perianth tube that, like the ovary and fruits, is naked except for very few hairs.

Growing in loose clumps or colonies, *S. icosagonus* (syns. *Borzicactus icosagonus, Binghamia icosagona*) has erect to prostrate stems 2 inches or slightly more in diameter, with sixteen to twenty ribs. The spine clusters are of many stiff, bristly, golden-yellow, ¼-inch-long radials and six to eight stouter, horn-yellow centrals, up to ¾ inch long. The scarlet blooms are about 3 inches in length. Variety *S. i. oehmeanus* has light brown spines, the one or two centrals in each group 1½ to 3 inches long. The blooms of *S. i. aurantiaciflorus* are orange-yellow. Closely allied to *S. icosagonus,* but with stems with only ten to twelve ribs and up to 3 feet long, **S. humboldtii** (syns. *Borzicactus humboldtii, Binghamia humboldtii*) has clusters of brownish-red to gray spines sprouting from woolly areoles. Each group consists of about twenty-five ½-inch-long radials and four to seven slightly longer centrals. The light pink to crimson blooms are about 2 inches long.

Garden and Landscape Uses and Cultivation. These are as for *Borzicactus.* For further information see the Encyclopedia entry Cactuses.

SEVEN STARS is *Ariocarpus retusus.*

SEVERINIA (Sever-ínia). Usually regarded as consisting of one species, although some botanists recognize more, *Severinia* belongs in the rue family RUTACEAE. It is closely related to the lime-berry (*Triphasia trifolia*) and is native in southeastern Asia and Taiwan. Its name commemorates an Italian lecturer on anatomy, M. A. Severino, who died in 1656. By some authorities *Severinia* is included in *Atalantia.* Its segregation is based on its fruits, which are black berries with succulent ovary walls.

A very spiny shrub, ordinarily about 6 feet tall, or a small tree, **S. buxifolia,** as its specific epithet suggests, has foliage resembling that of boxwood (*Buxus*). Its short-stalked, alternate, ovate-oblong leaves, rounded or notched at their apexes, evergreen and leathery, are up to 1½ inches long. Few together or solitary in the leaf axils, the small, white, nearly stalkless flowers have five sepals, five petals, and ten stamens. The fruits are shining berries about ⅓ inch in diameter. This species is sometimes misidentified as *Triphasia monophylla.*

Garden and Landscape Uses and Cultivation. The chief landscape value of this species is as a hedge shrub in the deep south and elsewhere in mild climates. It stands shearing well and thrives in ordinary soil in full sun under conditions that suit citruses. Propagation is by seed and by summer cuttings.

SHADBLOW or SHAD BUSH. See Amelanchier.

SHADDOCK. Also known as pomelo, pumelo, pummelo, and pompelous, the grapefruit relative shaddock (*Citrus maxima*) is popular as an edible fruit in some warm parts of eastern Asia, including China. In southern Florida it is sometimes grown as an ornamental and curiosity. Much more tender to cold than the orange, it has fruits sometimes weighing almost twenty pounds. Its soil and requirements and general cultivation needs are similar to those of grapefruits.

SHADE TREES. See Trees.

SHADY GARDENS. Shade can both limit and, if not too dense, afford unique opportunities for gardening. Frequently regarded as a problem, and this it can be if one's objectives are to grow vegetables, roses, and many other sorts of plants, shade makes the cultivation of a wealth of woodlanders, mostly spring-bloomers, as well as ferns and a number of other attractive kinds easier. The most lovely shady gardens are informal, but it is quite possible to design more structured ones. Here we have under consideration not only entire gardens that are shaded, but also shady parts of sunny landscapes.

There are several types of shade, produced by trees or shrubs or by buildings, walls, gully sides, or even large rocks. Shade may persist throughout the year, as under dense or closely spaced evergreens or near north-facing walls, or it may be seasonal, as that cast by deciduous trees or shrubs. Other variables are its daily duration and, of course, its density. All these and other factors need consideration when deciding what to plant.

Dappled shade that results from sun filtering through a canopy of branches of deciduous trees is most agreeable. It allows little patches of bright sunlight to reach and play across the plants below as the sun traverses the sky and as breezes disturb the foliage. In this manner enough light to adequately energize photosynthesis reaches underplantings, but it is not of sufficient overall intensity to harm plants averse to fuller exposure.

Azaleas thrive in dappled shade

This type of shade, which can fairly be designated light to medium shade, or half-shade, may exist or may be achieved by judiciously thinning out woodlands or by removing lower branches from trees to let in more side light.

Full shade provided by a heavier canopy of deciduous trees and so dense that in summer no direct sunlight reaches the ground is more limiting, but by no means hopeless. It usually allows for the growth of a selection of ferns and some other woodland plants satisfied with low light intensities as well as of a variety of choice flowering plants that make most of their growth early in the season before the shade becomes too heavy, and then often die down until the following spring. The majority of such plants in North American gardens are native woodlanders, but a not inconsiderable number hail from Japan and some from Europe.

All-year shade, such as occurs beneath evergreens and on the north sides of buildings, walls, cliffs, and large rocks, severely reduces possibilities among flowering plants. Beneath such evergreens as firs, pines, and spruces further restriction may come from root competition and from the acidifying or other changes in the soil wrought by accumulations of fallen leaves. Year-round shade from buildings, walls, cliffs, and big rocks, because it interferes less with sky light even though no direct sun reaches the plants, allows for success with a greater selection of plants. Still, kinds admired chiefly for their foliage must be the mainstay for areas deprived of sun throughout the year.

Part-day shade is agreeable to many plants. Even roses and many other sun-lovers give pretty good accounts of themselves with five or six hours of direct sun daily and some get along with three or four. A great many sorts actually benefit from protection from middle-of-the-day summer sun, but few locations admit of this and also allow exposure to less intense morning and afternoon sun. The time of day exposure comes may have a bearing on results. This is especially true of evergreens in regions of cold winters. Subjected to morning sun following intensely cold nights, these are much more likely to suffer from scorch or winter burn than are specimens that receive only afternoon sun.

Insufficient light is not always the only or even the most important discouragement to the satisfactory growth of plants in shade. Poor drainage, unsuitable soil, inadequate air circulation, and, commonly, hungry surface roots of such trees as beeches and maples may be more limiting.

For best results it is important to minimize all adverse factors. To this end, before planting take stock of existing conditions and initiate whatever steps are necessary to better them. These, except sometimes in natural woodlands, will almost surely include incorporating with the soil liberal amounts of such organic material as compost, leaf mold, or peat moss and may involve pruning to admit more light.

Overcrowding, planting too closely together, detracts from the appearance of shaded landscapes. This, of course, does not apply to such groundcovers as English ivy, lily-of-the-valley, or pachysandra,

Bearded irises, normally sun-lovers, here flourish in part-day shade

which are intended to hide the earth completely, but with other plants it is likely to result in weak, lanky growth and sparse flowering. Just as plants in deserts are usually rather widely spaced so that each has a generous area to draw upon for moisture, so in woodlands, spacing is optimal when it admits of each individual receiving the most available light without interruption by its neighbors.

Maintenance of plants in shade is not greatly different from that needed in sunny gardens, although emphasis on various phases may vary to some extent. Unless abhorent kinds such as catbriers or poison-ivy become established, weeding is likely to require less attention and so is disease and pest control. Watering, depending upon the kind of plants, may be more or less necessary than in sunnier locations and this is also true of fertilizing. For most shade plants slow-acting organic fertilizers are preferable to chemicals. Mulching with compost, leaf mold, peat moss, or other suitable organic material is generally highly beneficial. In shaded areas plants are less likely to need winter protection than in sunnier, more exposed places.

The lists now presented are of plants generally adapted for particular purposes in shade or partial shade. For groundcovers suitable for such environments see the Encyclopedia entry Groundcovers.

Evergreen flowering shrubs for light to medium shade include camellias, hypericums, mahonias, mountain-laurel (*Kalmia*), pierises, pittosporums, privets (*Ligustrum*), rhododendrons including azaleas, sweet-bay (*Magnolia virginiana*), and Yeddo-hawthorn (*Raphiolepis*).

Evergreen shrubs without conspicuous blooms, but some with attractive berries, useful in light to medium shade include *Acanthopanax*, ardisias, aucubas, euonymuses, *Fatsia*, *Gaultheria*, *Gaylussacia*, hollies (*Ilex*), *Illicium*, inkberry (*Ilex*), laurel (*Laurus nobilis*), leucothoes, nandinas, *Osmanthus fragrans*, pyracanthas, *Sarcococca*, *Skimmia*, *Torreya*, vincas, and yews (*Taxus*).

Deciduous shrubs appropriate for light to medium shade include abelias, amelanchiers, aronias, azaleas, bush honeysuckles (*Lonicera*), *Calycanthus*, *Chimonanthus*, clethras, coralberry (*Symphoricarpos*), Cornelian-cherry (*Cornus*), dogwoods (*Cornus*), *Daphne mezereum*, *Daphne odora*, enkianthuses, flowering raspberry (*Rubus odoratus*), fothergillas, fuchsias, *Hydrangea macrophylla*, *Hydrangea quercifolia*, hypericums, jetbead (*Rhodotypos*), kerrias, privets (*Ligustrum*), snowberry (*Symphoricarpos*), spicebush (*Lindera*), *Viburnum tomentosum* and some other viburnums, witch-hazels (*Hamamelis*), and yellow-root (*Xanthorhiza*).

Vines for shade include akebias, *Asparagus plumosus*, Boston-ivy (*Parthenocissus*), climbing hydrangea, English ivy (*Hedera*), Dutchman's pipe (*Aristolochia*), some kinds of honeysuckles (*Lonicera*), philodendrons, *Scindapsus pictus*, silver lace vine (*Polygonum*), star-jasmine (*Trachelospermum*), and Virginia creeper (*Parthenocissus*).

Herbaceous perennials including bulb plants that prefer or tolerate more or less shade include anemones, astilbes, balloon flowers (*Platycodon*), bellflowers (*Campanula*), bleeding hearts (*Dicentra*), bloodroot (*Sanguinaria*), camassias, Christmas-rose (*Helleborus*), cimicifugas, columbines (*Aquilegia*), daffodils (*Narcissus*), daylilies (*Hemerocallis*), English bluebells (*Endymion*), epimediums, eupatoriums, false-dragonhead (*Physostegia*), false-Solomon's-seal (*Smilacina*), many kinds of ferns, forget-me-nots (*Myosotis*), gas plants (*Dictamnus*), globe flowers (*Trollius*), glory-of-the-snow (*Chion-*

Light shade is favored by daffodils, which complete their growth before the foliage of deciduous trees becomes too dense

odoxa), grape-hyacinths (*Muscari*), heucheras, *Iris cristata*, ligularias, a few kinds of lilies (*Lilium*), lobelias, lungworts (*Pulmonaria*), meadow-rues (*Thalictrum*), monkshoods (*Aconitum*), *Phlox divaricata*, plantain-lilies (*Hosta*), polemoniums, primroses (*Primula*), a few kinds of saxifrages (*Saxifraga*), scillas, shooting stars (*Dodecatheon*), snowdrops (*Galanthus*), snowflakes (*Leucojum*), Solomon's-seal (*Polygonatum*), Spanish bluebells (*Endymion*), sweet rocket (*Hesperis*), tradescantias, trilliums, violets (*Viola*), Virginia bluebells (*Mertensia*), and winter-aconites (*Eranthis*).

Annuals and plants treated as annuals, including nonhardy perennials used for summer beds, and biennials that endure even fairly light shade are not numerous. They include balsams (*Impatiens*), begonias, caladiums, forget-me-nots (*Myosotis*), foxgloves (*Digitalis*), fuchsias, honesty (*Lunaria*), lobelias, nicotianas, and torenias.

SHALLOTS. The shallot is a kind of onion esteemed for pickling and also, especially in the south, for scallions. In the past usually identified as *Allium ascalonicum*, this vegetable according to recent studies is not a form of that species, but of *A. cepa*, also the parent of the common onion, the top or Egyptian tree onion, and the multiplier or potato onion. From the last, the shallot differs chiefly in the smaller sizes of its bulbs and in the half dozen or more offset bulbs that separate as individuals instead of remaining aggregated inside one large bulb.

Shallots

The best soil for shallots is a deep, moderately fertile one fairly moist throughout during the season of active growth. A sunny site is needed.

Plant as early in spring as it is possible to get the soil into condition, or in mild climates in fall or winter. Simply press the small bulbs (sets) into the soil surface until buried to about one-half their depths. Place them about 6 inches apart in rows about 1 foot apart.

Subsequent care consists of keeping weeds down by frequent shallow hoeing or cultivating and during dry weather watering copiously at about weekly inter-

vals. When the leaves begin to die naturally stop watering and when the foliage has completely browned dig the bulbs, spread them in a dry place to dry for a few days, separate the bulbs, and store in a cool dry cellar or similar place, in trays, baskets, or suspended from the roof in net bags or old nylon stockings.

SHALLOW is *Gaultheria shallon*.

SHAMROCK. No one plant stands unchallenged as shamrock, the national emblem of Ireland. Nor, despite claims of natives of that land, is there any plant identified as shamrock that grows only there. All contenders for the honor have a much wider natural distribution.

The first mention of shamrock in English language literature occurs in Edmond Campion's *Historie of Ireland*, published in 1571. The Irish form, seamrog, diminutive of seamar, clover, did not appear in print until 1707. In the *Historie*, it is noted that the Irish used the plant for food. This confirms a statement published a year earlier by the Flemish botanist Matthias Lobel in *Stirpium Adversaria Nova*. Lobel says Irish freebooters ate cakes made of hop clover. From then on many references to eating shamroke, shamrogh, shamrug, shamroote, and even chamroch occurred. The Earl of Antrim, in 1638, proposed to feed an army of 8,000 men on shamrock. A little over forty years later the Oxford physician Henry Mundy wrote "The Irish that nourish themselves with their shamrocks, which is the purple clover, are swift of foot and of nimble strength."

That shamrocks were eaten, at least when other foods were scarce, there can be no doubt. The Irish botanist Nathaniel Colgan, author of the definitive *Flora of County Dublin*, and responsible for publishing the second edition of *Cybele Hibernica*, concluded that the plants so used were one or both of two clovers, *Trifolium pratense* and *T. repens*, and that they were not used for food after about 1682.

In 1892 and 1893 Colgan, in an attempt to settle the identity of shamrock, conducted surveys, the results of which were published in the *Journal of the Royal Society of Antiquaries of Ireland* (Vol. 26, 1896). He asked to have sent to him from every county in Ireland specimens of "true shamrock." These he planted and later identified. Of the counties that responded in 1892, six sent the yellow-flowered small hop clover (*Trifolium procumbens*), three sent white clover (*T. repens*), and two both. The following year twenty counties sent him specimens of "true shamrock." This time twelve sent the small hop clover, nineteen white clover, two red or purple clover (*Trifolium pratense*), and two spotted medick (*Medicago arabica*). None sent wood sorrel (*Oxalis acetosella*), which like several other species has often been suggested for

the honor. The earliest reference traced by Colgate to shamrock's use as a national emblem was dated 1681.

According to legend, folklore, or fact, depending upon one's belief, the missionary Patrick, later canonized Saint Patrick, shortly after his arrival in Ireland in A.D. 432 preached to the pagan natives from the Hill of Tara in County Meath. Picking a leaf with three leaflets from the sod at his feet he used it so effectively to illustrate the doctrine of the Holy Trinity that many of his listeners were converted to Christianity.

Saint Patrick's plant is considered to be the true shamrock. But determining its identity with certainty is impossible. Because the Hill of Tara is open and exposed, wood sorrel, which grows only in heavily shaded, cool, moist woodlands, can almost certainly be eliminated. Less surely, but nevertheless with considerable probability, red or purple clover, which is much less rugged than white clover and small hop clover, should be discarded. Of the last two, which appear to be now most commonly accepted as "true shamrock," the small hop clover is perhaps the one most likely to have been plucked by the saint, because, first, there is doubt that white clover is an original native of Ireland and second, the small hop clover notoriously colonizes poor stony ground, such as that of the Hill of Tara.

Garden Uses and Cultivation. In regions where considerable populations of Irish people or people of Irish ancestry live shamrocks are raised as emblems and decorations for Saint Patrick's Day (March 17th). Seeds, usually of small hop clover, but sometimes of white clover, are sown three or four in a 2½-inch pot in greenhouses or sunny windows about the beginning of February. They soon germinate and the young plants grow sturdily in a temperature of 50 to 60°F at night and a few degrees warmer by day.

SHASTA-DAISY. Previously considered to be varieties of *Chrysanthemum maximum*, the popular hardy herbaceous perennials known as Shasta-daisies are now believed to represent hybrids between that species, a native of the Pyrenees, and *C. lacustre*, of Portugal. The correct name for the hybrids is *C. superbum*.

These are robust, hardy, clump-forming, essentially hairless perennials, 2 to 3 feet tall or sometimes taller, with many erect, stiffish stems. Their lower leaves, 6 inches to 1 foot long and coarsely-toothed, are oblanceolate. Those higher on the stems are stalkless, lanceolate, and considerably smaller. Borne singly on long, stiff stalks, the daisy-type flower heads, 2 to 6 inches in diameter, have, in single varieties, a bold yellow eye of disk florets encircled by many spreading, pure white ray florets. There are also double-flowered varieties in which the yellow eye is

Shasta-daisies: (a) Single-flowered

(b) Double-flowered

replaced by white petal-like florets, and varieties with frilled florets. Propagation is by division in early spring or fall and by spring-sown seed.

For long, favorites for garden decoration and cut flowers, Shasta-daisies accommodate well to cultivation in most temperate climates, although where hot, dry summers prevail, they are not long-lived and frequent propagation is necessary. In some regions it is advisable to treat them as biennials.

Any fairly good garden soil, neither excessively dry nor wet, suits Shasta-daisies. They give of their best in full sun, but will stand a little part-day shade. For cut flowers space them 1½ to 2 feet apart in rows about 3 feet apart. In mixed flower beds grow them in clumps developed by setting three or five small plants about 1 foot apart to form a group. Propagation is easily achieved by division in early fall or spring and by spring-sown seed.

SHAVING BRUSH TREE is *Pseudobombax ellipticum*.

SHE-OAK. See Casuarina.

SHEARS. Chiefly used for pruning and trimming, shears are essential garden tools.

An ordinary pruning shear, designed to be held in one hand, is practically indispensable for routine pruning of roses, shrubs, vines, and a variety of other plants the stems of which are not too thick or hard for the tool to sever fairly easily. If undue force is required, the shear is likely to be damaged by the unacceptable strain. Pruning shears come in several designs and sizes. The two main types are those in which a pair of usually curved cutting blades slide past each other like the blades of a pair of scissors and those with one straight cutting blade that closes against a broader bed or "anvil" blade, which serves as a stop for the cutting blade. Because the latter type is more apt to crush the tissues than pruning shears with a scissor-like action, the former are preferred.

Loping shears are operated with two hands. Because of the added leverage their much longer handles provide, their strong, curved blades, which in use pass each other in scissor fashion, are capable of slicing through much thicker stems and branches than regular pruning shears. The long handles also make it easily possible to reach well into bushes and to cut stems and branches not conveniently reachable by other means.

Hedge shears, designed to be held in two hands, have comparatively short handles and long, straight blades that operate with a scissor action. As the name implies, they are used chiefly for trimming hedges, topiary work, and the like, where each cut severs many slender stems. They are also useful for trimming low shrubs and cutting back herbaceous perennials. Electric hedge trimmers have, to a considerable extent, taken the place of hedge shears for trimming hedges, but many garden uses are still likely to be found for the hand tool.

Grass shears for trimming the edges and other small areas of lawns not easily reachable by mowers, and operated by one hand, come in a variety of patterns, at least one of which is useful to have. Professionals often favor the sheep-shear model, which can be used not only for trimming grass, but for such tasks as cutting back the leaves of irises that are being divided. Electric and gasoline-powered grass trimmers are available to accomplish much of the work formerly done with hand-operated grass shears.

Invest in good quality shears. Such tools are not the cheapest, but are not necessarily the most expensive. Respect them by not using them for tasks beyond their capacities. Clean them thoroughly after every use and wipe their metal parts with an oily rag. Sharpen them as needed and keep them in a dry place.

SHEBA VALLEY DEATH TREE is *Synadenium cupulare*.

SHEEP-LAUREL is *Kalmia angustifolia*.

SHEEPBERRY is a common name of *Viburnum lentago* and *V. prunifolium*.

SHEEP'S-BIT-SCABIOUS is *Jasione montana*.

SHELL FLOWER. This name is used for *Alpinia zerumbet* and *Molucella laevis*. Mexican shell flower is *Tigridia pavonia*.

SHELL GINGER is *Alpinia zerumbet*. Small shell ginger is *A. mutica*.

SHEPHERDIA (Shep-hérdia) — Buffalo-Berry. Three North American species of the oleaster family ELAEAGNACEAE compose *Shepherdia*, the name of which honors John Shepherd, English botanist and horticulturist, who died in 1836.

From related *Elaeagnus* shepherdias are readily distinguished by their opposite leaves and their flowers, which appear in spring, having eight stamens. They are shrubs or small trees with yellowish, petalless blooms. Male and female flowers are on separate plants. The males have four sepals and eight stamens and are in many-flowered spikes; the females, urn-shaped, four-cleft, and with a solitary style, enclose the ovary and are solitary or in pairs. The fruits, fleshy and drupelike, are produced by female plants only, and only when a male plant is growing near enough to effect pollination.

Buffalo-berry (*S. argentea*) occurs from Minnesota and Iowa to the Pacific coast. A broad, erect, deciduous shrub or small tree, up to 20 feet in height, it has rigid, often spine-tipped branches. Both surfaces of its blunt, oblong to oblanceolate, ¾- to 2-inch-long leaves are attractively covered

Shepherdia argentea (flowers)

Shallots

Silene acaulis

Sidalcea malvaeflora variety

Silene armeria

Sinningia cardinalis

Sinningia hirsuta

Sinningia speciosa varieties

Sisyrinchium bellum

Smilacina racemosa

Shepherdia argentea (fruits)

with silvery scales. The sour, scarlet fruits, about ⅕ inch long, are edible.

From the buffalo-berry *S. canadensis* differs in not being thorny and in its deciduous leaves having a dense coating of silvery scales on their undersides only. Up to about 9 feet tall, but often lower, this species has blunt leaves up to 2 inches in length and narrowly-lanceolate to ovate. Its insipid, yellowish-red fruits are about ¼ inch long. Native of dry, often alkaline soils, this species occurs from Newfoundland to Alaska, New York, Indiana, South Dakota, New Mexico, and Arizona. In *S. c. xanthocarpa* the fruits are yellow.

Garden and Landscape Uses and Cultivation. Extremely hardy and capable of surviving harsh winters and considerable drought, the shepherdias discussed are useful shrubs, chiefly esteemed for their habits of growth and ornamental foliage and berries. The buffalo-berry is very satisfactory as a hedge plant, and its fruits are made into jellies and conserves. Few shrubs are better adapted to dry, rocky, inhospitable, and alkaline soils than *S. canadensis*. Propagation of shepherdias is usually by seeds sown outdoors or in a cold frame as soon as they are ripe or after being stratified for three months at 40°F. The seeds must not be permitted to dry out before they are sown or stratified. Increase can also be by grafting scions from bushes of the desired sex onto seedlings of *Shepherdia* or *Elaeagnus*, and by root cuttings.

SHEPHERD'S NEEDLE is *Scandix pecten-veneris*.

SHEPHERD'S-SCABIOUS is *Jasione montana*.

SHIBATAEA (Shibat-aèa). Two or perhaps more species of Asian bamboos, of the grass family GRAMINEAE, constitute *Shibataea*. The name honors the distinguished twentieth-century Japanese botanist and student of bamboos Keita Shibata. From *Phyllostachys*, to which it is closely related and in which it was once included, *Shibataea* differs in having shorter, very zigzagged, nearly solid canes and ovate-oblong to ovate-lanceolate leaves.

An attractive native of Japan, *S. kumasaca* (syns. *Bambusa kumasaca, Phyllostachys kumasaca*) has 1¼-inch-thick canes 3 to 6 feet tall, elliptic or triangular in section and grooved. At first green, later turning dull brown, they retain their leaf sheaths for a considerable time. The branches, mostly paired, but occasionally in threes, have one or sometimes two leaves at the end of each twig. The leaves, 4 or 5 inches long by about 1 inch wide, are fringed on both margins with fine, bristly hairs. The upper surfaces of young leaves are lustrous dark green, those of older ones yellowish-green. The undersides are grayish-green.

Garden and Landscape Uses and Cultivation. This interesting bamboo, which in gardens is sometimes misnamed *Sasa kumasaca*, is hardy in sheltered locations in southern New York. Fairly compact, it is not likely to prove invasive. For its best success it needs a moist soil. For further information see Bamboos.

SHIELDWORT. See Peltaria.

SHIGEURAARA. This is the name of orchid hybrids the parents of which include *Ascocentrum, Ascoglossum, Renanthera,* and *Vanda*.

SHINGLE PLANT is *Raphidophora celatocaulis*.

SHINLEAF. See Pyrola. The one-flowered shinleaf is *Moneses uniflora*.

SHITTIMWOOD. This is a common name for *Acacia seyal* and *Bumelia lanuginosa*.

SHIZOCODON SOLDANELLOIDES is *Shortia soldanelloides*.

SHOE BUTTON PLANT is *Ardisia humilis*.

SHOO-FLY PLANT is *Nicandra physalodes*.

SHOOT. Young stems are often called shoots. Those that terminate the main axis or trunk and those at the ends of major branches are designated terminal or leading shoots. Others are known as lateral or side shoots.

SHOOTING STAR. See Dodecatheon.

SHORTIA (Shórt-ia) — Oconee Bells, Nippon Bells. Ten or fewer species, of the

mountains of Japan, Taiwan, and China, and one of the eastern United States, constitute *Shortia*, a genus named in honor of Dr. Charles Wilkins Short, a Kentucky botanist, who died in 1863. The group belongs in the diapensia family DIAPENSIACEAE and is kin with *Diapensia, Pyxidanthera,* and *Galax*.

Shortias are stemless, evergreen herbaceous perennials with creeping rootstocks, long-stalked leaves with rounded heart-shaped blades, and solitary or few, nodding bell-shaped flowers on leafless stalks. The corollas are five-lobed and the five stamens are joined to the inside of the bell for the greater parts of their lengths. They alternate with five scalelike staminodes (abortive stamens). There is one style with a three-lobed stigma. The fruits are globular capsules. The cultivated kinds are hardy near New York City.

Best known of the group and with a quite interesting history, Oconee bells is indigenous along shady banks of streams from North Carolina to Georgia, where it has survived since it was isolated from other members of the genus by the last great ice age. In prehistoric times its ancestors undoubtedly occupied much more of North America and even merged with ancestral stocks of their Asian relatives. The earliest record of Oconee bells is of its finding by Andre Michaux in 1788. The specimen he collected was pressed and dried and placed in his herbarium in Paris, France, where it remained until 1839 when the American botanist Asa Gray discovered it. Although the material consisted of only a few leaves and a single seed pod, Gray recognized its botanical affinities and predicted what its flowers would be like. Upon his return to America, Gray explored the mountains of North Carolina in an unsuccessful attempt to locate the plant and in 1842 he described it from the specimen he had examined in France and named it. In 1879 the plant was rediscovered on the banks of the Catawba River in McDowell County, North Carolina, by a boy, George Hymens, who brought specimens to his father, a herbalist, who in turn brought it to the notice of scientists and Gray's projections were substantiated. In 1886, almost a century after its original discovery, the colony of plants from which Michaux collected his specimen was relocated by Professor Charles S. Sargent near the source of the Keowee River. The popular name refers to its abundance along the Oconee River.

Oconee bells (*S. galacifolia*), 6 to 8 inches tall, is handsome. All basal, its leaves have glossy, nearly circular blades often slightly heart-shaped at their bases and with shallow, round teeth often with spiny tips. They are 1½ to 2 inches wide. The slender flower stalks have a few bracts near their tops and are up to 8 inches tall. The flowers, white or slightly pinkish, ¾ to 1 inch long and wide, nod or are inclined down-

Shortia galacifolia

ward. The margins of their petals are irregularly toothed.

Nippon bells (**S. uniflora**) is a Japanese species that differs from Oconee bells chiefly in its thinner, more heart-shaped leaves, 1 inch to 3 inches long and wide, with more conspicuously wavy margins. Its flowers vary from white to pale rose-pink. Variety *S. u. grandiflora* is said to have bigger flowers. The fringe bell of Japan (**S. soldanelloides** syn. *Schizocodon soldanelloides*) differs from the two described above in having three to about twelve blooms near the top of each 4-inch- to 1-foot-high stalk and in their petals being cleft into a deep fringe rather than only toothed. A loosely-branched creeping perennial, this has, mostly toward the ends of the stems, nearly circular to oblong, glossy leaves, with blades up to a little over 2 inches long, that have heart-shaped bases. Deep rose-pink, they become paler or white toward the apexes of their 1-inch-long and -wide flowers. Variety *S. s. ilicifolia* is distinguished by its more conspicuously sharp-toothed leaves, variety *S. s. magna* by the larger size of its parts.

Shortia soldanelloides ilicifolia

Garden Uses and Cultivation. Shortias are suitable for woodland and rock gardens. In such environments they may be used as groundcovers and to colonize in open places among shrubs, especially rho-

dodendrons, mountain laurels, and *Pieris.* Their greatest need is for a loose, spongy, acid soil that contains an abundance of leaf mold or other organic debris and that is never excessively dry, and shade from direct sun. Sunlight filtered through an overhead canopy of leaves is beneficial. Sheltered locations protected from drying winds suit best.

Planting may be done in spring or fall. It is helpful to keep the ground mulched with compost, peat moss, or other partially decayed organic material. Shortias can be increased by careful division in early spring or early fall or by sowing freshly gathered seeds. It is of the utmost importance that the seeds be sown as soon as they are ripe, without being allowed to dry. If sowing must be delayed for even twenty-four hours, store them in damp moss. Sow in well-drained pots or flats containing acid, sandy, peaty soil and put these in a shaded cold frame or cool greenhouse. Be sure the soil is always kept moderately moist, but not excessively wet.

SHOWER. The names apple-blossom shower, bronze shower, coral shower, golden shower, pink shower, pink-and-white shower, and rainbow shower are applied to sorts of *Cassia*.

SHRIMP PLANT is *Justicia brandegeana*.

SHRUB-ALTHEA is *Hibiscus syriacus*.

SHRUB YELLOW-ROOT is *Xanthorhiza simplicissima*.

SHRUBS. Important components of most gardens and many landscape plantings, shrubs are woody-stemmed perennials with usually from or near their bases several to many stems of approximately equal importance. They are without conspicuous trunks and are ordinarily under, and often much under, 20 feet tall. There is no sharp line of distinction between shrubs and trees at one extreme or shrubs and subshrubs at the other. The groups merge. In form shrubs vary according to kind from tall and narrow to rounded or broader, low and spreading, or even more or less pendulous. Climbing shrubs, such as allamandas, bougainvilleas, and wisterias, distinguished as vines, are discussed under the entry Vines in this Encyclopedia. Some low shrubs are treated under Groundcovers.

Thousands of species and varieties of shrubs are cultivated, the vast majority as ornamentals, but some, such as blueberries, currants, and gooseberries, for their edible fruits. They include evergreen and deciduous sorts from among which choices can be made for a wide variety of climates, purposes, and sites. In choosing, climate must be a first consideration. Prospective planters should familiarize themselves with

the sorts that prosper in gardens and nurseries in the vicinity and rely largely upon those and kinds believed to be as hardy and adaptable. This need not preclude some testing of doubtfully suitable sorts that make special appeal, but let this be on an experimental scale that will not disappoint too much if failure results.

Many purposes are served effectively by shrubs. A great number of kinds provide splendid floral displays. Among such are abelias, azaleas, daphnes, deutzias, forsythias, fothergillas, mock-oranges (*Philadelphus*), rhododendrons, and weigelas. Others, including barberries (*Berberis*), callicarpas, loniceras, nandinas, pyracanthas, snowberries (*Symphoricarpos*), and viburnums, are esteemed for their handsome fruits, many of which are attractive to birds. Colorful fall foliage is a decided asset of some shrubs, among them certain azaleas, barberries (*Berberis*), enkianthuses, euonymuses, fothergillas, rhuses, and vacciniums. And a few kinds, some dogwoods (*Cornus*), for example, are appreciated for their brightly colored stems displayed to best advantage in winter.

As "living furniture," shrubs give a sense of permanence to landscapes. They may be used to define boundaries and discrete areas within larger gardens, to emphasize vistas, to direct attention to interesting views, to screen less desirable views, and as components of foundation plantings, to "marry" buildings to the ground and to provide backgrounds to flower beds. Single specimens advantageously located can be employed with telling effects, as can well-planned and well-planted borders of shrubs.

Tall shrubs that stand exposure well, such sorts as caraganas, junipers (*Juniperus*), lilacs (*Syringa*), Russian-olive (*Elaeagnus angustifolia*), and tamarisks (*Tamarix*), serve excellently as windbreaks, and many kinds lend themselves to shearing and make splendid hedges.

Evergreen sorts, even boxwoods (*Buxus*), junipers (*Juniperus*), mugo pines (*Pinus*), yews (*Taxus*), and some others that make no showy display of bloom and are esteemed chiefly for their mostly green foliage, are of great value for giving "life" to winter landscapes and for shielding views and affording privacy when deciduous shrubs are leafless.

Site suitability must be the uppermost consideration when selecting shrubs for planting. If the soil is alkaline it is obviously unwise to set out such acid-soil sorts as azaleas, heaths, and rhododendrons. If it is dry, azaleas, rhododendrons or such shrubs as amelanchiers or clethras, will not flourish. It is unreasonable to expect success with cytisuses, genistas, junipers, and many other sorts in constantly moist locations, and few kinds tolerate wet soils. Some shrubs stand considerable shade, some need a certain amount of sun, whereas others do best in full sun. Shelter from strong winds is often important. Many shrubs, camellias and rhododendrons, for instance, succeed in sheltered sites, but fail in exposed ones.

Ultimate size, unless plants are to be sheared as hedges or topiary specimens, should be high on the list of considerations when matching shrubs to locations. Too often, small plants of large shrubs are afforded inadequate space for development, with the result that later they become miserable and scrawny, instead of fine, shapely specimens.

Examples of serious overcrowding are common in suburban gardens and especially in foundation plantings. The desire of planters to achieve immediate effects, even at the expense of future well-being, is understandable, but reprehensible. When setting out shrubs take into account their future spreads as well as the heights they are likely to attain and make appropriate, generous allowances. Annuals, perennials, or even other shrubs can serve as temporary fillers to flesh out installations that because of wide spacing at first seem skimpy.

Susceptibility to pests and diseases is another consideration. Most kinds are reasonably free of such troubles, but some, particularly in some regions, are regularly infested or infected, and growers of them must be prepared to take adequate control measures.

Maintenance needed varies from almost none to regular annual attentions, depending upon the kind of shrub, the purpose or purposes it is intended to serve, and perhaps its location. Included may be mulching, pruning or shearing, watering, fertilizing, controlling disease and pests, and protecting in winter. Recommendations for meeting these needs and about methods of propagation as well as other information are offered in the Encyclopedia entries of the genera to which the shrubs belong.

Suggestions for shrubs especially suited for particular purposes are provided in the Encyclopedia entries City Gardening, Desert Gardens, Hedges, Seaside Gardens, Shady Gardens, and Roof and Terrace Gardens. The lists that follow are of genera that include attractive shrubs. This does not mean that all members of such genera are necessarily shrubs, although in many cases they are. Some genera contain trees or herbaceous perennials as well as shrubs. These lists are intended as guides to Encyclopedia entries of shrub-containing genera.

Deciduous flowering shrubs without notable displays of berries or other fruits are to be found in these genera. Most, but not all, are hardy in the north: *Abelia*, *Abeliophyllum* (white-forsythia), *Aesculus*, *Amorpha* (lead plant), *Aralia*, *Buddleia*, *Caragana* (pea-shrub), *Caryopteris* (blue-spirea), *Ceanothus*, *Chimonanthus* (winter sweet), *Clethra*, *Corokia*, *Corylopsis*, *Cytisus* (broom), *Daphne*, *Desfontainea*, *Deutzia*, *Diervilla*, *Dipelta*, *Enkianthus*, *Elsholtzia*, *Escallonia*, *Exochorda* (pearl bush), *Forsythia*, *Fothergilla*, *Genista*, *Hamamelis* (witch-hazel), *Hibiscus*, *Holodiscus* (ocean spray), *Hydrangea*, *Hypericum* (St.-John's wort), *Indigofera*, *Kerria*, *Kolkwitzia* (beauty bush), *Lagerstroemia* (crape-myrtle), *Lespedeza*, *Lindera* (spice bush), *Loropetalum*, *Magnolia*, *Neillia*, *Neviusia* (snow wreath), *Paeonia* (tree peony), *Philadelphus* (mock-orange), *Physocarpus* (ninebark), *Potentilla*, *Rhododendron* (azalea), *Robinia* (rose-acacia), *Rubus* (flowering raspberry), *Salix* (willow), *Sorbaria* (false-spirea), *Spartium* (Spanish-broom), *Spiraea* (spirea), *Stephanandra*, *Stachyurus*, *Styrax*, *Syringa* (lilac), *Tamarix* (tamarisk), *Vitex*, *Weigela*, and *Xanthorhiza* (shrub yellow-root).

Deciduous shrubs with attractive displays of flowers and berries or other fruits occur in these genera: *Amelanchier*, *Aronia*, *Berberis* (barberry), *Callicarpa* (beauty-berry), *Chaenomeles* (flowering-quince), *Clerodendrum*, *Cotoneaster*, *Ligustrum* (privet), *Lonicera* (bush honeysuckle), *Photinia*, *Poncirus* (trifoliate-orange), *Prunus*, *Punica* (pomegranate), *Rhamnus* (buckthorn), *Rhodotypos* (jetbead), *Ribes* (flowering currant), *Rosa* (rose), *Sambucus* (elderberry), *Shepherdia* (buffalo-berry), *Symplocos* (sweetleaf), *Vaccinium*, and *Viburnum*.

Deciduous, mostly hardy shrubs, notable for their attractive berries or other fruits, but not for their floral displays, are found in these genera: *Baccharis* (groundsel bush), *Elaeagnus*, *Euonymus*, *Hippophae* (sea-buckthorn), *Ilex* (holly), *Leycesteria*, *Myrica* (bayberry), *Rhus* (sumac), and *Symphoricarpos* (coralberry, snowberry).

Deciduous shrubs with colorful fall foliage occur in these genera: *Abelia*, *Acer* (maple), *Amelanchier*, *Aronia*, *Berberis* (barberry), *Callicarpa*, *Clethra*, *Cornus*, *Cotinus*, *Cotoneaster*, *Enkianthus*, *Euonymus*, *Forsythia*, *Fothergilla*, *Hamamelis* (witch-hazel), *Ilex* (holly), *Itea*, *Kerria*, *Lindera*, *Nandina*, *Photinia*, *Physocarpus*, *Poncirus* (trifoliate-orange), *Prinsepia*, *Prunus*, *Rhododendron* (azalea), *Rhus* (sumac), *Ribes* (flowering currant), *Rosa* (rose), *Vaccinium*, and *Viburnum*.

Deciduous shrubs, notable for colored stems displayed to great advantage during winter, are to be found in *Cornus* (dogwood), *Rosa* (rose), and *Rubus* (blackberry).

Evergreen shrubs attractive in bloom, but without notable displays of berries or other fruits, occur in these genera, many of which are not hardy in the north: *Abelia*, *Abutilon*, *Acalypha*, *Aphelandra*, *Azara*, *Brunfelsia*, *Buddleia*, *Calliandra*, *Calluna* (heather), *Camellia*, *Carpenteria*, *Cassia*, *Ceanothus*, *Cestrum*, *Choisya* (Mexican-orange), *Cistus* (rock-rose), *Cytisus* (broom), *Daphne*, *Eranthemum*, *Erica* (heath), *Escallonia*, *Fuchsia*, *Gardenia*, *Garrya*, *Genista*, *Halimium*, *Hebe*, *Hibiscus*, *Holmskioldia*, *Illicium*, *Ixora*, *Justica*, *Kalmia*, *Lantana*, *Lavandula* (lavender), *Leptospermum*, *Leucothoe*, *Loropetalum*, *Lupinus*, *Malvaviscus*, *Medinilla*, *Michelia* (banana-shrub), *Mussaenda*, *Myrtus* (myrtle), *Nerium* (oleander), *Olearia* (daisy bush), *Osmanthus*, *Pachystachys*, *Phlomis*, *Pieris*, *Plumbago*, *Pseuderanthemum*, *Rondeletia*, *Rosmarinus*, *Rhododendron* (including azaleas), *Russelia*, *Sanchezia*, *Serissa*, *Tabernaemontana*, *Thunbergia*, and *Yucca*.

Evergreen shrubs esteemed chiefly for their foliage, but without notable displays of flowers or fruits, are to be found in these genera, not all of which are hardy in the north: *Acalypha*, *Acer* (maple), *Aucuba*, *Breynia*, *Buxus* (boxwood), *Cephalotaxus* (plum-yew), *Chamaecyparis* (false-cypress), *Coprosma*, *Danae*, *Eurya*, *Fatshedera*, *Fatsia*, *Gaultheria*, *Homalocladium*, *Juniperus* (juniper), *Laurus* (sweet bay), *Myrica*, *Picea* (spruce), *Pinus* (pine), *Polyscias*, *Taxus* (yew), and *Thuja* (arbor-vitae).

Evergreen shrubs with attractive flowers and berries or other fruits are included in these genera, not all of which are hardy in the north: *Arctostaphylos* (manzanita), *Berberis* (barberry), *Carissa* (Natal-plum), *Cotoneaster*, *Galphimia*, *Ligustrum* (privet), *Mahonia*, *Malpighia*, *Ochna*, *Photinia*, *Pittosporum*, *Pyracantha*, *Raphiolepis*, *Vaccinium*, and *Viburnum*.

Evergreen shrubs, with attractive berries or other fruits, but without notable displays of flowers, are to be found in these genera, not all of which are hardy in the north: *Ardisia*, *Euonymus*, *Ficus*, *Ilex* (holly), *Juniperus* (juniper), *Myrica*, *Nandina*, *Pernettya*, *Rhamnus* (buckthorn), and *Taxus* (yew).

SIBBALDIA (Sibbáld-ia). Closely allied to *Potentilla*, the genus *Sibbaldia*, of the rose family ROSACEAE, consists of about eight species of arctic, subarctic, and other cold parts of the northern hemisphere. Its name commemorates the Scottish botanist Sir Robert Sibbald, who died in 1722.

Sibbaldias are low, hardy herbaceous perennials of more or less tufted growth. Their leaves are alternate and have three leaflets. The small, yellow flowers, displayed in branched clusters have a five-cleft calyx, usually five, rarely four or ten petals, or sometimes none. The stamens and pistils are numerous. The fruits are tiny achenes.

Native of the far north of North America and southward along the mountains in alpine and subalpine regions to Quebec, New Hampshire, Colorado, and California, *S. procumbens* also is a native of northern Europe and Asia. Up to about 4 inches tall, it has long-stalked leaves with wedge-shaped or ovate, sparsely-hairy leaflets with three to five coarse teeth at their blunt ends. Similar leaves are borne toward the tops of the flowering stems. The flowers, which normally have tiny petals much exceeded by the green sepals, sometimes are without petals. Similar *S. parviflora*, of Europe and Asia, up to 10 inches tall, is less tufted than *S. procumbens*, and its leaflets have usually three apical teeth.

Garden Uses and Cultivation. Although of no great floral merit, the species described are occasionally grown by rock garden enthusiasts for their attractive evergreen foliage. They need a cool, sunny location. They are easily raised from seed sown in a greenhouse or cold frame, and by division in early spring or fall.

SIBERIAN PEA-TREE is *Caragana arborescens.*

SIBERIAN-WALLFLOWER is *Erysimum hieraciifolium.*

SIBIRAEA (Sibir-aèa). Once included in *Spiraea*, to which they are closely related, the two species of *Sibiraea*, of the rose family ROSACEAE, differ in that individual plants are functionally unisexual, although they have a few bisexual flowers of the opposite sex as well as those of the predominant one. Another difference is that the pair of usually two-seeded follicles or small pods that are the fruit are joined at their bases. The name refers to Siberia, a home territory of the genus.

Deciduous shrubs with alternate, short-stalked, undivided leaves, and flowers in terminal panicles, sibiraeas are natives of temperate Asia and eastern Europe. Their small, short-stalked flowers have five short sepals, five roundish white petals, and about twenty-five stamens. The stamens of the males are longer than the petals, the nonfunctional ones of the females are much shorter. The usually five pistils are joined at their bottoms.

The only species in cultivation is *S. laevigata* (syns. *S. altaiensis*, *Spiraea laevigata*). In the wild procumbent and about 3 feet tall, but as known in cultivation erect and taller, this inhabits limestone cliffs in a few locations in eastern Europe, and is native in eastern Siberia. Attempts have been made to separate the European population as *S. l. croatica*, but no sharp line can be drawn between it and plants that grow 4,000 miles away in Asia. As known in cultivation, *S. laevigata* is a stiffish, rather sparsely-branched, distinctively foliaged shrub usually much broader than tall. Its dull green or bluish-green, hairless leaves, are alternate and, on old shoots, clustered. They are oblanceolate to oblong-wedge-shaped and 1 inch to 1½ inches long, or longer on young vigorous shoots. The flowers, greenish-white, come in spring and are in hairless panicles 3 to 5 inches long. Variety *S. l. angustata* has narrower leaves.

Garden and Landscape Uses. Inferior in decorative value to the better species of *Spiraea*, these plants are most likely to interest only collectors and to be planted in arboretums and similar places. The species described is hardy through most of New England, the variety in southern New England.

Cultivation. Ordinary garden soil and sunny locations suit these shrubs. They need little routine care. Any pruning required is done as soon as blooming is through and consists of removing old, worn-out, crowded, and weak branches. Propagation is by seed, cuttings, and layering.

SIBTHORPIA (Sib-thórpia). Although its most familiar members have much the aspect of common ground-ivy (*Glechoma hederacea*), the genus under discussion belongs to a different family, that of the figworts, the SCROPHULARIACEAE. Ground-ivy is accommodated in the mint family LABIATAE. The resemblance, then, is chiefly one of manner of growth and foliage, rather than in the more classificatory significant details of floral structure. The opposite leaves of *Glechoma* readily distinguish it from *Sibthorpia*.

There are five species of *Sibthorpia*, a genus represented in the native floras of Mexico, Central America, South America, the Azores, Madeira, Europe, and the mountains of tropical Africa, and named to commemorate Dr. John Sibthorp, an English professor of botany, who died in 1796. They are evergreen, hairy, carpeting trailers, with slender, herbaceous stems that root at the nodes, and stalked, alternate or clustered, kidney-shaped to nearly round, prominently toothed leaves. Their small yellow, reddish, or purple blooms are in the leaf axils. They have bell-shaped calyxes with four to eight lobes, corollas with short tubes, as many spreading lobes (petals) as those of the calyx, and as many stamens or fewer by one than there are petals.

Cornish-moneywort (*S. europaea*), of Europe including the British Isles, is a neat, extremely low trailer with very slender stems furnished along their lengths with thin, rounded, round-toothed leaves up to ¾ inch in diameter and shallowly seven- to nine-lobed. Its minute, yellowish or reddish blooms have four-parted calyxes and corollas and four stamens. Variety *S. e. variegata* is distinguished by its leaves being margined with creamy-white. With larger flowers, ⅓ inch across, and with five to eight calyx and corolla lobes, on stalks up to 2 inches long, *S. peregrina* is native to Madeira. It has small, round-toothed leaves with scalloped margins and five- to eight-petaled yellow flowers about ⅓ inch across. Indigenous to the Andes of Colombia and Ecuador, *S. repens* (syn. *S. pi-*

Sibthorpia europaea variegata

Sibthorpia repens

chinchensis) has finely-hairy, kidney-shaped leaves up to 1 inch wide but often smaller, with conspicuously crenated margins. The up-facing flowers, purple to dark violet, or buff-yellow, and about ⅓ inch across, usually have five petals.

Garden Uses. Sibthorpias are undemanding plants adaptable for groundcovers and rock gardens in mild climates and for growing as trailers in pots and hanging baskets in cool greenhouses. The hardiest of the kinds described above, *S. europaea* survives outdoors in southern England and in eastern North America probably about as far north as Virginia. The others are less tolerant of cold and can be expected to be perennial only where little or no frost is experienced.

Cultivation. Very little care is needed. These plants prosper in porous soils kept evenly moist, and shaded from strong sun. A greenhouse with a minimum night temperature of 40 to 50°F is better than one warmer. Propagation is rapidly achieved by division and cuttings. The species can also be raised from seed.

SICANA (Sicà-na) — Cassabanana or Curuba. The one or, according to some authorities, two or three species of *Sicana*, of the gourd family CUCURBITACEAE, is a vigorous perennial vine usually cultivated as an annual. Its generic name is a Peruvian colloquial one.

The cassabanana or curuba (*S. odorifera*), probably native to Brazil, but now naturalized elsewhere, has angled stems up to 50 feet long. Its leaves, up to 1 foot in diameter and rough, but not hairy, are nearly circular to kidney-shaped and strongly-lobed or angled. The solitary, yellowish to orange-crimson flowers, the males ¾ inch long and the females about 2 inches long, unlike those of the white gourd (*Benincasa hispida*) to which the name cassabanana is often wrongly applied, are urn- or bell-shaped and not deeply divided into five separate petals. They have three stamens and three two-lobed styles. From the blooms of nearly related pumpkins and squashes they differ in having anthers that, although converging, do not cohere or unite, and sepals that are reflexed or spreading. The 1- to 2-foot-long fruits, which resemble long, slender squashes, are almost cylindrical, and black-purple to orange-crimson when ripe. They are pleasantly and often strongly fragrant.

Garden Uses and Cultivation. The cassabanana is grown chiefly for ornament, but its fruits are sometimes used as a vegetable or are eaten after pickling. This vine is an interesting subject for temporary screens and for clothing fences, arbors, and other supports. Its cultivation is as for Lagenaria. For additional information see Gourds, Ornamental.

SICYOS (Sícy-os)—Bur-Cucumber or Star-Cucumber. The genus *Sicyos*, its name derived from the Greek *sikys*, a cucumber, in allusion to the fruits, consists of about thirty-five species of annual climbing vines native to America, the Pacific Islands, Australia, and Africa. It belongs to the gourd family CUCURBITACEAE.

The sorts of this genus have broad, undivided, lobed or angular leaves and branched tendrils. Small and white or greenish, the flowers are unisexual. They have a small five-toothed calyx, a five-lobed, wheel-shaped corolla, stamens united in a column, and a short, slender style with three stigmas. The female flowers are in tight heads, the males in looser clusters. The fruits are small and usually spiny.

The eastern American bur-cucumber or star-cucumber (*S. angulatus*), a native of damp soils from Quebec to Minnesota, Florida, Arizona, and Texas, is a high climbing vine with stems many feet long, and rounded-heart-shaped, sharply palmately-angled or -lobed, toothed leaves. Its

Sicyos angulatus

starry, white or greenish blooms are in clusters at the ends of long stalks from the leaf axils. The male flowers are about ⅓ inch across. The fleshy fruits, about ½ inch long, are in tight clusters and contain one seed. They have pointed ends and are covered with long prickles.

Garden and Landscape Uses and Cultivation. The bur-cucumber is sometimes used as a fast-growing screen, but is not choice. Appropriate in native plant gardens, it may tend to become something of a weed. It is easily raised from seeds sown in spring and thrives in any ordinary reasonably fertile soil.

SIDA (Sì-da) — Virginia-Mallow. Of small horticultural significance, *Sida*, of the mallow family MALVACEAE, is native chiefly to warm parts of the Old World and the New World. It consists of possibly 200 species of annuals, herbaceous perennials, and shrubby plants. From related *Abutilon* it differs in having only one seed in each of the five to fifteen carpels (pistils) of each flower. The name is a Greek one used by Theophrastus for a different kind of plant.

Sidas have alternate, undivided, usually lobeless leaves. The solitary flowers, in clusters from the leaf axils or in spikes, racemes, or panicles, have five-lobed calyxes that persist and enclose the divided, dry fruits. They have five petals, numerous stamens joined into a tube, and five or more styles.

The Virginia-mallow (*S. hermaphrodita*) is a perennial 3 to 10 feet tall. Native in moist soils from Pennsylvania to Michigan and Tennessee, its young parts have stellate (star-shaped) hairs, but later are hairless or nearly so. In outline broadly-ovate to rounded, the leaves, up to 10 inches long, are deeply-cleft into three to seven pointed-lanceolate, irregularly toothed lobes of which the center one is the longest. The flowers, in clusters from the axils of the upper leaves, form considerable terminal panicles. They are white and about 1 inch in diameter. Each fruit

usually has ten carpels (divisions), each tipped with one or two short, pointed beaks. This species blooms in summer and fall.

Garden Uses and Cultivation. The Virginia-mallow is occasionally planted in semiwild places and native plant gardens. It succeeds in damp, fertile soil in sun or part-shade. It is increased by seed.

SIDALCEA (Sidál-cea)—Checker or Checkerbloom. This western North American genus of the mallow family MALVACEAE comprises about twenty-two species of annuals and herbaceous perennials. Its name is formed from those of two related genera, *Sida* and *Alcea*. The names checker and checkerbloom, here restricted to *S. malvaeflora*, are not uncommonly applied to other species.

Sidalceas have alternate, rounded, usually lobed or divided, stalked leaves, with the lobes or leaflets spreading in hand-fashion. Their mallow-like blooms are in terminal spikes or racemes and are mostly bisexual, but sometimes unisexual females, which are smaller than the bisexual flowers, develop. The blooms have five-lobed calyxes, five pink, purplish, or white petals cut squarely across or slightly indented at their apexes, a tube composed of two rows of united stamens, and a style with threadlike branches with the stigmas on their inner sides and not forming knobs at their ends, as they do in *Sida* and *Sphaeralcea*. The dry, kidney-shaped fruits, at first united, eventually separate. On the flower stem just below the calyx is one or no bractlets, which distinguishes *Sidalcea* from *Malva*, in which there are three bractlets.

The most important species horticulturally, the source of improved garden varieties more common in Europe than America, is the highly variable checker or checkerbloom (*S. malvaeflora*), of which there are many botanical varieties. Plants grown in gardens as *S. rosea* usually belong here. Checkerbloom is endemic to

Sidalcea, garden variety

California, where it decorates grassy slopes, and open areas in forests. Perennial, it has spreading rootstocks and hairy, erect stems 1 foot to 2 feet tall. The hairs, especially on the upper parts of the stems, are mostly stellate (star-shaped). From 1 inch to 3 inches across, the often fleshy, long-stalked, toothed leaves are roundish to kidney-shaped. The lower ones are shallowly, the upper ones more deeply, five-to nine-lobed. Those near the flowers are often divided to their bases. Usually the crowded or loose spikes of blooms are not branched. The flowers, 1½ to 2 inches across and pink or rosy-purple, usually have white veins. Variety *S. m. listeri* (syn. *S. m.* 'Pink Beauty') is distinguished by its beautiful, satiny-pink blooms.

Another decorative perennial is *S. candida,* of the Rocky Mountain region. This sort, with stems 2 to 3 feet tall that branch above, is nearly or quite hairless. It has broad, blunt-lobed or toothed basal leaves, 2 to 6 inches across, and upper ones with five or seven narrow lobes often toothed or cleft. Its abundant flowers, 1 inch or sometimes more in width, are in spikelike racemes. They are white. Variety *S. c. incarnata* has pink blooms.

Native from Montana to Wyoming, Washington, and California, *S. oregana* (syn. *S. nervata*) is a variable perennial of which botanists recognize several varieties. One previously named *S. spicata* is *S. o. spicata*. It has many hairless or sparsely-hairy, usually glaucous stems and hairy foliage. The long-stalked, round, basal leaves are up to 4 inches across and lobed and toothed. The upper leaves have three or five narrow, scarcely-toothed lobes. The rose-purple flowers are in spikelike racemes up to 1 foot long. They are 1 inch to 1½ inches in diameter. The horticultural variety 'Rosy Gem' is a variant of this species.

Generally with delicate pink, pale lavender, or nearly white blooms in loose-flowered, branched, or branchless racemes, *S. campestris,* of Oregon, is 3 to 6 feet tall. A perennial, its basal leaves are fairly deeply seven- to nine-lobed, and up to 6 inches in diameter. The stem leaves are divided usually nearly or quite to their bases into seven or sometimes five lobes. The petals are ½ to 1 inch long. Bright pinkish-lavender to rose-pink flowers in crowded, spikelike racemes are characteristic of perennial *S. hendersonii,* a native from Oregon to British Columbia. Its basal leaves, up to 6 inches wide, are very shallowly five-lobed and have round-toothed margins. The stem leaves are more deeply-cleft. A distinguishing characteristic of *S. neomexicana* is its much enlarged, fleshy, but not fibrous roots. A variable perennial, this occurs natively over a wide range in western North America and Mexico. It has hairy stems 1 foot to 2 or occasionally 3 feet tall. The basal leaves, about 4 inches wide, are shallowly five- to seven-lobed and cleft. The stem leaves are divided into narrow lobes. The light rose-pink flowers have petals up to ¾ inch long.

Garden and Landscape Uses and Cultivation. Sidalceas, especially cultivated varieties such as 'Rosy Gem', 'Rose Queen', 'Pink Beauty', and 'Scarlet Beauty', are excellent furnishings for perennial borders. They make a fine summer display and are useful as cut flowers. They grow best in full sun, or where there is a little shade during the hottest part of the day, and respond to deep, fertile soil that is well drained, but does not lack for moisture. As soon as the blooms fade the flowering stems should be cut partway back to encourage a second crop of flowers. Increase of garden varieties is by division in spring or early fall, of wild species by division or by seed. Seeds give good results if sown in May or June in a cold frame or protected spot outdoors. The seedlings are transferred to nursery beds from whence they are moved to their flowering locations in fall or the following spring. Sidalceas are little grown in northeastern North America. They are better suited to regions of milder winters and cooler summers.

SIDE SADDLE FLOWER is *Sarracenia purpurea.*

SIDERANTHUS. See Haplopappus.

SIDERASIS (Sider-ásis). The only species of *Siderasis,* of the spiderwort family COM-MELINACEAE, a native of Brazil, was for a long time named *Tradescantia fuscata.* It has also been known as *Pyrrheima fuscatum.* Its present name, from the Greek *sideros,* iron, alludes to the rust-colored hairs.

A low, evergreen herbaceous perennial, *S. fuscata* has rosettes of spreading, broad-elliptic leaves that, like the flower stalks

Siderasis fuscata

and sepals, are thickly clothed on both sides with short, erect, reddish-brown, velvety hairs. The upper surfaces of the leaves are dark green relieved by a central longitudinal band of silvery-white; their undersides are suffused with wine-red. From the centers of the rosettes arise short stalks with one to four, but most commonly two, 1-inch-wide, rose-purple to nearly violet, upturned blooms that open in succession. Each flower has three sepals, three broad petals, six stamens, and a solitary style. The fruits are capsules.

Garden Uses. This plant is well worth cultivating for the beauty of its foliage. Its quite showy blooms, which come in spring, are an added attraction. Its chief value is as an ornament in tropical greenhouses and terrariums. In the tropics it can be used effectively in rock gardens.

Cultivation. To assure success with this easy-to-grow species, fertile, porous soil that contains an abundance of organic matter and that is always moderately moist without being saturated for long periods is needed. A minimum winter temperature of 60°F, with a rise of a few degrees by day, and considerably more warmth at other seasons, and a decidedly humid atmosphere, provide an encouraging environment. Shade from strong sun is necessary. Propagation is by division and by seed.

SIDERITIS (Sider-ìtis). Belonging to the mint family LABIATAE, the genus *Sideritis* inhabits the Canary Islands, Madeira, Europe, and temperate Asia. It has 100 species of herbaceous plants, subshrubs, and shrubs, of which few are cultivated. The name, one used by Dioscorides, from the Greek *sideros,* iron, was given in recognition of an ancient belief that these plants could be employed to heal wounds caused by iron.

Sideritises are softly-hairy or woolly. They have opposite, undivided, toothed or toothless leaves and small, usually yellowish flowers in clusters of three or more from the axils of the upper leaves or bracts. The whorls (circles) of blooms, distant or close together are in spikelike arrangements along the upper parts of the stems. Each bloom has a five-toothed calyx, the teeth often spiny, and a two-lipped, tubular corolla with the upper lip notched or two-lobed and the lower with a central lobe flanked by two smaller ones. There are four stamens. The fruits consist of four seedlike nutlets.

Attractive natives of the Canary Islands are *S. canariensis, S. candicans,* and *S. dasygnaphala.* A shrub several feet tall, *S. canariensis* has long-stalked, round-toothed, ovate to heart-shaped, wrinkled, leaves 2 to 4 inches long and clothed with a velvet covering of yellow hairs. Its flowers, in circles of twenty to thirty, are in branchless spikes. They have a yellow corolla with the lower lip distinctly darker than the upper lip. Differing from the last in being only about 3 feet tall, in having stems and foliage densely clothed with white wool, and in its pale yellow flowers, with light brown to orange-red lower lips, being about ten in each circle, **S. candicans** is an especially lovely endemic of Tener-

Sideritis candicans

ife. Much like *S. candicans,* but differing in its flowers having a spine at the tip of each calyx lobe and yellow corollas without a darker lower lip, **S. dasygnaphala** is endemic to Gran Canaria.

Sideritis dasygnaphala

Other Canary Island natives cultivated include *S. argosphacelus, S. macrostachys,* and *S. massoniana,* the latter also indigenous in Madeira. From 6 inches to 1½ feet tall, **S. argosphacelus** has white-felty-hairy stems. The leaves are 2 to 4 inches long, round-toothed, grayish-hairy to greenish on their upper surfaces, and white-hairy beneath. The flowers, yellowish with brown lower lips, are in densely-white-hairy spikes. A shrub about 3 feet tall, **S. macrostachys** has large, round-toothed, ovate to nearly circular leaves that have gray-green upper sides and are white-hairy beneath. The crowded, erect flower spikes are 2 to 3 inches long. Approximately as tall, **S. massoniana** has blunt-pointed, slightly-round-toothed, oblong-ovate to heart-shaped leaves with greenish-pubescent upper surfaces and gray-hairy un-

Sideritis argosphacelus

dersides. The flower spikes are of rather widely-spaced whorls of pale yellow blooms. Variety *S. m. albida,* less hairy, has broader, more pointed leaves and paler flowers.

Native to southern Europe, **S. hyssopifolia** is a variable, much-branched subshrub 4 inches to a little over 1 foot tall. Its three-veined leaves, elliptic to linear, and sometimes toothed, are up to 1 inch long or a little longer. Pale yellow, and often spotted with purple, the blooms are in circles of six. They form short, dense, cylindrical spikes up to 4½ inches long. This sort inhabits rocky places in mountains.

Sideritis hyssopifolia

Garden and Landscape Uses and Cultivation. The kinds discussed are not hardy in the north, but for sunny sites where the soil is well drained and on the dryish side, they are appropriate in warm, semiarid climates such as those of parts of California and the southwest. They are fitting furnishings for shrub borders and beds, and the low growing ones for rock gardens. In Europe *S. candicans* is sometimes used in temporary summer plantings in flower beds, the plants being carried over the winter in cool greenhouses. Propagation is by cuttings and by seed.

SIDEROXYLON. See Mastichodendron, and Planchonella.

SIEVERSIA. See Geum.

SIGMATOSTALIX (Sigmato-stàlix). Small epiphytic (tree-perching) orchids constitute *Sigmatostalix.* Natives from Mexico to Brazil, they belong to the orchid family ORCHIDACEAE. There are about twenty species. The name, from the Greek letter *sigma,* and *stalix,* a stake, alludes to the column of the flower.

Sigmatostalixes have pseudobulbs with one or two leaves, and racemes or panicles of small blooms. The sepals and petals are similar. The lip narrows at its base to a claw or shaft. The column, suggesting that of the swan orchid (*Cycnoches*), is long and curved.

Peruvian **S. graminea** (syns. *S. bicornuta, S. peruviana*) has clusters of ovoid, about ½-inch-long pseudobulbs, each with a solitary linear leaf up to 2 inches long. The flowers, in loose racemes of few, have light yellow sepals and petals not over ⅛ inch long, the latter with a hornlike projection on the back. The petals and upper sepal are banded or striped with purple. The lip, triangular-kidney-shaped, is up to ¼ inch long.

Native from Mexico to Panama, **S. guatemalensis** (syn *S. costaricensis*) has clusters of flattened, 1½-inch-long pseudobulbs, each with one strap-shaped to elliptic-lanceolate leaf up to 5 inches long. The slender, erect flower stalks, with few to many rather distantly-spaced blooms, are up to 1 foot long. They sometimes branch. The reflexed sepals and petals are about ¼ inch long. They are pale green to yellow, usually marked with brown. Rarely yellow, the indistinctly three-lobed lip is more commonly reddish-brown with a yellow apex. There is a short spur at its base. With much the aspect of the last, **S. hymenantha,** of Costa Rica and Panama, has flowers under ¼ inch long in racemes not over 6 inches long that have short spreading branches. They have greenish to light brown, usually reflexed sepals and petals, and an indistinctly three-lobed, short-clawed, ovate lip with a fleshy callus.

Garden Uses and Cultivation. Of practical interest only to collectors of orchids, these plants are not difficult to grow. They succeed in humid, intermediate- or tropical-temperature greenhouses where they are shaded from strong sun. They are best kept in smallish, well-drained pots or pans (shallow pots) in osmunda or tree fern fiber or in tree bark of a type suitable for orchids. Except for periods of two or three weeks following the completion of growth of the new pseudobulbs, the rooting medium must be kept evenly moist, but not saturated. For further information see Orchids.

SILENE (Sil-lè-ne) — Catchfly, Campion, Cushion-Pink, Wild-Pink, Fire-Pink, Indian-Pink. This genus, of the pink family CAROPHYLLACEAE, is so closely related to *Lychnis* that it is difficult to draw sure lines of separation between them, and sorts placed in one genus by some authorities are sometimes accepted in the other genus. As treated here, *Silene* includes about 500 species. Its name is an ancient Greek one for a related plant.

Silenes are annuals, biennials, and herbaceous perennials widely distributed in temperate and cold regions throughout most parts of the world. They are low and cushion-forming or tufted, or have longer, erect or sprawling stems. Their leaves are opposite. The white, pink, or red flowers, solitary or in clusters or sprays, have five-toothed or -cleft, sometimes much-inflated cylindrical, egg- or bell-shaped calyxes; five petals with blades narrowed at their bases into shafts or claws, commonly, but not always, with a scalelike appendage at the base of the blade; ten stamens; and usually three, although sometimes five, styles. The fruits are capsules with generally six, or rarely three, teeth at their apexes.

Annual or biennial silenes fairly commonly cultivated include the sweet william catchfly (*S. armeria*) and *S. pendula,* both natives of southern Europe. Naturalized in parts of North America, **S. armeria** is 1 foot to 2 feet tall, erect, branched, hairless or minutely-hairy, and glaucous. The upper parts of its stems are sticky. The leaves, ovate-lanceolate to elliptic-oblong and 1 inch to 3 inches long or sometimes longer, have heart-shaped, stem-clasping bases. In crowded, branched clusters the short-stalked pink blooms, about ¾ inch across, have petals notched at their apexes. Varieties *S. a. grandiflora* and *S. a. splendida* have larger blooms. Those of *S. a. alba* are white. Similar **S. compacta** (syn. *S. orientalis*), native from

southeast Europe to the Ukraine, has stouter stems and broader leaves than sweet william catchfly. Its petals are not notched at their apexes. Showy **S. pendula** has erect, pubescent stems, about 9 inches tall, with oblong, spatula-shaped or lanceolate, softly-hairy leaves and more or less pendulous racemes of ½-inch-wide, light pink flowers. White flowers are borne by *S. p. alba,* pale pink ones by *S. p. carnea,* rose-pink ones by *S. p. rosea,* and purple blooms by *S. p. bonnettii.* There are also varieties with double flowers and some of especially compact habit.

Biennial or perhaps sometimes perennial, **S. rupestris,** a mountain species of central and western Europe, is up to 10 inches tall. It has erect, branched stems, oblanceolate basal leaves, and lanceolate stem ones. Its milky-white or sometimes pink-tinged flowers have broad-obovate, deeply notched petals with pointed scales at their bases.

Wild-pink (**S. caroliniana**), a glandular-hairy perennial native of rocky and grav-

Silene caroliniana

elly soils in dry open woodlands from New Hampshire to Ohio, North Carolina, and Tennessee, has a strong taproot and erect, slender, branchless stems 4 to 8 inches tall with two or three pairs of leaves. Broadly- to narrowly-oblanceolate, the leaves are 2 to 4½ inches long. The up-facing, deep pink to white blooms have densely-glandular-hairy calyxes. Sometimes treated as separate species, *S. c. pensylvanica* (syn. *S. pensylvanica*) differs in minute floral details, whereas *S. c. wherryi* (syn. *S. wherryi*), an attractive inhabitant of limestone woodlands from Kentucky to Ohio, Alabama, and Missouri, is distinct by reason of having flowers with calyxes densely-clothed with nonglandular hairs.

Fire-pink (**S. virginica**) inhabits rocky slopes and rich open woodlands from New York to Ontario, Georgia, and Oklahoma. A perennial in cultivation sometimes rather short-lived, this has glandular stems 6 inches to 2 feet tall or sometimes taller. Its basal leaves, oblanceolate to spatula-

shaped and up to 4 inches long and ¾ inch wide, are hairless or short-hairy. The stem leaves, of which there are two to four pairs almost or quite stalkless, may be as much as 1 foot long by 1¼ inches wide. In loose clusters, the brilliant scarlet-crimson, up-facing blooms, 1½ to 2 inches wide, have shallowly- to deeply-notched petals. From the fire-pink, **S. rotundifolia,** a perennial native of rocky banks and cliffs from West Virginia to Ohio, Georgia, and Alabama, differs in having weak, decumbent, freely-branched, thinly-hairy stems and much broader to nearly round leaves up to 4 inches long. Its crimson blooms, in clusters of few, which face upward and are 1½ to 2 inches wide, have petals deeply notched at their apexes.

Native to California and Oregon, **S. californica** (syn. *Melandrium californicum*), sometimes called Indian-pink, is a thick-rooted perennial with decumbent to erect, leafy, glandular-hairy stems 6 inches to 1 foot long or somewhat longer. Ovate to oblanceolate, the leaves are 1½ to 3½ inches long by up to a little over 1 inch wide. The few to many crimson blooms, about 1¼ inches wide, have deeply-four-lobed petals.

White and red campions, pleasant natives of Europe, North Africa, and temperate Asia, are naturalized in North America. By many authorities they are included in *Lychnis.* The white campion (**S. alba** syns. *Lychnis alba, Melandrium album*) is hairy and 1 foot to 2 feet tall. It has oblong leaves, 1 inch to 1½ inches long, and white or creamy-white flowers, male and female mostly on separate plants. A double-flowered variety is known. The red campion (**S. dioica** syns. *Lychnis dioica, Melandrium rubrum*) is similar, but is not glandular. It has smaller, purplish-red or rarely white flowers. Hybrids between the two occur.

Silene dioica

Bladder campion and sea campion are *S. vulgaris* (syns. *S. latifolia, S. cucubalus*) and *S. v. maritima* (syn. *S. maritima*), respectively. A very variable perennial of

Silene compacta

which several subspecies are recognized, *S. vulgaris* has usually branched, hairy or hairless, often glaucous stems up to 2 feet long and ovate to linear leaves. The solitary or clustered flowers have persistent, inflated calyxes with about twenty veins. The sizable corollas have usually white or whitish, deeply-notched petals narrowed to clawed bases, and usually scales that form a little crown or corona at the center of the bloom. The sea campion is an attractive, easy-to-grow native of sea coasts and cliffs in Europe. Forming mats of horizontally-spreading stems, it has very glaucous, linear-lanceolate to somewhat spatula-shaped leaves and white flowers. A double-flowered form is in common cultivation. There is also one with pinkish blooms.

Attractive magenta-pink-flowered *S. schafta*, of the Caucasus, is a perennial 3 to 6 inches tall with a woody rootstock and numerous weak, more or less procumbent, little-branched or branchless stems. The leaves are pointed-ovate-oblong. Solitary or in clusters of up to five, the pink to magenta-pink flowers have broadly-obovate petals notched at their apexes, each with two scales.

Low perennial sorts with white or whitish flowers, suitable for rock gardens and similar places, include, besides the sea campion described earlier, *S. quadrifida*, *S. quadridentata*, *S. saxifraga*, and *S. zawadskii*. A mountain plant of much beauty and from 6 to 9 inches or less often 1 foot tall, the alpine catchfly (*S. quadrifida* syn. *S. alpestris*) favors dampish places chiefly in

Silene quadrifida

limestone soils. Somewhat hairy, it has linear-lanceolate to narrow-obovate leaves ½ inch to 1½ inches long by up to ⅓ inch wide, and more or less sticky, lacy flower clusters. The individual flowers are ½-inch-wide and glossy-white and have four- to six-toothed petals with hair-fringed claws. There is also a double-flowered variety named *S. a. flore-pleno*. From the alpine catchfly, *S. quadridentata* (syn. *S. pusilla*), which grows wild under similar condi-

tions, differs in not exceeding 6 inches in height and in the claws of its petals not being fringed with hairs. Usually dwarf and densely-tufted, pretty *S. saxifraga* is a native of mountains in southern and central Europe and adjacent Asia. A perennial 3 to 8 inches tall and sometimes taller, it forms a loose cushion of usually branched, slender stems, sticky in their upper parts and pubescent below, and linear to linear-lanceolate, grassy-green leaves hair-fringed at their bases. The solitary or sometimes paired flowers have white or greenish-white, two-lobed petals brownish on the outsides. A native of central Europe, *S. zawadskii* (syn. *Melandrium zawadskii*) usually attains the middle

Silene zawadskii

reaches of its 3- to 8-inch height. It has fairly erect stems, hairy on their upper parts, and basal rosettes of lustrous, lanceolate leaves, with their lower margins fringed with hairs. The few stem leaves are linear-lanceolate. In few-flowered racemes, the blooms are white.

Moss campion or cushion-pink (*S. acaulis*) is native at high altitudes throughout the northern hemisphere and at lower elevations in subarctic and arctic regions. A charming alpine, this has a stout, woody rootstock. It forms compact, bright green,

Silene acaulis

mosslike mats or mounds, 1 inch to 3 inches high, of densely-crowded, fine foliage. In season these are studded with little, rose-pink to white, short-stalked, starry blooms with notched, oblanceolate petals with or without a two-lobed scale. The short-hair-fringed but otherwise hairless leaves ⅛ to ½ inch long are in rosettes. The American form of this species, native as far south as mountain tops in New Hampshire, is sometimes distinguished as *S. a. exscapa*.

Among the loveliest and choicest endemic American alpines is *S. hookeri* (syn. *S. ingramii*). This has a perpendicular stout

Silene hookeri

root from the top of which come shoots that sprawl in starfish-like fashion and have gray-downy, elliptic-spatula-shaped to pointed-elliptic-lanceolate leaves 2 to 4 inches long. Solitary from the leaf axils or few together from the ends of the stems, the flowers, 2 to 2½ inches wide, have spreading petals so deeply-lobed that each almost appears to be two slender petals. They vary in color from white to pink, cherry-red, purple, or violet.

Garden Uses. These are various depending upon sorts. The moss-campion and other high mountain kinds described are worthy of the best attentions of skilled growers of alpine plants. Even when happily placed, at least to the extent that it is permanent and grows well, *S. acaulis* is bothersome in being often reluctant to bloom with anything like the freedom it does in its native mountains. A sparse sprinkling of flowers decorating its mossy cushions is accounted as a horticultural achievement.

The other low perennials presented are equally as appropriate in rock gardens, but fortunately respond to less special treatment. Other sorts including the white and red campions and fire-pink are adapted to naturalistic plantings.

Except the wild-pink, fire-pink, *S. rotundifolia*, and the white and red campions, all of which crave a measure of shade in which the fiercest rays are filtered without committing the plants to sunlessness, these easier silenes prosper in full sun. The ones that prefer a little shade are as useful in woodland gardens and native plant gardens as rock gardens. Annual and biennial catchflys are simple-to-grow plants for displaying to good advantage in flower beds and borders.

Cultivation. Annual and biennial silenes prosper in ordinary garden soil and are easily raised from seed. Sow annuals in spring or in mild climates in fall where the plants are to bloom and thin the seedlings sufficiently to allow adequate space for their development. Sow biennnials in June and July and transplant the seedlings to nursery beds or cold frames to make their first season's growth. In early fall or spring lift the plants from the nursery beds or cold frames and transfer them to sites where they are to bloom.

Perennial silenes are mostly easy to manage. Those that appreciate some shade generally prefer slightly dampish woodland soil. Alpine or mountain species prefer poorer, gritty earth well-drained, but not excessively dry. The perennials may be increased by seed and by division.

SILK and SILKY. The word silk forms parts of the names of these plants: Chinese silk plant (*Boehmeria nivea*), floss-silk tree (*Chorisia speciosa*), red-silk-cotton tree (*Bombax ceiba*), silk-cotton tree (*Ceiba pentandra* and *Cochlospermum religiosum*), silk grass (*Agrostis hiemalis*), silk- or silky-oak (*Grevillea robusta*), silk tassel bush (*Garrya*), silk tree (*Albizia julibrissin*), silk vine (*Periploca*), and white silky-oak (*Grevillea hilliana*).

SILKWEED. See Asclepias.

SILPHIUM (Sílph-ium)—Rosinweed, Compass Plant, Cup Plant, Prairie-Dock. The genus *Silphium* accounts for possibly twenty species of coarse, vigorous, hardy herbaceous perennials, natives of eastern and midwestern North America. They are summer- and fall-bloomers and belong in the daisy family COMPOSITAE. The name is modified from *silphion*, which the ancient Greeks applied to a North African plant, the source of a resin.

Silphiums are sunflower-like plants with flower heads that have a central eye or disk of sterile florets, and petal-like, yellow or rarely white ray florets that are fertile. The leaves are alternate, opposite, or whorled (in circles of more than two). Some kinds have leafy stems, in others the foliage is chiefly basal. From sunflowers (*Helianthus*) silphiums differ in having sterile disk florets with undivided styles.

The compass plant (*S. laciniatum*) is so called because of a tendency of its erect basal leaves to align themselves in a north–south direction. Native from Ohio to

Minnesota, South Dakota, Alabama, and Tennessee, it is a conspicuous element in the prairie flora. From 5 to 10 feet tall, it has bristly stems and alternate, deeply once- or twice-pinnately-lobed leaves that are hairy chiefly along the midrib and veins beneath. The lower ones may be 1 foot long or longer. From the base upward, the leaves become gradually smaller. The several to many flower heads, in narrow clusters, have disks from nearly to a little over 1 inch wide and fifteen to thirty ray florets ¾ inch to 2 inches long.

The cup plant (*S. perfoliatum*) differs from the last in its leaves being only

Silphium perfoliatum

coarsely-toothed. The bases of the opposite upper ones envelop the hairless, square stems to form the cups alluded to in the common name. Roughly-hairy, the leaves are broadly-ovate to triangular and up to 1 foot in length. The flower heads, in loose clusters of several to many, have disks about 1 inch across and fifteen to thirty ray florets ¾ inch to 1½ inches long. This species inhabits open, fertile woodlands and low ground from Ontario to South Dakota, Georgia, and Louisiana.

Native chiefly to open woodlands, but also to prairies, *S. trifoliatum*, 3 to 6 feet in height, has hairless, glaucous stems. Its leaves, usually in circles of three or four, but sometimes opposite or alternate, mostly have short stalks; sometimes they are stalkless. Lanceolate, and more or less irregularly toothed, they are 3½ to 8 inches long by ¾ inch to 2 inches broad and are commonly short-bristly-hairy above and more or less hairy on their undersides; occasionally they are without hairs. The loose flower clusters consist of several to many

flower heads with disks up to ⅝ inch wide, and eight to fifteen ray florets ¾ inch to 1½ inch long.

From the previous kinds the prairie-dock (*S. terebinthinaceum*) differs in having nearly leafless, hairless stems; its leaves are almost entirely basal. They are long-stalked, narrowly- to broadly-ovate to elliptic, and usually heart-shaped at their bases. Rarely lobed, more commonly they are only sharply-toothed and may be hairless or have short, bristly hairs. The bloom clusters consist of several to many flower heads with disks ¾ to 1 inch wide, and twelve to twenty rays from somewhat under to somewhat over 1 inch in length.

Garden and Landscape Uses. Silphiums are stately, bold plants well suited for wild gardens and naturalistic plantings and for occasional use in the rears of large flower borders. In late summer they provide welcome color. They prefer deep, moderately fertile, not-too-dry soil and prosper in sun and, *S. laciniatum* and *S. trifoliatum*, in part-shade.

Cultivation. Little routine care is needed. A spring application of fertilizer is in order, but care must be taken not to apply too much nitrogen because of the risk of encouraging too rank growth. Staking is rarely needed, but a little unobtrusive support of this kind may be desirable. Propagation can be effected by division in early fall or spring and by seed. With kinds such as *S. laciniatum*, which have massive rootstocks that they are difficult to divide, seeds are more practicable.

SILT. This is the fraction of the soil consisting of particles of mineral matter larger than those of clay but smaller than those of sand. Silt particles range from 0.002 to 0.05 millimeters in diameter. Silt soils are those in which the mineral content consists of at least 80 percent silt, less than 12 percent clay. Such soils have characteristics intermediate between those of clayey and sandy soils. They are difficult to work because of their tendency to become compact and poorly aerated and because of the fact that crumb structure cannot be attained because silt particles, unlike clay particles, cannot be flocculated.

SILVER. The word silver forms parts of the names of these plants: silver lace vine (*Polygonum aubertii*), silver leaf (*Alphitonia excelsa*), silver-panamiga (*Pilea pubescens*), silver tree (*Leucodendron argenteum*), and silver vine (*Actinidia polygama*).

SILVERBELL. See Halesia.

SILVERBERRY is *Elaeagnus commutata*.

SILVERROD is *Solidago bicolor*.

SILVERSWORD. See Argyroxiphium.

SILYBUM (Síly-bum). Two species of thistle-like annuals or biennials of the Old World belong in *Silybum,* of the daisy family COMPOSITAE. The name is an ancient Greek one used by Dioscorides for some thistle-like plant.

Silybums are hairless and form rosettes of basal leaves from which rise branching, leafy flower stalks to a height of 3 or 4 feet. The glossy-green leaves are lobed, spiny-toothed, and conspicuously spotted or marbled with white. The flower heads are terminal, fairly fragrant, rose-purple, and 1 inch to 2½ inches across, with a collar or stiff, leafy, spiny bracts beneath each. The fruits are achenes.

Blessed-thistle, Holy-thistle, St.-Mary's-thistle, and milk-thistle are all vernacular names of *S. marianum,* a native of the Mediterranean region. Since this plant is

Silybum marianum

Silybum marianum (flower head)

common in the Holy Land, it is considered to be one of the several species included in the biblical meaning of the word thistle. This plant has beautiful foliage and

quite showy flower heads. The blessed-thistle is naturalized in California and extensively on the pampas of South America. It has been cultivated in Europe for its edible leaves and roots as a potherb, salad, and vegetable.

The other species *S. eburneum,* a native of North Africa, differs from *S. marianum* chiefly in the outer bracts of its flower heads being erect and short-pointed.

Garden and Landscape Uses. Silybums are sufficiently ornamental to warrant their inclusion to a modest extent in flower beds and borders where their blooms can be seen. Because the flower heads are on tall stalks, the need to appreciate the plants when they are low as well as when they are much higher sometimes presents a problem in locating them in small flower beds. They are especially appropriate for use in summer beds planted for subtropical effects. Silybums can also be used effectively in informal areas, especially on slopes and in association with such plants as yuccas, agaves, sedums, and others that take kindly to sunny, dryish conditions. It is also appropriate to include them in herb gardens.

Cultivation. These plants, raised from seed, are grown as annuals or biennials. The former treatment involves sowing indoors about eight weeks before the young plants are to be set in the garden, which is done about the time it is safe to plant out tomatoes, and growing them until then in flats or pots. When grown as biennials, the seeds are sown in June or July and the young plants transplanted to nursery beds or cold frames and in the following early spring to their flowering quarters. Beyond keeping down weeds, no particular care is required. Silybums need full sun and succeed in any fertile garden soil. They will grow even in poor soils, but do not then have the lush foliage that is largely responsible for their beauty. Their sturdy flower stalks stand without staking.

SIMAROUBACEAE — Quassia Family. The chiefly tropical family SIMAROUBACEAE comprises some 200 species of dicotyledons distributed among thirty genera. Its sorts, trees and shrubs, sometimes have very bitter bark. The alternate leaves, usually pinnate, are rarely undivided or rudimentary. The symmetrical, unisexual or bisexual small flowers are in terminal or axillary spikelike arrangements, racemes, or panicles. Generally they have five each sepals and petals, less frequently as few as three or up to eight. Rarely there are no petals. There are as many or twice as many stamens as petals (or sepals) or sometimes more and one to eight separate or united styles. The fruits are capsules, berries, drupes, or samaras. Genera of this family included in this Encyclopedia are *Ailanthus* and *Quassia.*

SIMMONDSIA (Simmónd-sia) — Goat Nut or Jojoba. The one species of this genus is the only member of the box family BUXACEAE that is native to California. Indigenous also in Baja California, it has a name that commemorates the nineteenth-century English naturalist, T. W. Simmonds. In view of its natural range and of its interest, it is unfortunate that the name has had to be changed from enlightening *Simmondsia californica* to completely misleading *S. chinensis* (meaning of China). But such are the quirks of the code for the application of botanical names that in the interest of uniformity must be accepted. Undoubtedly the first botanist to apply the epithet *chinensis* was sincere in his belief that the plant had its home in China.

A rigid, much-branched, evergreen shrub, 2 to 6 feet tall, with opposite, leathery, undivided, toothless leaves, *S. chinensis* has hairy young shoots. Its very short-stalked, dull green, oblong-ovate

Simmondsia chinensis

leaves are ¾ inch to 1½ inches long, and to a greater or lesser degree minutely-grayish-hairy. Male and female flowers are on separate plants. They have usually five, rarely four or six, greenish sepals and no petals. The males are somewhat cupped in shape and have ten or twelve stamens. The females are bell-shaped and have a prominent ovary and three styles. The flowers are on short stalks from the leaf axils, the females solitary, the males clustered. The fruits are acorn-like, three-angled, ovoid, one-seeded capsules about ¾ inch long, partially enclosed by the enlarged, persistent sepals.

In the 1970s this species became the subject of intensive research, investigation, and trial as the source of an oil that has properties so similar to those of sperm whale oil that it can be used as an adequate substitute for that increasingly scarce commodity. Among the many uses of jojoba oil are as a lubricant for high-speed machinery, as an additive to other lubricants, and as an ingredient of soaps, shampoos, face creams, hair oils, and similar products, as well as of furniture polishes, floor waxes, and automobile waxes. It may also be employed as a stabilizer of penicillin products and for cooking.

Garden and Landscape Uses and Cultivation. This boxwood-like native of arid hills in southwest North America is not hardy in the north. It is used to some extent for landscaping within its native range and in places that provide somewhat similar climates and environments. Propagation, usually by seed, can probably also be achieved by cuttings. Young plants are grown in containers until of a size that can be set in their permanent locations.

SINAPIS. See Brassica.

SINARUNDINARIA (Sin-arundinària). East Asian *Sinarundinaria*, sometimes spelled *Sinoarundinaria*, of the grass family GRAMINEAE, is closely allied to *Arundinaria* and *Semiarundinaria*, and by some authorities is included in the first. Unlike those of *Arundinaria*, the leaf sheaths of *Sinarundinaria* are not long persistent, but remain until the spring of the second year. They differ from those of *Semiarundinaria* in having pliable instead of rigid bristles. The name comes from the Latin *sino*, of China, and *Arundinaria*, the name of another genus of bamboos. It alludes to the similarity and geographical origin.

Sinarundinarias, of which there are about twenty species, form dense clumps of canes. Perhaps the hardiest and one of the most graceful of bamboos, *S. nitida*, of China, can be grown outdoors in sheltered sites in southern New York and southern New England. Under optimum conditions it attains a height of 20 feet, but often is not over 12 feet tall. This bamboo has slender, greenish-purple or purple canes and pubescent, purplish leaf sheaths. Its stems do not branch until their second season when they produce four or five branches from each node. In succeeding seasons the branches increase in number. When young the canes are covered with a waxy bloom. The leaves are small, thin, and fringed with fine bristly hairs all along both margins. They are up to 5 inches long, about ½ inch wide, and not strongly tessellated. The Chinese believe, probably mistakenly, that this species flowers only at intervals of 100 years.

Much more tender *S. murieliae* (syn. *Arundinaria murieliae*), also of China, has slender, yellow canes with a waxy bloom when young that branch earlier than do those of *S. nitida*. During the first season three or four branches develop, more subsequently. About 12 feet tall, this has leaves up to 5 inches long by about ½ to ¾ inch wide, green above, glaucous beneath, and with one margin edged with fine bristles, the other partially so. This

highly ornamental bamboo is not hardy in the north.

Garden and Landscape Uses and Cultivation. These plants thrive in moist, but not waterlogged soil and partial shade. They are handsome plants for containers. For more information on their uses and cultivation see Bamboos.

SINEPHROPTERIS (Sinephró-pteris). The only species of *Sinephropteris*, of the asplenium family ASPLENIACEAE, is native from southern China to Burma. Its name, meaning Chinese kidney fern, is derived from the Latin *sino*, of China, and the Greek *nephros*, a kidney, and *pteris*, a fern.

A small carpeting plant with brief, ascending rhizomes, *S. delavayi* (syn. *Scolopendrium delavayi*) has brown-stalked, kid-

Sinephropteris delavayi

ney-shaped fronds (leaves) ¾ inch to 1½ inches wide, heart-shaped at their bases and often with wavy margins. The spore clusters are mostly in pairs.

Garden Uses and Cultivation. An interesting species for inclusion in collections of ferns, *S. delavayi* thrives in humid environments outdoors in the tropics and warm subtropics, and in greenhouses and terrariums. It prospers in well-drained soil with a high humus content, kept evenly moist. Shade from direct sun is needed. Propagation is by division and by spores.

SINGHARA NUT is *Trapa bispinosa*.

SINK GARDENING. This phase of gardening in containers, popular in the British Isles, is sometimes done in North America. The receptacles are old stone sinks or troughs of sorts once common in rural districts, or because of the increasing scarcity of these, are newly cut from stone or are carefully made of concrete to simulate old sinks. It is important that they have drainage holes in their bottoms.

Filling is started by installing a layer of crocks, gravel, or other suitable coarse material and covering this with coarse leaves

or straw. Then a porous soil mix suited to the needs of the plants is filled in, firmed, and brought to about the level of the rim of the container or slightly higher. A few pieces of rock are usually positioned at the surface, which is contoured to suggest part of a miniature alpine landscape. Finally the plants are set and the soil surface is mulched with chips of stone.

SINNINGIA (Sin-níngia) — Gloxinia. The beautiful flowering plants commonly known to florists and gardeners as gloxinias do not belong in the botanists' genus *Gloxinia*, but in *Sinningia*, which is another member of the gesneria family GESNERIACEAE, and as such has contributed to a remarkable, widespread popular interest in that family that has been evident in North America since approximately the middle of the twentieth century.

Sinningias are native from Mexico to Argentina. Their name commemorates head gardener and instructor Wilhelm Sinning, of the University of Bonn, Germany, who died in 1874. As now understood the genus, comprising more than 75 species, includes the plants previously segregated as *Rechsteineria*.

Sinningias are nonhardy, nearly stemless to long-stemmed, deciduous or evergreen perennials and subshrubs. Most kinds have tubers, some do not; two species have rhizomes. Their stems and foliage are more or less softly-hairy. The leaves, undivided and opposite, in whorls (circles) of six or more, crowded at the base on short stems or arising directly from the tubers, are often fairly long-stalked. Those of many kinds form rosettes. Large or small, on long or shortish stalks, the flowers, except those of *S. tubiflora*, which are in racemes, are solitary or in branched, often long-stalked clusters from the leaf axils. They have five-lobed, leafy calyxes and tubular, cylindrical to nearly bell-shaped, frequently more or less two-lipped corollas with five unequal or nearly equal, rounded, flaring lobes (petals). There are four nonprotruding stamens with their anthers cohering, and a long style ending in a usually mouth-shaped stigma. Two to five prominent glands are located at the bottom of the ovary. The fruits are capsules.

Gloxinias of florists and gardens are derivatives of *S. speciosa*, a variable, deciduous, tuberous species with or without stems, perhaps no longer cultivated in its wild form. Its round-toothed, ovate to oblong-ovate leaves in flat rosettes, are up to 6 inches or more in length. The asymmetrical, nodding, white to purple and perhaps red but most commonly lavender blooms are about 2½ inches in length, but less in diameter. Horticultural varieties include, in addition to kinds with nodding, slipper-type blooms, the even more famil-

Sinningia speciosa

iar and popular sorts that have up-facing, bell- to bowl-shaped, symmetrical flowers up to 3 inches, or more, long and wide, in a wide color range including rich velvety reds, pinks, purples, blues, lavenders, and spotted and bicolor as well as white kinds. Vigorous specimens may have leaves 1 foot long. They produce large numbers of magnificent blooms. Double- as well as single-flowered kinds are popular. Quite like the wild form of *S. speciosa*, but its leaves longer-stalked and toward their apexes concave, tuberous *S. discolor* is charming. This has nodding, clear lavender-blue flowers, paler toward the bases of their corolla tubes, lifted on erect or arching stems well above the flat rosette of foliage. They are about 2¼ inches long by 1¼ inches wide. Beautiful *S. regina* is a tuberous kind not as large as *S. discolor* or the wild form of *S. speciosa*. In rosettes of

Sinningia regina

few, its velvety-hairy, dark green leaves, 4 to 8 inches long and reddish on their undersides, spread flatly. They have clearly defined white veins. The rich purple, 2-inch-long blooms, paler and spotted in their throats, measure about 1¼ inches across their faces.

Another choice tuberous kind, *S. eumorpha* is distinguished from *S. speciosa* and its varieties by its flowers having more slender calyx lobes and two instead of five prominent glands at the base of the ovary. This has broad, heart-shaped, round-toothed leaves some 4 inches long, lustrous green above and reddish on their undersides. The nodding blooms are about 1¾ inches long by 1½ inches across their faces. They are white with a band of yellow and with sometimes lavender markings in their throats. Remarkable because of the abundant, long, soft hairs that clothe its flower stalks and calyxes as well as its leaves, tuberous *S. hirsuta* has reddish-veined, dull olive-green, heart-shaped

Sinningia hirsuta

leaves with reddish undersides. They are up to 6 inches long. In compact clusters from the leaf axils, the violet-dotted, purple-throated, white flowers are borne in astonishing profusion. Asymmetrical and held more or less horizontally, the blooms have faces about ¾ inch wide.

Miniatures, *S. pusilla* and *S. concinna* are especially charming. Evergreen **S. pusilla** has tiny tubers difficult to start into growth

Sinningia pusilla

again if the plant is allowed to go dormant. This species has dark olive-green, broad-elliptic or oval leaves with reddish veins. They are in rosettes about 2½ inches in diameter. Funnel-shaped, the ½-inch-wide white-throated, lavender blooms have corolla tubes pouched or spurred at their lower ends and ¾ to 1 inch long. The petals are faintly marked with darker lines. White-flowered *S. p.* 'White Sprite' is just as pretty and so is *S. p.* 'Snowflake', which has fringed white blooms. With rosettes of foliage scarcely exceeding 2 inches in diameter, *S. concinna* has tiny, round tubers. Its slightly nodding, red-stalked flowers, except for their narrower corolla tubes, are equal in size of those of *S. pusilla*. The corolla tubes, bright purple along their tops, are white on their undersides. The two upper petals are purple, the others white with purple edges. Their throats are densely spotted with purple.

Very different from the kinds described above, *S. richii* does not form definite rosettes. It has prostrate stems and because of this has been called the creeping gloxinia. In addition to a sizable tuber, little ones are strung like beads along underground rhizomes. The oblong leaves, up to 8 inches long, are lustrous. The white flowers, spotted in their throats with delicate purple, are 1½ inches long and nearly as much across their asymmetrical faces. Their petals bend backward.

Tall-stemmed sinningias, very different in appearance from florists' gloxinias, include remarkable *S. tubiflora*, the only strongly scented member of the gesneria

Sinningia tubiflora

family. Intensely fragrant of tuberoses, its blooms, unlike those of other sinningias, are in racemes. This species, which looks much more like an achimenes than a sinningia, was once named *Achimenes tubiflora*. Attractive, it has a large, potato-like tuber and slender rhizomes that often bear smaller tubers. The stem, its leafy portion from 6 inches to over 1 foot tall, continues as an erect, slender, leafless flower stalk that may attain a height of 3 feet, and its upper part is a one-sided raceme of blooms. The leaves have scalloped edges and are up to 5 inches long by 1½ inches wide. The white or creamy-white, drooping blooms are shortly spurred at the bottoms of their 3½-inch-long corolla tubes. They are 1½ inches across their faces.

Kinds without tubers, or in the case of *S. barbata* sometimes with very poorly developed ones, include that species and *S. schiffneri*. Up to about 2 feet tall, **S. barbata** has branched, square, reddish stems,

Sinningia schiffneri

Sinningia leucotricha

Sinningia barbata

their upper parts furnished with arching to more or less erect, lustrous, oblong-lanceolate leaves, tapered at both ends, 4 to 6 inches long, and with reddish-purple undersides. Solitary or in pairs from the leaf axils, the white or creamy-white flowers, 1½ to 2 inches long, have very markedly pouched, hairy corolla tubes, and small, narrow-throated faces. There are two prominent glands at the bottom of the ovary. This has much the aspect of *Nautilocalyx*. Less decorative than most sinningias, *S. schiffneri* has several squarish, branchless stems, up to 5 feet tall, and very short-stalked, asymmetrical, pointed-elliptic, round-toothed leaves up to 6 inches long and about one-half as wide. Trumpet-shaped, the asymmetrical flowers are more or less hidden by the foliage. About ¾ inch long, they are in short-stalked clusters of seven or fewer. They are white with, inside, a pale yellow stripe and purple dots.

Among sorts previously segregated as *Rechsteineria*, one of the showiest and most attractive is **S. cardinalis** (syns. *Rechstein-*

Sinningia cardinalis

eria cardinalis, Gesneria cardinalis, G. macrantha, Corytholoma cardinalis). A native of Brazil, this is from 6 inches to nearly 1 foot tall. It has softly-hairy stems and leaves, the latter ovate-heart-shaped, shallowly-toothed, and up to 6 inches long. More or less angled upward, the showy flowers sprout from the axils of the leaves or are crowded at the summits of the stems. Their brilliant scarlet, 2½- to 3-inch-long corollas, velvety-hairy on their outsides, have a long-projecting, hooded upper lip. A variant with creamy-white flowers is sometimes cultivated.

Another Brazilian, handsome **S. leucotricha** (syn. *Rechsteineria leucotricha*), is remarkable for its stems, foliage, and blooms being clothed with a wool of hairs at first white that later become brown. This has tubers up to 1 foot in diameter and fleshy stems with one or two whorls of three or four obovate leaves up to 6 inches long by 4 inches wide. Its narrowly-tubular, salmon-red to rosy-pink, 1¼-inch-long flowers are in clusters of three to five at the ends of the stems or stalks from the leaf axils. Somewhat similar *S. macropoda* (syns. *Rechsteineria cyclophylla, R. lineata*) differs in its up to 2-foot-tall stems and stalks of its fleshy leaves being without dark reddish-purple lines. As its botanical

Sinningia leucotricha (flowers)

Sinningia macrorrhiza

epithet indicates, **S. macrorrhiza** (syn. *Rechsteineria macrorrhiza*), of Brazil, has a large root (actually a more or less globular, somewhat woody tuber). Its erect to somewhat lax stems, like the leaves, are furnished with fine, white hairs. The ovate-heart-shaped, very short-stalked leaves are green. Narrowly-tubular, the flowers are in panicles at the ends of the stems and branches. From other low species in cultivation that have flowers without a projecting hood, *S. verticillata* (syns. *Rechsteineria verticillata, R. purpurea*) differs in having terminal umbels of shell-pink flowers heavily spotted with deep maroon. The leaves of young plants are in pairs, those of older ones in two whorls of six near the centers of stems about 3 feet tall. Completely stemless *S. tuberosa* (syn. *Rechsteineria tuberosa*) develops from its tuber one or two broad leaves up to 1 foot in length and a stalkless, dense cluster of 1¼-inch-long, yellow-throated, red flowers with corolla lobes of equal size, the two uppermost projecting forward.

Tall sorts formerly named *Rechsteineria* include *S. claybergiana* (syn. *Rechsteineria lindleyi*). This attains a height of about 5 feet and has elliptic to elliptic-oblong, round-toothed leaves and slender terminal racemes of nodding, 1- to 1½-inch-long, cherry-red flowers with nearly equal-sized corolla lobes. Like the last, but not as tall and with leaves with a strong odor, *S. aggregata* (syn. *Rechsteineria aggregata*) has similarly-shaped, but rather smaller, orange-spotted, yellow blooms. Much like *S. claybergiana*, but with flowers with a distinctly hooded upper lip, *S. warscewiczii* (syns. *Rechsteineria warscewiczii, Corytholoma warscewiczii*), of Mexico and Central America, has elliptic to pointed-ovate, round-toothed leaves and terminal spikes of 1½-inch-long, red or orange flowers with yellow throats.

Sinningia warscewiczii

Hybrid sinningias other than florists' gloxinias include a number of charming miniatures. Notable among these is *S. 'Dollbaby'*, the parents of which are *S. pusilla* and *S. eumorpha*. This resembles *S. pusilla*, but has bigger blooms. Of the same lineage, *S. 'Tetra'* has rosettes of foliage about 4 inches across, and 1-inch-long, pale violet blooms almost as wide across their faces. Attractive *S. 'Cindy'* resulted from mating *S. concinna* and *S. eumorpha*. The

offspring is a free-blooming, sturdy, intermediate miniature. One of the smallest sinningias, *S. 'Bright Eyes'*, a cross between *S. concinna* and *S. pusilla*, has comparatively large blooms. More erect than other miniatures, *S. 'Freckles'* has small leaves and comparatively large blooms. It is a hybrid between *S. concinna* and *S. hirsuta*.

Sinningia 'Bright Eyes'

Garden Uses and Cultivation. The cultivation of the showy florists' gloxinias (*S. speciosa* varieties) is dealt with under Gloxinia, Florists'. Here our discussion is limited to other kinds. Sinningias are attractive greenhouse plants and houseplants that appeal strongly to gardeners who like to specialize in particular plant groups. Fanciers of gesneriads are much interested in sinningias. Their cultural needs differ only in detail from those of African-violets, episcias, and other plants of the same family. Specifically, whereas the plants just mentioned are evergreen and have no season of dormancy, many but not all sinningias die down and rest for a period of each year.

The chief environmental needs are warmth, high humidity, suitable soil, and good light with shade from strong sun. They do well under fluorescent light where the day length is about sixteen hours. The soil must be well drained. It should contain a liberal proportion of organic matter, such as leaf mold or peat moss, and enough coarse sand or perlite to ensure good porosity. The addition of a little dried cow manure or sheep manure and some bonemeal to the mix is helpful. Except during the resting seasons of kinds that go dormant, the soil should be kept always fairly moist. Specimens that have filled their containers with roots benefit from regular applications of mild liquid fertilizer. A winter night temperature of about 60°F, with a daytime rise of ten to fifteen degrees, is satisfactory. When kinds with tubers show evident signs of going to rest, gradually lengthen the periods between applications of water, allowing the soil to

practically dry before giving any. Finally, withhold water altogether and store the plants in their pots laid on their sides in a place a few degrees cooler than where the plants are grown, but not below 55°F. Some kinds take only a short rest, others are dormant for longer periods. While resting they must be inspected frequently for signs of new growth. At the very first evidence of this shake them free of old soil, repot them, water them, and start them into growth under warmer conditions. Seeds are a ready means of multiplying species sinningias, as are leaf cuttings and, in some cases, stem cuttings, natural multiplication, and artificial division of the tubers. Choice varieties and hybrids do not come true from seeds; with them one of the other methods must be used. Sinningias are subject to the pests and diseases that affect African-violets and other gesneriads. For additional information see the entry Gesneriads in this Encyclopedia.

SINOCRASSULA. Five species of *Sedum*, native from western China to the Himalayas, are by some botanists separated as this genus. See Sedum.

SINOJACKIA (Sino-jáckia). First discovered in the outskirts of populous Nanking, China, *Sinojackia* was unknown to botanists until 1925 and was not scientifically described and named until three years later. It is thus a newcomer among the vast store of fine trees and shrubs to which China is home. Its name commemorates John George Jack, of the Arnold Arboretum, who died in 1949. Belonging to the storax family STYRACACEAE, this genus is related to *Styrax* and *Halesia*. There are three species.

Sinojackias are deciduous small trees or shrubs with short-stalked, toothed leaves, and leafy racemes of slender-stalked white flowers with calyxes with five to seven small lobes, corollas deeply divided into five to seven lobes (petals), twice as many stamens as petals, and a slender style longer than the petals. The fruits are woody and generally one-seeded.

The first species discovered, *S. xylocarpa*, is up to 20 feet tall. Its younger shoots are thinly furnished with stellate (starlike) hairs. The elliptic to somewhat obovate leaves may be nearly 3 inches in length and, except when young and on the mid-veins on their undersides, are without hairs. An inch in diameter, the flowers have stalks over 1 inch long with mostly five to six each calyx lobes and petals. The egg-shaped fruits are ½ to ¾ inch long by two-thirds as wide.

From 7 to 15 feet in height, *S. rehderana* has young shoots with stellate (starry) hairs. The short-stalked leaves are obovate to elliptic and 2 to 4 inches long by approximately as wide. Their edges are

Sinojackia rehderana

furnished with glandular teeth, their upper surfaces with scattered, stellate hairs. The undersides of the leaves are lustrous. The semipendulous, long-stalked, starry flowers, with bright yellow anthers, are in loose racemes of three to eight. They develop from the previous year's shoots and are 1½ to 2½ inches long. The flowers are accompanied by green bracts up to 1½ inches long by one-half as broad and resembling in color and shape regular leaves. The calyx is five- or six-toothed and the corolla deeply five- or six-cleft into lobes (petals) ⅓ to ½ inch long. There are eight or ten erect stamens, shorter than the petals, a longer, slender style, and a slightly three-lobed stigma. The one-seeded, wingless, approximately cylindrical fruits, 1 inch long, taper to their bases and are long-beaked.

Garden and Landscape Uses. Although scarcely outstanding as ornamentals, sinojackias are sufficiently decorative to have garden appeal, especially to admirers of the rare and unusual. They are quite pretty in bloom. In fall their foliage becomes brown. They are hardy about as far north as Virginia.

Cultivation. Sinojackias are not demanding in their needs. They appreciate reasonably fertile and well-drained soil and are propagated by seed and by cuttings. No regular program of pruning is needed.

SINOMENIUM (Sino-mènium). A single species from Japan and China is the only representative of this genus of the moonseed family MENISPERMACEAE. It is nearly allied to moonseed (*Menispermum*) and Carolina-moonseed (*Cocculus*) and bears a name derived from the Greek *sinai*, the Chinese, and *men*, moon, in allusion to the shape of its seeds.

Not satisfactorily hardy in the north, *Sinomenium acutum* (syn. *S. diversifolium*) is a deciduous, twining, woody vine up to 20 feet tall with hairless or nearly hairless stems, and variable foliage. Its long-stalked, alternate leaves are round to round-ovate and 2¼ to 4 inches long. They may be three- to seven-angled or lobed, or sometimes plain-margined. They have five to seven main veins. The undersides of the young leaves are slightly glaucous and pubescent, their upper sides lustrous green and hairless. In terminal and axillary, drooping, many-flowered, pyramidal, more or less downy-stalked panicles 4 to 8 inches long, the inconspicuous, yellow or pale green unisexual flowers, less than ¼ inch across, are borne in summer. They have six sepals and six petals, the latter embracing the nine to twelve stamens (or in the female flowers nonfunctional stamens called staminodes). The styles of the female blooms are recurved. The black, compressed fruits, about ⅓ inch in diameter, are covered with a blue bloom. They contain a flattened, crescent-shaped stone or seed, ribbed along its back. Variety *S. a. cinereum* is distinguished by the undersides of its leaves being densely-gray-pubescent.

Garden and Landscape Uses and Cultivation. Where winters are not excessively cold, this handsome vine is attractive for furnishing arbors, fences, and other supports around which its stems can twine. It retains its foliage until late in the fall. Satisfied with reasonably fertile soil, and prospering in sun or part-day shade, *Sinomenium* is propagated by seed and by cuttings.

SINOWILSONIA (Sino-wilsònia). Established in honor of the great plant hunter Ernest Henry Wilson, affectionately known as "Chinese" Wilson, who died in 1930, the name *Sinowilsonia* derives from the Greek *sinai*, the Chinese, and Wilson's name. It constitutes a genus of only one species contained in the witch-hazel family HAMAMELIDACEAE.

Native to western China, *S. henryi* is a deciduous large shrub or tree up to 25 feet tall with alternate, elliptic to broad-ovate, bristle-toothed leaves up to 6 inches long. The small, greenish flowers are in slender, pendulous racemes, those consisting of male flowers catkin-like and 2 to 2½ inches long, those of female flowers up to 1¼ inches long. The blooms, with an urn-shaped calyx of five spreading sepals, are without petals. Males have five stamens, females five staminodes (nonfunctional stamens). The styles protrude. The fruits are capsules.

Garden Uses and Cultivation. This rare species is of chiefly botanical interest. Hardy in southern New England, it prospers in ordinary well-drained, fertile soil and is propagated by seed and by cuttings. Except for the removal of an ill-placed branch, no pruning is needed.

SIPHONOSMANTHUS DELAVAYI is *Osmanthus delavayi*.

SISAL HEMP. See *Agave sisalana*.

SISSOO is *Dalbergia sissoo*.

SISYRINCHIUM (Sisy-rínchium) — Blue-Eyed-Grass, Golden-Eyed-Grass, Satin Flower. Entirely New World in origin, but with some of its members now naturalized elsewhere, *Sisyrinchium*, of the iris family IRIDACEAE, contains approximately 100 species. Its name is an ancient Greek one originally applied to some plant of the *Iris* relationship.

Sisyrinchiums are fibrous-rooted or have short rhizomes as rootstocks. They are perennial herbaceous plants with grassy foliage and usually flattened and often winged, less often cylindrical and wingless, flower stalks that carry smallish, short-lived, starry, blue-purple or yellow flowers in a long succession. Bell- to wheel-shaped, the flowers have six spreading perianth segments (petals), three stamens, and one style. The fruits are globose capsules.

Perhaps the best flower garden kind, *S. striatum*, of southern Chile and Argentina, has sword-shaped basal leaves 9

Sisyrinchium striatum

inches to 1½ feet long by up to ½ inch wide. Its two-edged, usually branched flower stalks, 1 foot to 3 feet tall and narrowly-winged, bear smaller leaves that gradually diminish in size upward. The upper one-third of the stalk is a narrow panicle of terminal and lateral clusters of stalked, 1-inch-wide, bell-shaped flowers with wide-spreading petals. They are straw-yellow with the outsides of the petals streaked with brown or purple.

Blue-eyed-grasses sometimes planted include *S. angustifolium*, an inhabitant of damp meadows and open woods in Newfoundland, Ontario, and Minnesota, and of mountains in North Carolina. Up to 1½ feet tall, this has leaves up to ¼ inch wide and about one-half as long as the winged, branched flower stalks, which are 6 inches to 1½ feet tall. The bright violet-blue blooms are ½ to ¾ inch wide. Similar, but with rather narrower leaves not over one-half as long as the flower stalks,

about six females to one male. Unless taken by birds, and they usually are not, the fruits remain bright and colorful throughout the winter. In pots well-fruited specimens of *S. reevesiana* are highly ornamental and are suitable for embellishing greenhouses and cool rooms.

Cultivation. Few shrubs need less care than these. Once established they require no routine attention. From time to time a little judicious pruning to shape them or to keep them from growing out of bounds may be desirable. This is best done in late winter or early spring. Old, overgrown specimens may be cut back severely and that rejuvenation treatment followed by fertilizing and watering freely during dry spells the following summer. Growth is encouraged by an application of fertilizer in spring, but unless the soil is poor this is not necessary. New plants are very easily had from late summer cuttings, taken after the new shoots have become quite firm, and planted under mist or in a greenhouse or cold frame propagating bed. Seeds germinate readily when sown in fall or stratified and planted in spring. If only a few new plants are needed layering may be practiced.

To have small, berried specimens in pots for winter use, cuttings of *S. reevesiana* are rooted in late summer and the young plants grown through the winter in a cool greenhouse (night temperature 45 to 50°F). In spring they are planted outdoors in fertile soil where they will be lightly shaded from the fiercest sun of summer, and are lifted, potted, and brought indoors the following fall.

SKIRRET. A vegetable garden crop of decidedly minor importance, skirret (*Sium sisarum*) was formerly more commonly cultivated for its edible roots.

Sow seeds in fertile soil, prepared without adding manure but with the addition of a fertilizer of a type appropriate for carrots, parsnips, and other root crops, in early spring, or in fall in the south. Have the rows 1¼ to 1½ feet apart. Scatter the seeds, which germinate slowly and often poorly, to allow for a spacing, after any necessary thinning, of 8 inches apart. Summer care consists of keeping weeds down and watering in dry weather. The roots may be dug up in fall and stored in a root cellar or similar place for later use or be left in the ground to be dug as needed. If the latter plan is adopted, it is advisable, after the ground has frozen to a depth of 2 inches or so, to cover the rows with a layer of salt hay, straw, or leaves to prevent much greater freezing and so facilitate digging.

SKULLCAP. See Scutellaria.

SKUNK BUSH. This name is applied to *Garrya fremontii* and *Oemleria cerasiformis*, sometimes to *Rhus trilobata*.

SKUNK-CABBAGE is the common name of *Symplocarpus foetidus* and *Veratrum californicum*. Yellow skunk-cabbage is *Lysichiton americanum*.

SKY FLOWER is *Duranta repens*.

SKYROCKET is *Ipomopsis aggregata*.

SLIP. This, another name for a cutting, is more rarely restricted to mean a shoot pulled from a plant and, without slicing across its base or other preparation, inserted as a cutting.

SLIPPER FLOWER is *Pedilanthus tithymaloides*.

SLIPPERWORT. See Calceolaria.

SLOE is *Prunus spinosa*.

SLUGS and SNAILS. These creatures, properly categorized as mollusks, are relatives of clams, oysters, and octopuses. They are not insects, but some insects that, in the larval stage much resemble slugs, are known by such names as rose-slug, bristly-rose-slug, and pear-slug.

Of true slugs and snails there is an estimated 50,000 known species, nearly one-half of them inhabitants of the oceans and seas (abalones, conches, cowries, finger shells, limpets, and whelks) or of fresh waters. Nearly all land species favor humid habitats, such as damp woods and meadows, but some manage to exist in deserts. Some tropical sorts even climb trees. Varying in length from ½₀ inch to 8 inches for land species, and with some sea snails considerably bigger, the different kinds all have soft, slimy bodies and travel by swimming, floating, or crawling.

Land snails have projecting from their heads two pairs of tentacle-like organs, one of which has at its tips eyes, the other organs of smell. Below these is a gland that exudes slime. Snails usually carry on their humped backs a conspicuous spiraled shell into which the creature retreats when danger threatens and during dry periods. In a few species the shell is rudimentary. European edible snails are gastronomic delicacies esteemed chiefly by the French and some other Europeans.

Slugs, which otherwise resemble snails, are without readily recognizable shells, although vestigial ones may be present. A few freshwater snails are alternate hosts to worms and flukes parasitic to humans.

Most land slugs and snails feed on decaying animal and vegetable matter, but some are voracious eaters of living plants, being especially partial to tender parts and seedlings, and are serious pests in gardens and greenhouses. They mostly feed at night and hide during the day, often leaving silvery, slimy trails as evidence of their travelings. Eggs are laid in clusters covered with slime that hardens around them.

Control is chiefly based on cleaning up accumulations of dead leaves, stones, planks, flower pots, and other materials and debris likely to afford daytime hiding places, cultivating outdoor soil in spring to destroy dormant slugs and their eggs, and by using metaldehyde sprays or dusts as directed by the manufacturer.

Skimmia reevesiana (fruits)

SMELOWSKIA (Smel-ówskia). The name of this genus of four or five species commemorates the Russian botanist Timotheus Smelowsky, who died in 1815. The group consists of alpine and arctic plants of the mustard family CRUCIFERAE that inhabit western North America and Asia.

Smelowskias are hardy, woody-rooted, more or less gray-hairy, tufted shrublets or herbaceous perennials. Their slender-stalked basal leaves are pinnate, pinnately-lobed, or lobeless. The stem leaves resemble them, but are smaller. The white, pale yellow, or purplish blooms are in flattish racemes that eventually become much elongated. Each flower has four sepals, four petals in the pattern of a cross, six stamens of which two are shorter than the others, and a rather prominent style tipped with a disk-shaped stigma. The fruits are podlike capsules.

A mountain species of western North America and eastern Asia, *Smelowskia calycina* forms low tufts or mats of foliage above which rise to heights of 2 to 8 inches the erect, mostly branchless, flowering stems. The leaves, ovate to obovate and pinnate or pinnately-lobed, are up to 4 inches long and have long slender stalks conspicuously fringed with stiff hairs. The white or purplish blooms are from ⅓ to ½ inch in diameter. The plant sometimes identified as *S. americana* belongs here.

Endemic to high mountains in California, Oregon, and Washington, *S. ovalis* has pinnate to pinnately-lobed, ovate to oblong leaves, up to 3 inches in length, with slender stalks not fringed with stiff hairs. The flowering stalks, 2½ to 6 inches long, have blooms much like those of *S. calycina*, but smaller.

Garden Uses and Cultivation. Moderately pretty, smelowskias are, in the main, suitable only for rock gardens. They are usually not long-lived in cultivation, and to maintain stocks it is necessary to raise new plants fairly frequently. This is done from seed. Gritty, well-drained, poorish soil and sunny exposures are likely to afford the best growing conditions for these plants, which prefer cool climates to those with hot summers.

SMILACINA (Smila-cìna) — False-Solomon's-Seal. The about twenty-five species of *Smilacina*, of the lily family LILIACEAE, are natives of North America, eastern Asia, or both. Their name is a diminutive of that of the genus *Smilax* of the same family.

False-Solomon's-seals are hardy herbaceous perennials with creeping underground rhizomes and upright stems that have few to many alternate, very short-stalked or stalkless, longitudinally-parallel-veined leaves. The tiny white or creamy-white flowers are in terminal panicles or racemes. They have six similar spreading perianth segments (petals, or more truly, tepals), six slender-stalked stamens, and a

very short style ending in an indistinctly three-lobed stigma. The fruits, usually containing one or two seeds, are spherical berries.

Native from Nova Scotia to British Columbia, Georgia, Mississippi, and Arizona, *S. racemosa* is a familiar and delightful inhabitant of rich woodlands. In late

Smilacina racemosa

Smilacina racemosa (fruits)

spring or early summer it displays its plumes of creamy blooms, later its attractive purple-speckled, red berries. In clumps, the usually arching, finely-pubescent stems are 1½ to 3 feet tall. They carry in two ranks several pointed-elliptic, horizontally-spreading, short-stalked leaves, pubescent on their undersides, broadest about their middles, and 3 to 6 inches long by ¾ inch to 3 inches wide. The numerous flowers are in feathery, usually stalked panicles up to 6 inches in length. Western North American *S. r. amplexicaulis* (syn. *S. amplexicaulis*) is distinguished by its leaves having stem-clasping bases and being broadest well below their middles. Another Western variant, *S. r. glabra* is slightly glaucous and without pubescence.

Smilacina stellata

With many fewer, but larger flowers in racemes rather than panicles, *S. stellata* is found in moist and wet soils in woods, prairies, shores, and mountains from the Atlantic to Pacific coasts of Canada, and southward to Virginia, Indiana, Missouri, and California. This has erect, pubescent or hairless stems 9 inches to 2 feet tall, with six or more erect or spreading, usually channeled, stalkless and somewhat stem-clasping, pointed-lanceolate leaves up to 6 inches long by one-sixth to one-fifth as broad. The fifteen or fewer flowers, in short-stalked racemes, are succeeded by berries that become black, or green with black stripes. Variety *S. s. sessilifolia* (syn. *S. sessilifolia*) has stems usually zigzagged in their upper parts and spreading, flat, lanceolate-ovate leaves not more than four times as long as wide, with three veins more prominent than the others. This is confined to western North America.

Smilacina stellata sessilifolia

Inhabiting wet woods and bogs across Canada, southward to New Jersey, Ohio, Michigan, and Minnesota, and in eastern Asia, *S. trifolia* differs from *S. stellata* in having stems with four or fewer, usually three, hairless leaves, and flowers in long-stalked, 2-inch-long racemes. The leaves are pointed, broad-elliptic to lanceolate, stalkless, and 2½ to 4½ inches long by up to 1½ inches broad. The usually three to eight blooms are succeeded by dark red berries.

Garden and Landscape Uses. By far the finest of the false-Solomon's-seals is *S. racemosa*. This is splendid for colonizing in woodlands and other shaded places sheltered from wind, for planting in garden beds and borders, and for forcing into early bloom indoors. It succeeds best in fertile, slightly to moderately acid soil. Both its sprays of flowers and berries are excellent for cutting for use in arrangements. Although smaller and not as showy, *S. stellata* serves the same purposes. It is less needful of shade and moisture and does well in neutral as well as slightly acid soil. The other species described above are adapted to wild gardens and rock gardens.

Cultivation. Smilacinas luxuriate under conditions similar to those under which they grow naturally. They are very easily increased by division and by seeds freed of the surrounding pulp and sown as soon as ripe in moist soil in a shaded cold frame or similar environment. Established colonies benefit from mulching each fall or spring with leaf mold, compost, or peat moss and, if the soil is not satisfyingly rich, from a spring application of a complete garden fertilizer.

Excellent for forcing into early spring bloom in greenhouses, sunrooms, and windows, *S. racemosa* is easy to manage for this purpose. Strong clumps are dug in fall and potted in containers just big enough to hold the roots comfortably. Then they are put in a cold frame. In January or February they are brought indoors where the night temperature is 40 to 50°F and that by day not more than about ten degrees higher. They are watered freely, and under this gentle forcing make sturdy growth and soon develop pretty foliage and flowers. After blooming is finished, watering is continued, and when danger of frost is over they may be replanted in the garden. Individual clumps should not be forced more often than every two or three years.

SMILAX (Smì-lax)—Wild Sarsaparilla, Carrion Flower, Greenbrier or Catbrier or Horsebrier. The smilax of the florist does not belong in this group. It is *Asparagus asparagoides*. The genus *Smilax*, with which we are concerned here, consists of about 350 species of woody and herbaceous climbers or scramblers of the lily family LILIACEAE. Most are natives of the tropics, some of temperate Asia and North America. The name was used by the ancient Greeks for various plants. Sarsaparilla is obtained from the roots of some tropical species. The foliage of others is employed ornamentally as cut greens.

Smilaxes often have prickly stems. Their evergreen or deciduous leaves, those low on the stems reduced to scales, are alternate. Normal leaves are undivided, toothless, and sometimes shallowly-lobed. They have three to nine conspicuous, longitu-

dinal veins and, unusual in the lily family, networks of other veins between them. At the bottom of the leafstalk is usually a pair of tendrils. The flowers on individual plants are of one sex. They are small, greenish or yellowish, and in stalked umbels from the leaf axils or at the ends of short leafless branchlets. They have six similar perianth segments (petals, or more correctly, tepals). Male blooms have six stamens, females six or fewer staminodes (abortive stamens). The pistils of female blooms, almost or quite without styles, have one or three stigmas. The fruits are berries with up to six seeds.

Evergreen sorts include these: *S. aspera,* of southern Europe and adjacent Asia, has zigzagged, angled, spiny stems and narrow-ovate to triangular leaves 1½ to 4 inches long with often very broad, heart-shaped bases and five to nine chief veins. The light green, fragrant flowers, in racemes 3 to 4 inches long, are succeeded by ¼-inch-wide, red fruits. The leaves of *S. a. maculata* are blotched with white. *S. lanceolata,* native from Virginia to Florida, Texas, the West Indies, Mexico, and Panama, is 30 feet tall. It has fleshy root tubers, stems with recurved prickles, pointed ovate-lanceolate to lanceolate leaves 2 to 3½ inches long, and approximately ¼-inch-wide dark red to brown berries with usually two seeds. *S. laurifolia,* native from New Jersey to Florida and Texas, is high-climbing. It has thorny, angled stems and elliptic or lanceolate leaves 2 to 5 inches long. Its black, one-seeded fruits ripen at the end of their second season. *S. megalantha,* of China, up to about 20 feet in height, has angled stems with stout prickles. Its glossy, leathery leaves, slightly glaucous on their undersides and up to 9 inches long by 6 inches wide, but often smaller, are broadly-ovate to narrowly-oblong. They have three or five chief veins. The showy coral-red fruits, nearly ½ inch in diameter, mostly contain only one seed. *S. ornata,* of Mexico, up to 40 feet tall, has four-angled stems with hooked thorns. The

Smilax ornata

leaves on long, vigorous shoots are heart-shaped and have five to seven chief veins. They are up to 1 foot long by one-half as wide and are plain green. Those on weaker shoots are smaller, ovate, three-veined, and blotched with light gray.

Deciduous species include these: *S. glauca,* the wild sarsaparilla, is native from New Jersey to Illinois, Florida, and Texas.

Smilax glauca (fruits)

This spreads vigorously by underground stolons. Its stems are prickly or not. The ovate to broadly-ovate leaves, 2 to 3 inches long, are glaucous on their lower sides. Up to ⅓ inch in diameter, the blue-black fruits have a waxy bloom. *S. herbacea,* the carrion flower, earns its vernacular name because of the unpleasant odor of its blooms. Native in southern Canada and much of the eastern and central United States, its nonwoody stems, up to about 6 feet long and without prickles, die to the ground each winter. Its ovate to nearly round leaves are up to about 5 inches long. Bluish-black, the fruits are ⅓ inch in diameter. *S. hispida,* native from Connecticut to Minnesota, Florida, and Texas, has stems up to about 15 feet long furnished in their lower parts with straight prickles. Its broad-ovate to heart-shaped, five- to nine-veined leaves are 3 to 4½ inches long and often nearly as wide. About ⅓ inch across, the fruits are black. This species scarcely spreads by underground stolons and so, unlike *S. glauca* and *S. rotundifolia,* is not troublesomely invasive. *S. rotundifolia,* the common catbrier, greenbrier, or horsebrier, and one of the most abundant species in North America, inhabits open woodlands and thickets from Nova Scotia to Michigan, Florida, and Texas. It has wiry, prickly, often four-angled stems and glossy, broad-ovate to nearly round leaves 2 to 6 inches long. Its blue-black to black fruits, ¼ inch in diameter, contain one to three seeds. Because this sends out long underground stolons from which new shoots arise far from the parent plant, it is often hard to control.

Garden and Landscape Uses and Cultivation. Smilaxes have no important place in American horticulture. Red-fruited *S. megalantha* is the most satisfactory ornamental. Several native kinds, including *S. glauca* and *S. rotundifolia*, are too aggressive for use in any landscapes but those where their tendency to soon form large, spreading, practically impenetrable tangles is not objectionable. In special situations they may be used for such purposes as covering large banks and to deter trespassers. The carrion flower is objectionable in many places because of the odor of its blooms.

Smilaxes grow with little difficulty in ordinary soil in sun or part-shade and are propagated by seed or by division. The hardiness of native kinds can be approximately deduced from their native ranges. Probably none of the others described here is hardy in the north.

SMITHIANTHA (Smith-iántha). Four beautiful species of the eight that belong in this Mexican and Guatemalan genus of the gesneria family GESNERIACEAE are cultivated. Their name honors one of the most distinguished women contributors to the science of botany. Matilda Smith, cousin of Sir Joseph Hooker, Director of the Royal Botanic Gardens, Kew, England, was an outstanding botanical illustrator who for nearly half a century made numerous splendid paintings of plants published in the Botanical Magazine. She died in 1926. For long smithianthas were known to gardeners by their synonym *Naegelia*, but as that name had been applied to a group of fungi earlier than to the plants that are our concern here, it became necessary to find a new name for this genus; this was done with the happy result indicated.

Smithianthas are tropical herbaceous perennials with large, scaly rhizomes and solitary or rarely two or three erect, fleshy stems with opposite, velvety, often richly colored, broadly-heart-shaped leaves with toothed margins. The lowest leaves are largest. Upward they gradually diminish to the base of the terminal pyramidal spike of obliquely pendulous, tubular, foxglove-like blooms. The blooms have rare beauty and charm and come in a range of colors that contrast delightfully with the foliage. They have five-parted calyxes. The tubular corollas, narrowed at their lower ends, have open mouths and five small lobes (petals). There are four stamens. The fruits are capsules. In many ways smithianthas suggest *Kohleria*, but differ in their flowers being in spikes with the blooms arising singly from tiny, alternate bracts, instead of being from the axils of opposite leaves. Also, the corollas of kohlerias do not slim markedly at their bases and their lobes (petals) are usually much longer and spread or reflex more obviously than those of *Smithiantha*.

Most beautiful, *S. cinnabarina* (syns. *Naegelia cinnabarina*, *Gesneria cinnabarina*) is from 1 foot to 2 feet tall. It has lustrous, brownish-red foliage, densely clothed with soft hairs, and brilliant cinnabar-red to or-

Smithiantha cinnabarina

ange-scarlet blooms 1½ inches long, paler or spotted with white in their throats, and less markedly narrowed at their bases than are most kinds.

Smithiantha zebrina

Most frequent in cultivation are *S. zebrina* (syns. *Naegelia zebrina*, *Gesneria zebrina*) and variations (most probably of hybrid origin) of it. The species characteristically is densely-hairy and up to 3 feet tall. Its leaves are green, heavily marbled with darker green and reddish-brown. The

Garden varieties of *Smithiantha*

1½-inch-long blooms, strongly constricted at their bases, are bright yellow on their undersides and brilliant red in their upper halves. Their throats are streaked and spotted with red.

Two with plain green foliage are *S. fulgida* (syn. *Naegelia fulgida*) and *S. multiflora* (syns. *Naegelia multiflora*, *Gesneria*

Smithiantha multiflora

amabilis). They are usually 2 to 2½ feet tall. The first has brilliant red flowers, the other unspotted blooms of creamy-yellow to white. The leaves of *S. multiflora* sometimes are margined wth lighter green.

Horticultural hybrids between species of *Smithiantha*, and some between it and related genera, have so proliferated in recent years that only by consulting current catalogs of specialists can one hope to keep informed about those available. They show considerable variation in foliage and flower color, the latter running from pure yellows, through yellows shaded with purple or flushed with pink, to apricot-pinks, deeper pinks, violets, and deep reds. All are lovely. Hybrids between *Smithiantha* and *Achimenes* are named *Achimenantha*.

Garden Uses and Cultivation. For their finest development smithianthas need to

be grown under the congenial conditions afforded by a warm, humid greenhouse; nevertheless keen amateurs without such a facility often succeed with them in terrariums and under fluorescent light setups that afford approximately ideal environments. The soil should be fertile, of coarse texture, and one that does not pack with repeated watering and so deny adequate supplies of air to the roots. It should contain a generous proportion of decayed organic matter, such as leaf mold or peat moss, and, except during the period of dormancy when the plants are leafless, be kept evenly moist, but not saturated. Fairly high humidity is necessary. Smithianthas need shade from strong sun, but as much light as they will stand without their foliage yellowing or becoming scorched. It is especially important that they have adequate illumination during their early stages, otherwise the shoots become weak and leggy and the plants never develop into strong, shapely specimens.

Smithianthas are usually grown singly in 4- or 5-inch pots or two or three in containers 6 inches in diameter. In natural light they are started into growth in spring and, after they flower in late summer or fall, are gradually dried off and stored quite dry in the soil in which they grew, in a temperature of 55 to 60°F over winter. Under artificial light, by varying planting time and other factors, they can be flowered at any season. During their time of active growth a minimum night temperature of 70°F is needed and day temperatures may be five to fifteen or more degrees higher. For further information see the Encyclopedia entry Gesneriads.

SMOKE BUSH. See Cotinus.

SMOKE TREE. See Cotinus, and Dalea.

SMUT AND WHITE SMUT DISEASES. Typical symptoms of smut diseases are the development on roots, bulbs, stems, leaves, flowers, or seeds of whitish blisters or galls containing great numbers of dark brown to black, sooty-looking spores. The funguses that cause these diseases often infect seedling plants and grow undetected in their tissues until they approach maturity. Among the numerous susceptible plants are aconites, anemones, carnations, chives, columbines, corn, delphiniums, dianthuses, garlic, gladioluses, lawn grasses, monkshoods, onions, pansies, silver lace vine, and sweet williams.

White smut diseases, also caused by funguses, are evidenced by white, yellowish, yellowish-green, or colorless spots that later become brown to nearly black and from which the tissues may drop to leave ragged holes. Rarely serious, white smuts affect a considerable variety of plants including anemones, asters, calendulas, dahlias, delphiniums, gaillardias, lawn grasses, lobelias, poppies, spinach, sunflowers, and water-lilies.

To control smuts and white smuts, practice good sanitation by promptly picking off and burning affected parts and at the end of the season cleaning up all debris. Spray with a fungicide at seven- to ten-day intervals. In some instances, soil too acid and late planting seems to favor the development of white smuts. For more information about smuts and white smuts consult local Cooperative Extension Agents or a State Agricultural Experiment Station.

SMYRNIUM (Smýrn-ium)—Alexanders or Black Potherb or Horse-Parsley. Except that for its historical interest herb gardeners may include one species in their plantings, this genus has no horticultural appeal. It belongs in the carrot family Umbelliferae and has eight species, all Old World. The name, used by Dioscorides, is derived from the Greek *smyrra*, myrrh, in allusion to the scent of the plants.

Biennials, smyrniums are erect and hairless natives of Europe, adjacent Asia, and North Africa. Their lower foliage consists of three- or four-times-pinnately-dissected leaves, the upper leaves have few divisions or are undivided. In compound umbels consisting of many smaller umbels, the tiny greenish-yellow flowers are borne in late spring or summer. The small fruits (commonly called seeds) are rounded, egg-shaped, or prominently ribbed.

Alexanders, black potherb, or horse-parsley (*Smyrnium olusatrum*) was at one time grown and used as a vegetable and salad plant, but it is completely superseded by celery, which is more pleasing to modern tastes. It is a stout plant, 3 to 4 feet tall, branching, and leafy. It has ribbed stems and dark green thrice-divided leaves, the lower ones stalked, the upper not. The leaflets are broadly-ovate and lobed or bluntly-toothed. The numerous tiny yellow flowers in crowded, roundish umbels are followed by broadly-ovoid fruits that have three sharp ribs on each side and are nearly black when ripe. This plant may be grown in the same manner as celery.

SNAIL FLOWER is *Vigna caracalla*.

SNAIL MEDICK is *Medicago scutellata*.

SNAKE or SNAKE'S. The words snake or snake's occur as parts of the common names of these plants: snake gourd (*Trichosanthes anguina*), snake-lily (*Dichelostemma volubile*), snake melon (*Cucumis melo flexuosus*), snake mouth (*Pogonia ophioglossoides*), snake-palm (*Amorphophallus rivieri*), snake plant (*Sansevieria*), snake's head (*Fritillaria meleagris*), snake's-head-iris (*Hermodactylus tuberosus*), and yellow snake tree (*Stereospermum chelonoides*).

SNAKEROOT. This word forms parts of the vernacular names of these plants: black snakeroot (*Cimicifuga racemosa*), button snakeroot (*Eryngium yuccifolium* and *Liatris*), Canada snakeroot (*Asarum canadense*), Seneca snakeroot (*Polygala senega*), Virginia snakeroot (*Aristolochia serpentaria*), and white snakeroot (*Eupatorium rugosum*).

SNAKEWEED. This is a common name of *Gutierrezia sarothrae* and *Polygonum bistorta*.

SNAKEWOOD is *Cecropia palmata*.

SNAPDRAGON. See Antirrhinum. The snapdragon-tree is *Gmelina arborea*.

SNEEZEWEED. See Achillea, and Helenium.

SNOW. This word forms parts of the common names of these plants: Chinese snowball bush (*Viburnum macrocephalum*), Japanese snowball bush (*Viburnum plicatum*), snowball bush (*Viburnum opulus roseum*), snow bush (*Breynia disticha*), snow creeper (*Porana paniculata* and *P. racemosa*), snow-in-summer (*Cerastium tomentosum*), snow-on-the-mountain (*Euphorbia marginata*), snow-poppy (*Eomecon chionantha*), and snow wreath (*Neviusia alabamensis*).

SNOWBELL. See Styrax.

SNOWBERRY. This is a common name for *Chiococca* and *Symphoricarpos albus*. Creeping-snowberry is *Gaultheria hispidula*.

SNOWDROP. See Galanthus, and Leucojum. For snowdrop-tree see Halesia.

SNOWFLAKE. For the spring snowflake and summer snowflake see Leucojum. The water snowflake is *Nymphoides indica*. The snowflake plant or snowflake tree is *Trevesia palmata micholitzii*.

SNOWY-MESPILUS is *Amelanchier ovalis*.

SOAP. This word forms parts of the common names of these plants: soap-bark tree (*Quillaja saponaria*), soap nut (*Sapindus mukorossii*), soap plant (*Chlorogalum pomeridianum*), and soap tree (*Yucca elata*).

SOAPBERRY. See Sapindus.

SOAPBUSH is *Noltea africana*.

SOAPWEED is a common name applied to *Yucca elata* and *Y. glauca*.

SOAPWELL is *Yucca glauca*.

SOAPWORT See Saponaria.

SOBRALIA (So-brà:lia). Few of the reported ninety species of *Sobralia*, of the orchid family Orchidaceae, are in cultivation. The group is indigenous chiefly in mountain regions from Mexico to tropical America. Its name commemorates the eighteenth-century Spanish physician and botanist Francisco Martinez Sobral, who died in 1790.

Sobralias are chiefly ground orchids rather than tree-perchers, although a few grow as epiphytes in the wild. They have leafy, reedlike stems and very beautiful flowers. Their more or less pleated leaves are disposed all the way along or to within a little distance of the tops of the stems, which they sheathe with their bases. Solitary or few together in short terminal racemes, the blooms have three spreading sepals, two spreading petals, and a forward-projecting lip that forms a tube around the column and has a big blade often waved or fringed at its margins.

From 1 foot to 2½ feet tall, *S. decora*, of Mexico to northern South America, has clustered stems with scattered, oblanceolate to narrowly-lanceolate leaves up to 9 inches long. Its blooms resemble those of cattleyas, but last only one day. From 3 to 4 inches across they have creamy-white sepals and petals slightly flushed with pink and a rose-purple lip with a disk streaked with yellow and brown.

Costa Rican *S. leucoxantha*, 3 to 4 feet tall, has clustered stems with pointed-lanceolate leaves somewhat scurfy on their undersides, and 4 to 8 inches long. The flowers are solitary, fragrant, and 4 to 6½ inches wide. Except in the throat of the lip, which is yellow to orange-yellow, and sometimes with brownish lines, they are white. The sepals are lanceolate-oblong and longer than the oblong petals. The lip, shorter than the sepals, has a wavy-edged, nearly circular blade.

Native from Mexico to Costa Rica, *S. macrantha* has tight clusters of slender stems, 5 to 8 feet tall, leafy to their tops. Its narrowly- to broadly-lanclate leaves, which taper to slender points, are 6 inches to 1 foot in length. Each stem produces several fragrant, short-lived, purple and crimson blooms, about 6 inches in diameter, with a lip with a long creamy-white tube, ridged and yellow in its throat, and a big, wavy, deep purple blade. Central American *S. wilsoniana* has slender-pointed, lanceolate leaves up to 7 inches long and fragrant blooms 5 to 6 inches across that are white suffused with delicate rosy-mauve to light-lavender-pink. They have a yellow throat.

Garden Uses and Cultivation. Admirable for collections of orchids outdoors and in lath houses in the tropics and warm subtropics, sobralias are not difficult to manage once their needs are understood. Environments that suit cattleyas and many other intermediate- and warm-greenhouse orchids are satisfactory. Although some shade from strong sun is necessary, too much is to be deplored; as with cattleyas,

Sobralia wilsoniana

this may result in fine-looking, lush green plants, but with blooming sharply inhibited.

Because they are for the most part terrestrial, sobralias succeed in rooting mediums of types agreeable to cymbidiums. They are extremely impatient of water-retentive, sour soil and so it is important the containers in which these orchids are grown be extremely well drained. It is not too much to fill one-third of their depths with crocks, broken brick, coarse gravel, or similar material.

Water freely during periods of active growth, more sparingly for one month to six weeks after the year's new stems attain maturity, but at no time allow the roots to dry completely. This season of partial rest aids in ripening the shoots and encouraging blooming. Regular applications of dilute fertilizer from the time new growth begins until the period of semirest approaches are decidedly beneficial.

Root disturbance is particularly abhorrent to sobralias. Delay repotting as long as reasonably necessary, as well as the division of plants that are prospering unless increase by this means is the objective. Large-specimen sobralias that have experienced little root disturbance through the years flower most satisfactorily and abundantly. For additional information see Orchids.

SODIUM CHLORIDE. This, common table salt, is used in coarser form in immense quantities in cold regions for deicing highways, roads, driveways, and sidewalks. The resulting melt is highly toxic to roots. Damage to trees, shrubs, and other plants including lawn grasses adjacent to treated areas is common. It may result in death or in less severe cases show as more or less severe scorching of the edges of leaves, premature fall coloring and dropping of foliage, and dying back of twigs and branches.

Tolerance of this substance varies considerably with different species of plants. Research at the University of New Hampshire has shown that among trees, beeches, hemlocks, red pine, white pine, and sugar maple are very susceptible to harm; Amer-

ican linden, Norway and red maples, and shagbark hickory are more resistant; black locust, gray birch, paper birch, yellow birch, and white ash are tolerant; and red cedar, red oak, and white oak are least subject to damage.

Practical measures to minimize danger to vegetation include the establishment of surface grades to carry the melt away from roots, extreme care in spreading salt so that it falls only on paved surfaces, the substitution of one of the newer deicing materials now available that are harmless to plants, or the use of sand or sawdust to prevent slipping on ice.

SOIL EROSION. In some regions and on some sites, loss of soil by erosion is a serious matter. By the action of water or wind, surface soil is removed, more or less suddenly and dramatically or gradually and sometimes nearly imperceptibly. The dust bowls of the western United States in the 1930s resulted from the blowing of soil from land unprotected by growing plants (the natural grass cover had been destroyed by plowing, and drought prevented the growth of agricultural crops that would have protected the disturbed soil). Wind erosion is common near the sea and in desert regions. Washing and gulleying of steep slopes by water is often observable where forest cover has been removed, along the sides of newly constructed roads, and in other places where the earth has been bared. More subtle is sheet erosion that gently but surely "floats" fine surface soil down long gentle slopes, leaving the coarser elements, including stones and rocks, that seem to multiply or "grow" as a result.

Control of large-scale erosion is a concern of conservationists, agricultural experts, foresters, engineers, and others concerned with preserving the land. Local problems often confront and must be overcome by gardeners, who are sometimes faced with the need for stabilizing banks of newly disturbed soil and for slowing down or diverting storm water that cascades mud from places where soil is needed to places where it is not. They also face worn lawn areas bared by romping children or other users and, in windy regions, blowing surface soil and sand.

Techniques available to gardeners to control erosion are in the main small-scale adaptations of those employed on larger areas. First and foremost is the establishment, wherever possible, of a cover of living plants, the roots of which will hold the soil. Lawn grass is frequently employed and in suitable places is highly effective. For plants, other than grasses, that are useful for soil stabilization see the Encyclopedia entry Banks and Steep Slopes, and also the one titled Groundcovers.

Mulching is a splendid means of forestalling erosion. It checks the ill effects of wind and water. Mulching serves well with many single-season crop plants and is especially important on newly seeded and newly planted steep banks.

Where the land slopes, take special precautions with areas devoted to vegetables and other plants that occupy the ground for only a part of each year. Erosion is likely to be particularly severe when the land is bare and especially after it has been broken by spade, rotary tiller, or plow. One of the oldest and most effective, but unfortunately expensive and so often impractical, ways of alleviating such a condition is by terracing. Contour plowing serves as a good alternative. When spading hand-worked plots, leave the surface as rough and lumpy as possible. Do not rake until immediately before seed sowing. Also, spade from the top of the slope downward, throwing the soil forward, and thus upward, as the work proceeds. This partially compensates for the movement of soil by downward wash. Because they leave such a fine surface, rotary tillers trigger greater loss by erosion than spades or plows. Do not use them on land susceptible to soil loss until planting time is at hand. On long slopes, and especially where such exist above a cultivated area, diversionary ditches to carry surplus water away can sometimes be used to good purpose.

Wind erosion can be alleviated by breaking the force of the wind with shelter belts, screens of trees or shrubs, hedges, fences, walls, and baffles.

If you are faced with serious soil erosion problems seek help from your Cooperative Extension Agent, Soil Conservation District, or from the United States Soil Conservation Service.

SOIL STERILIZATION. Soils, especially fertile ones, are homes of vast multitudes of living organisms, the great majority beneficial to plants, a small minority harmful. Among the latter are the funguses, bacteria, and protozoa that can cause serious diseases, as well as insects and other small creatures, such as nematodes, that injure roots and other underground parts, transmit diseases, or, in other ways, are inimicable to growth. Beneficial organisms include those that break down complex organic substances to make their components available to plants as nutrients. These organisms are highly desirable. Soil devoid of them is more or less sterile and unsuited to the growth of plants.

Soil sterilization, or more properly, partial sterilization, given that its objective is so far as practicable to kill such offensive organisms as nematodes and disease-causing bacteria and funguses, without eliminating all others, is commonly practiced in commercial greenhouses and for special purposes commercially on outdoor plots. It is employed less by amateurs and in the main is not as essential for their

operations. Frequently professional operators of greenhouses use the same soil for several successive crops of the same kind, carnations or roses, for example, and find sterilizing less expensive than substituting new soil. For the amateur, the alternative is often more practicable. Moreover, operators of amateur greenhouses are more likely to grow a considerable variety of plants with the result that diseases specific to one are not likely to be as devastating as if the greenhouse were filled with that sort.

Perhaps the most practical consistent use of sterilization is when soil is prepared for sowing seeds and transplanting seedlings indoors. Sterilization can greatly reduce the incidence of damping-off disease and also kill weed seeds. It is well to remember, however, that greenhouses and other places where plants are grown are not as aseptic as hospital operating rooms and that reinfection of the soil can occur. This is especially true with damping-off disease among seedlings growing in soil kept too wet or in a place where humidity is too high or air circulation or light are inadequate.

Methods of sterilization are broadly thermal and chemical. Where practicable, the first is preferable and moist heat generated by forcing steam through the soil is usually more controllable and hence better than dry heat (baking).

Heat sterilization by steaming, commonly used in commercial greenhouses, but generally impracticable for amateurs, involves the positioning of perforated steam pipes beneath the soil and raising the temperature of the soil to a minimum of 180°F and maintaining that for at least thirty minutes.

Baking can be effective with small amounts of soil, but must be done carefully to achieve satisfactory results. If the temperature is too high the humus content of the soil and probably favorable organisms are destroyed, if too low, harmful organisms are left alive. Place the soil in a shallow pan and bake it for forty-five minutes to one hour at 200 to 225°F. As a check, insert a potato in the center of the pile of soil. When it is well cooked it may be assumed that the soil has been heated sufficiently throughout. Electric sterilizers that deal with a bushel or two of soil at a time are effective and practicable for amateurs.

Heat sterilization causes chemical changes in soil. For the first three weeks or so following heat sterilization, the level of available nitrogen is reduced. Because of this, the growth of plants set in newly sterilized soil may be retarded. Gradually the population of nitrifying bacteria increases and in five or six weeks the level of available nitrogen is restored. For best results, it is advisable to sterilize soil well in advance of using it for potting or planting.

Chemical methods of freeing soils of harmful organisms are often impractical for amateurs, either because of the toxicity of the substances employed or the complexity of the equipment needed. They include the use of formaldehyde, tear gas, methyl bromide, and preparations known as DD and Vapam. It may be well to obtain professional advice before using these. See also the Encyclopedia entry Fumigation.

SOIL TESTS AND ANALYSES. It is often helpful to have the soil tested to determine acidity or alkalinity, and so its suitability for kinds of plants that are fussy about such matters. Tests can be made with reasonable accuracy with readily available and inexpensive amateur kits sold commercially, perhaps more precisely by Cooperative Extension Agents. A soil analysis to determine organic content and the relative amounts of various nutrients and perhaps of clay, silt, sand, and other fractions is much more complicated. Do-it-yourself kits are less adequate for this purpose. Fortunately, except when large amounts of topsoil are to be purchased, or under other special circumstances, such analyses are rarely necessary. If one is to be made, take seven to ten cores of soil from different parts of the plot to be tested, each 6 to 8 inches deep and 2 to 4 inches or more in diameter. Mix these very thoroughly together. Then seal about a pint of the mix in a can or stout plastic bag and send it, together with as much information as you have about any fertilizing or liming that has been done over the past couple of years, to your State Agricultural Experiment Station or to a commercial laboratory specializing in such work. Their report should be accompanied by recommendations for any needed treatment.

SOILLESS GARDENING. See Hydroponics or Nutriculture.

SOILS AND THEIR MANAGEMENT. The meaning of the term soil is generally well understood as alluding to the more or less loose upper layer of relatively fine particles that constitutes the solid surface of the earth, except where bedrock protrudes or sand, gravel, or larger stones form a cover or pavement. It is the environment in which the roots and sometimes other parts of the vast majority of plants live (epiphytes and floating aquatics are obvious exceptions).

In most places, clear distinction is evident between the uppermost layer of soil, generally referred to as topsoil, and the layer immediately below it called subsoil. The topsoil varies greatly in depth from region to region, locality to locality, and sometimes even within the same small garden. From subsoil it differs most obviously in being of a different, usually darker color due to its higher organic content.

Subsoil, besides differing in color from topsoil, generally is more compact and very often has a different texture. It may be much more clayey or, at the other extreme, much sandier, or it may even consist largely of gravel or stones. Even though rich in potential nutrients, as some, but by no means all subsoils are, because of poor aeration, absence or paucity of humus and consequently of microorganisms that use that as a source of energy and in doing so release nutrients in form usable by roots, and sometimes because of accumulations of substances toxic to plants, subsoils are generally much less fertile than topsoil. However, as we shall learn, by intelligent management the quality of many subsoils can be improved and their upper layers gradually converted into topsoil. Even without such treatment, some roots of some plants extend into the subsoil in search of moisture and additional anchorage. They may even extract some nutrients.

Topsoil, and throughout the remainder of this discussion that is what we mean by the term soil (subsoil is designated as such), is of primary importance to plants.

Rich topsoil is an ideal medium for most plants to root into

It is their chief or only source of many nutrients as well as of most of the water they need. In addition it anchors the roots. Topsoil is truly "living soil," for if fertile, it literally teems with almost unbelievable numbers of macroscopic and microscopic organisms that by their living, procreation, and death profoundly affect the character of the soil.

Soils are of many types and qualities. Not all in their natural conditions are well adapted to the growth of a wide selection of plants, although practically all will support some. Still less well suited for gardening are unkindly subsoils often uncovered in grading and building operations and by builders and landscapers, and often hidden by covering them with 3 or 4 inches

of somewhat more agreeable earth. An encouraging truth is that the vast majority of soils, no matter how inhospitable they are to the growth of plants, can be brought into fertile condition by appropriate management.

Some understanding of the soil and its physical, chemical, and biological characteristics is necessary to improve and maintain its fertility intelligently. Briefly, soil consists of solid particles, spaces between them filled with air or water or both, and a living fauna and flora ranging from earthworms and much smaller creatures to fungi, bacteria, and other microscopic organisms.

The solid particles are of two kinds, mineral or inorganic and organic. The first, resulting from the weathering and disintegration of rock over vast periods of time are essentially stable, remaining unchanged for periods of many lifetimes. The organic particles, the remains of the bodies of animals and plants that have died, except in such highly specialized environments as peat bogs, where decay is arrested, are gradually broken down as the result of the activities of the soil's fauna and flora (especially microorganisms) until reduced to their constituent elements. Under conditions favorable to the growth of the vast majority of plants, organic matter is constantly lost from the soil and, for fertility to be maintained, must be replenished.

Inorganic material constitutes by far the greater bulk and weight of the vast majority of soils. Only of peat bogs and mucks (accumulations of organic debris) is this not true. The type of rock from which its inorganic portion is derived, notably whether acidic, neutral, or alkaline, affects the character of soil, and so most profoundly does the size of its particles.

Particle size ranges progressively, from largest to smallest, from easily observable stones, gravel, and sand to silt and clay, with those of the colloidal fraction of the clay so extremely minute that they cannot be seen even with the most powerful compound microscope. Only with an electron microscope are they observable.

Classification of soils for horticultural and agricultural purposes is usually done with some reference to the sizes of the particles chiefly responsible for their physical condition. Thus we have gravelly, sandy, silty, and clayey soils, none of which consists of only gravel, sand, silt, or clay, but which contain enough of one of these so that its characteristics are imparted to the whole. Obviously, all gradations occur between gravelly and very sandy soils and very clayey soils. Those intermediate in their characteristics between clays and sands are called loams, and may further be designated as sandy (or light) loam, medium loam, or clayey (or heavy) loam depending upon the de-

gree to which the components influence their characteristics. The words light and heavy applied to soils do not refer to their weights, nor does light allude to color. The criterion rather is ease of manipulation. A light soil works readily, yields with minimum effort to the spade, plow, and other tools of husbandry. The reverse is true of heavy soils. Any soil that contains a large proportion of stones may be designated as stony.

Clay is the most important soil fraction. This is because of its ability to absorb and retain water and because its particles have on their surfaces negatively (electrically) charged atoms or groups of atoms called anions. In a process called cation exchange, these are balanced by the adsorption (attracting to and holding on the surface) of various positively charged atoms or groups of atoms called cations. In this way such nutritive elements as calcium, magnesium, potassium, and sodium are retained instead of being leached from the soil and become available to the roots of plants.

Consisting chiefly of hydrated silicates of aluminum, clay is composed of particles 0.005 millimeters or less in diameter, the larger microscopic, the smaller ultramicroscopic. The latter constitute the colloidal fraction that is responsible for the plasticity of clay. An important characteristic of clay, or at least of colloidal clay, is that it can assume two states. When flocculated its minute particles cling together to form crumblike aggregates that permit water and air to pass between them, when deflocculated neither water nor air can penetrate.

Kneading (puddling) clay when it is moist causes deflocculation and it can then be molded into various shapes, including fairly thin leaves that even after drying hold their forms. Because of this, clay is admirable for making bricks, tiles, and chinaware. So long as puddled clay is not allowed to dry and crack or to be washed away by a running stream, quite thin layers hold water indefinitely. It can be used to line ponds, pools, and dams. Clearly, clay in a deflocculated condition is not favorable to root growth or to the well-being of plants; therefore, the management of clay soils involves heavy emphasis on maintaining the clay in a flocculated state.

Adobe and gumbo soils are special types of clay and silt soils found over extensive areas of the southwestern and western United States. They are usually rich in nutrients, but because of their physical properties are difficult to work. Consult the local Cooperative Extension Agent or the appropriate State Agricultural Experiment Station for suggestions on the management of such soils in specific regions.

Sand, in contrast to clay, consists of small, loose grains of rock, frequently quartz, large enough to be seen by the

Adobe soils typical of desert and semidesert regions are pasty when wet, badly cracked when dry

naked eye. Particles of very fine sand range from 0.05 to 0.10 millimeters in diameter, those of very coarse sand from 1.00 to 2.00 millimeters. Medium sands are of in-between sizes. Unlike clay particles, those of sand neither cohere nor adsorb and retain nutrients that can later be released and made available to the roots. But sand has the advantage of permitting the free passage of water and air, both necessary for the development of roots.

Silt is composed of particles of rock intermediate in size (from 0.002 to 0.05 millimeters in diameter) between those of clay and those of sand, and it possesses in-between qualities. It compacts to a much greater degree than sand, to such an extent that the free passage of water and air through it may be severely restricted. Although under some conditions silt flocculates, in general, it does not do this readily; thus, it rarely forms crumblike aggregates.

The organic content of the soil consists of plant and animal remains in various stages of decomposition. Only the portion that represents the next-to-the-end product of decay, the completion of a long series of changes brought about the activities of soil microorganisms under favorable conditions of warmth, moisture, and air, is properly termed humus. Manure, compost, straw, peat moss, and the black material sold commercially as humus are, more correctly, humus-forming materials.

Humus, like clay, includes a colloidal fraction capable of flocculation and, like clay, has the ability to retain nutrients derived from other sources so that they become available to plants over a longer period than they would otherwise. In addition, by breakdown into the elements of which it is composed, humus enriches the soil with nitrogen compounds and other plant nutrients.

But organic material functions importantly in other ways. It improves the structure of soils so that loose, sandy ones become more retentive of water and nutrients and compact clays and silts are made more porous. In addition, it is the food of the multitude of beneficial soil bacteria that work to release chemical nutrients that would otherwise remain unavailable to the plants. Under natural conditions, organic matter is replenished by roots dying, by the death and decay of the upper parts of plants, and to a lesser extent by the deaths of animals and by their feces, and by fallen leaves. In horticultural practice, manures, composts, and sometimes green manures (crops grown specially to be plowed under), as well as other sources, are used to supply organic material to soils.

The living organisms of the soil are, for the most part, highly beneficial in promoting its fertility, but there are some, including nematodes and the agents of certain plant diseases, that are decidedly obnoxious. In practice, good tillage and other management procedures are relied upon to encourage favorable organisms to multiply and these, too, adversely affect some unfavorable organisms. Others can be discouraged by crop rotations, but for a few, soil sterilization is the only solution.

Soils inhospitable to the growth of garden plants, and this may be their native condition or the result of mishandling, can usually be greatly improved. Besides the standard tillage and fertilizing practices, to be considered later, the most likely treatments needed are drainage to lower high-water tables and operations that deepen the layer of topsoil. About the first consult the Encyclopedia entry Drainage and Drain-

Topsoil brought from other areas is frequently used when landscaping around dwellings

ing. Deepening topsoil can be achieved in two ways. The most obvious is to bring in more from outside. This has the advantage of immediate results, but the disadvantage of high cost. The alternative, slower to achieve, but almost always practicable, is to improve the upper layer of subsoil so that it becomes topsoil. This cannot be done in one operation, although considerable betterment can generally be had from mixing with the subsoil large amounts of coarse organic materials, such as compost, partly rotted leaves, straw, or peat moss, which is practicable when holes of comparatively large size are dug for planting trees and shrubs. For larger areas such as flower beds, double digging (double spading) is effective. See the Encyclopedia entry Spading.

Ground given over to vegetables and annual flowers that occupy it for only one season, or to biennials, perennials, or young nursery stock, such as shrubs that are vacated from it every two or three years, can be very effectively gradually deepened each time it is prepared for a new planting by spading, rotary tilling, or plowing it a little deeper than before. In this way some of the subsoil is incorporated with the topsoil and with whatever organic material is added, and so becomes better aerated and subject to the ameliorating influences of the soil organisms present. It is important not to bring up more than 1 inch to 2 inches of subsoil at any one time.

Preparing ground for seed sowing or planting normally involves tilling (loosening it mechanically), supplementing its organic content, and fertilizing. In gardens, the spade, spading fork, rotary tiller, and less often the plow are the basic tillage implements. With them the soil is disturbed to a depth of 6 to 10 inches or more, manure, compost, and other additives are incorporated, and crop residues and weeds are buried. A word of warning about the use of rotary tillers. Employed with good judgment they are excellent for loosening ground and incorporating bulk organic materials and other amendments. But unlike spades, spading forks, and plows, which leave the soil comparatively lumpy, the whirling blades of rotary tillers mix and "fluff up" its entire mass to the depth they reach and, if done too frequently, may damage the soil by reducing aggregates to a much finer condition. Properly carried out, deep tillage is highly beneficial, thoughtlessly or carelessly done it can cause much harm to soil structure. For more information see the Encyclopedia entry Spading.

Clayey soils are especially susceptible to physical damage resulting from mismanagement. If worked or subjected to heavy weights when wet, as a result of the deflocculation of the colloidal clay, they become pasty, poorly aerated, and more or less impervious to water. When they dry they shrink, crack, and form hard clods. As an illustration of this, note how water collects and lies in wheel tracks across a clayey field, how a hog wallowing in such ground soon achieves a water-holding depression, and how effectively wet clay can be kneaded to make a waterproof lining for a pond or a dam. The golden rule with clayey soils is to keep off them when they are so wet that they stick to shoes and tools, to work them only when they are reasonably dry. Soil structure changed by deflocculation cannot be restored by mechanically loosening the ground with a spading fork or harrow. Seeming benefit from such manipulation is lost after the first rain or watering, which causes the surface layer to run together and cake and, when it dries, to crack. Good structure, the ag-

Surface cracks in dry soil indicate poor soil structure

gregation of the finer soil particles into larger crumbs that behave much like particles of a coarser textured soil in that they permit the free passage of air and water, must ever be the aim of gardeners operating on clayey soils.

Means of promoting good structure, besides such negatives as avoiding working them, not allowing trucks or other heavy equipment on them, or not walking over them when wet, include spading or plowing in fall and leaving the surface in a rough, cloddy condition so that alternate freezing and thawing can work its wonders. In regions of cold winters, even the most pasty clay soil will be improved to

Alternate freezing and thawing greatly improves the physical condition of soil spaded in fall and left with a rough surface

such an extent by this treatment that after a few drying spring days under the influence of spading fork or harrow it will break down readily into a delightful tilth.

Coarse organic material, such as compost, strawy manure, and green manures, added to clay soils also encourages satisfactory crumb structure, but beware of using peat moss in excess, as this may tend to hold too much water and not decay rapidly enough. Mulches are effective in reducing the need for frequent hoeing or other cultivation, which tends to powder the surface, and by eliminating the harmful packing effect of heavy rains and sprinkler irrigation. The addition of lime benefits crumb structure by flocculating colloids, but it also reduces acidity and may cause alkalinity unacceptable to such acid-soil plants as heaths and rhododendrons. Under such circumstances gypsum may

The addition of lime to clay soils improves their structure and reduces their acidity

serve in place of lime. The addition of coarse sand or, better still, fine coal cinders, not ash, but cokey pieces that will pass through a ½-inch mesh and that when rubbed in the hand give out a crunchy sound, improves the aeration and porosity of clay soils.

Silty soils respond, in the main, to management practices that are favorable for clayey soils. However, because their particles tend not to flocculate and form crumblike aggregates it is of even greater importance to incorporate with them at fairly frequent intervals considerable amounts of coarse organic materials, such as strawy manure, compost, or green manures, to keep them permeable to air and water.

Sandy soils are the easiest to work mechanically and to keep loose enough to assure that water percolates through them freely and that roots receive adequate supplies of air. No structural damage is likely to be done to these soils by the use of heavy equipment or by working them shortly after rain. They tend to warm up

quickly in spring and because of this are well suited for the production of early crops.

But sandy soils have some disadvantages; chiefly, they are deficient in plant nutrients, they do not retain well those applied in fertilizers and manures, and they have little water-holding capacity. Also, organic material mixed into them breaks down and is lost much more rapidly than from heavier soils. Because of these characteristics, sandy soils are called "hungry" soils.

The management of such soils calls for special emphasis on keeping up their organic content by mixing in, whenever opportunity permits, considerable bulks of manures, green manures, compost, and other humus-forming materials. It is beneficial, but not always practicable, to mix a 2- or 3-inch layer of heavier clay soil with the upper 6 inches or so of a sandy one. The free use of mulches is also very helpful. See that fertilizing is adequate to meet the plants' nutritional needs. In comparison with practices appropriate for heavier soils, more frequent applications of smaller amounts of fertilizer are likely to be advantageous.

Loams, especially medium loams, are ideal garden soils. They have many of the virtues of both clay and sandy soils without as much of the disadvantages of either. To obtain the best results from them, intelligent management practices, including incorporating such organic materials as compost, peat moss, manure, or green manure crops and fertilizing, are needed. Also it is not nearly as necessary to exercise the caution about manipulating them when wet as it is with clay and silt soils, nor is it necessary to give such frequent attention to fertilizing and watering as is demanded if the best results are to be had from sandy and gravelly soils.

Special soil types include mucks and alkaline and saline soils. These occur in limited regions. Mucks have usually 70 to 90 percent organic content and, as they occur naturally, high water tables. Such bog and swamp soils are fairly frequent in northern North America. Many, after draining, have been developed as productive agricultural lands suitable for such selected crops as carrots, celery, horse-radish, onions, potatoes, and spinach. But not all muck lands are so adaptable. To be amenable their water tables must be lowered to about 2½ feet below the surface and their acidity-alkalinity range must be maintained at approximately pH 6 to 7.5. It is sometimes practicable to raise the natural pH by liming or to lower it by applying aluminum sulfate or finely powdered sulfur. When comparatively small areas of muck soils exist in ornamental landscapes, it is often better to take advantage of their unique character and plant them with trees, shrubs, and other plants known to require or tolerate bog or swamp environments than to undertake draining and conversion to dry-land areas.

Saline soils exist in desert and coastal areas, alkaline soils in deserts and semi-deserts. For management practices best suited to these consult the local Cooperative Extension Agent or the State Agricultural Experiment Station of the state in which they are located.

Fertilizing, the provision of additional nutrients, is a very old and well-tried way of promoting plant growth. Until a little over a century ago, such soil enrichment was essentially confined to the use of raw animal manures and, to a lesser extent, a few other organics. The use of processed and formulated commercial fertilizers, including some synthetics, is of much later origin.

In modern practice, most gardeners and others who grow plants rely to a large extent or exclusively upon fertilizers. Comparatively few have access to outputs of local cow barns, stables, or stockyards. The

Many garden soils are improved by routine fertilizing

common nonavailability of manures (excluding packaged, dehydrated cow and sheep manures, which, unlike untreated manures, are applied in small amounts and are properly considered fertilizers) or, at best, the impracticability of depending upon them to any considerable extent has brought about general reliance upon fertilizers as the means of supplying nutrients to the soil. Fertilizers are much more convenient to store and handle than manures, they are standardized as to their nutrient contents, and nearly everywhere they are less expensive in relation to the nutrients they supply. Unlike manures they add little or no organic matter and so, for satisfactory results with most soils, they must be supplemented by the use of compost, peat moss, green manures, or other bulky organics that decay to form humus.

The times and rates of applications of fertilizers should be adjusted to the sorts

of plants and the character and inherent fertility of the soil. The latter can be determined most accurately by a soil test, which you can arrange to have done through your local Cooperative Extension Agent or State Agricultural Experiment Station. However, with a little experience with any particular soil the need for fertilizing can usually be determined from observation of the plants growing upon it or the behavior of previous crops; it is not necessary to have frequent soil tests made. Because of its deflocculating effect it is important not to use nitrate of soda on clay soils.

As a general rule, fertilization is done as part of the initial preparation of the ground for seeding or planting. For vegetables, annual and biennial flowering plants, and such crops as chrysanthemums, dahlias, and gladioluses, it is often desirable to supplement this with one or more applications broadcast over the surface or supplied as side dressings during the growing season. Permanent plantings, such as lawns, hardy herbaceous perennials, roses, and deciduous and evergreen shrubs and trees, may be fertilized at the beginning of their season of growth and sometimes later too, but not so late that the growth of soft shoots especially susceptible to winter killing is stimulated. For more information consult the Encyclopedia entry Fertilizers.

The pH value of the soil, the measure of its acidity or alkalinity, must be given reasonable attention, although inexperienced gardeners not uncommonly stress this unduly and at the same time exhibit too little concern about the importance of promoting a good physical condition.

Whether a soil is acid or alkaline and to what degree has an important bearing upon the sorts of plants that will grow satisfactorily in it. Acidity and alkalinity are measured on a pH scale from 1 to 14, with a pH of 7 representing the neutral point for a soil that is neither acid nor alkaline. For more information about this, about methods of changing the pH, and especially about the common practice of liming, which reduces acidity, consult the Encyclopedia entries Acid and Alkaline Soils, and Lime and Liming.

Surface cultivation with hoes, cultivators, and similar implements can be extremely helpful or harmful depending upon how it is done. Its chief benefit is suppression of weeds that otherwise would compete with desirable plants for water, nutrients, and light. Supplementary benefits may include improved aeration of the soil, which stimulates the activity of favorable soil organisms and root growth, allows for better water penetration, and conserves moisture by establishing a shallow layer of dry soil on the surface that checks the capillary rise of water from below.

Thoughtlessly done, surface cultivation can harm soil structure by pulverizing aggregates. This may occur as the result of too much tramping on the ground, of too frequent stirring of the surface, or of hoeing or cultivating when the ground is too moist. But most often damage comes from cultivating too deeply. Many garden plants have fine feeder roots near the surface and if these are destroyed by cultivating implements the growth of the plants is likely to be severely restricted.

Shallow cultivation, the stirring of the soil to not more than an inch deep at times

Stirring the surface shallowly with a hoe or cultivator benefits most soils and destroys weeds

when it is dry enough not to stick to tools and shoes, if done without unnecessary tramping (especially if the ground is clayey), is generally beneficial except around such notorious surface-rooting plants as azaleas and rhododendrons. Deeper disturbance is harmful. The scuffle hoe is the best hand tool to use for most garden cultivation. Mulching ranks high as a substitute for surface cultivation.

For plants in pots and other containers it is usually necessary or desirable to modify natural soil by adding appreciable

Mulching is an excellent substitute for shallow surface cultivation

quantities of a bulk organic material, such as peat moss or leaf mold, and substantial amounts of sand, perlite, or other inert inorganic material. Other amendments, including fertilizers, may be added. Soils so modified are called potting soils or potting mixes. The last term covers both soil-based and soilless potting media. See the Encyclopedia entry Potting Soils and Potting Mixes.

SOLANACEAE — Nightshade Family. An important source of ornamentals as well as foods, including eggplants and potatoes, and drugs, including atropine and hyoscamine, the SOLANACEAE is a family of approximately 2,000 species of dicotyledons dispersed among ninety genera. Its members are small trees, shrubs, and herbaceous plants, among them some vines. Some, deadly nightshade (*Atropa belladonna*) and jimson weed (*Datura stramonium*), for example, are virulently poisonous. Prevailingly alternate, but those on the flowering parts sometimes opposite, the leaves are undivided and lobeless, or variously cleft or pinnate. The flowers, mostly bisexual and symmetrical, are less often asymmetrical. They have a five-lobed calyx and a five-lobed, most often wheel-shaped, but sometimes bell-, funnel-, or trumpet-shaped, corolla. Usually they have five stamens with their anthers joined to form a cone surrounding the pistil. The fruits are berries.

Cultivated genera include *Acnistus, Atropa, Browallia, Brugmansia, Brunfelsia, Capsicum, Cestrum, Cyphomandra, Datura, Fabiana, Grabowskia, Hyoscyamus, Iochroma, Jaborosa, Juanulloa, Lycium, Lycopersicon, Mandragora, Nicandra, Nicotiana, Nierembergia, Petunia, Physalis, Salpichroa, Salpiglossis, Schizanthus, Scopolia, Solandra, Solanum, Streptosolen,* and *Vestia.*

SOLANDRA (Solánd-ra) — Chalice Vine, Copa-de-Oro or Cup-of-Gold. The ten species of *Solandra*, of the nightshade family SOLANACEAE, are climbing shrubs or woody vines native from the West Indies and Mexico to Central America and tropical South America. A few are cultivated outdoors in tropical and subtropical climates and in greenhouses. Their name honors Daniel C. Solander, a Swedish naturalist and traveler, who died in 1782.

Chalice vines are so called because of the form of their large, handsome, showy, white or yellow flowers. These have long, funnel-shaped corolla tubes that become bell- or goblet-shaped toward their mouths and five spreading or rolled back lobes (petals). The five stamens are attached close to the base of the corolla. The fruits are spherical or elongated pulpy berries containing large smooth seeds.

The copa-de-oro or cup-of-gold (*S. maxima* syn. *S. nitida*), in gardens often misidentified as *S. guttata*, is Mexican. This

Solandra maxima

grows 40 feet tall, is hairless, and has more or less lustrous, ovate or obovate leaves. Its flowers, up to 10 inches long, deep bronzy-yellow, with a few conspicuous brown-purple stripes in the throat, have reflexed corolla lobes. True *S. guttata* grows to about the same height, but has downy shoots, and leaves up to 6 inches long that are conspicuously downy beneath especially near the mid-vein. The flowers, as big as those of *S. maxima*, are cream-colored at first, but soon change to rich ochre-yellow. They are lined, feathered, or spotted with purple. This sort is Mexican.

West Indian *S. grandiflora,* up to 40 feet high, has leaves up to 5 inches long and fragrant flowers that when they first open are white tinged with violet, later changing to tawny-yellow. They are 6 to 10 inches long and have calyxes 2 to 3 inches long that enclose most or all of the narrow part of the corolla tube. Another West Indian, *S. longiflora,* has white flowers that turn yellow soon after opening, with purplish lines inside their throats and frilled margins to the petals. This favors limestone soils.

Solandra longiflora

Garden and Landscape Uses. Chalice vines are most effective where there is ample room for them to develop. Over-

restrictive pruning tends to produce awkward, ungainly specimens. They are appropriate for pergolas and tall pillars and for training against large wall spaces. Under favorable conditions single plants may spread horizontally for 150 feet or more, but they can be kept within lesser bounds by judicious pruning. Solandras are rapid growers and produce many vigorous long shoots each year and a good show of quite astonishing blooms. They are excellent for the adornment of large greenhouses and conservatories.

Cultivation. These plants must have a very well-drained soil, but too high fertility is likely to result in excessive vegetative growth at the expense of bloom. Unless they are obviously not making adequate growth, nitrogenous fertilizers should not be given. They flourish in full sun as well as where they receive a little part-day shade. The blooms are borne on young shoots and pruning consists of thinning out weak shoots and shortening others in late winter or spring. Only well-ripened shoots are likely to bloom. In greenhouses, and outdoors in some regions, it is advisable to withhold water for a few weeks in fall to the extent that the foliage wilts slightly as a means of encouraging the wood to ripen. Propagation is very easy by cuttings and by seed. In many warm regions seedlings from self-sown seeds spring up abundantly. Mealybugs, aphids, scale insects, and red spider mites are the chief pests.

SOLANUM (Sol-ànum)—Nightshade, Christmas-Cherry, Jerusalem-Cherry, Potato Vine, Potato-Tree, Garden-Huckleberry. The horticulturally important genus *Solanum*, of the nightshade family SOLANACEAE, contains 1,700 or more species and is practically cosmopolitan in its natural distribution, with its greatest concentration of species in warm parts of the Americas. It includes such familiar sources of food as eggplants and potatoes and is related to genera that contain sinister substances, such as deadly nightshade (*Atropa belladonna*), highly toxic jimson weed (*Datura stramonium*), and poisonous henbane (*Hyoscyamus niger*) from all of which important medicinal drugs are obtained. Tobacco (*Nicotiana tabacum*) is another well-known relative. The name *Solanum* is believed to derive from the Latin *solamen*, quieting, and to allude to the sedative properties of some kinds.

Annuals, biennials, herbaceous perennials, shrubs, vines, and a few trees comprise this genus. Some are hardy, others not. Some are formidably spiny. All have alternate, divided or undivided, lobed or lobeless leaves. The flowers, often showy, come from the leaf axils or from opposite the leaves. They are in clusters or solitary. They have a usually five-toothed, but sometimes four- or up to ten-toothed calyx, a five-lobed, wheel- to bell-shaped corolla, and most commonly five stamens with their anthers united to form a cone enclosing the style. The fruits, even those of eggplants, are technically berries. In the treatment that follows, eggplants and potatoes are omitted, since these are the subjects of separate articles in this Encyclopedia.

A hardy vine, the woody nightshade or bittersweet (*S. dulcamara*) of Europe and temperate Asia, is naturalized in North America where it is not infrequently mis-

Solanum dulcamara (flowers)

Solanum dulcamara (fruits)

identified as deadly nightshade. Not to be confused with quite different *Celastrus,* which in America is called bittersweet, this is too weedy to be worthy of general cultivation, but is interesting enough to leave undisturbed in some wild settings. Attaining heights up to 10 or 12 feet, it has ovate leaves 2 to 4 inches long that are sometimes lobed at their bases. In long-stalked clusters, the starry flowers, about ½ inch wide, have a bright blue-purple corolla and yellow stamens. The nearly ½-inch-long, ovoid fruits, at first bright green, change to brilliant scarlet at maturity. All parts of the plant are believed to be poisonous if they are eaten raw.

Nonhardy vines of much ornamental merit include two that bear the common name potato vine, *S. jasminoides* and *S.*

Solanum jasminoides

wendlandii, and *S. seaforthianum.* Native to Brazil, **S. jasminoides** has slender stems devoid of prickles and ovate-lanceolate leaves 1 inch to 3 inches long, sometimes pinnately-lobed or divided at their bases. In branched clusters, the about 1-inch-wide, starry, bluish-white flowers have yellow anthers. Those of *S. j. grandiflorum* are in bigger clusters. The other potato vine, **S. wendlandii,** is more vigorous, has stouter stems, and is bigger in its parts. A native of Costa Rica, and attaining heights up to 20 feet, this has stems with hooked prickles and leaves 4 inches to 1 foot long, mostly pinnate, with four or six pairs of lateral leaflets and a terminal one conspicuously larger, but often with the upper leaves three-lobed or heart-shaped instead of having separate leaflets. In large, showy, branched clusters, the open-faced, 2½-inch-wide, lilac-blue flowers are succeeded by orange, spherical to ovoid fruits almost ½ inch in diameter. Native to tropical America, **S. seaforthianum** is a slender, spineless, hairless vine 10 to 20 feet tall. Its leaves, of three to nine usually unequal-sized, lobed leaflets, are 4 to 8 inches long. In many-flowered, showy clusters from the leaf axils, the starry, blue to purple blooms, about 1 inch across, are succeeded by spherical to egg-shaped red fruits about ⅓ inch in diameter.

African-holly (**S. giganteum**), of India and Ceylon, is a shrub 4 to 10 feet tall furnished with stout prickles. Mostly 4 to 8 inches long, its oblong-lanceolate leaves have white-hairy undersurfaces. The ¾-inch-wide, pale violet to blue flowers in clusters of many are followed by showy, bright red, spherical fruits about ⁵⁄₁₆ inch in diameter.

The Chilean potato-tree (**S. crispum**), an evergreen or partially evergreen shrub or small tree up to 15 feet high, is a native of Chile and Peru that survives outdoors in southern England and in other climates where not more than a few degrees of frost are experienced. It has ovate leaves up to 2 inches long, downy on both surfaces, and in generous clusters, deep-purplish-blue flowers up to 1 inch across, with yellow

Solanum crispum

anthers. The fruits are yellow, spherical, and about ⅓ inch in diameter. Variety *S. c. autumnale* (syn. *S. c.* 'Glasnevin') has larger blooms.

The kangaroo apple or poro-poro (**S. aviculare** syn. *S. laciniatum*), of Australia and New Zealand, is a hairless shrub without spines or prickles and up to 10 feet tall. It has narrow-lanceolate to ovate leaves 5 inches to 1 foot long, irregularly-lobed or not. In clusters of many, the violet-blue to lilac or sometimes white flowers, 1 inch to 1½ inches across, have pointed corolla lobes (petals) about as long as the corolla tube. The large egg-shaped fruits change from green to yellow as they ripen.

Other shrubby sorts grown for ornament include several adaptable for outdoor cultivation in mild climates and in greenhouses, but not hardy in the north. Native to Argentina, Bolivia, and Peru, **S. abutiloides** is a shrub 6 to 12 feet tall with

Solanum abutiloides

shoots, leaves, and flower clusters densely clothed with stellate (starlike) yellowish hairs. Its broad-elliptic to elliptic-ovate, lobeless, toothless leaves have stalks 1 inch to 3 inches long and blades 4 to 6 inches in length. The whitish to light purple to deeper purple flowers, about 1 inch wide, have yellow anthers. In racemes, they are succeeded by fruits, about ⅝ inch in diameter, that are described as sweet-tasting. Western Australian **S. lasiophyllum** is a prickly-stemmed shrub 3 to 6 feet tall with short-stalked, lobeless, wavy-margined, ovate leaves, clothed with a felt of white

Solanum lasiophyllum

Solanum pyracanthum

Solanum subinerme

to gray, stellate (starry) hairs. The rich purple flowers, 1 inch to 1½ inches wide, have bright yellow anthers. The fruits are enclosed by the densely-felted, globular calyx. Known by the vernacular names potato-tree and Brazilian potato-tree, *S. macranthum,* of Brazil, in its homeland is a tree 20 to 30 feet in height, but as known in cultivation is a hairy, spiny shrub 5 to 8 feet tall. It has broadly-ovate, round-lobed or sinuately-toothed leaves prickly along the veins, up to 1¼ feet long by 2 inches wide, and dark bluish-violet flowers that become whitish as they age. Because its curious fruits suggest a breast, *S. mammosum,* of tropical America, is known as nipple fruit. A downy, prickly shrub 2 to

Solanum mammosum

3 feet tall and generally grown as an annual, this has broad-ovate, irregularly round-lobed leaves up to 6 inches long, and solitary or in clusters of few, violet flowers about 1½ inches in diameter. Its yellow or orange, conical, waxy fruits, approximately 2 inches long, have generally several nipple-like protrusions that spread outward from their bases. The fruits are reported to be poisonous. A subshrub native to Malagasy (Madagascar) and tropical Africa, *S. pyracanthum* is thought by some to be of hybrid origin. Up to about 5 feet tall and with scattered, orange to reddish, prominent spines, it has stalked,

narrow-pinnately-lobed leaves margined with white and with white-felty undersides. The light to dark violet flowers, sometimes striped with white and with white centers, have yellow anthers. The spherical fruits are yellow. Called blue potato-bush, *S. rantonnetii* is native to Argentina and Paraguay. Without spines or

Solanum rantonnetii

prickles and up to 6 feet high, this nearly hairless shrub has somewhat wavy, mostly pointed, ovate leaves, 2½ to 4 inches long, and attractive clusters of pale-eyed, dark blue to violet flowers nearly ½ inch in diameter. The bright red, heart-shaped fruits are pendulous and ¾ to 1 inch long. More commonly cultivated than the typical species, *S. r. grandiflorum* has flowers up to 1 inch across. The apple-of-Sodom, Dead-Sea-apple, or yellow popolo (*S. sodomeum*), of the Mediterranean region, is a somewhat straggly, conspicuously-spiny, pubescent shrub up to 6 feet in height. It has pinnate or deeply-pinnately-lobed leaves with wavy, toothless leaflets and clusters of 1-inch-wide, violet flowers succeeded by glossy, yellow, more or less poisonous, spherical fruits of strange appearance. They are 1½ inches in diameter. Very variable *S. subinerme* (syn. *S. laurifolium*), of Central America, is a shrub 3

to 10 feet tall with stems, leaves, and floral parts clothed with a felt of stellate (starlike), gray to tawny hairs. The stems and mid-veins of the leaves are sometimes prickly. In outline lanceolate to ovate or triangular-ovate, the more or less coarsely-lobed leaves have stalks 1½ to 4 inches long and blades 4½ to 8 inches long. About 1½ inches wide, the clear lavender to purple or less often white flowers are in branched clusters. They have yellow anthers and are succeeded by fruits ½ inch in diameter. Subshrubby *S. xantii,* of California, is a somewhat clammy-hairy subshrub or shrub with erect or prostrate, branched, slender stems 1 foot to 3 feet long, and soft, variously-shaped leaves 1 inch to 2½ inches long. In clusters at the stem ends or on short side branches, the nodding, wheel-to shallowly-bell-shaped, light purple-blue flowers, ¾ inch to 1½ inches across, have yellow anthers. The spherical fruits are green to purple.

The Jerusalem-cherry or Christmas-cherry (*S. pseudocapsicum*), popular as a pot plant for indoor decoration, is a native of the Old World tropics. An erect, bushy, hairless

Solanum pseudocapsicum

shrub 1½ to 4 feet tall, it is often grown as an annual. It has oblong to lanceolate, wavy leaves 2 to 4 inches long, with glossy upper surfaces. Solitary or in clusters of few and ½ inch wide or slightly wider, the white flowers are followed by long-persistent, spherical, red or yellow fruits about

Spathodea campanulata

Soldanella alpina

Sophronitis coccinea

Solanum pseudocapsicum

Sphyrospermum buxifolium

Solanum mammosum

Sparaxis grandiflora

Stachys byzantina

Stachyurus praecox

Stanhopea wardii

½ inch in diameter, or in cultivated varieties larger. The fruits are poisonous. Garden varieties of compact growth and superior fruiting qualities include *S. p.* 'Clevelandii', *S. p. nanum*, *S. p. pattersonii*, and *S. p.* 'Tom Thumb'. False-Jerusalem-cherry or false-Christmas-cherry (*S. capsicastrum*), of Brazil, resembles the Jerusalem-cherry, but its young stems and duller, grayish-green leaves are furnished with stellate (starlike) hairs, and its fruits, which tend to be not as lasting as those of the Jerusalem-cherry, are generally somewhat conical rather than spherical.

A delicious fruit little known in North America or Europe, the naranjilla or lulo (*S. quitoense*) is greatly esteemed in parts of South America, where its fruits are eaten out of hand and are used to make a refreshing, nonalcoholic beverage. A na-

Solanum quitoense

Solanum quitoense (fruits)

tive of the northern Andes, this is a coarse, spiny or spineless subshrub or shrub, 4 to 8 feet tall, with large eggplant-like, broadly-ovate, shallowly-lobed, purple-veined leaves, 8 inches to 1½ feet long, that, especially when young, are clothed with purple hairs. More or less hidden by the foliage, the ¼-inch-wide, white flowers are in clusters. The fruits, which resemble small oranges, have thin rinds at first orange, but becoming redder and fragrant as they ripen. They contain, depending upon the variety, bitter-sweet or acid pulp.

The pepino (*S. muricatum*), also called melon-shrub, melon-pear, and pear-melon, is esteemed for its crisp, juicy, aromatic fruits, the flesh of which suggests that of an acid cantaloupe melon. They are eaten fresh. Native in the Andes, this is an erect, spiny subshrub, 2 to 3 feet tall, with long-stalked, finely-hairy, oblong to ovate, lobeless, toothless, often wavy, 2- to 3-inch-long leaves. Bright blue, starry flowers, ½ to ¾ inch wide, are succeeded by violet-purple, ovoid fruits 4 to 6 inches long.

Annual solanums with edible, small, berry-like fruits include those called garden-huckleberry, wonderberry, sunberry or orange sunberry, and with some reservation, the common or black nightshade. The garden huckleberry (*S. melanocerasum* syn. *S. nigrum guineense*), perhaps of

Solanum melanocerasum

garden origin, 1½ to 2 feet tall, has broadly-ovate, toothless or lightly-toothed leaves 3 to 7 inches long. Its flowers, white with brown anthers, are about ⅜ inch wide. The fruits, black, spherical, and ½ inch or a little more in diameter, are slightly bitter. They are eaten after stewing, or in pies and preserves. Introduced by Luther Burbank early in the twentieth century, the wonderberry, sunberry, or orange sunberry (*S. burbankii*) is of uncertain, possibly hybrid, origin. From 1 foot to 1½ feet tall and short-hairy, this has ovate leaves 1 inch to 1½ inches long and ¼-inch-wide, white flowers with orange anthers. Its black or orange fruits, about ½ inch in diameter, are used similarly to those of the garden huckleberry. The foliage and fully ripe fruits of the common or black nightshade (*S. nigrum*), of Europe (also freely naturalized in North America), are cooked and eaten in some regions, but because this is a more or less poisonous species it may be hazardous to do this, especially if the fruits are unripened. Up to 2½ feet tall to nearly prostrate, this has lobeless or angular-lobed, wavy, ovate to ovate-lanceolate leaves, glossy on their upper surfaces and 3 to 7 inches long. The ¼-inch-wide, white flowers produce dull black or sometimes greenish, spherical fruits ¼ inch in diameter.

Annuals grown for ornament are the tomato- or scarlet-fruited eggplant and the soda-apple nightshade or cockroach berry. The first, *S. integrifolium,* is probably of African origin. Up to 2 to 3 feet tall, it is coarse, spiny, and pubescent. It has wavy-toothed, ovate to oblong-ovate leaves, up to about 10 inches long, with often prickly midribs, and in clusters of few, white flowers about ¾ inch wide. The longitudinally-ribbed, spherical, scarlet or yellow fruits are approximately 2 inches in diameter. Not unlike the last and about as tall, the soda-apple nightshade or cockroach berry (*S. aculeatissimum*), of the Old World tropics, is naturalized in the southern United States. The stems and foliage of this are clothed with yellowish-brown prickles as well as deciduous hairs. The five- to seven-lobed, broadly-ovate leaves are 4 to 6 inches long. Starry, white, and 1 inch wide, the flowers are succeeded by spherical, 2-inch-wide, brownish-orange to brownish-red, ribbed fruits, with skins that become parchment-like at maturity.

Other annuals sometimes cultivated include *S. citrullifolium* and *S. rostratum.* Native from Texas to Arizona and Mexico, *S. citrullifolium* is 1 foot to 3 feet tall, spiny,

Solanum citrullifolium

and pubescent. It much resembles *S. rostratum* from which it differs most noticeably in having mostly twice-pinnately-lobed leaves ovate in outline and up to 6 or 7 inches long. The violet to blue or purple flowers, about 1¼ inches wide, have one anther much longer than the others. They are succeeded by small fruits enclosed in the spiny calyx. Native from North Dakota to Wyoming, Utah, California, and Mexico, *S. rostratum,* 1 foot to 3 feet tall, has stems and leaves with conspicuous yellow

Solanum rostratum

spines interspersed with stellate (star-shaped) hairs. Its ovate to oblongish leaves, usually spiny along the principal veins, are pinnately-lobed, or sometimes a few are twice-pinnately-lobed. The yellow flowers, from ¾ inch to 1¼ inches wide and with one stamen much longer than the others, are in racemes of five to eight. The spherical fruits are completely enclosed by the spiny calyx.

Garden and Landscape Uses. Depending upon their individual growth habits and other characteristics, cultivated solanums serve a variety of garden purposes. The garden huckleberry and related annual sorts are cultivated to a limited extent for their edible fruits. In time, perhaps, the naranjilla or lulo and the pepino will also be grown in North America for theirs, but that time is not yet. Meanwhile, gardeners may enjoy experimenting with them, chiefly for fun.

The Jerusalem-cherry or Christmas-cherry, raised in great numbers in pots to supply the florist trade and also grown in greenhouses and on windowsills by amateurs, is undoubtedly one of the best-known ornamental solanums. Its fruits, somewhat like those of cherry tomatoes, but less juicy and much longer-lasting, in a fairly cool room remain attractive for several weeks. The false-Christmas-cherry has similar uses.

The shrubs, subshrubs, and vines are excellent furnishings for outdoors in the tropics and subtropics and for greenhouses. The vines lend themselves to training up trellis, poles, pillars, and along wires stretched a few inches beneath the roof glass of greenhouses. Good standard (tree-form) specimens of *S. rantonnetii* can be had by limiting their early growth to one shoot kept tied to an erect stake and, when this has attained a suitable height to form a "trunk," pinching out its tip to induce branching from near its top. These branches are pinched again when they are 6 inches or so long and this is repeated until a good head is developed. Any side shoots that sprout from the trunk are picked off when very small.

Cultivation. Accommodating plants, solanums for the most part cause gardeners no undue worries. The shrubs, subshrubs, and vines prosper in any reasonably fertile, well-drained soil that is not excessively dry. In greenhouses they may be accommodated in large pots or tubs or ground beds. They are not shade plants, but most appreciate a little shade from the strongest, hottest sun of summer. This is especially true of specimens in greenhouses. In too exposed locations, their foliage is apt to yellow somewhat and the flowers of some to fade or bleach.

Keep well-rooted, healthy specimens watered adequately to stimulate vigor and prevent wilting of the foliage or premature leaf drop. Those in containers that have filled their available soil with healthy roots greatly benefit from fertilizing regularly from spring to fall.

Pruning, to be done as soon as flowering is through or in spring just before new growth begins, is a much needed attention if most of these plants are to be kept shapely and of acceptable size. It involves shortening strong stems or even removing some, if they are too crowded, and cutting out or cutting hard back weak shoots. Propagation of solanums is easily accomplished by seed and by cuttings.

The Jerusalem-cherry or Christmas-cherry is usually raised from seed. It is not difficult to root cuttings, but seedlings are likely to give the best results. Seeds are readily available commercially, or it is a simple matter to save one's own by squashing one or more fully ripe fruits, washing the seeds free of the pulpy material around them, allowing them to dry, and storing them in a cool, frost-free, dry place until sowing time.

Sow from February to April in pots or pans of sandy soil in a greenhouse or similar accommodation where the temperature is 55 to 60°F. Within a few days of their emergence gradually accustom the seedlings to full sun. As soon as they have developed their first true leaves, transplant them individually to small pots or space them 1½ to 2 inches apart in flats. When they have attained heights of 3 inches or so, pinch out their tips to encourage branching and soon afterward pot them into 4-inch pots, using a coarse, porous, fertile soil. Grow them from now on in temperatures of 50°F at night and from 55 to 65°F by day. Keep the atmosphere moderately moist, but not dank and stagnant.

After the weather becomes warm and settled, about two weeks after it is safe to plant tomatoes in the garden, set the Christmas-cherries outdoors, either removing them from their pots and planting them in rows 2 feet apart and 1 foot to 1½ feet between individuals in the rows in moderately fertile soil, or repotting them in 5-inch pots and sinking these to their rims in a bed of sand or peat moss or in the ground. Summer care consists of weeding and watering and for specimens kept in pots moderate, but regular fertilizing.

Before the first light frost of fall, bring the plants indoors. In preparation for this, dig those planted in beds and, taking care not to disturb their roots more than necessary, pot them in containers just big enough to hold them. Water very thoroughly and until they recover from the shock of transplanting protect them from drafts and direct sun. This can be done by putting them into a shaded cold frame at first ventilated only enough to make sure the temperature does not rise unduly on warm days. In sunny weather, mist the newly potted plants two or three times a day with water. When they have recovered from the shock of transplanting, ventilate the frame more freely. Specimens that have been in pots all summer may also be accommodated temporarily to a cold frame. This is especially convenient if, as is often the case, the greenhouses are chock-a-block full of chrysanthemums and other plants that will soon be out.

Christmas-cherries must not be subjected to freezing. Before danger of this, transfer them to a cool, sunny greenhouse to complete the ripening of their fruits. Make sure they do not suffer from lack of moisture, but avoid keeping the soil constantly saturated. Either condition causes the foliage to wilt. Temperatures at this time may be 45 to 50°F at night and preferably not more than 60°F by day; an airy rather than heavily humid atmosphere is most favorable.

If the plants are to be kept over, either as sources of cuttings or to be grown on a second year, shortly after Christmas rest them by keeping the soil decidedly drier, but not completely dry. In February prune all branches to within an inch or two of their bases, resume moderate watering, and on sunny days mist the plants two or three times a day with water. This will encourage young shoots, which when about 2 inches long, can be used as cuttings. They root readily in sand or perlite in a temperature of about 60°F. Treat plants so raised as for seedlings.

Specimens to be grown on a second year, a procedure usually less satisfactory than raising new plants annually, are removed from their pots when the new shoots that come after pruning are about or just under 1 inch long. Shake most of the old soil from their roots, cut back the roots somewhat, and repot into containers just large enough to accommodate them.

The garden huckleberry and wonderberry or sunberry respond to conditions that suit tomatoes. Sow directly outdoors after the weather is warm and settled, or earlier indoors, and transplant the resulting plants about 2 feet apart in rows 2½ to 3 feet asunder. Summer care consists of eliminating weeds and, during dry spells, watering. Harvest the fruits as they ripen.

SOLDANELLA (Soldan-élla). Soldanellas are not widely known in America. A few sorts are treasured by devotees of alpine gardening, but otherwise they are little grown. The about eight species of *Soldanella*, of the primrose family PRIMULACEAE, inhabit the mountains of southern Europe, with one species, it is thought, inhabiting the Caucasus. Difficulty is experienced in defining the botanical limits of the species. Where they overlap geographically, hybrids occur. The name, derived from the Italian *soldo*, a coin, alludes to the shape of the leaves.

Soldanellas are low, hardy, herbaceous perennials that spread slowly by creeping rhizomes. Their often leathery, kidney-shaped to nearly circular leaves, with long, slender stalks, are in loose basal rosettes. Erect leafless stalks carry in early spring, often well before the last snows have gone, one to eight nodding, fringed, funnel- or bell-shaped, dainty violet to lavender-blue or more rarely white flowers. They have five-lobed persistent calyxes, corollas with five fringed lobes, five stamens, and a slender style tipped with a knoblike stigma. There may or may not be five scales alternating with the stamens in the throats of the blooms. The fruits are approximately cylindrical capsules.

Soldanellas are divided into two groups, one of which has leaves under ½ inch across and one or rarely a pair of narrowly-funnel-shaped flowers on each stalk, with the fringes of their corollas extending for not over one-third of their lengths, and usually without scales in their throats. The second group is distinguished by its leaves being ¾ inch or more across, and its flower stalks having normally two or more broadly-funnel- to bell-shaped blooms with corollas fringed for at least one-half their length, and with scales in their throats.

A favorite of the first group is *S. pusilla,* a native of moist meadows above 6,000 feet in central and eastern Europe. Its solitary or sometimes paired blooms, on stalks mostly 2 to 4 inches long, are reddish-violet to lavender-blue and are from a little under to a little over ½ inch long. There are no scales in their throats, and the frills extend for only about one-quarter the lengths of the corollas. Kidney-shaped, smooth-edged, and about ⅓ inch wide, the leaves are dotted with glands on their undersides. The leafstalks and flower stalks at first have stalkless glands, but these soon disappear. The upper sides of the leaves are conspicuously veined. Differing from the last in that its leafstalks and flower stalks have persistent stalked glands and the upper sides of the leaves are without evident veins, *S. minima,* a native of the southern Alps, has thick, round leaves, less than ½ inch in diameter, and solitary funnel-shaped blooms, on stalks up to 3 inches long, pale blue or white, with violet lines.

Belonging to the group with larger leaves and more flowers on the stalks, *S. montana* inhabits the Pyrenees, Alps, and Carpathian mountains. Attaining a height of 4 to 8 inches, it has shallowly-scalloped leaves ¾ inch to 2½ inches in diameter, with bluish undersides, and stalks, that, like those of the lavender-blue to lilac blooms, are densely clothed with glandular hairs. There are up to eight bell-shaped flowers on each stalk. They are fringed to below their middles and have widely out-curved corolla lobes. Not as tall

Soldanella montana

and more delicate in appearance, *S. alpina* has two or more blooms to each stalk. They are lavender-blue streaked on their insides with red, or more rarely are white. Their corollas, which are up to ½ inch long, have scales in their throats and are fringed at least to their middles. The thick, round-kidney-shaped leaves are up to 2¼ inches in diameter. The underground parts of this plant are purgative. Pretty *S. hungarica* (syn. *S. carpatica*) has roundish-kidney-shaped leaves up to 1 inch across and, on stalks 3 to 4 inches tall, one to three lavender or bluish flowers up to ¾ inch long. Native to the Pyrenees, *S. villosa* closely resembles *S. montana,* but differs most obviously in having more persistently hairy leaves and in the lobes of the calyxes of its flowers having three veins instead of one. Its leaves are approximately circular. Its flowers, up to four on each stalk, are blue.

Garden Uses and Cultivation. At their best only where summers are cool, these gems of the alpine world are treasured by rock gardeners and alpine greenhouse enthusiasts. They grow with abandon in environments to their liking, but elsewhere sulk and give poor accounts of themselves, or even perish. They are not very particular as to soil, provided it is well drained, it is satisfactorily humid from spring to fall, and it is not arid even in winter. On the whole a soil fairly well supplied with leaf mold or other decayed organic matter that is neutral or slightly acid is most to their liking. Although soldanellas are light-lovers, a little shade from the intensity of bright summer sun comes not amiss and helps to establish the cool conditions so necessary for them. Propagation is by careful division, as soon as flowering is through, and by seed. The latter often is of low viability and a fairly large percentage even of fresh seeds may fail to germinate.

SOLDIER WEED is *Hibiscus militaris.*

SOLEIROLIA (Soleir-òlia) — Baby's Tears. One low-creeping plant of the nettle family URTICACEAE, long common in cultivation under its synonymous name *Helxine soleirolii* and endemic to Corsica and Sardinia, is the only representative of this genus. It is named after Captain Soleirol, an early nineteenth-century collector of plants in Corsica.

The charm of baby's tears (*Soleirolia soleirolii*) does not lie in its unisexual

Soleirolia soleirolii

blooms, solitary in the leaf axils, as they are almost too small to see. With the aid of a lens it may be observed that they are without petals and that the males have a four-parted calyx and four stamens and the females a four-lobed calyx and a tiny, three-lobed, leafy involucre (collar). Its foliage does not have any color to offer other than a uniform bright green, and its minute fruits are completely without decorative merit. It is, however, the unbelievable neatness of the plant and minuteness of its foliage that attract. Almost mosslike in aspect and scarcely 1 inch high, it spreads quite rapidly and soon forms a perfect carpet of slender stems and numerous almost round, short-stalked leaves up to ¼ inch in diameter. It somewhat resembles *Nertera granadensis,* but that has opposite leaves, whereas those of baby's tears are alternate. It also lacks the lovely berries of *Nertera.* Variety *S. s. aurea* has yellow foliage.

Garden and Landscape Uses. The baby's tears is popular in greenhouses, for growing in windows and terrariums, and, in climates almost or quite frost-free, for planting in rock gardens and similar places. It is sometimes used to carpet the ground beneath greenhouse benches or to form a narrow band of greenery along the fronts of benches and beds in conservatories and display greenhouses. It can also be employed to cover the soil surface of plants, such as palms, cultivated in tubs. An interesting way of displaying it in window gardens and greenhouses is to crock and fill with porous soil three or four different-sized pans (shallow pots) and stand them one on top of the other with the largest at the bottom and the smallest at the top, then to plant the terrace-like spaces between the bottom of each pot and the top of the one below with small pieces of baby's tears. Within a comparatively short time the creeper will form an unbroken mat covering the soil surfaces and cascading down the sides of the pans to meet the terrace next below. Eventually a stepped cone of beautiful green foliage results which, with ordinary care, will remain attractive for several years. In mild climates, baby's tears may be used in rock gardens over deciduous bulbs and as a miniature groundcover.

Cultivation. An extremely adaptable plant, baby's tears prospers in any soil through which water passes readily. It is easily propagated by division. It flourishes in quite a wide range of greenhouse temperatures and is best where it receives good light with a little shade from strong sun. Too much shade causes it to become weak and develop comparatively long thin stems that reach toward the light. Sufficient water should be given to keep the soil always fairly moist. Old established plantings are helped by the occasional application of dilute liquid fertilizer.

SOLENANTHUS (Solen-ánthus). Occurring in the wild from the Mediterranean region to the Himalayas, *Solenanthus*, of the borage family BORAGINACEAE, comprises about fifteen species of biennials and hardy herbaceous perennials. It is closely similar to *Cynoglossum*, differing chiefly in having anthers that protrude from the corollas. The name derives from the Greek *solen*, a tube, and *anthos*, a flower, and alludes to the form of the corolla.

Solenanthuses usually have hollow stems, undivided basal leaves with long stalks, and alternate stem leaves. The cylindrical or funnel-shaped, purple, blue, or pinkish flowers are in panicles. They have persistent five-parted calyxes and tubular corollas with five small, blunt, usually erect lobes (petals). There are five stamens and a distinctly four-lobed ovary. The fruits are of four seedlike nutlets.

Native to southern Europe, *S. apenninus* is 2 to 3 feet tall or somewhat taller. It has stout, hollow stems, and coarse, ovate-oblong to elliptic basal leaves 9 inches to 1¼ feet in length, and hairy on their upper sides. The stem leaves are much narrower and stalkless. Purplish-blue and about ⅓ inch long, the numerous flowers are in racemes arranged in panicle-like clusters.

Garden Uses and Cultivation. The species described is adapted for flower borders, fronts of shrub plantings, and semiformal areas. In well-drained, reasonably fertile soil in sunny locations, it thrives with little care. A perennial, it is readily increased by seed sown in spring, and by division in spring or early fall.

SOLIDAGO (Solid-àgo) — Goldenrod, Silverrod. North America, especially eastern North America, is the provenance of the vast majority of the about 100 species of goldenrods and the silverrod (*Solidago*). A few kinds extend the genus into South America. One species inhabits Europe and one is native to the Azores. This genus belongs in the great daisy family COMPOSITAE. Its name is derived from the Latin *solidus*, whole, and *ago*, to make, and refers to healing virtues attributed to some of its species.

Solidagos are mostly hardy, herbaceous perennials. They have undivided, alternate leaves, mostly wandlike stems, and panicles, racemes, or spikes of numerous small cylindrical or narrowly-bell-shaped flower heads with bisexual disk florets surrounded by a single row of ray florets that are female. In the vast majority of species, the flowers are yellow, in a few they are whitish. The fruits are seedlike achenes.

Despite, or because of, their commonness in the wild and of many Americans' familiarity with them, solidagos are not highly regarded as garden plants in their principal homeland and indeed are little cultivated. This is not true in Europe. Throughout the northern part of that continent, gardens everywhere are aglow with goldenrods, the progeny of American species, from midsummer or a little later until the arrival of killing frost. They accompany in bloom and rival in display the numerous varieties of Michaelmas-daisies (*Aster*), another American group that European plant breeders have developed magnificently. But in Europe it is not only in gardens that one finds goldenrods. They are used freely as cut flowers, often for decorating tables in hotels and restaurants, as well as in many other ways. Europeans are unfamiliar with the unfounded American belief that goldenrods are a serious cause of hay fever; they sniff them without apprehension. The kinds cultivated in Europe are not our wild species, but hybrids, and selections from them in an array of garden varieties show tremendous variety in form, height, size of flower, and other details of interest to gardeners.

Although goldenrods are occasionally cultivated in North America, especially in native plant gardens, it seems unlikely indeed that they will ever attain even a fraction of the popularity that is theirs in Europe. Some of the finest improved horticultural varieties raised on the other side of the Atlantic and imported into the United States have, rather strangely, proved less handsome and less adaptable than in Europe. At The New York Botanical Garden several such introductions made in the 1950s did not behave particularly well; they were very susceptible to mildew diseases, and the flowers of some varieties faded badly under the strong American

sun. In successive years they tended to deteriorate. This seems to indicate that the European varieties have been bred and selected for European conditions and that if Americans want improved horticultural varieties it would be better to breed their own than rely on the products of European raisers. Until that is done, the best plan is to rely upon the wild species and, as individuals among these show considerable variation, to select only the finest ones for garden planting. This is easily done when the plants are in flower and, if cut back and carefully dug and replanted at that time, they can be transferred from the wild to the garden successfully. Alternatively, desirable specimens can be marked when in bloom and transplanted later.

The kinds of goldenrods are so numerous and gardeners' interest in them so limited that any lengthy discussion or descriptions of them here cannot be justified. For fuller information, regional floras and books on wild flowers should be consulted. In addition to the wild species, natural hybrids occur. Among the most attractive species are *S. caesia*, which thrives in part-day shade; *S. graminifolia*, a kind that prefers moist ground; *S. nemoralis*, the flowers of which last longer than those of many kinds and which does well in full sun in dryish soil; *S. odora*, which also has long-lasting flowers and anise-scented foliage; *S. sempervirens*, which is one of the handsomest and is excellent for seaside planting and for sa-

Solidago sempervirens

line soils; and *S. speciosa*, notable for its very large and handsome panicles of bloom, and which does well in part-shade. Two other kinds must be mentioned, the silverrod (*S. bicolor*), an inhabitant of open woodlands, remarkable for its slender, but not very showy spires of cream-colored flowers, and *S. cutleri*, which is very much like the European *S. virgaurea*. It is a high mountain species 2 inches to about 1 foot tall.

Garden and Landscape Uses. In addition to their adaptability for naturalistic plantings, the handsomest goldenrods can

Solidago speciosa

Solidaster luteus

Solidago cutleri

be used with good effect in bold clumps in perennial borders. They complement and provide a good foil for perennial asters, boltonias, and other late-blooming perennials, especially those that do not have yellow flowers. The alpine *S. cutleri* is suitable for rock gardens.

Cultivation. Goldenrods improve when taken from the wild and cultivated. The provision of more fertile soil is undoubtedly in part responsible, but freeing them from the necessity of competing too strenuously with neighboring vigorous plants is also an important factor. They respond to deep, moderately fertile soil and, for the best results, should be divided and replanted every two or three years. Too rich soil causes an unwanted exuberance of growth. A few kinds are comparatively short-lived, they behave almost as biennials; this is true of *S. nemoralis*. Routine care is minimal. Faded flowers should be removed promptly to prevent seed formation and self-sowing to the extent that the seedlings become a nuisance and are likely to smother out the choice variety.

SOLIDASTER (Solid-áster). The name of this bigeneric hybrid is composed of those of its parent genera, *Solidago* and *Aster*, of the daisy family COMPOSITAE.

Fairly frequent in cultivation, *Solidaster luteus* (syns. *Aster hybridus luteus, Asterago*

lutea), is a hardy, herbaceous perennial raised in France early in the twentieth century. Its parents are *Aster ptarmicoides* and a species of *Solidago*. From 1½ to 2½ feet in height, *S. luteus* has stems that branch freely above. Its upper parts are pubescent. The lowermost leaves are long-stalked, narrowly-oblanceolate, pointed, and up to about 4 inches in length. Those on the stems are linear-elliptic and have three main veins. The flower heads, in flattish clusters about 4 inches wide, are about ½ inch in diameter. When they first open both the disk florets that form the eye of each little daisy and the surrounding petal-like ray florets are golden-yellow, but the rays soon fade to cream-yellow.

Garden Uses and Cultivation. Easily grown, *S. luteus* is a pleasing summer-bloomer for flower beds and borders. It succeeds in ordinary soil in sunny locations and is readily increased by division in early fall or spring.

SOLISIA (Sol-ísia). The one Mexican species that constitutes *Solisia* is by some botanists included in nearly related *Pelecyphora*. It belongs in the cactus family CACTACEAE and bears a name honoring Octavio Solis, a twentieth century Mexican student of the cactus family.

A tiny species containing milky juice, *S. pectinata* has usually solitary, globular plant bodies under ½ to slightly over 1 inch across. They are covered with overlapping, white spines in groups of twenty to forty that are very much like those of *Pelecyphora*. They form double-edged combs lying flat on the plant surfaces. The whitish to yellow blooms originate not centrally, but near the edges of the tops of the stems, in the axils of protrusions of the plant body called tubercles. There is a cristate (crested) variety of this species.

Garden Uses and Cultivation. This rather rare cactus is often difficult to grow on its own roots. It usually thrives better when grafted onto a columnar type of cactus. It is chiefly a plant for keen collectors of succulents. Its general cultivation is that of the smaller cactuses. For a discussion of this see Cactuses.

SOLLYA (Sól-lya) — Australian Bluebell-Creeper. Two or three species of evergreen, vining shrubs, endemic to Australia, are the only representatives of *Sollya*, of the pittosporum family PITTOSPORACEAE. The name of the genus honors Richard Horsman Solly, a botanist, who died in 1858.

Sollyas have many slender stems and alternate, undivided, narrow leaves. Their pretty bright blue flowers have five small sepals, and five petals arranged in bell-shaped fashion. The stamens, of which there are five, form a cone surrounding the pistil. The blooms, rarely solitary, are much more commonly in few-flowered, loose clusters at the ends of slender stalks from the leaf axils. The fruits are approximately cylindrical berries containing several seeds.

Only one species is generally cultivated, the Australian bluebell-creeper (*S. heterophylla* syn. *S. fusiformis*). It is 6 feet tall or

Sollya heterophylla

taller and has leaves ranging from narrowly-lanceolate to elliptic-oblong. Their undersides are much paler than their upper sides and they are up to 2 inches in length. The charming, nodding flowers, freely borne over a long period in summer and fall, are up to ½ inch long.

Garden and Landscape Uses. The Australian bluebell-creeper is a pleasant plant for outdoors in California and places with climates equally as mild, and for greenhouses.

Cultivation. Neither outdoors nor in greenhouses do sollyas give much trouble. They need some support, such as a trellis or wires stretched tautly, around which their stems can twine. Soil must be well drained, with a generous proportion of organic matter, and not allowed to dry excessively. Sollyas do not need a great deal of soil and in greenhouses are as readily accommodated in pots as in ground beds. From spring through fall their soil is kept moderately moist; in winter, drier, but never excessively so. Good light with little shade from strong summer sun is satisfactory, as is part-shade. On all favorable occasions the greenhouse must be ventilated freely. A winter night temperature of 40 to 50°F is appropriate. By day an increase of five to ten degrees is desirable. Occasional applications of dilute liquid fertilizer are made in summer to specimens that have filled their containers with roots. Pruning to shape and repotting or top dressing is done in spring. Propagation is by cuttings, preferably consisting of short shoots with heels (slivers of the stems from which the shoots arise) attached at their bases. They are taken in spring and planted in a greenhouse propagating bench. Young plants may have the tips of their shoots pinched out once or twice to encourage branching.

SOLOMON'S SEAL. See Polygonatum. For false-Solomon's-seal see Smilacina.

SONCHUS (Sónch-us) — Sow-Thistle. Little known as cultivated plants in America, this group, of the daisy family COMPOSITAE, comprises fifty species of milky-juiced annuals, herbaceous perennials, and subshrubs native to Europe, Asia, Africa, and islands of the Atlantic. Its name, used by Theophrastus, is an ancient Greek one.

The leaves of sonchuses are all basal or are alternate, with their edges usually toothed or lobed and, very commonly, the bases of the stem leaves clasping the stems. The yellow flower heads, generally in clusters, more rarely are solitary. Like those of dandelions, they consist of strap-shaped florets only; there is no central eye of disk florets as in daisies. The backs of the flower heads are involucres (collars) of overlapping bracts. The seedlike fruits are accompanied by conspicuous hairs.

A few European species of Sonchus that have become cosmopolitan weeds are common in North America. Here belong **S. arvensis** and **S. oleraceus.** In times past both were employed medicinally and were used as salads. Their foliage is greatly enjoyed by rabbits, and in Europe it is common practice to gather it for domesticated ones. The plants are equally relished by hogs, which grub up the thick roots and feed upon them, and thus give reason for the common name sow-thistle.

In California and similar mild climate regions, species native to the Canary Islands may sometimes be grown, chiefly for their bold foliage. One of these, **S. congestus,** is the most likely to be cultivated. Woody toward its base and with stout, upright, few-branched stems, this attains a height of about 2 feet and has many spreading, recurved, partially stem-clasping, oblanceolate leaves 1 foot to 2 feet in length, up to 3 inches broad, and deeply-triangular-lobed and toothed. Their margins are fringed with hairs. From 2 to 3 inches in diameter, the flower heads are bright yellow.

Garden Uses and Cultivation. In practically frost-free, dryish climates, the spe-

cies described and others succeed in ordinary soil in full sun. They are easy to raise from seed and cuttings and may be displayed in flower borders and informal, naturalistic landscapes. They are also attractive as foliage pot plants for conservatories and greenhouses. For this use they are grown in well-drained containers in fertile, porous soil in a sunny greenhouse where the winter night temperature is 45 to 50°F, and daytime temperatures are not more than five to ten degrees higher. In summer the plants may be stood outdoors or be kept in a greenhouse ventilated as freely as possible. Generous amounts of water must be given and, after the pots in which they are to bloom are well filled with roots, dilute liquid fertilizer applied regularly. Repotting and rehabilitation of one-year-old and older specimens is done in spring as soon as flowering is over.

SONERILA (Soneril-a). Of the 100 or more species of this tropical Asian genus of the melastoma family MELASTOMATACEAE, only one and varieties of it appear to be cultivated in North America. The generic name is derived from the native Malabar name for one kind.

Sonerilas are herbaceous plants and small shrubs with opposite or whorled, lobeless leaves with three or five prominent veins. The flowers, in curved racemes or spikes, have usually three each sepals, petals, and stamens, and one style. The fruits are capsules. In closely related South American Bertolonia, the blooms have five petals. Bigeneric hybrids between Sonerila and Bertolonia are named Bertonerila.

Herbaceous **S. margaritacea** has slender, succulent, sparsely-hairy, freely-branched stems up to about 9 inches high.

Sonerila margaritacea

Its leaves, opposite and long-stalked, are ovate-lanceolate with blades up to 3 inches long by nearly 1½ inches wide, and with bristle-toothed margins. Their upper surfaces are dark coppery-green marked with lines of silvery spots between the veins.

Their undersides are wine-purple. The flowers are borne freely in short clusters that just top the foliage at the ends of the main stem and branches. They have spreading, rich lavender-pink petals, and stamens with conspicuous, slender, curved, lemon-yellow anthers that contrast pleasingly with the petals. Varieties are S. m. argentea, with the upper sides of its leaves covered very thickly with silvery dots so that only the main veins are clear; S. m. hendersonii, compact and taller than the typical kind and with its leaves more heavily covered with silvery spots; S. m. 'Mme. Baextele', a dwarfer kind with ovate, silvery-gray leaves densely covered with silvery, often confluent spots; and S. m. marmorata, its leaves banded with silvery-gray.

Garden Uses and Cultivation. Sonerilas are strictly plants for very warm and very humid conditions and can be expected to thrive only in tropical greenhouses and similar environments. They can be successfully grown in terrariums in warm rooms and when so cultivated benefit from being lighted artificaly. The light not only improves the plants, but is of great aid in displaying them to fullest advantage. Given the atmospheric conditions suggested, they grow freely in a coarse, loose, porous soil that contains an abundance of leaf mold or other organic matter and that is kept always moist, but not constantly saturated. Sonerilas may be grown individually in 3-inch pots or three to five together in 5- or 6-inch pans (shallow flower pots). They are very pleasing when grown in the latter way.

Cuttings rooted in late winter or very early spring and kept growing without check make good plants by fall. The plants branch naturally and need no pinching, but as they grow they need light staking to support their rather weak stems. When they have filled their final containers with roots, they benefit from weekly applications of dilute liquid fertilizer. The temperature range most beneficial for these plants is 70 to 90°F, with a relative humidity from 75 to 90 percent. To achieve such high humidity constantly, even in greenhouses, it is often advisable to grow these plants in a closed case or under a bell jar. Good light, but with shade from strong direct sun is necessary. Sonerilas may also be raised from seeds sown in pots of sandy peaty soil and scarcely covered with soil. The seeds germinate readily in a temperature of 75°F.

SONNERATIACEAE — Sonneratia Family. This family of dicotyledonous trees and shrubs, native chiefly to coastal regions of the tropics from East Africa to Polynesia and Australia, consists of seven species. They have opposite, undivided, lobeless and toothless leaves and, solitary or in threes forming clusters, symmetrical bisexual or unisexual flowers. The blooms have a four- to eight-lobed, persistent, sometimes colored calyx or none, four to eight or no small petals, twelve to numerous stamens, and a long, slender style. The fruits are capsules or berries. Of the two genera that constitute this family only *Dubanga* is sometimes cultivated.

SOOT. Now rarely used, soft coal soot was much employed by old-time gardeners, especially those of European background, as a fertilizer and to discourage slugs, snails, and some other pests. A bushel of good soot weighs about 28 pounds; if appreciably heavier it contains an excess of mineral matter. The nutrient content of soot varies from 0.5 to 6 percent nitrogen, the average being about 4 percent. Soot was chiefly used in two ways, as a top-dressing for growing plants, and steeped in water to make what was called soot water. The odor of soot undoubtedly serves as a deterrent to pests.

SOPHORA (Sóph-ora) — Japanese Pagoda Tree or Chinese Scholar Tree, Coral-Bean or Mescal-Bean or Texas-Mountain-Laurel, Yellow Kowhai, Eve's Necklace. A diverse group of some eighty species of deciduous and evergreen shrubs, trees, and rarely herbaceous plants of the pea family LEGUMINOSAE, the genus *Sophora* inhabits many mild and warm regions, including parts of North America. Its name is an adaptation of an Arabian one, *sophero*, for some tree with pea-like flowers. A few of its kinds are hardy in the north. All described here are decorative.

Sophoras have alternate, pinnate leaves with opposite leaflets and a terminal one. Their blooms, in leafy panicles or racemes, are pea-like or have their five petals all directed forward. Each bloom has a five-toothed calyx, a rounded or oblong-ovate standard or banner petal, ten stamens usually separate, rarely united at their bases, and an incurved style with a minute stigma. The usually cylindrical, more rarely flattened, sometimes four-angled or four-winged seed pods are conspicuously constricted between the seeds. The lumber of certain sophoras, including that of the yellow kowhai and the mamane, is hard and durable and is employed for fence posts and similar purposes. That of the Japanese pagoda tree closely resembles chestnut and is used similarly. The leaves and pods of the last mentioned are employed to adulterate opium, and in the Orient a yellow dye is extracted from its bark and buds. The flowers and seeds of some kinds, among them the mescal-bean and Eve's necklace, are reported to be poisonous. The bright red seeds of the former are used for beads and other adornments.

Japanese pagoda tree or Chinese scholar tree (*S. japonica*) is a handsome, fast-growing, deciduous species especially es-

Sophora japonica

Sophora japonica (fruits)

teemed because it flowers in late summer well after almost all other trees hardy in the north are through blooming. It provides an attractive display of large terminal panicles of small creamy-white blooms. Shapely and broad-headed, the Japanese pagoda tree attains heights of 50 to 90 feet and has good-looking foliage that remains green late in fall. The leaves, 6 to 10 inches long, are composed of seven to seventeen stalked, ovate to lanceolate-ovate leaflets up to 2 inches in length, lustrous above and finely-hairy on their undersides. The flowers, ⅓ to ½ inch long, in broad pyramidal panicles up to 1 foot in length, are succeeded by hairless one- to six-seeded pods so strongly constricted between the seeds that they look like strings of beads. Despite the implications of its botanical name and one of its common names,

Japanese pagoda tree is not native to Japan, but to China and Korea. Noteworthy varieties are *S. j. violacea*, which blooms even later than the typical kind and has purplish-tinged flowers; *S. j. columnaris*, which has a much narrower than typical top; and *S. j. pendula*, which has picturesquely contorted, down-sweeping branches, and in its most familiar form has the disadvantage of not blooming. However, there is a variant with strongly-pendulous branches that flowers freely and is sufficiently different in other respects, especially in its loose habit of growth, to warrant receiving a distinctive name. Fine specimens of this are reported to be in the old botanical garden at Basle, Switzerland, and in the garden of a Mr. Hare in Majorca, of the Balearic Islands. The name *S. j.* 'White Dome' has been suggested as appropriate for the flowering variety. *S. j. pubescens* is distinguished by its leaves, softly-hairy on their undersides, having leaflets about 3 inches in length and blooms often purple-tinged. Japanese pagoda tree and its varieties are reliably hardy about as far north as southern New England.

Eve's necklace (*S. affinis*) is deciduous and sometimes 30 feet, but often not over 6 to 15 feet tall. Native from Oklahoma to Arkansas, Louisiana, and Texas, it has leaves 3 to 9 inches long with nine to nineteen elliptic leaflets up to 1½-inches in length that, when young, are silky hairy. White or pink, its ½-inch-long, somewhat fragrant flowers appear in racemes, up to 6 inches long, with the new foliage in spring. The slender, much twisted, black pods, strongly constricted between the brown seeds, are 2 to 6 inches long. The coral-bean, mescal-bean, or Texas-mountain-laurel (**S. secundiflora**) is a narrow-headed, densely-foliaged evergreen, native to Texas and New Mexico, that attains heights up to 35 feet. Its firm-textured leaves, 4 to 6 inches long, are of five to thirteen lustrous, leathery, elliptic to elliptic-oblong leaflets ½ inch to 1½ inches long. Very decorative, the fragrant, blue-purple blooms, up to ¾ inch long, are in racemes 2 to 6 inches in length. The pods, moderately constricted between the bright red seeds, are up to 4½ inches long. Neither *S. affinis* nor *S. secundiflora*, both of which prosper in limestone soils, are hardy in the north.

A beautiful New Zealander, also native to Chile and some Pacific islands, the yellow kowhai (**S. tetraptera**) is adaptable for

Sophora tetraptera

cultivation in the Pacific Northwest and similar favored regions. Evergreen or deciduous depending upon climate, it attains heights up to 40 feet and has leaves with leaflets about 1 inch long. From four to eight together in racemes, its sulfur-yellow blooms have deeper-colored calyxes and are 1 inch to 2 inches in length. They contain an abundance of nectar so attractive to parson birds that the birds tear the flowers apart to obtain it. The 8-inch-long seed pods of the yellow kowhai are four-winged. Closely allied **S. microphylla** (syn.

Sophora microphylla

S. tetraptera microphylla) has leaflets not over ⅓ inch long, flowers up to 1¾ inches long, and the banner or standard petal nearly as long as the wing petals, instead of much shorter, as in *S. tetraptera*. Up to 15 feet tall, *S. m. longicarinata* has ⅛-inch-long leaflets and 2-inch-long, lemon-yellow flowers.

Native to Hawaii, the mamane (**S. chrysophylla**) is evergreen and much like yellow kowhai. Up to 40 feet tall it has pale yellow blooms in small axillary clusters and four-winged pods with yellow seeds.

A hardy, graceful, deciduous shrub up to 8 feet in height, **S. davidii** (syn. *S. viciifolia*), of China, has blue to almost white blooms and spreading, spiny, lacy-foliaged branches. Its leaves are up to 2 inches long and have thirteen to nineteen elliptic to elliptic-oblong leaflets under ½ inch in

Sophora davidii

length. Their undersides are silky-hairy or nearly hairless. The blooms, up to ¾ inch long, are up to twelve together in racemes from short lateral branchlets. The long-beaked seed pods are about 2 inches long.

Garden and Landscape Uses and Cultivation. The Japanese pagoda tree makes a fine lawn specimen and, because it stands heat, dryness, and other city conditions unfavorable to the growth of many trees, is satisfactory for street planting. Like others of its genus it does best in full sun, in fertile, sandy loam, but if drainage is good it adapts to a wide variety of soil types. Shrubby *S. davidii* is useful for beds, slopes, and similar locations. With the exception of the mamane, which is suitable only for the tropics, the nonhardy sophoras discussed here are handsome ornamentals for the south, California, and other mild-climate regions. They have attractive foliage and rewarding displays of bloom. Sophoras are easily raised from seed and this is the preferred method with tree kinds other than varieties of *S. japonica* that do not come true from seed and that are ordinarily increased by grafting onto seed-

ling understocks. Shrubby sophoras can be raised from summer cuttings and by layering.

SOPHRONITELLA. See Sophronitis.

SOPHRONITIS (Sophron-ìtis). Half a dozen species, native to Brazil, are the only members of *Sophronitis*, of the orchid family ORCHIDACEAE. They are small plants of rather varying aspects that grow as epiphytes (tree-perchers) or occasionally on mossy rocks. The name, from the Greek *sophron*, modest, was given because of the unassuming appearance of the first species discovered.

Related to *Cattleya*, but very much smaller than the vast majority of members of that familiar group, species of *Sophronitis* are rarely over 3 inches in height. They have clusters of little pseudobulbs ending in one or occasionally two leaves. The blooms, often many, usually solitary, are on stalks from the tops of the pseudobulbs. They have the two lower sepals joined at their bases and united to the short, thick, winged column. The lip protrudes forward. Hybrids of *Sophronitis* and *Cattleya* are *Sophrocatleya*; those between *Sophronitis* and *Laelia* are *Sophrolaelia*; those involving *Sophronitis*, *Cattleya*, and *Laelia* are *Sophrolaeliocattleya*; those between *Sophronitis* and *Epidendrum* are *Epiphronitis*; and those between *Sophronitis* and *Broughtonia* are *Sophrobroughtonia*.

Its blooms 1½ to 3 inches or sometimes more in diameter, **S. coccinea** (syn. *S. grandiflora*) is a beautiful kind. Its blooms are usually bright scarlet, with the lobes and base of the lip orange-yellow streaked

Sophronitis coccinea

with red, but the species is variable and includes plants with rosy-purple and carmine-purple flowers. The crowded, spindle-shaped pseudobulbs, 1 inch to 1½ inches tall, are topped by stiff, leathery, lustrous, oblong-lanceolate to broad-elliptic leaves up to 3 inches long. The flowers have blunt, elliptic-oblong sepals, about one-half as wide as the broad-elliptic to rhombic petals. The side lobes of the three-lobed lip are raised and generally partially enclose the usually white column. The middle lobe is concave. From the last, *S. cernua* differs in having tightly clustered pseudobulbs, somewhat flattened at their tops and nearly cylindrical. Like the leaves, which are sometimes 2 inches, but mostly not over 1 inch long, they are generally grayish-green. The flowers, commonly two to five on a stem, but sometimes solitary, are 1 inch or a little more wide. Variable in color, they are usually bright cinnabar-red with the base of the lip and the column orange-yellow.

Brazilian *S. violacea* (syn. *Sophronitella violacea*), which blooms in winter, has dense clusters of narrowly- to more broadly-egg-shaped pseudobulbs, ½ to somewhat over 1 inch long, and from the top of each a single, lustrous, leathery, pointed-linear leaf 1¼ to slightly over 3 inches in length. The short-stalked flowers, solitary or in pairs, are from a little under to a little over 1 inch in width. They are rich violet-pink, with the lip usually darker than the spreading, narrowly-oblong sepals and petals, which it about equals in length.

Garden Uses and Cultivation. Not all growers find these charming orchids easy to manage. Difficulty in maintaining them in permanent good health is reported. Choice plants for the collector, they need high humidity and a fair amount of shade, but not so much that weak growth or poorly colored blooms result. A mixture of tree fern fiber and chopped sphagnum moss, with some crushed charcoal added, is a satisfactory rooting medium. The plants succeed better in fairly small pans (shallow pots) than in deeper containers or those large for the sizes of the specimens. They may also be attached to suspended slabs of tree fern trunks. Good drainage is essential, but at no time must the compost become dry. Generous watering is especially important when new growth is being made. Excessive warmth is not to the liking of these orchids. They do best in cool-temperature greenhouses such as suit oncidiums. For more information see Orchids.

SORBACH is *Heteropterys beecheyana.*

SORBARIA (Sorb-ària) — False-Spirea. Deciduous, summer-flowering, Asian shrubs, once included in *Spiraea*, but easily distinguished from the sorts of that genus by their pinnate leaves, compose *Sorbaria*, of the rose family ROSACEAE. There are about ten species. The name is derived from that of the genus *Sorbus* and alludes to their mountain-ash-like foliage.

Sorbarias have pithy shoots and large, alternate, deciduous leaves of opposite, toothed or double-toothed leaflets and a terminal one. The white, often slightly disagreeably scented flowers, up to ⅓ inch across, are in large, showy terminal panicles. Each has a cupped calyx tube, five short, broad, reflexed sepals, five broadly-elliptic to nearly round petals, twenty to fifty stamens as long or longer than the petals, and five pistils. The capsule-like fruits are technically follicles.

A favorite is *S. sorbifolia.* Native in

Sorbaria sorbifolia

northern Asia from the Ural Mountains to Japan, this is upright, 3 to 6 feet in height, and spreads vigorously by suckers. Its young shoots and young foliage have stellate (star-shaped) hairs. The leaves, up to 1 foot long, are of thirteen to twenty-three ovate-lanceolate to lanceolate leaflets, ½ to 1 inch wide by 2 to 3½ inches long, with sharply-double-toothed margins. The dense, upright, flower panicles, 5 to 10 inches long, have erect branches. They are composed of numerous blooms, about ⅓ inch wide, with forty to fifty stamens twice as long as the petals. The fruits are hairless. Hardy well into eastern Canada, this attractive shrub is naturalized in parts of North America. Variety *S. s. stellipila* has pubescent fruits, and leaves with stellate (star-shaped) hairs on their undersides.

Three rather similar species are *S. arborea, S. tomentosa,* and *S. assurgens.* The first two attain heights of about 20 feet, the last is about one-half as tall and more erect than the others. A native of China, *S. arborea* has shoots furnished with stellate

Sorbaria arborea

down, and leaves 9 inches to 1¼ feet long, with thirteen to nineteen double-toothed, long-pointed, ovate-oblong to lanceolate leaflets, 2 to 4 inches long, and usually hairy beneath when young. The ¼-inch-wide flowers are in loose panicles up to 1 foot long by two-thirds as broad, and with wide-spreading branches. In length the stamens much exceed the petals. The fruits are pubescent. This species is hardy in southern New England. In *S. a. subtomentosa,* the branches, leafstalks, and undersides of the leaves are conspicuously pubescent. In *S. a. glabrata,* the branches and leafstalks are hairless and often purplish and the leaflets are narrower than those of the typical species. The stamens are two to three times as long as the petals. The Himalayan *S. tomentosa* (syn. *S. lindleyana*) is not hardy in a climate more severe than that of Virginia. An elegant shrub, this has widely-spreading branches, and leaves 10 inches to 1½ feet long with thirteen to twenty-one, long-pointed, lanceolate leaflets, 2 to 4 inches long, with double-toothed margins. The terminal leaflet is often larger than the others and pinnately-lobed. When young the leaves have branchless hairs on their undersides, especially on the midribs and veins. The flowers, scarcely ¼ inch wide, have stamens about as long as the petals. Often nodding, the loose panicles of bloom are 9 inches to 1½ feet long by two-thirds as broad. They have downy stalks and branches, the latter spreading widely. The fruits are without hairs. A native of China, *S. assurgens* is hardy in southern New England. More upright than the others discussed, it has hairless shoots, and leaves up to 1 foot long or longer with thirteen to seventeen long-pointed, oblong-lanceolate to narrowly-lanceolate, sharply-double-toothed leaflets, 2 to 3½ inches long, and hairless or with hairs on the veins of the undersides. The loose, narrow panicles of bloom, 6 inches to 1 foot long, have erect branches, and flowers ⅓ inch wide with about twenty stamens a little longer than the petals. The fruits are hairless.

Graceful *S. aitchisonii* differs from all other sorbarias described here in having leaves with leaflets single-toothed or at most very indistinctly double-toothed. Its branches are hairless and, when young, generally purplish-red. The leaves have fifteen to twenty-one narrow-lanceolate to linear, long-pointed leaflets 2 to 3½ inches long. About ⅓ inch wide, the flowers have stamens longer than the petals. They are in upright, hairless panicles up to 1 foot long or sometimes longer by about two-thirds as wide. This native of Kashmir and Afghanistan is hardy about as far north as New York City.

Garden and Landscape Uses. Easy to grow, beautiful in bloom, and providing masses of good-looking, coarsely-patterned, lively green foliage, sorbarias are vigorous and well adapted for grouping and massing in beds, at the fringes of woodlands, and by watersides and, the taller ones, for screening. They are especially effective in large masses viewed from a little distance and are particularly appreciated because they flower chiefly in July and August when few shrubs are in bloom. Some exhibit a strong ambition to spread by suckers and should not be planted where this may interfere with less vigorous plants or in other ways be objectionable. In general these are plants for broad, open landscapes rather than for small, intimate gardens.

Sorbarias prosper in sun or part-day shade and thrive in comparatively poor soil. To give of their best, however, they need fertile earth that is not excessively dry.

Cultivation. Once planted, sorbarias need little care other than the removal of faded flower panicles, which have an untidy appearance, and every few years a rather drastic rehabilitation pruning. This is done in late winter or very early spring and involves the removal of old worn-out shoots as well as any that are weak or overcrowded, and the shortening of others. Propagation is by seed and by digging up and transplanting rooted suckers.

SORBARONIA (Sorb-arònia). Hybrids between *Sorbus* and *Aronia*, both of the rose family ROSACEAE, are called *Sorbaronia*. Several are known, the oldest since before 1785.

Named **S. hybrida** (syn. *Sorbus spuria*), this is a shrub or small tree up to 12 feet tall or sometimes taller. Its parents are said to be *Sorbus aucuparia* and *Aronia arbutifolia*, but the fact that its fruits are black-purple and those of both its supposed parents red is cause for some doubt as to the accuracy of this. Possibly *Aronia melanocarpa*, rather than *A. arbutifolia*, is one parent. In any case, *S. hybrida*, slender-branched, has downy shoots, and leaves, at first slightly hairy beneath, that vary greatly in shape and size. Most are oblong to oblong-ovate, 2 to 3½ inches in length, and pinnate or pinnately-lobed toward their bases, with the lobes overlapping, but some are without lobes, and all kinds of intermediates occur. The flowers, white or pinkish, about ⅜ inch across, and in small clusters, come in May. The fruits are slightly under ½ inch long and pear-shaped to nearly spherical. Several similar hybrids are known between various species of *Sorbus* and *Aronia*.

Two that differ in having toothed, but not lobed, elliptic to oblanceolate leaves are *S. alpina* (syn. *Sorbus alpina*), a hybrid between *Sorbus aria* and *Aronia arbutifolia*, and *S. dipelii* (syn. *Sorbus dippelii*), a hybrid between *Sorbus aria* and *Aronia melanocarpa*. These are bushy shrubs with much the aspect of *Sorbus aria*. The oldest, **S. alpina**,

has been in cultivation since before 1809. From *Sorbus aria* these kinds are distinguished by their smaller leaves with fewer, less straight veins and their smaller clusters of smaller blooms. The leaves, 1½ to 3½ inches long and felted beneath, have glandular-toothed margins and glands on the midribs above. Those of **S. dippelii** lose much of their hairiness as they age. Their five-petaled flowers have two or three styles. The fruits are about ⅓ inch in diameter, those of *S. alpina* red or brownish-red and those of *S. dippelii* blackish-purple.

Garden and Landscape Uses and Cultivation. These hybrids, hardy in southern New England, are not much cultivated except in arboretums and similar places where plants of special botanical interest are appreciated, yet they are decidedly pleasing in form, pretty in bloom, and easy to grow. They succeed in ordinary soil in sunny locations and need no particular care other than any occasional pruning that may be needed to keep them shapely and tidy. Propagation is by grafting onto mountain-ash (*Sorbus*) or hawthorn (*Crataegus*).

SORBOPYRUS (Sorbo-pỳrus)—Bollwyller-Pear. As the name implies, *Sorbopyrus* consists of bigeneric hybrids between *Sorbus* and *Pyrus*, of the rose family ROSACEAE. They are deciduous trees, intermediate in appearance and characteristics between their parents.

Known since before 1620, the Boll-wyller-pear (**S. auricularis** syns. *Pyrus auricularis*, *Sorbus bollwylleriana*) has as parents *Pyrus communis* and *Sorbus aria*. Up to 60 feet in height and round-headed, it has pubescent twigs and stalked, broad-elliptic, coarsely- or double-toothed leaves, pubescent on their undersides and 2½ to 4 inches long. The lower leaf surfaces are covered with gray felt, the upper, hairy at first, later are hairless or nearly so. Borne in May, and ¾ to 1 inch in diameter, the white, five-petaled blooms are in terminal, many-flowered clusters. They have white-woolly calyxes and rose-red stamens. The pear-shaped fruits have yellowish, sweet flesh and are 1 inch to 1½ inches long. More closely resembling a pear (*Pyrus*) and somewhat more attractive than *S. auricularis*, of which it may be a seedling, *S. a. bulbiformis* (syn. *Pyrus malifolia*) has been known since before 1834. It has fruits about 2 inches long.

Garden and Landscape Uses and Cultivation. These quite handsome and botanically intriguing hybrids, little known except in arboretums and special collections, are hardy in southern New England. They are effective ornamentals and succeed in ordinary fertile soil in open, sunny locations. Although they sometimes produce a very few fertile seeds, these do not give plants true to the types of the trees that bear them; grafting is the most practical method of reproduction.

SORBUS (Sór-bus)—Mountain Ash, White Beam Tree. Closely related to apples (*Malus*), pears (*Pyrus*), and hawthorns (*Crataegus*), mountain-ashes (*Sorbus*) number possibly 100 species of deciduous trees and shrubs, natives of the northern hemisphere. Some are well-known ornamentals especially esteemed for their attractive flowers, clusters of brightly colored fruits, and colorful autumn foliage. Others are worthy of more attention than they presently receive from gardeners and landscapers. The mountain-ashes belong in the rose family ROSACEAE. Their name, *Sorbus*, is an ancient Latin one. The common name refers to the ashlike foliage of some kinds and to the fact that some inhabit mountain regions.

Mountain-ashes have alternate, undivided or pinnately-divided, sharply-toothed or lobed leaves and usually showy terminal clusters of small white or rarely pinkish, mostly bisexual, five-petaled flowers, each with fifteen to twenty stamens and one to five pistils. The fruits are technically pomes, which is to say they have the same structure as those of apples. Because they are small and clustered they resemble berries in gross appearance. For convenience the mountain-ashes may be divided into two groups, those in which all of the leaves are only toothed or lobed.

The most popular species in North America is the European mountain-ash or rowan tree (*S. aucuparia*), a native of northern Europe and northern Asia. Since colonial times this has been a great favorite and freely planted. Extremely hardy, it is naturalized to some extent in North America, including Alaska.

As a young tree, **S. aucuparia** is rather

Sorbus aucuparia (flowers)

Sorbus aucuparia (fruits)

narrow and erect, but with age it develops an open, rounded head and attains a height of 45 or 50 feet. Its young shoots and buds are pubescent, but the latter are not sticky. The leaves consist of nine to fifteen oblong-lanceolate, sharply-toothed leaflets up to 2 inches long. Borne in great numbers in dense, fuzzy-looking, flattish to somewhat rounded clusters, 4 to 6 inches in diameter, the creamy-white flowers are about ⅓ inch across. They are succeeded by great clusters of brilliant vermilion, long-lasting fruits, each about ⅓ inch in diameter. As is to be expected with a tree for so long cultivated, several distinct varieties have been selected and given varietal names. Chief of these are *S. a. asplenifolia,* sometimes called the cutleaf European mountain-ash because its leaflets are conspicuously deeply-double-toothed; *S. a. fastigiata,* which forms an erect, narrow head; *S. a. pendula,* with stiff, rather awkwardly disposed, drooping branches; and *S. a. xanthocarpa,* with clear yellow fruits. Another variety, *S. a. edulis* (syn. *S. a. moravica*), a native of Czechoslovakia, has fruits slightly bigger than those of the typical species. In Europe they are used for making preserves.

The American mountain-ash (*S. americana*) differs from its European relative mainly in having sticky winter buds and in its leaves soon losing the pubescence from their undersides. It occurs as a native from Newfoundland to North Carolina and Michigan and attains a maximum height of about 30 feet; often it is shrubby. Its flowers, about ¼ inch in diameter, are in flat-topped clusters up to 6 inches across; they are succeeded by bright red, glossy fruits ¼ inch in diameter. The leaves of this kind have eleven to seventeen oblong-lanceolate to lanceolate, sharp-toothed leaflets 1½ to 4 inches long. Another very similar and very hardy native of the northeastern United States and southeastern Canada is *S. decora.* The chief differences between this and *S. americana* are its more conspicuous red fruits and the slight reddish rather than whitish pubescence of its winter buds. Because of its showier fruits this species is superior as an ornamental to *S. americana.* It is a shrubby tree up to 30 feet tall.

The service tree (*S. domestica,* of the Mediterranean region and western Asia, also has pinnate leaves. It grows 60 to 80 feet tall and has broad-pyramidal, pointed flower clusters, each flower ⅝ inch across and with five styles. The lustrous winter buds are sticky and, at their tips, are pubescent. This species has its ½-inch-wide white flowers in broad-pyramidal clusters 4 to 6 inches across. The fruits are apple- or pear-shaped, dull yellowish-green to brownish, and when ripe tinged with red. The form with apple-shaped fruits is distinguished as *S. d. pomifera,* the one with pear-shaped fruits as *S. d. pyrifera.* They are 1 inch to 1½ inches long. In Europe

Sorbus decora

Sorbus domestica

they are used for making cider and sometimes, after they have been subjected to frost, for eating. The service tree is hardy in southern New England.

The white beam tree (*S. aria*) is a handsome kind that does not have pinnate

Sorbus aria

leaves. They are undivided, elliptic to ovate-oblong, double-toothed at their margins, 2 to 4½ inches long, and very white-pubescent on their undersides. The white flowers, in flattish clusters 2 to 3 inches across, are succeeded by brown-dotted red fruits. Before the foliage falls it becomes reddish. A native of Europe, this sort has a rounded, rather open, crown and attains a height of 45 or 50 feet. Its buds are sticky. It is hardy in southern New England. There are several varieties. Those named *S. a. aurea, S. a. chrysophylla,* and *S. a. lutescens* have yellow foliage. The best is *S. a. majestica* (syn. *S. a. decaisneana*), which has bigger leaves, flowers, and fruits.

Other kinds with leaves not pinnately divided include the very handsome Korean mountain-ash (*S. alnifolia*) This,

Sorbus alnifolia

when young, is pyramidal, becoming round-topped with age. A native of Korea, China, and Japan, it attains a maximum height of about 20 feet. It has lustrous, bright green, ovate to elliptic-ovate leaves, with unequally-toothed margins. Above, they are without hairs, their undersurfaces are hairless or nearly so. The small white flowers, in flat clusters, are succeeded by orange-scarlet fruits. The Korean mountain-ash is hardy in southern New England. Also belonging to the simple-leaved group is Chinese *S. folgneri,* a smaller tree than the last named, but equally or perhaps more handsome and about as hardy. It attains a height of some 25 feet and forms a graceful head of spreading branches. Its ovate to elliptic-ovate leaves are 2 to 3 inches long or slightly longer, finely-toothed and sometimes somewhat lobed. Their upper sides are dark green and hairless, while beneath they are covered with a felt of white hairs that shows to good advantage when the leaves are turned by the wind. The clusters, about 4 inches in diameter, of white flowers are not conspicuous. They are followed by red fruits. In fall the foliage becomes russet-red. Variety *S. f. pendula* has drooping branches.

The wild service tree, *S. torminalis,* a native of Europe, North Africa, and Asia Minor, and hardy in southern New England, is handsome, round-headed, and up to 75 feet tall. It has spreading branches and broadly-ovate leaves 3 to 5 inches long. Its flowers, ½ inch in diameter and in clusters 3 to 4 inches across, are succeeded by brown-speckled, ovate fruits about ½ inch long. In fall the foliage turns red or golden-yellow. The name *S. intermedia* is that of the Swedish white beam, a kind sometimes confused with *S. hybrida,* perhaps because of the similar implications of their names. From *S. hybrida,* the Swedish white beam, which is not a hybrid, differs in its leaves never having any separate leaflets; the clefts between the leaf lobes do not extend more than one-third of the way from margin to mid-vein. Up to about 30 feet tall, this species is a native of northern Europe. Sometimes it is not more than a large shrub. It has sticky buds and elliptic to obovate-oblong leaves with irregularly-toothed lobes. They are grayish or yellowish-gray-hairy beneath. The flowers, a little over ½ inch wide, are in clusters about 4 inches wide. The ½-inch-long, ovoid fruits are bright scarlet. The Swedish white beam is hardy in southern New England. A handsome shrub or small tree up to about 15 feet in height, *S. tianshanica* is hardy in southern New England. Native to Turkestan, it has pinnate leaves of nine to fifteen leaflets, flowers almost ¾ inch wide, and 3- to 5-inch-wide clusters of bright red fruits ⅓ inch in diameter.

As its name indicates, *S. hybrida* is of mixed parentage, the result of a cross between pinnate-leaved *S. aucuparia* and simple-leaved *S. intermedia.* It shows in-between characteristics. Up to 40 feet tall and with quite upright branches, it has sticky buds and ovate to ovate-oblong leaves with, at their bases, one to four pairs of separate leaflets. The fruits are red. More compact *S. h. gibsii* has larger red fruits. A very upright-growing variety is *S. h. fastigiata.* Variety *S. h. meinichii* has four to six pairs of distinct leaflets. Often confused with *S. hybrida,* a hybrid between *S. aucuparia* and *S. aria* correctly named *S. thuringiaca* is more erect and compact than *S. hybrida* and has somewhat longer leaves with smaller leaflets. Its light pink fruits outstanding, *S. arnoldiana* is a hybrid between *S. discolor* and *S. aucuparia.* This has pinnate leaves of eleven to seventeen leaflets. It is hardy in southern New England. Other hybrids chiefly selected for their colorful fruits and mostly introduced to North America from Holland bear such names as 'Apricot Queen', 'Carpet of Gold', 'Maidenblush', 'Old Pink', 'Pink Coral', 'Red Tip', and 'Scarlet King'.

Not all mountain-ashes have red or red-brown fruits. Some of the loveliest, alas, little known in cultivation in North America, have fruits of other colors. There are,

of course, yellow-fruited varieties of species that normally have red fruits such as *S. aucuparia xanthocarpa* (listed earlier under the species) and *S. esserteauiana flava.* But there are others. One of the most charming is *S. vilmorinii,* a western Chinese shrub or small tree with pinnate leaves and clusters of beautiful fruits that at maturity are rosy-pink. Flower buds tinged pink are characteristic of *S. cashmiriana,* a native of the Himalayas and hardy in much of New England. After opening, its blooms fade to creamy-white. Among the largest flowers in the genus, they are ¾ inch wide. They are succeeded by red-stalked, loose, pendulous clusters of gleaming white or pink-tinged, marble-like fruits ⅜ inch in diameter. The leaves of this, a bushy tree up to 20 feet tall, are of fifteen to nineteen leaflets. Pink-fruited or sometimes white-fruited *S. harrowiana,* of western China, is pinnate-leaved. This is much more tender to cold than the others we have discussed. Of other kinds with white fruits mention may be made of *S. hupehensis, S. prattii,* and *S. koehneana,* all Chinese. Their hardiness is not fully known, but except for the last named they probably would not survive in climates as harsh as that of New England.

A noteworthy dwarf, *S. reducta* is said not to exceed 1 foot to 2 feet in height in England, where in some places it is employed as a large-scale groundcover. In the vicinity of New York City there are specimens 4 feet tall. Native to western China and Burma, this suckering shrub has red-stalked leaves with thirteen to fifteen sharply-toothed leaflets. Dark green in summer, they turn bronze in fall. The small, spherical fruits are white flushed with pink.

Garden and Landscape Uses. Unfortunately, in some sections and especially in the east, mountain-ashes are much susceptible to infestations of borers, which, unless adequately controlled, can seriously weaken and kill trees. Otherwise they are among the best of ornamental trees and are especially effective when carrying profuse crops of fruits. Their maximum sizes are such that they are suitable for small and medium-sized properties. Effective as single-lawn specimens, they are also useful along boundaries and in avenues. As a general rule the kinds with pinnate leaves that are natives of northern habitats dislike hot summers and especially dry ones, but those from more southern regions, characterized by nonpinnate leaves, endure heat and drought well. As to soils, they are not fussy provided the root-run is well drained. Those with nonpinnate leaves prosper especially well on limestone. All need full sun.

Cultivation. The propagation of these trees is achieved by seeds taken from the pulp that surrounds them and sown in well-drained soil kept moderately moist. Sowing may be done in fall, or the seeds

may be stratified by mixing them with slightly moist peat moss, enclosing them in polyethylene bags, and storing them in a temperataure of 35 to 40°F until spring. Rare species and horticultural varieties may be increased by grafting or budding onto *S. aucuparia* or *S. americana* and by layering. No regular pruning is needed, but if it becomes desirable to reduce the size of a specimen this may be done in late winter or early spring. These trees renew themselves quickly after even drastic cutting back.

Pests and Diseases. The chief pests are borers, scales, leafhoppers, caterpillars, and the pear leaf blister mite, which causes galls to develop on the leaves. Canker diseases and leaf rusts not uncommonly affect these trees.

SORGHUM (Sorgh-um). This genus of forty species of the grass family GRAMINEAE, native to Africa, warm parts of Asia, Australia, and the Mediterranean region, is widely naturalized elsewhere, including North America. Its most familiar members are important annual grain crops and Johnson grass (*Sorghum halepense*), a perennial used for forage and pasture, which is often a pestiferous weed. The name is from the Italian *sorgho,* applied to one kind.

Sorghums are strong-growing annuals and perennials with usually long, flat leaf blades and loose or compact panicles of flowers, generally formed of many spike-like racemes. The spikelets are in pairs, one of which is stalkless and fertile, the other stalked and male or barren.

Sorghum (*S. bicolor* syn. *S. vulgare*) is cultivated agriculturally in numerous varieties. Here belong kinds esteemed as sources of sweet syrup, as well as the grain producers called Kafir-corn, chicken-corn, and durra-corn, broom-corn for making brooms, and Sudan grass for forage. These are annuals from 6 to 14 feet in height, with leaves up to 2 feet long by 2 inches broad, and large flower panicles. This species was probably originally African.

Garden Uses and Cultivation. Varieties of *S. bicolor* are occasionally included in educational displays of plants useful to man. To mature they need a long, warm growing season. Seeds are sown in spring in fertile soil where the plants are to remain.

SORREL, HERB PATIENCE, and SPINACH-RHUBARB. The plants known by these names are grown as greens for salads and for cooking. They are perennial species of *Rumex,* of the buckwheat family POLYGONACEAE, and include garden sorrel (*R. acetosa*), French sorrel (*R. scutatus*), herb patience or spinach-dock (*R. patientia*), and spinach-rhubarb (*R. abyssinicus*). All are easy to grow in sunny locations in fertile soil. Sow seed outdoors in spring, that of garden sorrel and French sorrel in rows about 1½ feet spart, that of herb patience and spinach-rhubarb in rows about 3 feet apart. Thin out the seedlings of the sorrels to about 1 foot apart and those of herb patience and spinach-rhubarb to 1½ to 2 feet apart. Keep free of weeds and water generously in dry weather. Harvest by picking youngish leaves while they are still tender. Jamaica-sorrel is *Hibiscus sabdariffa*, mountain-sorrel is *Oxyria digyna*, and sorrel tree is *Oxydendrum arboreum*.

SORROWLESS TREE is *Saraca indica*.

SOTOL. See Dasylirion.

SOUR GUM is *Nyssa sylvatica*.

SOURBERRY is *Rhus integrifolia*.

SOURSOP is *Annona muricata*.

SOURWOOD is *Oxydendrum arboreum*.

SOUTHERN-BEECH. See Nothofagus.

SOUTHERN CANE is *Arundinaria gigantea*.

SOUTHERNWOOD is *Artemisia abrotanum*.

SOW-THISTLE. See Sonchus. Blue-sow-thistle is *Lactuca alpina*.

SOWBREAD. See Cyclamen.

SOWBUGS or PILLBUGS. Surprising as it may seem to the uninitiated, sowbugs or pillbugs (the designations are interchangeable), also called woodlice, are not insects but crustaceans, relatives of crabs, crayfish, and lobsters. They have elliptic to oval, slightly arched brown or gray bodies with seven pairs of legs and two pairs of antennae. A common sort, one species is covered with gray, armour-like plates and rolls itself into a ball when disturbed, but not all kinds do this.

These pests live in dark, moist places and feed chiefly on decayed organic matter. They also often eat the roots and stems of plants and sometimes the foliage, particularly in greenhouses. Control measures consist of removing all decaying wood and treating wood that remains with a preservative, by trapping with slightly hollowed-out halves of potatoes laid cut side downward in infested areas and then scraping the creatures into a receptacle containing kerosene or a concentrated solution of salt water, by using commercial baits, and by spraying greenhouse benches and soil with malathion or Sevin.

SOYBEAN is *Glycine max*. See also Beans.

SPADING. Called digging in the British Isles, the operation known as spading in North America is the basic hand-tool method of turning over ground in preparation for seed sowing and planting. It is the gardener's equivalent of the farmer's plowing. Properly done, the end result equals or exceeds the best that can be achieved with a plow or rotary tiller.

But spading involves considerable labor and for large areas may be too costly, too time-consuming, or beyond the capabilities of those not in fairly good physical condition. Most gardeners find it practicable and pleasant to spade small beds.

In modern garden practice, power-driven rotary tillers are used to accomplish much of the soil preparation formerly done with the spade or spading fork and, on areas of suitable size, plows may be employed. But rotary tillers do a somewhat different job from spades and plows and sometimes, either because they are underpowered and not capable of disturbing the soil deeply enough or because instead of turning it over they churn it into too fine a condition, are less satisfactory.

The basic tools for spading are the spade (not to be confused with the shovel, which has a hollow blade designed for lifting and transferring loose material from place to place) and the spading fork. The spade has an almost flat, square-bottomed blade about 10 inches long by 8 inches wide, designed to slice into the ground when pushed vigorously with the foot. The spading fork is similar except that in place of a solid blade it has four prongs or tines. Both tools may be had in short-handled (handles 2 feet, 4 inches long) or long-handled (handles 4 feet long) models. By those experienced in their use, best results are had with the short-handled tools. With these the soil can be inverted more completely than by those with long handles.

The chief purposes of spading are to loosen the ground to permit better aeration and percolation of water, to incorporate bulky materials, such as compost and manure, to bury weeds and other trash, and to bring to the surface, to be acted upon by weathering agents, portions of the soil previously buried. It may be done at any time in advance of planting, preferably long enough before to allow the soil to settle somewhat. In regions of short springs and long pleasant fall weather, such as are typical of much of North America, the fall affords marvelous opportunity to spade ground in readiness for spring sowing or planting and in mild regions the work can continue through the winter. It should be an orderly process without the fuss and mess that often characterizes the attempts of the inexperienced and done in such a way that maximum results are achieved with minimum efforts. Except in stony soil and sometimes in very heavy clay soils the spade is superior to the spading fork as a tool for spading.

Simple spading or single digging consists of turning the ground over to the full depth of the spade blade or prongs of the fork, or if the topsoil is shallower than that,

possibly to a lesser depth. Begin by digging a trench or ditch across one end of the plot or bed and depositing the excavated soil just beyond the opposite end where the spading will finish. Have the trench 1 foot wide, its sides vertical, and as deep as the length of the blade of the spade, or if the topsoil be shallower then 1 inch to 2 inches deeper than the topsoil. Spread compost, manure, or other bulk organic material to be incorporated, evenly over the surface.

Now turn over a strip of soil adjacent to the trench and 6 to 8 inches wide by slicing off successive spadefuls and depositing them against the opposite side of the trench. As you do this, with a quick twist of the wrist turn the soil upside down. When the end of the trench is reached return to its beginning and repeat the performance with the next 6- to 8-inch strip and repeat this until the job is finished and the last trench is filled with the soil excavated from the first.

While working, the spader has his back to the finish end and faces the completed part of his work. The advantages of the trench (inexperienced gardeners often spade without this refinement and because of this, work much harder to attain less satisfactory results) are several. It facilitates the burial of organic material, weeds, and surface trash. Because nothing is pressing against the spadeful of soil being moved (it is simply lifted into empty space), resistance to its transfer forward is eliminated. Also it is easier to produce a level surface than if no trench is used. Adjustments in levels can be made as the task proceeds by allowing the trench to become a little more filled where the surface is to be lowered, a little larger where it is to be built up.

Drive the spade into the ground with its blade nearly vertical, not at a long backward slant, by jabbing its bottom edge into the surface and then pressing with one foot and all the weight of the body on the upper edge of the blade. Do not kick it into the ground. That is exhausting. Refrain from taking larger spadefuls than you can

When spading: (a) Work backward from the newly turned soil

(b) Drive the spade nearly vertically into the ground with a thrust of the foot

(c) Lift each spadeful of earth and then turn it over (here the backside of the trench can be clearly seen)

conveniently manage, and lift each no higher than is quite necessary to deposit it in its proper place. Do not chop and push the soil around after it is deposited. Simply lay spadeful after spadeful down to achieve as even a surface as possible and leave any further pulverizing to a later operation (just as the farmer plows, and later harrows).

Double digging involves moving and improving the soil to almost twice the depth achieved in single spading. It is an excellent method of readying ground for roses, perennials, and, indeed, if labor can be provided, for practically all plants, but because of the amount of work involved (four or five times as much as for the same area of single spading), its use is usually reserved for special purpose plantings, such as rose beds.

Begin double digging by taking out a trench as for single spading, but make it 2 feet wide. Deposit the soil taken out at the finish end of the plot. Clear all loose earth from the bottom of the trench and spread a generous layer of coarse organic material along its bottom. Fork this deeply into the under soil. Next stretch a line (cord) par-

allel to and 2 feet back from the edge of the trench, and to mark off this strip slice along the line by pushing the blade of the spade vertically into the ground.

Follow this by spading the topsoil of the 2-foot strip so delimited onto the top of the 2-foot-wide strip of forked-over bottom soil, at the same time mixing with it compost, peat moss, manure, or other decayed organic material. Remove all crumbs

Double digging: (a) The finished surface to the left, the soil yet to be spaded to the right, and the gardener tossing compost into the trench

(c) Moving the line 2 feet back from the edge of the trench to mark the next strip to be spaded

(e) Spading the new strip of soil onto the loosened soil in the bottom of the previous trench, thus starting a new trench

from the bottom of the trench and make a neat, vertical wall-like face to the soil moved over. Repeat this in successive 2-foot-wide strips until the end of the bed or plot is reached, then fill the final trench with earth removed from the first.

If ground to be spaded or double dug is grass sod, skim off the upper couple of inches and lay it, grass-side down, in each trench as the work proceeds.

(b) Forking the compost into the bottom of the trench

(d) Slicing deeply along the taut line with a spade so that the soil to be turned over will break evenly from the unspaded portion

(f) Shoveling the loose soil from the bottom of the new trench onto the top of the old trench

SPADIX. A spadix (plural spadices) is a thick, spikelike organ that bears small, more or less insignificant flowers and is usually surrounded by or has coming from its base a spathe. The "jack" in the "jack-in-a-pulpit" and the central yellow column in an arum-lily are spadices.

SPANIARDS. See Aciphylla.

SPANISH. This word forms parts of the names of these plants: Spanish bayonet (*Yucca aloifolia* and *Y. baccata*), Spanish bluebell (*Endymion hispanicus*), Spanish broom (*Cytisus multiflorus*), Spanish-broom (*Spartium junceum*), Spanish-buckeye (*Ungnadia speciosa*), Spanish-cedar (*Cedrela odorata*), Spanish-cherry (*Mimusops elengi*), Spanish dagger (*Yucca carnerosana*, *Y. gloriosa*, and *Y. treculeana*), Spanish-gorse (*Genista hispanica*), Spanish-lime (*Melicoccus bijugatus*), Spanish-moss (*Tillandsia usneoides*), Spanish-oak (*Catalpa longissima*), Spanish oyster plant (*Scolymus hispanicus*), Spanish-plum (*Spondias purpurea*), Spanish shawl (*Heterocentron elegans*), and Spanish-thyme (*Coleus amboinicus*).

SPANWORMS. The larvae or caterpillars of certain kinds of moths are called spanworms. They have the measuring-worm or inchworm manner of walking by a succession of looping movements. See Caterpillars.

SPARAXIS (Spar-áxis)—Wand Flower. Consisting of about six species native in South Africa, *Sparaxis* belongs in the iris family IRIDACEAE. Its name, from the Greek *sparasso*, to tear, refers to the lacerated floral bracts. Plants treated in this Encyclopedia as *Streptanthera* are by some authorities included in *Sparaxis*.

The corms (bulblike underground organs that, unlike bulbs, are solid instead of being composed of concentric layers like onions or of separate scales as are lilies) of *Sparaxis* are small and globose. They are renewed each year, the corm of the previous season withering as top growth is made and a new one forming at the base of the stem. In addition, toward the end of the growing season, little cormlets develop in the axils of some or all the leaves. The slightly silvery-green, sword- or rarely sickle-shaped, usually soft leaves, vary considerably in size and shape according to environment. They number five to twelve. The flowering stems, usually two or three from each corm, branch close to their bases or are branchless, except those of *S. bulbifera*, which usually have one or more branches well up from the ground. The stalks carry in loose, spikelike fashion few to rarely as many as ten, generally brilliantly colored blooms, often strikingly patterned with contrasting colors, coming from the axils of membranous bracts. The flowers have broadly-funnel-shaped perianths with short, straight tubes and six equal or nearly equal, more or less spreading lobes (petals). There are three stamens, the arrangement of which is of importance in identifying species, and a single three-branched style. The fruits are globose capsules.

In two species, *S. grandiflora* and *S. bulbifera*, the stamens are arranged asymmetrically and the style arches and lies behind them. With branchless stems up to 1½ feet tall and six to ten two-ranked leaves, *S. grandiflora* is variable and four

Sparaxis grandiflora

subspecies are recognized. Its leaves, up to 1 foot long by ½ inch or considerably less wide, are all basal. The six or fewer blooms have yellow, purple, or black perianth tubes and lanceolate, ovate or spatula-shaped petals that are cream-colored, yellow, or purple, with or without dark markings. The petals are 1 inch long or longer by nearly one-half as wide. In *S. g. fimbriata* the flowers resemble those of *S. bulbifera* in having cream-colored or white petals with black markings at their bases and purple markings outside.

Differing from *S. grandiflora* in having usually branched stems with a stem leaf at each fork as well as basal foliage, and in producing after flowering, cormlets in the axils of all leaves, *S. bulbifera* has cream-colored to white blooms rarely dotted with black at the base and often streaked on their outsides with purple. The perianth tubes are yellow. Rarely the blooms are entirely plum-purple.

The remaining species have erect styles with the stamens evenly spaced around them. Among these is *S. pillansii*, the tallest kind. Up to 2 feet in height, this has branchless stems and eight to ten two-ranked leaves up to 1 foot long or a little longer, the lower ones developing cormlets in their axils. The four to nine blooms with petals from a little under to a little over 1 inch long, are old-rose-colored, with the bases of the petals yellow, margined with a narrow purple band. The slightly twisted, red-purple anthers extend beyond the style branches.

Popular in cultivation, *S. tricolor* is similar to *S. pillansii*, but shorter, and has more intensely colored flowers with straight, yellow or white anthers. Its stems are branchless and rarely exceed 1 foot in length. The leaves, up to ¾ inch wide, are in fans that do not reach the lowermost of the two to five flowers that each stem bears. The perianth has a yellow tube, and pointed petals 1 inch to 1¼ inches long, salmon-pink to orange-vermilion and distinctly marked with arrow-shaped black to red blotches, or rarely without marks.

Less attractive horticulturally, *S. fragrans* (a name poorly applied because the blooms are malodorous rather than pleasantly scented) has branchless stems up to 1 foot long and fans of up to ten usually very slender leaves. The blooms, dull yellow, cream-colored or beige, and mostly unmarked, but sometimes with two dark spots and externally purple or brown central streaks, have petals up to 1 inch long.

Hybrids of *Sparaxis* are frequent in cultivation. The species most commonly involved appear to be *S. tricolor*, *S. pillansii*, and *S. grandiflora*. Hybrids have also been made between *Sparaxis* and related *Synnotia*.

Garden Uses and Cultivation. These are as for *Ixia*.

Sparaxis bulbifera

Sparaxis tricolor

Sparaxis tricolor varieties

SPARMANNIA (Sparmánn-ia) — African-Hemp. Andreas Sparmann, who died in 1820, is commemorated by the name of this genus of the linden family TILIACEAE. A Swedish naturalist, he accompanied Captain Cook on his second voyage to explore the Pacific. The genus comprises seven African species of trees or shrubs, none of which is hardy.

Sparmannias have large, palmately-lobed or toothed leaves. Their flowers, in terminal clusters, have four each sepals and petals and numerous stamens. These flowers are especially interesting because of their sensitive stamens and petals. The former move outward when touched; if the petals of a closed bloom are gently stroked, they open partially. The fruits are spiny capsules.

The African-hemp (*S. africana*) is most familiar. From 10 to 20 feet in height, it is a branching shrub or small tree with alternate, pointed, heart-shaped, long-stalked, unequally-toothed and sometimes slightly-lobed leaves up to 6½ inches long by 4½ inches wide. Except for the petals, all its parts are covered with soft, downy hairs. The flower clusters are erect. They are composed of many attractive, stalked blooms, about 1½ inches in diameter, with large, narrow sepals and, alternating with the sepals, obovate petals, white with pink-tinged bases. The stamens are red. The seed capsules have five compartments. Variety *S. a. flore-pleno*, with double flowers, is less ornamental.

Smaller in all its parts, *S. ricinicarpa* (syn. *S. palmata*) has long-stalked, deeply-five- to

seven-lobed leaves. The lobes are long-pointed. Its white to purplish blooms are in dense heads near the ends of the shoots. The seed capsules have four compartments.

Garden and Landscape Uses. These plants are admirable for outdoors in subtropical climates, such as that of southern California. There, *S. africana* is accounted one of the most beautiful flowering trees. Sparmannias are also excellent for winter and spring blooming in large greenhouses and conservatories.

Cultivation. Outdoors, any ordinary, well-drained, garden soil is agreeable. When grown in containers, coarse, loamy, nourishing earth that permits the free passage of water is best. A kind that suits chrysanthemums and geraniums is ideal. Sparmannias need full sun and sufficient water to keep their leaves from wilting. In greenhouses a winter night temperature of 50°F is adequate; too high temperatures at that season are detrimental. By day, winter temperatures may be five to ten degrees above those at night. In summer the greenhouse should be as cool and airy as possible. At that season, container-grown specimens benefit from being placed outdoors with their pots or tubs buried to their rims in a bed of sand, ashes, or similar material. Any needed pruning is done immediately flowering is over. If the plants are to be restricted in size, this consists of cutting out all crowded and weak branches and drastically shortening those that remain. At this time, too, repotting should be done. Sparmannias are gross feeders and regular applications of dilute liquid fertilizer throughout the growing season are highly beneficial. Cuttings root readily. Taken in spring they make good plants in 7- or 8-inch pots for blooming the following winter.

SPARTIUM (Spárt-ium) — Spanish-Broom or Weavers' Broom. Resembling a glorified Scotch broom (*Cytisus scoparius*), the Spanish-broom or weavers'-broom is the only species of its genus. It belongs in the pea family LEGUMINOSAE and is readily distinguished from true brooms (*Cytisus*) as well as from nearly related *Genista* by the one- rather than two-lipped calyxes of its flowers. The name *Spartium* is an ancient Greek one.

Spanish-broom or weavers' broom (**Spartium junceum**) is an upright, rather gaunt shrub, native to the Mediterranean region and the Canary Islands and widely naturalized through the Andes of South America and in some other parts of the world. It has round, slender, green, rush-like stems that function in the manner of leaves, of which it has few or none, that carry on photosynthesis. The leaves are alternate, undivided, linear to lanceolate, bluish-green, somewhat hairy, and up to 1½ inches long. The fragrant, showy flow-

Sparmannia africana

Spartium junceum

ers, in loose, terminal racemes 1 foot to 1½ feet long, resemble small golden-yellow sweet peas. They are about 1 inch long and almost as wide across the erect, flaring, upright petal called the standard. The flattened, hairy seed pods are 2 to 4 inches long by ¼ inch wide. Variety *S. j. ochroleucum* has whitish, and *S. j. plenum* double, blooms. Although not generally considered hardy north of about Washington, D.C., plants lived and bloomed in a sheltered place outdoors at The New York Botanical Garden for many years. In regions where native, the stems of Spanish-broom are used for making baskets and mats and formerly were employed as a source of fiber for rope-making and other purposes.

Garden and Landscape Uses. In climates as favorable as that of California, this showy ornamental blooms for most of the year, elsewhere for most of the summer, and is at its best at or shortly after midsummer. It revels in sun and flourishes in dry soils. Because of its many green stems it is evergreen in appearance. Its lower parts are likely to become bare and leggy, and so it is well to interplant it with lower shrubs, such as dwarf brooms, that need similar conditions.

Cultivation. Seeds afford the most practical way of securing new plants, but the double-flowered variety must be grafted onto seedlings of the single-flowered kind. Soak the seeds for twenty-four hours in water and then sow them in a cold frame or cool greenhouse in well-drained pots of sandy, peaty soil. The seeds may be placed individually or in twos or threes in small pots, or more in larger pots or pans (shallow pots). If small pots are used with more than one seed in each, pull out all except the strongest seedling as soon as the second leaves begin to develop. If sowing is done in a larger container transplant the young plants individually into small pots as soon as they are large enough to handle. Spartiums greatly resent root disturbance, but as small seedlings they can be transplanted with impunity and so are grown in pots, repotting them as growth necessitates to larger ones, until they are planted

in their permanent locations. This may be when they are one or two years old. Unless they are to be interplanted with other shrubs, when a greater distance is needed, spacing of about 3 feet apart is satisfactory. Routine care is minimal. To keep the plants shapely prune judiciously in early spring. Some growers shear the plants formally then, but specimens so treated lose much of their natural grace.

SPATHE. A bract or leaf, sometimes petal-like, that comes from the bottom of a spadix or flower cluster, which it sometimes encloses, is called a spathe. They are common in the arum family ARACEAE and palm family PALMAE. The white, yellow, or pink, trumpet-shaped flowering plants of the calla-lilies are spathes.

SPATHICARPA (Spathicàrp-a). Here belong seven species of curious South American plants closely related to Jack-in-the-pulpits, caladiums, and philodendrons and, like them, members of the arum family ARACEAE. The name *Spathicarpa* is derived from the Greek *spathe*, a spathe, and *karpos*, fruit. It refers to the flowers and fruits appearing to be borne directly on the spathes. Actually, the spadix (the part that in the calla-lily, jack-in-the-pulpit, and most other members of the ARACEAE is a free standing central column) is completely fused to the spathe (the bractlike or petal-like sheath that in the calla-lily and jack-in-the-pulpit surrounds the spadix), the whole forming an inflorescense.

The only species cultivated is *S. sagittifolia*, of Brazil, which forms a slowly-spreading clump about 8 inches tall. From below ground it sends up an abundance of rich glossy-green, arrow-shaped leaves. Between them and rising above them a continuous succession of inflorescences is produced. Pale green and slender-stalked, these end in recurved, pointed-paddle- or pointed-oar-shaped spathes down the centers of which are strung, reminiscent of the legs of a caterpillar, a fringe of tiny, petal-less, yellow-green flowers.

Garden Uses and Cultivation. This makes an attractive and interesting pot specimen for growing in greenhouses and

Spathicarpa sagittifolia

should be worth trying as a houseplant. The environmental needs of this plant are uncomplicated. It thrives in any fertile, porous potting soil, one that contains an abundance of organic matter being advantageous. Keep the soil always moderately moist. Give specimens that have filled their containers with healthy roots applications of dilute liquid fertilizer at about two-week intervals. A minimum night temperature of 60°F, a minimum day one of 70°F, a humid atmosphere, and shade from direct sun encourage good growth. Propagation is by division, preferably in late winter or spring.

SPATHIPHYLLUM (Spathi-phýllum). This genus of thirty-six species, of the arum family ARACEAE, inhabits the tropics of the eastern and western hemispheres. By the noncritical observer, its members are sometimes confused with anthuriums, to which they are closely related, but to the more experienced botanical or horticultural eye they are quite different. The name *Spathiphyllum* is from the Greek *spathe*, a spathe, and *phyllon*, a leaf, and refers to the appearance of the spathes.

Spathiphyllums are tender, evergreen herbaceous perennials that form dense clumps of dark green foliage arising from horizontal rooting rhizomes. The leaves, never with lobed or strongly heart-shaped bases, have long stalks that broaden into wings or sheaths for the lower one-third or more of their lengths and are distinctly bent at their tops. The upper parts of the lanceolate, oblong, elliptic, or ovate leaf blades generally spread outward. As with all aroids (members of the arum family), the parts usually called flowers are really inflorescences. They are aggregations of true flowers and attendant parts. Their structure is basically that of the calla-lily (*Zantedeschia*) and jack-in-the-pulpit (*Arisaema*). Each inflorescence consists of a spadix (spike or central column) crowded with many tiny flowers, the males at the top and the females below, and a spathe (bract) that arises from below the spadix (plural spadices). In the calla-lily and jack-in-the-pulpit, the spathe partly encloses the spadix, but this is not true of *Spathiphyllum*. Its white or greenish spathes are flat or nearly so and to one side of the spadix. They spread outward, upward, or downward. Typically, the spathes of spathiphyllums are thinner than those of anthuriums. In some kinds, the lower part of the spathe is fused to the stalk for some distance below the spadix so that the latter appears to arise from the midrib of the spathe some distance in from its base. The spadices of *Spathiphyllum* are smooth or rough. The stigmas of the tiny flowers of *Spathiphyllum* are three- to four-lobed, those of *Anthurium* are obscurely two-lobed. The fruits of *Spathiphyllum* are berries.

Species of *Spathiphyllum* with spathes joined continuously along the stem for some distance below the spadix are *S. blandum*, *S. cochlearispathum*, *S. phryniifolium*, *S. kochii*, and *S. clevelandii*. Of these the first has leaves with tapered bases. Those of the others have squarish or slightly heart-shaped bases. Native to Central America, *S. blandum*, 1 foot to 2 feet tall, has elliptic leaves narrowed equally at both ends, not more than three times as long as wide, and with petioles winged for almost their entire length. The white spathes, up to 10 inches long, are shaped like the leaves, but are smaller. The leaf blades of *S. cochlearispathum*, which attains a height of up to 5 feet or more and is the largest species, are oblong and markedly undulated along their margins. They have broadly-winged, sheathing stalks, finely mottled with white. The inflorescences have an erect, hooded, oblanceolate to elliptic spathe up to 1 foot long and a nearly stalkless, rough spadix. This is a native of southern Mexico. Lower and with blunt-based, long-elliptic to lanceolate leaf blades, *S. phryniifolium*, of Panama and Costa Rica, is sometimes confused with *S. friedrichsthalii*, a species not known to be in cultivation. From the latter, *S. phryniifolium* is distinguished by its spadices having very short stalks and by the long, tapering bases of its leaves. In the first of these details it differs also from *S. kochii*, which has spadices lifted away from the spathe on stalks 1 inch long or longer, but otherwise is similar to *S. phryniifolium*. True *S. kochii* seems not to be in cultivation, the plant usually cultivated under that name being the hybrid *S. clevelandii*. Native to Colombia and Venezuela, *S. wallisii* is a robust kind with lustrous, oblong-lanceolate, wavy-edged leaves. On reedy stalks, the inflorescences have spadices joined in the lower parts to the bottoms of the ovate, white spathes, which gradually turn green as they age.

Species in which the spathe is separate from the spadix, or at least is not joined continuously to its stalk for a considerable distance, include very lovely *S. floribundum*, of Colombia. Up to 1 foot tall, this has broad, velvety, dark green leaves with elliptic to oblanceolate blades up to three times as long as broad, and with paler midribs. Its inflorescences have reflexed spathes with pure white upper surfaces, and green and white spadices. A sort with very similar inflorescences is *S. patinii*. Known only as a cultivated plant, and up to 1½ feet tall, this has leaves rather like those of hybrid *S. clevelandii*, but narrower, and narrower too than those of *S. floribundum*. Their blades are four times as long as wide and, although glossy, lack the velvety appearance of those of *S. floribundum*. Others in this group are *S. cannaefolium*, *S. commutatum*, and *S. cuspidatum*. Very beautiful *S. cannaefolium*, of northern South America and Trinidad, is about 2½ feet tall. It has leaves with oblanceolate to broad-elliptic blades 7 inches to 1 foot long. Its fragrant inflorescences have erect to spreading, lanceolate to pointed-elliptic spathes 3½ to 5½ inches long, white on their upper surfaces, greenish beneath. The spadixes, when mature, are white. Very similar *S. commutatum*, of the Philippine Islands and Molucca Islands, much resembles *S. cannaefolium*, differing most noticeably in its leaves being more broadly elliptic. Native to northeastern South America, *S. cuspidatum* is 1½ to 3½ feet tall. It has long-stalked leaves with lanceolate to pointed-elliptic blades 6 inches to 1 foot long or longer. The slender-stalked inflorescences have cream-colored spadices 1½ to 4 inches long and a narrow, pointed-elliptic to oblongish, spreading to reflexed, white spathe 5 to 9 inches long, with a green center line down its back. With age the spathe changes to greenish-yellow.

Several hybrid spathiphyllums of excellence are cultivated. Foremost is *S. clevelandii*, often misnamed *S. kochii*, which is properly the name of a kind apparently not in cultivation. The hybrid has thin, lanceolate, glossy-green leaves with somewhat wavy margins and thin stalks. It has reedlike flower stalks and pure white spathes, with a green line up their backs, that turn green as they age. The spadices are white and rough. Their stalks are attached to the lower inch or so of the spathe. This plant is similar to *S. wallisii*, but is larger in all its parts. The handsome hybrid 'Marion Wagner' has *S. cochlearispathum* and *S. wallisii* as parents. This has glossy, satiny, quilted leaves and fragrant inflorescences with greenish-white spathes that shade to green. They are up to 1¼ feet long by about one-half as wide. The lower parts of the spadices are joined to the spathes. Another fine variety, with spathes from 5 to 8 inches long, 'Mauna Loa' is probably a hybrid between variety 'McCoy' and *S. floribundum*. It is vigorous, compact, and has dark, glossy-green foliage and inflorescences with white spathes slightly concave on their upper sides. The hybrid 'McCoy', raised in Hawaii, with probably *S. cochlearispathum* and *S. clevelandii* as its parents, is exceptionally vigorous and attains a height of 5 feet. Its spathes, 8 inches to 1½ feet long, are creamy-white or white, changing to green as they age. The stalk of the rough spadix is attached for about 1 inch of its length to the spathe.

Garden Uses. In tropical and subtropical regions unafflicted by frosts, spathiphyllums are excellent for shaded or partially shaded areas where they can be given rich, moist soil. Under similar conditions they prosper when planted in beds in tropical greenhouses. They make good underplanting beneath trees and are fine for bordering paths. Their blooms mostly wilt and do not last well when cut. Spathiphyllums are fine pot plants and most kinds thrive remarkably well under house conditions. This is especially true of *S. clevelandii*. Even in poorly lighted locations, they remain attractive for extended periods, but are then less likely to bloom. The production of inflorescences also seems to be checked by inadequate humidity.

Cultivation. These are tolerant tropicals. They adapt easily to a variety of conditions, including soil, light intensity, and relative humidity. They must have warmth. A minimum temperature of 60 to 70°F is recommended and, provided the air is reasonably humid, maximums may exceed these levels by at least twenty degrees. Best results are obtained with fairly high humidity and in good light, but with shade from strong sun. Rich, well-drained soil, kept constantly moist, favors strong, healthy growth. Specimens that have filled their available soil with roots are benefited by regular applications of dilute liquid fertilizer from spring through fall. Plants in pots need transferring to larger containers or dividing and repotting periodically, perhaps every three or four years. Propagation is easily done by division, best carried out in late winter or spring. Fresh seeds may also be used; sow them in sandy, peaty soil or in milled sphagnum moss in a temperature of 75 to 80°F.

Spathiphyllum wallisii

Spathiphyllum floribundum

Spathiphyllum 'Mauna Loa'

Spathiphyllum cannaefolium

Spathiphyllum cuspidatum

Spathiphyllum clevelandii

Spathiphyllum 'McCoy'

SPATHODEA (Spath-òdea) — African-Tulip-Tree, Fountain Tree. The African-tulip-tree (*Spathodea campanulata*) is not related to the American tulip tree (*Liriodendron tulipifera*). It and the only other representative of its genus, *S. nilotica*, belong in the bignonia family BIGNONIACEAE. They are kissing cousins of anemopaegmas, jacarandas, the sausage tree, and catalpas. The name, meaning spathelike, and referring to the calyx, is from the Greek *spathe*, a sheath or spathe, and *odes*, similar to.

Natives of tropical Africa, spathodeas are highly ornamental, normally evergreen, flowering trees with large opposite leaves, usually pinnate with five or more leaflets but sometimes with only three leaflets. The lopsided, brilliant orange-red to scarlet, cup-shaped, erect blooms are in dense terminal panicles or racemes. Fancifully tulip-like when viewed from some distance, they have strongly recurved calyxes cleft to their bases on one side, and bell-shaped corollas markedly swollen at one side and with five spreading, frilled lobes. The four stamens are clearly visible. The slender style ends in a two-lobed stigma. The broad-elliptic, flaky, winged seeds are contained in woody capsules.

The African-tulip-tree (*S. campanulata*) attains a maximum height of 70 feet, but often is not half that height in cultivation. Its leaves may be somewhat hairy when young, but later are hairless. They have nine to nineteen leaflets and are up to 1½ feet in length. The short-pointed leaflets are elliptic to ovate-lanceolate and 2 to 5 inches long by about one-half as wide. At their bases are two or three glands. The fiery-red flowers, in tight clusters of a dozen or so at the branch ends, are 4 inches long or sometimes longer. Their calyxes are more or less boat-shaped, leathery, and some 2½ inches in length. The ovate lobes of the corolla are pleated, wavy, and narrowly margined with yellow. The insides of the blooms, which have a foxy odor, are yellowish with streaks of red. As buds the blooms secrete great amounts of liquid that spills if the branches are shaken. This gives reason for the common name fountain tree. About 8 inches long by nearly one-quarter as wide, the flattened seed pods are without hairs or prickles. They contain many 1-inch-wide seeds with silvery wings.

Similar, but at best not much over 20 feet tall, is East African *S. nilotica*. Although this has even more brilliant blooms than its west African relative, its foliage is paler and it is less commonly planted.

Garden and Landscape Uses. In most parts of the humid tropics and warm subtropics African-tulip-trees are favorites. They are among the most beautiful and satisfactory trees for private gardens, parks, roadsides, and other landscaped places. With royal poincianas and such-

Spathodea campanulata

Spathodea campanulata (flowers)

like spectaculars they rank as the most gorgeous vegetation the tropics afford. For their well being, African-tulip-trees need fertile soil that does not dry out for long periods and a sunny location. In most places they are evergreen, but in some climates they lose their foliage for a brief period each year.

Cultivation. No particular problems attend the cultivation of these trees. They are readily increased by seed and by cuttings.

SPATHOGLOTTIS (Spatho-glóttis). Of the same relationship as *Calanthe* and *Phaius,* the genus *Spathoglottis* comprises nearly fifty species of evergreen and deciduous ground orchids of the orchid family OR-CHIDACEAE. It is indigenous to the warmer parts of Asia, Indonesia, the Philippine Islands, and New Caledonia. Its name, referring to the form of the lip of the flower, comes from the Greek *spathe,* a spathe, and *glotta,* a tongue.

Handsome ornamentals, these have usually ovoid pseudobulbs and one to several longitudinally-corrugated, often narrow, grasslike leaves. The flower stalks, terminating in racemes of blooms, originate from the bases of the pseudobulbs. The flowers open in succession over a very long period. Each has three separate,

nearly identical, spreading sepals and two similar broader or longer, spreading petals. The lip is concave or pouched at its base and deeply-three-lobed. The center lobe broadens from a narrow base to its apex and has a pair of prominent calluses and two small, lateral teeth. The side lobes curve upward. The column is slender and curved.

Most frequently cultivated, **S. plicata** is native from Malaya to New Guinea, the Philippine Islands, and the Caroline Islands. It is naturalized in Hawaii and perhaps somewhat in southern Florida. This has crowded, more or less ovoid pseudobulbs about 1½ inches long, and many linear-lanceolate leaves, sheathing at their bases and up to 2 feet or sometimes more in length. The racemes, carried to heights of 2½ feet and with lanceolate, pinkish bracts, have five to twenty-five rather crowded blooms each up to 1½ inches wide. The color varies considerably in individuals. Closely related **S. vieillardii,** of New Caledonia, is similar, but larger in all its parts, its blooms being about 2 inches in diameter. Malayan **S. aurea** has pseudobulbs up to 8 inches long and leaves, mostly purple-tinged, 2 to 3 feet long. The golden-yellow flowers, about 3 inches in diameter, have similar sepals and petals and a lip spotted and streaked with crimson. Other species are sometimes grown by orchid fanciers and a number of very beautiful hybrids between species within the genus have been raised, as well as intergeneric hybrids with *Phaius.*

Garden and Landscape Uses and Cultivation. This genus is attracting increased attention from orchid collectors. Its kinds bloom profusely over long seasons. They succeed outdoors in the humid tropics, warm subtropics, and in greenhouses under conditions and care that suit *Phaius* and *Calanthe.* The pseudobulbs must be set aboveground, not partly buried. Bright light or even full sun is needed. For more information see Orchids.

SPATTERDOCK is *Nuphar advena.*

SPATULA-SHAPED. As used in this Encyclopedia, spatula-shaped is equated with the botanical terms spatulate and spathulate. It describes organs, most often leaves, oblongish in outline, or somewhat broadened toward a more or less rounded apex and gradually narrowed at the base.

SPEARMINT is *Mentha spicata.*

SPECIES. Nineteenth-century British botanist George Bentham defined a species as "all the individual plants which resemble each other sufficiently to make us conclude that all are or all may have been descended from a common parent." More recently and succinctly, American botanist Arthur Cronquist wrote "a species is a

particular kind of plant or animal, which retains its distinction from other kinds in nature over a period of many successive generations." Because, in an evolutionary sense, species descend from other species, the Bentham definition must be amended to read "essentially identical common parent" for "common parent." Key words in the Cronquist definition are "in nature." There are numerous horticultural varieties or cultivars of plants that "retain their distinction from other kinds over a period of many successive generations," but only as a result of intervention by man.

A species, then, is a natural population of basic taxonomic importance that differs sufficiently from all other species to be accepted as distinct.

In the wild, species are often variable to the extent that they include populations that persistently differ from the norm or accepted type in minor characteristics. Such deviant populations are often identified as subspecies and botanical varieties.

Determination of the degree and consistency of variation that is acceptable within the concept of a species is a matter of botanical taxonomic judgment. Botanists may and not infrequently do differ in their opinions to the extent that one authority may, because of what he considers adequate differences, describe as two or more species a population of plants that another botanist, who lays more emphasis on the similarities, accepts as one species, with perhaps the variants considered as subspecies or varieties.

With some partial exceptions, in the wild, individuals of the same species interbreed freely, whereas those of different species, again with some exceptions, never or rarely. Natural hybrids may occur where the geographical ranges of compatible species overlap; however, because hybrids are usually less adapted to their environment than their parental species, they rarely persist in the wild. Geographic isolation and other causes, such as different flowering times, are sometimes responsible for keeping species pure by preventing cross-pollination. In such cases man's intervention to bridge the barrier may result in hybrids. A classic example is *Primula kewensis,* which came into being in the greenhouses of the Royal Botanic Garden, Kew, England, because of the fortuitous circumstance that *P. floribunda,* of China, and *P. verticillata,* of Ethiopia, were in close proximity and in bloom at the same time. Obviously this could not happen in the wild.

SPECULARIA. See Legousia.

SPEEDWELL. See Veronica.

SPEIRANTHA (Speiránth-a). A single species of the lily family LILIACEAE constitutes *Speirantha.* Its name, from the Greek *speira,* a coil or spire, and *anthos,* a flower, was applied because the blooms are in spire-like racemes.

Native to China, **S. gardenii** (syn. *S. convallarioides*) bears some resemblance to

Speirantha gardenii

lily-of-the-valley (*Convallaria majalis*) to which it is closely related. It has creeping rhizomes that spread rather slowly, deciduous, pointed-elliptic leaves, and stalked clusters of starry, white, scentless flowers that nestle among the foliage. The flowers are borne in spring.

Garden Uses and Cultivation. Hardy outdoors in England, but probably not in much severer climates, it is an interesting plant to use as a groundcover or as specimen clumps in rock gardens and other informal areas. In addition to its usefulness for outdoor planting, *S. gardenii* is a quite delightful plant for growing in cool greenhouses, either planted in pots or in ground beds. This plant thrives in part-shade in rich, moderately moist soil that contains an abundance of organic matter. It is easily propagated by division in fall or spring.

SPENCERIA (Spen-cèria). One of two western Chinese species of herbaceous perennials related to *Agrimonia* and belonging to the rose family ROSACEAE constitute this genus. The name honors the British botanist Spencer le Marchant, who died in 1931.

Spencerias differ from agrimonias in their flowers having thirty to forty stamens, instead of fifteen or fewer; in their calyx tubes being hairy, but not having hooked bristles; and in the slender stigmas not being knob-tipped.

A robust, erect, many-stemmed, silvery-hairy species 6 inches to over 1 foot tall, **Spenceria ramalana** forms a rosette of spreading basal leaves much like those of some potentillas. Each has up to about fifteen broadly-elliptic leaflets of which the largest, toward the leaf ends, may be a little over ½ inch long. The leaflets are notched or toothed at their apexes. The stem leaves are much smaller than the basal ones. They have one or two pairs of leaflets or may be undivided. About 1 inch in diameter, the bright yellow to reddish-yellow blooms, on individual stalks up to 1¾ inches in length, are in long, fairly dense racemes.

Garden Uses and Cultivation. The species described is reported to be hardy, but little is known about its cultivation in North America and it well may not be tolerant of hot summers. Not finicky as to soil, it likes sunny locations and is easily increased by seed and by division. It is suitable for rock gardens and other places where low flowering plants are appropriate.

SPHACELE CALYCINA is *Lepechinia calycina.*

SPHAERADENIA (Sphaera-dènia). Previously included in *Carludovica,* the genus *Sphaeradenia,* of the cyclanthus family CYCLANTHACEAE, comprises thirty-eight species, natives of Central America and northwestern South America. The name, from the Greek *sphaira,* a ball, and *aden,* a gland, alludes to secretion globules on the anthers.

Stemless or with very short stems, sphaeradenias have two-ranked, palmlike leaves with stalks usually about as long as the blades, but in some kinds considerably longer or shorter. The blades are cleft into two primary lobes, which in older leaves are often again cleft. The flowers, much like those of *Carludovica,* are similarly arranged in spikelike spadixes. Below each spadix are three to five spathes (bracts). The fruits are berries.

Occasionally cultivated, **S. laucheana** (syn. *Carludovica laucheana*) is believed to be native to Colombia. It has a very short stem and leaves with stalks shorter than the blade, which may be 8 inches to over 1½ feet long, and is cleft for one-third to two-thirds of its length. The spathes of the flower spikes are yellowish or greenish-white.

Garden and Landscape Uses and Cultivation. These are as for *Carludovica.*

SPHAERALCEA (Sphaer-álcea) — Globe-Mallow, Desert-Mallow or Desert-Hollyhock, Prairie-Mallow. Belonging to the mallow family MALVACEAE, the genus *Sphaeralcea* contains about fifty species, natives of the Americas. The name comes from the Greek *sphaera,* a globe, and *aklea,* a mallow. It alludes to the shape of the clusters of fruits. From related *Iliamna, Malvastrum,* and *Malacothamnus,* the genus here considered differs in the carpels that form its fruits being clearly differentiated into two parts.

Globe-mallows include shrubs, sub-shrubs, herbaceous perennials, and annuals, mostly natives of warm, dry regions. Their stems and their usually strongly-angled or lobed leaves are furnished with gray, stellate (star-shaped) hairs. Sometimes in terminal spikes or racemes, but more often in clusters or solitary in the leaf axils, the flowers are pink, red, or violet-purple. Beneath the calyx there is usually an early deciduous collar of two or three bracts. The calyx is five-cleft. There are five petals. The column of many stamens, the lower parts of their stalks united, frays above into a separate stalk for each anther. The stigmas are knob-shaped. The fruits are of many dry, one- to three-seeded carpels. The species previously known as *S. acerifolia* is *Iliamna rivularis,* those previously named *S. rosea* and *S. umbellata* belong in *Phymosia.*

South American **S. bonariensis,** a herbaceous perennial 2 to 3 feet tall, has three-lobed, ovate leaves and from the leaf axils crowded clusters of apricot-colored, salmon-pink, or brick-red, ½- to ¾-inch-long flowers with usually a dark spot near the base of each petal. Quite different **S. philippiana,** of Argentina, is a gray-hairy herbaceous perennial with trailing stems and small three- or five-lobed leaves with wavy, toothed margins. About 1 inch in diameter, the rose-pink flowers are solitary or in twos or threes.

Desert-mallow or desert-hollyhock (**S. ambigua**), native to dry parts of western

Sphaeralcea ambigua

North America, often is puzzling to the would-be identifier because of its great variability and because it hybridizes with other species. Unsullied by such dalliance, it is a whitish- or yellowish-hairy, herbaceous perennial 2 to 3 feet tall, with many stems and thickish, broadly-ovate to triangular, usually three-lobed leaves up to about 3 inches long. Its grenadine-red to bright pink blooms are about 2 inches in diameter. Native to the southwestern United States, **S. fendleri** is an erect to spreading subshrub up to 2½ feet tall, with leaves, scarcely-lobed to deeply-lobed or sometimes twice-lobed, that are extremely variable in shape. They are 1 inch to 2

Sphaeralcea fendleri

inches long and commonly velvety or downy with whitish, stellate (star-shaped) hairs. From ¾ to 1 inch in diameter, the orange-red to pink or mauve flowers are rather distantly spaced in erect spikes.

A herbaceous perennial 1 foot to 3 feet tall or sometimes taller, native from Idaho to British Columbia and California, *S. munroana* is slender-stemmed and clothed with minute, starry hairs. It has grayish, shallowly-three- to five-lobed, broadly-ovate, toothed leaves wider than their 1- to 2-inch lengths. The grenadine-red to apricot-pink flowers, about 1 inch wide, are many together in terminal or axillary clusters.

Prairie-mallow (*S. coccinea* syn. *Malvastrum coccineum*) is an attractive, usually rather densely-gray- or white-hairy herbaceous perennial. Its rather sprawling stems sometimes, but not commonly, exceed 9 inches in length. The thickish, conspicuously three-veined leaves are ½ inch to 2½ inches long and broader than long. They are prettily cleft into narrow lobes, with the primary lobes often again cleft. The short-stalked, brick-red blooms, in short, terminal racemes, are up to 1 inch wide. There are generally no bracts below the calyxes. Variety *S. c. dissecta* has more finely-cut foliage, usually more erect stems, and commonly is more conspicuously white-hairy.

Generally with delicate pink, pale lavender, or nearly white flowers, perennial *S. campestris*, of Oregon, is 3 to 6 feet tall. It has stems with their lower parts usually hairy, and basal leaves commonly fairly deeply-divided into seven or sometimes five lobes. In loose racemes, branched or not, the flowers have petals ½ to 1 inch long. Much enlarged, fleshy, but not fibrous or tough roots are characteristic of *S. neomexicana*. This variable perennial of Wyoming to Oregon, New Mexico, Arizona, California, and Mexico is from 9 inches to 2 feet tall or sometimes taller. It has hairy stems, and leaves with blades usually under, but sometimes over, 2 inches wide. They are shallowly-five- or

seven-lobed. The light rose-pink flowers have petals up to ¾ inch long. Usually with several stems 2 to 5 feet tall, hairless or sparsely-hairy at their bases, *S. hendersonii* is native from Oregon to British Columbia. A perennial, it has shallowly-five-lobed, round-toothed basal leaves up to 6 inches wide and stem leaves more deeply-cleft. In crowded, spikelike racemes, the flowers have bright pinkish-lavender to deep rose-pink petals approximately ½ inch long.

Garden and Landscape Uses. Sphaeralceas are best suited for gardens in warm, dry regions. Except for the prairie-mallow, they do not stand much cold and are very intolerant of wet soils. The prairie-mallow survives outdoors in the vicinity of New York City, but is happier in drier climates. It is adapted for rock gardens and similar places, as is *S. philippiana* in milder climates. The taller herbaceous perennials are useful for flower beds, informal plantings, and native plant gardens.

Cultivation. Well-drained soils and sunny sites are required by sphaeralceas. Because most kinds are tap-rooted, transplanting established specimens is often hazardous to success. It is better to set out young plants from containers. Once established, routine care is minimal. Propagation is by seed and by cuttings.

SPHAEROGYNE. See Tococa.

SPHAEROPTERIS. See Cyathea.

SPHAGNUM MOSS. See Moss, Sphagnum.

SPHALMANTHUS (Sphalm-ánthus). This genus of seventeen species of South African succulent plants, of the *Mesembryanthemum* complex of the carpetweed family AIZOACEAE, is, by some botanists, combined with *Aridaria* to form the genus *Nycteranthus*. The name *Sphalmanthus*, from the Greek *sphalma*, an error, and *anthos*, a flower, is unexplained.

Sphalmanthuses are low subshrubs with tuberous rootstocks and prostrate rooting stems. Their linear, cylindrical or subcylindrical, opposite or alternate, stalkless leaves are finely warted. The flowers, solitary or in twos or threes, and light pink to violet-pink, greenish, or yellow, have the appearance of daisies, but unlike daisies are not flower heads of many florets, but individual blooms each with five sepals, many petals, numerous stamens, and four or five stigmas. The fruits are capsules.

Its tubers partly aboveground and ½ to 1 inch thick, *S. longispinulus* (syns. *Nycteranthus longispinulus, Aridaria longispinula, Mesembryanthemum longispinulum*) has trailing stems up to 1 foot in length. Its slender leaves are semicylindrical, pointed, and up to ½ inch long or sometimes longer. They are persistent, remaining attached to

the stems and becoming rigid and spiny. The light yellow flowers are solitary, terminal, and up to approximately ½ inch in diameter.

Garden Uses and Cultivation. Rare in cultivation, members of this genus require the general conditions and care satisfactory for *Aridaria*. They must have well-drained, preferably sandy soil.

SPHENOGYNE. See Ursinia.

SPHENOMERIS (Spheno-mèris)—Lace Fern. From *Davallia*, this genus of ferns of the pteris family PTERIDACEAE is distinguished by scalelike coverings (indusia) forming tubular pockets for its clusters of spore capsules and by the ultimate segments of its fronds (leaves) being shortly wedge-shaped. This last characteristic accounts for the name, derived from the Greek *sphen*, a wedge, and *meris*, part.

The eighteen species of *Sphenomeris* are chiefly tropical and subtropical, but the genus is also represented in the native floras of Japan and New Zealand. Its members have creeping, scaly rhizomes, and erect, hairless fronds two- or more-times-pinnately-divided. The clusters of spore capsules, at the vein ends at the edges of the segments, have coverings (indusia) that allow the spores to escape through openings at their apexes.

Inhabiting warm parts of Asia and Polynesia, the lace fern (*S. chusana* syns. *Odontosoria chinensis, Davallia tenuifolia*) is one of the most abundant native ferns of Hawaii. It has underground, creeping rhizomes. Its graceful fronds with glossy, smooth stalks, up to 1 foot long, have broad-ovate to ovate-oblong blades, as long or longer than the stalks, three- or four-times-divided into more or less flat-apexed segments approximately ⅛ inch long. The spore clusters, broader than long and usually solitary, but sometimes paired, are at the apexes of lobes of the segments. Hawaiians obtained a dark brown dye from this species.

Garden and Landscape Uses and Cultivation. In the humid tropics, warm subtropics, and greenhouses the elegant species described here is easy to grow. It revels in well-aerated, coarse soil that contains an abundance of organic matter and is always moderately moist. Shade from strong sun is needed. Indoors a winter night temperature of 60°F suits. By day this may be increased by up to fifteen degrees. From spring to fall higher temperatures are in order. The atmosphere should be decidedly humid. Increase is easy by division in late winter or spring and by spores. For more information see the Encyclopedia entry Ferns.

SPHENOSCIADIUM (Spheno-sciàdium) — Ranger's Button or White Heads. Previously included in *Selinum*, the one species of this genus of the carrot family UMBEL-LIFERAE is a native of swampy places in mountains from California to Baja California, Oregon, Idaho, and Nevada. Its name comes from the Greek *sphenos*, a wedge, and *sciadios*, an umbrella, and alludes to the umbels of flowers.

Ranger's button or white heads (*Sphenosciadium capitellatum*) is an erect, thick-rooted, little-branched, stout-stemmed, herbaceous perennial, rough to the feel and 3 to 5 feet tall. Except for its flowering parts, it is hairless. The leaves have sheathing stalks and mostly twice-pinnate blades, in outline ovate to oblong and 6 inches to 1¼ feet in length. The leaflets, linear-oblong to lanceolate-ovate, are ½ inch to 5 inches long and toothed. The tiny, white to purplish, stalkless flowers are in umbels of button-like crowded heads attached to the enlarged ends (receptacles) of the rays of the umbels. This is a variable species; some botanists recognize several varieties. The little seedlike fruits are flattened and ribbed.

Garden Uses and Cultivation. For naturalistic plantings at watersides and in moist soils, ranger's button has some merit. It is not commonly cultivated and the limits of its hardiness are uncertain. It is probably best adapted to western parts of the United States and, within its natural range, is well worth including in collections of native plants. It may be raised from seed and by division.

SPHENOSTIGMA (Spheno-stígma). In 1791 William Bartram, pioneer American botanist, first described and illustrated the species described below. ''Behold'' he wrote, alluding to the landscape of northern Florida, ''the azure fields of cerulean Ixea.'' Following its discovery, Bartram's *Ixea* (the modern spelling is *Ixia*) was lost to science and not seen again for more than a century. Some botanists thought that it was extinct, others that it had never existed. In 1931 it was rediscovered and, as it was clearly not an *Ixia* as that genus is presently understood, it was given the name *Salpingostylis coelestina*. Later, botanists decided that the plant is really a northern representative of the chiefly tropical American genus *Sphenostigma*, and its name was changed to *S. coelestinum*. A genus of seventeen species, *Sphenostigma* belongs to the iris family IRIDACEAE. The name comes from the Greek *spheno*, a wedge, and stigma.

The rediscovery of *S. coelestinum* revealed an important reason why this quite showy plant remained hidden from searching botanists for so long. Its blooms open a little before dawn and close by eight to ten o'clock in the morning. As may be readily imagined, more than one comment concerning the rising habits of botanical collectors were occasioned by this discovery.

Lovely in bloom, *S. coelestinum* is 1 foot to 1½ feet tall. It has a corm (bulblike organ that is solid rather than composed of concentric layers or overlapping scales as are onion and lily bulbs). The corm, ½ to ¾ inch in diameter, produces narrow-linear, pleated leaves 5 to 6 inches in length. The flowers are nodding and 2 to 3 inches wide. They are violet, lavender-violet, or purple, sometimes with a white eye, or rarely are white. They have six perianth parts (commonly called petals, but more correctly, tepals) and three stamens, which are alternate with the three branches of the style, not opposite them as in *Nemastylis*. The fruits are capsules containing small, brick-red seeds.

Garden and Landscape Uses. Because of its limited natural distribution the possibility exists that this rare endemic of the United States will become extinct in the wild in the face of advancing agriculture and other operations of man. Fortunately it is easily raised from seeds and cultivated. A delightful plant for those allured by the rare and botanically interesting, it is adaptable to flower beds, rock gardens, and greenhouse cultivation.

Cultivation. Fertile, sandy, somewhat acid soil that contains an abundance of decayed organic matter and is well drained, but uniformly moist during the spring to fall season of growth, suits *S. coelestinum*. New growth starts in spring and ripens and dies after the seeds mature. Propagation by seed is the most practical means of increase. Under good cultivation plants can be had in bloom in their second year from seed sowing. In greenhouses the soil should be kept dry during the bulbs' dormant season. In late winter or spring repotting is done and watering resumed. A night temperature of 50°F, with a daytime rise of five to fifteen degrees, depending on the brightness of the day, is appropriate. On all favorable occasions the greenhouse is ventilated freely. Very light shade in summer, just sufficient to break the full intensity of the strongest sunlight, is beneficial. It seems probable that in the north this interesting species could be handled like gladioluses, by storing the bulbs over winter and planting them outdoors in spring.

SPHYROSPERMUM (Sphyro-spérmum). Native from Mexico to tropical America, Trinidad, and Haiti, *Sphyrospermum* belongs in the heath family ERICACEAE or, according to authorities who accept the split, in the blueberry family VACCINI-ACEAE. Sixteen species are recognized. The name, from the Greek *sphyron*, an ankle, and *sperma*, a seed, alludes to the seeds being bent like an ankle.

The sorts of this genus are usually epiphytic (tree-perching) shrubs with long, slender, often pendent, branched stems. They have alternate, small, short-stalked,

more or less leathery leaves. Solitary or rarely in pairs from the leaf axils, the flowers have a four- or five-lobed calyx, a subcylindrical, four- or five-lobed corolla, and as many or twice as many stamens as corolla lobes. The slender style is about as long as the corolla. The fruits are nearly spherical to ellipsoid berries.

The first species described and the only one known to be cultivated, *S. buxifolium*,

Sphyrospermum buxifolium in a hanging basket

native from Nicaragua to Bolivia, is a very attractive ornamental. It has prostrate to drooping stems up to 6 feet long, and fleshy, suborbicular, short-stalked leaves ⅓ to ⅔ inch long with dark green upper surfaces and paler lower ones. About ¼ inch long, the long-stalked flowers are white flecked with lilac. They are succeeded by pea-sized, lead-colored to pale bluish-violet fruits.

Garden Uses and Cultivation. These are as for *Columnea*.

SPICE BUSH is *Lindera benzoin*.

SPIDER FLOWER. See Cleome.

SPIDER-LILY. See Hymenocallis.

SPIDER PLANT is *Chlorophytum comosum*.

SPIDERLING. See Boerhavia.

SPIDERWORT. See Tradescantia.

SPIGELIA (Spi-gèlia)—Pinkroot or Worm-Grass. The fifty species of *Spigelia* are confined to the Americas, most to the tropics, subtropics, and warm-temperate parts. They are annuals and perennial herbaceous plants of the logania family LOGA-NIACEAE or, under an alternative classification, of the spigelia family SPIGELIACEAE. Their name commemorates the Dutch botanist Adrien Van den Spieghel, who died in 1625.

Spigelias have opposite, undivided leaves and tubular, red, purplish, or yellow flow-

Spigelia marilandica

ers in terminal, one-sided clusters called cymes. The blooms have five-lobed calyxes, narrowly-cylindrical or funnel-shaped corollas with five lobes (petals), and five stamens. The fruits are capsules.

The species most likely to be cultivated is the pinkroot or worm-grass (*S. marilandica*) which inhabits moist woods and partly shaded places from North Carolina to Indiana, Missouri, Oklahoma, Florida, and Texas. A perennial 1 foot to 2 feet tall, it has stalkless, pointed leaves, lanceolate to broadly-ovate-lanceolate and 2 to 4½ inches long. Mostly without branches, the attractive, raceme-like, few-flowered clusters of bloom are displayed in spring and early summer. Funnel-shaped and up to 2 inches long, the corollas are red outside and yellow inside. Their lobes spread. The seed capsules are nearly spherical and up to ⅓ inch long.

Garden and Landscape Uses. Pinkroot contains a poisonous alkaloid and has been used medicinally. Because of this, it is appropriate for inclusion in gardens given over to species that are or have been employed in medicine. In addition, it is worth planting as a decorative in flower beds and naturalistic areas. It is hardy north of its native range, but how far is not clearly determined.

Cultivation. Pinkroot grows without difficulty in fertile, garden soil in part-shade or, if the soil is not excessively dry, full sun, and may be propagated by division in spring or early fall and by seed.

SPIGNEL is *Meum athamanticum*.

SPIKE-HEATH is *Bruckenthalia spiculifolia*.

SPIKENARD. See Aralia.

SPILANTHES (Spilánth-es). This horticulturally little-known genus of the daisy family COMPOSITAE consists of sixty species of often weedy annual and perennial herbaceous plants widely distributed through tropical and subtropical America, Africa, Malaya, Borneo, and northern Australia. One, *S. americana*, is native in

the United States. The name *Spilanthes* is derived from the Greek *spilos*, a stain or spot, and *anthos*, a flower. The reference is to the disk that appears as a central spot in the flower heads of some kinds.

Para-cress or Brazil-cress (*S. oleracea*) is

Spilanthes oleracea

a tropical species of which the original habitat is in some doubt. It is compact, prostrate, and up to 1½ feet in height with opposite, approximately triangular, toothed leaves of crisp texture. Stalked flower heads develop in profusion from the leaf axils. They are scarcely raised above the foliage mass, but are in sufficient numbers to assure an attractive display that continues through the summer and fall until frost. The heads, suggestive of ovoid or cylindrical buttons ½ inch or so in diameter, are solitary and without ray florets. They are yellow with intensely orange centers. There is some evidence that this plant possesses some insecticidal properties, and, according to reports, it has something of an anesthetizing effect on the tongue.

Garden Uses and Cultivation. Para-cress or Brazil-cress is a pungent-flavored herb used in salads. It is also effective as an ornamental for use as in borders and edgings. It may be raised from seeds sown directly outdoors as soon as danger from frost has passed and the ground has warmed, or seeds may be sown indoors at about the same time as those of petunias and many other garden annuals, and the resulting plants be set in the garden later.

SPILOXENE. See Hypoxis.

SPINACH. A favorite healthful leaf vegetable, spinach is a member of the goosefoot family CHENOPODIACEAE. Garden varieties are derivatives of *Spinacia oleracea* and of its botanical variety *S. o. inermis*. Because of their spiny seeds (technically fruits), the former are grouped as prickly-seeded spinach, and the latter, which have spineless seeds, are distinguished as

Spinach

smooth- or round-seeded spinach. Prickly-seeded varieties, sometimes called winter spinach, are more cold-tolerant than round-seeded varieties.

Easy to grow, but intolerant of hot weather, spinach should be sown when there is reasonable assurance that relatively low temperatures and comparatively short days will prevail until it attains cutting size, which it does in six to seven weeks. Long days and, especially, a few really warm days soon cause the plants to bolt, sending up flowering stalks and becoming essentially useless for eating. Make the first sowing as early in spring as possible. Where climate permits, sowings of prickly-seeded spinach for late fall and winter harvesting are made in late summer and fall. This is practicable in sheltered locations as far north as New York City. When freezing weather comes, protect the rows by covering them with salt hay or similar loose material or with polyethylene plastic film supported on hoops of wire or a light wooden framework to form long, tentlike covers lengthwise over the rows of plants.

Fertile, slightly acid to neutral soil that never becomes unduly dry best suits this crop. In poor, dry earth it runs prematurely to seed. Spade or rotary till the ground deeply, incorporating compost, rotted manure, or other organic matter. Apply a complete fertilizer and immediately before sowing rake the surface to a fine tilth.

Do not plant too much seed at one time. Two or more smaller sowings at intervals of ten days or two weeks ensure longer harvesting than does one bigger sowing. Sow in drills 1 foot apart, about ½ inch deep. Thin seedlings from spring sowings to 4 to 5 inches apart. Allow about 6 inches between those from late sowings for winter harvesting.

Spinach is a good catch crop to sow between rows of tall peas. The little shade peas afford is advantageous to the spinach, and both crops respond to generous watering when the weather is dry. Harvest by cutting the entire plant at ground level. Popular varieties are 'America', 'Bloomsdale Long-Standing', 'Hybrid No. 7', and 'Viking'.

New-Zealand-spinach, an entirely different plant, is treated under that name in this Encyclopedia. Spinach-beet and perpetual-spinach are names sometimes used for Swiss chard. Mountain-spinach or orach is *Atriplex hortensis*. Tahitian spinach is *Xanthosoma brasiliense*.

SPINACH-DOCK is *Rumex patientia*.

SPINACH-RHUBARB is *Rumex abyssinicus*.

SPINACIA (Spin-àcia) — Spinach. Three or four species of annuals or biennials constitute *Spinacia*, of the goosefoot family CHENOPODIACEAE. Native to western Asia, it includes the species from which the familiar garden vegetable has been derived. The name, from the Latin *spina*, spiny, alludes to the fruits.

Spinacias are hairless plants with alternate, flat leaves, and unisexual flowers of no ornamental merit. The male blooms, in crowded spikes or panicles, are four- or five-parted. The females, without perianth parts, but with two or sometimes four persistent, small bracts that enlarge as the fruits (utricles) develop, come in the leaf axils. They have four or five each stamens and stigmas.

The wild progenitor of cultivated spinach, **S. oleracea** has rounded to triangular or arrowhead-shaped leaves, and erect, flowering stems up to three feet tall or taller. Its basal leaves are in rosettes and are narrowly-oblong to nearly circular. The stem leaves progressively diminish in size from below upward. The flowers are green. The fruits have two to four spines. Those of *S. o. inermis* are spineless. Except for the garden vegetable, *Spinacia* is not cultivated. For more information see Spinach.

SPINDLE TREE is *Euonymus europaea*.

SPIRAEA (Spir-aèa)—Spirea, Bridal Wreath. The botanical name of this genus is spelled *Spiraea*, its common name spirea. The latter is also used as a common name for certain other genera including *Astilbe*, *Filipendula*, and *Aruncus*. Species of these as well as of *Holodiscus*, *Physocarpus*, and *Sibiraea* have in the past been included in *Spiraea*. Belonging in the rose family ROSACEAE, the genus *Spiraea* comprises approximately 100 species of deciduous shrubs, some very popular and many highly ornamental in bloom. They are natives of the northern hemisphere, reaching their southern limits in Mexico and the Himalayas. The name probably comes from the Greek *speira*, a wreath, and refers, as does the English name bridal wreath, to the branches of many kinds being garlanded with clusters of blooms.

The genus *Spiraea* has alternate, undivided, but sometimes lobed leaves and numerous small, white, pink, or red flowers in clusters, racemes, or panicles. There are usually five sepals, five spreading petals, more in double-flowered varieties, and many separate stamens. The pistils usually number five. The fruits are small, dry, and capsule-like. In rare instances only does the foliage show attractive fall color.

In addition to the spireas dealt with below, some others are cultivated, but they are generally inferior to those discussed here. Ways in which these plants can be grouped include flower color, time of blooming, and approximate height. From the landscape planters' point of view, the last seems most useful and is followed here.

Low spireas, those that do not normally exceed 3 feet in height, include a number that are useful. Among the best known are varieties of the hybrid **S. bumalda.** These

Spiraea bumalda 'Anthony Waterer'

resulted from crossing *S. japonica* and *S. albiflora*. Their leaves are ovate-lanceolate, double-toothed, hairless, and 2 to 3 inches long. They have whitish, pink, or red flowers in flat clusters in summer. Those with colored blooms are usually preferred. Some of the *S. bumalda* kinds are closely similar to *S. japonica*, differing only in being lower, more upright, and in having slightly angled twigs. The oldest of the group, *S. b.* 'Anthony Waterer', which originated in 1890, is 2 feet tall, has young foliage tinged with red, and about midsummer bears crimson blooms. Similar, but 3 feet in height and blooming somewhat later, is *S. b. froebelii*. This has the advantage of, after flowering, producing secondary shoots that hide the faded flower heads. In *S. b. crispa*, about 2 feet tall, the leaves are slightly crinkled and the heads of bright pink flowers up to 6 inches in diameter. Even dwarfer is *S. b.* 'Norman'. It forms 10-inch-high mounds and has foliage that becomes reddish-purple in fall. Its flowers are rosy-pink.

Other low hybrids include 'Summer Snow' with flat panicles of white blooms from June to late August. About 2 feet tall, its parents are *S. betulifolia* and *S. media*. Some 3 feet in height, **S. conspicua,** the parents of which are *S. albiflora* and probably *S. latifolia*, is rather less meritorious. Upright, it has elliptic, short-stalked leaves up to 2½ inches long, once- or twice-toothed, and hairless except on the veins beneath. The rounded or conical clusters of whitish to pinkish tiny blooms, with stamens longer than the petals, are displayed from summer to fall. A hybrid between *S. albiflora* and *S. corymbosa*, named **S. superba,** has pale pink flowers in June. About 3 feet tall, it has upright, nearly hairless branches, and elliptic to elliptic-oblong leaves up to 3 inches long. The flowers, in solitary terminal clusters, have stamens about twice as long as the petals.

A good white-flowered Asian species, 1 foot to 2 feet tall, **S. albiflora** (syn. *S. japonica alba*), associates well with the *S. bumalda* varieties and the taller *S. japonica*. It blooms in July, is of upright growth, and has somewhat angled, hairless twigs. Its lanceolate leaves, 1½ to 3 inches long, are toothed or double-toothed and hairless. The flowers are in clusters, 1½ to 2 inches wide, that are grouped in flattish heads.

Two more low summer-bloomers are *S. bullata* (syn. *S. japonica bullata*) and *S. decumbens*. About 1¼ feet tall, *S. bullata* has erect branches that when young are hairy. Its leaves are short-stalked, broad-ovate, thickish, puckered, ½ inch to 1¼ inches long, grayish on their undersides, and toothed. It has compound clusters, up to 3 inches wide, of rosy pink blooms with reddish stamens a little longer than the petals. This Japanese spirea, one of the most delightful of its clan, covers itself with bloom in summer. Native to northern Italy, **S. decumbens,** a procumbent, hairless plant 6 to 10 inches tall, has erect branches, and elliptic to elliptic-oblong, toothed or double-toothed leaves ½ inch to 1¼ inches long. Its clusters of white flowers, 1 inch to 2 inches in diameter, are terminal on leafy branches in June. The stamens approximate the petals in length.

Flowering in May or June, Chinese **S. cantoniensis,** 3 to 4 feet tall, a parent of popular *S. vanhouttei*, is equally as fine as its hybrid, but unfortunately is less hardy. It survives in sheltered locations about as far north as New York City. It is also lower than *S. vanhouttei* and in mild climates such as that of California retains its foliage through most of the winter. Its lozenge-shaped leaves, 1 inch to 2½ inches long by up to ¾ inch wide, are irregularly deeply-toothed. This spirea has arching stems wreathed in spring with hemispherical, stalked clusters, up to 2 inches wide, of pure white flowers, the stamens of which are shorter than the petals. Variety *S. c.*

Spiraea trilobata

Spiraea alba

Spiraea tomentosa

Spiraea trichocarpa

lanceata, with double flowers nearly ½ inch in diameter, is especially lovely. Native from Korea and northern China to Siberia and Turkestan, and hardy in southern New England, **S. trilobata** is a fairly compact, broad shrub 3 to 4 feet tall. Its roundish, coarsely-toothed, bluish-green leaves, ½ to 1 inch long or a little longer, are sometimes slightly three- or five-lobed. The small, white, slender-stalked flowers are many together in umbels up to 1½ inches wide that terminate short, leafy shoots that sprout from stems of the previous year's growth.

Medium-sized spireas, ordinarily from 3½ to 6 feet tall, include some of the best as well as some of lesser horticultural merit. Among the latter are three natives of eastern North America, familiar as wildlings and not without a certain charm in natural surroundings, but of limited appeal as garden plants. They are two species called meadowsweet (*S. alba* and *S. latifolia*), and the hardhack or steeplebush (*S. tomentosa*). The blooms of *S. alba* are white, those of *S. latifolia* white or pinkish, those of *S. tomentosa* rose-pink to purplish red, except that in variety *S. t. alba* they are white. All have their flowers in pyramidal panicles, longer than wide, and bloom over a long period in summer. Up to 6 feet in height, **S. alba** inhabits bogs and wet soils and has nearly hairless, oblanceolate, finely-toothed leaves up to 2¼ inches long by up to one-third as wide. From it **S. latifolia** differs in usually not being taller than 4½ feet and having coarsely and often double-toothed, lanceolate or ovate-lanceolate leaves usually over one-third as broad as long, which may be up to 3 inches. Normally from 3 to 4 feet tall, **S. tomentosa** has ovate to lanceolate, irregularly-toothed leaves, up to 2½ inches long, that differ from those of the other two by being densely-hairy on their undersides.

Related to *S. tomentosa* and indigenous from Alaska to Oregon, **S. menziesii**, erect and about 5 feet tall, is hardy in southern New England. Its blunt, oblong-obovate

leaves, 2 to 3 inches long and irregularly-coarse-toothed above their centers, may be hairy on the veins beneath. The flowers, crowded in slender, pyramidal panicles 4 to 8 inches long, are pink and have stamens more than twice the length of the petals. This quite good-looking species blooms in summer.

Three outstanding Asian species of medium size are the Korean bridal wreath (*S. trichocarpa*), *S. thunbergii*, and *S. japonica*. As its common name suggests, the first is indigenous to Korea, while the second inhabits China and Japan and the third is endemic to Japan. Closely related to *S. nipponica* but scarcely as tall, **S. trichocarpa** is hardy in southern New England. It forms a compact shrub with stiffish, arching branches, and oblongish, hairless leaves, 1 inch to 2 inches in length, sometimes with a few teeth toward their ends. Its white flowers are in rounded clusters with pubescent stalks. The clusters are about 2 inches across and terminate short

leafy shoots that in June wreathe the stems of the previous year's growth.

Often broader than high, **S. thunbergii** is a very bushy, twiggy, graceful shrub with arching branches, slender, downy branchlets, and linear-lanceolate leaves, up to 1¾ inches long by not over ¼ inch wide, that become orange and scarlet in fall. Pale green on both surfaces, they taper to pointed apexes and have a few incurved teeth. In stalkless clusters of two to five, its slender-stalked, pure white flowers, with stamens shorter than the petals, open in spring earlier than those of any other spirea, so early that in parts of the northeast they may be injured by late frosts. Because of this, although it lives through New England winters, it usually blooms better further south. Quite different from the last two, **S. japonica** has erect stems and blooms in early summer. A parent of the *S. bumalda* group of hybrids, it resembles them, but is taller. Its pointed, ovate-oblong leaves, 1 inch to 3 inches long, are sharply-double-toothed. Their undersides, paler than the upper, may be hairy on the veins. Ranging from deep to pale pink or rarely white, the blooms, ¼ inch wide and with stamens much longer than the petals, are in clusters aggregated into much larger flattish-topped ones. Variety *S. j. atrosanguinea* has crimson flowers. Taller than the typical species, *S. j. fortunei* has

Spiraea japonica

oblong-lanceolate leaves up to 4 inches long and glaucous beneath. In *S. j. ovalifolia* the leaves are elliptic, the flowers white. Cultivated in North America since colonial times, *S. salicifolia* is native from Europe to Japan. Strictly erect, 4 to 6 feet tall, and densely-bushy, this has very short-stalked, toothed or double-toothed, hairless, lanceolate to oblong-lanceolate leaves up to 3 inches in length. Its ¼-inch-wide, rose-pink flowers, in crowded, elongated terminal panicles, are displayed in summer. This is hardy in New England.

Several hybrids of medium size are excellent. One of the most noteworthy, *S. arguta* has as parents *S. thunbergii* and *S. multiflora*. As the latter is itself a hybrid, the parentage of *S. arguta* involves three species. It is hardy through most of New England and in habit much resembles *S. thunbergii*, from which it differs in being taller and more vigorous, in having ovate to oblong-lanceolate leaves, and in blooming later in spring. Because of this, its flowers are not subject to damage by late frosts. Certainly *S. arguta* is one of the most free-blooming and handsome spireas. Its leaves, up to 1¾ inches long, are sharply- and sometimes doubly-toothed and, when mature, are without hairs. In many-flowered clusters, usually with a few leaves at their bases, the pure white blooms wreathe the arching stems. They have petals almost twice as long as the stamens.

A parent of the last, *S. multiflora* is a hybrid between *S. crenata* and *S. hypericifolia*. It has long, somewhat arching branches and obovate leaves toothed in their upper halves. The white flowers are in clusters, the lower ones only usually having short, leafy stalks. This kind attains a height of about 5 feet and is hardy in most of New England.

The vanhoutte spirea (*S. vanhouttei*) is one of the most popular and beautiful. With gracefully arching branches, in late spring smothered beneath clusters of pure white blooms, this hybrid attains a 5- or 6-foot height. Its parents are *S. cantoniensis* and *S. trilobata*. Its leaves are lozenge-shaped to obovate, coarsely-toothed in their upper halves, sometimes three-lobed, and without hairs. Their upper surfaces are dark green, beneath they are somewhat glaucous. They are up to 1½ inches long.

A hybrid between *S. douglasii* and *S. salicifolia*, variable *S. billiardii* has pointed, elliptic to oblong-elliptic leaves 2 to 3 inches long, sharply-toothed, and when young grayish-hairy on their undersides. Bright pink, its flowers are in slender, fluffy, spirelike panicles 4 to 8 inches long. Varieties are *S. b. alba*, with white flowers; *S. b. lenneana*, the leaves of which are lanceolate-elliptic to ovate; and *S. b. macrothyrsa*, with 2-inch-long broad-obovate leaves with green undersurfaces.

Spiraea vanhouttei (flowers)

Spiraea billiardii

Summer-blooming and pink-flowered, *S. margaritae* resulted from the intermingling of three species. It is a hybrid between *S. japonica* and *S. superba*, the latter a hybrid of *S. albiflora* and *S. corymbosa*. It blooms freely in high summer and sparsely later. About 5 feet tall, it has erect stems, downy when young, and elliptic-ovate to narrowly-elliptic leaves up to 3½ inches long by nearly one-half as wide. They are coarsely-double-toothed in their upper parts and are sometimes pubescent on the veins on their undersides. The small, bright pink flowers are in flat clusters 3 to 6 inches in diameter. This is one of the best summer-blooming spireas.

Tall spireas, normally exceeding 6 feet in height are available. In late spring *S. nipponica* and its variety *S. n. rotundifolia* bloom. Because of its larger blooms the latter is the more showy. Variety *S. n. tosaensis* has densely-clustered smaller flowers than the species. A rather rigid, spreading shrub, *S. nipponica*, native to Japan, has angled branches and is up to 8 feet tall. Its hairless leaves, oblanceolate to obovate, are ¾ inch to 1½ inches long with rounded, usually round-toothed apexes.

They are glaucous on their undersides. The clusters of many small, white blooms have leafy stalks, and stamens shorter than the petals. These kinds are hardy through most of New England.

Flowering later than the last, not coming into bloom until June, are three Chinese species, *S. wilsonii*, *S. henryi*, and *S. veitchii*, all hardy in southern New England. With the general aspect of the vanhoutte spirea (*S. vanhouttei*), but somewhat taller and blooming a little later, *S. wilsonii* attains a height of 7 feet. It has gracefully arching branches, pubescent when young and dullish purple, and ovate to obovate leaves ¾ inch to 2¼ inches long and sometimes toothed at their ends. They are hairy on both sides, dull green above and grayish-green beneath. In crowded clusters 1½ to 2 inches across, the white flowers have stamens and petals of approximately the same length. A closely similar species, the vigorous *S. henryi* is distinguished by the markedly pubescent branches of its flower clusters and its more spreading branches. Also, its leaves are somewhat bigger, less pubescent on their upper sides, and usually more conspicu-

Spiraea nipponica

Spiraea henryi

ously toothed at their apexes. Perhaps the tallest of the spireas, *S. veitchii,* attains a height of 12 feet. A vigorous grower, it has gracefully arched stems, on their younger parts slightly downy. The oblong to obovate, toothless leaves are hairless except, possibly, for a little down beneath. They are ¾ inch to 1½ inches long. The leafy stalks of the flower clusters, 1½ to 2½ inches across, are also downy. The stamens are longer than the petals. This is an elegant and handsome species.

The bridal wreath (*S. prunifolia*) enjoys a well-deserved popularity. Because of the botanical rule of priority the name *S. prunifolia* is correctly applied to the dou-

Spiraea prunifolia (flowers)

ble-flowered kind, and the genetic species, the single-flowered and horticulturally very inferior type, is *S. p. simpliciflora.* Only the first is worth considering for planting. It was introduced to America and Europe from Japan where, as in China, Korea, and Taiwan, the single-flowered species is native. Bridal wreath is hardy throughout most of New England. It becomes 8 or 9 feet tall by almost or quite as broad, and has many slender, arching branches. The young shoots are slightly pubescent. The leaves are elliptic to ovate, 1 inch to 2 inches long, and finely-toothed. They have lustrous upper sides and are pubescent beneath. The pure white blooms are nearly all double and are almost or quite

½ inch across. They are borne, before the leaves, in few-flowered, stalkless clusters. This is one of the very few spireas that provide some show of fall color. Its foliage turns orange before it drops.

The best tall summer-blooming spirea is **S. brachybotrys,** a hybrid between *S. canescens* and *S. douglasii* that grows to about 8 feet tall. It has quite bright pink flowers in stout, dense panicles, 1½ to 3½ inches long by about as wide, borne on leafy stems 3 inches to 1 foot long. Its arching branches are pubescent when young. The leaves are narrow-elliptic to oblongish and 1 inch to 1¾ inches long. They are toothed above their middles, slightly hairy above, and felted on their lower sides. The pink-flowered parent of the last mentioned, **S. douglasii** also blooms in high summer. Native from California to British Columbia, it is allied to, but taller than *S. menziesii.* It attains a height of 6 or 7 feet, spreads by suckers, and has rose-pink flowers in usually long and narrow panicles. The stamens are twice as long as the petals. The leaves are oblongish and often rather narrow, irregularly-toothed above their middles, and white-hairy on their undersides.

Tender in the north, the white-flowered parent of *S. brachybotrys* is **S. canescens.** This native of the Himalayas, up to 10 feet tall or taller, has arching branches, the younger

Spiraea canescens

parts of which are pubescent, and grayish-green, broad-ovate leaves up to ¾ inch long, round-toothed above their middles and pubescent to nearly hairless on their undersides. The dense flower clusters, 1½ to 2 inches in diameter, are produced profusely along the branches. The stamens are as long as or slightly longer than the petals.

Garden and Landscape Uses. Ease of cultivation and copious displays of flowers recommend spireas to gardeners and creators of landscapes. They are also inexpensive, grow rapidly under a wide variety of conditions, and are simple to propagate. Nor are they only useful outdoors; some can be easily forced in green-

houses to bloom in late winter. These shrubs are not notable for their foliage. In the main they are neutral in the landscape, neither especially attractive nor disturbing. Only in a very few cases do they assume fall coloring of interest, and then only to a mild degree. Spireas are without attractive fruits.

Because of their various sizes and blooming seasons spireas can serve a variety of purposes well. The low ones certainly have a place in rock gardens and similar intimate developments. Medium-sized kinds can be used to good effect in beds, borders, and foundation plantings, as lawn specimens, and for informal hedges as well. For the latter purpose and for screening, the tall growers can also be used to advantage. Their other uses are those suggested for medium-height ones, but, of course, they need more space to display themselves effectively and so generally are more suitable for extensive landscapes than for small home gardens. The kinds native to North America suggest themselves as being appropriate for native plant gardens and similar naturalistic developments.

Although rightful places can be found in most gardens for spireas, it is a mistake to plant too many. As a group they fail to bring definition and emphasis to the landscape. Except when in bloom, their effect is undistinguished. They are better foils than accents and, with few exceptions, cannot be rated as first-class or choice shrubs.

Spireas prefer fertile soils not lacking in moisture, but will settle for less. They stand city conditions surprisingly well. All need full sun. Unless they are planted to form a hedge, ample space should be allowed for their full development. A spirea that must be cut back frequently to accommodate to a limited space is not an object of beauty.

Cultivation. Cuttings often supply the most convenient way of increasing spireas. Both leafy summer cuttings of firm shoots and leafless hardwood cuttings taken in fall root with facility. Spireas also come readily from seed, but as the various kinds hybridize with some enthusiasm, results obtained from seeds collected from specimens growing near other kinds that bloom at the same time are likely to be an undistinguished and inferior hybrid swarm. Many spireas lend themselves to increase by removing suckers or even by dividing the plants when they are transplanted. Layering is an easy way of multiplying many kinds.

Pruning is one of the important routines in maintaining spireas in good condition. It varies according to kind. These shrubs fall into two groups, those that bloom early in the season from shoots formed the previous year and those that flower later on current season's shoots.

The former are pruned immediately after they are through blooming, the latter in late winter or very early spring. Pruning the first group, examples of which are *S. arguta, S. thunbergii, S. trichocarpa,* and *S. vanhouttei,* consists of cutting back or completely removing old flowering stems and thinning out new shoots if they threaten to crowd each other. The objectives are to allow plenty of light and air to reach strong, developing shoots that will bloom the following year, and to preserve the graceful, natural shapes of the shrubs. Kinds that flower on shoots of the current year, including *S. bumalda, S. douglasii, S. japonica,* and *S. tomentosa,* are pruned by cutting out all weak and crowded shoots and shortening those that remain. The extent to which they are shortened depends upon the height the plants are required to attain and the strength of the shoots. Generally thin stems are cut back more drastically than thick ones. If desired, they can be pruned to within a few inches of the ground.

For forcing into bloom in late winter and early spring in greenhouses, spireas that produce their flowers from shoots of the previous year are well adapted. Especially suitable are *S. arguta, S. thunbergii, S. trichocarpa,* and *S. vanhouttei.* For further information see Forcing.

Pests and Diseases. Pests that sometimes infest spireas are aphids, leaf rollers, and scale insects. They are sometimes infected with leaf spot diseases, powdery mildews, root rot, and fire blight.

SPIRAL FLAG. See Costus.

SPIRANTHES (Spi-ránthes)—Ladies' Tresses. This genus, for which the name *Ibidium* has been used, is of nearly cosmopolitan distribution. It does not occur in Central America, tropical South America, tropical Africa, or South Africa. It comprises twenty-five species of ground orchids of the orchid family ORCHIDACEAE. Its name, from the Greek *speira,* a coil, and *anthos,* a flower, refers to the usually twisted racemes of blooms.

Ladies' tresses have often clustered, fleshy or tuberous roots and slender, erect, branchless stems with terminal, more or less spirally-twisted racemes of mostly small flowers. The usually narrow leaves are mostly basal or are confined to the lower parts of the stems. Above the leaves are a few stem-sheathing bracts. The flowers are without spurs. The sepals and petals are essentially similar, with the petals joined to the upper sepal or to all three sepals to form a hood over the lip and column. The portion of the oblong to ovate lip beyond its middle bends downward. The margins of its lower part curve upward around the column. At its base are two small callosities (thickenings of the tissues).

Spiranthes cernua

Nodding ladies' tresses (**Spiranthes cernua** grows in fields, meadows, and open woodlands in moist, acid soils from Newfoundland to Minnesota, Florida, and Texas. From 9 inches to 3 feet tall or taller, it usually has basal as well as stem leaves, narrowly-oblanceolate and up to 1 foot in length. Its fragrant, white flowers, in three or sometimes two longitudinal rows, are crowded in racemes 1½ to 6 inches long. They have petals joined with the upper sepal and a lip with two conspicuous, projecting, rounded callosities up to ½ inch long. An especially robust variety with larger blooms and generally with leaves extending up the stems is *S. c. odorata.*

Also with flowers in two or three rows, *S. romanzoffiana* and *S. lucida* differ from nodding ladies' tresses in the callosities of their flowers being inconspicuous and not projecting. Wild in meadows, swamps, and thickets from Labrador to Alaska, Pennsylvania, and California, and in Ireland and Scotland, thickish-stemmed **S. romanzoffiana,** up to 1½ feet tall and with or without basal foliage, inhabits swamps, bogs, and other wetlands. Its leaves are linear to narrowly-spatula-shaped and 4 to 8 inches long. White or cream-colored, the flowers have all their sepals and petals joined to form a hood. The strongly down-turned, ovate lip, narrowed to a waist above its middle, is under ½ inch long. From the last, **S. lucida** differs in the lateral sepals of its blooms being separate from the other sepals and petals and in their yellow-centered lips not being constricted. It is up to 10 inches tall and has narrowly-oblanceolate basal leaves up to 6 inches long, with much smaller ones on the stems. The racemes are ¾ inch to 2 inches long or sometimes longer. This inhabits moist and wet soils, often of limestone character, from Nova Scotia to Wisconsin, Virginia, and Missouri.

Slender ladies' tresses (**S. gracilis**) has very slender stems and racemes, 8 inches to 2½ feet tall, with a single spiraled row of ¼-inch-long white flowers with a bright green area at the center of the lip. Usually

Spiranthes lucida

wilted or absent at flowering time, the ovate to oblong leaves are basal and up to 2 inches long. This orchid is an inhabitant of dry or damp, often sterile soil in woods and thickets from Nova Scotia to Minnesota, Florida, and Texas. From it, **S. longilabris** differs in its flowers, nearly ½ inch long, being in one-sided or very slightly spiraled racemes. Up to 1½ feet tall, this inhabits moist soils from North Carolina to Florida, and Louisiana.

Native to Brazil and the West Indies, variable **S. elata,** 1 foot to 2 feet tall, has

Spiranthes elata

pointed, elliptic to elliptic-oblong, stalked leaves up to 9 inches long, often attractively variegated with longitudinal silvery bands. Its slender-stalked, one-sided, erect racemes, which much overtop the foliage, are of many greenish-white or whitish, ¼- to ½-inch-long flowers, each with a blunt, linear lip. Also native to Brazil, **S. bracteosa** has a basal rosette of spreading, oblong-ovate leaves from the center of which arises an erect flower spike with conspicuous scarlet bracts and scarlet flowers. Tropical American **S. speciosa** (syn. *Stenorrhynchus speciosus*) has orbicular-ovate to obovate or oblanceolate, spreading basal leaves up to 8 inches long, decorated with

Spiranthes bracteosa

Spiranthes speciosa

grayish blotches or spots. Its bright red to purple-red flowers are in bracted spikes 3 to 4 inches long that terminate erect stalks 1 foot to 1½ feet long. Native to Guate-

Spiranthes cerina

mala, *S. cerina* blooms when without leaves. Its pinkish flowering stalks arise from a cluster of tuberous roots. They are erect, fuzzy, and 1 foot to 1½ feet long. The yellow-brown to greenish-yellow flowers have sepals and petals over 1 inch long, streaked at their tips with green veins.

Garden and Landscape Uses and Cultivation. Ladies' tresses are appropriate for native plant gardens, naturalistic landscapes, and rock gardens where environments approximating those under which they grow in the wild prevail. Some, including *S. cernua odorata* and *S. elata*, succeed as permanent plants in greenhouses, accommodated in pots in soils similar to those in which they grow in the wild, kept always moist. Propagation is by division. For further information see Orchids.

SPIREA. This is the common name for members of the genus *Spiraea* and is also sometimes applied to those of the genus *Astilbe*. For blue-spirea see Caryopteris, for false-spirea see Sorbaria, and for rock-spirea see *Holodiscus discolor*.

SPIRODELA (Spiro-déla). From the closely related duckweeds (*Lemna*), the six species of *Spirodela* differ in that each thallus (plant body not consisting of separate stems and leaves) has three or more roots extending downward from its underside. Spirodelas are floating aquatics belonging in the duckweed family LEMNACEAE, and hence, strange as it may seem, they are fairly close relatives of the arum family ARACEAE. The genus occurs in temperate and tropical America and much of the Old World. Its name, alluding to its conspicuous roots, is derived from the Greek *speira*, a cord, and *delos*, evident.

The common American species is *S. polyrhiza*. This has an ovate to obovate thallus, usually not over ⅓ inch across and purple-red on its underside, and four to nine roots. There are two reproductive pouches on the margins of the thallus, but flowers, similar to those of *Lemna*, are rare. Increase is mostly by offsets.

Garden Uses and Cultivation. These are identical with those of *Lemna*.

SPIRONEMA. See Callisia, and Hadrodemas.

SPITTLEBUGS. Also called froghoppers, these little, soft-bodied insects are conspicuous in their young (nymph) stage because of the frothy, spittle-like masses with which they cover themselves. This they do by exuding a "soapy" liquid, pumping air into it, and using their tails to whip it into foam. They feed by sucking the juices of the plants on which they live. After molting for the final time, they emerge looking and behaving much like leafhoppers.

Most sorts of spittlebugs are relatively harmless, but some are less so. A common sort may infest chrysanthemums, strawberries, and a fairly wide range of other garden plants, while others live on hollies and pines. Recommended controls are to spray forcibly with malathion or other contact insecticides.

SPLEENWORT. See Asplenium, and Athyrium.

SPONDIAS (Spón-dias) — Mombin, Hog-Plum, Spanish-Plum, Ambarella or Otaheite-Apple. This group of ten to twelve trees contains a few cultivated for their edible fruits. They are members of the cashew family ANACARDIACEAE, which means that, like their relatives the cashew nut and mango, they are botanically close to sumac and poison-ivy. The genus is widely distributed in the wild in the tropics. The cultivated kinds are common in many warm countries. The name is an ancient Greek one used by Theophrastus for the plum; the fruits of *Spondias* resemble those of plums.

Members of this genus have their alternate, usually pinnate leaves, with an odd number of leaflets, usually clustered toward the branch ends. In one species the leaves are undivided and in another are twice-pinnate. Their small, short-stalked flowers are unisexual or bisexual, each tree bearing male, female, and bisexual blooms. They have a calyx cleft in four or five parts, the same number of spreading petals, and usually the same number of styles. There are eight to ten stamens. The fruits are drupes.

The yellow mombin or hog-plum (*S. mombin* syn. *S. lutea*), an elegant tree up to 60 feet in height, has leaves, 1½ feet long or longer, with seven to twenty-one glossy leaflets with sixteen to twenty pairs of almost parallel, straight lateral veins, mostly forking at their ends, running from the midrib to a connecting vein that parallels the margin. Individual leaflets are mostly elliptic, sometimes lanceolate or ovate, and 3 to 5 inches long. The fragrant, yellowish flowers, in showy termi-

Spondias mombin (fruits)

nal panicles 6 inches to 1 foot long, are succeeded by thin-skinned, yellow, ovoid fruits, ¾ inch to 2 inches long, that contain a large angular seed surrounded by a thin layer of juicy, rather acid flesh that has a slight flavor of turpentine. The eating quality of the fruit varies considerably on different trees. The yellow mombin is native from Florida to Mexico and Brazil, and in the West Indies.

The purple or red mombin or Spanish-plum (*S. purpurea*) is indigenous to tropical America. Attaining a height of about 30 feet, it branches low and has a spreading head. Its leaves, up to 1 foot long, consist of seven to twenty-three lanceolate, elliptic, or obovate leaflets, 1 inch to 2 inches long. There are six to ten lateral veins to each leaflet and these branch near their ends and join a connecting vein that borders the margin of the leaflet. The greenish to purplish flowers are in clusters 2 to 4 inches long in the leaf axils. Red, or yellow in the variety *S. p. lutea*, the fruits are nearly spherical, obovoid, or ellipsoid and 1 inch to 2 inches long. They contain a large seed and have somewhat the flavor of plums.

The ambarella, Otaheite-apple, or Vi (*S. cytherea* syn. *S. dulcis*) is a semideciduous to deciduous native of the Society Islands believed to have been introduced to Jamaica by Captain Bligh of the *Bounty*. It attains a height of 60 feet and is graceful. It forms a spreading crown that has brittle twigs and glossy bright green leaves, 8 inches to 2½ feet in length, of eleven to twenty-three leaflets. Individual leaflets are pointed oval-oblong and have eighteen to twenty-two pairs of side veins that do not branch at their ends; they are 2½ to 3½ inches long. The flowers, in terminal panicles, are whitish. They are succeeded by orange-yellow or amber-colored fruits with firm, sweet to acid, slightly turpentiny, juicy flesh with fibers projecting into it from the large stone in the manner of some mangoes. The fruits are obovoid or ellipsoid, 1 inch to 3 inches long, and slightly ill-smelling. They contain one to five seeds.

Two other kinds, the imbú (*S. tuberosa*), a tuberous-rooted species of Brazil, and the amra (*S. pinnata*), of tropical Asia, are occasionally cultivated. Both are small trees. The former has leaves with five to nine toothless, ovate leaflets, whereas the leaves of the latter are 1 foot to 1¼ feet long and have five to seven ovate leaflets. The fruits of the imbú are pale yellow and about 1½ inches long, those of the amra are yellow-green and 1½ to 2½ inches long.

Garden and Landscape Uses. As fruit trees, members of this genus are not of primary importance. Considerable variation in the quality of the fruits exists within each species and only superior strains should be propagated and planted if their production for eating is important. The most palatable species is the purple mombin or Spanish-plum, the best fruits of which are agreeably flavored. They are eaten raw, cooked, and in jellies and drinks. The fruits of the yellow mombin or hog-plum are used in similar ways. The fruits of the imbú and amra are scarcely known in the United States. As ornamental landscape subjects, all of the kinds mentioned have some value for planting in essentially frost-free climates. They are attractive as single specimens and the yellow mombin makes good hedges and shelter belts. The imbú is especially well suited to dry climates.

Cultivation. Members of this genus grow satisfactorily in a wide variety of soils and are very easily propagated by seed and by cuttings, which root satisfactorily even if they consist of quite large pieces of branch.

SPORE. A spore is a tiny, often microscopic, usually one-celled, reproductive body of plants considered to be more primitive than seed plants. Many plant diseases are spread by spores of fungi that cause them. In horticultural practice, ferns are often raised from spores.

SPORT. See Mutant or Sport.

SPOTTED. This word forms parts of the common names of these plants: spotted cowbane (*Cicuta maculata*), spotted-laurel (*Aucuba japonica variegata*), and spotted-wintergreen (*Chimaphila maculata*).

SPRAGUEA. See Calyptridium.

SPRAYS and SPRAYING. Sprays, used chiefly to control diseases, pests, and weeds, use water, to which sometimes a spreader is added to improve its wetting effectiveness, or some other liquid, as in aerosols, as vehicles to deposit insecticides, miticides, fungicides, weed killers, and sometimes other materials on plants. Under most conditions they are preferred to dry dusts used for similar purposes.

Equipment for applying water-based sprays ranges from atomizers that hold no more than a pint and those of the flit-gun type, to power-driven machines that discharge streams of liquid under high pressure to the tops of tall trees. Power equipment includes also mist sprayers that break the liquid into tiny droplets and blow them in a broad, foglike stream to the plants.

Aerosols, or aerosol bombs as they are often called, are nonreusable canisters that contain the material to be applied as a gas, pressurized to a liquid state. Convenient to hold in one's hand, the canisters release a very fine mist when a button is pressed. Hold aerosols 1 foot to 1½ feet away from the plants. Closer application may cause injury resulting from a freezing effect of the spray.

Sprayers appropriate for home gardens include hand-held ones suitable for use indoors and selective spot spraying outdoors, as well as larger capacity, more sophisticated types generally adequate for all outdoor use except for treating tall vines and trees. Choose equipment best suited to the size of the garden and the physique of the user. A knapsack sprayer holding only a couple of gallons, and the larger ones accommodate five or six, can be burdensome to one not accustomed to such backpacking.

The chief types of hand-pumped sprayers, besides the one-operator knapsacks just mentioned, include one-person slide-pump or trombone models (these names allude to the action needed to operate them) and barrel or wheelbarrow sprayers that function best with two operators, one to pump, the other to direct the spray.

Spray guns operated by a stream of water have a jar to hold concentrated spray. After it is filled, the jar is screwed onto the gun, to which a hose is then connected. When

Small atomizer sprayers are useful when treating a few plants

Power sprays are used for tall trees and in extensive landscapes

the water is turned on, the concentrate is diluted and forcibly propelled as a spray. Guns fitted with a shutoff valve are decidedly superior to those without. It is also advantageous if the nozzle is a short pipe equipped at its end with a deflector that makes it easier to direct the spray to the underside of foliage.

Power sprayers of small to medium size (capacity five to fifty gallons) are convenient for gardens big enough to warrant their cost. Many designs are available, some with gasoline engines, others operated by an electric motor. The desirability of large wheels and easy maneuverability should be considered when purchasing these.

Quality of equipment is important. The cheapest is rarely satisfactory and often, over the long run, not the least expensive. Because they do not rust, sprayers with parts of brass, copper, or stainless steel are superior to those made with galvanized steel.

Good equipment deserves good care. Rinse sprayers after each use by pumping two or three changes of clean water through them, and a couple of times a year do a more thorough job by, where design permits, taking apart the pump and cleaning it, the extention tubes, the shutoff valve, and the strainers thoroughly. Oil parts that need this attention and replace any worn washers, gaskets, or hoses. With power sprayers follow the manufacturer's direction regarding operation, lubrication, and other maintenance.

What to spray with and when depends upon where you garden, what you grow, and a great many other variables. But do not spray haphazardly. If you are uninformed find out. Likely sources of information are Cooperative Extension Agents, botanic gardens, local nurserymen, experienced gardeners, up-to-date publications of the federal and state governments, and books and articles by specialists.

Use sprays only at recommended dilutions, which may vary for different kinds of plants and for use on the same kinds at different times of the year. Directions are usually given on packages of commercial spray materials. Pay particular attention to compatibilities and incompatibilities. Materials that can be mixed and applied together are compatible, those that cannot, and there are many, are incompatible. There is always an element of danger, no matter how well the equipment is cleaned, in spraying cherished plants with a sprayer previously used for weed killer. It is much wiser to have separate equipment for these purposes, the weed killer sprayer plainly marked.

Timeliness of application is often critical. In some cases, as with black spot of roses, the spray prevents rather than cures, and therefore must cover the foliage and be renewed as often as necessary

before symptoms develop. Many pests are vulnerable for very brief periods only. With some it is useless to spray until the pests are in evidence. And so it goes; effective spraying is based on sound knowledge.

Choose so far as possible calm days, certainly not gusty or windy ones, for spraying. Some sprays, notably dormant oils, may cause harm if shortly after application the temperature drops to freezing or below. Certain others, including those based on sulfur, are harmful if applied when the temperature is above 85°F. Read the directions that come with commercial sprays carefully. Precautions are usually spelled out.

Try to cover all parts of the plant, giving special attention to the undersides of foliage and difficult-to-reach parts, with an even coating of spray, without wasting the spray by causing an excessive amount to drip off. To do this you must keep the spray nozzle moving and constantly watch what you are doing.

SPREADER. See Sprays and Spraying.

SPREKELIA (Sprek-èlia) — Jacobean-Lily or St.-James-Lily or Aztec-Lily. Despite its common names, the only species of *Sprekelia* is not a lily and does not belong in the lily family. A member of the amaryllis family AMARYLLIDACEAE, and a native of Mexico and Guatemala, it has a name that commemorates J. H. Sprekelsen, a German, who first sent specimens of it to the great Swedish botanist Linnaeus. He died in 1764.

A tender bulb plant, the Jacobean-lily, St.-James-lily, or Aztec-lily (*S. formosissima*) is easy to grow and handsome in bloom. It has a globose bulb about 2 inches in diameter and several narrow, deciduous leaves, usually in evidence when the plant is in bloom. The leafless, hollow flower stalks terminate in a solitary, curious, spidery flower that looks like an asymmetrical, narrow-petaled amaryllis

Sprekelia formosissima

(*Hippeastrum*). The solitary, very asymmetrical blooms distinguish *Sprekelia* from *Hippeastrum*. Their six-petaled flowers are typically deep crimson. The placement and color of the petals suggest the cross embroidered on the cloaks of the Knights of St. James of Calatrova and thus, are reason for the name St.-James-lily. The flowers are 3 to 4 inches long. They are without perianth tubes, but the basal parts of the three lower perianth segments (petals), although completely separate, curl to form a short cylinder. The other petals are nearly or quite upright. The broadest, upper one may be 1 inch wide. The six stamens protrude from the throat of the bloom, but are shorter than the three-branched stigma. The top-shaped ovary is six-angled. The fruits are capsules containing flat, winged, black seeds.

Garden and Landscape Uses. In the south, the Jacobean-lily is a fine permanent plant for outdoor beds and borders and for rock gardens. It is not hardy in the north. It is also well worth growing in pots in greenhouses and window gardens.

Cultivation. Outdoors this bulb does well planted with its apex about 2 inches below the surface in well-drained soil in sunny locations. It blooms in summer. Indoors it flowers more commonly in late winter or spring. The bulbs may be planted singly in pots about 4 inches in diameter or accommodated three together in a 6-inch container. Good drainage and a fertile, sandy, loamy soil are needed. The bulbs are potted so that their necks stick out a little way from the soil surface. Winter or early spring, before new growth begins, is the time to pot. Established bulbs need repotting at intervals of four or five years only. Watering, both of newly potted and older established bulbs, is begun as soon as new growth starts and is increased as the leaves become larger. Throughout the entire period when foliage is in evidence, water is given freely, but when the leaves, by beginning to yellow preparatory to dying down, signal the approach of the winter dormant season, watering should be gradually reduced and finally stopped. During the winter the soil is kept quite dry and the plants kept where a temperature of 45° to 50°F is maintained. Specimens that have filled their pots with roots should be given weekly applications of dilute liquid fertilizer throughout their period of active growth. Propagation is usually by offsets, but bulb cuttings and seed are also satisfactory methods of increase.

SPRIGS. Small pieces of stolons with roots and leafy shoots attached of certain grasses used for planting lawns are called sprigs. Bermuda, carpet, centipede, and St. Augustine lawns are often established by sprigging. See Lawns, Their Making and Renovation.

SPRING. The word spring forms parts of the common names of these plants: spring beauty (*Claytonia virginica*), spring gold (*Lomatium utriculatum*), spring snowflake (*Leucojum vernum*), spring starflower (*Ipheion uniflorum*), and spring vetchling (*Lathyrus vernus*).

SPRINGTAILS. Tiny, wingless, primitive insects that congregate in damp places, springtails have a hinged tail that enables them to jump like fleas when disturbed. At most, they are about ¹⁄₁₆ inch long. They occur in greenhouses and not infrequently inhabit the soil of houseplants where they may be found active on the surface following watering. They do little or no damage to sizable plants, but can inflict severe injury by chewing delicate seedlings near the soil line. Control may be had by drenching the soil and places where they congregate with a contact insecticide. Another procedure is to soak the soil with water to which Clorox, at the rate of one tablespoonful to a quart of water, has been added.

SPROUTS. See Brussels Sprouts.

SPRUCE. See Picea. Hemlock-spruce is a name used in the British Isles for the genus *Tsuga.*

SPUR. Short lateral branches of trees, shrubs, and woody vines that have closely spaced nodes and elongate very little in any one growing season are called spurs. Flowers, followed by fruits, often develop from them. Natural spurs are characteristic of apples, ginkgoes, pears, and some other plants.

Artificial spurs can be induced in some plants by pruning. This is common practice when apples and pears are trained as espaliers and with vinifera grapes in greenhouses. The same procedure can also be applied to wisterias and some other woody plants. Such spurs are developed by cutting a one-year-old side shoot back to within an inch or less of its base and,

in summer, pruning secondary shoots that arise following this back to within five or six leaves of their bases. The next spring the secondary shoots are pruned to within an inch or less of their bases and the procedure is repeated yearly.

Another use of spur is as the name of a hollow, projecting appendage of the flowers of some plants. Those of columbines, delphiniums, and many orchids are good examples.

SPURGE. See Euphorbia. The Alleghany-spurge is *Pachysandra procumbens*, the Japanese-spurge is *Pachysandra terminalis*, the spurge-laurel is *Daphne laureola*, and the spurge-olive is *Cneorum.*

SPYRIDIUM (Spy-rídium). The name of this genus of thirty species of Australian and Tasmanian shrubs of the buckthorn family RHAMNACEAE alludes to the shape of the calyx. It derives from the Greek *spyris*, a basket, and *eidos*, a resemblance. Spyridiums are hardy only where little or no frost occurs. Downy or hairy, they have alternate, generally small leaves, and little, stalkless flowers clustered in heads surrounded by persistent, dry, small bracts. Each bloom has its parts in fives. The fruits are small capsules.

Evergreen and 6 to 8 feet tall, *Spyridium globulosum*, a native of western Australia, is planted as an ornamental in California and other mild-climate areas where dryish summers prevail. This has ovate, broad-elliptic, or obovate, short-stalked leaves, 1 inch to nearly 2 inches long by ½ to ¾ inch wide, with their undersides, like the young shoots, flower stalks, and calyxes, densely-white-felted. The upper surfaces are green and hairless. Abundant, the tight clusters of white flowers are rounded and about 1 inch across. They are in panicles at the branch ends and on short shoots from the leaf axils.

Garden and Landscape Uses and Cultivation. The interesting and attractive species described above is worth planting for its appearance and to add variety. It grows satisfactorily in ordinary soils, and may be increased by seed, and by cuttings under mist or in a greenhouse propagating bench. The only pruning ordinarily needed is any required to contain it to size or to keep it shapely.

SQUASH. The vegetable garden and field crops called squashes (this an adaptation of an American Indian name) belong in *Cucurbita*, of the gourd family CUCURBITACEAE. Their kinds are referable to four species, but not all of the varieties of any of these are squashes, some are pumpkins and some are gourds grown for ornament. Because no clear botanical distinction exists between squashes and pumpkins, common usage determines the application of these names. In general pumpkins are

sorts with large, usually more or less spherical fruits, orange when ripe, that when fully mature are used for making pies and jack-o'-lanterns and as stock feed. The seeds of some varieties are eaten. Squashes have fruits of various shapes and colors that are chiefly employed as human food. The flowers are also cooked and eaten. They are classed as summer (and early autumn) squashes and winter squashes. The fruits of the first, practically all varieties of *C. pepo*, are eaten well before they attain full maturity and before their skins harden. The fruits of winter squashes, varieties of *C. pepo*, *C. mixta*, *C. maxima*, and *C. moschata*, are allowed to mature on the vine and then are often stored for long periods before eating.

Annuals that revel in warm weather, sunny locations, and fertile, well-drained soil, squashes are vigorous growers and heavy croppers. Except where the growing season is so short that for satisfactory results an early start indoors is advisable, the usual procedure is to sow the seeds directly outdoors in spring as soon as there is no longer danger of frost and the weather is warm and settled, or sow about two weeks earlier under hotcaps or similar protection. Sow bush varieties (those without long, vining stems) in hills 3 to 4 feet apart in rows 4 to 6 feet asunder. Hills for running or vining varieties need to be 3 to 4 feet apart, with 8 to 10 feet between rows of hills. Ready the hills, which unless the soil is clayey or subsurface drainage is poor need not be raised above the surrounding level, by digging into each a bushel or two of rich compost or rotted manure and about half a pound of a 5-10-5 fertilizer or its equivalent in another formulation. Plant six to ten seeds 3 to 4 inches apart and 1 inch deep in each hill.

Alternatively, to have plants to set out from pots or other containers as soon as the weather is sufficiently warm, sow in a greenhouse or other suitable place indoors where a temperature of 60 to 70°F can be maintained. Make this sowing about three weeks before you expect to set the plants

Spurs on an apple

A healthy bush squash

in the garden. Allow three plants to each hill and take great care not to disturb their roots at planting time.

Subsequent care is minimal. Thin out the seedlings before they crowd, leaving only three in each hill. A black plastic mulch spread over the ground around the plants greatly reduces the need for weeding. If instead of a mulch you rely on cultivation to keep down weeds, be careful not to stir the soil to a depth of more than 1 inch. Generous watering is needed if the weather is dry. If practicable, do this without wetting the foliage. A light application of a readily available nitrogenous fertilizer twice during the growing season is likely to be helpful.

Harvest summer squashes while they are young, small, and tender regularly throughout the season before they are 8 inches long or, the 'Patty Pan' sort, more than 3 or 4 inches in diameter. If allowed to become too big, summer squashes toughen and become less palatable. Without subjecting them to frost, let winter squashes become thoroughly ripe before harvesting. Their rinds should be tough enough to strongly resist a thumb nail being pressed into them. If the fruits are to be stored, handle them to prevent bruising, leave a short piece of stalk attached, and put them in a dry, airy, dark or dimly-lighted place where the temperature is 50 to 60°F. Some authorities recommend storing varieties, except 'Table Queen', for the first two to three weeks in a temperature of 70 to 80°F. Immature fruits or those that have been bruised do not store satisfactorily.

Popular summer squashes are 'Cocozelle', 'Early Prolific Straightneck', 'Early White Bush Scallop', 'Golden Summer Crookneck', 'Patty Pan', and 'Zucchini'. Winter squashes include 'Banana', 'Blue Hubbard', 'Buttercup', 'Butternut', 'Hercules', 'Hubbard', and 'Table Queen'.

Pests, including aphids, borers, squash bugs, and striped cucumber beetle, are controllable with rotenone or a general purpose vegetable garden insecticide. Mildew is the most prevalent disease. To limit it, avoid wetting the foliage when water-

Popular varieties of squash: (a) 'Golden Summer Crookneck'

(b) 'Patty Pan'

(c) 'Zucchini'

ing and, if necessary, use an appropriate dust or spray. Other diseases include bacterial wilt and mosaic virus disease, neither of which have effective cures. Prompt removal of affected plants is important.

SQUAW. This word is employed in the common names of these plants: squaw-apple (*Peraphyllum ramosissimum*) squaw-berry (*Mitchella repens*), squaw-bush (*Viburnum trilobum*), squaw-cabbage (*Caulanthus inflatus*), squaw carpet (*Ceanothus prostratus*), squaw-grass (*Xerophyllum tenax*), and squaw-root (*Caulophyllum thalictroides, Hedeoma, Perideridia gairdneri*).

SQUILL. This is a common name for *Scilla* and *Urginea*. The striped-squill is *Puschkinia scilloides*.

SQUIRREL-CORN is *Dicentra canadensis.*

SQUIRRELS. These small animals are often nuisances in gardens. They sometimes destroy the young fruits of apples, pears, and peaches by feasting upon their seeds, and they have a considerable appetite for sweet corn as well as for nuts as filberts, tropical-almonds, and walnuts. Trapping or shooting are the only practicable controls.

SQUIRREL'S FOOT FERN is *Davallia mariesii.*

SQUIRTING-CUCUMBER is *Ecballium elaterium.*

ST. The abbreviation for saint forms parts of the names of these plants; marsh-St.-John's-wort (*Triadenum*), St.-Andrew's-cross (*Hypericum hypericoides*), St. Augustine grass (*Stenotaphrum secundatum*), St.-Bernard's-lily (*Anthericum liliago*), St.-Bruno's-lily (*Paradisea liliastrum*), St.-Catherine's-lace (*Eriogonum giganteum*), St.-Dabeoc's-heath (*Daboecia*), St.-James-lily (*Sprekelia*), St.-James-trefoil (*Lotus jacobaeus*), St.-John's-bread (*Ceratonia siliqua*), St.-John's-lily (*Crinum asiaticum sinicum*), St.-John's-wort (*Hypericum*), St.-Joseph's-lily (*Cybistetes longifolia* and *Hippeastrum johnsonii*), St. Martin's flower (*Alstroemeria ligtu*), St.-Mary's-thistle (*Silybum marianum*), St. Patrick's cabbage (a common name for *Saxifraga umbrosa* and *S. urbium*), St.-Peter's-wort (*Hypericum stans*), and St. Thomas tree (*Bauhinia tomentosa*).

STACHYS (Stàch-ys)—Woundwort, Hedge-Nettle, Betony, Lamb's Ears, Chinese Artichoke or Japanese Artichoke or Crosnes or Knotroot. Pronounced stak-is, the genus *Stachys*, of the mint family LABIATAE, contains some 300 species, natives of chiefly temperate and warm-temperate regions of most parts of the world, except Australia and New Zealand, and with a few kinds in mountains in the tropics. The name, an ancient Greek one used by Dioscorides, comes from *stachys*, a spike, and alludes to the arrangement of the blooms. Some American species, most not sufficiently attractive to be admitted as garden plants, are called hedge-nettles.

Woundworts are annuals, herbaceous perennials, or rarely shrubs, commonly hairy. They have opposite, toothed or toothless leaves that extend upward into the flowering spikes or are replaced there by smaller ones or bracts. The stalkless or short-stalked, asymmetrical flowers are in whorls (tiers) of two to many from the axils of the leaves or the bracts of terminal spikes. They are white, yellow, pink, red, or purplish. Each has a tubular-bell-shaped, rarely two-lipped, five-toothed calyx, and a strongly-two-lipped corolla with a cylindrical tube, an erect, usually arched and concave upper lip that may or may not be notched at its apex, and a spreading or down-pointing, three-lobed lower lip. There are four stamens in pairs of nearly equal lengths, one style, and two stigmas. The fruits are of four seedlike nutlets.

Handsome in bloom, *S. grandiflora* (syns. *S. macrantha, Betonica grandiflora*) is a native of Asia Minor. From 1 foot to 2 feet tall, it has erect stems and broadly-heart-shaped, wrinkled-surfaced, hairy leaves, the lower stalked, the upper stalkless. The rosy-purple, hairless flowers, 1 inch or so long, are in whorls of many. The upper tiers form a fairly dense spike, the lower ones are more distantly spaced with portions of stem showing between them. Variety *S. g. rosea* has pink blooms; those of

Stachys grandiflora

Stachys byzantina

Stachys citrina

S. g. *superba*, rich purple-violet; those of *S. g. violacea*, violet; and those of *S. g. alba*, white.

Betony (**S. officinalis** syn. *Betonica officinalis*), of Europe and 10 inches to 3½ feet

Stachys officinalis

Stachys byzantina (foliage)

tall, has erect stems, and stalked, coarsely-toothed, blunt, chiefly oblong-heart-shaped leaves 1 inch to 4 inches in length. The stem leaves are few and much narrower than the basal ones. Those immediately beneath the flowers may be stalkless. The reddish-purple blooms, in dense spikes 1 inch to 3 inches long, have about ¾-inch-long corollas that protrude conspicuously from the calyxes. An especially fine dwarf variety, about 9 inches high, with pure white flowers, is cultivated as *S. o. alba*.

Lamb's ears (*S. byzantina* syns. *S. lanata*, *S. olympica*) is admired for its beautiful, densely-softly-white-hairy stems and foliage rather than for its not especially showy spikes of bloom. Native from the Caucasus to Iran and one of the most popular kinds, this spreads rather slowly. It has stalked, oblong-elliptic to lanceolate, inconspicuously round-toothed, wrinkled-

surfaced leaves with blades about 3 to 4 inches long. From 9 inches to 1½ feet tall or sometimes taller, the flower stems have leaves similar to, but smaller than the basal ones, and shorter-stalked or, the uppermost, stalkless. Only the rosy-purple, ½-inch-long corollas of the flowers project beyond the thick matted white hairs that clothe the stems and bracts of the flower spikes. Variety *S. b.* 'Silver Carpet' does not produce flower spikes.

Gardeners who expect all plants with *alpina* as part of their names to be low and suitable for rock gardens are likely to be disappointed with *S. alpina* because this native of Europe has erect stems 4 to 6 feet tall or taller. Its leaves are coarsely-toothed, the lower ones long-stalked and ovate to ovate-oblong, the upper ones narrower. The rosy-purple flowers are in distantly-spaced tiers that furnish the upper parts of the stems for long distances.

Other kinds cultivated for ornament include the following: Native from Oregon to British Columbia, *S. ciliata* is a hairy to nearly hairless perennial 3 to 4 feet tall. It has stalked, toothed leaves, heart-shaped or ovate, with a heart-shaped base, up to 3½ inches long. The ¾-inch-long, reddish-purple flowers are in whorls (circles) of few. Sulfur-yellow blooms in small heads, the lowermost flowers in interrupted tiers, are borne by beautiful *S. citrina*, of Greece. This

is a spreading subshrub with hairy, sage-green, blunt, broad-elliptic, long-stalked leaves, minutely-round-toothed at their margins and 1 inch to 1½ inches long. Brilliant scarlet flowers, ¾ to 1 inch long or slightly longer and protruding far from their calyxes, are borne in loosely tiered spikes by softly-hairy, salvia-like *S. coccinea*, native to Texas and Arizona. From 6 inches to 2 feet in height, this has ovate-lanceolate to triangular, coarsely-round-toothed leaves. A carpeting or mat-forming species 3 to 6 inches tall, *S. corsica*, a native of damp soils in the mountains of Corsica and Sardinia and sparingly-hairy, has stalked, broadly-ovate to nearly heart-shaped, toothed, blunt leaves up to ½ inch long. Its white to purple, solitary or paired flowers are about as long. This, a short-lived perennial, is usually most satisfactory when treated as an annual. Up to 1 foot tall, *S. discolor*, of the Caucasus, has in gardens been misnamed *S. nivea*. Attractive, it is woody at the base and has stalked, oblong-lanceolate, wrinkled-surfaced, round-toothed leaves, 1 inch to 1½ inches long and white-woolly beneath. Its showy, flesh-colored to yellowish-white or white flowers have corollas twice as long as the calyxes. They are in crowded spikes up to 2 inches long. European, North African, and Asian *S. germanica* is a variable, woolly-hairy sort 1 foot to 4 feet high.

Stachys discolor

It has stalked, blunt or pointed, toothed, lanceolate to ovate-lanceolate leaves, up to 4½ inches long, with heart-shaped bases. Their upper surfaces are green, their undersides gray-hairy. The flowers, in separated whorls (tiers), are pink to purple and ½ to ¾ inch long. A subshrub of Asia Minor 1 foot to 1½ feet tall, **S. lavandulaefolia** spreads by underground runners and has gray-hairy, oblong-lanceolate, toothless basal leaves, the upper ones stalkless and ovate-lanceolate. Its rose-purple blooms in whorls of two to six are in very hairy spikes. **S. saxicola** is an attractive native of Morocco, where it occurs among limestone rocks. A lax, subshrubby perennial up to 1 foot or so tall, its stems and leaves are densely-clothed with soft, white hairs. The long-stalked leaves have round-toothed, broad-heart-shaped blades 1 inch to 1½ inches long or perhaps sometimes longer. The flowers are white.

Stachys saxicola

The Chinese or Japanese artichoke, crosnes, or knotroot (**S. affinis** syns **S. sieboldii**, **S. tuberifera**) may be sometimes cultivated as a novelty vegetable for its edible tubers. A native of China and cultivated there, in Japan, and to some extent in Europe, this is a herbaceous perennial 1 foot to 1½ feet tall. It has rough-surfaced, ovate leaves and, at least in cultivated plants, rarely produced spikes of pink or white flowers. Its tubers are slender, knobby, and white.

Garden and Landscape Uses. Stachyses, with the exception of the Chinese or Japanese artichoke, are cultivated as ornamentals. Those of low stature, such as lamb's ears and *S. citrina*, find favor as edgings and for rock gardens, the taller ones in flower beds and borders. Some, notably *S. grandiflora*, are useful for cut flowers. All the kinds described above are perennials and most are hardy in the north, but the precise degree of hardiness of all kinds is not adequately recorded and it is certain that not all will survive northern winters.

Stachys, undetermined species

Here belong *S. coccinea*, probably *S. lavandulaefolia*, *S. saxicola*, and some others.

Cultivation. Stachyses respond best to deep, fertile, well-drained, moderately moist soil. The silvery-leaved kinds, such as lamb's ears and *S. citrina*, need full sun, the others stand a little part-day shade, but are as happy in sunny locations. As a general rule they benefit from being taken up, divided, and replanted every third or fourth year, but if they are thriving and blooming well this is not necessary and it may be better or more convenient to wait until initial signs of decline become apparent before doing this. The natural species are very easily raised from seed, by cuttings taken in early summer and rooted in a cold frame or greenhouse propagating bench, and by division in spring or early fall. The last two methods are the only practicable ones for improved garden varieties. The Chinese or Japanese artichoke is grown by planting tubers in spring, much in the manner potatoes are, in rows 1½ feet apart with 6 inches to 1 foot of space between tubers, in fertile soil. The tubers are set at a depth of 4 to 6 inches. Other than regular cultivation to keep down weeds, no special care is needed. The tubers are dug in the fall as needed for cooking and eating.

STACHYTARPHETA (Stachy-tarphèta). Of minor horticultural importance, *Stachytarpheta*, of the vervain family VERBENACEAE, contains about 100 species. It inhabits warm regions of the Americas. Some species are naturalized in other parts of the tropics. It includes herbaceous plants and shrubs. The name, derived from the Greek *stachys*, a spike, and *tarphys*, thick, refers to the manner in which the flowers are borne.

Stachytarphetas are shrubs, subshrubs, and herbaceous perennials and annuals. They have opposite or alternate, toothed leaves and terminal spikes of white, blue, purple, or red tubular flowers that are without individual stalks and often are partly sunk in the stalk of the spike upon which they are borne. Their calyxes have four or five longitudinal ridges and as many teeth. The corollas have five

spreading lobes (petals). There are two stamens. The fruits, enclosed in the calyxes, are of two small nutlets that, when mature, separate.

The most familiar kind is **S. jamaicensis** (syn. *S. indica*). This is herbaceous or subshrubby and attains a height of 1 foot to 4 feet. It has squarish stems, and elliptic leaves 1 inch to 3 inches long. The erect flower spikes, up to 1 foot long, are mostly shorter. The blooms are blue-purple and about ¼ inch across. Only a few open on each spike at one time. Mexican **S. purpurea** is a low subshrub with slightly four-

Stachytarpheta purpurea

angled stems and opposite, ovate leaves, coarsely toothed, deeply-veined, and up to 2 inches long. The purple flowers are in slender, terminal spikes up to 10 inches long. South American **S. urticaefolia** is a subshrub 1½ to 2 feet tall. It has toothed, ovate to triangular-ovate or oblong leaves 3 to 4 inches long. They are hairless except sometimes for a few hairs on the veins on their undersides. Slender and 6 inches to 1½ feet long, the flowering spikes display small purple-blue blooms.

Garden Uses and Cultivation. Occasionally cultivated in warm regions in flower beds and elsewhere in greenhouses, these plants grow with great ease and are readily raised from seed. They withstand considerable dryness and need well-drained soil and full sun, or in greenhouses just sufficient shade to break the full intensity of summer sun. A minimum greenhouse night temperature of 55 to 60°F is favorable. During their early stages the young plants should have the tips of their shoots pinched out occasionally to induce branching.

STACHYURACEAE — Stachyurus Family. The characteristics of this family of dicotyledons are those of *Stachyurus*, its only genus.

STACHYURUS (Stachy-ùrus). The stachyurus family STACHYURACEAE consists of only *Stachyurus*, a genus of perhaps ten species of deciduous and evergreen shrubs and trees, native from Japan and Taiwan to the Himalayas. The name comes from the Greek *stachys*, a spike, and *oura*, a tail, and alludes to the racemes of flowers.

Stachyuruses have shoots with thick pith. They have alternate, undivided, toothed, stalked leaves, and usually bisexual, sometimes unisexual, nearly stalkless flowers in racemes drooping from the leaf axils. Each flower has four sepals, four petals, eight stamens, and a style capped with a four-lobed stigma. The berry-like fruits are many-seeded.

The species best known in cultivation, *S. praecox* is a common native in thickets

Stachyurus praecox

and open woods in mountains in Japan. Its variety *S. p. matsuzakii* is a seashore variant with thicker branches, leaves 4 to 6 inches long, and fruits averaging somewhat larger than those of the typical species. It hails from Japan and the Ryuku Islands. These are deciduous or semievergreen shrubs. In Japan called ki-bushi, *S. praecox*, up to 12 feet tall, has slender-pointed, elliptic-ovate to narrowly-ovate or oblong leaves 3 to 4½ inches long and about one-half as wide. They are hairless, or sparsely-pubescent, especially on the veins on their undersides. They have stalks from less than ½ to 1 inch long. In winter or very early spring, the reddish twigs are decorated along their lengths with numerous racemes of pale yellow or greenish-yellow, bell-shaped flowers, about ⅓ inch wide, with petals twice as long as the sepals. The racemes form in the fall and await fairly clement weather before their twelve to twenty blooms open. They are 1½ to 4½ inches long. The reddish-cheeked, yellow, nearly spherical to ellipsoidal fruits are ⅓ to ½ inch long. This species is hardy in sheltered places as far north as southern New England.

Native to China, *S. chinensis*, very much like *S. praecox*, but usually lower, has greenish or brownish branches, and flowers that spread more widely and have styles at least as long as, instead of shorter than,

the petals. This is hardy in sheltered locations near New York City.

Garden and Landscape Uses. The chief merit of these shrubs is their early blooming propensities. Because they flower when few other plants are in bloom they are doubly welcome. They offer a taste of joys to come. To be seen at their best, stachyuruses should be planted in front of dark evergreens, which make a splendid background for them at flowering time. They grow in sun or light shade and are grateful for porous, peaty soil of reasonable fertility that does not lack for moisture, yet is not saturated.

Cultivation. Given deep, agreeable soil and, toward the northern limits of their hardiness, locations sheltered from the blasts of winter, stachyuruses give little trouble. They require no systematic pruning. Any cutting needed to shape or restrain them is done as soon as they are through blooming. Propagation is by seeds sown in summer, as soon as they are ripe, in a cold frame or cool greenhouse. They can also be raised from summer cuttings inserted in a propagating bed in a greenhouse or under mist, and by layering. They are benefited by a mulch of compost or other suitable material.

STAG-BUSH is *Viburnum prunifolium*.

STAG-HEADED. This term is applied to old trees the upper branches of which have died back partway. The condition may be caused by permanent lowering or raising of the water level by draining, grading (especially filling considerable depths of soil over the roots of trees), or extensive construction work.

Stag-headiness usually first manifests itself by young shoots becoming progressively shorter and successive leaves smaller. Then, branchlets and branches gradually die back. If the trees are otherwise healthy, some improvement may be had by cutting

A stag-headed *Robinia*

the branches back to about 1 foot below the point where they are dead and just above a live side branch. Loosening the surface soil to allow for the admission of air, applying fertilizer, mulching, and watering deeply in dry weather may also be helpful.

STAGGERBUSH is *Lyonia mariana*.

STAKING and TYING. To encourage shapeliness, to favor the production of straight stems, or to prevent storm damage, many plants need support, often most appropriately and conveniently provided by staking. The requirement may be temporary, as with newly transplanted trees; seasonal, as for annuals, biennials, and such perennials as chrysanthemums, dahlias, and delphiniums, the tops of which die down each year; or permanent, as may be needed by some vines.

Various types of stakes are used. Among the more common are bamboo canes and wooden ones of square or round section, the latter often tapered slightly toward their tops. Sometimes, chiefly to support plants in greenhouse benches, lengths of stout, rigid wire are employed, but unless these have their tops suitably bent over

Bamboo canes are appropriate for staking: (a) Delphiniums

(b) Cordon-trained sweet peas

(c) Freesias

The best wooden stakes are of redwood, cypress, red-cedar, or other lumbers that in contact with moist soil resist decay and remain serviceable for several seasons. They may be from ½ inch to 2 inches in diameter, or considerably more for trees. Their bottoms should be sharpened and the portion that will be in the ground treated with a wood preservative not toxic to plants. This eliminates creosote. To render them less conspicuous, wooden stakes are often painted or stained green or brown. Bamboo stakes, varying in diameter from less than pencil thickness to an inch or more, are often colored in this way.

(c) Newly planted conifers

never use them where they can possibly enter an eye or in other ways injure a person who unwittingly bends over quickly. Twiggy brushwood, with the bottom of each piece sharpened for easy insertion into the ground, is fine for peas, sweet peas, and some other vining plants and for groups of chrysanthemums and many other perennials as well as annuals in flower beds. For vines in flower borders it may be arranged in "tepees."

Brushwood stakes are unobtrusive: (a) Sharpen the bottoms of pieces of brushwood to use as stakes

(b) Inserting the stakes among chrysanthemums

Poles of red-cedar may be used to support: (a) Pole beans

Simple as the operation sounds, staking is often poorly done, with the result unsightly, inadequate, or both. Of first importance is to select stakes suitable for the jobs. To do this intelligently some knowledge of the growth habits of the plants is required. Quite clearly, a slender bamboo

(b) Strong-growing vines

cane capable of supporting a young dahlia or tomato becomes totally inadequate when the plant has grown taller and bushier and presents a great deal more surface to the wind. But unnecessarily stout stakes can distract from beauty and be disturbing. Imagine a graceful lily supported by a ¾- or 1-inch-thick dahlia stake or even a much-too-thick bamboo cane.

Judgment as to lengths of the stakes to be used can be as important as balancing their thickness to actual needs. If they are seriously too short, they will not adequately serve their purposes. It may become necessary to tie or wire extensions to them, but this is an awkward, time-consuming procedure. Stakes taller than necessary, which poke up among the flowers or top the plants themselves, are intrusive and ugly. Shortening such stakes as the plants approach maximum height is wasteful.

When to stake is highly important. Inexperienced and careless gardeners often leave it until too late, attempting, as it were, to lock the stable door after the horse has departed. Probably no one ever staked too soon. When planting young, bare-rooted trees to be given a single support, or dahlias and other plants the roots of which may be injured by staking after planting, drive the stakes first and plant against them. Attend to other staking well before the plants begin to fall apart from lack of support or before their stems become twisted.

Neatness and so far as possible unobtrusiveness should be the chief aims after effectiveness when staking ornamental plantings. In vegetable gardens, nursery plots, and other utilitarian areas the second may be less necessary, but neatness still has merit. Use no more supports than necessary and position them, depending upon the type of plant, to best advantage. Try to do this so that as the plants grow the stakes will be hidden by foliage as much as possible. This is often best done by inserting the stakes in somewhat from the outsides of the plants but never so close to their centers that bulbs, tubers, or tuberous roots are pierced. The most horrible of bad staking procedures fairly commonly seen include those in which a bunch of stems is more or less loosely tied to a single stake and when three or four stakes are inserted around a plant and encircled with twine or other tie material.

A variant of this last method, that of employing a ring of wire held above the ground on three wooden or metal stakes can be effective with peonies because their foliage falls to largely conceal the support. In cut flower gardens, gladioluses and many other crops can be sufficiently supported by inserting stakes at intervals of a few feet along both sides of the row and connecting these with strings.

Pot plants of many kinds need staking. Some, such as tall begonias and vining and semivining sorts, require permanent supports, others, including chrysanthemums, freesias, and sometimes tulips, temporary ones. For many, thin bamboo canes, the slenderest available commercially, split from larger canes; thin wooden stakes; or shoots cut from dormant willows are satisfactory.

To support such sorts as freesias and ixias, when they are about half-grown, push a few slender canes, willow shoots, or wires among them and lace between these with strong thread or insert a few pieces of twiggy brushwood (birch is excellent for the purpose) among them. If the flowers are for cutting, it is enough to push three or four stakes around the inside rim of the pot and circle these with thread or thin string.

Tying staked plants for maximum effect is something of an art. Just as too many, unwieldy or awkwardly placed stakes detract from beauty, so do unsuitable, ill-placed or overabundant ties. Yet, except when brushwood is used, with other than those that twine around their supports in the fashion of morning glories or that, like sweet peas, attach themselves by tendrils, some means of securing stems to stakes must usually be employed.

Materials that serve this purpose include soft string (the hard-surfaced sort does not tie as readily and is likely to cut into stems) and a commercially available pliable wire embedded in thin strips of plastic. This last comes in spools and also in convenient short, single-tie lengths. It is secured by twisting the two ends of each tie together. Formerly, raffia, a really excellent tying material, and strong thread or special florists' string dyed green and of almost threadlike thickness were popular, but these are not readily available.

Raffia, most easily manipulated if soaked in water for a short time before use, has the advantage of being readily split into strips of varying thicknesses as the work proceeds and as the operator deems most appropriate for each tie. Almost nostalgic is the picture of a gardener with a bunch of raffia hanging from his belt as he engages in tying chrysanthemums or other plants.

Whatever material is favored, tying should begin well before stems become twisted or fall over from neglect of this, and before storm damage occurs. Generally it is best done in several stages as stems lengthen. It is important that ties are secure. This is simply accomplished with the Twist-em type, or with string ties by making sure that square or reef knots instead of "grannies" are used.

Other points to bear in mind are to tie so that the natural habit of the plant is preserved or enhanced and the ties will neither cut into or strangle stems as they thicken nor pull them out of place as they lengthen. As insurance against the last, it is usually advisable to have string-type ties angle downward from the stakes to the stems.

Tying a herbaceous perennial without destroying its natural growth habit

When tying with string or similar material, wrap it once or twice around the stake, cross it in between the stake and stem, bring both ends to the front of the stem, knot them there, and cut the ends off short. By crossing the string between stake and stem the latter is held more firmly and danger of it being bruised as a result of rubbing against the stake is greatly reduced. With woody stems, such

Tying a dahlia to a square wooden stake with soft string

as those of espaliered trees and shrubs and of some vines that must be tied closely to stakes or similar supports, it may be desirable to take the further precaution of wrapping the stem under the tie with burlap or other suitable cushioning material.

Trees ordinarily need support for only a few months or perhaps a year or two after transplanting, less frequently as very young plants in nurseries. A stout dahlia-type

This neat arrangement, used at the Royal Botanic Garden, Edinburgh, Scotland, to support phloxes and other sorts of herbaceous perennials, is fashioned out of wire and consists of three vertical stakes surmounted by two horizontal circles held together by four cross wires. The shoots grow up through the wires.

A young tree tied to a stout wooden stake; a wrapping of burlap around the trunk prevents abrasion of the bark

(b) The wires, where they encircle the trunk, are threaded through short lengths of hose

A recently planted tree is secured here with guy wires stretched to the short protruding tops of stakes driven deeply into the ground; the wires have been threaded through pieces of hose where they encircle the tree

stake is likely to be adequate for these last. Bigger, newly transplanted specimens, especially in wind-swept locations, are likely to need more sophisticated means of support. This may be provided for bare-rooted specimens by driving a single heavy stake into the center of the planting hole before positioning the tree. For trees transplanted with a ball of soil, three or four or sometimes two stout stakes are driven into the ground just outside the circumference of the root ball and from near the top of each a horizontal tie of two wires, twisted together to assure a reasonable strain between stake and trunk, are passed through pieces of hose where they encircle the trunk and have their other ends wound around the stake.

Newly-planted conifers, each wired temporarily with two tall, stout stakes

An alternative method especially suitable for large trees is to use guy wires stretched at an angle of approximately forty-five degrees from an appropriate height on the trunk to three or four stout stakes or deadmen (heavy pieces of concrete, tree trunk, or other suitable material buried in the ground to serve as anchors) equally spaced outside the perimeter of the root ball. If stakes are used, angle them so their lower ends point inward, drive them in deeply, and have their upper foot protrude above the surface. Have each wire in two sections connected by a turnbuckle and use this to stretch the wires tautly. The portion of the wire that encircles the trunk is threaded through a section of rubber hose.

An unusual way of securing newly transplanted balled trees, described in the *Gardeners' Chronicle* of England in 1876, has merit where aboveground stakes and ties are objectionable. After the tree is positioned, three sharp-pointed stakes, 3 to 3½

feet long, are driven vertically into the planting hole around and just outside the ball, with their upper ends approximately level with its top. The ends of the stakes are then connected by a triangle of three sturdy wooden members, which are fastened securely to them. The job is finished by backfilling to cover the ball and its supports.

STAMEN. The male organ of a flower consisting of an anther (pollen-bearing part) and usually a stalk called a filament is called a stamen.

STAND. The growth of a particular category of plants occupying a given area may be called a stand, as a stand of evergreens or of oak trees. Or one may refer, for instance, to a good stand of corn or a poor stand of cabbages.

STANDARD. In horticultural usage, a standard is a plant, such as a fuchsia, geranium (*Pelargonium*), lantana, oleander, rose, or wisteria, trained to tree form. It has a clear trunk, usually 2 to 4 feet tall, topped by a rounded, moplike head of branches, foliage, and often flowers. For methods of training standards see Pruning.

Standard is also used as a name for the usually erect upper or banner petal of the flowers of peas, sweet peas, and other members of the section of the family LEGUMINOSAE to which these sorts belong. The three erect petals of the flowers of irises are also called standards.

STANFIELDARA. This is the name of orchid hybrids the parents of which include *Epidendrum, Laelia,* and *Sophronitis.*

A newly-planted young tree: (a) Supported by wires secured to three tall, stout stakes

A standard lantana

STANGERIA

STANGERIA (Stan-gèria). The genus *Stangeria*, of the cycad family CYCADACEAE, rare in cultivation and endemic to South Africa, consists of one variable species. Its name commemorates a surveyor-general of Natal, William Stanger, who died in 1854. The name *Stangeria paradoxa* was once applied to this rare plant in recognition of a botanical error. When the plant was first discovered, because the arrangement of the veins of the leaflets is fernlike, it was thought to be a fern. Not until cones of the plant were found was the true relationship of the species understood. It is the only member of the cycad family with the veins of the leaflets running from the midribs to their margins.

The turnip-shaped to cylindrical stem of *S. eriopus* (syn. *S. paradoxa*), 1 foot to 2 feet

Stangeria eriopus

long, is mostly or entirely subterranean. From its top sprout few to several pinnate, hairless leaves, about 2 feet long by one-half as wide, with opposite and alternate, spiny-toothed, or rarely pinnately-lobed, linear-lanceolate leaflets. The cones are cylindrical; the males, considerably longer than the females, about 6 inches in length by 1 inch in diameter. Their hairy stalks are clothed with overlapping scales.

Garden and Landscape Uses and Cultivation. A collectors' item, *Stangeria* needs tropical or warm subtropical conditions and succeeds under the general care appropriate for other cycads. As a well-cared-for cultivated specimen it develops more foliage and is more handsome than in the wild. Shade from strong sun is advantageous. For further information see Cycads.

STANHOPEA (Stan-hòpea). The curious, sometimes almost grotesque, showy blooms of *Stanhopea* are not infrequently as bizarre as any to be found in a group noted for the unusual appearance of its flowers, the orchid family ORCHIDACEAE, to which *Stanhopea* belongs. The name commemorates Philip Henry Stanhope, fourth Earl Stanhope, president of the Medico-Botanical Society of London, who died in 1855. As is not unusual with orchid genera, considerable confusion exists as to the number of species involved, their identification, and the correct application of names. A conservative appraisal suggests there are about twenty-five. In the wild, stanhopeas are found only in Central America and tropical South America.

Stanhopeas are evergreen epiphytes (tree-perchers), but individual plants sometimes substitute for the arboreal life existence as lithophytes (plants that perch on rocks), or even grow in the ground. They have short rhizomes and many usually ribbed, ovoid pseudobulbs, 2 to 3 inches long, clothed with scales, with at their apexes a single longitudinally-pleated, strongly-veined, short-stalked, broadly-elliptic-lanceolate leaf. The flowers, nearly always intensely and usually pleasantly scented, have individual stalks. They are two or more together in thick-stalked, pendulous or sometimes laterally-spreading, bracted racemes that originate from the bottom of the pseudobulb. The papery bracts are often much like the sepals and petals in aspect and color. The blooms have three sepals, the lateral pair usually bigger than the other, and two usually smaller and thinner petals. The sepals and petals spread or are reflexed. The most remarkable feature of the flower is the thick, fleshy lip, often of great importance in identifying species. Typically it is composed of three more or less fleshy parts, a globular to boat-shaped, concave basal portion called the hypochil that may or may not have a pair of short, hornlike protuberances, a short central part that generally has two long, forward-pointing or out-curving horns and is called the mesochil, and a terminal portion, jointed to the mesochil and usually ovate, called the epichil. A few species break this most common pattern and have a less complicated lip consisting of only one or two of these parts. All have a long, slender, winged or wingless column that arches over the lip.

Flowers normally two or more together, with thin, reflexed petals and a lip with a globose or pouched, hornless hypochil not joined to the column, a conspicuous mesochil, with horns at least ¾ inch long, and an epichil are characteristic of *S. insignis*, *S. hernandezii*, and *S. tigrina*. Native to Mexico and Guatemala, *S. insignis* has elliptic-lanceolate leaves and, in fall or winter, 8-inch-long racemes each of usually two flowers. The purple-spotted, dull yellowish-white blooms are about 5 inches wide. From the mesochil sprout two curved horns longer than the epichil. The column is broadly-winged. The leaves of Mexican summer-blooming *S. hernandezii* (syn. *S. devoniensis*) are 9 inches to 1 foot long by one-quarter as wide. The about 4-inch-wide flowers, in racemes of two or three, have pale yellow to yellow-orange sepals, petals with reddish-brown spots, and a purple-spotted whitish lip, obscurely toothed at its apex and with the base of its hypochil stained purple. The column is narrowly-winged to essentially wingless. This blooms in summer. The 6- to 8-inch-wide blooms, in racemes of two to four, of *S. tigrina* have spreading, dark red sepals and petals blotched with yellow. The sepals are ovate, the petals strap-shaped. The lower portion of the orange-yellow lip is blotched with purple, the mesochil and three-toothed epichil are whitish spotted with purple. This early-summer-blooming orchid ranges in the wild from Mexico to northern South America.

Sorts with the hypochils of the lip of the flower elongated or squarish instead of globular include *S. oculata*, *S. jenishiana*, and *S. wardii*. Native from Mexico to Honduras, *S. oculata* has elliptic-lanceolate leaves up to 1¾ feet in length. The racemes, sometimes exceeding 1 foot in length, are of two to eight vanilla-scented blooms approximately 5 inches wide. They have reddish-purple-dotted, whitish to yellowish, reflexed, elliptic-lanceolate sepals and wavy-edged, linear-lanceolate petals. There are two deep purple eyelike

Stanhopea oculata

spots on the sides of the hypochil, and on its underside a transverse cleft. The remainder of the lip is whitish, generally spotted with purple. Its epichil is stalked. This variable species blooms from spring to fall. Summer-blooming *S. jenishiana* (syn. *S. bucephalus*), native from Mexico to Ecuador, has leaves up to a little over 1½ feet long. Its crimson-spotted, tawny-orange flowers, about 5 inches across, have turned-back sepals and petals, and lips with two prominent curved horns. From Central America and northern South America comes *S. wardii,* which blooms

Stanhopea wardii

Stanhopea wardii (flowers)

from late summer to midwinter. Its fragrant flowers, five to seven to a raceme, are up to 5 inches wide. They have pointed-oblong sepals and much slenderer, pointed petals with rolled-back, crisped margins. Like the sepals they are creamy- or greenish-white with reddish-purple dots. The fleshy lip has an orange-yellow to maroon hypochil with a purple-brown blotch on each side, a yellow or white mesochil, and a red-spotted, yellow, stalkless epichil. From closely related *S. oculata* this is distinguishable by the lack of a cross cleft on the underside of the hypochil.

From the kinds discussed above, *S. graveolens* (syn. *S. connata*) differs in the mesochil of the lip of the flower being poorly developed or absent and in the hypochil being obviously joined to the column. A South American, this has leaves up to 2 feet long and about one-quarter as wide. The flowers, approximately 5 inches wide, are whitish to pale or deeper yellow dotted with reddish-brown to purple. The lateral sepals and petals, the latter with wavy margins, are reflexed. The lip has two eyelike marks on the hypochil.

The less complex lips of its flowers without horns and consisting only of the hypochil and a nonjointed epichil distinguish *S. ecornuta* from other species considered here. Native to Central America, this has leaves up to 1½ feet long by 7 inches wide. Its one- to three-flowered racemes are up to 1 foot long. The flowers, about 4½ inches wide, are creamy-white, the petals spotted with purple toward their bases. The lip is yellow deepening to orange-yellow at its bottom and with swellings there and at its apex. The column is yellow and about ¾ inch long.

Other sorts cultivated include these: *S. grandiflora* (syn. *S. eburnea*), of Colombia, Guyana, and Venezuela, has leaves 9 inches to 1 foot long. The flowers, usually two together in pendulous racemes, are up to 5 inches wide. Ivory-white, they commonly have few purple marks on the 3-

Stanhopea grandiflora

inch-long, narrow lip, which has two horns at the base of the hypochil and a hornless mesochil. *S. shuttleworthii*, of Colombia, has leaves up to 1¼ feet long. The pendulous racemes, up to 2 feet long, are of three to seven flowers 4 to 5 inches across. They have a chocolate-like fragrance and are creamy-yellow to apricot-yellow, conspicuously spotted with light chocolate-brown, and with a prominent almost black blotch on the lip. The latter has a boat-shaped hypochil, a sickle-shaped mesochil, and a pointed-ovate epichil. *S. tricornis,* of Colombia, has leaves up to 1 foot long. The racemes, up to 2 feet long, are

Stanhopea tricornis

of two or three curious birdlike flowers, 4 to 5 inches wide, with spreading or reflexed ovate sepals and oblong petals that parallel the column. The blooms are yellow to creamy-white with a purple-spotted, bright yellow area on the lip, which has a globose hypochil, a strap-shaped mesochil, and a squarish epichil.

Garden Uses and Cultivation. In greenhouses where humid tropical conditions are maintained, stanhopeas are among the easiest orchids to satisfy and are rewarding in their production of beautiful, usually fragrant flowers. Unfortunately, their loveliness is fleeting. They fade after two or three days. Because of the way the racemes develop, the only practicable means of accommodating stanhopeas are in latticework wooden baskets, on latticework rafts, attached to slabs of tree fern trunk, or on some other suitable support that permits the pendent racemes to hang without interference. The best location for these orchids is close under the greenhouse roof. However accommodated, perfect drainage with consequent adequate aeration around the roots is imperative. Suitable materials in which to plant are tree fern and osmunda fibers. Except for about a month following the completion of the growth of the new pseudobulbs, during which water is withheld, the rooting medium should be kept evenly moist. During the growing season regular applications of mild fertilizer are beneficial. Shade sufficient to keep the foliage from scorching or becoming yellow, which it quickly does if exposed to sun, is needed. A winter night temperature of about 55°F, with a daytime rise of five to fifteen degrees, depending upon the weather, is generally satisfactory. Stanhopeas that become too large rarely flower satisfactorily. They should be divided and replanted or repotted before that occurs. For more information see Orchids.

STANLEYA (Stán-leya) — Prince's Plume. Stanleyas are mostly large, usually glaucous annuals, biennials, and herbaceous perennials, natives of western North

America. They number eight species and belong to the mustard family CRUCIFERAE. Their name commemorates Lord Edward Smith Stanley, the thirteenth Earl of Derby, one-time president of the Linnaean Society of England. He died in 1851.

The leaves of *Stanleya* are alternate, undivided, and lobeless, or they may be divided or lobed. The yellow flowers, in form characteristic of their family, are in terminal plumelike racemes. They have four sepals, four spreading petals that narrow sharply to claws or shafts at their bases and are displayed in the form of a cross, six stamens with curved, spirally coiled anthers (two of the stamens are slightly shorter than the others), and a small, stalkless, undivided stigma. The fruits are slender, podlike capsules. The presence of *S. pinnata* and perhaps other species is considered a good indication that the poisonous element selenium is present in the soil.

Prince's plume (*S. pinnata*), a variable perennial species, inhabits dry plains from South Dakota to Oregon and New Mexico. Its stems usually branch freely below and are 1 foot to 3 feet tall or taller. The lower leaves, with longish stalks, are up to 8 inches in length and pinnately-divided, with the divisions sometimes lobed. The upper leaves are smaller, narrow-lanceolate to linear, and undivided. Lemon-yellow to golden-yellow, the 1-inch-wide flowers are in long, showy, elongating racemes, that from a little distance suggest those of *Asphodeline lutea*. The numerous seed capsules stand out from the stems much like those of *Cleome*. There is, of course, no botanical similarity. Plants previously treated separately as *S. bipinnata* and *S. glauca* are considered varieties of *S. pinnata*.

Garden and Landscape Uses and Cultivation. Little is recorded about the garden uses or cultivation of this showy species. Undoubtedly in regions where it is native it would adapt to domesticity, but as is often the case with abundant wild plants, they are least likely to be welcomed into gardens in their home territories. This is worth trying in other regions where conditions approaching those of a sunny semidesert can be given. Seeds should germinate readily. Because these are deep-rooted plants it would be wise to grow the seedlings in pots up to the time of planting them in their permanent locations.

STAPELIA (Sta-pèlia)—Carrion Flower. Endemic to dry regions in southern Africa and tropical Africa, the genus *Stapelia*, of the milkweed family ASCLEPIADACEAE, has a name commemorating the Dutch physician Johannes Bodaeus van Stapel, who died in 1636. There are seventy-five species.

Stapelias are low, fleshy-stemmed succulents that the nonbotanical often mistake for cactuses. But their flower structure (upon which botanical relationships are based) differs greatly from that of cactuses, and among commonly cultivated plants stapelias are more closely akin to hoyas and milkweeds. Their four-angled stems, branched from their bases, are usually toothed, the teeth tipped with rudimentary or rarely more obvious, tiny fleshy leaves. The flowers of some species are of astonishing size, those of others are smaller, but all are intriguing. They develop from large, more or less spherical buds that open with a faint, but audible plop.

The blooms of many sorts emit as an insect attractant a nauseating stench that fully justifies the colloquial name carrion flower. But not all do this, and many are beautifully marked with bands or mottlings of a dark, rich color. They have a five-cleft calyx, a wheel- or bell-shaped, five-lobed corolla with a central cavity containing a double crown or corona and with or without a raised ring, called an annulus, surrounding it. The outer circle of the corona is usually of five smooth-edged or variously cleft, toothed lobes, more rarely of ten or more free parts. The inner corona is of five sometimes lobed, horned, winged, or crested lobes. The stalks of the five stamens are united into a very short tube. The anthers are erect or inclined inward over the tip of the style. Spindle-shaped and in pairs, the fruits are podlike follicles. From allied *Caralluma* the genus *Stapelia* is separated on the basis of the inner and outer circles of the corona being completely free from each other or, at most, rarely being connected for a short distance at their bases rather than being more obviously united, and the lobes of the outer circle of the corona not being joined at their bases as usually are those of *Caralluma*. But these distinctions are not always clear, and there are occasional examples of intermediates.

Most commonly grown, *S. variegata* has clusters of erect, bluntly-angled, hairless stems, often more or less mottled or suffused with purple and 2 to 6 inches long by about ½ inch wide. The freely-produced, star-shaped flowers, 2 to 3 inches in diameter, come from the bases of young stems; they are solitary or up to five on a stalk. They are pale greenish-yellow, conspicuously decorated with dark purple-brown spots and with a slightly five-sided annulus covered with granule-like warts or tubercles. Many varieties of this highly variable species have been given names.

Here is a selection, presented alphabetically, of other stapelias that appear to be most common in cultivation. More may be found in collections of specialists. *S. asterias,* a 4- to 10-inch-tall species with velvety-pubescent stems without conspicuous teeth, has possibly not been collected in the wild since its discovery in 1792. Plants in cultivation under its name are almost certainly hybrids derived from the original plants or represent variety *S. a. lucida.* This last differs from the typical sort in its blooms being without transverse yellow lines. Both species and variety are remarkable for their glossy or shining, purplish-red or purplish-brown flowers. These, starfish-like in form and about 4 inches wide, are margined with purple hairs. Those of the species have yellow or whitish cross lines that do not quite extend to the petal margins. *S. bella* is a popular sort, probably a hybrid between *S. revoluta* and *S. deflexa.* It has erect stems 5 to 7 inches tall by ½ to ¾ inch square, their sides concave, the angles slightly compressed. Coming from the bottoms of young stems and three or four together, the star-shaped, fleshy, deep purplish-red flowers, 1¾ to 2 inches in diameter and brownish toward the tips of their petals, are neither glossy (plants called *S. bella* that have shiny blooms are almost surely *S. asterias lucida*) nor, except along their margins, hairy. The annulus is slightly raised and rounded. *S. berlinensis* is a name without botanical acceptance. It is applied to a cultivated plant that perhaps is a very dark-flowered variant of *S. maculosa.* It has four-angled, purplish-tinged stems with small, spreading teeth.

Stapelia variegata

Stapelia berlinensis

The black-purple, star-shaped flowers, 3½ inches across, have pale green stamens and a purple-spotted pistil. *S. clavicorona* is a robust native of just north of the Tropic of Capricorn. It has velvety-hairy stems with deeply concave sides and winglike, notched angles. Produced about midway along the stems, the star-shaped flowers, slightly over 2 inches in diameter, have a few white hairs near their centers on the inside and are velvety-pubescent on their outsides; their margins are fringed with hairs. They are pale yellow to greenish-yellow with fine transverse, purple-brown lines. The corona is dark-purple. The lobes of its inner ring each have two club-shaped horns. *S. erectiflora,* 4 to 7 inches tall, has stems decumbent at their bases, then erect. Up to ½ inch square, they have channeled sides and very rounded angles. Freely produced all along the stems, the odorless or nearly odorless, long-lasting flowers, in clusters of up to four or rarely more or occasionally solitary, have slender, purplish, 2- to 5-inch-long stalks. Purple and densely-clothed with white hairs, the upward-facing blooms are less than ½ inch in diameter. Their petals recurve so strongly that the back of the corolla is hidden. *S. gettleffii* is a beautiful tropical species remarkable for the length of its rudimentary leaves, which point upward and are pressed against the angles of the stems. The latter, erect from decumbent bases and 8 to 10 inches high, are velvety-pubescent and have concave sides. In ones, twos, or threes, and opening in succession, the star-shaped flowers, which come from near the bottoms of the stems, are 6 inches or a little more in diameter. Greenish-yellow, marked with transverse purple lines and solid purple at their centers and petal tips, they have lanceolate petals with their lower parts and margins densely-clothed with long hairs. *S. gigantea* well deserves its name. Except by uncultivated and probably uncultivatable *Rafflesia* and perhaps some species of *Aristolochia*, it has the largest flower of any known plant. A native of tropical Africa and South Africa, this sort has erect, pubescent stems up to 9 inches long by ¾ inch to 1¼ inches square, with much-compressed angles. Solitary or in pairs, the flowers come from close to the bottoms or middles of the stems. Commonly 9 inches to 1 foot, more rarely up to 1½ feet in diameter, star-shaped, pale ochre-yellow, and freely marked with slender, crimson, transverse lines, they have a thin covering of hairs and hair-fringed margins to the petals. *S. glabricaulis* has completely hairless stems decumbent at their bases, then erect, 4 to 8 inches tall by ½ to ⅔ inch square, with much-compressed, notched angles. In clusters of five or fewer from near the bottoms of young stems, the starlike flowers, 2½ to 3½ inches across, have rolled-back, hair-fringed margins.

Stapelia glabricaulis

Stapelia leendertziae

Pinkish to reddish-purple becoming paler or yellowish toward their centers, they are without markings. The annulus and lower halves of the petals are thickly covered with silky, purple or gray-purple hairs. *S. grandiflora* is a name often misapplied in regard to cultivated plants that not infrequently are hybrids or even other species. True *S. grandiflora* has erect stems 6 inches to 1 foot in height by 1 inch to 1¼ inches square. They are deeply-channeled, with much-compressed angles. Coming from near the bottoms of the stems, the flowers, 5 to 6 inches in diameter, are dark purple-brown and without markings. Densely-clothed with soft, purple hairs toward their centers, along the edges of the petals they are thickly fringed with longer, purple or whitish hairs. *S. hirsuta* is very variable and several varieties and hybrids of it have been described. It has erect stems, 5 to 8 inches or occasionally up to 1 foot tall by ½ to ¾ inch square, clothed with very fine, short hairs. The starry flowers, solitary or in twos or threes, from near the bottoms of the stems, are 2½ to 5 inches wide and cream-colored suffused with purple toward their centers. Their petals have purple-brown apexes and are marked transversely with lines of the same color. The basal quarters of the petals are densely-clothed with long, soft, silky, purple hairs and the margins are fringed with similarly colored or whitish, long hairs. *S. leendertziae* has velvety-short-hairy stems decumbent at their bases, then erect. They are 4 to 6 inches long with slightly channeled sides and toothed angles. The short-stalked, bell-shaped, ill-scented blooms come from near the middles of the stems usually in pairs, less often singly. Brownish- to blackish-purple, short-hairy on their outsides, and with long purple hairs in the lower half of the insides of the bells, they have spreading petals and are about 2½ inches long by 3½ inches wide from petal tip to petal tip. The petals are not fringed with hairs. *S. longipes* has obscurely-angled, slightly-toothed, hairless stems, up to about 8 inches long, from a little under to

Stapelia leendertziae (flower)

a little over ½ inch square. Its 2½-inch wide flowers, terminating procumbent or pendulous, slender stalks 4½ to 7 inches long, are starlike. Their centers are white, spotted and lined with purple. The outer halves of the petals are deep black-purple, their lower margins hair-fringed. Variety *S. l. namaquensis* has flowers with both horns of the inner corona ending in large knobs, instead of the inner horn being spatula-shaped and concave below its apex. *S. maculosa,* possibly of hybrid origin, has grayish-green, hairless, roundish stems with small, pointed, spreading teeth. Solitary or two or three together, the star-shaped flowers, nearly or quite 3 to 4 inches in diameter, are greenish-yellow with the petals cross-lined with purple and spotted with purple and their tips and margins brownish. *S. pedunculata* much resembles *S. longipes,* but its flowers have erect instead of sprawling or drooping stalks and are lighter in color and slightly smaller. *S. nobilis* is much like *S. gigantea* and sometimes passes for that species. It differs chiefly in being more compact and in having shorter, less deeply-channeled stems. Also, its flowers are mostly smaller, averaging perhaps 8 inches in diameter, but sometimes are considerably larger. They come singly or in groups of up to five from the middles, or below, of young stems and differ from

Stapelia nobilis

those of *S. gigantea*, which they resemble in color, in having a well-marked saucer-like depression at their middles instead of being practically flat and also in the more abundant hairs that decorate their centers. *S. pillansii* has stinking, star-shaped flowers remarkable for the long-pointed, tail-like apexes of their hair-fringed petals. Coming from near the bases of the stems, they are up to 6 inches in diameter and dark purplish-brown to rusty-brown with a silky sheen. The velvety-pubescent stems are 4 to 6 inches long by ½ to 1 inch wide. They have channeled sides and slightly compressed angles and are inconspicuously-toothed. *S. pulvinata*, approximately 4 inches tall, has stems about ½ inch square, with compressed, notched angles and upward-pointing rudimentary leaves. Appearing singly from near the bottoms of the stems, the quite beautiful starry flowers, from 3½ to 4½ inches wide or a little wider, are remarkable for the large cushion of soft purple hairs that fills their centers. In color the blooms are dark purple-brown with a tiger-skin pattern of yellow cross lines on the lower two-thirds of the petals. *S. revoluta* has sparingly-branched, sharply-angled, glaucous-green, hairless stems up to 1¼ feet tall or sometimes taller. Solitary or in twos or threes, the very short-stalked flowers are borne near the tops of the stems. Wheel-shaped, they have short, strongly backward-curved petals. Without spreading the petals, the smooth, hairless blooms are 1¼ to 1½ inches in diameter. From light to a dull purple or purple-brown they are paler toward their depressed centers. There are a few varieties, some possibly hybrids. The blooms of *S. r. tigridia* have the disk around the central cup marked with yellow dots. *S. rubiginosa* has clumps of erect, minutely-hairy stems, 1½ to 2 inches tall by up to ½ inch thick and purple near their apexes. Their sides are scarcely hollowed, the notched angles obscure. In clusters of three to five, the very short-stalked blooms come from the center portions of the stems. They are starlike and ¾ inch in diameter and have a greenish-yellow central disk and yellowish-purple, hair-fringed petals, dotted

with purple. *S. schinzii* is tropical, and unusual because of the long-tapered petals of its blooms. It has stems about 3 inches tall by up to ¾ inch square, with compressed angles. The solitary, star-shaped flowers, from near the bottoms of young stems, are 4½ to 9 inches in diameter. They are dark brown, and hairless except along the margins of the petals. *S. semota* has hairless stems, about 3 inches long by ½ to ¾ inch thick, spotted with chocolate or dark green spots. In groups of several, the flowers, 1½ inches or somewhat more in diameter, are star-shaped. They are dark chocolate-colored, handsomely and conspicuously variegated with yellow, hairless except along the margins of the petals. *S. senilis* has stems 1 foot tall by ¾ inch to 1¼ inches square, with much-compressed angles. From 4½ to 5 inches in diameter, the starry blooms have transversely-ridged petals the apexes of which are purple-gray with a small yellowish or greenish patch. The remainder of the upper surface of the bloom is light purple with numerous short, transverse yellowish lines that do not extend to the edges. The annulus and lower halves or more of the petals are thickly covered with white hairs, which justifies *senilis* as the specific epithet. *S. tsomoensis* is very similar to *S. glabricaulis*, differing mainly in its stems being slightly pubescent and its flowers being smaller, duller, sometimes with yellowish markings, and petals often with strongly-recurved tips. *S. verrucosa*, very variable, is commonly cultivated in several varieties, the most frequent of which is *S. v. pulchra*. This species has hairless stems with prominent, projecting teeth, decumbent at their bases, then erect. They are up to 3 inches long by up to ½ inch square. Solitary or in twos or threes from the bases of young stems, the flowers, 1¾ to 2½ inches wide, are rough with small wart-like tubercles and have a distinct five-sided annulus with five distinct channels radiating from it. They are pale yellow generously spotted with crimson. Those of *S. v. pulchra*, pale yellow with purple to purple-brown spots, are without the radiating channels. *S. wilmaniae* resembles *S. leendertziae* in having bell-shaped blooms with spreading petals. It differs in that they are more rotund, have corolla tubes more richly colored and less hairy, and in the lower parts of the petals being fringed with hairs.

Garden Uses. Stapelias are among the most intriguing of the numerous sorts of plants cultivated by fanciers of succulents. They are useful in rock gardens and suchlike developments in warm desert and semidesert regions, but are most commonly grown in greenhouses. Wherever they are, their strange and beautiful blooms attract interest and attention.

Cultivation. These plants are not difficult to grow. They revel in fertile, porous

soil that contains rather more organic matter, such as leaf mold, well decayed cow manure, or peat moss, than suits many succulents, and some chips of limestone, crushed oyster or clam shells, or other source of lime. Sharp drainage is essential; stagnant water in the soil soon causes the roots to rot.

Because in relation to the heights of the plants, the roots and tops spread widely, shallow containers (pans) are more suitable for stapelias than standard flower pots. Repot when needed in spring just as new growth begins. Light shade from strong summer sun is needed. In winter keep night temperatures of 50 to 55°F, with an increase of five to ten degrees or on sunny days as much as fifteen degrees permitted. Maintain a dry atmosphere and water with some caution at all times, but especially in winter when the plants are resting. But even then do not let the soil remain dry for such periods that the stems shrivel, but do permit it to become distinctly dryish before soaking, and even in the spring and summer period of active growth, allow it to dry a little between applications.

Propagation is usually by dividing entire plants or by carefully cutting from their peripheries rooted pieces or entire stems to be used as cuttings. Spring, just as new growth begins, is the best time to attend to these matters. Seeds sown in pots or pans and covered only slightly or not at all with soil, then shaded and kept in a temperature of 60 to 65°F, germinate readily. However, because stapelias are much given to hybridizing, unless the seeds are from isolated plants that are not themselves hybrids, they are likely to result in mixed progeny.

STAPHYLEA (Staphy-lèa) — Bladder Nut. The only hardy members of the small bladder nut family STAPHYLEACEAE belong in *Staphylea*, a genus of ten species of deciduous shrubs and small trees that inhabit temperate regions of the northern hemisphere. The name, in allusion to the manner in which the flowers are borne, comes from the Greek *staphyle*, a cluster.

Staphyleas have smooth, striped bark and opposite leaves of three, five, or seven pinnately-arranged, toothed leaflets. The small, white, creamy-white, or pink-tinged flowers are in terminal panicles or racemes. They have five each sepals, petals, and stamens and an ovary divided to its base into two or three parts, each with a style. The styles are free, or united at their apexes. The fruits are much-inflated, bladdery, angled or lobed capsules containing several bony seeds.

North American species are *S. trifolia* and *S. bolanderi*, the first native from Quebec to Minnesota, Georgia, and Missouri, the other a Californian hardy in southern New England. These are rather similar shrubs, up to about 15 feet tall, with leaves of three leaflets, the center one with a stalk over ½ inch long. The flowers, about ⅓ inch long, which appear after the foliage, are in nodding panicles or umbel-like racemes. The Californian differs from the eastern species in its leaves having broader, elliptic to suborbicular instead of elliptic to ovate leaflets, hairless instead of pubescent on their undersides, and flowers with stamens longer than the petals. The stamens of *S. trifolia* are hairy below their middles, those of the other hairless. The leaflets are 1½ to approximately 3 inches long. The usually three-lobed fruits of *S. trifolia* are about 1½ inches long, those of *S. bolanderi* 2 inches long or longer.

Asian bladder nuts include Japanese *S. bumalda*, Chinese *S. holocarpa*, and Caucasian *S. colchica*. The two first have leaves of three leaflets. The leaves of the last mostly have five leaflets, but those on the flowering branchlets have usually only three. About 6 feet tall, and hardy through most of New England, *S. bumalda* has

Staphylea bumalda

slender branches, and leaves with short-pointed, elliptic to elliptic-ovate leaflets, 1½ to slightly over 2 inches long, on their undersides slightly hairy only along the veins. The center leaflet has a stalk under ½ inch long. The flowers, about ⅓ inch long and appearing after the foliage, are in loose, erect panicles 2 to 3 inches long. They have yellowish-white sepals and white petals. The flattened, usually two-lobed fruits are ¾ to 1 inch long. The white to pinkish flowers of **S. holocarpa,** a shrub or tree up to 30 feet tall and hardy in southern New England, come before the leaves. Somewhat over ⅓ inch long, they are in stalked, pendulous panicles, 1½ to 4 inches long, from shoots of the previous year. The leaves, hairless except at their bases, have elliptic to oblong leaflets 1½ to 4 inches long, the center one with a stalk over ½ inch in length. The pear-shaped to ellipsoid fruits, rarely lobed, are 1½ to 2 inches long. Variety *S. h. rosea* has pale pink flowers. The most beautiful bladder nut, **S. colchica** is an erect shrub up to 12 feet in height. Less hardy than other species considered here, it survives outdoors about as far north as New York City. This has leaves with ovate-oblong, hairless leaflets, 2 to 3½ inches long, with lustrous undersurfaces. The flowers, in broad, erect pan-

Staphylea colchica coulombieri

icles 2 to 4 inches long, suggest tiny daffodils. From slightly under to a little over ½ inch in length, they have spreading, yellowish-white sepals and erect, white petals. The egg-shaped, two- to three-lobed fruits are 1½ to 3½ inches long. More robust than the typical species, *S. c. coulombieri* has larger, longer-pointed leaves. The flowers of *S. c. kochiana* have stamens with hairy stalks. The leaves of *S. c. laxiflora* generally have only three leaflets. Its flowers are in longer, slenderer, drooping racemes. An attractive hybrid between *S. colchica* and *S. pinnata* named **S. elegans** has leaves with usually five leaflets, and drooping panicles of white blooms. In *S. e. hessei* the flowers are suffused with red-purple.

European **S. pinnata,** an upright shrub 10 to 15 feet in height, has leaves of five or seven pointed-oblong-ovate, hairless leaflets, 2 to 4 inches long, with dull undersides. The flowers, in stalked, raceme-like, drooping panicles 2 to 4 inches in length, are about ⅓ inch long. Whitish, they have upright sepals with greenish bases and red apexes. The two- to three-lobed fruits are 1 inch to 1½ inches long. This is hardy in southern New England.

Staphylea pinnata

Garden and Landscape Uses. Although not without merit on either count, bladder nuts cannot be included among the best or most showy flowering or fruiting shrubs. In the main they are suitable only for less important parts of landscapes and as fillers. Exceptions are *S. colchica* and its varieties, which have considerable merit in bloom and are interesting in fruit. These

are excellent for forcing into early flower in big pots or tubs to decorate large conservatories. The American species are suitable for native plant gardens.

Cultivation. Bladder nuts are easy to satisfy. They respond to ordinary, not-too-dry soils and flourish in sun or light shade. Little pruning is required, just sufficient, done immediately after flowering, to shape the bushes. Should they become too rangy or big they can be restored by cutting back with considerable severity in late winter, a procedure that results in the loss of one season's bloom. Propagation is easy by seeds sown as soon as they are ripe in a cold frame or in a greenhouse in winter or spring. Summer cuttings about 4 inches long, made from firm, but not hard shoots, can be rooted in a greenhouse propagating bench, preferably with a little bottom heat, or under mist. Layering provides yet another means of increase.

STAPHYLEACEAE — Bladder Nut Family. This assemblage of dicotyledons, of the northern hemisphere and South America, comprises some sixty species of trees and shrubs of five genera. Its members have opposite or alternate leaves, rarely of one leaflet, more often of three or pinnate. The flowers, symmetrical, in few- to many-flowered panicles, and bisexual or unisexual, have a calyx of five overlapped sepals, five overlapped petals, five stamens, and two, three, or less often four styles. The fruits are capsules, sometimes much inflated and bladder-like. Genera cultivated are *Euscaphis* and *Staphylea*.

STAR or STARS. One or other of these words is part of the common names of these plants: desert star (*Monoptilon*), earth star (*Cryptanthus*), golden star (*Chrysogonum virginianum, Hypoxis hygrometrica, Triteleia ixioides*), golden stars (*Bloomeria*), Mexican star (*Milla biflora*), prairie star (*Lithophragma*), seven stars (*Ariocarpus retusus*), shooting star (*Dodecatheon*), star-anise (*Illicium verum*), star-apple (*Chrysophyllum cainito*), star-bush (*Turraea obtusifolia*), star-cucumber (*Sicyos angulatus*), star flower (*Trientalis*), star-grass (*Aletris, Hypoxis*), star-hyacinth (*Scilla amoena*), star-jasmine (*Trachelospermum jasminoides*), star-lily (*Erythronium, Leucocrinum montanum*), star of Bethlehem (*Campanula isophylla, Ornithogalum*), star-of-Texas (*Xanthisma texana*), star-tulip (*Calochortus*), water-star-grass (*Heterathera dubia*), and woodland star (*Lithophragma*).

STARCH-HYACINTH is *Muscari neglectum*.

STARTER SOLUTION. Poured around young plants immediately after transplanting to supply water and quickly available nutrients such as nitrogen, starter solutions are prepared by dissolving suitable fertilizers in water in amounts sufficient to provide a mild stimulant.

STARWORT. See Aster. For water-starwort see Callitriche.

STATE AGRICULTURAL EXPERIMENT STATIONS. It is important for gardeners to know of available sources of up-to-date, reliable, commercially unbiased information about plants and plant growing, particularly with reference to soil management, uses of fertilizers, selection of plant kinds and varieties, and pest, disease, and weed controls. Such information and much more, oriented to local conditions and needs, is readily available from State Agricultural Experiment Stations either free, or for certain booklets, soil testing services, and the like, at nominal fees.

State Agricultural Experiment Stations are funded by the United States and by state governments. Frequently they are associated with State Agricultural Colleges. In addition to disseminating information by bulletins, circulars, and other publications, by organizing lectures and displays, and by consultation services available to agriculturists, orchardists, gardeners, and others interested in cultivated plants, these stations engage in extensive research programs.

Locations of State Agricultural Experiment Stations are as follows:

ALABAMA
  Auburn
ALASKA
  College
ARIZONA
  Tucson
ARKANSAS
  Fayetteville
CALIFORNIA
  Berkeley
  Davis
  Los Angeles
  Riverside
  Parlier
COLORADO
  Fort Collins
CONNECTICUT
  New Haven
  Storrs
DELAWARE
  Newark
FLORIDA
  Gainesville
GEORGIA
  Athens
  Experiment
  Tifton
HAWAII
  Honolulu
IDAHO
  Moscow
ILLINOIS
  Urbana
INDIANA
  LaFayette
IOWA
  Ames
KANSAS
  Manhattan
KENTUCKY
  Lexington
LOUISIANA
  Baton Rouge
MAINE
  Orono
MARYLAND
  College Park
MASSACHUSETTS
  Amherst
MICHIGAN
  East Lansing
MINNESOTA
  St. Paul
MISSISSIPPI
  State College
MISSOURI
  Columbia
MONTANA
  Bozeman
NEBRASKA
  Lincoln
NEVADA
  Reno
NEW HAMPSHIRE
  Durham
NEW JERSEY
  New Brunswick
NEW MEXICO
  Las Cruces
NEW YORK
  Geneva
  Ithaca
NORTH CAROLINA
  Raleigh
NORTH DAKOTA
  Fargo
OHIO
  Columbus
  Wooster
OKLAHOMA
  Stillwater
OREGON
  Corvallis
PENNSYLVANIA
  University Park
PUERTO RICO
  Mayaguez
  Rio Piedras
RHODE ISLAND
  Kingston
SOUTH CAROLINA
  Clemson
SOUTH DAKOTA
  Brookings
TENNESSEE
  Knoxville
TEXAS
  College Station
UTAH
  Logan
VERMONT
  Burlington
VIRGINIA
  Blacksburg
WASHINGTON
  Pullman
WEST VIRGINIA
  Morgantown
WISCONSIN
  Madison
WYOMING
  Laramie

In Canada the government maintains similar facilities called Experimental Farms, Research Stations, and Research Institutes, with one or more located each in Alberta, British Columbia, Manitoba, New Brunswick, Nova Scotia, Prince Edward Island, Saskatchewan, and Yukon and Northwest territories. For more information about these, for publications and literature they offer, and for information about gardening in Canada write to the Information Division, Agriculture Canada, Sir John Carling Building, Ottawa, Ontario, Canada K1A 0C5.

STATE FLOWERS. This listing is of flowers that either by acts of legislature or by statewide votes of school children have been selected as state flowers:

ALABAMA — goldenrod (*Solidago serotina*)
ALASKA — forget-me-not (*Myosotis sylvatica*)
ARIZONA — sahuaro (*Carnegiea gigantea*)
ARKANSAS — apple blossom (*Malus sylvestris*)
CALIFORNIA — California-poppy (*Eschscholzia californica*)
COLORADO — columbine (*Aquilegia caerulea*)
CONNECTICUT — mountain-laurel (*Kalmia latifolia*)
DELAWARE — peach blossom (*Prunus persica*)
DISTRICT OF COLUMBIA — rose 'American Beauty' (*Rosa*)
FLORIDA — orange blossom (*Citrus sinensis*)
GEORGIA — Cherokee rose (*Rosa laevigata*)
HAWAII — Hawaiian hibiscus (*Hibiscus rosa-sinensis*)
IDAHO — mock-orange (*Philadelphus lewisii*)
ILLINOIS — native violet (*Viola*)
INDIANA — zinnia (*Zinnia elegans*)
IOWA — wild rose (*Rosa arkansana*)
KANSAS — sunflower (*Helianthus annuus*)
KENTUCKY — goldenrod (*Solidago serotina*)
LOUISIANA — Southern magnolia (*Magnolia grandiflora*)
MAINE — white pine cone and tassel (*Pinus strobus*)
MARYLAND — black-eyed-Susan (*Rudbeckia hirta*)
MASSACHUSETTS — trailing arbutus (*Epigaea repens*)
MICHIGAN — apple blossom (*Malus sylvestris*)
MINNESOTA — showy lady slipper (*Cypripedium reginae*)

MISSISSIPPI — Southern magnolia (*Magnolia grandiflora*)

MISSOURI — hawthorn (*Crataegus mollis*)

MONTANA — bitter root (*Lewisia rediviva*)

NEBRASKA — goldenrod (*Solidago serotina*)

NEVADA — sagebrush (*Artemisia tridentata*)

NEW HAMPSHIRE — purple lilac (*Syringa vulgaris*)

NEW JERSEY — violet (*Viola*)

NEW MEXICO — yucca (*Yucca*)

NEW YORK — wild rose (*Rosa*)

NORTH CAROLINA — flowering dogwood (*Cornus florida*)

NORTH DAKOTA — wild rose (*Rosa arkansana*)

OHIO — scarlet carnation (*Dianthus caryophyllus*)

OKLAHOMA — mistletoe (*Phoradendron flavescens*)

OREGON — Oregon-grape (*Mahonia aquifolium*)

PENNSYLVANIA — mountain-laurel (*Kalmia latifolia*)

RHODE ISLAND — violet (*Viola*)

SOUTH CAROLINA — Carolina yellow-jessamine (*Gelseminum sempervirens*)

SOUTH DAKOTA — American pasque flower (*Anemone patens*)

TENNESSEE — iris (*Iris*)

TEXAS — bluebonnet (*Lupinus subcarnosus*)

UTAH — sego-lily (*Calochortus nuttallii*)

VERMONT — red clover (*Trifolium pratense*)

VIRGINIA — flowering dogwood (*Cornus*)

WASHINGTON — rhododendron (*Rhododendron macrophyllum*)

WEST VIRGINIA — rhododendron (*Rhododendron maximum*)

WISCONSIN — violet (*Viola*)

WYOMING — Indian paintbrush (*Castilleja lineariaefolia*)

STATE TREES.

This listing is of trees that either by acts of legislation or by popular vote in elections sponsored by statewide organizations have been designated as state trees:

ALABAMA — Cuban pine (*Pinus caribaea*), longleaf pine (*P. palustris*), loblolly pine (*P. taeda*)

ALASKA — Sitka spruce (*Picea sitchensis*)

ARIZONA — Arizona cypress (*Cupressus arizonica*)

ARKANSAS — pine (*Pinus*)

CALIFORNIA — redwood (*Sequoia sempervirens*)

COLORADO — Colorado blue spruce (*Picea pungens glauca*)

CONNECTICUT — white oak (*Quercus alba*)

DELAWARE — American holly (*Ilex opaca*)

FLORIDA — cabbage palmetto (*Sabal palmetto*)

GEORGIA — live oak (*Quercus virginiana*)

HAWAII — candlenut (*Aleurites moluccana*)

IDAHO — Western white pine (*Pinus monticola*)

INDIANA — tulip tree (*Liriodendron tulipifera*)

IOWA — oak (*Quercus*)

KANSAS — cottonwood and balsam poplar (*Populus deltoides* and *P. balsamifera*)

KENTUCKY — tulip tree (*Liriodendron tulipifera*)

LOUISIANA — Southern magnolia (*Magnolia grandiflora*)

MAINE — white pine (*Pinus strobus*)

MARYLAND — white oak (*Quercus alba*)

MASSACHUSETTS — American elm (*Ulmus americana*)

MICHIGAN — apple (*Malus*)

MINNESOTA — white pine (*Pinus strobus*)

MISSISSIPPI — Southern magnolia (*Magnolia grandiflora*)

MISSOURI — flowering dogwood (*Cornus florida*)

MONTANA — Western yellow pine (*Pinus ponderosa*)

NEBRASKA — American elm (*Ulmus americana*)

NEVADA — American quaking aspen (*Populus tremuloides*)

NEW HAMPSHIRE — canoe birch (*Betula papyrifera*)

NEW JERSEY — red oak (*Quercus rubra*)

NEW MEXICO — nut pine (*Pinus edulis*)

NEW YORK — sugar maple (*Acer saccharum*)

NORTH CAROLINA — tulip tree (*Liriodendron tulipifera*)

NORTH DAKOTA — green ash (*Fraxinus pennsylvanica lanceolata*)

OHIO — Ohio buckeye (*Aesculus glabra*)

OKLAHOMA — redbud (*Cercis canadensis*)

OREGON — Douglas-fir (*Pseudotsuga menziesii*)

PENNSYLVANIA — Eastern hemlock (*Tsuga canadensis*)

RHODE ISLAND — sugar maple (*Acer saccharum*)

SOUTH CAROLINA — cabbage palmetto (*Sabal palmetto*)

SOUTH DAKOTA — cottonwood and balsam poplar (*Populus deltoides* and *P. balsamifera*)

TENNESSEE — tulip tree (*Liriodendron tulipifera*)

TEXAS — pecan (*Carya illinoinensis*)

UTAH — Colorado blue spruce (*Picea pungens glauca*)

VERMONT — sugar maple (*Acer saccharum*)

VIRGINIA — flowering dogwood (*Cornus florida*)

WASHINGTON — Western hemlock (*Tsuga heterophylla*)

WEST VIRGINIA — sugar maple (*Acer saccharum*)

WISCONSIN — sugar maple (*Acer saccharum*)

WYOMING — cottonwood and balsam poplar (*Populus deltoides* and *P. balsamifera*)

STATICE. See Limonium.

STAUNTONIA (Staunt-ònia). Composed of about fifteen species of eastern Asia, *Stauntonia*, of the lardizabala family LARDIZABALACEAE, is closely related to *Akebia* and *Holboellia*. It differs from the first in its blooms having more than three sepals and from both in the stamens cohering. The female flowers have staminodes (nonfunctional stamens). There are no petals. The name commemorates Sir George Leonard Staunton, Irish physician and traveler in China, who died in 1801.

Stauntonias are evergreen, twining, woody climbers, with leaves of several leaflets arranged palmately (spreading from a common point at the top of the leafstalk). Their unisexual flowers are in clusters from the leaf axils, both sexes on the same plant. They are without petals, but have six sepals, the outer three broader than the others, and six stamens or three pistils. The fruits are berries.

Native to the warmer parts of Japan, the Ryukyu Islands, and southern Korea, handsome *S. hexaphylla*, up to 40 feet tall, has hairless stems and foliage. Its long-stalked leaves have five to seven, more rarely three, leathery, stalked, ovate, broadly-elliptic to obovate leaflets 2 to 4 inches long. The fragrant flowers, white to yellowish, are streaked with violet. They appear in spring. Their sepals are about ¾ inch long. The roundish to egg-shaped fruits are purplish, about 2 inches in length, and contain pulpy, edible flesh.

Garden and Landscape Uses and Cultivation. An excellent vine, not hardy in the north, this can be used effectively in the south and other mild-climate regions. It may be provided with wires or other suitable supports for its stems to entwine or be allowed to cover stumps and low walls. It succeeds in ordinary soil and needs little attention other than, if the soil is deficient in nutrients, fertilizing from time to time. To maintain neatness, unruly shoots may be trimmed in winter. Cuttings and seed are easy means of increase.